MW01617982

The Hirsch Chumash

חמשה חומשי תורה

מתורגם ומבואר

מאת

הגאון כמוהר״ר **שמשון**

בן כמוהר״ר **רפאל הירש** פ״פ זללה״ה

שומר משמרת הקודש בק״ק עדת ישורון בפפד״ם

ספר במדבר

תורגם לאנגלית

ע״י

דניאל הברמן

הוצאת פלדהיים — יודאיקא פרעסס

ירושלים - ניו יארק, תשס״ח לפ״ק

The Hirsch Chumash

THE FIVE BOOKS OF THE TORAH

Translation and Commentary by

RAV SAMSON RAPHAEL HIRSCH

English Translation
by
Daniel Haberman

FELDHEIM PUBLISHERS — JUDAICA PRESS
Jerusalem - New York

ISBN 978-1-58330-295-8

First printing, 2007
Second printing, 2008

FELDHEIM PUBLISHERS
POB 35002, Jerusalem, Israel 91350
208 Airport Executive Park, Nanuet, N.Y. 10954

www.feldheim.com

Typography by:
Simcha Graphics, Brooklyn, N.Y.

Printed in Israel

10 9 8 7 6 5 4 3 2 1

Editors' Note

The new English language version of Rav Samson Raphael Hirsch's Translation and Commentary to ספר במדבר was first published in the year תשס"ז. A complete introduction to this version of the "Hirsch Chumash" is presented in the Editors' Foreword to ספר בראשית. As stated in the Foreword, the following stylistic points should be noted:

• Unless specified, the word "Commentary" in the text refers to the Hirsch Commentary.
• In accordance with Rav Hirsch's Commentary to Bereshis 2:4, translation of the Divine Name in the Scriptural verse is distinguished with regular type when referring to the שם הוי', as opposed to italicized type when referring to אלקים.
• Transliterated Hebrew words in the Commentary are italicized if the words are not common to English usage. For example, "mitzvos" is italicized; "mitzvah" is not italicized.
• Differentiation is made between the "Halachah" as the corpus of the Law, and the "halachah" referring to a specific law in a particular case.
• References to sources in the same ספר of the חומש are referred to as being "above" or "below" the verse under discussion.
• To facilitate learning of the Commentary, the first occurrence of a word or phrase in a פסוק for which Rav Hirsch writes commentary is printed in bold. This should encourage the reader to refer back to the לשון הקרא, which is so crucial to Rav Hirsch's approach. Punctuation has been added for פסוקים from נביאים and כתובים. In a few places, brief explanatory remarks have been inserted in square brackets to clarify Rav Hirsch's words.

Elliott Bondi
David Bechhofer

לז״נ

ר׳ יעקב בן ר׳ יצחק שוואלבע
ואשתו מ׳ חנה בת מוה״ר ר׳ לוי יוסף ברייער
זכרונם לברכה

מאת בניהם ובנותיהם

The Hirsch Chumash

ספר במדבר

1 1 God *spoke to Moshe in the wilderness of Sinai, in the Tent of Appointed Meeting, on the first day of the second month in the second year of their exodus from the land of Egypt, saying:*	**א** א וַיְדַבֵּ֨ר יְהֹוָ֧ה אֶל־מֹשֶׁ֛ה בְּמִדְבַּ֥ר סִינַ֖י בְּאֹ֣הֶל מוֹעֵ֑ד בְּאֶחָד֩ לַחֹ֨דֶשׁ הַשֵּׁנִ֜י בַּשָּׁנָ֣ה הַשֵּׁנִ֗ית לְצֵאתָ֛ם מֵאֶ֥רֶץ מִצְרַ֖יִם לֵאמֹֽר׃

במדבר

CHAPTER 1

1 The end of the second book of the *Chumash* tells of the construction of the Sanctuary of the Torah. The third book is devoted entirely to the standards set for Israel by this Sanctuary — in symbolic terms, by the offerings, and in practical terms, by the laws that sanctify every aspect of daily life. Thus an outline is presented of the ideal to be translated into reality by every individual member of the nation as well as by the nation as a whole. The concluding chapter [of the third book], which deals with נדרי הקדש, allows room, within the framework of the Halachah, for one who might feel the need to express his personal relationship to the Sanctuary by a symbolic dedication of man's value, or by the dedication of personal property to the Sanctuary.

The fourth book now returns to the national reality. It shows us Israel as it actually is; it presents before us the actual nation in its relationship to the ideal of its calling as outlined in the third book. It opens with the command to take a census of the nation as an עדה, a community united by its common calling. All the independent members of the nation are to be counted, one by one. A census of this nature makes it clear to the nation's representatives that the community is not merely an idea but, rather, exists only in the actual totality of all its members. At the same time, every individual is made aware that he personally "counts" as an important member of the community, and that the task that devolves on the nation as a whole requires the faithfulness and devotion of each individual to the common calling.

The third book concludes with the dedicatory counting of the flocks, which pass in groups under the staff of their owners. The fourth book

2 *Take the total count of the entire community of the Children of Israel, according to their families, according to their fathers' house, counting the names, all males, according to their heads.*

ב שְׂא֗וּ אֶת־רֹאשׁ֙ כָּל־עֲדַ֣ת בְּנֵֽי־
יִשְׂרָאֵ֔ל לְמִשְׁפְּחֹתָ֖ם לְבֵ֣ית אֲבֹתָ֑ם
בְּמִסְפַּ֣ר שֵׁמ֔וֹת כָּל־זָכָ֖ר לְגֻלְגְּלֹתָֽם׃

now opens with the counting of the nation as "God's flock" for its Shepherd. The nation, too, is counted according to groups of families and tribes, all of which belong to God; and every individual passes under the staff of his Shepherd and is counted as an independent member of the flock.

במדבר סיני. The census is conducted in the wilderness. This proves that the purpose of this census is neither economic nor political — because economics and politics have no relevance to life in the wilderness. Rather, the addition of the words סיני and אהל מועד indicates that this census is to be made in the service of the Torah which was given on Sinai, and to which homage is to be paid in the אהל מועד. First, the Torah was given at Sinai. Then, on the first day of the month of Nissan, the Testimony of the Torah, which was restored to Israel as a sign that they were purified of the sin of the golden calf, found its ideal place. Now, on the first day of the month of Iyar, all the tribes, the families and the men are to be counted for the sake of this Torah. From now onward they are to gather and encamp around the Torah as its guardians and keepers.

2 **שאו את ראש**. See Commentary, *Shemos* 30:12ff. There, in verses 12 and 16, it says that everyone who is to be counted is to give half a shekel, and the total sum collected is to be given to בדק הבית for the upkeep of the Sanctuary — על עבדת אהל מועד. Thus, every Jewish man is counted and valued only on the basis of his commitment to the Torah; and *every* census is taken only in the service of, and for the purposes of, the Sanctuary.

This method of counting the people connects the beginning of the fourth book with the conclusion of the third book; for there, too, the discussion is of ערכים ונדרי הקדש.

כל עדת בני ישראל. עֵדָה — following the pattern of דֵעָה, לֵדָה, שֵׁנָה, and the like — stems from the root יעד, which is related to יחד, which means: to unite for the sake of a common purpose. עדה, then, denotes people who have joined together for the sake of a common calling, and who are united by the solidarity of that calling: a community. Individuals become a community not by means of an order that comes to them from without, but by means of a shared concern that calls them from within their own hearts.

בני ישראל are the entire Jewish people; and within the framework of this people, עדה denotes all the independent bearers and guardians of the common mission, which is none other than fulfilling the Torah.

The concept expressed here by the term "עדה" is expressed above (*Shemos* 30:12) by the term "לפקדיהם." פקודי בני ישראל are those whom the mission of the Jewish national community "thinks of," "appoints" and "entrusts"; these are the "men" of Israel. Accordingly, we are not dealing here with a population census. What is sought is not the number of people, but the number of "men" whom the Torah can reckon on.

למשפחתם לבית אבתם. But the individual men do not form the community of Israel directly; rather, the all-encompassing national community contains two inner circles. For the community consists of tribes, and every tribe consists of families. Accordingly, the men are to be counted according to their families, and the families according to their tribes, and the tribes combine to form the sum total of עדת בני ישראל.

משפחה stems from the root שפח, which is related to ספח and also to שפע (see Commentary, *Bereshis* 8:19). שפע — as in שִׁפְעַת יֵהוּא (*Melachim* II, 9:17), שִׁפְעַת גְּמַלִּים (*Yeshayahu* 60:6), שִׁפְעַת סוּסָיו (*Yechezkel* 26:10) — denotes the gathering of a multitude in one place. With the addition of a מ, the משפחה is the element that joins individuals into natural groups. What forms the family is common descent, and also marriage, which transfers the wife to the home of her husband.

לבית אבתם. From various places (e.g., below, 2:2, 32, 34; 7:2; 17:17, 18, et al.) it is clear that בית אב denotes the unity of a tribe. The individuals together form families; the families, which descend from one common home, together form tribes; and the tribes, which likewise descend from one common home, together form the "House of Israel," בית ישראל. These tribes are called "מטות" ("branches"; cf. *Yechezkel* 19:11-14) on account of their one common stem, and they are called "בתי

אבות" on account of the numerous families issuing from each tribe. בית ישראל, then, consists of twelve בתי אבות; each בית אב consists of various משפחות; and the משפחות comprise the first unit which joins the individuals into groups.

This method of grouping is found also in the tribe of Levi, which was separated out from the rest of the nation in order to be treated as an independent unit. Levi is Israel in miniature. לוי's sons — גרשון קהת ומררי — form בתי אבות (below, 3:24, 30, 35). Their sons — לבני ושמעי, עמרם ויצהר חברון ועוזיאל, מחלי ומושי — form משפחות הלוי לבית אבותם (below, 3:18-20).

This is the uniqueness of Jewish nationalism: The nation as a whole is always considered one house, the House of Israel, and the members of the nation are always called the "children of one man," the Children of Israel. At the same time, however, separate units remain, which are subordinate to and encompassed by the larger whole: בתי אבות and משפחות.

The conception of the nation as the "House of Israel" and of all its members as the "Children of Israel" ensures that the concept of the Jewish nation does not become a mere abstract idea without real union and does not exist merely as a fiction, as an imaginary union of elite representatives. The Jewish nation is always conceived of in the actual unified entirety of its members. They are united by a common inner element, and each one of them is an actual and integral part of this unity.

Our forefather Yisrael was one man; but even when his descendants had grown to six hundred thousand men, they all were still members of "one house," sons of "one man," bearing in their hearts and souls the impress of the same stamp, bearing through the ages their heritage of one mission and one destiny.

But amidst this fundamental unity and under its influence, a diversity of qualities unique to tribes and families is preserved and nurtured. In this way, the goal — which we have already pointed to several times in *Bereshis* (17:6, 35:11-12, 49:25) — will be attained: The one mission shared by all will be accomplished by every individual — despite his uniqueness; it will be accomplished by a diversity of special qualities and character traits, a diversity of professions and positions in life. And this accomplishment will be a model for the entire human race.

Each tribe in its specialty and each family with its special qualities

3 *From twenty years old and upward, everyone who goes forth into communal service in Israel, you shall number them according to their serving divisions, you and Aharon.*	ג מִבֶּ֨ן עֶשְׂרִ֤ים שָׁנָה֙ וָמַ֔עְלָה כָּל־יֹצֵ֥א צָבָ֖א בְּיִשְׂרָאֵ֑ל תִּפְקְד֥וּ אֹתָ֛ם לְצִבְאֹתָ֖ם אַתָּ֥ה וְאַהֲרֹֽן׃

are to work at the common task of the House of Israel; they are to give shape to this task, educate their children to it, and pass it on to the next generation. That is why the hundreds of thousands of members of the House of Israel do not come to the nation as an unorganized multitude, but למשפחתם לבית אבתם — i.e., as family groups which in turn are grouped according to the tribes to which they belong. The men of each tribe are counted, and the families in each tribe are kept separately. And each family is counted:

במספר שמות. Each individual is counted by *name*. Thus, each one joins the whole while conscious of the importance of his *personality.*

כל זכר לגלגלתם. Each one had to personally hand in his half-shekel and report as so-and-so from such-and-such a family, of such-and-such a tribe. Alternatively, the lineage — both family and tribal — had already come to expression through the preceding division into groups. In any case, everyone who came to be counted was made aware of his personal, family and tribal status, and "as such" he was counted among the whole.

In addition, the expression למשפחתם לבית אבתם implies that a person's tribal lineage (כהן, לוי, יהודי, שמעוני, etc.), as well as his family lineage in respect to the law of inheritance, are determined by the father, not by the mother: משפחת אב קרויה משפחה, משפחת אם אינה קרויה משפחה (*Bava Basra* 109b and 110b).

גלגלת. In a census, גלגלת (lit., "skull") represents the concrete, physically present individual. When a mass of people assemble, the heads offer the best means of counting them. In Judaism, however, we count not the heads, but בקע לגלגלת (*Shemos* 38:26), the half-shekel corresponding to each head.

3 **מבן עשרים וגו׳ כל יצא צבא בישראל**. The term "צבא" in Scripture does not necessarily, or even primarily, denote an army or military service

4 *And alongside you shall be one man for each tribe, each one the head of his fathers' house.*	ד וְאִתְּכֶם יִהְיוּ אִישׁ אִישׁ לַמַּטֶּה אִישׁ רֹאשׁ לְבֵית־אֲבֹתָיו הוּא׃
5 *These are the names of the men who shall stand alongside you: For Reuven, Elitzur, son of Shedei'ur.*	ה וְאֵלֶּה שְׁמוֹת הָאֲנָשִׁים אֲשֶׁר יַעַמְדוּ אִתְּכֶם לִרְאוּבֵן אֱלִיצוּר בֶּן־שְׁדֵיאוּר׃
6 *For Shimon, Shelumi'el, son of Tzurishaddai.*	ו לְשִׁמְעוֹן שְׁלֻמִיאֵל בֶּן־צוּרִישַׁדָּי׃

(see Commentary, *Bereshis* 2:1). Consider כל בא לצבא לעשות מלאכה באהל מועד (below, 4:3), לצבא צבא לעבד וגו' (below, 4:23), and elsewhere in chapter 4, where צבא denotes the service of the *Levi'im* in the אהל מועד. The same is true in chapter 8 verses 24-25 (below). From all these sources, it is clear that צבא denotes a multitude united for communal service under the command of a higher authority, or the service that is performed by such a multitude.

In our verse as well, צבא does not necessarily denote military service. Rather, יצא צבא בישראל denotes anyone who, when needed, is obligated to emerge from private life and enlist in the service of the community; that is to say, anyone whom the community can count on to carry out its objectives — namely, כל זכר, every man, מבן עשרים שנה ומעלה. Hence, in the section on the *Levi'im* (below, chap. 4), it does not say יוצא צבא but בא לצבא; for their entire lives are devoted to the service of the community.

תפקדו אתם — see Commentary, *Shemos* 30:13.

לצבאתם — see Commentary, ibid. 12:51.

4 **ואתכם וגו'**. Apparently, the heads of all the tribes assisted [Moshe and Aharon] throughout the entire census; it was not just the head of each tribe assisting at the census of his particular tribe (see Commentary below, 7:2).

5 The ל- in לראובן, לשמעון, and so on, apparently means: for Reuven and in its stead; i.e., the tribe was represented by its prince.

7 *For Yehudah, Nachshon, son of Amminadav.*

ז לִיהוּדָ֕ה נַחְשׁ֖וֹן בֶּן־עַמִּֽינָדָֽב׃

8 *For Yissachar, Nesan'el, son of Tzu'ar.*

ח לְיִ֨שָּׂשכָ֔ר נְתַנְאֵ֖ל בֶּן־צוּעָֽר׃

9 *For Zevulun, Eli'av, son of Chelon.*

ט לִזְבוּלֻ֕ן אֱלִיאָ֖ב בֶּן־חֵלֹֽן׃

10 *For the sons of Yosef: for Efrayim, Elishama, son of Ammihud; for Menashe, Gamli'el, son of Pedah-tzur.*

י לִבְנֵ֣י יוֹסֵ֔ף לְאֶפְרַ֕יִם אֱלִישָׁמָ֖ע בֶּן־
עַמִּיה֑וּד לִמְנַשֶּׁ֕ה גַּמְלִיאֵ֖ל בֶּן־
פְּדָהצֽוּר׃

11 *For Binyamin, Avidan, son of Gid'oni.*

יא לְבִ֨נְיָמִ֔ן אֲבִידָ֖ן בֶּן־גִּדְעֹנִֽי׃

12 *For Dan, Achi'ezer, son of Ammi-shaddai.*

יב לְדָ֕ן אֲחִיעֶ֖זֶר בֶּן־עַמִּֽישַׁדָּֽי׃

13 *For Asher, Pag'i'el, son of Ochran.*

יג לְאָשֵׁ֕ר פַּגְעִיאֵ֖ל בֶּן־עָכְרָֽן׃

14 *For Gad, Elyasaf, son of De'u'el.*

יד לְגָ֕ד אֶלְיָסָ֖ף בֶּן־דְּעוּאֵֽל׃

15 *For Naftali, Achira, son of Einan.*

טו לְנַ֨פְתָּלִ֔י אֲחִירַ֖ע בֶּן־עֵינָֽן׃

16 *These are the ones called from the community, princes of the tribes of their fathers; they are heads of the thousands of Israel.*

טז אֵ֚לֶּה קְרִיאֵ֣י הָעֵדָ֔ה נְשִׂיאֵ֖י מַטּ֣וֹת
אֲבוֹתָ֑ם רָאשֵׁ֛י אַלְפֵ֥י יִשְׂרָאֵ֖ל הֵֽם׃
קְרוּאֵי קרי

---

16 **קרואי העדה**. The written form is קריאי העדה. קָרִיא is a noun form, following the pattern of שָׂכִיר, נָדִיב. This form implies that the person is constantly being called, and that for him "being called" is a permanent characteristic. By contrast, קָרוּא is a verbal form, passive participle. This form indicates that the person is called ad hoc, for the needs of the moment, for the purpose in question.

The men named here were those whom the community generally called on to direct community affairs; they were קריאי העדה, who had

17 *Moshe took, and [so did] Aharon, these men, who had been designated by name.*

יז וַיִּקַּח מֹשֶׁה וְאַהֲרֹן אֵת הָאֲנָשִׁים
הָאֵלֶּה אֲשֶׁר נִקְּבוּ בְּשֵׁמוֹת׃

18 *And they assembled the entire community on the first day of the second month, and they declared themselves by their births in their families, according to the house of their fathers, numbering the names from twenty years old and upward, according to their heads.*

יח וְאֵת כָּל־הָעֵדָה הִקְהִילוּ בְּאֶחָד
לַחֹדֶשׁ הַשֵּׁנִי וַיִּתְיַלְדוּ עַל־
מִשְׁפְּחֹתָם לְבֵית אֲבֹתָם בְּמִסְפַּר
שֵׁמוֹת מִבֶּן עֶשְׂרִים שָׁנָה וָמַעְלָה
לְגֻלְגְּלֹתָם׃

19 *Even as* God *had commanded Moshe, so did he number them in the wilderness of Sinai.*

יט כַּאֲשֶׁר צִוָּה יְהוָה אֶת־מֹשֶׁה
וַיִּפְקְדֵם בְּמִדְבַּר סִינָי׃ ס שני

---

the confidence and recognition of the public. In addition, they were קרואי העדה: they were called on especially for this census.

They were also **נשיאי מטות אבותם**: Within their own tribes they were, by virtue of their social position, "raised" and exalted above the common people. Accordingly, they were **ראשי אלפי ישראל**: The *whole nation* regarded them as its leaders, on account of their character and their position.

18 **ויתילדו על משפחתם**. They presented themselves by giving their names and declaring their lineage, both family and tribal.

ואת כל העדה וגו׳ ויתילדו וגו׳ מבן עשרים וגו׳. The entire עדה assembled there, for the עדה consisted of all the men over 20 years (see Commentary above, v. 2).

19 **ויפקדם במדבר סיני**. This repetition brings to mind again — before the beginning of the census — the idea and meaning of the census (see Commentary above, v. 1).

כ וַיִּהְי֣וּ בְנֵֽי־רְאוּבֵן֮ בְּכֹ֣ר יִשְׂרָאֵל֒
תּוֹלְדֹתָ֥ם לְמִשְׁפְּחֹתָ֖ם לְבֵ֣ית
אֲבֹתָ֑ם בְּמִסְפַּ֣ר שֵׁמוֹת֙ לְגֻלְגְּלֹתָ֔ם
כָּל־זָכָ֗ר מִבֶּ֨ן עֶשְׂרִ֤ים שָׁנָה֙ וָמַ֔עְלָה
כֹּ֖ל יֹצֵ֥א צָבָֽא׃

20 *There were the sons of Reuven, the firstborn of Israel, their births according to their families according to the house of their fathers, numbering the names, according to their heads, all males from twenty years old and upward, each one who goes forth into communal service:*

כא פְּקֻדֵיהֶ֖ם לְמַטֵּ֣ה רְאוּבֵ֑ן שִׁשָּׁ֧ה
וְאַרְבָּעִ֛ים אֶ֖לֶף וַחֲמֵ֥שׁ מֵאֽוֹת׃ פ

21 *Their numbered ones of the tribe of Reuven: forty-six thousand, five hundred.*

כב לִבְנֵ֣י שִׁמְע֔וֹן תּוֹלְדֹתָ֥ם לְמִשְׁפְּחֹתָ֖ם
לְבֵ֣ית אֲבֹתָ֑ם פְּקֻדָ֞יו בְּמִסְפַּ֤ר
שֵׁמוֹת֙ לְגֻלְגְּלֹתָ֔ם כָּל־זָכָ֗ר מִבֶּ֨ן
עֶשְׂרִ֤ים שָׁנָה֙ וָמַ֔עְלָה כֹּ֖ל יֹצֵ֥א
צָבָֽא׃

22 *To the sons of Shimon, their births according to their families according to the house of their fathers; also his numbered ones, numbering the names, according to their heads, all males from twenty years old and upward, each one who goes forth into communal service:*

20 **ויהיו בני ראובן וגו'**. The order of the tribes in the census corresponds to their grouping in מחנות, as will be explained in chapter 2 (see Commentary there).

22 **תולדתם וגו'**. These details characterize this census, and when the census is taken they are brought to the awareness of each person who is counted. Hence they are repeated with each tribe. This repetition expresses the complete equality and the equal valuation of all the tribes and their members, as regards their importance to the nation. This is specially emphasized already with the second tribe, Shimon, by the extra word פקדיו. After Reuven's census, that of Shimon was also done as prescribed in exactly the same manner, and the same applies, of course, to the censuses of all the following tribes. In every case, these details, which are essential to this census, are repeated.

23 *Their numbered ones of the tribe of Shimon: fifty-nine thousand, three hundred.*

כג פְּקֻדֵיהֶ֖ם לְמַטֵּ֣ה שִׁמְע֑וֹן תִּשְׁעָ֧ה
וַחֲמִשִּׁ֛ים אֶ֖לֶף וּשְׁלֹ֥שׁ מֵאֽוֹת׃ פ

24 *To the sons of Gad, their births according to their families according to the house of their fathers; numbering the names from twenty years old and upward, each one who goes forth into communal service:*

כד לִבְנֵ֣י גָ֔ד תּוֹלְדֹתָ֖ם לְמִשְׁפְּחֹתָ֣ם
לְבֵ֣ית אֲבֹתָ֑ם בְּמִסְפַּ֣ר שֵׁמ֗וֹת מִבֶּ֨ן
עֶשְׂרִ֤ים שָׁנָה֙ וָמַ֔עְלָה כֹּ֖ל יֹצֵ֥א
צָבָֽא׃

25 *Their numbered ones of the tribe of Gad: forty-five thousand, six hundred and fifty.*

כה פְּקֻדֵיהֶ֖ם לְמַטֵּ֣ה גָ֑ד חֲמִשָּׁ֤ה
וְאַרְבָּעִים֙ אֶ֔לֶף וְשֵׁ֥שׁ מֵא֖וֹת
וַחֲמִשִּֽׁים׃ פ

26 *To the sons of Yehudah, their births according to their families according to the house of their fathers; numbering the names from twenty years old and upward, each one who goes forth into communal service:*

כו לִבְנֵ֣י יְהוּדָ֔ה תּוֹלְדֹתָ֖ם לְמִשְׁפְּחֹתָ֣ם
לְבֵ֣ית אֲבֹתָ֑ם בְּמִסְפַּ֣ר שֵׁמֹ֗ת מִבֶּ֨ן
עֶשְׂרִ֤ים שָׁנָה֙ וָמַ֔עְלָה כֹּ֖ל יֹצֵ֥א
צָבָֽא׃

27 *Their numbered ones of the tribe of Yehudah: seventy-four thousand, six hundred.*

כז פְּקֻדֵיהֶ֖ם לְמַטֵּ֣ה יְהוּדָ֑ה אַרְבָּעָ֧ה
וְשִׁבְעִ֛ים אֶ֖לֶף וְשֵׁ֥שׁ מֵאֽוֹת׃ פ

28 *To the sons of Yissachar, their births according to their families according to the house of their fathers; numbering the names from twenty years old and upward, each one who goes forth into communal service:*

כח לִבְנֵ֣י יִשָּׂשכָ֔ר תּוֹלְדֹתָ֖ם לְמִשְׁפְּחֹתָ֣ם
לְבֵ֣ית אֲבֹתָ֑ם בְּמִסְפַּ֣ר שֵׁמֹ֗ת מִבֶּ֨ן
עֶשְׂרִ֤ים שָׁנָה֙ וָמַ֔עְלָה כֹּ֖ל יֹצֵ֥א
צָבָֽא׃

29 *Their numbered ones of the tribe of Yissachar: fifty-four thousand, four hundred.*

כט פְּקֻדֵיהֶ֖ם לְמַטֵּ֣ה יִשָּׂשכָ֑ר אַרְבָּעָ֧ה
וַחֲמִשִּׁ֛ים אֶ֖לֶף וְאַרְבַּ֥ע מֵאֽוֹת׃ פ

30 *To the sons of Zevulun, their births according to their families according to the house of their fathers, numbering the names from twenty years old and upward, each one who goes forth into communal service:*

ל לִבְנֵ֥י זְבוּלֻ֖ן תּֽוֹלְדֹתָ֣ם לְמִשְׁפְּחֹתָ֣ם
לְבֵ֣ית אֲבֹתָ֑ם בְּמִסְפַּ֣ר שֵׁמֹ֗ת מִבֶּ֨ן
עֶשְׂרִ֤ים שָׁנָה֙ וָמַ֔עְלָה כֹּ֖ל יֹצֵ֥א
צָבָֽא׃

31 *Their numbered ones of the tribe of Zevulun: fifty-seven thousand, four hundred.*

לא פְּקֻדֵיהֶ֖ם לְמַטֵּ֣ה זְבוּלֻ֑ן שִׁבְעָ֧ה
וַחֲמִשִּׁ֛ים אֶ֖לֶף וְאַרְבַּ֥ע מֵאֽוֹת׃ פ

32 *To the sons of Yosef, to the sons of Efrayim, their births according to the house of their fathers; numbering the names from twenty years old and upward, each one who goes forth into communal service:*

לב לִבְנֵ֤י יוֹסֵף֙ לִבְנֵ֣י אֶפְרַ֔יִם תּֽוֹלְדֹתָ֥ם
לְמִשְׁפְּחֹתָ֖ם לְבֵ֣ית אֲבֹתָ֑ם בְּמִסְפַּ֣ר
שֵׁמֹ֗ת מִבֶּ֨ן עֶשְׂרִ֤ים שָׁנָה֙ וָמַ֔עְלָה
כֹּ֖ל יֹצֵ֥א צָבָֽא׃

33 *Their numbered ones of the tribe of Efrayim: forty thousand, five hundred.*

לג פְּקֻדֵיהֶ֖ם לְמַטֵּ֣ה אֶפְרָ֑יִם אַרְבָּעִ֥ים
אֶ֖לֶף וַחֲמֵ֥שׁ מֵאֽוֹת׃ פ

34 *To the sons of Menashe, their births according to their families according to the house of their fathers; numbering the names from twenty years old and upward, each one who goes forth into communal service:*

לד לִבְנֵ֣י מְנַשֶּׁ֔ה תּֽוֹלְדֹתָ֥ם לְמִשְׁפְּחֹתָ֖ם
לְבֵ֣ית אֲבֹתָ֑ם בְּמִסְפַּ֣ר שֵׁמ֗וֹת מִבֶּ֨ן
עֶשְׂרִ֤ים שָׁנָה֙ וָמַ֔עְלָה כֹּ֖ל יֹצֵ֥א
צָבָֽא׃

35 *Their numbered ones of the tribe of Menashe: thirty-two thousand, two hundred.*

לה פְּקֻדֵיהֶ֖ם לְמַטֵּ֣ה מְנַשֶּׁ֑ה שְׁנַ֧יִם
וּשְׁלֹשִׁ֛ים אֶ֖לֶף וּמָאתָֽיִם׃ פ

36 *To the sons of Binyamin, their births according to their families according to the house of their fa-*

לו לִבְנֵ֣י בִנְיָמִ֔ן תּֽוֹלְדֹתָ֥ם לְמִשְׁפְּחֹתָ֖ם
לְבֵ֣ית אֲבֹתָ֑ם בְּמִסְפַּ֣ר שֵׁמֹ֗ת מִבֶּ֨ן

thers; numbering the names from twenty years old and upward, each one who goes forth into communal service:

עֶשְׂרִים שָׁנָה וָמַעְלָה כֹּל יֹצֵא
צָבָא׃

37 *Their numbered ones of the tribe of Binyamin: thirty-five thousand, four hundred.*

לז פְּקֻדֵיהֶם לְמַטֵּה בִנְיָמִן חֲמִשָּׁה
וּשְׁלֹשִׁים אֶלֶף וְאַרְבַּע מֵאוֹת׃ פ

38 *To the sons of Dan, their births according to their families according to the house of their fathers; numbering the names from twenty years old and upward; each one who goes forth into communal service:*

לח לִבְנֵי דָן תּוֹלְדֹתָם לְמִשְׁפְּחֹתָם
לְבֵית אֲבֹתָם בְּמִסְפַּר שֵׁמֹת מִבֶּן
עֶשְׂרִים שָׁנָה וָמַעְלָה כֹּל יֹצֵא
צָבָא׃

39 *Their numbered ones of the tribe of Dan: sixty-two thousand, seven hundred.*

לט פְּקֻדֵיהֶם לְמַטֵּה דָן שְׁנַיִם וְשִׁשִּׁים
אֶלֶף וּשְׁבַע מֵאוֹת׃ פ

40 *To the sons of Asher, their births according to their families according to the house of their fathers; numbering the names from twenty years old and upward, each one who goes forth into communal service:*

מ לִבְנֵי אָשֵׁר תּוֹלְדֹתָם לְמִשְׁפְּחֹתָם
לְבֵית אֲבֹתָם בְּמִסְפַּר שֵׁמֹת מִבֶּן
עֶשְׂרִים שָׁנָה וָמַעְלָה כֹּל יֹצֵא
צָבָא׃

41 *Their numbered ones of the tribe of Asher: forty-one thousand, five hundred.*

מא פְּקֻדֵיהֶם לְמַטֵּה אָשֵׁר אֶחָד
וְאַרְבָּעִים אֶלֶף וַחֲמֵשׁ מֵאוֹת׃ פ

42 *Lastly, the sons of Naftali, their*

מב בְּנֵי נַפְתָּלִי תּוֹלְדֹתָם לְמִשְׁפְּחֹתָם

---

42 **בני נפתלי**. Here it does not say לבני נפתלי as in the cases of the preceding tribes. From this it follows that לבני שמעון, לבני גד, and the like, do not mean "of the sons of Shimon" but "*to* the sons of Shimon." That is to

births according to their families according to the house of their fathers; numbering the names from twenty years old and upward, each one who goes forth into communal service:

לְבֵית אֲבֹתָם בְּמִסְפַּר שֵׁמֹת מִבֶּן עֶשְׂרִים שָׁנָה וָמַעְלָה כֹּל יֹצֵא צָבָא׃

43 *Their numbered ones of the tribe of Naftali: fifty-three thousand, four hundred.*

מג פְּקֻדֵיהֶם לְמַטֵּה נַפְתָּלִי שְׁלֹשָׁה וַחֲמִשִּׁים אֶלֶף וְאַרְבַּע מֵאוֹת׃ פ

44 *These were the numberings that Moshe counted, and [so did] Aharon and the twelve princes of Israel. They were one man each for his fathers' house.*

מד אֵלֶּה הַפְּקֻדִים אֲשֶׁר פָּקַד מֹשֶׁה וְאַהֲרֹן וּנְשִׂיאֵי יִשְׂרָאֵל שְׁנֵים עָשָׂר אִישׁ אִישׁ־אֶחָד לְבֵית־אֲבֹתָיו הָיוּ׃

45 *All the numberings of the Children of Israel were according to their fathers' house, from twenty years old and upward, each one who goes forth into communal service in Israel.*

מה וַיִּהְיוּ כָּל־פְּקוּדֵי בְנֵי־יִשְׂרָאֵל לְבֵית אֲבֹתָם מִבֶּן עֶשְׂרִים שָׁנָה וָמַעְלָה כָּל־יֹצֵא צָבָא בְּיִשְׂרָאֵל׃

46 *All their numbered ones were six hundred and three thousand, five hundred and fifty.*

מו וַיִּהְיוּ כָּל־הַפְּקֻדִים שֵׁשׁ־מֵאוֹת אֶלֶף וּשְׁלֹשֶׁת אֲלָפִים וַחֲמֵשׁ מֵאוֹת וַחֲמִשִּׁים׃

---

say, they stepped forth from the midst of the assembly (see v. 18) and went to the tribe of Shimon; by going to that tribe, they were recognized as belonging to it. After eleven tribes had been counted in this manner, those that remained, who had not yet been counted, of themselves constituted the twelfth tribe; hence, there was no need for them to go to their tribe to be recognized as belonging to it. Accordingly, it does not say here לבני נפתלי but בני נפתלי. This lack of the -ל is a sure sign of the description of an event by an eyewitness.

47 *But the* Levi'im *according to the tribe of their fathers were not allowed to number themselves among them.*	מז וְהַלְוִיִּם לְמַטֵּה אֲבֹתָם לֹא הָתְפָּקְדוּ בְּתוֹכָם: פ
48 *For* God *spoke to Moshe [saying]:*	מח וַיְדַבֵּר יְהוָה אֶל־מֹשֶׁה לֵּאמֹר:

47 **לא התפקדו**. This form is a combination of the התפעל and הָפעל: They were not allowed or were not required to number themselves among the rest of the nation. Not of their own will — because they considered themselves superior to the people — did they stay out of the census. They would have counted themselves together with their brethren, but this was denied to them by God's command, as Scripture now goes on to explain.

48 We have already remarked on verse 2 that the concept of עדה implies a common mission, which is the reason and purpose of the people's unity. Now, the element that unites the Jewish people is none other than God's Torah. This uniting element is to be given visible expression — even during the encampment and the journeying in the wilderness.

The concrete evidence of the revelation of the Torah, which unites Israel, consisted in the Tablets of the Covenant, which later on were joined by a copy of the Written Law itself. The Torah's Dwelling Place — the Tent of Meeting — symbolized the Torah's demands and the reward for fulfilling the Torah. The "Dwelling Place of the Testimony" was the center point about which the Children of Israel encamped in their families and tribes.

However, at the Lawgiving the people were subjected to הגבלה and התקדשות, a distancing and sanctifying boundary. As we explained in our Commentary on *Shemos* (19:10-13 and 19:20-25), this signified that the Torah did not emanate *from* the people, but was given *to* the people; its origin is Divine, not human-earthly. The Torah is the lofty inviolable ideal which, by eternal Divine power, draws to itself the individuals of Israel and the community of Israel; but we can never draw so near to the Torah and stand so close to it as to lay our hands on it and control it.

As the רמב"ן in his commentary (introduction to *Sefer Bemidbar*; *Shemos* 25:1) already remarks, a parallel is drawn between the Lawgiving

49 *Only the tribe of Levi you shall not number and you shall not take up their total number among the Children of Israel.*

מט אַךְ אֶת־מַטֵּה לֵוִי לֹא תִפְקֹד וְאֶת־רֹאשָׁם לֹא תִשָּׂא בְּתוֹךְ בְּנֵי יִשְׂרָאֵל׃

and the Dwelling Place. Thus, later, when the Torah dwelled in Israel's midst, ה׳ בָם סִינַי בַּקֹּדֶשׁ (*Tehillim* 68:18): The Shechinah rested in Israel's midst, and Sinai could be found in the Sanctuary. Then, too, the Torah and its Sanctuary, the "Dwelling Place of the Testimony," rested in an area apart from the people. The Dwelling Place was a separate center point, around which Israel encamped מנגד סביב (below, 2:2): They camped around it at a distance, from which they directed their hearts to the center. This circle, which surrounded the Tent from afar, kept the Torah as something that remains *given* to us. For the Torah forever draws us to itself, but never merges with us. The Torah rules us and leads us on paths indicated by it.

At the sin of the golden calf, however, the people of Israel turned away precisely from this principle. They overlooked the "given" nature of the Torah, and so they made for themselves a divine "Moshe figure" of their own devising.

There was one tribe that remained faithful to God and to His Torah, defending the inviolability of the Torah against the rest of the nation, even against its own kin. This tribe, the tribe of Levi, is now appointed "guardian" of the Torah, and for this purpose is to remain apart from the rest of the nation. Levi does not belong to the community, but solely to the Testimony, which is the ruling soul of the community. For this reason the tribe of Levi is not to be counted בתוך בני ישראל, as already stated in the previous verse, and as will be explained in greater detail in the verses that follow.

49 **אך את מטה לוי לא תפקד וגו׳ בתוך בני ישראל**. Levi's individual members shall not receive their mission in the framework of the community; ואת ראשם לא תשא וגו׳: and the tribe as a whole shall be separate from the community. For the *Levi'im* do not belong to the עדה, but to the עדות.

נ וְאַתָּה הַפְקֵד אֶת־הַלְוִיִּם עַל־
מִשְׁכַּן הָעֵדֻת וְעַל כָּל־כֵּלָיו וְעַל
כָּל־אֲשֶׁר־לוֹ הֵמָּה יִשְׂאוּ אֶת־
הַמִּשְׁכָּן וְאֶת־כָּל־כֵּלָיו וְהֵם
יְשָׁרְתֻהוּ וְסָבִיב לַמִּשְׁכָּן יַחֲנוּ׃

נא וּבִנְסֹעַ הַמִּשְׁכָּן יוֹרִידוּ אֹתוֹ הַלְוִיִּם
וּבַחֲנֹת הַמִּשְׁכָּן יָקִימוּ אֹתוֹ הַלְוִיִּם
וְהַזָּר הַקָּרֵב יוּמָת׃

50 *And you shall appoint the* Levi'im *over the Dwelling Place of the Testimony, over all its utensils and over all that belongs to it; they are to carry the Dwelling Place and all its utensils and they are to minister to it, and they shall camp around the Dwelling Place.*

51 *When the Dwelling Place journeys forth, the* Levi'im *are to take it down, and when the Dwelling Place comes to rest, the* Levi'im *are to set it up; any outsider who comes near is liable to the death penalty.*

---

50 **ואתה הפקד וגו׳**. Just as they serve and represent the Torah in their personal lives, so are they to serve and represent the Sanctuary of the Torah. The service consists in bearing the Sanctuary and its furnishings when the nation is on the march, and in reassembling the Sanctuary when the nation sets up camp — ישרתהו. The representation consists in camping around the משכן and guarding it — וסביב למשכן יחנו.

51 **והזר הקרב יומת**: מיתה בידי שמים.

In the preceding verse, it says: ואתה הפקד את הלוים. Only as a result of an appointment by God's command were even the לויים allowed to approach the service of the משכן. Whoever was not *obligated* to do so was unauthorized to do so and was considered a זר. Even a לוי was authorized to perform only the particular task allotted to him, and it was forbidden for a לוי to transfer from one task to another: נקיטינן משורר ששיער בשל חבירו במיתה (*Arachin* 11b). Moreover, just as the לוי was obligated to abstain from the service of the כהונה, the כהן was prohibited from the service of the לויים (ibid.).

Thus, the whole service of the משכן was stamped with the character of being prescribed, ordained and inviolable. Indeed, the whole purpose of the separation of the משכן and the setting apart of its servants was

52 *The Children of Israel shall camp, each man near his [own] camp and each one near his [own] standard, according to their serving divisions.*

נב וְחָנ֖וּ בְּנֵ֣י יִשְׂרָאֵ֑ל אִ֤ישׁ עַל־מַחֲנֵ֙הוּ֙ וְאִ֥ישׁ עַל־דִּגְל֖וֹ לְצִבְאֹתָֽם׃

to constantly remind Israel of this character of the Service of the Sanctuary (see Commentary below, 3:10).

52 **וחנו בני ישראל וגו׳**. As we will see in the next chapter, the people encamped and journeyed in four camps. Each camp consisted of three tribes, one of which was the camp leader. There was the camp of Yehudah, the camp of Reuven, the camp of Efrayim, and the camp of Dan.

Although the next chapter expressly mentions only the standards of the leading tribes — דגל מחנה יהודה, דגל מחנה ראובן, and so on — nevertheless, in verse 2 it says: איש על דגלו באתת לבית אבתם, which implies that each tribe had its own flag. In our verse, too, it is clear that מחנהו and דגלו are not identical; rather, what it says here is: each man shall encamp near his own camp and, in the camp, each man by his flag — i.e., near his tribe. So it is also explained in *Bemidbar Rabbah* (2:6): Each tribe had its own flag, and the color of the flag corresponded with the color of the stone in the חושן on which the name of that tribe was engraved.

Perhaps there is also a difference, in verse 2 of the next chapter, between דגלו and אתת לבית אבתם. Perhaps דגל denotes the standard of the camp, the large flag of the leading tribe, to which two other tribes were attached, whereas אתת לבית אבתם are the smaller flags of each individual tribe.

In any case, it appears that ואיש על דגלו of our verse can denote only the tribal flags; accordingly, לצבאתם would denote the still smaller groups of families. Also, in verse 2 of the next chapter, the accentuation supports the first interpretation [viz., that דגל denotes a tribal flag].

דגל is apparently related to דקל, which is the Aramaic term for the palm tree, which is a tall tree that rises straight up. The branches at the top of the דקל are visible far away. In this respect they resemble a military standard. Thus, pillars of smoke rising high up are likewise called תִּימְרוֹת עָשָׁן, "palms of smoke" (*Yo'el* 3:3; *Shir Ha-Shirim* 3:6).

53 *But the* Levi'im *shall camp around the Dwelling Place of the Testimony, so that no wrath shall come upon the community of the Children of Israel, and the* Levi'im *shall keep the charge of the Dwelling Place of the Testimony.*

נג וְהַלְוִיִּם יַחֲנוּ סָבִיב לְמִשְׁכַּן הָעֵדֻת
וְלֹא־יִהְיֶה קֶצֶף עַל־עֲדַת בְּנֵי
יִשְׂרָאֵל וְשָׁמְרוּ הַלְוִיִּם אֶת־
מִשְׁמֶרֶת מִשְׁכַּן הָעֵדוּת׃

54 *The Children of Israel did so; according to all that* God *had commanded Moshe, thus did they do.*

נד וַיַּעֲשׂוּ בְּנֵי יִשְׂרָאֵל כְּכֹל אֲשֶׁר צִוָּה
יְהוָה אֶת־מֹשֶׁה כֵּן עָשׂוּ׃ פ שלישי

2 1 God *spoke to Moshe and Aharon, saying:*

ב א וַיְדַבֵּר יְהוָה אֶל־מֹשֶׁה וְאֶל־אַהֲרֹן
לֵאמֹר׃

2 *Every man shall camp next to his*

ב אִישׁ עַל־דִּגְלוֹ בְאֹתֹת לְבֵית

53 **ולא יהיה קצף וגו'**. Cf. below, 17:11 and 18:5. This was the essence of the rebellion of Korach: He denied the Divine origin of the order ordained in the Torah, and thus he denied the inviolability of the Torah (see Commentary below, 16:4). Conversely, the law that an unauthorized person may not approach the Sanctuary of the Torah is intended to instill this belief [in the inviolability of the Torah] in the people's hearts forever.

54 **ויעשו וגו'**: שריחקו עצמן מן המשכן ונתנו מקום ללוים לחנות סביב למשכן (*Bemidbar Rabbah* 1, end). They drew back from the Sanctuary and made room for the *Levi'im* to encamp around the Sanctuary.

CHAPTER 2

1-2 At the end of the preceding chapter, it says that the Children of Israel are to be grouped into camps, whereas the *Levi'im* and the Dwelling Place of the Testimony are to be apart from them. These instructions will now be discussed in detail.

The order to count the nation according to tribes and families was given to Moshe alone, whereas the directive of this chapter is given to

אֲבֹתָם יַחֲנוּ בְּנֵי יִשְׂרָאֵל מִנֶּגֶד סָבִיב לְאֹהֶל־מוֹעֵד יַחֲנוּ׃

standard, each designated with the insignia of their fathers' house, [so] shall the Children of Israel camp; they shall camp at some distance around the Tent of Appointed Meeting.

Moshe and to Aharon: They both are commanded to group the counted tribes into camps, located at a distance around the Dwelling Place of the Testimony. This indicates that the grouping into camps around the Tent of the Testimony is the purpose of the entire census.

We have already analyzed (Commentary, *Vayikra* 11:1 and 13:1) the nature of the *mitzvos* communicated to both Moshe and Aharon. Their importance goes beyond theoretical knowledge and practical fulfillment, which are represented by Moshe. Rather, their great importance is primarily in educating individuals for observance of the *mitzvos*, which is the life mission of the כהן.

Similarly, the mitzvah outlined here directs every individual to his family and tribe, and every tribe to its camp; and all the camps encamp and journey מנגד סביב לאהל מועד. The directive is given both to Moshe and to Aharon, which indicates its great importance for the education of the individuals, the families, and the tribes to the Torah.

The flag of the prince, the head of the camp, would fly מנגד סביב — at a distance but within the circle of the Sanctuary. To this flag, the prince would gather his tribes; each tribe would gather its families, and each family its members. Thus the prince would proclaim to himself, to his tribes, to his families, and to all the members of the families, to every man and woman, child and infant: The משכן העדות (above, 1:53) is the אהל מועד (v. 2); the place of the Testimony is the place of the common mission, which unites them all.

Thus, the Testimony — attested to by God — becomes the life soul of the entire people. All of them — the head of the camp and the prince of the tribe, together with the infant babbling in the midst of his family — camp מנגד סביב לעדות. For all of them, the Testimony is the most exalted holy of holies (מנגד); at the same time, it is near to them all, embracing all of them and drawing them to itself with great power (סביב).

3 *Those camping in the front, toward the east: the standard of the camp of Yehudah according to their serving divisions, and the prince of the sons of Yehudah: Nachshon, son of Amminadav.*

ג וְהַחֹנִים֙ קֵ֣דְמָה מִזְרָ֔חָה דֶּ֛גֶל מַחֲנֵ֥ה יְהוּדָ֖ה לְצִבְאֹתָ֑ם וְנָשִׂיא֙ לִבְנֵ֣י יְהוּדָ֔ה נַחְשׁ֖וֹן בֶּן־עַמִּינָדָֽב׃

4 *His division and their numbered ones: seventy-four thousand, six hundred.*

ד וּצְבָא֖וֹ וּפְקֻדֵיהֶ֑ם אַרְבָּעָ֧ה וְשִׁבְעִ֛ים אֶ֖לֶף וְשֵׁ֥שׁ מֵאֽוֹת׃

The foregoing explains why, above (1:50 and 53), the משכן is called "משכן העדת," whereas here, in the chapter that establishes the positions of the camps, it is called "אהל מועד." In itself it is משכן העדת, the Dwelling Place of the Testimony; for the people it is אהל מועד, which, before their very eyes, travels with them wherever they go, the center of the common mission which unites them all (יחד ,יעד :מועד).

איש על דגלו באתת וגו׳. As we have stated (above, 1:52), the accentuation connects באתת with דגלו. The flag of each בית אב — i.e., the flag of each tribe — had an אות, a distinguishing emblem, representing the tribe. According to *Bemidbar Rabbah* (here), each tribal flag was of the same color as that tribe's stone on the חושן, and each tribal flag had a characteristic emblem on it. The Midrash even identifies the distinctive emblem of each tribe.

מנגד: at a distance of a מיל, corresponding to the two thousand cubits of תחום שבת, so that they could go to the אהל מועד on Shabbos (*Bemidbar Rabbah* 2:9). So we find in *Yehoshua* 3:4.

3 **קדמה**: the front of the entire camp of Israel. The entrance to the אהל מועד also faced to the east: קדמה מזרחה. There, in the east, was the position of the camp of Yehudah. This camp would be the first to break camp and would lead the way.

4 **וצבאו ופקדיהם**. The men of each tribe are called here and in the following verses: צבאו and פקדיהם; or, as in the three following tribes: צבאו and פקדיו. On the one hand, as a whole they are called צבא הנשיא; they obey his orders, and this makes them a **צבא** (see Commentary, *Bereshis* 2:1).

5 *Those camping next to him: the tribe of Yissachar; and the prince of the sons of Yissachar: Nesan'el, son of Tzu'ar.*	ה וְהַחֹנִ֥ים עָלָ֖יו מַטֵּ֣ה יִשָּׂשכָ֑ר וְנָשִׂיא֙ לִבְנֵ֣י יִשָּׂשכָ֔ר נְתַנְאֵ֖ל בֶּן־צוּעָֽר׃
6 *His division and its numbered ones: fifty-four thousand, four hundred.*	ו וּצְבָא֖וֹ וּפְקֻדָ֑יו אַרְבָּעָ֧ה וַחֲמִשִּׁ֛ים אֶ֖לֶף וְאַרְבַּ֥ע מֵאֽוֹת׃
7 *The tribe of Zevulun; and the prince of the sons of Zevulun: Eli'av, son of Chelon.*	ז מַטֵּ֖ה זְבוּלֻ֑ן וְנָשִׂיא֙ לִבְנֵ֣י זְבוּלֻ֔ן אֱלִיאָ֖ב בֶּן־חֵלֹֽן׃
8 *His division and its numbered ones: fifty-seven thousand, four hundred.*	ח וּצְבָא֖וֹ וּפְקֻדָ֑יו שִׁבְעָ֧ה וַחֲמִשִּׁ֛ים אֶ֖לֶף וְאַרְבַּ֥ע מֵאֽוֹת׃
9 *All the numbered ones belonging to the camp of Yehudah: one hundred eighty-six thousand, four hundred, according to their serving divisions; they shall journey forth first.*	ט כָּל־הַפְּקֻדִ֞ים לְמַחֲנֵ֣ה יְהוּדָ֗ה מְאַ֨ת אֶ֜לֶף וּשְׁמֹנִ֨ים אֶ֜לֶף וְשֵֽׁשֶׁת־אֲלָפִ֛ים וְאַרְבַּע־מֵא֖וֹת לְצִבְאֹתָ֑ם רִאשֹׁנָ֖ה יִסָּֽעוּ׃ ס

On the other hand, he and they must bear in mind that they are פקודים: Before coming under his command, they had already been counted. This count was not for the purpose of obedience to the נשיא; rather, they were counted for their tribe and for the nation as a whole. They belong to themselves and to the mission of their tribe and nation. Their obedience to the נשיא is only for the sake of accomplishing this mission; his orders are binding only for the sake of this mission.

Thus, the addition of ופקדיו, ופקדיהם limits the concept of צבאו and assures all the members of the צבא an inalienable independence. That is why, in the majority of cases here, it says וצבאו ופקדיהם. The possessive suffix of פקודים is in the plural; the צבא, then, is considered a plurality consisting of a multitude of individuals. What requires further investi-

10 *The standard of the camp of Reuven, toward the south, according to their serving divisions; and the prince of the sons of Reuven: Elitzur, son of Shedei'ur.*

י דֶּגֶל מַחֲנֵה רְאוּבֵן תֵּימָנָה לְצִבְאֹתָם וְנָשִׂיא לִבְנֵי רְאוּבֵן אֱלִיצוּר בֶּן־שְׁדֵיאוּר׃

11 *His division and its numbered ones: forty-six thousand, five hundred.*

יא וּצְבָאוֹ וּפְקֻדָיו שִׁשָּׁה וְאַרְבָּעִים אֶלֶף וַחֲמֵשׁ מֵאוֹת׃

12 *Those camping next to him: the tribe of Shimon; and the prince of the sons of Shimon: Shelumi'el, son of Tzurishaddai.*

יב וְהַחוֹנִם עָלָיו מַטֵּה שִׁמְעוֹן וְנָשִׂיא לִבְנֵי שִׁמְעוֹן שְׁלֻמִיאֵל בֶּן־צוּרִישַׁדָּי׃

13 *His division and their numbered ones: fifty-nine thousand, three hundred.*

יג וּצְבָאוֹ וּפְקֻדֵיהֶם תִּשְׁעָה וַחֲמִשִּׁים אֶלֶף וּשְׁלֹשׁ מֵאוֹת׃

14 *And the tribe of Gad; and the prince of the sons of Gad: Elyasaf, son of Re'u'el.*

יד וּמַטֵּה גָּד וְנָשִׂיא לִבְנֵי גָד אֶלְיָסָף בֶּן־רְעוּאֵל׃

---

gation, however, is why, in the cases of the tribes of Yissachar, Zevulun and Reuven, צבא is considered a single unit: צבאו ופקדיו.

14 The רמב"ן points out that, above (1:14), the father of Elyasaf, the prince of the tribe of Gad, is called דעואל whereas here he is called רעואל. The רמב"ן explains this discrepancy — the like of which occurs not infrequently in Scripture — as follows:

People's names are not merely sounds that identify them; names have meaning. Hence, a name that expresses a certain idea is commonly interchanged with a different but synonymous name. Thus, one person is commonly called by two names similar in their meaning. The name זֶרַח (*Divrei Ha-Yamim* I, 4:24) is interchangeable with the name צוחר (*Bereshis* 46:10), for both names denote splendor and radiance. Thus, too, דעואל and רעואל, which mean: to direct one's mind (דעת) or thoughts (רעיון) to God. (See also our Commentary on *Bereshis* 36:1.)

15 *His division and their numbered ones: forty-five thousand, six hundred and fifty.*

טו וּצְבָאוֹ וּפְקֻדֵיהֶם חֲמִשָּׁה וְאַרְבָּעִים אֶלֶף וְשֵׁשׁ מֵאוֹת וַחֲמִשִּׁים׃

16 *All the numbered ones belonging to the camp of Reuven: one hundred fifty-one thousand, four hundred and fifty according to their serving divisions; they shall journey forth second.*

טז כָּל־הַפְּקֻדִים לְמַחֲנֵה רְאוּבֵן מְאַת אֶלֶף וְאֶחָד וַחֲמִשִּׁים אֶלֶף וְאַרְבַּע־מֵאוֹת וַחֲמִשִּׁים לְצִבְאֹתָם וּשְׁנִיִּם יִסָּעוּ׃ ס

17 *Then the Tent of Appointed Meeting shall journey forth, the camp of the* Levi'im *in the midst of the camp; even as they camp, so shall they journey, everyone in his position, according to their standards.*

יז וְנָסַע אֹהֶל־מוֹעֵד מַחֲנֵה הַלְוִיִּם בְּתוֹךְ הַמַּחֲנֹת כַּאֲשֶׁר יַחֲנוּ כֵּן יִסָּעוּ אִישׁ עַל־יָדוֹ לְדִגְלֵיהֶם׃ ס

17 **ונסע אהל מועד**: אף על פי שנסע אהל מועד הוא. Even after it was dismantled and even in transit on the journeys, the Dwelling Place of the Testimony remained the center of the national mission; the camps were still considered מחנה ישראל, such that קדשים קלים could be eaten in them. Even after the אהל מועד had been dismantled, the place still enclosed by the curtains retained קדושת עזרה; hence קדשי קדשים could still be eaten there. Even on the journeys, מצורעים were banned from מחנות ישראל, and זבים were banned from מחנה לוייה; see below, 5:2 and 3. (See *Menachos* 95a; *Zevachim* 61b, 116b-117a and תוספות there.)

כאשר יחנו כן יסעו. On the journeys, too, the arrangement of the camps was the same: the אהל מועד, surrounded by *Levi'im*, in the center; the camp of Yehudah in the lead, at an appropriate distance from the משכן; the camp of Reuven on the right; the camp of Dan on the left; and the camp of Efrayim in the rear. Also according to the view that the camps would travel in one straight line (see Commentary below, 10:25), the same order was kept, the various tribes keeping in the groups ordered here and following in the same succession, with the אהל מועד entrusted to the *Levi'im* in the center of the line.

18 *The standard of the camp of Efrayim according to their serving divisions toward the west; and the prince of the sons of Efrayim: Elishama, son of Ammihud.*

יח דֶּגֶל מַחֲנֵה אֶפְרַיִם לְצִבְאֹתָם יָמָּה
וְנָשִׂיא לִבְנֵי אֶפְרַיִם אֱלִישָׁמָע בֶּן־
עַמִּיהוּד׃

19 *His division and their numbered ones: forty thousand, five hundred.*

יט וּצְבָאוֹ וּפְקֻדֵיהֶם אַרְבָּעִים אֶלֶף
וַחֲמֵשׁ מֵאוֹת׃

20 *Next to him the tribe of Menashe; and the prince of the sons of Menashe: Gamli'el, son of Pedah-tzur.*

כ וְעָלָיו מַטֵּה מְנַשֶּׁה וְנָשִׂיא לִבְנֵי
מְנַשֶּׁה גַּמְלִיאֵל בֶּן־פְּדָהצוּר׃

21 *His division and their numbered ones: thirty-two thousand, two hundred.*

כא וּצְבָאוֹ וּפְקֻדֵיהֶם שְׁנַיִם וּשְׁלֹשִׁים
אֶלֶף וּמָאתָיִם׃

22 *And the tribe of Binyamin; and the prince of the sons of Binyamin: Avidan, son of Gid'oni.*

כב וּמַטֵּה בִּנְיָמִן וְנָשִׂיא לִבְנֵי בִנְיָמִן
אֲבִידָן בֶּן־גִּדְעֹנִי׃

23 *His division and their numbered ones: thirty-five thousand, four hundred.*

כג וּצְבָאוֹ וּפְקֻדֵיהֶם חֲמִשָּׁה וּשְׁלֹשִׁים
אֶלֶף וְאַרְבַּע מֵאוֹת׃

24 *All the numbered ones belonging to the camp of Efrayim: one hundred eight thousand, one hundred according to their serving divisions; they shall journey forth third.*

כד כָּל־הַפְּקֻדִים לְמַחֲנֵה אֶפְרַיִם
מְאַת אֶלֶף וּשְׁמֹנַת־אֲלָפִים וּמֵאָה
לְצִבְאֹתָם וּשְׁלִשִׁים יִסָּעוּ׃ ס

25 *The standard of the camp of Dan to the north according to their serving divisions; and the prince of the sons of Dan: Achi'ezer, son of Ammishaddai.*

כה דֶּגֶל מַחֲנֵה דָן צָפֹנָה לְצִבְאֹתָם
וְנָשִׂיא לִבְנֵי דָן אֲחִיעֶזֶר בֶּן־
עַמִּישַׁדָּי׃

26 *His division and their numbered ones: sixty-two thousand, seven hundred.*

כו וּצְבָא֖וֹ וּפְקֻדֵיהֶ֑ם שְׁנַ֧יִם וְשִׁשִּׁ֛ים אֶ֖לֶף וּשְׁבַ֥ע מֵאֽוֹת׃

27 *Those camping next to him: the tribe of Asher; and the prince of the sons of Asher: Pag'i'el, son of Ochran.*

כז וְהַחֹנִ֥ים עָלָ֖יו מַטֵּ֣ה אָשֵׁ֑ר וְנָשִׂיא֙ לִבְנֵ֣י אָשֵׁ֔ר פַּגְעִיאֵ֖ל בֶּן־עָכְרָֽן׃

28 *His division and their numbered ones: forty-one thousand, five hundred.*

כח וּצְבָא֖וֹ וּפְקֻדֵיהֶ֑ם אֶחָ֧ד וְאַרְבָּעִ֛ים אֶ֖לֶף וַחֲמֵ֥שׁ מֵאֽוֹת׃

29 *And the tribe of Naftali; and the prince of the sons of Naftali: Achira, son of Einan.*

כט וּמַטֵּ֖ה נַפְתָּלִ֑י וְנָשִׂיא֙ לִבְנֵ֣י נַפְתָּלִ֔י אֲחִירַ֖ע בֶּן־עֵינָֽן׃

30 *His division and their numbered ones: fifty-three thousand, four hundred.*

ל וּצְבָא֖וֹ וּפְקֻדֵיהֶ֑ם שְׁלֹשָׁ֧ה וַחֲמִשִּׁ֛ים אֶ֖לֶף וְאַרְבַּ֥ע מֵאֽוֹת׃

31 *All the numbered ones belonging to the tribe of Dan: one hundred fifty-seven thousand, six hundred; they shall journey forth last, according to their standards.*

לא כָּל־הַפְּקֻדִים֙ לְמַחֲנֵ֣ה דָ֔ן מְאַ֣ת אֶ֗לֶף וְשִׁבְעָ֧ה וַחֲמִשִּׁ֛ים אֶ֖לֶף וְשֵׁ֣שׁ מֵא֑וֹת לָאַחֲרֹנָ֥ה יִסְע֖וּ לְדִגְלֵיהֶֽם׃ פ

32 *These are the numbered ones of the Children of Israel according to their fathers' houses. All the numbered ones of the camps according to their serving divisions: six hundred three thousand, five hundred and fifty.*

לב אֵ֛לֶּה פְּקוּדֵ֥י בְנֵֽי־יִשְׂרָאֵ֖ל לְבֵ֣ית אֲבֹתָ֑ם כָּל־פְּקוּדֵ֤י הַֽמַּחֲנֹת֙ לְצִבְאֹתָ֔ם שֵׁשׁ־מֵא֤וֹת אֶ֙לֶף֙ וּשְׁלֹ֣שֶׁת אֲלָפִ֔ים וַחֲמֵ֥שׁ מֵא֖וֹת וַחֲמִשִּֽׁים׃

33 *The* Levi'im *were not directed to number themselves among the Children of Israel, [it was] as* God *had commanded Moshe.*

לג וְהַ֨לְוִיִּ֔ם לֹ֣א הָתְפָּקְד֔וּ בְּת֖וֹךְ בְּנֵ֣י יִשְׂרָאֵ֑ל כַּאֲשֶׁ֛ר צִוָּ֥ה יְהֹוָ֖ה אֶת־מֹשֶֽׁה׃

34 *The Children of Israel did so. According to all that* God *had commanded Moshe, so did they camp next to their standards, and so did they journey, each one according to his families, according to his fathers' house.*

לד וַיַּעֲשׂוּ בְּנֵי יִשְׂרָאֵל כְּכֹל אֲשֶׁר־צִוָּה יְהוָה אֶת־מֹשֶׁה כֵּן־חָנוּ לְדִגְלֵיהֶם וְכֵן נָסָעוּ אִישׁ לְמִשְׁפְּחֹתָיו עַל־בֵּית אֲבֹתָיו: פ רביעי

34 **ויעשו בני ישראל וגו'**. If we picture to ourselves the grouping of the Jewish people according to camps as directed in these verses, we will see, in the front, to the east, under the standard of Yehudah, the tribes of Yehudah, Yissachar and Zevulun. To the right, in the south, under the standard of Reuven, are the tribes of Reuven, Shimon and Gad. To the left, in the north, under the standard of Dan, are the tribes of Dan, Asher and Naftali. In the rear, opposite Yehudah, under the standard of Efrayim, are the tribes of Efrayim, Menashe and Binyamin.

Each of the three tribes of the camp of Yehudah was noted for two qualities. Already the patriarch Ya'akov, on his deathbed (*Bereshis* 49:8-10), visualized Yehudah as the leader striding at the head, with both שבט and מחוקק — i.e., with a *ruler*'s scepter and a *lawmaker*'s stylus. Yissachar was the tribe of *agriculture*, with sufficient leisure also to engage in *learning* (ibid. 49:14-15). Zevulun (ibid. 49:13) was the tribe of *commerce*; at the same time, according to the Song of Devorah (*Shoftim* 5:14), his sons produced *literature*, מֹשְׁכִים בְּשֵׁבֶט סֹפֵר. Thus, the camp of Yehudah, which traveled in the lead, united all the basic elements on which the material and spiritual welfare of the nation depends: the scepter and the law, agriculture and scholarship, commerce and literature.

These two factors, the spiritual and the material, *united* in the leading camp, are *divided* into two subordinate camps, which follow the leading camp on either side.

Reuven, Shimon and Gad comprise Yehudah's right hand, as it were. Reuven is endowed with all the intellectual gifts and with a keen sense of justice, but the softness of his character makes him unfit for national leadership. Assigned to flank him are Shimon, the impetuous avenger of honor, and Gad, the avenger of unprovoked attacks (see *Bereshis* 49:3-7 and 19). These, then, are the attributes represented by the tribes on Yehudah's right: the courage to fend off insults and attacks, but all under the aegis of gentle mercy.

Marching at Yehudah's left were Dan, the tribe of adroit cunning (ibid. 49:16-17); Asher, representing refinement of taste (ibid. 49:20; cf. חמרא וריחני פקחין, *Yoma* 76b); and Naftali (Bereshis 49:21), representing eloquence. Thus, on the left side, under the aegis of Dan, there was rich development in the direction of spiritual creativity, just as on the right side, under the aegis of Reuven, there was development in the direction of strength and force.

The tribes camped to the west, under the standard of Efrayim, opposite the camp of Yehudah in the east, were Efrayim, Menashe and Binyamin. Their national significance is not characterized as clearly as that of the other tribes. Actually, Efrayim and Menashe together represent the tribe of Yosef. But what Ya'akov said on his deathbed with regard to Yosef (ibid. 49:22ff.) refers to Yosef personally, more than to the tribe. What Ya'akov said (ibid. 48:19) about Efrayim and Menashe indicates an unfolding of power; particularly of Efrayim, Ya'akov said that he would become very great and that his descendants would become מלא הגוים, which we (ibid.) took to mean that Efrayim would become the "armor" reinforcing the defenses of the other tribes.

Thus, in the camp of Efrayim we should look for *strength* and *courage*, which, for the national well-being, were positioned facing the camp of Yehudah in the lead. Yehudah was in the east and Efrayim in the west. Thus, too, the Song of Asaf (*Tehillim* 80:2-3) sees Israel's salvation as depending on the achievements of Yosef. Asaf prays: רֹעֵה יִשְׂרָאֵל הַאֲזִינָה נֹהֵג כַּצֹּאן יוֹסֵף יֹשֵׁב הַכְּרֻבִים הוֹפִיעָה, לִפְנֵי אֶפְרַיִם וּבִנְיָמִן וּמְנַשֶּׁה עוֹרְרָה אֶת־גְּבוּרָתֶךָ וּלְכָה לִישֻׁעָתָה לָּנוּ; "O Shepherd of Israel, incline Your ear! You Who leads Yosef like a flock, You Who are enthroned upon the cherubim, shine forth! Before Efrayim and Binyamin and Menashe [the very tribes of the camp of Efrayim], rouse Your omnipotence and come to our aid!" (cf. Commentary there).

Later in our history, instead of complementing Yehudah, the House of Yosef came into conflict with Yehudah and usurped the crown of leadership; it planted its standard not behind Yehudah, but at the head of the nation. This spelled disaster and brought about the nation's downfall. Estranged from the Testimony and from its Dwelling Place, the House of Yosef perished, dragging down to ruin with it ten of the twelve tribes of Israel.

3 1 *And these were the descendants of Aharon and Moshe on the day that* God *spoke with Moshe on Mount Sinai.*	**ג** א וְאֵלֶּה תּוֹלְדֹת אַהֲרֹן וּמֹשֶׁה בְּיוֹם דִּבֶּר יְהוָה אֶת־מֹשֶׁה בְּהַר סִינָי׃
2 *These are the names of the sons of Aharon: Nadav, the firstborn, and Avihu, Elazar and Isamar.*	ב וְאֵלֶּה שְׁמוֹת בְּנֵי־אַהֲרֹן הַבְּכֹר ׀ נָדָב וַאֲבִיהוּא אֶלְעָזָר וְאִיתָמָר׃

Bemidbar Rabbah, too, characterizes the four camps in accordance with their national significance (see there, 2:10).

CHAPTER 3

1 The Children of Israel have already been counted as the עדה, the community, and the *Levi'im* — as the guardians of the עדות — are about to be counted. First, however, Moshe and Aharon are mentioned, those who are not among the counted but are the counters. In addition, the members of Aharon's family are mentioned; for Aharon's descendants are not actually *Levi'im*, but form a special national group: כהנים. It must be established that only two of Aharon's sons — Elazar and Isamar — are to carry on their father's כהונה; hence, forevermore, only those who descend from either Elazar or Isamar are fit for the כהונה.

It is significant that although Scripture refers also to the תולדות of Moshe, his sons are not named. For in these chapters on censuses, only those who hold an official public position — נשיאים or כהנים — are *named*. But this man Moshe did not cloak his sons in the mantle of office; he let them fade into the crowd, without any special title or distinction.

ביום דבר וגו'. It was necessary to mention also Nadav and Avihu, to inform us that no priestly families descended from them. But since at the time of the census they had already died, it was necessary here to refer back to an earlier date. When God spoke with Moshe on Mount Sinai, and Aharon and his sons were appointed to the priesthood, Aharon had four sons, all four of whom were consecrated and appointed as priests.

2 The accentuation is unusual. It is as though the report pauses painfully over Nadav, and then over Avihu, and then quickly adds Elazar and Isamar.

3 *These are the names of the sons of Aharon, those who were anointed as priests, who were invested with full authority to minister as priests.*	ג אֵלֶּה שְׁמוֹת בְּנֵי אַהֲרֹן הַכֹּהֲנִים הַמְּשֻׁחִים אֲשֶׁר־מִלֵּא יָדָם לְכַהֵן׃
4 *But Nadav and Avihu died before* God *when they brought near strange fire before* God *in the wilderness of Sinai, and they had no sons, and so only Elazar and Isamar remained to minister as priests before the countenance of Aharon, their father.*	ד וַיָּמָת נָדָב וַאֲבִיהוּא לִפְנֵי יְהוָה בְּהַקְרִבָם אֵשׁ זָרָה לִפְנֵי יְהוָה בְּמִדְבַּר סִינַי וּבָנִים לֹא־הָיוּ לָהֶם וַיְכַהֵן אֶלְעָזָר וְאִיתָמָר עַל־פְּנֵי אַהֲרֹן אֲבִיהֶם׃ פ
5 God *spoke to Moshe, saying:*	ה וַיְדַבֵּר יְהוָה אֶל־מֹשֶׁה לֵּאמֹר׃

4 **וימת נדב וגו׳** (see Commentary, *Vayikra* 10:1-2).

ובנים לא היו להם. Had sons been born to them after they had been appointed כהנים, these would have become כהנים by birth, and the כהונה would have been a legacy bequeathed also in the families of Nadav and Avihu. But they left no sons when they died; hence ויכהן אלעזר ואיתמר על פני אהרן אביהם.

We have already noted (Commentary, *Bereshis* 16:12) that the expression "על פני" is often used in connection with unpleasant and undesirable feelings and experiences. Here, too, על פני should be understood in this sense. Since his two elder sons died childless, Aharon was left with only Elazar and Isamar to carry on the priesthood.

5 **וידבר וגו׳**. In the preceding verses the family appointed to the priesthood is established; in addition, the death of the two elder sons is mentioned: They died upon the completion of the consecration of the priesthood, at the beginning of the priestly service, because they brought אש זרה before God. They introduced arbitrariness into the priestly service — contrary to the whole meaning of the Service of the Sanctuary. The whole essence of the Service of the Sanctuary is *service*, and as *service* it is based on obedience. It teaches us that our whole mission in life is

6 *Let the tribe of Levi come near, and place it before Aharon the priest; they shall minister to him.*

ו הַקְרֵב֙ אֶת־מַטֵּ֣ה לֵוִ֔י וְהַעֲמַדְתָּ֣ אֹת֔וֹ לִפְנֵ֖י אַהֲרֹ֣ן הַכֹּהֵ֑ן וְשֵׁרְת֖וּ אֹתֽוֹ׃

joyful obedience: joyful submission to God's Will by setting aside all subjective arbitrariness.

As already explained (Commentary above, 1:48ff.), the accomplishment of this mission depends on our remaining ever aware that God's Will, which determines our life mission, expresses itself in the Testimony which rests in the Dwelling Place, and that this expression derives *from* God, came *to* us from God, and remains for us a "given." We also explained (ibid.) that the given nature of the Torah's Testimony is symbolized by its position in the center of the nation and by the distance the nation must keep from this center, and that the *Levi'im* were appointed *guardians* of the Testimony given by God.

Above, however, this guarding of the Sanctuary is described only as flowing from the nature and needs of the Sanctuary, whereas here this guarding is considered in its relation to the כהנים and to the nation. Accordingly, here the relative position of the *Levi'im*, the guardians of the Sanctuary, to the other two national circles — the כהנים and the community — is detailed. First, Scripture outlines the position of the *Levi'im* in relation to the כהנים.

6 **הקרב**. The Testimony of the Torah and its demands have already received a living representative in the כהן. Through the symbolical service of the offerings inside the Sanctuary, as well as by living his whole life outside the Sanctuary in accordance with the laws of the כהונה, the כהן prepares (מכין) and directs (מכונן) the nation (see Commentary, *Bereshis* 14:18) to carry out the Torah's demands.

Preparing the nation for, and educating it to, the Sanctuary is an integral part of the "Levite *guard*"; and the inviolability of the Sanctuary is the starting point of the task of the כהן. The כהן is the foremost guardian of the Testimony of the Torah; he guards it against the nation — and against himself. Hence, the guard that the *Levi'im* keep over the Sanctuary of the Torah is characterized here as assistance to the כהן; it

7 *And they shall keep his charge and the charge of the entire community before the Tent of Appointed Meeting, to perform the Service of the Dwelling Place.*

ז וְשָׁמְרוּ אֶת־מִשְׁמַרְתּוֹ וְאֶת־מִשְׁמֶרֶת כָּל־הָעֵדָה לִפְנֵי אֹהֶל מוֹעֵד לַעֲבֹד אֶת־עֲבֹדַת הַמִּשְׁכָּן׃

is service that helps the כהן fulfill the task assigned to him. Thus, the task of the *Levi'im* is intimately connected with the mission of the כהן: to direct and to educate the people.

It says הקרב, let the *Levi'im* "come near" to you and to Aharon, והעמדת אתו לפני אהרן הכהן. (Cf. *Esther* 4:5, *Daniyel* 1:5, *Shemuel* I, 16:22, *Melachim* I, 1:2, et al. In all these case, עמד לפני denotes personal service.)

ושרתו אתו. In our Commentary on *Shemos* 31:10 we noted the relation of שרת and שרד, and we suggested that שרת always denotes personal service. The שירות frees the other person from work that otherwise he would have had to do himself in order to fulfill his wishes, his duties, etc.

This, then, is the nature of the לוייה, the office of the לוי, as defined here by the two expressions והעמדת אתו לפני וגו׳ and ושרתו אתו: The לוי assists the כהן and participates in his service.

7 **ושמרו את משמרתו**. The guard that the *Levi'im* are to keep is a charge that devolves upon them in the name of the כהנים; at the same time, however, it is also משמרת כל העדה. For the כהנים themselves are nothing but the representatives of the national community in the Sanctuary. The Torah was not given to the כהנים and לויים; it was entrusted to the whole community. It is not the כהנים and the לויים who are to build for the Torah a Sanctuary; rather, ועשו לי מקדש ושכנתי בתוכם (*Shemos* 25:8): the whole community was commanded to build a Sanctuary for the Torah, so that God should dwell בתוכם, among *them*.

Thus, the כהנים and the לויים stand there in the name of the nation; in particular, the watch of the לויים about the Sanctuary must be done on behalf of the nation. For the Torah and its Sanctuary are a sacred charge entrusted to the nation, and the שמירה, the guard, over the Torah — against infringement by others and by themselves — is the foremost duty of the Torah's keepers. Hence, for its own good and to fulfill its duty, the nation sends the לויים to their watch, to guard the Dwelling

8 *They are to be in charge of all the utensils of the Tent of Appointed Meeting and to keep the charge of the Children of Israel to perform the Service of the Dwelling Place.*

ח וְשָׁמְרוּ אֶת־כָּל־כְּלֵי אֹהֶל מוֹעֵד וְאֶת־מִשְׁמֶרֶת בְּנֵי יִשְׂרָאֵל לַעֲבֹד אֶת־עֲבֹדַת הַמִּשְׁכָּן׃

9 *You shall give the* Levi'im *to Aharon and to his sons; they shall be given, [indeed] given to him from among the Children of Israel.*

ט וְנָתַתָּה אֶת־הַלְוִיִּם לְאַהֲרֹן וּלְבָנָיו נְתוּנִם נְתוּנִם הֵמָּה לוֹ מֵאֵת בְּנֵי יִשְׂרָאֵל׃

Place of the Testimony of the Torah against the nation as a whole and against each of its individual members.

This watch must be kept not only against the nation, but even against the כהנים. For the mitzvah of והזר הקרב יומת (above, 1:51) precludes every unauthorized person from officiating as a לוי. It not only bars the people, but also precludes the לויים from encroaching on one another's service; and it warns the כהנים against encroaching on the functions of the לויים. All must keep within the bounds set by the Torah for its keepers. We have already noted this above (ibid.).

לעבד את עבדת המשכן. The לויים are commissioned by the כהן (משמרתו) and by the entire community (משמרת כל העדה) to perform the Service of the Dwelling Place, לעבד את עבדת המשכן. They serve in the Dwelling Place on behalf of Aharon and on behalf of the entire community.

8 **ושמרו את כל כלי אהל מועד**. The ארון, the שולחן, the מנורה and the מזבחות are כלי אהל מועד; they make the משכן the central assembly point where the community finds the common mission that unites all its members. For these furnishings represent the task that is incumbent on Israel (ארון), and they symbolize what is given to every soul and what is required of every soul in accordance with this task (מזבחות, שולחן, מנורה).

The משכן entrusts these כלים to the לויים. At the same time, these כלים are a charge entrusted to the לויים by every individual Jew; they are משמרת בני ישראל; every Jewish soul has a right in them. With this in mind, the לויים are to perform the Service of the Dwelling Place.

9 **ונתתה**. The service of the לויים is performed in the name of the כהנים and the people; nevertheless, the כהן and the community do not control

י וְאֶת־אַהֲרֹן וְאֶת־בָּנָיו תִּפְקֹד
וְשָׁמְרוּ אֶת־כְּהֻנָּתָם וְהַזָּר הַקָּרֵב
יוּמָת׃ פ

10 *You shall appoint Aharon and his sons that they may keep [watch over] their priesthood; any outsider who comes near becomes liable to the death penalty.*

the לויים by some power they possess or by the force of their own will. Rather, ונתתָּה: God ordains it through Moshe. It is by a Divine command, to be carried out by Moshe, that the duties of standing guard over the Sanctuary and ministering to it — duties incumbent upon the community and upon the כהן on the community's behalf — are to be turned over to the לויים. Moshe is to remove the לויים from among the people — or take them as "given" by the people — and give them to the כהנים for this purpose.

Aside from this specific purpose and aside from the duties implicit in this Divine command, the כהנים have no authority over the לויים. נתונם נתונם המה לו — they are "*given*" to him. The position of the לויים in relation to the כהנים does not stem from any general superiority of the כהנים; the relationship between the two goes no further than what is stipulated in this command — in its content and its purpose.

10 **ואת אהרן**. Having been relieved of the responsibility of guarding the Sanctuary, the כהנים were left only with the duty of the כהונה itself. The Sanctuary, like an object requiring safekeeping, was entrusted to the לויים. It was their responsibility to protect it against unauthorized intruders, to care for it on the journeys, and to erect it upon encampment. It was their job to ensure that the Sanctuary was fit and ready to be reassembled as prescribed. The sons of Aharon, on the other hand, were responsible for the כהונה, whose procedures are performed *inside* the Sanctuary. Through these procedures the כהנים give expression to the *preparation and direction* of the people (see Commentary, *Bereshis* 14:18); the כהנים are to direct the people's attention to the demands of the Sanctuary, which seek to be fulfilled in life.

11 God *spoke to Moshe, saying:*

12 *As for Me, lo! I have taken the* Levi'im *from amidst the Children of Israel in place of every firstborn, the opening of a mother's womb, from among the Children of Israel, and the* Levi'im *shall be Mine.*

יא וַיְדַבֵּר יְהֹוָה אֶל־מֹשֶׁה לֵּאמֹר׃

יב וַאֲנִ֞י הִנֵּ֧ה לָקַ֣חְתִּי אֶת־הַלְוִיִּ֗ם מִתּוֹךְ֙ בְּנֵ֣י יִשְׂרָאֵ֔ל תַּ֧חַת כָּל־בְּכ֛וֹר פֶּ֥טֶר רֶ֖חֶם מִבְּנֵ֣י יִשְׂרָאֵ֑ל וְהָ֥יוּ לִ֖י הַלְוִיִּֽם׃

11 The position of the לויים in relation to the community and in relation to the כהנים has just been characterized as based on God's command. This command, which indicates the special relationship of the לויים to God, is now explained in greater detail.

12 **ואני**. It was God Who took the לויים from amidst the people and established a special relationship with them; for, more than all the others, the לויים belong to God.

Such a relationship had formerly existed between the firstborn and God. As we have already explained (Commentary, *Shemos* 13:2), the meaning of the sanctification of the firstborn is as follows: The firstborn son in each family represents the Divine; that is to say, he is responsible for fulfilling God's Will within his family circle. Accordingly, the common element that unites all צבאות ה' depends on the firstborn. The firstborn sons unify all the different groups, turning them into the one united people of God.

When this common element was given symbolical expression through the Sanctuary of the Torah, which dwells in the midst of the people, it was necessary to appoint guards for the Sanctuary. The firstborn, who had already been sanctified unto God, were the automatic candidates, for they were the natural representatives of the common Divine element.

But on the fateful day of the sin of the עגל, the firstborn did not prove themselves as the champions and guardians of the Torah. What was expected of them was done by the לויים; instead of the firstborn, the sons of Levi rallied to do battle לה'. Already then, Moshe exhorted the לויים to hold on to their standing among the people as fighters for the Torah, and promised them that by doing so they would merit God's blessing (see Commentary, *Shemos* 32:29).

13 *For all that is firstborn is Mine; on the day I struck down all the firstborn in the land of Egypt, I sanctified for Myself all that is firstborn in Israel from man to beast; Mine they shall remain; I,* God.

יג כִּ֣י לִי֮ כָּל־בְּכוֹר֒ בְּיוֹם֩ הַכֹּתִ֨י כָל־
בְּכ֜וֹר בְּאֶ֣רֶץ מִצְרַ֗יִם הִקְדַּ֨שְׁתִּי לִ֤י
כָל־בְּכוֹר֙ בְּיִשְׂרָאֵ֔ל מֵאָדָ֖ם עַד־
בְּהֵמָ֑ה לִ֥י יִהְי֖וּ אֲנִ֥י יְהוָֽה׃ פ חמישי

Here, too, we see the לויים taken by God from the midst of the Children of Israel in place of the firstborn and given the vocation והיו לי, to be God's — i.e., to be representatives of His Sanctuary in the midst of the people.

According to what has been said thus far, the guardianship and service assigned to the לויים are משמרת משכן העדות (above, 1:53), משמרת אהרן, and משמרת כל העדה (above, 3:7). That is to say, they are to guard and serve in the name of the Sanctuary, in the name of the כהנים, and in the name of the community. Above all, however, they are to serve בשם ה׳, in the name of God; for they belong to Him. It was He Who appointed them for His Sanctuary and assigned them duties for the sake of this Sanctuary. And were it not for the לויים, these duties would be incumbent on the whole community, on its natural representatives [the firstborn], and on the כהנים.

13 **כי לי כל בכור** — (cf. *Shemos* 13:15).

לי יהיו. With the transfer of the service in the Sanctuary from the firstborn to the *Levi'im*, the consecration of the firstborn does not cease. Despite this transfer, they remain consecrated to God. The transfer only nullifies their status as the nation's representatives in the Sanctuary; their status within the family, however, remains intact, and they continue to represent the family's belonging to God. Likewise, the consecration of the firstborn of בהמה טהורה and the consecration of פטר חמור continue, signifying that the family's food and possessions belong to God. Thus, ר׳ יוחנן expounds לי יהיו as בהוייתן יהו (*Bechoros* 5a); that is to say, the sanctification of the firstborn which started with the exodus from Egypt continued without interruption: קדשו ולא פסקו (ibid. 4b). This contrasts with the view of ריש לקיש that the sanctification of the firstborn resumed with the entry into the Land (see Commentary, *Shemos* 13:5).

14 God *spoke to Moshe in the wilderness of Sinai, saying:*

15 *Number the sons of Levi according to their fathers' house, according to their families; every male from one month old and upward shall you number them.*

יד וַיְדַבֵּ֤ר יְהוָה֙ אֶל־מֹשֶׁ֔ה בְּמִדְבַּ֥ר
סִינַ֖י לֵאמֹֽר׃
טו פְּקֹד֙ אֶת־בְּנֵ֣י לֵוִ֔י לְבֵ֥ית אֲבֹתָ֖ם
לְמִשְׁפְּחֹתָ֑ם כָּל־זָכָ֛ר מִבֶּן־חֹ֥דֶשׁ
וָמַ֖עְלָה תִּפְקְדֵֽם׃

הקדשתי לי כל בכור בישראל. The consecration of the firstborn does not reflect physical reality. Rather, it has moral, national significance of the highest import. Accordingly, בכור בהמה applies only בישראל; the בכור has sanctity only in a sphere of holiness that is exclusively Jewish. If a non-Jew owns a share in the animal — whether in the mother animal or in the young — קדושת בכורה is not applicable: כל זמן שיד נכרי באמצע פטורה מן הבכורה (*Bechoros* 2b).

14 In the preceding verses (5-13) it is stated generally that the *Levi'im* are designated to serve in the Sanctuary. Now they are counted according to their fathers' houses and their families. Each "house" receives as its charge specific parts of the Sanctuary and is assigned its position in the camp around the Dwelling Place.

במדבר סיני. Here, too, as in 1:1 (above), Scripture mentions the site of the census. This mention indicates the significance of this census: It has an inner relation to the Torah, and has no external political significance.

15 **פקד וגו'**. We have already stated (above, 1:2) that the tribe of Levi is analogous to the House of Israel in miniature; like the House of Israel, it, too, is divided into groupings. The sons of Ya'akov formed בתי אבות (tribes), and their sons in turn formed family branches, so that the whole nation was divided into tribes (ראובן, שמעון, לוי, etc.) descended from the sons of Ya'akov, and these tribes in turn were divided into families (משפחת החנכי, משפחת הפלאי, etc.; cf. below, 26:5ff.) descended from the sons of these sons. In the same manner, Levi's three sons (גרשון קהת ומררי) formed three בתי אבות of *Levi'im*, and their sons (לבני, שמעי, etc.) formed the משפחות of the *Levi'im*.

מבן חדש ומעלה תפקדם. The *Levi'im* are counted from the age of one month and upward, when an infant is no longer considered only doubtfully viable. This indicates that their calling as *Levi'im* entails far more than the mere performance of the service assigned to them here. This service — guarding the Sanctuary during the encampments and journeys — is only a logical outgrowth and practical expression of their general calling. For the actual entry into this service, they will be counted again (below, chap. 4), and in that census they will be counted from the age of thirty years and upward. It follows, then, that the census from the age of one month and upward relates to a more general calling, a calling that goes beyond this practical service. It must be a calling that even a youth might be qualified to serve; in any case, it must be a calling for which the individual requires training from earliest childhood and boyhood onward.

Indeed, the tribe of Levi not only guards the Dwelling Place of the Torah, which is made of wood and gold, linen and purple wool, but guards and teaches the Torah itself and defends its observance. The *Levi'im*, then, serve to promote the realization in life of all those ideals embodied in the physical Dwelling Place that was entrusted to their care. (See Moshe's blessing of the tribe of Levi, *Devarim* 33:9-11.)

This general calling devolves upon every male לוי from the first month of his life onward, and his training for it must begin when he first becomes aware of his surroundings.

Besides their service to the Sanctuary building and furnishings, the *Levi'im* also serve *inside the Sanctuary*. These two forms of service differ in character. The service to the Sanctuary building is called "משמרת המשכן," "משמרת אהרן הכהן," and "משמרת כל העדה." Accordingly, it is performed in the name of the Sanctuary, in the name of the כהנים, and in the name of the community. Nevertheless, as we said above (on v. 12), it is performed first and foremost in the name of God. By contrast, the *Levi'im*'s service inside the Sanctuary is performed exclusively in the name of God.

Of the *Levi'im*'s service inside the Sanctuary, it says: ושרת בשם ה׳ אלקיו (*Devarim* 18:7), and our Sages expound: איזהו שירות שבשם הוי אומר זה שירה, "Which service is performed in the name of God and with the Name of God? It is song" (*Arachin* 11a). For *song* is service בשם ה׳ in a dual sense: The singer sings in the name of God and at His bidding, and he pronounces the Name of God with his lips.

16 *Moshe numbered them at the behest of* God, *as he had been commanded.*

טז וַיִּפְקֹד אֹתָם מֹשֶׁה עַל־פִּי יְהֹוָה
כַּאֲשֶׁר צֻוָּה׃

17 *These were the sons of Levi, by their names: Gershon, Kehas and Merari.*

יז וַיִּהְיוּ־אֵלֶּה בְנֵי־לֵוִי בִּשְׁמֹתָם
גֵּרְשׁוֹן וּקְהָת וּמְרָרִי׃

18 *And these are the names of the sons of Gershon, according to their families: Livni and Shim'i.*

יח וְאֵלֶּה שְׁמוֹת בְּנֵי־גֵרְשׁוֹן לְמִשְׁפְּחֹתָם
לִבְנִי וְשִׁמְעִי׃

19 *The sons of Kehas, according to their families: Amram, Yitzhar, Chevron and Uzzi'el.*

יט וּבְנֵי קְהָת לְמִשְׁפְּחֹתָם עַמְרָם
וְיִצְהָר חֶבְרוֹן וְעֻזִּיאֵל׃

20 *The sons of Merari according to their families: Machli and Mushi. These are the families of the* Levi'im *according to their fathers' house.*

כ וּבְנֵי מְרָרִי לְמִשְׁפְּחֹתָם מַחְלִי
וּמוּשִׁי אֵלֶּה הֵם מִשְׁפְּחֹת הַלֵּוִי
לְבֵית אֲבֹתָם׃

Thus do our Sages fathom the deep meaning of the song with which the *Levi'im* accompanied קרבנות הציבור, the communal offerings. David, Asaf, and the sons of Korach produced song that was Divinely inspired. Their song, proceeding from the mouths of the *Levi'im,* is literally שירות בשם ה׳. The singer speaks in the name of God. He says what God Himself would say to us, had He not made the singer His instrument, inspired him with His holy spirit, and placed His Word on the singer's tongue. As the "sweet singer of Israel" says, looking back on his life and work as a singer: רוּחַ ה׳ דִּבֶּר־בִּי וּמִלָּתוֹ עַל־לְשׁוֹנִי, "The spirit of God spoke through me, and His Word was on my tongue" (*Shemuel* II, 23:1-2). At the same time, the singer's influence is by the power of God's Name, which he pronounces with his lips. For this is the whole essence of his song: putting God's Name on all aspects of man and the world; he regards every aspect from the standpoint of this Name (see also Commentary, *Bereshis* 49:22; *Shemos* 15:1).

21 *Of Gershon: the family of the Livni branch and the family of the Shim'i branch. These are the families of the Gershuni house.*	כא לְגֵרְשׁוֹן מִשְׁפַּחַת הַלִּבְנִי וּמִשְׁפַּחַת הַשִּׁמְעִי אֵלֶּה הֵם מִשְׁפְּחֹת הַגֵּרְשֻׁנִּי׃
22 *Their numberings were carried out according to the number of all males from one month old and upward. Their numbered ones were seven thousand, five hundred.*	כב פְּקֻדֵיהֶם בְּמִסְפַּר כָּל־זָכָר מִבֶּן־חֹדֶשׁ וָמָעְלָה פְּקֻדֵיהֶם שִׁבְעַת אֲלָפִים וַחֲמֵשׁ מֵאוֹת׃
23 *The families of the Gershuni house shall camp behind the Dwelling Place, to the west.*	כג מִשְׁפְּחֹת הַגֵּרְשֻׁנִּי אַחֲרֵי הַמִּשְׁכָּן יַחֲנוּ יָמָּה׃

In this service of song in the Sanctuary, even young Levite boys are allowed to participate: אין הקטן נכנס לעזרה לעבודה אלא בשעה שהלוים אומרים בשיר (*Arachin* 13b).

23 **משפחת הגרשני וגו׳**. The *Levi'im* fall into three groups: the sons of Gershon, the sons of Kehas, the sons of Merari.

The sons of Gershon encamp in the west. They are placed in charge of the cherubim-tapestry of the Dwelling Place, the goats'-hair tapestries of the tent-covering, the rams' skins and תחש-skins of the roof, the hangings of the forecourt, and the curtains of the entrances of the Dwelling Place and of the forecourt. In short, they are in charge of the partitions around the Sanctuary and the roof above it.

The sons of Kehas encamp in the south. They are placed in charge of the Ark, the Table, the Menorah, the altars and the utensils required for their service, and the dividing curtain. In short, they are in charge of the Sanctuary furnishings and the dividing curtain.

The sons of Merari encamp in the north. They are placed in charge of the beams, bars, pillars and sockets of the Dwelling Place as well as the pillars and sockets of the forecourt and the accessories for both. In short, they are in charge of the wooden structure of the Sanctuary.

Let us now consider the parts of the Sanctuary and the places assigned to the bearers and keepers of each part. First let us note that the

Sanctuary is divided into three parts: (a) the Dwelling Place, i.e., the tapestries that cover and surround the Sanctuary; (b) the Sanctuary furnishings, which comprise the main content of the Dwelling Place; (c) the beams, i.e., the wooden framework of the Dwelling Place.

The purpose of the ארון, שולחן, מנורה, and מזבח, and the purpose of the acts performed with them, is to lead to God's Presence abiding among us. This is represented by the tapestries of the Dwelling Place woven in the pattern of cherubim, which symbolize God's providence. To the foregoing, the coverings of the tent, of the roof, and the curtains of the forecourt are added as supplementary parts (see Commentary, *Shemos* 26:36). But the essential *dwelling* place is on the side opposite the entrance, as we have noted elsewhere. One thinks of dwellers as residing in the innermost room, the one furthest from the entrance; all the outer rooms lead to this room. The hindmost room is the real interior of the house. Hence, the expression יַרְכְּתֵי הַבַּיִת refers to the innermost room (see Commentary, *Tehillim* 48:3 and 128:3; *Amos* 6:10). Now, since the entrance to the Sanctuary is in the east, the essential part of the משכן is in the west. That is where the קודש הקדשים is located; thus שכינה לעולם במערב (*Bemidbar Rabbah* 2:10). For this reason the bearers of the משכן are directed to encamp in the west.

To the right of the bearers of the משכן, in the south, the side of the light, which is the side of the spiritual life in the Sanctuary, is the place of the bearers of the ארון, שולחן, מנורה, and מזבחות. For the purpose of these furnishings is to cause spiritual life to develop and thrive under the rays of light of God's spirit. Related to these is the פרוכת, the cherubim-curtain, which divides and protects: Its purpose is to guard the ארון — the life soul of the whole people — against the possible degeneration of שולחן and מנורה life (see Commentary, *Shemos* 26:36).

To the left of the bearers of the משכן, in the north, the midnight side which awaits the light, opposite the camp of the ארון, שולחן, מנורה and מזבחות, is the place of the bearers of the קרשים (the beams) and their accessories. As we have seen (ibid.), the cedar beams covered with gold represent the tribes of Israel in the Sanctuary. For the "wood" and "gold" of Israel correspond to the wood and gold of the ארון, שולחן, מנורה and מזבחות — meaning: Israel is to devote its development and strength to the realization of the tasks embodied by these furnishings, which in turn restore to Israel vibrant life and renewed strength, under the protection of the sheltering cherubim (see ibid.). Accordingly, the assigned

24 *The prince of the fathers' house of the Gershuni house [was] Elyasaf, son of La'el.*

25 *The charge of the sons of Gershon in the Tent of Appointed Meeting is the Dwelling Place and the Tent, its covering and the protective curtain of the entrance of the Tent of Appointed Meeting;*

26 *The hangings of the forecourt and the protective curtain of the entrance of the forecourt, which is round about the Dwelling Place and the altar, and its ropes, for all its requirements.*

27 *Of Kehas: the family of the Amrami branch, the family of the Yitzhari branch, the family of the Chevroni branch, and the family of the Uzzi'eli branch. These are the families of the Kehasi house.*

כד וּנְשִׂ֥יא בֵית־אָ֖ב לַגֵּרְשֻׁנִּ֑י אֶלְיָסָ֖ף בֶּן־לָאֵֽל׃

כה וּמִשְׁמֶ֤רֶת בְּנֵֽי־גֵרְשׁוֹן֙ בְּאֹ֣הֶל מוֹעֵ֔ד הַמִּשְׁכָּ֖ן וְהָאֹ֑הֶל מִכְסֵ֕הוּ וּמָסַ֕ךְ פֶּ֖תַח אֹ֥הֶל מוֹעֵֽד׃

כו וְקַלְעֵ֣י הֶֽחָצֵ֗ר וְאֶת־מָסַךְ֙ פֶּ֣תַח הֶֽחָצֵ֔ר אֲשֶׁ֛ר עַל־הַמִּשְׁכָּ֥ן וְעַל־הַמִּזְבֵּ֖חַ סָבִ֑יב וְאֵת֙ מֵֽיתָרָ֔יו לְכֹ֖ל עֲבֹדָתֽוֹ׃ ס

כז וְלִקְהָ֗ת מִשְׁפַּ֤חַת הָֽעַמְרָמִי֙ וּמִשְׁפַּ֣חַת הַיִּצְהָרִ֔י וּמִשְׁפַּ֙חַת֙ הַֽחֶבְרֹנִ֔י וּמִשְׁפַּ֖חַת הָֽעָזִּיאֵלִ֑י אֵ֥לֶּה הֵ֖ם מִשְׁפְּחֹ֥ת הַקְּהָתִֽי׃

place of the bearers of the קרשים is opposite the bearers of the ארון, שולחן, מזבחות and מנורה.

In front of the משכן, in the east, is the camping place of Moshe, Aharon, and his sons. For they are the first to be summoned to enter the Dwelling Place, and they are to represent the Sanctuary of the Torah and mediate between it [the Sanctuary] and the people.

26 **ואת מיתריו**. The possessive pronoun refers to the משכן: The מיתרים, like the forecourt itself, are an appendage to the משכן. In verse 37 the ropes of the forecourt are an appendage to the pillars, on which the hangings of the forecourt are fixed [thus, in v. 37 it says מיתריהם].

לכל עבדתו: עבודת המשכן is everything that is required for the construction and dismantling of the משכן.

28 *According to the number of all males from one month old and upward: eight thousand six hundred, keepers of the charge of the Sanctuary.*

כח בְּמִסְפַּר֙ כָּל־זָכָ֔ר מִבֶּן־חֹ֖דֶשׁ וָמָ֑עְלָה שְׁמֹנַ֤ת אֲלָפִים֙ וְשֵׁ֣שׁ מֵא֔וֹת שֹֽׁמְרֵ֖י מִשְׁמֶ֥רֶת הַקֹּֽדֶשׁ׃

29 *The families of the sons of Kehas shall camp at the side of the Dwelling Place, to the south.*

כט מִשְׁפְּחֹ֥ת בְּנֵֽי־קְהָ֖ת יַחֲנ֑וּ עַ֛ל יֶ֥רֶךְ הַמִּשְׁכָּ֖ן תֵּימָֽנָה׃

30 *The prince of the fathers' house of the families of the Kehasi house: Elitzafan, son of Uzzi'el.*

ל וּנְשִׂ֥יא בֵית־אָ֖ב לְמִשְׁפְּחֹ֣ת הַקְּהָתִ֑י אֱלִיצָפָ֖ן בֶּן־עֻזִּיאֵֽל׃

31 *Their charge: the Ark, the Table, the Menorah, the altars, and the utensils of the Sanctuary with which one ministers, and the protective curtain and all its requirements.*

לא וּמִשְׁמַרְתָּ֗ם הָאָרֹ֤ן וְהַשֻּׁלְחָן֙ וְהַמְּנֹרָ֣ה וְהַֽמִּזְבְּחֹ֔ת וּכְלֵ֣י הַקֹּ֔דֶשׁ אֲשֶׁ֥ר יְשָֽׁרְת֖וּ בָּהֶ֑ם וְהַמָּסָ֔ךְ וְכֹ֖ל עֲבֹדָתֽוֹ׃

32 *The prince of the princes of the* Levi'im*: Elazar, son of Aharon the priest. He was appointed over the keepers of the charge of the Sanctuary.*

לב וּנְשִׂיא֙ נְשִׂיאֵ֣י הַלֵּוִ֔י אֶלְעָזָ֖ר בֶּן־אַהֲרֹ֣ן הַכֹּהֵ֑ן פְּקֻדַּ֕ת שֹׁמְרֵ֖י מִשְׁמֶ֥רֶת הַקֹּֽדֶשׁ׃

---

31 **והמסך** here is the פרכת המסך (*Shemos* 39:34), the curtain that divides off, covers, and shields the ארון.

32 **פקדת וגו'.** פקודה is a noun from the root פקד in the sense of appointing someone to an office, to assign him a task, as in verse 10 above. It was Elazar's job to appoint the שמרי משמרת הקדש to their service and to instruct them in their tasks, and it stands to reason that he also supervised their service.

33 *Of Merari: The family of the Machli branch, and the family of the Mushi branch; these [are] the families of the Merari house.*

לג לִמְרָרִ֕י מִשְׁפַּ֙חַת֙ הַמַּחְלִ֔י וּמִשְׁפַּ֖חַת הַמּוּשִׁ֑י אֵ֥לֶּה הֵ֖ם מִשְׁפְּחֹ֥ת מְרָרִֽי׃

34 *Their numbered ones according to the number of all males from one month old and upward: six thousand, two hundred.*

לד וּפְקֻדֵיהֶם֙ בְּמִסְפַּ֣ר כָּל־זָכָ֔ר מִבֶּן־חֹ֖דֶשׁ וָמָ֑עְלָה שֵׁ֥שֶׁת אֲלָפִ֖ים וּמָאתָֽיִם׃

35 *The prince of the fathers' house of the Merari branch: Tzuri'el, son of Avichayil; they shall camp at the side of the Dwelling Place, to the north.*

לה וּנְשִׂ֤יא בֵית־אָב֙ לְמִשְׁפְּחֹ֣ת מְרָרִ֔י צוּרִיאֵ֖ל בֶּן־אֲבִיחָ֑יִל עַ֣ל יֶ֧רֶךְ הַמִּשְׁכָּ֛ן יַחֲנ֖וּ צָפֹֽנָה׃

36 *The appointment of the charge of the sons of the Merari branch: the beams of the Dwelling Place, its bars, its pillars and its sockets, its utensils and all its requirements;*

לו וּפְקֻדַּ֣ת מִשְׁמֶ֘רֶת֮ בְּנֵ֣י מְרָרִי֒ קַרְשֵׁי֙ הַמִּשְׁכָּ֔ן וּבְרִיחָ֖יו וְעַמֻּדָ֣יו וַאֲדָנָ֑יו וְכָל־כֵּלָ֔יו וְכֹ֖ל עֲבֹדָתֽוֹ׃

37 *Also the pillars of the forecourt round about, and their sockets, their stakes and their ropes.*

לז וְעַמֻּדֵ֧י הֶחָצֵ֛ר סָבִ֖יב וְאַדְנֵיהֶ֑ם וִיתֵדֹתָ֖ם וּמֵיתְרֵיהֶֽם׃

---

36 **ופקדת וגו'**. The assignment of the charge of the sons of Merari is called here especially "פקודה," probably because they were the last division of *Levi'im*, and Scripture wants to rule out the idea that they received their charge simply because no other task remained. Hence the assignment of the sons of Merari is called a "פקודה": They were appointed to their task no less than the other sons of Levi were appointed to theirs; their assignment was a special charge entrusted especially to them.

לח וְהַחֹנִים לִפְנֵי הַמִּשְׁכָּן קֵדְמָה לִפְנֵי
אֹהֶל־מוֹעֵד ׀ מִזְרָחָה מֹשֶׁה ׀
וְאַהֲרֹן וּבָנָיו שֹׁמְרִים מִשְׁמֶרֶת
הַמִּקְדָּשׁ לְמִשְׁמֶרֶת בְּנֵי יִשְׂרָאֵל
וְהַזָּר הַקָּרֵב יוּמָת׃

38 *But those who are to camp in front of the Dwelling Place, to the east, [are] Moshe and Aharon and his sons, keeping the charge of the entire Sanctuary as the charge of the Children of Israel. Any outsider who comes near is liable to the death penalty.*

לט כָּל־פְּקוּדֵי הַלְוִיִּם אֲשֶׁר פָּקַד
מֹשֶׁה וְאַהֲרֹן עַל־פִּי יְהוָה
לְמִשְׁפְּחֹתָם כָּל־זָכָר מִבֶּן־חֹדֶשׁ
וָמַעְלָה שְׁנַיִם וְעֶשְׂרִים אָלֶף׃ ס

ששי נקוד על ואהרן

39 *All the numbered ones of the* Levi'im, *whom Moshe numbered, and [so did] Aharon, at the behest of* God, *according to their families — all males from one month old and upward — were twenty-two thousand.*

38 **שמרים משמרת המקדש.** בני קהת (v. 28), as the bearers of the furnishings of the Sanctuary, and also the other *Levi'im* (v. 32), are שמרי משמרת הקדש. For each one of the parts of the Sanctuary is called "קדש," whereas the Sanctuary as a whole is usually called "מקדש" — e.g., מקדש ה׳ כוננו ידך (*Shemos* 15:17), ועשו לי מקדש (ibid. 25:8), את מקדש ה׳ טמא (below, 19:20). In addition, the *Levi'im* are called שמרי וגו׳ [not שומרים]; that is their office, the whole content of their assigned task. Moreover, since they were counted מבן חודש, all those that were counted here are not yet שומרים וגו׳; rather, they are שמרי משמרת הקדש — i.e., משמרת הקדש is the calling to which they are destined. But for Moshe and Aharon, the care of the Sanctuary is only one of their *activities*; [it does not define their office, their whole function]. They are שמרים משמרת המקדש.

39 **אשר פקד משה ואהרן.** נקוד על אהרן שבחמש הפקודים, the dots over the word "ואהרן" are to remind us שלא היה באותו מנין, that he himself was not included in this count of the *Levi'im* (see *Bechoros* 4a). Aharon's appointment to the priesthood was not like the appointment of the *Levi'im*; it did not result from the replacement of the firstborn. He and his sons were appointed as כהנים at once with the command to erect

40 God *said to Moshe: Number all the male firstborn of the Children of Israel from one month old and upward, and take the number of their names.*

מ וַיֹּאמֶר יְהוָה אֶל־מֹשֶׁה פְּקֹד כָּל־
בְּכֹר זָכָר לִבְנֵי יִשְׂרָאֵל מִבֶּן־חֹדֶשׁ
וָמָעְלָה וְשָׂא אֵת מִסְפַּר שְׁמֹתָם:

the Dwelling Place, before the firstborn had forfeited their position in the Sanctuary; for the sin of the golden calf occurred only later (see *Shemos* 28:1). Had it not been for that sin, the firstborn would presumably have occupied the position of the *Levi'im*, yet the service of the offerings would have been entrusted to the sons of Aharon immediately upon the construction of the Dwelling Place, at least in respect to קרבנות ציבור and קרבנות חובה; for even בשעת היתר במות, these עבודות were permissible only in the משכן (see *Zevachim* 117a).

שנים ועשרים אלף. The total sum of all the *Levi'im* counted here is twenty-two thousand, three hundred. But these three hundred were (according to *Bechoros* 5a) firstborn sons, and are not included in the total mentioned in our verse. For the numbers given here are preparatory to the replacement of the firstborn by the *Levi'im*, whereas the firstborn of the *Levi'im* are to replace themselves, so to speak. They are to perform as *Levi'im* the duties they were hitherto called on to perform as firstborn; דיו לבכור שיפקיע קדושת עצמו (ibid.).

40 **ויאמר ה' וגו'**. The appointment of the *Levi'im* to replace the firstborn is to be expressed also by a concrete act, the counting of the firstborn corresponding to the counting of the *Levi'im*. This counting of the firstborn is merely a complementing act; it complements the appointment already ordained by God. It is not a mitzvah for all time; all future firstborn will be automatically discharged from עבודת המשכן, and will be responsible only for פדיון, which was required of them beforehand at the introduction of קדושת בכור (see Commentary, *Shemos* 13:2 and 13). Perhaps that is why this section begins with ויאמר and not with the usual וידבר. It provides only an additional explanation of an ordinance which had already been given.

ושא את מספר שמתם. Counting by individual names will remind each one of them personally of his loss: he forfeited the distinction of

41 *And take the* Levi'im *for Me — I,* God *— in place of every firstborn among the Children of Israel, and the livestock of the* Levi'im *in place of every firstborn among the livestock of the Children of Israel.*

מא וְלָקַחְתָּ֨ אֶת־הַלְוִיִּ֥ם לִי֙ אֲנִ֣י יְהֹוָ֔ה תַּ֥חַת כָּל־בְּכֹ֖ר בִּבְנֵ֣י יִשְׂרָאֵ֑ל וְאֵ֨ת בֶּהֱמַ֤ת הַלְוִיִּם֙ תַּ֣חַת כָּל־בְּכ֔וֹר בְּבֶהֱמַ֖ת בְּנֵ֥י יִשְׂרָאֵֽל׃

the בכורה because, at the sin of the golden calf, he did not live up to his responsibility as firstborn.

41 **לי אני ה׳**: the Name of God is stamped on the election of the *Levi'im*. **ואת בהמת הלוים וגו׳.** (מפשט הסוגיא דבכורות ד א׳ ב׳ משמע דלא פטרו בהמת הלוים במדבר אלא פטרי חמורן של ישראל, ולא בכור בהמה טהורה שלהן שהוא גופא דבר תמוה שיהא פדיון לקדושת הגוף שאינו בעל מום והלא אפי׳ בכור ב״מ אין לו פדיון וכן פירש״י הכא בחומש וכן נלע״ד פשט לשונו שם בבכורות. והא דפריך רבא התם אם איתא אפי׳ מבהמה טהורה ניפטרי ופרש״י אם איתא דדרשינן ק״ו גבי בהמה מבכור בהמה טהורה ניפטרי לוים דהא בהמה טהורה דידהו הפקיעה בהמת ישראל אי לאו דמסתפינא הייתי אומר דה״ק בהמה טהורה דידהו כלומר שה של בן לוי הפקיעה בכורה של בהמת ישראל כלומר פטר חמור של ישראל ואם הפקיע שה של בן לוי בכורה בבהמת ישראל אינו דין שיפקיע בכורה של עצמו שהיא בכורה בהמה טהורה. אלא התוספות לא פירשו הכי וס״ל דבהמה טהורה של בן לוי הפקיעה בכור בהמה טהורה של ישראל במדבר, וצע״ג.)

In our Commentary on *Shemos* (13:13) we explained that the חמור, the beast of burden, represents movable property, and קדושת פטר חמור expresses the idea that all of the family's lifeless property belongs to God. The redemption of פטר חמור by means of a שה given to the כהן signifies that lifeless property has no value or meaning unless it comes alive through the living personality of man and is used to further the purposes of the Sanctuary.

We have here, then, a clear admonition to the *Levi'im*, who are now entering the service of the Sanctuary: Through their personalities, they redeem the firstborn of Israel, releasing them from the service of the Sanctuary. At the same time, however, they also redeem, through their lambs, all the פטרי חמורים of the entire people. The implication is that the לוי should consider himself a servant of the Sanctuary not only in respect to the spiritual-moral side of his personality, but also in respect to the means of his livelihood. Bear in mind that the *Levi'im* had to

42 *And Moshe numbered, as* God *had commanded him, all the firstborn among the Children of Israel.*

מב וַיִּפְקֹד מֹשֶׁה כַּאֲשֶׁר צִוָּה יְהוָה אֹתוֹ אֶת־כָּל־בְּכוֹר בִּבְנֵי יִשְׂרָאֵל׃

43 *All the male firstborn, according to the number of names of those one month old and upward who were numbered, were twenty-two thousand, two hundred and seventy-three.*

מג וַיְהִי כָל־בְּכוֹר זָכָר בְּמִסְפַּר שֵׁמֹת מִבֶּן־חֹדֶשׁ וָמַעְלָה לִפְקֻדֵיהֶם שְׁנַיִם וְעֶשְׂרִים אֶלֶף שְׁלֹשָׁה וְשִׁבְעִים וּמָאתָיִם׃ פ

44 God *spoke to Moshe, saying:*

מד וַיְדַבֵּר יְהוָה אֶל־מֹשֶׁה לֵּאמֹר׃

45 *Take the* Levi'im *in place of all the firstborn among the Children of Israel, and the livestock of the* Levi'im *in place of their livestock; so the* Levi'im *shall be Mine, I,* God.

מה קַח אֶת־הַלְוִיִּם תַּחַת כָּל־בְּכוֹר בִּבְנֵי יִשְׂרָאֵל וְאֶת־בֶּהֱמַת הַלְוִיִּם תַּחַת בְּהֶמְתָּם וְהָיוּ־לִי הַלְוִיִּם אֲנִי יְהוָה׃

renounce their share in the land which was the means of the national livelihood; they were dependent for their livelihood on gifts which the nation set aside from its property, as an expression of its subordination to God, for the study of Torah and its fulfillment.

This, then, is the duty of the *Levi'im*: They are servants of the Sanctuary with the whole of their persons and possessions, with life and property. In the future as well, the tribe of Levi must never lose sight of this duty. Toward this end, the law is that their firstborn and their פטרי חמורים do not require redemption. כהנים ולויים פטורים מק״ו, אם פטרו את של ישראל במדבר דין הוא שיפטרו את של עצמן (*Bechoros* 3b). This law encompasses and applies to the whole tribe of Levi, including its daughters. Hence, if the daughter of a כהן or a לוי marries a ישראל, her firstborn son does not require redemption, this despite the fact that the son himself belongs to the tribe of the father and is not considered a לוי. So, too, the פטרי חמור of a כהנת or a לוייה do not require redemption, in accordance with the principle: כל שישנו בבכור אדם ישנו בבכור בהמה טמאה וכו׳ (ibid. 4a).

46 *But as regards the redemption of the two hundred and seventy-three of the firstborn of the Children of Israel who are over and above the [number of the]* Levi'im,	מו וְאֵת פְּדוּיֵי הַשְּׁלֹשָׁה וְהַשִּׁבְעִים וְהַמָּאתָיִם הָעֹדְפִים עַל־הַלְוִיִּם מִבְּכוֹר בְּנֵי יִשְׂרָאֵל׃
47 *You shall take five shekels per head; according to the weight of the Sanctuary you shall take [them], twenty* gerah *to the shekel.*	מז וְלָקַחְתָּ חֲמֵשֶׁת חֲמֵשֶׁת שְׁקָלִים לַגֻּלְגֹּלֶת בְּשֶׁקֶל הַקֹּדֶשׁ תִּקָּח עֶשְׂרִים גֵּרָה הַשָּׁקֶל׃
48 *And you shall give the money to Aharon and his sons as a redemption for those [firstborn] who are over and above [the number of* Levi'im*].*	מח וְנָתַתָּה הַכֶּסֶף לְאַהֲרֹן וּלְבָנָיו פְּדוּיֵי הָעֹדְפִים בָּהֶם׃
49 *Moshe took the redemption money from those who were over and above [the number of] those who were redeemed through the* Levi'im.	מט וַיִּקַּח מֹשֶׁה אֵת כֶּסֶף הַפִּדְיוֹם מֵאֵת הָעֹדְפִים עַל פְּדוּיֵי הַלְוִיִּם׃
50 *From the firstborn of the Children of Israel did he take the money: one thousand, three hundred and sixty-five according to the weight of the Sanctuary.*	נ מֵאֵת בְּכוֹר בְּנֵי יִשְׂרָאֵל לָקַח אֶת־הַכָּסֶף חֲמִשָּׁה וְשִׁשִּׁים וּשְׁלֹשׁ מֵאוֹת וָאֶלֶף בְּשֶׁקֶל הַקֹּדֶשׁ׃

47-48 **ולקחת וגו׳**. This is the amount set below (18:16) for the redemption of the firstborn, and this is always the manner in which the mitzvah of redemption — which was already mentioned in *Shemos* 13:13 — is fulfilled. The amount corresponds to the first ערך of a boy after the first month of life (see *Vayikra* 27:6). For each of the other firstborn [i.e., the 22,000 corresponding to the number of לויים], a לוי was "given" to the כהן (see v. 9). The [273] firstborn for whom there were no corresponding *Levi'im*

51 *And Moshe gave the redemption money to Aharon and his sons at the behest of* God, *as* God *had commanded Moshe.*

נא וַיִּתֵּ֨ן מֹשֶׁ֜ה אֶת־כֶּ֣סֶף הַפְּדֻיִ֗ם
לְאַהֲרֹ֛ן וּלְבָנָ֖יו עַל־פִּ֣י יְהֹוָ֑ה כַּאֲשֶׁ֛ר
צִוָּ֥ה יְהֹוָ֖ה אֶת־מֹשֶֽׁה׃ פ שביעי

4 1 God *spoke to Moshe and Aharon, saying:*

ד א וַיְדַבֵּ֣ר יְהֹוָ֔ה אֶל־מֹשֶׁ֥ה וְאֶֽל־אַהֲרֹ֖ן
לֵאמֹֽר׃

2 *Take the total count of the sons of Kehas from among the sons of Levi, according to their families, according to their fathers' house,*

ב נָשֹׂ֗א אֶת־רֹאשׁ֙ בְּנֵ֣י קְהָ֔ת מִתּ֖וֹךְ
בְּנֵ֣י לֵוִ֑י לְמִשְׁפְּחֹתָ֖ם לְבֵ֥ית אֲבֹתָֽם׃

---

were redeemed in the manner described here. They gave to the כהן the "ערך" of five shekels. This amount is the symbolic expression of the ideal value of a young male child in his relation to the Sanctuary.

CHAPTER 4

1 In the preceding chapter, all those destined for the Levite vocation were counted — a count that included all *Levi'im* from the age of one month and upward. Now follows the counting of the bearers and guardians of the Sanctuary — i.e., only those called upon for active service in the Sanctuary. And Scripture explains in greater detail the duties assigned to each of the three Levite "houses" during the years of wandering. The work of lifting and carrying the parts and contents of the Sanctuary demanded an expenditure of strength and was therefore limited to the age of thirty to fifty years. We have already noted (Commentary above, 2:17) that the sanctity of the Sanctuary did not cease in transit on the journeys, even after it was dismantled.

2 **נשא וגו' מתוך וגו'**. Treated first are the sons of Kehas, for, as already stated above (3:31), they were put in charge of the holiest parts of the משכן.

3 *From thirty years old and upward until fifty years old, each one who comes to communal service, to do [sacred] work in the Tent of Appointed Meeting.*

ג מִבֶּן שְׁלֹשִׁים שָׁנָה וָמַעְלָה וְעַד
בֶּן־חֲמִשִּׁים שָׁנָה כָּל־בָּא לַצָּבָא
לַעֲשׂוֹת מְלָאכָה בְּאֹהֶל מוֹעֵד׃

4 *This is the service of the sons of Kehas in the Tent of Appointed Meeting: the Holy of Holies.*

ד זֹאת עֲבֹדַת בְּנֵי־קְהָת בְּאֹהֶל
מוֹעֵד קֹדֶשׁ הַקֳּדָשִׁים׃

5 *And Aharon and his sons shall come when the camp journeys forth, and they shall take off the protective curtain and cover the Ark of the Testimony with it.*

ה וּבָא אַהֲרֹן וּבָנָיו בִּנְסֹעַ הַמַּחֲנֶה
וְהוֹרִדוּ אֵת פָּרֹכֶת הַמָּסָךְ וְכִסּוּ־
בָהּ אֵת אֲרֹן הָעֵדֻת׃

6 *They shall place upon this a cover of* tachash *skin, spread over it a cloth entirely of sky-blue wool, and adjust its [carrying] poles.*

ו וְנָתְנוּ עָלָיו כְּסוּי עוֹר תַּחַשׁ וּפָרְשׂוּ
בֶגֶד־כְּלִיל תְּכֵלֶת מִלְמָעְלָה וְשָׂמוּ
בַּדָּיו׃

3 **כל בא לצבא**. See Commentary above, 1:3.

5-6 **ובא אהרן**. Not even the לויים are allowed to touch the sacred objects of the Sanctuary — the ארון, שולחן, מנורה, and מזבחות (v. 15). The לויים receive the objects from the כהנים when the objects are already wrapped in their protective covers for transport. Let us recall what has already been stated above: Even when dismantled and in transit, the "Dwelling Place of the Testimony" retains its holy and sanctifying significance as the unifying gathering point of the nation. Thus, the very act of wrapping and preparing the objects for transport is a priestly act of great significance.

The covers themselves correspond to the character of the covered object. The protective exterior covering of all the objects is made of עור תחש, the pelt of an animal distinguished by its outstanding speed (Commentary, *Shemos* 26:14). This symbolizes the speed of the journey, which must not be slowed by any hindrance. The objects that stand in the קודש הקדשים and in the קודש — the ארון, שולחן, מנורה, and מזבח הזהב —

7 *And upon the Table of the Countenance they shall spread a cloth of sky-blue wool and shall place upon it the dishes, the spoons, the purification tubes and the supports of the covering, and the continual bread shall be upon it.*

ז וְעַ֣ל ׀ שֻׁלְחַ֣ן הַפָּנִ֗ים יִפְרְשׂוּ֮ בֶּ֣גֶד
תְּכֵלֶת֒ וְנָתְנ֣וּ עָלָ֗יו אֶת־הַקְּעָרֹ֤ת
וְאֶת־הַכַּפֹּת֙ וְאֶת־הַמְּנַקִּיֹּ֔ת וְאֵ֖ת
קְשׂ֣וֹת הַנָּ֑סֶךְ וְלֶ֧חֶם הַתָּמִ֛יד עָלָ֥יו
יִהְיֶֽה׃

are covered with a cloth of תכלת, the color of holiness and closeness to God (Commentary, ibid. 25:3-8).

The ארון is first wrapped in the cherubim-cover which shields it in the Sanctuary, whereas the sky-blue cloth is on top, the ארון's outer, visible covering. Thus, its character is reflected by its cover: the Ark of the Testimony is כליל תכלת, close to God in highest holiness.

On the "Table of God's special care" — which likewise is covered with a תכלת-covering of holiness — rests the bread of Divine providence (v. 7), together with the appurtenances symbolizing the necessary conditions for this providence; they show how to shape, dedicate to God, and preserve what is granted to man by God (Commentary, ibid. 25:23-28).

The "bread" of Jewish national prosperity is covered with a cloth of תולעת שָׁני (v. 8), whereas the מזבח העולה is covered with one of ארגמן (v. 13). We have already explained (Commentary, *Shemos* 25:3-8) that the color red represents life, only that שָׁני represents the lower, *animal* side of life and ארגמן the higher, *human* side. The means of existence and prosperity are granted by God's "Countenance," but all these ensure only "שָׁני," animal-bodily life. "ארגמן," on the other hand, the higher, human level of life, is not *granted* by God. Rather, man must attain this level himself by freely mastering his own desires; he must harness all his animal-bodily powers and subordinate them to God's Will. This is symbolized by the offering altar and by the offering procedures performed on it.

The meaning of ושמו בדיו here (v. 6) differs from its meaning in connection with the other כלים. Here it does not mean to insert the poles, for according to *Shemos* 25:15 the poles were never to be removed from the rings of the Ark. Rather, here it means to adjust the poles.

7 **ולחם התמיד עליו יהיה**. As a rule, כל המקודש בכלי פסול ביוצא (רש"י *Zevachim* 20b ד"ה יציאה; see תוספות there ד"ה יציאה מהו): anything received in a

8 *Over this they shall spread a cloth of crimson wool, cover it with a cover of* tachash *skin, and insert its [carrying] poles.*

ח וּפָרְשׂוּ עֲלֵיהֶם בֶּגֶד תּוֹלַעַת שָׁנִי
וְכִסּוּ אֹתוֹ בְּמִכְסֵה עוֹר תָּחַשׁ
וְשָׂמוּ אֶת־בַּדָּיו׃

9 *They shall then take a cloth of sky-blue wool and cover the Menorah of the light and its lamps, its tongs and its pans and also all its oil vessels with which they minister to it.*

ט וְלָקְחוּ ׀ בֶּגֶד תְּכֵלֶת וְכִסּוּ אֶת־
מְנֹרַת הַמָּאוֹר וְאֶת־נֵרֹתֶיהָ וְאֶת־
מַלְקָחֶיהָ וְאֶת־מַחְתֹּתֶיהָ וְאֵת כָּל־
כְּלֵי שַׁמְנָהּ אֲשֶׁר יְשָׁרְתוּ־לָהּ
בָּהֶם׃

10 *They shall place it [i.e., the Menorah] and all its utensils into a cover of* tachash *skins, and place it upon the carrying frame.*

י וְנָתְנוּ אֹתָהּ וְאֶת־כָּל־כֵּלֶיהָ אֶל־
מִכְסֵה עוֹר תָּחַשׁ וְנָתְנוּ עַל־
הַמּוֹט׃

11 *Over the golden altar they shall spread a cloth of sky-blue wool, cover it with a cover of* tachash *skin, and insert its [carrying] poles.*

יא וְעַל ׀ מִזְבַּח הַזָּהָב יִפְרְשׂוּ בֶּגֶד
תְּכֵלֶת וְכִסּוּ אֹתוֹ בְּמִכְסֵה עוֹר
תָּחַשׁ וְשָׂמוּ אֶת־בַּדָּיו׃

12 *They shall then take all the utensils of ministry with which they minister in the Sanctuary, place them into a cloth of sky-blue wool, cover them with a cover of* tachash *skin, and place them upon the carrying frame.*

יב וְלָקְחוּ אֶת־כָּל־כְּלֵי הַשָּׁרֵת אֲשֶׁר
יְשָׁרְתוּ־בָם בַּקֹּדֶשׁ וְנָתְנוּ אֶל־בֶּגֶד
תְּכֵלֶת וְכִסּוּ אוֹתָם בְּמִכְסֵה עוֹר
תָּחַשׁ וְנָתְנוּ עַל־הַמּוֹט׃

13 *They shall clear the altar of ashes and spread over it a cloth of purple wool.*

יג וְדִשְּׁנוּ אֶת־הַמִּזְבֵּחַ וּפָרְשׂוּ עָלָיו
בֶּגֶד אַרְגָּמָן׃

14 *And they shall place upon it all its*

יד וְנָתְנוּ עָלָיו אֶת־כָּל־כֵּלָיו אֲשֶׁר

utensils with which they minister upon it — the pans, the forks, the shovels, the bowls for dashing [the blood of the animal offerings] — all the utensils of the altar, and spread over this a cover of tachash *skin and insert its [carrying] poles.*

יְשָׁרְתוּ עָלָיו בָּהֶם אֶת־הַמַּחְתֹּת
אֶת־הַמִּזְלָגֹת וְאֶת־הַיָּעִים וְאֶת־
הַמִּזְרָקֹת כֹּל כְּלֵי הַמִּזְבֵּחַ וּפָרְשׂוּ
עָלָיו כְּסוּי עוֹר תַּחַשׁ וְשָׂמוּ בַדָּיו:

15 *When Aharon and his sons have finished covering the holy [objects] and all the utensils of the Sanctuary when the camp journeys forth — only after that shall the sons of Kehas come to carry [them] so that they will not touch the holy [objects] and die. These constitute the burden to be carried by the sons of Kehas for the Tent of Appointed Meeting.*

טו וְכִלָּה אַהֲרֹן־וּבָנָיו לְכַסֹּת אֶת־
הַקֹּדֶשׁ וְאֶת־כָּל־כְּלֵי הַקֹּדֶשׁ
בִּנְסֹעַ הַמַּחֲנֶה וְאַחֲרֵי־כֵן יָבֹאוּ
בְנֵי־קְהָת לָשֵׂאת וְלֹא־יִגְּעוּ אֶל־
הַקֹּדֶשׁ וָמֵתוּ אֵלֶּה מַשָּׂא בְנֵי־
קְהָת בְּאֹהֶל מוֹעֵד:

16 *But the responsibility of Elazar, the son of Aharon the priest, is the oil for lighting, the spicy incense, the*

טז וּפְקֻדַּת אֶלְעָזָר ׀ בֶּן־אַהֲרֹן הַכֹּהֵן
שֶׁמֶן הַמָּאוֹר וּקְטֹרֶת הַסַּמִּים

service vessel for the purposes of the Sanctuary is disqualified upon its removal from the area of the Sanctuary (see Commentary, *Shemos* 22:30). Nevertheless, the showbread on the Table retains its intimate connection with the Sanctuary even on the journeys and is not נפסל ביוצא (*Menachos* 95a; see Commentary above, 2:17).

15 **את הקדש** refers to ארון העדות. For the ארון is the essence of the קודש; the ארון gives all the others their קדושה. כלי הקדש are the שולחן, מנורה and מזבחות. Their relation to the ארון is that of a כלי to the object it serves: the כלי accomplishes the purpose set by the object.

16 **ופקדת וגו׳ פקדת וגו׳**. The order of these statements indicates that the second statement explains the first. Elazar's responsibility is the oil for

homage gift of the daily offering and the anointing oil; the responsibility for the entire Dwelling Place and its entire contents of holy [objects] and its utensils.	וּמִנְחַת הַתָּמִיד וְשֶׁמֶן הַמִּשְׁחָה פְּקֻדַּת כָּל־הַמִּשְׁכָּן וְכָל־אֲשֶׁר־בּוֹ בְּקֹדֶשׁ וּבְכֵלָיו: פ מפטיר
17 God *spoke to Moshe and Aharon, saying:*	יז וַיְדַבֵּר יְהֹוָה אֶל־מֹשֶׁה וְאֶל־אַהֲרֹן לֵאמֹר:

lighting, and so forth; but this in fact means responsibility for the entire Dwelling Place. That is to say, Elazar is put in charge of the oil for lighting, the spicy incense, the homage gift of the daily offering (this is the offering of flour, the מנחת סולת, which accompanies every תמיד [*Yerushalmi*, *Shabbos* 10:3]; according to the version of the *Yalkut* here, these are the חביתי כהן גדול; see *Vayikra* 6:13), and the anointing oil. Thereby, he is entrusted with the purpose and mission of the Dwelling Place and of its contents — i.e., of the ארון (בקדש) and of the שולחן, the מנורה, and the מזבחות (ובכליו — see above, v. 15).

שמן המאור, קטורת הסמים, מנחת התמיד, שמן המשחה: Spiritual enlightenment, complete self-surrender to God's Will and God's satisfaction, rendering homage to God in every moment of one's life, holiness — these are the goals to strive for through the Ark, the Table, the Menorah, and the altars. The mere existence of the objects entrusted to the sons of Kehas is not sufficient. Only the *avodos* connected with these goals — whose symbolic representations are entrusted to Elazar — give life and purpose to the משכן. Since Elazar is entrusted with the materials of these *avodos*, he is in effect entrusted with the entire משכן, its entire contents, and its whole purpose.

17 **וידבר וגו׳**. In the preceding verses it is stated that the sacred objects are to be handed over to the sons of Kehas only after these objects have been completely covered, so that the bearers should have no direct physical contact with them. Now we are told that the sons of Kehas may not even be present while the covering is done. They must not *see* the sacred objects while they are being covered. If we are not mistaken, the intent of this prohibition is as follows: The Sanctuary is meant to be a

יח אַל־תַּכְרִ֕יתוּ אֶת־שֵׁ֖בֶט מִשְׁפְּחֹ֣ת הַקְּהָתִ֑י מִתּ֖וֹךְ הַלְוִיִּֽם׃

18 *Do not permit the tribe of the Kehasi families to become extinct from among the* Levi'im.

יט וְזֹ֣את ׀ עֲשׂ֣וּ לָהֶ֗ם וְחָיוּ֙ וְלֹ֣א יָמֻ֔תוּ בְּגִשְׁתָּ֖ם אֶת־קֹ֣דֶשׁ הַקֳּדָשִׁ֑ים אַהֲרֹ֤ן וּבָנָיו֙ יָבֹ֔אוּ וְשָׂמ֣וּ אוֹתָ֗ם אִ֥ישׁ אִ֛ישׁ עַל־עֲבֹדָת֖וֹ וְאֶל־מַשָּׂאֽוֹ׃

19 *Do this for them so that they will live and not die when they approach the Holy of Holies: Aharon and his sons shall come and set them, every single one [separately], to his service and to his burden.*

כ וְלֹא־יָבֹ֧אוּ לִרְא֛וֹת כְּבַלַּ֥ע אֶת־הַקֹּ֖דֶשׁ וָמֵֽתוּ׃ פפפ

20 *They shall not go in to see when the holy [objects] are completely wrapped, and die.*

---

subject for thought, not an object of physical sight. The bearers of the Sanctuary should direct their minds to it, not feast their eyes on it. They should contemplate the meaning of the Sanctuary, and not divert their attention from this meaning. This is an essential aspect of their duties. Hence, to feast their eyes on the Sanctuary during the covering would be to desecrate it in their hearts.

18 **שבט**. See Commentary above, 3:15.

20 **כבלע**. בָּלַע means "to sink something into another body," hence "to swallow." בלע is related to פלא (cf. Commentary, *Shemos* 3:20; 8:18): something concealed from one's understanding, inaccessible to the mind. Thus, too, בַּלֵּעַ means: to conceal something from view, to prevent the eye from perceiving it. Thus וְדֶרֶךְ אֹרְחֹתֶיךָ בִּלֵּעוּ (*Yeshayahu* 3:12): they hid from your sight the only path you should take among all the paths that lie before you.

21 God *spoke to Moshe, saying:*	כא וַיְדַבֵּר יְהוָה אֶל־מֹשֶׁה לֵּאמֹר׃
22 *Take also the total count of the sons of Gershon, according to their fathers' house, according to their families.*	כב נָשֹׂא אֶת־רֹאשׁ בְּנֵי גֵרְשׁוֹן גַּם־הֵם לְבֵית אֲבֹתָם לְמִשְׁפְּחֹתָם׃
23 *From thirty years old and upward until fifty years old shall you number them, every one who comes to perform communal service, to minister at the Tent of Appointed Meeting.*	כג מִבֶּן שְׁלֹשִׁים שָׁנָה וָמַעְלָה עַד בֶּן־חֲמִשִּׁים שָׁנָה תִּפְקֹד אוֹתָם כָּל־הַבָּא לִצְבֹא צָבָא לַעֲבֹד עֲבֹדָה בְּאֹהֶל מוֹעֵד׃

נשא

22 **נשא וגו'**. The counting of the sons of Kehas came first. Although Gershon was the eldest, it was necessary to deal first with the sons of Kehas. For Scripture was establishing the order of handing over the sacred objects of the Sanctuary at the breaking of camp, and the sons of Kehas are in charge of the sacred objects. Even at the breaking of camp, the wrapping and handing over of the most sacred objects of the Sanctuary precedes everything else. Thus, when commanding the counting of the sons of Kehas, Scripture employs the expression "מתוך בני לוי" (above, v. 2), for that count singled them out and gave them prominence.

Now Scripture mentions the counting of the sons of Gershon and sets down their assignment. The words "גם הם" stand in relation to that first count. They indicate that the precedence of the sons of Kehas is not meant to discriminate against the sons of Gershon. Perhaps that is why it also says here — as it says of the whole tribe of Levi (above, 3:15) — לבית אבתם למשפחתם, whereas everywhere else it says למשפחתם לבית אבתם. The implication is that the sons of Gershon — no less than the others — form a "house" in their own right. Accordingly, it says in the Midrash (*Bemidbar Rabbah* 6:2): מהו שאמר הכתוב גם הם? שלא תאמר שלכך

24 *This is the service of the families of the Gershuni house to minister and to carry:*

כד זֹאת עֲבֹדַת מִשְׁפְּחֹת הַגֵּרְשֻׁנִּי
לַעֲבֹד וּלְמַשָּׂא:

25 *They shall carry the tapestries of the Dwelling Place and the Tent of Appointed Meeting, its covering and the covering of* tachash *skin which is above it; and the protective curtain of the entrance to the Tent of Appointed Meeting;*

כה וְנָשְׂאוּ אֶת־יְרִיעֹת הַמִּשְׁכָּן וְאֶת־
אֹהֶל מוֹעֵד מִכְסֵהוּ וּמִכְסֵה
הַתַּחַשׁ אֲשֶׁר־עָלָיו מִלְמָעְלָה
וְאֶת־מָסַךְ פֶּתַח אֹהֶל מוֹעֵד:

26 *The hangings of the forecourt; the protective curtain of the gate of the forecourt, which is round about the Dwelling Place and around the altar, their ropes and all the utensils of ministry — and whatever must be done for these objects they shall serve.*

כו וְאֵת קַלְעֵי הֶחָצֵר וְאֶת־מָסַךְ ׀
פֶּתַח ׀ שַׁעַר הֶחָצֵר אֲשֶׁר עַל־
הַמִּשְׁכָּן וְעַל־הַמִּזְבֵּחַ סָבִיב וְאֵת
מֵיתְרֵיהֶם וְאֶת־כָּל־כְּלֵי עֲבֹדָתָם
וְאֵת כָּל־אֲשֶׁר יֵעָשֶׂה לָהֶם
וְעָבָדוּ:

27 *All the service of the Gershuni house shall be according to Aharon's and his sons' instruc-*

כז עַל־פִּי אַהֲרֹן וּבָנָיו תִּהְיֶה כָּל־
עֲבֹדַת בְּנֵי הַגֵּרְשֻׁנִּי לְכָל־מַשָּׂאָם

מנה בני גרשון שניים שהם פחותים מבני קהת, לאו, אלא כתב גם הם שאף בני גרשון כיוצא בהם של בני קהת אלא שהקדימם הכתוב כאן בשביל כבוד התורה (לפי שקהת היה מטועני הארון) וכו'.

26 **ואת כל אשר וגו'**. It is their responsibility to care for and to transport the parts of the Dwelling Place and forecourt that are entrusted to them. Hence, it is their duty to perform any service that is needed to meet this responsibility. As it says in the Midrash (*Bemidbar Rabbah* 6:3): כל מה שהיה נעשה לכל הכלים יהיו בני גרשון עושים.

tions, with regard to everything they have to carry and to serve. Everything that they have to carry you must appoint for them, along with the duty to take charge of them.

וּלְכֹל֙ עֲבֹדָתָ֔ם וּפְקַדְתֶּ֤ם עֲלֵהֶם֙ בְּמִשְׁמֶ֔רֶת אֵ֖ת כָּל־מַשָּׂאָֽם׃

28 *This is the service of the sons of the Gershuni house for the Tent of Appointed Meeting, and their charge shall be under the direction of Isamar, son of Aharon the priest.*

כח זֹ֣את עֲבֹדַ֗ת מִשְׁפְּחֹ֛ת בְּנֵ֥י הַגֵּרְשֻׁנִּ֖י בְּאֹ֣הֶל מוֹעֵ֑ד וּמִ֨שְׁמַרְתָּ֔ם בְּיַד֙ אִֽיתָמָ֔ר בֶּֽן־אַהֲרֹ֖ן הַכֹּהֵֽן׃ ס

29 *As for the sons of Merari, you shall number them according to their families, according to their fathers' house.*

כט בְּנֵ֖י מְרָרִ֑י לְמִשְׁפְּחֹתָ֥ם לְבֵית־אֲבֹתָ֖ם תִּפְקֹ֥ד אֹתָֽם׃

30 *From thirty years old and upward until fifty years old shall you number them, every one who comes to communal service, to perform the service for the Tent of Appointed Meeting.*

ל מִבֶּן֩ שְׁלֹשִׁ֨ים שָׁנָ֜ה וָמַ֗עְלָה וְעַ֛ד בֶּן־חֲמִשִּׁ֥ים שָׁנָ֖ה תִּפְקְדֵ֑ם כָּל־הַבָּא֙ לַצָּבָ֔א לַעֲבֹ֕ד אֶת־עֲבֹדַ֖ת אֹ֥הֶל מוֹעֵֽד׃

31 *And this is the charge of their burden for all their service at the Tent of Appointed Meeting: the beams of the Dwelling Place, its bars, pillars and sockets;*

לא וְזֹאת֙ מִשְׁמֶ֣רֶת מַשָּׂאָ֔ם לְכָל־עֲבֹדָתָ֖ם בְּאֹ֣הֶל מוֹעֵ֑ד קַרְשֵׁי֙ הַמִּשְׁכָּ֔ן וּבְרִיחָ֖יו וְעַמּוּדָ֥יו וַאֲדָנָֽיו׃

27 **ופקדתם עלהם במשמרת את כל משאם**. They are not to be mere porters; rather, they are to serve with intelligence and awareness. For their charge includes the responsibility of custodianship: שיהיו מצווים עליהם שיהיו שומרים על כל מה שנושאים (ibid.).

28 **ומשמרתם**: Initially they were directed by Aharon and his sons (v. 27), but subsequently they were under the direction of Isamar (*Bemidbar Rabbah* 6:3).

32 *The pillars of the forecourt round about, their sockets, stakes and ropes, along with all their utensils and all that is required for their service. And [you shall refer to these objects] by their name when you turn over the utensils to their charge in carrying.*

לב וְעַמּוּדֵי הֶחָצֵר סָבִיב וְאַדְנֵיהֶם
וִיתֵדֹתָם וּמֵיתְרֵיהֶם לְכָל־כְּלֵיהֶם
וּלְכֹל עֲבֹדָתָם וּבְשֵׁמֹת תִּפְקְדוּ
אֶת־כְּלֵי מִשְׁמֶרֶת מַשָּׂאָם׃

33 *This is the service of the families of the sons of Merari, for all their service at the Tent of Appointed Meeting, under the direction of Isamar, son of Aharon the priest.*

לג זֹאת עֲבֹדַת מִשְׁפְּחֹת בְּנֵי מְרָרִי
לְכָל־עֲבֹדָתָם בְּאֹהֶל מוֹעֵד בְּיַד
אִיתָמָר בֶּן־אַהֲרֹן הַכֹּהֵן׃

34 *And Moshe and Aharon and the princes of the community numbered the sons of the Kehasi house according to their families and according to their fathers' house,*

לד וַיִּפְקֹד מֹשֶׁה וְאַהֲרֹן וּנְשִׂיאֵי הָעֵדָה
אֶת־בְּנֵי הַקְּהָתִי לְמִשְׁפְּחֹתָם
וּלְבֵית אֲבֹתָם׃

35 *From thirty years old and upward until fifty years old, every one who comes to communal service, to the service at the Tent of Appointed Meeting.*

לה מִבֶּן שְׁלֹשִׁים שָׁנָה וָמַעְלָה וְעַד
בֶּן־חֲמִשִּׁים שָׁנָה כָּל־הַבָּא לַצָּבָא
לַעֲבֹדָה בְּאֹהֶל מוֹעֵד׃

36 *The numbered ones according to their families were two thousand, seven hundred and fifty.*

לו וַיִּהְיוּ פְקֻדֵיהֶם לְמִשְׁפְּחֹתָם
אַלְפַּיִם שְׁבַע מֵאוֹת וַחֲמִשִּׁים׃

32 **ובשמת תפקדו את כלי משמרת משאם**. The [structural] parts entrusted to the sons of Merari are also of symbolic meaning (see Commentary above, 3:23). Hence, when you hand them over, you shall refer to them by their names, which reflect their meaning.

37 *These are the numbered ones of the families of the Kehasi house, every one ministering at the Tent of Appointed Meeting, whom Moshe and Aharon numbered, at the behest of* God *through Moshe.*

לז אֵלֶּה פְקוּדֵי מִשְׁפְּחֹת הַקְּהָתִי כָּל־
הָעֹבֵד בְּאֹהֶל מוֹעֵד אֲשֶׁר פָּקַד
מֹשֶׁה וְאַהֲרֹן עַל־פִּי יְהוָה
בְּיַד־מֹשֶׁה׃ ס שני

38 *And the numbered ones of the sons of Gershon according to their families and according to their fathers' house,*

לח וּפְקוּדֵי בְּנֵי גֵּרְשׁוֹן לְמִשְׁפְּחוֹתָם
וּלְבֵית אֲבֹתָם׃

39 *From thirty years old and upward until fifty years old, everyone who comes to communal service, to the service at the Tent of Appointed Meeting —*

לט מִבֶּן שְׁלֹשִׁים שָׁנָה וָמַעְלָה וְעַד
בֶּן־חֲמִשִּׁים שָׁנָה כָּל־הַבָּא לַצָּבָא
לַעֲבֹדָה בְּאֹהֶל מוֹעֵד׃

40 *Their numbered ones according to their families, according to their fathers' house, were two thousand, six hundred and thirty.*

מ וַיִּהְיוּ פְּקֻדֵיהֶם לְמִשְׁפְּחֹתָם לְבֵית
אֲבֹתָם אַלְפַּיִם וְשֵׁשׁ מֵאוֹת
וּשְׁלֹשִׁים׃

41 *These are the numbered ones of the families of the sons of Gershon, every one ministering at the Tent of Appointed Meeting, whom Moshe and Aharon numbered, at the behest of* God.

מא אֵלֶּה פְקוּדֵי מִשְׁפְּחֹת בְּנֵי גֵרְשׁוֹן
כָּל־הָעֹבֵד בְּאֹהֶל מוֹעֵד אֲשֶׁר
פָּקַד מֹשֶׁה וְאַהֲרֹן עַל־פִּי יְהוָה׃

42 *And the numbered ones of the families of the sons of Merari according to their families and according to their fathers' house,*

מב וּפְקוּדֵי מִשְׁפְּחֹת בְּנֵי מְרָרִי
לְמִשְׁפְּחֹתָם לְבֵית אֲבֹתָם׃

43 *From thirty years old and upward until fifty years old, every one who comes to communal service, to the service at the Tent of Appointed Meeting —*

מג מִבֶּן שְׁלֹשִׁים שָׁנָה וָמַעְלָה וְעַד
בֶּן־חֲמִשִּׁים שָׁנָה כָּל־הַבָּא לַצָּבָא
לַעֲבֹדָה בְּאֹהֶל מוֹעֵד׃

44 *Their numbered ones according to their families were three thousand, two hundred.*

מד וַיִּהְי֥וּ פְקֻדֵיהֶ֖ם לְמִשְׁפְּחֹתָ֑ם
שְׁלֹ֥שֶׁת אֲלָפִ֖ים וּמָאתָֽיִם׃

45 *These are the numbered ones of the families of the sons of Merari, whom Moshe and Aharon numbered, at the behest of* God *through Moshe.*

מה אֵ֣לֶּה פְקוּדֵ֔י מִשְׁפְּחֹ֖ת בְּנֵ֣י מְרָרִ֑י
אֲשֶׁ֨ר פָּקַ֤ד מֹשֶׁה֙ וְאַהֲרֹ֔ן עַל־פִּ֥י
יְהוָ֖ה בְּיַד־מֹשֶֽׁה׃

46 *All the numbered ones, whom Moshe and Aharon and the princes of Israel numbered of the* Levi'im *according to their families and according to their fathers' house,*

מו כָּל־הַפְּקֻדִ֡ים אֲשֶׁר֩ פָּקַ֨ד מֹשֶׁ֧ה
וְאַהֲרֹ֛ן וּנְשִׂיאֵ֥י יִשְׂרָאֵ֖ל אֶת־הַלְוִיִּ֑ם
לְמִשְׁפְּחֹתָ֖ם וּלְבֵ֥ית אֲבֹתָֽם׃

47 *From thirty years old and upward until fifty years old, every one who comes to perform the service of the service and the service of carrying burdens for the Tent of Appointed Meeting —*

מז מִבֶּ֨ן שְׁלֹשִׁ֥ים שָׁנָה֙ וָמַ֔עְלָה וְעַ֖ד
בֶּן־חֲמִשִּׁ֣ים שָׁנָ֑ה כָּל־הַבָּ֗א לַעֲבֹ֨ד
עֲבֹדַ֧ת עֲבֹדָ֛ה וַעֲבֹדַ֥ת מַשָּׂ֖א
בְּאֹ֥הֶל מוֹעֵֽד׃

47 **עבדת עבדה ועבדת משא**. According to the Gemara in *Arachin* 11a, עבודת עבודה is the song that accompanies the offerings: איזהו עבודה שצריכה עבודה הוי אומר זו שירה. It is עבודה, service, that is merely an accompaniment to another עבודה. Thus, the bringing of offerings is here called "עבודה" (see Commentary, *Shemos* 12:25), even though this term is generally not applied in the Torah to offerings, and the song that accompanies the offering is conceived of as assisting the offering and furthering its ultimate purpose.

The meaning of an offering, when it is designated by the term "עבודה," is complete subordination to God's Will; not passive submission, but the creative and active subordination of one who joyfully undertakes to serve God's purposes on earth. The blissfulness of this עבודה finds its highest expression at the bringing of נסכים; for at that time all the yearning of our hearts and the cup of our joy overflow down to the

48 *Their numbered ones were eight thousand five hundred and eighty.*

מח וַיִּהְיוּ פְּקֻדֵיהֶם שְׁמֹנַת אֲלָפִים
וַחֲמֵשׁ מֵאוֹת וּשְׁמֹנִים׃

49 *At the behest of* God *through Moshe did he appoint each one to his service and to his carrying, and they were His numbered ones, since* God *had commanded it to Moshe.*

מט עַל־פִּי יְהֹוָה פָּקַד אוֹתָם בְּיַד־
מֹשֶׁה אִישׁ אִישׁ עַל־עֲבֹדָתוֹ וְעַל־
מַשָּׂאוֹ וּפְקֻדָיו אֲשֶׁר־צִוָּה יְהֹוָה
אֶת־מֹשֶׁה׃ פ שלישי

5 1 God *spoke to Moshe, saying:*

ה א וַיְדַבֵּר יְהֹוָה אֶל־מֹשֶׁה לֵּאמֹר׃

---

base of the altar of the Torah. Human thought knows no happiness comparable to the happiness of one who lives his life in faithfulness to the service of God. The song of the Sanctuary springs from the heart that is filled with the awareness of this happiness; it expresses in words the thoughts and emotions that the offering symbolizes in acts.

49 **ופקדיו**: God's counted ones, who were counted at His command and for His sake (cf. *Bemidbar Rabbah* 6, end).

CHAPTER 5

1 In the preceding chapters (1-4) the people were counted as an עדה, a community for the Torah, and were assigned camping places. In separate camps, they are to encamp at a distance around the Dwelling Place of the Torah, their common center. The *Levi'im*, who were chosen to serve in the Sanctuary, are to encamp in the immediate surroundings of the Dwelling Place.

This arrangement of the nation — the Sanctuary of the Torah in the center, surrounded by the camp of the *Levi'im*, who are the guardians and representatives of the Sanctuary, and surrounding them the camp of the people — expresses unequivocally the nature and calling of this nation. The Torah is the nation's soul, giving existence to the people and uniting its members. God gave the Torah not so as to found with it a temple- or church-congregation, but to establish with it a people, a community, that would base its whole social life on God's

ב צַו אֶת־בְּנֵי יִשְׂרָאֵל וִישַׁלְּחוּ מִן־הַמַּחֲנֶה כָּל־צָרוּעַ וְכָל־זָב וְכֹל טָמֵא לָנָפֶשׁ׃

2 *Command the Children of Israel that they send away from the camp every leper and everyone with a discharge and everyone who has become impure [by contact] with a [dead] person.*

ג מִזָּכָר עַד־נְקֵבָה תְּשַׁלֵּחוּ אֶל־מִחוּץ לַמַּחֲנֶה תְּשַׁלְּחוּם וְלֹא יְטַמְּאוּ אֶת־מַחֲנֵיהֶם אֲשֶׁר אֲנִי שֹׁכֵן בְּתוֹכָם׃

3 *Both male and female shall you send away, outside the camp shall you send them, and they shall not desecrate their camps, in whose midst I dwell.*

Torah. In giving the Torah to Israel, God set the fulfillment of this Torah as the condition on which His Presence would dwell among them. The *Levi'im* are the guardians and bearers of the Torah. They represent the Torah and promote the fulfillment of its commandments. They are separated from the people and "given" to the Sanctuary of the Torah, so that through them the people should be united with the spirit of the Torah.

The laws that now follow are a result of this division of the nation and arrangement of the camps around the Dwelling Place. First: שילוח מחנה.

2-3 **צו וגו'**. The words "דבר אל בני ישראל" are also appropriate for introducing a commandment; for God's Word expresses His Will, which in itself obligates a person. Hence, if a commandment is specially introduced by the words "צו את בני ישראל," the implication is that one should be specially conscientious in its performance. Our Sages say (*Sifre*) that the term "ציווי" always denotes זירוז מיד ולדורות, urging on the performance of a duty that is effective immediately and for all generations to come, and that this term is applied especially to *mitzvos* that entail חסרון כיס — i.e., sacrificing material assets [in this case, having to leave the camp] (see Commentary, *Shemos* 27:20).

צו את בני ישראל וגו'. The preceding commands regarding the census and the division of the camps were directed to Moshe, Aharon, and the elders of Israel. The consequences of this division, which now follow, are directed to every individual among the people; everyone is obligated to abide by them.

וישלחו מן המחנה. The טומאה of the צרוע is set forth in *Vayikra* chapter 13, and already there in verse 46 it says: כל ימי אשר הנגע בו יטמא טמא הוא בדד ישב מחוץ למחנה מושבו; during the whole time that he is טמא, he must remain outside the camp.

The טומאה of the זב is likewise set forth in *Vayikra* chapter 15; it includes all the states of טומאה discussed there and in *Vayikra* 12:2 (see הל׳ ביאת המקדש, 3:3 on משנה למלך) — namely, זב וזבה נדה ויולדת ובעל קרי, and of בעל קרי it also says in *Devarim* (23:11): ויצא אל מחוץ למחנה לא יבא אל תוך המחנה.

טמא לנפש is one who has become טמא by having come into contact with a human corpse. This טומאה will be discussed in detail in chapter 19 of this book. It is mentioned already in *Vayikra* 5:3, in connection with all the other טומאות-by-contact, such as מגע שרץ ונבלה, which are discussed in detail in *Vayikra* chapter 11. The duty to keep away from the precincts of the Sanctuary and to avoid touching sacred objects — a duty incumbent upon all who become טמא by contact — is the underlying assumption of what is said there (in *Vayikra* 5:2-3).

The general duty of keeping away from the Sanctuary when in any state of טומאה is already expressed in *Vayikra* 15:31: והזרתם את בני ישראל מטמאתם ולא ימתו בטמאתם בטמאם את משכני אשר בתוכם. This duty will now be explained more precisely.

The three categories of טומאה mentioned here — מצורע, זב, and טמא מת — are not alike in their *halachos*. מצורע is more severe than זב, in that a מצורע is מטמא בביאה (see Commentary, ibid. 13:46). זב is more severe than טמא מת, in that a זב is מטמא משכב ומושב and even תחת אבן מסמא (Commentary, ibid. 15:4). And the Halachah teaches that they are also not alike in respect to the expulsion stated here (*Sifre* here; *Pesachim* 68a).

As already stated above (Commentary, v. 1), and as is evident from the arrangement of the camps described in the preceding chapters, the national circle is divided into three spheres. In the center is the sphere of the Sanctuary, מחנה שכינה; immediately surrounding it is the camp of the *Levi'im*, מחנה לוייה, which is then surrounded by the camp of the people, מחנה ישראל. Correspondingly, later, in the city of God, the sphere of the Sanctuary, beginning at עזרת ישראל, is מחנה שכינה; from הר הבית to עזרת ישראל, which begins at the Nikanor Gateway, is מחנה לוייה; the whole of the rest of the city, up to הר הבית, is מחנה ישראל.

The מצורע, whose טומאה is the severest of the three levels of טומאה, is banned from all three camps, משתלח חוץ לשלוש מחנות. Thus, he is excluded even from מחנה ישראל.

טמאים of the second level — זב וזבה נדה ויולדת ובעל קרי; any טומאות היוצאת עליו מגופו, i.e., anyone whose טומאה stems from his own bodily condition — are banned from two camps, משתלח חוץ לשתי מחנות: they must keep out of מחנה שכינה ומחנה לוייה, but may remain in מחנה ישראל.

טמאים of the third level — טמא מת and also מגע שרץ ונבלה and in general anyone who contracts טומאת מגע — are banned only from מחנה שכינה but may stay in מחנה לוייה and מחנה ישראל.

In our opinion, the first sentence, וישלחו מן המחנה כל צרוע וכל זב וכל טמא לנפש, refers especially to מחנה שכינה, which is prohibited to all three of these categories, including even טמא מת. The second sentence, מזכר עד נקבה תשלחו, refers especially to מחנה לוייה, from which זב וזבה etc. are expelled. For these טומאות differ for male and female; hence it says here: מזכר עד נקבה תשלחו (see *Niddah* 28b: מזכר עד נקבה תשלחו זכר ודאי נקבה ודאית וכו׳ אי הכי כי איטמי בשאר טומאות לא לישלחו, אמר קרא מזכר, מטומאה הפורשת מן הזכר, ע״ש ברש״י). Accordingly, the third sentence, אל מחוץ למחנה תשלחום, refers especially to מצורע, who is expelled from the entire camp, even from מחנה ישראל. And then the concluding sentence says of all of them: ולא יטמאו את מחניהם, which denotes a plurality of camps. Each one of them must be careful not to desecrate the camp specially suited to him, from which he is commanded to keep away.

אשר אני שכן בתוכם: My Presence dwells in all three camps — in מחנה ישראל and in מחנה לוייה no less than in מחנה שכינה. These טמאים shall keep away from the various camps, out of reverence for the Shechinah which dwells in them.

If we now compare the meanings of these three classes of טמאים, we find that they correspond to the three camps from which they are banned. We have already seen (Commentary, *Vayikra* chaps. 13 and 14) that נגעי צרעת with their associated laws are the finger of God pointing to *social* wrongdoing. The expulsion of the מצורע is meant to bring about *social purity*; hence, it is understandable that the מצורע is expelled also from מחנה ישראל.

זב וזבה are connected to the sphere of *sexual* purity (see Commentary, ibid. chap. 15). But *sexual purity*, purity in sexual life, is the very first duty of all those who seek to spiritually uplift themselves and draw near to God. In Judaism's view, spiritual distinction is no license for moral lapses. On the contrary, the greater the spiritual gifts and the higher the spiritual calling, the more serious and the more sweeping are the demands for moral purity. *Our* poets, *our* singers, and so forth, men of vision and eloquence, are not to devote their minds to God — and their bodies to lustful sensuality. We have been told that the Shechinah departs because of ערוה: ולא יראה בך ערות דבר (*Devarim* 23:15) — מלמד שהעריות מסלקות את השכינה (*Sifre* ad loc.). In Judaism, the אורים and the תומים go together (see Commentary, *Shemos* 28:43); יחוס, which depends on sexual purity, already adorned the cradle in which our priests and the singers of our Sanctuary choir awakened to life (see *Arachin* 11a, מעלין מדוכן ליוחסין). That is the spirit that prevailed in מחנה לוייה, and that is what is symbolized by the mitzvah of שילוח זב וכו׳ ממחנה לוייה.

In *Vayikra* (Commentary, 5:13, 21:5, et al.) we focused several times on the contrast between טומאת מת and the true conception of God taught by the Torah and its Sanctuary. According to the heathen conception, death and the dead attest to god. They reveal the power of god, to whom proud man must submit. This power, the irresistible power of the forces of nature, is the heathen's god. But the truth of the Torah says: אֵין בַּמָּוֶת זִכְרֶךָ בִּשְׁאוֹל מִי יוֹדֶה־לָּךְ (*Tehillim* 6:6; see Commentary there). Death and the grave are not the signature of God. The power to which man submits in life, and which digs a grave for his bodily shell, is itself subject to God's authority, and is also given over to the authority of man who has sanctified himself in God's sanctity. In life he subdues this power, and even in death he does not submit to it: לֹא־תַעֲזֹב נַפְשִׁי לִשְׁאוֹל (ibid. 16:10); he merely surrenders to it his bodily shell, whose origin is dust and whose nature is earthly. Man himself is close to God even in life, by virtue of the moral power of his Divine freedom which God has breathed into him; and in death, unchained, the whole of him returns to God. Not the dead man, but the living man who resembles his God, who masters himself with his moral power, and who freely rules over his earthly drives — he, the living man who does his duty, is the one who tells of God's glory and offers praise to Him.

This power in man, which enables him to rule over himself in freedom, is the core of his personality; it is a portion of God from on high, by which God imparts to man a portion of His power and freedom. This power manifests itself whenever man does his duty in freedom, for it is a fruit that has ripened, with God's help, on the tree of life of man's Divine nature.

4 *The Children of Israel did so, they sent them away outside the camp; as* God *had spoken to Moshe, so did the Children of Israel do.*

ד וַיַּעֲשׂוּ־כֵן֙ בְּנֵ֣י יִשְׂרָאֵ֔ל וַיְשַׁלְּח֣וּ
אוֹתָ֔ם אֶל־מִח֖וּץ לַֽמַּחֲנֶ֑ה כַּאֲשֶׁ֨ר
דִּבֶּ֤ר יְהוָה֙ אֶל־מֹשֶׁ֔ה כֵּ֥ן עָשׂ֖וּ בְּנֵ֥י
יִשְׂרָאֵֽל׃ פ

5 God *spoke to Moshe, saying:*

ה וַיְדַבֵּ֥ר יְהוָ֖ה אֶל־מֹשֶׁ֥ה לֵּאמֹֽר׃

6 *Speak to the Children of Israel,*

ו דַּבֵּר֮ אֶל־בְּנֵ֣י יִשְׂרָאֵל֒ אִ֣ישׁ אֽוֹ־

"For it is not the grave that praises You, not death that extols You . . . [rather] חַי חַי הוּא יוֹדֶךָ" (*Yeshayahu* 38:18-19). This is Judaism's joyous message. Living man is to praise אלקים חיים. Anyone who is טמא מת and all similar טמאים such as one rendered טמא by מגע שרץ ונבלה (see Commentary, *Vayikra* 11:46-47) — in short, anyone who contracts טומאה that comes from without by contact — all these must he (living man) keep away from the sphere of God's Sanctuary: טמא מת משתלח חוץ למחנה שכינה (see also Commentary below, chap. 19, end).

5 **וידבר וגו'**. Now follow three laws: גזל הגר, סוטה, and נזיר. Later, we will see that these laws are closely linked to the three national spheres discussed above — מחנה ישראל, מחנה לוייה, and מחנה שכינה — and to the three classes of טמאים who are expelled from these spheres: צרוע, זב, and טמא מת.

The mitzvah of שילוח מחנה shows symbolically what the laws of גזל הגר, סוטה, and נזיר seek to realize in the actual reality of life. The law of גזל הגר parallels the mitzvah of שילוח מצורע ממחנה ישראל; it shows that God dwells wherever the people have *social* dealings. The law of סוטה parallels the mitzvah of שילוח זב ממחנה לוייה; it teaches that the Shechinah resides with husband and wife in the sexual life of the *family.* The law of נזיר parallels the mitzvah of שילוח טמא מת ממחנה שכינה; it shows the presence of God in the life of each *individual* who aspires to moral freedom.

Scripture begins with פרשת גזל הגר.

6 **דבר אל בני ישראל וגו'**. The basic principles of this law have already been set forth in *Vayikra* 5:20ff. We are dealing here with אשם גזילה. It

saying: If a man or a woman commits a sin from among all the sins of man, committing a breach of trust against God, *and that person has incurred guilt.*	אִשָּׁה כִּי יַעֲשׂוּ מִכָּל־חַטֹּאת הָאָדָם לִמְעֹל מַעַל בַּיהוָה וְאָשְׁמָה הַנֶּפֶשׁ הַהִוא׃

says there that if one denies a debt owed to another for whatever reason, and denies it under oath, whether in court or out of court, he must pay קרן (the principal) and חומש (a quarter of the principal) to the rightful claimant, and he must also bring an אשם offering. For a full discussion of this law, see our Commentary in *Vayikra* (ibid.).

This law is repeated here in order to supplement it with two *halachos*. First (v. 7), that one does not bring the אשם or add the חומש unless he voluntarily admits his guilt. But if witnesses testify against him that he had sworn falsely, he pays only קרן; on the other hand, the full weight of the pronouncement לא ינקה ה׳ (*Shemos* 20:7) rests on him, without mitigation (see Commentary, *Vayikra* 5:23). Second (v. 8), that if, after the defendant has sworn falsely, the claimant dies and leaves no heirs, the debtor pays קרן and חומש to the כהנים.

מכל חטאת האדם. Just as עון הקדשים (*Shemos* 28:38) and עון המקדש (below, 18:1) denote sins against the holy things and against the Sanctuary, so, too, here חטאת האדם could denote sin *against* other people. More likely, however, is that it is the ordinary possessive, "sins of man," and Scripture here is relying on the detailed presentation in *Vayikra*, which begins with a similar formulation. For from the continuation it is clear here, too, that we are dealing with an unpaid debt — i.e., a sin relating to another person's assets.

למעל מעל בה׳. Every such sin against one's fellow man is also a breach of trust against God; for God is the Guarantor of honesty in business dealings between men. The breach of trust is especially serious if the person takes an oath and invokes the Name of God in order to prove his honesty. In such a case, the appeal to God is exploited in order to conceal an injustice. The debt owed to one's fellow man becomes, as a result of the oath, a debt owed to God. It is elevated to sacred status because the oath-taker claims that he is "close to God"; he, as it were, wraps himself in the מעיל of a כהן, and his treachery

ז וְהִתְוַדּ֗וּ אֶֽת־חַטָּאתָם֮ אֲשֶׁ֣ר עָשׂוּ֒ וְהֵשִׁ֤יב אֶת־אֲשָׁמוֹ֙ בְּרֹאשׁ֔וֹ וַחֲמִישִׁת֖וֹ יֹסֵ֣ף עָלָ֑יו וְנָתַ֕ן לַאֲשֶׁ֖ר אָשַׁ֥ם לֽוֹ׃

7 *They must acknowledge to themselves the sin they committed, and he must then make restitution for the object of his guilt in its [full] capital value and add to it one fifth, and give it to the one with regard to whom he has been guilty.*

against his fellow man thereby becomes מעילה (see Commentary, *Vayikra* 5:15 and 5:21-22ff.). There (*Vayikra* 5:21) it says similarly: נפש כי תחטא ומעלה וגו׳, and the sin is explained in detail: וכחש בעמיתו בפקדון וגו׳ או מכל אשר ישבע עליו לשקר וגו׳ (ibid. 5:21, 24).

ואשמה הנפש ההיא. He who increases his assets by means of a false oath has laden himself with the guilt that brings desolation in its wake (see Commentary, ibid. 5:13 and 26).

איש או אשה וגו׳. Thus the far-reaching legal principle: השוה הכתוב אשה לאיש לכל עונשין שבתורה (*Bava Kamma* 15a, *Pesachim* 43a, et al.).

7 **והתודו** (see Commentary, *Vayikra* 5:5). This is the first halachah which supplements the *halachos* already set forth in *Vayikra*. Only one who admits his guilt brings an אשם and pays חומש. As regards אשם, this goes without saying; for one does not bring an אשם or any other offering unless he has confessed and pledged to mend his ways (see Commentary, ibid.). The foregoing halachah, however, applies to חומש as well: Only one's own confession — not the testimony of witnesses — makes one liable to חומש. Witnesses obligate one to pay only the principal, whereas confession — whether arising voluntarily or after the testimony of witnesses — makes one liable to חומש and אשם (see *Bava Kamma* 108a-b).

והשיב את אשמו בראשו וגו׳: ממון המשתלם בראש מוסיף חומש, ממון שאין משתלם בראש אין מוסיף חומש (*Bava Kamma* 65b). If the testimony of witnesses makes him liable only to the principal, his confession makes him liable also to חומש; but if the testimony of witnesses makes him liable to כפל — as in cases of גניבה or טען טענת גנב (see Commentary, *Shemos* 22:6) — his confession does not make him liable to חומש; rather, in such a case he is liable only to כפל and אשם.

Moreover, כפל excludes חומש in every case. One does not become

8 *But if a man has no legal heir to whom restitution could be made for the object of the guilt, then the object of guilt for which restitution is made to* God *shall be the priest's, besides the ram of the atonements with which atonement is effected for him.*

ח וְאִם־אֵין לָאִישׁ גֹּאֵל לְהָשִׁיב הָאָשָׁם אֵלָיו הָאָשָׁם הַמּוּשָׁב לַיהוָה לַכֹּהֵן מִלְּבַד אֵיל הַכִּפֻּרִים אֲשֶׁר יְכַפֶּר־בּוֹ עָלָיו׃

liable to חומש on account of an object for which one has already become liable to כפל, not even if one takes an oath (about the object) totally unrelated to the matter of כפל — e.g., טען טענת גנב ונשבע וחזר וטען טענת אבד ונשבע ובאו עדים אקמייתא והודה אבתרייתא; because, as it says there: ממון המחייבתו כפל פוטרו מן החומש (*Bava Kamma* 107b-108a).

ונתן לאשר אשם לו. According to ר׳ נתן (*Gittin* 37a), sometimes he does not pay his direct creditor but, rather, someone to whom he became indebted indirectly: נושה בחבירו מנה וחבירו בחבירו, מוציאין מזה ונותנין לזה.

8 **ואם אין לאיש גאל**. A גואל is a relative who is entitled to inherit [his blood relation] (cf. *Vayikra* 25:25).

The Torah does not mention the self-evident halachah that if the claimant dies, the debt is paid to his heirs. That Scripture passes over this case in silence and immediately takes up the case of a claimant who dies and leaves no heirs is particularly understandable in view of the explanation given by ר׳ נתן to the end of the preceding verse, ונתן לאשר אשם לו. For according to that explanation, the debt can be collected not only by the original claimant, but also by one who has a legal claim to the claimant's property — e.g., one of his creditors. By *a fortiori* argument, this would include the claimant's heir, for he is the natural claimant to the claimant's property. Scripture then adds ואם אין לאיש גאל, as he left no heirs.

Now, according to Jewish law (as explained in *Bava Kamma* 109a), such a case [that a person should die and leave no heirs] can arise only in the instance of a גר who dies leaving no children. Everyone else has relatives — however distant — entitled to inherit him; for the right of inheritance is transmitted through one's ancestors down to their descendants. But a גר enters a new existence at the moment of his conversion, is considered as newly born: גר שנתגייר כקטן שנולד דמי (*Yevamos* 22a, et al.); hence, only children born to him after his conversion are entitled to inherit him. If he dies leaving no such children, he leaves no legal heirs, and there exists no creditor entitled to claim the debts owed to him. As ownerless assets, they belong to the first person who takes them into his possession; and since they now are in the possession of the debtors, the debtors precede all others in possessing them.

It is different in the case described here, and this is the second halachah supplementing the *halachos* already set forth in *Vayikra*. If the defendant denies the debt and swears falsely, and *then* the claimant dies, האשם המושב לה׳ לכהן: As soon as the defendant admits that he swore falsely, the asset becomes God's, and God turns it over to the כהן: קנאו ה׳ ונתנו לכהן שבאותו משמר (*Bava Kamma* 109b). It must be returned to God; for his oath constituted a denial not only to his fellow man, but also to God, and His confession was an admission to God.

He must pay both קרן and חומש: אשם זה קרן, המושב זה חומש (ibid. 110a). אשם cannot refer to the offering, for the offering is mentioned specially afterward: מלבד איל וגו׳. Thus, the קרן to be restored is called here "אשם," whereas המושב לה׳ refers to חומש; for the fact that the asset became sanctified unto God at the time of the oath is evidenced by the requirement to pay a חומש.

We see, then, that an asset of someone who dies leaving no heirs — and which is now restored to God — is called by Scripture "אשם." Thus, the restoration of the asset is considered an offering. Hence, restitution for גזל הגר must be made in the daytime, cannot be made in installments, each member of the division of כהנים on duty at the time is entitled to an equal share, and the כהנים cannot come to any mutual arrangement of exchange at such distribution: מה אשם אין חולקין אשם כנגד אשם, אף גזל אין חולקין גזל הגר כנגד גזל הגר (ibid. 110a-b).

מלבד איל הכיפורים אשר יכפר בו עליו. The offering may not be brought until the money has been repaid; and both — the money and the offering — belong together: they both go to the division of כהנים on duty at the time (משמר, see Commentary, *Vayikra* 6:19).

9 *Also any uplifted donation with regard to all the holy things of the Children of Israel, which they bring to the priest to be near [to* God*], shall be his.*

ט וְכָל־תְּרוּמָ֞ה לְכָל־קָדְשֵׁ֧י בְנֵֽי־
יִשְׂרָאֵ֛ל אֲשֶׁר־יַקְרִ֥יבוּ לַכֹּהֵ֖ן ל֥וֹ
יִהְיֶֽה׃

10 *But [as for] every man's holy things, they are his; only that which a man gives to the priest shall be his [i.e., the priest's].*

י וְאִ֥ישׁ אֶת־קֳדָשָׁ֖יו ל֣וֹ יִהְי֑וּ אִ֛ישׁ
אֲשֶׁר־יִתֵּ֥ן לַכֹּהֵ֖ן ל֥וֹ יִהְיֶֽה׃ פ רביעי

9 **וכל תרומה וגו׳**. This verse and the following verse are incidental remarks on the gifts that are directed to the כהנים; thus their connection to the preceding verses.

It says in the preceding verse: המושב לה׳ לכהן; that which is to be restored to God is to be given to the כהנים. To that, Scripture adds the remark: וכל תרומה וגו׳ אשר יקריבו לכהן. תרומה literally means: something uplifted to God. It denotes, then, anything dedicated to God. Hence Scripture uses here the term "הקרבה," which usually is used only in connection with offerings: אשר יקריבו לכהן. One brings it to the כהן, but one really wants to "bring it near" to God.

Now, it says here that every תרומה given to a כהן as הקרבה becomes the כהן's property, for it has been transferred to him by God. That is exactly what was just said regarding גזל הגר: קנאו השם ונתנו לכהן; or, as it generally says of the holy things given to the כהנים: כהנים משולחן גבוה קא זכו (*Beitzah* 21a). Similarly, our Sages (*Sifre*) derive from here that בכורים — regarding the disposition of which nothing is said in *Devarim* 26 — are to be given to the כהנים.

10 **ואיש את קדשיו לו יהיו וגו׳**. The grammatical construction indicates that there are two sentences in the first half of this verse. ואיש את קדשיו, but every man has holy things! That is to say, every man has the right of disposition of his holy things, לו יהיו. Although dedicated to God and transferred to the כהנים, they are still his in one respect — namely, that only what is *given* to the כהן belongs to him: איש אשר יתן לכהן לו יהיה. No כהן has any direct claim to any of the priestly gifts. Rather, whoever is obligated to give a gift is entitled to give it to any כהן he chooses. No

כהן can demand it from him. This right of disposal of one's holy things is called "טובת הנאה." As it says in the *Sifre*: ואיש את קדשיו לו יהיו למה נאמר? לפי שהוא אומר כל תרומת הקדשים אשר ירימו בני ישראל (להלן יח, ט) שומע אני יטלם בזרוע ת״ל ואיש את קדשיו לו יהיו, מגיד שטובת הנאת קדשים לבעליהם. The right of disposition and deriving benefit thereby is called "טובת הנאה." A person is entitled to show favor to any כהן he chooses by enabling him to benefit from his holy things.

Let us now consider the two novel *halachos* derived here in פרשת גזל הגר, namely: One does not bring the אשם or add the חומש unless he voluntarily admitted (והתודו) his sin. And if the claimant dies and leaves no heirs, the defendant must restore the asset to God — if he denied the claim and swore falsely. These two *halachos* are the practical outgrowth of קדושת מחנה ישראל, the holiness of the camp of Israel. They show that God's gaze is ever-watchful when people do business.

The oath-taker's very appeal to God already shows this; for he submits all his worldly possessions to Divine judgment, in order to prove his honesty and to exonerate himself in this specific case. He thereby assumes that God pays close attention to every word spoken and to every deed done when people do business. Through his oath he declares that Divine providence and Divine rule are the power that governs the world, and that where human justice falls short — out of limited knowledge or power — Divine justice takes over.

When the person confesses his sin, this shows God's power exerting its influence even within man's own mind. God's power reveals itself in the Divine voice that we call "conscience," and which Scripture calls the "lamp of God," by which God "searches even the most secret, innermost chambers of our minds" (*Mishlei* 20:27).

When he denied the claim by invoking the Name of God, the asset thereby became sanctified unto God. As in the case of all holy things, a fifth must be added to it. If the claimant dies leaving no heirs, the defendant must return it to God.

This, then, is the whole import of this law: God dwells in the *social* life of the people, sanctifying that life with His sanctity.

In light of the foregoing, the tension between כפל and חומש — that ממון המחייבו כפל פוטרו מן החומש (see Commentary above, v. 7) — is easy to understand. We have already explained (Commentary, *Shemos* 21:37) that כפל represents *human* justice, which is the firm foundation of social life. The property owner relied on this foundation, whereas the thief

11 God *spoke to Moshe, saying:*

12 *Speak to the Children of Israel and say to them: Any man whose wife strays from the right path and commits a breach of trust against him,*

יא וַיְדַבֵּר יְהוָה אֶל־מֹשֶׁה לֵּאמֹר׃

יב דַּבֵּר אֶל־בְּנֵי יִשְׂרָאֵל וְאָמַרְתָּ
אֲלֵהֶם אִישׁ אִישׁ כִּי־תִשְׂטֶה
אִשְׁתּוֹ וּמָעֲלָה בוֹ מָעַל׃

scorned it and exploited it. By contrast, חומש represents *Divine* justice, which is the basis of the world and of its continued existence. It is necessary to give expression to this basis precisely after an oath, for in such a case human justice falls short. Thus, only confession makes him liable to חומש. קנס, on the other hand, is not imposed if a person confesses and incriminates himself. קנס, then, is emblematic of the power of human justice. Hence, where the court has full authority and the defendant has already been charged with a קנס, liability to חומש is excluded.

פרשת גזל הגר is nothing but the practical outgrowth of שילוח מצורע ממחנה ישראל.

11 Scripture follows with פרשת סוטה. This section teaches that the Shechinah resides with husband and wife in the sexual life of the family; it parallels the mitzvah of שילוח זב וזבה ממחנה לוייה.

12 **איש איש כי תשטה אשתו**. שטה: to stray from the path; thus שְׂטֵה מֵעָלָיו (*Mishlei* 4:15), and thus here: to deviate from the path of morality. Similarly, in Aramaic שטה denotes deviating from the path of rationality; i.e., a mental aberration, insanity. Our Sages linked the two concepts: אין אדם עובר עבירה אלא אם כן נכנס בו רוח שטות (*Sotah* 3a). Every moral lapse is also a mental aberration; moral truth and logical truth are interconnected; and no one sins unless he has lost the true perspective of things.

ומעלה בו מעל. In the preceding פרשה (5:6) the term "מעילה" (למעל מעל בה') is used to teach us that social relationships between man and his fellow man are also sacred to God. Here, too, the use of the term "מעילה" teaches us that the marital relationship between husband and wife is sacred to God. Hence, in the following verse it says והיא נטמאה; for a woman who is unfit to continue in her marriage is called "טמאה."

13 *[In that another] man has lain with her carnally, but it has remained hidden from her husband, and she went to a secret place so that she has forfeited her purity, then no complete testimony is required against her; all that matters is that she was not forced.*

יג וְשָׁכַ֨ב אִ֣ישׁ אֹתָהּ֮ שִׁכְבַת־זֶ֒רַע֒ וְנֶעְלַם֙ מֵעֵינֵ֣י אִישָׁ֔הּ וְנִסְתְּרָ֖ה וְהִ֣יא נִטְמָ֑אָה וְעֵד֙ אֵ֣ין בָּ֔הּ וְהִ֖וא לֹ֥א נִתְפָּֽשָׂה׃

Marriage is קודש. Marital fidelity — with proper moral behavior — is called "טהרה" (v. 28), and the opposite is called "טומאה"; if a woman becomes אסורה to her husband, it is said of her that נטמאה: טומאה excludes her from her marriage, just as טומאה always means exclusion from the Sanctuary and its holy things.

The wife's conduct described here in verse 12 is not yet outright adultery. However, it does constitute a deviation from the path of morality and modesty; hence, it has already given her husband just cause to warn her about her conduct (v. 14).

13 **ושכב וגו'**. This verse concludes with the words והִוא לא נתפשה : The act was not done *to* her by force but, rather, was willingly done *by* her; she cannot claim that it was a case of אונס.

From this conclusion we learn that our verse speaks of a case where her guilt has already been proven [by the testimony of a single witness; see below]; hence the continuance of the marriage is legally forbidden, and there exists no doubt requiring a Divine decision. The Halachah understands this conclusion — והיא לא נתפשה — as a statement that establishes a categorical איסור. Hence, whenever it cites this statement, the Halachah adds the explanatory word אסורה: והיא לא נתפשה אסורה.

From the limiting pronoun והיא we learn that although in general תפישה, i.e., אונס, does not prohibit the continuance of the marriage, with an אשת כהן the continuance of the marriage is forbidden even in the case of אונס: והיא לא נתפשה אסורה הא נתפשה מותרת ויש לך אחרת שאף על פי שנתפשה אסורה ואיזו זו אשת כהן (*Kesubos* 51b; *Yevamos* 56b).

Indeed, the case discussed here involves adultery: ושכב איש וגו'; but this was not proven [by the testimony of two witnesses]: ונעלם וגו'. What

14 *But if the spirit has come over him that he must maintain his [marital] claim, and he has warned his wife, but she may nevertheless have forfeited her purity, or there has come over him the spirit to maintain his [marital] claim, and he has warned his wife, but she may not have forfeited her purity,*

יד וְעָבַ֨ר עָלָ֧יו רֽוּחַ־קִנְאָ֛ה וְקִנֵּ֥א אֶת־אִשְׁתּ֖וֹ וְהִ֣וא נִטְמָ֑אָה אֽוֹ־עָבַ֨ר עָלָ֤יו רֽוּחַ־קִנְאָה֙ וְקִנֵּ֣א אֶת־אִשְׁתּ֔וֹ וְהִ֖יא לֹ֥א נִטְמָֽאָה׃

was proven was only: ונסתרה; she secluded herself with another man; and beforehand she had deviated from the ways of modesty (v. 12), thereby giving her husband cause to warn her about that man (v. 14), and now she was found together with him בסתר, secluded, in such a manner that she may have had sexual relations with him: והיא נטמאה.

The סתירה (seclusion) and the קינוי (warning — see v. 14) must be certified by two witnesses, like any דבר שבממון and דבר שבערוה (see Commentary, *Devarim* 19:15 and 24:1; *Sotah* 2a and 31a-b). But thereafter ועד אין בה, complete testimony against her is not required. Even if there are not two witnesses, but only one witness who states that she was defiled, everything depends on whether there was תפישה. והיא לא נתפשה: If she cannot claim that the sexual relations were באונס, she is אסורה לבעלה.

This law — that in this case a single witness suffices — is attributed to רגלים לדבר (*Sotah* 3a): The fact determined on the basis of one witness has already been proven by the circumstances established by complete testimony; for two witnesses testified to קינוי and סתירה. As our Sages say (ibid.): מפני מה האמינה תורה עד אחד בסוטה, שרגלים לדבר, שהרי קינא לה ונסתרה ועד אחד מעידה שהיא טמאה. Let us note, however, that, despite the רגלים לדבר, the testimony of the one witness effects only the breakup of the marriage and all that that entails in civil law, but it has no effect whatsoever in criminal law.

14 **ועבר עליו רוח קנאה**. We have already noted (Commentary, *Shemos* 20:5) the relation of קנא to קנה, to acquire something and possess it as your own. We explained that קִנֵּא means to claim something as rightfully

yours; to demand something as rightfully belonging to you. Hence קנא -ב: to demand for yourself something belonging to someone else, claiming that it should be yours; to envy someone because of something he possesses.

Accordingly, קנא את אשתו means: he asserts his rights over his wife; he demands her as belonging to him; he reminds her of his rights as her husband and warns her against violating them. Thus, our Sages say: אין קנוי אלא לשון התראה (*Sotah* 3a). They say further: כיצד מקנא להּ? אומר לה בפני שנים אל תדברי עם פלוני (ibid. 2a), and רש״י (on the Gemara ibid. 5b) explains that קינוי is: אל תסתרי עם פלוני.

רוח קנאה, then, is the husband's feeling that his conjugal rights have been violated by his wife; or it is his suspicion that these rights are likely to be violated. It is the suspicion of unfaithfulness.

Of this רוח קנאה it says ועבר עליו: it comes over him "from without." That is to say, it is not just an inner feeling; it is not the figment of a morbid imagination. Rather, his suspicions were forced on him by his wife's immodest behavior, as already described by Scripture (v. 12). Hence וקנא את אשתו: he warns her not to violate her obligations as a married woman.

Our verse introduces a new possibility. The new element does not lie in the words ועבר עליו וגו׳ וקנא וגו׳ themselves. For the Halachah teaches (*Sotah* 3a) that already in the case described in the preceding verse — where the decision is made on the evidence of a single witness — קינוי is necessary: the woman must be warned in the presence of two witnesses. It is this warning and the סתירה that follows in spite of it which together form the circumstantial evidence (רגלים לדבר) on the basis of which the testimony of a single witness of טומאה is accepted. Rather, what is new about our verse is that it describes a case in which there is not even a single witness of טומאה; hence, even after קינוי and סתירה, it is still in doubt whether נטמאה or לא נטמאה. Our verse gives expression to this doubt by placing the two possibilities side by side: The woman aroused his suspicion by improper behavior; he warned her against סתירה, she ignored the warning ונסתרה — and also נטמאה. Or the woman aroused his suspicion by improper behavior; he warned her against סתירה, she ignored the warning ונסתרה — but nevertheless לא נטמאה.

The two verses 13 and 14 complement each other. Verse 13 mentions סתירה, and must be supplied with the קינוי mentioned in verse 14; for only a warning certified by two witnesses, followed by the testimony of

טו וְהֵבִ֨יא הָאִ֣ישׁ אֶת־אִשְׁתּוֹ֮ אֶל־
הַכֹּהֵן֒ וְהֵבִ֤יא אֶת־קָרְבָּנָהּ֙ עָלֶ֔יהָ

15 *Then the man shall bring his wife*
to the priest and bring her offering
for her: one tenth of an efah *of bar-*

two witnesses that the warning was disregarded, constitute the circumstantial evidence (רגלים לדבר) on the basis of which the testimony of a single witness of טומאה is accepted. Similarly, verse 14 mentions קינוי, and must be supplied with the סתירה mentioned in verse 13; for a mere warning without evidence that the woman disregarded the warning does not justify casting doubt on her טהרה, and there is no need for a Divine decision to allow the continuance of the marriage.

This, then, is the rule: If there was קינוי וסתירה על פי שני עדים, then a single witness testifying that adultery took place is sufficient to make her אסורה לבעלה. If there is no witness of adultery, she is אסורה לבעלה until her unbroken innocence is determined by Heaven. This determination comes as a result of the procedure described here in the continuation.

Our verse states that the wife is אסורה לבעלה as long as there is doubt — because of the סתירה — whether נטמאה or לא נטמאה. Thus, the Torah here treats ספק טומאה stringently, only that the טומאה in question here is actual moral טומאה; but from here we extrapolate to cases of doubt regarding symbolical טומאה. For the following is a major principle in הלכות טומאה: דבר שיש בו דעת לישאל, ברשות היחיד ספיקו טמא, ברשות הרבים ספיקו טהור, ושאין בו דעת לישאל, בין ברשות היחיד בין ברשות הרבים ספיקו טהור (*Sotah* 28b). This halachah is derived from סוטה, and we have already explained it in detail (Commentary, *Vayikra* 7:19-21). Here we would only note that the equating of these two טומאות — moral, sexual טומאה and symbolical טומאה — indicates that they are one and the same. This constitutes an emphatic statement: The Torah uses terms of טומאה and טהרה to describe the demands of marriage as regards moral purity. The implication is that the Torah regards marriage as a מקדש, a Sanctuary. Conversely, הלכות טומאה are derived from the laws regarding moral purity. The implication is that הלכות טומאה are merely the symbolic representation of moral purity which is based on moral freedom.

15 **והביא האיש**. As already stated above, once there are witnesses to קינוי and סתירה, doubt arises whether נטמאה האשה; from that point onward she is אסורה לבעלה, until the question is decided by God. However, placing

עֲשִׂירִת הָאֵיפָה קֶמַח שְׂעֹרִים לֹא־יִצֹק עָלָיו שֶׁמֶן וְלֹא־יִתֵּן עָלָיו לְבֹנָה כִּי־מִנְחַת קְנָאֹת הוּא מִנְחַת זִכָּרוֹן מַזְכֶּרֶת עָוֺן׃

ley meal. He shall not pour oil upon it and shall not place frankincense upon it, for it is a gift symbolizing that he subordinates the maintaining of his (marital) claim to God*; it is a gift symbolizing that he subordinates the remembrance to* God*, to recall a sin.*

the decision in the hands of God depends on the willingness of both husband and wife. The husband can opt for cancellation of the marriage rather than putting the woman to this test. And the wife, without admitting any guilt, can opt for termination of the marriage rather than undergoing the test. The test cannot be forced on the husband nor on the wife (*Sotah* 6a). Also, if the husband dies in the meantime, the test is not administered; for its main purpose — to allow for the continuance of the marriage — is no longer applicable (*Kesubos* 81a).

Let us also note that the procedure prescribed here for a woman whose fidelity is suspect can be carried out only by the highest court, בית דין הגדול בירושלים (*Sotah* 7a); the husband must bring his wife to Yerushalayim.

והביא את קרבנה עליה. A husband must bring all of his wife's obligatory offerings (*Nedarim* 35b). This expresses the intimate unity of souls which exists in marriage. Here, too, the husband brings his wife's offering: He wants the marriage to continue, if only God will decide favorably.

Her offering consists of עשירית האיפה קמח שערים; not סולת, but unsifted קמח, the coarsest sort of flour; and not חטים, but שעורים, barley, the commonest kind of grain, usually used only for animal fodder. It is a question here of simple existence, to be or not to be; and since it is the husband bringing the מנחה of the wife, it is a question of the existence or nonexistence of the marriage. For in the case of every מנחה, a person places his sustenance at God's feet, thereby surrendering to Him in homage his future existence (see Commentary, *Vayikra* 2:1).

According to *Sotah* 14a, שעורים, as מאכל בהמה, also represents the doubt about the wife's moral respectability and human dignity: כשם שמעשיה מעשה בהמה כך קרבנה מאכל בהמה. In any case, she deserves this char-

16 *The priest shall have her come nearer and have her stand before* **God.**	טז וְהִקְרִיב אֹתָהּ הַכֹּהֵן וְהֶעֱמִדָהּ לִפְנֵי יְהוָה׃

acterization; for even if her guilt did not reach the point of complete טומאה, she did deviate from the ways of modesty (vv. 12, 14).

לא יצק עליו שמן ולא יתן עליו לבנה: No sign of well-being and no sign of satisfaction should be on it; כי מנחת קנאת הוא מנחת זכרון מזכרת עון: for the seriousness of the doubt represented by this מנחה excludes שמן and לבונה.

The two sides of the doubt, which is the cause of this מנחה, are expressed here by the dual designation "מנחת קנאת" and "מנחת זכרון."

קנאות: On the one hand, the husband *wishes to vindicate his wife*; he wants her to remain his, if she still is his. This intention is made clear by the fact that he brings her before God for a decision. If he were interested in dissolving the marriage, there would be no need for him to take this action, since she is already אסורה to him. He is seeking from God a היתר.

On the other hand, the מנחה is **מנחת זכרון מזכרת עון**. We have already explained (Commentary, *Vayikra* 2:2) that the concept of זכירה and אזכרה [actualized by הקטרת קומץ] is an essential part of the meaning of the מנחה. The מנחה conceives of a person's existence as given over to God's providence; and if the מנחה consists also of שמן and לבונה, it also conceives of a person's well-being and satisfaction as given over to God. One who brings a מנחה asks of God to remember and bless his possessions, which provide him with all of the above. Here, however, the מנחת זכרון becomes a מזכרת עון: He to Whom all things are known is to decide on the question of this woman's continuance in the marriage; if He knows of her guilt, He will punish her. This is the other side of the doubt. Here, it is not a question of granting well-being and happiness. The basic question of the existence or nonexistence of the marriage is what is brought before God for a decision. Hence לא יצק עליו שמן ולא יתן עליו לבנה (cf. *Vayikra* 5:11 and Commentary there, 5:13).

כי מנחת קנאת הוא. הוא refers to the קמח (רש״י).

16 **והקריב אתה הכהן והעמדה לפני ה׳**. לפני ה׳: in the eastern entrance of the Nikanor Gateway, through which all who enter or exit the Temple pass: והוא הפתח שבו דרך כניסה ויציאה לכל באי עזרה (*Sotah* 7a; 8a and רש״י there).

יז וְלָקַח הַכֹּהֵן מַיִם קְדֹשִׁים בִּכְלִי־
חָרֶשׂ וּמִן־הֶעָפָר אֲשֶׁר יִהְיֶה
בְּקַרְקַע הַמִּשְׁכָּן יִקַּח הַכֹּהֵן וְנָתַן
אֶל־הַמָּיִם׃

17 *The priest shall take holy water in an earthen vessel, and the priest shall take [some] of the dust from the ground that is on the floor of the Dwelling Place and put it in the water:*

עמד לפני פלוני means: to place yourself at someone's disposal. העמיד לפני פלוני means: to place someone at someone else's disposal. Compare above, 3:6; below, 27:19; *Melachim* I, 17:1, 18:15, et al. Here, too, the כהן places her before God, at His disposal.

17 **מים קדשים**: water sanctified in the כיור for קידוש ידים ורגלים of the כהנים (*Shemos* 30:18-21).

אשר יהיה בקרקע המשכן. If no dust is found there, some dust must be brought into the היכל, and must first be spread over the floor (*Sotah* 15b).

קרקע stems from the root רקע, just as כרכב stems from the root רכב (cf. Commentary, *Shemos* 27:5). Regarding רקע, see וּרְקַע בְּרַגְלְךָ (*Yechezkel* 6:11), וְרַקְעֲךָ בְּרָגֶל (ibid. 25:6). Thus, רקע means: to stamp down forcefully, to trample with the feet. (By extension, it also means: to flatten, to hammer out — and thereby to stretch.) Accordingly, the primary meaning of קרקע is the earth trodden on by people, the ground, the floor. Thus, we find repeatedly: קַרְקַע הַבַּיִת, "the floor of the Temple" (*Melachim* I, chap. 6). But קרקע is also used in a general sense: בְּקַרְקַע הַיָּם (*Amos* 9:3).

The כהן enters the היכל and lifts from the floor a marble tile which was specially designated for this purpose and takes some of the dust from beneath it (see *Sotah* 15b).

ונתן אל המים. Not במים but אל המים: כדי שיראה על המים (ibid.). The dust is not to be stirred and mixed into the water, in the way that אפר הפרה is mixed into מים חיים (see Commentary below, 19:17). Rather, the dust is to remain visible on the water, כדי שיראה על המים; and if the dust is put in before the water, it is invalid: הקדים עפר למים פסול (*Sotah* 15b, 16b).

There, in the case of the sprinkling of מי חטאת, a person who has become טמא by contact with a corpse is reminded that although his body will ultimately decay and revert to **אפר**, dust, his true essence is מים **חיים**, drawn from the source of eternal life (see Commentary below, 19:17).

18 *And the priest shall have the* יח וְהֶעֱמִיד הַכֹּהֵן אֶת־הָאִשָּׁה לִפְנֵי

Here, in the case of סוטה, a woman who is suspected of moral טומאה is reminded that although her earthly body is **עפר**, and is gifted with powers of motherhood and with natural urges — like fertile earth yearning to bear fruit — nevertheless, she herself is analogous to **מים קדושים**: The purpose of her true essence is purity of moral holiness. Her sensual bodily energies, whose nature is like that of עפר, are to form only the external, outwardly visible side of herself. She is to bear them and rule over them, but they are never to mix with her and muddy her purity. (Cf. *Sotah* 17a: אמר רבא מפני מה אמרה תורה הבא עפר לסוטה? זכתה, יוצא ממנה בן כאברהם אבינו דכתיב ביה עפר ואפר, לא זכתה, תחזור לעפרה.)

Just as here the earthly, sensuous side of woman's nature is represented by עפר, so in *Tehillim* 139:15 the woman's womb, in which the fetus is formed, is called "the depths of the earth": רֻקַּמְתִּי בְּתַחְתִּיּוֹת אָרֶץ.

But this עפר is part of the ground on which people stand in God's Sanctuary. For the Sanctuary does not address its demands to people possessed of a superhuman nature; it does not address people whose nature is antithetical to human nature. Rather, the earthly, bodily, sensual side forms the קרקע המשכן; it is the foundation on which the Sanctuary establishes the whole mode of life of its holy *mitzvos*.

The מים הקדושים are taken from the כיור, by which the כהנים prepare themselves for every holy act they perform (ידים) and for every holy step they take (רגלים). This vessel for the sanctification of the כהנים is made of the מראות הצובאות, the mirrors of the women who would throng to the entrance of the Sanctuary (*Shemos* 38:8). In the past, women congregated here to donate their mirrors; and in this very place, their sister — so unlike them in her deeds — now stands, awaiting God's decision. Truly, the modesty that is expected of the Jewish woman is the source of the holiness that emanates from the Sanctuary; it is this modesty that imbues all of Jewish life with priestlike sanctity (see Commentary there).

18 **והעמיד הכהן את האשה לפני ה׳**. It has already been said above (v. 16): והעמידה לפני ה׳. The repetition here indicates that she is to be led from place to place in order to prolong the procedure (לייגעה), giving her time to confess (*Sotah* 8a).

יְהוָה וּפָרַע אֶת־רֹאשׁ הָאִשָּׁה וְנָתַן עַל־כַּפֶּיהָ אֵת מִנְחַת הַזִּכָּרוֹן מִנְחַת קְנָאֹת הִוא וּבְיַד הַכֹּהֵן יִהְיוּ מֵי הַמָּרִים הַמְאָרְרִים׃

woman stand before God *again, and he shall uncover the woman's head and place upon her hands the gift symbolizing that her husband subordinates the remembrance [to* God*]; it is a gift symbolizing that he subordinates the maintaining of the [marital] claim [to* God*], and in the priest's hand shall be the curse-bearing waters of bitternesses.*

ופרע את ראש. A modest woman wears a covering on her head to prevent her hair from being seen by others. Hence, the uncovering of her hair is called "פריעה," literally, "freeing" (cf. Commentary, *Bereshis* 16:11-12 and *Shemos* 32:25).

According to *Sotah* 7a, a rent is made in the neckline of her dress, which is then tied into place over her bosom with a bast ribbon; and the uncovering of her hair is completed by undoing her braids.

Uncovering the hair contravenes the modesty of a married Jewish woman. Thus, from here our Sages derive: אזהרה לבנות ישראל שלא יצאו בפרוע ראש, "The daughters of Israel are forbidden to appear in public with their hair uncovered" (*Kesubos* 72a). If a married woman uncovers her hair, it is ערוה in the literal sense of the term. In our case, the uncovering of the woman's hair is intended to expose the woman as immodest. The head covering that hides the woman's hair is an external symbol of her marital fidelity. A woman who by her conduct has forsaken the path of modesty is no longer worthy of this diadem of צניעות. By removing the covering from her head, the כהן gives sharp expression to the blame that attaches to her.

Remember that although it is still a question — now in the process of being decided — whether she actually committed adultery, in any case there *was* a סטייה מדרכי צניעות (v. 12) ; by straying from the path of modesty, the woman gave her husband cause to warn her (קינוי), and it was then proven that she disregarded his warning by secluding herself with the man involved (סתירה). Thus, in any case, she deserves reproach for her frivolity and immodesty.

19 *The priest shall adjure her and* יט וְהִשְׁבִּיעַ אֹתָהּ הַכֹּהֵן וְאָמַר אֶל־

ונתן על כפיה את מנחת הזכרון מנחת קנאת הִוא. The one aspect of the meaning of this מנחה is stated first here; it is a מנחת זכרון, and God will decide whether the woman is guilty. This aspect is in the foreground, because only this Divine decision — and the retribution that comes in its wake — makes the water "curse-bearing" (see Commentary, v. 26). But the other aspect is also mentioned; for the husband, who brings the woman's מנחה, seeks to vindicate her as his future wife: מנחת קנאת היא.

וביד הכהן יהיו וגו׳. The מנחה in the hand of the woman and the water in the hand of the כהן go together. By dint of the מנחה, the water becomes מי המרים המאררים. The מנחה is מזכרת עון; כמה דלא קרבה מנחתה לא בדקי לה מיא (*Sotah* 14a, 20b).

מי המרים המאררים. It does not say here המים המרים, "the bitter water"; rather, Scripture employs the construct state, מי המרים, "the water of bitterness." מרים are bitternesses, the bitter facts which the מי סוטה hold up to the woman. We have already seen (in v. 17) that the מים קדשים בכלי חרש and the עפר מקרקע המשכן signify that moral purity and holiness must be kept, in spite of the body's earthly nature; what is more, bodily sensuality is the basic assumption of the mitzvah to purify and sanctify oneself. If this truth is a "bitter" one for the woman — i.e., if it contradicts her behavior until now -- then drinking the water representing this bitterness will bring a curse upon her. מאררים is an active form: the waters are מאררים if what they represent is מר.

These two aspects — "המרים" and "המאררים" — are also given material expression by the addition of something bitter to the water. צריך שיתן מר לתוך המים, מאי טעמא? דאמר קרא מי המרים, שמרים כבר (*Sotah* 20a; see רש״י there). It seems to us that this expresses the following: The water is bitter on account of its content and meaning, not on account of its fateful effect. Its fateful effect is only the result of the bitterness of its content. Similarly, the curse-bearing aspect of the water is given material expression: The dissolution of the curse written on the parchment (v. 23) signifies that this water brings retribution.

19 **והשביע אותה וגו׳ אם לא שכב וגו׳ ואם לא שטית וגו׳**. The explanatory repetition — ואם לא שטית וגו׳ — is apparently intended to avert a mis-

הָאִשָּׁה אִם־לֹא שָׁכַב אִישׁ אֹתָךְ וְאִם־לֹא שָׂטִית טֻמְאָה תַּחַת אִישֵׁךְ הִנָּקִי מִמֵּי הַמָּרִים הַמְאָרְרִים הָאֵלֶּה׃

shall say to the woman: If no man has lain with you, and if you have not strayed in your relationship to your husband so as to forfeit your purity, then you shall remain untouched by the waters of these curse-bearing bitternesses.

understanding. Were it only to say אם לא שכב וגו׳, this could be taken to mean that the Torah censures only full-fledged adultery; but as long as the woman does not complete the crime, the Torah does not censure her for acting frivolously and deviating from the ways of modesty. Hence, first it says אם לא שכב וגו׳: To be sure, the curse that comes by way of the water of bitterness depends on the completion of the crime. At the same time, however, the Torah refers to the woman's immodest actions by the expression ואם לא שטית טומאה; for in any case it was proven that she deviated from the ways of modesty which the Sanctuary prescribes for its people. She is in any case a סוטה, even if she did not reach the point of complete טומאה. Similarly, both actions are stressed in the affirmative case (v. 20): ואת כי שטית תחת אישך וכי נטמאת ויתן וגו׳.

תחת אישך apparently describes the relationship between a loyal wife and her husband. Had she kept in mind this relationship, she would have been saved from sin. Consider: וְתַחַת כְּנָפָיו תֶּחְסֶה (*Tehillim* 91:4), וּפָרַשְׂתָּ כְנָפֶךָ עַל־אֲמָתְךָ (*Ruth* 3:9), רַק יִקָּרֵא שִׁמְךָ עָלֵינוּ (*Yeshayahu* 4:1). A wife is under the protection of her husband, and she has obligations to him. She is bound to respect his exclusive conjugal rights. She bears his name. She belongs to him in this status which she attained at her marriage. When she deviated from the moral duties imposed on her by her status, she became a סוטה.

הנקי. Consider the ascending scale of נגע, נגח, נכה, נקה (cf. Commentary, *Bereshis* 20:5, 24:8). The implication is that נקה denotes a forceful movement of diverting something from oneself. הנקי, then, means: you shall remain untouched by the power of this water.

20 *But if you have strayed in your relationship to your husband and have forfeited your purity, in that a man other than your husband has lain with you —*

כ וְאַ֗תְּ כִּ֥י שָׂטִ֛ית תַּ֥חַת אִישֵׁ֖ךְ וְכִ֣י
נִטְמֵ֑את וַיִּתֵּ֨ן אִ֥ישׁ בָּךְ֙ אֶת־
שְׁכָבְתּ֔וֹ מִֽבַּלְעֲדֵ֖י אִישֵֽׁךְ׃

21 *At this point the priest shall adjure the woman with an oath of the curse, and the priest shall say to the woman: Thus may* God *make you into a curse-word and an oath among your people, in that* God *will cause your thigh to fall away and your belly to swell.*

כא וְהִשְׁבִּ֨יעַ הַכֹּהֵ֥ן אֶֽת־הָאִשָּׁה֮
בִּשְׁבֻעַ֣ת הָאָלָה֒ וְאָמַ֤ר הַכֹּהֵן֙
לָֽאִשָּׁ֔ה יִתֵּ֨ן יְהוָ֥ה אוֹתָ֛ךְ לְאָלָ֥ה
וְלִשְׁבֻעָ֖ה בְּת֣וֹךְ עַמֵּ֑ךְ בְּתֵ֨ת יְהוָ֤ה
אֶת־יְרֵכֵךְ֙ נֹפֶ֔לֶת וְאֶת־בִּטְנֵ֖ךְ צָבָֽה׃

22 *And these curse-bearing waters shall enter into your bowels and cause your belly to swell and your thigh to fall away. The woman shall say: Amen, amen.*

כב וּ֠בָאוּ הַמַּ֨יִם הַמְאָרְרִ֤ים הָאֵ֙לֶּה֙
בְּֽמֵעַ֔יִךְ לַצְבּ֥וֹת בֶּ֖טֶן וְלַנְפִּ֣ל יָרֵ֑ךְ
וְאָמְרָ֥ה הָאִשָּׁ֖ה אָמֵ֥ן ׀ אָמֵֽן׃

20-21 **ואת כי וגו׳ והשביע וגו׳ בשבעת האלה**. Here, in the affirmative case, the כהן has the woman accept the curse: יתן ה׳ וגו׳. Her condition will be such that anyone wishing to express an אלה and a שבועה will say: May God do to so-and-so as He did to this woman.

Note that throughout this whole section Scripture repeatedly states that it is the כהן who performs the procedure. This procedure is not an act of the court, but an appeal to the Sanctuary. The כהן is the Sanctuary's emissary and representative, and God will demonstrate Himself as its Founder and as the Guarantor of its demands. That is why the Name ה׳ is also mentioned here: The retribution is expected from God, Who, in His love, dispenses life and blessing. For the ultimate purpose of this procedure is not the destruction of the sinner; rather, its purpose is to ensure modesty, on which Israel's salvation and blessing depend.

22 **ואמרה האשה אמן אמן**. For our discussion of "אמן," see Commentary, *Bereshis* 15:6.

One who responds to an oath by saying אמן commits himself entirely to that oath and makes the oath his own. The subordination of his whole being to the judgment of God — subordination which comes to expression in an oath (see Commentary, ibid. 21:23 and *Shemos* 20:7) — becomes, through the response of אמן, the firm foundation on which his whole future depends. כל העונה אמן אחר שבועה כמוציא שבועה בפיו דמי (*Shevuos* 29b); אמן בו שבועה, בו קבלת דברים, בו האמנת דברים (ibid. 36a).

By responding with אמן, the woman takes upon herself all that the כהן has said: the simple oath without the אלה (v. 19) as well as the oath linked with אלה (v. 21). According to תוספות (*Kiddushin* 27b ד"ה אמן), by this אמן she also takes upon herself the oath that she did not commit adultery with the man with whom she secluded herself, as well as the oath that during the whole time that she was תחת אישה she was never unfaithful to her husband; but since she responds with a second אמן, her oath is expanded to include even the time when she was not yet completely תחת אישה, but was only ארוסה or שומרת יבם (see *Devarim* 25:5). Infidelity during that time, too, constitutes adultery which prohibits the consummation of the marriage, but such infidelity cannot by itself make her liable to the סוטה oath. על מה היא אומרת אמן אמן? אמן על האלה, אמן על השבועה, אמן מאיש זה, אמן מאיש אחר, אמן שלא סטיתי ארוסה ונשואה ושומרת יבם וכנוסה (*Sotah* 18a).

Thus, we are dealing here with a case where an oath to which a person becomes liable is extended and applied also to things in which there was no cause for an oath. Moreover, the oath is extended to include things that by themselves can in no way effect an oath. The husband suspects his wife with regard to a specific man. Once she becomes obligated to clear herself of suspicion by means of an oath, the oath is extended to include any infidelity, regarding which there is no specific suspicion. What is more, the oath is extended to include even times that are excluded from the סוטה oath, where the incidents that may have occurred cannot by themselves effect an oath.

Such an extension of an oath's applicability is called "גלגול שבועה": An extended oath is imposed on the defendant, if he is obligated to take an oath about something, and the claimant thinks or suspects — or sometimes the court suspects — that he misappropriated or became liable also to something unrelated to the original claim. What is more, an oath can be superimposed also on something excluded from Torah oaths — e.g., קרקעות (see Commentary, *Shemos* 22:8). Thus the principle:

23 *The priest shall then write these curses upon a piece of parchment, and dissolve them in the waters of bitternesses.*

כג וְכָתַב אֶת־הָאָלֹת הָאֵלֶּה הַכֹּהֵן בַּסֵּפֶר וּמָחָה אֶל־מֵי הַמָּרִים׃

נכסים שאין להם אחריות זוקקין את הנכסים שיש להם אחריות לישבע עליהן, even though אין נשבעין על הקרקעות (*Kiddushin* 26a, רש״י there).

It appears that the law of גלגול שבועה stems from the deep inner nature of the oath. For this is the meaning of every oath administered before the court: Man, of limited insight, appeals to omniscient God; and the oath-taker submits himself and all his possessions to Divine judgment: Let God punish him if, as is claimed, some of these possessions were obtained illegally. This appeal is not permitted unless there is objective legal doubt as to the legality of some possession. Once the matter is referred to God's court of justice, however, the focus shifts from the object to the person. Henceforth, the whole person must vindicate his entire personality; that is to say, his honesty is judged in *all* matters in which he ever owed fidelity to the claimant.

23 **וכתב וגו׳**. The whole סוטה procedure is called "תורה," "Law" (v. 30); hence, it bears the character of דיני נפשות (*Sotah* 17b), the most serious application of the Law, and every step in this procedure — from beginning to end, בין גמר בין תחילה (תוספות there ד״ה מה משפט) — must be done in broad daylight. What is at work here is not the dark powers of night. Rather, it is the Divine power of God's Torah intervening in order to protect the interests of "man" and to protect the moral freedom of human society (cf. *Collected Writings*, vol. III, p. 86ff.). Hence, all the laws pertaining to the writing of a ספר תורה apply also to the writing of מגילת סוטה (*Sotah* 17b).

בספר — on a piece of parchment (ibid.).

את האלת האלה. He writes: אם לא שכב איש אתך וגו׳ (v. 19), ואת כי שטית וגו׳ (v. 20), יתן ה׳ אותך וגו׳ (v. 21), ובאו המים וגו׳ ולנפל ירך (v. 22). But he does not write: והשביע אתה הכהן וגו׳ (v. 19), nor does he write: ואמרה האשה אמן אמן (v. 22) [*Sotah* 17a]. He writes the adjuration only after the woman has accepted it by saying "Amen," and he must write it לשמה, having in mind the particular woman who is standing here (ibid. 18a).

24 *And he shall make the woman drink the curse-bearing waters of bitternesses, and the curse-bearing waters shall enter into her as bitternesses.*

כד וְהִשְׁקָה֙ אֶת־הָ֣אִשָּׁ֔ה אֶת־מֵ֥י הַמָּרִ֖ים הַמְאָרְרִ֑ים וּבָ֥אוּ בָ֛הּ הַמַּ֥יִם הַמְאָרְרִ֖ים לְמָרִֽים׃

25 *The priest shall then take from the*

כה וְלָקַ֣ח הַכֹּהֵן֙ מִיַּ֣ד הָֽאִשָּׁ֔ה אֵ֖ת

This writing, then, is nothing but the fixation in writing of the שבועה and אלה which already rest upon the woman. First she accepted them verbally, and now they are also set down in writing.

ומחה אל וגו׳. This is not a blotting out *by* the water, but a dissolving *into* the water. The lines of writing are completely mixed into the water, and thereby the bitter truths symbolized by the drink's ingredients — מים קדושים and עפר — are complemented by the retribution which she accepted upon herself in the written אלות. This retribution will come upon her as punishment for having violated these truths. Through the dissolving of the אלות-writing into the water, מי המרים become מאררים.

24 **והשקה וגו׳**. "To drink of the cup of fate" or "to drink of the cup of God's wrath" are common expressions in Scripture, and even שתה alone — simply the word "drinking" — can denote receiving punishment from the hand of God: כִּי כַּאֲשֶׁר שְׁתִיתֶם עַל־הַר קָדְשִׁי יִשְׁתּוּ כָל־הַגּוֹיִם תָּמִיד וגו׳ (*Ovadyah* 1:16). It is plausible, then, that here, too, the drinking is a concrete act representing an abstract idea: She accepts her fate, which depends on her guilt or innocence. In *Tehillim* 75:9 we find that the cup in God's hand is "mixed." Here, too, the cup in her hand holds a mixture of the truths of her destiny and the reward or punishment for her fulfillment or nonfulfillment of this destiny.

ובאו בה וגו׳. First, the curse-bearing water enters into her למרים; it does not yet have a fateful effect, for that depends on what follows. For now, the water enters into her למרים: like bitter truths, they are tested on her past.

25 **ולקח וגו׳ והניף וגו׳ והקריב וגו׳**. והניף, and he shall perform the movements of תנופה and תרומה: מוליך ומביא מעלה ומוריד (see Commentary, *Shemos* 29:22-25). Heaven and earth and all that dwell on earth are summoned

woman the gift symbolizing [her husband's] subordination of the maintaining of [his] claim, and he shall wave the gift of subordination before God *and bring it near to the altar.*

מִנְחַ֣ת הַקְּנָאֹ֑ת וְהֵנִ֤יף אֶת־הַמִּנְחָה֙ לִפְנֵ֣י יְהוָ֔ה וְהִקְרִ֥יב אֹתָ֖הּ אֶל־הַמִּזְבֵּֽחַ׃

26 *The priest shall then scoop out the remembrance portion of the gift of subordination and give it to the altar to go up in smoke. Only after that can he make the woman drink the waters.*

כו וְקָמַ֨ץ הַכֹּהֵ֤ן מִן־הַמִּנְחָה֙ אֶת־אַזְכָּ֣רָתָ֔הּ וְהִקְטִ֖יר הַמִּזְבֵּ֑חָה וְאַחַ֛ר יַשְׁקֶ֥ה אֶת־הָאִשָּׁ֖ה אֶת־הַמָּֽיִם׃

to act as witnesses of the procedure and to participate in the vindication of the woman's morality. It is to them that the מנחה vindicating the marriage is directed in the presence of God.

Thereafter והקריב אתה אל המזבח via הגשה ברוח מערבית דרומית (see *Sotah* 14b): He shall bring the מנחה to the side of the altar that is dedicated to the spiritual life deriving from the Torah (see Commentary, *Vayikra* 2:8-10). Thus the verdict now sought from God is sought not from the viewpoint of this one marriage alone, but in the name of heaven and earth, in the name of all of human society, and in the name of the spiritual life flowing from the Torah, all of which have an equal share in maintaining the morality of womanhood.

The woman and the כהן wave the מנחה together (as in *Vayikra* 7:30; see *Sotah* 19a). The woman is interested in proving her innocence, and the כהן represents the Sanctuary's interest in preserving the sanctity of marriage. Hence, both together perform the act that will lead to God's decision.

26 **וקמץ וגו׳**. He seeks the decision by means of הקטרת הקומץ, which here is called "אזכרתה," whereas above it is called "מזכרת עון" (see v. 15).

ואחר ישקה את האשה. The drinking of the water was already mentioned above (v. 24), before the offering of the מנחה. And in fact that is the halachah, which was reached by majority decision: משקה ואחר כך מקריב (*Sotah* 19a). Nevertheless, here, after the הקרבה, Scripture again

27 *He shall give her the waters to* כז וְהִשְׁקָהּ אֶת־הַמַּיִם וְהָיְתָה אִם־

mentions the drinking. According to תוספות (ibid.), this teaches us that it is a mitzvah to precede the offering of the מנחה with the drinking, but that this order is not indispensable; hence it says in the *Yerushalmi* (ibid. 3:2) שאם הקריב מנחתה ואחר כך השקה שהיא כשרה. A similar case that could occur is the case described in the *Bavli* (ibid. 19b): If, after the הקרבה, it becomes clear that the writing did not dissolve properly, and traces of it are still visible (שרישומו ניכר), the dissolution and the drinking must be repeated.

We have already stated that the drinking of the water and the offering of the מנחה go together. The water in itself has no effect whatsoever. Only the Divine decision, which comes through the offering of the מנחה, gives potency to the water: דכמה דלא קרבה מנחתה לא בדקי לה מיא (ibid. 20b). This can be clearly seen when the drinking precedes the offering of the מנחה and yet the water has its effect only after the offering. By drinking the water, the woman performs a symbolic act, taking into herself the content of the oath. Thereby she puts her whole bodily self under the power of the bitter truths that are being tested on her past, and thereby she also takes upon herself the consequences of these truths. Then the מנחת קנאות מזכרת עון calls for God to decide in accordance with her guilt or her innocence whether the drink is to bring blessing or ruin. Although she drank beforehand, the drinking is concluded — from a conceptual standpoint — only after the offering of the מנחה. The drinking is therefore mentioned both before the offering of the מנחה and after it; Scripture thereby links these two procedures and explains the nature of the connection between them.

27 **והשקה**. From this further repetition that she is to be given the water to drink, our Sages (ibid. 19b) derive that, once the inscription with the Name of God has been obliterated in the water, they make her drink the water against her will, unless she admits her guilt. Until the inscription is obliterated, she drinks of her own free will. She need not admit her guilt; she may insist on her innocence, and if she declares herself unwilling to drink the water, the procedure is simply stopped. Her guilt remains in doubt, and the marriage must be dissolved (see Commentary,

נִטְמְאָה וַתִּמְעֹל מַעַל בְּאִישָׁהּ וּבָאוּ בָהּ הַמַּיִם הַמְאָרְרִים לְמָרִים וְצָבְתָה בִטְנָהּ וְנָפְלָה יְרֵכָהּ וְהָיְתָה הָאִשָּׁה לְאָלָה בְּקֶרֶב עַמָּהּ׃

drink, and then it shall come to pass that if she has forfeited her purity by committing a breach of trust against her husband, the curse-bearing waters will enter her and become bitter ones; her belly will swell and her thigh will fall away, and the woman will become a curse-word among her people.

כח וְאִם־לֹא נִטְמְאָה הָאִשָּׁה וּטְהֹרָה הִוא וְנִקְּתָה וְנִזְרְעָה זָרַע׃

28 *But if the woman has not forfeited her purity and is still pure, she will remain untouched by it and, in fact, she will be blessed with off-spring.*

v. 13). However, once the inscription has been obliterated, she has no alternative but to admit her guilt or to drink the סוטה water, knowing that she is innocent (*Sotah* 20a).

ובאו בה המים המאררים למרים: the curse-bearing water will enter into her as water of bitterness; or: it will become evident that the water is water of bitterness. The truths expressed by this water, which consists of מים קדושים and עפר מקרקע המשכן, are bitter to her, and this will become manifest through the realization of the curse, which was transmitted to the water upon the dissolving of the אלות (v. 23).

However, the foregoing applies only אם נטמאה וגו׳, only if she has lost her purity and so stands in contradiction to the moral holiness demanded by the content of these truths. If the contents of this water suit her, such that the water is not "bitter" to her, then it has no bitter results; on the contrary, it brings blessing to the sexual future of the woman, as will immediately be made clear in the next verse.

28 **ונקתה** (see Commentary on v. 19): She will remain unharmed by the curse, for the water brought it to her only conditionally. Her innocence wards off the curse completely.

ונזרעה זרע: Her purity, which is in harmony with the מים קדושים, will be demonstrated by an increase of her עפר force and by fulfillment

29 *This is the teaching concerning the maintaining of [the husband's marital] claim, when a woman strays in her relationship to her husband and has forfeited her purity;*

כט זֹ֛את תּוֹרַ֥ת הַקְּנָאֹ֖ת אֲשֶׁ֨ר תִּשְׂטֶ֥ה
אִשָּׁ֛ה תַּ֥חַת אִישָׁ֖הּ וְנִטְמָֽאָה׃

30 *Or when the spirit has come over him that he must maintain his [marital] claim and he has warned his wife, and he has the woman stand before* God, *and the priest implements all this teaching upon her.*

ל א֣וֹ אִ֗ישׁ אֲשֶׁ֨ר תַּעֲבֹ֥ר עָלָ֛יו ר֥וּחַ
קִנְאָ֖ה וְקִנֵּ֣א אֶת־אִשְׁתּ֑וֹ וְהֶעֱמִ֤יד
אֶת־הָֽאִשָּׁה֙ לִפְנֵ֣י יְהוָ֔ה וְעָ֤שָׂה לָהּ֙
הַכֹּהֵ֔ן אֵ֥ת כָּל־הַתּוֹרָ֖ה הַזֹּֽאת׃

31 *If the man is free of iniquity, the woman must bear her iniquity.*

לא וְנִקָּ֥ה הָאִ֖ישׁ מֵעָוֺ֑ן וְהָאִשָּׁ֣ה הַהִ֔וא
תִּשָּׂ֖א אֶת־עֲוֺנָֽהּ׃ פ

---

of the destiny of עפר מקרקע המשכן. Blessing will come to the woman's womb, for which "fertile earth" is a metaphor. If until now she has been childless, now she will receive the blessing of children. If until now she would give birth in pain, now she will give birth with ease (*Sotah* 26a).

29 **אשר תשטה וגו׳ ונטמאה**. This is the case described in verse 13. Evidence of adultery given by even one witness suffices, if his testimony is supported by the preceding circumstances [two witnesses having testified to קינוי and סתירה]. In such a case the marriage must be dissolved immediately.

30 **או איש וגו׳**. If there is no witness to adultery, the woman is subjected to the procedure that begins in verses 14 and 15.

ועשה לה הכהן את כל התורה הזאת. The procedure of השקאת סוטה is called here "תורה." Scripture thus equates it with the most important laws devolving on the nation's highest representative. Hence, the whole procedure must be done under the authority of בית דין הגדול (*Sotah* 7b; see vv. 15 and 23).

31 **ונקה האיש מעון וגו׳**. A man can expect a Divine verdict concerning his wife's guilt or innocence, only if he himself is innocent of all sexual

crimes. If he himself deliberately or inadvertently violated the laws of sexual purity — e.g., he had sexual relations with his wife after קינוי וסתירה — the water has no effect on his wife. So, too, if a man, since coming of age with regard to mitzvah observance, ever had forbidden sexual relations, or even if he simply turned a blind eye to sexual excesses committed by members of his family, he has no right to make his wife drink the סוטה water. ת״ר ונקה האיש מעון, בזמן שהאיש מנוקה מעון המים בודקין את אשתו, אין האיש מנוקה מעון אין המים בודקין את אשתו, ואומר (הושע ד, יד) לא אפקוד על בנותיכם כי תזנינה ועל כלותיכם כי תנאפנה כי הם עם הזנות יפרדו ועם הקדשות יזבחו ועם לא יבין ילבט, מאי ואומר? וכי תימא עון דידיה אין, דבניה ובנתיה לא, תא שמע לא אפקוד וגו׳, וכי תימא עון אשת איש אין, עון דפנויה לא, תא שמע כי הם עם הזנות יפרדו וגו׳, מאי ועם לא יבין ילבט? אמר רבי אלעזר אמר להם נביא לישראל, אם אתם מקפידים על עצמכם מים בודקין נשותיכם, ואם לאו אין המים בודקין נשותיכם (*Sotah* 47b; see *Yevamos* 58a and תוספות there ד״ה ונקה). God's laws of morality are not indulgent toward men who are sexually unrestrained; they are not more tolerant of men than of women.

The Halachah teaches further that just as the wife who is suspected of adultery is אסורה to her husband as long as the water has not proven her innocence, the man who is suspected of being her partner in adultery may never marry her, not even after she has been divorced: כשם שאסורה לבעל כך אסורה לבועל (*Sotah* 27b). Scripture repeatedly says of the woman: "נטמאה" (vv. 14, 27, 29), to teach us that she forfeited her purity as regards the sanctuary of marriage and as regards the Sanctuary in general; that is to say, she is אסורה לבעל לבועל ולתרומה (*Sotah* 28a; see Commentary, *Vayikra* 21:7 and 22:12-13).

The Halachah also teaches: כשם שהמים בודקין אותה כך המים בודקין אותו (*Sotah* 27b). The fateful effect of the water does not strike the woman alone. Rather, the man with whom she committed the sin is also stricken with the same punishment. For in the adjuration it does not say לצבות בטנך ולנפל ירכך, but לצבות בטן ולנפל ירך (v. 22). The fateful effect strikes also the בועל (*Sotah* 28a).

Once the woman's purity becomes suspect as a result of קינוי and סתירה, the survival of the marriage requires a Divine decision. But this does not apply in every case. There are marriages that must be dissolved immediately, once they have reached this stage. The Halachah derives from the text of our chapter that only if, at the time of קינוי and סתירה, the marriage has already been brought to completion — אשה תחת אישה — can the survival of the marriage be decided by the סוטה water, but not if the suspicion about the woman's purity arises while she is ארוסה or שומרת יבם (ibid. 23b). The Halachah also derives that the Torah is speaking here of a couple who both have use of all their physical faculties; but if one of them is blind, lame or dumb, the woman is forbidden immediately after קינוי and סתירה, and the marriage must be dissolved (ibid. 27a-b). Also, if the husband has no children, and the wife is infertile, the marriage must be dissolved immediately after קינוי and סתירה (ibid. 25b). The same is true if the woman's behavior, which led to קינוי and סתירה, has not only aroused the suspicion of her husband, but has caused a public scandal and is the "the talk of the women at their spinning wheels." As our Sages expound (ibid. 6b): וטהרה . . . ולא שישאו ויתנו בה מוזרות בלבנה. The סוטה test is administered if, apart from the suspicion of her husband, she is still pure. But if the woman has become the focus of gossip, the continuance of the marriage would be a moral scandal; מכוער הדבר ותצא (see רש״י ibid. 31a).

If we take all these laws together, we see that what we have here is not an inquisition into the private affairs of a marital relationship. What we have here are matters that are open to everyone — some of which are matters that are purely external — which, because the wife has given just cause for suspicion by קינוי and סתירה, call for the dissolution of the marriage.

In the case of ארוסה and שומרת יבם, only the personal bond which will lead to marriage has been formed, but the woman has not yet moved into the man's home. In the case of איילונית and עקרה, one of the most essential purposes of marriage cannot be attained. Hence, קינוי and סתירה suffice to prevent the completion of the marriage (in the case of ארוסה and שומרת יבם), or to dissolve the marriage (in the case of איילונית and עקרה). We can explain the case of ארוסה, since adultery committed by an ארוסה is deserving of punishment more severe than is adultery committed by a נשואה [see Commentary, *Devarim* 22:13ff.] It is also not difficult to explain the consideration of the physical integrity of the marital partners (in the case of איילונית and עקרה). Bodily disablement brings with it greater dependence on the one partner and a lack of independence for the other. Such a situation is likely to deepen the love between partners possessed of noble characters, but it can also lead to fickleness. If, in such circumstances, the wife — by deviating from the ways of modesty — gives occasion to קינוי, and then nevertheless shows, through סתירה, that she disregards this warning, such behavior in these circumstances indicates such a high degree of fickleness that it is no longer proper for the marriage to continue.

6 1 God *spoke to Moshe, saying:*	ו א וַיְדַבֵּר יְהוָה אֶל־מֹשֶׁה לֵּאמֹר׃
2 *Speak to the Children of Israel and say to them: When anyone, man or woman, makes the express resolve to take the vow of a* nazir, *to fulfill the task of a* nazir *for* God.	ב דַּבֵּר אֶל־בְּנֵי יִשְׂרָאֵל וְאָמַרְתָּ אֲלֵהֶם אִישׁ אוֹ־אִשָּׁה כִּי יַפְלִא לִנְדֹּר נֶדֶר נָזִיר לְהַזִּיר לַיהוָה׃

The רמב״ן, in his commentary on פרשת סוטה, remarks: אין בכל משפטי התורה דבר תלוי בנס זולתי הענין הזה שהוא פלא ונס קבוע שיעשה בישראל בהיותם רובם עושים רצונו של מקום. Among all the legal institutions of Biblical law, only here does the outcome regularly depend on God's direct intervention by a miracle. Indeed, this section shows that God — Who created the whole institution of marriage — is the witness and judge of every Jewish couple that enters into the union of marriage. This, then, is the principle on which the section of סוטה is based: God is present in every Jewish marriage, and He directs His special attention not only to the marital fidelity of the wife, but also to that of the husband. Sexual morality is the root of all spiritual and moral welfare. Only a question concerning the purity of sexual life may be brought directly before all-seeing God for a decision. This is the basis of פרשת סוטה.

Thus, the institution of סוטה realizes in the actual life of the people what the expulsion of זב וזבה וכו׳ from מחנה לויה shows the people symbolically. שילוח זב וזבה from מחנה לויה shows that sexual purity is the first prerequisite for all spiritual self-elevation toward God, and השקאת סוטה teaches that the sexual purity of family life is the object of God's special attention. The relation of פרשת סוטה to שילוח זב וזבה ממחנה לויה resembles the relation of פרשת גזל הגר to שילוח מצורע ממחנה ישראל.

CHAPTER 6

1 What now follows is the third פרשה, פרשת נזיר, which parallels שילוח טמא מת from מחנה שכינה.

2 **כי יפלא**. See Commentary, *Vayikra* 22:21.

נזיר. The basic meaning of נזר is undoubtedly "keeping far from," "separation," and הִנָּזֵר (ibid. 22:2 — see Commentary there; *Zecharyah*

7:3) means "to abstain from something." Since a נזיר is commanded to abstain from wine (v. 3), it would be most natural to interpret נזיר as an "abstainer" or "abstemious person."

However, the fact that the נזיר is forbidden to partake not only of wine and grapes, but even of wine vinegar and of the seeds and skins of grapes — restrictions that do not seem to entail great personal sacrifice — already suggests that the meaning of נזירות goes beyond mere abstinence.

Moreover, consider this: When a נזיר is rendered ritually impure by contact with a corpse, even if it happens by accident, this invalidates the period he has already spent in fulfilling his vow of נזירות, whereas his partaking of wine does not have this invalidating effect. From this we learn that although abstention from wine is indeed one of the obligations of a נזיר, no less than avoiding contact with a corpse and letting his hair grow, it does not by any means constitute the essence of נזירות, nor is it the distinguishing feature of נזירות. Hence, a נזיר is not primarily an abstainer.

A study of verses 4-6 and of the summation in verse 8 makes it clear that not even all three of these restrictions together constitute the essence of נזירות; rather, they are merely external manifestations by which the נזירות expresses itself. The very essence of נזירות is described in verse 8: קדש הוא לה׳; and the שלשה מינין אסורין בנזיר הטומאה והתגלחת והיוצא מן היין (*Nazir* 34a) are only consequences of this קדושה. Indeed, in *Amos* (2:11) we find נזירים mentioned alongside נביאים, and the presence of both in Israel's midst is a sign of special Divine favor.

In any case, נזיר does not denote one who keeps away from others, but one from whom others must keep away [because he is seeking to be alone with God (see below)]. This is borne out by the term נזירים (*Vayikra* 25:5 and 11), which denotes vines which must be left untended — i.e., left to grow on their own during the Sabbatical and Jubilee years.

Just as the נֵזֶר (crown) that adorns the head of the king puts the rest of the people a distance away from him, the same is true of the נֵזֶר of the נָזִיר, which is a specific regimen of living and striving. He who voluntarily undertakes this regimen distinguishes himself from his contemporaries and elevates himself above them. He sets himself the task of being completely קדוש לאלוקיו, of belonging exclusively to God — with his whole being and with all his aspirations. He seeks, as it were, to draw around himself a נֵזֶר, a circle, within which God alone is to be

3 *Then he must fulfill his* nazirship, *abstaining from weak and strong wine; he shall not drink vinegar from weak [wine] or vinegar from strong wine; he shall not drink any [liquid] in which grapes were steeped, and he shall not eat grapes, fresh or dried.*

ג מִיַּ֤יִן וְשֵׁכָר֙ יַזִּ֔יר חֹ֥מֶץ יַ֛יִן וְחֹ֥מֶץ שֵׁכָ֖ר לֹ֣א יִשְׁתֶּ֑ה וְכָל־מִשְׁרַ֤ת עֲנָבִים֙ לֹ֣א יִשְׁתֶּ֔ה וַעֲנָבִ֛ים לַחִ֥ים וִיבֵשִׁ֖ים לֹ֥א יֹאכֵֽל׃

present. This self-isolation with God is called להזיר לה׳, and one who isolates himself in this manner — one who, as it were, draws a circle and stands inside it with God — is called a נזיר. Note, however, that this is not physical isolation, a hermit's life in the wilderness, but a mental and spiritual isolation with God — in the midst of the bustle of everyday life.

3 **מיין ושכר יזיר**: he shall draw the distance-keeping circle to exclude יין and שכר. כהנים before serving in the Sanctuary and teachers of the Law before deciding halachic questions are forbidden to drink anything intoxicating (*Vayikra* 10:9-11). A similar prohibition — of a wider scope — is imposed on the נזיר during his נזירות: he is commanded to abstain from wine and from all products of the grapevine. כהנים and teachers of the Law must refrain — when serving in the Sanctuary and deciding the halachah — from anything intoxicating, even from drinking the small quantity of a רביעית. By contrast, the prohibition imposed on the נזיר is limited to wine, but this prohibition is extended to everything produced by the grapevine: he must refrain from everything that reminds one of wine, even if it is not in the slightest degree intoxicating.

As long as he is a נזיר, he should direct his mind to the Sanctuary and to the Torah; as long as he is a נזיר, it devolves upon him to be a כהן and a teacher at all times. And the prohibition of everything produced by the grapevine serves him as a constant warning: As a נזיר, he is given the task of refining his thoughts and emotions; hence, he is obligated to maintain the clarity of mind and tranquility of disposition that are required for this task.

מיין ושכר. An analogous expression is found in *Vayikra* 10:9. There — according to the halachah as stated by the רמב"ם (הל' ביאת המקדש, 1:1) — שכר serves as an amplification of יין, and means: כדרך שכרותו; in addition, it serves to extend the prohibition to שאר משכרין, all intoxicating drinks (see *Kerisos* 13b; שו"ת רשב"א, I:363). Here, however, Scripture adds various details: חומץ, ענבים, חרצנים, זג; hence שכר, too, is to be understood here only as a פרט of the כלל, which is stated in verse 4: מכל אשר יעשה מגפן היין. Thus, יין is יין מגיתו, new wine, which is in the first forty days of its formation, whereas שכר is old wine, which has already reached the stage of being intoxicating. Thus Onkelos translates: מחמר חדת ועתיק.

The whole structure of verses 3 and 4 is a פרט וכלל ופרט structure: מיין ושכר יזיר פרט, מכל אשר יעשה מגפן היין כלל, מחרצנים ועד זג חזר ופרט, פרט וכלל ופרט אי אתה דן אלא כעין הפרט מה הפרט מפורש פרי ופסולת פרי (כגון חומץ [רש"י]) אף כל פרי ופסולת פרי (*Nazir* 34b). (Such a structure is treated like a כלל ופרט וכלל — see Commentary, *Vayikra* 11:9 — only that in a פרט וכלל ופרט structure, the כלל expanded from the פרט is more limited: אי איכא פרטא דדמי משני צדדין מרבינן, בחד צד לא מרבינן [*Nazir* 35b].)

וכל משרת ענבים. In Aramaic, שרה means to slacken, to dissolve, to loosen (hence to allow, like הַתֵּר), to soak. In Scripture the word occurs only here, and is to be understood in the latter sense. שִׁרְיוֹן, too, apparently stems from this root. שִׁרְיוֹן, armor, is made of soft metal — i.e., metal made flexible by the loose connection of metal plates.

Nazir 37a cites two interpretations of משרת ענבים. One interpretation is: שרה ענבים במים ויש בהם טעם יין, one soaks grapes in water until the water has the taste of wine. According to this interpretation, we have here an example of the general law that טעם כעיקר: If איסור material is absorbed into permitted material, and is recognizable there by its taste alone, its איסור remains in effect. The other interpretation is: שרה פיתו ביין ואכל כזית מפת ומיין, a נזיר soaks his bread in wine and eats a כזית of bread and wine together. In such a case היתר מצטרף לאיסור: the permitted bread combines with the prohibited wine to complete the שיעור of כזית. According to this interpretation, the law stated here applies only to איסורי נזיר (see Commentary, *Vayikra* 6:11; below, 31:23).

4 *All the days of his* nazirship *he shall not eat anything prepared from the wine-producing grapevine, from [its] seeds to [its] skin.*

ד כֹּל יְמֵי נִזְרוֹ מִכֹּל אֲשֶׁר יֵעָשֶׂה
מִגֶּפֶן הַיַּיִן מֵחַרְצַנִּים וְעַד־זָג לֹא
יֹאכֵל׃

5 *All the days of his* nazir *vow no razor shall come upon his head; until the days are completed in which he took upon himself to fulfill the task of* nazirship *for* God, *it [i.e., his head] shall be holy, in that he shall allow the hair of his head to grow wild.*

ה כָּל־יְמֵי נֶדֶר נִזְרוֹ תַּעַר לֹא־יַעֲבֹר
עַל־רֹאשׁוֹ עַד־מְלֹאת הַיָּמִם
אֲשֶׁר־יַזִּיר לַיהוָה קָדֹשׁ יִהְיֶה גַּדֵּל
פֶּרַע שְׂעַר רֹאשׁוֹ׃

4 **מחרצנים ועד זג**. According to ר׳ יוסי (*Nazir* 34b), the חרצנים are the pips, and the זג is the outer skin.

It is possible that the grape pips are called חרצנים, from the root חרץ, because of their characteristic notches, while זג — related to זך — denotes the clear and transparent skin.

5 **כל ימי נדר נזרו**. At the prohibitions of drinking wine and of becoming טמא by contact with a corpse, it says כל ימי הזירו, כל ימי נזרו. For these two prohibitions instruct the נזיר to keep away from things. Thus, they themselves constitute a concrete realization of the נזר that surrounds the נזיר; they limit him to the narrow sphere of the נזיר circle. By contrast, the prohibition of cutting the hair entails no such limitation. It is not itself a concrete נזר. Rather, it expresses the נֶדֶר נֵזֶר; it characterizes the person who took upon himself the vow of נזירות.

תער stems from the root ערה, "to be uncovered," just as תבל stems from the root בלה. A תער is an instrument that uncovers the skin, makes it naked.

The Halachah teaches (*Nazir* 39a-b) that the prohibition of תער לא יעבר על ראשו includes all removal of hair, even if not done with a תער, a razor. For the sake of this expansion, Scripture here does not use the usual term גלח, but the circumlocution לא יעבר על ראשו. The limitation implied by the term תער is nullified by the expansion implied by the following phrase לא יעבר על ראשו. This in contrast to והעבירו תער (below, 8:7), where the general sense of והעבירו is limited by the following term תער (see Commentary there). The prohibition here does not lie in the

6 *All the days of his* nazir *task to be fulfilled for* God *he must not come near to the person of one who has died.*

ו כָּל־יְמֵ֛י הַזִּיר֥וֹ לַֽיהוָ֖ה עַל־נֶ֥פֶשׁ מֵ֖ת לֹ֥א יָבֹֽא׃

תער, but in its effect, in removing the hair of the head. This prohibited effect is specially stressed by its contrast: The effect that will be achieved by not cutting the hair will be קדש יהיה גדל פרע וגו׳.

Thus, cutting the hair is forbidden to the נזיר by a לא תעשה and an עשה. He violates both by the removal of even a *single* hair (תוספות *Nazir* 39a ד״ה נזיר).

קדש יהיה: it — i.e., his head — shall be holy; cf. verse 11: וקדש את ראשו, he shall let his head have the stamp of holiness.

גדל פרע שער ראשו: the hair of his head shall be allowed to grow wild. The hair attains this character of wild growth after at least thirty days (רש״י *Nazir* 39a ד״ה סותר). Hence סתם נזירות ל׳ יום (*Nazir* 5a, 39a): If the duration of the נזירות is not specified in the vow, the נזירות lasts for thirty days. For Scripture says here that the growth of his hair is the expression of נדר נזרו, the vow of his נזירות.

We have already said (Commentary, *Vayikra* 14:8) that hair serves to insulate, to reduce receptiveness to external influences; hence, admission into, or devoting oneself to, the community — while giving up the aspiration to live only for oneself — is symbolized by תגלחת מצורע and תגלחת לויים. The reverse — allowing the hair to grow untrimmed — would then represent self-isolation and withdrawal into oneself.

Indeed, that is the task that the נזיר undertakes, with his vow, for the period of the נזירות: He seeks to withdraw into himself, to sink into himself. He does not want to detach himself from the world physically; rather, he wants to work on himself spiritually and morally (see Commentary, v. 3). He seeks connection with God, with His Sanctuary, with His Torah — and with himself.

The insulating growth of his hair reminds him of this vow. Hence his head becomes קדוש, holy, for it bears the sign of his holy vow. Similarly, everything that is meant to bring us closer to spiritual and moral perfection is קודש and is called קדוש (see Commentary, *Shemos* 29:37 and *Vayikra* 23:3).

6 **כל ימי הזירו לה׳ וגו׳**. Here it does not say simply כל ימי נזרו or כל ימי נדר נזרו, as it says in verses 4 and 5. For the טומאה prohibition imposed on

the נזיר comes from the relation of the נזירות to *God.* The whole purpose of the prohibition is to preserve the purity of this relation.

על נפש מת וגו׳. As a rule, נפש is feminine. Hence, מת is probably not an adjective modifying נפש, but either is possessive in relation to נפש — as in נפשׁת מת (*Vayikra* 21:11) [the נפש of a dead person] — or is in apposition with it: a נפש, which now lies there as a מת. Similarly, we find במת בנפש (below, 19:13), where בנפש is in apposition with במת.

The נפש חיה of a human being is never מתה. But the נפש, a man's individual personality (see Commentary, *Bereshis* 1:20), is represented during his lifetime in the image of the body, and the same is true after death: When confronted with a corpse, we involuntarily see the נפש represented. Actually, what lies before us is not the נפש, but the מת. Nevertheless, the מת represents to us the נפש; and so that we should not ascribe the מיתה to the נפש, we have been given the laws of טומאת מת (see Commentary, *Vayikra* 11, end; below, chap. 19).

Scripture is therefore very careful in its choice of expressions and placement of words. The case here is not one of contact, but of ביאה: a person comes incidentally to a place where there is a corpse. Hence, Scripture allows itself to say first that the person comes to a place in which there is a נפש, and then it says — as though to correct itself — that he comes to אהל המת. In the case of נגיעה, however, it never says נגע בנפש מת but, rather, הַנֹּגֵעַ במת בנפש (below, 19:13) or, with still greater clarity: הַנֹּגֵעַ במת לכל נפש (below, 19:11). For the נפש — in the sense assigned to it here — is inaccessible to touch.

The foregoing would explain the distinctive approach of Onkelos in his *Targum.* He always translates טמא לנפש as דמסאב לטמי נפשא דאנשא; he avoids saying דמסאב לנפשא, and adds the word "טמי," which, as רש״י says (above, 5:2), is Aramaic for עצמות אדם, human bones. This is Onkelos' practice also in regard to the concept of God. Wherever Scripture employs anthropomorphic expressions, Onkelos translates them with paraphrases, seeking thereby to keep us from ascribing to God material features. Similarly, regarding the נפש, Onkelos seeks to keep us from the mistaken notion that the נפש can be מטמא. For from the expression טמא נפש it would seem as though the נפש itself transmits טומאה; as though the person touched the נפש, and the נפש transmitted טומאה to him. To keep us from this error, Onkelos adds the word טמי, to teach us that the person touched the bones of the מת, and the corpse transmitted טומאה to him.

Actually, though, the text of Scripture itself has already ruled out such a notion by using the construction ל-. For it never says טמא בנפש but, rather, טמא לנפש. The טומאה derives from the *relation* to the נפש. One who comes in contact with the corpse is reminded of the נפש; through the contact, he *relates* to the נפש.

Generally speaking, the symbolical טומאה arising from contact differs from the concrete טומאה of מאכלות אסורות and עריות. This difference expresses itself also in the different grammatical constructions: טמא ל- versus טמא ב-. We have already discussed this in our Commentary on *Vayikra* 11:24-25.

From the analogy between verse 3 and *Vayikra* 10:9-11 we concluded that, in his relation to the Torah, the נזיר is like a כהן. The prohibition stated here — על נפש מת לא יבא וגו׳, which is analogous to the prohibition stated in regard to the כהן גדול: ועל כל נפשת מת לא יבא לאביו ולאמו לא יטמא (ibid. 21:11) — elevates the נזיר to the level of a כהן גדול. As long as he is in the Naziritic circle — in isolation with God and for God — he may not come near a corpse.

As we have seen several times, a corpse evokes the idea that man is subjugated to his bodily nature. A corpse also evokes the idea of the forces of nature overpowering everything by irresistible compulsion. It is to this idea that heathen thought builds its altars.

The Sanctuary of the Torah — and the God-idea that prevails in it — is based on the very opposite of this heathen conception. It is based on the idea of the free God and free man, who was created in the image of God. That is why death and everything evocative of death is banned from His Sanctuary. That is why the Sanctuary's servants may not come in contact with a corpse, and why the כהן גדול — who is first among the Sanctuary's servants and who represents it in the midst of the people — is charged in this regard with special stringency.

The inscription קדש לה׳ on the כהן גדול's forehead (*Shemos* 28:36) is a vigorous protest against those heathen ideas. It proclaims: The Sanctuary was not erected for the power of death, which lays low even free man. The Sanctuary is dedicated לה׳, to the living God, Who eternally gives life and Who grants eternal life, Who imparts to man personality from His Personality, freedom from His freedom, life from His life. Even the angel of death is but one of His messengers, a messenger who delivers man to complete freedom (see Commentary, ibid. 28:38).

Now, just as טומאת מת must be kept out of מחנה שכינה, so must it be

7 *Not even with regard to his father* ז לְאָבִיו וּלְאִמּוֹ לְאָחִיו וּלְאַחֹתוֹ לֹא־

kept out of the Naziritic circle. The meaning of these two exclusions is identical, only that the exclusion of טומאה from מחנה שכינה is for the sake of the national Sanctuary, as the Sanctuary is meant to educate the nation to moral perfection, whereas the exclusion of טומאה from the נזיר's circle is for the sake of his limited individual sphere, within which he seeks to attain his moral perfection.

Human society — from which the נזיר temporarily withdraws in order to live more in himself and his relationship to God — fulfills itself through the synthesis of two elements: moral freedom and physical compulsion. For the synthesis of these two elements — the physical and the moral — is what makes a human being. Partial withdrawal from human society can help a person devote himself more fully to his moral freedom. However, it can just as easily lead him to concern himself primarily with his physical needs; and the God to whom the נזיר in his self-isolation devotes his thoughts and meditations can easily become the all-powerful force of nature, which celebrates its triumphs in the sensual grave of morality's absence, and which bears its flag in the wasteland of graves and tombstones.

But that should not be the case. Rather, the God to Whom the נזיר dedicates the isolating circle of his נזירות is the free and personal God, Who enables man to become a free and moral personality. The God of the נזיר is ה׳, and it is to His Torah that the נזיר should devote his thoughts and aspirations. In limiting himself, he should increase his personal holiness, so as to live in God's presence in moral freedom. His withdrawal into himself should be dedicated to life at its fullest, not to death and dying. His מחנה is to be a מחנה שכינה of אלקים חיים.

So that he should bear all of this in mind, he must, like a כהן גדול, keep away from death and dead bodies.

7 **כי נזר אלקיו על ראשו**. The growth of the hair of his head signifies that he has limited himself to his circle; he thereby expresses the fact that he has devoted himself to "his God." His keeping away from טומאה signifies *Who it is* he considers his God; it signifies that אלקים חיים ה׳ הוא

יִטַּמָּא לָהֶם בְּמֹתָם כִּי נֵזֶר אֱלֹהָיו
עַל־רֹאשׁוֹ׃

and his mother, his brother and his sister — even with regard to these he must not allow himself to become impure when they have died, because the diadem of his God is upon his head.

ח כֹּל יְמֵי נִזְרוֹ קָדֹשׁ הוּא לַיהוָה׃

8 *All the days of his* nazirship *he is holy to* God.

ט וְכִי־יָמוּת מֵת עָלָיו בְּפֶתַע פִּתְאֹם
וְטִמֵּא רֹאשׁ נִזְרוֹ וְגִלַּח רֹאשׁוֹ בְּיוֹם
טָהֳרָתוֹ בַּיּוֹם הַשְּׁבִיעִי יְגַלְּחֶנּוּ׃

9 *And if someone dies very suddenly beside him, and this deprives his* nazir *head of its purity, he shall shave his head on the day he regains his purity; on the seventh day shall he shave it.*

אלקיו! Similarly, the ציץ on the forehead of the כהן גדול is called נזר הקדש (*Shemos* 29:6 et al.; cf. *Vayikra* 21:12).

The general formulation of the preceding verse — על נפש מת לא יבא — would have been sufficient to prohibit the נזיר from allowing himself to become טמא upon the death of his nearest relatives. If nevertheless Scripture here expressly stresses לאביו וגו׳, this indicates that although family duties — even the most sacred, such as duties to father and mother, etc. — do not override the prohibition against allowing oneself to become טמא, the humane duty of burying a מת מצוה, an unattended corpse, does override this prohibition (*Nazir* 48a-b). Even where various קדושות accumulate — e.g., a כהן גדול who is also a נזיר, who is engaged in the most serious of *mitzvos*, שהיה הולך לשחוט את פסחו ולמול את בנו — there, too, the law is: לאביו ולאמו לאחיו ולאחתו לא יטמא, אבל מטמא הוא למת מצוה (ibid.).

8 **כל ימי נזרו וגו׳**. This verse sums up the whole meaning of נזירות, and it especially expresses the connection between נזירות and the prohibition against allowing oneself to become טמא; for the whole purpose of this prohibition is to give expression to the meaning of the נזירות (see Commentary, v. 2).

9 **בפתע פתאם**. In *Kerisos* 9a, our Sages say: פתע denotes שוגג, as in ואם בפתע בלא איבה הדפו (below, 35:22); פתאום denotes אונס, as in ויאמר ה׳ פתאם

אל משה (below, 12:4). Our Sages also say there: פתאום denotes מזיד, as in עָרוּם רָאָה רָעָה וְנִסְתָּר וּפְתָיִים עָבְרוּ וְנֶעֱנָשׁוּ (*Mishlei* 22:3). רש״י (*Kerisos* 9a) explains that from ונענשו we infer that the פתיים transgressed במזיד. Hence the Halachah teaches (ibid.) that the consequences stated here in verses 9-12 apply also to one who becomes impure במזיד. Thus, נזיר is one of the few cases where מביאין על הזדון כשוגג (ibid.), where an offering must be brought even where the transgression was done במזיד, with full awareness and intention.

From this halachah it appears that the underlying conception of both פתע and פתאום derives from פתה, the root of פתי. פתה, related to פתח, denotes a mind that is open, unguarded, and hence vulnerable to outside influences (cf. Commentary, *Bereshis* 9:27). Accordingly, it also denotes inexperience, lack of judgment, and lack of caution in matters of practical and moral behavior. פֶּתִי יַאֲמִין לְכָל־דָּבָר, "a פתי will believe anything" (*Mishlei* 14:15), וּפְתָיִים עָבְרוּ וְנֶעֱנָשׁוּ (ibid. 22:3), and פתיים knowingly transgress the law because they do not consider the consequences.

The difference between פתע and פתאום can be explained as follows: פתע is a state of carelessness, in which one is surprised by results and events which he could have foreseen, had he only thought of what was to be expected according to the laws of probability and possibility. Thus, in the moral sphere, פתע corresponds to שוגג (see Commentary, *Vayikra* 4:2). פתאום, on the other hand, denotes an occurrence that was beyond all reasonable expectation, regarding which human judgment was פתי and people were פתיים; they could not have been prepared for this occurrence. It came suddenly, unexpectedly. In the moral sphere, this corresponds to אונס.

Thus the combination לְפֶתַע פִּתְאֹם (*Yeshayahu* 29:5) and פִּתְאֹם לְפֶתַע (ibid. 30:13), denoting the collapse of tyranny and wrongdoing, a collapse brought about by God. The event in itself comes פתאום, against all reasonable expectation, and it reveals the finger of God. And it is all the more powerful because it comes לפתע: The tyrants were calm and at ease and unworried; they did not give a thought to the normal consequences of their tyranny and wrongdoing.

In the moral sphere, the Halachah views the phenomenon of מזיד, too, as something that happens פתאום, against all expectation. That a man who knows the nature of the deed and its consequences — for that is the halachic conception of מזיד, as is shown by התראה — should nevertheless transgress the Torah is against all reasonable assumptions.

פתע is subjective; it denotes the relation of a person's consciousness to events that befall him and to deeds done by him. By contrast, פתאום is objective; it denotes the nature of the event or deed in itself. For this reason פתאם can denote אונס as well as מזיד. It denotes an event that occurs באונס, totally unexpected: the person affected by it could not have foreseen it. And it also denotes a transgression committed במזיד: the transgressor certainly acted with full awareness, but *precisely for this reason* the act *in itself* was beyond all expectation.

Thus, according to the Halachah, the term בפתע פתאם includes all three states of consciousness: אונס, שוגג, and מזיד. And no matter how he came near to a corpse, whether by being under the same roof (אהל; see below, 19:14) or by contact, the נזירות he observed until now is annulled, and he is obligated to shave his head (תגלחת), bring the offering (קרבן), and begin again to fulfill his vow.

One case of אונס is an exception to this rule: He already completed his נזירות and even brought his offerings, and then he found out that he had touched a corpse or had stood over a corpse (had himself formed the אהל) during the period of the נזירות; and when he became טמא, no one in the world knew that a corpse was lying hidden in that place. This case is called "טומאת התהום": איזהו טומאת התהום כל שאינה מכירה אחד בסוף העולם. If he finds out afterward that he was rendered טמא by טומאת התהום, his נזירות is not annulled retroactively, provided that he has already completed all the obligations of the נזירות (*Nazir* 63a).

The law of טומאת התהום applies only to נזיר ועושה פסח, one who has completed the obligations of נזירות, or one who has completed the obligations of the פסח offering. And it applies only to טומאת מת: לא אמרו טומאת התהום אלא במת בלבד (ibid. 63b); it does not apply to other טומאות that can invalidate עושה פסח.

וטמא ראש נזרו. The טומאה-idea represented by a corpse is totally antithetical to נזירות, which is proclaimed by the growth of the hair (v. 6). Therefore, the טומאה-idea must be rejected by a complete stoppage of the נזירות that has been observed until now. Otherwise, the טומאה-idea will transform the consecration of the נזירות into its opposite. Hence —

וגלח ראשו ביום טהרתו. After he returns to the stage of טהרה by means of הזייה בשלישי ובשביעי (below, 19:12), he must shave off all the hair of his נזירות and thereby proclaim that the טומאה has cancelled all of the נזירות observed until now.

However, it says: ביום השביעי יגלחנו; he need not wait until he becomes

10 *And on the eighth day he shall bring two turtledoves or two young doves to the priest to the entrance of the Tent of Appointed Meeting.*

י וּבַיּוֹם הַשְּׁמִינִי יָבִא שְׁתֵּי תֹרִים אוֹ
שְׁנֵי בְּנֵי יוֹנָה אֶל־הַכֹּהֵן אֶל־פֶּתַח
אֹהֶל מוֹעֵד׃

11 *The priest shall offer the one as an offering that clears of sin and the other as an ascent offering, and he shall effect atonement for him for that which he sinned concerning the person, and he shall reconsecrate his head on that day.*

יא וְעָשָׂה הַכֹּהֵן אֶחָד לְחַטָּאת וְאֶחָד
לְעֹלָה וְכִפֶּר עָלָיו מֵאֲשֶׁר חָטָא
עַל־הַנָּפֶשׁ וְקִדַּשׁ אֶת־רֹאשׁוֹ בַּיּוֹם
הַהוּא׃

completely טהור by means of טבילה and הערב שמש. For תגלחת הטומאה represents the נזירות that must be removed, once the נזירות has been damaged by טומאה; תגלחת הטומאה is not connected to the entry into the stage of טהרה. In this respect, תגלחת הטומאה differs from the offerings, which can be brought on the eighth day only after הערב שמש [of the seventh day].

The law here differs from the law that applies in the case of the second תגלחת of the מצורע (*Vayikra* 14:9). That תגלחת is connected to the restoration of טהרה; hence, הערב שמש is required following the תגלחת, before the offerings may be brought. Here, however, the law is: נזיר שגילח בשמיני מביא קרבנותיו בו ביום (*Nazir* 44b).

10-11 **וביום השמיני וגו׳**. A טמא מת is not reckoned among the מחוסרי כפרה, such as זב וזבה and the like. His טהרה vis-à-vis מקדש וקדשיו does not depend on his bringing certain offerings; rather, immediately after הזיית שלישי ושביעי, טבילה, and הערב שמש he is טהור also vis-à-vis מקדש וקדשיו.

Likewise, a נזיר whose נזירות has been interrupted by טומאת מת is טהור vis-à-vis מקדש וקדשיו after הערב שמש of the seventh day, and is not מחוסר כפרה in the main sense of this term. Nevertheless, regarding the renewal of נזירות הטהרה he is considered מחוסר כפרה: נזירות הטומאה continues until the offerings are brought. Hence, if after הערב שמש and before he has brought his offerings (see below) he again becomes טמא מת, the whole is considered as one prolonged טומאה אריכתא, and on the second eighth day he brings only one קרבן (*Nazir* 18a-b; *Kerisos* 8b).

12 *He shall then fulfill for* God *the* nazir *task during the days of his* nazirship, *but he shall bring a sheep in its first year as a guilt offering; the previous days become void because his* nazirship *had lost its purity.*	יב וְהִזִּ֤יר לַֽיהוָה֙ אֶת־יְמֵ֣י נִזְר֔וֹ וְהֵבִ֛יא כֶּ֥בֶשׂ בֶּן־שְׁנָת֖וֹ לְאָשָׁ֑ם וְהַיָּמִ֤ים הָֽרִאשֹׁנִים֙ יִפְּל֔וּ כִּ֥י טָמֵ֖א נִזְרֽוֹ׃

After the תגלחת הטומאה, the נזיר טמא shall bring two turtledoves or two young doves, and the כהן shall offer one לחטאת and the other לעולה.

We have already seen such a bird offering in the cases of יולדת זב וזבה (*Vayikra* 12:8; 15:14 and 29). There, it serves as a positive expression of טהרה at the transition from the state of טומאה, and its meaning is as follows: Although the bodily side of man submits to its nature, man is capable of soaring upward to moral freedom and moral perfection (חטאת העוף). And despite the submission of the bodily side of man, he is obligated to maintain his high level and to adhere to the heights of every moral perfection (עולת העוף; see Commentary, ibid. 1:17, 5:13, 12:6-8). With this positive expression of טהרה, the נזיר starts his fresh period of נזירות.

וכפר עליו מאשר חטא על הנפש: By silencing the טומאה-idea through the expression of its opposite, he clears himself of his sin against the טהרה-idea of the נזירות; he removes the sin into which he stumbled when he came near a corpse. ("חטא": he sinned against the נזירות; "על הנפש": by coming near a corpse, about which he was warned: על נפש מת לא יבא [v. 6]; "הנפש," the מת, which מת עליו וגו׳ [v. 9]. So we find that a טמא מת is called simply "טמא לנפש.")

וקדש את ראשו ביום ההוא: Thereby he reconsecrates his head to נזירות, and the consecration begins on that day, which is the eighth day, not on the seventh day, which is connected with the טומאה to be removed.

Scripture makes the renewal of the נזירות contingent on the bringing of the offerings, on the one hand, and on the day itself, on the other. From this the Halachah derives that the renewal of the נזירות is not contingent on the bringing of all the offerings — חטאת, עולה, אשם (see below) — but only on the bringing of חטאת העוף (*Nazir* 18b).

12 **והזיר לה׳ את ימי נזרו והביא כבש בן שנתו לאשם**. He shall fulfill anew the days of the נזירות, but first he must bring an אשם for the past. Scrip-

ture clearly distinguishes between this אשם and the חטאת and עולה, which are brought at the same time (v. 11). The אשם is in no way connected to the bird offerings, which introduce the new נזירות. The entry to the new נזירות in no way depends on this אשם. Before mention is made of the אשם, Scripture says: וקדש את ראשו ביום ההוא והזיר לה׳ את ימי נזרו, and only then does it say: והביא כבש וגו׳ לאשם (see *Nazir* 18b). Rather, by its meaning, this אשם is connected with the past; for only after mention is made of the אשם is the past concluded with the words והימים הראשונים יפלו.

We have already seen אשמות in *Vayikra*: אשם מעילה, אשם גזילות, אשם תלוי, אשם מצורע, אשם שפחה חרופה; and we have already recognized the common denominator of the sins atoned for by these אשמות: egoistic behavior toward people and things, behavior which is likely to bring desolation to the selfish personality.

All these אשמות — except for אשם מצורע — consist of אילים; for they are brought to atone for a person who aspires to stride at the head of society, yet acts selfishly when it comes to his own self-interest and power. They teach the sinner that, in striding at the head of his brothers, he must sanctify himself by dedication to duty (see Commentary, *Vayikra* 5:26 and 19:21-22).

Only אשם מצורע consists of a כבש; for the מצורע's sin was not selfish advancement in society, but selfish opposition to society. His behavior was antisocial; as a result, desolation came upon him, to improve his character. When he re-enters the social community, he must learn to be a "כבש," a simple member of God's flock. As an ordinary member he must fit into the community, which "grazes" under the guidance of its Shepherd. While renouncing selfishness and with selfless devotion to God's purposes, he must direct his aspirations and aims in accordance with God's Will and hallow his achievements and enjoyments with priestlike sanctity.

Like the מצורע, the נזיר טמא here brings a כבש as an אשם. This אשם is the final result of the נזירות הטומאה just now concluded, and it stands to reason that it has almost the same meaning as the אשם brought by the מצורע upon his re-entry into society. To be sure, the נזיר טמא did not commit an actual sin against the social community. But the נזירות vow in itself appears like antisocial arrogance, like the presumption of one who separates himself from the community in order to stand out, and it is only the goal to which the נזיר aspires — spiritual and moral en-

יג וְזֹ֥את תּוֹרַ֖ת הַנָּזִ֑יר בְּי֗וֹם מְלֹאת֙ יְמֵ֣י נִזְר֔וֹ יָבִ֣יא אֹת֔וֹ אֶל־פֶּ֖תַח אֹ֥הֶל מוֹעֵֽד׃

13 *But this is the teaching concerning the* nazir*: On the day when his* nazir *days are completed, he shall take himself to the entrance of the Tent of Appointed Meeting.*

noblement — that purges the vow of this reprehensible semblance. However, this aspiration was now frustrated by טומאה; the נזירות observed until now will not attain its goal, and is null and void: והימים הראשונים יפלו. Thus, all that was done until now amounts to antisocial, purposeless, and unjustified presumption; all that remains is the separation from the community, and that requires atonement via כבש לאשם.

והימים הראשונים יפלו כי טמא נזרו. Only טומאה interrupts the נזירות to such an extent that the previous days become void and the נזירות must begin anew: הטומאה סותרת את הכל (*Sifre*). By contrast, if the נזיר violates the other two prohibitions of the נזירות — viz., היוצא מן הגפן and תגלחת — in no case do the previous days become void. Drinking wine does not even entail an interruption of the נזירות (*Nazir* 44a). Cutting off most of his hair (תגלחת רוב ראשו) — if within thirty days of the end of his term of נזירות — obligates him to observe another thirty days of נזירות (תוספות *Nazir* 39a ד״ה סתם נזירות). According to the רמב״ם, however, תגלחת רוב ראשו in every case prolongs the period of the נזירות by an additional thirty days (הל׳ נזירות, 6:2, לחם משנה there; see Commentary, v. 2).

13 **וזאת תורת הנזיר**: But this is the normal teaching for the נזיר; i.e., this is what should be done, after the נזירות has been properly completed according to regulation.

יביא אתו: himself, as in *Vayikra* 22:16: והשיאו אותם עון אשמה (*Sifre*). Indeed, he is obligated to "bring himself" — i.e., to present himself before the Sanctuary with all the spiritual and moral strength that he has gained from the נזירות for his life. Thus, he shall bring himself to the entrance of the Tent of Appointed Meeting, and then —

14 *And he shall bring near his offering to God: one sheep in its first year, whole, for an ascent offering; and one female sheep in its first year, whole, for an offering that clears of sin, and one ram, whole, for a peace offering;*

יד וְהִקְרִ֣יב אֶת־קָרְבָּנ֣וֹ לַֽיהוָ֡ה כֶּ֣בֶשׂ
בֶּן־שְׁנָת֨וֹ תָמִ֤ים אֶחָד֙ לְעֹלָ֔ה
וְכַבְשָׂ֨ה אַחַ֧ת בַּת־שְׁנָתָ֛הּ תְּמִימָ֖ה
לְחַטָּ֑את וְאַֽיִל־אֶחָ֥ד תָּמִ֖ים
לִשְׁלָמִֽים׃

14 **והקריב וגו׳**: in an offering seeking closeness to God he shall give expression to the meaning of his life from then onward. With youthful vitality (בן שנתו) and with his whole being and will (תמים), he shall draw near to God. He shall be strong and be a man and aspire to ascend toward God in a life of action (לעולה). He shall maintain his high level and remain steadily on the lofty heights of his moral standing (לחטאת). He shall take his place as a simple member in God's flock, the social community (כבש and כבשה).

But the focal point of the נזיר's offering is the איל לשלמים, which constitutes the antithesis of the נזירות. For the נזיר withdraws from social contact and abstains from wine, which gladdens the heart. He thereby seeks to attain closeness to God through the inwardness of spiritual and moral refinement. But this effort, directed primarily inward, does not reflect a permanent state; its whole purpose is to educate. True נזירות leads only to a temporary withdrawal from communal life; one temporarily withdraws from society, so that afterward one can dedicate himself with redoubled force to fulfilling the tasks set for him by God. Just as formerly he distinguished himself by his withdrawal and renunciation, now he is to lead the people. With flawless strength (איל אחד תמים) he is to be a model for his people in the fulfillment of the Jewish ideal, which is essentially this: In the midst of the aspirations and enjoyments of social communal life, upheld by the עולה- and חטאת-sanctification of a life rich in deeds and morally pure, one attains the blissful harmony of a life lived in the presence of God. This is what is expressed by the distinctively Jewish offering, the קרבן שלמים (see Commentary, *Vayikra* 3:1).

Here, Scripture puts the עולה before the חטאת, whereas above (v. 11) it puts the חטאת before the עולה. In the order of offering, the חטאת always precedes the עולה, because being free of sin is a precondition for sanctifying one's actions: First סור מרע and then עשה טוב. But in the text of the Torah's command, the order varies. So we find in these two verses here, and so also in *Vayikra* 5:7, והביא וגו׳ אחד לחטאת ואחד לעלה, and then in 12:8 there, אחד לעלה ואחד לחטאת. So also earlier there in 12:6, כבש וגו׳ לעלה ובן יונה וגו׳ לחטאת, and then in 14:22 there, והיה אחד חטאת והאחד עלה.

Where the חטאת serves to atone for an actual חטא, the stress is on the חטאת; hence, also in the text of the command, the חטאת appears first. That is the case with קרבן עולה ויורד and קרבן מצורע, and that is also the case here, with נזיר טמא (v. 11). Conversely, where no actual sin was committed, and the חטאת is only the expression of the commitment for the future — to stand firm against sin — there the stress is on the עולה, to which the חטאת is secondary, like a prerequisite; hence, in the text the חטאת appears after the עולה. That is the case with יולדת, and that is also the case here, with נזיר טהור.

Accordingly, it is characteristic that in the command of the מילואים of Aharon, Scripture puts the חטאת before the עולה (*Vayikra* 9:2), whereas in the command of the מילואים of the לויים, Scripture puts the עולה before the חטאת (below, 8:8). This confirms the view of our Sages — which we examined in our Commentary on *Vayikra* 9:2 — that the עגל בן בקר לחטאת of Aharon was brought to atone for Aharon's role in the sin of the golden calf. As for the לויים, however, מעשה העגל was precisely where they displayed their impeccable devotion and faithfulness, and that display was the reason for their election afterward. In contrast to the מילואים of Aharon, חטאת המילואים of the לויים refers only to the future; hence, the חטאת is mentioned after the עולה.

The foregoing could resolve two striking problems that arise in the מילואים of the לויים. In verse 8 there (8:8, below), the עולה is not explicitly mentioned; and the פר החטאת, even though it is a חטאת חיצונה, is not eaten by Aharon and his sons (*Horayos* 5a). The explanation is probably as follows: Out of regard for Aharon's dignity, the עולה is not mentioned; the contrast between Aharon and the לויים is only hinted at. And the פר החטאת was not eaten because there was no כהן there worthy of eating this חטאת, which is also the reason פרים הנשרפים are not eaten (see Commentary below, 8:8).

15 *And one basket of matzos from fine wheat flour, cakes mixed with oil, and thin matzos brushed with oil, and their homage offerings and their libations.*	טו וְסַל מַצּוֹת סֹלֶת חַלֹּת בְּלוּלֹת בַּשֶּׁמֶן וּרְקִיקֵי מַצּוֹת מְשֻׁחִים בַּשָּׁמֶן וּמִנְחָתָם וְנִסְכֵּיהֶם׃

15 **וסל מצות**. From verse 17 it is clear that the basket of *matzos* is connected with איל השלמים.

Whoever brings עולה and שלמים — and thus surrenders his personality to God — also surrenders with homage the assets of sustenance, prosperity, and joy, and this comes to expression through מנחה ונסכים. These two are not missing here either, as it says at the end of our verse: ומנחתם ונסכיהם.

In addition, the נזיר brings a סל מצות with the שלמים; for by bringing איל השלמים he vows as follows: He will stride before the people and be a model to others through a joyful life dedicated to God. He therefore gives special expression to the proper relationship to life's possessions, and for this purpose he brings the סל המצות with the איל השלמים (cf. the מילואים of the כהנים, *Shemos* 29:2 and Commentary there). For נזירות is an anomaly, and איל הנזיר — representing the antithesis of נזירות — signifies the following: When the נזיר returns to full communal life, he must be made aware of the fullness of normal life with all its relationships. Among these relationships, all of which must be properly appreciated, the relationship to material possessions, which determine the external measure of one's happiness, deserves due consideration.

Material possessions are represented by the סל מצות. The "basket of *matzos*" includes all possessions designed to bring us happiness. Everything should be "matzah" in our hands; everything should bear for us the stamp of our lack of independence and our dependence on God (see Commentary, ibid. 12:15).

It is significant that the basket of the נזיר includes only חלת בלולת בשמן and רקיקי מצות משחים בשמן. Missing is מורבכת, the rich, fancy oil-bread of the תודה and of the מילואים of the כהנים. The נזיר brings the חלה of affluence, which is soaked in the oil of prosperity, and he also brings the thin wafer of limited means, which is merely brushed with oil. But he does not bring the מורבכת; he does not give expression to the excep-

16 *And the priest shall bring [it] near to* God *and shall make his offering that clears of sin and his ascent offering.*

טז וְהִקְרִ֥יב הַכֹּהֵ֖ן לִפְנֵ֣י יְהוָ֑ה וְעָשָׂ֥ה אֶת־חַטָּאת֖וֹ וְאֶת־עֹלָתֽוֹ׃

17 *And he shall make the ram for a meal-of-peace offering to* God *for the basket of matzos, and the priest shall make his homage offering and his libation.*

יז וְאֶת־הָאַ֜יִל יַעֲשֶׂ֨ה זֶ֤בַח שְׁלָמִים֙ לַֽיהוָ֔ה עַ֖ל סַ֣ל הַמַּצּ֑וֹת וְעָשָׂה֙ הַכֹּהֵ֔ן אֶת־מִנְחָת֖וֹ וְאֶת־נִסְכּֽוֹ׃

tional prosperity that allows for luxurious and elaborate pleasures. For exceptional prosperity is not included among the normal goals of God-serving people; preferably, a נזיר should not direct his attention to extreme wealth. The spirit of שלמים and the happiness of שלמים do not require the rich bread that is prepared artificially. Sustenance and a greater or lesser degree of prosperity are included in the שלמים-way of life, and only these are represented in the basket of the נזיר (see *Menachos* 78a).

ומנחתם ונסכיהם. The מנחות ונסכים which are always brought with עולה and שלמים are specially mentioned here; for the סל המצות, which is brought here unusually, might have led to the mistaken notion that the usual מנחות ונסכים are not brought. As our Sages say: מפני שהיה בכלל ויצא לידון בלחם, החזירו הכתוב לכללן (*Sifre*), in accordance with the hermeneutic rule: כל דבר שהיה בכלל ויצא לידון בדבר החדש אי אתה יכול להחזירו לכללו עד שיחזירנו הכתוב לכללו בפירוש.

17 **ואת האיל וגו׳ על סל המצות**. From this wording our Sages derive (*Menachos* 46b): מלמד שהסל בא חובה לאיל ושחיטת איל מקדשן. Hence, the קדושה of the *matzos* depends on the legality of the שחיטה of the איל. At the שחיטה, the personality represented by the איל relinquishes his whole egocentric being, in order to devote himself selflessly to God; in doing so, he also devotes to God the material means of his existence and prosperity. The קדושה of our daily bread depends on whether we relinquish our whole egocentric being.

ועשה הכהן את מנחתו ואת נסכו. The סולת בלולה בשמן of the מנחת נסכים

18 *And the* nazir *shall shave his* nazir *head at the opened Tent of Appointed Meeting, and he shall take the hair from his* nazir *head and place it upon the fire that is underneath the meal-of-peace offering.*

יח וְגִלַּח הַנָּזִיר פֶּתַח אֹהֶל מוֹעֵד אֶת־רֹאשׁ נִזְרוֹ וְלָקַח אֶת־שְׂעַר רֹאשׁ נִזְרוֹ וְנָתַן עַל־הָאֵשׁ אֲשֶׁר־תַּחַת זֶבַח הַשְּׁלָמִים:

is to be given over entirely to the altar fire, and all the wine of the נסכים is to be poured down from the top of the altar to the base of the altar. These two procedures signify that our whole existence and all our prosperity are to further godliness on earth and give satisfaction to God, and all the joy of our life shall be integrated with the joy that God takes in the upbuilding of humanity. Along with the integration of our whole existence and happiness with God, our daily bread shall then be consecrated: the כהן shall consecrate it through his eating, and the one who brings the קרבן shall partake of it in priestlike sanctity. This will come to expression through the procedures performed with the סל המצות (vv. 19-20).

18 **וגלח הנזיר וגו׳**. The shaving of the hair and its placement on the fire that is cooking the שלמים meal gives fine expression to the meaning of the נזירות just ended: Its value was only relative — compared with the life of enjoyment in God's presence, now beginning. The נזירות was only preparatory training for that life. Letting the hair grow was a sign of separation from the community and of self-isolation (v. 5), whereas head-shaving signifies that this self-isolation is now ended, and that the נזיר now re-enters the social community.

Re-entering the social life of the community is not only permissible, it is a mitzvah, a duty. It is a mitzvah to rejoice and enjoy life in God's presence, and to live a life imbued with the spirit of שלמים. Such a life is greater than נזירות, which demonstrates its moral strength merely through self-isolation and separation; only if it leads to such a life does נזירות have value.

Therefore, when the Sanctuary is open for the שלמים offering, the נזיר's hair is subjected to the razor and is then placed as fuel in the fire

19 *The priest shall then take the cooked foreleg of the ram and one matzah cake from the basket and one thin matzah, and then place it upon the hands of the* nazir, *after he has shaved his* nazir *head,*

יט וְלָקַח הַכֹּהֵן אֶת־הַזְּרֹעַ בְּשֵׁלָה
מִן־הָאַיִל וְחַלַּת מַצָּה אַחַת מִן־
הַסַּל וּרְקִיק מַצָּה אֶחָד וְנָתַן עַל־
כַּפֵּי הַנָּזִיר אַחַר הִתְגַּלְּחוֹ אֶת־
נִזְרוֹ׃

20 *And the priest shall wave them in a waving before* God; *as a holy thing, it is the priest's, along with the breast of the wave [offering] and the thigh of the uplifted donation; after that, the* nazir *may drink wine.*

כ וְהֵנִיף אוֹתָם הַכֹּהֵן ׀ תְּנוּפָה לִפְנֵי
יְהוָה קֹדֶשׁ הוּא לַכֹּהֵן עַל חֲזֵה
הַתְּנוּפָה וְעַל שׁוֹק הַתְּרוּמָה
וְאַחַר יִשְׁתֶּה הַנָּזִיר יָיִן׃

under the pot in which the שלמים meal is being cooked. Thereby the נזירות is subordinated to the שלמים spirit and to the שלמים life, as means to the end.

פתח אהל מועד means: not actually in the entrance to the Sanctuary, but while the entrance is open, when the doors of the Sanctuary are open for the sake of bringing the שלמים offering. For a שלמים may be offered only when the doors of the Sanctuary are open (*Vayikra* 3:2 and see Commentary there; *Nazir* 45a).

19-20 **ולקח הכהן וגו׳**. הזרוע, the two upper joints of the right foreleg, corresponding to שוק הימין, the two upper joints of the right hindleg (*Chullin* 134b). שוק הימין and the חזה from every שלמים offering are given to the כהן even before the cooking. In the case of איל הנזיר, the זרוע is added to them, but it is separated only after the cooking, and is given to the כהן after it has been cooked, בשלה.

According to one opinion (ibid. 98b), בשלה means "whole": אין בשלה אלא שלימה (apparently from the root שלה, as in אֹיְבֶיהָ שָׁלוּ [*Eichah* 1:5], her foes are at ease, undisturbed. שֵׁלָה, then, would denote a state of wholeness, and בְּשֵׁלָה would mean "in a state of wholeness"). The majority opinion, however, is that בשלה is the feminine of בשל, as in וּבָשֵׁל

מבשל במים (*Shemos* 12:9). But even the first opinion agrees that the זרוע of איל הנזיר is given to the כהן only after the cooking.

The difference between חזה ושוק and זרוע בשלה can be explained as follows. The offering animal is meant to be eaten by the בעלים, but the Sanctuary retains for itself the חזה ושוק for the sake of the כהן. The בעלים are entitled to enjoy their portion, only *after* they have dedicated their thoughts and feelings (חזה) and their active efforts (שוק) to God's Torah, represented by the כהן. By contrast, the זרוע בשלה is given to the כהן from the animal that has already been prepared for the enjoyment of the בעלים. It is the כהן's portion in the שלמים meal of the בעלים. It is part, as it were, of their own enjoyment; they will not be happy with their own portion unless they provide the כהן with the זרוע in their possession.

The זרוע is an organ that exercises power; hence, it is always the symbolic expression of power. The זרוע is מושל over everything the שוק has striven for. Accordingly, the זרוע belongs to the conceptual sphere of the איל, which represents striving for and possessing material assets.

If, then, the נזיר — before enjoying his שלמים meal — must give to the כהן the זרוע, this teaches him the following: The purpose of mastery over all that God grants us is to uphold God's Torah, represented by the כהן; our זרוע should be זרוע התורה. It also teaches him that in the spirit of שלמים we can enjoy God's blessing, only if we are aware that our זרוע includes the זרוע of the Torah, and that the success of our power includes the success of the Torah's power.

The זרוע, which may be eaten only by the כהנים, is cooked here together with the rest of the meat, which is eaten by the בעלים. Thus, איסור (for זרים) is cooked here together with היתר. From here our Sages derive the law of ביטול איסור בששים (see *Chullin* 98a-b; and see Commentary, *Vayikra* 11:8).

ונתן וגו' אחר התגלחו את נזרו וגו'. Only after the תגלחת, after the נזיר has removed the sign of the self-isolation in which he lived until this point, does the כהן take the זרוע בשלה and חלת מצה אחת and רקיק מצה אחד and place them on the hands of the נזיר; together with the חזה ושוק, he performs with them תנופה and תרומה before God in the east of the forecourt, opposite the Holy of Holies.

Not in isolation, but only by full participation in the social community do we receive from the Sanctuary the right to our own ideas and aspirations (חזה ושוק); only thus are we entitled to exercise our own power (זרוע) and gain our own bread and prosperity (חלת מצה ורקיק מצה);

21 *This is the teaching concerning the* nazir *who vowed his offering to* God *for his* nazirship, *in addition to anything that his means make possible; according to his vow which he has vowed, thus shall he do in addition to that which is prescribed for his* nazir*ship.*

כא זֹ֣את תּוֹרַ֣ת הַנָּזִיר֮ אֲשֶׁ֣ר יִדֹּר֒ קָרְבָּנ֤וֹ לַֽיהוָה֙ עַל־נִזְר֔וֹ מִלְּבַ֖ד אֲשֶׁר־תַּשִּׂ֣יג יָד֑וֹ כְּפִ֤י נִדְרוֹ֙ אֲשֶׁ֣ר יִדֹּ֔ר כֵּ֣ן יַעֲשֶׂ֔ה עַ֖ל תּוֹרַ֥ת נִזְרֽוֹ׃ פ

only by our full participation in the social community are all these invested with sacred significance — for heaven and earth (מעלה ומוריד) and for the whole community of God on earth (מוליך ומביא). Only by our full participation in the social community do all these become a holy thing directed to the Torah: קדש הוא לכהן.

ואחר ישתה הנזיר יין: Only then does the נזיר return to a normal life of enjoyment.

Nevertheless, in *Nazir* 46a our Sages rule that all these procedures are מצוה but are not מעכבים; rather, once the first קרבן is offered, the נזיר may drink wine and is not restricted as regards טומאת מת.

21 **זאת תורת וגו׳ מלבד וגו׳ כן יעשה על תורת נזרו**. These are the נזיר's duties for the conclusion of his vow. He is free, however, to bring עולות ושלמי נדר ונדבה על תורת נזרו: In addition to the duties stated here, he may give expression to his own special thoughts, emotions, meditations, and vows.

This, then, is the principle that emerges from the institution of נזירות: Any individual among the people is permitted to elevate himself temporarily to the level of כהונה — and become like a כהן גדול — if he feels the need for spiritual and moral ennoblement. His aspiration for God's nearness is manifested primarily by his keeping away from טומאת מת. Thus, נזירות clearly parallels שילוח טמא מת from מחנה שכינה.

Accordingly, the three פרשיות — גזל הגר, סוטה, and נזיר — seen in connection with the preceding פרשה, that of שילוח מחנה, yield the following parallel concepts:

שילוח מצורע from מחנה ישראל finds its concrete realization in פרשת גזל

22 God *spoke to Moshe, saying:*	כב וַיְדַבֵּר יְהֹוָה אֶל־מֹשֶׁה לֵּאמֹר:
23 *Speak to Aharon and to his sons as follows: Thus shall you bless the Children of Israel — this is to be said to them:*	כג דַּבֵּר אֶל־אַהֲרֹן וְאֶל־בָּנָיו לֵאמֹר כֹּה תְבָרְכוּ אֶת־בְּנֵי יִשְׂרָאֵל אָמוֹר לָהֶם: ס

הגר. For that section proclaims the presence of God in the social life of the *nation*.

שילוח זב וזבה from מחנה לוייה finds its concrete realization in פרשת סוטה. For that section proclaims the presence of God in the sexual purity of the *family*.

שילוח טמא מת from מחנה שכינה finds its concrete realization in פרשת נזיר. For that section proclaims the presence of God wherever the *individual* aspires to spiritual and moral holiness with God.

All three together impress upon society, family, and individual the stamp of God's holiness.

23 **דבר אל אהרן וגו׳**. This is not an authorization, but a duty assigned to Aharon's descendants to bless the Children of Israel. The priestly blessing does not emanate from the personal benevolence of the כהנים; rather, it is part of their service in the Sanctuary. For Scripture defines the priestly service as follows: לעמד לפני ה׳ לשרתו ולברך בשמו (*Devarim* 10:8); and similarly: כי בם בחר ה׳ אלקיך לשרתו ולברך בשם ה׳ (ibid. 21:5). ברכת כהנים, then, is part of the שרת and is intimately connected with it. The כהן *stands* in service before God and pronounces the blessing at His bidding and in His Name. Hence, only בעבודה, at the completion of the communal offerings, do the כהנים pronounce the blessing — just as it says of Aharon: וישא אהרן את ידיו אל העם ויברכם וירד מעשת החטאת והעלה והשלמים (*Vayikra* 9:22; see Commentary there).

Also בגבולין, when the people assemble for prayer outside the Sanctuary — nowadays as well — ברכת כהנים is attached to עבודה. Hence כל כהן שאינו עולה בעבודה שוב אינו עולה (*Sotah* 38b): Any כהן who does not start moving toward the raised platform (דוכן) during the recital of the prayer for the עבודה (רצה) may not ascend to pronounce the blessing during that prayer service.

Since ברכת כהנים is part of the שרת and the עבודה, it also has the character of the עבודה procedures. Its meaning lies in its objective prescribed content. The כהן who recites the blessing is merely the appointed instrument through which, there [in the Sanctuary] the procedures, here the words, come to expression. The death of Aharon's sons (*Vayikra* 10:2) has already established a rule regarding the entire עבודה: Only an act performed *as prescribed* is true עבודה; service that one concocts on his own — אשר לא צוה (ibid. 10:1) — is considered זרה, the very opposite of God's service. This rule applies also to ברכת כהנים.

The Torah says: כה תברכו את בני ישראל; כה, "thus," in the prescribed words, in the prescribed manner, and the Halachah teaches (*Sotah* 38a): כה — i.e., בלשון הקודש, בלשון הזה, in the same words in the original language; בעמידה, standing, in the manner of service; בנשיאות כפים, with upraised hands, as though pointing to God, not with horizontally outstretched hands, as though intending to bestow (Jewish priests do not *bestow* blessing); פנים כנגד פנים, face to face with the congregation; בקול רם, in a loud voice. The priestly blessing has no magic power deriving from the priest or from the formula. The attitude of the one who pronounces the blessing is an essential part of the blessing; indeed, it is his attitude that turns the formula he recites into a blessing (v. 27). The *halachos* בעמידה, בלשון הקודש, פנים כנגד פנים, בקול רם (not בלחש) are all indicated by the word "כה": Just as I transmit the command to you in the name of God, so must you fulfill it in the name of God (לבוש אורח חיים 128). And if part of these *halachos* are also derived (*Sotah* 38a) from the words "אמור להם" — which is a call to the כהנים to pronounce the blessing — then these derivations spring from the same concept [both the command to the כהנים and the fulfillment by the כהנים are in the name of God].

Finally, אמור להם: Just as you, Moshe, are to give the order to Aharon and his sons to pronounce the blessing, that shall always be the practice. Whenever it is time to pronounce the blessing, the כהנים should be requested to bless the people; otherwise, they are not obligated and are not authorized to pronounce the blessing. The חזן הכנסת who represents the congregation shall call to them in a loud voice to bless the people. (חזן הכנסת: In the Talmud, "חזן" denotes the superintendent or beadle of the synagogue, המתעסק בצרכי בית הכנסת or שמש הכנסת, not to be confused with the שליח ציבור, the ש״ץ, who leads the prayers and represents the congregation in prayer; see תוספות *Berachos* 34a ד״ה לא יענה אמן. Our custom is that the one who leads the prayers calls to the כהנים, but he does so as חזן — at the bidding and in the name of the congregation.)

24 *May* God *bless you and keep you.*

כד יְבָרֶכְךָ֥ יְהֹוָ֖ה וְיִשְׁמְרֶֽךָ׃ ס

Even after the כהנים have responded to this call and have already pronounced the first word, every succeeding word of the blessing (according to our custom even the first word, too) is dictated to them. Thus, they merely repeat the blessing that was already dictated to them by the representative of the congregation being blessed, and according to the רמב״ם (הל׳ תפלה, 14:3) this, too, is part of the mitzvah of אמור להם. In pronouncing the blessing, the כהנים are a completely passive instrument. Only when summoned by the congregation do they pronounce it, and they pronounce only the blessing dictated to them in the name of the congregation. In truth it is the congregation that brings upon itself the blessing prescribed by God and pronounced by the כהנים.

The summons "כהן" is not directed to a single individual: לשנים קורא כהנים ולאחד אינו קורא כהן (*Sotah* 38a). A blessing pronounced by a *single* person is likely to highlight that single personality and give him an aura of exaggerated importance. Perhaps that is the reason the call "כהן" is not addressed to him.

Let us note that the passivity required by אמור להם is maintained also in the case of the individual כהן by the dictation of יברכך (see מגן אברהם on אורח חיים 128:13). (According to some opinions, a single כהן is not obligated מן התורה to pronounce ברכת כהנים; see ט״ז on אורח חיים 128 ס״ק ג.)

אמור להם. Our Sages (*Sotah* 38a) derive from here that the כהנים should be addressed with a request to bless the people. Onkelos, too, translates: כד תימרון להון (see above).

24 **יברכך וגו׳**. Since יברכך is then complemented by וישמרך, we infer that this blessing refers primarily to possessions that require שמירה, protection, even after they have been granted. They need to be protected so that they remain in our possession and thus prove to be a true blessing. Thus, too, our Sages say in the *Sifre* (here): יברכך ה׳ – בברכה המפורשת, וכן הוא אומר (דברים כח, ג) ברוך אתה בעיר וברוך אתה בשדה ברוך טנאך ומשארתך וגו׳, יברכך ה׳ בנכסים וישמרך בנכסים; ר׳ נתן אומר יברכך בנכסים וישמרך בגוף; ר׳ יצחק אומר וישמרך מיצר הרע וכו׳; ד״א וישמרך שלא ישלטו אחרים עליך וכו׳; ד״א וישמרך מן המזיקים. The first blessing, then, blesses Israel with the prosperity of all

25 *May* God *illuminate His Countenance for you and favor you.*

כה יָאֵ֨ר יְהֹוָ֧ה ׀ פָּנָ֛יו אֵלֶ֖יךָ וִֽיחֻנֶּֽךָּ׃ ס

their *bodily* and *material* possessions and with protection from anything that might harm them.

25 **יאר וגו׳**. Cf. בעמוד אש להאיר להם (*Shemos* 13:21), לְהָאִיר לָהֶם אֶת־הַדֶּרֶךְ (*Nechemyah* 9:12), הֵאִירוּ בְרָקִים תֵּבֵל (*Tehillim* 77:19), הֵאִירוּ בְרָקָיו תֵּבֵל (ibid. 97:4). In all these verses, האיר means: to illuminate something so that it can be seen. Thus נָאוֹר אַתָּה (ibid. 76:5; see Commentary there): God was revealed by the almighty deeds of His rule. The world events emanating from Him radiate back on the One Who caused them, revealing Him in the almighty power of His rule.

פניו. פני ה׳ are God's aims, toward which God "directs His Countenance." These aims are achieved by God's rule and by people who do God's Will in freedom. As it says in *Tehillim* (89:15): צֶדֶק וּמִשְׁפָּט מְכוֹן כִּסְאֶךָ חֶסֶד וֶאֱמֶת יְקַדְּמוּ פָנֶיךָ "God's throne is founded upon righteousness and justice; His Countenance is directed to love and truth."

ויחנך. We have already analyzed (Commentary, *Bereshis* 6:8) the meaning of חנן, based on its relation to ענן and הנן. חנן means: to grant someone his wishes.

In our verse, ויחנך complements the preceding יאר וגו׳. Accordingly, the granting spoken of here is God's granting of the spiritual abilities required in order to behold פני ה׳ which have been illuminated before our eyes; i.e., in order to recognize and understand פני ה׳ which have been revealed to us. יאר ה׳ פניו אליך would accordingly mean: May God reveal to you the aims of His rule and the aims to be achieved through you. The aims of His rule are illuminated by His prophets, and the aims to be achieved through you are illuminated by His Torah. ויחנך: May He equip you with the *spiritual abilities* to understand His Words in תורה and in נבואה and to perceive from these His work in history and your own tasks in life. Similarly, our Sages interpret in the *Sifre*: יאר זה מאור תורה שנא׳ כי נר מצוה ותורה אור, ויחונך בדעת ובבינה ובהשכל ובמוסר ובחכמה; ד״א ויחונך – יחנך בתלמוד תורה. A similar interpretation is found in *Bemidbar Rabbah* (11:6), which finds confirmation in the text of the שמונה עשרה prayer, that חנינה denotes the granting of spiritual gifts. The Midrash

26 *May* God *turn His Countenance toward you and establish peace for you.*

כו יִשָּׂא יְהוָה ׀ פָּנָיו אֵלֶיךָ וְיָשֵׂם לְךָ שָׁלוֹם׃ ס

interprets: ויחנך – הרי הם מבורכים ושמורים ושכינה ביניהן, ומנין אף חנוני בדעת ובבינה תלמוד לומר ויחנך – כמה דמצלינן אתה חונן לאדם דעת ומלמד לאנוש בינה.

It is to the granting of this spiritual blessing that the Psalmist refers in *Tehillim* 67 (see Commentary there). The psalm states that Israel's enlightenment, enabling it to recognize "God's way" on earth (דרך ה׳ includes both the way of God's rule and the way of duty which God has commanded us to follow), is a means to the enlightenment of all mankind. In the words of the Psalmist: אֱלֹקִים **יְחָנֵּנוּ** וִיבָרְכֵנוּ **יָאֵר פָּנָיו** אִתָּנוּ סֶלָה. **לָדַעַת** בָּאָרֶץ **דַּרְכֶּךָ** בְּכָל־גּוֹיִם יְשׁוּעָתֶךָ. יוֹדוּךָ עַמִּים אֱלֹקִים יוֹדוּךָ עַמִּים כֻּלָּם. יִשְׂמְחוּ וִירַנְּנוּ לְאֻמִּים כִּי־תִשְׁפֹּט עַמִּים מִישׁוֹר וּלְאֻמִּים בָּאָרֶץ תַּנְחֵם סֶלָה וגו׳. The entire psalm is a commentary on our verse.

26 **ישא וגו׳**. The expression **נשא פנים אל-** does not occur elsewhere referring to God. Our Sages (*Bemidbar Rabbah* 11:7) interpret: **יהפך פניו כלפי אצלך כמה דתימא ופניתי אליכם**, "He will turn His Countenance toward you, as it says: 'And I will turn to you' (*Vayikra* 26:9)." Accordingly, this expression is another way of saying **יפנה ה׳ אליך**. Indeed, there too, **ופניתי אליכם** introduces a zenith of Divine blessings (see Commentary there). Onkelos, too, translates (here): **יסב ה׳ אפיה לותך**.

There [in *Vayikra* 26], an abundance of blessings had already been promised: fertility, peace, victory; and after these it says: **ופניתי אליכם**, which can mean nothing other than a still more intimate personal relationship of God to Israel, a relationship which then reaches its climax in the blessing **ונתתי משכני בתוככם וגו׳ והתהלכתי בתוככם**.

Here, too, material and spiritual blessing has already been pronounced, and the generality of the terminology [in vv. 24-25] indicates that the blessing is most comprehensive. To this is now added the blessing **ישא וגו׳**, which is the final product crowning the preceding blessing of **יברכך** and **יאר**. The meaning of this blessing (**ישא וגו׳**) is God's closeness. We will attain it, if we properly utilize all the material and spiritual assets granted to us by God, using them in the spirit of the "illumination of God's Countenance." After our eyes have been enlightened to recog-

27 *They shall place My Name upon the Children of Israel; and as for Me, I will bless them.*	כז וְשָׂמ֥וּ אֶת־שְׁמִ֖י עַל־בְּנֵ֣י יִשְׂרָאֵ֑ל וַאֲנִ֖י אֲבָרְכֵֽם׃ ס חמישי

nize His Will, we are to channel our material and spiritual assets solely toward the fulfillment of the Divine aims revealed to us by God.

We do not yearn for God's closeness in order to attain through it material and spiritual blessing; rather, we seek material and spiritual blessing in order to do with it God's Will — so as to be worthy of God's closeness. קִרְבַת אֱלֹקִים, God's closeness, is טוֹב in itself, is the absolute good (*Tehillim* 73:28).

"פנים" in ישא וגו׳ can be taken in the same sense as "פנים" in יאר וגו׳, and it expresses even more clearly God's intimate relationship with Israel. This, then, is the meaning of the blessing: God illuminated His Countenance for you and revealed to you His aims, and you have already been granted the spiritual abilities and material means with which to recognize and achieve these aims. If you properly utilize all these gifts, then ישא ה׳ פניו אליך: He will direct to you all the aims of His rule in nature and in history. For God is interested in the formation, continuance, and development of a God-serving circle of people; and since you embody this circle, the purpose of God's whole rule on earth will be focused on you. ישא ה׳ פניו אליך: God will direct His Countenance toward you, and you will be the object of His providence.

וישם לך שלום. Do not think that, because your endeavors are directed solely to God, and because God's providence seems directed solely to you, you will be isolated and at odds with the world; in fact, precisely for you God ישם שלום, will establish peace and supreme harmonious accord. If you will be a true servant of God with all your physical and spiritual powers, so that God will see in you the fulfillment of all His aims, then all those around you who are sensitive and thoughtful will consider you their perfect complement, the element that spurs them on to good endeavors and sustains them in existence. Every breath drawn by an individual who truly serves God will elicit a responsive chord from the universe around him.

27 **ושמו את שמי וגו׳**. It is not the כהנים who bless Israel; their words have no power of conferring blessing. Their job is only לשום שמי על בני ישראל;

as for Me — ואני אברכם, *I* will bless them. Their job is to "place" God's Name on Israel, so that the people of Israel become bearers of the Shechinah. The כהנים are to impress the Name "God" on Israel's every aspect. They are to proclaim that Israel looks to God and to God alone for all blessing and all protection, all revelation and all ability, all elevation and all peace. Israel expects all these from God alone, so that the blessing and protection, revelation and ability, elevation and peace will themselves constitute a "Name of God"; they will form a book of awesome deeds, by which God reveals Himself. As God has assured us: לא תעשון אתי וגו׳ בכל מקום אשר וגו׳ (*Shemos* 20:20-21). Not in images, but in the blessing that He will bestow on us, will His Presence be revealed to us. Wherever He would have His Name remembered, God will reveal Himself in the blessing bestowed to Israel (see Commentary, ibid. 20:21).

The כהן is meant to be the instrument by which God's Name is pronounced over Israel. The congregation to be blessed shall summon the כהן to be an instrument of blessing, and then God will bless them.

ברכת כהנים in the מקדש differs from ברכת כהנים outside the מקדש in three ways: במדינה אומר אותה שלש ברכות ובמקדש ברכה אחת; במקדש אומר את השם ככתבו ובמדינה בכינויו; במדינה כהנים נושאים את ידיהן כנגד כתפיהן ובמקדש על גבי ראשיהן (*Sotah* 37b). Outside the Sanctuary, ברכת כהנים is said in three separate verses, as it is done today; in the Sanctuary, the three verses are said together as one verse. In the Sanctuary, the Name of God is pronounced as it is written; outside the Sanctuary, it is pronounced in its attributive form (אדנ-י). Outside the Sanctuary, the כהנים raise their hands to the height of their shoulders; in the Sanctuary, they raise their hands above their heads.

The law that the three verses of ברכת כהנים are said in the Sanctuary as one verse is explained (ibid. 40b) as follows: לפי שאין עונין אמן במקדש. ברכות pronounced in the Sanctuary are not responded to with "Amen"; instead, the congregation says: ברוך שם כבוד מלכותו לעולם ועד (see תוספות ibid. ד״ה וכל כך). תוספות suggest the possibility that the response ברוך שם כבוד מלכותו לעולם ועד is made immediately after the Name of God is pronounced. But from the wording of the Gemara (*Ta'anis* 16b) it appears that this response is made at the end of every ברכה in lieu of "Amen"; for it says there regarding the מקדש: והן עונין אחריו בשכמל״ו, just as it says regarding בגבולין: והן עונין אחריו אמן.

The law that the response "Amen" is not made after the ברכות pronounced in the Sanctuary but, rather, the congregation joins itself to the ברכה by saying ברוך שם כבוד מלכותו לעולם ועד is proven (*Berachos* 63a, *Ta'anis* 16b, *Sotah* 40b) from what is stated in *Nechemyah* 9:5, where the לויים call to the assembly: קוּמוּ בָּרְכוּ אֶת־ה׳ אֱלֹקֵיכֶם מִן־הָעוֹלָם עַד־הָעוֹלָם, and the response to this call is expressed — in an address to God — as וִיבָרְכוּ שֵׁם כְּבוֹדֶךָ וּמְרוֹמַם עַל־כָּל־בְּרָכָה וּתְהִלָּה. This proof is ingeniously explained by the commentator ר׳ אליהו מפולדא at the end of *Yerushalmi Berachos*: מנין שלא היו עונין אמן במקדש ת״ל קומו ברכו וגו׳ משמע כולם היו מן המברכין ולא היה בהן שאינו מברך אלא עונה אמן ש״מ שהמברך אומר בא״י וכו׳ והעונים בשכמל״ו וה״ל שפיר כולן מברכין. Outside the Sanctuary, the reader says the ברכה primarily for the assembled congregation: He recites it out loud so that the words will be taken to heart and appropriated by the listeners. This appropriation is accomplished by the response "Amen" (see Commentary above, 5:22). What is said in the Sanctuary, however, is of national significance, and is said for the whole nation, just as the Sanctuary itself and the offerings at which the ברכות are recited are of broad national significance. In general, what is said in the Sanctuary is but a verbal expression of the acts performed there, and these acts are always directed to the consciousness of the whole national community (cf. *Collected Writings*, vol. III, p. 235ff.: the שמונה עשרה). For this reason "Amen" is not said in the Sanctuary. Responding "Amen" would limit the import of the ברכה, as though it were directed not to the consciousness of the whole community, but to a negligible fraction of the nation [i.e., to those who are physically present in the Sanctuary]. Therefore all those who are present join the reader, and they too are considered pronouncers of the blessing. Thus the character of the blessing as directed to the entire community is preserved.

Similarly, ברכת כהנים in the מקדש differs from ברכת כהנים שבגבולין, which likewise is pronounced only for the limited circle of the fraction of the nation actually in attendance. So as to exclude this limited import, "Amen" is not pronounced in the מקדש after ברכת כהנים also.

This is also the reason that ברכת כהנים in the מקדש is said as one single ברכה. In the מקדש, ברכת כהנים is not directed primarily to the consciousness of those present. Its idea transcends the narrow confines of the Sanctuary. It expresses the מקדש-idea that encompasses the whole nation and ultimately all of humanity. And since this idea is *one* unified idea, ברכת כהנים in the מקדש is likewise said as *one* single ברכה.

For at the very first glance one can see how the three verses of ברכת

כהנים are but the verbal expression of what is represented by מקדש וכליו, the Sanctuary and its contents. יברכך, יאר, and ישא correspond to the שולחן, מנורה, and ארון. יברכך expresses the idea of the שולחן, יאר the idea of the מנורה. They teach that the nation's material prosperity and spiritual enlightenment depend on God's dispensation and care. ישא expresses the idea of the ארון and the כפורת: that God's Presence dwells wherever the material and the spiritual unite (יברכך = שולחן, יאר = מנורה) to receive and fulfill God's revealed Will (ארון). And just as the focal point of the Sanctuary is the ארון, to which the שולחן and מנורה are subordinate as prerequisites, so, too, in ברכת כהנים: the ברכה of ישא is the focal point of ברכת כהנים in the Sanctuary, to which the ברכות of יברכך and יאר are attached as antecedent clauses. This is the meaning of ברכת כהנים in the Sanctuary: May God grant you blessing and protection, enlightenment and ability, and may He then let His Presence dwell in your midst and grant you everlasting peace.

Outside the Sanctuary, it is different. There, everything is oriented toward the actual realization of these blessings. The nation's various classes and circles strive to attain the goal of the blessing. There, special attention must be paid to each one of the blessings: The circles seeking blessing must first learn that God alone grants them material blessing and preservation; and when they grasp this truth, they shall appropriate it by answering "Amen." Then let them hear that the longing for peace can be satisfied only through God's closeness, and by answering "Amen" they shall appropriate this truth as well.

In this respect, the relation between ברכת כהנים בגבולין and ברכת כהנים במקדש resembles the relation between תפלין של יד and תפלין של ראש (see Commentary, *Devarim* 6:8).

If this interpretation is not mistaken, it could also resolve the question raised by תוספות (*Sotah* 40b ד״ה וכל כך [regarding the absence of a response after each ברכה of ברכת כהנים in the ביהמ״ק]). The Gemara's statement אין עונים אמן במקדש implies that what is pronounced in the Sanctuary is not directed solely to those present; they are not the only ones who are to appropriate those pronouncements. Accordingly, ברכת כהנים in the Sanctuary is only one ברכה, and if those present are to make a response, they can do so only at the conclusion of the third verse. According to the רמב״ם (הל׳ תפלה, 14:9), those who are present respond at the end of the one ברכה: ברוך ה׳ אלקים אלקי ישראל מן העולם ועד העולם; according to others (תוי״ט, *Sotah* 7:6), they respond: ברוך שם כבוד מלכותו

לעולם ועד (see באר שבע on *Sotah* 40b), and thus link the awaited blessing from God with our ברכה-dedication to Him (see חורב, chap. 111). None of the above excludes the possibility suggested by תוספות that the law applicable to יום הכיפורים applies also to ברכת כהנים, and when they would hear God's Name pronounced by the כהנים the people would respond: ברוך שם כבוד מלכותו לעולם ועד.

The foregoing also explains the other differences between מקדש and גבולין. In ברכת כהנים in the Sanctuary, God's Name (the שם המפורש) is pronounced, whereas בגבולין the usual practice for גבולין is followed, and the Name is pronounced in its attributive form (אדנ-י). For the ברכה in the Sanctuary is a pronouncement, in which the מקדש comes to expression, whereas בגבולין the ברכה is something appropriated by the listeners, hence God's Name, too, is pronounced there in the form of the attribute by which we conceive of Him.

Finally, בגבולין the כהנים raise their hands to the height of their shoulders, whereas in the Sanctuary they raise their hands above their heads. In the Sanctuary, it is necessary to negate the idea that God's Presence is limited to the Temple. Hence, the כהנים's hands, pointing to God, are raised heavenward; they point to the universe, where the heavens are God's throne, and the earth His footstool. By contrast, outside the Temple it must be recalled that here, too, God is present; that מלא כל הארץ כבודו, that שכינה למעלה מראשינו, God's Presence is just above our heads wherever we are, and God is close to man; and where man's realm ends, the holy Divine realm begins (see *Kiddushin* 31a). Hence, the כהנים's hands, pointing to God, are raised only to the height of their shoulders.

If we now consider פרשת ברכת כהנים in connection with the preceding פרשיות, what strikes us first is that

the ברכה of יברכך is realized in מחנה ישראל,
the ברכה of יאר is realized at first in מחנה לוייה,
the ברכה of ישא is realized in מחנה שכינה.

Thus, the three מחנות of the Jewish people form the integrated fundamental idea for the order and connection of the following laws:

שילוח מחנות
גזל הגר, סוטה, נזיר
ברכת כהנים

7 1 *It came to pass even on the day when Moshe had finished setting up the Dwelling Place, when he had anointed it and sanctified it and its utensils, the altar and all its utensils, when he had anointed and sanctified them all together,*

ז א וַיְהִי בְּיוֹם כַּלּוֹת מֹשֶׁה לְהָקִים אֶת־הַמִּשְׁכָּן וַיִּמְשַׁח אֹתוֹ וַיְקַדֵּשׁ אֹתוֹ וְאֶת־כָּל־כֵּלָיו וְאֶת־הַמִּזְבֵּחַ וְאֶת־כָּל־כֵּלָיו וַיִּמְשָׁחֵם וַיְקַדֵּשׁ אֹתָם׃

CHAPTER 7

1 At the beginning of this fourth book we noted that the content of the third book is connected with the construction of the Sanctuary, which is described at the end of the second book; for *Vayikra* teaches the *mitzvos* of holiness, which are the *mitzvos* that the Sanctuary — and the Testimony of the Torah, for whose sake the Sanctuary was erected — set as the task of our lives. This, now, is the content of *Bemidbar*: It describes the relationship and conduct of the nation toward the Sanctuary of the Torah.

The first six chapters counted the whole nation in all its members, families and tribes. Each individual member was counted, to serve the purposes of the Sanctuary. Then they gathered around the משכן in closer or more distant circles — כהנים, לויים, ישראלים — with the Sanctuary as their common center point. שילוח מחנות showed symbolically the effect of the center on the surrounding national sphere, whereas סוטה, גזל הגר and נזיר showed the actual, concrete effect of the center on this sphere. Finally, the assurances signified by the Sanctuary and its contents came to expression in ברכת כהנים, which promises thriving national prosperity, attesting to God's Presence.

Chapter 7 now returns to the day already mentioned at the end of *Shemos* (40:17), the first of Nissan of the second year, the day on which the construction of the משכן was conclusively completed. Scripture returned to this day once before, in *Vayikra* (9:1), whereas at the beginning of *Bemidbar* Scripture passed over it by a month, to complete the instructions connected with the construction of the משכן; hence Scripture described the census and the division of the camps, and added the regulations connected with these.

This chapter now returns to the day on which the משכן was erected.

2 *That the princes of Israel, the heads of their fathers' house brought near — these were the princes of the tribes, the same ones who had assisted in the numberings.*	ב וַיַּקְרִיבוּ נְשִׂיאֵי יִשְׂרָאֵל רָאשֵׁי בֵּית אֲבֹתָם הֵם נְשִׂיאֵי הַמַּטֹּת הֵם הָעֹמְדִים עַל־הַפְּקֻדִים׃

Against the background of the instructions at the beginning of the book, Scripture informs us that even before these instructions were given, already on the day the משכן was erected, the princes understood their position in relation to the משכן, and Scripture describes how they showed this understanding in their deeds.

ויהי ביום כלות משה להקים וגו׳. See Commentary, *Shemos* 40:17ff.

וימשח אותו וגו׳. See Commentary, ibid. 30:23-29.

וימשחם ויקדש אתם. This repetition is explained in the *Sifre* as follows: וימשח אותו ויקדש אותו ואת כל כליו, שומע אני ראשון ראשון שנמשח היה קדוש ת״ל וימשחם ויקדש אותם, מגיד שלא קידש אחד מהם עד שנמשחו כולם. The act of וימשח אתו ויקדש אתו ואת כל כליו was completed only when וימשחם ויקדש אתם; the sanctification of the individual parts of the Sanctuary was accomplished only by the sanctification of the whole. For the Sanctuary in its totality forms *one* integrated idea, and this all-encompassing idea invests each part with its sacred meaning. Each part by itself is incomplete and one-sided, and is not fit to fulfill the purpose on which its sanctity depends. The sanctity of each part depends on that part being complemented by all the other parts. So, too, the whole cannot do without even its least important part. Nothing is superfluous to the whole.

The Sanctuary as a whole is the embodiment of the sentence: ועשו לי מקדש ושכנתי בתוכם (*Shemos* 25:8). But just as a sentence is incomplete if missing a word, syllable, or letter, yet no letter, no syllable, no word conveys any meaning by itself, so, too, in the case of the Sanctuary, the symbolical embodiment of this sentence: The Sanctuary, too, is a single symbolical whole; the whole needs each part, and the part needs the whole.

ויקדש אתו ואת כל כליו ואת המזבח ואת כל כליו. The Sanctuary as a whole is divided here into its two main parts: המשכן וכל כליו symbolize the task; המזבח וכל כליו (the חצר) symbolize the way to accomplish this task.

2 **ויקריבו וגו׳**. The object of ויקריבו is קרבנם of the next verse. Thus, the meaning is: ויקריבו ויביאו את קרבנם וגו׳, and the interruption in the middle

3 *They brought their offering before* God*: six covered wagons and twelve oxen, one wagon each for two princes and one ox for each one. They brought them near in front of the Dwelling Place.*

ג וַיָּבִ֨יאוּ אֶת־קָרְבָּנָ֜ם לִפְנֵ֣י יְהוָ֗ה
שֵׁשׁ־עֶגְלֹ֥ת צָב֙ וּשְׁנֵ֣י עָשָׂ֣ר בָּקָ֔ר
עֲגָלָ֛ה עַל־שְׁנֵ֥י הַנְּשִׂאִ֖ים וְשׁ֣וֹר
לְאֶחָ֑ד וַיַּקְרִ֥יבוּ אוֹתָ֖ם לִפְנֵ֥י
הַמִּשְׁכָּֽן׃

is designed to give a more detailed description of the subject, נשיאי ישראל.

They were נשיאי ישראל, eminent people who bear the people's burden. By virtue of their position, they stood at the height of the national mission, and it was their task to elevate the nation to the heights of their own position.

And they were ראשי בית אבתם. בית אב includes all the families descending from one ancestor and united by tribal unity. These prominent men, who stood out as נשיאי ישראל, stood out also within the united families of the tribe. Their personalities and social character gave them influence, and the community had confidence in them; hence, they were called upon to represent the interests of their respective tribes in all matters affecting the tribe.

Their dual character — as נשיאי ישראל and as ראשי בית אבתם — qualified them to be נשיאי המטת. The tribe is called "בית אב" because of its internal relations and is called "מטה" because it is a "branch" of the national community. As "מטה," the tribe imbibes the national spirit from the common root and trunk and conveys that spirit to the particular spirit of the tribe. Thus, the community's common mission is carried out within the framework of the tribe's individuality.

As נשיאי ישראל they were connected with the nation; as ראשי בית אב they were connected with their respective tribes; therefore, they were fit to represent the national interests within their particular tribes, which is the task that devolved upon them as נשיאי המטת. Hence, they were הם העמדים על הפקדים: a month later, they were to assist in taking the census, in which individuals were counted according to their families and tribes — for the sake of the whole nation (see Commentary above, 1:2-4).

3 **ויביאו את קרבנם**. We have already noted in our Commentary on *Vayikra* (1:2) that anything by which one seeks to draw near to God is called

4 *Then* God *spoke to Moshe, saying:*

ד וַיְדַבֵּ֥ר יְהוָ֖ה אֶל־מֹשֶׁ֥ה לֵּאמֹֽר׃

5 *Take it from them; they shall be in order to serve for the service of the Tent of Appointed Meeting, and you shall give them to the* Levi'im, *to each man according to his service.*

ה קַ֚ח מֵֽאִתָּ֔ם וְהָי֕וּ לַעֲבֹ֕ד אֶת־עֲבֹדַ֖ת
אֹ֣הֶל מוֹעֵ֑ד וְנָתַתָּ֤ה אוֹתָם֙ אֶל־
הַלְוִיִּ֔ם אִ֖ישׁ כְּפִ֥י עֲבֹדָתֽוֹ׃

6 *And Moshe took the wagons and the oxen and gave them to the* Levi'im.

ו וַיִּקַּ֣ח מֹשֶׁ֔ה אֶת־הָעֲגָלֹ֖ת וְאֶת־
הַבָּקָ֑ר וַיִּתֵּ֥ן אוֹתָ֖ם אֶל־הַלְוִיִּֽם׃

7 *Two of the wagons and four of the oxen he gave to the sons of Gershon, according to their service.*

ז אֵ֣ת ׀ שְׁתֵּ֣י הָעֲגָל֗וֹת וְאֵת֙ אַרְבַּ֣עַת
הַבָּקָ֔ר נָתַ֖ן לִבְנֵ֣י גֵרְשׁ֑וֹן כְּפִ֖י
עֲבֹדָתָֽם׃

"קרבן." These wagons, too, were a form of קרבן, considering the purpose for which they were brought. They were gifts by which the giver demonstrated his God-seeking spirit.

עגלת צב. צב occurs also in *Yeshayahu* 66:20 as a means of transport. Phonetically related to סבב, צב apparently denotes the surround on all sides of the wagon, by which people or articles placed in the wagon are protected. The component parts of the משכן were not covered when loaded onto wagons; hence, there was a need for covers over the wagons. Onkelos, too, translates: כד מחפין.

These wagons they brought as נשיאי ישראל. Through this gift they activated the nation's awareness that the Sanctuary of the Torah is the national treasure which the nation is to carry with it on all its journeys, just as the body carries the soul which gives it life. Not as ראשי בית אבותם and not as נשיאי המטות, but as נשיאי ישראל did they dedicate the wagons to the Sanctuary, and this came to expression in the fact that every two נשיאים brought one wagon and its team of oxen. Thus, no נשיא made the presentation for his own tribe alone.

ויקריבו אותם לפני המשכן: מלמד שהביאום ומסרום לציבור (*Bemidbar Rabbah* 12:18); they made the wagons national property.

8 *And four of the wagons and eight of the oxen he gave to the sons of Merari, according to their service under the direction of Isamar, son of Aharon the priest.*

ח וְאֵ֣ת ׀ אַרְבַּ֣ע הָעֲגָלֹ֗ת וְאֵת֙ שְׁמֹנַ֣ת
הַבָּקָ֔ר נָתַ֖ן לִבְנֵ֣י מְרָרִ֑י כְּפִי֙
עֲבֹ֣דָתָ֔ם בְּיַד֙ אִֽיתָמָ֔ר בֶּֽן־אַהֲרֹ֖ן
הַכֹּהֵֽן׃

9 *He did not give any to the sons of Kehas because the service of the Sanctuary devolved upon them; they had to carry [the holy things] upon their shoulders.*

ט וְלִבְנֵ֥י קְהָ֖ת לֹ֣א נָתָ֑ן כִּֽי־עֲבֹדַ֤ת
הַקֹּ֙דֶשׁ֙ עֲלֵהֶ֔ם בַּכָּתֵ֖ף יִשָּֽׂאוּ׃

10 *Thereupon the princes brought near the dedication [offering] of the altar, on the day it was anointed; the princes brought near their offering before the altar.*

י וַיַּקְרִ֣יבוּ הַנְּשִׂאִ֗ים אֵ֚ת חֲנֻכַּ֣ת
הַמִּזְבֵּ֔חַ בְּי֖וֹם הִמָּשַׁ֣ח אֹת֑וֹ וַיַּקְרִ֧יבוּ
הַנְּשִׂיאִ֛ם אֶת־קָרְבָּנָ֖ם לִפְנֵ֥י
הַמִּזְבֵּֽחַ׃

9 **כי עבדת הקדש עלהם** — as opposed to עבדת אהל מועד in the limited sense of verse 5. The בני קהת were assigned the service of the קודש — in the primary sense of this term. Their service related to those parts for whose sake the אהל מועד had been erected, the parts that constitute the essence of the קודש, the parts whose sanctity sanctifies all the other sacred objects. They are the קודש of the קדשים, and for this reason they are called "קדש הקדשים" (above, 4:4). They are that קודש that gives expression to the task that devolves upon us; hence to them we must devote our very own energies, the essence of our own power. Therefore בכתף ישאו.

10 **ויקריבו הנשאים**. Not as נשיאי ישראל (v. 2), but as ראשי בית אבותם and as נשיאי המטות did the נשיאים bring חנכת המזבח: as princes of the tribes, not as princes of the nation.

In our Commentary on *Bereshis* (14:14) we explained that חנך denotes introducing something into its calling. We noted there that this concept has a negative feature and a positive feature. All חינוך entails limitation which negates, but precisely thereby it enables more intensive positive activity.

11 *And* God *said to Moshe: One prince each on a [given] day, one prince each on a [given] day shall they bring near their offering for the dedication of the altar.*

יא וַיֹּאמֶר יְהוָה אֶל־מֹשֶׁה נָשִׂיא אֶחָד לַיּוֹם נָשִׂיא אֶחָד לַיּוֹם יַקְרִיבוּ אֶת־קָרְבָּנָם לַחֲנֻכַּת הַמִּזְבֵּחַ: ס

The sanctification, which excludes the altar from any other use or purpose, already came to expression through the משיחה, whereas the positive aspect of the altar's purpose was merely indicated by the aromatic ingredients of the שמן המשחה (see Commentary, *Shemos* 30:25).

The princes of the tribes wanted to initiate the positive purpose of the altar immediately after its משיחה [ביום המשח אתו]. For the אש דת burning on the altar as אש אוכלה (see Commentary, *Vayikra* 1:7) summons everyone to devote to the Torah everything that comprises his "self"; thereby he shall sustain the holy on earth and fashion all the earthly material to bring with it satisfaction to God. The princes of the tribes wanted to answer this silent summons issuing from the altar, immediately upon the completion of its משיחה. At the same time, they wanted to demonstrate thereby that they understood the Sanctuary's effect on the nation, that the Sanctuary's impact was felt immediately at the משיחה of the altar.

Hence ויקריבו הנשיאם את קרבנם לפני המזבח: They brought their offering, all of them together, simultaneously, thus demonstrating that the tribes represented by them are equal in their relation to the Sanctuary of the Torah, and they come to it with one attitude.

11 **ויאמר ה׳ וגו׳**. God, however, commanded that each tribal prince should make his offering on his own particular day. For each tribe represents a unique configuration of social characteristics, which, if purified, pervaded with the spirit of the Torah, and employed in the fulfillment of the Torah's commandments, will enable each tribe to make its own contribution to the accomplishment of the mission assigned to the nation as a whole.

12 *And the one who brought near his offering on the first day was Nachshon, son of Amminadav, of the tribe of Yehudah.*

יב וַיְהִ֗י הַמַּקְרִ֛יב בַּיּ֥וֹם הָרִאשׁ֖וֹן אֶת־
קָרְבָּנ֑וֹ נַחְשׁ֥וֹן בֶּן־עַמִּינָדָ֖ב לְמַטֵּ֥ה
יְהוּדָֽה׃

13 *And his offering was one silver dish weighing one hundred and thirty, one silver sprinkling basin [weighing] seventy shekels by the weight of the Sanctuary, both filled with fine wheat flour mixed with oil for an homage offering;*

יג וְקָרְבָּנ֞וֹ קַֽעֲרַת־כֶּ֣סֶף אַחַ֗ת
שְׁלֹשִׁ֣ים וּמֵאָה֮ מִשְׁקָלָהּ֒ מִזְרָ֤ק
אֶחָד֙ כֶּ֔סֶף שִׁבְעִ֥ים שֶׁ֖קֶל בְּשֶׁ֣קֶל
הַקֹּ֑דֶשׁ שְׁנֵיהֶ֣ם ׀ מְלֵאִ֗ים סֹ֛לֶת
בְּלוּלָ֥ה בַשֶּׁ֖מֶן לְמִנְחָֽה׃

12 The order in which they brought their offerings was the same as that prescribed for the tribes for encamping and journeying (see chap. 2).

13 **וקרבנו וגו׳.** קערת כסף is a כלי שרת in which a מנחה offering is received for the purposes of the Sanctuary and thus the מנחה becomes sacred. With this vessel, the הגשה of the מנחה to the southwest corner of the altar is then performed, the corner representing the spirit directed to the Torah and illuminated by the spirit of the Torah (see Commentary, *Vayikra* 1:5). מזרק is a vessel for זריקה, i.e., for throwing the blood to the heights of the altar. According to *Sifre* (here), these two vessels differed only in their weight, but were of equal capacity; it was only that the מזרק was much thinner, גלדו דק, and so weighed less, but they contained an identical quantity, a similarity that is indicated by the expression **שניהם** מלאים (cf. *Vayikra* 16:5).

As ראש בית אבותיו and as נשיא מטהו, the tribal prince brought *both* vessels filled with flour and oil for a מנחה offering. Thereby he expressed the following: All means of sustenance and prosperity which his tribe will acquire through its own special qualities shall be dedicated and subordinated to the spirit of the Torah. His tribe must never attach importance to the sheer production and acquisition of possessions. The dead capital of social prosperity should not be regarded as a sign of greatness. His tribe should attach importance to the material wealth of possessions, only if the dead capital is brought to life, if the flour and oil is transformed into "blood," into דם הנפש, and the נפש ascends to the

14 *One spoon [weighing] ten shekels of gold, filled with incense;*	יד כַּף אַחַת עֲשָׂרָה זָהָב מְלֵאָה קְטֹרֶת׃

height of its calling. For the דם that is destined to be received in the מזרקות shall give life also to the שמן and the סולת, ennobling them with life that strives to ascend to God.

14 **כף וגו׳**. כף is a vessel that is used for the presentation and offering of the incense that accompanies the לחם הפנים (*Shemos* 25:29) as well as for the offering of קטורת daily and on יום הכיפורים (*Yoma* 47a; *Tamid* 5:4). Normally, לבונה is offered with מנחת סולת (see Commentary, *Vayikra* 2:1). Here, however, the הקטרה לריח ניחוח is independent, and what is offered up in smoke is קטורת, which is the intensified and highest expression of the incense offering.

We have already stated (Commentary, *Shemos* 30:34ff.) that the קטורת is the highest expression of ideal devotion, of total self-surrender to God; it is the ריח ניחוח itself, to which all the other procedures performed on the altar in the עזרה only pave the way. Hence, קטורת is offered only on the מזבח הזהב and is never brought בנדבה. For the קטורת represents the highest ideal which is set before man as a goal. This exalted goal can only be set before us, and only the Sanctuary can set it. To offer קטורת as נדבה would constitute arrogance that ignores the exaltedness of the goal.

Here, קטורת was brought בנדבה and on the מזבח החיצון; it was a הוראת שעה (*Menachos* 50a), an offering dependent on the significance of the moment and the momentary purpose. As part of חנוכת המזבח, that קטורת showed the ריח ניחוח in its complete perfection. Ever since, the מזבח החיצון shows the way to that ריח ניחוח.

When the נשיא brings the קטורת as prince of the tribe, he expresses the following vow: This highest goal of Jewish perfection shall shine before his tribe as the ideal to which it shall aspire with all the assets granted to it. All the aspirations of his tribe shall be absorbed in the aspiration to do God's Will. All its ריח ניחוח shall be ריח ניחוח לה׳.

The combination of קערה, מזרק, and כף represents the three fundamental procedures of the קרבנות: קבלה, זריקה, and הקטרה. These three procedures are performed on or at the side of the altar, and so form the basis of חנוכת המזבח. The entry to the sphere of the Sanctuary (קבלה)

15 *One young bull, one ram, one sheep in its first year for an ascent offering;*	טו פַּר אֶחָד בֶּן־בָּקָר אַיִל אֶחָד כֶּבֶשׂ־אֶחָד בֶּן־שְׁנָתוֹ לְעֹלָה׃
16 *One male goat for an offering that clears of sin;*	טז שְׂעִיר־עִזִּים אֶחָד לְחַטָּאת׃

begins already with one's external possessions: קערה. The self-devotion (זריקה) is done with the living personality: מזרק. And the total absorption in God (הקטרה) is accomplished mainly with the Divine element in man, an element whose source is in God and whose aspiration is to God: כף.

These or similar considerations may have affected the determination of the vessels' weight; for these are the figures stated in connection with the weights: קערה: 130; מזרק: 70; כף: 10. Taking 10 as one unit, we get the numbers 13, 7, 1. These numbers appear here in descending order, and the difference between each pair of adjacent numbers is 6: 13 - 6 = 7; 7 -6 = 1.

Now, 6 is the sign of the created world. Man, however, is a created thing in two respects, for he consists of the vegetative element and the animal element, and the Divine soul in him binds him to the unity of the Creator. Expressed in terms of numbers, man, then, is 6 + 6 + 1 = 13.

The קערה consecrates the means of sustenance and enjoyment, and is assigned the full number: 13. For שמן and סולת are of the vegetative element, and they represent one aspect of the created world. Their purpose is to be integrated with the body and converted into the animal element [6], whose combination with the Divine soul creates man [6+1]. Hence, their sign is 6 and 7 = 13.

The נפש, which in the blood of the מזרק is devoted to the holy, finds its expression in the number 7. For in the נפש the vegetative element, which is *one* aspect of the created world, has already been converted into the animal element, whose combination with the Divine soul creates man. The נפש, then, is 13 - 6 = 7. Hence, the sign of the מזרק is 7.

The קטורת symbolizes man's total absorption in God. Accordingly, it symbolizes the Divine element, which in man is joined to the animal element. The קטורת is the Divine soul itself, without the animal element of the created world; it is 7 - 6 = 1. Hence, the sign of the כף is 1.

15-16 After the מנחה has dedicated the tribe's assets, the עולה and the חטאת dedicate the tribe's activities. This dedication is to be performed with

17 *And for the meal-of-peace offering: two oxen, five rams, five bucks, five yearling sheep. This was the offering of Nachshon, son of Amminadav.*

יז וּלְזֶ֣בַח הַשְּׁלָמִים֮ בָּקָ֣ר שְׁנַ֒יִם֒ אֵילִ֤ם
חֲמִשָּׁה֙ עַתּוּדִ֣ים חֲמִשָּׁ֔ה כְּבָשִׂ֥ים
בְּנֵי־שָׁנָ֖ה חֲמִשָּׁ֑ה זֶ֛ה קָרְבַּ֥ן נַחְשׁ֖וֹן
בֶּן־עַמִּינָדָֽב׃ פ

the moral earnestness of the חטאת. The tribe shall boldly resist all temptation (שעיר) and adhere to the heights of all moral standards already attained. The tribe shall serve God with unwavering strength (פר אחד בן בקר), stride ahead of its brother tribes, showing them the way of progress (איל), and faithfully follow God, never arrogantly assuming that it does not need His guidance (כבש). The tribe shall demonstrate these capabilities in its deeds and in its endeavors to ascend toward God (עולה). (See our Commentary above, 6:14.)

This offering of חטאת נדבה was likewise a הוראת שעה, connected with the חנוכה-aspect of these offerings (see Commentary, *Vayikra* 4:24).

17 **ולזבח השלמים וגו׳**. But the culmination of חנוכת המזבח, the dedication of the altar, is with the זבח השלמים: Having dedicated its assets and its deeds, the tribe rejoices before God in its own existence and volition; and in rejoicing in God, it merits to enjoy and rejoice in itself.

Mentioned here is an animal that appears nowhere else as an offering animal: עתודים. Instead, Scripture generally mentions שעירים, the characteristic offerings brought from goats. According to the רד״ק, שעירים are smaller and younger than עתודים. It appears, then, that the עֵז- and שעיר-character manifests itself in עתודים to a heightened degree. They are always "מעותדים"; they are the largest and strongest of the herd, always ready for the fray. Thus, עַתּוּדֵי אָרֶץ (*Yeshayahu* 14:9) are the great military world-powers, which — like Bavel — pass across the stage of history.

This, then, is the meaning of the שלמים of חנוכת המזבח: The tribe rejoices before God in its existence and volition; for it participates as a co-worker with God in His great work in the world (בקר), strides at the head of its national contemporaries (אילם), defends against the outside (עתודים), and faithfully commits itself to the guidance of the "Shepherd of Israel" (כבשים).

18 *On the second day Nesan'el, son of Tzu'ar, prince of Yissachar, brought near.*	יח בַּיּוֹם הַשֵּׁנִי הִקְרִיב נְתַנְאֵל בֶּן־צוּעָר נְשִׂיא יִשָּׂשכָר׃
19 *He brought near his offering: one*	יט הִקְרִב אֶת־קָרְבָּנוֹ קַעֲרַת־כֶּסֶף

The numbers are characteristic. Appearing here is a number that occurs nowhere else as a number of offerings — namely, the number five. Ten is the basic number of an עדה, a plurality that has been completed and transformed into a unit. Accordingly, five is a half, a plurality not completed. Now we understand why this number appears in שלמים. For the שלמים offering expresses that the tribe rejoices before God in its existence and volition; but, in this joy, the tribe does not present itself as a complete unit, but as a half that has not yet reached completion, and that will be complete only if it joins one of its brother tribes.

In the עולה, which expresses what the tribe *should* be and *ought* to do, the tribe can draw near as פר אחד וגו׳. For each tribe is *obligated* to be its own distinctive "one" within the broader framework of God's people.

The שלמים, however, expresses the tribe's joy in what it *is*; the שלמים does not relate to the tribe's *obligation*, but to its *being*. In the case of שלמים, the tribe does not consider itself a unit or a completed plurality which has become a unit. Hence, not by "one" and not by "ten" does it count its offerings. In its activity in God's service, it regards itself as a "plurality," בקר שנים; it is mindful that every household and every individual of the tribe makes its contribution to God's work, and every member of its masses is reckoned among the "thousands and ten thousands of Israel." And when the tribe rejoices in its influence directed inward (איל), in its power directed outward (עתודים), and in its consciousness that God is its Shepherd (כבש), it considers itself only a part of the whole, considers itself complete only in brotherly union. When it expresses this joy, the tribe appears as אילם חמשה עתודים חמשה כבשים בני שנה חמשה.

18-19 **ביום השני הקריב וגו׳ הקרב וגו׳**. The offering on the second day is introduced twice by the term "הקריב," to teach us that, although this offering is merely a repetition of the first, it is of equal importance, and the same applies to all the following offerings, which are reported in *silver dish weighing one hundred and thirty, one silver sprinkling basin [weighing] seventy shekels by the weight of the Sanctuary, both filled with fine wheat flour mixed with oil for an homage offering;*

אַחַת שְׁלֹשִׁים וּמֵאָה מִשְׁקָלָהּ
מִזְרָק אֶחָד כֶּסֶף שִׁבְעִים שֶׁקֶל
בְּשֶׁקֶל הַקֹּדֶשׁ שְׁנֵיהֶם ׀ מְלֵאִים
סֹלֶת בְּלוּלָה בַשֶּׁמֶן לְמִנְחָה׃

20 *One spoon [weighing] ten shekels of gold, filled with incense;*

כ כַּף אַחַת עֲשָׂרָה זָהָב מְלֵאָה
קְטֹרֶת׃

21 *One young bull, one ram, one sheep in its first year for an ascent offering;*

כא פַּר אֶחָד בֶּן־בָּקָר אַיִל אֶחָד
כֶּבֶשׂ־אֶחָד בֶּן־שְׁנָתוֹ לְעֹלָה׃

22 *One male goat for an offering that clears of sin;*

כב שְׂעִיר־עִזִּים אֶחָד לְחַטָּאת׃

23 *And for the meal-of-peace offering: two oxen, five rams, five bucks, five yearling sheep. This was the offering of Nesan'el, son of Tzu'ar.*

כג וּלְזֶבַח הַשְּׁלָמִים בָּקָר שְׁנַיִם אֵילִם
חֲמִשָּׁה עַתֻּדִים חֲמִשָּׁה כְּבָשִׂים
בְּנֵי־שָׁנָה חֲמִשָּׁה זֶה קָרְבַּן נְתַנְאֵל
בֶּן־צוּעָר׃ פ

24 *On the third day the prince of the sons of Zevulun: Eli'av, son of Chelon.*

כד בַּיּוֹם הַשְּׁלִישִׁי נָשִׂיא לִבְנֵי זְבוּלֻן
אֱלִיאָב בֶּן־חֵלֹן׃

---

the abbreviated style: ביום השלישי נשיא וגו׳, ביום הרביעי נשיא וגו׳, and so on. According to the *Sifre* (here), Scripture here [by the repetition הקריב, הקרב] recognizes a mark of distinction for the tribe of Yissachar, which distinguished itself with יוֹדְעֵי בִינָה לָעִתִּים לָדַעַת מַה־יַּעֲשֶׂה יִשְׂרָאֵל (*Divrei Ha-Yamim* I, 12:33): Nesan'el, prince of Yissachar, inspired his fellow princes to make these offerings for חנוכת המזבח.

25 *His offering was one silver dish weighing one hundred and thirty, one silver sprinkling basin [weighing] seventy shekels by the weight of the Sanctuary, both filled with fine wheat flour mixed with oil for an homage offering;*

כה קָרְבָּנוֹ קַעֲרַת־כֶּסֶף אַחַת שְׁלֹשִׁים
וּמֵאָה מִשְׁקָלָהּ מִזְרָק אֶחָד כֶּסֶף
שִׁבְעִים שֶׁקֶל בְּשֶׁקֶל הַקֹּדֶשׁ
שְׁנֵיהֶם ׀ מְלֵאִים סֹלֶת בְּלוּלָה
בַשֶּׁמֶן לְמִנְחָה׃

26 *One spoon [weighing] ten shekels of gold, filled with incense;*

כו כַּף אַחַת עֲשָׂרָה זָהָב מְלֵאָה
קְטֹרֶת׃

27 *One young bull, one ram, one sheep in its first year for an ascent offering;*

כז פַּר אֶחָד בֶּן־בָּקָר אַיִל אֶחָד
כֶּבֶשׂ־אֶחָד בֶּן־שְׁנָתוֹ לְעֹלָה׃

28 *One male goat for an offering that clears of sin;*

כח שְׂעִיר־עִזִּים אֶחָד לְחַטָּאת׃

29 *And for the meal-of-peace offering: two oxen, five rams, five bucks, five yearling sheep. This was the offering of Eli'av, son of Chelon.*

כט וּלְזֶבַח הַשְּׁלָמִים בָּקָר שְׁנַיִם אֵילִם
חֲמִשָּׁה עַתֻּדִים חֲמִשָּׁה כְּבָשִׂים
בְּנֵי־שָׁנָה חֲמִשָּׁה זֶה קָרְבַּן אֱלִיאָב
בֶּן־חֵלֹן׃ פ

30 *On the fourth day the prince of the sons of Reuven: Elitzur, son of Shedei'ur.*

ל בַּיּוֹם הָרְבִיעִי נָשִׂיא לִבְנֵי רְאוּבֵן
אֱלִיצוּר בֶּן־שְׁדֵיאוּר׃

31 *His offering was one silver dish weighing one hundred and thirty, one silver sprinkling basin [weighing] seventy shekels by the weight of the Sanctuary, both filled with fine wheat flour mixed with oil for an homage offering;*

לא קָרְבָּנוֹ קַעֲרַת־כֶּסֶף אַחַת שְׁלֹשִׁים
וּמֵאָה מִשְׁקָלָהּ מִזְרָק אֶחָד כֶּסֶף
שִׁבְעִים שֶׁקֶל בְּשֶׁקֶל הַקֹּדֶשׁ
שְׁנֵיהֶם ׀ מְלֵאִים סֹלֶת בְּלוּלָה
בַשֶּׁמֶן לְמִנְחָה׃

32 *One spoon [weighing] ten shekels of gold, filled with incense;*

לב כַּף אַחַת עֲשָׂרָה זָהָב מְלֵאָה קְטֹרֶת׃

33 *One young bull, one ram, one sheep in its first year for an ascent offering;*

לג פַּר אֶחָד בֶּן־בָּקָר אַיִל אֶחָד כֶּבֶשׂ־אֶחָד בֶּן־שְׁנָתוֹ לְעֹלָה׃

34 *One male goat for an offering that clears of sin;*

לד שְׂעִיר־עִזִּים אֶחָד לְחַטָּאת׃

35 *And for the meal-of-peace offering: two oxen, five rams, five bucks, five yearling sheep. This was the offering of Elitzur, son of Shedei'ur.*

לה וּלְזֶבַח הַשְּׁלָמִים בָּקָר שְׁנַיִם אֵילִם חֲמִשָּׁה עַתֻּדִים חֲמִשָּׁה כְּבָשִׂים בְּנֵי־שָׁנָה חֲמִשָּׁה זֶה קָרְבַּן אֱלִיצוּר בֶּן־שְׁדֵיאוּר׃ פ

36 *On the fifth day the prince of the sons of Shimon: Shelumi'el, son of Tzurishaddai.*

לו בַּיּוֹם הַחֲמִישִׁי נָשִׂיא לִבְנֵי שִׁמְעוֹן שְׁלֻמִיאֵל בֶּן־צוּרִישַׁדָּי׃

37 *His offering was one silver dish weighing one hundred and thirty, one silver sprinkling basin [weighing] seventy shekels by the weight of the Sanctuary, both filled with fine wheat flour mixed with oil for an homage offering;*

לז קָרְבָּנוֹ קַעֲרַת־כֶּסֶף אַחַת שְׁלֹשִׁים וּמֵאָה מִשְׁקָלָהּ מִזְרָק אֶחָד כֶּסֶף שִׁבְעִים שֶׁקֶל בְּשֶׁקֶל הַקֹּדֶשׁ שְׁנֵיהֶם ׀ מְלֵאִים סֹלֶת בְּלוּלָה בַשֶּׁמֶן לְמִנְחָה׃

38 *One spoon [weighing] ten shekels of gold, filled with incense;*

לח כַּף אַחַת עֲשָׂרָה זָהָב מְלֵאָה קְטֹרֶת׃

39 *One young bull, one ram, one sheep in its first year for an ascent offering;*

לט פַּר אֶחָד בֶּן־בָּקָר אַיִל אֶחָד כֶּבֶשׂ־אֶחָד בֶּן־שְׁנָתוֹ לְעֹלָה׃

40 *One male goat for an offering that clears of sin;*

מ שְׂעִיר־עִזִּים אֶחָד לְחַטָּאת׃

41 *And for the meal-of-peace offering: two oxen, five rams, five bucks, five yearling sheep. This was the offering of Shelumi'el, son of Tzurishaddai.*

מא וּלְזֶבַח הַשְּׁלָמִים בָּקָר שְׁנַיִם אֵילִם
חֲמִשָּׁה עַתֻּדִים חֲמִשָּׁה כְּבָשִׂים
בְּנֵי־שָׁנָה חֲמִשָּׁה זֶה קָרְבַּן
שְׁלֻמִיאֵל בֶּן־צוּרִישַׁדָּי׃ פ ששי

42 *On the sixth day the prince of the sons of Gad: Elyasaf, son of De'u'el.*

מב בַּיּוֹם הַשִּׁשִּׁי נָשִׂיא לִבְנֵי גָד אֶלְיָסָף
בֶּן־דְּעוּאֵל׃

43 *His offering: one silver dish weighing one hundred and thirty, one silver sprinkling basin [weighing] seventy shekels by the weight of the Sanctuary, both filled with fine wheat flour mixed with oil for an homage offering;*

מג קָרְבָּנוֹ קַעֲרַת־כֶּסֶף אַחַת שְׁלֹשִׁים
וּמֵאָה מִשְׁקָלָהּ מִזְרָק אֶחָד כֶּסֶף
שִׁבְעִים שֶׁקֶל בְּשֶׁקֶל הַקֹּדֶשׁ
שְׁנֵיהֶם ׀ מְלֵאִים סֹלֶת בְּלוּלָה
בַשֶּׁמֶן לְמִנְחָה׃

44 *One spoon [weighing] ten shekels of gold, filled with incense;*

מד כַּף אַחַת עֲשָׂרָה זָהָב מְלֵאָה
קְטֹרֶת׃

45 *One young bull, one ram, one sheep in its first year for an ascent offering;*

מה פַּר אֶחָד בֶּן־בָּקָר אַיִל אֶחָד
כֶּבֶשׂ־אֶחָד בֶּן־שְׁנָתוֹ לְעֹלָה׃

46 *One male goat for an offering that clears of sin;*

מו שְׂעִיר־עִזִּים אֶחָד לְחַטָּאת׃

47 *And for the meal-of-peace offering: two oxen, five rams, five bucks, five yearling sheep. This was the offering of Elyasaf, son of De'u'el.*

מז וּלְזֶבַח הַשְּׁלָמִים בָּקָר שְׁנַיִם אֵילִם
חֲמִשָּׁה עַתֻּדִים חֲמִשָּׁה כְּבָשִׂים
בְּנֵי־שָׁנָה חֲמִשָּׁה זֶה קָרְבַּן אֶלְיָסָף
בֶּן־דְּעוּאֵל׃ פ

48 *On the seventh day the prince of the sons of Efrayim: Elishama, son of Ammihud.*

מח בַּיּוֹם הַשְּׁבִיעִי נָשִׂיא לִבְנֵי אֶפְרָיִם
אֱלִישָׁמָע בֶּן־עַמִּיהוּד׃

49 *His offering: one silver dish weighing one hundred and thirty, one silver sprinkling basin [weighing] seventy shekels by the weight of the Sanctuary, both filled with fine wheat flour mixed with oil for an homage offering;*

מט קָרְבָּנוֹ קְעָרַת־כֶּסֶף אַחַת שְׁלֹשִׁים
וּמֵאָה מִשְׁקָלָהּ מִזְרָק אֶחָד כֶּסֶף
שִׁבְעִים שֶׁקֶל בְּשֶׁקֶל הַקֹּדֶשׁ
שְׁנֵיהֶם ׀ מְלֵאִים סֹלֶת בְּלוּלָה
בַשֶּׁמֶן לְמִנְחָה׃

50 *One spoon [weighing] ten shekels of gold, filled with incense;*

נ כַּף אַחַת עֲשָׂרָה זָהָב מְלֵאָה
קְטֹרֶת׃

51 *One young bull, one ram, one sheep in its first year for an ascent offering;*

נא פַּר אֶחָד בֶּן־בָּקָר אַיִל אֶחָד
כֶּבֶשׂ־אֶחָד בֶּן־שְׁנָתוֹ לְעֹלָה׃

52 *One male goat for an offering that clears of sin;*

נב שְׂעִיר־עִזִּים אֶחָד לְחַטָּאת׃

53 *And for the meal-of-peace offering: two oxen, five rams, five bucks, five yearling sheep. This was the offering of Elishama, son of Ammihud.*

נג וּלְזֶבַח הַשְּׁלָמִים בָּקָר שְׁנַיִם אֵילִם
חֲמִשָּׁה עַתֻּדִים חֲמִשָּׁה כְּבָשִׂים
בְּנֵי־שָׁנָה חֲמִשָּׁה זֶה קָרְבַּן
אֱלִישָׁמָע בֶּן־עַמִּיהוּד׃ פ

54 *On the eighth day the prince of the sons of Menashe: Gamli'el, son of Pedahtzur.*

נד בַּיּוֹם הַשְּׁמִינִי נָשִׂיא לִבְנֵי מְנַשֶּׁה
גַּמְלִיאֵל בֶּן־פְּדָהצוּר׃

55 *His offering: one silver dish weighing one hundred and thirty, one silver sprinkling basin [weighing] seventy shekels by the weight of the Sanctuary, both filled with fine wheat flour mixed with oil for an homage offering;*

נה קָרְבָּנוֹ קְעָרַת־כֶּסֶף אַחַת שְׁלֹשִׁים
וּמֵאָה מִשְׁקָלָהּ מִזְרָק אֶחָד כֶּסֶף
שִׁבְעִים שֶׁקֶל בְּשֶׁקֶל הַקֹּדֶשׁ
שְׁנֵיהֶם ׀ מְלֵאִים סֹלֶת בְּלוּלָה
בַשֶּׁמֶן לְמִנְחָה׃

56 *One spoon [weighing] ten shekels of gold, filled with incense.*

נו כַּף אַחַת עֲשָׂרָה זָהָב מְלֵאָה קְטֹרֶת׃

57 *One young bull, one ram, one sheep in its first year for an ascent offering;*

נז פַּר אֶחָד בֶּן־בָּקָר אַיִל אֶחָד כֶּבֶשׂ־אֶחָד בֶּן־שְׁנָתוֹ לְעֹלָה׃

58 *One male goat for an offering that clears of sin;*

נח שְׂעִיר־עִזִּים אֶחָד לְחַטָּאת׃

59 *And for the meal-of-peace offering: two oxen, five rams, five bucks, five yearling sheep. This was the offering of Gamli'el, son of Pedahtzur.*

נט וּלְזֶבַח הַשְּׁלָמִים בָּקָר שְׁנַיִם אֵילִם חֲמִשָּׁה עַתֻּדִים חֲמִשָּׁה כְּבָשִׂים בְּנֵי־שָׁנָה חֲמִשָּׁה זֶה קָרְבַּן גַּמְלִיאֵל בֶּן־פְּדָהצוּר׃ פ

60 *On the ninth day the prince of the sons of Binyamin: Avidan, son of Gid'oni.*

ס בַּיּוֹם הַתְּשִׁיעִי נָשִׂיא לִבְנֵי בִנְיָמִן אֲבִידָן בֶּן־גִּדְעֹנִי׃

61 *His offering: one silver dish weighing one hundred and thirty, one silver sprinkling basin [weighing] seventy shekels by the weight of the Sanctuary, both filled with fine wheat flour mixed with oil for an homage offering;*

סא קָרְבָּנוֹ קַעֲרַת־כֶּסֶף אַחַת שְׁלֹשִׁים וּמֵאָה מִשְׁקָלָהּ מִזְרָק אֶחָד כֶּסֶף שִׁבְעִים שֶׁקֶל בְּשֶׁקֶל הַקֹּדֶשׁ שְׁנֵיהֶם ׀ מְלֵאִים סֹלֶת בְּלוּלָה בַשֶּׁמֶן לְמִנְחָה׃

62 *One spoon [weighing] ten shekels of gold, filled with incense;*

סב כַּף אַחַת עֲשָׂרָה זָהָב מְלֵאָה קְטֹרֶת׃

63 *One young bull, one ram, one sheep in its first year for an ascent offering;*

סג פַּר אֶחָד בֶּן־בָּקָר אַיִל אֶחָד כֶּבֶשׂ־אֶחָד בֶּן־שְׁנָתוֹ לְעֹלָה׃

64 *One male goat for an offering that clears of sin;*

סד שְׂעִיר־עִזִּים אֶחָד לְחַטָּאת׃

65 *And for the meal-of-peace offering: two oxen, five rams, five bucks, five yearling sheep. This was the offering of Avidan, son of Gid'oni.*

סה וּלְזֶבַח הַשְּׁלָמִים בָּקָר שְׁנַיִם אֵילִם חֲמִשָּׁה עַתֻּדִים חֲמִשָּׁה כְּבָשִׂים בְּנֵי־שָׁנָה חֲמִשָּׁה זֶה קָרְבַּן אֲבִידָן בֶּן־גִּדְעֹנִי׃ פ

66 *On the tenth day the prince of the sons of Dan: Achi'ezer, son of Ammishaddai.*

סו בַּיּוֹם הָעֲשִׂירִי נָשִׂיא לִבְנֵי דָן אֲחִיעֶזֶר בֶּן־עַמִּישַׁדָּי׃

67 *His offering: one silver dish weighing one hundred and thirty, one silver sprinkling basin [weighing] seventy shekels by the weight of the Sanctuary, both filled with fine wheat flour mixed with oil for an homage offering;*

סז קָרְבָּנוֹ קַעֲרַת־כֶּסֶף אַחַת שְׁלֹשִׁים וּמֵאָה מִשְׁקָלָהּ מִזְרָק אֶחָד כֶּסֶף שִׁבְעִים שֶׁקֶל בְּשֶׁקֶל הַקֹּדֶשׁ שְׁנֵיהֶם ׀ מְלֵאִים סֹלֶת בְּלוּלָה בַשֶּׁמֶן לְמִנְחָה׃

68 *One spoon [weighing] ten shekels of gold, filled with incense;*

סח כַּף אַחַת עֲשָׂרָה זָהָב מְלֵאָה קְטֹרֶת׃

69 *One young bull, one ram, one sheep in its first year for an ascent offering;*

סט פַּר אֶחָד בֶּן־בָּקָר אַיִל אֶחָד כֶּבֶשׂ־אֶחָד בֶּן־שְׁנָתוֹ לְעֹלָה׃

70 *One male goat for an offering that clears of sin;*

ע שְׂעִיר־עִזִּים אֶחָד לְחַטָּאת׃

71 *And for the meal-of-peace offering: two oxen, five rams, five bucks, five yearling sheep. This was the offering of Achi'ezer, son of Ammishaddai.*

עא וּלְזֶבַח הַשְּׁלָמִים בָּקָר שְׁנַיִם אֵילִם חֲמִשָּׁה עַתֻּדִים חֲמִשָּׁה כְּבָשִׂים בְּנֵי־שָׁנָה חֲמִשָּׁה זֶה קָרְבַּן אֲחִיעֶזֶר בֶּן־עַמִּישַׁדָּי׃ פ שביעי

72 *On the eleventh day the prince of the sons of Asher: Pag'i'el, son of Ochran.*

עב בְּיוֹם עַשְׁתֵּי עָשָׂר יוֹם נָשִׂיא לִבְנֵי אָשֵׁר פַּגְעִיאֵל בֶּן־עָכְרָן׃

73 *His offering: one silver dish weighing one hundred and thirty, one silver sprinkling basin [weighing] seventy shekels by the weight of the Sanctuary, both filled with fine wheat flour mixed with oil for an homage offering;*

עג קָרְבָּנ֞וֹ קַֽעֲרַת־כֶּ֣סֶף אַחַ֗ת שְׁלֹשִׁ֣ים
וּמֵאָה֮ מִשְׁקָלָהּ֒ מִזְרָ֤ק אֶחָד֙ כֶּ֔סֶף
שִׁבְעִ֥ים שֶׁ֖קֶל בְּשֶׁ֣קֶל הַקֹּ֑דֶשׁ
שְׁנֵיהֶ֣ם ׀ מְלֵאִ֗ים סֹ֛לֶת בְּלוּלָ֥ה
בַשֶּׁ֖מֶן לְמִנְחָֽה׃

74 *One spoon [weighing] ten shekels of gold, filled with incense;*

עד כַּ֥ף אַחַ֛ת עֲשָׂרָ֥ה זָהָ֖ב מְלֵאָ֥ה
קְטֹֽרֶת׃

75 *One young bull, one ram, one sheep in its first year for an ascent offering;*

עה פַּ֣ר אֶחָ֞ד בֶּן־בָּקָ֗ר אַ֧יִל אֶחָ֛ד
כֶּֽבֶשׂ־אֶחָ֥ד בֶּן־שְׁנָת֖וֹ לְעֹלָֽה׃

76 *One male goat for an offering that clears of sin;*

עו שְׂעִיר־עִזִּ֥ים אֶחָ֖ד לְחַטָּֽאת׃

77 *And for the meal-of-peace offering: two oxen, five rams, five bucks, five yearling sheep. This was the offering of Pag'i'el, son of Ochran.*

עז וּלְזֶ֣בַח הַשְּׁלָמִים֮ בָּקָ֣ר שְׁנַיִם֒ אֵילִ֤ם
חֲמִשָּׁה֙ עַתֻּדִ֣ים חֲמִשָּׁ֔ה כְּבָשִׂ֥ים
בְּנֵי־שָׁנָ֖ה חֲמִשָּׁ֑ה זֶ֛ה קָרְבַּ֥ן
פַּגְעִיאֵ֖ל בֶּן־עָכְרָֽן׃ פ

78 *On the twelfth day the prince of the sons of Naftali: Achira, son of Einan.*

עח בְּיוֹם֙ שְׁנֵ֣ים עָשָׂ֣ר י֔וֹם נָשִׂ֖יא לִבְנֵ֣י
נַפְתָּלִ֑י אֲחִירַ֖ע בֶּן־עֵינָֽן׃

79 *His offering: one silver dish weighing one hundred and thirty, one silver sprinkling basin [weighing] seventy shekels by the weight of the Sanctuary, both filled with fine wheat flour mixed with oil for an homage offering;*

עט קָרְבָּנ֞וֹ קַֽעֲרַת־כֶּ֣סֶף אַחַ֗ת שְׁלֹשִׁ֣ים
וּמֵאָה֮ מִשְׁקָלָהּ֒ מִזְרָ֤ק אֶחָד֙ כֶּ֔סֶף
שִׁבְעִ֥ים שֶׁ֖קֶל בְּשֶׁ֣קֶל הַקֹּ֑דֶשׁ
שְׁנֵיהֶ֣ם ׀ מְלֵאִ֗ים סֹ֛לֶת בְּלוּלָ֥ה
בַשֶּׁ֖מֶן לְמִנְחָֽה׃

80 *One spoon [weighing] ten shekels of gold, filled with incense;*

פ כַּף אַחַת עֲשָׂרָה זָהָב מְלֵאָה קְטֹרֶת׃

81 *One young bull, one ram, one sheep in its first year for an ascent offering;*

פא פַּר אֶחָד בֶּן־בָּקָר אַיִל אֶחָד כֶּבֶשׂ־אֶחָד בֶּן־שְׁנָתוֹ לְעֹלָה׃

82 *One male goat for an offering that clears of sin;*

פב שְׂעִיר־עִזִּים אֶחָד לְחַטָּאת׃

83 *And for the meal-of-peace offering: two oxen, five rams, five bucks, five yearling sheep. This was the offering of Achira, son of Einan.*

פג וּלְזֶבַח הַשְּׁלָמִים בָּקָר שְׁנַיִם אֵילִם חֲמִשָּׁה עַתֻּדִים חֲמִשָּׁה כְּבָשִׂים בְּנֵי־שָׁנָה חֲמִשָּׁה זֶה קָרְבַּן אֲחִירַע בֶּן־עֵינָן׃ פ

84 *This was the dedication [offering] of the altar, on the day it was anointed by the princes of Israel: twelve silver dishes, twelve sprinkling basins, twelve gold spoons.*

פד זֹאת ׀ חֲנֻכַּת הַמִּזְבֵּחַ בְּיוֹם הִמָּשַׁח אֹתוֹ מֵאֵת נְשִׂיאֵי יִשְׂרָאֵל קַעֲרֹת כֶּסֶף שְׁתֵּים עֶשְׂרֵה מִזְרְקֵי־כֶסֶף שְׁנֵים עָשָׂר כַּפּוֹת זָהָב שְׁתֵּים עֶשְׂרֵה׃

85 *Each dish [weighed] one hundred and thirty in silver and each sprinkling basin [weighed] seventy; all the silver of the vessels was two thousand, four hundred, by the weight of the Sanctuary.*

פה שְׁלֹשִׁים וּמֵאָה הַקְּעָרָה הָאַחַת כֶּסֶף וְשִׁבְעִים הַמִּזְרָק הָאֶחָד כֹּל כֶּסֶף הַכֵּלִים אַלְפַּיִם וְאַרְבַּע־מֵאוֹת בְּשֶׁקֶל הַקֹּדֶשׁ׃

84 **זאת חנכת וגו'**. This recapitulation expresses the complete unanimity of the princes of Israel. In חנוכת המזבח they expressed the attitude of each individual tribe toward the common Sanctuary of the people, and they expressed this attitude in harmony and in complete accord.

86 *Twelve gold spoons filled with incense, each spoon [weighing] ten by the weight of the Sanctuary; all the gold of the spoons [amounted to] one hundred and twenty.*

פו כַּפּוֹת זָהָב שְׁתֵּים־עֶשְׂרֵה מְלֵאֹת קְטֹרֶת עֲשָׂרָה עֲשָׂרָה הַכַּף בְּשֶׁקֶל הַקֹּדֶשׁ כָּל־זְהַב הַכַּפּוֹת עֶשְׂרִים וּמֵאָה׃ מפטיר

87 *All the oxen for the ascent offering [totalled] twelve bulls, [with] twelve rams [and] twelve yearling sheep along with their homage offering, and twelve male goats for an offering that clears of sin.*

פז כָּל־הַבָּקָר לָעֹלָה שְׁנֵים עָשָׂר פָּרִים אֵילִם שְׁנֵים־עָשָׂר כְּבָשִׂים בְּנֵי־שָׁנָה שְׁנֵים עָשָׂר וּמִנְחָתָם וּשְׂעִירֵי עִזִּים שְׁנֵים עָשָׂר לְחַטָּאת׃

88 *And all the cattle for the meal-of-peace offering: twenty-four bulls, sixty rams, sixty bucks, [and] sixty yearling sheep. This was the dedication [offering] of the altar after it had been anointed.*

פח וְכֹל בְּקַר ׀ זֶבַח הַשְּׁלָמִים עֶשְׂרִים וְאַרְבָּעָה פָּרִים אֵילִם שִׁשִּׁים עַתֻּדִים שִׁשִּׁים כְּבָשִׂים בְּנֵי־שָׁנָה שִׁשִּׁים זֹאת חֲנֻכַּת הַמִּזְבֵּחַ אַחֲרֵי הִמָּשַׁח אֹתוֹ׃

89 *And when Moshe went into the Tent of Appointed Meeting to speak with Him, he heard the voice speaking to him from above the cover that was upon the Ark of the Testimony, from between the two cherubim; thus did He speak to him.*

פט וּבְבֹא מֹשֶׁה אֶל־אֹהֶל מוֹעֵד לְדַבֵּר אִתּוֹ וַיִּשְׁמַע אֶת־הַקּוֹל מִדַּבֵּר אֵלָיו מֵעַל הַכַּפֹּרֶת אֲשֶׁר עַל־אֲרֹן הָעֵדֻת מִבֵּין שְׁנֵי הַכְּרֻבִים וַיְדַבֵּר אֵלָיו׃ פפפ

---

89 **ובבא משה וגו'** — cf. *Shemos* 25:22 and Commentary there.

This verse immediately follows חנוכת המזבח of נשיאי ישראל. This חנוכה demonstrated that the *tribes of Israel* unanimously agreed that the Sanctuary of the Torah would be *their* Sanctuary of the Torah, and they resolved that this Sanctuary would guide and direct their national ex-

8 1 God *spoke to Moshe, saying:* **ח** א וַיְדַבֵּר יְהוָה אֶל־מֹשֶׁה לֵּאמֹר׃

istence. Correspondingly, our verse now adds that when Moshe went into the Sanctuary לדבר אתו because God wished to say something to him, וישמע וגו׳ מעל הכפרת אשר על ארן העדת מבין שני הכרבים. For, as we already stated (ibid.), God's Word is heard by Moshe not by virtue of a special personal relationship of Moshe to God but, rather, by virtue of God's covenantal closeness to Israel — as expressed by the ארון and the כפורת; God sends His Word to Moshe because *He dwells in the midst of the people that keeps His Torah.*

בהעלתך

CHAPTER 8

1 This section returns to the narrative of the people redeemed from Egypt who are developing into the people of God. This narrative was interrupted with chapter 34 of *Shemos*, which describes the renewal of the covenant after the atonement for the sin of the golden calf. The purpose of the interruption was to tell of the משכן's construction and its associated laws, which form the contents of the whole book of *Vayikra* and the beginning of the book of *Bemidbar* (until here). Thereby Scripture set down the ideal for which Israel was to become the people of God. However, Israel would have to be trained and shaped for that ideal over hundreds, indeed thousands of years, extending beyond our own present day.

In our Commentary on *Shemos* (19:10-13; 32:1) we noted the contrast between Israel at the Lawgiving and the Torah itself, with all its assumptions and requirements, a contrast that could be overcome only by centuries of training. This is a clear proof of the Divine origin of the Torah, for the relation between Israel and its Law is unique in the history of mankind. All other codes of law originate in the needs of the generation and accommodate the conditions of the times. This Law, however, presents man with the supreme goal of human conduct, and awaits a generation sufficiently mature to translate its ideals into reality.

The transition to the continuation of this developmental history is

2 *Speak to Aharon and say to him: When you light up the lights, the seven lights shall shine toward the [center of] the Menorah.*	ב דַּבֵּר֙ אֶֽל־אַהֲרֹ֔ן וְאָמַרְתָּ֖ אֵלָ֑יו בְּהַעֲלֹֽתְךָ֙ אֶת־הַנֵּרֹ֔ת אֶל־מוּל֙ פְּנֵ֣י הַמְּנוֹרָ֔ה יָאִ֖ירוּ שִׁבְעַ֥ת הַנֵּרֽוֹת׃

made by several sections: the kindling of the lights by the כהנים; the induction of the לויים into their service in the Sanctuary; the offering up of the Pesach offering, which revives the people's national consciousness that they are destined to be God's people, and that toward this end they are to lay anew each year the foundation of Israel's mission. And finally there is the first breaking of camp and moving on from Mount Sinai, a march that in the ordinary course of events should have led them directly to the Promised Land, the land that was destined — and still is destined — for Israel, so that it should fulfill there God's Torah. Then — with verses 35 and 36 of chapter 10 — Scripture makes a "break" and takes us down into the midst of the camp to see how much the people still needed to develop in order to fulfill the lofty aims set for it.

2 **בהעלתך**. See Commentary, *Shemos* 27:20.

אל מול פני המנורה. The primary meaning of מנורה is the central shaft bearing the central light. Six branches issue from this shaft — three on each side — with a light on each branch. Here Aharon is commanded to direct the lights on both sides toward the central light on the central shaft, so that all seven lights cast their light in this one direction. This is nothing but a detailed explanation of what is stated in *Shemos* 25:37: והאיר על עבר פניה.

We have already explained (Commentary, *Shemos* 25:39, end) the dispute regarding the Menorah's position in the Sanctuary. According to one view, the Menorah was placed in a north-south direction; the central light was directed westward toward the Holy of Holies; the three lights on the right were directed from north to south, and the three lights on the left were directed from south to north. According to the other view, the Menorah was placed in an east-west direction, and the central light on the central shaft rose straight upward; the three lights in the east were directed westward, and the three lights in the west were directed eastward.

According to the first view, the Menorah's position symbolizes the spirit fostered in the Sanctuary, the spirit that seeks God in His Torah and in the covenant that He established with Israel regarding the Torah. The southern lights shining northward symbolize that the purpose of all spiritual awareness is the suffusion of the material with the spiritual. The northern lights shining southward symbolize that the purpose of the material is its consignment to the spiritual, so that the material should be fertile ground for the light of the good and the upright, which is sown upon it. These two lights — of the spirit suffusing the material and of the material consigned to the spiritual — have this in common: they both strive to fulfill the Torah, which rests in the Holy of Holies, and they both seek God's nearness, which lies there as a promise.

According to the second view, the light burning in the Sanctuary symbolizes the spirit rising upward to God. The western lights shining eastward symbolize the following: From the Torah in the Holy of Holies and from God's nearness which is assured there, an outpouring of knowledge will radiate to the people of Israel, who await in the east the light of holiness. The eastern lights shining westward symbolize the following: The people of Israel, who await the light of holiness, shall enlighten their eyes and revitalize their hearts in God's Torah and its promises. The Torah's spirit, which is realized in the life of Israel, and Israel's impassioned devotion to this spirit are both directed solely to one goal: rising and ascending to God.

In whichever position the Menorah stood, its seven lights, shining toward the center of the Menorah and united in the central light, represent the following: The practical spirit of בינה, גבורה, and יראת ה׳ shall join the theoretical spirit of חכמה, עצה, and דעת, and the spirit of יראת ה׳ shall bear them all, leading to such a spiritual flowering and unfolding that the holy spirit will rest on man: וְנָחָה עָלָיו רוּחַ ה׳ (*Yeshayahu* 11:2). (See Commentary, *Shemos* 25, end, on the Menorah.)

As reported in the preceding chapter, the princes of Israel's tribes brought to the Sanctuary the best and choicest of their belongings: silver and gold, oil and fragrant spices, and the best of their herds and flocks. Thereby they expressed that they were devoting to God all their possessions and their whole existence and volition. They also expressed — on their own behalf and on behalf of their tribes — their happiness in devoting all these to God and His Sanctuary. By thus demonstrating —

3 *Aharon did so; he lit up its lights toward the [center of] the Menorah, as* God *had commanded Moshe.*

ג וַיַּ֤עַשׂ כֵּן֙ אַהֲרֹ֔ן אֶל־מוּל֙ פְּנֵ֣י הַמְּנוֹרָ֔ה הֶעֱלָ֖ה נֵרֹתֶ֑יהָ כַּאֲשֶׁ֛ר צִוָּ֥ה יְהֹוָ֖ה אֶת־מֹשֶֽׁה׃

4 *And this is the workmanship of the*

ד וְזֶ֨ה מַעֲשֵׂ֤ה הַמְּנֹרָה֙ מִקְשָׁ֣ה זָהָ֔ב

in harmony and in complete accord — their attitude toward the Sanctuary, they completed חנוכת המזבח.

The tribe of Levi and Aharon its prince (below, 17:18) did not participate in this dedication by the tribes of Israel and their princes. They did not possess the flour and the oil, the silver, the gold, and the spices; they did not possess the wealth of herds and flocks. For their position was not *toward* the Sanctuary; rather, they stood *beside* the Sanctuary, and the Sanctuary itself was their portion and inheritance.

Thus, while the princes of Israel brought the חנוכה-offering of the altar and thereby gave expression to the nation's relationship to the Sanctuary, Aharon and then his tribe (v. 5ff.) were told what their relationship was to the Sanctuary in the midst of the nation. להעלות את הנרות so that אל מול פני המנורה יאירו שבעת הנרות. To tend the "lights" in such a way that the whole diversity of spiritual aspirations is united in the aspiration to God — *that* is the mission of the כהן and the meaning of the service of the לויים. What the princes expressed in the exalted days of the dedication is what the כהנים must attend to daily; they must see to it that this spirit rests among the people every day, and that the nation's life continually matures toward its spiritual and moral perfection. This is the task assigned to the כהנים, and Aharon is to give expression to it by directing all the lights to the central light. And Scripture immediately adds:

3 **ויעש כן אהרן**. Aharon gave expression to the task assigned to the כהן: to direct all of the nation's spiritual aspirations to God and to His Torah. Aharon gave expression to this by correspondingly directing the lights of the Menorah. This was not priestly arrogance; he merely did as God had commanded Moshe.

4 **וזה מעשה וגו׳**. The repetition of the mitzvah of kindling the lights (v. 2) can be explained by its relation to the חנוכה offerings and by Aharon's

Menorah: hammered out of one piece of gold, to its rootstock, to its blossom, it is beaten work. Like the vision that God *had let Moshe behold, so did he make the Menorah.*	עַד־יְרֵכָהּ עַד־פִּרְחָהּ מִקְשָׁה הִוא כַּמַּרְאֶה אֲשֶׁר הֶרְאָה יְהוָה אֶת־מֹשֶׁה כֵּן עָשָׂה אֶת־הַמְּנֹרָה: פ

relation to them. But this can hardly be the only reason for the repetition, as it does not explain why Scripture repeats the work of constructing the Menorah and describes the manner in which it was carried out (v. 4); for the whole work of constructing the Menorah was already presented in full detail in *Shemos*.

Hence, in our view, there is additional significance to this repetition of the task of Aharon and the tribe of Levi. Scripture repeats it at the beginning of the פרשה as preparation for what will follow: the continuation of the history of Israel's development for its great mission. This history shows how vast was the gulf between Israel at its inception and the ideal of its mission; how far the people were from the lofty heights of complete devotion and total commitment to God and His Torah. Nevertheless, a whole tribe in Israel demonstrated its faithfulness to God and His Torah, and for this reason it was to be the servant, representative, and champion of this ideal. To this tribe God entrusted His Urim and Tummim — the ideal of moral integrity and intellectual enlightenment; He could expect that just as in the past שמרו אמרתו, so in the future ינצרו בריתו and יורו משפטיו ליעקב ותורתו לישראל (see *Devarim* 33:8-10 and Commentary there).

Let us now look at the Menorah and consider its construction: מקשה זהב עד ירכה עד פרחה מקשה הִוא! The Menorah is *a tree of gold, made of one piece, hammered out by repeated blows of the hammer, from rootstock to blossom.* This is the appearance of the bearer of the light sown in the Sanctuary, and thus it rises and blossoms out to God and to His Torah. The spiritual element nurtured in the Sanctuary is pure gold, through and through, requiring no refinement. But its bearer is a tree that grows and develops from the rootstock below to the blossom above. In individuals, also in nations, development to the highest spiritual blossoming requires time. For the individual it takes years, for the nation centuries. The tree is formed of one mass, which already includes the

5 God *spoke to Moshe, saying:*	ה וַיְדַבֵּר יְהוָה אֶל־מֹשֶׁה לֵּאמֹר:
6 *Take the* Levi'im *from the midst of the Children of Israel and purify them.*	ו קַח אֶת־הַלְוִיִּם מִתּוֹךְ בְּנֵי יִשְׂרָאֵל וְטִהַרְתָּ אֹתָם:

material for everything — material for the rootstock, material for the blossom. מקשה, heavy blows from the God of Israel, formed the raw material into the rootstock and will ultimately produce the final blossom at the top of the tree of light: מקשה זהב עד ירכה עד פרחה מקשה הִוא.

What Moshe wrought with the Sanctuary presents a picture of Israel; for God showed him the tree of life of Israel's whole future: כמראה אשר הראה ה׳ את משה כן עשה את המנרה. However, הַמַּאֲמִין לֹא יָחִישׁ, "let the believer not expect it soon" (*Yeshayahu* 28:16).

5-6 We have already noted (above, vv. 2 and 4) the significance of the consecration of the לויים in connection with the preceding חנוכה of the princes and the succeeding continuation of the history of Israel's development. This פרשה was communicated on the day on which the construction of the משכן was completed, the first of Nissan, the eighth day of the מילואים. On that day, the consecration of the כהנים was concluded and the חנוכה of the princes began; and on that day, too, the consecration of the לויים was prescribed (*Gittin* 60a). On the second of Nissan the פרה אדומה was burned (below, chap. 19), and the consecration of the לויים was carried out on the third day of the month (*Sifre* on נשא, 7:1).

וטהרת אתם. טמא מת was not banished from מחנה לויה; and had the service of the לויים consisted only in being guards outside the Sanctuary and in carrying the parts of the משכן after its dismantling, the לויים would not have required הזיית מי חטאת so as to achieve טהרה from טומאת מת. For the לויים were allowed to approach the sacred objects only after they were covered; and although the idea of the Sanctuary retained its influence even after it was dismantled (see Commentary above, 2:17) — hence even in transit קדושת מחנה לויה and קדושת מחנה ישראל were not nullified — nevertheless, קדושת מחנה שכינה was then in abeyance (see תוספות *Zevachim* 61a ד"ה קדשים). Presumably, their guard duty, too, was held only outside קלעי החצר — i.e., in מחנה לויה. And it appears that, in

7 *Thus shall you do with them to purify them: sprinkle upon them waters that clear of sin. They shall then have a razor pass over all their flesh; they shall rinse their garments and purify themselves.*	ז וְכֹה־תַעֲשֶׂה לָהֶם לְטַהֲרָם הַזֵּה עֲלֵיהֶם מֵי חַטָּאת וְהֶעֱבִירוּ תַעַר עַל־כָּל־בְּשָׂרָם וְכִבְּסוּ בִגְדֵיהֶם וְהִטֶּהָרוּ׃

the Temple as well, their guard duty was carried out outside the עזרת ישראל — in מחנה לוייה (see *Middos* 1:1; but see משנה למלך on הל׳ בית הבחירה, 8:4).

However, as already noted above (4:47), the song that accompanied the communal offerings was an essential part of the service of the לויים; and in order to carry out this service, they had to enter daily into the inner areas around the altar, where no טמא מת may tread.

7 **הזה עליהם מי חטאת וגו׳** — see below (19:19). The sprinkling of מי חטאת is invalid before the third day of טומאה. The sprinkling is repeated on the seventh day: הזיית שלישי ושביעי. If the first הזייה is performed on a later day, that day is considered the third day of טומאה; hence, the second sprinkling is valid only if performed four days later, and that day is considered the seventh day of טומאה. We have already noted this in our Commentary on *Bereshis* 1:11.

The טהרה that is to be attained here is undoubtedly טהרה from טומאת מת, as is evident from the words הזה עליהם וגו׳. It follows that what is stated afterward — והעבירו וגו׳ וכבסו וגו׳ – is connected with the הזייה and completes the טהרה, as is evident also from the end of the verse: והטהרו. This latter term indicates that the טהרה is a result of all the preceding procedures. Indeed, טבילה is always connected with הזייה, and is performed on the seventh day, after the second הזייה. This טבילה is called here (as in *Vayikra* 11:25, 11:28, et al.) "כיבוס בגדים," and it includes טבילה of the body and of the clothes (see Commentary, *Vayikra* 11:25).

However, here they are commanded to perform an act which does not appear in the other cases of טמאי מת: והעבירו תער וגו׳. Its position makes it clear that this act is connected with the טהרה, and the accentuation indicates that it is to be added before the טבילה, which is generally performed on the seventh day. [Thus, גילוח is performed instead of the

8 *They shall then take a young bull and its homage offering, fine wheat flour mixed with oil, and you shall take a second young bull for an offering that clears of sin.*

ח וְלָקְחוּ֙ פַּ֣ר בֶּן־בָּקָ֔ר וּמִנְחָת֔וֹ סֹ֖לֶת בְּלוּלָ֣ה בַשָּׁ֑מֶן וּפַר־שֵׁנִ֥י בֶן־בָּקָ֖ר תִּקַּ֥ח לְחַטָּֽאת׃

second הזייה.] In agreement with this, our Sages say in the *Sifre* (נשא 7:1): תחת הזאה שניה גילחו. (In the edition of the *Sifre* published recently with the הגהות הגר״א, these four words are bracketed as an interpolation.) In *Bemidbar Rabbah* (12:15), our Sages elaborate: ותחת הזיה שניה שהיו צריכים הלויים להזות מפני שהיו כולם טמאי מתים במה שהרגו בעובדי העגל . . . צוה המקום לגלחם במקום הזייה של יום שביעי.

In our Commentary on *Bereshis* 1:11, we expressed the following view: The first sprinkling relates to man's vegetative aspect, to his sexual life, and it lifts him out of the realm of moral subjugation. By contrast, the second sprinkling, on the seventh day, relates to man's dynamic aspect, and it elevates him into the realm of moral freedom.

We have already stated several times that העברת תער symbolizes the nullification of isolating selfishness (see Commentary, *Vayikra* 14:8; above, 6:5). Here, the *Levi'im* shaved their whole bodies. This indicated to them at their induction into office that they must cease from living only for themselves; rather, they are obligated to devote their whole lives to the service of the community. This message was brought to their attention in the most impressive manner. The man of action sheds all selfish desire and devotes himself to the service of national aims. Thereby, he enters the realm of moral freedom. Thus, in the purification of the *Levi'im*, גילוח takes the place of the הזייה שניה.

8 **ולקחו פר בן בקר וגו'**. The *Levi'im* come here as a "פר": Aware of the work assigned to them in the capacity of their office, they will be working in the service of God. Through the חטאת they vow to remain steadily on the moral heights of this calling. Through the עולה and its attendant מנחה they vow to act boldly and vigorously, to always strive with all the power of their being to ascend to the lofty goal of their office, and they vow that only from the viewpoint of this aspiration will they attach value to the food and property in their possession.

9 *You shall have the* Levi'im *come near before the Tent of Appointed Meeting, and you shall assemble the whole community of the Children of Israel.*

ט וְהִקְרַבְתָּ֙ אֶת־הַלְוִיִּ֔ם לִפְנֵ֖י אֹ֣הֶל מוֹעֵ֑ד וְהִ֨קְהַלְתָּ֔ אֶֽת־כָּל־עֲדַ֖ת בְּנֵ֥י יִשְׂרָאֵֽל׃

10 *You shall have the* Levi'im *come near before* God, *and the Children of Israel shall lean their hands upon the* Levi'im.

י וְהִקְרַבְתָּ֥ אֶת־הַלְוִיִּ֖ם לִפְנֵ֣י יְהֹוָ֑ה וְסָֽמְכ֧וּ בְנֵֽי־יִשְׂרָאֵ֛ל אֶת־יְדֵיהֶ֖ם עַל־הַלְוִיִּֽם׃

11 *Aharon shall then perform with*

יא וְהֵנִ֨יף אַהֲרֹ֤ן אֶת־הַלְוִיִּם֙ תְּנוּפָה֙

In several respects, the prescription of this induction of the *Levi'im* and its laws differ from the norm. The purpose of the first פר is not stated; only from verse 12 do we learn that it is to be offered as an עולה. Whereas in the מילואים of Aharon (*Vayikra* 9:2) the חטאת is prescribed first, here the עולה is prescribed first. As a rule, a חטאת חיצונה is eaten by the כהנים; here, however, the חטאת is not to be eaten but burned (*Horayo*s 5b).

As we have already discussed (above, 6:14), the reason for all these peculiarities lies in the historical event that led to the election of the *Levi'im*. Here let us add that this can also explain the change from third person to second person: ולקחו וגו׳ ופר שני וגו׳ תקח. Scripture thereby makes it clear that this חטאת does not derive *from them*, on account of anything in their past, but is out of consideration of their future mission, which now is being brought to them by Moshe. Hence it does not say here ולקחו, but תקח.

10 **וסמכו וגו׳** — see Commentary, *Vayikra* 1:4. By this סמיכה the nation expresses that all the procedures that will be done here with the *Levi'im* will be done in the name of the nation. It is the nation's will that the *Levi'im* should be its representative toward the Sanctuary.

11 **והניף אהרן וגו׳**. תנופה occurs three times in this induction of the *Levi'im*: in verses 11, 13, and 15. The meaning of תנופה is known as the expression of dedication, designation, direction (see Commentary, *Shemos* 29:22-

the Levi'im *a waving before* God *for the Children of Israel; in this manner they shall be consecrated to do the service of* God.

לִפְנֵי יְהוָה מֵאֵת בְּנֵי יִשְׂרָאֵל וְהָיוּ
לַעֲבֹד אֶת־עֲבֹדַת יְהוָה׃

12 *And the* Levi'im *shall lean their hands upon the heads of the bulls, and you shall make the one as an offering that clears of sin, and the other as an ascent offering, to* God, *to effect atonement for the* Levi'im.

יב וְהַלְוִיִּם יִסְמְכוּ אֶת־יְדֵיהֶם עַל
רֹאשׁ הַפָּרִים וַעֲשֵׂה אֶת־הָאֶחָד
חַטָּאת וְאֶת־הָאֶחָד עֹלָה לַיהוָה
לְכַפֵּר עַל־הַלְוִיִּם׃

13 *You shall then have the* Levi'im *stand before Aharon and his sons, and you shall perform with them a waving before* God.

יג וְהַעֲמַדְתָּ אֶת־הַלְוִיִּם לִפְנֵי אַהֲרֹן
וְלִפְנֵי בָנָיו וְהֵנַפְתָּ אֹתָם תְּנוּפָה
לַיהוָה׃

25). The *Levi'im* here are inducted into their service by three dedications, as is explained in verses 16-19: Israel dedicates them to God, God dedicates them to Aharon, Aharon and his sons dedicate them to the Service of the Sanctuary. Thus, it is in the name of God, in the name of the nation, and in the name of Aharon that the *Levi'im* take up their position and carry out their mission, and these three aspects of their calling are brought to their attention by the three תנופות. Here, in our verse, we first have Israel's dedication of the *Levi'im* to God: והניף וגו׳ לפני ה׳ מאת בני ישראל והיו לעבד את עבדת ה׳.

12 **והלוים יסמכו וגו׳**. The bulls of the חטאת and עולה represent how the *Levi'im* shall perform "the service of God": They shall faithfully adhere to their lofty level, and act powerfully to strive upward. Thus they now enter a new future that will not be dimmed by any past weakness (לכפר על הלוים).

13 **והעמדת וגו׳**. The עבודת ה׳ devolving upon the *Levi'im* includes more than their relationship to Aharon and their service in the Sanctuary. It also includes representing the Torah and "keeping the covenant" with Israel, in both of which the *Levi'im* have already ennobled themselves by standing up for God at the sin of the golden calf. But within the

14 *Thus shall you set apart the* Levi'im *from out of the midst of the Children of Israel, and the* Levi'im *shall become Mine.*

יד וְהִבְדַּלְתָּ֙ אֶת־הַלְוִיִּ֔ם מִתּ֖וֹךְ בְּנֵ֣י
יִשְׂרָאֵ֑ל וְהָ֥יוּ לִ֖י הַלְוִיִּֽם׃ שני

15 *Thereafter the* Levi'im *shall come to do the service at the Tent of Appointed Meeting; it is for this purpose that you shall purify them, and for this purpose shall you perform a waving with them.*

טו וְאַחֲרֵי־כֵן֙ יָבֹ֣אוּ הַלְוִיִּ֔ם לַעֲבֹ֖ד
אֶת־אֹ֣הֶל מוֹעֵ֑ד וְטִֽהַרְתָּ֙ אֹתָ֔ם
וְהֵנַפְתָּ֥ אֹתָ֖ם תְּנוּפָֽה׃

16 *For they are given, [indeed] given to Me from out of the midst of the Children of Israel; in place of the opening of every mother's womb, the firstborn of all the Children of Israel, have I taken them for Myself.*

טז כִּי֩ נְתֻנִ֨ים נְתֻנִ֥ים הֵ֨מָּה֙ לִ֔י מִתּ֖וֹךְ
בְּנֵ֣י יִשְׂרָאֵ֑ל תַּחַת֩ פִּטְרַ֨ת כָּל־רֶ֜חֶם
בְּכ֥וֹר כֹּל֙ מִבְּנֵ֣י יִשְׂרָאֵ֔ל לָקַ֥חְתִּי
אֹתָ֖ם לִֽי׃

general framework of their belonging to God, they are especially committed to those purposes of which the כהנים are in charge. Hence והעמדת וגו׳ לפני אהרן וגו׳ והנפת אתם תנופה לה׳.

This תנופה represents their dedication to Aharon. Nevertheless, it remains a תנופה לה׳: Only for sacred purposes, not for private purposes, are they subordinated to the כהנים.

14-15 **והבדלת וגו׳**. Thus shall you set the *Levi'im* apart from the nation and signify that they belong to God.

ואחרי כן יבאו וגו׳: Only after they have been subordinated to Aharon and his sons — as stated in verse 13 — shall they come to do the service of the Tent of Appointed Meeting; and for this service, טהרה must precede their תנופה.

16 **כי נתנים וגו׳**. In every "נתינה," the giver renounces — in favor of the receiver — a right that he has in the object. Hence, here, too, it must be that the nation had a claim on the *Levi'im*; for only the renunciation

17 *For every firstborn among the Children of Israel among men and among beast became Mine; on the day I struck every firstborn in the land of Egypt I sanctified them for Myself.*	יז כִּ֣י לִ֤י כָל־בְּכוֹר֙ בִּבְנֵ֣י יִשְׂרָאֵ֔ל בָּאָדָ֖ם וּבַבְּהֵמָ֑ה בְּי֗וֹם הַכֹּתִ֤י כָל־בְּכוֹר֙ בְּאֶ֣רֶץ מִצְרַ֔יִם הִקְדַּ֥שְׁתִּי אֹתָ֖ם לִֽי׃
18 *Now I have taken the* Levi'im *in place of every firstborn among the Children of Israel.*	יח וָאֶקַּח֙ אֶת־הַלְוִיִּ֔ם תַּ֥חַת כָּל־בְּכ֖וֹר בִּבְנֵ֥י יִשְׂרָאֵֽל׃
19 *And I have given the* Levi'im *to*	יט וָאֶתְּנָ֨ה אֶת־הַלְוִיִּ֜ם נְתֻנִ֣ים ׀ לְאַהֲרֹ֣ן

of such a claim for the benefit of their new calling justifies the application of the term מתוך בני ישראל to the dedication of the *Levi'im*. This claim might be found in the following idea.

Every national community is entitled to demand that each of its individual members be as productive as he can — i.e., that he should contribute to increasing the means of existence and prosperity; as our Sages put it: יהא מתעסק ביישובו של עולם. Only at that price is the community obligated to let the individual share in the general prosperity.

Here, the nation dedicates an entire tribe to God and to His service, thereby releasing the tribe from the obligation to work for its own existence and for that of the society. What is more, the nation undertakes, on its part, to provide for the material existence of the tribe. In this respect, the dedication of the *Levi'im* can be regarded as the nation's מתנה to God and to His Sanctuary.

Thus, תנופת הלויים obligates the nation toward the tribe, and for this reason the concept of מתנה is stressed by the repetition נתנים נתנים. The nation should know what it is undertaking with this תנופה. Without such an undertaking, the תנופה on the part of the nation would make no sense.

בכור כל. The word "כל" includes אדם ובהמה, as in verse 17. Cf. above, 3:45.

19 **נתנים לאהרן וגו'**. Aharon and his descendants have no original claim on the *Levi'im*; rather, the *Levi'im* are "given" to them for the purposes ordained by God.

וּלְבָנָיו מִתּוֹךְ֮ בְּנֵ֣י יִשְׂרָאֵל֒ לַעֲבֹ֞ד אֶת־עֲבֹדַ֤ת בְּנֵֽי־יִשְׂרָאֵל֙ בְּאֹ֣הֶל מוֹעֵ֔ד וּלְכַפֵּ֖ר עַל־בְּנֵ֣י יִשְׂרָאֵ֑ל וְלֹ֨א יִהְיֶ֜ה בִּבְנֵ֤י יִשְׂרָאֵל֙ נֶ֔גֶף בְּגֶ֥שֶׁת בְּנֵֽי־יִשְׂרָאֵ֖ל אֶל־הַקֹּֽדֶשׁ׃

Aharon and to his sons from out of the midst of the Children of Israel, to do the service of the Children of Israel at the Tent of Appointed Meeting and to effect atonement for the Children of Israel. Thus there shall be no [sudden] death among the Children of Israel when the Children of Israel approach the Sanctuary.

לעבד וגו': The Service of the Sanctuary devolves first and foremost on all of Israel. Formerly they performed it through their firstborn sons; henceforth it shall be done by the *Levi'im*.

ולכפר על בני ישראל. If we understand this expression correctly, the dismissal of the firstborn and their replacement by the *Levi'im* are a continuous כפרה for the sin of golden calf. It is a warning for future generations to remember that first great sin; for that sin showed how vast was the gulf between the actual state of the people and their great mission, and it became clear that the nation still needed to be educated. The nation acknowledged this when it willingly replaced the firstborn with the *Levi'im*.

ולא יהיה בבני ישראל וגו'. At the same time, the removal of the Children of Israel from the Sanctuary is a continuation of the הגבלה ordered at Sinai. Already on the day of the Lawgiving, it was brought to the people's attention that they were still far from achieving the ultimate purpose ordained for them in the Torah. Thus the fact was established for all time that the Torah is in the category of something *given*: it was brought *to* the people; it did not emanate *from* the people. Hence, it may never be tampered with, and Israel is neither obligated nor permitted to subjectively devise any form of worshipping God. The disregard of this fact is the root of the sin of the golden calf (see our discussion in *Shemos* on the mitzvah of הגבלה and on the incident of the עגל).

20 *Moshe, Aharon and the whole community of the Children of Israel did with the* Levi'im *according to all that* God *had commanded Moshe regarding the* Levi'im; *thus did the Children of Israel do with them.*

כ וַיַּעַשׂ מֹשֶׁה וְאַהֲרֹן וְכָל־עֲדַת
בְּנֵי־יִשְׂרָאֵל לַלְוִיִּם כְּכֹל אֲשֶׁר־
צִוָּה יְהוָה אֶת־מֹשֶׁה לַלְוִיִּם כֵּן־
עָשׂוּ לָהֶם בְּנֵי יִשְׂרָאֵל׃

21 *The* Levi'im *cleared themselves of sin and rinsed their garments, and Aharon performed with them a waving before* God. *Aharon then effected atonement for them, to purify them.*

כא וַיִּתְחַטְּאוּ הַלְוִיִּם וַיְכַבְּסוּ בִּגְדֵיהֶם
וַיָּנֶף אַהֲרֹן אֹתָם תְּנוּפָה לִפְנֵי יְהוָה
וַיְכַפֵּר עֲלֵיהֶם אַהֲרֹן לְטַהֲרָם׃

22 *Afterward the* Levi'im *came to do their service at the Tent of Appointed Meeting before Aharon and before his sons; as* God *had commanded Moshe with regard to the* Levi'im, *thus did they do with them.*

כב וְאַחֲרֵי־כֵן בָּאוּ הַלְוִיִּם לַעֲבֹד אֶת־
עֲבֹדָתָם בְּאֹהֶל מוֹעֵד לִפְנֵי אַהֲרֹן
וְלִפְנֵי בָנָיו כַּאֲשֶׁר צִוָּה יְהוָה אֶת־
מֹשֶׁה עַל־הַלְוִיִּם כֵּן עָשׂוּ לָהֶם׃ ס

23 God *spoke to Moshe, saying:*

כג וַיְדַבֵּר יְהוָה אֶל־מֹשֶׁה לֵּאמֹר׃

24 *This is what pertains to the*

כד זֹאת אֲשֶׁר לַלְוִיִּם מִבֶּן חָמֵשׁ

---

21 **ויתחטאו הלוים** refers to הזייה במי חטאת; cf. below, 19:12. **ויכבסו בגדיהם** refers to טבילה; see verse 7.

ויכפר עליהם אהרן — by offering the חטאת and the עולה (v. 12).

לטהרם: With these offerings, the טהרה reached its positive completion. Without them, the *Levi'im* would have still been מחוסרי כפרה and would not have been allowed to enter the Sanctuary.

24 **זאת וגו'**. Above (4:2-3), it says that the sons of Kehas enter service after reaching the age of thirty years (see רמב"ן, v. 25), whereas here it says in general that all the *Levi'im* serve after reaching the age of twenty-five.

וְעֶשְׂרִים שָׁנָה וָמַעְלָה יָבוֹא לִצְבֹא
צָבָא בַּעֲבֹדַת אֹהֶל מוֹעֵד׃

Levi'im: *From twenty-five years old and upward he shall come to perform communal service in the service of the Tent of Appointed Meeting.*

כה וּמִבֶּן חֲמִשִּׁים שָׁנָה יָשׁוּב מִצְּבָא
הָעֲבֹדָה וְלֹא יַעֲבֹד עוֹד׃

25 *And after the age of fifty years he shall retire from the public performance of the service and need no longer do service.*

כו וְשֵׁרֵת אֶת־אֶחָיו בְּאֹהֶל מוֹעֵד
לִשְׁמֹר מִשְׁמֶרֶת וַעֲבֹדָה לֹא יַעֲבֹד
כָּכָה תַּעֲשֶׂה לַלְוִיִּם בְּמִשְׁמְרֹתָם׃ פ
שלישי

26 *[Nevertheless] he shall serve with his brethren to keep watch at the Tent of Appointed Meeting, but he shall no longer do service. Thus shall you do with the* Levi'im *concerning the obligations of their office.*

This contradiction is resolved (in *Chullin* 24a) as follows: חמש ועשרים ללמוד ושלשים לעבודה. That is to say, after reaching the age of twenty-five they begin to learn the service, but only after reaching the age of thirty are they allowed to perform service.

26 The difference between שרת and עבודה is open to question. In the *Sifre* it says: מלמד שחוזר לנעילת שערים ולעבודת בני גרשון. The inference from this statement is that עבודה includes only the harder physical labor of the sons of Kehas, who carried the sacred objects on their shoulders, and the work of the sons of Merari, who loaded the heavy beams of the משכן. By contrast, the service of the sons of Gershon was done by all of them even after the age of fifty: choir and guard duty, which devolves upon all *Levi'im*, as well as loading the tapestries and the like. However, the commentators differ on this point; see מזרחי ad loc.

Let us also note that the limitation of the service of the *Levi'im* to certain years applied only in the wilderness, where they erected and dismantled the משכן and transported it from place to place, whereas in

9 1 God *spoke to Moshe in the wilderness of Sinai, in the second year after their exodus from the land of Egypt, in the first month, saying:*	**ט** א וַיְדַבֵּ֨ר יְהוָ֤ה אֶל־מֹשֶׁה֙ בְמִדְבַּר־סִ֠ינַ֠י בַּשָּׁנָ֨ה הַשֵּׁנִ֜ית לְצֵאתָ֨ם מֵאֶ֧רֶץ מִצְרַ֛יִם בַּחֹ֥דֶשׁ הָרִאשׁ֖וֹן לֵאמֹֽר׃

Shilo and in the Temple the only thing that could disqualify a *Levi* from service was his voice: בשילה ובבית עולמים אין נפסלים אלא בקול (*Chullin* 24a).

CHAPTER 9

1 While still encamped in view of the mountain of the Lawgiving, before journeying on to the land intended for the Torah, the Children of Israel are to bring the Pesach offering, which renews the consciousness of their mission and places this consciousness on its first basis. Facing Mount Sinai and on the basis of the redemption from Egypt, every household in Israel and every person in every household shall be made conscious of the calling that rests on these two pillars, and their consciousness shall express itself in practice through the Pesach offering.

For various reasons, a special reminder of the mitzvah of קרבן פסח was necessary here. According to the *Mechilta* (on *Shemos* 12:25), the command to bring the Pesach offering every year applied only after they had entered the Land. Thus the need here for a special command; for unless they were specially commanded to bring it, they were exempt from bringing the Pesach offering during the whole period they were in the wilderness. The reason for this law can be well understood from our Commentary there in *Shemos*.

It appears, however, that this opinion of the *Mechilta* is not the generally accepted opinion (see תוספות *Kiddushin* 37b ד״ה הואיל). But even without the *Mechilta*, one can explain as follows:

At the first repetition of the Pesach offering, all the *halachos* by which פסח דורות differs from פסח מצרים came into effect: מקחו בעשור, הזאה באגודת אזוב על המשקוף ועל שתי המזוזות, אכילה בחפזון — none of these apply to פסח דורות, whereas שפיכת דם ליסוד המזבח and הקטר חלבים על גבי המזבח apply only to פסח דורות. And whereas in the case of פסח מצרים the prohibition of חמץ lasted only one day, in the case of פסח דורות it lasts for

2 *Let the Children of Israel make the Pesach [offering] at its appointed season.*	ב וְיַעֲשׂוּ בְנֵי־יִשְׂרָאֵל אֶת־הַפָּסַח בְּמוֹעֲדוֹ׃

seven days (see *Pesachim* 96a-b; *Shemos* 12:34). Hence, with the return of the fourteenth of Nissan for the first time after פסח מצרים, it was necessary to remind the people of the *halachos* now coming into effect. These *halachos* of פסח דורות are apparently indicated by the words ככל חקתיו וככל משפטיו וגו׳ (v. 3).

There was yet another reason for a special command to offer the Pesach that year. According to *Seder Olam* (*Shabbos* 87b), the first of Nissan of the second year fell on the first day of the week, and on that day the construction of the משכן was completed. Now if the first of Nissan fell on the first day of the week, then the fourteenth of Nissan, which is the day on which the Pesach is offered, fell on Shabbos. Hence, it was necessary to teach the novel halachah that פסח דוחה שבת, the duty of bringing the Pesach offering overrides the prohibition of מלאכה on Shabbos. Indeed, this halachah is indicated only here by the term "במועדו" of verse 2.

בחדש הראשון: We have already seen above, 7:1, that Scripture there returns to the first month, after having already reported at the beginning of the book events of the second month, and we noted there the reason for this order. This practice of Scripture -- to disregard the chronological order and to arrange the events according to their inner meaning — is called in the *Sifre* (here) and in *Pesachim* 6b "אין מוקדם ומאוחר בתורה."

This principle especially determines the order of the *mitzvos* in the Torah: they, too, are frequently written in an order dictated by their content. Hence it frequently happens that an earlier chapter will mention a halachah that is explained in detail only in a later chapter. Thus, for example, הזייה במי חטאת, which is mentioned above (8:7), but is discussed in detail only later, in chapter 19. The Torah, after all, was written only at the end of the fortieth year (see *Gittin* 60a), after it had already been transmitted orally in all its detail. Hence, in the case of every mitzvah set down in writing, it could be assumed that the entire Torah was already known to the people.

2 **ויעשו בני ישראל וגו׳**. Just as it says here regarding the Pesach offering that it should be offered במועדו, it also says below (28:2) regarding the

תמיד offering: תשמרו להקריב לי במועדו. From the term "במועדו," our Sages derive in respect to both cases: במועדו ואפילו בשבת, במועדו ואפילו בטומאה (*Pesachim* 77a). That is to say, when the appointed time of the offering arrives, it should be offered no matter what, even if its appointed time falls on Shabbos, and even if it can be brought only בטומאה — e.g., if the כהנים or the כלי שרת were טמאים, or, in the case of Pesach, if the community of offerers or the majority of the community was טמא. Our Sages say further there that this halachah applies also to the other קרבנות ציבור, for of all of them it says: אלה תעשו לה׳ במועדיכם (below, 29:39), וידבר משה את מעדי ה׳ אל בני ישראל (*Vayikra* 23:44); thus, the law of "במועדו" applies generally to all these offerings: הכתוב קבעו מועד אחד לכולן.

In *Pesachim* 66-67 our Sages adduce another special proof from Scripture that קרבן תמיד is to be offered even on Shabbos, and קרבן פסח even בטומאה. Regarding תמיד on Shabbos it says: עלת שבת בשבתו על עלת התמיד (below, 28:10). Regarding פסח בטומאה it says: איש איש כי יהיה טמא לנפש (v. 10), which implies: Only individuals who are טמאים לנפש bring פסח שני in the month of Iyar, but a צבור, a community that is טמא brings the פסח in its proper time, in Nissan. Thus, the פסח is brought בטומאה. As our Sages say there: איש נדחה לפסח שני ואין ציבור נדחין לפסח שני אלא עבדי בטומאה. Then these two laws are transferred by גזירה שוה of במועדו במועדו from תמיד to פסח and from פסח to תמיד.

It appears that these two סוגיות (*Pesachim* 66ff. and 77a) complement each other, and only by the גזירה שוה does the term "במועדו" receive its precise definition. Were it not for this גזירה שוה, which transfers the law of טומאה from פסח to תמיד, the law implied by the term "במועדו" would have applied to all טומאות, in which case the offering would have been brought at its appointed time even בטומאת זב וכדומה. The גזירה שוה from פסח limits this halachah strictly to טומאת מת. If all we had were the גזירה שוה, the halachah would have been limited to תמיד and to פסח; but since the גזירה שוה merely establishes the משמעות of "במועדו," the halachah evidently applies to all קרבנות ציבור, for Scripture includes them all in the concept of מועד. This resolution of the two סוגיות seems also to be at the basis of תוספות in *Menachos* 72b ד״ה שנאמר.

Indeed, the concept inherent in the term "במועדו" — an offering that must be brought at a fixed time, שזמנו קבוע — is the decisive factor for דחיית שבת וטומאה. Although the common expression טומאה הותרה בציבור or טומאה דחויה בציבור (see below) seems to stress the factor of ציבור, and similarly the סוגיות cited above consistently speak of קרבנות ציבור, our

Sages point out in *Temurah* 14a and in *Yoma* 50a that the פר יום הכיפורים of the כהן גדול and the חביתי כהן גדול (*Vayikra* 6:13) are קרבנות יחיד and yet are דוחים שבת וטומאה, whereas פר העלם דבר של ציבור (ibid. 4:13) and שעירי עבודה זרה (*Bemidbar* 15:24) are קרבנות ציבור and yet are not דוחים טומאה. Hence our Sages conclude there that everything depends solely on זמנו קבוע: נקוט האי כללא בידך, כל שזמנו קבוע דוחה את השבת ואת הטומאה אפילו ביחיד, וכל שאין זמנו קבוע אינו דוחה לא את השבת ולא את הטומאה אפילו בציבור (*Yoma* 50a).

Closer analysis, however, reveals that the concepts "זמנו קבוע" and "ציבור" overlap to a certain extent. For although it cannot be said of all קרבנות ציבור that זמנם קבוע, nevertheless all קרבנות שזמנם קבוע are קרבנות ציבור in the wider sense of this term. For it appears that a distinction should be drawn between offerings that the כהן גדול brings in his official capacity — the חביתין and פר יום הכיפורים — and offerings that he brings for personal, private reasons — e.g., he was מחוסר כפרה after being purified of his טומאה. Offerings of this latter kind are true קרבנות יחיד. By contrast, the חביתין and פר יום הכיפורים are unique to the כהן גדול; he who brings them is marked by them as the כהן גדול, as the ideal representative of the nation in the Sanctuary. This representation does not depend on the individual personality of this particular כהן גדול; for if he is rendered impure or if he dies, the nation replaces him with someone else. Thus, although *Yoma* 50a does not accept the view that פר יום הכיפורים is a קרבן ציבור in the narrower sense, it seems to us — for the reasons explained above — that the aforementioned halachah may be summarized as follows: כל קרבנות ציבור שזמנן קבוע דוחין את השבת ואת הטומאה.

Let us now try to understand the reason for these *halachos*. It appears that the factors included in the concept "במועדו" — as defined above — express the same truths demonstrated also by the laws of שבת and טומאה; and they express these truths in such a positive manner that their realization can set aside שבת and טומאה.

For מועד (see Commentary, *Shemos* 12:1-2) is a time designated by God for us to meet with Him, and we respond to this summons with a קרבן לה׳. All these times are based on some special act of God's providence, which invested each of these times with its own special meaning for our moral elevation. This meaning is in addition to the significance of each moment in time; for every moment has significance through its integration into the natural unfolding of the times.

Each one of these מועדים, then, reveals God as a free, personal and omnipotent God, Who not only created the world, but also rules it after the Creation, shaping it by free rule. Thus all מועדי ה׳ — including ראש חדש (see Commentary, *Shemos* 12:1-2) — are connected to the revelatory acts of the period of Israel's founding. All these מועדים attest to the fundamental fact of God's creation and guidance of the world, and they attest to it on the basis of the historical experience of our own development. Shabbos is the first and the universal memorial to this same fundamental truth, only that its testimony goes beyond all personal experience. Accordingly, all מועדי ה׳ are merely new attestations to Shabbos.

This explains the halachah regarding קרבנות המועדים on Shabbos. These קרבנות are offered on the day of remembrance of God's acts of revelation; we offer them to God Who was revealed to us on this day. Hence מלאכות, which as a rule are prohibited on Shabbos, are permitted for the sake of these offerings. For מלאכה done for this purpose does not desecrate the Sabbath, but, rather, sanctifies it.

The foregoing applies not only to the times of revelation, which summon us to meet with God; rather, the קרבן תמיד, too — of morning and of evening — is linked with these מועדי ה׳; the קרבן תמיד is equated with the קרבן פסח, for in connection with both of them it says במועדו. (These are the only two instances in which this word is written מלא. Thus, the root יעד, which is the decisive conception here, is stressed here in full clarity.) From this we learn that every day should be considered a special act of God. The ordinary and everyday joins the unique event, and both together declare God's glory. The rising sun and the setting sun each become a מועד, a time that attests to God's presence. At these times, we bring a קרבן לה׳, to seek His closeness at the time of His revelation. Accordingly, the time of the תמיד is a revelation of God in the present, just as the Sabbath attests to His revelation through מעשה בראשית. Hence offering the תמיד on the Sabbath does not desecrate the Sabbath but, rather, sanctifies it.

The same is true of דחיית הטומאה. For טומאת מת — in contrast to the Sanctuary — is a denial of the free and personal God and a denial of the human personality possessed of moral freedom. But the מועדו aspect of a קרבן שזמנו קבוע attests to both of these truths, and this positive testimony nullifies טומאה's denial. For a specific moment in time becomes a מועד, a זמן קבוע, only by a special act of the free God. Through this act, God affirms of Himself that He is a free and personal God —

this the indispensable precondition for the free personality of man. In summoning us on the מועד, He lays down His personal freedom as the basis of our freedom, and thus He guarantees us our moral freedom, which finds its highest expression in a קרבן לה׳. God's free act, which underlies every זמן קבוע, summons us to a free human act, whose appropriate expression is the קרבן.

But the concept of ציבור also has special significance here. For it seems to us that a קרבן שזמנו קבוע can devolve only on a ציבור; hence all קרבנות שזמנן קבוע are קרבנות ציבור. Only the community can offer a קרבן at a designated time, year after year, for only the community will always exist at this time every year. The individual ultimately dies, whereas אין הציבור מתים (*Temurah* 15b), the community as a whole is immortal. But thereby the community — as it is represented in קרבנות שזמנן קבוע — is indisputable evidence of the spiritual-godlike standing of morally free man, a standing that is above טומאת מת and over which death has no dominion. For what unites the multitudes and makes them a ציבור is not the bodily side, which is destined to disappear in death, but the spiritual, godly element. Through this element, the individual member who devotes himself to the community also lives forever through the community. His life continues even after his bodily death; for the spiritual, Divine values that he imparted to the community during his earthly lifetime live on, and through them he still lives in this world, and his good work endures forever. Hence טומאה דחויה בציבור or טומאה הותרה בציבור, and this דחייה is limited to טומאת מת.

(According to the foregoing, there is significance also to the concept of ציבור beside the concept of זמנו קבוע, and that is the reason שלמי חגיגה and עולות ראייה are not דוחים שבת וטומאה. For although they are limited to the רגל [זמנם קבוע לרגל] and אם יעבור רגל אין להם תקנה, still, since יש להם תשלומין כל שבעה, they do not resemble פסח, which is brought בכנופיא, by the whole congregation of Israel at one time. Hence, the concept of ציבור in its precise sense is not realized in them. This would answer the questions raised by תוספות *Pesachim* 76b ד״ה קא. Cf. לחם משנה on הל׳ חגיגה, 1:8, who answers these questions in a somewhat different manner.)

However, the idea evoked by טומאת מת is so antithetical to the meaning and purpose of the Sanctuary that טומאה is not overridden בציבור automatically; rather, against the minority opinion that טומאה הותרה בציבור, the accepted view is that טומאה דחויה בציבור. Hence, wherever טומאה is overridden — in the case of a קרבן ציבור שזמנו קבוע — the positive

3 *On the fourteenth day of this month, between the two evenings, you shall make it at its appointed season. According to all its laws and all the regulations pertaining to it shall you make it.*	ג בְּאַרְבָּעָה עָשָׂר־יוֹם בַּחֹדֶשׁ הַזֶּה בֵּין הָעַרְבַּיִם תַּעֲשׂוּ אֹתוֹ בְּמֹעֲדוֹ כְּכָל־חֻקֹּתָיו וּכְכָל־מִשְׁפָּטָיו תַּעֲשׂוּ אֹתוֹ׃

effect of the ציץ is required: בעיא ציץ לרצות (*Pesachim* 77a). On the significance of the ציץ in connection with the overriding of טומאה, see our Commentary on *Shemos* 28:38.

3 **בארבעה עשר וגו' תעשו אתו**. This is a rare case — perhaps the only case — where two consecutive verses treat the same mitzvah, only that the first commands the nation in the third person (ויעשו בני ישראל), whereas the second commands it in the second person and so also includes Moshe.

Our Sages say in the *Sifre* that במועדו of the first verse teaches us of דחיית שבת, whereas במעדו of our verse teaches us of דחיית טומאה.

Now, we have already explained the great importance of the concept of ציבור as regards the law of במועדו אפילו בטומאה. More than anything else, the inclusion of Moshe — particularly of Moshe -– in the national community attests to the immortality of the national community. Who is like Moshe, present and alive forever, in the nation and through the nation! Who, like Moshe, participates in earthly immortality through the immortality of the community! Who, although physically dead, remains undominated by death, like Moshe!

בארבעה עשר וגו' בחדש הזה בין הערבים — see our Commentary on *Shemos* 12:6 and 13:3.

ככל חקתיו וככל משפטיו. In the case of פסח שני (v. 12) it says only ככל חקת הפסח יעשו אתו, with no mention of משפטיו.

Now, from *Pesachim* 95a we know the differences between פסח ראשון and פסח שני. At פסח שני, the מצוות **שבגופו** are in force: אל תאכלו ממנו נא וגו' כי אם צלי אש, עצם לא תשברו בו, לא ישאירו ממנו עד בקר. Also in force are the מצוות **שעל גופו**: על מצות ומרורים יאכלהו. Not in force, however, are the מצוות **שלא על גופו**: לא תשחט על חמץ, תשביתו שאור, לא יראה לך. Rather, פסח שני חמץ ומצה עמו בבית. (It is uncertain whether איסור הוצאה מחבורה applies to פסח

4 *And Moshe spoke to the Children of Israel that they might make the Pesach [offering].*

ד וַיְדַבֵּר מֹשֶׁה אֶל־בְּנֵי יִשְׂרָאֵל לַעֲשֹׂת הַפָּסַח׃

5 *And they made the Pesach [offering] in the first month, on the fourteenth day of the month, between the two evenings, in the wilderness of Sinai; in accordance with all that* God *had commanded Moshe, thus did the Children of Israel do.*

ה וַיַּעֲשׂוּ אֶת־הַפֶּסַח בָּרִאשׁוֹן בְּאַרְבָּעָה עָשָׂר יוֹם לַחֹדֶשׁ בֵּין הָעַרְבַּיִם בְּמִדְבַּר סִינָי כְּכֹל אֲשֶׁר צִוָּה יְהוָה אֶת־מֹשֶׁה כֵּן עָשׂוּ בְּנֵי יִשְׂרָאֵל׃

6 *But there were [some] men who were impure by the person of a man, and therefore they could not make the Pesach [offering] on that day; and they appeared before Moshe and Aharon on that day.*

ו וַיְהִי אֲנָשִׁים אֲשֶׁר הָיוּ טְמֵאִים לְנֶפֶשׁ אָדָם וְלֹא־יָכְלוּ לַעֲשֹׂת־הַפֶּסַח בַּיּוֹם הַהוּא וַיִּקְרְבוּ לִפְנֵי מֹשֶׁה וְלִפְנֵי אַהֲרֹן בַּיּוֹם הַהוּא׃

שני. According to the רמב"ם in הל' קרבן פסח 10:15, it does not apply; see כסף משנה there.)

Clearly, then, חקתיו are the מצוות שבגופו as well as those שעל גופו, i.e., all the laws relating to the קרבן פסח itself, including the laws pertaining to the eating thereof and, of course, to סדר עבודותיו, whereas משפטיו are the מצוות שלא על גופו: laws in which the קרבן פסח affects matters that lie beyond the offering itself, such as the prohibition of חמץ at שחיטת הפסח. In the case of חקתיו, the קרבן פסח is the object; in the case of משפטיו, the קרבן פסח is the effecting cause.

Here, in the case of פסח ראשון, the laws of Pesach come into full force, and we have already noted (above, v. 1) that at this Pesach, the first פסח דורות, there was a special need for the reminder: ככל חקתיו וככל משפטיו תעשו אתו.

6 **ולא יכלו לעשת הפסח וגו'**. Even though we have already learned from the term "במועדו" (vv. 2 and 3) that the פסח is not to be omitted because of טומאה, there was a question that remained to be resolved.

We have already seen that, beside the concept of שזמנו קבוע, the concept of קרבן ציבור also is of significance. Although a קרבן יחיד שזמנו קבוע — חביתי כהן גדול and פר יום הכיפורים — is not omitted because of טומאה, in such offerings the כהן גדול is not regarded as an individual, but as the representative of the whole community. Moreover, were these offerings to be omitted because of טומאה, the effect would be that they would not be brought at all at the appointed time.

However, the פסח is the sole קרבן ציבור in which the ציבור appears not as a community, but as a *plurality.* Therefore it was necessary to clarify the status of the individual vis-à-vis the offering within the framework of this plurality.

Presumably it was clear that if the community or the majority of the community becomes טמא, the טומאה recedes in favor of במועדו; for otherwise the קרבן ציבור would not be brought במועדו. A question remained, however, regarding the case where only some individuals become טמא. For in that case the קרבן ציבור is offered במועדו, at its appointed time, and only the obligations of the individual are not fulfilled; hence his offering could be set aside in the face of טומאה. On the other hand, since the individual's obligation is integrated in the general obligation of the whole community to bring the offering במועדו, his obligation to bring the Pesach offering במועדו might be an integral part of the community's obligation; hence perhaps טומאה recedes also in favor of his במועדו, and he should bring his offering בטומאה together with the rest of the community.

To this question a negative answer was given (v. 10), and in such a case the individual brings a פסח שני.

From the words ביום ההוא — ולא יכלו לעשות הפסח ביום ההוא — our Sages deduce (*Pesachim* 90b) that these men were fit to offer the פסח on the following day: טמאי מת מצוה היו שחל שביעי שלהן להיות בערב הפסח, שנאמר ולא יכלו לעשות הפסח ביום ההוא, ביום ההוא הוא דאינן יכולין לעשות אבל למחר יכולין לעשות. They were in the seventh day of their טומאה; on this day a טמא מת can undergo הזייה and טבילה and become טהור with הערב שמש. Thus, they could have eaten the פסח that evening; nevertheless, they were unfit to offer it, since at the time of שחיטה they had not yet undergone טבילה. This is in accordance with the principle (ibid.) that אין שוחטין וזורקין על טמא שרץ, even if he can undergo טבילה and become טהור after הערב שמש. According to this view, these men brought their פסח, and then underwent הזייה and טבילה; only after the prescribed time for bringing the פסח passed, and they could no longer bring another פסח on that day, did

7 *And these men said to him: We are impure by the person of a man; why should we stand back so as not to bring near the offering of* God *at its appointed season in the midst of the Children of Israel?*	ז וַיֹּ֨אמְר֜וּ הָאֲנָשִׁ֤ים הָהֵ֙מָּה֙ אֵלָ֔יו אֲנַ֥חְנוּ טְמֵאִ֖ים לְנֶ֣פֶשׁ אָדָ֑ם לָ֣מָּה נִגָּרַ֗ע לְבִלְתִּ֨י הַקְרִ֜יב אֶת־קָרְבַּ֤ן יְהוָה֙ בְּמֹ֣עֲד֔וֹ בְּת֖וֹךְ בְּנֵ֥י יִשְׂרָאֵֽל׃
8 *And Moshe said to them: Wait; I wish to hear what* God *will command with regard to you.*	ח וַיֹּ֤אמֶר אֲלֵהֶם֙ מֹשֶׁ֔ה עִמְד֖וּ וְאֶשְׁמְעָ֕ה מַה־יְצַוֶּ֥ה יְהוָ֖ה לָכֶֽם׃ פ
9 *And* God *spoke to Moshe, saying:*	ט וַיְדַבֵּ֥ר יְהוָ֖ה אֶל־מֹשֶׁ֥ה לֵּאמֹֽר׃
10 *Speak to the Children of Israel,*	י דַּבֵּ֛ר אֶל־בְּנֵ֥י יִשְׂרָאֵ֖ל לֵאמֹ֑ר אִ֣ישׁ

their question occur to them. (See ראב״ד on הל׳ קרבן פסח, 6:2. A different view is taken by the רמב״ם. See משנה למלך there.)

7 **ויאמרו האנשים ההמה אליו אנחנו וגו׳**. In their question, they demonstrated that they understood all sides of the issue. Hence Scripture stresses that האנשים ההמה, these men, although just ordinary men of the people, asked this question on their own. They argued as follows:

אנחנו טמאים לנפש אדם. Had they contracted any other טומאה, they would not have asked, for they had already been taught that only טומאת מת recedes in favor of קרבן פסח.

למה נגרע וגו׳ קרבן ה׳ במעדו: It is a קרבן שזמנו קבוע, and it is offered בתוך בני ישראל: it is a קרבן ציבור, and they are part of the ציבור. As we have seen (v. 6), these are the two factors that could allow them to bring the פסח.

8 **עמדו ואשמעה וגו׳**. This is concrete evidence that the *mitzvos* of the Torah were given to Moshe not just in their general principles (כללים); rather, also the details of the laws (פרטים) were given to him by God's direct revelation. Here was a particular case where the law was in question, and Moshe awaited a special pronouncement by God to resolve the question.

10 **איש איש וגו׳**. The Halachah teaches (*Pesachim* 93a) that the law of פסח שני is not limited to cases of טומאה and distance; rather, anyone who is

saying: If anyone will be impure by a person or will be on a distant journey — among you or among your descendants — and he must make the Pesach offering to God.	אִ֣ישׁ אִ֣ישׁ כִּֽי־יִהְיֶ֣ה טָמֵ֣א ׀ לָנֶ֡פֶשׁ א֠וֹ בְדֶ֨רֶךְ רְחֹקָ֜ה לָכֶ֗ם א֚וֹ לְדֹרֹ֣תֵיכֶ֔ם וְעָ֥שָׂה פֶ֖סַח לַֽיהוָֽה׃ נקוד על ה'

prevented — for any reason — from offering the פסח brings a פסח שני. What is more, even if one refrains במזיד from offering the קרבן פסח in Nissan, one is obligated in פסח שני. Other טומאות and other hindrances are included in דרך רחוקה, which is cited here merely as an example. טמא לנפש — i.e., טומאת מת — is mentioned only as a contrast to other טומאות, whose law is different with respect to a ציבור. For from איש איש we derive that only individuals who constitute a minority of the ציבור bring פסח שני. By contrast, if the community was טמא on the מועד of the פסח, the people bring the offering בטומאה in the month of Nissan: איש נדחה לפסח שני ואין ציבור נדחין לפסח שני אלא עבדי בטומאה (ibid. 66b). But this applies only to טומאת מת, whereas other טומאות override the offering even בציבור: וכי עבדי ציבור בטומאה, בטמא מת, אבל שאר טומאות לא עבדי (ibid. 67a). If the ציבור or the majority of the ציבור contracts other טומאות, the people bring neither פסח ראשון nor פסח שני.

בדרך רחקה. The ה of רחקה has a dot above it, to teach us that the journey need not be distant in an absolute sense, but only distant relative to offering the פסח. If, at the beginning of the time of offering, at midday of the 14th of Nissan, someone is at a distance from which he cannot reach the עזרה during the course of בין הערבים, before the end of the prescribed time of offering, this is considered "בדרך רחוקה," and he cannot offer the פסח; nor can anyone else perform the שחיטה and so forth on his behalf, even if he could arrive בערב in time for the eating. Just as היה בדרך רחוקה ושחטו וזרקו עליו . . . לא ,אין שוחטין וזורקין על טמא שרץ, so, too, הורצה (ibid. 92b). A distance of fifteen מיל, the distance between Modi'in and Yerushalayim, is considered "דרך רחוקה" in this regard (ibid. 93b).

(According to the רמב"ם [הל' קרבן פסח, 5:9], דרך רחוקה is defined as follows: At sunrise on the 14th of Nissan, someone is so distant from the עזרה that he cannot reach the עזרה at the *beginning* of the time of offering. רש"י and תוספות [*Pesachim* 93b], and also the wording of the *Yerushalmi*, *Pesachim* 9:2, are opposed to this view.)

יא בַּחֹ֨דֶשׁ הַשֵּׁנִ֜י בְּאַרְבָּעָ֨ה עָשָׂ֥ר י֛וֹם
בֵּ֥ין הָעַרְבַּ֖יִם יַעֲשׂ֣וּ אֹת֑וֹ עַל־מַצּ֥וֹת
וּמְרֹרִ֖ים יֹאכְלֻֽהוּ׃

11 *They shall make it in the second month, on the fourteenth day between the two evenings; with* matzos *and bitter herbs shall they eat it.*

יב לֹֽא־יַשְׁאִ֤ירוּ מִמֶּ֙נּוּ֙ עַד־בֹּ֔קֶר וְעֶ֖צֶם
לֹ֣א יִשְׁבְּרוּ־ב֑וֹ כְּכָל־חֻקַּ֥ת הַפֶּ֖סַח
יַעֲשׂ֥וּ אֹתֽוֹ׃

12 *They shall not leave any of it until the morning and not break any of its bones; according to all the law of the Pesach offering shall they make it.*

יג וְהָאִ֨ישׁ אֲשֶׁר־ה֜וּא טָה֗וֹר וּבְדֶ֙רֶךְ֙
לֹא־הָיָ֔ה וְחָדַל֙ לַעֲשׂ֣וֹת הַפֶּ֔סַח
וְנִכְרְתָ֛ה הַנֶּ֥פֶשׁ הַהִ֖וא מֵעַמֶּ֑יהָ כִּ֣י ׀
קָרְבַּ֣ן יְהוָ֗ה לֹ֤א הִקְרִיב֙ בְּמֹ֣עֲד֔וֹ
חֶטְא֥וֹ יִשָּׂ֖א הָאִ֥ישׁ הַהֽוּא׃

13 *But one who is pure and was not on a journey and neglects to make the Pesach offering, that person shall be uprooted from among his people; that same man, if he has not brought near the offering of* God *at its appointed season, must bear his sin.*

11-12 We have already stated (above, v. 3) that all the מצוות שעל גופו, which are included under the term חקת הפסח, apply also at פסח שני, whereas the מצוות שלא על גופו (לא יראה לך, השבתת שאור, לא תשחט על חמץ), which are included under משפטי הפסח, do not apply at פסח שני; rather, the law for פסח שני is: חמץ ומצה עמו בבית.

13 **והאיש אשר הוא טהור**. In *Pesachim* 93a, three opinions are cited as to the relation of פסח שני to פסח ראשון. According to רבי, פסח שני is a רגל בפני עצמו, an independent institution; hence, even שגג בראשון והזיד בשני חייב כרת. According to רבי נתן, שני is תשלומין דראשון; hence, שגג בראשון והזיד בשני פטור. [However, ר׳ נתן agrees with רבי that הזיד בראשון ושגג בשני חייב.] According to רבי חנניה בן עקביא, שני is תקנתא דראשון; that is to say, the two פסחים are interconnected; hence, he is חייב only if he missed both במזיד, whereas even הזיד בראשון ושגג בשני פטור (ibid. 93b).

The רמב״ם (הל׳ קרבן פסח, 5:2) rules in accordance with the first opinion, that each one of the two פסחים is an independent institution. According to this view, גר שנתגייר בין שני פסחים וכן קטן שהגדיל בין שני פסחים חייב לעשות פסח שני (*Pesachim* 93a); even a person on whom the duty to bring the offering was not at all incumbent on the first would still have to bring the offering on the second.

According to this opinion, our verse mentions the penalty of כרת separately for each one of the two פסחים, first for פסח ראשון and then for פסח שני. Accordingly, האיש ההוא of our verse would mean as follows: If someone, for any reason, fails to offer the פסח ראשון and then neglects to bring the פסח שני, חטאו ישא. חטאו ישא is כרת, as in ונשא חטאו (*Vayikra* 24:15) in the case of מברך ה׳ (see below, 15:30).

It says: והאיש אשר הוא טהור ובדרך לא היה. Perhaps the change of tense can be explained by what is said in *Pesachim* 94a. There it appears that the concept of דרך רחוקה is defined absolutely: A radius of fifteen מיל around the city of the Temple is the radius within which the duty of bringing the Pesach offering applies. Anyone who was outside this radius at the beginning of the time of offering is not liable to כרת for neglecting to bring the פסח, even if he could have arrived in time by means of riding or transport.

In this respect אונס דרך רחוקה differs from אונס טומאה. A טמא who could have been טהור via טבילה on the fourteenth but neglected to immerse — and thereby was unable to bring the פסח — is חייב כרת (*Pesachim* 69b).

It could be, then, that if one is exempt from the duty of פסח at the beginning of the time of offering because he is בדרך רחוקה, he remains exempt under all circumstances; even if he later arrives — by riding or transport — during the time of offering and yet does not bring the פסח, he is not liable to the penalty of כרת.

If that is indeed the law, then the change of tense in our verse is quite precise. He who *during* the time of offering is טהור or could be טהור, and one who *was* not בדרך at the beginning of the time of offering . . .

Although פסח שני, according to the accepted Halachah, is a רגל בפני עצמו, its character as a substitute dependent on פסח ראשון is preserved. We have already stated that only individuals can bring a פסח שני; they attach themselves subsequently to the national offering which the nation offered at the proper time: איש נדחה ואין ציבור נדחין לפסח שני. And the individuals can bring פסח שני, only if the ציבור brought פסח ראשון at the designated time and in טהרה. Conversely, if the ציבור was prevented from offering the פסח in Nissan because of טומאה that does not recede in favor

14 *And if someone from outside will have entered among you, he must make the Pesach offering to God; according to the law of the Pesach offering and according to the regulations pertaining to it, thus shall he make it. There shall be one and the same law for him who has entered from outside and the native-born of the land.*	יד וְכִי־יָגוּר אִתְּכֶם גֵּר וְעָשָׂה פֶסַח לַיהוָה כְּחֻקַּת הַפֶּסַח וּכְמִשְׁפָּטוֹ כֵּן יַעֲשֶׂה חֻקָּה אַחַת יִהְיֶה לָכֶם וְלַגֵּר וּלְאֶזְרַח הָאָרֶץ׃ ס רביעי
15 *And on the day that the Dwelling*	טו וּבְיוֹם הָקִים אֶת־הַמִּשְׁכָּן כִּסָּה

of the פסח, or if the ציבור offered it בטומאת מת, the individuals cannot bring פסח שני: אין תשלומין לפסח הבא בטומאה (ibid. 80a).

14 **וכי יגור וגו׳**. See Commentary, *Shemos* 12:48. Scripture emphasizes several times that, in respect to הלכות הפסח, the גר and the native-born are equal, and this equality can be considered the basis of the גר's equal rights in general. For by making the Pesach offering, he attaches himself to the entire Jewish past, which henceforth becomes his own; thus — as we already explained there — any differences that might derive from differences in origin are eliminated. Here, at פסח שני, this equality must be emphasized especially, for here it could happen that a גר would have to offer the פסח by himself [גר שנתגייר בין שני פסחים].

Regarding פסח ראשון it says only that he is not to be excluded from the community, whereas here it says that a גר שנתגייר בין שני פסחים is obligated to bring פסח שני, even though the national obligation to bring the פסח ראשון did not apply to him at all; we already noted this above, v. 13.

כחקת הפסח וכמשפטו וגו׳ teaches us that he is obligated in פסח in general, and in פסח ראשון in particular, whereas his obligation to bring פסח שני is included in the statement חקה אחת וגו׳ (see Commentary, v. 3).

15 **וביום**. The ו of וביום connects this section with the preceding, indicating that the present section is the natural continuation of the preceding section and is intimately bound up with it. For the פסח of the preceding section brought to expression Israel's mission and the vow they took

Place was erected, the cloud covered the Dwelling Place in the direction of the Tent of the Testimony, and in the evening there was above the Dwelling Place a fire-like glow until the morning.	הֶעָנָן֙ אֶת־הַמִּשְׁכָּ֔ן לְאֹ֖הֶל הָעֵדֻ֑ת וּבָעֶ֜רֶב יִהְיֶ֧ה עַל־הַמִּשְׁכָּ֛ן כְּמַרְאֵה־אֵ֖שׁ עַד־בֹּֽקֶר׃
16 *Thus it was always; the cloud covered it, and [there was] a fire-like glow at night.*	טז כֵּ֚ן יִהְיֶ֣ה תָמִ֔יד הֶעָנָ֖ן יְכַסֶּ֑נּוּ וּמַרְאֵה־אֵ֖שׁ לָֽיְלָה׃

upon themselves, whereas what follows is nothing but the actualization of the idea symbolized by the פסח. For the fundamental idea of פסח מצרים (see Commentary, *Shemos* 12:3-6) is this: Israel, as God's flock, is to follow its Shepherd and place itself under God's guidance. This idea recurs each Pesach every year and is renewed in the hearts of all Israel. But what all the families of Israel express, by drawing near to God with their Paschal lambs, is nothing other than that על פי ה׳ יחנו ועל פי ה׳ יסעו: they shall dwell in the place that God will mark for them, and go to the place to which He will lead them. The verses that now follow show how they learned and fulfilled this mission and followed God with devotion.

וביום הקים. Immediately after the משכן was erected, the cloud rested upon it. By this cloud God caused His Presence to dwell among Israel and guided them on their way (*Shemos* 13:21-22). The cloud testified that God dwells in the משכן, and the people are to encamp around it and to regard it as their common center.

לאהל העדת. The expression אהל העדות (below, 17:22-23) occurs as a term for the Holy of Holies: the place that contained the ארון העדות.

The ל of לחוף ימים ישכן (*Bereshis* 49:13) denotes the direction, and it appears that here too the ל of לאהל העדת denotes the direction of כסה הענן: The cloud covered the Dwelling Place in the direction of the site of the Testimony. The base of the cloud resting upon the משכן was on the אהל העדות, on the western side of the משכן. Thereby it was revealed that God's Presence in Israel hinges on the Torah.

16-22 The cloud was the shepherd's staff, by means of which God, רועה ישראל, revealed to His flock where and when to camp, and when and in which

יז וּלְפִי הֵעָלוֹת הֶעָנָן מֵעַל הָאֹהֶל וְאַחֲרֵי כֵן יִסְעוּ בְּנֵי יִשְׂרָאֵל וּבִמְקוֹם אֲשֶׁר יִשְׁכָּן־שָׁם הֶעָנָן שָׁם יַחֲנוּ בְּנֵי יִשְׂרָאֵל׃

17 *And only when the cloud rose from the Tent did the Children of Israel journey forth; and at the place where the cloud settled, there did the Children of Israel camp.*

יח עַל־פִּי יְהוָה יִסְעוּ בְּנֵי יִשְׂרָאֵל וְעַל־פִּי יְהוָה יַחֲנוּ כָּל־יְמֵי אֲשֶׁר יִשְׁכֹּן הֶעָנָן עַל־הַמִּשְׁכָּן יַחֲנוּ׃

18 *At the behest of* God *did the Children of Israel journey forth, and at the behest of* God *did they camp; as long as the cloud rested upon the Dwelling Place, did they remain encamped.*

יט וּבְהַאֲרִיךְ הֶעָנָן עַל־הַמִּשְׁכָּן יָמִים רַבִּים וְשָׁמְרוּ בְנֵי־יִשְׂרָאֵל אֶת־מִשְׁמֶרֶת יְהוָה וְלֹא יִסָּעוּ׃

19 *Even when the cloud remained over the Dwelling Place for many days, the Children of Israel kept* God*'s charge and did not journey forth.*

כ וְיֵשׁ אֲשֶׁר יִהְיֶה הֶעָנָן יָמִים מִסְפָּר עַל־הַמִּשְׁכָּן עַל־פִּי יְהוָה יַחֲנוּ וְעַל־פִּי יְהוָה יִסָּעוּ׃

20 *It happened some times that the cloud remained upon the Dwelling Place for only a few days; at the behest of* God *did they camp, and at the behest of* God *did they journey forth.*

direction they were to journey forth. And we are told here that the will and intention of this guidance was unpredictable. There were times when the people had to stay in one place for a long period; at other times, they were allowed to remain at rest for a few days only. Some of their rest periods lasted only one night, or one day and one night, and then again there were times when they had to remain encamped for a whole month, or even a year.

The רמב״ן explains that since they never had advance indication of how long each rest period would be, whenever the cloud would give the signal to encamp they would have to make all the arrangements for

21 *It also happened sometimes that the cloud remained [only] from evening until morning, and the cloud rose in the morning and they journeyed forth; or [it remained] for a day and a night, and [then] the cloud rose and they journeyed forth.*

כא וְיֵ֞שׁ אֲשֶׁר יִהְיֶ֤ה הֶֽעָנָן֙ מֵעֶ֣רֶב עַד־
בֹּ֔קֶר וְנַעֲלָ֧ה הֶֽעָנָ֛ן בַּבֹּ֖קֶר וְנָסָ֑עוּ א֚וֹ
יוֹמָ֣ם וָלַ֔יְלָה וְנַעֲלָ֥ה הֶעָנָ֖ן וְנָסָֽעוּ׃

22 *Or [it remained] two days or a month or a year; when the cloud remained over the Dwelling Place for a long time and rested upon it, the Children of Israel remained encamped and did not journey forth; when it rose, they journeyed forth.*

כב אֽוֹ־יֹמַ֜יִם אוֹ־חֹ֣דֶשׁ אֽוֹ־יָמִ֗ים
בְּהַאֲרִ֨יךְ הֶעָנָ֤ן עַל־הַמִּשְׁכָּן֙ לִשְׁכֹּ֣ן
עָלָ֔יו יַחֲנ֥וּ בְנֵֽי־יִשְׂרָאֵ֖ל וְלֹ֣א יִסָּ֑עוּ
וּבְהֵעָלֹת֖וֹ יִסָּֽעוּ׃

an extended encampment, knowing that in a few hours they might have to break camp to follow the movement of the cloud.

This is the teaching of the journey through the wilderness, from which we learned for all time to follow God's guidance with devotion and trust, no matter how incomprehensible it may seem to us. At times He instructs us to leave what we have just now begun to love, and at times He requires of us to remain steadfast in an undesirable situation; nevertheless, we accept and fulfill with joy whatever He commands us. For beneath the shepherd's staff of His guidance, we will always be happy, and it is our faithfulness and obedience to God that bring us happiness. We will always be ready to put all our trust in God and to follow Him to unknown destinations, along mysterious paths; to wait and long for Him patiently, or to follow Him boldly — all according to the direction of His guidance.

However, closer consideration of these exercises and tests, by which God sought to train His people for all time, reveals that not the strain of long journeys, but primarily the patient waiting in lengthy stops is what is stressed here as the test to the people. Nothing is said of the

23 *At the behest of* God *did they camp, and at the behest of* God *did they journey forth; they kept* God's *charge at* God's *behest through Moshe.*

כג עַל־פִּ֤י יְהוָה֙ יַחֲנ֔וּ וְעַל־פִּ֥י יְהוָ֖ה יִסָּ֑עוּ אֶת־מִשְׁמֶ֤רֶת יְהוָה֙ שָׁמָ֔רוּ עַל־פִּ֥י יְהוָ֖ה בְּיַד־מֹשֶֽׁה׃ פ

duration of the journeys, but the prolonged waiting is mentioned several times. Already in verse 17, it says: ואחרי כן יסעו וגו׳; they journeyed forth only after — not before — the cloud lifted. And in verse 18 — after it has already said על פי ה׳ יסעו וגו׳ ועל פי ה׳ יחנו — it repeats: כל ימי אשר ישכן הענן וגו׳ יחנו. Finally, in verse 19, the fact that לא יסעו, they did not journey forth, even when the cloud rested there for a long time, is what is called שמירת משמרת ה׳, keeping God's charge, and it is the proof of their obedience to Him.

Clearly, then, particular stress is placed on Israel's endurance and patience. This is all the more understandable if one considers the inhospitableness of the wilderness, and particularly the fact that the people — not yet condemned to forty years of wandering — were fully aware that their destination lay not in the wilderness but beyond it, and that every stop they made in the wilderness served only to keep them from their promised destination.

Through these exercises the people acquired the virtue of quiet, serene resignation and trusting patience, which they would need on their wanderings in the "wilderness of the nations" (*Yechezkel* 20:35) through so many centuries of גלות. It was of this virtue that the prophet said: אִם־יִתְמַהְמָהּ חַכֵּה־לוֹ (*Havakkuk* 2:3).

23 **על פי ה׳ ביד משה**. They camped and journeyed forth at God's bidding, as He revealed His Will by means of the cloud. Moshe, however, was the mediator: It was he who demanded of them to obey God, whenever He revealed His Will by means of the cloud. This will be explained immediately in the verses that follow.

10 1 God *spoke to Moshe, saying:*

2 *Make yourself two silver trumpets, hammered of one piece shall you make them, and they shall serve you to call the community together and to cause the camps to journey forth.*

י א וַיְדַבֵּר יְהֹוָה אֶל־מֹשֶׁה לֵּאמֹר׃

ב עֲשֵׂה לְךָ שְׁתֵּי חֲצוֹצְרֹת כֶּסֶף מִקְשָׁה תַּעֲשֶׂה אֹתָם וְהָיוּ לְךָ לְמִקְרָא הָעֵדָה וּלְמַסַּע אֶת־הַמַּחֲנוֹת׃

CHAPTER 10

2 **חצוצרת**. The root is undoubtedly חצר, and the second root letter is doubled instead of a דגש חזק: חֲצוֹרָה. So we find (in *Divrei Ha-Yamim* II, 5:13) מְחַצְּצְרִים instead of מְחַצְּרִים. From our comments on *Bereshis* 2:18 and *Shemos* 27:9 it is clear that חָצֵר denotes the immediate surroundings of a main center; the חצר surrounds the center and serves its needs. The verb חַצֵּר means: to form a court around oneself. When applied to musical instruments, חַצֵּר means: to produce a sound as a signal to others, and the חצוצרה is the instrument that produces this sound. For this is the meaning of the sound of the חצוצרה: it calls others to personally turn to, or to direct their attention to, the one who produces the sound. Thus, the one who blows the חצוצרה becomes the center of a circle about him, the sound of the חצוצרה "forms a court," and the חצוצרה is the instrument for forming a court; it summons others to come to the court.

שתי חצוצרת: שיהו שוות במראה ובקומה ובנוי (*Sifre* here). As always in the Torah, whenever a mitzvah involves only two objects, and the number "two" is mentioned beside the plural, the number serves to teach that the two objects should be alike in every respect (see *Vayikra* 16:5).

In verses 3-4 it says that blowing *one* trumpet is the signal for calling the princes, the heads of thousands, as one national *unit*, whereas blowing *two* trumpets summons the nation in the whole *plurality* of its members. Hence, the complete alikeness of the two חצוצרות is required here for two reasons: to equate the honor of the people with the honor of the princes, and to indicate the complete equality of all the members of the national plurality.

3 *When they will blow with them, the whole community shall be ordered to you to the entrance of the Tent of Appointed Meeting.*

ג וְתָקְע֖וּ בָּהֵ֑ן וְנוֹעֲד֤וּ אֵלֶ֙יךָ֙ כָּל־הָ֣עֵדָ֔ה אֶל־פֶּ֖תַח אֹ֥הֶל מוֹעֵֽד׃

4 *But if they blow [only] with one [of them], the princes will be ordered to you, the heads of the thousands of Israel.*

ד וְאִם־בְּאַחַ֖ת יִתְקָ֑עוּ וְנוֹעֲד֤וּ אֵלֶ֙יךָ֙ הַנְּשִׂיאִ֔ים רָאשֵׁ֖י אַלְפֵ֥י יִשְׂרָאֵֽל׃

5 *And if you blow a* teruah, *the camps that camp to the east shall journey forth.*

ה וּתְקַעְתֶּ֖ם תְּרוּעָ֑ה וְנָֽסְעוּ֙ הַֽמַּחֲנ֔וֹת הַחֹנִ֖ים קֵֽדְמָה׃

כסף: the precious metal characteristic of the חצר (see Commentary, *Shemos* 27, end).

מקשה: hammered out of one piece, representing the unity and equality of the caller and the called. However, מקשה is not מעכב in the case of the חצוצרות (*Menachos* 28a).

עשה לך — והיו לך. The repetition of לך teaches that כל הכלים שעשה משה כשרים לו וכשרים לדורות, חצוצרות כשרות לו ופסולות לדורות (ibid.). All the things that were made through Moshe could be used also after his death, except the חצוצרות. Thus the difference between Moshe and all those that came after him was brought to the attention of all those that followed Moshe. The fact that לא קם נביא עוד בישראל כמשה (*Devarim* 34:10) comes to expression in this halachah. The trumpets, by which Moshe summoned the people and its leaders, were unsuitable for anyone else after his death.

ולמסע את המחנות. מסע can be interpreted as a verb: to set in motion; this would explain the phrase ולמסע את המחנות. Thus the *Sifre*: שתהא מזמן העדה ומסיע את המחנות.

3-7 **ותקעו וגו׳**. From verse 7 it is clear that תקיעה and תרועה are two different tones. Nevertheless, in verse 5 it says ותקעתם תרועה and not והרעותם, which would correspond to תריעו of verse 7. This teaches us that these two notes should be combined, and that the תרועה should be introduced by a תקיעה. Accordingly, תרועה יתקעו of verse 6 teaches that the תרועה should

6 *And if you blow a* teruah *a second time, the camps that camp to the south shall journey forth; they shall blow* teruah *for their journeyings forth.*	ו וּתְקַעְתֶּם תְּרוּעָה שֵׁנִית וְנָסְעוּ הַמַּחֲנוֹת הַחֹנִים תֵּימָנָה תְּרוּעָה יִתְקְעוּ לְמַסְעֵיהֶם׃
7 *When the assembly of the community is to be assembled, you shall blow, but do not blow a* teruah.	ז וּבְהַקְהִיל אֶת־הַקָּהָל תִּתְקְעוּ וְלֹא תָרִיעוּ׃

be concluded with a תקיעה. This concurs also with the Halachah (*Rosh Hashanah* 34a; cf. *Vayikra* 23:24).

The original meaning of תקע is to thrust, to forcefully insert something — e.g., to drive a nail into the wall or a peg into the ground. A person thrusts his hand into the hand of another, to symbolize a promise. A handshake symbolizes that, as the doer — or more accurately, as the owner; for the usual expression is תקיעת כף, not תקיעת יד — one energetically and unreservedly puts oneself at the disposal of another; one's hand is subordinated to the other person and is at his service. In this expression, the hand symbolizes the personality of the doer — or more accurately, of the owner; thus יִתָּקֵעַ (*Iyov* 17:3) in the reflexive sense: to clasp oneself. And of one who shook hands with another, it says: בָּאתָ בְכַף־רֵעֶךָ (*Mishlei* 6:3).

Transferred to the sphere of music, תקע denotes the forceful and prolonged blowing of a column of air into a wind instrument, and תקיעה denotes the strong, sustained tone produced thereby, which penetrates the ear. Thus the special meaning of תקיעה: the even, continuous, unbroken tone of a wind instrument: פשוטה.

The meaning of רוע, רעע is to break. Thus: תְּרֹעֵם בְּשֵׁבֶט בַּרְזֶל (*Tehillim* 2:9). In connection with music, the root denotes the broken, trembling tone, composed of several short blasts: תרועה.

In verse 2 it says that the main purpose of the חצוצרות is למקרא העדה and למסע את המחנות: to signal the community to assemble and the camps to journey forth. תקיעה, the even, calling tone, serves as the signal for assembly (vv. 3, 4, 7). תרועה, the broken tone of alarm, serves as the signal for breaking camp (vv. 5, 6), only that it says ותקעתם תרועה and

תרועה יתקעו, which implies that the תרועה does not stand alone, but is introduced by a תקיעה and is followed by a תקיעה (*Rosh Hashanah* 34a).

To call the nation together as a unit — represented by the princes, the heads of the thousands of Israel — they would blow a single trumpet (v. 4), thereby giving expression to the concept of the unit. But if the nation was to assemble in the plurality of its members, they would blow two trumpets, thereby giving expression to the concept of plurality.

The signal to break camp was, as already stated, תרועה, which was preceded and followed by תקיעה. Now, since תקיעה is a call signal and תרועה is an alarm signal, the combination of these tones works as follows: The first תקיעה summons them all to the nation's chief commander. If no תרועה follows the תקיעה, the order is: report to the head of the nation, to receive orders from him. But if a תרועה is sounded following the תקיעה, it gives the order to set everything in motion, to dismantle the camp and prepare it for journeying. The final תקיעה orders them as follows: After breaking camp, they should go wherever the leader directs them. This is apparently the meaning of תרועה יתקעו למסעיהם (v. 6): A תקיעה should follow the תרועה and thereby give the order to journey on.

From the wording of the text (vv. 5 and 6), it appears that the signal to break camp would be repeated only for the second camp, encamped to the south, whereas the camps encamped to the west and to the north would set out automatically, without any additional signal. Indeed, if we consider the description of the journeying in verse 14, we see that only the first camp and the second camp needed the signal of the trumpets in order to set out. For the order of the decampment was as follows:

First to set out [after the initial signal] would be the camp of Yehudah. At the same time — as we see in verse 17 and in 4:4-15, above — the sacred objects would be covered in cloths and delivered to the sons of Kehas. Then the sons of Gershon and the sons of Merari would come to dismantle the Tent and the courtyard and to load them on the wagons. It was important that first the dismantling of the Sanctuary would be completed, and the sons of Gershon and the sons of Merari would set out in the wake of the camp of Yehudah, and only then [after the second signal] would the second camp set out. Only at this point would the sons of Kehas — who would be ready with the sacred objects when the first camp set out — join the second camp and follow in its footsteps. The reason for this is explained in verse 21: At the new encampment, the sons of Gershon and the sons of Merari should arrive

8 *Aharon's sons, the priests, shall blow with the trumpets; they shall remain for you an everlasting statute for your descendants.*	ח וּבְנֵי אַהֲרֹן הַכֹּהֲנִים יִתְקְעוּ בַּחֲצֹצְרוֹת וְהָיוּ לָכֶם לְחֻקַּת עוֹלָם לְדֹרֹתֵיכֶם:
9 *And if you will come into war in*	ט וְכִי־תָבֹאוּ מִלְחָמָה בְּאַרְצְכֶם עַל־

in advance and thus be able to erect the Tent and the courtyard and prepare them to receive the sacred objects, and only then should the sons of Kehas arrive. The other camps, which by then would be ready to set out, would follow automatically [without the need for further signals].

Nevertheless, according to the *Sifre* (here), the trumpets would sound yet a third signal for the decampment of the last two camps, as indicated by the sentence תרועה יתקעו למסעיהם. According to another opinion cited in the *Sifre*, the trumpets were sounded for the departure of each one of the four camps.

8 **ובני אהרן הכהנים**. It is highly significant that the signals had to be sounded by כהנים. Indeed, according to ר׳ עקיבא in the *Sifre*, these were כהנים תמימים, who were fit for עבודה, for that is always the meaning of the expression בני אהרן הכהנים (Commentary, *Vayikra* 1:5, et al.). The same people who worked in the name of the Torah inside the Sanctuary of the Torah, performing there the symbolic acts of the nation's devotion to the Torah, were the ones by means of whom the nation's leader would call the nation or its heads to hear the Torah's commandments. Here as well as there, they were the Torah's heralds to the nation; and when the leader sounded his call by means of the כהנים, he thereby indicated that he was not calling them on the strength of his own personality, but strictly on the strength of his position in relation to the Torah.

והיו לכם לחקת עולם. The חצוצרות are not limited to the period of the wilderness, as explained thus far; rather, they also have meaning for future generations; and then, too, only כהנים are to sound them (see Commentary, vv. 9 and 10).

9 **וכי תבאו מלחמה**. As a rule, Scripture uses the expression "יצא למלחמה," whereas "בא למלחמה" is rare. It occurs again, notably, in Moshe's speech to the sons of Gad and the sons of Reuven: האחיכם יבאו למלחמה (below, 32:6).

הַצַּר הַצֹּרֵר אֶתְכֶם וַהֲרֵעֹתֶם בַּחֲצֹצְרֹת וְנִזְכַּרְתֶּם לִפְנֵי יְהֹוָה אֱלֹהֵיכֶם וְנוֹשַׁעְתֶּם מֵאֹיְבֵיכֶם:

your land against the oppressor that oppresses you, then you shall blow teruos *with the trumpets and you will be remembered before* God, *your God, and you will be delivered from your enemies.*

A יוצא למלחמה is one who goes to war vigorously, of his own volition; he is eager to do battle and goes off to fight even outside his own territory.

By contrast, a בא למלחמה — especially a בא מלחמה, as in our verse — is one who resigns himself to the dangers of battle after having become embroiled in war. Unprovoked, war has come, and one has no choice but to face the danger. Hence Moshe asks (ibid.): האחיכם יבאו למלחמה — and in contrast to that: ואתם תשבו פה! Your brothers, as much as you, would prefer to have already reached a state of rest and security. But the war is a necessity; it has reached us, and your brothers must enter the fray — and you wish to evade your duty?

Similarly, when it says (below, 31:21) אנשי הצבא הבאים למלחמה, Scripture there is dealing with results of איסור and of טומאה, which were produced by the soldiers' participation in the war, and which had to be removed at the war's conclusion. These results were not produced because יצאו למלחמה, but because באו למלחמה; for the war brought it about that they came into contact with corpses and seized as booty utensils of איסור. Apart from this, the *Sifre* (on verse 5, there) explains that they participated in this war unwillingly, for it was known beforehand that this was to be the last act of Moshe's life (see *Sifre* there).

וכי תבאו מלחמה of our verse undoubtedly speaks of a defensive war forced on Israel without any provocation on their part. For it says that the enemy is בארצכם. This is no war of conquest beyond the borders of the Land; rather, the enemy is in the Land. He has invaded your country and presses hard on you in your own land. He is הצר הצרר אתכם, and you are in trouble.

In such distress והרעתם בחצצרת, "you shall blow תרועות with the trumpets." The purpose of the תרועה with the חצוצרות is ונזכרתם וגו׳ ונושעתם, from which it follows that the תרועה is a cry for help, directed to God.

10 *And on the day of your rejoicing, and in your festive seasons, and at the beginning of your months, you shall blow with the trumpets over*

י וּבְיוֹם שִׂמְחַתְכֶם וּבְמוֹעֲדֵיכֶם וּבְרָאשֵׁי חָדְשֵׁכֶם וּתְקַעְתֶּם בַּחֲצֹצְרֹת עַל עֹלֹתֵיכֶם וְעַל זִבְחֵי

In the preceding verses, the tones signalled the leader's commands to the nation; here, it is the nation that, by these tones, calls to God. And since here, too, the tones are sounded by the כהנים (see Commentary, v. 8), who are the servants of the Torah in the Sanctuary, it is evident that deliverance is hoped for on the merit of the Torah, which forms the bond between God and Israel. And just as the תרועה that calls for decampment demands of the people to move with vigor, the תרועה directed to God in times of distress is nothing but the cry: קומה והושיעה נא, or as it says in verse 35: קומה ה׳ ויפצו איביך וגו׳.

However, it does not say here simply והרעתם וגו׳ ונושעתם וגו׳ but, rather, ונזכרתם וגו׳ ונושעתם וגו׳. The inference from ונזכרתם is that hitherto זכירה has been lacking. God had forsaken them, had left them to the natural course of events, and their natural weakness compared to the superior strength of the enemy had brought upon them their trouble. Hence, the first thought of their urgent cry to God is: Turn to us again, watch over us with Your providence, stand by us! The hoped-for deliverance is then simply the direct result of God turning again to His people.

Since the Halachah teaches that a תקיעה precedes each תרועה, this תרועה, too, of calling for help is introduced by a תקיעה. Now, we have already seen that the תקיעה introducing the תרועה of decampment calls upon the nation to turn to its leader and pay attention to his commands. Here, too, the introductory תקיעה is a call to God to direct His Countenance to us again; it is nothing but an imploring cry: זכרנו! And the תקיעה that concludes the תרועה expresses the prayer: Remain with us even after You have delivered us; do not forsake us again; travel with us!

10 **וביום שמחתכם**. In *Sukkah* 53b it is made clear that blasts are blown daily at the morning and afternoon תמיד and also at all the מוספים on Sabbaths and festivals. The only question under discussion there (54a et seq.) is the following: When a day has the character of a combined

שַׁלְמֵיכֶם וְהָיוּ לָכֶם לְזִכָּרוֹן לִפְנֵי אֱלֹהֵיכֶם אֲנִי יְהֹוָה אֱלֹהֵיכֶם: פ
חמישי

your ascent offerings and over your meal-of-peace offerings, and they will become for you a remembrance before your God; I, God, *your God.*

festival, and accordingly two or three מוספים are brought — e.g., a New Moon that falls on a Sabbath, or Rosh Hashanah that falls on Sabbath, in which case three מוספים are offered: one for Sabbath, one for the New Moon, and one for Rosh Hashanah — are תקיעות blown separately for each one of the מוספים, or is only one series of תקיעות blown for all of the מוספים together? The Halachah decides in favor of the latter alternative.

According to this, however, it is difficult to understand our verse. Mentioned explicitly in our verse are מועדים, ראשי חדשים, and in addition "יום שמחתכם." The question is, on the one hand, what is the meaning of "יום שמחתכם"? Clearly, it designates something other than the מועדים, for it is mentioned in addition to them. On the other hand, which of these categories includes שבת and תמיד? In the *Sifre*, there are two opinions. The one explains: וביום שמחתכם אלו שבתות, but does not explain which category includes the תמידים. The second opinion understands יום שמחתכם as an allusion to the תמידים, but does not explain which category includes the שבתות.

First let us note that שמחה need not necessarily denote a mood of elation brought about by some special occasion; rather, it also includes the inner mood of serenity and good cheer which should always be the keynote of our lives. This is evident from many verses, such as *Tehillim* 90:14, 4:8, 97:11, 100:2, 104:34; *Koheles* 9:7, 3:12, 5:18, 11:9; *Mishlei* 5:18, 23:24-25, 13:9.

And certainly this applies to the nation as a whole, with which our text is concerned. For the nation knows neither death nor impoverishment: אין ציבור מת ואין ציבור עני (*Temurah* 15b; see *Yerushalmi*, *Gittin* 3:7, end). Constant joy prevails especially in God's House, the Sanctuary of the Torah, at whose threshold death and mourning must be left behind; where, beneath the rays of God's Presence, only שמחה של מצוה can flourish. There, the idea שהשמחה במעונו becomes a reality, and everyone receives the call: עִבְדוּ אֶת־ה׳ בְּשִׂמְחָה (*Tehillim* 100:2). There, every ordinary day is fit to be designated "יום שמחה." This designation is used here in contrast to יום צרה of the preceding verse, which speaks of the trouble and oppression that befall the nation because God has forsaken it.

It is certainly possible, then, that יום שמחתכם refers to the daily תמיד offering, whereas שבתות are included under מועדיכם. After all, the verse that deals with the offerings of the מועדים includes שבת in the general concept of מועד: According to *Pesachim* 77a, the summation אלה תעשו לה׳ במועדיכם (below, 29:39) includes all קרבנות ציבור that קבוע להם זמן; hence, it also includes מוספי שבת (see Commentary above, 9:2).

However, if every ordinary day not clouded by some special sorrow is fit to be designated a יום שמחה by virtue of our awareness of God which accompanies its every moment, then certainly the Sabbath is fit to be so designated. For the Sabbath is especially dedicated to God-consciousness, and the idea that infuses a spirit of שמחה into all the work of the other days of the week is the very essence of the Sabbath. Hence, the Sabbath is fit to be called "יום שמחתנו," *the* day of our joy. Whichever state of mind the Sabbath may find us in, be it a state of "full flowering," or a "withered" state of sadness, or a state of deep contemplation in which we meditate on the mysteries of life — עֲלֵי־עָשׂוֹר וַעֲלֵי־נָבֶל עֲלֵי הִגָּיוֹן בְּכִנּוֹר (*Tehillim* 92:4; cf. Commentary there) — the Sabbath evokes the same idea, namely, that we live in God's world, together with His creatures, under the influence of His works and deeds. This idea of the Sabbath will always move us to exclaim: שִׂמַּחְתַּנִי ה׳ בְּפָעֳלֶךָ בְּמַעֲשֵׂי יָדֶיךָ אֲרַנֵּן, "You have given me joy in Your work, O God; I will exult in the works of Your hands" (*Tehillim* 92:5); or as it says in our *Siddur*: ישמחו במלכותך שומרי שבת!

Therefore it is possible that יום שמחתכם refers to the Sabbath, in which case תמידים would be included under מועדיכם; for also in the laws of דחיית הטומאה, the תמידים are included under the concept of מועד (see Commentary above, 9:3).

Thus, the Torah tells us: On the joyous days of God-awareness, at seasons when special memories invite us to commune with God, on days that summon us to self-renewal, we are to give expression, through קרבן, to this awareness, to the aspiration toward God, to self-renewal. Through עולות, תמידים, and מוספים, and שלמי ציבור of כבשי עצרת, we are to give expression to the consecration of actions and to the joy of living, which lead to God's nearness. On all these occasions, we are to call out to God through תקיעת חצוצרות; we are to ask Him to hear the vows to which we were inspired by the particular season and look upon our devotion in seeking קרבת אלקים; we are to call to Him to draw near to us, even as we, heeding His voice, seek His nearness.

Accordingly, תקיעת חצוצרות of the communal offerings is likewise (as in v. 9) Israel's call to God: We call to Him to draw near to us, and thereby we express the very essence of the idea of a קרבן. And when we strive to draw near to God, and God responds and draws near to us, the whole idea of the מועד offering becomes a reality; for the time of the offering is transformed thereby into a מועד, a time of union between Israel and God. We have already stated (above, 9:2) that שבתות and תמידים are also מועדים of offerings.

The Halachah teaches that the תקיעה at the offerings was also not a single tone, but תקיעה-תרועה-תקיעה, similar to the cry for help in the preceding verse. Although there it says והרעתם and here it says ותקעתם, the רמב"ן has already explained that there the emphasis is on תרועה, whereas here the emphasis is on תקיעה. There, it is a תרועה introduced and accompanied by תקיעה, whereas here it is תקיעות introducing and accompanying the תרועה. There, the Divine intervention is the purpose, and the hoped-for nearness of God is the means; here, God's nearness is the purpose, and the Divine intervention is the means. For God's constant closeness is likewise dependent on the intervention of His almighty power; it depends on כפרה, which is a miraculous act of Divine lovingkindness. כפרה eliminates from our past everything that is counter to our aspiration to be worthy of God's nearness. By virtue of the כפרה, we will be reborn, and we will be worthy of a new and pure future. Thus, the תקיעה-תרועה-תקיעה of the offerings calls to God to come to us (תקיעה), to effect כפרה for us (תרועה), in order to remain close to us from now on and to guide us through life (תקיעה).

It is possible that the different meaning of the תקיעה-תרועה-תקיעה — as a call for help or as a call with the offerings — was reflected also in the manner of producing the tones: There the תרועה was emphasized by prolonging it and sounding it loudly, while here by the same method the תקיעות were emphasized. Analogous is the Halachah's teaching regarding the combination of חצוצרות and שופר on a תענית and on ראש השנה (*Rosh Hashanah* 26b) [see below].

והיו לכם לזכרון לפני אלקיכם. The precise meaning of the term "זכרון" is evident from various places, such as והיה היום הזה לזכרון (*Shemos* 12:14), from what is said of the names on the אפוד and the חושן (ibid. 28:12 and 29), and also from what is said of the *tefillin*: ולזכרון בין עיניך (ibid. 13:9). From all these it is evident that זכרון is not the means of remembrance, but the thing that should be remembered. Here, too, it appears that the subject of והיו is not the חצוצרות but the עולות וזבחי שלמים, which, through the תקיעות, will become a remembrance before God. The תקיעות are a call to God to take note of our actions on earth and to remember the vows of devotion expressed thereby. Thus והיו לכם וגו׳: God will listen to the sound of our תקיעות and grant our request, and as a result אני ה׳ אלקיכם: He will forever fulfill the covenant He established with us.

Closer consideration reveals that the three sentences — ותקעתם, והיו לכם לזכרון, אני ה׳ אלקיכם — correspond to the meaning of תקיעה-תרועה-תקיעה. ותקעתם is the call to God that emerges from the תקיעה; זכרון is the favorable acceptance of our offerings, for God will grant us כפרה as we requested in the תרועה; אני ה׳ אלקיכם is the closeness of the covenant which will accompany us in life, and it is that for which we prayed in the final תקיעה on the basis of the כפרה. (See our Commentary, *Vayikra* 23:24, on תקיעת שופר of ראש השנה and יובל.)

In *Rosh Hashanah* 26b and 27a our Sages say that, in the Temple, שופר and חצוצרות were always blown simultaneously. On ראש השנה, the חצוצרות were on either side of the שופר, and the sound of the שופר was prolonged, whereas the sound of the חצוצרה was shortened, since the mitzvah of the day is with שופר. On תעניות, the two חצוצרות were in the middle, with an accompanying שופר on either side, and the sound of the חצוצרות was prolonged, whereas the sound of the שופר was shortened, since the mitzvah of the day is with חצוצרות. The combination of חצוצרות and שופר appears in the verse: בַּחֲצֹצְרוֹת וְקוֹל שׁוֹפָר הָרִיעוּ לִפְנֵי הַמֶּלֶךְ ה׳ (*Tehillim* 98:6).

If we now recall that the שופר represents God's call to us, whereas the חצוצרות represent our call to Him, their combination in the מקדש, the abode of the Torah and of God's promises, signifies the following: The חצוצרות accompany the שופר, and the שופר must accompany the חצוצרות. That is to say, if we heed God's call to us (שופר), God will listen to our call to Him (חצוצרות); so, too, we will be able to call to God in times of distress (חצוצרות), only if we undertake to obey His voice (שופר).

The תקיעות of the offerings are given verbal expression in the ברכת העבודה (רצה) of the שמונה עשרה — which was instituted in correspondence to the תמידים — and especially in the insertion of יעלה ויבא on the מועדים and ראשי חדשים.

11 *It came to pass in the second year, in the second month, on the twentieth [day] of the month, that the cloud rose from its site over the Dwelling Place of the Testimony.*

יא וַיְהִ֞י בַּשָּׁנָ֧ה הַשֵּׁנִ֛ית בַּחֹ֥דֶשׁ הַשֵּׁנִ֖י בְּעֶשְׂרִ֣ים בַּחֹ֑דֶשׁ נַעֲלָה֙ הֶֽעָנָ֔ן מֵעַ֖ל מִשְׁכַּ֥ן הָעֵדֻֽת׃

12 *Then the Children of Israel journeyed forth upon their journeys out of the wilderness of Sinai, and the cloud came to rest in the wilderness of Paran.*

יב וַיִּסְע֧וּ בְנֵֽי־יִשְׂרָאֵ֛ל לְמַסְעֵיהֶ֖ם מִמִּדְבַּ֣ר סִינָ֑י וַיִּשְׁכֹּ֥ן הֶעָנָ֖ן בְּמִדְבַּ֥ר פָּארָֽן׃

11 **ויהי בשנה וגו׳ מעל משכן העדת** — see Commentary above, 9:15. The cloud rested on the משכן because it was the "Dwelling Place of the Testimony." Actually, it rested on the Testimony, for the Testimony of the Torah formed the bond between God and Israel and led to God's Presence abiding in the people's midst.

בחדש השני בעשרים וגו׳. The 14th of the month was פסח שני; anyone who had been prevented from offering the Pesach in Nissan offered it on that day and thus made himself aware again that Israel is a people guided by God. Only then, after encamping at Sinai for nearly twelve months, did they journey on towards entering the promised land of the Torah.

12 **ויסעו וגו׳ למסעיהם**. נסע — related to נסח: וְיִסָּחֲךָ מֵאֹהֶל (*Tehillim* 52:7) — primarily means to rise from a resting place one has hitherto occupied; hence: to leave the place, to set oneself in motion. (Thus also the meaning of the related root נסה; נִסָּה: to assign someone an activity, to test and train him.) **נסע** then also denotes uprooting oneself continuously; to constantly get up, move forward, relocate. **נסע** is used particularly in this sense when the discussion is about a great multitude, which is difficult to set in motion, as in our case here, where we are dealing with an entire camp, and as in the case of Avraham, who travelled with his entire household (*Bereshis* 12:9). The progress of such a multitude is really a continuous act of "moving house" (cf. Commentary, ibid. 11:2).

In our chapter, **נסע** is used in both senses: to uproot from the place

יג וַיִּסְע֖וּ בָּרִאשֹׁנָ֑ה עַל־פִּ֥י יְהֹוָ֖ה בְּיַד־מֹשֶֽׁה׃

13 *This was the first time that they journeyed according to the order imparted by* God *through Moshe.*

יד וַיִּסַּ֞ע דֶּ֣גֶל מַחֲנֵ֧ה בְנֵֽי־יְהוּדָ֛ה בָּרִאשֹׁנָ֖ה לְצִבְאֹתָ֑ם וְעַ֨ל־צְבָא֔וֹ נַחְשׁ֖וֹן בֶּן־עַמִּינָדָֽב׃

14 *The standard of the camp of the sons of Yehudah journeyed forth first, according to their serving divisions, and over its division was Nachshon, son of Amminadav.*

טו וְעַ֨ל־צְבָ֔א מַטֵּ֖ה בְּנֵ֣י יִשָּׂשכָ֑ר נְתַנְאֵ֖ל בֶּן־צוּעָֽר׃

15 *And over the division of the tribe of the sons of Yissachar [was] Nesan'el, son of Tzu'ar.*

---

and to relocate. Here, ויסעו means: they set out from their place, to commence the journeys that would bring them to the Land.

ויסעו וגו׳ ממדבר סיני וישכן הענן במדבר פארן. For the present, it was just a move from one wilderness to another.

13 **ויסעו בראשונה על פי ה׳ ביד משה**. Their journey from Egypt to Sinai had also been under Divine guidance through the agency of Moshe. But this was the first time that they travelled as described here: as the people of the Torah, in camps around the Dwelling Place of the Torah, with the cloud — resting on, or rising from, the Testimony of the Torah — directing them to encamp or to journey forth, and with the Ark of the Covenant of the Testimony of the Torah going before them to seek out a resting place. Never before had they travelled in this manner.

14 **לצבאתם**: in orderly divisions. Presumably the families were organized in groups within the framework of each tribe as well, and the term "לצבאתם," which is repeated in the cases of all the camps, refers to these groups. Had it said לצבאותיו, the singular pronominal suffix would have referred to the דגל or the מחנה, and we would have interpreted צבאותיו as the three divisions of the tribes assigned to each standard. It says, however, לצבאתם, and the plural pronominal suffix can refer only to the preceding בני יהודה. Hence, we must assume that within the framework of בני יהודה as well there were several צבאות.

טז וְעַל־צְבָ֕א מַטֵּ֖ה בְּנֵ֣י זְבוּלֻ֑ן אֱלִיאָ֖ב
בֶּן־חֵלֹֽן׃

16 *And over the division of the tribe of the sons of Zevulun [was] Eli'av, son of Chelon.*

יז וְהוּרַ֖ד הַמִּשְׁכָּ֑ן וְנָסְע֤וּ בְנֵֽי־גֵרְשׁוֹן֙
וּבְנֵ֣י מְרָרִ֔י נֹשְׂאֵ֖י הַמִּשְׁכָּֽן׃

17 *When the Dwelling Place was taken down, the sons of Gershon and the sons of Merari, the bearers of the Dwelling Place, journeyed forth.*

יח וְנָסַ֗ע דֶּ֛גֶל מַחֲנֵ֥ה רְאוּבֵ֖ן לְצִבְאֹתָ֑ם
וְעַל־צְבָא֔וֹ אֱלִיצ֖וּר בֶּן־שְׁדֵיאֽוּר׃

18 *Then the standard of the camp of Reuven journeyed forth according to their serving divisions, and over its division [was] Elitzur, son of Shedei'ur.*

יט וְעַל־צְבָ֕א מַטֵּ֖ה בְּנֵ֣י שִׁמְע֑וֹן
שְׁלֻמִיאֵ֖ל בֶּן־צוּרִֽישַׁדָּֽי׃

19 *And over the division of the tribe of the sons of Shimon [was] Shelumi'el, son of Tzurishaddai.*

כ וְעַל־צְבָ֕א מַטֵּ֖ה בְּנֵי־גָ֑ד אֶלְיָסָ֖ף
בֶּן־דְּעוּאֵֽל׃

20 *And over the division of the tribe of the sons of Gad [was] Elyasaf, son of De'u'el.*

כא וְנָסְעוּ֙ הַקְּהָתִ֔ים נֹשְׂאֵ֖י הַמִּקְדָּ֑שׁ
וְהֵקִ֥ימוּ אֶת־הַמִּשְׁכָּ֖ן עַד־בֹּאָֽם׃

21 *Then the Kehasi, the bearers of the Sanctuary, journeyed forth first, so that the Dwelling Place would be set up by the time they arrived.*

כב וְנָסַ֗ע דֶּ֛גֶל מַחֲנֵ֥ה בְנֵֽי־אֶפְרַ֖יִם
לְצִבְאֹתָ֑ם וְעַל־צְבָא֔וֹ אֱלִישָׁמָ֖ע
בֶּן־עַמִּיהֽוּד׃

22 *Thereafter the standard of the camp of Efrayim journeyed forth according to their serving divisions, and over its division [was] Elishama, son of Ammihud.*

17-21 **והורד המשכן וגו׳ ונסעו הקהתים וגו׳** — see Commentary, vv. 3-7.

23 *And over the division of the tribe of the sons of Menashe [was] Gamli'el, son of Pedahtzur.*

כג וְעַ֨ל־צְבָ֔א מַטֵּ֖ה בְּנֵ֣י מְנַשֶּׁ֑ה גַּמְלִיאֵ֖ל בֶּן־פְּדָהצֽוּר׃

24 *And over the division of the tribe of the sons of Binyamin [was] Avidan, son of Gid'oni.*

כד וְעַ֨ל־צְבָ֔א מַטֵּ֖ה בְּנֵ֣י בִנְיָמִ֑ן אֲבִידָ֖ן בֶּן־גִּדְעוֹנִֽי׃

25 *Then the standard of the camp of the sons of Dan journeyed forth according to their serving divisions, the rear guard of all the camps, and over its division [was] Achi'ezer, son of Ammishaddai.*

כה וְנָסַ֗ע דֶּ֚גֶל מַחֲנֵ֣ה בְנֵי־דָ֔ן מְאַסֵּ֥ף לְכָל־הַמַּחֲנֹ֖ת לְצִבְאֹתָ֑ם וְעַל־צְבָא֕וֹ אֲחִיעֶ֖זֶר בֶּן־עַמִּישַׁדָּֽי׃

---

25 **מאסף לכל המחנת**. The underlying concept of the root אסף is: to take something and absorb it entirely, or in general: to take something for a distinct purpose. Like many פ״א verbs — e.g., אכל, אבד, etc. — אסף is none other than סף with an individualizing א prefixed to it (see Commentary, *Bereshis* 1:29-30, et al.). Accordingly, its meaning is: to end, to cease, in order to be given over exclusively to another purpose (cf. Commentary, ibid. 49:1). אסף also means simply to remove, without directing the object to any other use or purpose; thus, for example: אסף ה׳ את חרפתי (*Bereshis* 30:23).

In an army column marching to war, the vanguard is called "החלוץ," literally a "detachment." It is the body of troops sent ahead of and detached from the main force, and it is ready for battle. It makes first contact with the enemy and, generally speaking, overcomes the first difficulties. The rear guard is called "מאסף." It is the body of troops that forms the end of the column of troops, keeps the troops together, and makes them a unit. It guards the rear from attack, as מאסף also denotes defensive protection (see *Yehoshua* 6:9ff.).

In the *Yerushalmi* (*Eruvin* 5:1), there are two opinions as to the formation in which the camps would move on the journeys. According to one view, they would travel כמין תיבה, in square formation, the same arrangement in which they encamped: Yehudah in the lead, Reuven to the right, Dan to the left, and Efrayim in the rear; for it says: כאשר יחנו

26 *And over the division of the tribe of the sons of Asher [was] Pag'i'el, son of Ochran.*	כו וְעַל־צְבָא מַטֵּה בְּנֵי אָשֵׁר פַּגְעִיאֵל בֶּן־עָכְרָן׃
27 *And over the division of the tribe of the sons of Naftali [was] Achira, son of Einan.*	כז וְעַל־צְבָא מַטֵּה בְּנֵי נַפְתָּלִי אֲחִירַע בֶּן־עֵינָן׃
28 *Thus were the journeyings of the Children of Israel according to their serving divisions, and now they journeyed forth.*	כח אֵלֶּה מַסְעֵי בְנֵי־יִשְׂרָאֵל לְצִבְאֹתָם וַיִּסָּעוּ׃ ס

כן יסעו (above, 2:17). The other opinion infers from our verse, מאסף לכל המחנות, that they would travel כקורה, in a straight line: Yehudah in the lead, followed by Reuven, Efrayim and Dan; thus, Dan was the מאסף in the straightforward sense of the term.

However, from what is stated above (10:14-21), it is clear and unequivocal that the sons of Kehas would follow the camp of Reuven, whereas the sons of Gershon and the sons of Merari would follow the camp of Yehudah, so as to be able to erect the משכן before the arrival of the sons of Kehas. It is also clear that the camp of Dan would begin to move only after the camp of Efrayim; this is evident from the order of the verses here, and is expressly stated above (2:31): לאחרונה יסעו. Accordingly, the view that they would travel כמין תיבה can hardly mean that, even on the march, they would keep the form of a closed square. Rather, it stands to reason that this view essentially holds as follows: Even while on the march, they would keep the relative positions they occupied in camp: Yehudah would take the lead, followed by Reuven, not directly behind but keeping to the right. Then Efrayim would follow in a straight line behind Yehudah, and finally Dan, keeping to the left. Thus, when the time would come to stop, each camp would arrive on the correct side for encampment.

28 **אלה מסעי**: This is the order they adopted on all their journeys; thus they would break camp, and thus they would travel from place to place. **ויסעו**: And now they journeyed forth.

29 *Moshe said to Chovav, son of Re'u'el the Midianite, father-in-law of Moshe: We are journeying to the place of which* God *said: I will give it to you. Please come with us and we will do good with you, for* God *has promised good concerning Israel.*

כט וַיֹּאמֶר מֹשֶׁה לְחֹבָב בֶּן־רְעוּאֵל הַמִּדְיָנִי חֹתֵן מֹשֶׁה נֹסְעִים | אֲנַחְנוּ אֶל־הַמָּקוֹם אֲשֶׁר אָמַר יְהוָה אֹתוֹ אֶתֵּן לָכֶם לְכָה אִתָּנוּ וְהֵטַבְנוּ לָךְ כִּי־יְהוָה דִּבֶּר־טוֹב עַל־יִשְׂרָאֵל:

29 **ויאמר משה**. In *Shoftim* 4:11 Chovav is called "חֹתֵן מֹשֶׁה," "Moshe's father-in-law." It appears, then, that here, too, חתן משה refers not to Re'u'el, but to Chovav; and if in *Shemos* 2:18 Re'u'el is called the father of Tzipporah and her sisters, "father" should be understood as "grandfather," comparable to אלקי אבי אברהם (*Bereshis* 32:10) and other places, as noted by the רמב"ן in *Shemos* 2:16.

His primary name was Yeser and Yisro; so we find in *Shemos* 3:1 and 4:18, and also in *Shemos* 18. According to the רמב"ן (ibid. 18:1; *Bemidbar* 10:29), Yisro received the name "Chovav" after his conversion to Judaism, and thereafter was called by that name. See also the *Sifre* ad loc.

The root חבב, common in Rabbinic Hebrew in the sense of love and esteem, occurs in תנ"ך only once: אף חבב עמים כל קדשיו בידך (*Devarim* 33:3). It appears that חבב is related to חוב, which likewise is common in Rabbinic Hebrew and occurs in תנ"ך only once: חֲבֹלָתוֹ חוֹב יָשִׁיב, "he carries out the return of the pledge like an obligation" (*Yechezkel* 18:7). Accordingly, חבב would denote love that obligates and love that springs from a sense of duty.

Perhaps this is the meaning of the verse אף חבב עמים: Even when You wish to obligate the nations by bestowing on them the highest kindness, You take all of Israel's holy ones into Your hands; that is to say, when You wish to act with supreme lovingkindness toward the nations, the holy ones of Israel serve as an instrument to this end. והם תכו לרגלך ישא מדברותיך: They, the nations, will be led to Your feet because it, Israel, will bear some of Your words to them. If this is the meaning of the verse, then חבב is the special expression for the Divine mode of rule that brings the nations to knowledge of God and obedience to Him

30 *Then he said to him: I will not go; rather, I will go to my [own] land and to my birthplace.*

ל וַיֹּ֥אמֶר אֵלָ֖יו לֹ֣א אֵלֵ֑ךְ כִּ֧י אִם־אֶל־אַרְצִ֛י וְאֶל־מוֹלַדְתִּ֖י אֵלֵֽךְ׃

31 *But he said: Please do not leave us! For I am asking this because you are familiar with the places of our camping in the wilderness and you can serve us as eyes.*

לא וַיֹּ֕אמֶר אַל־נָ֖א תַּעֲזֹ֣ב אֹתָ֑נוּ כִּ֣י ׀ עַל־כֵּ֣ן יָדַ֗עְתָּ חֲנֹתֵ֙נוּ֙ בַּמִּדְבָּ֔ר וְהָיִ֥יתָ לָּ֖נוּ לְעֵינָֽיִם׃

32 *If you go with us, it shall be that the same good that* God *in His goodness will do for us, we will do for you.*

לב וְהָיָ֖ה כִּֽי־תֵלֵ֣ךְ עִמָּ֑נוּ וְהָיָ֣ה ׀ הַטּ֣וֹב הַה֗וּא אֲשֶׁ֨ר יֵיטִ֧יב יְהוָ֛ה עִמָּ֖נוּ וְהֵטַ֥בְנוּ לָֽךְ׃

through Israel, the mode of rule that shows love to the nations and thereby obligates them.

Accordingly, חוֹבָב (cf. the forms שׁוֹבָב, שׁוֹלָל, עוֹלָל, all of which occur in the passive) is a person whom God's love obligates, one who feels that he is duty bound to God by this love. It is a fitting name for Yisro, who consciously made the transition from heathenism to Judaism. We will see that Yisro's descendants inherited from him this sense of duty and acted upon it (see Commentary below, vv. 31-32).

נסעים אנחנו. They set out, then, under the assumption that they would enter the Land immediately. For the Lawgiving had been completed, and the time had come to take possession of the land in which the Torah would find its full realization.

31-32 **ויאמר אל נא וגו'**. In the previous verse, the request is made from the standpoint of Yisro's own interest: לכה אתנו והטבנו לך. That request, Yisro rejects: לא אלך וגו'; there is no price at which I would give up my home and fatherland. Moshe therefore repeats the request and explains it more precisely: אל נא תעזב אתנו, your staying with us is for *our* good; for you to leave us would be to *forsake* us. כי על כן וגו' (see Commentary, *Bereshis* 18:5): For I am appealing to you not out of consideration of your own interest but, rather, because ידעת וגו', you are familiar with the terrain of the areas in which we must encamp, you know the paths of the wilderness; and wherever we will be directed by God to encamp, you know all the possible advantages to be had from that particular spot; והיית לנו לעינים, your knowledge of the region would benefit us. When I said והטבנו לך, I was not thinking of material recompense. Rather, הטוב ההוא וגו׳ והטבנו לך, you would find with us a replacement for the home and fatherland you gave up for our sake. The sacrifice you will make for us, and the great benefit we will gain from you, will entitle you to, and obligate us to grant you, land and a home in our midst. We will give you a share in the land that God will give to us (that is the טוב mentioned in Moshe's first appeal, in v. 29).

Moshe says that the good promised to Yisro mirrors the good that God will do for Israel, for he employs the same language in reference to both: אשר ייטיב ה׳ עמנו והטבנו לך. What is delicately implied is: Do not be shy about accepting from us this bounty, for we ourselves are receiving the Land only as a gracious gift from the hand of God; and that which for us is purely a gift, טובה **עמנו**, for you is something thoroughly deserved, טובה **לך**.

From *Shoftim* 1:16 it is clear that descendants of Moshe's father-in-law inhabited עיר התמרים, the City of Date-Palms, which is Yericho (cf. *Divrei Ha-Yamim* II, 28:15, יְרֵחוֹ עִיר־הַתְּמָרִים). It must be, then, that Chovav acceded to Moshe's request and journeyed with Israel to the Land. Although he first returned to his homeland (*Shemos* 18:27), he later rejoined Moshe in the wilderness.

In *Shoftim* there (1:16), Moshe's father-in-law is called קֵינִי, apparently on account of his origin. In any case, בני קיני descend from חובב, Moshe's father-in-law; for in *Shoftim* 4:11 it says explicitly: וְחֶבֶר הַקֵּינִי נִפְרָד מִקַּיִן מִבְּנֵי חֹבָב חֹתֵן מֹשֶׁה. And when Sha'ul went to war against Amalek and found a branch of the Keini living among the Amaleki, he requested of them (*Shemuel* I, 15:6) to depart from among the Amaleki, to avoid being destroyed along with them, and he explained this request as follows: וְאַתָּה עָשִׂיתָה חֶסֶד עִם־כָּל־בְּנֵי יִשְׂרָאֵל בַּעֲלוֹתָם מִמִּצְרָיִם. Thus Israel remembered the kindness showed to them by Moshe's father-in-law. According to the *Sifre* (here), the most fruitful district around Yericho, דושנה של יריחו, was allotted to Yisro's descendants, who inhabited it for 440 years until the Temple was built.

Yisro also bequeathed to his descendants the trait for which he was called "חובב." They, הַקֵּינִים הַבָּאִים מֵחַמַּת אֲבִי בֵית־רֵכָב, were not only מִשְׁפְּחוֹת

33 *So they journeyed forth from the* לג וַיִּסְעוּ מֵהַר יְהוָה דֶּרֶךְ שְׁלֹשֶׁת

סוֹפְרִים, who excelled in study and learning; they were not only יֹשְׁבֵי יַעְבֵּץ, who left the most fertile part of Yericho and went off to learn Torah from the esteemed Yabetz (*Divrei Ha-Yamim* I, 2:55 and 4:9-10; *Shoftim* 1:16 and *Sifre* here); rather — as is evident from the verse cited above — they were also בית רכב, who carried out the dictates of their great ancestor Yonadav (see *Yirmeyahu* 35:2-19). Long before the destruction of the Temple, they recognized the depravity of the cities and the government and avoided them; they renounced field and vineyard, did not build themselves houses to live in, abstained from wine, and vowed to live a nomadic life forever, to preserve liberty and moral purity for themselves and their descendants. Perhaps they are living to this very day among the Rechavites of the Arabian desert, in fulfillment of the Divine promise: לֹא־יִכָּרֵת אִישׁ לְיוֹנָדָב בֶּן־רֵכָב עֹמֵד לְפָנַי כָּל־הַיָּמִים (ibid. 35:19).

This request that Moshe made of his father-in-law and recorded for all time is of great importance, for the request that his father-in-law should help them with his judgment and with his knowledge of the terrain can bring us to a correct evaluation of Moshe's mission.

As we have already seen (*Shemos* 18:13-27), Yisro's organizational advice proves that Moshe did not have the organizational skills required of a state-building lawmaker. Likewise, the fact related here refutes all the idle chatter about Moshe's knowledge of the ways of the wilderness, according to which the Divine wonder of our journeying in the wilderness is merely the result of clever and shrewd leadership. Moshe, who needed the advice of his father-in-law in order to organize the judicial system and to make proper arrangements for the camps, and recorded both of these instances for everlasting memory among his people — this man could not have led his people and given it Torah on his own; he could have accomplished it only as the instrument of God. He would have been the very last person to ascribe to himself a halo of superhuman insight and miraculous power (cf. Commentary, *Shemos* 18:24).

33-34 **ויסעו וגו׳**. It does not say ויסעו . . . שלשת ימים, but ויסעו . . . דרך שלשת ימים. This is an indication of the hardship and strain entailed in such a three-days' journey. Nevertheless וארון ברית ה׳ נסע לפניהם דרך שלשת ימים: Through-

יָמִ֑ים וַאֲר֨וֹן בְּרִית־יְהֹוָ֜ה נֹסֵ֣עַ לִפְנֵיהֶ֗ם דֶּ֚רֶךְ שְׁלֹ֣שֶׁת יָמִ֔ים לָת֥וּר לָהֶ֖ם מְנוּחָֽה׃

mountain of God *a journey of three days, and the Ark of* God's *Covenant traveled ahead of them a three days' journey to seek out a resting place for them.*

לד וַעֲנַ֧ן יְהֹוָ֛ה עֲלֵיהֶ֖ם יוֹמָ֑ם בְּנָסְעָ֖ם מִן־הַֽמַּחֲנֶֽה׃ ס ששי

34 *And the cloud of* God *was over them by day, when they journeyed forth from the camp.*

לה ׆ וַיְהִ֛י בִּנְסֹ֥עַ הָאָרֹ֖ן וַיֹּ֣אמֶר מֹשֶׁ֑ה קוּמָ֣ה ׀ יְהֹוָ֗ה וְיָפֻ֙צוּ֙ אֹֽיְבֶ֔יךָ וְיָנֻ֥סוּ מְשַׂנְאֶ֖יךָ מִפָּנֶֽיךָ׃
נו״ן הפוכה

35 *It came to pass, when the Ark journeyed forth, that Moshe said: Arise, 0* God, *so that Your enemies may be scattered and those that hate You flee from before Your Countenance.*

לו וּבְנֻחֹ֖ה יֹאמַ֑ר שׁוּבָ֣ה יְהֹוָ֔ה רִֽבְב֖וֹת אַלְפֵ֥י יִשְׂרָאֵֽל׃ ׆ פ
ובנחו קרי נו״ן הפוכה

36 *And when it gently came to rest, he said: Return, 0* God, *to the myriads of the thousands of Israel.*

out this three-day journey, they saw before their eyes the Ark of God's Covenant, traveling ahead of them to seek out a resting place for them. The sight of the Ark maintained in them the vibrancy and cheerfulness that come from the awareness of walking in the ways of God. Similarly, וענן ה' עליהם: God's cloud, which hovered above them and moved with them when they journeyed forth, assured them of God's protection throughout their journeys.

35-36 **ויהי בנסע הארן**. As already noted in our introduction (above, 8:1), the history of Israel's development was interrupted in *Shemos* 34 with the renewal of God's covenant after the sin of the golden calf. Here Scripture returns to that narrative and describes the continuation of this development.

The Lawgiving at Sinai had been completed. Had the people already attained the lofty level required for the fulfillment of the Torah, their subsequent history would have been completely different and less complicated. From God's *mountain* they would have travelled immediately to God's *land*, to fulfill the Torah in the Land. The Sanctuary of the Torah and the people of the Torah would have reached their zenith in the Land, casting light far out to all the nations. Now this is but a vision for the end of days. Like Israel's history, the history of mankind would have taken a different course.

But the people had not yet reached the lofty heights of their calling. The verses that follow take us into the midst of the camp and introduce a series of aberrations. Ultimately it will become clear that this entire generation was unworthy of entering the land of the Torah, that the possession of the Land over the succeeding centuries was only part of the educational period of Israel's history (see *Tehillim* 106:27 [and Commentary below, 14:23]), and that even this period of Israel's education to its calling could begin only after the generation [that left Egypt] died out and a new generation grew up in its stead.

Consequently, the preceding verse 34 constitutes a parting of the ways, a true turning point in Jewish history. What is more, verse 34 is considered the end of a book, the following chapter 11 is considered the beginning of a new book, and the verses in between (vv. 35-36) are regarded as an important book unto itself: ספר חשוב הוא בפני עצמו. That is why these two verses are framed by סימניות מלמעלה ולמטה. Thus, not just five books were given to Moshe; rather, the number of the books of the Torah is really seven (*Shabbos* 115b and 116a).

Let us try to get at the meaning of these pivotal verses.

It says: בנסע הארן ויאמר משה קומה וגו׳ and ובנחה יאמר שובה וגו׳. When the Ark set out, Moshe called upon it to set out; and when the Ark came to rest, he called upon it to come to rest. Now, we know that the Ark neither set out nor came to rest at Moshe's behest. Yet Moshe called upon it to set out and to come to rest, as though what had already been done had yet to be done. Here we have an expression of man's total identification with the Will of God. One who reaches this level accepts God's Will as though it were his own. This is רבן גמליאל's principle: עשה רצונו כרצונך (*Avos* 2:4). Similarly, it says in the *Sifre* (here): ויאמר משה קומה ה׳, וכתוב אחד אומר על פי ה׳ יחנו וכו׳, משל למלך שאמר לעבדו הנראה שתעמידני בשביל שאני הולך ליתן ירושה לבני. Here, too, the implication is that Moshe's will was in perfect harmony with the Will of God.

But this exalted quality of selfless acquiescence in, and self-identification with, the Will of God is the very antithesis of the low state of mind in which Moshe's generation was still mired, as will be shown by the events about to be related. Moshe reached the pinnacle of total identification with the Will of God, but only in the end of days will this be a national characteristic of the entire Jewish people. The attainment of this quality is a prerequisite for the fulfillment of the vision of the end of days, to which Israel and its Torah are paving the way, whereas the lack of this quality led to a turning point in Israel's history. For this reason, the verses containing this statement by Moshe are an intermediate point and divider between two books of Jewish history.

It was regarding הארן, the Ark of the Torah, that Moshe made his statement; when the Ark would journey forth and when it would come to rest, Moshe would call to God Himself to arise or to return. Thus, the Torah's journeys were in his sight God's expeditions on earth. Where the Torah finds no home, there is no home for God's Presence; and where there is a dwelling place for the Torah, there is a dwelling place for God's Presence.

Moshe knew that אויבים and משנאים would be waiting for the Torah immediately upon its entry into the world. Its demands for justice and love stand in sharp opposition to the dictates of force and selfishness, whose curse is felt so keenly by the weak and needy. The people in power band together in order to ensure one another of the enforcement of their dictates. These are the Torah's enemies, אויבים, who tacitly conspire to form an all-encompassing barrier to the Torah, which seeks to dwell on earth.

And the Torah's demands for self-control and moral sanctification stand in sharp opposition to the allurements of vulgar sensuality. Hence, the individuals in the ignoble masses of all classes are not only the Torah's שונאים but its משנאים; the Torah is not only hated by them, it is persecuted by them. (שִׂנֵּא in the *pi'el* is indicative of hateful propaganda, which arouses hatred of the hated object.)

Nevertheless, Moshe knew that ultimately the Torah would prevail. Because the Torah's journeys are God's expeditions in society and in people's hearts, and because the Torah's enemies and haters are enemies and haters of God's kingdom on earth — that is precisely why Moshe made his statement. When the Ark of the Torah set out, he was confident that the Torah would complete its course on earth, and that when the Torah would intervene in the world, the coalition of enemies would disperse, and the hateful persecutors would take flight in panic. As it says in the *Sifre*: קומה ה׳ ויפוצו אויביך אלו המכונסים, וינוסו משנאיך אלו הרודפים, מפניך הם נסים ואין אנו כלום לפניהם וכו׳. (The contrast between מכונסים and רודפים derives from the contrast between ויפוצו and וינוסו.)

ובנחה: And when the Ark of the Torah came to its resting place, Moshe saw in his mind's eye not נָחוֹ but נְחָה. He envisioned that the day will come when the Torah will not stand in manly opposition (נחו, masculine) to human society; rather, with all its power, which will remain undiminished, the Torah will be מאורסה (נחה, feminine; see *Sifre* on *Devarim* 33:4), the "betrothed" of individual man and of mankind in general, and all men will become bearers of the Torah in all their endeavors, both individual and general. Then the day will come when the thousands of Israel will become myriads [see below]; and of that day, one of the last prophets, Moshe's successors, says: וְנִלְווּ גוֹיִם רַבִּים אֶל־ה׳ בַּיּוֹם הַהוּא וְהָיוּ לִי לְעָם וְשָׁכַנְתִּי בְתוֹכֵךְ (*Zecharyah* 2:15). Thus, when the Ark gently came to rest, Moshe said: "Return, O God, to the myriads of the thousands of Israel."

רבבות אלפי ישראל cannot mean "ten thousand times a thousand" or "twice ten thousand times a thousand"; for if that were the case, the smaller number would come first, אלפי רבבות, as in אחותנו את היי לאלפי רבבה (*Bereshis* 24:60). Besides, in Moshe's time, Israel numbered no more than 2.5 million souls, whereas the number רבבות אלפים is twenty million.

Hence, in our view, the meaning of רבבות אלפי ישראל is "the myriads of the thousands of Israel" — i.e., the myriads that will arise and develop from the thousands of Israel; for a thousand will become ten thousand, due to the great number of descendants and of those who will attach themselves to Israel. In any case, אלף is not just a precise number; rather, אלפי ישראל are the masses united in the framework of the nation and the tribes; cf. ראשי אלפי ישראל (above, 1:16 et al.), אַלְפִּי הַדַּל בִּמְנַשֶּׁה (*Shoftim* 6:15).

If our approach is not mistaken, these two verses capsulize the history of Israel and mankind, a history that began with Moshe's Divine mission. It is therefore fitting that these two verses form "an important book unto itself."

A commentary on these two verses is found, in our opinion, in *Tehillim* 68; for this psalm recounts the history of the triumph of God's kingdom, a triumph that will be achieved by virtue of Israel and by the power of the Torah. Even the words of this psalm indicate that it is

11 1 *But the people were as though in mourning over themselves; they were bad in the ears of* God. God *heard it, His anger was kindled, and* God's *fire broke out against them and devoured at one edge of the camp.*

יא א וַיְהִ֤י הָעָם֙ כְּמִתְאֹ֣נְנִ֔ים רַ֖ע בְּאׇזְנֵ֣י יְהֹוָ֑ה וַיִּשְׁמַ֤ע יְהֹוָה֙ וַיִּ֣חַר אַפּ֔וֹ וַתִּבְעַר־בָּם֙ אֵ֣שׁ יְהֹוָ֔ה וַתֹּ֖אכַל בִּקְצֵ֥ה הַֽמַּחֲנֶֽה׃

none other than an echo of our two verses. It is worth comparing verses 2 and 18, there, to the two verses here. Verse 18 there says: רֶכֶב אֱלֹקִים רִבֹּתַיִם אַלְפֵי שִׁנְאָן אֲדֹנָ-י בָם סִינַי בַּקֹּדֶשׁ. That is to say: Hitherto, two myriads of thousands of blessed heavenly beings were the bearers of God's glory; henceforth, God is among them and Sinai is in the Sanctuary (see Commentary, *Shemos* 27:8). The whole essence of this verse is none other than a paraphrased explanation of what is said here: שובה ה׳ רבבות אלפי ישראל. (Hitherto, רבתים אלפי שנאן were the bearers of God's glory; now chosen in their stead are רבבות אלפי ישראל. שנאן is the same as שאנן [an undisturbed rest, used here to denote the unchanged nature of heavenly beings — see Commentary, *Tehillim* 68:18]; cf. צונה and צאן, and see Commentary below, 32:24.) So, too, יָקוּם אֱלֹקִים יָפוּצוּ אוֹיְבָיו וגו׳ (*Tehillim* 68:2) is a direct repetition of what is said here: קומה ה׳ ויפצו איביך וגו׳.

CHAPTER 11

1 Moshe joyfully accepted God's guidance, and he was ready to follow Him through wilderness and wasteland, then and forevermore. With complete and selfless devotion, he merged his own will with God's Will, and thereby demonstrated the spirit and outlook on life which should have been common to all the members of the nation.

The people, however, were still far removed from such spiritual and moral perfection. The *people* — in contrast to Moshe — were כמתאננים! They were as though in mourning over themselves (see Commentary, *Bereshis* 35:18); they regarded themselves as though already dead, and, as it were, mourned over themselves. The cloud of God above them and the Ark of God's Covenant traveling before them made them feel cut off from the rest of the world, its manifestations, and its conditions of life. The unique bond with God, the presence of God's Sanctuary in

2 *And the people cried out to Moshe; Moshe prayed to* God, *and the fire died down.*

ב וַיִּצְעַק הָעָם אֶל־מֹשֶׁה וַיִּתְפַּלֵּל
מֹשֶׁה אֶל־יְהוָה וַתִּשְׁקַע הָאֵשׁ׃

3 *He named the place Tav'erah, because the fire of* God *had broken out against them.*

ג וַיִּקְרָא שֵׁם־הַמָּקוֹם הַהוּא
תַּבְעֵרָה כִּי־בָעֲרָה בָם אֵשׁ יְהוָה׃

4 *But the rabble whom they had taken up into their midst had worked themselves into a lust, and then the Children of Israel, too, began to weep again and said: Would that someone gave us meat to eat!*

ד וְהָאסַפְסֻף אֲשֶׁר בְּקִרְבּוֹ הִתְאַוּוּ
תַּאֲוָה וַיָּשֻׁבוּ וַיִּבְכּוּ גַּם בְּנֵי יִשְׂרָאֵל
וַיֹּאמְרוּ מִי יַאֲכִלֵנוּ בָּשָׂר׃

their midst, the Divine calling toward which they were headed — all this was of no value to them and did not seem to them to be adequate compensation. They did not feel that they had attained a loftier, happier mode of life; rather, they felt as though they had been placed in a coffin, and they mourned over themselves.

They were "bad": Far from God, they were at odds with the spirit appropriate to their Divine destiny. They were not רע בעיני ה'; they were רע באזני ה': They knew that God heard the voice in their hearts, and they directed this voice to Him; they complained that He had made their lives worthless and meaningless.

ותבער בם וגו': The destruction that threatened them reminded them of their existence and of the value of their existence. They had no right yet to mourn over themselves.

בקצה המחנה. The fire did not break out in the middle of the camp, nor in several places; rather, it began at one end of the camp and threatened to spread and destroy the entire camp.

2 **ותשקע האש**: The fire died down where it was burning and did not continue to spread.

4 **וְהָאסַפְסֻף**, like וְהָאֲסַפְסוּף, is the **ערב רב** that came with them when they left Egypt and which was absorbed in their midst. The doubling of the root

5 *We still remember the fish we used to eat in Egypt at no cost; the cucumbers and the melons, the leeks and the onions and the garlic.*	ה זָכַרְנוּ אֶת־הַדָּגָה אֲשֶׁר־נֹאכַל בְּמִצְרַיִם חִנָּם אֵת הַקִּשֻּׁאִים וְאֵת הָאֲבַטִּחִים וְאֶת־הֶחָצִיר וְאֶת־הַבְּצָלִים וְאֶת־הַשּׁוּמִים׃
6 *And now our soul is dried out, without anything; we have nothing except this manna before our eyes.*	ו וְעַתָּה נַפְשֵׁנוּ יְבֵשָׁה אֵין כֹּל בִּלְתִּי אֶל־הַמָּן עֵינֵינוּ׃

letters indicates that it was a repeated absorption, meaning that a multitude was absorbed. The quiescent **א** adds the nuance of meaning that the absorption was primarily external [the prefix **א** usually means internalizing; here, the **א** is not vocalized], and that those who were absorbed did not identify with the essence of the national union that absorbed them. It was a ספף more than an אסף. Israel was for them a סף, a "container," a "vessel," and a "threshold"; they lived in Israel's midst, but did not assimilate and did not integrate into its inner essence.

התאוו תאוה: This was not lust that was aroused in them without their intention by external circumstances; rather, willingly and indulgently they fanned the flame of lust.

וישבו ויבכו וגו׳. התאונן of verse 1 is also indicative of inner weeping. Hence, it is appropriate to say here: וישבו ויבכו, "they started weeping again."

If our interpretation of **רבבות אלפי ישראל** (above, 10:36) is correct, then there is a sharp contrast between the incitement of the people by **האספסוף אשר בקרבו** and Israel's destiny as expressed there. Israel, the smallest of all peoples, is destined to be the spiritual and moral nucleus to which the nations returning to God will attach themselves, yet here Israel itself falls under the destructive influence of an alien minority staying in its midst!

5 **את הקשאים וגו׳**. We translated these names in accordance with the conventional interpretation, but we have no etymological substantiation to justify this interpretation.

6 **נפשנו יבשה** — cf. יָבֵשׁ כַּחֶרֶשׂ כֹּחִי (*Tehillim* 22:16).

We do not lack nutrition. (The vegetables they mentioned in the

7 *And yet the manna was like the seed of* gad, *and its luster was as the appearance of crystal!*	ז וְהַמָּן כִּזְרַע־גַּד הוּא וְעֵינוֹ כְּעֵין הַבְּדֹלַח׃
8 *The people roamed about and gathered [it], and they ground it in mills and crushed it in mortars; they cooked it in a pot or made it into cakes, and its taste was like that of an oil-cake.*	ח שָׁטוּ הָעָם וְלָקְטוּ וְטָחֲנוּ בָרֵחַיִם אוֹ דָכוּ בַּמְּדֹכָה וּבִשְּׁלוּ בַּפָּרוּר וְעָשׂוּ אֹתוֹ עֻגוֹת וְהָיָה טַעְמוֹ כְּטַעַם לְשַׁד הַשָּׁמֶן׃

previous verse are of no special nutritional value.) What we lack are stimulating foods that excite the appetite. To remain in good health, one must occasionally vary one's diet.

בלתי אל המן עינינו: To always eat the same kind of food is unbearable.

7-8 **והמן וגו׳**. Against this apparently justified complaint, Scripture describes the manna's special qualities, which demonstrate the baselessness of this complaint.

The manna was כזרע גד וגו׳, it was appealing to the eye. כזרע גד (see *Shemos* 16:31) — according to *Yoma* 75a: עגול כגידא ולבן כמרגלית, round and pearl white.

ועינו כעין הבדלח: An object's color makes a certain impression on the eye, and this impression is called "עין." If we compare the other places where עין occurs in this sense, we find that the subject there is always a shiny object. Thus: כְּעֵין הַקֶּרַח הַנּוֹרָא, כְּעֵין תַּרְשִׁישׁ, כְּעֵין נְחֹשֶׁת קָלָל (*Yechezkel* 1 and 10). Since בדלח, according to רש״י, is crystal, Scripture here is apparently describing its transparency (see Commentary, *Shemos* 16:14).

שטו העם: The manna did not come to them without any effort on their part but, rather, as a result of activity, and the term "שטו" indicates that this activity was not monotonous: they roamed in various directions in order to obtain the manna, and this provided mental stimulation.

וטחנו ברחים וגו׳: They ground it fine or pounded it into coarse flakes; they ate it cooked or baked. The various ways of preparing the manna for consumption ensured that it was not lacking in variety.

9 *When the dew fell upon the camp during the night, the manna fell upon it.*	ט וּבְרֶדֶת הַטַּל עַל־הַמַּחֲנֶה לָיְלָה יֵרֵד הַמָּן עָלָיו׃
10 *Moshe heard the people weeping within their families, each one at the entrance of his tent. God's wrath was kindled greatly, and in Moshe's eyes it was bad.*	י וַיִּשְׁמַע מֹשֶׁה אֶת־הָעָם בֹּכֶה לְמִשְׁפְּחֹתָיו אִישׁ לְפֶתַח אָהֳלוֹ וַיִּחַר־אַף יְהוָה מְאֹד וּבְעֵינֵי מֹשֶׁה רָע׃

לשד occurs elsewhere only in *Tehillim* 32:4, נֶהְפַּךְ לְשַׁדִּי, where it denotes moisture and bodily fluids. Accordingly, here, too, לשד would denote the richness of oil, the moisture of oil.

In *Shemos* 16:31 the taste of the manna is described as כצפיחת בדבש (see Commentary there). Here it does not say וטעמו וגו׳ but והיה טעמו וגו׳, and the רשב״ם explains that this was the taste of manna after it was cooked or baked, whereas there Scripture describes the taste of manna eaten raw.

9 **וברדת הטל וגו׳** — see Commentary, *Shemos* 16:13-14. In addition to all this, the manner in which the manna fell showed the special care with which it was given. Thus, each day it lay there as מן, as a gift of God granted especially to them. This fact should have made the manna sweet to people of even lesser intelligence.

10 **למשפחתיו**: It was not an open rebellion; they did not gather in groups against Moshe; rather, they wept and complained among their families. Everyone remained in his own home. But they stood at the entrances of their tents and wailed, and the wailing and complaining were heard everywhere.

ובעיני משה רע. To Moshe, this attested to the failure of his mission. He was to have won the people's hearts to the supreme ideal of moral and spiritual perfection — and here the people were wailing about the lack of leeks and onions!

11 *And Moshe said to* God*: For what purpose have You ordered such evil for Your servant, and why have I not found favor in Your eyes — to place the burden of this entire people upon me?*	יא וַיֹּאמֶר מֹשֶׁה אֶל־יְהוָה לָמָה הֲרֵעֹתָ לְעַבְדֶּךָ וְלָמָּה לֹא־מָצָתִי חֵן בְּעֵינֶיךָ לָשׂוּם אֶת־מַשָּׂא כָּל־הָעָם הַזֶּה עָלָי׃ חסר א׳
12 *Have I been pregnant with this en-*	יב הֶאָנֹכִי הָרִיתִי אֵת כָּל־הָעָם הַזֶּה

11 **למה הרעת**. From the very outset I considered myself unfit for this mission. Now it has brought disaster upon me. I would gladly bear it if I could see some benefit resulting from it for others. But through my ineptitude the people will perish, and so all my suffering is without purpose.

ולמה לא מצתי וגו': מצתי is written without an א, suggesting מצה, which means: to suck, to drink avidly to the very last drop (cf. *Tehillim* 73:10, 75:9, et al.). I insistently pleaded with You not to entrust me with this lofty mission because I did not consider myself capable of carrying it out. Should not my own misgivings about my talents have been sufficient reason for You to grant my request? Is not self-confidence the very first prerequisite for the mission of leading a nation, and was not, therefore, my lack of confidence in my own ability sufficient proof that I am truly not qualified for this task? Why, then, did You refuse my request?

ולמה לא מצתי חן בעיניך can be interpreted as a parenthesis, in which case לשום וגו' is the continuation of למה הרעת וגו'. Alternatively, perhaps this is the meaning of למה לא מצתי וגו': "Why have I found so little favor in Your eyes that You have placed the burden of this entire people upon me?" Or perhaps לשום וגו' is an independent elliptical sentence: "To lay the burden of this entire nation on me!" That is to say: "Who could understood that!" (See also Commentary, *Shemos* 32:11.)

12 **האנכי הריתי**: Am I its mother? אם אנכי ילדתיהו: or am I its father? (Cf. *Bereshis* 4:18; 10:8ff.) If a father and mother are not adequate to the task of educating their children, it is a misfortune for the parents as well as for the children. But such a case is something natural that goes

tire people, or have I begotten them, that You should say to me: Carry them in your bosom as a nurse carries the suckling infant, up to the land that You have sworn to their ancestors?

אִם־אָנֹכִי יְלִדְתִּיהוּ כִּי־תֹאמַר
אֵלַי שָׂאֵהוּ בְחֵיקֶךָ כַּאֲשֶׁר יִשָּׂא
הָאֹמֵן אֶת־הַיֹּנֵק עַל הָאֲדָמָה
אֲשֶׁר נִשְׁבַּעְתָּ לַאֲבֹתָיו׃

13 *From where should I have meat to give to this entire people? For they weep to me and say: Please give us meat so that we may eat.*

מֵאַיִן לִי בָּשָׂר לָתֵת לְכָל־הָעָם יג
הַזֶּה כִּי־יִבְכּוּ עָלַי לֵאמֹר תְּנָה־לָּנוּ
בָשָׂר וְנֹאכֵלָה׃

with the birth of children; it is but one of the life situations into which, and for which, people are born, and it is the totality of these situations that creates the diversity of roles to be fulfilled by every person. Moreover, from the beginning, the bond between parent and child engenders in the child a natural love, respect, and trust for his parents, which makes the parents' task of educating him considerably easier. I, however, am not the natural educator of this people. You *chose* me to be their educator, and, alas, You chose Yourself a man who has neither the eloquence, nor the imposing personality, nor any of the other skills needed to influence and win the respect of a whole nation.

13 **מאין לי בשר וגו׳**. They know very well that it is beyond my power to fulfill their request. Moreover, what they are demanding from me is something dispensable and superfluous, for they already have sufficient and satisfying food in the manna. Their demand, then, has no other purpose but to torment the man whom they regard as the guide of their fate. Had he been a proper leader, he would long ago have won their love and respect, which would never have allowed such vexatious desires to arise.

Precisely because the demand was for something dispensable and superfluous, neither Moshe nor the people could expect that God would do their will in a miraculous manner.

14 *I alone am not able to carry this entire people, for it is too heavy for me.*	יד לֹא־אוּכַ֤ל אָנֹכִי֙ לְבַדִּ֔י לָשֵׂ֖את אֶת־כָּל־הָעָ֣ם הַזֶּ֑ה כִּ֥י כָבֵ֖ד מִמֶּֽנִּי׃
15 *And if You will deal with me in this manner, withdrawing from me, then let me die at once, if I have found favor in Your eyes, and do not let me see my misfortune.*	טו וְאִם־כָּ֣כָה׀ אַתְּ־עֹ֣שֶׂה לִּ֗י הָרְגֵ֤נִי נָא֙ הָרֹ֔ג אִם־מָצָ֥אתִי חֵ֖ן בְּעֵינֶ֑יךָ וְאַל־אֶרְאֶ֖ה בְּרָעָתִֽי׃ פ

14 **לא אוכל וגו׳**. I cannot carry out by myself the task You have assigned to me. I lack not only the required ability to influence others, but also the skill to acquire this ability. I am only half the right man for this task. I can receive Your Torah, and I can teach Your Torah, but I am not capable of training for You a people for this Torah. The people's hearts are not under my control, and I cannot exercise over them the educative and formative mastery that will lead to this goal (cf. *Shemos* 3:11 and Commentary there).

15 **ואם ככה את וגו׳**. The feminine form את alludes to weakness, and what is implied by its use here is the following: If You leave me in my weakness, of which I am well aware, and if You do not help me with Your power, which can transform a weak person into a strong one -- this help is apparently hinted at by the expression אנכי לבדי of the previous verse — I prefer to die before my time, so that I do not live to see my misfortune, i.e., the complete failure of my mission, when the people degenerates completely.

Similarly, at the very outset of his mission (*Shemos* 4:10), Moshe expected that God would equip him with the necessary power and force of eloquence, immediately upon assigning him the mission. And when the Divine help did not materialize — גם מאז דברך אל עבדך — he saw this as further proof of his unworthiness for his mission. It did not occur to him, however, that precisely this constant weakness of his, combined with the extreme modesty of his character, would be the everlasting proof of the Divine nature of his mission (cf. Commentary, *Shemos* 4:13).

Perhaps this is also the meaning of the interpretation by our Sages

16 *And* God *said to Moshe: Gather for Me seventy men from among the elders of Israel [of] whom you know that they are the elders of the people and its overseers, and take them to the Tent of Appointed Meeting and have them stand there with you.*	טז וַיֹּאמֶר יְהֹוָה אֶל־מֹשֶׁה אֶסְפָה־לִּי שִׁבְעִים אִישׁ מִזִּקְנֵי יִשְׂרָאֵל אֲשֶׁר יָדַעְתָּ כִּי־הֵם זִקְנֵי הָעָם וְשֹׁטְרָיו וְלָקַחְתָּ אֹתָם אֶל־אֹהֶל מוֹעֵד וְהִתְיַצְּבוּ שָׁם עִמָּךְ׃

here (see רש״י): תשש כחו של משה כנקבה; Moshe expressed his own weakness through the weakness of the Divine assistance: If God does not exert His saving power, Moshe cannot be a powerful man.

16 **אספה לי שבעים איש**. We find in later periods that prophets and people endowed with the holy spirit appeared in Israel's midst even in times of spiritual decline. This attests to the preservation of a large circle of spiritually and morally pure families, from whose midst such men could have emerged.

Here, too, Moshe is ordered to choose seventy men who will be worthy of receiving the holy spirit and of being appointed among those who do His bidding; yet at this time the *people* do not appear in a positive light. From this we may infer that knowledge of God and devotion to God were deeply rooted in a large circle of the noblest among the people; the masses, however, still needed to be educated to this level.

מזקני ישראל. From the dawn of its history as a nation, Israel had זקנים, "elders," who occupied a position of prominence and authority among the people (see *Shemos* 3:16, 4:29, and Commentary there; *Vayikra* 9:1). Moreover, they already served in an active capacity: they were שוטריו, the overseers who monitored the people's life of duty. As a result of the natural trust that the people placed in them, the elders had considerable influence over the community. Thus, they had a parental relationship to the people; and since Moshe complained that he lacked this relationship (v. 12), he was instructed to choose seventy of these elders, so that they should collaborate with him in the education of the people. This task was to be conferred upon them publicly by God.

17 *I will descend and will speak with you there, and will keep back [part] of the spirit that has come upon you and put it upon them. They will then bear the burden of the people with you, and you will not have to bear it alone.*	יז וְיָרַדְתִּ֗י וְדִבַּרְתִּ֣י עִמְּךָ֮ שָׁם֒ וְאָצַלְתִּ֗י מִן־הָר֛וּחַ אֲשֶׁ֥ר עָלֶ֖יךָ וְשַׂמְתִּ֣י עֲלֵיהֶ֑ם וְנָשְׂא֤וּ אִתְּךָ֙ בְּמַשָּׂ֣א הָעָ֔ם וְלֹא־תִשָּׂ֥א אַתָּ֖ה לְבַדֶּֽךָ׃

אספה לי. It does not say אספה in general; nor does it say אספה לך — to satisfy a need that you personally feel. Rather, it says אספה לי: With these elders a permanent institution shall be founded, in order to realize an eternal purpose of Mine.

Thus the Sanhedrin was founded. It consists of seventy members besides a presiding elder, just as here it consists of Moshe and the seventy elders. They must always regard themselves as merely assistants to Moshe, and their job is to see to it that the task transmitted by Moshe is accomplished by the nation.

17 **וירדתי ודברתי עמך שם ואצלתי**. The basic meaning of אצל is: something that is left free from something else, not taken up by it. Hence the spacial term אֵצֶל, "next to," where the space occupied by something comes to an end. Hence also אצילי ידים, where the arms border on the body, the armpit. By extension, this term also denotes the places that remain outside a sphere or province (*Yeshayahu* 41:9), or people who are separated from others (*Shemos* 24:11; see Commentary there).

Let us now compare the places where אצל appears as a verb: הלא אצלת לי ברכה (*Bereshis* 27:36), לֹא אָצַלְתִּי מֵהֶם (*Koheles* 2:10). In both these cases, the meaning of אצל is not "to remove something from someone's possession, to take from someone something already in his possession," but, rather, "to deny someone something, to prevent something from coming into his possession, to hold back part of the things due him (to keep them next to him, אצלו, outside him)." Hence, presumably here too, ואצלתי וגו׳ does not mean: I will take part of the spirit that is on you and put it on them; rather, it means: When the spirit comes over you (when I speak with you), I will hold back part of it and put it on them. When I speak with you, the spirit that otherwise comes to rest on you alone shall rest also on them. Thereby they will become spiritual partners of your personality and will join you in a close spiritual bond.

מן הרוח אשר עליך. In its terminology, Scripture clearly distinguishes between the conferral of the prophetic spirit and every other conferral of spirit by God. The spirit of God was *in* Yosef (*Bereshis* 41:38). God *filled* Betzalel with the spirit of God (*Shemos* 31:3, 35:31). Yehoshua was *filled* with the spirit of wisdom (*Devarim* 34:9). God sent Moshe to put His holy spirit *in the midst* of the people (*Yeshayahu* 63:11). Yechezkel relates that a spirit came *into* him and stood him on his feet (*Yechezkel* 2:2; 3:24). Regarding the spirit of God that emboldened Gideon (*Shoftim* 6:34), the spirit of God that gave Zecharyah the courage to admonish the people for forsaking God (*Divrei Ha-Yamim* II, 24:20), and the spirit that encouraged Amasai to bless David with peace (ibid. I, 12:19), Scripture says that the spirit *clothed* (לבשה) the man. In all these verses, the common denominator is that the spirit was given to the person in order to increase and to exalt his *inner* spiritual state. What the person did as a result of this special inspiration did not transcend human capability. The words and deeds remained human, only that they were borne and elevated by a special capability given by God.

By contrast, the *prophetic* spirit is *not* an *inner* process. It comes *upon* a person, over him, rests *on* him. Thus the prophetic spirit that came or will come over Sha'ul (*Shemuel* I, 10:6 and 10), over his messengers (ibid. 19:20), over Azaryah (*Divrei Ha-Yamim* II, 15:1), over Yechezkel (*Yechezkel* 11:5), over Yeshayahu (*Yeshayahu* 61:1), over God's servant (ibid. 42:1), over Israel (ibid. 44:3 and 59:21), over all mankind (*Yo'el* 3:1). Prophecy is a power of God, a hand of God, יד ה׳, which comes *over* a person (*Yechezkel* 1:3, 3:22, 37:1). It is *God's Word*, of which a man becomes the bearer, conveyer, and herald. It comes to him from *without*, from above, and raises him above the normal human level. Through prophecy, the human element in man becomes a step for the Divine on earth. What is said and done by man is God's Word and God's deed; the man is merely its conveyer and agent. Also of Shimshon's feats of strength it says that God's spirit came *over* him (*Shoftim* 14:6 and 19; 15:14), to teach us that these were supernatural, superhuman acts.

18 *And to the people you shall say: Hold yourselves in readiness for tomorrow, and you shall eat meat, for you have wept before the ears of* God *and said: Would that someone give us meat to eat! For we were better off in Egypt. Therefore* God *will give you meat to eat.*

יח וְאֶל־הָעָם תֹּאמַר הִתְקַדְּשׁוּ
לְמָחָר וַאֲכַלְתֶּם בָּשָׂר כִּי בְּכִיתֶם
בְּאָזְנֵי יְהוָה לֵאמֹר מִי יַאֲכִלֵנוּ
בָּשָׂר כִּי־טוֹב לָנוּ בְּמִצְרָיִם וְנָתַן
יְהוָה לָכֶם בָּשָׂר וַאֲכַלְתֶּם:

19 *You shall have [meat] to eat not for one day and not for two days, not for five days and not for ten days and not for twenty days;*

יט לֹא יוֹם אֶחָד תֹּאכְלוּן וְלֹא יוֹמָיִם
וְלֹא | חֲמִשָּׁה יָמִים וְלֹא עֲשָׂרָה
יָמִים וְלֹא עֶשְׂרִים יוֹם:

18 **התקדשו וגו'**. We have already noted several times (see Commentary, *Bereshis* 2:3 et al.) that the basic meaning of קדש is to be absolutely ready for some purpose. This meaning is rather general; hence קָדֵשׁ (*Devarim* 23:18; see Commentary there) can also denote giving oneself up completely to gross sensual degeneration. Thus, התקדשו here can also be taken in a general sense: "Be ready."

Nevertheless, since everywhere else in Scripture התקדש always denotes preparing oneself for a serious moment, that could be the meaning of the term here as well, and its underlying idea would be as follows:

When we get to enjoy a treasure that was long withheld from us and that was finally granted to us only after we implored God excessively, such a time is always a time for introspection. It was not for lack of power or for lack of goodwill that God denied us this treasure; He denied it from us for our own good. And if finally He grants our request — after we have implored Him inappropriately — we should carefully consider whether today's granting will prove more beneficial for us than yesterday's denial. So, too רש"י: הזמינו עצמכם לפורענות.

19-20 **לא יום וגו'**. You will have meat in such quantity that you will not only satisfy your momentary craving, but you will be able to eat of it for a whole month, until you are sick of it. **יצא מאפכם** is a hyperbolic expression, to describe the abundance. You will be so full of meat that it will seek all possible means of egress.

כ עַד ׀ חֹדֶשׁ יָמִים עַד אֲשֶׁר־יֵצֵא מֵאַפְּכֶם וְהָיָה לָכֶם לְזָרָא יַעַן כִּי־מְאַסְתֶּם אֶת־יְהוָה אֲשֶׁר בְּקִרְבְּכֶם וַתִּבְכּוּ לְפָנָיו לֵאמֹר לָמָּה זֶּה יָצָאנוּ מִמִּצְרָיִם׃

20 *For a full month [you will eat meat], until it comes out of your nostrils and will make you nauseated. This is because you have rejected* God *Who dwells in your midst, and have wept before Him, saying: Why did we ever go out from Egypt?*

כא וַיֹּאמֶר מֹשֶׁה שֵׁשׁ־מֵאוֹת אֶלֶף רַגְלִי הָעָם אֲשֶׁר אָנֹכִי בְּקִרְבּוֹ וְאַתָּה אָמַרְתָּ בָּשָׂר אֶתֵּן לָהֶם וְאָכְלוּ חֹדֶשׁ יָמִים׃

21 *Then Moshe said: The people in whose midst I am are six hundred thousand men on foot, and You say I shall give them meat so that they may have to eat for a whole month!*

כב הֲצֹאן וּבָקָר יִשָּׁחֵט לָהֶם וּמָצָא לָהֶם אִם אֶת־כָּל־דְּגֵי הַיָּם יֵאָסֵף לָהֶם וּמָצָא לָהֶם׃ פ

22 *Shall sheep and cattle be slaughtered for them so that it may be enough for them, or shall all the fish of the sea be gathered so that it may be enough for them?*

לזרא. זרה means: to throw and cast away; cf. תִּזְרֵם כְּמוֹ דָוָה צֵא תֹּאמַר לוֹ (*Yeshayahu* 30:22). Hence, it is not far-fetched to say that זרא means "to vomit."

יען כי מאסתם את ה׳ אשר בקרבכם. In your detachment from the world, you merited to attain an intimate spiritual relationship with God. This relationship more than compensates you for any deprivations you may be suffering, as you claim. You, however, did not value this relationship. You wept לפניו: The sight of His Presence did not remind you of the attainment you merited; rather, you weepingly asked: למה זה יצאנו ממצרים — i.e., we see nothing in our present circumstances that could justify our exodus from Egypt.

21-22 **ויאמר משה וגו׳**. Moshe's complaint (vv. 11-15) expressed the urgency of the hour, but in His response (vv. 16-20) God mentioned only the appointment of the elders, to which He then attached the message for

23 *And* God *said to Moshe: Will the hand of* God *not suffice? You shall see at once whether My word will come to pass for you or not.*

כג וַיֹּאמֶר יְהוָה אֶל־מֹשֶׁה הֲיַד יְהוָה תִּקְצָר עַתָּה תִרְאֶה הֲיִקְרְךָ דְבָרִי אִם־לֹא׃

the people that they would receive satisfaction the next day. Moshe could have inferred from this that the appointment of the elders was itself the means for meeting the people's needs, and that he, with the help of his new associates, was to attend to the feeding of the people. He could have assumed that providing for the people would be the first task in which the seventy elders would collaborate with him. For the immediate urgency was to meet the people's needs, whereas the assistance that Moshe requested to compensate for his deficiency (v. 14) was a matter for the future. If this assistance had no connection with satisfying the immediate needs, then providing for the people should have preceded the appointment of the elders.

Thus, Moshe could have assumed that he and the elders were expected to feed the people by natural means. Hence his amazed question: *שש מאות וגו׳!*

ואתה אמרת בשר אתן וגו׳ is not a direct quotation of God's Word, but a report of its implication: You said *that* I should give them meat. Similar is אֱלֹקִים דִּבֶּר בְּקָדְשׁוֹ אֶעְלֹזָה אֲחַלְּקָה שְׁכֶם, "God has spoken in His Sanctuary that I will exult, I will divide Shechem" (*Tehillim* 60:8).

הצאן וגו׳. צאן and בקר require שחיטה, whereas for fish אסיפה suffices (see *Chullin* 27b).

23 **היד ה׳ תקצר.** Here it does not say היפלא מה׳ דבר, as it does in *Bereshis* 18:14, for Moshe correctly recognized that here they could not expect a miracle from God's strong hand. Had it been a question of a miracle, Moshe would not have doubted its success. He thought, however, that he was supposed to act within the framework of the natural possibilities available to him, and therefore he asked for an explanation. God's reply to him was that He has the power to carry out His Word even within the framework of natural possibilities.

היקרך (see Commentary, *Bereshis* 24:12): Although My Word is beyond all your calculations, it will come "toward you." The term "יקרך"

aptly describes the nature of the coming event: It is an event that is beyond all human reckoning, yet it will occur by natural causes, which are directed solely by God toward the accomplishment of His purpose.

We have noted that the appointment of the seventy elders to assist Moshe in leading the nation constituted the basis for the future Sanhedrin (*Sanhedrin* 2a and 16b), which, through all future generations, would lead the people and ensure the fulfillment of God's Word in times of changing ways of God's providence. The elders would be messengers of God's Word long after Moshe had died, when there would be no more revealed miracles to fulfill God's Word.

In light of the foregoing, it appears that there is a close relationship between the appointment of these elders and the nature of the event that follows it. For this was an event that even Moshe could not foresee, and it occurred within the framework of natural conditions directed solely by God toward the fulfillment of His purposes. The foregoing also explains why the appointment of the elders preceded the event, when, in fact, the event was intended only to satisfy an immediate, temporary need. For, in years to come, whenever circumstances do not seem to favor the realization of God's Word, and the battle of Israel's future זקנים for the fulfillment of God's Word does not seem — by human reckoning — to stand a chance, they will be able to look back for moral support upon that initial moment, upon the events surrounding the appointment of the very first זקנים of the Jewish people. Those events should always serve to reassure these men that, as long as the message they represent and convey is truly the Word of God, they can trust in His hidden providence. It is not necessary for God to tear open the heavens or to make the sun stand still, for He will realize His Word even within the framework of natural causality. Even if it is beyond the purview of shortsighted man, and he cannot foresee it, God will orchestrate circumstances in such a way that His Word will be realized by them. The very first event in which they were asked to participate gave our זקנים a firm foundation of confidence for all their future activity.

24 **ויצא משה וגו'**. Moshe spoke with God in private, perhaps in the אהל משה, and from there he went out into the public sphere of the people.

דִּבְרֵ֣י יְהֹוָ֑ה וַיֶּאֱסֹ֞ף שִׁבְעִ֥ים אִישׁ֙
מִזִּקְנֵ֣י הָעָ֔ם וַיַּעֲמֵ֥ד אֹתָ֖ם סְבִיבֹ֥ת
הָאֹֽהֶל׃

of God *to the people. He then gathered seventy men from among the elders of the people and had them stand round about the Tent.*

כה וַיֵּ֨רֶד יְהֹוָ֥ה ׀ בֶּעָנָן֮ וַיְדַבֵּ֣ר אֵלָיו֒
וַיָּ֗אצֶל מִן־הָר֙וּחַ֙ אֲשֶׁ֣ר עָלָ֔יו וַיִּתֵּ֕ן
עַל־שִׁבְעִ֥ים אִ֖ישׁ הַזְּקֵנִ֑ים וַיְהִ֗י
כְּנ֤וֹחַ עֲלֵיהֶם֙ הָר֔וּחַ וַיִּֽתְנַבְּא֖וּ וְלֹ֥א
יָסָֽפוּ׃

25 *And* God *descended in the cloud and spoke with him, and He held back some of the spirit that came upon him and placed a shadow of it upon the seventy men [who had been] appointed as elders. And it came to pass that when the spirit had come to rest upon them, they prophesied, and never did so again.*

He stood in the people's midst and transmitted to them the words of God (vv. 18-20), which could bring every thoughtful person in the nation to his senses.

25 **וירד וגו׳ וידבר אליו**. Scripture does not tell us what it was that God said to Moshe. Is this omission perhaps intended to make clear to all future Sanhedrins that not everything God said to Moshe is recorded in the Written Law? Is it to indicate to them that the basis of the activity for which they were just appointed is the Oral Law, the תורה שבעל פה?

וַיָּאצֶל is an unusual form. If Scripture's intention had been the *kal* of the root אצל, it would say ויאצל. The form וַיָּצֶל indicated by the vowelization that we have before us is the *hif'il* of צול, which is the root of מצולה, and which is related to צלל, which signifies dark depths. Perhaps the intention in using this form is to indicate the disparity between the spirit imparted to the elders and the spirit bestowed upon Moshe. Only a shadow of Moshe's spirit reached the elders.

ויתנבאו. For a discussion of the root נבא, see our Commentary on *Bereshis* 20:7. נבא is related to נבע, for נבואה (prophecy) emanates from the Source of life like water gushing from a spring. Hence הִנָּבֵא, in the passive, means: to be made into a vessel through which God's Word flows out to man; to be an instrument of God's Word.

26 *But two men remained behind in the camp; the name of the one [was] Eldad and the name of the second, Meidad; the spirit rested upon them. They were among those who had been registered, but they had not gone out to the Tent. They prophesied in the camp.*

כו וַיִּשָּׁאֲרוּ שְׁנֵי־אֲנָשִׁים ׀ בַּמַּחֲנֶה שֵׁם הָאֶחָד ׀ אֶלְדָּד וְשֵׁם הַשֵּׁנִי מֵידָד וַתָּנַח עֲלֵהֶם הָרוּחַ וְהֵמָּה בַּכְּתֻבִים וְלֹא יָצְאוּ הָאֹהֱלָה וַיִּתְנַבְּאוּ בַּמַּחֲנֶה׃

27 *And the lad ran and reported it to Moshe and said: Eldad and Meidad are prophesying in the camp.*

כז וַיָּרָץ הַנַּעַר וַיַּגֵּד לְמֹשֶׁה וַיֹּאמַר אֶלְדָּד וּמֵידָד מִתְנַבְּאִים בַּמַּחֲנֶה׃

הִתְנַבֵּא, then, means: to present oneself to be an overflowing vessel — i.e., to prepare oneself to be an instrument of God's Word. In the overwhelming majority of cases, the התפעל form denotes a low level of prophecy, a preliminary stage of prophecy or an isolated instance of it (cf. *Shemuel* I, 10:5-6, 10 and 19:23-24). Hence also the denotation: to make oneself an instrument of a spirit that is not God's spirit but a false vision, a deceit of one's own contriving; to bring upon oneself an evil spirit (cf. *Yirmeyahu* 14:14; *Melachim* I, 22:10 and 18:29; *Shemuel* I, 18:10). Genuine prophecy that comes regularly is always mentioned in the נפעל form: הנבא.

ולא יספו: and never did so again. Only at this moment of their appointment were they privileged with participating in the spirit that rested upon Moshe, and this participation attested to their calling: Henceforth, they were to work together with Moshe in complete accord. They were to regard every word addressed by God to Moshe as addressed to them also, and their task would be to see that it is carried out.

26-27 **וישארו וגו׳**. Seventy elders were gathered by Moshe, and they stood around the Tent. Verse 26 implies that also Eldad and Meidad were summoned to go out to the Tent; they, too, were included in the list drawn up by Moshe for that purpose (בכתבים). But since only seventy could be elected, our assumption is that Moshe summoned seventy-two — six from each tribe, so as not to sow envy among the tribes — and

28 *And Yehoshua, son of Nun, the attendant of Moshe from his youth, replied and said: My lord Moshe, restrain them.*

29 *And Moshe said to him: Are you jealous for my sake? Would that all of* God's *people were prophets, so that* God *would place His spirit upon them.*

כח וַיַּעַן יְהוֹשֻׁעַ בִּן־נוּן מְשָׁרֵת מֹשֶׁה מִבְּחֻרָיו וַיֹּאמַר אֲדֹנִי מֹשֶׁה כְּלָאֵם׃

כט וַיֹּאמֶר לוֹ מֹשֶׁה הַמְקַנֵּא אַתָּה לִי וּמִי יִתֵּן כָּל־עַם יְהוָה נְבִיאִים כִּי־יִתֵּן יְהוָה אֶת־רוּחוֹ עֲלֵיהֶם׃ שביעי

left it to God to decide which two would not be elected. However, Eldad and Meidad decided on their own to remain behind in the camp. Out of modesty they thought that, among the whole group, they were the least worthy, and precisely because of this modesty the prophetic spirit rested upon them, even though they remained in the camp among the people. This is in accordance with one opinion in *Sanhedrin* 17a. According to another opinion (there), Moshe cast lots for the seventy-two elders, and Eldad and Meidad were the two who were eliminated by the lottery.

28 **מבחריו**. בְּחוּרִים, following the pattern of נְעוּרִים (in *Koheles* 11:9 and 12:1 we find the form בְּחוּרוֹת), means: the time of youth.

אדני משה כלאם. Yehoshua thought that Eldad and Meidad were undermining Moshe's authority and infringing upon his rights. The seventy elders received their share of prophecy only as participants with Moshe, whereas Eldad and Meidad appeared as independent chosen ones.

29 **המקנא אתה לי**. Do you feel that you must champion my cause and defend my rights? Do you think that Eldad and Meidad have infringed on my rights and that you must stand up for my rights? (See Commentary above, 5:14.)

The appearance of Eldad and Meidad at the appointment of the elders to the first Sanhedrin and Moshe's remarks at that time are of profound significance for all their successors. For we are shown here that the appointment of the supreme spiritual authority in Israel is not intended to establish a spiritual monopoly. Spiritual aptitude granted by God is not dependent on any special office or vocation. The humblest in the nation may be deemed just as worthy of a portion of God's spirit as the foremost holder of the most exalted office.

At the same time, Moshe's reply to Yehoshua serves as an eternal example whose purpose is to show all teachers and leaders in Israel that the supreme ideal of their endeavors will be realized when they render their own services superfluous, when all classes of the people attain such a spiritual level that they no longer require teachers and leaders! Indeed, the successors of these elders have been true heirs of the spirit of Moshe their master: They have understood that their supreme task is להרביץ תורה בישראל, to make the knowledge of God's Law the foundation of Israel's life, and they have transmitted to all the spiritual leaders of their people a major principle: והעמידו תלמידים הרבה (*Avos* 1:1). When Moshe said "המקנא אתה לי?!," he eliminated the basis for any possible division between sacred clergy and profane laity.

In *Sanhedrin* 17a, various opinions are given as to the content of the prophecy of Eldad and Meidad. According to one opinion, it concerned the coming event of the quails. Another opinion presents the content of their prophecy in these words: משה מת יהושע מכניס את ישראל לארץ. A third opinion says: על עסקי גוג ומגוג היו מתנבאין. The war of Gog and Magog is described in *Yechezkel* and in *Zecharyah* as the final development of the history of the ages, and of this it says in *Yechezkel* (38:17): הַאַתָּה־הוּא אֲשֶׁר־דִּבַּרְתִּי בְּיָמִים קַדְמוֹנִים בְּיַד עֲבָדַי נְבִיאֵי יִשְׂרָאֵל הַנִּבְּאִים בַּיָּמִים הָהֵם שָׁנִים, לְהָבִיא אֹתְךָ עֲלֵיהֶם, "Are you the one I spoke of in the days of yore, through My servants the prophets of Israel, who prophesied in those days that in years to come I would bring you against them?" According to this third opinion, Eldad and Meidad are the men who prophesied in days of yore about the end of days.

Elsewhere (see Commentary below, 29:13) we develop the idea that Gog and Magog represent the גוג principle, the "roof-principle," of concentrating all leadership at the topmost summit of the nation. This principle will be defeated in the end of days, and the city of the opposing principle of democracy will be called "הֲמוֹנָה," the "City of the Masses" (*Yechezkel* 39:16).

If there is any truth in this idea, it can explain the meaning of the prophecy of Eldad and Meidad. They heralded the ultimate victory of the principle of democracy over that of Gog and Magog; or they foresaw

30 *And Moshe withdrew into the camp, he and the elders of Israel.*

ל וַיֵּאָסֵ֥ף מֹשֶׁ֖ה אֶל־הַֽמַּחֲנֶ֑ה ה֖וּא וְזִקְנֵ֥י יִשְׂרָאֵֽל׃

31 *But a wind went forth from* God *and drove quails up from the sea, and let them down upon the camp at [a distance of] about one day's journey in one direction and one day's journey in the other direction round about the camp, and about two cubits above the ground.*

לא וְר֜וּחַ נָסַ֣ע ׀ מֵאֵ֣ת יְהֹוָ֗ה וַיָּ֣גָז שַׂלְוִים֮ מִן־הַיָּם֒ וַיִּטֹּ֨שׁ עַל־הַֽמַּחֲנֶ֜ה כְּדֶ֨רֶךְ י֥וֹם כֹּה֙ וּכְדֶ֣רֶךְ י֣וֹם כֹּ֔ה סְבִיב֖וֹת הַֽמַּחֲנֶ֑ה וּכְאַמָּתַ֖יִם עַל־פְּנֵ֥י הָאָֽרֶץ׃

32 *And the people arose all that day*

לב וַיָּ֣קָם הָעָ֡ם כָּל־הַיּוֹם֩ הַה֨וּא וְכָל־

the nearer event of Moshe's death and Yehoshua's leadership. These prophecies were pronounced by the most modest of men, who were found worthy of leading the people. Out of their great modesty, they declined influential posts and preferred to remain במחנה, in the midst of the people. For this reason they merited to bear the message of an ideal democratic future, in which the focal point of world social salvation will not be in the "אהל," but in the "מחנה," not in "גוג ומגוג" but in the "המון." Or they prophesied about Moshe's death and the culmination of the national destiny through Yehoshua. For from this prophecy we learn a profound truth: No man is indispensable, not even Moshe. His contemporaries, too, must recognize that the nation will continue to exist even without him. Moshe dies — and yet the nation's destiny will be fulfilled.

31 **ויגז שלוים מן הים**. It seems that the quails were in the midst of a mass migratory flight over the sea. A strong wind or undercurrent cut (גזז) under them, between them and the sea. This wind lifted the quails and cast them down all around the camp.

32-33 **ויקם וגו'**. They felt a gluttonous craving to eat, and in addition they lacked confidence in the assurance relayed to them by Moshe. Thus the

הַלַּ֣יְלָה וְכֹ֣ל ׀ י֣וֹם הַמָּחֳרָ֗ת וַיַּֽאַסְפוּ֙
אֶת־הַשְּׂלָ֔ו הַמַּמְעִ֕יט אָסַ֖ף עֲשָׂרָ֣ה
חֳמָרִ֑ים וַיִּשְׁטְח֤וּ לָהֶם֙ שָׁט֔וֹחַ
סְבִיב֖וֹת הַֽמַּחֲנֶֽה׃
השליו קרי

and all the night and all the next day, and they gathered the quails. The one who had gathered the least gathered ten chomers, *and they spread them out round about the camp.*

לג הַבָּשָׂ֗ר עוֹדֶ֙נּוּ֙ בֵּ֣ין שִׁנֵּיהֶ֔ם טֶ֖רֶם
יִכָּרֵ֑ת וְאַ֤ף יְהוָה֙ חָרָ֣ה בָעָ֔ם וַיַּ֤ךְ
יְהוָה֙ בָּעָ֔ם מַכָּ֖ה רַבָּ֥ה מְאֹֽד׃

33 *The meat was still between their teeth, not yet chewed, and the anger of* God *broke out against the people, and* God *struck the people a heavy blow.*

לד וַיִּקְרָ֛א אֶֽת־שֵׁם־הַמָּק֥וֹם הַה֖וּא
קִבְר֣וֹת הַֽתַּאֲוָ֑ה כִּי־שָׁם֙ קָֽבְר֔וּ
אֶת־הָעָ֖ם הַמִּתְאַוִּֽים׃

34 *He named this place Kivros Hata'avah (Graves of Lust), for there they had buried the people who had lusted.*

לה מִקִּבְר֧וֹת הַֽתַּאֲוָ֛ה נָסְע֥וּ הָעָ֖ם
חֲצֵר֑וֹת וַיִּהְי֖וּ בַּחֲצֵרֽוֹת׃ פ

35 *From Kivros Hata'avah the people journeyed to Chatzeros, and they stayed at Chatzeros.*

---

frenzied rush to gather the quails. Bear in mind that they had been assured that they would be able to enjoy meat for a whole month. Perhaps that is why it says (v. 33): **ואף ה׳ חרה בעם**.

35 **ויהיו בחצרות**. These words probably serve as an introduction to the incident of the following chapter, for they report the place where it happened.

12 1 *And Miriam and Aharon spoke against Moshe regarding the "dark-skinned woman" whom he had married, for he had [indeed] married a "dark-skinned woman."*

יב א וַתְּדַבֵּ֨ר מִרְיָ֤ם וְאַהֲרֹן֙ בְּמֹשֶׁ֔ה עַל־
אֹד֛וֹת הָאִשָּׁ֥ה הַכֻּשִׁ֖ית אֲשֶׁ֣ר לָקָ֑ח
כִּֽי־אִשָּׁ֥ה כֻשִׁ֖ית לָקָֽח׃

2 *They said: Has* God *indeed spoken only with Moshe? Has He not also spoken to us? And* God *heard it.*

ב וַיֹּאמְר֗וּ הֲרַ֤ק אַךְ־בְּמֹשֶׁה֙ דִּבֶּ֣ר
יְהוָ֔ה הֲלֹ֖א גַּם־בָּ֣נוּ דִבֵּ֑ר וַיִּשְׁמַ֖ע
יְהוָֽה׃

CHAPTER 12

1-2 **ותדבר מרים**. These verses present many difficulties. They report that Miriam and Aharon censured Moshe because of האשה הכשית אשר לקח, and Scripture adds that the fact in itself is really true, כי, "for indeed" אשה כשית לקח, "he had married an Ethiopian woman." So far, the meaning would be clear, and more puzzling than the fact that Miriam and Aharon took offense at this marriage would be why Moshe should indeed have married an Ethiopian woman. If you posit that this Ethiopian (or Abyssinian) woman is none other than Tzipporah the Midianite, then, apart from the fact that כוש is not identical with Midyan, there are two problems: First, what did Miriam and Aharon find wrong with this marriage? Furthermore, the fact of this marriage has long been known to us, and need not be stated as though it were a fresh disclosure: כי אשה כשית לקח.

Now, the words of Miriam and Aharon, which are reported in verse 2, refute the assumption that they denounced the marriage with the אשה כשית — whomever she may have been — in itself. For the words הרק אך במשה דבר ה׳ clearly indicate a close connection between Moshe's prophecy and the fact כי אשה כשית לקח; they clearly imply that Moshe married an אשה כשית because ה׳ דיבר בו. Miriam and Aharon, however, thought that the fact that ה׳ דיבר במשה was no justification for לקיחת אשה כשית. After all, Moshe was not the only one to whom God had spoken, and yet none of the others — themselves (Miriam and Aharon) included — had married an אשה כשית, even though they, too, had attained prophecy.

Now it is absolutely unthinkable that Moshe — or anyone else in the world — *because* he had been endowed by God with prophecy would "therefore" marry an Ethiopian woman! Since the entire context indicates that Moshe's prophecy was the cause of כי אשה כשית לקח, these words must signify something other than that he had married an Ethiopian.

When we search through the whole Torah for the relation between prophecy and marital matters, we find only one place containing a clear directive in this regard. In *Shemos* 19:15 the people are commanded to abstain from sexual intercourse with their wives, in order to be worthy of hearing God's Word directly from Him. This abstention is an essential precondition for prophecy; hence, it is tacitly included in the general directive וקדשתם וגו׳ והיו נכונים וגו׳ (ibid. 19:10 and 11).

Indeed, the *Sifre* conveys to us the tradition that Miriam and Aharon denounced Moshe because פרש מן האשה, he abstained from sexual intercourse with his wife, a fact that only now became known to them, when the prophetic spirit rested upon the seventy elders [see *Rashi* ד״ה ותדבר מרים ואהרן]. They considered this abstention an injustice committed against the wife, for they thought that Moshe's prophecy did not obligate him to abstain from sexual relations, as they themselves and the patriarchs before them had been found worthy of hearing God's Word without thereby having to suffer limitation on their married life.

They overlooked the difference between Moshe's level and their own level, and they were not aware of the instructions that were given after the Lawgiving. The people were told: שובו לכם לאהליכם (*Devarim* 5:27), and thus were allowed to return to family life and marital intimacy, whereas Moshe was commanded to maintain abstention, for he was told: ואתה פה עמד עמדי ואדברה אליך וגו׳ (ibid. 5:28).

The entire context unequivocally indicates that this is the meaning of our verse. Support for this interpretation can also be adduced from the following fact: Wherever the expression על אדות occurs in the Torah in a similar connection, it always refers to a person or thing suffering from deprivation, whose interests one now wishes to promote. Thus: וירע וגו׳ על אודת בנו (*Bereshis* 21:11), והוכח וגו׳ על אדות באר (ibid. 21:25), אשר עשה ה׳ לפרעה ולמצרים על אודת ישראל (*Shemos* 18:8). Here, too, in the case of the אשה הכשית, the complaint is not about her, but in her interest.

Now all that remains is to explain the words האשה הכשית אשר לקח according to their unequivocal meaning. We would venture to offer a theory that to us does not seem impossible. The expression "לקיחת אשה כושית" is nothing but a descriptive term for "marriage without sexual relations."

3 *And the man Moshe was extremely humble, more than any other man on earth.*	ג וְהָאִ֥ישׁ מֹשֶׁ֖ה עָנָ֣ו מְאֹ֑ד מִכֹּל֙ הָֽאָדָ֔ם אֲשֶׁ֖ר עַל־פְּנֵ֥י הָאֲדָמָֽה׃ ס ענָו קרי

The term "כושי" occurs several times in a characteristic sense. In הֲיַהֲפֹךְ כּוּשִׁי עוֹרוֹ (*Yirmeyahu* 13:23) it denotes black people in general. In הֲלוֹא כִבְנֵי כֻשִׁיִּים אַתֶּם לִי (*Amos* 9:7) it denotes the lowest of peoples: "Even if you were כושים, would you not be equally Mine!" In שִׁגָּיוֹן לְדָוִד אֲשֶׁר־שָׁר לַה׳ עַל־דִּבְרֵי־כוּשׁ בֶּן־יְמִינִי (*Tehillim* 7:1) it denotes the great discrepancy between the deeds of Sha'ul and what would be expected of a בן ימיני, the son of a Jewish tribe. Sha'ul's degeneration was analogous to the physiological degeneration that would be entailed by the birth of a כושי to a Jewish tribe. Perhaps a similar explanation applies here as well. Marriage with a כושית is considered unnatural and intolerable. Hence, if someone married a woman and yet lived apart from her, it would be said of him that "he married an אשה כושית." We can only offer this explanation as a suggestion, but in our view what we have posited here is not unreasonable, and if we have hit upon the truth, we have found the natural interpretation of our verse.

הרק אך וגו׳. The doubling of the limiting particle expresses the exclusive status that Moshe — as they imagined — ascribed to himself, such that he saw the need to act this way toward his wife. "Has God indeed spoken only and solely with Moshe?" Avraham, Yitzchak and Ya'akov also were considered worthy of hearing God's Word, and yet they did not abstain from sexual relations with their wives! הלא גם בנו דבר: We, too, have merited to hear God's Word, and we have not had to give up marital life!

וישמע ה׳. They spoke only to each other, but God heard what they said.

3 **והאיש משה ענו**. In reference to mental activity, ענה means: to say something precipitated by the circumstances, speech elicited by something said or by an existing fact, a fitting response to something said or to some reality. In other words, ענה means: to reply, to initiate speech in correspondence to something, to give testimony in accordance with what actually happened (see Commentary, *Shemos* 20:13); thus למען ,יען, terms of cause and consequence.

4 *And* God *suddenly said to Moshe,*
to Aharon and to Miriam: Go out,
all three of you, to the Tent of Ap-
pointed Meeting. All three of them
went out.

ד וַיֹּאמֶר יְהוָה פִּתְאֹם אֶל־מֹשֶׁה
וְאֶל־אַהֲרֹן וְאֶל־מִרְיָם צְאוּ
שְׁלָשְׁתְּכֶם אֶל־אֹהֶל מוֹעֵד וַיֵּצְאוּ
שְׁלָשְׁתָּם׃

In the social sphere, ענה denotes complete dependence on the will of another. Hence, ענו and ענוה denote the trait of complete selflessness. One who has attained this trait has banished from his mind any thought of his own worth and his own greatness. Towards God, ענוה means: to nullify one's own being and will before God's Will. This trait is the negative prerequisite for the positive trait of חסידות, whose whole essence is total self-sacrifice for the practical fulfillment of God's Will. These two virtues together are the pinnacle of greatness of character and deeds. Hence our Sages (in *Avodah Zarah* 20b) waver as to which of the two is the greatest of all virtues: חסידות or ענוה.

For various reasons, Scripture mentions here Moshe's humility. Had his sister and brother considered this trait of Moshe — which surely must have been known to them — they would not have judged him unfavorably and would not have attributed his conduct to presumption. For no one was further from presumption than Moshe! Furthermore, Moshe, in his humility, would not have defended himself; hence God took up his cause. Finally, perhaps the words והאיש משה וגו׳ indicate how they came to such a judgment of Moshe. Because of his extreme ענוה, they knew nothing of his special and unique relationship to God. He always presented himself as their equal, never said anything about the preeminence of his prophecy. What is more, it is possible that in his ענוה he was totally unaware of the uniqueness of his prophecy, and thought that other prophets, too, reached this level.

4 **פתאם** — see Commentary above, 6:9.

God's Word in verse 6 is connected with what was said in verse 2 and constitutes a reply to the words of Miriam and Aharon. Hence the subject (Moshe) is not explicitly mentioned in God's reply (v. 6), but is obvious from the previous words (in v. 2). Accordingly, we may assume that God

5 *Then* God *descended in a pillar of cloud and stood at the entrance of the Tent. He called Aharon and Miriam, and both of them went out.*

ה וַיֵּ֤רֶד יְהוָה֙ בְּעַמּ֣וּד עָנָ֔ן וַֽיַּעֲמֹ֖ד
פֶּ֣תַח הָאֹ֑הֶל וַיִּקְרָא֙ אַהֲרֹ֣ן וּמִרְיָ֔ם
וַיֵּצְא֖וּ שְׁנֵיהֶֽם׃

6 *He said: Hear, now, My words; if he were your prophet, then* God*— I — would make Myself known to him in a vision; I would speak to him in a dream.*

ו וַיֹּ֖אמֶר שִׁמְעוּ־נָ֣א דְבָרָ֑י אִם־יִֽהְיֶה֙
נְבִ֣יאֲכֶ֔ם יְהוָ֗ה בַּמַּרְאָה֙ אֵלָ֣יו
אֶתְוַדָּ֔ע בַּחֲל֖וֹם אֲדַבֶּר־בּֽוֹ׃

summoned the three of them (here) immediately after Miriam and Aharon finished speaking.

6 **אם יהיה נביאכם**: If he, Moshe, were "your" prophet — i.e., if he were the kind of prophet you take him to be. Or: If Moshe were a prophet like yourselves, on the same level of prophecy as you are.

במראָה. There is a distinction between מראָה (here) and מראֶה. A מראֶה is seen directly and without intermediation; cf. עץ נחמד למראֶה (*Bereshis* 2:9), אשה יפת מראֶה (ibid. 12:11 et al.). A מראָה, however, is seen by reflection; thus מראָה in the sense of "mirror" (*Shemos* 38:8).

במראה . . . בחלום In two respects, the prophecy of נביאכם does not come directly, but by intermediation: objectively and subjectively. Objectively: the Divine which is revealed to the prophet is not shown to him directly, but is reflected to him, as in a mirror, and the prophet perceives the One revealed to him according to the vision in which He reveals Himself to him. Subjectively: he does not receive the prophecy in his normal wakeful state, in which he is active and in conscious control of his faculties; rather, בחלום אדבר בו: he is capable of hearing God's Word only in a dream-like state, and after he awakes he ponders over it and absorbs it. The Divine comes down to him indirectly and raises him out of his normal state, so that God's Word will reach him.

For these two reasons his moral-sensual life can run its usual course, and no restrictions need be imposed.

7 *Not so is My servant Moshe; he is trusted in all My house.*

ז לֹא־כֵן עַבְדִּי מֹשֶׁה בְּכָל־בֵּיתִי נֶאֱמָן הוּא׃

8 *Mouth to mouth do I speak with*

ח פֶּה אֶל־פֶּה אֲדַבֶּר־בּוֹ וּמַרְאֶה

7 **לא כן עבדי משה**: Not so is My servant, not so is Moshe. Not so is My *servant*, for he is more than a prophet, he is permanently in My service; and he is *Moshe* in the singularity of his personality, which raises him as a human being above all other human beings.

בכל ביתי נאמן הוא. If we have any inkling of what is expressed by this sentence, its meaning is as follows: He has access to everything; everything is unlocked and uncovered for him. God's rule of the world is hidden from the eyes of all living; but to the extent that His rule can be comprehended by a mortal, it is openly revealed to Moshe and accessible to his full consciousness without intermediation.

A servant who is not "entrusted with the whole house" is not familiar with all of its inner recesses. He does not know where certain things are located, or is not given access to them, and there are other things whose very existence has never been revealed to him. There are still other things of whose existence he is aware and whose location is known to him, but he has never seen them with his own eyes, or he may have seen them only when they were covered up. He has an idea of what the house contains, and he can put this idea into words and communicate it to others; and in certain elevated moments the master of the house shows him some of the things that otherwise must remain hidden from him, so that he should tell his brothers outside about the glories of his master in his house.

Not so with a servant who is נאמן בכל ביתו. He wanders freely always in the Light of the house. His knowledge is complete and constant, and nothing is hidden from him.

8 **פה אל פה אדבר בו**. פה אל פה — in contrast to the objective (במראָה) and subjective (בחלום) intermediation indicated in verse 6. Moshe attains direct revelation objectively and subjectively. פה speaks to פה; God's mouth speaks to him when he himself is "in possession of a פה" — i.e., is able to speak; in other words, not במראָה and not בחלום.

וְלֹ֣א בְחִידֹ֔ת וּתְמֻנַ֥ת יְהֹוָ֖ה יַבִּ֑יט וּמַדּ֙וּעַ֙ לֹ֣א יְרֵאתֶ֔ם לְדַבֵּ֖ר בְּעַבְדִּ֥י בְמֹשֶֽׁה׃

him, in a vision and not in riddles, and he beholds the image of God*; why, then, were you not afraid to speak against My servant, against Moshe?*

ט וַיִּֽחַר־אַ֧ף יְהֹוָ֛ה בָּ֖ם וַיֵּלַֽךְ׃

9 *The anger of* God *was kindled against them and He went.*

י וְהֶעָנָ֗ן סָ֚ר מֵעַ֣ל הָאֹ֔הֶל וְהִנֵּ֥ה מִרְיָ֖ם מְצֹרַ֣עַת כַּשָּׁ֑לֶג וַיִּ֧פֶן אַהֲרֹ֛ן אֶל־מִרְיָ֖ם וְהִנֵּ֥ה מְצֹרָֽעַת׃

10 *But when the cloud had departed from the Tent, Miriam was leprous as snow. And Aharon turned to Miriam and lo! she was a leper.*

ומראֶה: What he is made aware of is revealed to him directly and openly, ולא בחידת: revelation is not communicated to him through an intermediating vision, through the interpretation of a symbol.

חידה stems from the root חוד (אָחוּדָה־נָּא לָכֶם חִידָה [*Shoftim* 14:12], חוּד חִידָה וּמְשֹׁל מָשָׁל [*Yechezkel* 17:2]), related to אוד, אות, which denote mechanical and mental mediation (see Commentary, *Bereshis* 1:1).

ותמנת ה׳ יביט — as opposed to ה׳ במראה אליו אתודע of verse 6 (see Commentary, ibid. 1:11).

ומדוע לא יראתם וגו׳. How did you dare to equate yourselves with עבדי, with Moshe! How did you dare to draw an analogy between yourselves and עבדי, between yourselves and Moshe? How could you imagine that you are able to judge what is befitting for My servant, what is befitting for Moshe?

10 **והענן וגו׳ והנה מרים מצרעת כשלג ויפן אהרן אל מרים והנה מצרעת**. As soon as the cloud had departed from the Tent, they saw that Miriam was leprous as snow. When Aharon turned to Miriam and examined the leprosy more closely, he recognized that it was one of the kinds of נגעים of צרעת mentioned in the Torah, which marks the person stricken by it as one who has incurred God's wrath (see Commentary, *Vayikra* 13, end).

יא וַיֹּאמֶר אַהֲרֹן אֶל־מֹשֶׁה בִּי אֲדֹנִי אַל־נָא תָשֵׁת עָלֵינוּ חַטָּאת אֲשֶׁר נוֹאַלְנוּ וַאֲשֶׁר חָטָאנוּ׃

11 *And Aharon said to Moshe: O my lord, do not count it as a grave sin against us what we have done thoughtlessly and wherein we have sinned.*

יב אַל־נָא תְהִי כַּמֵּת אֲשֶׁר בְּצֵאתוֹ מֵרֶחֶם אִמּוֹ וַיֵּאָכֵל חֲצִי בְשָׂרוֹ׃

12 *Let her not remain like a corpse! For since she came forth from your mother's womb, it would be [as though] half of your [own] flesh had been consumed.*

11 **אל נא תשת עלינו חטאת וגו׳**. The meaning of this request is not sufficiently clear. Since Aharon admits that they sinned, it is difficult to understand what is intended by the request אל נא וגו׳. If they have sinned, the sin is there and it rests upon them.

Perhaps the emphasis of the request lies in the term שות, as in אם כפר יושת עליו (*Shemos* 21:30), and the meaning of the expression אל נא תשת עלינו חטאת is: let our sin not be placed upon us as a sin that entails punishment. It is also possible that this expression should be taken in connection with what is stated in the preceding verse — ויפן אהרן וגו׳ והנה מצרעת — and means: let us not be stamped with sin, the imprint of our deed; let the נגע not be a sign of the sin we thoughtlessly committed.

נואלנו — see Commentary, ibid. 2:21.

12 **אל נא תהי כמת**. מצורע חשוב כמת (see Commentary, *Vayikra* 13:46). מה המת מטמא באהל אף מצורע מטמא בביאה (*Sifre*). The נגע is a sign of her exclusion from the social community.

Our Sages say in the *Sifre*: There was no כהן there — besides Aharon and his sons — who could treat her in accordance with the laws of נגע צרעת: לסוגרה לטמאה ולטהרה. Thus, since קרובים פסולים לראות נגעים (see *Nega'im* 2:5 and *Sifre* ad loc.), there was no one there who could restore her to טהרה. Accordingly, however, the טומאה and the consequent obligation of seclusion likewise could not have taken effect at all, for they, too, take effect only by the declaration of a כהן (see *Vayikra* 13:3). We must say, then, that in this case טומאת הנגע was declared by God Himself, and the

13 *And Moshe cried to* God: *O* God! *Do heal her, I beseech You!*

יג וַיִּצְעַק מֹשֶׁה אֶל־יְהֹוָה לֵאמֹר אֵל
נָא רְפָא נָא לָהּ׃ פ מפטיר

14 *And* God *said to Moshe: If her father had spat before her, would she not have been ashamed for seven days? Let her be confined outside the camp for seven days, and afterwards she shall be taken in again.*

יד וַיֹּאמֶר יְהֹוָה אֶל־מֹשֶׁה וְאָבִיהָ יָרֹק
יָרַק בְּפָנֶיהָ הֲלֹא תִכָּלֵם שִׁבְעַת
יָמִים תִּסָּגֵר שִׁבְעַת יָמִים מִחוּץ
לַמַּחֲנֶה וְאַחַר תֵּאָסֵף׃

15 *And Miriam was confined outside the camp for seven days, and the people did not journey on until Miriam had been taken in again.*

טו וַתִּסָּגֵר מִרְיָם מִחוּץ לַמַּחֲנֶה
שִׁבְעַת יָמִים וְהָעָם לֹא נָסַע עַד־
הֵאָסֵף מִרְיָם׃

---

declaration of a כהן was unnecessary. Hence her טהרה, too, could be restored to her only directly by God, for there was no כהן מטהר. In the words of the *Sifre*: הקב״ה הסגירה והקב״ה טימאה והקב״ה טיהרה (see *Zevachim* 102a).

אשר בצאתו מרחם אמו. The pronominal suffix of בצאתו refers to מת, whereas those of אמו and of בשרו refer back to אדני (v. 11). Thus, out of respect, Aharon, when addressing Moshe, refers to him in the third person, as in: אדני יֹדֵעַ (*Bereshis* 33:13), יעבר נא אדני (ibid. 33:14). In such addresses, second person and third person frequently occur side by side; for example: יִזְכָּר־נָא הַמֶּלֶךְ אֶת־ה׳ אֱלֹקֶיךָ (*Shemuel* II, 14:11) and then again repeatedly in the continuation there.

For clarity's sake we have translated אמו and בשרו in the second person. Aharon here appeals to Moshe's brotherly feelings: Miriam is, after all, Moshe's sister, his own flesh and blood. If she were to remain in the same condition, rotting and resembling a corpse, it would be as though his own flesh were being consumed!

ויאכל חצי בשרו — as in אחינו בשרנו הוא (*Bereshis* 37:27 — *Sifre*).

14 **ואביה ירק וגו׳** — see Commentary, *Vayikra* 13, end.

בפניה, "before her," as in לא יתיצב איש בפניך (*Devarim* 7:24).

16 *Afterwards the people journeyed from Chatzeros and encamped in the wilderness of Paran.*

טז וְאַחַר נָסְעוּ הָעָם מֵחֲצֵרוֹת וַיַּחֲנוּ
בְּמִדְבַּר פָּארָן׃ פפפ

13 1 God *spoke to Moshe, saying:*

יג א וַיְדַבֵּר יְהוָה אֶל־מֹשֶׁה לֵּאמֹר׃

2 *Send out men for yourself to explore the land of Canaan, which I am giving to the Children of Israel. You shall send out one man each for every tribe of his fathers; each an outstanding person in their midst.*

ב שְׁלַח־לְךָ אֲנָשִׁים וְיָתֻרוּ אֶת־אֶרֶץ
כְּנַעַן אֲשֶׁר־אֲנִי נֹתֵן לִבְנֵי יִשְׂרָאֵל
אִישׁ אֶחָד אִישׁ אֶחָד לְמַטֵּה
אֲבֹתָיו תִּשְׁלָחוּ כֹּל נָשִׂיא בָהֶם׃

16 **ויחנו במדבר פארן**. The רמב״ן points out that חצרות, too, was in the wilderness of Paran. They had entered this wilderness already in קברות התאוה, as is evident from what is stated in 10:12 (above). Accordingly, ויחנו וגו׳ can only mean: and they continued to camp — i.e., further on — in the wilderness of Paran.

If we now look back on the events that especially stand out in פרשת בהעלותך, we find that they can be subsumed under one concept: They show many degrees of endowment with the Divine spirit and of relationship to the Divine. First we see Moshe and the nation as a whole (10:35-36), then Moshe, the elders, and Eldad and Meidad (11:24ff.), then Aharon, Miriam, and the other prophets (12:4ff.).

Perhaps in this respect, too, it is significant that the פרשה opens with the mitzvah of the Menorah. For there is a profound underlying link between the contents of the פרשה and the "Tree of Light" of Jewish spiritual development, the Menorah, which stands at the beginning of the פרשה [cf. Commentary, *Shemos*, p. 375ff.].

שלח לך

CHAPTER 13

1-2 **שלח לך**. Compare עשה לך שתי חצוצרת (above, 10:2), קח לך בשמים (*Shemos* 30:23), and other similar places where the addition of the word "לך" does not detract from the statement's meaning as a command. Here, too, it appears that שלח לך is a full-fledged command. Thus, in the following verse it says that the men were sent על פי ה׳.

In a later period, Moshe reviewed these events, speaking of them from his memory of them (*Devarim* 1:19ff.). From this retrospect we know that they had already traversed the wilderness of Paran, which is there described as המדבר הגדול והנורא, and had already reached Kadesh Barnea, which is at the border of the land to be conquered. The Emori mountain range lay before them, and they had already been commanded to climb it and thus begin their conquest of the land (ibid. 1:7-8). The people then asked Moshe to send before them a group of men ויחפרו לנו את הארץ; in order, as it were, to raise the land out of the dark depths of concealment and unawareness into the clear light of knowledge and awareness. The expressed purpose of the mission was to find the best route by which to enter the land and to familiarize themselves with the cities they would come to first.

In this request itself there was nothing improper. Moshe himself says there: וייטב בעיני הדבר. For immediately upon the people's entry into the Promised Land, the miraculous mode of God's rule would come to an end, and from then onward they would have to actively participate in shaping their fate. What is more, even during the journeying in the wilderness, Moshe sought to draw upon his father-in-law's knowledge of the region — this despite the fact that this journeying was conducted under the immediate direction of God.

According to Sforno, שלח לך of our verse differs from the request of the people in only one respect: They said נשלחה אנשים לפנינו, they asked for permission to send men of their own choosing, whereas God commanded that Moshe himself should send the men, and that he should choose from each tribe the most qualified for this mission.

It is likely that also the substance of the mission was changed in several respects. The mission's goal, as formulated by the people, was: ויחפרו וגו׳. The primary meaning of חפר את הארץ is apparently to spy out a country's vulnerable points in order to later conquer it. Thus in *Yehoshua* 2:2-3, and thus also in *Iyov* 39:29 regarding the eagle searching out its prey: מִשָּׁם חָפַר אֹכֶל. This is also the meaning of חפר in the intransitive sense: it denotes the shame felt when faults are brought to light. The underlying conception of all these meanings is חפירה in the sense of excavation: to bring to light what should remain hidden.

By contrast, God's command was ויתרו וגו׳. תור is related to טור, תפר,

דבר (cf. Commentary, *Bereshis* 1:22-23). טור: a row of various things arranged side by side. תפר: to sew together pieces of fabric and the like; to join them, as it were, in one row. דבר: different signifiers arranged side by side and combined into one concept, or a word expressed verbally. תור can denote investigation that is strictly objective: the investigator observes the special qualities of a thing and puts them together as expressions of one concept. This is the sense of תור in *Koheles* 1:13, 2:3, 7:25. But תור can also denote exploration with a subjective purpose, and in such a case it primarily denotes searching out the good points suitable for some intended purpose. Thus לתור להם מנוחה (above, 10:33), לתור לכם מקום לחנתכם (*Devarim* 1:33), and thus especially regarding the choice of the Promised Land, which was chosen because it is the best and most suited for Israel's calling: אֶרֶץ אֲשֶׁר־תַּרְתִּי לָהֶם זָבַת חָלָב וּדְבַשׁ צְבִי הִיא לְכָל־הָאֲרָצוֹת (*Yechezkel* 20:6).

Accordingly, God's command ויתרו את הארץ וגו׳ changed and expanded their mission. They were not charged only with searching out the best way to conquer the land. That goal was now secondary. Rather, their mission was to come to know the land itself as a base for the development of a nation, and it was indicated to them that they were to consider the land from a dual standpoint: ארץ כנען אשר אני נתן לבני ישראל. Today it is ארץ כנען, a land whose inhabitants have corrupted their way, and God is the One Who now gives it to the Children of Israel, so that they should develop in it a national life in accordance with His Will.

כל נשיא בהם. The accentuation indicates that נשיא is the predicate of כל: every one of them shall be a נשיא among the members of his tribe. These were not נשיאי מטות אבותם, the "princes of the tribes of their fathers," who are called (above, 1:4 and 16) ראש לבית אבתיו and ראשי אלפי ישראל, individuals who were at the head of each tribe and who are therefore called ראשי בית אבתם (above, 7:2). Rather, each one of them was נשיא בהם: they were בהם, not at the head of the tribes, but in the midst of the people, individuals who, though not in official positions of leadership, stood out from all the rest by virtue of their character and ability. They were not ראשי המטות or ראשי אלפי ישראל; they were not high-ranking officials. They were, as it says in the next verse, ראשי בני ישראל: they were heads of the people, influential leaders among the people.

ג וַיִּשְׁלַ֨ח אֹתָ֥ם מֹשֶׁ֛ה מִמִּדְבַּ֥ר פָּארָ֖ן
עַל־פִּ֣י יְהֹוָ֑ה כֻּלָּ֣ם אֲנָשִׁ֔ים רָאשֵׁ֥י
בְנֵֽי־יִשְׂרָאֵ֖ל הֵֽמָּה׃

3 *And Moshe sent them out from the wilderness of Paran according to the command of* God. *They were all of them men, heads of the Children of Israel.*

ד וְאֵ֖לֶּה שְׁמוֹתָ֑ם לְמַטֵּ֣ה רְאוּבֵ֔ן
שַׁמּ֖וּעַ בֶּן־זַכּֽוּר׃

4 *And these were their names: For the tribe of Reuven, Shammu'a, son of Zakkur.*

ה לְמַטֵּ֣ה שִׁמְע֔וֹן שָׁפָ֖ט בֶּן־חוֹרִֽי׃

5 *For the tribe of Shimon, Shafat, son of Chori.*

ו לְמַטֵּ֣ה יְהוּדָ֔ה כָּלֵ֖ב בֶּן־יְפֻנֶּֽה׃

6 *For the tribe of Yehudah, Kalev, son of Yefunneh.*

ז לְמַטֵּ֣ה יִשָּׂשכָ֔ר יִגְאָ֖ל בֶּן־יוֹסֵֽף׃

7 *For the tribe of Yissachar, Yig'al, son of Yosef.*

ח לְמַטֵּ֥ה אֶפְרָ֖יִם הוֹשֵׁ֥עַ בִּן־נֽוּן׃

8 *For the tribe of Efrayim, Hoshea, son of Nun.*

ט לְמַטֵּ֣ה בִנְיָמִ֔ן פַּלְטִ֖י בֶּן־רָפֽוּא׃

9 *For the tribe of Binyamin, Palti, son of Rafu.*

י לְמַטֵּ֣ה זְבוּלֻ֔ן גַּדִּיאֵ֖ל בֶּן־סוֹדִֽי׃

10 *For the tribe of Zevulun, Gaddi'el, son of Sodi.*

יא לְמַטֵּ֥ה יוֹסֵ֖ף לְמַטֵּ֣ה מְנַשֶּׁ֑ה גַּדִּ֖י בֶּן־
סוּסִֽי׃

11 *For the tribe of Yosef, [of] the tribe of Menashe, Gaddi, son of Susi.*

יב לְמַטֵּ֣ה דָ֔ן עַמִּיאֵ֖ל בֶּן־גְּמַלִּֽי׃

12 *For the tribe of Dan, Ammi'el, son of Gemalli.*

---

3 **כלם אנשים**. They were all "men," capable and outstanding individual personalities. Cf. מי שמך לאיש (*Shemos* 2:14). Thus the Midianites called Gideon "אִישׁ יִשְׂרָאֵל" (*Shoftim* 7:14), and thus David said to Avner: הֲלוֹא־אִישׁ אַתָּה וּמִי כָמוֹךָ בְּיִשְׂרָאֵל (*Shemuel* I, 26:15), and thus also: הִתְחַזְּקוּ וִהְיוּ לַאֲנָשִׁים (ibid. I, 4:9). (See above, v. 2).

13 *For the tribe of Asher, Sesur, son of Micha'el.*

יג לְמַטֵּ֣ה אָשֵׁ֔ר סְת֖וּר בֶּן־מִֽיכָאֵֽל׃

14 *For the tribe of Naftali, Nachbi, son of Vafsi.*

יד לְמַטֵּ֣ה נַפְתָּלִ֔י נַחְבִּ֖י בֶּן־וָפְסִֽי׃

15 *For the tribe of Gad, Ge'u'el, son of Machi.*

טו לְמַטֵּ֣ה גָ֔ד גְּאוּאֵ֖ל בֶּן־מָכִֽי׃

16 *These are the names of the men whom Moshe sent out to explore the land. And Moshe called Hoshea the son of Nun, Yehoshua.*

טז אֵ֚לֶּה שְׁמ֣וֹת הָֽאֲנָשִׁ֔ים אֲשֶׁר־שָׁלַ֥ח
מֹשֶׁ֖ה לָת֣וּר אֶת־הָאָ֑רֶץ וַיִּקְרָ֥א
מֹשֶׁ֛ה לְהוֹשֵׁ֥עַ בִּן־נ֖וּן יְהוֹשֻֽׁעַ׃

16 **ויקרא משה להושע בן נון יהושע**. The change of name bears an implied message to him and also to his companions; for each time they addressed him by his new name, they, too, were to remember the message implied by this name, and in carrying out their mission they were not to lose sight of this message. For this name indicates to him and to them that הוֹשֵׁעַ is יהושע: He Who saved us in the past will also save us in the future. What is more, יְהוֹשֻׁעַ: God is our wealth, our power, the sum and substance of our aspirations; without Him, all these things have no meaning. For it does not say here יהושיע but, rather, יְהוֹשֻׁעַ; thus, this name not only changes past (הושע) to future but replaces ישע — which is the root of הושע — with שוע, preceded by God's Name.

ישע — related to ישה, which is the root of יש and תושיה — denotes the essence of existence, whereas שוע, related to שבע and שפע, denotes ownership and possession; thus שׁוֹעַ, the well-to-do. Cf. Commentary, *Shemos* 14:13. It is possible that שַׁוַּעַ is primarily a cry for help against robbery, and תשועה is help to gain victory in a war of defense of country, whereas ישועה is the saving of life.

There is a close relation between the change of name and the mission assigned to Yehoshua and his companions. This is evident from the point in Scripture where we are told of the change of name. If the change had only private, personal meaning, it would have been reported above in verse 8. But the new name is reported here, after mention of the mission in general — אשר שלח וגו׳ ויקרא וגו׳ — and before the elaboration upon the

17 *Moshe sent them out to explore the land of Canaan and he said to them: Go up here in the south and ascend the mountain.*	יז וַיִּשְׁלַח אֹתָם מֹשֶׁה לָתוּר אֶת־אֶרֶץ כְּנָעַן וַיֹּאמֶר אֲלֵהֶם עֲלוּ זֶה בַּנֶּגֶב וַעֲלִיתֶם אֶת־הָהָר׃
18 *And look at the land, what it is like, and at the people that dwell upon it, whether they are strong or weak, whether they are few or many.*	יח וּרְאִיתֶם אֶת־הָאָרֶץ מַה־הִוא וְאֶת־הָעָם הַיֹּשֵׁב עָלֶיהָ הֶחָזָק הוּא הֲרָפֶה הַמְעַט הוּא אִם־רָב׃

mission in detail. The change of name, then, is the mission's "seal" and also its basic introduction. It indicates to Yehoshua and his companions that they are not being sent to examine the possibility and value of conquering the land. Their תשועה and שוע is *God*; the certainty of victory and of success does not rise or fall with the land's positive or negative qualities. Accordingly, with this change of name Moshe accompanied his emissaries in spirit, and gave them a compass to direct them to an understanding of their mission.

17 **לתור את ארץ כנען**. They are to explore the land in its present condition as the land of Canaanite inhabitants.

עלו זה, literally, "Go up this here." For your mission, it is immaterial from where you enter the land.

בנגב: they were encamped to the southeast of Eretz Yisrael.

ועליתם את ההר: the Emori mountains, which they had reached (*Devarim* 1:20).

18 **וראיתם את הארץ מה הִוא**. This is a question about the topographical nature of the land in general, whether it is mountainous or flat, well watered or not, and so forth. ואת העם הישב עליה is an ethnological question on the physical, spiritual, and moral qualities of the inhabitants. החזק הוא הרפה וגו' stresses the various points to be probed in this connection.

In our view, it is significant that the question is formulated as: החזק הוא הרפה. In contrast to all the following questions, here the form of opposition, -ה followed by אם, is not employed.

19 *And what the land is like in which they dwell, whether it is good or bad, and what the cities are like in which they dwell, whether [they are] in open or in fortified places.*

יט וּמָ֣ה הָאָ֗רֶץ אֲשֶׁר־הוּא֙ יֹשֵׁ֣ב בָּ֔הּ
הֲטוֹבָ֥ה הִ֖וא אִם־רָעָ֑ה וּמָ֣ה
הֶעָרִ֗ים אֲשֶׁר־הוּא֙ יוֹשֵׁ֣ב בָּהֵ֔נָּה
הַבְּמַחֲנִ֖ים אִ֥ם בְּמִבְצָרִֽים׃

If we consider the import of this question, at first glance it would appear to be the decisive question for the mission of conquering the land. If the inhabitants are strong, it will be difficult, perhaps impossible, to conquer the land; if the inhabitants are weak, these doubts do not arise. However, it is precisely this conception of the question that Scripture seeks to rule out. From the standpoint of Israel's interests, it is totally irrelevant whether the inhabitants are weak or strong. [The conquest] is not a question of either/or. Hence, the two sides of the question are presented not as opposites, but only side by side as different possibilities.

Thereby the mission was invested with a character completely different from what was originally intended by the people. They are to come to know the land in its present condition, not for sake of the conquest, but in order to learn a lesson for all time. If they find deficiencies in the land and in its inhabitants, let them tell of them to their descendants after them, who will merit to see the difference; for the land and its inhabitants are destined to flourish — through the protection and blessing of God. If they find wealth and abundance in the land, they will well be able to imagine the degree of blessing that will yet be granted to the land when God watches over it with His benevolence. And above all, when they see the power of the land's Canaanite inhabitants, let this serve as a warning to them for all generations: Power and might will not save a nation from ruin, if it violates the Divine law of morality. Thus does Amos (2:9) warn his contemporaries, who, heedless of the future, corrupt their way: וְאָנֹכִי הִשְׁמַדְתִּי אֶת־הָאֱמֹרִי מִפְּנֵיהֶם אֲשֶׁר כְּגֹבַהּ אֲרָזִים גָּבְהוֹ וְחָסֹן הוּא כָּאַלּוֹנִים וָאַשְׁמִיד פִּרְיוֹ מִמַּעַל וְשָׁרָשָׁיו מִתָּחַת!

19 **ומה הארץ אשר הוא ישב בה**. This is a question about the nature of the land as a dwelling place for man. Above (v. 18), it says: ואת העם הישב עליה. The people are viewed apart from the land: In what manner do the people

כ וּמָ֣ה הָאָ֗רֶץ הַשְּׁמֵנָ֨ה הִ֜וא אִם־רָזָ֗ה
הֲיֵֽשׁ־בָּ֥הּ עֵץ֙ אִם־אַ֔יִן וְהִ֨תְחַזַּקְתֶּ֔ם
וּלְקַחְתֶּ֖ם מִפְּרִ֣י הָאָ֑רֶץ וְהַ֨יָּמִ֔ים יְמֵ֖י
בִּכּוּרֵ֥י עֲנָבִֽים׃ שני

20 *And what the soil is like, whether it is fat or lean, whether there is woodland in it or not. Take courage and take [some] of the fruit of the land. The season was the season when the first grapes become ripe.*

live and develop *on* it? Here, however, it says: ומה הארץ אשר הוא ישב בה. The people are considered *in* the land: In what way do the land's special qualities influence its inhabitants and shape their character? What is the value of the land as a source of national development? In this respect הטובה הִוא אם רעה, is the land "good" or "bad"? Will it serve to promote the spiritual and moral cultural life of the nation, or hinder it? In this connection, we would call to mind the saying of our Sages, which was gleaned from experience: אוירא דארץ ישראל מחכים (*Bava Basra* 158b).

ומה הערים וגו׳ הבמחנים אם במבצרים. This contrast is like the contrast between עיר חומה and חצרים אשר אין להם חמה (*Vayikra* 25:29 and 31). מחנים: open cities; מבצרים: fortified cities; only that the difference here is considered from the aspect of its strategic importance. To the enemy, an open city is of the nature of a מחנה, its defense depends solely on the bravery of its residents. By contrast, a walled city is a מבצר, which is difficult to conquer (cf. Commentary, *Bereshis* 11:6). In *Shemuel* I, 6:18, all the Philistine cities are included by this contrast: מֵעִיר מִבְצָר וְעַד כֹּפֶר הַפְּרָזִי. In *Bemidbar Rabbah* (16:12) it says that settlement in open cities is a sign of courage, whereas settlement in fortified cities is a sign of cowardice: מנין אתם יודעים כחם? אם במחנים הם שרויין הם גבורים בוטחין על כחם אם במבצרים חלשים הם ולבם רך. Of open cities it says: על שדה הארץ יחשב (*Vayikra* 25:31). These cities, then, are considered as pertaining to fields. From a historical-cultural standpoint, we have here an intrinsic difference between the nature of open cities and walled cities, which stems from difference in livelihood, as already noted in our Commentary on *Vayikra* 25:34.

20 **ומה הארץ**. This is a question about the nature of the soil as a source of food and of national prosperity. The question השמנה הִוא אם רזה already exhausts the issue of the soil's fertility; hence, it is difficult to say that the question היש בה עץ refers to fruit trees. Nor can it be assumed that the

21 *They went up and explored the land, from the wilderness of Tzin to Rechov, toward Chamas.*

כא וַיַּעֲלוּ וַיָּתֻרוּ אֶת־הָאָרֶץ מִמִּדְבַּר־
צִן עַד־רְחֹב לְבֹא חֲמָת׃

22 *They went up in the south and came as one man as far as Chevron; [and] there were Achiman, Sheshai and Talmai, the offspring of Anak. And Chevron had been built in seven years, long before Tzo'an Mitzrayim.*

כב וַיַּעֲלוּ בַנֶּגֶב וַיָּבֹא עַד־חֶבְרוֹן וְשָׁם
אֲחִימַן שֵׁשַׁי וְתַלְמַי יְלִידֵי הָעֲנָק
וְחֶבְרוֹן שֶׁבַע שָׁנִים נִבְנְתָה לִפְנֵי
צֹעַן מִצְרָיִם׃

term "עץ" without specification denotes fruit trees. Rather, היש בה עץ means: does the land also contain forests besides fields and orchards? In forested regions, industry inevitably develops, since other sources of livelihood — e.g., agriculture and sheep and cattle breeding — are lacking.

והתחזקתם: have the courage to take fruit openly, even though the result will be that the purpose of your mission will become clear to everyone.

והימים ימי בכורי ענבים. At harvest time, it would have been possible to ascribe the taking of fruit to a different intention. However, it was the season when the first grapes become ripe; harvest time had not yet arrived.

21 **ממדבר צן**. From the description of the borders of the land in chapter 34 it appears that the wilderness of Tzin forms the southeast border, for it says there in verse 3: פאת נגב ממדבר צן על ידי אדום. It also appears from verses 7-9 there that חמת is part of the northwest border, for the northern border is described there as a line extending from the Mediterranean Sea, on the west, over הר ההר, חמת, צדד, זפרן, חצר עינן. Since חצר עינן is in the northeast, it follows that חמת lies to the northwest. Accordingly, they traversed the whole land diagonally from southeast to northwest.

22 **ויעלו וגו' ויבא וגו'**. The singular of ויבא is striking. The common interpretation — based on *Sotah* 34b — is that ויבא refers to Kalev, who went there alone and prostrated himself on the graves of the patriarchs, praying for strength to resist the counsel of his colleagues. Support for this inter-

pretation is adduced from what is said of Kalev: ולו אתן את הארץ אשר דרך בה (*Devarim* 1:36), and in fact Chevron was given to him as an inheritance, as it says: וַיִּתְּנוּ לְכָלֵב אֶת־חֶבְרוֹן כַּאֲשֶׁר דִּבֶּר מֹשֶׁה (*Shoftim* 1:20).

However, upon their return the emissaries say: וגם ילידי הענק ראינו שם (v. 28). Accordingly, it was not only Kalev who went to Chevron, the home of the ענקים. It is precisely his colleagues who tell of ילידי הענק, and it is they who describe the powerful impression made on them by the sight of the ענקים (v. 33). Moreover, in *Devarim* 1:28 it says that it was precisely the description of the ענקים that caused the people to lose heart and took away their courage. In any case, in the preceding verses, there is nothing at all to support making Kalev — or any other individual — the subject of ויבא. Also, the accentuation connects ויבא to ויעלו, indicating that they share a common subject.

Hence, in our opinion, ויעלו as well as ויבא refer to all of the emissaries together. ויבא is put in the singular to indicate that they went together and reached as far as Chevron — as one man in complete accord. "They went up from the south and in unison reached Chevron." There, however, they saw ילידי הענק, and the sight of the giants — and, as we shall see, the strangeness and the huge dimensions of the buildings — made a powerful impression on them; that is when they had a change of heart and their views began to change.

It is possible to reconcile this interpretation with the comments of our Sages in *Sotah*, cited above. Kalev's powerful influence on his colleagues kept them all united until they reached Chevron. There, the conflict broke out, and that is what prompted Kalev to pray at the graves of the patriarchs for the strength to resist the counsel of his colleagues. Since Kalev's faithfulness — as opposed to his colleagues' treachery — was proven in Chevron, he was later given Chevron as an inheritance, and it was Kalev who prevailed over the ענקים, the mere sight of whom had caused his colleagues to lose heart (*Yehoshua* 15:14).

ילידי הענק. Verse 33 states that בני הענק are הנפילים and מן הנפילים; thus they themselves are נפילים (see Commentary, *Bereshis* 6:4) or descendants of נפילים, a gigantic race of giants who are a remnant of the ancient נפילים or their descendants.

An ענק is a necklace worn for pride and glory (see Commentary, ibid. 14:14). Here it denotes the neck, which extends upward and is held high out of pride.

Now, from *Yehoshua* 11:21 we know that ענקים lived in various cities and districts in the Land. They constituted a considerable part of the population, such that Moshe could say of the Land's inhabitants: עם גדול ורם בני ענקים אשר אתה ידעת ואתה שמעת מי יתיצב לפני בני ענק! (*Devarim* 9:2). Understandably, the cities are described as ערים גדלת ובצרת בשמים (ibid. 9:1), for it is only natural that the houses and cities correspond to the huge dimensions of the inhabitants.

Here it says that Chevron was distinguished with these three giants, and they are called "ילידי הענק"; the מרגלים, too, specially emphasize: וגם ילידי הענק ראינו שם (v. 28). These three, then, must have been giants even among giants. This is indicated by the expression "ילידי הענק," which is not identical with the general expression "בני הענק." בני הענק, like בני ישראל, means "descendants of ענק." They might be generations removed from the ancient נפילים. Their lineage was evident in their gigantic height, yet they still might have been much shorter than their early ancestor. By contrast, ילידי הענק — like ילידי בית (*Bereshis* 17:12; *Vayikra* 22:11) — were those born to the first ענק, remnants of the second generation. By their gigantic height and their extreme old age, they exceeded all the other נפילים and thus made an overwhelming impression on all who saw them. From *Yehoshua* (11:21), too, it appears that the others are called simply "הָעֲנָקִים," whereas the three who lived in Chevron — אחימן, ששי, and תלמי — are called "יְלִידֵי הָעֲנָק"; Scripture adds this term especially to distinguish them from the others (ibid. 15:14), after having already called them "בְּנֵי הָעֲנָק." It also says there (v. 13) that their father was called "אַרְבַּע": אַרְבַּע אֲבִי הָעֲנָק; thus the original name of Chevron, "קִרְיַת אַרְבַּע." And it says there (14:15) that this man ארבע was הָאָדָם הַגָּדוֹל בָּעֲנָקִים, the giant among the giants. His immediate descendants were still living in Chevron.

וחברון שבע וגו'. צען מצרים must have been known as a very ancient city, and here it says that Chevron was even older. It is possible that שבע שנים נבנתה does not mean that Chevron was built seven years before Tzo'an but, rather, means: It took seven years to build Chevron — cf. וַיִּבְנֵהוּ שֶׁבַע שָׁנִים (*Melachim* I, 6:38) — and it was built long before Tzo'an, which likewise was well known as an ancient city. Chevron's earlier name "קרית ארבע" indicates that it was built by Arba, the ancestor of the race of giants. קריה is a city protected by strong fortifications; cf. לא היתה קריה אשר שגבה ממנו (*Devarim* 2:36). Accordingly, those who came to Chevron saw before them an imposing stronghold that was built with great diligence by giant hands. This sight intensified the powerful impression that the giant inhabitants made on the newcomers.

23 *They came as far as the Valley of Grapes, and from there they cut down one vine and one cluster of grapes and carried it between two [of them] upon a carrying-pole, and [they] also [took some] of the pomegranates and of the figs.*

כג וַיָּבֹאוּ עַד־נַחַל אֶשְׁכֹּל וַיִּכְרְתוּ
מִשָּׁם זְמוֹרָה וְאֶשְׁכּוֹל עֲנָבִים אֶחָד
וַיִּשָּׂאֻהוּ בַמּוֹט בִּשְׁנָיִם וּמִן־
הָרִמֹּנִים וּמִן־הַתְּאֵנִים׃

24 *This place was called Valley of Grapes because of the cluster of grapes that the Children of Israel had cut from there.*

כד לַמָּקוֹם הַהוּא קָרָא נַחַל אֶשְׁכּוֹל
עַל אֹדוֹת הָאֶשְׁכּוֹל אֲשֶׁר־כָּרְתוּ
מִשָּׁם בְּנֵי יִשְׂרָאֵל׃

25 *They returned from the exploration of the land at the end of forty days.*

כה וַיָּשֻׁבוּ מִתּוּר הָאָרֶץ מִקֵּץ
אַרְבָּעִים יוֹם׃

26 *They went and they came to Moshe and to Aharon and to the entire community of the Children of Israel, to the wilderness of Paran, toward Kadesh. They brought back word to them and to the entire community, and showed them the fruit of the land.*

כו וַיֵּלְכוּ וַיָּבֹאוּ אֶל־מֹשֶׁה וְאֶל־אַהֲרֹן
וְאֶל־כָּל־עֲדַת בְּנֵי־יִשְׂרָאֵל אֶל־
מִדְבַּר פָּארָן קָדֵשָׁה וַיָּשִׁיבוּ אֹתָם
דָּבָר וְאֶת־כָּל־הָעֵדָה וַיַּרְאוּם
אֶת־פְּרִי הָאָרֶץ׃

---

23 **אשכל** — see Commentary, *Bereshis* 27:45. **זמרה** — see Commentary, ibid. 43:11. **מוט** — see Commentary, *Vayikra* 26:13.

26 **וילכו ויבאו וגו׳**. On their way back they had decided that they would not go directly to Moshe and Aharon with their report, but would report immediately their findings to the entire nation. This showed their evil intentions. Had their intentions been good, they would have reported first to Moshe and Aharon and sought their advice and instructions. But that was just what they did not want. They thought that the only means for their own and the people's salvation lay in opposition to Moshe and Aharon. Their report therefore took the form of an accusation against

27 *They told him and said: We came into the land where you sent us, and it is indeed flowing with milk and honey, and this is its fruit.*

כז וַיְסַפְּרוּ־לוֹ וַיֹּאמְרוּ בָּאנוּ אֶל־
הָאָרֶץ אֲשֶׁר שְׁלַחְתָּנוּ וְגַם זָבַת
חָלָב וּדְבַשׁ הִוא וְזֶה־פִּרְיָהּ׃

28 *However, the people that dwell in the land are too strong, and the cities are exceedingly great fortresses, and we also saw offspring of Anak there.*

כח אֶפֶס כִּי־עַז הָעָם הַיֹּשֵׁב בָּאָרֶץ
וְהֶעָרִים בְּצֻרוֹת גְּדֹלֹת מְאֹד וְגַם־
יְלִדֵי הָעֲנָק רָאִינוּ שָׁם׃

29 *Amalek dwells in the land of the south; the Chitti, the Yevusi and the Emori dwell in the mountains; and the Kena'ani dwell by the sea and on the banks of the Yarden.*

כט עֲמָלֵק יוֹשֵׁב בְּאֶרֶץ הַנֶּגֶב וְהַחִתִּי
וְהַיְבוּסִי וְהָאֱמֹרִי יוֹשֵׁב בָּהָר
וְהַכְּנַעֲנִי יוֹשֵׁב עַל־הַיָּם וְעַל יַד
הַיַּרְדֵּן׃

Moshe and Aharon in the presence of the entire nation; they appealed to the people to save themselves from Moshe and Aharon, who would bring ruin upon them.

ויראום את פרי הארץ: Their whole report is nothing but an explanation of what they believed to be their incontestable argument. From the extraordinary size of the fruit, the people could picture to themselves the frightening size of the men and the corresponding size of everything connected with them.

28 **אפס וגו׳**: All this is nothing, loses all value to us, for the people are too strong for us. בצרות גדלת מאד, not just בצורות גדולות: The cities are exceedingly great fortresses, built by giants to resist giants. Hence, against ordinary people they are impregnable.

וגם ילדי הענק — see Commentary, verse 22.

29 **עמלק וגו׳**. The whole land is sketched. Amalek dwells in the south; the Chitti, etc., dwell in the mountains of Lebanon, the range that crosses the land from north to south; the Mediterranean seashore and the banks of the Yarden form the bulwarks on the west and on the east.

They had already felt the sword of Amalek on their own flesh. The

30 *Then Kalev quieted the people for Moshe and said: We can indeed go up and take possession of it, for we are truly able to do so.*

ל וַיַּהַס כָּלֵב אֶת־הָעָם אֶל־מֹשֶׁה וַיֹּאמֶר עָלֹה נַעֲלֶה וְיָרַשְׁנוּ אֹתָהּ כִּי־יָכוֹל נוּכַל לָהּ׃

31 *But the men who had gone up with him said: We cannot go up against this people, for they are too strong for us.*

לא וְהָאֲנָשִׁים אֲשֶׁר־עָלוּ עִמּוֹ אָמְרוּ לֹא נוּכַל לַעֲלוֹת אֶל־הָעָם כִּי־חָזָק הוּא מִמֶּנּוּ׃

32 *They then produced a slanderous report for the Children of Israel about the land they had explored, saying: The land through which we passed, to explore it, is a land that destroys its inhabitants, and the entire population that we saw are big in stature.*

לב וַיֹּצִיאוּ דִּבַּת הָאָרֶץ אֲשֶׁר תָּרוּ אֹתָהּ אֶל־בְּנֵי יִשְׂרָאֵל לֵאמֹר הָאָרֶץ אֲשֶׁר עָבַרְנוּ בָהּ לָתוּר אֹתָהּ אֶרֶץ אֹכֶלֶת יוֹשְׁבֶיהָ הִוא וְכָל־הָעָם אֲשֶׁר־רָאִינוּ בְתוֹכָהּ אַנְשֵׁי מִדּוֹת׃

Amaleki were not inhabitants of the land, but they lived close by, and there was reason to fear that they would suddenly attack during the attempt to conquer the land.

30 **ויהס** is the *hif'il* of הסה, which is related to חשה, to be silent. הסה means: to refrain — or to prevent others — from speaking. Thus in *Chavakkuk* 2:20, *Zecharyah* 2:17, et al.

Kalev tried to prevent the people from speaking against Moshe. As soon as the מרגלים had finished speaking, the people's anger burst out against Moshe. We can understand why it was not Yehoshua but Kalev who rose to speak. For at that time it was necessary to defend Moshe, and the people — aware of Yehoshua's close relationship with Moshe — would not have attached much weight to Yehoshua's assurances.

32 **ויציאו דבת וגו׳** — see Commentary, *Bereshis* 37:2.

They produced a slanderous report about the land, and thus their sin reached its height. Not ויביאו — as it says in the case of Yosef [ויבא יוסף;

33 *We saw giants there, the sons of Anak, descendants of the giants. We were in our own eyes like grasshoppers, and so, too, were we in their eyes.*

לג וְשָׁ֣ם רָאִ֗ינוּ אֶת־הַנְּפִילִ֛ים בְּנֵ֥י עֲנָ֖ק מִן־הַנְּפִלִ֑ים וַנְּהִ֤י בְעֵינֵ֙ינוּ֙ כַּחֲגָבִ֔ים וְכֵ֥ן הָיִ֖ינוּ בְּעֵינֵיהֶֽם׃

Bereshis 37:2]— but ויציאו: they produced, fabricated an evil report about the land (רמב"ן). By doing so, they frightened the people and brought them to the point of complete despair. They told them: Even if you were to succeed in conquering the land, to live there would be a disaster. It is a land that brings ruin upon its inhabitants. It is not suitable for people of ordinary size. Only giants can live in it; ordinary people soon die there. This accounts for the extraordinary size of the people — אנשי מדות. The small and the weak do not survive there (רמב"ן).

33 **ושם ראינו את הנפילים**, those ancient giants אשר מעולם אנשי השם (*Bereshis* 6:4), of whose enormous size and strength ancient legends tell — we truly and actually saw them with our own eyes. These are ילידי הענק (vv. 22 and 28), the three giant brothers living in Chevron. בני ענק מן הנפלים are the other ענקים living in the land; they, too, are descendants of the נפילים (see Commentary above, v. 22).

Thus, there were still remnants of the antediluvian נפילים living in Eretz Yisrael. This fact fits well with the opinion (*Zevachim* 113a) that לא ירד מבול לארץ ישראל, Eretz Yisrael was spared from the flood. In Eretz Yisrael, then, the land's original power remained intact. When the land was under a Canaanite population, this power showed itself only in production of ענקים, men possessed of great physical stature. But this power can also make the land suitable to be the soil for God's people; for this people will observe God's Torah in this land and aspire to the ideal of man's spiritual and moral greatness, and thus the world will rejuvenate and the land will be like a paradise (see Commentary, *Bereshis* 3:19). Let us not forget the statement by our Sages that bodily health and strength are among the preliminary conditions for the highest spiritual development (see *Shabbos* 92a). Perhaps we are not mistaken in saying that the relation between the power of the land and the character of its inhabitants is as follows: Where the mind lies fallow, the land's power is apt to produce

14 1 *Then the entire community lifted up their voice and gave it free rein, and the people wept all through that night.*

יד א וַתִּשָּׂא֙ כָּל־הָ֣עֵדָ֔ה וַֽיִּתְּנ֖וּ אֶת־
קוֹלָ֑ם וַיִּבְכּ֥וּ הָעָ֖ם בַּלַּ֥יְלָה הַהֽוּא׃

2 *Then all the Children of Israel murmured against Moshe and against Aharon, and the entire community said to them: Would that we had died in the land of Egypt, or in this wilderness — would that we had died there!*

ב וַיִּלֹּ֙נוּ֙ עַל־מֹשֶׁ֣ה וְעַֽל־אַהֲרֹ֔ן כֹּ֖ל בְּנֵ֣י
יִשְׂרָאֵ֑ל וַיֹּאמְר֨וּ אֲלֵהֶ֜ם כָּל־הָעֵדָ֗ה
לוּ־מַ֙תְנוּ֙ בְּאֶ֣רֶץ מִצְרַ֔יִם א֛וֹ
בַּמִּדְבָּ֥ר הַזֶּ֖ה לוּ־מָֽתְנוּ׃

3 *Why is* God *bringing us to this land to fall by the sword? Our wives and our children will become prey! Truly it would be better for us to return to Egypt.*

ג וְלָמָ֣ה יְ֠הֹוָ֠ה מֵבִ֨יא אֹתָ֜נוּ אֶל־
הָאָ֣רֶץ הַזֹּ֗את לִנְפֹּ֣ל בַּחֶ֔רֶב נָשֵׁ֥ינוּ
וְטַפֵּ֖נוּ יִהְי֣וּ לָבַ֑ז הֲל֧וֹא ט֛וֹב לָ֖נוּ
שׁ֥וּב מִצְרָֽיְמָה׃

giants possessed of great physical stature; but if the land's inhabitants are people whose direction is spiritual, the land's power is used for spiritual activity and not for giant bodily stature.

CHAPTER 14

1 **ותשא וגו׳** means: ותשא כל העדה את קולם ויתנו את קולם. They first broke out in a great cry and then continued the outcry without letup.

בלילה ההוא. According to *Ta'anis* 29a, it was the night of the ninth of Av, the day on which, in a later period as well, the bitterest tragedies of the national downfall occurred. This could explain the word "ההוא." It indicates that this night is to be remembered in the future.

2 **וילנו וגו׳**. The complaining was universal; all the men who had a say, who formed the "community," came directly to Moshe and Aharon with accusations.

4 *And they said to one another: Let us appoint a leader, and return to Egypt.*

ד וַיֹּאמְרוּ אִישׁ אֶל־אָחִיו נִתְּנָה רֹאשׁ וְנָשׁוּבָה מִצְרָיְמָה׃

5 *Then Moshe and Aharon fell upon their faces before the whole assembly of the community of the Children of Israel.*

ה וַיִּפֹּל מֹשֶׁה וְאַהֲרֹן עַל־פְּנֵיהֶם לִפְנֵי כָּל־קְהַל עֲדַת בְּנֵי יִשְׂרָאֵל׃

6 *But Yehoshua, son of Nun, and Kalev, son of Yefunneh, of those who had explored the land, had rent their garments.*

ו וִיהוֹשֻׁעַ בִּן־נוּן וְכָלֵב בֶּן־יְפֻנֶּה מִן־הַתָּרִים אֶת־הָאָרֶץ קָרְעוּ בִּגְדֵיהֶם׃

7 *And they said to the entire community of the Children of Israel: The land through which we passed, to explore it, is an exceedingly good land.*

ז וַיֹּאמְרוּ אֶל־כָּל־עֲדַת בְּנֵי־יִשְׂרָאֵל לֵאמֹר הָאָרֶץ אֲשֶׁר עָבַרְנוּ בָהּ לָתוּר אֹתָהּ טוֹבָה הָאָרֶץ מְאֹד מְאֹד׃ שלישי

5 **ויפל וגו'**. By saying נתנה ראש ונשובה מצרימה, as stated in the preceding verse, the people had served notice on Moshe and Aharon that they would no longer follow their orders. Moshe and Aharon took this to mean that their mission was at an end. They cast themselves down לפני כל קהל וגו'.

קהל עדת וגו' is the council entrusted with the leadership of the community: the elders (see Commentary, *Shemos* 12:3-6). By casting themselves down before the elders, Moshe and Aharon indicated that the leadership of the people had now reverted to the elders. They expressed thereby that since the people would no longer obey them, their authority was at an end, and there was nothing more they could do for the people.

6 **ויהושע וגו'**. Here, in the קריעה, in the feeling of grief over Moshe, over the complete failure of his mission, and over the fateful sin of the people — here Yehoshua takes the lead.

קרעו בגדיהם. As soon as they saw the direction in which the events were developing, they — in contrast to their colleagues — rent their garments.

7 **טובה הארץ מאד מאד**: Not only is it not a land that אוכלת את יושביה, but it is טובה מאד מאד.

8 *If* God *is pleased with us, He will bring us into this land and give it to us, a land truly flowing with milk and honey.*

9 *Only do not rebel against* God*! And* you, *you should not fear the people of this land, for they are our bread! Their shade has departed from them, because* God *is with us; do not fear them.*

ח אִם־חָפֵץ בָּנוּ יְהוָה וְהֵבִיא אֹתָנוּ
אֶל־הָאָרֶץ הַזֹּאת וּנְתָנָהּ לָנוּ אֶרֶץ
אֲשֶׁר־הִוא זָבַת חָלָב וּדְבָשׁ׃
ט אַךְ בַּיהוָה אַל־תִּמְרֹדוּ וְאַתֶּם אַל־
תִּירְאוּ אֶת־עַם הָאָרֶץ כִּי לַחְמֵנוּ
הֵם סָר צִלָּם מֵעֲלֵיהֶם וַיהוָה אִתָּנוּ
אַל־תִּירָאֻם׃

8 **אם חפץ וגו׳**. Conquering the land depends solely on our being worthy of God's satisfaction with us.

ארץ אשר הִוא וגו׳. These words express their great anger at the slanderous report about the land. They saw the land, and found that it is indeed זבת חלב ודבש — as always promised to them.

9 **ואתם**, "And *you.*" All the spiritual greatness and moral nobility, the whole God-ordained vocation and closeness of the covenant, associated with Israel's past and future — all these are included in this "*you.*" Even if these people are the most terrifying giants, with fortresses of solid granite, *you* should have no fear of them. Knowing your spiritual and moral power, which is sustained by God and which takes strength in God, they will all melt away. You should be ashamed to fear them!

כי לחמנו הם. They are spiritually and morally degenerated, and are imposing only in their material physique. Hence, they can offer no resistance and amount to nothing against the Divine spiritual and moral principle, which will fight against them through Israel.

סר צלם וגו׳. They can survive only as long as they hide in the shadows and remain unnoticed. But when we enter into their midst, God, with His truth and His justice, which brings salvation to mankind, will enter along with us. Before the brilliance of this truth, their shade will vanish, and their depravity will stand fully exposed. Because of this depravity, they will be judged and destroyed. Therefore, do not fear them!

10 *The entire community spoke of stoning them to death, when the glory of* God *appeared in the Tent of Appointed Meeting to all the Children of Israel.*

י וַיֹּאמְרוּ֙ כָּל־הָ֣עֵדָ֔ה לִרְגּ֥וֹם אֹתָ֖ם
בָּאֲבָנִ֑ים וּכְב֣וֹד יְהֹוָ֗ה נִרְאָה֙ בְּאֹ֣הֶל
מוֹעֵ֔ד אֶֽל־כָּל־בְּנֵ֖י יִשְׂרָאֵֽל׃ פ

11 *And* God *said to Moshe: How long will this people mock Me? And how long will they put no trust in Me, despite all the signs that I have performed in their midst?*

יא וַיֹּ֤אמֶר יְהֹוָה֙ אֶל־מֹשֶׁ֔ה עַד־אָ֥נָה
יְנַאֲצֻ֖נִי הָעָ֣ם הַזֶּ֑ה וְעַד־אָ֙נָה֙ לֹא־
יַאֲמִ֣ינוּ בִ֔י בְּכֹל֙ הָֽאֹתֹ֔ת אֲשֶׁ֥ר
עָשִׂ֖יתִי בְּקִרְבּֽוֹ׃

12 *I will strike them with pestilence and drive them out of existence, and make you into a greater, mightier nation than they are.*

יב אַכֶּ֥נּוּ בַדֶּ֖בֶר וְאוֹרִשֶׁ֑נּוּ וְאֶֽעֱשֶׂה֙
אֹֽתְךָ֔ לְגוֹי־גָּד֥וֹל וְעָצ֖וּם מִמֶּֽנּוּ׃

13 *And Moshe said to* God*: Then the*

יג וַיֹּ֥אמֶר מֹשֶׁ֖ה אֶל־יְהֹוָ֑ה וְשָׁמְע֣וּ

---

10 **נראה באהל מועד**: When the entire people was condemned to destruction because it was no longer worthy of its mission, God's glory found a place for itself on earth only *within* the Sanctuary of the Torah. God's Torah, which is deposited there, and the future that was promised for it there, will endure forever — even if an entire generation is lost to it.

11 **ינאצני**. נאץ is related to נחץ, which means: to urgently press on in haste. נאץ, then, means: to hastily skip over something, because it is not worthy of any consideration. It is the highest degree of scorn and abuse: the מנאץ does not consider the object worthy of any consideration whatsoever.

ניאוץ exactly describes the people's feelings shown here. In planning their future, they did not include God in their considerations.

12 **ואורשנו**: I will drive them out of existence in this world.

3-16 **ויאמר משה וגו׳**. Moshe accepts God's words, but he foresees their direct consequences: a setback to God's project, in which Moshe and the people serve as implements. It is to this that he now gives expression.

If the present generation is wiped out, God's project for the future of

Egyptians will hear this — for, after all, it is with Your might that You have brought out this people from their midst.	מִצְרַ֔יִם כִּֽי־הֶעֱלִ֧יתָ בְכֹחֲךָ֛ אֶת־הָעָ֥ם הַזֶּ֖ה מִקִּרְבּֽוֹ׃
14 *And they will say to the inhabitants of this land — they, too, have already heard that You, O God,*	יד וְאָמְר֗וּ אֶל־יוֹשֵׁב֮ הָאָ֣רֶץ הַזֹּאת֒ שָֽׁמְעוּ֙ כִּֽי־אַתָּ֣ה יְהוָ֔ה בְּקֶ֖רֶב הָעָ֣ם

mankind will not be lost. After four hundred years, a new Abrahamitic people can emerge from Moshe, and through it the promise given to Avraham will be fulfilled. But in the present, the destruction of the people would work against the Divine objective of enlightening the nations, which is one of the main purposes for which Israel was chosen.

Even now, the eyes of the two cultured nations of our time — the Egyptians and the Phoenicians — are directed to this people which is God's people. With anxious tension they are following its national history, for from it they have received some idea of the one, omnipotent God Who freely rules His world and fights for justice and humanity on earth; and Who, by introducing this people into the midst of the nations, has already declared war on their gods. The Egyptians — because they saw and felt Your power directly, for You took this people out of their midst and raised it up to You, so that it should go up to the land that You promised it. The Phoenicians — because they, too, have already heard of God's power manifesting itself in the midst of this people which threatens them; His protection and guidance of this people attest to His power.

כי העלית until מקרבו (in v. 13) and שמעו until לילה (in v. 14) are parenthetical statements. והמתה וגו׳ (in v. 15) resumes the train of thought; but since there has been a long interruption, Scripture repeats the content of God's previous statement (אכנו בדבר, v. 12), to which Moshe (in v. 13, ושמעו) had begun to respond, and then (the latter part of v. 15) reiterates: ואמרו. Thus, these sentences run as follows: If You do this, the Egyptians will say to the Phoenicians — both of them have already become aware of You, and they are anxiously following Your continuing guidance of this people — indeed, if You now suddenly kill this people all at once, the nations that have heard this news of You will say: מבלתי יכלת וגו׳.

This result would be antithetical to the whole purpose of Israel's elec-

dwell in the midst of this people, that You, O God, *are seen eye to eye, that Your cloud rests over them, and You go before them in a pillar of cloud by day and in a pillar of fire by night —*	הַזֶּה אֲשֶׁר־עַ֨יִן בְּעַ֜יִן נִרְאָ֣ה ׀ אַתָּ֣ה יְהוָ֗ה וַעֲנָֽנְךָ֙ עֹמֵ֣ד עֲלֵהֶ֔ם וּבְעַמֻּ֣ד עָנָ֗ן אַתָּ֨ה הֹלֵ֤ךְ לִפְנֵיהֶם֙ יוֹמָ֔ם וּבְעַמּ֥וּד אֵ֖שׁ לָֽיְלָה׃
15 *If you now kill this people as one man, then these nations that have heard this news of You will say:*	טו וְהֵמַתָּ֛ה אֶת־הָעָ֥ם הַזֶּ֖ה כְּאִ֣ישׁ אֶחָ֑ד וְאָֽמְרוּ֙ הַגּוֹיִ֔ם אֲשֶׁר־שָׁמְע֥וּ אֶת־שִׁמְעֲךָ֖ לֵאמֹֽר׃
16 *It is beyond the capacity of* God *to bring these people into the land that He has sworn to them. That is why He slaughtered them in the wilderness.*	טז מִבִּלְתִּ֞י יְכֹ֣לֶת יְהוָ֗ה לְהָבִיא֙ אֶת־הָעָ֣ם הַזֶּ֔ה אֶל־הָאָ֖רֶץ אֲשֶׁר־נִשְׁבַּ֣ע לָהֶ֑ם וַיִּשְׁחָטֵ֖ם בַּמִּדְבָּֽר׃

tion, and would only strengthen the nations' denial of Your power. The initiative for taking this mistaken view of the event would come from Egypt, which has already been forced by painful afflictions to recognize Your power.

עין בעין: the human eye sees Your eye; people see that You see; they discover that You watch over the earth with Your providence.

ובעמד ענן אתה הלך לפניהם: You go before them and show them the way to the Promised Land.

והמתָה: If now *You*, Who have already revealed to all eyes Your intention of bringing this people into the Land, instead kill this people כאיש אחד, suddenly and all at once, in a miraculous manner . . .

כאיש אחד assumes that if the fathers, who have become unworthy of the Land, die off gradually in a natural manner, and only their children enter the Land, this will not detract from the recognition of God among the nations. Only if the people die suddenly, all at once, and as a result God's promise will not be fulfilled until centuries hence — only in such a case will the nations fall into error.

יכלת is a noun, like יְבֹשֶׁת המים (*Bereshis* 8:7), קְטֹרֶת, and so forth.

יז וְעַתָּה יִגְדַּל־נָא כֹּחַ אֲדֹנָי כַּאֲשֶׁר
דִּבַּרְתָּ לֵאמֹר:
י׳ רבתי

17 *And now, do let the power of my Lord be great, as You did once say it:*

יח יְהוָה אֶרֶךְ אַפַּיִם וְרַב־חֶסֶד נֹשֵׂא
עָוֹן וָפָשַׁע וְנַקֵּה לֹא יְנַקֶּה פֹּקֵד עֲוֹן
אָבוֹת עַל־בָּנִים עַל־שִׁלֵּשִׁים
וְעַל־רִבֵּעִים:

18 God, *long-suffering and abundant in lovingkindness, lifting away crookedness and rebellion, yet He excuses nothing; He remembers the crookedness of parents for the children, to the third and fourth generation.*

17-18 **ועתה**. Now is the time to demonstrate the greatness of Your power. For although the people deserve to be destroyed, other considerations (as just stated) oppose the carrying out of this punishment. You have granted me insight into the ways of Your rule and have taught me to recognize the infinite greatness and diversity of Your "goodness" (cf. Commentary, *Shemos* 33:19-20). And now, this is a case that clearly calls for the exercise of Your power in all its greatness.

יגדל נא. The sign of the future tense is stressed by a large י. All the greatness of the miracles and the power that You have shown thus far, in Egypt and in the wilderness — all this does not reach that greatness of כח that will now be shown if You will forgive their sin. For Your power is world-creating and world-bearing, and in order to accomplish Your purposes it overcomes the world and shapes the world — all this is inherent in the concept of כח. This כח will now be demonstrated if, in the face of *such* defection, You will act in accordance with Your attributes, according to the mode of rule that You revealed to me; if You will be ארך אפים ורב חסד נושא עון ופשע, and while upholding ונקה לא ינקה You nevertheless will be פקד עון אבות על בנים על שלשים ועל רבעים!

According to heathen thought, the great might of its gods lies in destruction. But the true God is great not in might, but in power, כח. כח is the ability to create light out of darkness, and to transform opposition into agreement. כח fans the tiny harmonious spark that lies hidden in the very midst of the opposition and, through this spark, blazes a trail by which, in the course of time, the opposition can be overcome and transformed into agreement. To the כח mode of God's rule which educates mankind, a thousand years are like one day of progressive development; "כח" has infinite patience, for it has the whole of eternity before it.

ועתה יגדל נא כח אדנ-י כאשר דברת לאמר. The sudden annihilation of the entire nation would demonstrate Your might, but Your *power* will be revealed in all its greatness if You let the people live, and through them and with their assistance You achieve the purpose they have scorned.

Here he calls God "אדנ-י," for whoever is called upon to be an instrument in God's service describes his relationship to God by this Name. It represents the כח mode of God's rule, by which He educates people and nations. God revealed this mode of rule to Moshe as the seal of the enterprise to be completed by him; this was after the sin of the golden calf, when Moshe asked that God reveal to him the mode of rule that would accompany him as he continued to carry out his mission (*Shemos* 33:12ff.; see Commentary there).

Among the Divine attributes revealed to him, Moshe stresses those whose activation he seeks in this case. Foremost among them is **ארך אפים**: God patiently awaits the satisfaction of His just demands. Instead of immediately annihilating the sinner, God gives him time, a long time, to reconsider, to mend his ways, to rise again after his fall, to rectify the wrong.

ורב חסד: He bestows love in abundance and is not stingy with it. His stores are full of love, which He dispenses again and again, and He is prepared to continue bestowing love even for the thousandth time, after the sinner has forfeited his right to it nine hundred and ninety-nine times.

נושא עון ופשע: He lifts away the onus of waywardness and rebellion from the one who left the straight path knowingly but motivated by passion [עון], or even from the one who rebelled openly [פשע], so that he should not be buried beneath the burden.

Finally, Moshe mentions the Divine attribute that reveals the greatness of His love in all its depth: God views the present in terms of the future, every man in terms of his children and grandchildren, and every generation in terms of its posterity. He wishes to purify all people, all generations, and all eras, to save them from moral ruin; nevertheless, **ונקה לא ינקה**, He will not allow even the slightest unrepented sin to go unpunished. Yet He will extend the opportunity for repentance over many generations; and before passing sentence on a man, He will look

19 *Forgive, I beseech You, the crookedness of this people according to the greatness of Your lovingkindness, and even as You have extended forbearance to this people from Egypt even until now.*

יט סְלַח־נָא לַעֲוֺן הָעָם הַזֶּה כְּגֹדֶל חַסְדֶּךָ וְכַאֲשֶׁר נָשָׂאתָה לָעָם הַזֶּה מִמִּצְרַיִם וְעַד־הֵנָּה׃

20 *And* God *said: I have forgiven, in accordance with your word.*

כ וַיֹּאמֶר יְהוָה סָלַחְתִּי כִּדְבָרֶךָ׃

upon that man's great-grandson, still unborn, who might come to his senses and ascend to that high level of morality from which his grandfather — in error, or perhaps deliberately — fell: ונקה לא ינקה פקד עון אבות על בנים על שלשים ועל רבעים (see Commentary, *Shemos* 34:6-7).

בנים here denotes descendants generally. Thus, first the Divine attribute itself is described by the words אבות על בנים, and then the attribute is limited by the addition of על שלשים ועל רבעים. For שלשים are great-grandchildren, and if בנים were meant to be taken literally as immediate children, then בני בנים should also be mentioned, just as they are mentioned in *Shemos* 34:7. (The wording in *Shemos* 20:5 resembles the wording here.)

19 **סלח וגו׳ כגדל חסדך**: Similarly, the psalm of providence in *Tehillim* 145 sings of God's "greatness," primarily by describing His love (see Commentary there).

וכאשר נשאת לעם הזה וגו׳: Its whole history, from Egypt until now, has been nothing but a revelation of God's forgiving love. He bears with the sinner's errant ways and does not let him collapse under the burden of his sin. Both of these ideas are included in the concept of נושא עון. One who is נושא עון takes the sin on himself, as it were, helps the sinner bear his burden, and grants atonement and heals in ways other than ruination of the wicked person.

Moshe repeats the expression העם הזה, לעם הזה: the people's present behavior is not unlike their previous behavior; it is only the highest level of defection. Heretofore as well, the people have been wavering and heading in this direction.

20 **ויאמר ה׳ סלחתי כדברך**. God had already beforehand decided to forgive — for the very reasons that Moshe stressed. In verse 12 He merely in-

כא וְאוּלָם חַי־אָנִי וְיִמָּלֵא כְבוֹד־יְהֹוָה אֶת־כָּל־הָאָרֶץ׃

21 *However, as surely as I live, and [as surely] as the whole earth will be full of* God's *glory,*

formed Moshe of the punishment that would be indicated for this defection, were it not for these external considerations. Thereby He afforded Moshe insight into the nature of God's rule, and at the same time also gave him the opportunity to demonstrate his own complete selflessness. Moshe did not harbor the slightest bitterness toward this people who were rebelling against him, nor was he tempted in the least by the brilliant prospect of becoming a second Avraham — the patriarch of the promised people of God! Only one who is possessed of such ענוה, who is completely selfless, will be privileged to attain so profound a perception of God's mode of rule. Only he will be elevated to a level of human insight that is attuned to Divine insight. Only he meets the condition for understanding God's ways, for only he can attain complete objectivity, unclouded by subjective motives (cf. Commentary, *Shemos* 6:14-30, on עושר as a prerequisite for נבואה).

In *Tehillim* 99:6, God's closeness to Moshe, Aharon, and Shemuel is described by the words קֹרְאִים אֶל־ה׳ וְהוּא יַעֲנֵם. The א of קראים is quiescent, and the word is read as קורים, as though stemming from the root קרה. In our view, this difference between what is written and what is read reveals the secret as to why they, more than other mortals, merited to receive a favorable response to their prayers. When they called to God, they "met" Him. They asked for nothing that was not suitable. In their prayers, they assumed the standpoint of the Divine mode of rule and attuned their thoughts to God's thoughts (see Commentary there). That is exactly what is expressed here by סלחתי כדברך.

סלחתי. We have already noted (Commentary, *Bereshis* 24:21) the relation of סלח to שלח and צלח. In our verse, סלח occurs in this special sense. The people's sin obstructed the people's progress. Thanks to God's kindness and the wisdom of His rule, the people can again advance and progress toward the fulfillment of its destiny.

21 **ואולם חי אני וגו׳**. These could be the two factors that we indicated above (on vv. 17-18), which in this case call for exercising the attribute of ארך

22 *All the men who have seen My glory and My signs that I performed in Egypt and in the wilderness, and who have nevertheless put Me to the test these ten times and still did not listen to My voice,*

23 *They shall not see the land that I swore to their fathers, and all those who mock Me shall not see it.*

כב כִּ֤י כָל־הָֽאֲנָשִׁים֙ הָֽרֹאִ֣ים אֶת־
כְּבֹדִ֔י וְאֶת־אֹ֣תֹתַ֔י אֲשֶׁר־עָשִׂ֥יתִי
בְמִצְרַ֖יִם וּבַמִּדְבָּ֑ר וַיְנַסּ֣וּ אֹתִ֗י זֶ֚ה
עֶ֣שֶׂר פְּעָמִ֔ים וְלֹ֥א שָׁמְע֖וּ בְּקוֹלִֽי׃

כג אִם־יִרְאוּ֙ אֶת־הָאָ֔רֶץ אֲשֶׁ֥ר
נִשְׁבַּ֖עְתִּי לַאֲבֹתָ֑ם וְכָל־מְנַאֲצַ֖י לֹ֥א
יִרְאֽוּהָ׃

אפים. As surely as חי אני — I am eternal and could postpone the achievement of My goals from era to era — and as surely as ימלא כבוד ה׳ את כל הארץ, Israel's fate stands in the service of enlightening all of mankind, and the realization of this ideal is the ultimate purpose of My rule. Indeed, these two factors are significant enough to speak against the annihilation of the people. But just as all this is true, so is the following:

22-23 **כי כל האנשים וגו׳**, the forgiveness cannot be absolute. For these men have seen all the Divine revelations until this point, and yet the revelations have not sufficed to win their hearts and minds to boundless devotion to God. They have thereby shown their unworthiness and unfitness for possessing the Land. הראים את כבדי: they have seen the whole "weight" of My greatness, and they have "seen" כבדי; God did not remain for them merely an abstract idea, based on reason, faith, or conjecture; rather, they had actual, perceptual experience of Him. From their experience they recognized that He is the supreme, omnipotent Force in the midst of all the concrete earthly forces. ואת אתתי אשר עשיתי וגו׳: They have seen His "signs," His deeds that enlighten the mind. These signs were revealed to them in Egypt and in the wilderness — i.e., in the sphere of power of the most highly developed human culture, and in a wasteland totally devoid of the support of human culture. It was made clear to them that a culture breaks down and comes to naught if man rebels against God's Will, and that a wasteland is transformed into a habitable place on the merit of faithful devotion to God's Will. They have seen all this, yet they doubt whether God actually intervenes in earthly affairs, and whether His intervention and the assistance of His providence are sufficient. Ten times, in many different situations, they put God to the test, as it were, trying out whether His promised help is reliable, actual, and adequate. Despite all this: ולא שמעו בקולי, they have not learned to obey God.

Hence אם יראו את הארץ (this is an oath formula; see Commentary, *Bereshis* 21:23): God swears irrevocably that *these* men shall *not* see the Land.

הראים — אם יראו. In our opinion, these two expressions are intimately connected, which explains the use here of the phraseology of "ראיית הארץ" instead of the common phraseology "ביאת הארץ." For the Land is זבת חלב ודבש, and, as the land of God's people, it will attain an unimagined fullness of blossom and blessing. But the Land can attain that destiny only if the people in control of the Land are worthy of elevating it to that level; if the people see God, His rule, and His providence as an actual reality that intervenes in earthly affairs and determines them — as no less a reality than the Land, its bounty, and its resources; in short, if they *see God* as much as they *see the Land.*

For this was the purpose of everything they experienced במצרים and במדבר until the day they entered the Land: it was all meant to bring them to this "seeing of God," to instill in their hearts and minds fear of God and trust in God, so that they should fear nothing other than God and place their trust solely in Him.

But the very opposite of this "seeing God" in the Land is ניאוץ ה׳. We have already explained (on v. 11) the nature of the מנאץ: In comparison with the elements of earthly success, God in his eyes is as nothing. When he considers the ways to success and prosperity, he skips over God as one unworthy of consideration. Hence: אם יראו את הארץ אשר נשבעתי לאבתם וכל מנאצי לא יראוה.

וכל מנאצי לא יראוה. The Psalmist (*Tehillim* 106:24-27) describes this stage in the development of our history as follows: וַיִּמְאֲסוּ בְּאֶרֶץ חֶמְדָּה לֹא־הֶאֱמִינוּ לִדְבָרוֹ. וַיֵּרָגְנוּ בְאָהֳלֵיהֶם לֹא שָׁמְעוּ בְּקוֹל ה׳. וַיִּשָּׂא יָדוֹ לָהֶם לְהַפִּיל אוֹתָם בַּמִּדְבָּר. וּלְהַפִּיל זַרְעָם בַּגּוֹיִם וּלְזָרוֹתָם בָּאֲרָצוֹת. This passage indicates that when it was decreed that the generation that had gone forth from Egypt would die in the wilderness, on that same day it was also decreed that Israel would be exiled from the Land and dispersed among the nations. It does indeed appear that the future exile is included in the words: וכל מנאצי לא יראוה (see רמב״ן here). For the same blindness that cost their forefathers the right to enter God's land will exile the children from the land if they do as their forefathers did.

24 *But as for My servant Kalev, because there was a different spirit with him, and [because], following Me, he fulfilled his duty, him I will bring into the land into which he went, and he will leave it to his descendants.*

כד וְעַבְדִּי כָּלֵב עֵקֶב הָיְתָה רוּחַ
אַחֶרֶת עִמּוֹ וַיְמַלֵּא אַחֲרָי
וַהֲבִיאֹתִיו אֶל־הָאָרֶץ אֲשֶׁר־בָּא
שָׁמָּה וְזַרְעוֹ יוֹרִשֶׁנָּה׃

We may well say that the ארך אפים mode of God's rule — thanks to which the immature generation was spared the fate of mass annihilation, and the sons born to and educated by this generation were led into the land — included in its educational plan all the subsequent centuries. In this plan, Divine providence envisioned that its purposes would be fully realized only in a future beyond our own present day. For the generation reared by the generation of the wilderness, which merited to enter the Land, likewise did not attain the mature height of its calling. Twice we attained statehood in the Land, and twice we were exiled from it, and all that has befallen us until this very day is nothing but an educational process directed by the attribute of ארך אפים, to train us for our spiritual and moral calling. The pure and complete realization of God's Torah is, even today, still a vision for the future. The decree of וכל מנאצי לא יראוה set the whole course of our history.

24 **ועבדי כלב**. He stood up faithfully and fearlessly for the Divine truth, and thus merited to be called "עבד ה׳," which is the highest designation of a person working for God's sake.

עקב — see Commentary, *Bereshis* 22:18.

היתה רוח אחרת עמו apparently means: a different spirit supported him; a different outlook and a different will saved him from the sin of his comrades.

וימלא אחרי. מלא occurs frequently in the sense of fulfilling a word, a promise, a wish. Thus לְמַלֵּא אֶת־דְּבַר ה׳ (*Melachim* I, 2:27), יְמַלֵּא ה׳ כָּל־מִשְׁאֲלוֹתֶיךָ (*Tehillim* 20:6). Hence, the meaning of the term here could be: he fulfilled his duty by following אחרי, by remaining faithful to Me, unlike his comrades, of whom it can be said that סרו מאחרי ה׳. Alternatively, אחרי could be the object of וימלא: he fulfilled the duty of following Me, of remaining faithful to Me.

25 *The Amaleki and the Kena'ani dwell in the valley; tomorrow you shall turn and journey into the wilderness toward the Sea of Reeds.*	כה וְהָעֲמָלֵקִי וְהַכְּנַעֲנִי יוֹשֵׁב בָּעֵמֶק מָחָר פְּנוּ וּסְעוּ לָכֶם הַמִּדְבָּר דֶּרֶךְ יַם־סוּף: פ רביעי
26 *And* God *spoke to Moshe and Aharon, saying:*	כו וַיְדַבֵּר יְהֹוָה אֶל־מֹשֶׁה וְאֶל־אַהֲרֹן לֵאמֹר:
27 *How long will this community be permitted to stir up revolt against Me? I have heard the murmurings of the Children of Israel, which they make in order to stir up revolt against Me.*	כז עַד־מָתַי לָעֵדָה הָרָעָה הַזֹּאת אֲשֶׁר הֵמָּה מַלִּינִים עָלָי אֶת־תְּלֻנּוֹת בְּנֵי יִשְׂרָאֵל אֲשֶׁר הֵמָּה מַלִּינִים עָלַי שָׁמָעְתִּי:

וזרעו יורשנה — cf. אֵת אֲשֶׁר יוֹרִישְׁךָ כְּמוֹשׁ (*Shoftim* 11:24). זרעו is the object and Kalev is the subject of יורשנה: He will bequeath the land to his children, whereas in the case of all the other members of the generation, the children will be the first possessors of the land.

25 **והעמלקי וגו׳ בעמק**: on the other side of the mountain ridge before which they were encamped. Thus, they could not proceed on their way without facing war, but God was not with them to help them in this war (רש״י). Hence they were commanded to immediately turn away from the Land and to return to the wilderness in the direction of the Red Sea, in accordance with the fate that had been decreed for them, that they would not enter the Land.

26 **וידבר ה׳ וגו׳**. In verses 11-25 Moshe is told in general of what was decreed upon the people. Here, the decree is explained in detail. The information is given to Moshe and to Aharon, for they were together appointed as leaders of the people (*Shemos* 6:26), whose fate was now changed for the worse; hence both are charged with the task of informing the people of this change, so that the people should understand it properly and digest its import.

27 **עד מתי לעדה וגו׳**. According to our Sages in *Megillah* 23b, the עדה mentioned here refers to the spies, who were "מלינים עלי" — i.e., inciting the

28 *Say to them: As surely as I live — thus is it said by* God*— even as you have spoken before My ears, so will I do to you.*

כח אֱמֹר אֲלֵהֶם חַי־אָנִי נְאֻם־יְהוָה
אִם־לֹא כַּאֲשֶׁר דִּבַּרְתֶּם בְּאָזְנָי כֵּן
אֶעֱשֶׂה לָכֶם׃

29 *Your corpses will fall in the wilderness and all your numbered ones at all your numberings from twenty years old and upward, those who brought you to revolt against Me.*

כט בַּמִּדְבָּר הַזֶּה יִפְּלוּ פִגְרֵיכֶם וְכָל־
פְּקֻדֵיכֶם לְכָל־מִסְפַּרְכֶם מִבֶּן
עֶשְׂרִים שָׁנָה וָמָעְלָה אֲשֶׁר
הֲלִינֹתֶם עָלָי׃

30 *You shall not come into the land concerning which I lifted up My hand to have you settle there to dwell, except for Kalev, son of Yefunneh, and Yehoshua, son of Nun.*

ל אִם־אַתֶּם תָּבֹאוּ אֶל־הָאָרֶץ אֲשֶׁר
נָשָׂאתִי אֶת־יָדִי לְשַׁכֵּן אֶתְכֶם בָּהּ
כִּי אִם־כָּלֵב בֶּן־יְפֻנֶּה וִיהוֹשֻׁעַ בִּן־
נוּן׃

---

people to rebel against God. And it is from here that we derive the general halachah that ten men joined together for a specific purpose are called an "עדה."

מלינים — see Commentary, *Shemos* 16:2.

28 **אמר אלהם**, to the two עדות mentioned in this section: to the עדה that cast accusations (v. 2), and to the עדה of inciters.

נאם ה' — see Commentary, *Bereshis* 5:29.

כאשר דברתם — in verse 2.

29 **פגריכם**: First He addresses the spokesmen (v. 2), for they formulated the accusations and hurled them at Moshe and Aharon. וכל פקדיכם are all the rest of the independent men, from the age of twenty and upward, who are obligated to serve the community, those whom the community counts on and who therefore are counted for the sake of the community (see chap. 1). This virile core of the nation should have foiled the machinations of the spies; particularly the intelligentsia and the spokesmen should have exerted their influence toward this end. Instead, however, precisely

31 *Your children, of whom you said that they would become prey, them I will bring in; they will come to know the land that you have scorned.*

לא וְטַפְּכֶם אֲשֶׁר אֲמַרְתֶּם לָבַז יִהְיֶה
וְהֵבֵיאתִי אֹתָם וְיָדְעוּ אֶת־הָאָרֶץ
אֲשֶׁר מְאַסְתֶּם בָּהּ׃

32 *But as for you, your corpses will fall in this wilderness.*

לב וּפִגְרֵיכֶם אַתֶּם יִפְּלוּ בַּמִּדְבָּר הַזֶּה׃

33 *And your sons will wander about in the wilderness for forty years and will bear your defection, until the last of your corpses has fallen in the wilderness.*

לג וּבְנֵיכֶם יִהְיוּ רֹעִים בַּמִּדְבָּר
אַרְבָּעִים שָׁנָה וְנָשְׂאוּ אֶת־זְנוּתֵיכֶם
עַד־תֹּם פִּגְרֵיכֶם בַּמִּדְבָּר׃

---

these influential men expressed the general discontent in a formulated complaint and inflamed this feeling to open rebellion (vv. 2-4). It is understandable, then, that all the men מבן עשרים ומעלה were considered guilty.

32 **ופגריכם אתם**. אתם re-emphasizes the contrast between them and their children.

33 **ובניכם יהיו רעים**. Scripture uses the term "רעייה" — being shepherded, tended — to describe the prolonged wandering in the wilderness, in which the children, too, will participate. Thereby Scripture indicates to us that this wandering will bring the children survival and success.

ונשאו את זנותיכם. Here we have a living commentary on the attribute of פקד עון אבות על בנים. As an inevitable natural consequence, the children, too, will be stricken by the punishment decreed upon their parents, but the children's participation in the suffering will be their salvation. For the forty years of wandering will instill in Israel the spirit of the Torah and the attribute of trust in God. This lesson continued to bear fruit — and will go on bearing fruit — for centuries.

זנותיכם: In discussing the children's participation in the suffering, Scripture describes the sin as a defection; for God's relationship to the parents had changed, and that is what brought upon them the decree

34 *According to the number of days in which you explored the land, forty days, for every day one year, you shall bear your iniquities, forty years, and you shall come to know [the consequences of] refusing Me.*

לד בְּמִסְפַּ֨ר הַיָּמִ֜ים אֲשֶׁר־תַּרְתֶּ֣ם אֶת־הָאָ֗רֶץ אַרְבָּעִ֣ים יוֹם֒ י֣וֹם לַשָּׁנָ֞ה י֣וֹם לַשָּׁנָ֗ה תִּשְׂאוּ֙ אֶת־עֲוֺנֹ֣תֵיכֶ֔ם אַרְבָּעִ֖ים שָׁנָ֑ה וִֽידַעְתֶּ֖ם אֶת־תְּנוּאָתִֽי׃

from which the children had to suffer. By contrast, in discussing the parents, who are the ones truly to blame, Scripture describes the sin objectively as עון (v. 34), a divergence from the straight path. In both cases, the plural form is used: זנותיכם, עונתיכם. The punishment decreed upon them is a consequence of many sins they had committed.

34 **במספר הימים אשר תרתם**: the nation, by means of its emissaries. Since the nation joined in the sin of its emissaries, it is equal to them.

יום לשנה וגו׳. The numerical relation between the duration of the punishment and the duration of the sin will remind them of the sin throughout the duration of the punishment. This method — indicating a relationship between two things by means of an external similarity of numbers — is used frequently in the institutions of our Sages. Thus: ג׳ קרואים, ז׳ קרואים כנגד וכו׳ (see *Megillah* 23a), י״ח ברכות כנגד וכו׳ (see *Berachos* 28b); and the question is always: הני כנגד מי. The external similarity of the numbers indicates an inner relation, as we find here.

תנואתי. The noun תנואה is found only here and in *Iyov* (33:10): הֵן תְּנוּאוֹת עָלַי יִמְצָא. הניא, in the *hif'il*, means: to prevent, to refuse. Accordingly, נוא, in the *kal*, means: to suffer from denial and refusal, to be unable to carry out an objective because of the denial or refusal of others (see Commentary, *Bereshis* 12:10-13, end). Thus, the verse in *Iyov* means: See, he wishes to find refusals from me; that is to say, he wishes to find things that I have denied him or that I have refused to do for him. תנואתי, then, means: the refusal I suffered from you. I wished to lead you on the way to happiness, but you refused to do My Will. Now you shall come to know the evils that befall a person who refuses to follow the ways of God.

35 *I,* God, *have spoken it. This I will do to all this evil community that gathered together against Me: In this wilderness they will meet their end, and there they shall die.*

לה אֲנִי יְהוָה דִּבַּרְתִּי אִם־לֹא | זֹאת אֶעֱשֶׂה לְכָל־הָעֵדָה הָרָעָה הַזֹּאת הַנּוֹעָדִים עָלָי בַּמִּדְבָּר הַזֶּה יִתַּמּוּ וְשָׁם יָמֻתוּ׃

36 *But [as for] the men whom Moshe sent out to explore the land, and who returned and incited the whole community against him by producing a slanderous report about the land —*

לו וְהָאֲנָשִׁים אֲשֶׁר־שָׁלַח מֹשֶׁה לָתוּר אֶת־הָאָרֶץ וַיָּשֻׁבוּ וַיַּלִּונוּ עָלָיו אֶת־כָּל־הָעֵדָה לְהוֹצִיא דִבָּה עַל־הָאָרֶץ׃

וילינו קרי

37 *Those men who produced an evil report on the land died by sudden death before* God.

לז וַיָּמֻתוּ הָאֲנָשִׁים מוֹצִאֵי דִבַּת־הָאָרֶץ רָעָה בַּמַּגֵּפָה לִפְנֵי יְהוָה׃

38 *But Yehoshua, son of Nun, and Kalev, son of Yefunneh, remained alive from among those men who had gone to explore the land.*

לח וִיהוֹשֻׁעַ בִּן־נוּן וְכָלֵב בֶּן־יְפֻנֶּה חָיוּ מִן־הָאֲנָשִׁים הָהֵם הַהֹלְכִים לָתוּר אֶת־הָאָרֶץ׃

39 *Moshe spoke these words to all the Children of Israel, and the people mourned greatly.*

לט וַיְדַבֵּר מֹשֶׁה אֶת־הַדְּבָרִים הָאֵלֶּה אֶל־כָּל־בְּנֵי יִשְׂרָאֵל וַיִּתְאַבְּלוּ הָעָם מְאֹד׃

---

35 **העדה הרעה וגו׳** are all the independent men הנועדים עלי, who united in the rebellion against God.

במדבר הזה יתמו: their destiny shall not extend beyond this wilderness; they shall not come out of this wilderness alive.

36 **וילינו וגו׳ להוציא וגו׳**. By slandering the Land, they incited the whole community to rebel against God.

40 *And they rose up early in the morning and went up to the top of the mountain, thereby saying: We are ready to go up to that place which* God *has described, for we have sinned.*

מ וַיַּשְׁכִּ֣מוּ בַבֹּ֔קֶר וַיַּעֲל֥וּ אֶל־רֹאשׁ־
הָהָ֖ר לֵאמֹ֑ר הִנֶּ֗נּוּ וְעָלִ֛ינוּ אֶל־
הַמָּק֛וֹם אֲשֶׁר־אָמַ֥ר יְהוָ֖ה כִּ֥י
חָטָֽאנוּ׃

41 *And Moshe said: Why do you now transgress the command of* God*? This will not succeed.*

מא וַיֹּ֣אמֶר מֹשֶׁ֔ה לָ֥מָּה זֶּ֛ה אַתֶּ֥ם
עֹבְרִ֖ים אֶת־פִּ֣י יְהוָ֑ה וְהִ֖וא לֹ֥א
תִצְלָֽח׃

42 *Do not go up, for* God *is not in your midst. Do not be struck down before your enemies!*

מב אַֽל־תַּעֲל֔וּ כִּ֛י אֵ֥ין יְהוָ֖ה בְּקִרְבְּכֶ֑ם
וְלֹא֙ תִּנָּ֣גְפ֔וּ לִפְנֵ֖י אֹיְבֵיכֶֽם׃

43 *For the Amaleki and the Kena'ani are there before you; you will fall by the sword! For since you have shrunk back from following* God, God *will not be with you.*

מג כִּי֩ הָעֲמָלֵקִ֨י וְהַכְּנַעֲנִ֥י שָׁם֙ לִפְנֵיכֶ֔ם
וּנְפַלְתֶּ֖ם בֶּחָ֑רֶב כִּֽי־עַל־כֵּ֤ן שַׁבְתֶּם֙
מֵאַחֲרֵ֣י יְהוָ֔ה וְלֹא־יִהְיֶ֥ה יְהוָ֖ה
עִמָּכֶֽם׃

44 *They insisted on going up to the top of the mountain, but the Ark of* God's *Covenant and Moshe did not depart from the camp.*

מד וַיַּעְפִּ֕לוּ לַעֲל֖וֹת אֶל־רֹ֣אשׁ הָהָ֑ר
וַאֲר֤וֹן בְּרִית־יְהוָה֙ וּמֹשֶׁ֔ה לֹא־
מָ֖שׁוּ מִקֶּ֥רֶב הַֽמַּחֲנֶֽה׃

45 *And the Amaleki and the Kena'ani*

מה וַיֵּ֤רֶד הָעֲמָלֵקִי֙ וְהַֽכְּנַעֲנִ֔י הַיֹּשֵׁ֖ב

---

43 **כי על כן** — see *Bereshis* 18:5. For this reason I say to you not to venture to go up: because you have turned back from following God.

44 **ויעפלו** — see Commentary, ibid. 4:1-2. They resisted forcefully, stubbornly insisting on having their own way.

45 **בהר ההוא** — in that mountain range. Above (v. 25), it says that the עמלקי and כנעני lived בעמק. It must be, then, that they lived not on the mountain,

who lived in that mountain range came down and struck them and crushed them all the way to Chormah.

בָּהָר הַהוּא וַיַּכּוּם וַיַּכְּתוּם עַד־הַחָרְמָה׃ פ

15 1 God *spoke to Moshe, saying:*

טו א וַיְדַבֵּר יְהוָה אֶל־מֹשֶׁה לֵּאמֹר׃

2 *Speak to the Children of Israel and say to them: When you enter the land of your habitations that I am giving you,*

ב דַּבֵּר אֶל־בְּנֵי יִשְׂרָאֵל וְאָמַרְתָּ אֲלֵהֶם כִּי תָבֹאוּ אֶל־אֶרֶץ מוֹשְׁבֹתֵיכֶם אֲשֶׁר אֲנִי נֹתֵן לָכֶם׃

---

but in the highlands, in a valley on the other side of the heights the Jewish people wished to climb.

ויכתום — like ויכתו אתכם (*Devarim* 1:44). This is apparently a deviant *hif'il* form of the root כתת, "to crush"; or perhaps it is a *kal* form of the root נכת, as in וָאֶכֹּת אתו טחון (ibid. 9:21), but in that case it should have said וַיַּכְּתוּם. Perhaps the פתח is used in the *kal* form in order to equalize the sounds of וַיַּכּוּם and וַיַּכְּתוּם (the use of the פתח is retained in *Devarim* 1:44, although וַיַּכְּתוּ appears there alone) and ויכום and ויכתום are a combination: they smashed them to smithereens.

CHAPTER 15

1 The *mitzvos* contained in this chapter are closely connected with the fateful events described in the two preceding chapters. The connection is so close that it appears that these *mitzvos* were given as a response to those events. This will become clear when we examine these *mitzvos* in detail.

The first mitzvah is פרשת נסכים, which teaches that מנחה and נסך are to be added to every עולה and to every שלמים.

2 **דבר וגו' כי תבאו וגו'**. It has already been stated in *Shemos* 29:40-41 that נסכים are to accompany the תמיד offering, and it also states in chapters 28-29 (below) that נסכים are to be offered with the מוספים. According to *Kiddushin* 37a-b (see רש"י there and תוספות ד"ה לא קרבו), our chapter deals primarily with קרבנות יחיד, and two opinions on this matter are reported there.

According to ר' ישמעאל, in the wilderness נסכים were offered only with

3 *And you make a fire offering, an ascent offering or a meal offering to* God, *for a vow, or in free-will dedication, or in your festive seasons, to make for* God *an expression of compliance from cattle or sheep,*

ג וַעֲשִׂיתֶ֨ם אִשֶּׁ֤ה לַֽיהוָה֙ עֹלָ֣ה אוֹ־זֶ֔בַח לְפַלֵּא־נֶ֙דֶר֙ א֣וֹ בִנְדָבָ֔ה א֖וֹ בְּמֹעֲדֵיכֶ֑ם לַעֲשׂ֞וֹת רֵ֤יחַ נִיחֹ֙חַ֙ לַֽיהוָ֔ה מִן־הַבָּקָ֖ר א֥וֹ מִן־הַצֹּֽאן׃

קרבנות ציבור (the תמיד and מוסף offerings — see *Menachos* 45b: מה שאמור בחומש הפקודים קרב במדבר). Here it says that נסכים are to be offered also with every קרבן יחיד that can be brought בנדר ונדבה — i.e., with עולה and שלמים; however, this duty applies only בארץ and only after ירושה וישיבה. This condition is derived from the clause כי תבאו אל ארץ מושבתיכם, from which we learn that the mitzvah stated here is contingent upon entry and settlement. During the fourteen years of conquest and division of the Land — שבע שכבשו ושבע שחלקו — the law was different. During that period, the משכן had only a temporary home, in Gilgal, and במות were still permitted (see Commentary, *Devarim* 12:8-9). At that time, נסכים were not yet offered with קרבנות יחיד. This duty, then, applied only משעת איסור במות, once the משכן reached its permanent home in Shilo. In short, according to ר׳ ישמעאל, לא קירבו נסכים (של יחיד) במדבר ולא בבמות יחיד.

According to ר׳ עקיבא, however, קירבו נסכים במדבר; the duty stated here, to offer נסכים with קרבנות יחיד, applied immediately, in the wilderness, just like the duty to offer נסכים with קרבנות ציבור. The clause כי תבאו אל ארץ מושבתיכם serves only להטעינה נסכים בבמה קטנה (*Zevachim* 111a). That is to say, even כי תבאו, when you enter the Land — during שבע שכבשו ושבע שחלקו, when the משכן stood in a temporary home, in Gilgal, and במות were permitted בכל מושבתיכם — then, too, it is a mitzvah to bring נסכים. And the mitzvah applies everywhere, even בבמת יחיד. (במת יחיד is also called "במה קטנה" — in contrast to the מזבח in the משכן, which served as במת ציבור during the period of היתר במות and which is also called "במה גדולה." See תוספות ibid. ד״ה במה.)

3 **ועשיתם אשה לה׳ וגו׳** is the continuation of the introductory clause which begins with the word "כי" of the preceding verse.

עלה או זבח. זבח includes שלמים and תודה. Although תודה is always ac-

ד וְהִקְרִיב הַמַּקְרִיב קָרְבָּנוֹ לַיהוָה מִנְחָה סֹלֶת עִשָּׂרוֹן בָּלוּל בִּרְבִעִית הַהִין שָׁמֶן׃

4 *Then one who brings his offering near to* God *shall at the same time bring an homage offering of a tenth of fine flour mixed with one-quarter of a* hin *of oil.*

ה וְיַיִן לַנֶּסֶךְ רְבִיעִית הַהִין תַּעֲשֶׂה

5 *And a quarter* hin *of wine for a*

---

companied by לחמי תודה, it requires — in addition — also the מנחה ונסך ordered here.

לפלא נדר. פלא נדר is the pronouncement "הרי עלי," whereas the bringing of the offering is nothing but the fulfillment of the נדר. Hence the -ל of לפלא can only mean "in connection with" the נדר, for it and for the sake of its fulfillment. By contrast, in the case of נדבה one says "הרי זו," and here the first act — the הקדשה, the dedication of the animal for use as an עולה or שלמים — is already considered an offering procedure and is termed "הקרבה" (see Commentary, *Vayikra* 1:3). Hence in this case it says בנדבה, meaning "in a dedication" or "through a dedication"; for the עשיית אשה begins when one dedicates an animal for use as an עולה or זבח.

לפלא נדר או בנדבה teaches that the mitzvah stated here applies only to those offerings that can be brought also בנדר ונדבה, and the mitzvah applies to these offerings even when they are brought as חובה. This is derived from the addition או במעדיכם, which refers to חובות הבאות מחמת הרגל, offerings that one is bound to bring on festivals: עולות ראייה ושלמי חגיגה. Thus, הבכור והמעשר והפסח והחטאת והאשם — offerings that are brought only as חובה — are exempt from מנחת נסכים. The only obligatory offering that requires מנחה ונסך is חטאתו של מצורע ואשמתו (see *Vayikra* 14:10; *Menachos* 90b et seq.).

מן הבקר או מן הצאן excludes עולת עוף (*Menachos* ibid.).

4 **והקריב המקריב וגו׳ מנחה וגו׳**. Even when the קרבן itself is a free-will offering, the מנחה that accompanies it is obligatory. The מנחה is an essential complement to the offering. Like its עולה or the אימורים of its שלמים, the מנחה is burnt entirely on the altar.

5 **ויין לנסך**. נסך never means "to pour away" (i.e., in disposal); rather, the מנסך's intention is always to get the liquid to a specific place. Thus the

עַל־הָעֹלָה אוֹ לַזָּבַח לַכֶּבֶשׂ הָאֶחָד׃

libation you shall offer with the ascent offering or for the meal offering; thus [shall it be] for each sheep.

ו אוֹ לָאַיִל תַּעֲשֶׂה מִנְחָה סֹלֶת שְׁנֵי עֶשְׂרֹנִים בְּלוּלָה בַשֶּׁמֶן שְׁלִשִׁית הַהִין׃

6 *Or for a ram you shall make an homage offering of two tenths of fine flour mixed with a third of a* hin *of oil.*

---

meaning: to cast liquid metal into a mold, or: to pour anointing oil on the head, from which we get נסיך, an anointed one, a prince.

The נסכים are offered as follows: The wine is poured into a bowl attached to the top of the altar on the southwest corner, from where it flows down through a cavity into the depths of the altar's foundation (שיתין — *Sukkah* 48b; see לחם משנה on הל׳ מעשה הקרבנות, 2:1).

ויין לנסך וגו׳. יין is not an additional object of והקריב of the preceding verse, but is the object of תעשה, which constitutes a separate mitzvah. This indicates that the יין is not to be subsumed together with the סולת and the שמן under one concept; rather, the יין represents an independent idea. Thus, too, the halachah: הסולת והשמן אין מעכבין את היין ולא היין מעכבן (*Menachos* 44b).

על העלה או לזבח: The idea that is represented by the wine is joined to (על) the עולה, but is added to (ל) the זבח.

6 **או לאיל**. In its first year a sheep is called "כבש." Once the first month of the second year has passed, it is called "איל," whereas during the first month of the second year it is called "פלגס" (see Commentary, *Shemos* 29:15). In *Chullin* 23a our Sages derive from the term "או" that as soon as it is no longer a כבש — even though it is not yet an איל, but is still a פלגס — it already requires נסכי איל: או לאיל לרבות את הפלגס.

(The precise term for the מנחה that accompanies the עולה and the שלמים is "מנחת נסכים," whereas the wine that accompanies the מנחה is called "נסכים." However, sometimes both together are called "נסכים" — see תוספות יום טוב on *Shekalim* 5:1.)

7 *And a third of a* hin *of wine for a libation shall you bring near to* God *as an expression of compliance.*	ז וְיַ֥יִן לַנֶּ֖סֶךְ שְׁלִשִׁ֣ית הַהִ֑ין תַּקְרִ֥יב רֵֽיחַ־נִיחֹ֖חַ לַיהוָֽה׃ חמישי
8 *And if you prepare an animal of the cattle species as an ascent offering or a meal offering to* God, *as a vow or as a peace offering,*	ח וְכִֽי־תַעֲשֶׂ֥ה בֶן־בָּקָ֖ר עֹלָ֣ה אוֹ־זָ֑בַח לְפַלֵּא־נֶ֛דֶר אוֹ־שְׁלָמִ֖ים לַיהוָֽה׃

7 **תקריב ריח ניחח לה׳**. Just as above, in verse 5, לכבש האחד refers back to all that is written before it, here too the object of תקריב is everything that is brought with the איל.

It says here that נסך, too, is offered as ריח ניחח, this despite the fact that the term "ריח ניחח" is usually applied only to things that go onto the altar fire. In this way Scripture indicates to us the נסכים's great importance to the offering: נסכים, too, are required in order for the offering to be לריח ניחוח.

8 **וכי תעשה וגו׳**. The איל and the כבש together constitute the קרבנות מן הצאן (cf. v. 3). Hence, the איל offering (vv. 6-7) is simply added (או לאיל תעשה וגו׳) to the עולה and the זבח of the כבש (vv. 4-5). Both together represent the ideas of the עולה and שלמים from the viewpoint of one who is in a state of "צאן": one whose fate is entrusted to God's care. By contrast, בן בקר represents these ideas from the viewpoint of participation in God's work on earth. Hence, the נסכים section of בן בקר begins with a fresh introduction (v. 8).

לפלא נדר או שלמים. This combination — נדר או שלמים — is very difficult to understand. שלמים and נדר present no contrast, for שלמים themselves can be brought בנדר or בנדבה. Besides, שלמים are already included in the term "זבח," which is the common designation for שלמים and תודה. The contrast to נדר is נדבה, as indeed they are paired in the parallel law in verse 3.

Perhaps the difficulty can be resolved in light of the meaning of the בן בקר offering. The mention of שלמים as the contrast to נדר proceeds from the assumption that *here* "נדר" without specification is an עולה, whereas שלמים are usually brought בנדבה. What this indicates to us may be this: As

9 *He must make, along with the animal of the cattle species, an homage offering: three tenths of fine flour mixed with half a* hin *of oil.*

ט וְהִקְרִ֣יב עַל־בֶּן־הַבָּקָ֗ר מִנְחָ֗ה סֹ֛לֶת שְׁלֹשָׁ֥ה עֶשְׂרֹנִ֖ים בָּל֥וּל בַּשֶּׁ֖מֶן חֲצִ֥י הַהִֽין׃

10 *And you shall bring near half a* hin *of wine for a libation; it is a fire offering to* God *as an expression of compliance.*

י וְיַ֛יִן תַּקְרִ֥יב לַנֶּ֖סֶךְ חֲצִ֣י הַהִ֑ין אִשֵּׁ֥ה רֵֽיחַ־נִיחֹ֖חַ לַיהוָֽה׃

11 *Thus shall be done for every ox or for every ram, or for the lamb among the sheep or goats.*

יא כָּ֣כָה יֵעָשֶׂ֗ה לַשּׁוֹר֙ הָֽאֶחָ֔ד א֖וֹ לָאַ֣יִל הָאֶחָ֑ד אֽוֹ־לַשֶּׂ֥ה בַכְּבָשִׂ֖ים א֥וֹ בָעִזִּֽים׃

a rule, it cannot be assumed that a person will bring שלמי נדר from בקר, but he is likely to bring שלמי נדבה from בקר. Hence, here נדבה can be designated by the term "שלמים." Let us remember that שלמי בקר represent the שלמים-idea from the viewpoint of "בקר"; that is to say, they represent the joy of life that comes from the awareness of participating in God's work. This joy in fulfilling life's purpose cannot be a permanent feeling. Rather, a person attains it momentarily, as a result of an especially gratifying experience. Such joy seeks immediate expression through שלמי נדבה, and the שלמי בקר that are immediately dedicated will afterward serve as an expression of that glorious moment. The case of נדר is different. One who makes a vow (נודר) to bring a בן בקר as שלמים is preparing for a future moment; he anticipates ahead of time that he will be happy and contented with his work. This is a feeling of complacent self-satisfaction, which the Torah would prefer to suppress and has no reason to encourage. Thus, the Torah uses the term שלמים [from בן בקר] to refer to נדבה, indicating that it is preferred to bring שלמים as a נדבה rather than as a נדר.

9 **והקריב וגו'** apparently refers to what is stated in verse 4 (see Commentary there), and is an abbreviation of והקריב המקריב.

10 **אשה ריח ניחח לה'** — see Commentary, verse 7.

11 **ככה יעשה**. ככה: מיעוטו מעכב את רובו (*Menachos* 27a). The quantities prescribed here must be strictly adhered to; the slightest deviation, whether

12 *Thus shall you do, in accordance with the number [of offerings] you make, one for each, according to their number.*

יב כַּמִּסְפָּר אֲשֶׁר תַּעֲשׂוּ כָּכָה תַּעֲשׂוּ לָאֶחָד כְּמִסְפָּרָם׃

13 *Every native-born can do these things also in this fashion, to bring near to God a fire offering as an expression of compliance.*

יג כָּל־הָאֶזְרָח יַעֲשֶׂה־כָּכָה אֶת־אֵלֶּה לְהַקְרִיב אִשֵּׁה רֵיחַ־נִיחֹחַ לַיהוָה׃

---

in deficiency or excess, invalidates the whole: ריבה שמנה חיסר שמנה פסולה (ibid. 11a).

לשור האחד. In the case of שור, there is no differentiation, from the standpoint of נסכים, between עגל and פר. Its significance lies in the character of the species.

או לשה וגו׳. Apart from איל (see Commentary, v. 6), with animals from the flock — כבשים and עזים — the quantity of נסכים is not affected by age or by sex.

12 **כמספר וגו׳**. The prescribed מנחה and נסך must be added to each animal. Even if one brings two offerings that are similar in every respect — e.g., two עולות פר בנדר or two בנדבה, or two שלמי כבש בנדר or two בנדבה — it is not sufficient to bring one מנחה and one נסך for the two of them (ibid. 91a). For the נסכים are not the personal obligation of the offerer, which he can fulfill by one offering. Rather, they are an obligation that attaches to every עולה and to every שלמים, and one does not fulfill his obligation in these offerings as long as he does not add to each offering its מנחה and its נסך. If he does not add them on the day the offering is made, he must supply what is missing at a later date (*Zevachim* 44a). This obligation is so strongly binding that such נסכים not brought directly with the offering — נסכים הבאים בפני עצמן — are offered even at night: מנחתם ונסכיהם בלילה, מנחתם ונסכיהם למחר (*Temurah* 14a-b).

13 **כל האזרח יעשה ככה את אלה להקריב וגו׳**. According to *Menachos* 104a, this verse means as follows: An אזרח may bring these נסכים not only as accompaniments to עולה and שלמים, but also as independent offerings, and he can even bring oil or wine by itself. He must adhere, however, to

14 *And if an outsider enters among* יד וְכִֽי־יָג֨וּר אִתְּכֶ֜ם גֵּ֗ר א֤וֹ אֲשֶׁר־

the prescribed measures stipulated here. When he brings wine, he can bring only 3, 4, or 6 לוגים (¼, ⅓, ½ הין), but not 1, 2, or 5 לוגים. When he brings oil, however, he can bring also one לוג, as that is the quantity prescribed for מנחת נדבה (*Vayikra* 2:1ff.; *Menachos* 104a and 107a). According to רבי, oil, too, may be brought only in the prescribed measure stipulated for נסכים — i.e., at least three לוגים as stipulated for נסכי כבש.

The foregoing dispute hinges on another dispute pertaining to the hermeneutic rules by which the Torah is expounded: whether דון מינה ומינה or דון מינה ואוקי באתרה. That is to say, in deriving a general halachah from some other law [for application to the law presently under discussion], do we also derive from that other law all of its detailed *halachos*: דון מינה ומינה, or are the detailed *halachos* determined according to the special character of the law presently under discussion: דון מינה ואוקי באתרה. The halachah that שמן — like the wine of נסכים — can be brought by itself is derived from מנחת נדבה. One who holds דון מינה ומינה will also derive the prescribed quantity of שמן from מנחת נדבה. By contrast, one who holds דון מינה ואוקי באתרה will set the quantity of שמן according to the quantity prescribed for נסכים, for שמן brought separately resembles יין נסכים.

The permission to bring נסכים as an independent קרבן נדבה is given exclusively to the אזרח of the Jewish nation: אזרח מביא נסכים ואין העובד כוכבים מביא נסכים (*Temurah* 3a). Although non-Jews may bring free-will offerings on the altar of the Jewish Sanctuary — נכרים נודרים נדרים ונדבות כישראל (see Commentary, *Vayikra* 1:2) — they are not entitled to bring נסכים. However, our Sages say: יכול לא תהא עולתו טעונה נסכים ת״ל ככה (*Temurah* 3a). That is to say, although they cannot bring independent נסכים, their offerings require נסכים, and these are brought by the Jewish community. According to one opinion (see רש״י ibid. and לחם משנה on הל׳ מעשה הקרבנות, 3:5), the non-Jews themselves may bring the נסכים that accompany their offerings, and "האזרח" here excludes them only from bringing נסכים as independent offerings.

14 **וכי יגור וגו׳**. "האזרח" of the preceding verse excludes the non-Jew from at least independent נסכים. Here it says that the גר, who is a גר צדק (see *Shemos* 12:48 and Commentary there), is not excluded; for the גר is made equal

you from abroad, or whoever shall enter into your midst among your descendants, and he makes a fire offering to God *as an expression of compliance, as you do it, thus shall he do.*	בְּתוֹכְכֶם לְדֹרֹתֵיכֶם וְעָשָׂה אִשֵּׁה רֵיחַ־נִיחֹחַ לַיהוָה כַּאֲשֶׁר תַּעֲשׂוּ כֵּן יַעֲשֶׂה׃
15 *O assembly! There shall be one and the same statute for you and for the outsider who has entered from abroad. It is an everlasting statute for your descendants: The outsider who has entered from abroad shall be equal with you before* God.	טו הַקָּהָל חֻקָּה אַחַת לָכֶם וְלַגֵּר הַגָּר חֻקַּת עוֹלָם לְדֹרֹתֵיכֶם כָּכֶם כַּגֵּר יִהְיֶה לִפְנֵי יְהוָה׃
16 *There shall be one Teaching and*	טז תּוֹרָה אַחַת וּמִשְׁפָּט אֶחָד יִהְיֶה

to the אזרח — the native-born Jew — in regard to the duty and the permission to bring נסכים.

וכי יגור אתכם גר: now; או אשר בתוכם לדרתיכם: if at any future time a גר joins you (see *Kerisos* 9a).

15 **הקהל** — as in מעיני הקהל (*Vayikra* 4:13; see Commentary there) — perhaps refers to the סנהדרין הגדולה, in whose hands the leadership of the national community is entrusted. From *Kiddushin* 73a, however, it appears that it refers to the Jewish people in general, as in בקהל ה׳ (*Devarim* 23:3).

חקה אחת וגו׳: the same rights; what you are entitled to, he is also entitled to, and what you by law deserve, he, too, deserves (see Commentary, *Bereshis* 47:22).

ככם כגר יהיה לפני ה׳. Just as they are equated here regarding the offerings, so are they equated in all respects before God — i.e., in all relations of man to God and God to man.

And finally:

16 **תורה אחת ומשפט וגו׳**: בא הכתוב והשוה הגר לאזרח בכל מצות שבתורה (*Sifre*). גר and אזרח are equated in all the laws of the Torah.

The sentence that declares the גר's equality in the offerings — כאשר

לָכֶם וְלַגֵּר הַגָּר אִתְּכֶם׃ פ ששי

one [standard of] right for you and for the outsider who has entered among you from abroad.

תעשו כן יעשה (v. 14) — is expounded in *Kerisos* 8b with regard to another halachah: For his complete entry into Judaism, a גר requires — besides מילה וטבילה — also הרצאת דמים through an offering, just as Israel entered into the covenant of the Torah through an offering (*Shemos* 24:5). When the Temple was standing, a גר, after undergoing מילה וטבילה, would bring an עולת בהמה or an עולת עוף (שני בני יונה או שני תורים), and as long as he had not brought this offering he was precluded from partaking of קדשים: מעוכב לאכול בקדשים עד שיביא קינו. However, when the Temple is not in existence, גירות is not impeded by the impossibility of bringing an offering, for Scripture expressly states that גרים are accepted in all generations: או אשר בתוככם לדרתיכם (v. 14; see *Kerisos* 9a).

Accordingly, by this institution of נסכים it is ordained that henceforth no עולת בהמה or שלמים may be brought unless the קרבן בהמה is accompanied by a מנחה of flour and a נסך of wine, and these must be joined — or added later — to each animal that one brings. The significance of this is as follows: The Jewish נפש — of the individual or of the community — approaches God in His Sanctuary. At this time, the Jewish נפש gives expression to the sanctification of actions out of consciousness of duty (עולה), or to the feeling of happiness in the heart (שלמים), and it devotes to the altar fire the *personality* and its powers. But to this same altar and to this same fire, it is also obligated to devote the *possessions* that afford the possibility for existence, prosperity, and happiness. This duty has already been established in the daily national offering (תמיד; see *Shemos* 29:40 and Commentary there), and henceforth it shall apply to all the communal offerings. What is more, this shall be a duty — or a conditional duty — in every עולה and in every זבח brought by an individual; a conditional duty, inasmuch as the duty to bring נסכים with a נדר or נדבה arises only as a consequence of the free decision to bring an עולה or זבח.

Thus, נסכים differ from all other מנחות נדבה, and they also differ from the offering they accompany. They do not express the ideas and resolutions by which the offerer seeks to draw near to God; rather, they express a warning issuing from the Sanctuary, and the Sanctuary demands that this warning be expressed with every offering that it receives for the sake of God and His Torah. This concurs with the fact that the duty of נסכים depends not on the person, but on the offering; hence, if the offerer is a non-Jew and is not obligated — or is not qualified — to bring נסכים, the ציבור brings them in the name of the Sanctuary (see Commentary, vv. 4, 12, 13).

Let us consider further that the Torah ascribes national significance to the duty and qualification to bring נסכים. Hence, the mitzvah of נסכים is given only to the אזרח, to the exclusion of the נכרי. On the other hand, the Torah finds it necessary to expressly state that the גר is obligated and qualified to bring נסכים. Moreover, the גר's obligation and qualification to bring נסכים are a touchstone of his rights and his status, to which the Torah attaches the solemn proclamation of the גר's equality before God and the Torah. It follows, then, that the נסכים-idea is one of the central pillars of Jewish nationality and of the Jewish calling. It is rooted in a factor that is lacking in a גר as such; hence, were it not for the Torah's explicit statement, we would have considered the גר excluded from the duty of נסכים and unqualified to perform it.

As we have seen, the Sanctuary demands that a מנחה and a נסך accompany every עולה and every שלמים. Thereby, the Sanctuary addresses as follows all who enter its gates: You are devoting to God the נפש, the personality that thinks and feels, aspires and acts. But not only the נפש belongs to God and His Torah; also all דגן, תירוש, and יצהר (סולת, יין, שמן) — all the elements necessary for existence, prosperity, and happiness — these, too, belong solely to God and His Torah; they depend on God alone, and no one can attain them except by doing God's Will and sustaining the holy on earth (see Commentary, *Vayikra* 1:9). Only if we fuel and keep the fire of the Torah burning on the altar will we, too, attain sustenance and endurance. As we say every day in קריאת שמע: והיה אם שמע וגו׳ ונתתי וגו׳ ואספת וגו׳.

נסכים, then, are an expression of the fact that God shapes Israel's fate with His direct providence and guidance. This truth is the basis of the covenant of Avraham, which is fulfilled in Israel, and is also the basis of the mission assigned to Israel for the sake of the Torah. Israel's fate is directly shaped by God's guidance, and it was the disregard of this truth which was the essence of the sin of which we just read; this was the sin of the people, the sin of its emissaries and men, in contrast to whom only Kalev recognized the truth and gave expression to it in his courageous words: אם חפץ בנו ה׳ (above, 14:8). The lesson to be learned from נסכים is that obedience to God is the sun that fertilizes our fields and the triumphant sword of our victories. Thus the close connection between פרשת נסכים and חטא המרגלים seems self-evident. This [the fact that Israel's fate in the Land depends on obedience to God] is also the implication of the introductory words "כי תבאו" (v. 2).

One opinion derives [from the words כי תבאו אל ארץ מושבתיכם] that the duty of נסכים applied to קרבנות יחיד only after the conquest of the Land, whereas the other opinion derives [from these words] just the opposite: this duty is so important for the conquest that it already applied during the war and before the conquest was completed, even בבמת יחיד (see Commentary, v. 2).

The foregoing also explains why it is necessary to specially state that גרים are obligated and qualified to bring נסכים, and why in this connection Scripture declares that the גר is like the native-born in every respect — in rights and in status. For God promised the patriarchs that He would directly shape the fate of their descendants, and that their descendants would inherit the land in which this promise was destined to be fulfilled. The גר, however, does not descend from the patriarchs and has no share in the Land. His very name attests that he is "landless" (see Commentary, *Bereshis* 23:4). Hence, just as at the Pesach offering (*Shemos* 12:48-49; see Commentary there), so here, too, it is necessary to specially state that the גר is like the native-born as regards נסכים. He, too, is under God's direct care: ככם כגר יהיה לפני ה׳, which guarantees him a humane and civil existence in the Land (see *Devarim* 10:18ff.), even though he has no share in it. Thus, the גר's equality as regards נסכים already includes his equality in every respect. The Torah in many places cautions about the rights of the גר, but פרשת נסכים is the principal source of his equal rights in all Torah matters. This indicates the great significance of the institution of נסכים.

The נסכים consist of two parts: the מנחה (סלת עשרון בלול ברבעית ההין שמן) and the נסכים themselves (יין לנסך רביעית ההין). The מנחה, then, is a מנחת סולת like the מנחת נדבה (*Vayikra* 2:1; see Commentary there), but it differs from מנחת נדבה in the quantity of oil. An ordinary מנחת נדבה contains only one לוג of oil, whereas a מנחת נסכים contains three times as much: ¼ הין = 3 לוגים. A מנחת נדבה requires הגשה and קמיצה. Only a קומץ of it reaches the altar; the remainder is given to be eaten by the כהנים (*Vayikra* 7:9-10). מנחת נסכים has neither הגשה nor קמיצה, and is burnt in its entirety on the altar.

It appears that the special *halachos* of מנחת נסכים can be explained on the basis of its meaning. One who brings a מנחת נדבה signifies that the means of subsistence and prosperity *that have been granted to him* are devoted to God with homage and dedication. The Sanctuary teaches him what to do with the property granted to him by God: he is to place it with homage before the altar (הגשה), fully satisfy the Sanctuary's demands (קמיצה), and enjoy the remainder under the influence of priestly holiness (אכילת כהנים). By contrast, מנחת נסכים is a general objective expression of the means of subsistence and prosperity given to the Jewish people directly by God. Therefore, these means belong exclusively to God and are dedicated to the fulfillment of His Torah. Hence this מנחה has no הגשה, קמיצה, or אכילת כהנים, but is entirely אשה ריח ניחח לה׳.

The foregoing also accounts for the rich fullness of oil in מנחת נסכים, triple the amount in an ordinary מנחת נדבה, an amount that is found elsewhere only in מנחת חביתים (see Commentary, ibid. 6:14-15). For this מנחה is not an expression of the individual's prosperity; rather, it signifies that prosperity in general — even in the fullness of the national wealth — is exclusively a gift from God. In this respect מנחת נסכים resembles חביתי כהן גדול, which likewise are three לוגים and are entirely given over to the altar fire. The common denominator of מנחת נסכים and חביתי כהן גדול is that their perspective is national. The quantity of the סולת, however, does not change. It represents simple existence, and so cannot be increased or decreased. Its prescribed measure, עשירית האיפה, is absolutely fixed historically by the measure of the manna (see Commentary, *Shemos* 16:36).

מנחת נדבה has also a קומץ לבונה, which represents satisfaction and contentment with the means of subsistence and prosperity. לבונה is lacking in מנחת נסכים, but it is replaced by the expression of supreme happiness, of perfect joy in the community's fate, which is guided by God's providence. The expression of this is the offering procedure unique to the institution of נסכים — namely, the libation of wine which accompanies מנחת נסכים.

There is no doubt that, in Scripture, wine represents man's highest joy. "Wine cheers the heart of man" (*Tehillim* 104:15). Wine is enjoyed with song (see *Yeshayahu* 24:9). "Wine makes life merry" (*Koheles* 10:19). "Give strong wine to the unhappy, wine to those that be of heavy hearts" (*Mishlei* 31:6). "Their hearts shall rejoice as with wine" (*Zecharyah* 10:7) is an expression of the highest joy. "Your love is more delightful than wine" (*Shir Ha-Shirim* 1:2) is an expression of the highest happiness of love. "Wine and milk" (*Yeshayahu* 55:1) are metaphors for the happiness and sustenance granted by God's Torah.

It is also well known that, in Scripture, wine commonly represents the portion of happiness that God grants to individuals and to nations. Hence, "cup" occurs in Scripture as an expression for the fate decreed by God. "For there is a cup in God's hand, and the wine is strong and fully mixed, and He dispenses therefrom, but the dregs thereof all the wicked of the earth shall wring them out and drink them" (*Tehillim* 75:9). Thus, there is a "cup of wrath" and a "cup of stupor" (*Yeshayahu* 51:17), but also a "cup of salvation" (*Tehillim* 116:13) and a "cup of consolation" (*Yirmeyahu* 16:7). The Babylonian superpower, which alters the fate of all the nations, is "a golden cup in God's hand" (ibid. 51:7). For the pious who merit to have God as their Shepherd, their cup is always overflowing (*Tehillim* 23:5), and God is their portion and their cup (ibid. 16:5).

Let us add that Scripture describes the offering of the נסכים with the words בקדש הסך נסך שכר לה׳ (below, 28:7). Thus, the wine of the נסכים is considered with regard to its strong spiritual power. In light of all the foregoing, it appears that the wine of נסכים represents the highest earthly happiness. This wine, the expression of man's perfect joy, is brought into the Sanctuary, where it is received in a vessel of the Sanctuary, a כלי שרת, and thereby is sanctified and belongs to God. During the ניסוך the wine is not poured out, but "poured into" the depths of the altar's foundation (Commentary, v. 5). This pouring down expresses the thought that our highest earthly happiness in itself is not the pinnacle of our aspirations, but, rather, just as it comes from God, so does it form the basis of upbuilding our lives toward God. The truth is that happiness becomes ours only if it is found in the depths of the altar's foundation.

The foregoing also explains why נסכים accompany only עולת בהמה and שלמים. For the consciousness of sin and guilt, which comes to expression in חטאת and אשם, is not compatible with the perfect joy that finds its expression in נסך. The מנחת חוטא lacks even oil and incense (*Vayikra* 5:11), and the state of depression and suffering, from which all קרבנות עוף spring (see Commentary, *Vayikra* 1:17), is equally unsuitable for מנחה ונסך.

In harmony with our conception of the נסכים is the halachah that שירי הלוים accompany ניסוך היין (*Arachin* 11a). For the לויים sing of man "beholding" [שׁוּר] God through contemplation of Israel's history [cf. Commentary, *Bereshis* 49:22]. These שירים, then, express verbally what is performed symbolically through בקדש הסך נסך שכר לה׳. In any case, we have already noted the linguistic and conceptual connection between שֵׁכָר and שיר (Commentary, ibid. 9:20-21).

This, then, is the meaning of the נסכים that accompany עולה and שלמים: They represent the affirmation of the basic fact of Jewish life and duty — namely, that existence, prosperity, and happiness on earth depend directly on God alone, and can be attained only by doing God's Will with joy. In short, the נסכים represent Israel's affirmation that its fate depends on God.

This affirmation rises in importance, the higher the social or national standing that an individual or community ascribes to himself or itself. An individual who regards himself as a "כבש," a simple member of God's flock — he, too, is obligated to take to heart this truth. But for one who regards himself as an איל, the obligation is double. For the integrity of his faith does not affect just his own adherence to duty; rather, the eyes of his contemporaries are upon him. Because of his social standing, he must take the lead as an "איל" and set an example in faithfully following God. If, however, he is a representative and an active partner in God's work, and his role is to be a "פר" in his circle, the affirmation of this fundamental truth is three times as important.

The מרגלים catastrophe, in whose wake פרשת נסכים was communicated, emphasizes the deviation from the נסכים-truth by just such a series of classes. The evil began with the מרגלים, whose role was that of "פרים." They were sent by the community to act for the sake of God's work, but they violated the task of "פר" and did just the opposite. The spokesmen of the community, the "אילים," were enticed by the מרגלים into open rebellion, and they in turn incited the whole people, the "כבשים," to join them in the apostasy.

We can understand, then, why the affirmation of the נסכים-truth is doubled and tripled for the "אילים" and for the "פרים" of Israel, as emphasized by the standard formula for the offerings: שלושה עשרונים לפר שני עשרונים לאיל ועשרון לכבש. For the fundamental truth of the Jewish faith must govern life and shape life and become the legacy of the entire people, and this will happen only if the nation's spokesmen and leaders uphold this truth in word and deed in double and triple force.

However, it is difficult to understand the relation between the amount of oil and wine and the amount of flour. For the flour increases in the proportion of 1, 2, 3 for כבש, איל, and פר respectively, and accordingly we would have expected the oil and wine, too, to increase in similar

17 God *spoke to Moshe, saying:* יז וַיְדַבֵּר יְהֹוָה אֶל־מֹשֶׁה לֵּאמֹר:

proportion: ¼, ½, ¾; yet they increase only in the proportion of ¼, ⅓, ½. Thus, the מנחה of a כבש is richer in oil than that of an איל or פר. The מנחה of a כבש has ¼ הין to an עשרון, whereas the מנחה of איל or פר has only ⅙ הין for each עשרון. Perhaps the reason is as follows: The oil — like the wine — in מנחת נסכים is not merely accessory to the flour and is not merely a modification of the concept "food": richer food, richest food; rather, it represents the independent concept of prosperity in general. Hence, the measure of oil does not parallel the measure of flour. So we find also in the Halachah: Although the flour and the oil of מנחת נסכים are מעכבין זה את זה (see תוספות *Menachos* 44b ד"ה הסולת), oil — as נדבה — can also be brought independently (see Commentary, v. 13). Scripture therefore lays down that the ¼ הין of wine and oil is to increase independently, and toward this end the usual rising scale for fractions is chosen: ¼, ⅓, ½.

The measure of wine — and, according to רבי, of oil also — that may be brought בנדבה is the same as the measure fixed for נסכים (see Commentary, v. 13). It appears that this halachah is rooted in the objective character that must be preserved in the מנחה offering. Even when a מנחה is brought in נדבת יחיד, it is to be given the form of affirmation by which the national Sanctuary expresses this fundamental truth [— that Israel's fate depends solely on God].

17 **וידבר וגו'**. פרשת חלה is intimately connected with פרשת נסכים. פרשת נסכים teaches us that the subsistence, well-being, and happiness of the national prosperity depend directly on God's rule, whereas פרשת חלה teaches us that also the livelihood of every household and of every individual is subject to God's special providence. Not only is the sunlight that ripens the produce of the nation's fields God's direct messenger in His Land, but the same applies also to the allotted portion of every household and of every person. Even the individual's share in the general prosperity is a special act of God — within the framework of God's providence that is directed to the community. This comes to expression in the mitzvah of חלה.

18 *Speak to the Children of Israel and say to them: When you come into the land to which I am bringing you,*	יח דַּבֵּר֙ אֶל־בְּנֵ֣י יִשְׂרָאֵ֔ל וְאָמַרְתָּ֖ אֲלֵהֶ֑ם בְּבֹֽאֲכֶם֙ אֶל־הָאָ֔רֶץ אֲשֶׁ֥ר אֲנִ֛י מֵבִ֥יא אֶתְכֶ֖ם שָֽׁמָּה׃

18 **בבאכם אל הארץ**. We have already noted above (v. 2) the different interpretations of the expression that is used there, כי תבאו אל ארץ מושבתיכם. As a result of that dispute, there are two interpretations here as well.

According to ר׳ ישמעאל, כי תבאו וגו׳ and the similar והיה כי יביאך always mean: לאחר ירושה וישיבה. Consequently, here he says that the unusual term "בבאכם" indicates that מצות חלה applied immediately, even during the fourteen years of conquest and division: שינה הכתוב ביאה זו מכל ביאות שבתורה ללמדך שכיון שנכנסו לארץ מיד נתחייבו בחלה (*Sifre* and רבנן בבי רב in *Kesubos* 25a).

According to רב הונא בריה דרב יהושע, however, the meaning of בבאכם is rather (— or more accurately, "is also"; see תוספות *Niddah* 47a ד״ה ל״ג, who explain that אי בבאכם is none other than the continuation of the ברייתא in the *Sifre*, from which רבנן בבי רב learn that חלה applied also during the fourteen years of conquest. This is also how the סמ״ג [עשין 141] cites the *Sifre*.): ביאת כולכם. Accordingly, the duty of חלה applies only if the whole nation dwells in its land: בביאת כלכם אמרתי ולא בביאת מקצתכם (*Niddah* 47a).

A further consequence of this dispute is that, according to רבנן בבי רב, חלה בזמן הזה דאורייתא, whereas, according to רב הונא בריה דרב יהושע, חלה בזמן הזה דרבנן.

The term "בזמן הזה" includes all the time after the resettlement under Ezra. For a ברייתא cited from סדר עולם (*Yevamos* 82b; *Niddah* 46b) derives from אשר ירשו אבתיך וירשתה (*Devarim* 30:5): ירושה ראשונה ושניה יש להן ושלישית אין להן, which according to most commentators (see רש״י and תוספות to *Yevamos* 82b) means as follows: Yehoshua's conquest sanctified the Land as the land of the Torah vis-à-vis *mitzvos* that are dependent on the sanctification of the Land — e.g., תרומות, מעשרות, שביעית, and the like. This sanctification was nullified by the Babylonian exile and had to be reestablished by the repossession under Ezra. This repossession sanctified the Land for that time and for all future time; the sanctification was not nullified by the second exile. Hence, when we return to the Land, a third sanctification will not be necessary. Thus, the Roman conquest and Israel's dispersion changed nothing as regards קדושת הארץ, and those מצוות

התלויות בארץ that applied מדאורייתא in the land of Israel in the period of בית שני apply there מדאורייתא today as well.

According to רב הונא בריה דרב יהושע, however, we derive from בבאכם that the mitzvah of חלה depends not only on קדושת הארץ, but also on whether the whole nation dwells in the Land. Hence, even if we say that תרומה ומעשר applied מדאורייתא in the period of בית שני and apply מדאורייתא today, חלה applies only מדרבנן; for this condition (the whole nation dwelling in the Land) was not fulfilled in the time of Ezra, as only a part of the nation returned to the Land: וכי אסקינהו עזרא לאו כולהו סלוק (*Kesubos* 25a).

Conversely, according to רבנן בבי רב, precisely from בבאכם we derive that, as regards חלה, an incomplete possession of the Land suffices. Hence, even if we say that תרומה ומעשר apply today only מדרבנן, because the re-possession under Ezra was incomplete, nevertheless, חלה applies מדאורייתא.

(כן נלע״ד דצריכין למימר לסברת רבנן בבי רב, דהא אי אפשר לומר דס״ל דטעמא דמ״ד דרבנן משום דבטלה קדושת הארץ, דאי בטלה לתרומה בטלה לחלה. ועוד מאי ראיה מביאין מהא דחלה היה נוהג בז׳ שכבשו וז׳ שחלקו. ואם כן י״ל דיש לימוד לתרומות ומעשרות שיהו דרבנן, אפי׳ לא דרשינן בבואכם ביאת כולכם גבי חלה. ונראה דס״ל לרבנן בבי רב דמ״ד תרומה בזה״ז דרבנן היינו משום דאין חיובה אלא אחר ירושה וישיבה, וירושת עזרא וישיבתו לא מקרי ירושה וישיבה, או משום שלא כבשו כל הארץ דשבקו הרבה כרכים, או משום שהיו משועבדים למלכי פרס, אע״פ כן חלה דאורי׳, דהא נתחייבו בחלה קודם ירושה וישיבה. ואפשר דלדינא מודה לזה רב הונא, אלא דקאמר אפי׳ למ״ד דזה מיקרי ירושה וישיבה ותרומה דאורי׳, מ״מ חלה עוד תנאי אחר לה והיא ביאת כולכם. ואפשר שזה עיקר טעם הרמב״ם [פ״א מהל׳ תרומות הכ״ו] וצע״ע.)

The רמב״ם rules in accordance with the view of רב הונא בריה דרב יהושע that חלה applies today only מדרבנן. And since חלה, too, is called "תרומה," the condition of ביאת כולכם applies, in his opinion, also to תרומות ומעשרות. Thus, חלה תרומה ומעשרות applied only מדרבנן — even in ארץ ישראל in the time of בית שני (see כסף משנה there).

Not everyone agrees, however, that the condition of ביאת כולכם applies also to תרומות ומעשרות. Rather, according to תוספות (*Yevamos* 82b ד״ה ירושה), the view that קדושת הארץ בזמן בית שני למעשרות ולכל מצוות התלויות בארץ היתה מדרבנן is completely unacceptable. We must say, then, that, this condition is characteristic of חלה.

The halachah that the sanctification of the ירושה שניה was not nullified by the second exile explains the nature of this ירושה שניה, and teaches us the following: The whole national life of the Second Temple period did not give Israel national independence which was then brought to an end by the subsequent exile. Rather, the significance of the Second Temple

19 *It shall be, when you eat of the bread of the land, you shall lift out an uplifted donation for* God.

יט וְהָיָ֕ה בַּאֲכָלְכֶ֖ם מִלֶּ֣חֶם הָאָ֑רֶץ תָּרִ֥ימוּ תְרוּמָ֖ה לַיהוָֽה׃

period was this: The people reassembled around the Sanctuary of the Torah to prepare itself for the centuries of exile that lay before them. The repossession and sanctification of the Land in the time of Ezra were purely for the sake of the exile, for they took place in the very midst of the exile, which even after Ezra's return did not come to a complete end. Thus, the catastrophe of Titus was just a bitter intensification of the fate that continued even in Ezra's time. The catastrophe did not constitute a complete contrast to Ezra's time, and therefore it could not nullify the sanctification effected by him. The effect of Ezra's possession of the Land continues to this very day: ירושה ראשונה ושניה יש להן, שלישית אין להן.

19 **והיה באכלכם מלחם הארץ**. The selective particle -מ indicates that חלה applies only to what is called "לחם" in the narrow sense of the term — viz., the five kinds of grain: חיטים, שעורים, כוסמין, שבולת שועל, ושיפון. These are the same five kinds of grain that can reach a state of חמץ and that are fit to be לחם עוני for [the fulfillment of the mitzvah of eating matzah on] Pesach (*Challah* 1:2; see ר״ש there). We also derive from the term "לחם" that dough becomes subject to חלה only if it is made like bread (*Challah* 1:4-5).

In the preceding verse it does not say בבאכם אל הארץ אשר אני נותן לכם but, rather, אשר אני מביא אתכם שמה. In our view, this already indicates that the laws that follow depend more on our presence in the Land than on the soil of the Land itself. What is more, from the expression "בבאכם" we derive that the presence of the whole nation in the Land is a condition for the mitzvah of חלה. Indeed, the Halachah teaches (ibid. 2:1) that חלה applies in the Land even to bread that is made from produce grown outside the Land, but does not apply outside the Land to bread that is made from produce grown in the Land: פירות חוצה לארץ שנכנסו לארץ חייבים בחלה, יצאו מכאן לשם ר׳ אליעזר מחייב ור׳ עקיבא פוטר. And the Halachah is in accordance with ר׳ עקיבא.

This halachah — that the decisive factor regarding חלה is not the origin of the produce but the place where the bread is made — is derived

20 *As the first portion from your kneading troughs you shall lift out a cake of bread as an uplifted donation. Like the uplifted donation from your threshing floor, so shall you lift up this one.*

כ רֵאשִׁית֙ עֲרִסֹ֣תֵכֶ֔ם חַלָּ֖ה תָּרִ֣ימוּ תְרוּמָ֑ה כִּתְרוּמַ֣ת גֹּ֔רֶן כֵּ֖ן תָּרִ֥ימוּ אֹתָֽהּ׃

from verse 18: הארץ אשר אני מביא אתכם שמה, שמה אתם חייבין בין בפירות חוצה לארץ בין בפירות הארץ (see ר״ש, *Challah* 2:1). Accordingly, לחם הארץ is not bread grown in the Land, but bread made in the Land, as is explained in the *Yerushalmi* (*Challah* 2:1) according to ר׳ עקיבא. Indeed, as a rule, all bread made in a land is indirectly given by the land, as the land provides the means to obtain it. Hence the bread can be called "לחם הארץ" in the wider sense of the term. This is especially the case if the whole nation is living in the Land.

(This halachah of חיוב פירות חו״ל in the Land and פטור פירות הארץ outside the Land — which is indicated by the words אשר אני מביא אתכם שמה — is expressly stated only regarding חלה. The רמב״ם, however, applies it also to תרומות ומעשרות. Accordingly, in these *mitzvos* as well, everything hinges not on the origin of the produce, but on the place of גמר מלאכה, of מירוח. In the case of פירות חו״ל שנכנסו לארץ, the [source of the] רמב״ם's position regarding תרומות ומעשרות [that the חיוב is דרבנן] is not clear. See הל׳ תרומות, 1:22, and כסף משנה there. This view of the רמב״ם is not found in the סמ״ג; he cites this halachah only as regards חלה [עשין 141].)

20 **ראשית ערסתכם**. There is room to speculate whether עריסה denotes the receptacle in which the dough is prepared or the dough itself.

Onkelos translates it as אצוותא, as he also translates ובמשארותיך (*Shemos* 7:28), which is adjacent to ובתנוריך and which undoubtedly means kneading-trough. Support for this interpretation can be adduced from the term "ערש," for a bed is a container for the bedding, the sheets, etc.

On the other hand, in Rabbinic language the root "ערס" is used for kneading: הכא במאי עסקינן בשערסן (*Berachos* 37b). Similarly the *Yerushalmi* (*Challah* 1:1): עירס ראשי עיסיות וכו׳ וההן נשוך לאו כמעורס הוא. Apparently also: כיון שהיא נותנת את המים זו היא ראשית and לא הוקשה וכו׳ אלא למלאכת העירוס בלבד עריסותיכם (ibid. 3:1). In all of the above, עירוס and עריסה apparently denote the act of preparing the dough. The meaning of ערס as the mixing of flour with water is clearest in the *Sifre*: מראשית עריסותיכם למה נאמר? לפי שהוא אומר והיה באכלכם מלחם הארץ שומע אני אף הקמחים במשמע ת״ל מראשית עריסותיכם משיתערס, מכאן אמרו אוכלין עראי מן העיסה עד שתתגלגל בחטים וטימטמה בשעורים.

In *Kilayim* (4:7) it says: אם ערסן מלמעלה. The meaning of ערס there is: an arbor-like binding together of vines over a partition; and lattice work made of reeds to which vines are tied is called "עריס" (ibid. 6:1). Let us also note the relation of ערס to ארס. אירוסין is the first act of joining together toward marriage.

From all of the foregoing it appears that the basic meaning of ערס is a mutual binding together. Thus ערש, whose primary meaning is a criss-cross bed frame whose side pieces are bound one to another by strong webbing (סירוג כרעי המטה — *Kelim* 16:1 et al.). Thus עריס: plaited work of vines or for vines, and thus finally the mixing of flour and water, which forms dough. And just as ארס does not denote the completion of the marriage bond, but only the first act toward this end, so ערס does not denote the completed act of dough-making, but the preliminary mixing of flour and water. At this stage — which the Mishnah calls "גלגול" for wheaten flour and "טמטום" for the less easily mixed barley flour — the dough becomes subject to the duty of חלה (*Challah* 3:1).

עריסה, then, is either the mixing of flour with water to make a dough, or, as Onkelos translates, the receptacle designed for that purpose. Once the dough is finished by לישה, kneading, it is called "בצק."

עריסתכם: According to the Halachah, we have here an indication of the minimum quantity that is subject to the duty of חלה: a mix containing at least one day's requirements for one person. In the case of the manna in the wilderness, this was one עומר = 1/10 איפה. 1 איפה = 3 סאה, 1 סאה = 6 קב, 1 קב = 4 לוג; hence, 1/10 איפה = 7 and 1/5 לוג. 1 לוג = 6 ביצים; accordingly, the שיעור חלה is 43 and 1/5 ביצים.

Since it does not say ראשית העריסת but ראשית ערסתיכם, only *our* dough is subject to the duty of חלה, but not the dough of נכרים or of הקדש (*Menachos* 67a).

כתרומת גרן. Just as the threshing floor shows us the abundance with which God has blessed our fields, the עריסה represents the prosperity He has bestowed on our households. Hence, what applies to the produce of the threshing floor applies also to the עריסה. The owner may not partake of the produce piled into a heap on his threshing floor, until he performs the symbolic act of separating תרומה גדולה for the כהן. By separating this

תרומה, he gives expression to his awareness that it is God Whom he has to thank for the blessing of his fields; hence, he first gives the homage levy to the כהן, who represents to him the Sanctuary of the Torah (see Commentary, *Vayikra* 22:9). This awareness is renewed in him when he prepares the daily bread for himself and for his family and considers the particular care that God extends to every household and to every soul in every home. The ears of corn ripen in the fields under the rays of the sun, which is a blessing to all people on earth. The portion of every individual in the general blessing, the bread given to him daily, is a result of God's special providence. Hence, just as he separates grain from the pile of produce, he must separate a piece of dough and "raise" it to God and to His Sanctuary.

This חלה becomes קודש and is like תרומה in every respect: חייבין עליה מיתה וחומש ואסורה לזרים, and it is the property of the כהן — just like תרומה (*Challah* 1:9; see *Vayikra*, chap. 22). Neither for תרומה nor for חלה is a minimum quantity stated; מן התורה one fulfills the obligation of חלה with the tiniest piece of dough (see Commentary, v. 21), just as to meet the obligation of תרומה even a single kernel from the whole pile is sufficient: חטה אחת פוטרת את הכרי. On the other hand, there is a maximum limit for both, as both are called "ראשית," and there can be no ראשית unless a considerable amount remains: בעינן ראשית ששיריה ניכרין. Hence the dictum: האומר כל גרני תרומה וכל עיסתי חלה לא אמר כלום, "If someone declares his whole barn to be תרומה or the whole of his dough to be חלה, his declaration is invalid and has no effect" (*Chullin* 136b).

From the foregoing halachah we learn an important lesson about the relationship of the people and of the individual to the Sanctuary of the Torah. No one may consider the priest's relation to the Torah to be a substitute for his own. No one should imagine that the Sanctuary is interested in the priest's existence, but that his own existence is immaterial in God's sight. Rather, the preservation of his own existence for the sake of the Sanctuary of the Torah is the condition for and purpose of maintaining the priest, with which he is charged by the mitzvah of חלה. By separating חלה for the priest, he affirms that his own existence and that of his household are dedicated to God and to His Torah. His gift of חלה becomes חלה only if he leaves something also for himself: בעינן ראשית ששיריה ניכרין.

כא מֵרֵאשִׁית֙ עֲרִסֹ֣תֵיכֶ֔ם תִּתְּנ֥וּ לַיהֹוָ֖ה תְּרוּמָ֑ה לְדֹרֹ֖תֵיכֶֽם׃ ס

21 *From the first portion from your kneading troughs shall you give to* God *an uplifted donation for your descendants.*

21 **מראשית ערסתיכם**. In the previous verse the י, the sign of the plural, is missing [from ערסתכם]. That verse deals only with the concept of עריסה in general. The plural ערסתיכם of our verse refers to different kinds of dough, to a plurality of doughs [see next paragraph]. The מ of מראשית, however, indicates a restriction of the duty of חלה, and, as mentioned in our Commentary to verse 19, only the חמשה מיני דגן are חייבים בחלה (*Sifre*).

In the previous verse, Scripture equates תרומת עריסה with תרומת גורן. Here, Scripture repeats תרומת עריסה by itself, to teach us its independence of תרומת גורן. Even if one prepares dough from produce that is exempt from תרומת גורן — e.g., it was הפקר, לקט, שכחה, or פאה, and hence had no בעלים — the dough is subject to the duty of חלה. What is more, Scripture adds לדרתיכם: the duty of חלה continues uninterruptedly and applies even during שביעית. Even though the produce of that year is exempt from תרומות ומעשרות, the dough prepared from that produce is subject to חלה (*Sifre*).

The foregoing emphasizes that aspect of God's providence that comes to expression in תרומת החלה — beside the aspect expressed in תרומת הגורן. Sometimes blessing is bestowed on the general harvest, but an individual and his household can hunger for bread; he can even participate in the general blessing, and yet the bread of his home may not be blessed. Sometimes, what happens is the reverse: In times of widespread scarcity and high prices, an individual and his household do not suffer from want; they are sustained by God's generosity, even without sharing in the blessing of the harvest. Taking חלה from the "manna measure" of the שיעור חלה signifies that the provision of manna continues, and that God, Who sustains His creatures, not only watches over worlds and countries, but in countries extends His care to the cities, and in cities to the households, and in households to the souls. He watches over every soul, whether young or old, who calls to Him and longs for His love. The mitzvah of חלה represents the special השגחה פרטית, and so forms an essential complement to the preceding mitzvah of מנחה ונסך, which is dedicated to God's general providence.

22 *And if one day you should fall into the error that you need no longer observe all these commandments that* God *has communicated to Moshe —*

כב וְכִ֣י תִשְׁגּ֔וּ וְלֹ֣א תַעֲשׂ֔וּ אֵ֥ת כָּל־הַמִּצְוֺ֖ת הָאֵ֑לֶּה אֲשֶׁר־דִּבֶּ֥ר יְהֹוָ֖ה אֶל־מֹשֶֽׁה׃

Accordingly, it seems to us that the halachah that ties the mitzvah of חלה to ביאת כולכם is of immeasurable significance. For it implies that precisely the mitzvah of חלה, which recalls God's providence over the individual in his individuality, depends on whether all of Israel reside in the land of this special providence. In this respect, חלה and יובל are similar: God's act of providence for Israel's sake — the rejuvenation of the nation during the יובל (see Commentary, *Vayikra* 25:10) — depends on whether all of Israel reside in the Land. So, too, God's special care for each individual — as signified by חלה — depends on whether all of Israel take refuge under the wings of God's grace and power. This halachah is a reminder to every individual member of Israel: When he is entitled and obligated to regard himself as being under God's special care — at that moment he must remember that his own well-being and that of every individual depend on the well-being of all of Israel. No man is entitled to sit happily "under his vine and under his fig tree," as long as one of his brethren is still "outside," an alien in another country.

We have already stated on verse 20 that מן התורה the smallest quantity is sufficient for the fulfillment of the duty of חלה. Nevertheless, it is a מצוה מדרבנן to give a quantity that is sufficient to constitute a נתינה, a "gift," as implied by the word "תתנו" in our verse. This quantity is fixed at 1/24 of the dough in domestic baking, and 1/48 of baker's dough in commercial baking (*Challah* 2:7 and ר״ש there).

Our חלה, outside of ארץ ישראל, is only a reminder of the duty that applied in our ancient homeland. It is burned in accordance with the law of חלה טמאה. One fulfills this obligation with the smallest amount, but the custom is to separate at least a כזית as חלה (שו״ע יו״ד 322:3, 5).

22-23 **וכי תשגו וגו׳**. The sin of the מרגלים was that they cast doubt on God's providence over our earthly existence and whether this providence is exclusive and sufficient. By saying נתנה ראש ונשובה מצרימה, they reached the

23 *All that* God *has commanded you through Moshe, from the day that* God *gave His commandments, and onward to your descendants* —

כג אֵת֩ כָּל־אֲשֶׁ֨ר צִוָּ֧ה יְהֹוָ֛ה אֲלֵיכֶ֖ם בְּיַד־מֹשֶׁ֑ה מִן־הַיּ֞וֹם אֲשֶׁ֨ר צִוָּ֧ה יְהֹוָ֛ה וָהָ֖לְאָה לְדֹרֹתֵיכֶֽם׃

point of complete rebellion and complete defection from God. As a result of this sin, the people were given two *mitzvos* — נסכים and חלה. And the very fact of this defection prompted the communication now of פרשת שעירי עבודה זרה; for the assumption of this פרשה is that this sin could be repeated — inadvertently even by the nation, or deliberately by individuals. When the nation repents of this inadvertence, it must bring—in addition to the חטאת, and even before the חטאת — an עולה accompanied by the prescribed נסכים.

וכי תשגו. We have already shown in our Commentary on *Vayikra* 4:13 that שגה is to be distinguished from שגג (see also Commentary, *Bereshis* 8:1). שגג denotes error in practice, whereas שגה denotes error in theory. From this linguistic proof it is already clear that the following words, ולא תעשו, are not the explanation of תשגו; they do not describe the error itself, but only the practical *result* of the theoretical error.

Furthermore, ולא תעשו cannot mean the actual sin brought about by the theoretical error, the sin for which atonement is required here. For לא תעשו denotes neglect of duty and *nonperformance*, whereas והיה אם וגו׳ נעשתה לשגגה (v. 24) and והנפש אשר תעשה ביד רמה (v. 30) clearly indicate that we are dealing here with an *active transgression*.

Moreover, from ולא תעשו את כל המצות וגו׳ את כל אשר צוה ה׳ וגו׳ it is clear that what is under discussion is the *nonfulfillment of the entire Torah*; yet the phrase נעשתה לשגגה (v. 24) and the expressions שגגה הוא, שגגתם, תחטא בשגגה (vv. 25, 27, 28) indicate *one* transgression committed inadvertently, and this is corroborated by analogous phraseology everywhere else in Scripture.

We must conclude, then, that ולא תעשו וגו׳ characterizes only this *one* inadvertence, its significance and its consequences; its point is that this one transgression represents an abandonment of all the Torah's commandments: "If you should fall into error, and by this error signify that you will no longer observe any of these commandments . . ." This is also what is stated in verse 31. One who does deliberately what is done here inadvertently does away with and nullifies God's commandments: כי דבר ה׳ בזה ואת מצותו הפר.

Indeed, the Halachah teaches (*Horayos* 8a) that our verse deals with an error in the sphere of idolatry, עבודה זרה. This is derived from Scripture's addition of the words ולא תעשו וגו׳: אמר קרא וכי תשגו ולא תעשו את כל המצות האלה, איזו היא מצוה שהיא שקולה ככל המצות, הוי אומר זו ע״ז. The prohibition of idolatry is the fundamental principle of all the Torah's commandments, and the whole Torah stands or falls by the fulfillment or nonfulfillment of this prohibition. In the *Sifre Zuta* (cited in *Yalkut Shimoni* ad loc.), the derivation from our verse is as follows: יכול שהוא מדבר בכל המצות, אמרת אם מעיני העדה נעשתה בשגגה, באחת מכל המצות דיבר ולא דיבר בכל המצות, אי אפשר לומר בכל המצות שכבר נאמר באחת ואי אפשר לומר באחת שכבר נאמר בכל המצות, הא מה מצוה שכל המצות תלויין בה, זו ע״ז. And according to ס׳ באר שבע on *Horayos* 8a, this interpretation of our verse also underlies the Gemara's interpretation there.

Accordingly, it is possible that ולא תעשו וגו׳ actually describes the theoretical error of וכי תשגו. Since it is a theoretical error, ולא תעשו would not mean: they do not fulfill all the commandments in practice; rather, ולא תעשו would mean: they hold that the commandments no longer obligate them. The verse והיה אם מעיני העדה then discusses the case resulting from the erroneous teaching of the Sanhedrin: As a result of this theoretical abandonment of all the commandments, they transgressed in practice. The meaning of verses 22-24, therefore, is as follows: If you should fall into the error of thinking that you are no longer obligated to observe any of these commandments that God has communicated to Moshe; if you should think that you are exempt from doing all that God has commanded you through Moshe from the day that He gave commandments and onward to your descendants; and if, then, the "eyes of the community" cause an act of inadvertence to be committed, then . . .

This act of inadvertence represents the theoretical nullification of all the commandments, and it can be none other than an inadvertent act of idolatry. Now, it is inconceivable that עיני העדה would permit an act of idolatry, for they are the nation's teachers and visionaries, and it cannot be that such men would permit the honoring of a non-god — unless the whole binding force of the Torah had first been nullified in their minds. For the recognition that God alone guides our fate and directs our actions is the foundation and basis of the entire Torah, and the proclamation of this fundamental principle began the revelation at Sinai (*Shemos* 20:2-3; see Commentary there). Abandoning this basis is tantamount to abandoning the whole Torah, and abandoning the Torah deliberately and on principle is identical with abandoning this basis.

As the רמב״ן points out in his Commentary (here), there have been times in Jewish history when a community representing the entire Jewish people fell into such an error. An erroneous understanding of the period misled them into thinking that the Torah had become antiquated. Sacrilegious policies of leaders or overwhelming catastrophes brought it about that the Torah was nearly forgotten. It was the "elders of Israel" who approached the prophet Yechezkel to inquire of God about the new age (*Yechezkel* 20:1), for they questioned whether they were still obligated to observe the Torah. They thought that once God had abandoned His people, He had dismissed them from His service and released them from the duties of the Torah. Hence, it was possible to call out to the "elders of Israel": "What has entered your minds shall never come to pass — what you say, 'Let us be like the other nations, like the families of the lands, worshiping wood and stone.' As sure as I live, says God, I will reign over you with a strong hand and with an outstretched arm and with outpoured fury" (ibid. 20:32-33; see *Sifre*, שלח לך, end). Under the influence of Yerav'am and his successors, 10/12 of the Jewish people were removed from Torah study and practice. Under the heavy pressure of the Babylonian exile, the greater part of the *lower* ranks of the people were so far from knowledge of the Torah that it was necessary to teach the Torah anew to those who returned from exile with Ezra.

And are we not witnessing a similar phenomenon in our own times? In wide circles, a generation of our people has been raised and educated in the spirit of those elders of Israel of Yechezkel's day, a generation that is ignorant of the Torah, and that considers the Torah's commandments irrelevant!

The theoretical abandonment of the Torah, expressed by an act of idolatry, is not described merely with the words ולא תעשו את כל המצות האלה; rather, Scripture specifies and distinguishes between the commandments, according to the mode of revelation and the time of revelation: אשר דבר ה׳ אל משה, את כל אשר צוה ה׳ אליכם ביד משה מן היום אשר צוה ה׳ והלאה לדרתיכם. The purpose of this specification is apparently to describe the abandonment of God and His Torah in its comprehensive totality. If one takes אשר דבר

אל משה 'ה as a relative clause modifying כל המצות האלה, then the reference is to the commandments written in the Torah, תורה שבכתב, whereas את כל אשר צוה ה' אליכם ביד משה refers to what was transmitted to Moshe so that he should communicate it orally: תורה שבעל פה. [But see below according to the *Sifre*.]

מן היום וגו'. Since it does not say אשר צוה ה' אליכם but אשר צוה ה' in general, Scripture here undoubtedly refers back to the time in which God first gave commandments to mankind, and thus includes also the general commandments revealed to Adam and to Noach, and also includes the commandments given to the **אבות**. Indeed, the prohibition of ע"ז is not only the foundation of the commandments given to Israel, but is the foundation of the general human sphere of duty. And by saying לדרתיכם, Scripture goes beyond the Mosaic period and includes all of God's words revealed to the Prophets in later periods (*Sifre*).

Scripture thereby teaches us that our relationship to God is indivisible; for the commandments are a unified whole, and it is impossible to choose some and reject some. One cannot assume the standpoint of a Noachide, retain only what is universal, and forgo what is distinctively Jewish. One cannot dispense with the Torah of Moshe and suffice oneself only with the "teaching of the Prophets." The choice before us is either/or: Either one is a complete Jew, observing all the commandments, or one has turned completely away from God. Not for naught does Scripture here equate abandoning God with abandoning His commandments — or more accurately, abandoning the commandments with abandoning God; not for naught is abandoning God — by turning to idolatry — euphemistically described as abandoning the commandments; for we can connect with God only by means of faithful adherence to His Torah (see Commentary, vv. 30 and 31).

In the *Sifre* our Sages say that אשר דבר ה' אל משה is not a relative clause modifying את כל המצות האלה; rather, אשר דבר ה' אל משה goes together with what is stated in the following verse: את כל אשר צוה וגו', מן היום אשר צוה וגו'; and the combination of all these phrases forms the complete contents of כל המצות האלה. For, as opposed to אשר צוה ה' אליכם ביד משה, the meaning of אשר דבר ה' אל משה is not: God's words transmitted to us *through Moshe*; rather, this phrase means: words revealed to us as commandments at the same moment that God spoke them to Moshe. These were the first two of עשרת הדברות — אנכי and לא יהיה לך — which מפי הגבורה שמענום. These two commandments were spoken in the first person to every soul in Israel —

אנכי ה׳ אלקיך אשר הוצאתיך, לא יהיה לך וגו׳ על פני וגו׳ — and each person heard them *directly*. In the case of the other דברות, however, God spoke of Himself in the third person; accordingly, He expressed them to Moshe in the same form in which they were to be transmitted by Moshe to the people. By the first two דברות it was made known to us כי ידבר אלקים את האדם וחי (*Devarim* 5:21); by the others it was made known to us that God chose Moshe as an intermediary to transmit to us His commandments. Although it says את הדברים האלה דבר ה׳ אל כל קהלכם (ibid. 5:19), from which it follows that at Sinai we heard all עשרת הדברות, only the first two were addressed directly to the people. Hence, only the first two overwhelmed the people with such power that they were unable to bear the intensity of God's direct address, and that is why the people requested Moshe's agency for all the rest of the Lawgiving (ibid. 5:19-24; see באר שבע on *Horayos* 8a).

According to the foregoing, אשר דבר ה׳ אל משה includes only אנכי and לא יהיה לך, which were received directly from God, whereas את כל וגו׳ ביד משה includes the rest of the דברות and all the rest of the commandments which were transmitted to us by Moshe in the form of the Oral Law and the Written Law; and ומן היום וגו׳ includes all that God communicated for us to Adam, Noach, the patriarchs, and the prophets — before and after Moshe's time.

אנכי and לא יהיה לך are the two pronouncements on which the entire Torah is based. They obligate us to acknowledge that God alone guides our fate and directs our actions, and by this very acknowledgement we detach ourselves from every form of heathenism. All the other commandments and all the words of the prophets are merely commentary on this. Perhaps that is why Scripture specially emphasizes here these two pronouncements, for we are dealing here with an act of idolatry attesting to the abandonment of the entire Torah. Perhaps this is the meaning of תני דבי רבי (*Horayos* 8a): אמר קרא אשר דבר ה׳ אל משה וכתיב אשר צוה ה׳ אליכם ביד משה, איזו היא מצוה שהיא בדיבורו של הקב״ה וצוה על ידי משה הוי אומר זו ע״ז, דתנא דבי רבי ישמעאל אנכי ולא יהיה לך מפי הגבורה שמענום. According to the foregoing, צוה על ידי refers not only to the explanation of the prohibition of עבודה זרה, but to the explanation of all the מצוות, for they all are corollaries of the עבודה זרה prohibition promulgated by אנכי and לא יהיה לך. תנא דבי רבי, then, is conceptually identical to the idea of רבא or ר׳ יהושע בן לוי (ibid.) that עבודה זרה is שקולה ככל המצוות.

כד וְהָיָה אִם מֵעֵינֵי הָעֵדָה נֶעֶשְׂתָה
לִשְׁגָגָה וְעָשׂוּ כָל־הָעֵדָה פַּר בֶּן־
בָּקָר אֶחָד לְעֹלָה לְרֵיחַ נִיחֹחַ
לַיהוָה וּמִנְחָתוֹ וְנִסְכּוֹ כַּמִּשְׁפָּט
וּשְׂעִיר־עִזִּים אֶחָד לְחַטָּת׃
חסר א'

24 *Then it shall be if, by the eyes of the community, an act of inadvertence has been committed, the entire community shall prepare one young bull each for an ascent offering as an expression of compliance to* God, *and its homage offering and its libation according to regulation, and one male goat as an offering that clears of sin.*

24 **והיה אם מעיני העדה וגו'**. עיני העדה are the nation's "intelligence": the בית דין הגדול.

This, then, is the case under discussion here: The supreme Torah authority erroneously (as a result of שגייה — v. 22) permits the performance of an act of עבודה זרה, and consequently נעשתה לשגגה: this theoretical error gives rise to an inadvertent sin in practice. That is to say, an act of idolatry — permitted by בית דין הגדול — is inadvertently committed. In accordance with what is stated in verse 26, לכל העם בשגגה, this act is committed by the whole nation or by a majority representing the whole nation — be it רוב הקהל במיעוט שבטים or רוב השבטים במיעוט הקהל (see Commentary, *Vayikra* 4:13).

This is the same case discussed in *Vayikra* 4:13-21 regarding all sins liable to the punishment of כרת. There, too, הוראת בית דין הגדול gives rise to an error in practice, and the community is obligated to bring a פר העלם דבר של ציבור. Only the offering is different. There, the national community — each of the tribes of Israel — brings a פר for a חטאת; thus, twelve פרים are brought. And זקני העדה — the court of seventy-one — express through סמיכה (ibid. v. 15) their special relation to these offerings. Here, the national community — each of the tribes of Israel — brings a פר for an עולה and a שעיר for a חטאת; thus, twelve פרים are brought as עולה and twelve שעירים as חטאת. Here — as in all other קרבנות ציבור — there is no סמיכה (*Horayos* 4b; *Menachos* 92a).

Thus, the national atonement for שגגת עבודה זרה differs not only from the national atonement for all other שגגות, but also from all other atonements. In all other offerings atoning for שגגות, the כפרה is attained only by חטאת, whereas here it is attained by עולה and חטאת, and the importance of the עולה is specially emphasized. Generally, חטאת precedes עולה; here, however, the עולה is offered first, and the חטאת is secondary and is offered after the עולה, which is also indicated by the abbreviated spelling, חסר א׳ חטת כתיב (*Zevachim* 90b).

The sin atoned for by פר העלם דבר של ציבור includes שגייה and שגגה: a הוראת בית דין and a מעשה ציבור. But the שגייה encompasses no more than the שגגה; hence, one כפרה is effected for both.

By contrast, here the שגייה is the theoretical abandonment of the whole Torah, as expressly stated in verses 22-23, whereas the שגגה — the one act of עבודה זרה — is only a special concrete consequence of the שגייה. Hence, each of them is atoned for by a special offering: the שגייה by עולה, and the שגגה by חטאת. First, the general bond with God and His Torah must be renewed; only then is it possible to atone for the single act of the sin. But purely mental lapses — הרהורי הלב — are atoned for by עולה; for the source of these lapses is intellectual slackness and a lack of devotion to knowledge of the truth, as a result of which the error *arises* and takes hold in the mind. Hence our Sages (*Yerushalmi Yoma*, 8:7) derive from the verse וְהָעֹלָה עַל־רוּחֲכֶם וגו׳ (*Yechezkel* 20:32, cited above on vv. 22-23) that עולה atones for הרהור הלב; for where the truth is not עולה על הרוח, the error is עולה (see Commentary, *Shemos* 27:8). Moreover, it is the עולה — not the חטאת — that is the expression of our normal relation to God (see Commentary, *Vayikra* 4:24). Hence, since here the whole bond with God has been severed because of the nation's intellectual error, and after repentance this bond must be renewed, this renewal of the bond with God *cannot be expressed other than by* עולה. Here, too, the נסכים accompany the עולה, and Scripture specially emphasizes them: ועשו כל העדה פר בן בקר אחד לעלה לריח ניחח לה׳ ומנחתו ונסכו כמשפט.

We have already stated several times that the fundamental axiom of Jewish truth is אנכי and לא יהיה לך. This axiom teaches us to recognize that God alone directs our actions and guides our fate, and the full expression of this recognition is פר לעולה and מנחתו ונסכו כמשפט. For the עולה teaches that God directs our actions, whereas the מנחה ונסך teach that God guides our fate. This, then, is the meaning of the offerings that are brought here:

The whole nation committed a great sin, and now it presents itself again as a "פר" before God. Thereby, it vows that henceforth it will be faithful to God's *service*, it will devote its whole existence and all its efforts to the fire of the Torah on the heights of the altar, and it will strive to

25 *The priest shall effect atonement for the entire community of Israel and they will be forgiven, for it is an act of inadvertence, and they*

כה וְכִפֶּר הַכֹּהֵן עַל־כָּל־עֲדַת בְּנֵי יִשְׂרָאֵל וְנִסְלַח לָהֶם כִּי־שְׁגָגָה הִוא וְהֵם הֵבִיאוּ אֶת־קָרְבָּנָם

carry out the whole of God's Will. In addition, it will pay homage to God alone, in all aspects of its fate and its happiness. Only then will it be able to rectify the one sin committed inadvertently.

This rectification will be accomplished by the חטאת-vow expressed through the שעיר: We shall never again thoughtlessly fall from the heights on which God has placed us. Rather, with the firmness of a שעיר we shall resist all the temptations that entice us to turn away from God, for God alone is our Guide and Leader.

In these offerings that are brought to atone for שגגת עבודה זרה, בית דין does not stand out but, rather, is merged with the nation. פר העלם דבר של ציבור is really an offering of בית דין הגדול. Each tribe puts its פר at the disposal of בית דין and thereby sends it a warning: From now on, בית דין must be more conscientious and more judicious in discharging the duties of its office. Through סמיכה, the members of בית דין adopt the offering as *their* חטאת. In the case of שגיית עבודה זרה, however, בית דין undermined its very existence [and thereby has merged with the nation]. The atonement offering is not פר חטאת, but שעיר חטאת. Accordingly, it has no סמיכה, and its whole essence is strictly atonement for the nation. Within the framework of the nation, בית דין, too, returns to God and to the fulfillment of its calling.

ועשו כל העדה פר וגו׳: According to the Halachah (*Horayos* 4b), each tribe brings one פר and one שעיר. שעירי עבודה זרה are treated as חטאות פנימיות. They have הזיה in the היכל toward the פרוכת, כנגד בין הבדים; נתינה על קרנות מזבח הזהב; and שפיכת שיריים אל יסוד מזבח העולה. After עבודות הדם, the אימורים are burned on the מזבח, and the rest of the offering is burned מחוץ למחנה (see Commentary, *Vayikra* 4:4-21).

25 **והם הביאו את קרבנם אשה לה׳**: the עולה and the נסכים.

וחטאתם לפני ה׳: the שעיר הנעשה בפנים as חטאת פנימית.

אִשֶּׁה לַיהוָה וְחַטָּאתָם לִפְנֵי יְהוָה
עַל־שִׁגְגָתָם׃

have renewed their nearness by bringing a fire offering to God, *and their sin offering that clears of sin, before* God *for their inadvertence.*

כו וְנִסְלַח לְכָל־עֲדַת בְּנֵי יִשְׂרָאֵל
וְלַגֵּר הַגָּר בְּתוֹכָם כִּי לְכָל־הָעָם
בִּשְׁגָגָה׃ ס שביעי

26 *The entire community of the Children of Israel and he who has entered into their midst from abroad shall be forgiven, because the entire people has acted in inadvertence.*

כז וְאִם־נֶפֶשׁ אַחַת תֶּחֱטָא בִשְׁגָגָה
וְהִקְרִיבָה עֵז בַּת־שְׁנָתָהּ לְחַטָּאת׃

27 *And if a person sins inadvertently, he shall bring a female goat in its first year as an offering that clears of sin.*

כח וְכִפֶּר הַכֹּהֵן עַל־הַנֶּפֶשׁ הַשֹּׁגֶגֶת
בְּחֶטְאָה בִשְׁגָגָה לִפְנֵי יְהוָה לְכַפֵּר
עָלָיו וְנִסְלַח לוֹ׃

28 *And the priest shall effect atonement before* God *for the person who was inadvertent in that he sinned inadvertently, and he shall be forgiven.*

---

26 Scripture here specially mentions ולגר הגר בתוכם. Perhaps the reason is as follows: This גר had renounced heathenism and converted to Judaism. Hence, one might have thought that his turning to עבודה זרה should be treated with special stringency, for it appears as though he reverted to heathenism. Scripture therefore emphasizes that he, too, is worthy of סליחה and כפרה for שגגת עבודה זרה. *כי לכל העם בשגגה*: the transgression came to the whole people through error.

27-28 **ואם נפש אחת וגו׳**. The community's עבודה זרה lapse was preceded by an intellectual-theoretical abandonment of the Torah and by an erroneous ruling by "עיני העדה." Hence — as we have tried to show — the community brings an עולה with מנחה and נסך, and hence the חטאת is a חטאת פנימית. However, בית דין הגדול does not present itself as "פר"; rather, the nation with its tribes presents itself as "שעיר." Through the הזיות and מתנות in the היכל, they admonish themselves and undertake the following: With boldness and manliness they will fulfill the task that awaits them between בדי הארון: as the bearers and keepers of the Torah, they will study and observe its commandments (הזיות על הפרוכת כנגד בדי הארון), and only on the heights of the ideal indicated by God will they expect the nation's material and spiritual blossoming (מתנות על קרנות מזבח הזהב).

In the normal course of national life, the כהן המשיח and בית דין הגדול act as the nation's emissaries in carrying out this task. However, the nation's שגגת עבודה זרה temporarily undermined the nation's relationship to God. Hence, upon the renewal of this relationship, this task reverts to the nation. The tribes of Israel — by their twelve שעירים — present themselves in the היכל as guardians and bearers of the task represented by the פרוכת and מזבח הקטורת.

However, the foregoing applies only if the national "intelligence" causes the community to inadvertently sin. It is different if נפש אחת תחטא בשגגה (v. 27). For an individual's inadvertent sin of עבודה זרה — without הוראת בית דין הגדול or שגגת רוב הציבור — is treated the same as all other שגגות יחיד in sins שזדונן כרת: they all are atoned for by a חטאת חיצונה (*Vayikra* 4:27ff.). The only difference is that there [in the case of other שגגות יחיד] one has a choice of שעירת עזים or כבשה, whereas here [שגגת עבודה זרה של יחיד] the one seeking atonement is נידון בקבוע (*Sifre*), and his offering is an עז בת שנתה. For there is but one law for everyone in the nation who inadvertently commits עבודה זרה: He is expected to display שעיר-like firmness and independence; for had he possessed these traits, he would not have fallen into an error deriving from carelessness and ignorance, and thus he would have guarded himself against such a far-reaching sin.

Even if an erroneous decision is issued by the highest authority, an individual who follows it is not freed from responsibility before God: יחיד שעשה בהוראת בית דין חייב (*Horayos* 5b). This principle should be taken to heart especially in our own time, in which conscience barricades itself behind erroneous declarations made by individual rabbis or by congresses of rabbis. An indication of this principle may perhaps be found in the "דגש-less" spelling of בְּחֶטְאָה בשגגה (and not בְּחֶטְאָהּ): Even when "the person" is not solely responsible and the sin is not strictly his own, for the erroneous views of a supposed authority also contributed to the sin, even then the person requires כפרה before God.

In one respect, however, the law for the individual resembles the law

29 *[As for both] the native-born among the Children of Israel and one who entered into their midst from abroad, there shall be one Teaching for one who committed anything inadvertently.*

כט הָאֶזְרָח֙ בִּבְנֵ֣י יִשְׂרָאֵ֔ל וְלַגֵּ֖ר הַגָּ֣ר בְּתוֹכָ֑ם תּוֹרָ֤ה אַחַת֙ יִהְיֶ֣ה לָכֶ֔ם לָעֹשֶׂ֖ה בִּשְׁגָגָֽה׃

for the community: In the case of שגגת עבודה זרה של ציבור, the בית דין הגדול as such is not represented in the offering; hence the national חטאת is not פר, but שעיר. So we find also in the case of שגגת עבודה זרה של יחיד: In this sin, the office and honor of the individual disappear, and neither the כהן משיח nor the נשיא has a special offering — this in contrast to the law applicable to all other חטאות היחיד (*Vayikra* 4:3 and 22). Rather, this is the halachah of חטאת יחיד של עבודה זרה: There is but one law for every individual — from the כהן משיח and the נשיא to the most ordinary commoner. They all appear before God as a "שעירה," not as a "שעיר." ובעבודת כוכבים היחיד והנשיא והמשיח מביאין שעירה (*Horayos* 9a).

29 **האזרח וגו׳** — see Commentary, v. 26.

תורה אחת יהיה לכם לעשה בשגגה. This generalization teaches that the laws stated here apply to the whole category, and that the sin of עבודה זרה treated here is the archetype for all other שגגות for which one is liable to a חטאת. The sin of עבודה זרה, for which Scripture here makes one liable to a חטאת if committed בשוגג, when done במזיד carries the penalty of כרת. This we learn from what is stated in the next verse: והנפש אשר תעשה וגו׳. Furthermore, the sin described here is committed by an action; it does not come to expression through omission alone. This, too, is indicated by what is stated there: אשר תעשה וגו׳. Hence our Sages say: הוקשו כולם לע״ז, מה להלן דבר שחייבים על זדונו כרת ושגגתו חטאת אף כל דבר שחייבין על זדונו כרת ועל שגגתו חטאת, and further מה עבודת כוכבים שב ואל תעשה אף כל שב ואל תעשה (*Shabbos* 69a, תוספות there ד״ה מה ע״ז; *Kerisos* 3a). Hence any sin for whose willful violation one would not be liable to כרת is excluded from חטאת in the case of שוגג. And hence פסח and מילה, although their willful violation carries the penalty of כרת, are also excluded from חטאת in the case of שוגג; for one who violates them merely refrains from fulfilling a positive precept, but does not actively violate a negative precept. מגדף, too, is excluded

30 *But as for the person who does this with an uplifted hand, either among the native-born or one who has entered from abroad, he has blasphemed* God *by so doing, and that soul shall be uprooted from the midst of its people.*	ל וְהַנֶּפֶשׁ אֲשֶׁר־תַּעֲשֶׂה ׀ בְּיָד רָמָה מִן־הָאֶזְרָח וּמִן־הַגֵּר אֶת־יְהֹוָה הוּא מְגַדֵּף וְנִכְרְתָה הַנֶּפֶשׁ הַהִוא מִקֶּרֶב עַמָּהּ׃

from חטאת. Even though he would be liable to כרת in the case of מזיד and he violates a negative precept, his sin entails no action but only speech, and so is not comparable to עבודה זרה (*Kerisos* 2a; see Commentary, *Vayikra* 4:2).

30 **והנפש אשר וגו׳**. ביד רמה denotes independence without subordination; הרים יד ב- is rebellion (cf. Commentary, *Shemos* 14:8). Here, the expression denotes simply מזיד, in contrast to שוגג which was discussed in the preceding verses (see *Shabbos* 68b, 69a). However, עבודה זרה במזיד, an act of worshipping an idol with full consciousness and intent, by definition, is מרד, rebellion against God, and זדון עבודה זרה becomes יד רמה.

מגדף. The meaning of גדף in relation to God is evident from *Melachim* II, 19:6 and 19:22. The גידוף mentioned there refers to the words of the emissaries of the king of Asshur (ibid. 18:32-36), who compared God to all the gods of heathenism and their powerless futility. That denial of God, which rejects God's power and existence, is termed "גידוף." In *Yechezkel* 20:27-28 it says that the people of Israel, dwelling in the land given to them by God, offer sacrifices to the gods. That worship, too, is termed "גידוף ה׳."

גדף may be related to קטף, "to bend" and "to detach," and is related also to קטב, "to kill" (cf. נקב; see Commentary, *Bereshis* 30:28).

Accordingly, this is what is said here: If someone deliberately performs עבודה זרה, even if it is עבודה זרה of the kind that בית דין הגדול might erroneously permit (as evident from the preceding verses), he has already committed גידוף: he has blasphemed God and denied His existence. From the wording here [which describes the עובד עבודה זרה במזיד as having reached the level of מגדף] it is clear that גידוף is the more comprehensive concept, the more reprehensible sin, yet Scripture equates עבודה זרה with

גידוף, and even one single act of עבודה זרה — if done במזיד — resembles גידוף. גידוף is blaspheming God, and Scripture is saying that every act of עבודה זרה is full-blown גידוף.

The relation between עבודה זרה and ברכת ה׳ is described in *Kerisos* 7b. However, to avoid desecration of God's holy Name, our Sages there do not put the idea into words, but speak metaphorically; and in a wordplay they replace גדף with the similarly sounding גרף. Of עבודה זרה they say there as follows: כאדם האומר לחברו גירפתה הקערה ולא חיסרתה — i.e., you emptied the vessel of all its contents, but you did not damage the vessel itself. But of ברכת ה׳ they say: כאדם האומר לחברו גירפתה הקערה וחיסרתה — i.e., you scraped the vessel clean, in the process of which you also damaged the vessel itself; or in the version of the *Sifre*: גררת את כל הקערה כולה ולא שיירת ממנה כלום; i.e., you scraped away the vessel itself, so that nothing remained of it.

To explain: The עובד עבודה זרה acknowledges another god and worships it. Thus, he denies God His due, for one ought to worship God alone. He may think, however, that his recognition of God does not suffer as a result. By contrast, the מברך את ה׳ turns directly against God with complete blasphemous denial. עבודה זרה is contradictory opposition, whereas ברכת ה׳ is contrary opposition; the מברך את ה׳ is כופר בעיקר.

According to the opinion of the חכמים, which is accepted as the halachah, the מגדף in our verse is מברך את ה׳, and Scripture here equates עובד עבודה זרה במזיד [והנפש אשר תעשה ביד רמה] with מברך את ה׳ [את ה׳ הוא מגדף]. This teaches us the following: The עובד עבודה זרה thinks that he merely performs one act of עבודה *also* to another god, but his act goes far beyond what his intention appears to be on the surface; for every עבודה to another god constitutes a complete denial of God. He wanted to be גורף את הקערה, but actually גירדה ולא שייר ממנה כלום. This stems from the concept of א-ל קנא, from the exclusiveness of the idea of God's unity.

Let us note further: In our verse it says that the עובד עבודה זרה is liable to כרת, and since Scripture here equates עבודה זרה with ברכת ה׳ — for it says את ה׳ הוא מגדף — the implication is that the מברך את ה׳ is likewise liable to כרת: לא בא הכתוב אלא ליתן כרת למברך השם (*Kerisos* 7b).

That מברך את ה׳ is punishable by סקילה is already mentioned in *Vayikra* 24:13ff. Here it says that he is liable to כרת if he transgresses במזיד without עדים and התראה. However, even though the מגדף במזיד is liable to כרת, the שוגג is not liable to a חטאת, for it is a sin שאין בו מעשה (see רמב״ם הל׳ שגגות, 1:2, and לחם משנה there). Proof of this is the following: The penalty of כרת

31 *For he has scorned a word of* God; *he has nullified a commandment of His; uprooted, uprooted shall that soul be; its iniquity shall turn against it.*

לא כִּ֤י דְבַר־יְהוָה֙ בָּזָ֔ה וְאֶת־מִצְוָת֖וֹ הֵפַ֑ר הִכָּרֵ֧ת ׀ תִּכָּרֵ֛ת הַנֶּ֥פֶשׁ הַהִ֖וא עֲוֺנָ֥ה בָֽהּ׃ פ

for the מגדף is derived from עבודה זרה, yet even the עובד עבודה זרה בשוגג is not liable to a חטאת unless he committed some act.

31 **כי דבר ה׳ בזה וגו׳**. The introduction of the section on שגגת עבודה זרה וזדונה (vv. 22-23) deals with the abandonment of all the commandments, and this abandonment comes to concrete expression in שגגת עבודה זרה, which is discussed in v. 24ff. Thereby Scripture has already described the full severity of the sin of עבודה זרה, which entails the abandonment of the entire Torah: כל המודה בע״ז ככופר בכל התורה כולה (רש״י, v. 23).

Indeed, the essence of the sin of עבודה זרה is not, as one might have thought, the scorn directed at God, but the concomitant abandonment of the Torah. This is expressed in those introductory sentences [vv. 22-23], which present before us the whole of God's revelation which obligates us, in all its parts and stages. This is so obvious that the sin of עבודה זרה is mentioned only indirectly — as the abandonment of all the commandments.

The foregoing also explains the conclusion of the עבודה זרה section, which provides the following reason for the כרת penalty of עבודה זרה and מגדף: כי דבר ה׳ בזה ואת מצותו הפר הכרת תכרת וגו׳. This sentence puts the stamp of God — on God's Torah! Ultimately, even the idolater or the blasphemer is not punished with כרת because he serves idols or blasphemes God, but because he thereby scorns God's *Word* and nullifies God's *commandment*. For he deliberately violates God's Word — אנכי and לא יהיה לך — and God's commandment, אלקים לא תקלל (*Shemos* 22:27), and the deliberate violation of *these* commandments is more serious than transgression במזיד of other commandments, since it entails מרד and transgression להכעיס and "הרמת יד" against God and against His Torah.

From this it follows that our objective metaphysical recognition of God, of His existence, is not sufficient; we must acknowledge Him subjectively and morally. We must acknowledge the relationship He established with us when He gave us His Torah, a relationship of which we are made aware by this Torah. In short, we must acknowledge God and accept Him as *our* God. That is exactly what is stated by the declaration that laid the foundation for our whole relationship to God: אנכי ה׳ אלקיך, not אנכי ה׳ אלקים (see Commentary, *Shemos* 20:2 and 3).

All of the foregoing also explains the halachah that אוכל נבילות להכעיס is a מין or a מומר (*Avodah Zarah* 26b). Whoever violates even one of God's commandments — not as a result of yielding to temptation (תיאבון), but out of basic contempt for the commandments — is already included in the category of those who renounce God and His Torah. For it explicitly says here that the severity of the penalty for זדון עבודה זרה is due to the contempt for God's Word and the nonobservance of His commandment ביד רמה: כי דבר ה׳ בזה ואת מצותו הפר. עבודה זרה is special only in the respect that even an ordinary case of מזיד is considered transgression להכעיס and מרד done ביד רמה (see בית יוסף יו״ד סוף סי׳ רסח). But every transgression להכעיס of God's commandment is likewise "הרמת יד" against God and against His Torah, and is therefore included in the same category.

Hence also the statement in *Sanhedrin* 99a: כי דבר ה׳ בזה, זה האומר אין תורה מן השמים, ואפילו אמר כל התורה כולה מן השמים חוץ מפסוק זה שלא אמרו הקב״ה אלא משה מפי עצמו, זהו כי דבר ה׳ בזה; ואפילו אמר כל התורה כולה מן השמים חוץ מדקדוק זה מקל וחומר זה מגזירה שוה זו, זהו כי דבר ה׳ בזה. That is to say, one who denies the Divine origin of the Torah — even if he accepts the entire Torah as Divine except for only one verse which he attributes to Moshe, not to God, or even if he denies the Divine origin of only one nuance expressed in one law, or the hermeneutic validity of only one קל וחומר or one גזירה שוה — is classed as a scorner of the Law, as expressed in our verse by the words כי דבר ה׳ בזה.

Not without good reason does this section open [vv. 22-23; see Commentary there] with the concept of revelation in all its components: תורה שבכתב; תורה שבעל פה; *mitzvos* communicated before Moshe's time, to Adam, Noach, the patriarchs; communications after Moshe's time, to the prophets. Of one who denies even one דבר of these דברי ה׳ or one מצוה of these מצות ה׳, Scripture says: כי דבר ה׳ בזה ואת מצותו הפר!

הפר. הפר generally occurs in connection with ברית, עצה, מחשבה, נדר, and means: to frustrate and to prevent something that should be done. Accordingly, הפר מצוה means: to nullify the mitzvah's force and effectiveness, not in general but as regards oneself; to treat the mitzvah as though it does not exist, to deny its binding force, to stubbornly discount its effectiveness.

32 *[While] the Children of Israel were in the wilderness, they discovered a man gathering sticks on the Sabbath day.*

לב וַיִּהְי֥וּ בְנֵֽי־יִשְׂרָאֵ֖ל בַּמִּדְבָּ֑ר וַֽיִּמְצְא֗וּ אִ֛ישׁ מְקֹשֵׁ֥שׁ עֵצִ֖ים בְּי֥וֹם הַשַּׁבָּֽת׃

עונה בה. His enmity toward God's commandment is futile. God's Torah endures forever, is inviolable; its sanctity cannot be nullified. But his iniquity falls back on *himself*. By scorning God's commandment, he forfeited his *own* future: הכרת תכרת הנפש ההִוא עונה בה. For this reason, apparently, עונה is רפה [the absence of the possessive דגש indicates a weakened נפש]. (See also Commentary, *Vayikra* 20:3.)

32 The preceding section dealt with the sin of עבודה זרה, presenting it as the abandonment of God and His Torah. The focal point of the offerings mentioned there is the acknowledgement that God directs our actions and guides our fate, and this comes to expression through עולה and מנחה ונסך. The section's conclusion dealt with someone who performs עבודה זרה deliberately (במזיד) but without עדים והתראה. Hence he is not brought before a human court of law, but is turned over to Divine judgment, which imposes כרת for עבודה זרה and ברכת ה׳.

Now, there is another mitzvah in which God has designated the performance of a specific act — or more accurately, refraining from a specific act — as an expression of our acknowledgement of God as Master of our fate and of our actions. Accordingly, one who observes this mitzvah acknowledges — and one who fails to observe it denies — that God is the Master of our fate and of our actions. For this reason, one who violates this mitzvah is subject to the penalties of כרת and סקילה — like an עובד עבודה זרה and like a מגדף. This mitzvah is שבת. For the Sabbath puts a halt — by God's command — to our labors, and by this one שביתה we place all our actions, along with the world in which we live, before God's throne. Our refraining from creative work on the Sabbath is a double acknowledgement — and the performance of any such work on the Sabbath is a double denial — of God's mastery.

Thus, there is a close connection between the instance of a חילול שבת, which is related in the verses that follow, and the laws and events mentioned in the preceding verses.

Indeed, we see here the same בני ישראל and the same עדה which we saw also at the beginning of the פרשה, only that there they rebelled against God and against His guidance, whereas here they resumed being faithful to God. And although they were במדבר, doomed to wander through the wilderness without any hope of arriving at their destination, they became aware again of their duty. They knew that they owed allegiance to God and to His Torah, and in the name of the Torah they defended its commandments against all members of the עדה.

The opening phrase ויהיו בני ישראל במדבר as well as the wording of this entire narrative — when compared with the narrative about the מקלל (*Vayikra* 24:10ff.) — indicate that here special emphasis is laid on the initiative taken by the people. It does not say here: ויצא איש ויקושש עצים ביום השבת ויביאו אותו אל משה וגו׳; rather, it says: ויהיו בני ישראל במדבר וימצאו וגו׳ ויקריבו אתו המצאים אתו וגו׳. Thereby, our attention is directed to the activity of the people and to their intervention for the sake of the Torah, more than to the sinner himself.

מקשש עצים. See our Commentary on *Shemos* 5:7, where we speculated whether the original meaning of קשש can be explained by its relation to קצץ, גזז, to cut off, to cut close, or by its relation to גשש, to grope about, to pick up something that can be taken by hand. Thus our Sages, too, speculate (*Shabbos* 96b) whether the מלאכה committed by the מקושש was that of תולש or מעמר or מעביר ד׳ אמות ברשות הרבים, cutting, gathering, or transporting the wood four אמות in רשות הרבים (see Commentary, *Shemos* 35:1-2).

If we accept the latter opinion, the opening remark ויהיו בני ישראל במדבר is intrinsically connected with the whole incident. For our Sages say in *Shabbos* 6b that the מדבר, the wilderness, was considered רשות הרבים, a public domain, only בזמן שישראל שרויין במדבר, only owing to Israel's presence there. If we now assume that the מקושש's offense was מעביר ד׳ אמות ברשות הרבים, then only from the opening remark — ויהיו בני ישראל במדבר — is it established that his action entailed prohibited מלאכה. In addition, the opening remark forestalls the error of regarding this case as a precedent for categorizing the מדבר בזמן הזה [as a רשות הרבים when Israel is not in the מדבר].

To this let us add a further comment. According to the accepted halachah (*Chullin* 5a), a מומר לחלל שבת בפרהסיא is treated the same as a מומר לעבודה זרה and is considered a מומר לכל התורה כולה. This, then, is the only transgression whose severity depends on it being committed in public, בפרהסיא, and only in such a case is it similar to עבודה זרה. Here [in our chapter] we learn from their juxtaposition that חילול שבת is similar in its

33 *Then those that had discovered him gathering sticks brought him to Moshe, to Aharon and to the entire community.*

לג וַיַּקְרִ֣יבוּ אֹת֔וֹ הַמֹּצְאִ֥ים אֹת֖וֹ מְקֹשֵׁ֣שׁ עֵצִ֑ים אֶל־מֹשֶׁה֙ וְאֶל־אַהֲרֹ֔ן וְאֶ֖ל כָּל־הָעֵדָֽה׃

severity to עבודה זרה. Hence, there is great importance to the Torah's remark that בני ישראל were at the site of the crime, and that the crime was committed in their presence: המצאים אתו מקשש עצים (see v. 33). Bear in mind that the concept of פרהסיא, פרסום, is not limited to the actual presence of עשרה מישראל, but applies also in a case where the sinner knows that his act will become publicly known, יודע שיתפרסם (שו״ת מהרי״ק, 160, based on *Sanhedrin* 74b). Accordingly, in this case of the מקושש — as well as in every case of חילול שבת punishable by a human court of law — the sin was committed in public and therefore is equal to עבודה זרה. For the עדים והתראה — the witnesses who remind the sinner of the law and of the punishment entailed by its transgression — make him aware, while the sin is being committed, of the publicity of the community. By his attitude of אף על פי כן, he submits himself to the court of this community, and at the time of the sin he is aware of the community. Thus, Scripture's emphasis that בני ישראל were present at the sin of the מקושש could explain the halachah that only חילול שבת בפרהסיא is equal to עבודה זרה.

This might also explain the difficult statement by ר׳ יצחק in the *Sifre* on the next verse: ויקריבו אתו המצאים אתו מקשש וכו׳ מגיד שהתרו בו מעין מלאכתו, מכאן לכל וכו׳; ר׳ יצחק אומר אינו צריך וכו׳ ומה ת״ל ויקריבו מלמד שהתרו בו ואחר כך (הקריבו) [הביאוהו]. In light of the foregoing, ר׳ יצחק's intention can be interpreted as follows: המצאים אתו מקשש (see Commentary, v. 33) does not serve to teach us of the התראה required in every testimony of criminal law, for that halachah is derived from another source. Rather, המצאים אתו מקשש teaches us the following: The התראה that was required to bring the מקושש to court was given at the time the sin was committed. His sin, then, constituted חילול שבת בפרהסיא, and thus the important halachic conclusion: The equation of חילול שבת with עבודה זרה — which is derived here from the juxtaposition of the two sections — applies only to חילול שבת בפרהסיא.

33 **ויקריבו אתו המצאים וגו׳**. Scripture repeats the description of the subject: המצאים אתו מקשש עצים, from which our Sages derive (*Sanhedrin* 41a) that

34 *They put him into custody, for it had not been explained what should be done with him.*

לד וַיַּנִּ֥יחוּ אֹת֖וֹ בַּמִּשְׁמָ֑ר כִּ֚י לֹ֣א פֹרַ֔שׁ מַה־יֵּעָשֶׂ֖ה לֽוֹ׃ ס

what is meant by this "finding" is that the people made a discovery: they not only saw him doing the act, but found that *he* did the act, and that it could be attributed to him in every respect. That is to say, he acted with clear knowledge of the prohibition and its penalty — a discovery they could have made only if he continued his act after due warning, התראה: שהתרו בו ועדיין הוא מקושש (cf. Commentary, *Shemos* 21:18 and *Vayikra* 20:17).

34 **ויניחו אתו במשמר**. This is detention pending further investigation, which is also alluded to in *Shemos* 21:19.

כי לא פרש מה יעשה לו. פרש — see Commentary, *Vayikra* 24:12. There it says of the מקלל: לפרש להם על פי ה׳, for it had not yet been stated that this act carries with it a penalty. Here, however, it says: כי לא פרש מה יעשה לו; that is to say, it had not yet been explained which form of the death penalty shall be administered. יודע היה משה רבינו שהמקושש במיתה שנא׳ מחלליה מות יומת (שמות לא, יד), אלא לא היה יודע באיזו מיתה נהרג (*Sanhedrin* 78b).

Nevertheless, the התראה that was given to the מקושש was sufficient, for all that is required is to inform the offender that he is liable to the death penalty; it is not necessary to inform him by which method he will be executed (ibid. 80b). According to ר׳ יהודה, however, the התראה is not complete until the offender is informed by which method he will be executed. According to this view, the מקושש was killed on the basis of a הוראת שעה.

This opinion of ר׳ יהודה may be the explanation of the statement in the *Sifre* here: מות יומת האיש – לדורות; רגום אותו באבנים – לשעה. This would mean as follows: According to the law that would ordinarily apply, a מקושש could be liable to the death penalty only from now onward — after it has been made clear by which form of the death penalty he shall be executed, and it is possible to properly warn him. Nonetheless, even this מקושש — who was not given a complete warning — shall be executed by סקילה on the basis of a הוראת שעה. (In any case, all agree that the מקלל [*Vayikra* 24:13] was executed only on the basis of a הוראת שעה, for it was not yet possible to warn him that he was liable to the death penalty [*Sanhedrin* 78b].)

35 *And* God *said to Moshe: The man shall be executed; let the entire community stone him with stones outside the camp.*

לה וַיֹּאמֶר יְהוָה אֶל־מֹשֶׁה מוֹת יוּמַת הָאִישׁ רָגוֹם אֹתוֹ בָאֲבָנִים כָּל־הָעֵדָה מִחוּץ לַמַּחֲנֶה:

36 *The entire community led him outside the camp and stoned him with stones so that he died, as* God *had commanded Moshe.*

לו וַיֹּצִיאוּ אֹתוֹ כָּל־הָעֵדָה אֶל־מִחוּץ לַמַּחֲנֶה וַיִּרְגְּמוּ אֹתוֹ בָּאֲבָנִים וַיָּמֹת כַּאֲשֶׁר צִוָּה יְהוָה אֶת־מֹשֶׁה: פ

מפטיר

Although they had already been told that מחלליה מות יומת and that סתם מיתה is חנק (see Commentary, *Vayikra* 20:10), nevertheless, they were in doubt as to the method of execution by which the מקושש was to be put to death. For חילול שבת בפרהסיא is equivalent to עבודה זרה; hence, it occurred to Moshe that the penalty [i.e., סקילה] would be the same for both (תוספות *Sanhedrin* 78b and *Bava Basra* 119a). Here again we see the close connection between פרשת המקושש and the preceding פרשת עבודה זרה.

(On the opening phrase ויהיו בני ישראל במדבר the *Sifre* states as follows: בגנות ישראל הכתוב מדבר שלא שמרו אלא שבת ראשונה ושניה חיללו. Since מחלליה מות יומת was communicated only after מתן תורה, it cannot be that the שבת ראשונה mentioned in the *Sifre* refers to the Shabbos given to them with the manna. Rather, it must refer to the Shabbos after מתן תורה, for only then were they given the comprehensive warning לא תעשה כל מלאכה. Indeed, there is room to speculate whether the prohibition of תולש and מעמר applied before מתן תורה; it is possible that at that time the prohibited מלאכות included only הוצאה and אפיה ובישול. Several of the difficulties raised by ר״א מזרחי on verse 32 could perhaps be resolved by this observation.) [The opinion of the *Sifre* is in contrast to the one followed in the Commentary on v. 32 that the מקושש incident occurred after the מרגלים episode.]

35-36 **ויאמר ה׳ וגו׳, רגום אתו וגו׳, כל העדה, מחוץ למחנה** — see Commentary, *Vayikra* 20:2, 24:14, 16, 23.

In the similar case of the מקלל (ibid. 24:13), it says: וידבר ה׳ וגו׳. There, an entirely new halachah was pronounced, for the death penalty had not yet been ordained for מברך את השם. Hence, there it says: וידבר ה׳ וגו׳. Here,

37 *And* God *said to Moshe:*	לז וַיֹּאמֶר יְהוָה אֶל־מֹשֶׁה לֵּאמֹר׃
38 *Speak to the Children of Israel and say it to them so that they will make themselves fringes upon the corners of their garments, for [the generations of] their descendants, and they shall place upon the fringes of the corner a thread of sky-blue wool.*	לח דַּבֵּר אֶל־בְּנֵי יִשְׂרָאֵל וְאָמַרְתָּ אֲלֵהֶם וְעָשׂוּ לָהֶם צִיצִת עַל־כַּנְפֵי בִגְדֵיהֶם לְדֹרֹתָם וְנָתְנוּ עַל־צִיצִת הַכָּנָף פְּתִיל תְּכֵלֶת׃

however, מות יומת had already been ordained, only that it was necessary to clarify by which method he was to be executed. Hence it says here: ויאמר ה׳ וגו׳.

37 **ויאמר וגו׳**. It is very rare that legal sections open with the term "ויאמר." Where they do open in this way, they are usually explanations of laws already given — thus: ויאמר וגו׳ זאת חקת הפסח (*Shemos* 12:43), ויאמר וגו׳ אך את שבתתי וגו׳ (ibid. 31:12), ויאמר וגו׳ (above, v. 35); or the law under discussion in that section is a consequence of a previous utterance — thus: וידבר וגו׳ אחרי מות וגו׳ ויאמר וגו׳ (*Vayikra* 16:1-2); or the laws under discussion are connected to previous events — thus: ויאמר ה׳ אל אהרן אתה וגו׳ (below, 18:1), and thus the first mitzvah communicated to Moshe: ויאמר וגו׳ החדש הזה וגו׳ (*Shemos* 12:1-2), where the opening serves to teach us that the mitzvah is the goal of all the preceding events and acts of Divine providence. (Regarding *Vayikra* 21:1, see Commentary there.) Here, too, the opening with the term "ויאמר" serves to teach us that the following mitzvah is connected with what preceded it. But it does not refer back solely to the event that immediately preceded it; rather, as we shall see, it is the summing-up of all the events and laws contained in פרשת שלח לך.

38 **דבר וגו׳ ואמרת וגו׳ ועשו להם וגו׳**. As we have already stated in *Collected Writings*, vol. III, p. 139-140, had this been a categorical command, it would have been worded: דבר וגו׳ ויעשו להם וגו׳. ועשו indicates that the performance is the result of ואמרת אלהם: the fulfillment will follow naturally, as a result of Moshe's instructions and explanations. Say to them all of the preceding and everything connected with it and make them conscious

of it, so that they take it to heart and gladly make fringes on the corners of their garments, as I bid them.

In *Menachos* 42a our Sages derive from the wording דבר אל בני ישראל וגו׳ ועשו וגו׳ that only בני ישראל are fit to make ציצית, whereas ציצית בנכרי פסולה. They also say in *Sukkah* 9a that ציצית גזולה פסולה, as ועשו להם משלהם. They also derive from גדלים תעשה לך (*Devarim* 22:12) that the whole preparation of the fringes — the spinning as well as the attachment to the garment — must be done for the sake of the mitzvah: בעינן טויה ועשיה לשמה.

ציצת stems from צוץ (related to זוז, שוש, סוס): a movement that bursts from inside outward. As a verb, ציץ denotes the bursting forth of the parts of a plant from the stem and branches: to sprout, to blossom. As a noun, ציץ denotes a shoot, a blossom. On animal bodies, ציץ is a wing and ציצת is a lock of hair. Thus the ציץ, which is an ornament that stands out upon the forehead of the כהן גדול. Similarly, זיז in Rabbinic Hebrew is a projection. הציץ means: to peer through a lattice, as though one's gaze penetrates to the other side. In our verse, according to the Halachah, ציצת denotes threads that protrude from a garment like sprouts, as our Sages say: אין ציצית אלא יוצא, "The term '*tzitzis*' means nothing other than something that comes out from something else" (*Menachos* 41b). They say further: אין ציצית אלא ענף, "*Tzitzis* denotes sprouting threads," as it says: וַיִּקָּחֵנִי בְּצִיצִת רֹאשִׁי (*Yechezkel* 8:3)"; that is to say, in our verse the term "*tzitzis*" denotes sprouts of threads, just as in *Yechezkel* it denotes a lock of hair (cf. Commentary, *Shemos* 28:36).

על כנפי בגדיהם: not על בגדיהם, anywhere on their garments, but על כנפי בגדיהם; where the garment ends, the ציצית threads are to begin, for they must protrude from the garment like sprouts. Accordingly, the ציצית is fastened on the corner of the garment, no farther than three thumbbreadths and no closer than a קשר גדול — the length of the upper joint of the thumb — from the edge. The ציצית is placed על כנפי וגו׳: it emerges from the garment above the edge, before the end of the garment; thus, it is נוטפת על הקרן: it emerges from the corner, from which it "flows" downward (*Menachos* 42a).

בגדיהם. We have already stated several times — in connection with בגדי כהונה (*Shemos* 28), נגעים (*Vayikra* 13, end), and כלאים (ibid. 19:19) — that the Torah views wool and linen as the primary materials of garments; hence, when בגדים סתם are mentioned in the Torah, as a rule only woolen or linen garments are to be understood. Accordingly, there is one opinion

(*Menachos* 39b) that the duty of *tzitzis* applies מדאורייתא only to garments of wool or linen, whereas garments made of other materials are subject to the duty only מדרבנן, and this opinion is accepted as the halachah by the רמב"ם (הל' ציצית, 3:1). According to another opinion, however (*Menachos* 39b), all garments are subject to the duty of *tzitzis* (see below).

בגדיהם: even garments of שותפים — for the common use of more than one owner — are subject to the duty of *tzitzis*. On the other hand, a טלית שאולה is exempt, for it is not כסותך (*Devarim* 22:12; *Chullin* 115a).

ונתנו על ציצת הכנף וגו'. Here it says הכנף categorically, not limited by the addition כנף הבגד, and from this the other opinion (*Menachos* 39b) derives an extension of the duty of *tzitzis*: the duty goes beyond the limited concept of בגד צמר ופשתים and includes garments made of all materials.

Regarding the material out of which the *tzitzis* is made, our verse is expounded as follows: ציצת הכנף, מין כנף. That is to say, the assumption is that the *tzitzis* that emerges from the corner of the garment is of the same material as the corner itself; and since we learn from the juxtaposition of the verses in *Devarim* 22:11-12 (see Commentary there) that there is significance to צמר ופשתים also as regards the mitzvah of *tzitzis*, the result is the following rule: צמר ופשתים פוטרין בין במינן בין שלא במינן, שאר מינין במינן פוטרין שלא במינן אין פוטרין. That is to say, since wool and linen are the primary materials of garments, they are fit for the mitzvah of *tzitzis* in all garments, whereas any other material is fit only in a garment made of the same material (see רשב"א on *Shabbos* 27a).

ועשו וגו' ונתנו וגו'. These two terms complement each other. Had it said only ועשו, one might have interpreted that the *tzitzis* can be made with the garment, and that the threads are left hanging at the ends of each corner. Against that, ונתנו על indicates that the *tzitzis* is a separate entity, and only afterward is placed on the corner of the garment; nevertheless, the *tzitzis* should be attached firmly to the garment, to meet the requirement of ועשו. Thus, from the combination of these two terms we learn that the *tzitzis* should be fastened to the corner of the garment by a firm knot (*Sifre*; see תוספות *Menachos* 39a ד"ה לא).

In *Menachos* 39a our Sages adduce further proof that קשר עליון דאורייתא — i.e., that the joining of the *tzitzis* to the garment by a firm knot is the way prescribed by the Torah. For a special derivation was required to allow סדין בציצית — i.e., to allow a linen garment to be provided with woolen *tzitzis*, overriding the prohibition of כלאים (*Devarim* 22:11-12). The implication is that the *tzitzis* is tied to the garment by a firm knot.

מדרבנן, however, סדין בציצית is prohibited, lest people transgress the prohibition of כלאים unlawfully (*Menachos* 40a-b).

The mitzvah of *tzitzis* contains two prescriptions: (a) ועשו להם ציצת, to make fringes on the corners of garments; (b) ונתנו על ציצת הכנף פתיל תכלת, to place on these fringes a thread of תכלת-colored wool. The Torah does not prescribe the color of ציצת הכנף. Since the fringes are ציצת הכנף, fringes of the garment, they are presumed to be מין הכנף, similar to the garment, also in respect to the color, and since garments were predominantly white, the fringes are called in the Halachah "לבן." But the color white is entirely immaterial, and לבן means only: not תכלת (ibid. 38a and רש״י there).

To the fringes of the garment, one thread of תכלת is to be added. But לבן and תכלת are not indispensable to each other; in the absence of one, the duty is fulfilled by the other: התכלת אינה מעכבת את הלבן והלבן אינו מעכב את התכלת (*Menachos* 38a).

The number of the threads and the numerical proportion of תכלת to לבן is the subject of a dispute, but the most generally accepted tradition is that the ציצית contains eight threads; that is to say, four threads are passed through a hole in the corner of the garment, are doubled in the middle, and are knotted together, so that eight threads hang down from the corner. According to the רמב״ם, half of one of these four threads is dyed תכלת, so that there are seven threads of לבן and one thread of תכלת (ibid. 41b; רמב״ם הל׳ ציצית, 1:6).

We have already analyzed (Commentary, *Bereshis* 30:8) the meaning of the root פתל in light of its relation to בתל ,בדל, which yields the meaning of פתיל: a thread which is "separated" (from the rest) by means of connection. Accordingly, פתיל הציצית, too, is not one single thread, but threads twisted into a cord; it is שוע טווי ונוז (see Commentary, *Vayikra* 19:19; תוספות *Yevamos* 4b, ד״ה ואמר). By contrast, "חוט" denotes a simple thread; cf. וְהַחוּט הַמְשֻׁלָּשׁ (*Koheles* 4:12).

A complement to the mitzvah of *tzitzis* stated here is found in *Devarim* 22:12: גדלים תעשה לך על ארבע כנפות כסותך אשר תכסה בה. What here is called "ציצת" and "פתיל" — threads hanging down freely (ענף, as in ציצת ראשי; see Commentary above) — is called there "גדלים." גדיל is cord, thick thread "enlarged" in circumference by tightly joining together several threads. (Thus in *Melachim* I, 7:17: גְּדִלִים מַעֲשֵׂה שַׁרְשְׁרוֹת; and thus מעשה עבת in *Shemos* 28:14 is translated by Onkelos as עובד גדילו. And in Rabbinic Hebrew גודל is not the great finger but the thick one, the thumb.)

The *tzitzis*, then, is גדיל as well as ענף. That is to say, after tying the

39 *And this shall be fringes for you, so that you may see them and remember all the commandments of* God *and carry them out, and not go exploring after your own heart and after your own eyes [and], following them, become unfaithful to Me.*

לט וְהָיָה לָכֶם לְצִיצִת וּרְאִיתֶם אֹתוֹ
וּזְכַרְתֶּם אֶת־כָּל־מִצְוֺת יְהוָה
וַעֲשִׂיתֶם אֹתָם וְלֹא־תָתֻרוּ אַחֲרֵי
לְבַבְכֶם וְאַחֲרֵי עֵינֵיכֶם אֲשֶׁר־
אַתֶּם זֹנִים אַחֲרֵיהֶם׃

threads to the corner of the garment, one takes one of the eight threads and winds it several times around the other threads, thereby turning the threads into a tight cord, גדיל, for part of their length, and the rest is allowed to hang free, ענף. The proper proportion is one third גדיל and two thirds ענף: נויי תכלת שליש גדיל ושני שלישי ענף (*Menachos* 39a)

From the complementing verse in *Devarim* it is also clear that only a garment that has four corners is subject to the duty of *tzitzis*; if it has only three corners, it is exempt, and if it has more than four corners, only four must be provided with *tzitzis* (ibid. 43b). However, the four ציציות form a single unit, and if on one corner the *tzitzis* is lacking or unfit, the mitzvah is not fulfilled at all: ארבע ציציות מעכבות זו את זו שארבעתן מצוה אחת (ibid. 37b).

תכלת is the special shade of sky-blue that is the basic color of the Sanctuary (see Commentary, *Shemos* 25:3-8 and 28:43). No other color may be substituted for it. In particular, one may not substitute for it the color of קלא אילן, which is deceptively similar. If תכלת is not available, one fulfills the mitzvah with the לבן threads, as already noted.

39 **והיה לכם לציצת**. After having already stated ונתנו על ציצת וגו׳, ועשו להם ציצת, the Torah continues: והיה לכם לציצת וגו׳. It must be, then, that the term "ציצת" expresses both the external character of these threads as well as their purpose [see Commentary v. 41], and this purpose is to be accomplished by וראיתם אתו וגו׳.

וראיתם אתו assumes that the time when the mitzvah of *tzitzis* applies is the daytime, for in the daytime one recognizes things by one's sense of sight: וראיתם אותו פרט לכסות לילה (*Menachos* 43a). Hence the mitzvah of *tzitzis* is a מצות עשה שהזמן גרמא, a positive mitzvah that is limited to a certain time, and therefore women are exempt from this mitzvah (ibid.; see Commentary, *Vayikra* 23:43).

Opinions differ regarding this halachah that limits the mitzvah of *tzitzis* to the day, excluding the night. According to רש״י and the רמב״ם, the time is the decisive factor: in daytime, even night clothes are subject to the duty; at night, even day clothes are exempt. According to רבינו תם and the רא״ש, however, the designation of the garment is the decisive factor: a night-garment is exempt even if worn in the daytime, and a day-garment is subject to the duty even if worn at night (see טור and בית יוסף, או״ח 18).

Relatedly, let us note that, according to the view that is accepted as the halachah, the mitzvah of *tzitzis* is חובת גברא and not חובת טלית. That is to say, the mitzvah applies only when a garment is worn, whereas כלי קופסא — a garment placed in the closet — is exempt from *tzitzis* (*Menachos* 41a). On the other hand, כסות סומא — the garment of a blind man — is subject to the duty of *tzitzis*. וראיתם אתו only assumes that daytime is the time of ראיה and only designates daytime in general, even if this particular individual lacks the power of sight; for ישנה בראיה אצל אחרים (ibid. 43a). But the mitzvah of *tzitzis* is not an absolute obligation. The Torah does not obligate us to wear a garment that is subject to the duty of *tzitzis*. The Torah ties the mitzvah to the assumption that we will wear a garment that is subject to *tzitzis*, and expects us to subject ourselves to this obligation willingly (ibid. 41a; see Commentary, v. 38).

וראיתם וגו׳ וזכרתם. By this ראיה the purpose assigned to the fringes in the preceding statement "והיה לכם לציצת" will be achieved. When you see them, you shall remember all of God's commandments and resolve to fulfill them: ראיה מביאה לידי זכירה, זכירה מביאה לידי עשיה (*Menachos* 43b).

ולא תתורו וגו׳. We have already stated in our Commentary above (13:2), that תור can denote exploration with a subjective purpose, and in such a case it signifies the aspiration to get to know things to the extent that they can be of use to us. The mental activity signified by תור seeks to find out what is good or not good for us. The לבב forms wishes, and the עינים seek the means to satisfy these wishes. When a person is left to himself, it is only the ego — with all its requirements, inclinations, and demands — which forms the motives of this wishing and desiring heart, and the eye sees only the sensual relationships of the sensual world. In the service of the desiring heart and the seeing eye, the mind — התר אחרי הלב והעין — judges and distinguishes between good and bad: it will pronounce something "good" if its sensual qualities are such that they give satisfaction to the heart, or "bad" if it does not offer this satisfaction or blocks the way to this satisfaction. The same is true of fulfilling the heart's wishes and avoiding the things that prevent their satisfaction: the mind that seeks after the heart and after the eyes will value things only according to their relationship to its own sphere, and it will cultivate fear and hope only according to the results of this judgment. But if a person draws near or rejects, fears or hopes, only according to the dictates of a mind that forms its judgments by following the heart and the eyes, he is not free to contemplate God and His Torah, and he does not occupy himself with God, Who directs his actions and guides his fate; God does not influence what he draws near or rejects, his hopes or his fears. Serving the heart and the eyes does not go together with serving God; אחרי לבבכם ואחרי עיניכם אתם זנים: whoever follows his heart and his eye betrays God and is unfaithful to Him.

It is quite a different matter, however, if God and His Torah form the basis and the starting point of all our considerations, thoughts, and judgments. If we regard ourselves as God's servants with our desiring hearts and our seeing eyes, if we subordinate the wishes of our hearts to God's wishes and set aside our will in deference to His, then our "eyes" too, our knowing and judging minds, will value things only according to their compatibility with God's Will. When we "explore" things in consideration of their value for satisfying the wishes of our hearts, we will investigate them only in consideration of their value for satisfying God's Will; for our will, purified by God's Will, will already be wholly absorbed in God's Will. So, too, in fulfilling the wishes of our hearts, we will not first weigh the power of things against our own power; for above us and above our world stand God and His holy Will. We will not ascribe greatness and power to sensual and intellectual greatness and power in and of themselves, for only to compliance with God's Will and to the performance of His Will — not to sensuality, not to intellect, but only to morality — will we ascribe greatness and power. When we are *with* God, we feel stronger than the whole world; *without* Him, even the most gigantic force that we have shrinks to pygmy-like nothingness. And just as our whole will to draw near or reject will be transformed, so will the fear and hope in our hearts be transformed. For instead of being in the service of our hearts and eyes, we will enter God's service with our hearts and our eyes, and we will regard Him alone as the Director of our actions and the Guide of our fate.

40 *[This is] in order that you may remember and carry out all My commandments and remain holy to your God.*	מ לְמַעַן תִּזְכְּרוּ וַעֲשִׂיתֶם אֶת־כָּל־מִצְוֹתָי וִהְיִיתֶם קְדֹשִׁים לֵאלֹהֵיכֶם׃

This transformation of our whole emotional and sensual being, which draws near and rejects, fears and hopes — *that* is the purpose of the *tzitzis*-sprouts on our garments.

Our verse is also thus explained in *Berachos* 12b: אחרי לבבכם זו מינות וכה״א אמר נבל בלבו אין אלקים, אחרי עיניכם זה הרהורי עבירה שנאמר אותה קח לי כי היא ישרה בעיני, אתם זונים זה הרהור ע״ז וכה״א ויזנו אחרי הבעלים. From this we learn a profound truth: The מינות that denies God's existence is not — as it boasts — the cause, but the result of the heart's release from the laws of morality. The נבל, who has morally withered, soothes himself by denying the existence of God (cf. Commentary, *Bereshis* 34:7, *Shemos* 18:18, *Tehillim* 14:1). We also learn that one who denies God will ultimately believe in many gods: מינות, denial of God, leads to עבודה זרה, polytheism. Indeed, only the awareness of God makes us spiritually free. The מין seeks to free himself from the mastery of one God; therefore, he simply denies His existence. Ultimately, he will serve the בעלים, who cast lots blindly; he will be ruled by the blind, compelling forces of nature, and will be kicked about like a ball by a host of masters.

Let us make one further observation. We have already had occasion several times to discuss the fact that the עולה is מכפרת both for עשה and for הרהור הלב, and it seemed to us that sinful thoughts are not the product of positively giving oneself up to illusion and sin, but of neglecting to study the truth and the good. Where the mental energy fails to be directed to the truth and to the good, thoughts of illusion and sin automatically arise. Here, too, it says that ולא תתורו אחרי לבבכם וגו׳ is only a result of the ראייה and the זכירה, which are directed to עשיית כל מצות ה׳.

40 **למען תזכרו וגו׳**. Verse 39 speaks of the sight of *tzitzis* reminding us of God and His commandments. But the purpose of this remembering is למען תזכרו וגו׳: From within our own selves we should remember God's commandments and we should do them — even without the reminding *tzitzis*. In verse 39 the *tzitzis*-symbol is in front of our eyes, reminding us

41 *I,* God, *am your God, Who brought you out from the land of Egypt to be God to you; I,* God, *your God.*

מא אֲנִ֞י יְהֹוָ֣ה אֱלֹהֵיכֶ֗ם אֲשֶׁ֨ר הוֹצֵ֤אתִי אֶתְכֶם֙ מֵאֶ֣רֶץ מִצְרַ֔יִם לִהְי֥וֹת לָכֶ֖ם לֵאלֹהִ֑ים אֲנִ֖י יְהֹוָ֥ה אֱלֹהֵיכֶֽם׃ פפפ

of God's commandments at a time when they are not on our minds; hence, there it says מצות ה׳ and not מצותי. Verse 40, however, sets a new goal: What we should keep in sight is not the symbol, but God Himself in His special relation to us — מצותי, לאלקיכם; He should fill our minds at all times, so that we act with the living awareness of our duty. With our whole selves, with our whole existence and will, we should belong to God. We should serve God wholeheartedly and unreservedly and be God's very Own — i.e., we should be *holy* unto our God. Verse 39 ensures us of the level of man; verse 40 uplifts us to the calling of Israel.

41 **אני ה׳ אלקיכם וגו׳.** יציאת מצרים is the source of our awareness that God guides our fate and ordains our actions; it is the source of our consciousness of our calling as man and as Israel. The *tzitzis*-symbol points to יציאת מצרים, from which we learned by historical experience that God is our Redeemer and Lawgiver: הוצאתי אתכם מארץ מצרים להיות לכם לאלקים. יציאת מצרים forms the unshakable basis of our whole consciousness in all times, and it is what gave us God's pronouncement which capsulizes all of this: אני ה׳ אלקיכם. And since ה׳ is אלקינו, it is He alone Who directs our thought and our will.

The meaning and the purpose of the *tzitzis* on our garments are unequivocal, for the Torah itself clearly spells them out. The *tzitzis* is a means of recalling the commandments; it makes us aware of God's commandments and of our commitment to them. Thereby, we may guard ourselves against erroneous views that could induce us to forsake God and His commandments; thus, we shall remain faithful and holy unto our mission — as human beings and as Jews.

The question still remains, however, as to the connection between the means, which the Torah has chosen, and the idea that it calls to mind. First of all, it seems to us that the *tzitzis* on our garments, the *milah* on our bodies, the *tefillin* on arm and forehead, and the *mezuzah* on our homes have a common denominator. For the *milah*, the *tefillin*, and the *mezuzah* sanctify the body, the head and arm, and the home, on which they have been placed as symbols, and this sanctification is accomplished by devoting our bodies and our homes to their Divine purpose. So, too, the *tzitzis* on our garments sanctifies the human garment by devoting it to the purpose God has indicated for it.

To find the meaning of the *tzitzis* on our garments, we must first investigate the significance of garments themselves. This is especially necessary since the name of the *tzitzis* describes not only its external appearance — threads "sprouting" from the garment — but also its symbolic purpose, as Scripture explicitly says: והיה לכם לציצת (v. 39; cf. ועליו יציץ נזרו [*Tehillim* 132:18]). The implication, then, is clear: Through the *tzitzis* the human garment should "sprout," that is, blossom forth and bear the fruit for which it is intended. ציצית הכנף tells us: Your garment should not be something barren; do not clothe yourselves vainly and thoughtlessly in human garments; let the garment fulfill the purpose for which it was given to you!

There is a close relation between our clothing and our moral calling as human beings. This is evident from the historical origin of clothing (*Bereshis* 3:7 and 3:21; see Commentary there). The sin that preceded [the giving of the first garments to Adam and Chavah] — against which the garment is meant to protect — mirrors the sin mentioned above in verse 39. Indeed, these two sins are not only related and similar, but are virtually identical. It appears, then, that the conceptual connection could hardly be more obvious. We need only consider what is stated there — ותרא האשה כי טוב העץ למאכל וכי תאוה הוא לעינים ונחמד העץ להשכיל (*Bereshis* 3:6) — to understand that man transgressed God's command because he strayed after his heart and eyes, תר אחרי לבבו ואחרי עיניו, and regarded as "good," טוב, anything that, in the judgment of his greedy eye and his sensual-gratification-seeking mind, would provide him with satisfaction. By thus following the dictates of his eyes and heart, he sank to the level of intelligence of the animal, which, in choosing what to pursue and what to avoid, is guided solely by the inclination of its heart and the perception of its eyes. Thereupon came the sense of shame, which is the Divine voice within man. This voice instructed man to cover his animal nakedness, and the instruction was confirmed by God when He provided man with garments. With a garment God banished man from Paradise, and with a garment He warns man at all times that his destiny is higher than that of an animal; he must submit his power of judgment to the dictates of a higher Authority, and learn from Him what is "good" and what is "evil."

This, then, is the admonition — translated into words — inherent in man's clothing: וזכרתם את כל מצות ה׳ ועשיתם אתם ולא תתורו אחרי לבבכם ואחרי עיניכם אשר אתם זנים אחריהם! That is also the message of the *tzitzis* "sprouting from the garment": it demands of man to obey the admonishment inherent in human clothing.

The most generally accepted tradition is that there are eight *tzitzis* threads. Seven of them are considered ציצת הכנף — "sprouts" emerging from the corner of the garment; hence their color is לבן, like the color of the garment, and they are included in the concept of the garment. To these the eighth thread — the פתיל תכלת — is added. After they have all been attached to the corner of the garment by a firm knot, the seventh "white" thread and the eighth thread which is colored תכלת are wound several times around the other threads. These windings form the cord [גדיל], whose length is a third of the length of the threads, and they are made permanent by a firm knot. The remaining two thirds are left to hang freely down.

All this indicates which energies we must exert to live up to the "admonition of the garment." "Six," "seven," "eight" — the sensual aspect of the created thing, the human-Divine aspect, and the Jewish-Divine aspect (see *Collected Writings*, vol. III, pp. 129-130) — these are the three elements of which our personality consists; they are the threads of our being and the components of our personality, the material from which is woven the fabric of our lives, and they are represented by the threads of the *tzitzis*. All three of these elements are given to us, all three are woven into our being, and they must be actualized for the fulfillment of our destiny. However, two of these three energies must be the rulers. The six must subordinate themselves to the seventh and the eighth, which are also given as part of us. The sensual element of the created thing must be subordinated to the Divine element of man and of the Jew; it must allow itself to be overcome, "wound round" and restrained by the bonds of duty. This being bound by the cords of duty is the indispensable prerequisite for the fulfillment of our human calling, regarding which the human garment admonishes us. It alone — the exercise of our moral freedom — makes us human beings; thanks to it alone are we worthy of human clothing; and only by its power will the animal element in us retreat and freely subordinate itself to man. But this subordination entails no suppression, and the binding is not suffocating. Once the sensual-animal element has submitted itself to the bonds of duty through the

Divine human and Jewish elements, it is completely equal in stature to these two elements, which are like brothers to it. Like them, it, too, shall develop freely within the limits of Jewish human duty. Moreover, the freedom is greater than the limitation, and not only the seventh and the eighth but all the sprouts of man's power — those that bind and those that are bound — unfold in complete equality to develop freely.

The eighth thread, however, representing the power of Judaism, is dipped in תכלת. This color, by its name and by its essence, points to the limit of our sensual perception and thus represents the Power that is beyond the range of the senses. This Power has entered into a covenant with man. He has revealed Himself to us in history and at the Lawgiving, and thus תכלת became the basic color of the Sanctuary of the Torah.

This פתיל תכלת, sanctified to be a symbol of the Torah, recalls the Torah even when it is not present on the garment; for the very absence of the פתיל תכלת attests that this color may not be replaced by any other color, no matter how similar. By its presence or by its absence, the פתיל תכלת delivers to us the following message: There is but one Torah, which rests in the Sanctuary. It was given only once, and it cannot be replaced by another. Only through the Torah can we accomplish the mission of Jewish man. Only through the Torah will God's covenant with us continue to exist; it alone creates the bond between us and God. The eighth thread of the *tzitzis* — whether awaiting the color תכלת or colored by it — marks all of us as אנשי קודש, as men of a holy calling, as members of the ממלכת כהנים וגוי קדוש!

However, the mitzvah of *tzitzis* — like most of the *mitzvos* that remind us of God and of our duty — applies only in the daytime, or it applies only to day-garments representing daytime activity (Commentary, v. 39). Our acknowledgement of God's sovereignty does not begin at the time of rest, when active man rests from his work. Rather, the standard of the symbol of the Torah is raised in the midst of man's daytime activity and mastery of the world. Upright, active, creative man is to pay homage to God and be close to Him in the very midst of his exaltedness and upright stature. Not through passivity, but through active accomplishment are we to make our contribution to God's altar of the Torah. In active, creative life are we to realize God's Torah: וראיתם אתו וזכרתם את כל מצות ה׳ ועשיתם אתם ולא תתורו וגו׳.

Since the mitzvah of *tzitzis* is limited to daytime, it is a מצות עשה שהזמן גרמא, and therefore women are exempt from this mitzvah (see Commentary, *Vayikra* 23:43).

Man's clothing has dual significance. It is בגד; by covering the animal aspect of the human body, it reveals that man has been endowed with a moral character. At the same time, it is also כסות; it covers the body and protects it against the elements of the physical world.

When man's moral weakness became apparent, he needed clothing to remind him of his moral clothing. At the same time, he also needed כסות. For God's educative love drove him out of the pleasant harmony of paradisaic nature. Thereupon the earth's nature became hostile to him, the earth producing for him only thorns and thistles. He now needed protective clothing, for he had to carry out the mission common to all mankind under the most diverse climatic conditions.

Hence the mitzvah of *tzitzis* applies both to בגד and to כסות. Of בגד, which conceals the sensual body, it says: ועשו להם ציצת על כנפי בגדיהם לדרתם; for the mission of Jewish man is for all time, *independent of changing times*; it applies לדרתם. Correspondingly, of כסות, which covers and protects, it says: גדלים תעשה לך על ארבע כנפות כסותך; for the mission of Jewish man is obligatory all over the world; it is not tied to a *place*, and it does not depend on the climate or on local conditions. Wherever you go, even if you are alone; in whichever direction you turn, east or west, north or south; in all ארבע כנפות, all four corners of the earth — you will be accompanied by the same reminder of the one mission which devolves upon you wherever you are. Everywhere, the גדיל shall be firmly tied. It will remind you that your human mission is to realize the ideal of your Jewish mission. It will demand of you self-control. It will obligate you to bind yourself in the cords of duty, and to subordinate all your sensual drives and powers to the restraints of the covenant. Neither time nor place can undo so much as one thread from the cords of your duty; לדרתם and בארבע כנפות, in every age and in every place, your human existence must be absorbed by your Jewish calling.

But just as God's educative love gave man his first garment only after the feeling of shame had already awakened in him the need for clothing, similarly, in case of the mitzvah of *tzitzis*, the fulfillment of the mitzvah depends on whether the heart has already awakened to feel the need for education. Only after we have, of our own free will, put on a garment that is subject to the requirement of *tzitzis* does the mitzvah of *tzitzis* apply to us (Commentary, v. 38). The *tzitzis* is a means of sanctifying us, but this sanctification depends on our own awareness of our requiring such a means.

We have described the mitzvah of *tzitzis* in greater detail in *Collected Writings*, vol. III, pp. 111-140, and we refer to our comments there.

If we now look back on the entire פרשה of שלח לך, which concludes with the mitzvah of *tzitzis*, it immediately becomes evident that this mitzvah is closely linked with the incident of the מרגלים, just as we saw that the group of *mitzvos* that follows it — נסכים, חלה, שגגת עבודה זרה ומגדף, with the attached פרשת המקושש — flows from that incident.

The מרגלים were sent לתור את הארץ, and Scripture repeatedly states that this was their mission. When they failed to accomplish this mission, they came to rebel openly against God and induced the people to follow them.

And now, at the end of the פרשה, the mitzvah of *tzitzis* appears, warning us each day and at every hour: ולא תתורו אחרי לבבכם ואחרי עיניכם אשר אתם זנים אחריהם. Is this not a warning to avoid the same error into which the תרים את הארץ fell? They explored the land only אחרי לבבם — to gratify their own desires. They investigated the land only אחרי עיניהם — their judgment of how to achieve the gratification of these desires was based on what they saw with their sensual eyes. On this basis they drew their conclusions. They forgot that they were to follow not אחרי לבבם but, rather — like Kalev — אחרי ה׳ [cf. above, 14:24]. They were to stand in the service of God, and they were to enter the Land in and for His service. There was only one yardstick by which they were to measure themselves against the land and its inhabitants as regards the future, and that yardstick was God and the performance of His holy Will, and whether they were worthy or unworthy of His hoped-for support. Only because they were תרים אחרי לבבם ואחרי עיניהם did they lose sight of the fact that God directs their actions and guides their fate. Hence, despite their moral relationship to God, in their own sight they were as small and as powerless as grasshoppers, while the land and its inhabitants, despite their moral depravity, assumed in their imagination gigantic proportions. What God rejected came to seem "good" in their eyes, and what God had promised them seemed "evil." As a result of this perverted judgment, the gates of the revived Paradise clanged shut before them, just as Adam had forfeited Paradise because of this same perversion of judgment.

Here, then, we have a further point which completes the analogy. Because it was תר אחרי הלב ואחרי העינים, mankind forfeited Paradise. Accordingly, mankind was given an educational means to warn it against similar errors and to remind it of its duty. This means is the garment. The people of Israel were meant to possess the Land, which is an ארץ זבת חלב ודבש, and upon their arrival in the Land a development was to begin that would

16 1 *Korach presumed — [he was] the son of Yitzhar, son of Kehas, son of Levi — and [so did] Dasan and Aviram, sons of Eli'av, and On, son of Peles, sons of Reuven.*

טז א וַיִּקַּח קֹרַח בֶּן־יִצְהָר בֶּן־קְהָת בֶּן־לֵוִי וְדָתָן וַאֲבִירָם בְּנֵי אֱלִיאָב וְאוֹן בֶּן־פֶּלֶת בְּנֵי רְאוּבֵן׃

2 *And they rose up before Moshe,*

ב וַיָּקֻמוּ לִפְנֵי מֹשֶׁה וַאֲנָשִׁים מִבְּנֵי־

restore Paradise on earth. But the generation of the wilderness forfeited its right to the Land, because it was תר אחרי הלב ואחרי העינים, and it was then given an educational means to warn it against similar errors and to remind it of its duty. This means is the *tzitzis* on the garment.

Adam denied God as Director of our actions; the מרגלים denied God as Guide of our fate. פרשת ציצית includes both these principles, and it concludes with יציאת מצרים, which vouches for both (see *She* 3:12): אני ה׳ אלקיכם אשר הוצאתי אתכם מארץ מצרים להיות לכם לאלקים אני ה׳ אלקיכם.

קרח

CHAPTER 16

1 שלח לך is the פרשה of the rebellion against God; קרח is the פרשה of the rebellion against Moshe.

ויקח קרח—without an object. Similar is: וְאַבְשָׁלֹם לָקַח וַיַּצֶּב־לוֹ בְחַיָּו אֶת־מַצֶּבֶת וגו׳ (*Shemuel* II, 18:18). Grammatically, all the action described thereafter is the object of the לקיחה. Logically, the לקיחה describes the improper behavior of someone acting in his own interest. Avshalom assumed the right, had the presumption, to have a monument to himself erected in his lifetime. Korach assumed the right, had the presumption, to reprove Moshe and Aharon regarding their position in the nation. And since Scripture employs the term "לקיחה," it indicates in addition that Korach was motivated by selfish considerations; he acted in his own interest, and his display of representing the interests of the community was nothing but sham and pretense.

2 **ויקמו לפני משה**. The order in which the rebels are introduced in the narrative seems to indicate the degree of their involvement in the uprising.

יִשְׂרָאֵל חֲמִשִּׁים וּמָאתָיִם נְשִׂיאֵי עֵדָה קְרִאֵי מוֹעֵד אַנְשֵׁי־שֵׁם׃

and so, too, [did] men from [among] the Children of Israel — two hundred and fifty — princes of the community, representatives of the assembly, men of renown.

ג וַיִּקָּהֲלוּ עַל־מֹשֶׁה וְעַל־אַהֲרֹן וַיֹּאמְרוּ אֲלֵהֶם רַב־לָכֶם כִּי כָל־הָעֵדָה כֻּלָּם קְדֹשִׁים וּבְתוֹכָם יְהוָה וּמַדּוּעַ תִּתְנַשְּׂאוּ עַל־קְהַל יְהוָה׃

3 *When these had assembled themselves against Moshe and Aharon, they said to them: You take too much upon yourselves, for the entire community, they all are holy and* God *is in their midst. And why do you lift yourselves up above the community of* God*?*

Korach was the instigator of the uprising; hence: ויקח קרח. Dasan, Aviram, and On joined him as additional agitators. These four rose up before Moshe (ויקמו וגו׳), after they had won over another 250 men from among the people, who supported them as a rebellious mob (ויקהלו על וגו׳).

3 **ויקהלו וגו׳ ויאמרו וגו׳**. Korach, Dasan and Aviram rose up before Moshe, and after the 250 men whom they had incited to support them in their reproaches and demands had gathered en masse, Korach and his companions, claiming to be spokesmen of the community, said: רב לכם וגו׳.

The word כי indicates that the declaration כל העדה וגו׳ explains the preceding assertion רב לכם. The following question [ומדוע תתנשאו על קהל ה׳], however, is not explained by the words that precede it, for it is not connected to them in the form of מדוע; rather, it is a new question, which is added to the preceding in the form of ומדוע. It appears, then, that they rose against Moshe with two claims, or rather with a claim and a reproach.

First they claimed: כל העדה וגו׳, and therefore רב לכם. The entire community — not only as a whole (כֻּלָּהּ), but כֻּלָּם, in all its individual members — they all are holy, and God is in their midst: each one of the six hundred thousand members of the community is holy and therefore close to God. Hence, no *priest* is required in order to express in the name of the individual his thoughts and his feelings and to bring them near to God in an offering. God promised to cause His Presence to dwell with these six hun-

4 *Moshe heard [it] and he fell upon his face.*

ד וַיִּשְׁמַע מֹשֶׁה וַיִּפֹּל עַל־פָּנָיו׃

dred thousand, not with any one person. Hence, God does not need a *prophet* in order to convey His Word to these six hundred thousand. Hence רב לכם; all of them are close to God, and God is close to all of them, and neither Aharon nor Moshe is required. Thus, the whole position of Moshe and Aharon is presumption based on falsehood.

Furthermore, even if it were true that there is a need for an individual who heads the community and represents it, why just Aharon and Moshe? Why should the people not be given the right to choose its own representatives? What justifies Aharon and Moshe placing *themselves* at the head of the nation?

4 **וישמע משה וגו׳**. Moshe heard, or rather, he understood the aim and the motive of the claims and accusations made against him. It was a denial of the Divine basis of his mission. Had they arrived at this opinion by way of erroneous thinking, it would have been possible to apprise them of their error and to correct them. But they arrived at it out of jealousy and the seeking of honor. Under the pretense of representing the public interest, they sought to satisfy their own selfish ambitions, and toward this end they employed dazzling sophisms that were flattering to the people's self-conceit. In this way they sought to oust Moshe and Aharon from their positions.

The basic premises of Korach's revolt are false, and the conclusions — in their application to the circumstances being considered — are no less false. כל העדה כולם are not קדושים already. They are אנשי קדש (*Shemos* 22:30; see Commentary there), men of a holy calling. קדשים תהיו (*Vayikra* 19:2; see Commentary there) — their calling is to be holy, and by this very calling they are קדשים לאלקיהם (above, 15:40), an עם קדוש לה׳ (see *Devarim* 7:6 et al.). They are men *sanctified* unto God, a people *sanctified* unto God, and with every fiber of their being, as individuals and as a people, they belong exclusively to God; but they are not yet קדושים, holy. Rather, their task is to ascend and to uplift themselves without letup to their holy calling. They must not confuse reality with destiny, imagining themselves already holy because they have been sanctified to a holy calling. Rather, their holy calling should be ever before them as a distant goal to which they aspire. To promote the realization of all this, the Sanctuary — which encompasses the Testimony given to them by God — was erected in their midst, giving their holy calling its ideal symbolic representation. That is why not everyone is worthy of having unrestricted access to the Sanctuary. Even Aharon may draw near only by God's express command, and even then not as a private individual, but only clad in the garments symbolizing his service. Precisely for this reason the people and the כהנים are told: והזר הקרב יומת, so that they should not substitute the reality for the destiny and thereby divest the Sanctuary of its soul, completely nullifying its radiating influence. The whole division of the people into ranks — כהנים, לויים, ישראלים — with the Sanctuary bounded and fenced off in the center, is an expression of the call: "קדושים תהיו," but you have not yet reached "קדושים אתם"!

Furthermore, even if it were true that already כולם קדושים and that in reality בתוכם ה׳ — even then Korach and his companions would have been justified only if the Lawgiving had already been completed and the nation had already reached a state of rest and security. Indeed, had the entire Torah already been given unto completion, so that the principle לא בשמים היא (*Devarim* 30:12; *Bava Metzia* 59b) already applied, from then onward the Torah would have awaited only its realization by the nation; and had the state of the nation, too, already reached the point where it should be, so that the nation's sole task was to realize the Torah, *in that case and for that purpose* the nation itself would have appointed the best and the most qualified in its midst to lead the community and to look after its interests. Actually, something similar to this appointment had occurred already, at the time of the rebellion, for the nation already had נשיאי עדה קראי מועד, of which the 250 rebels were living examples (v. 2). Thus — in passing let us note — their very appearance contradicted the first part of their accusation [כי כל העדה כלם קדושים], for they themselves constituted clear proof of the need for representatives who are outstanding personalities, even in those areas where the equality of all is undisputed. But when it comes to matters not originated or done by the people, where the initiative does not lie with the people or in any human sphere, matters that do not arise *from within* the people but come *to* the people — when it comes to *God's messages to the people*, where is the man or nation brazen enough to ask, "Why did God choose you, just you?" What basis could there be for the brazenness thereby directed to God: "Choose this one and no other to be Your messenger"?

5 *And he spoke to Korach and to his company, saying: Let morning come and then* God *will make*

ה וַיְדַבֵּר אֶל־קֹרַח וְאֶל־כָּל־עֲדָתוֹ לֵאמֹר בֹּקֶר וְיֹדַע יְהוָה אֶת־

A true, authentic messenger of God — and none more so than Moshe — will surely be the first to admit that he is unworthy of the task, and he will beg God to choose as His messenger someone worthier, better, and more capable. But if, despite his protests, God has sent him and none other as the one most worthy and qualified to bear His message, who would dare to come before him and ask him: מדוע תתנשא על קהל ה׳?! The charge "תתנשאו" constitutes a denial that God has sent him; it implies that Moshe is a fraud and that his mission is a lie. Therefore:

וישמע משה ויפל על פניו. The truth of a fact can be confirmed only by another fact, not by reasoning. Reasoning can establish a fact's probability or necessity, but it can never establish that the fact is true. The veracity of a messenger's message can be confirmed only by the one who sent him; so, too, the authenticity of Moshe's mission can be confirmed only by God Himself. For this reason Moshe does not utter a word to counter Korach's accusations. If God would not consider it proper to reconfirm the authenticity of Moshe's mission, then his mission was indeed at an end — ויפל על פניו.

From the continuation we will see that Korach's envy was aroused primarily by Aharon's priestly position, and he sought to undermine Moshe's authority only in order to put an end to Aharon's privileged position, which was upheld by that authority. Nevertheless, Aharon remained passive throughout this incident. Only at Moshe's behest did he accept the office and the honor. To him also, the office and the honor were not a personal matter. *He* would not bear his sword to defend them and would not waste a word for them. The matter hinged on the authenticity of his brother's mission, and it was up to God alone to demonstrate that authenticity to the people once again.

5 **וידבר וגו׳ בקר וגו׳**. בקר: not מחר, tomorrow, but בקר, in the morning; i.e., let today and the night pass. Since the dispute would be decided by the destruction of the rebels, they were to be given time to come to their senses, particularly in the quiet and seclusion of the night, when everyone

known who is His, and who is the holy one, so that He will allow him to come near to Him. Whoever He will choose, He will allow him to come near to Him.

אֲשֶׁר־ל֛וֹ וְאֶת־הַקָּד֖וֹשׁ וְהִקְרִ֣יב אֵלָ֑יו וְאֵ֛ת אֲשֶׁ֥ר יִבְחַר־בּ֖וֹ יַקְרִ֥יב אֵלָֽיו׃

is relegated to the company of his own family and is free to commune with himself, and thus is removed from the influence of inciting companions. At the same time, Moshe wanted to utilize this time to remonstrate with those who had gone astray, as will be seen from what now follows. Indeed, at the fateful moment of decision, On, son of Peles, was not present, for according to tradition his wife prevented him from taking further part in the rebellion (*Bemidbar Rabbah* 18:20). Similarly, at the moment of decision the sons of Korach righted themselves and thus were spared the fate decreed upon their father (*Yalkut Shimoni, Korach*, 752).

וידע ה׳ את אשר לו: God will make known who is His — i.e., who is His instrument, His messenger and servant; these are the credentials of Moshe. **ואת הקדוש והקריב אליו**: who, if not absolutely holy, is still the holy one — i.e., is so holy that God grants him the privilege of drawing near to Him as the people's representative; these are the credentials of Aharon. Moshe's credentials refute the false deduction from the true premise that בתוכם ה׳. Aharon's credentials refute the false deduction from the false premise that כל העדה כלם קדשים.

ואת אשר יבחר בו יקריב אליו explains the manner in which God's decision will be revealed. God will choose and designate the one who is entitled to draw near to Him, and thereby the whole matter will be decided in all its aspects. It will be decided whether *everyone*, or only one designated by God, may draw near, as כהן, to God; at the same time, it will also be decided who the chosen one is. And if it becomes clear that Moshe had already, on a former occasion, announced in the Name of God that this man was chosen for the priesthood, then Moshe's mission, too, will be authenticated. The decision will be revealed in this manner: The chosen one will be the one whom God *allows* to approach Him, whose approach He tolerates. The inference is that God will not tolerate the approach of one who was not chosen. The implicit warning is that if it is revealed that they have been rejected, this revelation is likely to be fateful for them.

6 *Do this: Take for yourselves fire pans, Korach and all his company.*

ו זֹאת עֲשׂוּ קְחוּ־לָכֶם מַחְתּוֹת קֹרַח וְכָל־עֲדָתוֹ׃

7 *Place fire into them and lay incense upon them tomorrow before* God, *and then it shall be [that] the man whom* God *will choose, he is the holy one. You want too much, O sons of Levi.*

ז וּתְנוּ בָהֵן ׀ אֵשׁ וְשִׂימוּ עֲלֵיהֶן ׀ קְטֹרֶת לִפְנֵי יְהוָה מָחָר וְהָיָה הָאִישׁ אֲשֶׁר־יִבְחַר יְהוָה הוּא הַקָּדוֹשׁ רַב־לָכֶם בְּנֵי לֵוִי׃

8 *And Moshe said to Korach: Hear now, O sons of Levi!*

ח וַיֹּאמֶר מֹשֶׁה אֶל־קֹרַח שִׁמְעוּ־נָא בְּנֵי לֵוִי׃

6-7 Moshe saw through Korach. What had brought him to rebellion was none other than the jealousy burning in his heart; for he envied the tribe of Aharon, which had been preferred over the other Levite families and privileged with the priesthood. He therefore sought to nullify Aharon's special status, in order to transfer it to himself and to his descendants by means of a popular vote. Toward this end he claimed that all were equally entitled to this honor, and he put forward this claim as the motive of his rebellion. Toward this same end he also expressed the suspicion that Aharon's special status was not ordained by God.

Very well, then, if they are really convinced of the truth of their assertions, let them dare to put them to the test by performing before God a function permitted only to the כהן גדול. The supreme function of the כהן גדול is to make the קטורת offering, the symbolic expression of complete, supreme devotion to God's Will and total absorption in bringing Him satisfaction. In accordance with their claim that they are worthy of the priesthood, let them approach God and submit themselves to His decision.

However, Moshe warns them: Your actions entail the most fateful presumption. The warning is not only for the rest of the tribes represented by the 250 men, but also for the *Levi'im*, whose position has already brought them near to the Sanctuary, and as whose representative Korach wished to be considered. Hence: רב לכם בני לוי!

8-11 In his first address to them, Moshe had already warned Korach and his entire company that dire consequences would ensue if they insisted on

9 *Is it too little for you that the God of Israel has set you apart from the community of Israel, to have you come near to Him, to do the Service of the Dwelling Place of* God *and to stand before the community to minister before them?*

ט הַמְעַט מִכֶּם כִּי־הִבְדִּיל אֱלֹהֵי
יִשְׂרָאֵל אֶתְכֶם מֵעֲדַת יִשְׂרָאֵל
לְהַקְרִיב אֶתְכֶם אֵלָיו לַעֲבֹד אֶת־
עֲבֹדַת מִשְׁכַּן יְהוָה וְלַעֲמֹד לִפְנֵי
הָעֵדָה לְשָׁרְתָם׃

10 *And since He has thus brought you and all your brothers, the sons of Levi, with you, near to Him, will you now seek the priesthood also?*

י וַיַּקְרֵב אֹתְךָ וְאֶת־כָּל־אַחֶיךָ בְנֵי־
לֵוִי אִתָּךְ וּבִקַּשְׁתֶּם גַּם־כְּהֻנָּה׃

11 *Therefore you and all your company, you are the ones who have assembled against* God. *But as for Aharon, what is he that you should stir up rebellion against him?*

יא לָכֵן אַתָּה וְכָל־עֲדָתְךָ הַנֹּעָדִים
עַל־יְהוָה וְאַהֲרֹן מַה־הוּא כִּי
תַלּוֹנוּ עָלָיו׃
°תלינו קרי

their assertions and submitted themselves to God's decision. Now, therefore, he does not refrain from trying persuasive remonstrances, and he spends the rest of the day doing so.

ויאמר, not **וידבר** as in verse 5: he addresses them with gentle words, in order to mollify them.

Since Moshe approached Korach, and Dasan and Aviram, separately, it appears that the rebellion formed from two groups with two different aims. Although they were united in rebelling against Moshe and Aharon, Korach's aim differed from that of Dasan and Aviram.

Korach, the Levi, stood up for the rights of his tribe, which were violated, as it were, by the preference given to Aharon. Korach, the pretended champion of equal rights for all, quite liked the privileges that he and his tribe were accorded. Had he been consistent, he would have waived them. But he was not content with these privileges, and, under the guise of equal rights for all, he also sought the honor of the priesthood.

By contrast, Dasan and Aviram attached no special importance to the office of the priesthood and its honor. In verse 17 as well, they are not listed among the incense-bringers. Only the 250 men and Korach and Aharon are expressly mentioned there. What Dasan and Aviram resented, however, was Moshe's political position, and they joined Korach under the assumption that once the people's trust in the Divine origin of Moshe's mission had been undermined, his position in the nation would be destroyed also.

המעט מכם: Is it less than you – i.e., is it, in your opinion, less than what you deserve?

לעבד את עבדת משכן ה׳ ולעמד לפני העדה לשרתם — cf. above, 3:6-8. עבדת משכן ה׳ is the service of erecting, maintaining, protecting, and transporting the Sanctuary and its contents. At the same time, it is also עבודה that is rendered in the service of the nation, in the course of which they stand לפני העדה לשרתם, to do that which is really the task of the entire nation.

In Jewish thought, public office dignifies the server because it entails "service of the community." The bearer of the office does not control others; he serves them. He does not assume שררה; he assumes עבדות (*Horayos* 10a). The dignity of public service lies in the fact that the individual is imbued with the idea of the community and its purposes, which he promotes in the spirit of the community and from its standpoint.

לכן וגו׳. In your accusation ומדוע תתנשאו על קהל ה׳, you accused me and Aharon of the greatest sin against God: the misuse of His Name and authority for selfish, ambitious purposes. According to your claim, our whole position is a rebellion against God and a violation of His Will. This accusation will fall back with double force on your own head and on the heads of your co-conspirators. They are not satisfied with being the people of God's Sanctuary, you are not satisfied with being a servant in the Sanctuary on the people's behalf. Rather, you also want to be priests *within* the Sanctuary; thus you rebel against orders given not by us but by God. You are the ones הנעדים על ה׳: you conspired to rebel against God.

הִוָּעֵד always denotes joining together for a common purpose. Thus, too, מועד (see Commentary, *Shemos* 12:1-2 and 25:22). Hence also עדה: a community united by a common mission. Hence also here, Korach's company, united in its spirit and in its aims, is an עדה. The sin does not lie in הִוָּעֵד and in עדה, but in the fact that they banded together על ה׳.

ואהרן וגו׳. You have directed your resentment also against Aharon, but there is no basis for that. He, in any event, does not deserve your

12 *Thereupon Moshe sent to call Dasan and Aviram, sons of Eli'av. But they said: We will not come up.*	יב וַיִּשְׁלַח מֹשֶׁה לִקְרֹא לְדָתָן וְלַאֲבִירָם בְּנֵי אֱלִיאָב וַיֹּאמְרוּ לֹא נַעֲלֶה׃

hostility. He received his position strictly on my orders, which I transmitted to him in the Name of God. If anyone is to blame, I alone bear the blame.

תלונו — see Commentary, *Shemos* 16:7. The כתיב is תלונו, and the קרי is תלינו: Basically, they had only their own interests in mind, they were נלונים. This, however, they did not stress. Rather, they incited general discontent, they were מלינים, to thereby conceal their own selfish תלונה.

12 **וישלח וגו׳**. We have already noted that Dasan and Aviram seem to have formed a faction of their own within Korach's conspiracy. Korach's rebellion was primarily against Aharon's priestly status; it was aimed only indirectly against the authority of Moshe, the source and support of Aharon's status. Dasan and Aviram, on the other hand, rebelled directly against Moshe; their aim was to remove his political leadership. The hostility — direct or indirect — to Moshe was the cement that united the two factions. That is why Moshe wanted to speak with Dasan and Aviram by themselves, but they replied: לא נעלה.

In this reply they expressed, in biting sarcasm, all the hatred they harbored. שלח לקרא ל- does not connote an order issued by a superior; it is not a summons to judgment or for clarification, but a friendly invitation (cf. below, 22:5, 20, 37; *Shemos* 2:20, 34:16; *Shemuel* I, 16:3; *Melachim* I, 1:19, et al.). עלה, however, denotes not only going up to a higher place, but also going to an exalted place, to a person who occupies a high position, to a superior, and it particularly denotes going to a court of law: ועלתה יבמתו השערה (*Devarim* 25:7), וּבֹעַז עָלָה הַשַּׁעַר (*Ruth* 4:1). Moshe called them in a friendly way, asking them to come to him. But they took his invitation as a summons, and replied: We will not go up to the "master"! That is to say, we will not take orders from him. It is presumptuous of him to order us to come to him. He has no right to give orders.

13 *Is it too little that you brought us out from a land flowing with milk and honey to let us perish in the wilderness, that you now would also set yourself up as a despot over us?*

יג הַמְעַ֗ט כִּ֤י הֶֽעֱלִיתָ֙נוּ֙ מֵאֶ֨רֶץ זָבַ֤ת
חָלָב֙ וּדְבַ֔שׁ לַהֲמִיתֵ֖נוּ בַּמִּדְבָּ֑ר כִּֽי־
תִשְׂתָּרֵ֥ר עָלֵ֖ינוּ גַּם־הִשְׂתָּרֵֽר׃ שני

14 *Moreover, you certainly have not brought us into a land flowing with milk and honey merely by giving us an inheritance of field and vineyard. Will you put out the eyes of these people? We will not go up.*

יד אַ֡ף לֹ֣א אֶל־אֶ֩רֶץ֩ זָבַ֨ת חָלָ֤ב וּדְבַשׁ֙
הֲבִ֣יאֹתָ֔נוּ וַתִּתֶּן־לָ֕נוּ נַחֲלַ֖ת שָׂדֶ֣ה
וָכָ֑רֶם הַעֵינֵ֞י הָאֲנָשִׁ֥ים הָהֵ֛ם תְּנַקֵּ֖ר
לֹ֥א נַעֲלֶֽה׃

13 **המעט וגו'**. You have already done us much harm in taking us out of Egypt, a land flowing with milk and honey. Is it not enough that you brought us up out of Egypt ("up" — i.e., promising to bringing us to a still better land, or because the Land of Israel is higher than all the other lands) to die here in the wilderness — by your latest evil decree — that you now would also תשתרר וגו'?

The three roots שרה, שור, and שרר sound very much alike but differ in their meanings. All three denote rule. שרה denotes ruling by superior power. שור denotes leading by moral influence, which sets the standard for others (see Commentary, *Bereshis* 17:15). שרר — related to סרר, intractable disobedience — denotes capricious tyranny, which does not submit to legal authority. *This* is the attribute they fault Moshe with, and they even cite a proof of it: Look, he takes the liberty of summoning them, even though he has no right whatsoever to do so!

14 **אף לא וגו'** appears to repeat the accusation of להמיתנו במדבר of the preceding verse: The whole generation that left Egypt has been doomed to perish in the wilderness without seeing the Promised Land. This accusation, however, has already been stated, and certainly our verse should not, in that case, be introduced by the term "אף," which indicates something additional, for our verse would then be nothing but repetition.

15 *This hurt Moshe exceedingly, and he said to God: Do not turn to their homage offering! I did not take [so much as] a donkey from any one of them, neither have I hurt any one of them.*

טו וַיִּחַר לְמֹשֶׁה מְאֹד וַיֹּאמֶר אֶל־יְהוָה אַל־תֵּפֶן אֶל־מִנְחָתָם לֹא חֲמוֹר אֶחָד מֵהֶם נָשָׂאתִי וְלֹא הֲרֵעֹתִי אֶת־אַחַד מֵהֶם׃

Rather, our verse should be interpreted as follows: Upon us, the generation that left Egypt, you have already brought great misfortune by breaking your word. We left the good land, and now we are going to die in the wilderness. As for your further promise that our children will possess the Promised Land, though we ourselves will not merit to do so — in this promise, too, we have no faith, no matter how glibly you speak to us of possessing fields and vineyards and give *mitzvos* concerning them (e.g., above, 15:2 and 18, immediately after the decree that they would die in the wilderness). Though you promise us נחלת שדה וכרם and even "give" it [ותתן לנו] in words (cf. *Bereshis* 1:17; below, 20:12; et al.), in reality you have not yet brought us into the Land. Your promise regarding the children will prove to be false, just as your promise to the fathers proved to be false. העיני וגו׳: Do you think you can blind us, not to see things as they are?

Sforno, in his commentary, explains ותתן לנו וגו׳ in a similar way.

15 **ויחר וגו׳**: It "burned" inside him, it hurt him deeply, that they dared to talk to him in this way, for they accused him of exploiting his position to rule arbitrarily and unlawfully.

אל תפן אל מנחתם. In trying to understand this sentence, we encounter many difficulties. The מנחה referred to here cannot be the incense which was to be brought the next day by Korach and his company, for, as we have already stated, Dasan and Aviram took no part in that offering. Rather, in our view, the מנחה referred to here should be understood as follows:

Korach and the 250 men rebelled directly against God, for they disputed the service of the offerings in the Sanctuary performed by Aharon at God's command. In their arrogance they dissociated themselves from the service of the offerings that is truly an expression of homage to God, and in their presumption were ready to offer to God incense of their own choosing.

Dasan and Aviram took no part in this aspect of the rebellion, which pertains to priestly matters. They did not sin with "their מנחה." As regards their מנחה they remained on the common basis of the whole nation; as regards their מנחה, symbol of their homage to God, they were properly connected to the national public offering in the Sanctuary. They did not seek to seize the priesthood for themselves and to perform priestly functions. Nevertheless אל תפן אל מנחתם: Although they did not sin in the symbolic expression of their homage to God, their actual behavior entailed a manifold violation of the homage due to God. For they blamed Moshe for their inability to enter the Promised Land, and mockingly cast doubt on whether they would enter the Land in the future. In everything that happened they saw only Moshe's helplessness, with Moshe masking his weakness in a supposed sin of the people. Thus, they presented Moshe as the unscrupulous deceiver of his people, and at the same time they also accused him of pursuing power and base tyranny. In their view, then, Moshe's whole mission was a low deceit, for they denied that he was sent by God, and they also denied the whole special relationship of God to Israel, which had become a fact through this mission. Thereby they declared that, as far as they were concerned, the whole basis of the Torah, the Sanctuary, and the offerings is null and void, and there is no longer any meaning to the testimony given to Moshe regarding the Torah that was revealed to him; there is no longer any meaning to the offerings dedicated to the Sanctuary of the Torah.

Thus, Dasan and Aviram refrained from joining the incense-bringers — not because they [Dasan and Aviram] recognized the lawful Sanctuary and its offerings, but, on the contrary, because they completely rejected them. Therefore אל תפן אל מנחתם!

This conception may underlie the explanation given in *Bemidbar Rabbah* (18:10) on this sentence: כך אמר משה לפני הקב״ה רבונו של עולם יודע אני שיש לאלו חלק באותה מנחה שהקריבו שנאמר מלבד עולת התמיד ומנחתה, והיתה של כל ישראל קריבה, הואיל ופירשו אלו מבניך אל תסתכל בחלקם, תניחנו האש ואל תאכלנה.

לא חמור אחד מהם נשאתי וגו׳. If I had blemished my character even by the slightest demonstration of self-interest or despotism, they would have a right not only to doubt, but to directly deny, the Divine basis of my mission. Your emissaries must be immaculate in their personal qual-

טז וַיֹּאמֶר מֹשֶׁה אֶל־קֹרַח אַתָּה וְכָל־
עֲדָתְךָ הֱיוּ לִפְנֵי יְהוָה אַתָּה וָהֵם
וְאַהֲרֹן מָחָר׃

16 *And Moshe said to Korach: Then you and your whole company shall be before* God, *you, and they, and also Aharon, tomorrow.*

ities. You do not send anyone who has even the slightest tendency toward improbity or tyranny. Purity of character is the first of the credentials of Your emissaries.

But I do not deserve the accusation that I undermined the people's confidence in my mission by capriciousness and despotism. Not only have I not overburdened any of the people, but I have not even placed my burden on any of their beasts of burden, and I have never knowingly or capriciously hurt any of them.

The meaning of **נשאתי** here is open to question. **נשא** does occur in the sense of "taking away": **וְנָשָׂא שֶׂה מֵהָעֵדֶר** (*Shemuel* I, 17:34), **נֹשֵׂא אֶת־פַּת־בָּגָם** (*Daniyel* 1:16). However, **מַשְׂאֵת** is a gift, generally a gift to show honor (*Bereshis* 43:34; *Yirmeyahu* 40:5; *Esther* 2:18). **משאת** is also a tax that is paid to a superior — in the sense of **תרומה** as in the shekel gift for the Sanctuary: **אֶת־מַשְׂאַת מֹשֶׁה עֶבֶד־ה'** (*Divrei Ha-Yamim* II, 24:6 and 9). Hence, here too, **נשא** could mean: to demand a mandatory payment. I have not even laid claim to the use of a donkey as my due. As Onkelos translates: **לא חמרא דחד מנהון שחרית**.

לא חמור אֶחָד מהם נשאתי: I have not taken the donkey of any one of them. **ולא הרעתי את אַחַד מהם**: I have not even hurt any particular person among them, one who, by his behavior, would have deserved such treatment (see Commentary, *Bereshis* 3:22).

16 **ויאמר וגו'**. The instructions in verses 6 and 7 were given only conditionally: this is what they were to do if they wished to submit their accusations to God's decision. Here, Moshe repeats these instructions categorically. After his attempts had achieved no results, he says to Korach: Since you do not accept human admonishment, **היו לפני ה'** and lay your demands before Him; dare to make your demands before God, so that He should decide between you and your company — and Aharon.

17 *And let each one of you take his pan and place incense upon it, and let each one bring near his pan before* God, *two hundred and fifty pans, and you also, and Aharon, each one his pan.*	יז וְקְחוּ ׀ אִ֣ישׁ מַחְתָּת֗וֹ וּנְתַתֶּ֤ם עֲלֵיהֶם֙ קְטֹ֔רֶת וְהִקְרַבְתֶּ֞ם לִפְנֵ֣י יְהֹוָ֗ה אִ֣ישׁ מַחְתָּת֔וֹ חֲמִשִּׁ֥ים וּמָאתַ֖יִם מַחְתֹּ֑ת וְאַתָּ֥ה וְאַהֲרֹ֖ן אִ֥ישׁ מַחְתָּתֽוֹ׃

17 **וקחו וגו׳**. By offering קטורת they would make their claim to the priesthood before God. Aharon, too, is mentioned here, only that the 250 men are grouped by themselves, whereas Korach is placed beside Aharon. For there was a dual claim regarding which judgment had to be rendered: They claimed the equal right and the equal worthiness of the whole nation to the priesthood. This claim was to be proved by the 250 מקריבי הקטורת. In addition, however, they claimed: If the community must be represented by a single individual serving in the priesthood before God, this role need not be fulfilled just by Aharon; rather, Korach, too, is worthy of this role. This claim was to be put to the test by Korach's appearance beside Aharon.

ונתתם עליהם קטרת וגו׳. Throughout this section — here and in verse 18 and also above in verse 7 — Scripture does not speak of laying the incense on the fire, but of laying the incense on the pans. This is striking, for in the case of the קטורת of Nadav and Avihu (*Vayikra* 10:1), and at the normal הקטרה of יום הכיפורים (ibid. 16:12-13), the קטורת is put on the fire. There it says: ויקחו וגו׳ איש מחתתו ויתנו בהן אש וישימו עליה קטרת and similarly ולקח מלא המחתה גחלי אש וגו׳ ונתן את הקטרת על האש, whereas here it says: קחו לכם מחתות וגו׳ ותנו בהן אש ושימו עליהן קטרת, וקחו איש מחתתו ונתתם עליהם קטרת, ויקחו איש מחתתו ויתנו עליהם אש וישימו עליהם קטרת.

Clearly, Scripture here emphasizes the מחתות, which represent the personalities bringing them. In the case of Nadav and Avihu, the people were fit to officiate; hence also the כלי in their hands — the מחתה — was ritually acceptable. The offering, however, was unlawful; it was אש זרה because it was אשר לא צוה אתם: they devised it on their own, based on their own subjective judgment. Here, however, the unlawfulness did not lie in the offering, for Aharon brought the identical קטורת. It may have been the regular קטורת which must be brought each morning, although that should

18 *They each took their pans, put fire on them, and laid incense on them, and they stood at the entrance of the Tent of Appointed Meeting, along with Moshe and Aharon.*

יח וַיִּקְחוּ אִישׁ מַחְתָּתוֹ וַיִּתְּנוּ עֲלֵיהֶם
אֵשׁ וַיָּשִׂימוּ עֲלֵיהֶם קְטֹרֶת
וַיַּעַמְדוּ פֶּתַח אֹהֶל מוֹעֵד וּמֹשֶׁה
וְאַהֲרֹן׃

19 *But Korach assembled the entire community against them to the entrance of the Tent of Appointed Meeting — then the glory of* God *appeared to the entire community.*

יט וַיַּקְהֵל עֲלֵיהֶם קֹרַח אֶת־כָּל־
הָעֵדָה אֶל־פֶּתַח אֹהֶל מוֹעֵד וַיֵּרָא
כְבוֹד־יְהֹוָה אֶל־כָּל־הָעֵדָה׃ ס
שלישי

have been offered on the מזבח הזהב. In any case, the unlawfulness lay in the people who came with their מחתות and regarded themselves as fit for the priesthood. Scripture therefore emphasizes the מחתות: Dare to come, with your מחתות in your hands, and burn קטורת before God. That is your test.

Hence we also find at the performance of the test that the suffixed pronoun referring to the [feminine] מחתות occurs three times in the masculine: ונתתם עליהם, ויתנו עליהם, וישימו עליהם. This is an allusion to the defiance and presumption of the act. Also when Scripture mentions the placement of the fire, it does not say ויתנו בהם — as in verse 7 above — but ויתנו עליהם אש. Thus the מחתות are not containers for the fire but the basis on which they would dare to bring the offering. Hence, too, Scripture does not mention the number of men, but the number of pans, חמשים ומאתים מחתת, as though to say: so many men, so many כהנים. This is the sharpest way of expressing the claim to equal rights.

19 **ויקהל וגו'**. Korach was so sure of himself, he must have forgotten so completely the truth of the relationships to God put in question here, that, even at the fateful moment of decision, he summoned the entire nation to join his cause and to witness his triumph — unless we assume that his motive in summoning the entire nation was to impose his will by sheer force of numbers, without waiting for Divine intervention.

In any event, this mass gathering was directed against Moshe and

20 *And* God *spoke to Moshe and Aharon, saying:*	כ וַיְדַבֵּר יְהוָה אֶל־מֹשֶׁה וְאֶל־אַהֲרֹן לֵאמֹר׃
21 *Separate yourselves from the midst of this community so that I may destroy them instantly.*	כא הִבָּדְלוּ מִתּוֹךְ הָעֵדָה הַזֹּאת וַאֲכַלֶּה אֹתָם כְּרָגַע׃
22 *And they fell upon their faces and said: O God, God of the spirits of all flesh! If one man sins, will You be angry with the whole community?*	כב וַיִּפְּלוּ עַל־פְּנֵיהֶם וַיֹּאמְרוּ אֵל אֱלֹהֵי הָרוּחֹת לְכָל־בָּשָׂר הָאִישׁ אֶחָד יֶחֱטָא וְעַל כָּל־הָעֵדָה תִּקְצֹף׃ ס

Aharon. Hence, all those who came demonstrated by their presence that they sided with Korach.

21 **הבדלו וגו׳**. As already noted on verse 19, by their very presence they sided with Korach. Thus, they, too, participated in the sin. Scripture explicitly says ויקהל עליהם, to teach us that they gathered על משה ואהרן.

22 **ויפלו וגו׳ א-ל אלקי הרוחת וגו׳**. You know how easily the masses can be inflamed by dazzling oratory, and that a man like Korach, who is intellectually superior to them and who has hitherto enjoyed their unbroken confidence, is likely to delude them and induce them to sin. As a rule, when the masses commit a crime, the ones really to blame are only a handful of inciters who stand above the rest. If human authorities then intervene, it often happens that the incited masses, who are less to blame, are made to suffer, whereas the inciters, who are the ones truly to blame, go unpunished. But You are א-ל אלקי הרוחת לכל בשר: Since You are the almighty א-ל, it is *within Your power* to punish anyone who is guilty; and since You are אלקי הרוחת לכל בשר, *in Your wisdom* You *know* how to determine who is truly guilty.

האיש אחד וגו׳. Only Korach is to blame, whereas the incited people should receive Your clemency. We have already noted on several previous occasions [e.g., Commentary *Bereshis* 18:23-30; *Shemos* 32:14, 33:12-23] that when God prompts Moshe to intercede in behalf of the people, He

23 *And* God *spoke to Moshe, saying:*

כג וַיְדַבֵּר יְהוָה אֶל־מֹשֶׁה לֵּאמֹר׃

24 *Speak to the community, saying: Raise yourselves up, away from the environs of the dwelling place of Korach, Dasan and Aviram.*

כד דַּבֵּר אֶל־הָעֵדָה לֵאמֹר הֵעָלוּ
מִסָּבִיב לְמִשְׁכַּן־קֹרַח דָּתָן
וַאֲבִירָם׃

25 *Moshe arose and went to Dasan and Aviram, and the elders of Israel followed him.*

כה וַיָּקָם מֹשֶׁה וַיֵּלֶךְ אֶל־דָּתָן וַאֲבִירָם
וַיֵּלְכוּ אַחֲרָיו זִקְנֵי יִשְׂרָאֵל׃

26 *And he spoke to the community, saying: Depart, I beseech you, from near the tents of those wicked people and do not touch anything that is theirs, lest you perish along with them in all their sins.*

כו וַיְדַבֵּר אֶל־הָעֵדָה לֵאמֹר סוּרוּ נָא
מֵעַל אָהֳלֵי הָאֲנָשִׁים הָרְשָׁעִים
הָאֵלֶּה וְאַל־תִּגְּעוּ בְּכָל־אֲשֶׁר
לָהֶם פֶּן־תִּסָּפוּ בְּכָל־חַטֹּאתָם׃

27 *And they raised themselves up, away from near the dwelling place of Korach, Dasan and Aviram, from every side. But Dasan and Aviram stepped out and stood upright at the entrance of their tents, with their wives, and their children, and their little ones.*

כז וַיֵּעָלוּ מֵעַל מִשְׁכַּן־קֹרַח דָּתָן
וַאֲבִירָם מִסָּבִיב וְדָתָן וַאֲבִירָם
יָצְאוּ נִצָּבִים פֶּתַח אָהֳלֵיהֶם
וּנְשֵׁיהֶם וּבְנֵיהֶם וְטַפָּם׃

---

helps him gain insight into the ways of His rule; He elevates his mind, as it were, to think along the lines of Divine providence.

24 **העלו וגו׳**: By this withdrawal they were to dissociate themselves from the rebels and thereby atone for the sin they committed — הִקְהִל על משה ואהרן.

25 **ויקם וגו׳**. Dasan and Aviram—more than all the other rebels—had directly insulted Moshe, yet Moshe makes a special effort to save precisely them and tries until the very last moment to bring them to a change of heart.

27 **נצבים**: standing defiantly, with erect posture.

28 *And Moshe said: By this you shall know that* God *has sent me to do all these deeds and [that I have] not [done them] of my own mind.*	כח וַיֹּאמֶר מֹשֶׁה בְּזֹאת תֵּדְעוּן כִּי־יְהֹוָה שְׁלָחַנִי לַעֲשׂוֹת אֵת כָּל־הַמַּעֲשִׂים הָאֵלֶּה כִּי־לֹא מִלִּבִּי׃
29 *If these [men] will die as all men die, and if a fate like that of all men will be visited upon them, then* God *has not sent me.*	כט אִם־כְּמוֹת כָּל־הָאָדָם יְמֻתוּן אֵלֶּה וּפְקֻדַּת כָּל־הָאָדָם יִפָּקֵד עֲלֵיהֶם לֹא יְהֹוָה שְׁלָחָנִי׃

28 **את כל המעשים האלה** refers, apparently, to all his previous activities, not just to the specific things mentioned by the rebels — viz., the elevation of Aharon to the priesthood and the decree that the older generation would die in the wilderness.

29 **אם כמות וגו׳.** מות כל אדם is a natural death that comes as a result of man's innate mortality. פקדת כל אדם is a "natural" death that comes as a result of a special event that can be fatal — e.g., death בחרב, ברעב, באש, במים. These events, too, occur in accordance with the laws of nature, which are regulated and sustained by God's Will; for God's decree exposes or abandons a person to the effects of these natural causes. A death of this kind, too, is פקדת כל האדם: it is an event that does not lie beyond the sphere of those circumstances to which all other men are likewise subject in the natural course of things. All the so-called natural events, which occur according to the natural order of the world, occur only by God's Will, for God established the natural order of the world, and this order works only as long as God wants it to do so. In addition, man is subject to God's special providence, which determines his fate for life or death, for success or failure, and nothing minor or major happens to him — even in the "ordinary course of things" — unless God's holy Will has decreed it upon him.

Hence, even if כמות כל האדם ימתון אלה ופקדת כל האדם יפקד עליהם, such a death and such a fate would fulfill God's direct pronouncement. Nevertheless, such a death and such a fate would not constitute certification of Moshe's Divine mission. For that mission is based on God's intervention, which is accomplished in a manner beyond the natural order of things, intervention by which God reveals Himself through the attribute of the

30 *But if* God *will create an entirely new thing, and the earth will open its mouth and swallow them up with all that is theirs, so that they go down into the grave alive, then you will know that [it is] these people [who] have scorned* God.

ל וְאִם־בְּרִיאָ֞ה יִבְרָ֣א יְהֹוָ֗ה וּפָצְתָ֨ה
הָאֲדָמָ֤ה אֶת־פִּ֙יהָ֙ וּבָלְעָ֤ה אֹתָם֙
וְאֶת־כָּל־אֲשֶׁ֣ר לָהֶ֔ם וְיָרְד֥וּ חַיִּ֖ים
שְׁאֹ֑לָה וִֽידַעְתֶּ֕ם כִּ֧י נִאֲצ֛וּ הָאֲנָשִׁ֥ים
הָאֵ֖לֶּה אֶת־יְהֹוָֽה׃

Name ה׳, which attests that He stands in the freedom of His Personality above the order of the world. That mission attests that the order of the world emanates *from Him* and exists *through Him*. All things that exist need Him, but He does not need them. He is not just אלקים, Who created and ordered the world one time. Rather, He is ה׳: He has the power to introduce at any time a new future not dependent on the past, and for man's sake He is ready to exercise His power which operates in freedom, for He breathed into man the breath of life from His Own Personality and freedom. Thereby He created man in His image, and thus man became a living being, possessed of freedom and personality. Man, created in the image of his Creator, must in moral freedom release himself from the compelling force of the world's natural causes, and he must recognize God's Will and do God's Will in freedom. In the province that he calls "his world," he is to serve God on earth, and he is to elevate himself and his world to the sphere of moral-Divine freedom. Through Moshe's mission, God wished to begin the education of mankind. This mission is meant to restore man to God, so that he may attain moral freedom (see Commentary, *Shemos* 6:3). Moshe's mission — as well as every Word of God sent to man — is an act of a Personality operating in freedom. Hence, the certification of this mission can only be by אות ומופת which attest to this free Personality.

Hence אם כמות כל האדם וגו׳ לא ה׳ שלחני. However:

30 **ואם בריאה וגו׳**. If their demise is brought about by a new creation that proclaims God as ה׳, in Whose Name I appeared and acted, וידעתם כי נאצו האנשים האלה את ה׳, then you will know that these people, who deny that God has sent me, have denied the rule of God Who acts in freedom and have denied all His works.

31 *And it came to pass when he had finished speaking all these words that the ground under them split.*

לא וַיְהִי כְּכַלֹּתוֹ לְדַבֵּר אֵת כָּל־
הַדְּבָרִים הָאֵלֶּה וַתִּבָּקַע הָאֲדָמָה
אֲשֶׁר תַּחְתֵּיהֶם׃

32 *The earth opened its mouth and swallowed them up and their houses and all the men who belonged to Korach, and all the property.*

לב וַתִּפְתַּח הָאָרֶץ אֶת־פִּיהָ וַתִּבְלַע
אֹתָם וְאֶת־בָּתֵּיהֶם וְאֵת כָּל־הָאָדָם
אֲשֶׁר לְקֹרַח וְאֵת כָּל־הָרְכוּשׁ׃

33 *They and all that was theirs went down alive into the grave; the earth closed over them and they vanished from the midst of the community.*

לג וַיֵּרְדוּ הֵם וְכָל־אֲשֶׁר לָהֶם חַיִּים
שְׁאֹלָה וַתְּכַס עֲלֵיהֶם הָאָרֶץ
וַיֹּאבְדוּ מִתּוֹךְ הַקָּהָל׃

34 *All of Israel who had been round about them fled at their cries, for they thought: The earth could swallow us up also.*

לד וְכָל־יִשְׂרָאֵל אֲשֶׁר סְבִיבֹתֵיהֶם
נָסוּ לְקֹלָם כִּי אָמְרוּ פֶּן־תִּבְלָעֵנוּ
הָאָרֶץ׃

32 **ואת כל האדם אשר לקרח**. According to verses 17-19, Korach was with מקריבי הקטורת [who died by fire (v. 35)], in which case it would appear that he was not included among those who met their death as described here. Below (26:10), however, it says: ותפתח הארץ וגו׳ ותבלע אתם ואת קרח וגו׳, according to which Korach, too, died by the ground splitting under him. Hence, in *Sanhedrin* 110a there are divergent opinions as to in which catastrophe he met his end, whether with the בלועין or with the שרופין. There is one opinion that he — as the originator of the whole disaster — was struck by both.

33 **ותכס וגו׳ ויאבדו וגו׳**. The earth closed over them in such a manner that no trace remained of their downfall. Thus they vanished completely from the midst of the community.

35 *But a fire had gone out from* God *and it consumed the two hundred and fifty men who had offered the incense.*

לה וְאֵשׁ יָצְאָה מֵאֵת יְהוָה וַתֹּאכַל אֵת הַחֲמִשִּׁים וּמָאתַיִם אִישׁ מַקְרִיבֵי הַקְּטֹרֶת׃ ס

17 1 God *spoke to Moshe, saying:*

יז א וַיְדַבֵּר יְהוָה אֶל־מֹשֶׁה לֵּאמֹר׃

2 *Say to Elazar, the son of Aharon the priest, that he shall lift the pans out from the conflagration, but you shall throw away the fire, for they have become holy.*

ב אֱמֹר אֶל־אֶלְעָזָר בֶּן־אַהֲרֹן הַכֹּהֵן וְיָרֵם אֶת־הַמַּחְתֹּת מִבֵּין הַשְּׂרֵפָה וְאֶת־הָאֵשׁ זְרֵה־הָלְאָה כִּי קָדֵשׁוּ׃

3 *The very pans of those who became sinners against their own persons, let them be made into thin beaten plates as an overlay for the altar; for since they brought them before* God, *they have become holy and shall remain as a sign for the Children of Israel.*

ג אֵת מַחְתּוֹת הַחַטָּאִים הָאֵלֶּה בְּנַפְשֹׁתָם וְעָשׂוּ אֹתָם רִקֻּעֵי פַחִים צִפּוּי לַמִּזְבֵּחַ כִּי־הִקְרִיבֻם לִפְנֵי־יְהוָה וַיִּקְדָּשׁוּ וְיִהְיוּ לְאוֹת לִבְנֵי יִשְׂרָאֵל׃

---

35 **ואש יצאה וגו׳**. At the same time that the ground split asunder in the camp, the מקריבי הקטורת were killed by אש מאת ה׳. The fire, which otherwise consumed the offerings, on this occasion consumed the offerers.

CHAPTER 17

1-3 **כי קדשו**. One might have thought that מקריבי הקטורת had first dedicated the מחתות to be כלי שרת, and this קדושה was not nullified, even though the מחתות were used unlawfully. However, in verse 3 it says: כי הקריבם לפני ה׳ ויקדשו, from which it appears that the קדושה took effect only by means of the הקרבה לפני ה׳. The רמב״ן, however, notes that, according to the Halachah in usual cases, a prohibited הקרבה such as this one cannot cause קדושה to apply to an object.

Perhaps the explanation is as follows: קדשו — they remained sacred unto the purpose for which they were dedicated. For הקריבם לפני ה׳, they

4 *Elazar the priest took the copper pans which those that were burned had brought near, and they were beaten thin as an overlay for the altar;*

ד וַיִּקַּ֞ח אֶלְעָזָ֣ר הַכֹּהֵ֗ן אֵ֚ת מַחְתּ֣וֹת הַנְּחֹ֔שֶׁת אֲשֶׁ֥ר הִקְרִ֖יבוּ הַשְּׂרֻפִ֑ים וַיְרַקְּע֖וּם צִפּ֥וּי לַמִּזְבֵּֽחַ׃

had brought them before God, so that through them God would show which priesthood He desires. The purpose of the הקרבה was attained, even though the offerers forfeited their lives through it. But the fact that this purpose was attained is important for God's Sanctuary and for its future, and the moral holiness that emanates from the Sanctuary depends on the remembrance of this fact. Hence, just as these מחתות served to achieve this sacred purpose, they are to remain dedicated to the maintenance of what was achieved through them; ויקדשו, they have become sacred in a dual sense. They remain dedicated to their original purpose, to serve as testimony to the true priesthood; and since this remains their permanent designation, they are connected with the sacred purposes of the Sanctuary. Therefore they themselves become sacred, like all the other objects connected with the Service of the Sanctuary.

ואת האש זרה הלאה. The fire that was brought on the מחתות is not acceptable, and precisely for this reason the מחתות are to be kept as an eternal reminder that the offering brought on them was rejected.

את מחתות וגו׳. Scripture puts the object before the predicate [ועשו] to specially emphasize the object, because Scripture wishes to emphasize the מחתות's character as a sign: The מחתות shall remain an אות, a sign of teaching and warning. With these מחתות the offerers became sinners against their own selves! They sinned against themselves and brought about their own ruin! Scripture here connects the sin against themselves with the designation of the מחתות to be an overlay for the altar: את מחתות החטאים וגו׳ ועשו אתם וגו׳. The meaning of this connection is as follows: In the pursuit of honor, they sought to undermine the service of the altar ordained by God. In this attempt they forfeited their lives, and their ruin only served to strengthen the altar founded by God (see Commentary, *Tehillim* 42:1).

5 *As a remembrance for the Children of Israel, so that no stranger who is not a descendant of Aharon will draw near to make incense go up in smoke before* God *and [that] he not fare like Korach and his company, as* God *had told him through Moshe.*	ה זִכָּרוֹן לִבְנֵי יִשְׂרָאֵל לְמַעַן אֲשֶׁר לֹא־יִקְרַב אִישׁ זָר אֲשֶׁר לֹא מִזֶּרַע אַהֲרֹן הוּא לְהַקְטִיר קְטֹרֶת לִפְנֵי יְהוָה וְלֹא־יִהְיֶה כְקֹרַח וְכַעֲדָתוֹ כַּאֲשֶׁר דִּבֶּר יְהוָה בְּיַד־מֹשֶׁה לוֹ׃ פ
6 *On the next day the whole community of the Children of Israel murmured against Moshe and Aharon and said: You have caused the death of the people of* God.	ו וַיִּלֹּנוּ כָּל־עֲדַת בְּנֵי־יִשְׂרָאֵל מִמָּחֳרָת עַל־מֹשֶׁה וְעַל־אַהֲרֹן לֵאמֹר אַתֶּם הֲמִתֶּם אֶת־עַם יְהוָה׃

5 **להקטיר קטרת**. It stands to reason that the term "קטרת" here does not denote incense in the ordinary sense, but includes everything that is delivered to the altar fire and is מוקטר לפני ה׳. Thus קְטֹרֶת אֵילִים (ibid. 66:15). For קטורת in the limited sense of the term is never offered on the מזבח הנחושת; hence, a warning attached to that altar cannot be referring to such incense.

כאשר דבר וגו׳. Moshe spoke to Korach at God's behest (above, 16:5-7), and his words also contained a warning to Korach: He had better not submit himself to God's decision; for that decision is likely to be fateful for someone who, like Korach, is not entitled to the priesthood. Just as the warning came true in the case of Korach, it will also come true in the case of any unauthorized person who dares to approach the altar as a priest. Later, this warning came true also in the case of King Uzziyahu (*Divrei Ha-Yamim* II, 26:16ff.).

6 **אתם המתם וגו׳**. From what is stated below (v. 17 et seq.), it appears that they did not understand the nature of the Divine decision. The death of the 250 men did not apprise them of the meaning of Aharon's election. They were not convinced that Aharon's election to the priesthood was by Divine decree exclusively. They did not believe that this decree had noth-

7 *And it came to pass as the community assembled against Moshe and Aharon that they turned toward the Tent of Appointed Meeting, and lo! the cloud had covered it, and the glory of* God *appeared.*

ז וַיְהִי בְּהִקָּהֵל הָעֵדָה עַל־מֹשֶׁה וְעַל־אַהֲרֹן וַיִּפְנוּ אֶל־אֹהֶל מוֹעֵד וְהִנֵּה כִסָּהוּ הֶעָנָן וַיֵּרָא כְּבוֹד יְהוָה׃

8 *Moshe and Aharon came to the front of the Tent of Appointed Meeting.*

ח וַיָּבֹא מֹשֶׁה וְאַהֲרֹן אֶל־פְּנֵי אֹהֶל מוֹעֵד׃ ס רביעי

9 *And* God *spoke to Moshe, saying:*

ט וַיְדַבֵּר יְהוָה אֶל־מֹשֶׁה לֵּאמֹר׃

10 *Lift yourselves up from the midst of this community so that I may destroy them instantly. But they fell upon their faces.*

י הֵרֹמּוּ מִתּוֹךְ הָעֵדָה הַזֹּאת וַאֲכַלֶּה אֹתָם כְּרָגַע וַיִּפְּלוּ עַל־פְּנֵיהֶם׃

ing to do with any personal interest, and that its whole purpose was to ensure the nature of the Sanctuary. They apparently thought that God chose Aharon so as to confer personal distinction on his brother Moshe, and that the 250 men were punished because of the personal insult to Moshe and Aharon. The community thought that, had Moshe and Aharon forgiven the insult, they could — and should — have prevented the death of so many fathers of families. They did not understand the true reality of the event, they failed to grasp that a pardon would not have rectified the sin, that a Divine decision was called for, and that only thus was it possible to save and sustain the Divine enterprise in whose service Moshe and Aharon were mere instruments.

10-13 **הרמו וגו׳**. The people's accusation was certainly a purely personal indictment, and in response God said to Moshe: If you wish, remove yourselves from them, and I will destroy the masses that rise up against you. But Moshe and Aharon did not go away; rather, they threw themselves down on their faces before God. They did not demonstrate the mentality ascribed to them by the rebellious masses. They did not demand the death of their offenders, and they refused to be the agents of death amidst God's

11 *And Moshe said to Aharon: Take the pan, put on it fire from the altar and add incense to it, and take it quickly to the community and effect atonement for them, for the anger has already gone forth from* God; *the plague has begun.*

יא וַיֹּאמֶר מֹשֶׁה אֶל־אַהֲרֹן קַח אֶת־
הַמַּחְתָּה וְתֶן־עָלֶיהָ אֵשׁ מֵעַל
הַמִּזְבֵּחַ וְשִׂים קְטֹרֶת וְהוֹלֵךְ מְהֵרָה
אֶל־הָעֵדָה וְכַפֵּר עֲלֵיהֶם כִּי־יָצָא
הַקֶּצֶף מִלִּפְנֵי יְהוָה הֵחֵל הַנָּגֶף׃

12 *Aharon took [the pan] as Moshe had spoken and ran into the midst of the community, and lo! the plague had begun among the people. He placed the incense there and effected atonement for the people.*

יב וַיִּקַּח אַהֲרֹן כַּאֲשֶׁר ׀ דִּבֶּר מֹשֶׁה
וַיָּרָץ אֶל־תּוֹךְ הַקָּהָל וְהִנֵּה הֵחֵל
הַנֶּגֶף בָּעָם וַיִּתֵּן אֶת־הַקְּטֹרֶת
וַיְכַפֵּר עַל־הָעָם׃

13 *And he stood between the dying and the living, and the plague was checked.*

יג וַיַּעֲמֹד בֵּין־הַמֵּתִים וּבֵין הַחַיִּים
וַתֵּעָצַר הַמַּגֵּפָה׃

14 *Those that died by the plague were fourteen thousand, seven hundred, in addition to those that had died because of the matter of Korach.*

יד וַיִּהְיוּ הַמֵּתִים בַּמַּגֵּפָה אַרְבָּעָה
עָשָׂר אֶלֶף וּשְׁבַע מֵאוֹת מִלְּבַד
הַמֵּתִים עַל־דְּבַר־קֹרַח׃

15 *Aharon returned to Moshe, to the entrance of the Tent of Appointed Meeting, and the plague was checked.*

טו וַיָּשָׁב אַהֲרֹן אֶל־מֹשֶׁה אֶל־פֶּתַח
אֹהֶל מוֹעֵד וְהַמַּגֵּפָה נֶעֱצָרָה׃ פ
חמישי

people. Rather, Aharon rushed into the midst of the community, which had already been condemned to death. With the קטורת rising up to God, he gave expression to devotion to God with heart and soul, and thus stood between the dying and the living as an agent of atonement and salvation. He thus demonstrated to the people his true nature and the true nature of his mission: to redeem and to conquer death.

16 *And* God *spoke to Moshe, saying:*

טז וַיְדַבֵּר יְהוָה אֶל־מֹשֶׁה לֵּאמֹר׃

17 *Speak to the Children of Israel and take from them one staff for each father's house, from all their princes of the house of their fathers, twelve staffs, and inscribe the name of each one upon his staff.*

יז דַּבֵּר ׀ אֶל־בְּנֵי יִשְׂרָאֵל וְקַח מֵאִתָּם מַטֶּה מַטֶּה לְבֵית אָב מֵאֵת כָּל־נְשִׂיאֵהֶם לְבֵית אֲבֹתָם שְׁנֵים עָשָׂר מַטּוֹת אִישׁ אֶת־שְׁמוֹ תִּכְתֹּב עַל־מַטֵּהוּ׃

18 *And you shall write the name of Aharon on the staff of Levi, for there shall be one staff for the head of the house of their fathers.*

יח וְאֵת שֵׁם אַהֲרֹן תִּכְתֹּב עַל־מַטֵּה לֵוִי כִּי מַטֶּה אֶחָד לְרֹאשׁ בֵּית אֲבוֹתָם׃

17 **דבר וגו'**. As already stated above (1:2), the tribes of Israel are called "מטות" (literally, "branches") because they branch out from one common stem. Hence, the twelve מטות taken here from the princes are apt symbols of the tribes of Israel. However, since each tribe transmits to its posterity its own unique traits within the ethos of the nation of which they all are a part, each tribe constitutes a separate בית אב within the one common בית ישראל. Thus, the tribes are called מטות on account of what is common to them all, and they are called בתי אבות on account of what is unique to each tribe.

The fact that here the twelve בתי אבות of Israel were to be represented by twelve מטות leaves room to consider whether, no matter what the differences between them, all the tribes should be considered equal regarding the matter about to be decided, since they do hold certain basic traits in common; or whether, regardless of the traits they all hold in common, they should *not* be considered as equals, since each tribe has unique traits that set it apart from all the others.

18 **ואת שם אהרן וגו'**. We have already stated (*Vayikra* 22:9) that the כהנים never ceased to belong to the tribe of Levi. They, too, are לויים; for the כהונה is merely לוייה in its highest degree of perfection, לוייה *par excellence*. Hence, the tribe of Levi should see in the tribe of כהנים only the elite of its indivisible totality, while the כהן should consider himself as having been sent to fulfill

19 *And you shall lay them down in the Tent of Appointed Meeting, in front of the Testimony, where I have set a time to meet with you.*

יט וְהִנַּחְתָּ֖ם בְּאֹ֣הֶל מוֹעֵ֑ד לִפְנֵי֙ הָֽעֵד֔וּת אֲשֶׁ֛ר אִוָּעֵ֥ד לָכֶ֖ם שָֽׁמָּה׃

20 *And it shall come to pass that the man whom I will choose, his staff will blossom. Thus will I calm down — turning [them] away from Me — the murmuring complaints of the Children of Israel which they stir up against you.*

כ וְהָיָ֗ה הָאִ֛ישׁ אֲשֶׁ֥ר אֶבְחַר־בּ֖וֹ מַטֵּ֣הוּ יִפְרָ֑ח וַהֲשִׁכֹּתִ֣י מֵעָלַ֗י אֶת־תְּלֻנּוֹת֙ בְּנֵ֣י יִשְׂרָאֵ֔ל אֲשֶׁ֛ר הֵ֥ם מַלִּינִ֖ם עֲלֵיכֶֽם׃

the task of the לויים on its highest level. Aharon, therefore, is none other than ראש לבית לוי, and his staff is the staff of Levi, מטה לוי.

19 **והנחתם וגו׳**. The מטות — in a dual sense: the staffs, and the stems (i.e., the tribes) — are to be laid down in front of the עדות אשר אועד לכם שמה. It is as though the question is to be turned over to the עדות to decide, and the answer is to be given from the standpoint of the עדות. Thereby the people are told: This is not a question of personal distinction, as they mistakenly thought (Commentary, v. 6). Rather, the matter pertains to עדות ה׳, which is the condition for God's presence in the people's midst, and it is this עדות and its activity amidst the people which is being considered here. What is to be determined is the מטה — the branch on the tree of the Jewish nation — that God has found worthy of being chosen, chosen because its special traits qualify it to represent the Testimony and to nurture the service of the Testimony among the people.

20 **והיה וגו׳**. He whose מטה blossoms, his מטה was chosen by God, for He found in it the germ for the future flowering and fruit-bearing of the עדות amidst the people. At the same time, the owner of that staff is marked as the right "bearer" [נשיא] of the chosen tribe.

והשכתי מעלי וגו׳. שכך means: to calm and to quiet something raging and roaring (cf. *Bereshis* 8:1 [see Commentary there] and *Esther* 2:1).

The distinction conferred on Aharon aroused the people's complaints against you. But these complaints are really against Me, for I am the One

21 *And Moshe spoke to the Children of Israel, and all their princes gave him one staff apiece, one for each prince of their fathers' houses, [altogether] twelve staffs. And the staff of Aharon was among their staffs.*

כא וַיְדַבֵּר מֹשֶׁה אֶל־בְּנֵי יִשְׂרָאֵל
וַיִּתְּנוּ אֵלָיו | כָּל־נְשִׂיאֵיהֶם מַטֶּה
לְנָשִׂיא אֶחָד מַטֶּה לְנָשִׂיא אֶחָד
לְבֵית אֲבֹתָם שְׁנֵים עָשָׂר מַטּוֹת
וּמַטֵּה אַהֲרֹן בְּתוֹךְ מַטּוֹתָם׃

22 *And Moshe laid down the staffs before* God *in the Tent of the Testimony.*

כב וַיַּנַּח מֹשֶׁה אֶת־הַמַּטֹּת לִפְנֵי יְהֹוָה
בְּאֹהֶל הָעֵדֻת׃

23 *And it came to pass on the next day, when Moshe came to the Tent of the Testimony, that lo! Aharon's staff from the house of Levi was blossoming. It produced blossoms, sprouted twigs, and bore almonds.*

כג וַיְהִי מִמָּחֳרָת וַיָּבֹא מֹשֶׁה אֶל־
אֹהֶל הָעֵדוּת וְהִנֵּה פָּרַח מַטֵּה־
אַהֲרֹן לְבֵית לֵוִי וַיֹּצֵא פֶרַח וַיָּצֵץ
צִיץ וַיִּגְמֹל שְׁקֵדִים׃

Who conferred this distinction on Aharon. Hence, the uproar of the complaints against you reflects back, as it were, on Me.

This, however, will now cease, for it will be shown that Aharon's priesthood is an act of God's choice, and that the motives of this choice are free of favoritism toward the chosen one.

21 **ומטה אהרן וגו׳**: Outwardly, Aharon's staff did not differ from the staffs of the other princes; it was "among their staffs" — just a staff like the others.

22 **לפני ה׳**: for God's decision.

23 **מטה אהרן לבית לוי**. Thus the tribe of Levi was chosen out of the other tribes, and at the same time Aharon was chosen out of the other *Levi'im* (see Commentary, v. 18).

ויצא פרח וגו׳. פרח (related to פרה — cf. Commentary, *Bereshis* 1:11-13) denotes the flower and blossom; hence, the verb פרח predominantly means: to blossom. As for ציץ, all the evidence supports the assumption that it denotes only the first sprouting. ציצים are the buds that push their way out. Hence, there is no justification for saying that ציץ here denotes an advanced stage of blossoming. However, the special quality of the almond tree is that it blossoms even before it grows leaves. This quality is apparent in almond trees even more than in apple trees (see *Shabbos* 88a) or other seed-bearing fruit trees. It hardly shows any leaf formation before it stands in all the glory of its blossoms.

Hence, in our opinion, ויצץ ציץ means: "put forth leaves" [i.e., twigs that bear leaves]. Aharon's staff blossomed here like an almond branch, giving expression to the ideas under consideration here. To elaborate:

Are not all branches of fruit trees similar to one another? They all produce leaf, blossom, and fruit. The same earth bears them all. The rain water that waters them comes to all of them from the same source. The same wind blows through them all, and they all thrive in the rays of the sun.

Nevertheless, the almond tree stands out among all its comrades in the field. And in what is its uniqueness? In שקידה, from which it gets its name; with zeal, keen devotion, and vigor, it performs its duty and thereby precedes all its brother trees. While they are still making up their minds, it has already completed its work, and it begins immediately with the goal — namely, the blossom, which produces the fruit; the whole purpose of the blossom is to produce fruit. For the sake of the fruit it [the almond tree] then produces its leaves, and toward this same goal it prepares and directs all its sap.

Now, is this not a perfect depiction of the Levite spirit, by virtue of which the tribe of Levi merited to be the representative of the Torah and the Sanctuary? For only the *Levi'im* responded to the call מי לה׳ אלי (*Shemos* 32:26) and gathered around Moshe, and this spirit is to be inherited by the elite of the Levite family — by Aharon and his sons (cf. Commentary, *Shemos* 25, end). At the same time, a consoling promise is expressed here. For the almond tree only precedes the others in blossoming and maturing its fruit. It leads the way before its comrades in the field, preceding them in development, but they, too, eventually follow its example. Similarly, the *Levi'im* and the sons of Aharon lead the way in spiritual development and way of life, and the rest of the tribes are called upon to follow their example and attain the same spiritual level.

(Cf. Commentary, *Shemos*, ibid. — There on p. 592 we translated the word ציץ of our verse as "pollen-stamens [filaments]." But we ques-

24 *Moshe brought out all the staffs from their place before* God *to all the Children of Israel. Each man saw and took his [own] staff.*

25 *And* God *said to Moshe: Put Aharon's staff back again in front of the Testimony, to be kept there as a sign for men of disobedience, so that it may put an end to their murmuring complaints — that were turned away by Me — and they will not die.*

כד וַיֹּצֵ֨א מֹשֶׁ֤ה אֶת־כָּל־הַמַּטֹּת֙
מִלִּפְנֵ֣י יְהֹוָ֔ה אֶל־כָּל־בְּנֵ֖י יִשְׂרָאֵ֑ל
וַיִּרְא֥וּ וַיִּקְח֖וּ אִ֥ישׁ מַטֵּֽהוּ׃ פ ששי
כה וַיֹּ֨אמֶר יְהֹוָ֜ה אֶל־מֹשֶׁ֗ה הָשֵׁ֞ב אֶת־
מַטֵּ֤ה אַהֲרֹן֙ לִפְנֵ֣י הָֽעֵד֔וּת
לְמִשְׁמֶ֛רֶת לְא֖וֹת לִבְנֵי־מֶ֑רִי וּתְכַ֧ל
תְּלוּנֹּתָ֛ם מֵעָלַ֖י וְלֹ֥א יָמֻֽתוּ׃

tion the accuracy of this translation since, when the blossom appears, the filaments are already in place; the filaments do not belong to a later stage of development [as is implied by the order of our verse: ויצא פרח ויצץ ציץ. We therefore translate ויצץ ציץ here as: "and sprouted twigs."])

25 **ויאמר וגו'**. Just as the לוחות העדות attest to the Divine origin of the Torah, מטה אהרן attests to the Divine origin of Aharon's election: only on the basis of God's choice do they serve as כהנים in the Sanctuary of the Torah.

מטה אהרן is placed beside לוחות העדות in the Sanctuary, and from this we learn the significance of the election of the sons of Aharon and the *Levi'im*: The sons of Aharon are chosen out of the *Levi'im*, the *Levi'im* are chosen out of the people, and thereby the people are kept at a distance from the Sanctuary of the Torah, a distancing which is none other than a continuation of the הגבלה mentioned in *Shemos* 19:10-13.

That הגבלה took place at the giving of the Torah, and on that occasion the לוחות, too, were given as eternal testimony to the Torah. The purpose of the הגבלה was to show that the Torah came *to* the people and did not develop *from within* the people. We have already shown there the profound significance of this fact, on which the Torah's whole character as eternal, immutable, and inviolable depends. But the same הגבלה is con-

26 *Moshe did so; as* God *had commanded him, so did he do.*

כו וַיַּ֖עַשׂ מֹשֶׁ֑ה כַּאֲשֶׁ֨ר צִוָּ֧ה יְהֹוָ֛ה אֹת֖וֹ
כֵּ֥ן עָשָֽׂה׃ פ

tinued by the encampment of the sons of Aharon and the *Levi'im* around the Sanctuary of the Torah and by the keeping of the people at a distance from this Sanctuary, and thereby the same fact of the Torah's superhuman origin and its validity independent of time and place is established for all time.

In the course of time, the need for asserting this fact will increase. For all classes of the Jewish people — irrespective of profession or occupation — are called upon to study the Torah, accept its authority, and fulfill its commandments, and the Torah is destined to accomplish its mission among the people. The Torah will penetrate every spirit and every heart, shape every thought and every feeling, every outlook and every accomplishment, and the people's spirit, energized by the Torah and growing stronger from generation to generation, will grow ever closer to the spirit of the Torah. Finally, the gap between the Torah's ideal and its realization amidst the people will close, and thus the presumptuousness in Korach's claim כי כל העדה כלם קדשים ובתוכם ה׳ will gradually diminish. And the more this ideal is realized, the more grounds there are to fear that man might rebel against the source of his enlightenment and, denying the Torah's Divine origin, consider the Torah a creation of the human mind. Thus, people will cease being disciples and servants of the Torah and will dare to act as its critical master.

For this reason the mitzvah of הגבלה was given, applying for all time. It keeps the people at a distance from the עדות and from its Sanctuary by means of the לויים and the כהנים, and it warns even the greatest of Torah sages, who is constantly preoccupied with the love of Torah: he, too, must grasp the Torah in its absolute objectivity. For the Torah is Divine and unapproachable, and even the כהנים may approach the עדות of the Torah only in the vestments symbolic of their service and only after קידוש ידים ורגלים. Throughout the centuries the warning of הגבלה issues from Sinai and declares: רד העד בעם פן יהרסו אל ה׳ לראות ונפל ממנו רב; וגם הכהנים הנגשים אל ה׳ יתקדשו פן יפרץ בהם ה׳! (*Shemos* 19:21-22).

27 *And the Children of Israel said to Moshe: So then we are about to die, we are lost, we are all lost!*	כז וַיֹּאמְרוּ בְּנֵי יִשְׂרָאֵל אֶל־מֹשֶׁה לֵאמֹר הֵן גָּוַעְנוּ אָבַדְנוּ כֻּלָּנוּ אָבָדְנוּ׃
28 *Whoever comes near, whoever comes too near to the Dwelling Place of* God, *dies — are we then altogether given to die?*	כח כֹּל הַקָּרֵב ׀ הַקָּרֵב אֶל־מִשְׁכַּן יְהוָה יָמוּת הַאִם תַּמְנוּ לִגְוֺעַ׃ ס

27-28 **ויאמרו וגו׳**. All these experiences — culminating with the testimony of Aharon's staff — accomplished their purpose. The people understood that only the sons of Aharon and the *Levi'im* are permitted to approach the Sanctuary, and that this restriction was ordained by God and is rooted in the sanctity of the עדות. Hence they feared they would die if they drew near unwittingly or unavoidably. They considered themselves near death, in a state of גויעה, which is the stage of transition to death, and in their anxiety they aptly described the narrow and dangerous path every Jew must tread in relation to God's Sanctuary. Everyone is קרב — and yet may not be too קרב! The Sanctuary was not erected to be the site of a self-contained cultic rite of the כהנים. Everyone is called upon to approach it — yet is forbidden to come too near. Indeed, God's Torah, whose Testimony rests in the Sanctuary, is compared to fire; as our Sages say: קרוב לה נכוה רחוק ממנה צונן, "He who comes too near gets burned, he who keeps afar remains cold" (*Sifre* on *Devarim* 33:2). One is obligated to draw near, but, in drawing near, one must keep at the required distance.

Actually, though, the gulf between כהן and non-כהן is not as wide as the people in their anxiety imagine. Regarding קריבה אל משכן ה׳ there is no difference between them; for any arbitrary entry into the היכל, not for the purpose of עבודה as prescribed, is forbidden also to the כהן, and he, too, incurs the penalty of מיתה בידי שמים if he needlessly enters the קודש הקדשים (see Commentary, *Vayikra* 16:2). Conversely, for the purposes of the Sanctuary — לבנות לתקן ולהוציא את הטומאה — even a non-כהן may, if necessary, enter the היכל (*Eruvin* 105a; see משנה למלך, end of הלכות ביאת מקדש). Only regarding the performance of the עבודה is there a difference between כהן and non-כהן: A non-כהן who במזיד, deliberately, performs עבודה incurs

18 1 *And* God *said to Aharon: You and your sons, and your father's house with you, you must bear the iniquity against the Sanctuary, and you and your sons with you must bear the iniquity against your priesthood.*	**יח** א וַיֹּאמֶר יְהֹוָה אֶל־אַהֲרֹן אַתָּה וּבָנֶיךָ וּבֵית־אָבִיךָ אִתָּךְ תִּשְׂאוּ אֶת־עֲוֺן הַמִּקְדָּשׁ וְאַתָּה וּבָנֶיךָ אִתָּךְ תִּשְׂאוּ אֶת־עֲוֺן כְּהֻנַּתְכֶם׃

the penalty of מיתה בידי שמים, and even then, only in certain cases (see Commentary below, 18:3-7).

CHAPTER 18

1 **ויאמר**. This is not a new law, but an elaboration on an already existing relationship ordained by God. The significance of this relationship must be explained to the people in order to set their minds at ease. It is not the people who need to feel threatened by the Sanctuary because of a thoughtless act or careless error on their part. It is Aharon, his sons and his House — all those designated to perform the Service of the Sanctuary — who bear the responsibility, which they can fulfill only by constant vigilance and attention to their duty.

Similarly, it says in the *Sifre* (here): ויאמר ה׳ אל אהרן אתה ובניך ובית אביך אתך תשאו את עון המקדש, ר׳ ישמעאל אומר למי שהדבר מסור (לאהרן) אותו הזהיר (גירסת הגר״א); ר׳ יאשיה אומר מנין אתה אומר שאם זרק את הדם כראוי ואינו יודע לשם מי זרקו והקטיר את החלב כראוי ואינו יודע לשם מי הקטירו, שהכהנים נושאים עון על כך, ת״ל אתה ובניך ובית אביך אתך תשאו את עון המקדש; ר׳ יונתן אומר מנין אתה אומר שאם זכה בבשר קודם זריקת דמים בחזה ושוק קודם הקטר חלבים, שהכהנים נושאים עון על כך, ת״ל אתה ובניך אתך תשאו את עון כהונתכם; וכן מצינו שלא נחתם גזר דינו של עלי אלא על שנהגו בזיון בקדשים וכן הוא אומר (שמואל א׳ ב, טו-יז) גם בטרם יקטירון את החלב וגו׳ ויאמר אליו האיש קטר יקטירון כיום החלב וגו׳ ותהי חטאת הנערים גדולה מאד; וכן מצינו שלא נחתם גזר דינם של אנשי ירושלים אלא על שנהגו מנהג בזיון בקדשים שנאמר (יחזקאל כב, ח) קדשי בזית. The *Sifre* apparently interprets תשאו את עון המקדש, תשאו את עון כהונתכם as follows: Aharon and his House are not responsible for keeping the people at a distance from the Sanctuary, for we have already stated above, and it is also clear from the continuation, that the people's entry into the halls of the Sanctuary (with the exception of the Holy of Holies, which even the כהן גדול may not enter except on יום הכיפורים) in itself entails no sin, and certainly no capital sin. Rather, Aharon and his House are responsible for sins that they themselves commit while performing their service. And since the people are not designated to serve in the Sanctuary, and they are excluded from the main duties of the עבודה (see v. 7), it is not the people who are to blame; rather, the responsibility lies with those who are designated for the עבודה. The people are not charged with the responsibility; rather, למי שהדבר מסור (לאהרן), he who is entrusted with the Service of the Sanctuary, אותו הזהיר, he is the one put under serious warning.

The outcome of Korach's rebellion clearly demonstrated that the people are excluded from the Service of the Sanctuary, but this exclusion protected the people more than it threatened them.

The examples by which the *Sifre* explains עון המקדש and עון כהנתכם are all taken from the sphere of the service of the offerings. The implication is that the term "המקדש" here denotes not the House and its furnishings, but the institution of the Sanctuary in its totality; for the purpose of the Sanctuary is realized primarily through the offering procedures, which express the Sanctuary's demands on us. It is a sin against the institution of the Sanctuary if the כהן does not give his full attention to the offering — e.g., he performs זריקת דמים and הקטר חלבים correctly (זרק את הדם כראוי הקטיר את החלב כראוי), but he does not know for whom the offering is made. As such, the כהן does not know who it is whose devotion to God — with his whole existence and will — is given expression through these procedures. This, too, is sin, even though כל הזבחים שנזבחו שלא לשמן כשרים אלא שלא עלו לבעלים לשם חובה (*Zevachim* 2a; see Commentary, *Vayikra* 1:9). Furthermore, if the כהן merely "forgets" לשם מי זרקו, the offerer does not have to bring another one, the offering is עלה לשם חובה, because סתמא עלו נמי לבעלים לשם חובה (*Zevachim* 2b). Even if the כהן offers it for the sake of another, but does so mistakenly, the validity of the offering is not compromised in any respect: עקירה בטעות לא הויא עקירה (*Menachos* 49a). Finally, in the case of הקטרה, which the *Sifre* mentions as one of the examples, שינוי בעלים has no effect whatsoever (תוספות *Zevachim* 2a ד"ה כל). According to the משנה למלך (הל' פסולי המוקדשים, 15:1), this is true even as regards זריקה: שינוי בעלים compromises the offering's validity only if שחט או קיבל או הילך קרבן ראובן על מנת לזרוק דמו לשם שמעון; at the זריקה, however, שינוי בעלים has no effect whatsoever. Even if זרק דם קרבן ראובן לשם שמעון — and even if he did so deliberately — the offering is valid and is עלה לשם חובה. Thus, forgetfulness, which the *Sifre* cites as an example of עון המקדש, has no negative effect whatsoever in the normal procedure of the Sanctuary. Nevertheless, it is considered a grave sin on the part of the כהן, for he in any case sins against the spirit of the canon לשם ששה דברים הזבח נזבח וכו׳ (see Commentary, *Vayikra* 1:9). Such forgetfulness comes close to the thoughtlessness that is called "מתעסק בקדשים," which actually invalidates the whole offering procedure (*Zevachim* 46b-47a).

עון המקדש, then, is a sin against the Sanctuary institution. By contrast, עון הכהונה is misuse of the priesthood for one's own selfish ends. A כהן who misuses his priesthood sins against his priesthood, for it is degraded thereby. Here, too, the *Sifre* cites an example of sin that to us seems slight, but which nevertheless is a grave sin. Obviously, the כהן sins if he takes something to which he is not entitled; but he sins even if he takes something to which he is entitled, if he takes it before the proper time. If he takes בשר before זריקת דמים, חזה ושוק before הקטר חלבים, he commits a grave sin. For the whole meaning of the Sanctuary and his service therein must have escaped his attention, he must have forgotten that כהנים משולחן גבוה קא זכו (*Chullin* 120a). He himself is foremost on his mind, whereas the whole Sanctuary is in his eyes merely a source of livelihood!

Through the thoughtlessness of עון המקדש and through the greed of עון הכהונה, the whole character of the Sanctuary is lost. The House of Eli was condemned to ruin because נהגו בזיון בקדשים. In the end, the people, too, ceased to value the Sanctuary properly. For them, it was no longer a place for sanctification, obligating the sanctification of national life. Rather, in the Temple they sought to reach an accommodation with God, whereby in exchange for attending to the needs of the Sanctuary, they allowed themselves to live without restraint. Thereupon they, too, were confronted with God's pronouncement: קָדָשַׁי בָּזִית (*Yechezkel* 22:8); consequently, the Sanctuary was destroyed, and the people were exiled.

Now it remains only to explain the meaning of ובית אביך in the first sentence of our verse. From the *Sifre* it appears that עון המקדש includes only the כהנים's sins against the procedures performed in the Sanctuary; hence, it is difficult to determine who is included in בית אביך. For it is clear from the second sentence of our verse that אתה ובניך already includes the whole tribe of כהנים; hence, בית אביך can refer only to the tribe of Levi, of which בית אהרן is one of the family branches. Indeed, this is also the view of the Midrash cited in the *Yalkut* (here). According to this Midrash, בית אביך refers to the *Levi'im*, for they, too, are responsible for the sins that the כהנים commit against the Sanctuary: ואתה ובניך הכהנים ובית אביך אלו הלוים, מלמד שהלוים מוזהרים על ידי הכהנים. This relationship is entirely in keep-

2 *But also your brothers, the branch of Levi, the tribe of your father — let them come near along with you; they shall join with you and minister to you while you and your sons with you keep watch before the Tent of the Testimony.*

ב וְגַ֨ם אֶת־אַחֶ֜יךָ מַטֵּ֨ה לֵוִ֜י שֵׁ֤בֶט אָבִ֙יךָ֙ הַקְרֵ֣ב אִתָּ֔ךְ וְיִלָּו֥וּ עָלֶ֖יךָ וִישָׁרְת֑וּךָ וְאַתָּה֙ וּבָנֶ֣יךָ אִתָּ֔ךְ לִפְנֵ֖י אֹ֥הֶל הָעֵדֻֽת׃

ing with the position of the כהנים vis-à-vis the לויים (see Commentary, *Vayikra* 22:9). However, this does not appear to be the view of the *Sifre*, which expressly says that the *Levi'im* are not responsible for the service assigned to the כהנים. It derives this from what is stated in verse 23: והם ישאו עונם.

Accordingly, in our opinion עון המקדש includes the whole Service of the Sanctuary, whether performed *in* the Sanctuary or *on behalf of* the Sanctuary; thus, it includes the whole institution of the Sanctuary in its totality. Hence, the *Levi'im*, too, are held responsible for thoughtless or improper performance of their service, analogous to what the *Sifre* states in its examples regarding the כהנים and their duties.

2 **וגם וגו'** refers back to the previous sentence. Although the כהונה itself devolves on you and your sons, also the *Levi'im* הקרב אתך.

הקרב אתך is to be distinguished from the following וילוו עליך. In the expression וילוו עליך וישרתוך the *Levi'im* are subsidiary and subordinate to Aharon, whereas in the expression הקרב אתך they draw near to God *together with* Aharon and parallel to him, and perform service side by side with the כהנים before God. As ר' עקיבא (*Sifre*) explains this expression: להזהיר את הלוים בשיר על דוכנם. The *Levi'im* recite song in the Sanctuary while standing beside the כהנים; they complement the nation's offering procedures with words that express fervor for God (see Commentary above, 3:15). This is the *Levi'im*'s specific task *inside* the Sanctuary. (ר' עקיבא's hermeneutic derivation נאמר כאן אתך ונאמר להלן אתך וכו' is not clear; also, our version of it is questionable. One thing, however, is certain: the interpretation that הקרב is indicative of שיר is derived from the term "אתך.")

וילוו עליך וישרתוך. The Gemara in *Tamid* 26b explains: וילוו עליך וישרתוך בעבודתך Whereas הקרב אתך confers on them the independent task of שיר, וילוו עליך וישרתוך involves them also בעבודתך: they participate — as auxiliaries and subordinates — in the very service that devolves on the כהנים, and in this service they are attached to the כהנים and minister to them. This priestly service in which the *Levi'im* participate as auxiliaries is the guard duty in the עזרה (see ibid.), a duty entrusted here to the כהנים by the words ואתה ובניך אתך לפני אהל העדת. In this service, the *Levi'im*, too, participate: כהנים שומרים מלמעלה ולוים מלמטה (ibid.). The *Sifre*'s version is: הכהנים מבפנים והלוים מבחוץ. In addition, the *Levi'im* stand guard at twenty-one locations in the Temple area (*Tamid* 27a; see משנה למלך on הל' בית הבחירה, 8:4). On the significance of this Levite guard, see Commentary above, 1:48. The *Levi'im* also performed supportive service — וישרתוך — as גזברים (administrators, treasurers, etc.) and אמרכלים (superintendents) (*Sifre*). Besides the foregoing, even in the service of the offerings, there are procedures — e.g., שחיטה, הפשט, ניתוח — that do not require a כהן (see רמב"ם הל' ביאת המקדש, 9:6), and these, in a case of exigency, can be performed by the *Levi'im*. It is possible that these, too, are included by the term "וישרתוך."

In defining the לויים's status vis-à-vis the כהנים, Scripture refers to the tribe of Levi — in relation to Aharon — by three designations: אחיך, מטה לוי, שבט אביך.

אחיך denotes equality, as a result of which the לויים can be compared with the כהנים in their standing before God. This would refer to the שירות בשם ה', which our Sages (see Commentary, *Devarim* 18:7-8) take to be the service of singing psalms while offerings are made. As it says here: הקרב אתך.

מטה — from the root נטה, pointing horizontally — conceives of the tribe as a "branch" of the stem. By this term the tribe is viewed from the standpoint of its equality to the other tribes. As a result, the *Levi'im* are allowed to perform only supportive services — as auxiliaries and subordinates — but are excluded from the service of the כהונה. As it says here: וילוו עליך וישרתוך.

שבט — as opposed to מטה — is not a branch of the stem, but an independent rod. The term "שבט" itself denotes grandeur and power, and as a rule it designates the tribes of Israel in their independent power and dignity; they are called "שבטי ישראל," not "מטות ישראל." Through שבט אביך your father [לוי] lives on, as it were, in his own unique characteristics; through שבט אביך your father contributed significantly to the formation of the Jewish national community. It is the tribe that distinguished itself

3 *They are to keep your charge and the charge of the entire Tent, but they must not come near the utensils of the Sanctuary or to the altar so that they will not die, neither they nor you.*

ג וְשָׁמְרוּ מִשְׁמַרְתְּךָ וּמִשְׁמֶרֶת כָּל־הָאֹהֶל אַךְ אֶל־כְּלֵי הַקֹּדֶשׁ וְאֶל־הַמִּזְבֵּחַ לֹא יִקְרָבוּ וְלֹא־יָמֻתוּ גַם־הֵם גַּם־אַתֶּם׃

in its devotion to God's Word, and thus it naturally became the "guardian of the Sanctuary"; clearly, this was its destiny. As a result, it received its position and mission towards the people, and as a concrete expression of this position it stood guard in the camp around the Sanctuary. This guardianship is included in משמרת אהל מועד of the next verse, and was later continued also in the Temple in the form of the outer watch, at the twenty-one locations around the Temple and the עזרות. The inner watch לפני אהל העדת, at the three inner locations before the Sanctuary itself, was carried out by the כהנים. In this watch, the כהנים are considered only as the elite of the לויים, and the כהנים manifest through it their Levite character. In these three watches of the כהנים, the לויים participate only as auxiliaries, as already noted above.

3 **ושמרו וגו'** — cf. above, 3:6-8, and Commentary there. משמרתך is the service that they perform at your request; משמרת כל האהל is the independent service of the *Levi'im* in erecting and guarding the Tent of Meeting which is entrusted to them.

אך אל כלי וגו': It is not merely touching or approaching that is forbidden here, but, rather, using the vessels for the purpose of עבודה. ואל המזבח לא יקרבו — for the purpose of עבודה; what is forbidden here is the עבודה (see ספר המצוות לרמב"ם, לא תעשה 72, and משנה למלך at the end of הל' ביאת המקדש; see also סמ"ג, לא תעשה 297).

ולא ימתו גם הם גם אתם: אתם בשלהם והם בשלכם במיתה (*Arachin* 11b). Just as the כהנים were given title to the service of the offerings, the לויים were given title to the service of song; and just as a לוי is forbidden to serve as a כהן, a כהן is forbidden to serve as a לוי. Both are forbidden under the penalty of מיתה בידי שמים. Moreover, even הם בשלהם: even among the לויים, it is forbidden to transfer from one task to another, and the change from

4 *They shall join you and keep the charge of the Tent of Appointed Meeting with regard to all the service of the Tent, and no stranger shall come near to you.*

ד וְנִלְוּ עָלֶיךָ וְשָׁמְרוּ אֶת־מִשְׁמֶרֶת אֹהֶל מוֹעֵד לְכֹל עֲבֹדַת הָאֹהֶל וְזָר לֹא־יִקְרַב אֲלֵיכֶם׃

5 *Keep the charge of the Sanctuary and the charge of the altar; then anger shall come no more upon the Children of Israel.*

ה וּשְׁמַרְתֶּם אֵת מִשְׁמֶרֶת הַקֹּדֶשׁ וְאֵת מִשְׁמֶרֶת הַמִּזְבֵּחַ וְלֹא־יִהְיֶה עוֹד קֶצֶף עַל־בְּנֵי יִשְׂרָאֵל׃

משורר to משוער, from the choir to the guard or vice versa, is forbidden באזהרה or even במיתה (ibid.; see Commentary above, 1:51).

4 **ונלוו עליך וגו׳** — cf. above, 3:7-8, and Commentary there.

וזר לא יקרב אליכם: לעבודה (*Sifre*). An unauthorized person may not come near to perform עבודה that has been assigned to you. This is the warning, and the penalty is מיתה בידי שמים, as explicitly stated in verse 7 (*Sifre*; see also *Zevachim* 16a).

5 **ושמרתם וגו׳**. הקדש is the Sanctuary, which represents Israel's mission, whereas the מזבח is designated for the acts of devotion to that mission. משמרת הקדש is the task that devolves on the לויים in association with the כהנים, whereas משמרת המזבח is the special task of the כהנים. In the *Sifre* our Sages say that ושמרתם is directed to the highest representative body in Israel, בית דין של ישראל: הרי זה אזהרה לב״ד של ישראל להזהיר את הכהנים שתהא העבודה כתיקונה, שכשעבודה נעשית כתיקונה הם כלים את הפורענות מלבא לעולם. This interpretation is supported by the *Sifre*'s position — as understood by רש״י — that this פרשה and the following פרשה were not communicated directly to Aharon, but were communicated to Moshe to be conveyed to Aharon.

To be sure, this שמירה also includes keeping all זרים away from the עבודה. The performance of the entire עבודה in the Sanctuary is stamped with the imprint of obedience to the Torah. Even the כהנים and the לויים, who are fit for the עבודה, are warned against any arbitrariness. The whole סדר העבודה expresses the fact that the Sanctuary and its Service down to the smallest detail — the procedures performed as well as the performers

ו וַאֲנִי הִנֵּה לָקַחְתִּי אֶת־אֲחֵיכֶם
הַלְוִיִּם מִתּוֹךְ בְּנֵי יִשְׂרָאֵל לָכֶם
מַתָּנָה נְתֻנִים לַיהוָה לַעֲבֹד אֶת־
עֲבֹדַת אֹהֶל מוֹעֵד׃

6 *I, lo! I have taken your brothers, the* Levi'im, *from out of the midst of the Children of Israel, to you are they given as a gift for* God's *purposes, to perform the service of the Tent of Appointed Meeting.*

ז וְאַתָּה וּבָנֶיךָ אִתְּךָ תִּשְׁמְרוּ אֶת־
כְּהֻנַּתְכֶם לְכָל־דְּבַר הַמִּזְבֵּחַ
וּלְמִבֵּית לַפָּרֹכֶת וַעֲבַדְתֶּם עֲבֹדַת
מַתָּנָה אֶתֵּן אֶת־כְּהֻנַּתְכֶם וְהַזָּר
הַקָּרֵב יוּמָת׃ פ

7 *But you and your sons with you must attend to your priesthood, with regard to everything pertaining to the altar and to anything behind the cloth partition you are to do the service; I am giving you your priesthood for a service of free-willed giving; the stranger that comes near shall die.*

of the procedures — are all dictated by God's Will; nothing may be done based on human judgment. Hence, the faithful performance of the עבודה will automatically prevent the recurrence of the sin that leads to ruin: ולא יהיה עוד קצף על בני ישראל.

6-7 In conclusion, Scripture declares once again that the exclusive authorization conferred upon the *Levi'im* and the sons of Aharon to serve in the Sanctuary derives from God alone. This declaration should obviate any presumptuousness or conceit on the part of those chosen to perform the עבודה. At the same time, it reconfirms the Divine origin of the Service, of the [choice of] servants, and of the Torah, to which the whole Sanctuary is dedicated and to which the whole Service refers.

ואני: the choice of these individuals derives from Me. **הנה לקחתי וגו'**: the *Levi'im* have played a completely passive role in their selection; they merely carry out a decree which God ordained for them. **לכם וגו'**: The כהנים's right to the לויים's services is not their original right and does not derive from their own authority. **מתנה וגו'**, the לויים are *given* to the כהנים as a gift for specific and limited purposes: **לה'**, only in the service of God, not in their own service, may the כהנים use the לויים: לה' הם מסורים ואין מסורים לכהנים (*Sifre*).

ואתה ובניך וגו'. לכל דבר המזבח includes everything that is done on the מזבח החיצון; מבית לפרכת includes all the עבודות הפנים done in the קודש הקדשים on יום הכיפורים; and the term ולמבית לפרכת includes also everything that is done on the מזבח הזהב in the היכל and on the פרכת כנגד בין הבדים (*Yoma* 24a). ועבדתם: all the עבודות that are done in the עזרה, in the היכל, or in the קודש הקדשים shall be done by you.

Above (v. 4), it says: וזר לא יקרב אליכם, from which we derive an אזהרה to the non-כהן not to perform anything that is called "עבודה." Here, it says: והזר הקרב יומת, from which we derive that a זר who performs a priestly עבודה incurs the penalty of מיתה בידי שמים. However, the Halachah teaches that here an עבודה is considered as such only in the stage of its completion (cf. Commentary, *Shemos* 28:35, 28:43): עבודה תמה ולא עבודה שיש אחריה עבודה (*Yoma* 24a). Thus, the חיוב מיתה for a זר is incurred only if he performs a concluding עבודה which completes an act of עבודה — e.g., זריקה which completes the עבודת הדם, הקטרת קומץ which completes the עבודת אש of the מנחה, and so also הקטרת אברים ואימורים. But a זר does not incur the penalty of מיתה if he performs an introductory עבודה — e.g., קבלה והולכה in עבודת הדם, קמיצה of the מנחה.

The עבודה specific to the כהנים is characterized as עבודת מתנה: it is עבודה of "giving," giving of oneself, devotion. All the acts performed in the Sanctuary center on the concept of מתנה; it is עבודה of giving oneself up, of devotion. Whereas the מקדש and its furnishings — the ארון, שולחן, and מנורה — represent what we *receive* from God through the Torah and for the sake of the Torah, the purpose of the עבודה in the Sanctuary is to teach us to *give* ourselves and our God-given possessions to God and to His Torah. The זריקה as well as the נתינה and the הזייה of דם הנפש on the altar, on the פרכת and on the כפורת; the הקטרה on the מזבח הנחושת of the חלב, כליות, and איברים, and of the קומץ and the מנחה; also the הקטרה of the קטורת on the מזבח הזהב and, on יום הכיפורים, in the קודש הקדשים; the ניסוך המים on חג הסוכות and the ניסוך היין daily — all these procedures, in which the עבודה in the Sanctuary culminates, are "מתנות" in which we surrender ourselves and our possessions, and in which the totality of our life mission is represented. The purpose of the כהן is to teach himself and the people the "direction" that God has set for our lives; his whole עבודה is nothing but עבודת מתנה, service conducive to self-devotion to God.

For this reason the hallmark of the עבודה specific to the כהנים is — in addition to עבודה תמה — also עבודת מתנה ולא עבודת סילוק (*Yoma* 24a); this excludes, for example, תרומת הדשן. A זר is not liable to מיתה בידי שמים unless he performs עבודה that includes both of these attributes: עבודה תמה and עבודת מתנה. Hence our Sages say: היוצק והבולל והפותת המולח והמניף המגיש והמסדר את השולחן המטיב את הנרות והקומץ והמקבל דמים בחוץ פטור ואין חייבין עליהן לא משום זרות ולא משום טומאה ולא משום מחוסר בגדים ולא משום ריחוץ ידים ורגלים (*Sanhedrin* 82b).

Now follows a most significant statement: **עבדת מתנה אתן את כהנתכם**. God wants to *give us our giving*. If we understand it correctly, the meaning of this statement is as follows: A gift certainly denotes an act motivated entirely by our own free will. Hence, the giving of ourselves and of our possessions to God emanates from the deepest wellsprings of our moral freedom of will. On the other hand, as regards its motivation and the manner in which it is to be performed, this giving of ourselves must not in any manner be guided by personal whim. It must conform with strict standards; it must be nothing other than *obedience in freedom*, עבודת מתנה, a free act of dedication to the fulfillment of life's purpose as set down in God's Torah. We must keep in mind not only that the things we give, namely, the possessions we call our own, are in fact God's possessions, so that we are merely giving back to God what we have received from Him (וּמִיָּדְךָ נָתַנּוּ לָךְ [*Divrei Ha-Yamim* I, 29:14]), but also that the very fact of our giving, and the nature, quality and purpose of our gift, are nothing more than the fulfillment of God's command. Thus, in truth, our מתנה becomes a נתינה from God, an act that *realizes God's Will through the medium of our own free-willed obedience.*

Free-willed obedience to the Will of God is the basis of Judaism. It rejects the mere inner impulse of "piety" or "devoutness" that seeks expression and gratification in self-devised practices, presumed to be "pleasing to God." That cannot be called "Divine service." Judaism maintains: God has *told* man what is "good" and what He requires of him (*Michah* 6:8). The Jew's עבודה, his Divine service, consists in "serving God," in obedience, in the faithful performance of God's expressed Will. The most sacred object in the Holy of Holies is God's Torah, with its laws and rules, and the acts that symbolize devotion to the Torah are themselves regulated by this Torah. The individuals who perform these acts are servants of the Torah, just as they are servants of the Sanctuary, and they were appointed to this charge by God. In the name of God and in the name of His Torah, they accept the symbols of our free-willed devotion to the dictates set down in the Torah. The sons of Aharon were appointed, to the exclusion of all others, to perform עבודת מתנה in the Sanctuary of the

8 God *spoke to Aharon: And I, lo! I have given you the charge of My uplifted donations; [this applies] also to all the holy things of the Children of Israel. I have given them to you as a consecration, and to your sons, as an everlasting due.*	ח וַיְדַבֵּר יְהֹוָה אֶל־אַהֲרֹן וַאֲנִי הִנֵּה נָתַתִּי לְךָ אֶת־מִשְׁמֶרֶת תְּרוּמֹתָי לְכָל־קָדְשֵׁי בְנֵי־יִשְׂרָאֵל לְךָ נְתַתִּים לְמָשְׁחָה וּלְבָנֶיךָ לְחָק־עוֹלָם׃

Torah, and their service is for the sake of fulfilling the Torah. Thereby the Torah itself and its Sanctuary are stamped with the impress of their Divine origin. At the same time, it is thereby shown that the fulfillment of our lives must be identical with the fulfillment of God's Will.

In Korach's statement כל העדה כלם קדשים ובתוכם ה׳, he proclaimed a rebellion against the appointment of the sons of Aharon as כהנים. He thereby denied the Divine origin of Moshe's mission and of the Torah transmitted by him. Korach sought to replace the Torah with the subjectivity of the individual. In his view, the individual need only follow his inner stirrings of holiness in order to attain God's nearness and approval.

As opposed to such subjectivism, which undermines the whole of Judaism, the Word of God concludes here with: עבדת מתנה אתן את כהנתכם והזר הקרב יומת; the punishment is מיתה בידי שמים (*Sanhedrin* 84a).

8 **וידבר וגו׳**. The foregoing established the privileged position of the כהנים and לויים in relation to the Sanctuary and also established the responsibility that devolves upon them by virtue of this position. To that, Scripture now adds a list of their rights in the nation, rights which likewise are stamped with the impress of Divine regulation. At the same time, Scripture also notes the duties that are attached to these rights.

ואני הנה נתתי וגו׳ תרומתי. According to our Sages (*Shabbos* 25a and 26a; *Bechoros* 34a), תרומתי are the gifts called "תרומה," which are separated from the produce that is ready to be used for human food.

תרומה מן התורה, applies only to דגן תירוש ויצהר (grain, wine, and oil), which are man's principal foods. This is the view of most commentators (see *Bechoros* 54a, תוספות there ד״ה ושני). The רמב״ם (הל׳ תרומות, 2:1) apparently holds that תרומות ומעשרות of all produce are דאורייתא, with the sole exception of ירקות, which are not included in the concept of תבואת זרעך,

the true crops [ibid. 2:6] (see משנה למלך ibid. 2:1; שולחן ערוך יו״ד 331:13 adopts the view of the רמב״ם).

We have already analyzed (on *Vayikra* 22:9) the meaning of תרומה, the "uplifted gift," with regard to the people and with regard to the כהן.

On the one hand, the people are obligated to separate תרומה from the produce that has reached a finished state, and so long as this has not been done, the produce is טבל and אסור. In this way, the people learn that their whole material existence depends on their observance of the Torah.

On the other hand, the כהן's whole existence depends on these gifts dedicated by the people to God and to His Torah. Every morsel of bread that the כהן eats reminds and admonishes him: The Torah and the Sanctuary, in whose service he stands, are not a monopoly of the כהנים; rather, they are the Sanctuary of the nation, and only as the representative of the nation was he appointed by God as the servant of the Torah and the Sanctuary. His whole existence depends on the Torah and its Sanctuary, and he is unworthy of this "bread" unless he and his household, which is supported by the bread of the Sanctuary, contribute to the blossoming of the Sanctuary of the Torah and set a shining example to the people.

Hence, he must regard the תרומה-bread as תרומתי; he must guard it as something belonging to God which has been entrusted to him למשמרת in accordance with its character and purpose. Although the תרומה is לך and is נכסי כהנים, it is קודש, and, as already stated in *Vayikra* (ibid.), it must be protected from טומאה and eaten only בטהרה. In its use, too, there are restrictions. He must protect it from טומאה, and as the Halachah in *Bechoros* 34a explains: תרומתָי, בשתי תרומות הכתוב מדבר, אחת תרומה טהורה ואחת תרומה תלויה, ואמר רחמנא עביד לה שימור. That is to say, even תרומה that is "תלויה," suspended in doubt, שנולד בה ספק טומאה, must be kept from טומאת ודאי.

Since we are dealing here with תרומה in both of its states, with תרומה טהורה and with תרומה טמאה, and of both it says לך, from this we derive (*Shabbos* 25a) that תרומה טמאה, too, is given over to the כהן, and he may benefit from it. Although תרומה טמאה — like all קודש שנטמא — must be burned, which is why שמן תרומה טמאה is called "שמן שריפה," the כהן is permitted to benefit from the תרומה as it is being burned: בשעת ביעורה תיהני ממנה — e.g., for lighting or for cooking; בשתי תרומות הכתוב מדבר, אחת תרומה טהורה ואחת תרומה טמאה, ואמר רחמנא לך שלך תהא להסיקה תחת תבשילך. This benefit is called הנאה של כילוי (תוספות *Yevamos* 66b ד״ה לא), and it is prohibited in the case of תרומה טהורה.

As already stated, the כהן is generally restricted in the benefit he may

ט זֶה יִהְיֶה לְךָ מִקֹּדֶשׁ הַקֳּדָשִׁים מִן־
הָאֵשׁ כָּל־קָרְבָּנָם לְכָל־מִנְחָתָם
וּלְכָל־חַטָּאתָם וּלְכָל־אֲשָׁמָם
אֲשֶׁר יָשִׁיבוּ לִי קֹדֶשׁ קָדָשִׁים לְךָ
הוּא וּלְבָנֶיךָ׃

9 *This shall be yours from the holy of holies reserved from the fire: everything that they bring near, their every homage offering, and their every offering that clears of sin, and their every guilt offering that they return to Me, a holy of holies shall it be to you and to your sons.*

derive from the תרומה. סחורה with תרומה is prohibited (*Shevi'is* 7:3). אסור לאבדה: Even in preparing food, it is forbidden to use תרומה in such a way that only part of it will be eaten and the rest — which likewise is fit to be eaten — will be thrown away (*Terumos* 11:1). A general rule that applies to תרומות is that אין משנין אותם מברייתן (ibid. 11:3): One may not make honey from dates, cider from apples, and so forth.

טהרה and obedience are the two ideas of which תרומה constantly reminds the כהן and his household, for the תרומה is the food they live on; they sustain themselves on bread that is sacred unto the service of God, and they must be worthy of it all the days of their lives through moral purity and faithfulness to duty.

לכל קדשי בני ישראל: The same responsibility and the same care that devolve upon you in respect to תרומה devolve upon you also in respect to all קדשי בני ישראל.

לך נתתים למשחה, God gave them to the כהנים for a continuous משיחה, "anointment": Whenever they partake of these holy things, they are to remember that they were separated and kept far from everything profane and base, which indeed is the meaning of anointing (see Commentary, *Shemos* 29:7). And only in anticipation of this consecration were these holy things given to them as חק עולם, as an everlasting due.

9 **זה יהיה לך וגו׳**. The list of the מתנות כהונה begins with what the preceding verse concluded with: the כהנים's share of the קדשים, which are the offerings. First: **מקדש הקדשים**, from offerings that consecrate actions (see Commentary, *Shemos* 29:37). **מן האש**: After לחם אשה has been delivered to the אש אוכלה, to the אש דת upon the altar, אכילת כהנים is added merely as a complementing and concluding consequence (see ibid. 29:31-32).

10 *In the holiness of holy things must you eat it; every male may eat it; it shall be a holy thing to you.*	י בְּקֹדֶשׁ הַקֳּדָשִׁים תֹּאכְלֶנּוּ כָּל־זָכָר יֹאכַל אֹתוֹ קֹדֶשׁ יִהְיֶה־לָּךְ׃

כל קרבנם וגו׳, everything that they bring near to God in order to attain His nearness.

In *Zevachim* 44b, the comprehensive terms כל קרבנם, לכל מנחתם, and so on, are explained: they serve to include those categories of offerings in which the כהנים's share has not yet been mentioned and cannot be deduced by analogy. **כל קרבנם** includes לוג שמן של מצורע (*Vayikra* 14:12 and 18), which likewise is called a קרבן, as the term והקריב is applied to it (ibid. 14:12) — even though it does not come מן האש. **לכל מנחתם** includes מנחת העומר (ibid. 23:10) and מנחת הקנאות (above, 5:15), even though their purpose is not כפרה and they are not included in the statement ואכלו אתם אשר כפר בהם (*Shemos* 29:33; see Commentary there). **ולכל חטאתם** includes חטאת העוף, even though it is killed by מליקה, which in general effects נבילה (see *Vayikra* 5:8). **ולכל אשמם** includes אשם נזיר (above, 6:12), even though it, too, does not spring from a need for כפרה, but, rather, concludes נזירות של טומאה and begins נזירות של טהרה. **ולכל אשמם אשר ישיבו לי**: As already stated in our Commentary on each one of the אשמות, every אשם was preceded by a sin in the realm of possessions; thus אשם מעילה, אשם תלוי, and אשם גזילות, and thus — in a wider sense — also the other אשמות. Hence it says here: ישיבו לי. In *Zevachim* 44b our Sages say that this expression includes especially גזל הגר, whose קרן is called "אשם," and to which ישיבו לי applies precisely (see above, 5:8, and Commentary there).

10 **בקדש הקדשים וגו׳**: not actually in the Holy of Holies, but in the עזרה, the place designated for the consumption of קדשי הקדשים, as already stated in connection with מנחה, חטאת, and אשם (*Vayikra* 6:9, 19 and 7:6).

It stands to reason that the term "קדש" here — as in שבת קדש, אדמת קדש — denotes not a holy place, but holiness. That is to say, these offerings must be eaten in the exceptionally holy manner of the holy things. This includes — as stated in the sources cited above — that they must be eaten only in the עזרה. The eating of these קדשים is a continuation and conclusion of the כפרה that started with the עבודות on the altar (see Commentary, *Shemos* 29:31-33). That is why they must be eaten only by זכרי כהונה. Our

יא וְזֶה־לְּךָ֞ תְּרוּמַ֣ת מַתָּנָ֗ם לְכָל־
תְּנוּפֹת֮ בְּנֵ֣י יִשְׂרָאֵל֒ לְךָ֣ נְתַתִּ֗ים
וּלְבָנֶ֧יךָ וְלִבְנֹתֶ֛יךָ אִתְּךָ֖ לְחָק־עוֹלָ֑ם
כָּל־טָה֥וֹר בְּבֵיתְךָ֖ יֹאכַ֥ל אֹתֽוֹ׃

11 *And this shall be for you as an uplifted donation from their gift, from all the [wave] offerings of the Children of Israel have I given them to you and to your sons and to your daughters with you as an everlasting due. Every one in your house who is [ritually] pure may eat it.*

Sages (*Zevachim* 97b) derive further from here that זבחי שלמי ציבור (*Vayikra* 23:19) as well must be eaten only by זכרי כהונה, for they, too, are subsumed under קדשי הקדשים.

11 **וזה לך וגו׳**. Now follow the קדשים קלים — שלמים and תודה — which are the offerings that consecrate our fate. After the חלב and the כליות have been offered, the שלמים and the תודה are eaten by the בעלים in their homes, and the כהנים take only the חזה and שוק. In the case of the תודה, they also take one loaf of each of the four kinds of לחמי תודה (see ibid. 7:14, 31-32). With all these parts taken from the שלמים for the altar and for the כהנים — with the אימורים and חזה ושוק of the שלמים, and in the case of תודה also with each one of the four kinds of bread — תרומה ותנופה are performed. The אימורים are offered upon the altar, whereas the חזה ושוק and לחמי תודה are characterized by תנופה ותרומה [alone], on account of which they are called "תרומה" and "תנופה" (ibid. 7:14, 32, 34).

The structure of וזה לך תרומת מתנם וגו׳ לך נתתים וגו׳ is difficult to understand. The object to which זה refers seems to be missing. In our view, the term "תרומה" in "תרומת מתנם" does double duty. This [the תרומה] shall be yours as תרומת מתנם: This shall be for you as a share, for it was uplifted to God to be a מתן, a gift, to the כהן, as opposed to the אימורים, which likewise are uplifted, but for a different purpose, namely, to be delivered to the altar fire. These are the תרומות of all the תנופות: the four לחמים of the לחמי תודה, חזה ושוק, and the זרוע בשלה of איל הנזיר (above, 6:19-20). Although both תנופה and תרומה are performed with all of them, they are called here "תרומה," for that is the usual term for the כהן's share.

These מתנות כהונה from זבחי השלמים may be eaten in the כהן's home by

12 *All the best of the oil and all the best of the new wine and of the grain, the first of that which they give to* God, *to you have I given them.*	יב כֹּל חֵלֶב יִצְהָר וְכָל־חֵלֶב תִּירוֹשׁ וְדָגָן רֵאשִׁיתָם אֲשֶׁר־יִתְּנוּ לַיהוָה לְךָ נְתַתִּים׃

all members of his household, just as the שלמים themselves may be eaten by the בעלים in their homes. They are נאכלין בכל העיר . . . לכהנים לנשיהם ולבניהם ולעבדיהם (*Zevachim* 55a).

12 **כל חלב וגו'**. Now follow the קדשי גבול. These קדשים are not eaten only in the עזרה as in the case of קדשי קדשים, nor are they eaten only in the city surrounding the Sanctuary as in the case of קדשים קלים; rather, they may be eaten anywhere in the Land.

First: תרומה (see Commentary, v. 1; *Vayikra* 22:9ff.). חלב יצהר: See *Bereshis* 45:18 (and Commentary there), where חלב הארץ serves as a metaphor for the choice and the best. Here, too — as will be explained on verse 32 — it is a duty to lift out the best as תרומה. מן התורה there is no שיעור, no prescribed measure, for תרומה. Even a single kernel from the whole pile is sufficient. However, it is appropriate to the idea represented by תרומה that this single kernel should come from the very best of the pile (see *Terumos* 2:4). Hence it says here: חלב יצהר.

From what is stated in verse 27 — כדגן מן הגרן וכמלאה מן היקב — it is clear that the duty of תרומה comes into effect only at גמר מלאכה, i.e., when the work for storing the produce has been completed. Hence גפן and זית are not mentioned here, but יצהר and תירוש; so, too, דגן is grain that has already been piled into a heap and smoothed over (see *Pesachim* 35b).

דגן is apparently related to תכן, which denotes a quantitative summing up, and is related also to תקן, which means: to bring something to completion, to put things in order.

If the fruits of the vine and the olive tree are to be eaten as they are — as grapes and olives — they are subject to תרומה when they are brought home as fruit (see *Bava Metzia* 88b).

Now it does not say here כל חלב יצהר תירוש ודגן, but, rather, כל חלב יצהר וכל חלב תירוש ודגן. From this we derive the halachah that אין תורמין ממין על שאינו מינו ואם תרם אין תרומתו תרומה וכו׳, אמרה תורה תן חלב לזה וחלב לזה (*Bechoros*

13 *The first fruit of all that is in their land, that they bring to God, shall be yours; every one in your house who is [ritually] pure may eat it.*	יג בִּכּוּרֵ֞י כָּל־אֲשֶׁ֧ר בְּאַרְצָ֛ם אֲשֶׁר־יָבִ֥יאוּ לַיהֹוָ֖ה לְךָ֣ יִהְיֶ֑ה כָּל־טָה֥וֹר בְּבֵיתְךָ֖ יֹאכְלֶֽנּוּ׃

53b). One cannot take תרומה collectively from different kinds of produce, but must give it separately from each kind. Each kind of produce should be regarded as a special gift from God; hence, with each kind, we should express our devotion to God's Torah, whose realization is indeed the purpose of every gift we receive from God's hand.

The law that אם תרם ממין על שאינו מינו אין תרומתו תרומה is — according to רבא — a result of the principle: כל מילתא דאמר רחמנא לא תעביד אי עביד לא מהני, any act performed against the Law has no legal effect. According to אביי, who disputes this principle, the aforementioned law is derived from the term "ראשיתם": ראשית לזה וראשית לזה (*Temurah* 4b-5a and רש״י there; see Commentary, *Vayikra* 22:23).

ראשיתם — similarly in *Devarim* (18:4): ראשית דגנך — is the first obligation on the produce at the end of the work of the harvest (see *Terumos* 3:7). At the same time, the term "ראשית" implies that מן התורה there is no prescribed minimum measure for תרומה, but there is a maximum. The Torah establishes only that תרומה is "ראשית": it is a "first" of the heap, whatever the quantity this first might be; hence חטה אחת פוטרת את הכרי. On the other hand, it is to be a ראשית of the whole: בעינן ראשית ששיריה ניכרין (*Chullin* 136b), a considerable amount must remain, and "If someone declares his whole barn to be תרומה . . . his declaration is invalid and has no effect" (ibid.). The same law applies also to חלה (ibid.; see Commentary above, 15:20).

13 **בכורי כל וגו׳** — see *Shemos* 23:19; *Devarim* 26:2.

כל אשר בארצם. In contrast to תרומה, the mitzvah of ביכורים applies already במחובר לקרקע (*Sifre*), once the produce becomes ripe, which is why ביכורים are called "מלאתך" (*Shemos* 22:28; see Commentary there). The difference between the expressions אשר יתנו לה׳, in the case of תרומה, and אשר יביאו לה׳, in the case of ביכורים, is significant. The produce that is subject to the duty of תרומה is already completely in man's possession, and before he partakes of it he *gives* to God the first part of what he took for

יד כָּל־חֵ֖רֶם בְּיִשְׂרָאֵ֥ל לְךָ֥ יִהְיֶֽה׃

14 *Whatever has been placed under a vow of interdiction in Israel shall be yours.*

טו כָּל־פֶּ֣טֶר רֶ֠חֶם לְכָל־בָּשָׂ֞ר אֲשֶׁר־
יַקְרִ֧יבוּ לַיהוָ֛ה בָּאָדָ֥ם וּבַבְּהֵמָ֖ה
יִֽהְיֶה־לָּ֑ךְ אַ֣ךְ ׀ פָּדֹ֣ה תִפְדֶּ֗ה אֵ֚ת
בְּכ֣וֹר הָֽאָדָ֔ם וְאֵ֛ת בְּכֽוֹר־הַבְּהֵמָ֥ה
הַטְּמֵאָ֖ה תִּפְדֶּֽה׃

15 *Whatever opens the womb of any creature that is brought near to* God, *whether it be of man or of beast, shall be yours; however, you must redeem the firstborn of man and you shall also redeem the firstborn of an impure animal.*

himself. By contrast, the produce subject to the duty of ביכורים is still standing in the field, but instead of bringing it home for his own needs, he *brings home* the first part for the purposes of the Sanctuary, thereby acknowledging that the produce that grows in Jewish fields is first and foremost תבואת הקדש (see *Shemos* 23:19 and Commentary there).

כל טהור בביתך יאכלנו. ביכורים resemble תרומה; both — as well as חלה — may be eaten by all members of the כהן's household: by his wife, by a בת ישראל המאורסת לכהן, by his sons and daughters, and also by his עבדים ושפחות הכנענים, who, as קנין כספו, are attached to the כהן by personal bond-service.

In this respect, חזה ושוק of קדשים קלים (v. 11) likewise resemble תרומה, with the one exception of a בת כהן who was married to a ישראל and is childless: Upon the termination of the marriage (by death of the husband or divorce), she may return to her father's home and resume eating תרומה, but not חזה ושוק (see Commentary, *Vayikra* 22:10-14).

14 **כל חרם וגו׳** — see *Vayikra* 27:21, 28, and Commentary there.

15 **כל פטר רחם וגו׳** — see *Shemos* 13:2, 12-15, and Commentary there. The expression פטר רחם לכל בשר includes all three categories of בכורות — viz., בכור אדם, בכור בהמה טהורה, and בכור בהמה טמאה — as is evident from the explanatory addition באדם ובבהמה. Thus, אשר יקריבו לה׳ cannot refer to bringing an offering, but only to general dedication to God. The בכורות of all three categories are brought into close relationship to God. The same idea is expressed elsewhere as והעברת כל פטר רחם לה׳ (ibid. 13:12).

אך פדה תפדה וגו׳: בכור אדם is equated here with בכור בהמה טמאה as regards the duty of redemption: כל שישנו בבכור אדם ישנו בבכור בהמה טמאה וכל שאינו בבכור אדם אינו בבכור בהמה טמאה. Hence כהנים ולוים פטורים both from בכור אדם as well as from פטר חמור (*Bechoros* 4a; see Commentary above, 3:41).

אך פדה תפדה וגו׳ ואת בכור הבהמה הטמאה תפדה. פדיון בכור אדם is an absolute duty, whereas פדיון פטר חמור is only a conditional one, for עריפה can be performed instead of פדיון, although the duty of פדיון takes precedence over the duty of עריפה (see *Shemos* 13:13 and Commentary there). This perhaps explains the change in the wording [from פדה תפדה of פדיון בכור אדם to תפדה of פדיון פטר חמור].

In *Kiddushin* 29a our Sages derive from the doubled form פדה תפדה that this mitzvah must be fulfilled in any case, and if the father did not fulfill it, it devolves upon the son as soon as he comes of age: היכא דלא פרקיה אבוה מיחייב איהו למפרקיה. And since the duty of redeeming one's son and the duty of redeeming oneself are included here in one expression, our Sages derive from this the following halachah: כל שמצווה לפדות את עצמו מצווה לפדות את אחרים וכל שאינו מצווה לפדות את עצמו אינו מצווה לפדות את אחרים (ibid.). Hence the duty of פדיון הבן devolves only upon the father, but not upon the mother.

Scripture here ascribes the act of redemption to the כהן, for תפדה (in this verse and the next) is addressed to Aharon, who is the representative of the כהונה. This is puzzling, for without a doubt the mitzvah of redeeming the firstborn devolves not upon the כהן but upon the father, and it can be fulfilled only by the father. So it says explicitly in *Shemos* 13:13 and 15: וכל בכור אדם בבניך תפדה, וכל בכור בני אפדה.

However, the Mishnah (*Bechoros* 51a) states a principle that applies in no other פדיון הקדש: המפריש פדיון בנו ואבד חייב באחריותו. If a father sets aside redemption money for his son, but the money is lost before he manages to give it to a כהן, no redemption has taken place. The redemption takes effect only when the כהן receives the money. From this it follows that the כהן's receipt of the money is an essential part of the redemption procedure. Accordingly, the כהן is considered a participant in the פדיון-act, and this could explain the second person of "תפדה," which refers to the כהן. This is apparently also the explanation of the proof adduced by the Mishnah (ibid.): שנאמר יהיה לך ופדה תפדה. (Bear in mind that the text reads: אך פדה תפדה.) For from יהיה לך it is clear that פדה תפדה, which follows, is addressed to the כהן, from which we may infer that the כהן is considered a participant in the פדיון-act.

16 *And you shall perform its redemption from the age of one month according to your valuation, five silver shekels of the shekel of the Sanctuary, [the shekel] being [worth] twenty* **gerah.**

טז וּפְדוּיָו מִבֶּן־חֹדֶשׁ תִּפְדֶּה בְּעֶרְכְּךָ כֶּסֶף חֲמֵשֶׁת שְׁקָלִים בְּשֶׁקֶל הַקֹּדֶשׁ עֶשְׂרִים גֵּרָה הוּא׃

This, then, is the meaning of פדיון בכור, as implied by this verse: יהיה לך — the firstborn really belongs to the Sanctuary represented by the כהן, and his original destiny was to assume a priestly or Levite position relative to the Sanctuary (see above, 3:12, and Commentary there). אך — by receiving the redemption money, the כהן, in the name of the Sanctuary, exempts and releases him from his position in the Sanctuary. Henceforth, his influence is to be felt in the family sphere, where he is to realize in the service of actual family life what he would have represented in the symbolical service in the Sanctuary, had he been given a priestly or Levite position. (Cf. שו״ת ריב״ש 131.)

But this special halachah does not apply to פדיון בכור בהמה טמאה. There — as in the פדיון of every other הקדש, e.g., פדיון מעשר שני — the פדיון takes effect even before the animal comes into the possession of the כהן, or before the money is brought to Yerushalayim (see *Bechoros* 12b). In the case of בכור בהמה טמאה, the second person of "תפדה" remains difficult.

In the *Sifre*, on the introduction to this mitzvah in verse 8, it says that the mitzvah was not communicated directly to Aharon, but to Moshe in order that he should convey it to Aharon. It is possible that this interpretation is based on the term "תפדה" in the case of בכור בהמה טמאה. If the mitzvah was communicated to Moshe, then this תפדה is addressed to the nation, and only פדה תפדה — which is connected by אך to the preceding יהיה לך — would undoubtedly refer to Aharon.

16 **ופדויו**: The pronominal suffix refers to בכור אדם, whose redemption was specially stressed in the preceding verse, whereas פדיון בכור בהמה טמאה was added there only secondarily, and has already been discussed in detail in *Shemos* 13:13 (see Commentary there). פדיון פטר חמור may be done immediately (*Bechoros* 12b).

מבן חדש תפדה — after thirty days have passed, as in the case of בכור

17 *However, the firstborn of an ox or the firstborn of a sheep or the firstborn of a goat you shall not redeem; they are holy. You shall dash their blood onto the altar, and you shall give its fat to go up in smoke as a fire offering, as an expression of compliance, to* God.

יז אַךְ בְּכוֹר־שׁוֹר אוֹ־בְכוֹר כֶּשֶׂב אוֹ־בְכוֹר עֵז לֹא תִפְדֶּה קֹדֶשׁ הֵם אֶת־דָּמָם תִּזְרֹק עַל־הַמִּזְבֵּחַ וְאֶת־חֶלְבָּם תַּקְטִיר אִשֶּׁה לְרֵיחַ נִיחֹחַ לַיהוָה׃

מדבר (above, chap. 3), of whom it says explicitly: מבן חדש ומעלה (above, 3:43). The child does not require פדיון until he reaches the thirty-first day: מת ביום שלושים כיום שלפניו (*Bechoros* 49a). Once the child has passed the thirtieth day, his viability is established: כל ששהה שלשים יום באדם אינו נפל (*Shabbos* 135b). Even if the child's viability is established on other grounds — קים לן ביה דכלו לו חדשיו — the פדיון cannot be made earlier (תוספות *Bechoros* 49a ד"ה מת בנו). The child's viability must be clearly apparent. Let no one think that פדיון protects against physical collapse; rather, its purely moral meaning is to be preserved.

בערכך כסף חמשת שקלים וגו׳. This is the ערך of a בן חודש (see *Vayikra* 27:6).

שקלים — see Commentary, *Shemos* 30:16 (end) and 22:15-16; also *Bechoros* 49b et seq. According to the נחלת שבעה (12:31), a shekel is 1¹⁄₁₅ *loth* [a measurement of weight; approximately half an ounce] of fine silver; hence the five shekels of פדיון הבן are 5⅓ *loth* of fine silver. But the structure of the sentence ופדויו וגו׳ תפדה וגו׳ כסף is that of כלל וכלל ופרט, which is treated as כלל ופרט וכלל; hence אי אתה דן אלא כעין הפרט, מה הפרט מפורש דבר המטלטל וגופו ממון אף כל דבר המטלטל וגופו ממון. Accordingly, כסף is to be taken as an example of anything that is movable and has intrinsic value. Excluded are קרקעות, which are immovable, עבדים, who are equated with קרקעות, and שטרות, which — although they are movable — have no intrinsic value, but only attest to the right to something that is of monetary value. Thus, פדיון הבן can be performed with any movable property that has intrinsic value and whose worth is כסף חמשת שקלים (*Bechoros* 51a; see also Commentary, *Vayikra* 11:9).

17 **אך בכור שור וגו׳**. עד שיהא הוא שור ובכורו שור (*Bechoros* 17a). The young is not considered a בכור if its appearance is at odds with the character of the

mother's species; hence רחל שילדה מין עז ועז שילדה מין רחל פטורה מן הבכורה ואם יש בו מקצת סימנין חייב (ibid. 16b).

We have already explained (Commentary, *Shemos* 13:2) that the consecration of the firstborn serves to consecrate the womb of the *mother*, and that consequently all those to be born afterward will be consecrated as well. In our view, the law stated here is an outgrowth of that concept, for sanctity does not rest upon the firstborn unless it represents its mother.

לא תפדה וגו׳. Its קדושה cannot be redeemed. Even as a בעל מום, it cannot be redeemed like all other פסולי המוקדשים, for which פדיון is provided in *Vayikra* 27:11-12. For the firstborn are not מוקדשים, and the קדושה did not come to rest upon them through man's free will. Rather, קדש הם, they are קדושים from the womb, and this קדושה remains upon them in all circumstances (see *Temurah* 5b; see *Vayikra* 27:26 and Commentary there). Hence, not even תמורה completely transfers קדושת בכור, and תמורת בכור — like תמורת מעשר — is not offered upon the altar (see *Zevachim* 37b; Commentary, *Vayikra* 27:33). בכור בהמה טהורה fully embodies the לי הוא of קדש לי כל בכור וגו׳ (*Shemos* 13:2), and in this respect it exceeds the other two בכורות, which is why it precedes them in verses 12-13 there (see Commentary there).

את דמם תזרק וגו׳. The term "סביב" [which means שתי מתנות שהן ארבע] is stated in connection with זריקת הדם of the עולה (*Vayikra* 1:5) and is then repeated in connection with the חטאת (ibid. 8:15) and with the אשם (ibid. 7:2). Hence, it is impossible to say that סביב is stated in connection with these offerings merely as an example [and סביב applies to all offerings], for שני כתובים — and certainly שלושה כתובים — הבאים כאחד אין מלמדין (*Zevachim* 57a). And since here Scripture does not say סביב, the blood requires only one מתנה, but that מתנה must be כנגד היסוד (see Commentary, *Vayikra* 1:5), as in the blood applications of the עולה (*Zevachim* 57a).

In this respect, בכור is similar to פסח and מעשר בהמה, whose blood likewise requires only מתנה אחת כנגד היסוד (see *Devarim* 12:27 and Commentary there). Their common denominator is that they signify the blessings of the home, which are granted by God and dedicated to Him. Hence, in all three cases, אכילת בעלים in the home is central.

In the cases of פסח and מעשר, only the דם and כליות וחלב come to the altar — the expression of dedicating life and will, with all its aims, to God; but the remainder of the offering is eaten by the בעלים in their home, for they have already renounced all selfish aims, and thereby even man's

18 *But their flesh shall be yours; like the breast of the wave [offering] and the right thigh, it shall be yours.*	יח וּבְשָׂרָם יִהְיֶה־לָּךְ כַּחֲזֵה הַתְּנוּפָה וּכְשׁוֹק הַיָּמִין לְךָ יִהְיֶה׃

enjoyment in his home is transformed into an act of Divine service and constitutes the realization of the task of the מקדש.

The same is true in the case of בכור בהמה טהורה: When it is handed over to the כהן, it becomes ממון כהן, and from then on the כהן is considered the בעלים of the בכור. Through it he shall come to understand the meaning of his own existence and that of his family, relative to the nation and to the Sanctuary. As כהן he shall devote to God's altar his own life and desires and those of his family, and in so doing he shall also elevate his own enjoyment in his home (ובשרם וגו׳ of the following verse) to the level of service in God's Sanctuary.

Since בכור מעשר ופסח represent dedication of existence more than dedication of actions, they have only מתנה אחת and do not require שתי מתנות שהן ארבע, which fully express the ideal of the altar: the aspiration of ascent to all the aims indicated by God. בכור requires only זריקה אחת כנגד היסוד: the blood is dashed against one of the altar corners rising upon the foundation of the Sanctuary. What this expresses in general is that the aspiration to ascend to God and to His purposes is a precondition for the sanctification of enjoyment. מעשר and פסח require only שפיכה onto the יסוד: one stands on the base of the altar and pours the blood onto the base, thereby signifying that his whole existence is rooted in the base of God's Sanctuary. What is more, from the רמב״ם's wording in הל׳ מעשה הקרבנות, 5:17, it appears that בכור, too, requires only שפיכה, but that is against the implication of our verse and hence seems unlikely (see לחם משנה there). After all, ר׳ יוסי הגלילי derives from our verse that מעשר and פסח also require זריקה (see *Pesachim* 64b).

18 **ובשרם יהיה לך**: To the כהן belong both תם, after זריקת הדם and הקטרת החלב as stated in the previous verse, and בעל מום, which is unfit for an offering but nevertheless is the כהן's property and is his to eat, only that it remains אסור בגיזה ובעבודה (see *Devarim* 15:19ff.; *Zevachim* 37a).

כחזה התנופה וכשוק הימין לך יהיה. The בכור בהמה טהרה belongs to the

19 *All the uplifted donations from the holy things that the Children of Israel lift up to* God *I have given to you and your sons and your daughters with you as an everlasting due. It is a covenant of everlasting salt before* God *for you and for your descendants with you.*

יט כֹּל ׀ תְּרוּמֹת הַקֳּדָשִׁים אֲשֶׁר יָרִימוּ בְנֵי־יִשְׂרָאֵל לַיהוָה נָתַתִּי לְךָ וּלְבָנֶיךָ וְלִבְנֹתֶיךָ אִתְּךָ לְחָק־עוֹלָם בְּרִית מֶלַח עוֹלָם הִוא לִפְנֵי יְהוָה לְךָ וּלְזַרְעֲךָ אִתָּךְ׃

כהן like חזה ושוק of שלמים, which are נאכלין לשני ימים ולילה אחד (see *Vayikra* 7:16 and Commentary there; *Zevachim* 57a), and of which it says above (v. 11) that they may be eaten by all members of the כהן's household (see *Bechoros* 32b).

19 **כל תרומת וגו'**. Scripture summarizes it all again. Everything that is "uplifted and sanctified" — i.e., everything that is directed to the Sanctuary because it has been dedicated to God and thus participates in the holy character of the Sanctuary — has been given by God to the כהן and his household as an everlasting due, for the כהן has been appointed by God to represent and to foster the people's relationship to God and His Sanctuary. The position of the sons of Aharon as representatives of the Torah and its Sanctuary among the people comes to expression in the people's sight, in every aspect of their national and domestic lives, through the מתנות כהונה given to them.

This position in itself is a ברית, something given by God as absolute, and it is מלח עולם. It reveals the character of the Torah and its Sanctuary as "given" and "immutable." At the same time, as it says in the *Sifre*, it is also like salt in another respect. For the כהן is to instill the eternal spirit of the eternal Torah in all the aspects and relationships of national and family life, preserving them so that they not decay but remain fresh and wholesome for God and His Sanctuary: כרת הכתוב ברית עם אהרן בדבר הבריא ולא עוד אלא שמבריא את אחרים (see also Commentary, *Vayikra* 2:13). Jewish priests are to regard themselves, their home, and their priesthood as the "eternal salt" in the people, and thus are to carry out their service under God's supervision and protection.

The מתנות כהונה — listed here in an order of כלל (v. 8), פרט (vv. 9-18), and כלל (v. 19), which is the usual order also in the case of the rest of the *mitzvos* — fall into three groups: (a) those that may be eaten only in the עזרה in the מקדש (vv. 9-10); (b) those that may be eaten only in ירושלים (v. 11. ביכורים [v. 13] also belong to this group, but since they resemble תרומה in other respects, they are listed here together with תרומה. Also belonging to this group is בכור בהמה טהורה [vv. 17-18], but it is listed here with the other two בכורות); (c) those that may be eaten and used בגבולין, anywhere in the Jewish domain (vv. 12-16).

The תוספתא (*Chullin* 133b) lists twenty-four מתנות כהונה, and they, too, fall into these groups: עשרים וארבע מתנות כהונה הן וכו׳ ואלו הן: **עשר במקדש וארבע בירושלים ועשר בגבולין. עשר במקדש:** חטאת וחטאת העוף אשם ודאי ואשם תלוי וזבחי שלמי צבור ולוג שמן של מצורע ושתי הלחם ולחם הפנים ושירי מנחות ומנחת העומר; **וארבע בירושלים:** הבכורה והבכורים ומורם מן התודה ומאיל הנזיר (ובכללם חזה ושוק של שאר שלמים) ועורות קדשים; **ועשר בגבולין:** תרומה ותרומת מעשר וחלה וראשית הגז ומתנות (הזרוע והלחיים והקיבה – דברים יח, ג-ד) ופדיון הבן ופדיון פטר חמור ושדה אחוזה (ויקרא כז, כא) ושדה חרמים וגזל הגר. In the second group — ארבע בירושלים — עורות קדשי קדשים are included also, even though their use is not limited to ירושלים, because only those who can participate in the division of the flesh participate in the division of the skins, as the רשב״א states (*Bava Kamma* 110b): אין נותנין אלא לכהנים הראוין לחלוק בבשר והכהנים האוכלים בבשר עומדין בירושלים [משום הכי] קרי להו מתנות ירושלים.

In an introduction, the תוספתא says as follows: עשרים וארבע מתנות כהונה הן וכולן ניתנו לאהרן ולבניו בכלל ופרט וברית מלח, כל המקיימן כאילו קיים בכלל ופרט וברית מלח וכל העובר עליהן כאילו עובר על בכלל ופרט וברית מלח. That is to say, the מתנות כהונה are written in an order of כלל ופרט, which is the usual order of all the *mitzvos*, and they were given as a ברית מלח, as a covenant of absoluteness and immutability. He who fulfills them merits to fulfill everything that was given בכלל ופרט, as an absolute and eternal covenant, and the opposite applies to one who violates them.

A cursory glance at these groups of מתנות כהונה suffices for us to see that through them the כהן's activity is brought into contact with all aspects of the people's life in all of its diverse manifestations. Each one of them assigns the כהן and his household with a task: to lead a model life in all the diversity of life's conditions. In addition, the כהן is admonished to totally devote himself to his people. He is charged with elevating them to the lofty heights of the Torah's moral ideal, the ideal he is to exemplify through his life and the lives of the members of his household. Thus the Torah will be realized בכלל ובפרט as a ברית

20 God *furthermore said to Aharon: You will receive no inheritance in their land, nor will you have any portion among them. I [Myself] am your portion and your inheritance in the midst of the Children of Israel.*

כ וַיֹּאמֶר יְהוָה אֶל־אַהֲרֹן בְּאַרְצָם
לֹא תִנְחָל וְחֵלֶק לֹא־יִהְיֶה לְךָ
בְּתוֹכָם אֲנִי חֶלְקְךָ וְנַחֲלָתְךָ בְּתוֹךְ
בְּנֵי יִשְׂרָאֵל: ס שביעי

מלח עולם — in all circumstances, irrespective of the condition of the times.

20 **ויאמר ה׳ וגו׳**. This is almost a self-understood result of all the preceding, and it is merely an explanatory addition. Hence it says ויאמר and not וידבר, which introduces a new command (cf. Commentary above, v. 1).

נחלה is property that flows like a stream from generation to generation: from ancestors to descendants and from them to their descendants. נחול means: to inherit property from one's parents in order to bequeath it to one's children (cf. Commentary, *Shemos* 15:17).

Here, נחלה is the land which has already been promised to the forefathers and which is considered their property on the strength of that promise. חלק בתוכם is the individual's share in the national prosperity, which increases as a result of cultivation of the land and other favorable opportunities. The priestly tribe has no direct right in either of these. It is not their mission to possess the Land and bequeath it; it is not their task to increase the national prosperity by working the land and increasing its produce. Rather,

אני חלקך ונחלתך וגו׳. They are to relate to *God* all the material elements of the people's lives; this is their office and task in the nation. The flourishing of this relationship in understanding and in practice is their חלק, their share in the nation's achievements, and handing down these spiritual achievements from the parents to the children is their נחלה, their spiritual heritage. Both together — the חלק and the נחלה — are the basis of their existence and of their material prosperity. In the second half of the verse, חלק comes first, because אני חלקך embodies the spiritual harvest of the work of every generation of כהנים.

In the *Sifre*, חלק [in the first half of the verse] is interpreted in the

21 *But to the sons of Levi, lo! I have given all the tithes in Israel as an inheritance, as a compensation for their service which they perform in the service of the Tent of Appointed Meeting,*

כא וְלִבְנֵי לֵוִי הִנֵּה נָתַתִּי כָּל־מַעֲשֵׂר בְּיִשְׂרָאֵל לְנַחֲלָה חֵלֶף עֲבֹדָתָם אֲשֶׁר־הֵם עֹבְדִים אֶת־עֲבֹדַת אֹהֶל מוֹעֵד׃

sense of a portion in the spoils of war. In our view, this is only an example of the totality of the nation's achievements — apart from taking possession of the Land.

21 **ולבני לוי וגו'**. כל מעשר: only the tithe from the produce of the soil, and according to most commentators — as stated in our Commentary on verse 8 — only from דגן תירוש ויצהר, which is also the assumption of verses 27 and 30. Although the *Levi'im* do not have a direct share in the Land, they have a fixed share of the Land's main produce. This share is given to them as a נחלה.

Scripture clearly distinguishes between this מעשר of the לויים and the preceding מתנות כהונה. מעשר is considered שכר ,חלף עבדתם (v. 31), "wages" for their service in the Sanctuary. The nation owes them these wages for their service, because this service originally devolved upon the people, and the *Levi'im* now serve in their stead. By contrast, the מתנות כהונה are not wages for עבודת הכהנים. Rather, God transferred to them holy things dedicated to Him and to His Sanctuary, for He appointed them as representatives and servants in His Sanctuary. Moreover, eating the מתנות במקדש is itself part of the עבודה: הכהנים אוכלים ובעלים מתכפרים (*Pesachim* 59b). For most of the מתנות כהונה are קודש, and of most of them it can be said: כהנים משולחן גבוה קא זכו (*Chullin* 120a). תרומה — the most widespread among the מתנות כהונה — cannot be considered שכר, for it is essentially only a symbolic gift, and therefore חטה אחת פוטרת את הכרי. We have already noted this several times (see Commentary above, v. 12).

Hence, there is a clear distinction between אני חלקך ונחלתך and ולבני לוי הנה נתתי כל מעשר בישראל לנחלה וגו'. Thus also in the *Sifre*: כל מצות כהונה קנאו ה' ונתנו לכהנים וזו חלף עבודתם. Hence the כהנים are not merely שלוחי דידן, but, rather, שלוחי דשמיא (*Nedarim* 35b), שלוחי דרחמנא (*Kiddushin* 23b). Elsewhere (*Chorev*, chap. 118), we expressed our view that it was not only

22 *So that the Children of Israel shall no longer come near to the Tent of Appointed Meeting to incur a sin deserving of death.*	כב וְלֹא־יִקְרְבוּ עוֹד בְּנֵי יִשְׂרָאֵל אֶל־אֹהֶל מוֹעֵד לָשֵׂאת חֵטְא לָמוּת׃
23 *As for the Levi, he must perform the service of the Tent of Appointed Meeting, and they must bear their iniquity. [It is] an everlasting statute for your descendants, but they shall receive no inheritance in the midst of the Children of Israel.*	כג וְעָבַד הַלֵּוִי הוּא אֶת־עֲבֹדַת אֹהֶל מוֹעֵד וְהֵם יִשְׂאוּ עֲוֺנָם חֻקַּת עוֹלָם לְדֹרֹתֵיכֶם וּבְתוֹךְ בְּנֵי יִשְׂרָאֵל לֹא יִנְחֲלוּ נַחֲלָה׃

after the sin of the עגל that the עבודה במקדש was entrusted to the כהנים. It appears that this conception is confirmed here by the distinction between the position of the כהנים and that of the לויים.

22 **ולא יקרבו וגו'**. The *Levi'im* do the service of the Children of Israel in the Sanctuary, and thereby they also keep the people far from those עבודות that are prohibited to the זר under the penalty of מיתה בידי שמים (v. 7).

23 **ועבד הלוי וגו'**. A לוי receives compensation for the service he performs, but he cannot evade this service by waiving his compensation. He must perform it even if he receives no מעשר, which is always a possibility, since no לוי has a direct claim to any tithe, but, rather, the one obligated in מעשר is entitled to give it to any לוי he chooses: טובת הנאה לבעלים (Commentary above, 5:10). The לוי must perform his service even during שמיטה and יובל, when no מעשר is distributed anywhere, since all produce is הפקר and hence not subject to מעשר (*Sifre*). In short, his duty to serve is absolute, even though his right to מעשר is conditional.

והם ישאו עונם: their service entails grave responsibilities (v. 3).

ובתוך בני ישראל לא ינחלו נחלה. Although the מעשר is due them as compensation for services they must render to the community, nevertheless they must renounce all claims to inherit any part of the Land. Thus, the *Levi'im* do not attain a privileged position from a material standpoint. Rather, the tribe's livelihood depends on the nation's good-

24 *For the tithe of the Children of Israel which they lift up to* God *as an uplifted donation have I given to the* Levi'im *as an inheritance. For this reason I have declared concerning them that they shall have no inheritance in the midst of the Children of Israel.*	כד כִּ֞י אֶת־מַעְשַׂ֣ר בְּנֵֽי־יִשְׂרָאֵ֗ל אֲשֶׁ֨ר יָרִ֤ימוּ לַֽיהוָה֙ תְּרוּמָ֔ה נָתַ֥תִּי לַלְוִיִּ֖ם לְנַחֲלָ֑ה עַל־כֵּן֙ אָמַ֣רְתִּי לָהֶ֔ם בְּת֙וֹךְ֙ בְּנֵ֣י יִשְׂרָאֵ֔ל לֹ֥א יִנְחֲל֖וּ נַחֲלָֽה׃ פ

will. Hence, the Torah repeatedly exhorts us to look after the *Levi'im*'s welfare (*Devarim* 12:12, 18-19), and in this regard they are mentioned together with the גר יתום ואלמנה (ibid. 26:11-13).

24 **כי את מעשר וגו׳**. One may not partake of the produce of one's own land unless one has separated מעשר for the upkeep of the tribe dedicated to the Service of the Sanctuary. In other words, before looking after one's own bodily subsistence, one must concern himself with maintaining the spirit of the Torah.

This מעשר given to the *Levi'im* is likewise designated here as תרומה לה׳, which is especially appropriate since all מעשר also includes תרומת מעשר; for it says in verse 26 that the לוי must separate מעשר from his מעשר and give it to the כהן. The לוי's מעשר is regarded as actual תרומה: קראו המקום תרומה עד שיוציא ממנו תרומת מעשר (*Sifre*). It appears, then, from the wording of Scripture that תרומת מעשר is given — indirectly — by the ישראל who is the first owner. As we shall see, this has halachic ramifications.

In *Menachos* 31a two opinions are discussed as to whether יש קנין לנכרי בארץ ישראל להפקיע מיד מעשר or אין קנין וכו׳; i.e., whether a non-Jew who acquires land in ארץ ישראל thereby removes the מעשר obligation from its produce. The majority opinion, accepted also by the רמב״ם (הל׳ תרומות, 1:10), is that אין קנין וכו׳; even produce grown on the property of a non-Jew is subject to the duty of מעשר. Even though our Sages derive (*Menachos* 67a) from מעשר דגנך (*Devarim* 12:17) that דיגון נכרי exempts the produce from tithes, that applies only if the produce is grown on a non-Jew's land and the final work on the produce is also done while it is in his possession, in which case מירוח נכרי פוטר. If, however, the produce comes into Jewish possession before the final process and is subjected to מירוח while in Jewish possession, it is subject to מעשרות.

In *Bechoros* 11b our Sages derive from the wording of verses 26 and 28 — כי תקחו מאת בני ישראל וגו׳ והרמתם וגו׳ ונתתם וגו׳ — that the mitzvah of מעשר and תרומת מעשר applies fully only to produce grown on land owned by Jews. If, however, the produce is grown ברשות נכרי and comes into Jewish possession before מירוח, the מירוח ברשות ישראל only turns the produce into טבל and makes it subject to תרומות ומעשרות because אין קנין וכו׳, but the מעשר that is separated remains in the ישראל's possession, and even the תרומת מעשר which is אסורה לזרים is given to the כהן in exchange for payment. This law, however, does not apply to תרומה גדולה, which in the event of מירוח ברשות ישראל must be separated and given to the כהן. The foregoing follows the view of רבינו תם (תוספות ibid. ד״ה טבלים), which is also the view of the רמב״ם (הל׳ תרומות, 1:10). (See also our Commentary on v. 27.)

Related to this discussion is another halachah, which we will consider in detail in our Commentary on *Devarim* 14:22ff., which is the main chapter on מעשר. According to the רמב״ם (הל׳ מעשר, 2:1), the mitzvah of מעשר applies only to produce that is subjected to מירוח for the sake of the owner's consumption; but if produce is subjected to מירוח for trade purposes and is sold to others, it is exempt from מעשר both in the possession of the seller and in the possession of the buyer: לוקח פטור. (See also the view of ר״ת and ריב״ם, *Bava Metzia* 88a, תוספות there and in *Bechoros* 11b, *Menachos* 31a. The ראב״ד has a different view; see כסף משנה on רמב״ם הל׳ מעשר, 2:1-2.) God willing, we will treat these *halachos* in connection with other *halachos* (see Commentary, *Devarim* 14:22ff.). We mention them here because they help resolve a question that has been raised regarding the proportion of the tithe to the relatively small number of *Levi'im*.

It has been claimed that the tithe gives the *Levi'im* much more than what is needed for their livelihood. For according to the census reported above (3:39), the number of *Levi'im* is twenty thousand out of a general population of six hundred thousand. The *Levi'im*, then, constitute 1/30 of the population. Moreover, those twenty thousand were counted from the age of one month and upward, whereas the six hundred thousand members of Israel were counted from the age of twenty years and upward!

However, one need only compare the inequality in the numbers of the other tribes to see that we have no means of reckoning the influence of Divine providence; hence, it is impossible to predict what the size of a tribe or family will be at a given time; and, in our case, it is impossible

25 God *spoke to Moshe, saying:*	כה וַיְדַבֵּר יְהוָה אֶל־מֹשֶׁה לֵּאמֹר:
26 *But speak to the* Levi'im *and say to them: When you take from the Children of Israel the tithe which I have given to you from them as your inheritance, you shall lift from it as* God's *uplifted donation one tenth of the tithe.*	כו וְאֶל־הַלְוִיִּם תְּדַבֵּר וְאָמַרְתָּ אֲלֵהֶם כִּי־תִקְחוּ מֵאֵת בְּנֵי־יִשְׂרָאֵל אֶת־הַמַּעֲשֵׂר אֲשֶׁר נָתַתִּי לָכֶם מֵאִתָּם בְּנַחֲלַתְכֶם וַהֲרֵמֹתֶם מִמֶּנּוּ תְּרוּמַת יְהוָה מַעֲשֵׂר מִן־הַמַּעֲשֵׂר:

to predict what the number of לויים or כהנים will be in the coming decades or centuries.

Additionally, let us bear in mind what we have already noted: According to most halachic authorities, only grain, wine, and oil are subject to מעשר. Thus, only part of the Land's produce is subject to tithing. Add to this what is stated above: Only produce whose final work has been completed for the owner's consumption is subject to מעשר. This excludes produce whose final work has been completed for trade purposes. Thus, even in the case of grain, wine, and oil, only the lesser part of the produce becomes subject to מעשר.

In any case, one cannot say that the tithe gives the *Levi'im* more than what is needed for their livelihood, for, as already mentioned above, the Torah finds it necessary to exhort Israel to support the *Levi'im* with generosity.

26 **בנחלתכם**: [בנחלתכם does not mean "in your נחלה " but] in the character of your נחלה, as your נחלה, similar to בקדש הקדשים in verse 10, above. In *Rosh Hashanah* 12b our Sages derive from the term "נחלה" that מעשר ראשון אין לו הפסק: We do not cease giving מעשר ראשון in any year, whereas מעשר שני is interrupted in the third and sixth years, in which it is replaced by מעשר עני (see Commentary, *Devarim* 14:22).

והרמתם ממנו תרומת ה' מעשר מן המעשר. In verse 29 it says: מכל מתנתיכם תרימו את כל תרומת ה', from which our Sages derive (*Beitzah* 13b) that if a לוי receives his מעשר from grain that became subject to תרומה, but the owner neglected to first give תרומה גדולה to a כהן and thus violated what is stated in *Shemos* 22:28, the לוי is obligated to separate from his tithe את כל תרומת ה'; he must give the כהן not only תרומת מעשר but also תרומה גדולה.

27 *And your uplifted donation shall be regarded by you like the grain from the threshing floor and the fullness of the wine press.*

כז וְנֶחְשַׁב לָכֶם תְּרוּמַתְכֶם כַּדָּגָן מִן־הַגֹּרֶן וְכַמְלֵאָה מִן־הַיָּקֶב׃

This case is called "הקדימו בכרי": the לוי preceded the כהן in receiving his share of grain that had already become subject to תרומה. It is different if הקדימו בשבלין — i.e., if the לוי receives מעשר from produce that has not reached the final process of grain preparation and thus has not yet become subject to תרומה. In such a case, he gives the כהן only תרומת מעשר but not תרומה גדולה. As it says in our verse (v. 26): והרמתם ממנו תרומת ה׳ מעשר מן המעשר, מעשר מן המעשר אמרתי לך ולא תרומה גדולה ותרומת מעשר מן המעשר (see תוספות *Shabbos* 127b ד״ה האי אידגן).

27 **ונחשב לכם תרומתכם וגו׳**: cf. נכריות נחשבנו לו (*Bereshis* 31:15). תרומתכם refers to תרומת מעשר; כדגן מן הגרן וגו׳ refers to תרומה גדולה which the ישראל separates from the threshing floor and the wine press; and Scripture here equates תרומת מעשר with תרומה גדולה (רש״י *Gittin* 31a and everywhere else this verse is cited).

Now since it does not say והיתה לכם תרומתכם but ונחשב לכם תרומתכם, the implication is that the designation of both תרומות is in the realm of מחשבה; both תרומת מעשר and תרומה גדולה are ניטלת במחשבה: Without saying or doing anything, but in thought alone, one can designate produce as תרומה or תרומת מעשר, and the result is that that produce is regarded as though it had actually been separated, and the rest of the produce is no longer טבל: נותן עיניו בצד זה ואוכל בצד זה (*Shabbos* 142a). In this respect, תרומה and תרומת מעשר differ essentially from מעשר and are similar only to קדשים (see Commentary, *Shemos* 35:5), whose sanctity likewise takes effect through thought alone (see *Menachos* 54b, 55a; רש״י and תוספות there; תוספות *Shevuos* 26b ד״ה משום).

We have already explained (above, v. 24) Scripture's wording כי את מעשר בני ישראל אשר ירימו לה׳ תרומה: תרומת מעשר is given to the כהן by the לוי, but indirectly it is given by the ישראל who gives the מעשר as obligated. In fact, as soon as the ישראל separates the מעשר, it becomes טבל containing תרומת מעשר. It is טבול לתרומת מעשר. Accordingly, our Sages say (*Gittin* 31a) that since Scripture here equates תרומת מעשר with תרומה גדולה, they are

28 *Thus you, too, shall lift out an uplifted donation from all of your tithes which you receive from the Children of Israel, and you shall then give* God's *uplifted donation to Aharon the priest.*	כח כֵּן תָּרִימוּ גַם־אַתֶּם תְּרוּמַת יְהֹוָה מִכֹּל מַעְשְׂרֹתֵיכֶם אֲשֶׁר תִּקְחוּ מֵאֵת בְּנֵי יִשְׂרָאֵל וּנְתַתֶּם מִמֶּנּוּ אֶת־תְּרוּמַת יְהֹוָה לְאַהֲרֹן הַכֹּהֵן׃

equated also as regards the donor: וכשם שיש לו רשות לבעל הבית לתרום תרומה גדולה, כך יש לו רשות לבעל הבית לתרום תרומת מעשר (see Commentary, v. 28).

However, although תרומת מעשר resembles תרומה גדולה in that it is אסורה לזרים וחייבים עליה מיתה וחומש, there are several differences between them: תרומה גדולה ניטלת באומד and has no prescribed measure מן התורה. Furthermore, אין תורמין אלא מן המוקף (*Challah* 1:9): the produce from which the תרומה is separated and other produce for which it is separated must be adjacent to each other. By contrast, תרומת מעשר must be an exact tenth, but may be separated שלא מן המוקף (*Beitzah* 13b; *Terumos* 4:6; *Bikkurim* 2:5; see תוספות *Gittin* 30b ד"ה וכי).

Our Sages draw a further inference from the term "תרומתכם": The תרומה that the לוי is obligated to give and which he is forbidden to eat is still called here "his," and from this we learn (*Pesachim* 23a) that תרומה is מותר בהנאה to a זר [in the case of הנאה שאינה של כילוי — see Commentary above, v. 8].

28 **כן תרימו גם אתם**. In *Kiddushin* 41b our Sages derive from the expression גם אתם that שלוחו של אדם כמותו, one person can authorize another to act on his behalf [see Commentary, *Shemos* 21:37]. The essence of the law of שליחות (agency) is established as a general rule in *Shemos* 12:5-6 (see Commentary there) and in *Devarim* 24:1-2 (see Commentary there). Here, the nature of the agent is defined: מה אתם בני ברית אף שלוחכם בני ברית — one person cannot become the agent of another unless they are alike from a national-religious standpoint. Hence אין שליחות לנכרי — a ישראל and a נכרי cannot become agents for one another (see ש"ך חושן משפט סי' רמג ס"ק ה). "גם" is taken as an extension of the concept "אתם": One can separate תרומה by means of someone who is "גם אתם" — namely, one's agent, who *also* may be regarded as "you" and who represents you for this act.

Let us recall what we stated in our Commentary on verses 24 and 27:

29 *From all that is given you, you shall lift out* God's *every uplifted donation, of all the best of it, that part of it which is to be sanctified.*

כט מִכֹּל֙ מַתְּנֹ֣תֵיכֶ֔ם תָּרִ֕ימוּ אֵ֖ת כָּל־תְּרוּמַ֣ת יְהוָ֑ה מִכָּל־חֶלְבּ֔וֹ אֶת־מִקְדְּשׁ֖וֹ מִמֶּֽנּוּ׃ מפטיר

תרומת מעשר is given indirectly by the ישראל; moreover, the ישראל may himself separate תרומת מעשר for the כהן. Accordingly, the לוי himself is basically only a שליח. It is the nation which — through the agency of the לוי — gives the מעשר מן המעשר to the כהן.

The foregoing provides us with an even deeper explanation of the law of שליחות that is derived from here. גם אתם means: Just as the ישראל appoints you to be his שליח to the כהן, you, too, can appoint someone else to perform this act on your behalf.

לאהרן הכהן. The כהנים who are entitled to receive תרומה are called here "אהרן הכהן." From this we learn (*Sanhedrin* 90b) that a כהן is unworthy of תרומה if his spiritual and moral character is inappropriate for his ancestry: לאהרן כאהרן, מה אהרן חבר אף בניו חברים, מכאן אמרו שאין נותנין מתנה לכהן עם הארץ. Similarly, *Divrei Ha-Yamim* II, 31:4 is expounded (ibid.) as follows: וַיֹּאמֶר לָעָם לְיוֹשְׁבֵי יְרוּשָׁלַם לָתֵת מְנָת הַכֹּהֲנִים וְהַלְוִיִּם, לְמַעַן יֶחֶזְקוּ בְּתוֹרַת ה׳ – כל המחזיק בתורת ה׳ יש לו מנת ושאינו מחזיק בתורת ה׳ אין לו מנת.

29 **מכל מתנתיכם** — see our Commentary on verse 24.

מכל חלבו: it is a duty to give the תרומה from the best of the produce; אין תורמין מן הרעה על היפה (*Temurah* 5a).

את מקדשו ממנו. To this expression our Sages attach a דרבנן law that תרומה עולה באחד ומאה (*Orlah* 2:1): If תרומה is mixed into חולין, and the mixture is of like kinds, מין במינו, the תרומה is בטלה if the mixture is one part of תרומה against a hundred parts of חולין. For תרומת מעשר is one out of a hundred, and this one which was separated out of a hundred is called here "מקדשו"; and if it is mixed again with the other ninety-nine, they all become קודש and are אסורים לזרים. But if the תרומה is mixed into a hundred parts of חולין, the תרומה is nullified. A mixture of תרומה and חולין in which the תרומה is not nullified is called "דמוע" (see Commentary, *Vayikra* 7:19); the act of mixing, along with its effect, is called "מְדַמֵּעַ" (*Orlah* 2:4).

30 *And furthermore say to them: When you lift out its best part from it, this is to be regarded as the property of the* Levi'im *like the produce of the threshing floor and the produce of the wine press.*	ל וְאָמַרְתָּ אֲלֵהֶם בַּהֲרִימְכֶם אֶת־חֶלְבּוֹ מִמֶּנּוּ וְנֶחְשַׁב לַלְוִיִּם כִּתְבוּאַת גֹּרֶן וְכִתְבוּאַת יָקֶב׃
31 *You may eat it at any place, you and your household; for it is your wages, a compensation for your service in the Tent of Appointed Meeting.*	לא וַאֲכַלְתֶּם אֹתוֹ בְּכָל־מָקוֹם אַתֶּם וּבֵיתְכֶם כִּי־שָׂכָר הוּא לָכֶם חֵלֶף עֲבֹדַתְכֶם בְּאֹהֶל מוֹעֵד׃
32 *Do not incur sin concerning it when you lift out its best part from it, and do not desecrate the holy things of the Children of Israel, so that you do not die.*	לב וְלֹא־תִשְׂאוּ עָלָיו חֵטְא בַּהֲרִימְכֶם אֶת־חֶלְבּוֹ מִמֶּנּוּ וְאֶת־קָדְשֵׁי בְנֵי־יִשְׂרָאֵל לֹא תְחַלְּלוּ וְלֹא תָמוּתוּ׃ פפפ

30 **ונחשב ללוים**. It does not say ונחשב לכם [as in v. 27]; thus ללוים is to be understood as an independent thought: מעשר ראשון shall be regarded as Levite property. מעשר ראשון has no further קדושה; it is like תבואת גרן וגו׳ after תרומות ומעשרות have been separated from it (*Sifre*; see Commentary, *Vayikra* 22:15). כתבואת גרן וגו׳ is the produce that remains in the גורן and יקב, as opposed to כדגן מן הגרן וגו׳ (v. 27), which is the תרומה that was taken therefrom. Hence:

31 **ואכלתם אתו בכל מקום וגו׳**: אפילו בקבר (*Sifre*), whereas תרומה may be eaten only בטהרה (*Vayikra* 22). Our Sages also learn from here דלא בעי חומה, unlike מעשר שני which may be eaten only in Yerushalayim (*Yevamos* 86b).

אתם וביתכם. Just as the מעשר is given to you, so it is given to your wives, and they, too, may separate from it תרומת מעשר or appoint an agent for this purpose: לימד על נשואה בת ישראל שנותנת רשות לתרום (ibid. 86a).

32 **ולא תשאו וגו׳ בהרימכם את חלבו ממנו**. It has already been indicated several times (vv. 12 and 30) that it is a duty לתרום מן היפה, to lift out the best, a

19 1 God *spoke to Moshe and Aharon, saying:*

2 *This is a basic statute of the Teach-*

יט א וַיְדַבֵּר יְהֹוָה אֶל־מֹשֶׁה וְאֶל־אַהֲרֹן
לֵאמֹר׃
ב זֹאת חֻקַּת הַתּוֹרָה אֲשֶׁר־צִוָּה

duty derived from the term "חלבו." Here it says that if one violated this duty ותרם מן הרעה על היפה, he is נושא חטא. From this our Sages derive (*Temurah* 5a) that התורם מן הרעה על היפה תרומתו תרומה — that if one violates this duty, his act is nevertheless valid — for אם אינו קדוש נשיאת חטא למה: Were it the case that the תרומה does not take effect and the whole heap remains טבל as before, it would be possible to rectify the transgression immediately by taking תרומה מן היפה; moreover, it would be obligatory to rectify the transgression so that the produce should not remain טבל.

ואת קדשי בני ישראל לא תחללו וגו׳. The distribution of the תרומות and מעשרות is entirely dependent on the goodwill of the owners. The כהן or לוי cannot claim these gifts directly; rather, those obligated to give them may give their gifts to any כהן or לוי they choose. Hence, the כהנים and לויים are likely to be tempted to curry favor with the owners, to do them favors and provide them with services in order to win their hearts, thereby degrading their office and the holy things. According to the Gemara in *Bechoros* 26b, our verse warns them against this: ת״ר הכהנים והלוים והעניים המסייעים בבית הרועים ובבית הגרנות ובבית המטבחיים אין נותנין להם תרומה ומעשר בשכרן, ואם עושין כן חיללו ועליהן הכתוב אומר (מלאכי ב, ח) שחתם ברית הלוי, ואומר ואת קדשי בני ישראל לא תחללו ולא תמותו.

For more on the mitzvah of תרומות ומעשרות, see our Commentary on *Vayikra* 22:9; for a summary of the mitzvah, see our Commentary on *Devarim* 14:22ff.

חקת

CHAPTER 19

1 **וידבר וגו׳** — see Commentary, *Vayikra* 11:1 and 13:1. This mode of address to Moshe and to Aharon indicates the great importance of the subject matter that follows, both for the understanding of the Law in theory and for the education of the people to observe the Law in practice.

2 **זאת חקת התורה**. This expression occurs in only one other place in Scripture: in *Bemidbar* 31:21, as the introduction to הכשר וטבילת כלי מדין. The

ing that God has commanded: Speak to the Children of Israel that they take for you a completely red cow on which there is no blemish and on which no yoke has ever come.

יְהֹוָה לֵאמֹר דַּבֵּר | אֶל־בְּנֵי יִשְׂרָאֵל וְיִקְחוּ אֵלֶיךָ פָרָה אֲדֻמָּה תְּמִימָה אֲשֶׁר אֵין־בָּהּ מוּם אֲשֶׁר לֹא־עָלָה עָלֶיהָ עֹל:

halachos stated there and the *halachos* of פרה אדומה stated here have this in common: The purpose of the law of כלי מדין is to qualify food vessels for טהרת גויות; the purpose of פרה אדומה is to qualify man for טהרת קדושות [see Commentary, *Vayikra* 11:4]. Both [sets of *halachos*] are fundamental to the entire Torah, and their laws are essential prerequisites for the observance of purity. If we had no means of restoring the כשרות of our vessels and the טהרה of our persons, it would be impossible for us to observe the Torah. Hence both are חוקות התורה, directives that are essential to the observance of the Torah.

Now, as we shall see and as can already be understood at first glance, פרה אדומה is a clear proclamation of the idea of טהרה, and טהרה is none other than moral freedom on which the entire Torah depends. Accordingly, we can understand all the more the reason for the categorical tone of the introductory words: זאת חקת התורה!

In *Menachos* 19a our Sages derive further from the term "חוקה" that every law stated here regarding פרה אדומה is essential for the validity of the whole procedure: כל מקום שנאמר חוקה אינו אלא לעכב.

ויקחו אליך: מתרומת הלשכה, from the national fund for offerings, which is replenished each year by the donation of מחצית השקל (*Shekalim* 4:2; see Commentary, *Shemos* 30:16).

פרה: בת שלוש, from the beginning of the third year and onward, after it is fit to bear offspring, as our Sages say: פחותה מבת ג׳ שנים מי קא ילדה (*Avodah Zarah* 24b).

פרה אדמה תמימה. The very next stipulation is אשר אין בה מום, which teaches us that a מום invalidates the פרה. From this we may infer that תמימה describes the redness: תמימה לאדמימות (*Sifre*). Even two black or white hairs invalidate the פרה (*Parah* 2:5).

אשר אין בה מום: Although the פרה אדומה is of קדשי בדק הבית and not of קדשי מזבח, it is invalidated by all the מומים and by all the other deficien-

3 *And you shall give it to Elazar the priest; he shall take it out, outside the camp, and he shall slaughter it before his countenance.*	ג וְנְתַתֶּם אֹתָהּ אֶל־אֶלְעָזָר הַכֹּהֵן וְהוֹצִיא אֹתָהּ אֶל־מִחוּץ לַמַּחֲנֶה וְשָׁחַט אֹתָהּ לְפָנָיו׃

cies that render an animal unfit for an offering: רובע ונרבע, מוקצה ונעבד, אתנן ומחיר and also יוצא דופן וטריפה (see Commentary, *Vayikra* 1:2); for פרה אדומה is called "חטאת" (v. 9) and is treated like a חטאת, even though it is of קדשי בדק הבית (see *Avodah Zarah* 23b; *Parah* 2:3).

אשר לא עלה עליה על׳. Had it said here אשר לא עלה עול עליה, only עול would invalidate the פרה. However, it says here אשר לא עלה עליה על׳: nothing that could be considered a yoke has been placed on the animal. Thus, not only an עול but also עבודה invalidates the פרה. From this we learn in *Sotah* 46a that the law of פרה is similar to that of עגלה ערופה (*Devarim* 21:3) of which it says: אשר לא עבד בה אשר לא משכה בעל׳ (see Commentary there); nevertheless, here, in the case of פרה, the law is defined precisely as follows: עול פוסל בין בשעת עבודה בין שלא בשעת עבודה, שאר עבודות אין פוסלות אלא בשעת עבודה. That is to say, putting an actual yoke on the cow invalidates it even if one has no intention of using it for work at this time; for a yoke is a sign of service. By contrast, any other use of the animal's power to work invalidates the cow only if one intends to use it for actual work. Accordingly, putting a yoke on the cow invalidates it even if one has no intention that the animal should pull the yoke now, whereas putting any other object on the cow invalidates it only if one intends that it should bear the burden.

3 **ונתתם** — apparently בני ישראל and משה, who are mentioned in the preceding verses.

אתה אל אלעזר. In *Yoma* 42b our Sages expound: אותה לאלעזר ולא לדורות לאלעזר, איכא דאמרי לדורות בכהן גדול ואיכא דאמרי לדורות בכהן הדיוט. The רמב״ם (הל׳ פרה, 1:11) adopts the latter view, that a כהן הדיוט may perform the procedure of the פרה. Nevertheless, as a rule it was the כהן גדול who would perform the procedure (see *Parah* 3:8).

The כהן who performs the procedure of the פרה must appear as a כהן — clothed in the priestly garments, and מחוסר בגדים invalidates the פרה, just as the פסול of מחוסר בגדים does at all the offerings (*Shemos* 28:43 and Commentary there).

The procedures of the פרה are performed בבגדי לבן like the עבודה of the יום הכיפורים on כהן גדול (*Parah* 4:1; see משנה למלך on הל׳ פרה, 1:12).

So, too, מעשי הפרה require קידוש ידים ורגלים כעין עבודה, only that the קידוש can be done also בחוץ and not בכלי שרת (*Zevachim* 20b).

What applies to the כהן גדול who serves on יום הכיפורים applies also to the כהן who performs the procedure of the פרה: שבעת ימים קודם לשריפת הפרה מפרישין כהן השורף את הפרה מביתו ללשכה שעל פני הבירה צפונה מזרחה (*Parah* 3:1). The chamber in which the כהן stays during the days of פרישה is in the northeast, to remind him of the two aspects of the procedures he is to perform. The פרה is called "חטאת" (v. 9); hence the לשכה is בצפון, for שחיטת קדשי קדשים is בצפון. In addition, the procedures of the פרה are performed outside the Sanctuary and even outside the city, and the כהן sees only the Sanctuary entrance, which is on the east side of the Sanctuary. Hence the לשכה is במזרח, signifying the gate that leads out of the Sanctuary. Likewise, the הזיות prescribed in verse 4 are directed toward the entrance to the Sanctuary. (See *Yoma* 2a; Commentary, *Vayikra* 8:34.)

והוציא אתה אל מחוץ למחנה: חוץ לשלש מחנות (*Yoma* 68a) — i.e., not only outside מחנה שכינה and מחנה לוייה, but also outside מחנה ישראל; correspondingly, in the case of the Temple: not only outside the מקדש and הר הבית, but also outside the wall of Yerushalayim (see Commentary above, 5:2-3; cf. Commentary, *Vayikra* 4:11-12). They would take the פרה out of Yerushalayim to הר המשחה, which lies to the east outside the city (*Parah* 3:6).

והוציא אותה – לבדה (ibid. 3:7): No other פרה אדומה may be taken out with it, nor may any other animal be taken out with it (ibid. and *Yoma* 43a). So, too, ושחט אותה – ולא אותה וחברתה (*Chullin* 32a): No other פרה אדומה may be slaughtered with it; and even if a בהמת חולין is slaughtered with it, the פרה is invalidated.

ושחט אתה לפניו: The שחיטה may be done only by a כהן — שחיטת פרה בזר פסולה; it says here לפניו only to teach us that he must keep his whole mind concentrated on the פרה and its procedures: שלא יסיח דעתו ממנה (*Yoma* 42a).

This is the only שחיטה that is valid only if done by a כהן. At all the offerings, שחיטה כשרה בזר (ibid. 27a) and שחיטה לאו עבודה היא (ibid. 42a; see Commentary, *Vayikra* 1:5), and even שחיטת פר כהן גדול ביום הכיפורים כשרה בזר (*Yoma* 42a). Although פרה belongs only to קדשי בדק הבית, its שחיטה, as well as all the procedures performed with it until it is reduced to ashes, are valid only if performed by a כהן. In this respect, it is compared to מראות נגעים (ibid.; see *Vayikra* 13:2 and Commentary there).

Furthermore, מעשיה ביום: all the procedures performed with the פרה are valid only during daytime (*Parah* 4:4). According to one version in the *Sifre*, the burning is valid also at night, similar to שריפת אימורי חטאת בלילה. However, that is against the Gemara in *Yoma* 42b, for it says there that שחיטתה וקבלת דמה והזאת דמה ושריפתה והשלכת עץ ארז ואזוב ושני תולעת are valid only during daytime, just as הזאת מימיה is valid only during daytime, as the Torah explicitly says of הזאת מי פרה: ביום השלשי וגו׳ (v. 12). Only אסיפת אפרה ומילוי מים וקידוש are valid also if done at night (קידוש is placing the ashes in the water and mixing them therein).

In *Parah* 4:4 it says: כל העוסקין בפרה מתחילה ועד סוף וכו׳ ופוסלין אותה במלאכה. It says further there: המלאכה פוסלת בה עד שתעשה אפר. That is to say, from beginning to end, i.e., until it is reduced to ashes, none of those who are occupied with the פרה may do any other מלאכה while performing any of the procedures of the פרה, and the פרה is invalidated by any other מלאכה done together with the procedures of the פרה. In the *Sifre*, this halachah is derived from the words of our text as follows: ושחט אותה, בא הכתוב ולמד על הפרה שתהא מלאכה פוסלת בשחיטתה; ושרף את הפרה וגו׳, בא הכתוב ולימד על הפרה שתהא מלאכה פוסלת בשריפתה וכו׳ אלא בא הכתוב ולימד על הפרה שתהא מלאכה פוסלת בה משעת שחיטתה עד שתעשה אפר.

Now we have already mentioned the halachah — derived in *Yoma* 42a from the wording ושחט אתה לפניו, ושרף את הפרה לעיניו — that שלא יסיח דעתו ממנה; one who deals with the פרה must concentrate on the פרה and may not divert his attention from it. Our Sages (ibid. 42a-b) say היסח הדעת is פוסל even during אסיפת אפרה and מילוי מים לקידוש. This law is derived from למשמרת למי נדה (v. 9); the שמירה entails giving one's undivided attention to the פרה until it is turned into מי נדה — i.e., until the ashes are mixed into the water. Only השלכת עץ ארז ואזוב ושני תולעת is not invalidated by היסח הדעת, because this procedure is not done to the פרה itself: דלאו גופה דפרה נינהו (ibid. 42b).

It is not clear whether the פסול היסח הדעת and the פסול מלאכה are identical or whether they are two different halachic concepts. Since it would seem that another מלאכה cannot be done without היסח הדעת, it stands to reason that the two are one and the same concept, with מלאכה being only an attestation of היסח הדעת. What is called in *Yoma* "היסח הדעת" is called in the Mishnah in *Parah* 4:4 "מלאכה"; in fact, in the *Sifre* the פסול מלאכה, too, is derived from למשמרת וגו׳. On the other hand, it is striking that the Gemara in *Yoma*, which discusses היסח הדעת בפרה, does not mention the *Sifre*. What is more, according to the Gemara in *Yoma* היסח הדעת is פוסל

4 *And Elazar the priest shall take [some] of its blood with his finger and sprinkle [some of] its blood toward the front of the Tent of Appointed Meeting, seven times.*

ד וְלָקַח אֶלְעָזָר הַכֹּהֵן מִדָּמָהּ בְּאֶצְבָּעוֹ וְהִזָּה אֶל־נֹכַח פְּנֵי אֹהֶל־מוֹעֵד מִדָּמָהּ שֶׁבַע פְּעָמִים׃

even during אסיפה, yet according to the תוספתא (*Parah* 4:6) — and this is also the ruling of the רמב״ם (הל׳ פרה, 4:17) — מלאכה is not פוסל during אסיפה. Also, nowhere do we find that השלכת עץ ארז וכו׳ is not invalidated by מלאכה, as we find (in *Yoma)* that it is not invalidated by היסח הדעת.

Strikingly, the רמב״ם omits the law that היסח הדעת is not פוסל during השלכת עץ ארז וכו׳, and this omission is not remarked on by the commentaries. Nor do they — or the רמב״ם — mention the law stated in *Yoma* that היסח הדעת is פוסל בשעת אסיפה. וצ״ע. (On היסח הדעת and מלאכה, cf. ראב״ד and כסף משנה to הל׳ פרה, 7:3.)

From *Gittin* 53b it appears that מלאכה can be done without היסח הדעת, and from תוספות there (ד״ה דאסח) it appears that היסח הדעת is פוסל even without מלאכה. וצע״ע in the מאירי, quoted in the שיטה מקובצת on *Bava Kamma* 56a.

4 **ולקח וגו׳ מדמה באצבעו**: מצותה מצות יד ולא מצות כלי (*Sifre*). The blood is not received in a vessel; rather, the כהן receives the blood in his hand and then, with the forefinger of his right hand, he sprinkles some of it toward the entrance to the Sanctuary. The remainder of the blood, which according to verse 5 is burned with the cow, is received in a vessel (ראב״ד הל׳ פרה, 3:2; cf. לוג שמן של מצורע, *Vayikra* 14:15).

והזה וגו׳ מדמה שבע פעמים: על כל הזיה טבילה, before each sprinkling he dips his finger in the blood, and before each dipping he cleanses his finger of the remaining blood (*Parah* 3:9; *Zevachim* 93b; cf. *Vayikra* 4:6 and Commentary there).

אל נכח פני אהל מועד: כנגד פתח ההיכל; and הזה ולא כיון כנגד הפתח פסולה (*Parah* 4:2). The Halachah teaches (*Zevachim* 113a) that what applies to הזיה applies also to the preceding שחיטה and to the succeeding שריפה: it must be done facing the entrance to the Sanctuary, and פרה ששחטה (או שרפה) שלא כנגד הפתח — or, as it says in the Mishnah, שרפה חוץ מגתה — is פסולה. A גת is a cavity prepared for the burning of the פרה. This

5 *The cow shall thereafter be burned before his eyes; its skin, its flesh, its blood, along with its dung, shall be burned.*

ה וְשָׂרַף אֶת־הַפָּרָה לְעֵינָיו אֶת־עֹרָהּ וְאֶת־בְּשָׂרָהּ וְאֶת־דָּמָהּ עַל־פִּרְשָׁהּ יִשְׂרֹף׃

6 *And the priest shall take a piece of cedar wood and hyssop and scarlet wool, and he shall throw it into the burning of the cow.*

ו וְלָקַח הַכֹּהֵן עֵץ אֶרֶז וְאֵזוֹב וּשְׁנִי תוֹלָעַת וְהִשְׁלִיךְ אֶל־תּוֹךְ שְׂרֵפַת הַפָּרָה׃

cavity, which resembles a wine press, is dug on the Mount of Olives facing the front of the Sanctuary.

5 **ושרף את הפרה לעיניו** — see Commentary, verse 3. שרפה חוץ מגתה או בשתי גתות או ששרף שתים בגת אחת פסולה (*Parah* 4:2).

את ערה ואת בשרה וגו׳. It must be burned entirely, with all its parts. It is immaterial whether one first flays it and sections it and then burns the skin and all the parts together, or one burns it as it is without flaying or sectioning: הפשיטה ונתחה כשרה (ibid. 4:3).

6 **ולקח הכהן וגו׳**. Similarly, it says: וכבס בגדיו הכהן (v. 7). Scripture emphasizes and reemphasizes that the one who deals with the פרה is a כהן, to teach us that any כהן is fit for the procedure of the פרה, providing that he appears בכהונתו, that his כהונה is recognizable through בגדי כהונה (see *Yoma* 43a).

עץ ארז ואזוב וגו׳. The אזוב must be at least one טפח long (*Niddah* 26a).

ושני תולעת: ששינתו תולעת ולא ששינתו דבר אחר (*Sifre*) — i.e., wool whose color has been changed by תולעת and not by anything else. This interpretation may throw some light on the term "שני." שני stems from the root שנה and denotes a change of color, a change of such a nature that the new color remains permanent, like the original natural color. שני, then, denotes a color that does not fade.

שלשה (מינים) שבפרה וכו׳ מעכבין זה את זה (*Menachos* 27a); each one of these three things is absolutely indispensable.

כרכן בשיירי הלשון (*Parah* 3:11): He ties them together with the ends of the שני תולעת wool. Our Sages differ as to whether he ties them כדי שיהיו כולן באגודה אחת, that the three items be joined as one object, or כדי שיהא

7 *And the priest shall rinse his garments and bathe his flesh in water, and only thereafter may he come into the camp. However, the priest will remain impure until the evening.*

ז וְכִבֶּ֨ס בְּגָדָ֜יו הַכֹּהֵ֗ן וְרָחַ֤ץ בְּשָׂרוֹ֙ בַּמַּ֔יִם וְאַחַ֖ר יָבֹ֣א אֶל־הַֽמַּחֲנֶ֑ה וְטָמֵ֥א הַכֹּהֵ֖ן עַד־הָעָֽרֶב׃

בהן כובד ויפלו לתוך שריפת הפרה, that the tying gives them a certain weight that they can fall into the fire of the פרה (*Yoma* 41b). In any case, according to the תוספתא (*Parah* 4:7), even if they are thrown into the fire one after the other, this does not invalidate the procedure (רמב״ם הל׳ פרה, 3:2). It is possible that the תוספתא adopts the latter view.

אל תוך שרפת הפרה, while it is already שרופה and yet is still called "פרה" — i.e., משיצית האור ברובה, after the greater part of the cow has caught fire, before it has been reduced to ashes (*Sifre*).

7 **וכבס בגדיו הכהן וגו׳** — the כהן המשליך who is mentioned in the preceding verse, even though he did not deal with the פרה itself; and so it says in verse 8 regarding השורף אותה who performed the main procedure of the פרה: לימד על העוסקים בפרה מתחילה ועד סוף שיהיו טעונים תכבוסת ורחיצת גוף והערב שמש; all who take part in any of the procedures of the פרה, from the beginning to the end, are טמאים and require כבוס בגדים, טבילה, and הערב שמש (*Sifre*; *Parah* 4:4). Thus, also the שוחט and the מזה are טמאים.

The עוסקים בפרה become טמאים only if the procedures were performed validly; but once the פרה is invalidated, those who deal with it do not become טמאים: אירע בה פסול בשחיטתה אינה מטמאה בגדים, אירע בה בהזייתה כל העוסק בה לפני פסולה מטמאה בגדים, לאחר פסולה אינה מטמאה בגדים (*Parah* 4:4).

Only one who is occupied with the פרה and performs with it one of the procedures prescribed by the Torah — the שוחט, the מזה, the שורף, and also the אוסף (v. 10) — is rendered טמא, whereas the נוגע is not rendered טמא: פרה עצמה אינה מטמאה (*Parah* 8:3; cf. פרים הנשרפים, *Vayikra* 4:12).

The עוסק בפרה is טמא בחיבורין like the נושא נבלה: As long as he is occupied with the פרה, he is not just מטמא בגדים שעליו; rather, he is מטמא all כלים that are in contact with him — to the exclusion of אדם וכלי חרס. And these כלים

8 *Also the one who burns it shall rinse his garments in water and bathe his flesh in water, and will remain impure until the evening.*

ח וְהַשֹּׂרֵף אֹתָהּ יְכַבֵּס בְּגָדָיו בַּמַּיִם וְרָחַץ בְּשָׂרוֹ בַּמָּיִם וְטָמֵא עַד־הָעָרֶב׃

that are in contact with him while he is occupied with the פרה become ראשונים לטומאה — like himself (see Commentary, *Vayikra* 11:24-25 and at the end of that chapter; but see the רמב״ם's commentary on *Zavim* 5:10 and תוספות יום טוב there).

וכבס בגדיו — see Commentary, *Vayikra* 11:24-25.

וכבס בגדיו הכהן וגו׳. The unusual word order apparently indicates that he requires this טהרה only as a כהן, and therefore the following statement ואחר יבוא אל המחנה refers only to the special מחנה of the כהנים, to the מחנה שכינה, which begins with the עזרת כהנים (see Commentary above, 5:2-3). It is necessary for Scripture to tell us this. For the כהן is sent with the cow חוץ לשלוש מחנות (v. 3), outside the מחנה ישראל also. Hence, one might have thought that, like a מצורע, until he becomes טהור the כהן may not enter מחנה ישראל and must stay outside the city. It therefore says here וכבס בגדיו הכהן: he requires this טהרה only as a כהן, in order to eat תרומה and to enter the Sanctuary.

The foregoing would also explain the fact — already noted by רש״י — that Scripture here inverts the order and puts first what actually comes later, for it says ואחר יבוא אל המחנה in close connection with וכבס בגדיו הכהן, even though it ought to have been stated after וטמא הכהן עד הערב. With this order, Scripture indicates that the מחנה referred to is מחנה כהונה. The sentence וטמא הכהן עד הערב is merely a self-understood supplement to everything connected with the כהונה; i.e., since he is a כהן, the טומאה departs from him only after sunset: a טבול יום — who is after טבילה but before הערב שמש — is considered טהור only as regards מעשר שני, whereas אכילת תרומה and ביאת מקדש וקדשים always require הערב שמש. A מחוסר כפרה requires in addition הבאת קרבנותיו in order to be permitted אכילת קדשים and ביאת מקדש (see Commentary, *Vayikra* 7:19-21).

8 **והשרף וגו׳** — see Commentary, verse 7.

9 *A man who is pure shall then gather up the ashes of the cow and lay them down outside the camp in a pure place. It shall remain for the Children of Israel to be kept as a water of separation; it is an offering that clears of sin.*

ט וְאָסַף ׀ אִישׁ טָהוֹר אֵת אֵפֶר הַפָּרָה וְהִנִּיחַ מִחוּץ לַמַּחֲנֶה בְּמָקוֹם טָהוֹר וְהָיְתָה לַעֲדַת בְּנֵי־יִשְׂרָאֵל לְמִשְׁמֶרֶת לְמֵי נִדָּה חַטָּאת הִוא׃

9 **ואסף איש וגו׳**. איש להכשיר את הזר, טהור להכשיר את האשה, והניח מי שיש בו דעת להניח יצא חרש שוטה וקטן (*Yoma* 43a). For gathering up the ashes, a כהן is not required; any sane adult is qualified. So, too, the ashes may be gathered up also at night, and doing some other מלאכה at the same time does not invalidate the act: אין מלאכה פוסלת בה (תוספתא, *Parah* 4:6).

והניח מחוץ למחנה וגו׳. Here, too, מחוץ למחנה refers only to מחנה שכינה (see v. 7). None of the ash is brought into the עזרה. Rather, it is divided into three portions: חולקין אותו לג׳ חלקים, אחד נותן בחיל ואחד נותן בהר המשחה ואחד היה מחלק לכל המשמרות. The portion that is placed in the חיל — within the inner wall of the Temple Mount — is kept לעדת בני ישראל למשמרת; the other two portions are made available for טהרה purposes (*Parah* 3:11; see רמב״ם and תוספות יום טוב there).

במקום טהור. The place in which the אפר הפרה is stored must be absolutely טהור. Even if the אפר is in a כלי חרס אשר צמיד פתיל עליו (see v. 15), it is not protected from the טומאה contracted in אהל המת (*Parah* 11:1; ר״ש there).

למשמרת למי נדה. נדה — see Commentary, *Vayikra* 12:2. There, the term "נדה" denotes a condition that brings about a temporary separation, and that reaches its conclusion by a period of seven days and טבילה. Here, too, "נדה" denotes separation from all קודש, a separation caused by טומאת מת, which likewise reaches its conclusion by a period of seven days and טבילה, except that in this case the טבילה must be preceded by הזיה with מים חיים and אפר פרה, as will be explained in the following verses. This מים חיים mixed with אפר פרה is called "מי נדה."

The essence of the act of שמירה, here called "משמרת," is keeping one's mind on the object without diverting one's attention from it. Hence, our Sages in the *Sifre* derive from the expression "למשמרת למי נדה" that מלאכה פוסלת במים just as it invalidates the פרה עד שתיעשה אפר. As already stated,

10 *And the one who gathers the ashes of the cow shall rinse his garments and will remain impure until the evening. And this shall be for the Children of Israel and for the stranger who has entered into their midst as an everlasting statute.*	י וְכִבֶּס הָאֹסֵף אֶת־אֵפֶר הַפָּרָה אֶת־בְּגָדָיו וְטָמֵא עַד־הָעָרֶב וְהָיְתָה לִבְנֵי יִשְׂרָאֵל וְלַגֵּר הַגָּר בְּתוֹכָם לְחֻקַּת עוֹלָם׃

the gathering up of the ashes is not נפסל במלאכה; however, their conversion into מי נדה is a different matter. The mind may not be diverted by any other מלאכה during the whole process of converting the ashes into מי נדה, i.e., until the ashes have been strewn on the drawn water. Therefore, if one engages in מלאכה during the drawing of the water or while the water is being conveyed or while one pours the water from vessel to vessel or while one sprinkles the ashes onto the water, one invalidates the water. The duty of משמרת extends until the water becomes מי נדה. Once the ashes have been strewn on the water and it has become מי נדה, then, even at the הזיה, מלאכה is not פוסלת: המלאכה פוסלת במים עד שיטילו את האפר (*Parah* 4:4).

חטאת הִוא. It has the character of a חטאת. Hence מעילה, מועלין בה is applicable to it, as to all קדשים. According to תוספות (*Menachos* 51b ד״ה חטאת), it is regarded — in this respect — as though it has קדושת הגוף, and therefore מועל אחר מועל is possible with it (see Commentary, *Vayikra* 5:15). However, מעילה is applicable to פרה only so long as it is a פרה but not after it has become ash: בה מועלין באפרה אין מועלין (*Menachos* 51b). We learn further from here that פרת חטאת ששחטה שלא לשמה קיבל והיזה שלא לשמה וכו׳ פסולה (*Parah* 4:1), as in the case of חטאת (Commentary, *Vayikra* 4:24). Hence, according to one version in the *Sifre*, אין נשרפת בלילה. According to another version נשרפת בלילה like אימורי חטאת (see Commentary, v. 3). Nevertheless אינה נפסלת בלינה and therefore נשחטה היום והזה דמה כהלכתו ונשרפה למחר כשרה (רמב״ם הל׳ פרה, 4:13, based on the תוספתא, *Parah* 4:1).

10 **וכבס האסף וגו׳**. See Commentary, verse 7. Only the אוסף, the one who gathers up the ashes, is טמא, but once he finishes gathering up the ashes, anyone who then engages in dividing or distributing them, or who comes into contact with them in any other way, is טהור (רמב״ם הל׳ פרה, 5:4).

The פרשה of פרה אדומה divides into two parts: the preparation of אפר

11 *One who touches the corpse of any human soul becomes impure for seven days.*

יא הַנֹּגֵ֥עַ בְּמֵ֖ת לְכָל־נֶ֣פֶשׁ אָדָ֑ם וְטָמֵ֖א שִׁבְעַ֥ת יָמִֽים׃

12 *He shall purify himself with it on the third day and on the seventh day so that he may become pure. If he does not purify himself on the third day and on the seventh day, he will not become pure.*

יב הֽוּא יִתְחַטָּא־ב֞וֹ בַּיּ֧וֹם הַשְּׁלִישִׁ֛י וּבַיּ֥וֹם הַשְּׁבִיעִ֖י יִטְהָ֑ר וְאִם־לֹ֨א יִתְחַטָּ֜א בַּיּ֧וֹם הַשְּׁלִישִׁ֛י וּבַיּ֥וֹם הַשְּׁבִיעִ֖י לֹ֥א יִטְהָֽר׃

הפרה and its use for טהרת טמא מת. The discussion of the preparation of the ashes concludes with the words וכבס וגו׳, and the discussion of its use begins in the verses that follow.

Both parts conclude — here in verse 10 and below in verse 21 — with the pronouncement: והיתה לבני ישראל וגו׳ לחקת עולם, והיתה להם לחקת עולם. Similar pronouncements are found elsewhere only in the פרשה of יום הכיפורים (*Vayikra* 16:29 and 34) and in the פרשה of the חצוצרות to be sounded by the כהנים (above, 10:8). In these places the Torah proclaims that the principle of כפרה and the principle that all authority and all hopes for Israel's salvation are based on the Law are חקת עולם. Similarly, here, too, the concept of the mitzvah of פרה אדומה is a basic principle of Jewish life, to which the repetition of the pronouncement והיתה וגו׳ lends sanction for all time to come. In addition, it is a concept of which it must be expressly stated that it applies also to גרים (see below).

11 **הנגע במת וגו׳**. Scripture clearly distinguishes between מת and נפש אדם. The dead body is in relationship to נפש האדם, comes from it, belongs to it, but is not identical to the נפש (see Commentary, v. 13).

לכל נפש: להביא את בן שמונה (*Sifre*), even a human being that was never viable.

12 **הוא יתחטא בו ביום וגו׳**. From verse 19 it is clear that the הזיה is done on the third day and on the seventh day, and then, after the הזיה of the seventh day, the טהרה is completed by טבילה and הערב שמש. It must be, then, that וביום השביעי refers back to ביום השלישי, whereas יטהר is either a clause that states a result or a clause that states a purpose: "He shall purify himself

13 *One who, by [touching] a corpse,* יג כָּל־הַנֹּגֵעַ בְּמֵת בְּנֶפֶשׁ הָאָדָם

with it on the third day and on the seventh day, and then he can become pure" (by טבילה), or "so that he may become pure" (by טבילה).

For the חיטוי through הזאה is a special characteristic of טומאת מת, the like of which is found only in the case of מצורע (*Vayikra* 14:7-8), whose טבילה likewise must be preceded by הזאה, only that the הזאה there differs from the הזאה here. In the case of all other טומאות — including those that last seven days, such as זב וזבה נדה ויולדת — טבילה alone after the lapse of the prescribed period suffices. Here, however, הזיית שלישי ושביעי must precede the טבילה in order for the טבילה to effect טהרה.

Thus, the הזאה of the third day and the seventh day is a prerequisite for the טבילה, which is the usual act of טהרה. Hence the טבילה is called here simply טהרה: "יטהר" and "לא יטהר." The חיטוי with אפר הפרה is a prerequisite for the טבילה's effectiveness, but the חיטוי itself effects no change whatsoever in the state of טומאה. Even after the הזאה is performed and then repeated, the טומאה remains in effect. The הזיה, then, cannot be taken as an act of טהרה. Rather, the הזיה represents a certain aspect of the טהרה, and makes the one striving for טהרה aware of this aspect.

Accordingly, the הזיה's name is in harmony with the character of the פרה. The פרה is חטאת, its effect is that the person is מתחטא, and the act itself is called "חַטֵּא" (v. 19). So, too, the הזאה-act done to בית המנוגע is called "חַטֵּא" (*Vayikra* 14:51-52).

According to רבינו תם (תוספות *Yevamos* 46b ד"ה דאין), טבילה must precede הזאה on the third day and on the seventh day, but this טבילה is considered part of the הזאה and does not affect the טומאה.

The first הזאה can be done also after the third day, and in such a case the law is as follows according to רש"י (*Kiddushin* 62a) and תוספות (*Yoma* 8a ד"ה מקשינן): The day of the הזאה is regarded as though it were the third day; hence the second הזאה can be done only on the fourth day after it. Thus, there are always four days between the first הזאה and the second הזאה — no more and no less than the number of days between the third day and the normal seventh day. The רמב"ם (הל' פרה, 11:2) has a different approach.

13 **כל הנגע במת בנפש האדם אשר ימות**. The expression and the construction are chosen here with extreme precision in order to define the concept of

אֲשֶׁר־יָמוּת וְלֹא יִתְחַטָּא אֶת־
מִשְׁכַּן יְהוָה טִמֵּא וְנִכְרְתָה הַנֶּפֶשׁ
הַהִוא מִיִּשְׂרָאֵל כִּי מֵי נִדָּה לֹא־
זֹרַק עָלָיו טָמֵא יִהְיֶה עוֹד טֻמְאָתוֹ
בוֹ׃

comes into contact with the soul of man, who is destined to die, and does not purify himself, has defiled the Dwelling Place of God; *that soul will be uprooted from Israel. If the water of separation was not dashed upon him, he will remain impure; his impurity is still upon him.*

טומאת מת. Had it said כל הנוגע בנפש אדם אשר מת, the implication would have been that the corpse represents the נפש that died or the נפש of a dead person. However, נפש האדם and נפש האדם אשר ימות are to be distinguished from נפש אדם and נפש אדם אשר מת. נפש אדם is the soul of an individual person, and if this person dies, then his soul is נפש אדם אשר מת. By contrast, נפש האדם is the soul of man in general, the soul of man in his character as a human being. האדם אשר ימות is not a man who has died, but who is destined to die, man as mortal. Accordingly, נפש האדם אשר ימות is the soul of man who is destined to die, the soul of mortal man.

Every corpse represents נפש האדם אשר ימות, man over whom death prevails. Whoever beholds the lack of physical freedom which death demonstrates is likely to extend the lack of freedom to man's psychological nature also, for the psyche is connected with the body. As a result, he will deny man's freedom even in life. נפש האדם אשר ימות is living man who cannot escape the fate of death which hangs over him, and every corpse demonstrates this fate which prevails over man as absolute necessity. Every dead man represents man at the time of his death; dead man represents living man who submits to bitter death. Hence the נוגע במת, one who comes in contact with a corpse, is regarded — conceptually speaking — as נוגע בנפש אדם אשר ימות; and not with the נפש of a specific person, but with נפש האדם וגו׳, for death is the fate of every man.

Thus, בנפש האדם וגו׳ provides the reason for the law that applies to הנגע במת. He requires חיטוי not because he is נוגע במת, but because the נגיעה במת makes him mindful of נפש האדם אשר ימות. Accordingly, בנפש האדם אשר ימות explains במת. Alternatively, as we have translated it, the ב of במת is the medium, the mediating ב: through the corpse, he comes in contact with נפש האדם אשר ימות (cf. Commentary above, 6:6).

Therefore, not only a complete corpse, but — as is clear from verse 16 — any part thereof conveys טומאה, for the part represents the whole.

Our Sages (*Niddah* 55a) say as follows: כל שנברא עמו ואין גזעו מחליף, anything that is born with the person and, if lost, does not completely reproduce itself, is מטמא. This excludes teeth, which are not born with the person, and excludes hair and nails, which, although born with the person, replace themselves. Flesh, however, is מטמא. Even though it does grow again, נעשה מקומו צלקת, a visible scar remains (ibid.).

According to the foregoing, one would think that blood is not מטמא, for blood that is lost is replaced by the body. However, since the blood represents the נפש, the Halachah derives from the wording הנגע במת בנפש וגו׳ that רביעית דם הבאה מן המת מטמאה (*Chullin* 72a; see Commentary, *Vayikra* 21:11).

את משכן ה׳ טמא — even if he underwent טבילה, but did not undergo the הזיות prescribed here, and entered the משכן without them. In verse 20 it says: כי את מקדש ה׳ טמא. משכן is the dwelling place for God's Presence; מקדש is the place where everything earthly is consecrated and elevated to God (see Commentary, *Shemos* 25:8). These two verses, then, give expression to the concept of טומאה from two different standpoints. טומאה is the antithesis of the idea of God that comes to expression in the משכן, and it is the antithesis of the consecration of earthly existence and earthly will that come to expression in the מקדש.

A person is not punished with כרת because he neglects to undergo הזאה, but because he enters the Sanctuary without first undergoing הזאה. According to the *Sifre*, this is evident already from the preceding verse. For it does not say there ואם לא יתחטא וגו׳ ונכרתה but, rather, ואם לא יתחטא וגו׳ לא יטהר: עונשו לא יטהר ואין עונשו כרת. The words את משכן ה׳ טמא, then, conclude the introductory clause of our verse: Whoever comes in contact with a corpse and enters the משכן without חיטוי and thereby is מטמא God's Dwelling Place, ונכרתה וגו׳.

More likely, however, is that the words את משכן וגו׳ begin the concluding clause, and ביאת מקדש without הזיה is already contained in ולא יתחטא. For in the preceding verse it is already stated that without first undergoing הזיית שלישי ושביעי, the person does not become טהור through the טבילה (expressly prescribed in v. 19) on the seventh day. To this, verse 13 adds the case where a person behaves as though he has become טהור through טבילה alone without הזיה, and that can mean only that he comes in contact with מקדש and קדשים without preceding טבילה with הזיה; that he considers

14 *Now this is the teaching: If a person dies in a tent, then all that comes into the tent, and all that is in the tent, shall be impure for seven days.*

יד זֹאת הַתּוֹרָה אָדָם כִּי־יָמוּת בְּאֹהֶל כָּל־הַבָּא אֶל־הָאֹהֶל וְכָל־אֲשֶׁר בָּאֹהֶל יִטְמָא שִׁבְעַת יָמִים׃

himself טהור is revealed only through such contact. Thus, לא יתחטא already contains the whole consequence of ביאת מקדש and אכילת קדשים without הזיה. Hence, the words את משכן וגו׳ can be the opening of the concluding clause.

טמא יהיה עוד טמאתו בו: If he did not undergo הזאה, it is as though he did not undergo טבילה. The law that excludes the טמא from the מקדש and from קדשים has already been stated above, 5:2-3, and in *Vayikra* 22:2ff, 15:31, 5:3. Here Scripture only adds the halachah that, without הזאה, טמאי מת who require הזאה remain in a state of טומאה even after טבילה.

14 **זאת התורה וגו׳**. טומאת מגע במת has already been discussed in the previous verses. This method of contracting טומאה is common to all טומאות, whereas זאת התורה is, as the *Sifre* puts it, תורה חדשה, unique to טומאת מת and analogous only to what is found in the case of מצורע who likewise is מטמא בביאה (see Commentary, *Vayikra* 13:46). This תורה is טומאת אהל, and according to one view (*Yevamos* 61a) it applies only to מת ישראל, but the Halachah is not clearly decided on this point (see תוספות ibid. ד״ה ממגע and רמב״ם הל׳ אבל, 3:3). By contrast, טומאת מגע ומשא applies to any human corpse (*Yevamos* 61a). Perhaps this is already indicated by the phrase הנגע במת לכל נפש אדם (v. 11). Furthermore, on או בקבר (v. 18) our Sages expound: זה קבר שלפני הדיבור (*Nazir* 54a), from which we learn that קבר שלפני הדיבור is included in טומאת מגע, and תוספות there hold that טומאת אהל does not apply to קבר שלפני הדיבור — i.e., to someone who died before the Lawgiving, for it says here אדם כי ימות באהל: if a person dies in a tent from now onward. מורי ורבי המנוח מהור״ר יעקב עטלינגר ז״ל in ערוך לנר to *Yevamos* 61a holds that this is also the opinion of the רמב״ם. רש״י (*Nazir* ibid.) interprets קבר שלפני הדיבור in a different way (cf. Commentary, *Vayikra* 13:2).

כל הבא אל האהל: זה הבא מקצתו (*Sifre*). One becomes טמא immediately upon entering the tent; even if only one limb or member of the body enters the tent in which there is a corpse, the whole person becomes טמא:

15 *And every open vessel that does not have a cover bound to it shall be impure.*	טו וְכֹל֙ כְּלִ֣י פָת֔וּחַ אֲשֶׁ֥ר אֵין־צָמִ֥יד פָּתִ֖יל עָלָ֑יו טָמֵ֖א הֽוּא׃

(*Nazir* 43a, תוספות there ד״ה בבית). דאהל המת כמליא טומאה דמי ומיד שהושיט ידו מבפנים כאלו נגע במת With this explanation, the question of the משנה למלך in הל׳ טומאת צרעת (16:6) can be resolved. One becomes טמא not because ביאה במקצת שמה ביאה, but because it is considered as though one actually touches the מת.

וכל אשר באהל: not only what is under the same roof, but also what lies buried in the ground beneath the אהל. The concept "house" extends down to the depths beneath the house, לעשות קרקעו של בית עד התהום כמוהו (*Sifre*; *Ohalos* 15:5).

כל הבא אל האהל: דרך פתחו הוא מטמא ואין מטמא בכל צדדיו כשהוא פתוח (*Sifre*). As long as the house has a door for entry and exit, one becomes טמא only upon entering the interior space of the house, not by touching the outer walls. But בית סתום, if the doorway is completely walled in, and פרץ את פצימיו, the beams that heretofore served as the door frame are removed, then the house is considered a sealed tomb, and it is מטמא כל סביביו (*Bava Basra* 12a; see Commentary, v. 16).

The space of an אהל is no less than one cubic טפח, and the concept of the אהל extends to all the places that are connected to the אהל המת by an opening of at least a square טפח (*Ohalos* 13:1ff.; see Commentary, v. 16).

Furthermore, just as an אהל טפח conveys the טומאה to all the objects beneath it, it also protects all the objects above it against the טומאה. The אהל is both מביא and חוצץ (*Ohalos* 8:1).

15 **וכל כלי פתוח וגו׳**. We have already learned from וכל אשר באהל of the preceding verse that everything susceptible to טומאה — which would include כלים — becomes טמא in אהל המת. Here, however, the inference is that a vessel does not become טמא if it is closed with a tightly sealed lid. We are dealing here, then, with a vessel to which טומאה can be conveyed only through its open inner space, שטומאתו קודמת לפתחו (*Chullin* 25a): the טומאה, as it were, waits for an opening, for the vessel cannot be rendered טמא by contact with its outer surface. Thus, we are dealing here with a כלי חרס,

of which it has already been stated (*Vayikra* 11:33) that it is מיטמא מאוירו but is not מיטמא מגבו.

If a כלי חרס is closed with a tightly sealed lid, אשר צמיד פתיל עליו — and as a result the טומאה cannot reach its inner space — it remains טהור in אהל המת and protects its contents from טומאה: a כלי חרס is מציל באהל המת (see *Sifre*).

טמא הוא. Here it does not say שבעת ימים as it says in the preceding verse and the succeeding verse, because here it is speaking of a כלי חרס, שאין לו טהרה במקוה (see Commentary, *Vayikra* 11, end); hence טמא הוא absolutely: אין לו טהרה מטומאתו (*Sifre*).

צמיד פתיל. Both roots צמד and פתל denote joining. We find צמד in צמד בקר, a pair of oxen bound together; צמידים על ידיה (*Bereshis* 24:22), bracelets; ויצמד ישראל לבעל פעור (below, 25:3), denoting close attachment to the evil-doings of Pe'or. פתל is found in פתיל: several threads twisted into a thin cord.

We have already noted several times that the relation of פתל to בתל and בדל indicates that the primary meaning of פתל is not connection, but isolation resulting from connection. For different things that are joined together are thereby isolated from others. Hence we find וקצץ פתילים (*Shemos* 39:3), which speaks of a single metal wire that is strong and stiff even by itself.

Now, a cover can close a vessel so hermetically that its contents are isolated from everything outside, without the cover being actually joined to the vessel. In such a case, it is פתיל although not צמיד. If one then cements the points of contact between cover and vessel with some soft material which hardens when set, it is פתיל and also צמיד: the closing cover is actually joined to the vessel. Thus the Mishnah says: במה מקיפין? בסיד ובגפסיס בזפת וכו׳ בכל דבר המתמרח; אין מקיפין לא בבעץ ולא בעופרת מפני שהוא פתיל ואינו צמיד (*Kelim* 10:2). This, then, is the meaning of אשר אין צמיד פתיל עליו: that is not tightly closed by a cover that is joined to it. It is self-understood that this cover, too, must be of חרס or of some other material that is not susceptible to טומאה.

We have already stated that a כלי חרס מציל באהל המת because it (the vessel) is sealed and the טומאה cannot reach it, for it is not מקבל טומאה מגבו. Certainly, then, this is true of vessels that are not susceptible to טומאה at all, on account of the material out of which they are made or on account of their size — e.g., כלי גללים כלי אבנים וכו׳ and כלי עץ הגדולים הבאים במידה שאינם מיטלטלין מלא וריקן וכו׳ (see Commentary, *Vayikra* 11, end); they, too, מצילים בצמיד פתיל (see *Kelim* 10:1).

16 *And all that which, in the open field, comes into contact with one who was slain by the sword, or with a dead body, or with a human bone, or with a grave, shall be impure for seven days.*	טז וְכֹל אֲשֶׁר־יִגַּע עַל־פְּנֵי הַשָּׂדֶה בַּחֲלַל־חֶרֶב אוֹ בְמֵת אוֹ־בְעֶצֶם אָדָם אוֹ בְקָבֶר יִטְמָא שִׁבְעַת יָמִים׃

16 **וכל אשר יגע וגו׳**. טומאת מגע has already been discussed and summarized in verses 11-13, whereas זאת התורה — which is the טומאת אהל-teaching unique to מת — begins in verse 14 and continues in verse 15. According to the order of the verses, verse 16, too, is connected with this teaching. Indeed, in *Nazir* 53b our Sages expound: על פני השדה זה המאהיל על פני המת; similarly, in *Chullin* 72a they expound: וכל אשר יגע על פני השדה לרבות גולל ודופק [גולל ודופק are the top and sides of the coffin or the stones marking the grave — see תוספות *Kesubos* 4b ד״ה עד]. For the two previous verses deal with the usual way of contracting טומאת אהל: a person or object is together with a corpse under the same roof. This verse deals with a second kind of טומאת אהל: a person or object is מאהיל על המת. Corresponding to this second kind, there is a third kind of טומאת אהל: מת מאהיל עליו. The three kinds of אהל are similar to one another as regards conveying the טומאה (see *Ohalos* 3:1).

That the טומאת אהל discussed in our verse — the טומאה of מאהיל על המת — is called here נגיעה confirms a view stated by רבא (*Chullin* 125b). For the Gemara (ibid.) says as follows: There is a type of טומאת אהל that is included in the concept of טומאת מגע. Thus, there are two types of אהל: אהל נגיעה and אהל גרידא. And רבא explains: אהל נגיעה refers to anything that is מאהיל על המת. This is the kind of אהל that is discussed in our verse: forming a roof over a corpse is considered to be like coming in direct contact with it. By contrast, אהל גרידא, רבא continues, is בהמשכה, and רש״י explains: דבר אחר מאהיל עליו ועל הטומאה וכו׳ ממשיך את הטומאה עליו. That is the kind of אהל discussed in verses 14 and 15.

The practical difference whether a type of טומאת אהל is considered טומאת מגע lies in צירוף, for זה הכלל: כל שהוא משם אחד טמא, משני שמות טהור (*Ohalos* 3:1). From the whole give-and-take of the discussion there in *Chullin* it appears that the distinction made by רבא is the halachah. (See תוספות *Chullin* 126a ד״ה מאן; רשב״א there; רא״ש on *Ohalos* 3:1. It is striking that the רמב״ם in הל׳ טומאת מת, 4:14, does not adopt this distinction of רבא, and the ר״ש in his commentary on *Ohalos* does not mention it; וצ״ע.)

בחלל חרב. It does not say here simply בחלל, as it says in verse 18; rather, it says בחלל חרב. The Torah suggests the presence of both the body and the instrument that caused its death, for only by the presence of the חרב does one know that a body lying על פני השדה is a חלל חרב. And since the Torah here notes the presence of both, it teaches, according to the Halachah (*Nazir* 53b), that חרב הרי זה כחלל: the status of one who touches a חרב is the same as that of one who touches a חלל; or, in accordance with what was explained above, the status of one who is מאהיל over a חרב is the same as that of one who is מאהיל over a חלל.

However, the Halachah equates the טומאה of the חרב with that of the חלל not because the חרב was the death-causing instrument, but because it came in contact with the corpse. Indeed, not only חרב, but any כלי מתכות that touches a corpse becomes אבי אבות הטומאה like the מת itself, and if the כלי מתכות touches a טמא מת it becomes, like it, אב הטומאה.

Only כלי באדם, an implement that touches a person, receives the same degree of טומאה as that of the person it touches. The same does not apply, however, in the case of כלי בכלי, one implement touching another.

Every אבי אבות הטומאה and every אב הטומאה is טמא שבעה, and every ראשון לטומאה is טמא טומאת ערב (see vv. 11 and 22).

אדם וכלים — as already stated in our Commentary on *Vayikra* 11, end — are מקבל טומאה only מאב הטומאה.

These *halachos* form the foundation of the laws stated in *Ohalos* 1:1-4: שנים טמאים במת, אחד טמא טומאת שבעה ואחד טמא טומאת ערב; שלשה וכו׳; ארבעה טמאים במת, שלשה טמאין טומאת שבעה ואחד טמא טומאת ערב; כיצד שנים וכו׳; כיצד שלשה וכו׳; כיצד ארבעה? כלים נוגעים במת (הם נעשים אבי אבות הטומאה) ואדם בכלים (הוא נעשה אב הטומאה) וכלים באדם (אף הם נעשים אב הטומאה) טמאים טומאת שבעה, הרביעי בין אדם בין כלים טמא טומאת ערב.

In accordance with what is explained above, these laws apply only to כלי מתכות. This is the view of רבינו תם (תוספות *Nazir* 54b ד״ה ת״ש). However, according to רבי יצחק מסימפונט (in תוספות there) — and this is also the view of the רמב״ם in הל׳ טומאת מת, 5:3 — the law of חרב הרי הוא כחלל applies to all כלים, with the sole exception of כלי חרס, which never become אב הטומאה and certainly not אבי אבות הטומאה. According to this view, the laws stated in the Mishnah apply to all כלים except כלי חרס (ר״ש on *Ohalos* 1:2; see Commentary, *Vayikra* 11, end).

או במת או בעצם אדם. Not only a complete corpse is מטמאה באהל, but

17 *And they shall take for the impure person [some] of the ash-dust from the burning of the offering that clears of sin, and he shall place upon them living water in a vessel.*

יז וְלָקְחוּ֙ לַטָּמֵ֔א מֵעֲפַ֖ר שְׂרֵפַ֣ת הַֽחַטָּ֑את וְנָתַ֥ן עָלָ֛יו מַ֥יִם חַיִּ֖ים אֶל־כֶּֽלִי׃ שני

even כזית מן המת ,השדרה ,הגלגלת, etc. (*Ohalos* 2:1). For טומאת מגע ומשא even smaller parts are sufficient; even עצם כשעורה etc. (ibid. 2:3) are מטמא במגע ובמשא although they are not מטמא באהל.

או בקבר. In *Nazir* 53b our Sages expound: או בקבר זה קבר סתום. The law stated here regarding מאהיל על המת applies only to a tomb that is sealed on all sides and שיש בו פותח טפח (תוספות there) — i.e., there is empty space of at least one cubic טפח between the corpse and the earth that covers it. Only by virtue of this empty space is the earth surrounding the corpse considered a "tomb." If the tomb is סתום, sealed on all sides, it is מטמא כל צדדין as a קבר, and anyone who is מאהיל over it — even שלא כנגד המת — becomes טמא. If, however, the layer of earth is directly upon the corpse and there is no empty space of one טפח, then it is not the קבר that is מטמא but the מת. In such a case, there is טומאה רצוצה which is בוקעת ועולה בוקעת ויורדת: the טומאה penetrates upward and downward to an unlimited height and depth, unless it is checked by an אהל whose empty space contains [at least] one cubic טפח. One who passes over a tomb containing טומאה רצוצה becomes טמא only if he passes directly over the spot that covers the corpse. It is not the tomb that renders him טמא, but the מת, which, as טומאה רצוצה, is בוקעת ועולה. This is also the view of the רמב״ם in הל׳ טומאת מת, 7:4. The ראב״ד takes a different approach.

A field in which plowing discloses a hidden grave from which splinters of bone could be scattered about in the area is called "בית הפרס" — deriving from פרס (פרש), to scatter, to spread. (For more on this, see *Ohalos* 17:1ff.)

17 **ולקחו לטמא וגו׳**. ולקחו: any sane adult is qualified for this, and the same applies to אסיפת האפר, which is described in verse 9 (see *Yoma* 43a).

ולקחו . . . ונתן. The change from plural to singular indicates that these two actions need not be done by the same person (ibid.).

מעפר וגו׳. The primary denotation of עפר is the dust of the earth, but it also denotes the material produced by burning — viz., ash; thus in *Melachim* II, 23:4ff., and thus also in *Devarim* 9:21; cf. *Shemos* 32:20. It is reasonable to assume that the term is chosen here with special intention (see below).

ונתן עליו מים חיים אל כלי denotes a complex act. מים חיים אל כלי indicates that first the water should be poured into the vessel, and that when the water comes into the vessel, nothing else should be there yet. Then ונתן עליו: the ashes should be placed into the water, but one should not leave them floating on the surface of the water; rather, one should mix them with the water by stirring, so that the water now comes over them. כתיב עליו אלמא אפר ברישא, וכתיב מים חיים אל כלי אלמא מים ברישא, הא כיצד? וכו׳ אל כלי דוקא – עליו לערבן (*Sotah* 16b). Putting the ash in the water and mixing it in the water is called "קידוש," and the water in which the ash is mixed is called "מי חטאת." אין מי חטאת נעשין מי חטאת אלא עם מתן האפר (*Temurah* 12a).

The water designated for מי חטאת must be received in a vessel. However, any vessel that has a כלי-character may be used: בכל הכלים מקדשים אפילו בכלי גללים וכו׳ אין ממלאין ואין מקדשין ואין מזין מי חטאת אלא בכלי (*Parah* 5:5). The water must be received in the vessel directly from a spring (ibid. 6:5). All water from springs that only rarely dry up is called "מים חיים," provided that it has not undergone any chemical change (מוכים) — i.e., not מלוחים and not פושרים (ibid. 8:9). Flowing water that comes from a distant source is valid, provided that there is no interruption to the flow (ibid. 8:11).

We have already mentioned above, in explaining the phrase "למשמרת למי נדה" (v. 9), that מלאכה פוסלת from the moment the water is drawn until the קידוש — i.e., until the ashes are mixed in the water. After the קידוש — even during the הזיה — מלאכה and היסח הדעת are not פוסלים.

The רמב״ם and the ראב״ד (הל׳ פרה, 10:2 and 4) differ in their interpretations of פסול מלאכה and היסח הדעת; see כסף משנה there (see Commentary, below and v. 3, above).

In *Bechoros* 29a it is taught that just as הנוטל שכרו לדון דיניו בטילין and הנוטל שכרו להעיד עדותיו בטילין, so also הנוטל שכרו להזות ולקדש, מימיו מי מערה אפרו אפר מקלה. The acts of קידוש and הזיה are invalid if one takes payment for them. On the other hand, one may take payment for הבאה ומילוי, bringing the ashes and filling the vessel with water. רש״י there and in *Kiddushin* 58b explains that the הבאה and the מילוי entail work that does not devolve upon him as an obligation and for which he may take compensation, whereas קידוש and הזאה are purely mitzvah acts — or as רש״י puts it in *Kiddushin*: שכר לימוד מצוה הוא נוטל, [being paid for the act of קידוש or הזאה,

which does not entail work, is payment for the knowledge of the Law] for which compensation may not be made, according to the dictum: ראה למדתי אתכם וגו' מה אני בחנם אף אתם בחנם (כתובות כט.).

What remains to be explained, however, is why הזיה and קידוש are invalidated if payment is taken for doing them, whereas שחיטה, טבילת כלי, קביעת מזוזה בבית, הטלת ציצית בבגד, כתיבת סת"ם, and the like are valid even if payment is taken for them (see תוספות *Kesubos* 105a ד"ה גוזרי).

Perhaps קידוש והזיה — more than other *mitzvos* — come under the concept of *teaching*, regarding which the principle מה אני בחנם וכו' was primarily stated, and perhaps this is indicated by the wording of the introduction זאת התורה (v. 14).

וצ"ע בצאן קדשים לבכורות כט. דמשמע דס"ל דהזיה וקידוש רמיא רחמנא על האי כהן דשייך בעבודה משום הכי אסור ליקח אפילו אגר בטלה דמוכח עכ"ל וצ"ע מאי קאמר. ועי' בריטב"א קידושין נח: דסבירא ליה דהא דדיניו בטלין קנסא דרבנן הוא וסבירא ליה נמי דשכר טבחים ובודקים שהוא מותר דהנהו פועלים נינהו ולא שכר הוראה הוא אלא שכר פעולה ועדיף משכר הבאה ומילוי וצ"ע.

[הגהה מכתב יד המחבר זצ"ל:] אפשר לענ"ד יש לחלק בין קידוש והזיה לשאר המצוות. כל שאר המצוות יש ביד המחויב לעשות המצוה ואינו מוטל על אחרים לעשות המצוה בעדו לכתוב לו ס"ת לשחוט לו בהמה וכיוצא אכן קידוש והזיה אי אפשר לטמא לעשות והזה הטהור על הטמא קאמר רחמנא ומצוה היא על חבירו לעשות ודומה ללימוד תורה עדות ודין שאי אפשר בלי אחר ודו"ק.

[Further explication by the author:] The difference between קידוש והזיה עדות ודין ותלמוד תורה and other מצות appears to be this: In the case of קידוש והזיה, the act is done essentially for the sake of someone else — by the טהור for the טמא: ולקחו לטמא וגו', והזה הטהור על הטמא (vv. 17 and 19). Likewise, עדות and דין are acts that can be done only by others [for the sake of the litigant]. So, too, תלמוד תורה שבעל פה depends — originally and essentially — on the reception of an oral tradition; hence, to receive the Torah, a person is dependent on his fellow man. In all these cases, the Torah obligates us to perform actions for the sake of others without taking payment. These actions are an integral part of the מצוה, they are a duty to the Torah, and it is forbidden to accept payment for them. Other מצוות — such as שחיטה, כתיבת סת"ם, etc. — every person can do by himself without the assistance of anyone else. In these cases, doing for others is not the essential nature of the מצוה. Hence, payment may be accepted.

ולקחו וגו' ונתן. The אפר must be strewn onto the water by conscious, intentional human action (*Parah* 6:1; רמב"ם there).

18 *And a man who is pure shall take hyssop, dip it into the water, and sprinkle [water] upon the tent and upon all the persons who were there, and upon the one who touched the bone or the one slain, or the dead body, or the grave.*	יח וְלָקַח אֵזוֹב וְטָבַל בַּמַּיִם אִישׁ טָהוֹר וְהִזָּה עַל־הָאֹהֶל וְעַל־כָּל־הַכֵּלִים וְעַל־הַנְּפָשׁוֹת אֲשֶׁר הָיוּ־שָׁם וְעַל־הַנֹּגֵעַ בַּעֶצֶם אוֹ בֶחָלָל אוֹ בַמֵּת אוֹ בַקָּבֶר:

18 **ולקח וגו׳ איש טהור וגו׳**. Every sane male — even if he is a minor — is qualified for הזיה, whereas the קידוש (v. 17) is valid only if performed by an adult, but women, too, are qualified for it (*Yoma* 43a).

אזוב: כל אזוב שיש לו שם לווי פסול, אזוב זה כשר (*Parah* 11:7). It must not bear a special name. Only the ordinary common hyssop — of which people say simply "אזוב זה," "this is hyssop" — is fit for הזאה.

It is a מצוה to take three hyssop stalks and to bind them together into one bunch, as at פסח מצרים (*Shemos* 12:22; see Commentary there). However, two stalks are also sufficient, and if — in the course of use — only one remains, the הזיה can still be performed with it (*Sukkah* 13a): מצות אזוב שלושה קלחים ובהן שלושה גבעולין וכו׳ תחלתו שנים ושיריו אחד כשר.

The prescribed length of the אזוב — at the first הזאה — is at least one טפח (see תוספות יום טוב, *Parah* 11:9); but if, in the course of use, it is worn down to less than the prescribed length, it may still be used: גרדומיו כל שהוא (*Sukkah* 13a).

והזה. The sprinkling must be done with כוונה, with intent. According to the רמב״ם, one must intend לטהר את הטמא, as suggested by the words והזה הטהור על הטמא of the following verse (*Parah* 12:3), whereas according to the ראב״ד (הל׳ פרה, 10:7) one need only intend to sprinkle and need not intend לטהר את הטמא.

In this respect הזיה differs from טבילה, for טבילה does not require כוונה: גל שנתלש ובו ארבעים סאה ונפל על האדם ועל הכלים טהורין (*Chullin* 31a).

הזאת מי חטאת differs from הזיות דם (*Vayikra* 4:6; Commentary there), of which it says: על כל הזיה טבילה. In the case of הזאת מי חטאת, as long as there is water on the אזוב, one can sprinkle again and again. Even the slightest amount of water that reaches the outer surface of the body suffices לטהר את הטמא: אגבא דגברא אין צריכה שיעור (*Yoma* 14a; *Kiddushin* 25a).

19 *The pure person shall sprinkle upon the impure person on the third day and on the seventh day and shall purify him on the seventh day; he shall wash his garments and bathe in water and will become pure in the evening.*	יט וְהִזָּה הַטָּהֹר עַל־הַטָּמֵא בַּיּוֹם הַשְּׁלִישִׁי וּבַיּוֹם הַשְּׁבִיעִי וְחִטְּאוֹ בַּיּוֹם הַשְּׁבִיעִי וְכִבֶּס בְּגָדָיו וְרָחַץ בַּמַּיִם וְטָהֵר בָּעָרֶב׃

The intention of the one who is to be purified is not required during the sprinkling: מזין על האדם מדעתו ושלא מדעתו (*Parah* 12:2).

על האהל. The אהל itself becomes טמא, even if it is מחובר and as such is otherwise not מקבל טומאה. But this applies only to the materials mentioned in the case of the roof of the משכן: wool, skins, goats'-hair and, of vegetable origin, linen. Thus the Mishnah says: כל היוצא מן העץ אינו מטמא טומאת אהלים אלא פשתן (*Shabbos* 27b). All other materials are מקבלים טומאה only if they are not מחוברים. But this distinction exists only regarding the טומאה of the roof itself. It does not exist in regard to conveying טומאה to the things inside the אהל המת; in this regard, all materials are equal, and there is no difference between מחובר and תלוש (תוספות there ד״ה ואין מטמא; רמב״ם, ראב״ד, and הל׳ טומאת מת, משנה למלך, 5:12).

19 **והזה הטהר על הטמא**. It has already been stated in verse 18: ולקח וגו׳ איש טהור וגו׳, from which we would have derived that absolute טהרה is required of the person who performs the procedure. However, here this requirement is defined more precisely: Only relative טהרה is required; טהרה is mentioned only as a contrast to טומאה. He is required only not to be טמא; it is sufficient if he takes one step out of טומאה and attains a degree of טהרה, even if he is not yet a complete טהור. From this our Sages derive the halachah that not only הזיה but all the procedures of the פרה are valid if performed by a טבול יום; for through the טבילה he has already attained the first degree of טהרה, and Scripture (*Vayikra* 14:8) calls him "טהור": ורחץ במים וטהר (see *Yoma* 43b).

The Sadducees, who denied the Oral Law, vehemently disputed the traditional halachah that טבול יום כשר בפרה. It was therefore necessary to attest to the authenticity of the Tradition and to uphold the authority of the Sages. And since all the procedures of the פרה were performed in pub-

כ וְאִ֤ישׁ אֲשֶׁר־יִטְמָא֙ וְלֹ֣א יִתְחַטָּ֔א
וְנִכְרְתָ֛ה הַנֶּ֥פֶשׁ הַהִ֖וא מִתּ֣וֹךְ
הַקָּהָ֑ל כִּ֡י אֶת־מִקְדַּ֨שׁ יְהוָ֜ה טִמֵּ֗א
מֵ֥י נִדָּ֛ה לֹא־זֹרַ֥ק עָלָ֖יו טָמֵ֥א הֽוּא׃

20 *But one who becomes impure and does not clear himself of sin, that soul will be uprooted from the midst of the community, for he has defiled the Sanctuary of* God*; water of separation has not been dashed upon him; he is impure.*

כא וְהָיְתָ֥ה לָהֶ֖ם לְחֻקַּ֣ת עוֹלָ֑ם וּמַזֵּ֤ה
מֵֽי־הַנִּדָּה֙ יְכַבֵּ֣ס בְּגָדָ֔יו וְהַנֹּגֵ֙עַ֙ בְּמֵ֣י
הַנִּדָּ֔ה יִטְמָ֖א עַד־הָעָֽרֶב׃

21 *It shall remain for them an everlasting statute. One who sprinkles water of separation for another purpose shall wash his garments, and one who touches water of separation becomes impure until the evening.*

lic, and the טהרה of every individual depended on them, the words of the Sages were upheld in public by doing as follows: Before the כהן would begin the פרה procedure, they would render him טמא in public on the Mount of Olives, and then he would undergo טבילה. In this way, all would see that every פרה אדומה process was carried out by a טבול יום: מטמאין היו הכהן השורף את הפרה ומטבילין אותו, להוציא מלבן של צדוקין שהיו אומרים במעורבי שמש היתה נעשית (*Yoma* 2a). On the other hand, throughout the process they would maintain a heightened degree of טהרה, and for that purpose they would take the most elaborate precautions (see ibid. and *Parah* 3).

20 See Commentary, verse 13.

21 **והיתה להם לחקת עולם**. This is a law that still affects us today. Since we are all טמאי מת and, having no אפר פרה, have no means of attaining טהרה, anyone who enters the site of the Temple on Mount Moriah incurs the penalty of כרת even today. The sanctity of the site was not nullified upon the destruction of the Temple: קדושה ראשונה קדשה לשעתה וקדשה לעתיד לבוא (רמב״ם הל׳ בית הבחירה, 6:15; but see ראב״ד there, 6:14).

ומזה מי הנדה וגו׳. The words והיתה להם לחקת עולם conclude the second part of פרשת פרה, which contains the הזיה procedure, just as the words והיתה

22 *Also anything that the impure person touches becomes impure, and also the person who touches him will be impure until the evening.*

כב וְכֹל אֲשֶׁר־יִגַּע־בּוֹ הַטָּמֵא יִטְמָא וְהַנֶּפֶשׁ הַנֹּגַעַת תִּטְמָא עַד־הָעָרֶב׃ פ

וגו׳ לחקת עולם (v. 10) conclude the first part, which contains the שריפה procedure. Accordingly, the continuation of our verse — ומזה וגו׳ — does not deal with one who sprinkles the water for טהרה purposes. Furthermore, here it does not say וכבס המזה על הטמא את בגדיו, similar to verse 19 and analogous to verse 10; rather, it says ומזה מי הנדה. Thus, there is no mention here of any person or object sprinkled upon, and the same is true of the continuation of the verse, והנגע במי הנדה, which without a doubt is not referring to an act of הזיה, for there is no need to touch the water during הזיה.

Rather, ומזה מי הנדה refers to someone who moves מי הנדה not for the purpose of טהרה. Thus the following contrast: The מזה על הטמא remains טהור, whereas the מזה מי הנדה not for טהרה purposes becomes טמא. However, this movement of the water is none other than משא, which is identical with היסט (see Commentary, *Vayikra* 11:24-25). Thus, the Halachah states (*Yoma* 14a) that the מזה of our verse is none other than a נושא, and Scripture calls him "מזה" to teach us that נושא מי חטאת is טמא only if the water is of sufficient quantity to be used for sprinkling: דבעינן שיעור הזאה, and that only one who carries such a quantity is טעון כיבוס בגדים. By contrast, one who merely is נוגע במי הנדה is not מטמא בגדים, but he is rendered טמא by this contact even if the quantity of the water is less than the שיעור הזיה. Thus the laws stated in *Kelim* (1:1-2): אבות הטומאות השרץ וכו׳ ומי חטאת שאין בהם כדי הזיה הרי אלו מטמאין אדם וכלים במגע וכלי חרש באויר ואינם מטמאין במשא; למעלה מהם נבלה ומי חטאת שיש בהם כדי הזיה שהם מטמאין את האדם במשא לטמא בגדים במגע וחשוכי בגדים במגע (see Commentary, *Vayikra* 11:24-25).

22 **וכל אשר יגע בו הטמא יטמא וגו׳**. In the first clause it says יטמא without a limiting addition, whereas in the second clause it says תטמא עד הערב. Hence in *Avodah Zarah* 37b our Sages say that the first clause deals with טומאת שבעה that results from טומאה בחיבורין, and contains the following law: One who is touched by the טמא while the latter is still touching the מת is טמא טומאת שבעה. The second clause, on the other hand, deals with טומאה שלא

בחיבורין, and contains the following law: One who touches the טמא מת after the latter has ceased to be in contact with the מת is טמא with only טומאת ערב. The מת is אבי אבות הטומאה, the one who touches it becomes אב הטומאה, and if he touches someone — שלא בחיבורין — that person becomes ראשון לטומאה and is טמא only until evening.

We have already mentioned (v. 16) the view that the law of חרב הרי הוא כחלל applies to all כלים, and if כלים come in contact with a מת or with a טמא מת, they receive the same degree of טומאה as that of what they touch. According to this view, we can understand why the second clause says והנפש, specially emphasizing the person. For כלים that come in contact with a טמא מת — even שלא בחיבורין —receive the same degree of טומאה as that of the טמא מת they touch; they, too, become אבות הטומאה and are טמאים טומאת שבעה.

According to the רמב״ם in הל׳ טומאת מת, 5:2, טומאה בחיבורין is only מדרבנן (see כסף משנה and משנה למלך there).

Let us consider the laws set forth here regarding פרה אדומה and טומאת מת, and let us attempt to ascertain the ideas they express. We should consider first the concept under which the Torah itself includes the whole mitzvah of פרה אדומה — namely, the concept of חטאת, which characterizes this mitzvah and which forms the basis for its *halachos.*

חטאת — a clearing away of sin, a cancellation of the sinful act — is a concept that belongs exclusively to the sphere of *morality.* Now the mitzvah of פרה אדומה is חוקת התורה, the fundamental institution of the whole teaching of טומאת מת, which in turn is the principal category of the whole teaching of טומאה altogether. And since the Torah refers to פרה אדומה as חטאת, it is clearly directing us to the sphere of *morality.* That is the sphere in which we should seek the meaning of the laws of טומאה and טהרה in general and of the mitzvah of פרה אדומה in particular.

The foregoing serves as clear confirmation of the conception we have already arrived at regarding all the laws of טומאה and טהרה discussed in the Torah thus far. *Moral freedom* — so we asserted — is the first and indispensable condition for the whole sanctification of life which the Torah obligates us to strive for.

This fundamental truth is threatened by the sight of man submitting to death, for the human corpse demonstrates the power of death for all to see, and the superficial observer perceives in the corpse the power of nature dominating everything, including man. If the *whole* man has succumbed to death; if the corpse lying before us, overwhelmed by the compelling forces of nature, represents all that there is to man, then man, even during his lifetime, is no different from any other living thing. He is under the spell of a universally compelling necessity. If all this were indeed so, then this physical "must" would not leave room for any moral "thou shalt." Then moral freedom would be an illusion, God's moral law would be inconceivable, and its demands to freely dedicate one's existence and will to the purifying and vivifying fire of the Sanctuary would rest on baseless suppositions (cf. Commentary, *Vayikra* 5:13 et al., on the identity of freedom of existence and of will with the concept of קדושה).

The whole purpose of the laws of טומאה and טהרה — as presented in the Book of *Vayikra* — is to negate this idea. These laws confront the demoralizing illusion of physical nonfreedom with the Divine guarantee that man does indeed have moral freedom. Throughout our lives, whenever the energy of moral awareness is threatened by reminders of bondage to physical forces, the Law reminds us of the טהרה-element of moral freedom, as we have already noted in the various elements of טומאה and טהרה in the sections dealing with them.

Here, this same טומאה and טהרה legislation seeks to proclaim the great concept of חטאת, publicly, before the eyes of all Israel, through the nation's priestly representative, in full view of the Sanctuary. Thereby it lays down, as the moral basis of the whole life of the people, the truth that man *can be free of sin, can clear himself of sin, and can remain free of sin.*

Such is the meaning of this חטאת, this symbolic "clearing of sin" that must be performed *outside* the Sanctuary. It is not to be equated with the sin offerings that are made *inside* the Sanctuary, for they atone for one particular individual from one particular sin, and the atonement is attained through an act symbolizing his vow to remain faithful to his duty henceforth. This חטאת, on the other hand, publicly proclaims that it is indeed possible to be free of sin, that man is indeed capable of controlling himself in the face of any physical temptation. This חטאת *proclaims the general fact that man is endowed with moral willpower.*

However, in proclaiming man's freedom, it recognizes that he is subject to physical forces; it demonstrates moral freedom in connection with physical subjection. It does not teach man to close his eyes and ignore the physical subjection which is a part of his nature. Rather, it shows man in the whole contrast of his nature. For he is mortal, and at the same time he is eternal; he is fettered, and at the same time he is free; he is endowed with physical powers along with moral powers. By placing him, in the totality of his dual nature, before the Sanctuary of the one sole God, Who is the only One with absolute freedom, this חטאת elevates man with his whole nature, with his transient physical powers and with his eternal moral powers, into the free, eternal sphere of the one, sole God, and says to him: Do not be misled by the sight of corpses and of death; become free, become immortal, not *despite*, but *along with* all those aspects of your existence that are mortal and physically fettered. Be the immortal master of your mortal body; in the midst of טומאה, preserve your טהרה!

From this perspective, which is attained through the concept of חטאת, we can understand the meaning of the mitzvah of פרה אדומה.

פרה אדומה תמימה אשר אין בה מום אשר לא עלה עליה עול is the physical, animal aspect. This aspect is represented here by full vitality (אדומה תמימה), by unblemished completeness (אין בה מום), and by maturity (בת ג׳ שנים). According to its purpose, it is פרה: it is meant to be a help to man in his work, but it has never used its strength in the service of man (פסול עבודה); what is more, it has never borne the sign of service (פסול עול — see v. 2). It represents, then, *physical* nature *not mastered* by man, and in this regard it shall be taken by the national community (דבר אל בני ישראל ויקחו אליך – מתרומת הלשכה) and handed over to the כהן who serves in the Sanctuary of the Torah.

The כהן, in the name of the Torah of the Sanctuary, shall show what is to be the position of physical nature uncontrolled by man; he shall show what meaning this nature is to have in the sphere of life of a human society that seeks to shape its life under the influence of the Torah. The פרה אדומה is to be handed over to the כהן — the מכין and מכונן, the one who "prepares" and "gives direction to" the life of the people toward its goal — when he is clad in בגדי כהונה, in the uniform of his office. The garments are to be בגדי לבן, white garments, like those of the כהן גדול in the Service of יום הכיפורים; for his task is to show the way of טהרה, the "purity" required by the Torah in whose service he stands.

והוציא אותה: This is the first lesson which he conveys by symbolic action: He shall take it חוץ לשלוש מחנות, outside the מחנה שכינה, outside the מחנה לוייה, and even outside מחנה ישראל. For פרה אדומה תמימה אשר אין בה מום אשר לא עלה עליה עול represents physical animal nature. This nature is meant to serve man, not after it has withered or is broken, but in its full vitality and completeness. But when it is not controlled by man, it *no longer has a place within the framework* of the Jewish national life of the people. Therefore the כהן who serves the Torah shall take the פרה וגו׳ אשר לא עלה

עליה עול outside the sphere of the people, where he shall prepare for it a place (גת) high up and at a distance but opposite the entrance to the Sanctuary of the Torah.

והוציא אותה: it should be taken out alone; no *other* animal should be taken out with it. For the meaning of another animal could only be concrete, not symbolic, and would divert attention from the symbolical meaning of all these procedures. However, neither may two פרות אדומות be taken out together, for two פרות would recall the idea of plurality, whereas here the objective is to represent man's uncontrolled animal nature by itself.

ושחט אותה is the second lesson which the כהן conveys through significant action. In the name of the Sanctuary of the Torah, as whose servant he stands here and to the entrance of which he looks — כנגד פתח ההיכל (see Commentary, v. 4) — he performs the act of שחיטה on the פרה אדומה תמימה אשר אין בה מום אשר לא עלה עליה עול. For this "animal" which stands here in the "fullness of its vitality and completeness" and on which no "yoke" has ever been placed, the only remedy is שחיטה. It requires total subordination through a sharp and decisive act of human free will. This is the sole intended purpose of the "animal" aspect, and only under this condition *can* and *should* it ascend into a hallowed relationship to God's Sanctuary. Otherwise it has no place in the human realm.

This is the only שחיטה that is valid only if performed by a כהן, and in that it differs essentially from all the שחיטות performed at the offerings in the Sanctuary. In all the קרבנות offered in the Sanctuary, שחיטה is not an עבודה. It does not represent the positive value that the seeker of God's closeness must learn and accept. Rather, it represents the negative *prerequisite* of self-renunciation. The seeker of God's closeness must first of all *renounce* all selfishness and all egocentric living; only then can his life (נפש) be *devoted* to God's Sanctuary and be *accepted* there in priestlike sanctity. Hence that שחיטה is כשרה בזר. Here, however, the שחיטה represents the central aspect that is to be given expression. It embodies man's free mastery over the physical-animal aspect of his nature; it proclaims the very opposite of the פרה אשר לא עלה עליה עול, and for that purpose the פרה is given over to the כהן, so that he may indicate this contrast. This שחיטה is כשרה only בכהן.

ולקח מדמה באצבעו. He does not receive the blood in a כלי שרת or in any other vessel; rather, he receives the blood in his hand. For it is not the Sanctuary that receives here the human נפש; rather, it is man who receives the animal נפש and introduces it into his free sphere of influence. The קרבן offered in the Sanctuary represents the whole man who devotes himself to the Sanctuary before the Presence of God. פרה אדומה, on the other hand, represents the animal aspect in man, which man takes in his hand while looking at God's Sanctuary.

והזה אל נכח פני אהל מועד מדמה שבע פעמים. With ever renewed energy — על כל הזיה טבילה (cf. *Vayikra* 4:6) — he shall direct the animal aspect of man to the Divine ideal of the Torah; seven times he shall direct it, until it reaches "completion," until it attains the Divine "closeness of the covenant." שחיטה and הזיה are the full expression of moral freedom. They represent mastery over the physical-sensual drives and their direction to the path of God's moral law.

ושרף את הפרה, את ערה ואת בשרה וגו׳ ישרף: Only what has been directed from the animal element to Divine morality by human power — *that alone will not become ash*: That alone will be saved by free man on his way to the moral ideal, and thus gain for it, too, the closeness of God's eternal covenant. Everything else will disintegrate and become ash, for its basis is dust.

Yet even the decaying of the unfree sensual aspect — no less than the movement toward God and toward the eternity of moral freedom — relates to God Who is the one God, for both belong to Him, both were created by Him, and both serve His purposes in the world and in man: the fleeting and the eternal, the mortal and the immortal, the fettered and the free. Like the שחיטה and the הזיה, so is גתה — the place for its conversion to ash — כנגד פתח ההיכל, in view of, and directed toward the gate of the Sanctuary of the Torah. One God has mixed these two antithetical elements in man's nature for one and the same moral purpose — namely, so that the Divine power of moral and free man's nature should manifest itself in the very struggle against physical compulsion, and so that the earthly frame which will ultimately decay should not drag man away from the gates of eternity and moral freedom: שרפה חוץ לגתה פסולה. The two aspects of man's nature were combined for one purpose: so that man should attain God's closeness on earth and build God's earthly Sanctuary by free-willed actualization of God's Torah. Man's eternal soul joined to a body destined to decay is the basic premise of God's whole Torah.

ולקח הכהן עץ ארז ואזוב ושני תולעת והשליך אל תוך שרפת הפרה. "Cedar," the highest and strongest of plants; "hyssop," the lowest and weakest of them;

"wool" dyed with the blood of a "worm"; worm and sheep, worm and mammal, the lowest and highest of animal life — do these not represent the whole of organic life? The כהן takes these representatives of the whole physical organic world and throws them into the fire of the פרה, at the moment when the פרה, which represents the physical organic part of man, is about to become ashes.

This, then, is the idea that the כהן brings to expression: The human body is destined by Divine decree to become dust, but the element that brings decay to the body is the same element that brings decay also to the whole rest of the physical organic world, and the decay grips only that part of man that comes to him from the general organic world to be joined — temporarily — with the eternal element.

Let us consider again what has been said until now. The פרה אדומה before the שחיטה represents the animal element in man which he failed to control as he should have. The שחיטה and the הזיה, and the שריפה which follows them, emphasize the contrast that inheres in man: The נפש, which is directed to Divine morality, is spared the fate of reverting to ash and is represented by the דם of the שחיטה and the הזיה, whereas the body reverts to ash, a fate symbolized by שריפת עורה בשרה דמה ופרשה.

Hence the relationship between שריפת הפרה באש and the preceding שחיטה והזיה differs from the relationship between שריפת האיברים והאימורים of the קרבנות in the אש על גבי המזבח and the preceding שחיטה ועבודות הדם.

שריפת האיברים והאימורים is the continuation, the result, and the completion of the שחיטה and מתנות הדם. After the נפש has aspired to ascend to the heights of the altar — or has held fast to those heights — the body, too, achieves its purpose: its desires and efforts, represented by the אימורים and איברים and controlled by the נפש, sustain the holy on earth and are pleasing before God. Hence, the שחיטה and the הקטרה may not be separated, for it is only the positive aspect of the הקטרה that completes the negative aspect of the שחיטה, and the positive aspect of the הקטרה is based on the preceding שחיטה. Both must be done on the same day, and איברים ואימורים that were not given over to the altar fire before the end of offering day are פסולים בלינה (see Commentary, *Vayikra* 7:18).

In the case of the פרה, the שחיטה and the שריפה have a different relationship. For the fire which burns the פרה בגתה and consumes the animal in its place on earth is not אש דת על המזבח; rather, it is the fire of the elements. This fire engulfs all organic matter and ultimately reduces it to ash and dust. Hence, the שריפה, too, is not the continuation and the result of the שחיטה and the הזיה כנגד פתח ההיכל; rather, it stands beside them and has a different object. It is the ash-future of the body *beside* the sanctuary-future of the soul. Hence the שריפה can be done on a different day, and the פרה is not פסולה בלינה.

אסיפה. With שריפת הפרה the function of the כהן is completed. In the name of the Sanctuary, facing the front of the Sanctuary, he expresses the duality in man: Man's free power subordinates the animal element within himself and humanizes it, thus elevating it toward God, to the realm of the Divine freedom of His Torah. This is represented by שחיטה and הזיה. The transient, fleeting element, the bodily animal frame, is represented by שריפת הפרה.

These procedures are performed in order to teach the people of the community. Hence the community is to take the ashes of the פרה and keep them למשמרת. These ashes are to remind the community of the fundamental teaching of man's dual nature. For man is an amalgam of the heavenly and the earthly, the godly and the animal, the eternal and the transitory, and the community is to use these ashes whenever it is necessary to set this teaching against the טומאה-illusion of man's nonfreedom.

ואסף איש טהור: The gathering of the ashes shall accordingly be done by an ordinary man of the people. He himself must be pure, and he is to take the ashes, which convey the teaching of purity, and deposit them outside the שכינה-sphere of the Sanctuary in an absolutely pure place.

This requirement of "purity" for the gathering and depositing of the ashes is of great significance. Although they represent the material that succumbs to death, the "ashes" — this is a point we shall have to come back to — do not convey טומאה by contact, and absolute purity is required for the place where they are kept. For the pernicious טומאה-illusion does not entail the death of mortals; rather, it lies in the erroneous notion that would drag the immortal, too, to death. This notion does not differentiate between the eternal and the body's material, which is subject to decay. Accordingly, this notion gives an affirmative reply to the exclamation of astonishment: אַךְ־כָּל־הֶבֶל כָּל־אָדָם נִצָּב סֶלָה "Is all of man a mere breath — however upright he may stand!" (*Tehillim* 39:6). Now, the eternal Divine element in man belongs to God and to His Sanctuary and is not destined to go the way of the mortal dust. This element was already removed מעפר שרפת החטאת at the הזיה כנגד פתח ההיכל, and what lies now in the ashes of the פרה is that part of man which is mortal. Hence [the ashes that remain do not convey the concept of טומאה and must remain pure] ואסף איש טהור את

אפר הפרה והניח במקום טהור. Nevertheless, it must be מחוץ למחנה, outside the מחנה שכינה. For only when the animal bodily element is joined with the human godly element does it have a place in God's Sanctuary. If, however, the animal bodily element is separated from the human element, it is then part of the physical world, whose place is outside of God's Sanctuary, which is dedicated to "man."

But this ash is destined to be mixed in "living water" (v. 17), and in that mixture it will evoke the idea of the "eternally living" which was temporarily combined with the "material subject to decay." It will evoke this idea for all those who come in contact with a corpse or with part of a corpse, an experience that casts a shadow in their minds over the idea of the eternally living element in man. As long as this idea is obscured in their minds, these people are barred from the Sanctuary and its holy things.

The community of Israel stands on the basis of the eternal Divine element, on which man's free moral willpower depends. For the community of Israel, this ash is to be kept למשמרת למי נדה. Not the ash in itself, but its purpose to be מי נדה — to banish the erroneous idea of moral nonfreedom — is what gives the mitzvah of פרה the character of חטאת (see above).

מים חיים: מילוי וקידוש, "living spring water," is drawn "directly and without a mediating means" from the spring, or from a stream flowing from the spring uninterruptedly, into a "vessel," and some of the ash is then strewn into the water [held by the vessel].

It is significant that the "ash" is called here "עפר" (v. 17). The organic body decomposes and becomes ashes, but these ashes are none other than the material from which the body originated — עפר אתה ואל עפר תשוב (*Bereshis* 3:19) — and it is as such that they are presented here. For what is man? An element of eternal life, drawn from the source of eternal life and confined in an earthly vessel. This element which lives forever — "מים חיים" — is the original, essential, and primary element, מים חיים אל כלי. To this element which lives forever, עפר, dust of the earth, is added, and, within the earthly confines of the vessel, these two elements shall not be next to each other or one above the other, but shall be מעורבים together: the "living" mixed with the "earthly." And the mixture shall be such that the "living," which is the primary and original element, shall overpower the "earthly" element, subordinate it, be seen through it, and contain it: עליו מים חיים. It is not something earthly containing life, but life containing something earthly: עפר שריפת החטאת עליו מים חיים אל כלי — that is what man is.

When the time of the mixture's end comes, the ash-dust sinks to the ground, and the מים חיים appears in its original clarity: וְיָשֹׁב הֶעָפָר עַל־הָאָרֶץ כְּשֶׁהָיָה וְהָרוּחַ תָּשׁוּב אֶל־הָאֱלֹקִים אֲשֶׁר נְתָנָהּ (*Koheles* 12:7; cf. *Collected Writings*, vol. I, pp.369-382 פרשת פרה).

At the moment in which the ash is strewn into the מים חיים, the water becomes מי חטאת, a medium for teaching man that he is capable of avoiding sin, and the act of the mixing is called "sanctification," קידוש.

מי סוטה and מי חטאת have a common denominator. For this is the meaning of מי סוטה: Although man is עפר and is provided with organic earthly urges, nevertheless, he is endowed with the element of "מים קדושים" and is capable of moral sanctification of life. The meaning of מי חטאת is similar. Although man is אפר, his life is eternal — "מים חיים"! (see Commentary above, 5:17).

מי חטאת .הזיה בשלישי ושביעי represent the transient yet nonetheless intimate combination of man's two aspects: the organic-material and the eternal-godly, and this very combination represents the idea of "man." Similarly, הזיה — whose purpose is to restore the concept of man to its former clarity, after its obfuscation in man's consciousness — is a dual act, dedicated to both these elements.

Moral freedom is man's ability to subordinate himself with the whole of his being to God's Torah, and the awareness of this freedom must be the basis for all aspects of man: for the organic and physical aspect no less than for the Divine and spiritual aspect of life. The gratification of one's physical urges, hunger and sexual drive, which is part of organic life, must be subjected of one's own free will to the guidance of God's Law, no less than the thoughts, aspirations and accomplishments in which the spiritual and Divine aspect of man unfolds. Both require free-willed devotion to the directives of God's Torah and His commandments.

Hence, before a טמא מת can attain טהרה through טבילה — after he has completed the טומאה period — he must be reminded of the fundamental teaching of moral freedom. This is done by הזיה, which is directed not only to the spiritual, godly aspect but also to the organic, physical aspect of human nature. The הזיה is performed on the third day and again on the seventh.

We have already shown in our Commentary on *Bereshis* 1:11-13 that the third day of Creation and the seventh day have a common denominator. On the third day, the physical-organic world was created, stamped with the impress of the Divine law of למינו. Hence the third day bears the seal of physical, organic life submitting to the Divine law. And so we find on the seventh day. For on this day man, with his Godlike powers of mastering the material world, places his use of these powers under the dominion of God. Therefore, the הזיה that is directed to man as a physical, organic creature is assigned to the third day, and the הזיה that is directed to man as a spiritual, Godlike being is assigned to the seventh day. On whatever day the first הזיה takes place — from the third day onward — that day is regarded as though it were the third day, and then four days must pass before the second הזיה can be performed, which is considered as having been performed on the seventh day. That the הזיה of מי חטאת alludes to the days of Creation, thus investing the days of הזיה with their special character, is not a far-fetched idea, for, as we have already stated, מי חטאת, which contain עפר ועליו מים חיים אל כלי, symbolize man in his genesis at the time of Creation.

In recapitulation, then, the first הזיה, that of the third day, paves the way for man's physical, bodily purification. The second, that of the seventh day, paves the way for spiritual, godly purification. Only then can the whole man — or human nature in its entirety — attain complete purity: הזיה וטבילה על אדם וכלים.

All that remains for us now is to consider various general laws that characterize the mitzvah of פרה or the relation between the mitzvah's parts. This is the summary stated in the תוספתא (*Parah* 4:6): כל מעשה הפרה ביום חוץ מאסיפת האפר והמילוי והקידוש, כל מעשיה בכהנים חוץ מאסיפת האפר והמילוי והקידוש והזאה, כל מעשיה מלאכה פוסלת בהן חוץ מאסיפת אפרה והזית מימיה.

ביום: All the procedures of the פרה must be performed in the daytime, except for gathering up the ashes, drawing the water into a vessel, and putting the ashes into the water. We are already familiar with the meaning of the halachah that limits certain *mitzvos* to the daytime. This halachah indicates that the act relates to wakeful, free, and moral life of conscious man, in contrast to the sphere of control of the unfree physical world (see *Collected Writings*, vol. III, p. 86ff.; cf. Commentary, *Vayikra* 6:2). It is understandable, then, that this halachah applies to the principal procedures of the mitzvah of פרה, which bear its message. אסיפה, מילוי, and קידוש, on the other hand, are merely preliminaries to the mitzvah; hence, they are not assigned a set time.

If — as is the case according to one version in the *Sifre* (see Commentary, v. 3) — שריפה, too, is valid at night, that corresponds entirely with our approach. For the conversion of the whole פרה — with the sole exception of the blood that was sprinkled toward the Sanctuary — into ashes represents the process of decay of all matter belonging to physical nature, a process that transpires in the framework of the physical world of the elements; and the halachah that does not limit the שריפה to daytime expresses this meaning clearly.

כהן: As we have already pointed out, שחיטה, הזיה, and שריפה proclaim in the name of the Sanctuary the fundamental principle of moral freedom. They teach that man's integrated being includes two elements: an eternal element belonging to God and to His Sanctuary, and a material element destined to decay by the elements of nature. This teaching is completed by these procedures. All the other procedures — אסיפה, מילוי, קידוש, הזיה [של מי חטאת] — are therefore valid even if done by a non-כהן.

מלאכה: The meaning of the פסול מלאכה is more difficult to understand, and this difficulty is magnified by the fact that — as already noted on v. 17 — various details of this halachah are in doubt. In particular, it is not clear whether פסול מלאכה and היסח הדעת are identical or are separate concepts. If we assume the latter, the halachah is as follows:

In all the פרה procedures — except for אסיפה and הזיה (but see Commentary, v. 3) — one must concentrate on the procedure; even a momentary diversion, היסח הדעת, invalidates the entire procedure. Likewise, one who performs any of the פרה procedures — except for אסיפה and הזיה — may not do other מלאכה at that time.

The requirement of concentration during the פרה procedures is indicated in Scripture by the term "לפניו": ושחט אתה לפניו; by the term "לעיניו": ושרף את הפרה לעיניו; and by the term "שמירה": למשמרת למי נדה. It appears that these terms describe three aspects of דעת. The intention, the purpose that one desires, the focus of one's concentration: לפניו; observation and awareness: לעיניו; keeping in one's consciousness: שמירה.

Let us now recall that שחיטה and הזיה signify man's freedom, which manifests itself in self-control and in devotion to God's purposes; by contrast, שריפה symbolizes the process of decay, to which only the unfree material element is subject; whereas מילוי וקידוש symbolize the normal combination of these two antithetical elements and their becoming one in man's being.

The foregoing enables us to understand the division of the various aspects of דעת among the various procedures of the פרה. The free moral activity symbolized by שחיטה והזיה requires פנים: directing all the energy of the mind to a purpose to be accomplished. The decomposition of the material, which is symbolized by שריפה, requires only objective observation, עינים. The combination of these two antithetical elements in a pure human being, a combination symbolized by מילוי וקידוש, is what is to be kept in one's consciousness and remembered at all times: שמירה.

However, when we consider that דעת, paying attention, is not only a מצוה but is מעכב, and that even only a momentary diversion, היסח הדעת, invalidates the entire procedure, it appears that דעת is an integral part of the idea that comes to expression here. For this reason we would venture the following speculation:

Man's דעת alludes here to the supreme דעת of the One Who speaks and does whatever He wishes, Whose eyes range over all, and Who preserves and watches over His world. With full דעת He completed His work, and He watches over His handiwork. The work of His hands is the Divine soul in man and also the material-organic nature of the physical world and the combination of both these elements — in man. Man's דעת is merely an earthly echo heralding the supreme דעת.

The foregoing enables us to clearly understand the distinction between פסול מלאכה and פסול היסח הדעת. If another מלאכה were to be done at the same time, it would appear as though the פרה procedure were being done "by chance." This, then, is what is being expressed here: The השגחה, Whose intelligence and will sustain man and the world, operates not with היסח הדעת and not with מלאכה אחרת — not "without thought" and not "by chance" — but with supreme intelligence and special intention.

The הזית מי חטאת itself is not invalidated by מלאכה אחרת. The one who performs the הזיה must intend to sprinkle the object requiring טהרה, but the one who is to be purified need not be aware of the act during its performance, and the one who performs the הזיה may engage in another מלאכה at the same time. The הזיה of מים חיים ועפר does not require a כהן; it can be performed by any sane male, and, as we have stated, he may engage in מלאכה אחרת during the הזיה. From all this it appears that the מים חיים ועפר, which are sprinkled even incidentally on the one requiring טהרה, symbolize the normal life that is reflected by the activity of any sane person; and from such activity, this life will be understood by one who must be apprised of the vast difference between a corpse and a body with a living soul.

What remains to be explained is why minors are qualified to perform

הזיה whereas women are excluded, as opposed to קידוש, which is valid if performed by a woman but invalid if performed by a minor (see below).

טומאה. The laws of טומאה that are unique to פרה, which apply at the various stages of its procedures, are of great significance. These laws are summarized by the following statements:

כל העוסקים בפרה מתחילה ועד סוף מטמאין בגדים: All those who are occupied with the פרה, from beginning to end — i.e., at the שחיטה, הזיה, שריפה, השלכת עץ ארז, אסיפת האפר — become טמא, and their טומאה resembles that of נושא נבילה (Commentary, *Vayikra* 11:25). They are מטמא also all the כלים that they touch while so *occupied*, but one who *touches* the פרה or the ashes does *not* become טמא (vv. 7, 8, 9).

On the other hand, כל העוסקים במילוי וקידוש והזיה: All those who engage in drawing the water and mixing the ashes for the purpose of the הזיה, as well as those who engage in the הזיה itself, do *not* become טמא, whereas one who *touches* מי חטאת not for the purpose of הזיה does become טמא. If אין במים כדי הזיה, one is rendered טמא by them only במגע; but if יש בהם כדי הזיה, one is rendered טמא by them also במשא לטמא בגדים.

Engaging in the פרה procedure and touching מי חטאת are מטמא only so long as the פרה and the מי חטאת are valid; but once the פרה or the water is invalidated, engaging in the procedure or touching the water does not make one טמא.

Touching the water or the ashes before they are mixed does not make one טמא. Only after they have become מקודשים by being mixed do they convey טומאה to one who touches them not for the purpose of הזיה.

This last halachah, that the מזה מי חטאת remains טהור, whereas the נוגע ונושא מי חטאת not for the purpose of הזיה becomes טמא provides the key to the whole matter. For this is the meaning of the פרה, as expressed also in its end product, the מים חיים ועפר of the מי חטאת:

פרה brings to mind the duality of the antithetical elements that constitute man — that in him which lives forever and that which will ultimately die as man. The awareness of this antithesis brings relief to a person who has come in contact with a corpse, for his sense of moral freedom has been numbed by this experience, and it must be restored. There lies the corpse, demonstrating one side of this antithesis — that part of man that is unfree and bound to die. Hence, the מי חטאת, which contain מים חיים and עפר, are a curative medicine, for they set up in contrast the other side — that part of man that is endowed with moral freedom.

However, that which is a healing drug for the sick can be deadly poison for a healthy person. Normally, one does *not* live thinking of this antithesis. In normal untroubled life, this antithesis is entirely in abeyance, should be in abeyance; the thought of death is not to lurk beside the thought of life, and the thought of life is not to flow beside the thought of death; feelings of death and thoughts of corpses are not to be present at all, for the normal, pure beat of the pulse is *entirely* that of life. The spirit of God in man masters the material and elevates it to the realm of morality and eternity, allowing it to participate in the eternity that lies in every moment of a pure person's life. A pure person is not divided into two; his heart is undivided, and the very consciousness of the antithetical elements in his being blunts his thought.

מי חטאת are medicine, not bread. Therefore, if someone's mind has been infected by thoughts prompted by a corpse, he should be confronted with מי חטאת in which מים חיים have been mixed with עפר, and this will help him find the way to spiritual and moral recovery. Accordingly, מי חטאת that have been used for such a purpose are a medium for טהרה and do not convey טומאה.

It is different in the case of a healthy person, whose thoughts have not dwelled on a corpse. If he comes in contact with or handles מי חטאת, he is rendered טמא, for the water brings to his mind the thought of his dual nature, of the עפר and the מים חיים.

In any case, the הזיה with the מים חיים ועפר of the מי חטאת does not effect טהרה directly. Even after the הזיה, the טמא is still טמא as he was before. The הזיה-idea is only a preparation for טהרה; it puts the antithetical elements in man in the right relation to one another, assigning them their proper place, and it says to man: Although you are עפר and will become אפר, מים חיים is the essential nature of your being. But man will become טהור only if he then immerses himself entirely, with the "whole" of his being, in the element of purity. With the setting of the sun, all thought of the corpse will recede, and he will begin a fresh new day, free of all inner conflict and not beset by morbid thoughts.

This idea itself comes to expression through the halachah that decrees טומאה upon all who take part in the פרה procedure. This procedure includes שחיטה והזיה on the one hand, and שריפה ואסיפה on the other. Accordingly, it represents before all eyes this antithesis of the two elements in man: the free eternal element and the fettered transient element. It represents this idea in a general sense, without there being a particular cause. Thus, it evokes for all the עוסקים בפרה מתחילה ועד סוף the idea of this antithesis, and thereby renders them טמא. Consciousness of the antithesis represented by the פרה אדומה is not the normal consciousness, and it is not with such consciousness that one discharges the duty assigned to man by the Sanctuary and its holy things, whose place is no place for meditations on death. Before those who were occupied with the פרה אדומה return to the Sanctuary and its holy things, they must free themselves of the thought of the antithesis evoked by the פרה procedure; through טבילה and הערב שמש they must recover the consistency of the pure idea of life.

The fact that פרה and מי חטאת do not convey טומאה after they have become פסולים is self-explanatory. Once they have become פסולים, they lose their symbolical meaning, and they revert to their concrete, non-symbolical character. They are not מטמא any more than ordinary water and ash.

Likewise, it is self-understood that אפר alone — and obviously מים חיים alone — are טהורים, and that one who touches them remains טהור. For the process of decay of all organic material is in itself a true and pure idea, bearing no trace of the טומאה-illusion. Only if the אפר is a component in a mixture in which it is antithetical to the מים חיים of human nature does it present the danger of טומאה-aberration. For the אפר-עפר in man is likely to cause him to lose sight of the מים חיים in him; or the עפר-אפר element becomes so predominant that the חי in man is no longer considered man's original essence and nature, but only an accident that befalls עפר ואפר; it is born with the עפר and is buried with the אפר, and within the framework of man who is עפר ואפר there is no room for the free and eternal Divine element. Therefore, neither one who touches the מים חיים nor one who touches the אפר פרה becomes טמא. Only when the אפר has been strewn onto the water and mixed in the water, and they have together become מי חטאת for the purpose of הזיה — only then, if one touches them not for the purpose of הזיה, does he become טמא.

Finally, the halachah whose impact is felt throughout the פרה-procedure: טבול יום כשר בפרה.

The degree of טהרה required of one who engages in the פרה procedures and in הזיה is only the lowest degree of טהרה. This degree is attained through טבילה, even before the טהרה is completed by הערב שמש.

The Sadducees, who denied the Oral Law, vehemently disputed this halachah. The Sages would therefore publicly uphold this halachah at every פרה procedure in which they engaged. In public on the Mount of Olives, they would do as follows: Before the כהן would begin to carry out his function, they would render him טמא. Having been rendered טמא by contact, he would require טבילה. Thus, he would engage in the פרה procedure as a טבול יום.

However, this טומאה which they would deliberately and publicly bring upon the כהן — so that he would require טבילה — could have undermined the meaning of all the procedures, and there was concern that people would not understand the פרה procedure as a mitzvah of טהרה, but would give it the opposite meaning. For this reason — כי היכא דלא לזלזלו בה — the Sages would publicly take the most elaborate precautions involving great sacrifices to keep the כהן far from any remote possibility of ספק טומאת מת. Thus it was made clear to all that absolute טהרה is required for these procedures.

Let us now consider the elaborateness of these precautions. For example: Courtyards were built on rock under which there was a hollow, to avoid any possibility of טומאה רצוצה (see Commentary, above, v. 16) penetrating upward to an unlimited height. Women who were near the end of their pregnancy were brought to these courtyards, where they raised their sons until their seventh or eighth year, so that these boys who could never have become טמא should perform the הזיות on the כהן who was preparing to burn the פרה. Consider the extent of these טהרה precautions, and bear in mind that they were done only with this end in mind: With the most scrupulous care, they would keep the כהן in a state of טהרה for seven days; and then, when the time would come for him to act, they would deliberately render him טמא, so that he should require טבילה, immerse, and perform the פרה procedures only as a טבול יום. Why did they go to such great lengths? להוציא מלבן של צדוקים שהיו אומרים במעורבי שמש היתה נעשית; to negate the view of the Sadducees, who held that the פרה procedures require complete טהרה. The implication is that great importance is attached to this halachah that טבול יום כשר בפרה, and that it was worthwhile adopting such elaborate measures — in a setting of national importance — for its public proclamation.

Closer consideration of this halachah reveals that the following is the principle on which it is based: The טהור is the opposite of the טמא not only after the טהור has completed his טהרה, but already in the first stage of טהרה. According to the Sadducean pretension, והזה הטהור על הטמא can refer only to the completely טהור, whereas the tradition of our Sages teaches that already a טבול יום is called "טהור" and he, too, is considered the opposite of the טמא. According to the Sadducean pretension, the difference between טבול יום and טמא is only a quantitative difference in degree, and the qualitative difference in kind begins only with הערב שמש. According to the tradition of our Sages, however, what distinguishes the טבול יום and the טמא is already a qualitative difference in kind, and the difference between טבול יום and הערב שמש is only a quantitative difference in degree of טהרה.

If we transpose all this to the conceptual sphere of the teaching of moral freedom proclaimed by the mitzvah of פרה, the rule according to Sadducean pride is as follows: Only one who is spiritually and morally perfect is free and immortal. Anyone on a lower level is still in the transient realm of physical constraint. The teaching of the Sages, however, says: Every human being — even on the lowest level — is endowed with Divine freedom, and this distinguishes him from all transient physical creatures and grants him moral freedom and a share of eternal life. Only a difference in degree separates him from the very height of spiritual and moral perfection. According to the erroneous view of the Sadducees, immortality and eternity is an ideal that is attainable only through spiritual and moral perfection; hence — perhaps — it cannot be attained by any human being. According to the wisdom of our Sages, immortality and eternity is a gift innate in every man as man, given by God to every man upon his entrance into this world. This gift enables him during his earthly lifetime to walk in the ways of freedom, which lead to his homecoming to eternity in a state of higher perfection. Is it remote to suggest that the Sadducees' opposition and view — במעורבי שמש היתה נעשית — are closely connected with their opposition to the עולם הבא teaching of those same Sages [cf. אבות דרבי נתן פ״ה]?

We are much inclined to believe that the acceptability of boys, even a child, for הזיה (see *Parah* 12:10) is connected with this acceptability of a טבול יום. The same wisdom that sees the טהור already in the טבול יום, the "pure" already in the beginning of purity, also sees the future "man" in the child, and therefore qualifies even a קטן טבול יום to demonstrate the vast difference between life and death, between a human being and a corpse. The idea from which the acceptability of a טבול יום stems is what teaches the acceptability of the קטן, and just as our Sages say that והזה הטהור על הטמא extends the concept of טהור — regarding פרה — to include also טבול יום, they also expound in *Yoma* 43a: ולקח אזוב וטבל במים איש טהור, איש ולא אשה, טהור להכשיר את הקטן.

That אשה כשרה לקידוש ופסולה להזיה is perhaps connected with the fact

20 1 *The Children of Israel — the entire community — came into the wilderness of Tzin in the first month, and the people settled down in Kadesh. There Miriam died, and there she was buried.*

כ א וַיָּבֹאוּ בְנֵי־יִשְׂרָאֵל כָּל־הָעֵדָה מִדְבַּר־צִן בַּחֹדֶשׁ הָרִאשׁוֹן וַיֵּשֶׁב הָעָם בְּקָדֵשׁ וַתָּמָת שָׁם מִרְיָם וַתִּקָּבֵר שָׁם׃

that קידוש כשר בלילה, whereas הזיה is valid only during daytime, which makes הזיה a מצות עשה שהזמן גרמה, a positive mitzvah that is limited to a certain time.

The halachah that limits the הזיה to daytime defines the meaning of the הזיה. It is included among those acts that attest to truths on which the life of the whole community depend. In every generation, teaching these truths and transmitting them from generation to generation is the responsibility of the male. The fact that הזיה is valid even if performed by a "future man" indicates the fundamental importance of this truth of all truths, which comes to expression in הזית מי חטאת. The Jewish boy — as a future man — should be educated to this truth in the dawn of his youth. As far as we know, הזיה במי חטאת is the only case in which the Halachah qualifies קטנים for the performance of a מצוה and disqualifies נשים.

CHAPTER 20

1 **ויבאו וגו'**. The meaning of the addition כל העדה is not that all the people reached the wilderness of Tzin and that none stayed behind. For there is no point in specially mentioning that all the people arrived there. Moreover, had Scripture wished to mention this, it would have simply stated ויבואו כל עדת בני ישראל, as it does in *Shemos* 16:1. There, too, the whole community is called "עדה" for a special reason (see Commentary there). Here, however, Scripture emphasizes this term. After they have already been called בני ישראל, they are then specially characterized as כל העדה. בני ישראל who entered the wilderness of Tzin were כל העדה, "the whole community," united for their common mission — as denoted by the term "עדה." The fate decreed upon them (above, 14:29-35) had already been fulfilled. All those who entered the wilderness of Tzin were the עדה before whom a new future had now opened up; they were עדה השלמה, as the term

"כל העדה" (below, v. 22; see there) is interpreted in מדרש רבה: עדה הנכנסת לארץ, לפי שמתו יוצאי מצרים ואלו מן אותן שכתוב בהן חיים כולכם היום.

בחדש הראשון: in a season when the land of an inhabited country blossoms, heralding the coming fruit.

וישב העם בקדש. It does not say ויחן, which always denotes a temporary stay during one of the stops of the journey; rather, it says וישב, indicating that they settled down there, as it also says below, 21:25 and 31. קדש is called in verse 16 "עיר קצה גבולך"; it was a city on the border of the land of Edom, and although they probably did not enter the city, they had already come to the province that bore its name. The people thought that they had already reached the end of the journeying in the wilderness, and that after forty years of wandering they had, by arriving in Kadesh, at last come to an inhabitable land. וישב העם בקדש: With this feeling they prepared to settle down there. They thought that they had reached their goal.

ותמת שם מרים ותקבר שם. "There Miriam died and there she was buried." She had completed her mission on earth. Her grave in Kadesh would show future generations that she did not leave this world until the new generation was ready for the future that had been promised to it.

During Israel's long wanderings, filled with so many difficult experiences, the women did not take part in the incidents of defection from God, which resulted from despair. They cheerfully trusted in God and devotedly waited for Him, and for this reason they were not included in the fateful decree of death in the wilderness (*Bemidbar Rabbah* 21:10). Now, mothers and grandmothers were about to go up with the new generation to the Promised Land. Bringing with them their personal recollections of the past in Egypt and of the journey in the wilderness under God's guidance, they could refresh the souls of their grandchildren and great-grandchildren from the spiritual wellspring of their experiences with God. The fact that these Jewish women were so deeply imbued with the Jewish spirit may be ascribed in no small part to Miriam, who set them a shining example as a prophetess (see Commentary, *Shemos* 15:20).

This chapter, which describes briefly and simply the deaths of Aharon and Miriam, is preceded by the great פרה אדומה chapter, which teaches the Jewish concept of immortality. That chapter is in itself an important introduction to these deaths. It declares that what made Miriam into Miriam and what made Aharon into Aharon did not die when Miriam and Aharon died. Just as their work lives on forever in their nation, their

2 *And there was no water for the community, and they assembled against Moshe and Aharon.*

ב וְלֹא־הָיָה מַיִם לָעֵדָה וַיִּקָּהֲלוּ עַל־מֹשֶׁה וְעַל־אַהֲרֹן׃

true essence is eternal: it has now departed transient earthliness and returned to God, the Source of all life.

Our Sages say: למה נסמכה מיתת מרים לפרשת פרה אדומה? לומר לך מה פרה אדומה מכפרת אף מיתתן של צדיקים מכפרת (*Mo'ed Katan* 28a). The juxtaposition of these two chapters teaches that just as the חטאת-character of the פרה אדומה effects atonement, so does the death of *tzadikim* effect atonement. This may well mean that just as the mitzvah of פרה אדומה teaches that the Divine aspect of human nature is immortal and endowed with moral freedom, so does the death of *tzadikim* teach us these truths.

Truly, the death of a *tzaddik* offers convincing proof of immortality. For only one who is spiritually blind would identify the *tzaddik* with his corpse, which lies inert, already marked by the traces of decay. How can one identify the corpse with what only a short time before had employed thought and will with spiritual strength and moral power? Only one who is blind would not see that the corpse of a *tzaddik* is merely the garment of a man who departed — and cast aside his cloak.

2 **ולא היה מים לעדה**. As already noted on *Shemos* 17:5-6, the spring that was opened from the rock at Chorev not only satisfied the requirements of the moment, but accompanied them on all their subsequent wanderings in the wilderness, and for this reason we did not hear of any complaints about a lack of water. Now, however, immediately after Miriam's death (see *Ta'anis* 9a), the spring dried up, and the עדה, which for the first time regarded itself as "the community of the future," lacked the most basic requirement for their survival: ולא היה מים לעדה!

Because of the juxtaposition ותמת שם מרים . . . ולא היה מים לעדה, our Sages say (ibid.) that באר בזכות מרים: the well that accompanied them from Chorev through the wilderness came to them on Miriam's merit. Miriam's unobtrusive work for the moral future of the people was now made known to all. Her death was a great loss to the nation as a whole, and this became apparent immediately after her death, when the Chorev-well dried up.

3 *The people contended with Moshe and said: Would that we had perished when our brothers perished before* God!	ג וַיָּ֥רֶב הָעָ֖ם עִם־מֹשֶׁ֑ה וַיֹּֽאמְר֣וּ לֵאמֹ֔ר וְל֥וּ גָוַ֛עְנוּ בִּגְוַ֥ע אַחֵ֖ינוּ לִפְנֵ֥י יְהֹוָֽה׃
4 *For what purpose did you bring the community of* God *into this wilderness, that we and our animals should die there?*	ד וְלָמָ֤ה הֲבֵאתֶם֙ אֶת־קְהַ֣ל יְהֹוָ֔ה אֶל־הַמִּדְבָּ֖ר הַזֶּ֑ה לָמ֣וּת שָׁ֔ם אֲנַ֖חְנוּ וּבְעִירֵֽנוּ׃

3 **וירב העם** — the same עם of whom it is said in verse 1: וישב העם בקדש. When they reached Kadesh, they were happy to have returned to an inhabitable country, and then suddenly they experienced a lack of water, which they had not suffered in all their wanderings in the wilderness. They felt that Moshe and Aharon had betrayed them — and misled them! Therefore וירב העם עם משה.

ולו גוענו וגו׳. גויעה denotes painless natural death (see Commentary, *Bereshis* 6:17).

All those who died in the wilderness, upon whom it was decreed that they would not enter the Land, died by גויעה. They all died לפני ה׳; to their very last breaths, God's care did not forsake them. Their deaths went the way of the natural law of human mortality and were not caused by any unusual calamity — whereas we shall die of thirst!

4 **ולמה הבאתם**. This is not *God's* Will; rather, *you* have brought it about, and by doing so you have committed treachery against קהל ה׳. *God* wants to sustain us, He wants us to remain alive and to enter the Promised Land; for we are a community of people that belongs to God, and He wants to preserve us in life for a happy future. *You*, however, have brought this whole קהל into this desert so that we and our beasts should die there in terrible suffering.

ובעירנו. Scripture employs here the term "בעיר," which is the designation for animals under the mastery of their natural instincts (see Commentary, *Shemos* 22:4). Here the animals are so designated in reference to the urgent need to drink. This is their complaint: You should have refrained from doing this, if not for our sake then for the sake of our animals; you should have had pity on the poor blameless creatures!

5 *For what purpose have you brought us up from Egypt? In order to bring us to this evil place? This is not a place of seed, or of figs, or of wine, or of pomegranates. There is not even water to drink!*

ה וְלָמָה הֶעֱלִיתֻנוּ מִמִּצְרַיִם לְהָבִיא
אֹתָנוּ אֶל־הַמָּקוֹם הָרָע הַזֶּה לֹא ׀
מְקוֹם זֶרַע וּתְאֵנָה וְגֶפֶן וְרִמּוֹן
וּמַיִם אַיִן לִשְׁתּוֹת׃

6 *And Moshe and Aharon withdrew from the assembly to the entrance of the Tent of Appointed Meeting, and they fell upon their faces. And the glory of* God *appeared to them.*

ו וַיָּבֹא מֹשֶׁה וְאַהֲרֹן מִפְּנֵי הַקָּהָל
אֶל־פֶּתַח אֹהֶל מוֹעֵד וַיִּפְּלוּ עַל־
פְּנֵיהֶם וַיֵּרָא כְבוֹד־יְהֹוָה אֲלֵיהֶם׃ פ
שלישי (שני כשהן מחוברין)

7 *And* God *spoke to Moshe, saying:*

ז וַיְדַבֵּר יְהֹוָה אֶל־מֹשֶׁה לֵּאמֹר׃

8 *Take the staff and assemble the*

ח קַח אֶת־הַמַּטֶּה וְהַקְהֵל אֶת־

5 **ולמה העליתנו וגו׳**. The period for which it was decreed that we should wander through the wilderness has come to an end. We should already be entering the flourishing land that was promised to us, a land that in this spring season should be resplendent with all the beauty of blossom and bud. What a contrast that is to the place where we are now, where there is not even water for us to drink! This is not the Will of God; this is your doing.

6 **ויבא וגו׳ מפני וגו׳**. Cf. *Bereshis* 7:7: ויבא נח וגו׳ אל התבה מפני מי המבול; *Yeshayahu* 2:19 and 21: וּבָאוּ בִּמְעָרוֹת וגו׳ לָבוֹא בְּנִקְרוֹת הַצֻּרִים וגו׳ מִפְּנֵי פַּחַד ה׳ וגו׳. They said nothing in response, but fled to the entrance of the אהל מועד, as they always did whenever doubt was cast on the Divine source of their mission.

8-9 **קח את המטה וגו׳**. We do not find the staff in Moshe's hand since the victory over Amalek (*Shemos* 17:9). As is evident from v. 9, the staff was "before God" [לפני ה׳], i.e., it had been deposited in the Sanctuary, next to the ארון העדות. The staff of God in the hand of Moshe identified Moshe as God's emissary. Whenever Moshe moved that staff of God, whenever he inclined it or struck a blow with it prior to an event of which advance *community, you and your brother Aharon, and speak to the rock before their eyes, that it may give forth its water; then you shall bring forth water to them from out of the rock, and you shall give the community and their animals to drink.*

הָעֵדָה אַתָּה וְאַהֲרֹן אָחִיךָ וְדִבַּרְתֶּם אֶל־הַסֶּלַע לְעֵינֵיהֶם וְנָתַן מֵימָיו וְהוֹצֵאתָ לָהֶם מַיִם מִן־הַסֶּלַע וְהִשְׁקִיתָ אֶת־הָעֵדָה וְאֶת־בְּעִירָם׃

9 *And Moshe took the staff that had been laid down before* God, *as He had commanded him.*

ט וַיִּקַּח מֹשֶׁה אֶת־הַמַּטֶּה מִלִּפְנֵי יְהוָה כַּאֲשֶׁר צִוָּהוּ׃

warning had been given, this meant that the event about to occur would be the result of an instantaneous, direct intervention by God.

The people had accused Moshe and Aharon of having betrayed their Divine mission. It could not have been in accordance with God's Will, they said, that they had been brought to this waterless place; rather, Moshe and Aharon had maliciously brought the people to this place in order to bring upon them a calamity. It is inconceivable that God wants them to die in the wilderness.

"Take the staff," God says to Moshe, and show them that you are still My emissary, and that you have never, not even for one moment, ceased to be in My service.

והקהל את העדה. By the authority of your Divine mission, as manifested by the staff in your hand, assemble this "community of the future." ודברתם אל הסלע לעיניהם: Do not use the staff; rather, speak to the rock לעיניהם — in the presence of the entire people — and order the rock to yield מימיו, its water, the water which is already contained within it.

If he were to strike the rock — as in *Shemos* 17:6 — that would give the impression that the water was coming forth as the result of a new Divine intervention provoked by the people's uproar. But that is precisely the impression that should not be given. Rather, the people should be made to understand that it was not Moshe and Aharon but God Who had brought them to this place, and since God had brought them to this place and His cloud had directed them to encamp in this place, their stormy agitation, which was meant to provoke God's intervention, was unnecessary. Rather, the required water was already provided by God at the place to which He had directed them. One word from Moshe and Aharon to the rock would suffice for it to yield its water, which was already ready and waiting for them, ונתן מימיו. Accordingly, והוצאת וגו׳ והשקית וגו׳: Their need shall be met not by a new miracle performed by God, but simply by a word from you. This manner of obtaining water from the rock would have convinced the people of the great wrong they had done to Moshe and to Aharon. For they had accused Moshe and Aharon of having led them to this waterless place against the Will of God, and this claim would now have been refuted.

It is different if the water gushes forth only after a blow of the staff upon the rock. This still leaves room for the assumption that Moshe and Aharon had, on their own initiative, brought them to the wilderness of Tzin, that they had been justified in revolting, and that only this revolt and their distress had caused God to have mercy on them and to perform a miracle for them.

Had the miracle come about as prescribed, the people would have learned that under God's guidance they could banish all worries; they could be certain of receiving the right help at the right time — even without Moshe's staff.

The following interpretation I heard from the late lamented Chacham Bernays נ״ע: Just now they reached the border of the Promised Land and a new era awaited them. The visible miracles of the wilderness were henceforth to be replaced by the invisible but just as close guidance of God through נסים נסתרים. This miracle [v. 8] was meant to be the transition to this [new mode of] guidance, and it was meant to teach the following: The *staff* of Moshe in the wilderness shall be replaced by the *word* of Moshe, henceforth and forever. The wandering in the wilderness began with the Marah miracle, which showed Israel — according to the profound understanding of our Sages — that דבר מן התורה, a Word of the Torah, is sufficient to sweeten all the bitter water (see Commentary, *Shemos* 15:25). The wandering in the wilderness was concluded — and a new future opened up for Israel — with the miracle described here, which was meant to show that the *word* of Moshe suffices to bring forth living water out of the rock (cf. also Commentary below, 27:14).

10 *And Moshe and Aharon assembled the community before the rock. And he said to them: Hear now, you rebels! Shall we bring forth water for you out of this rock?*

י וַיַּקְהִלוּ מֹשֶׁה וְאַהֲרֹן אֶת־הַקָּהָל
אֶל־פְּנֵי הַסָּלַע וַיֹּאמֶר לָהֶם
שִׁמְעוּ־נָא הַמֹּרִים הֲמִן־הַסֶּלַע
הַזֶּה נוֹצִיא לָכֶם מָיִם׃

11 *And Moshe raised his hand and struck the rock with his staff twice. Water came forth abundantly, and the community and their animals drank.*

יא וַיָּרֶם מֹשֶׁה אֶת־יָדוֹ וַיַּךְ אֶת־
הַסֶּלַע בְּמַטֵּהוּ פַּעֲמָיִם וַיֵּצְאוּ מַיִם
רַבִּים וַתֵּשְׁתְּ הָעֵדָה וּבְעִירָם׃ ס

10-11 **ויקהלו וגו׳ ויאמר וגו׳ וירם וגו׳**. May we presume to explore the impulses that could have influenced the emotions of one such as Moshe, the servant of God, of whom God Himself said: בכל ביתי נאמן הוא (above, 12:7)? What could have distracted him, for even one moment in his life, from carrying out his mission properly?

Our conjecture would be as follows: In accordance with God's command, Moshe removed the staff from the Sanctuary, where it had lain for nearly forty years, and took it into his hand, and with this symbol of his Divine mission he assembled the people. Thus he again stood before the people — after nearly forty years — with the staff of God in his hand. At the start of his mission, forty years earlier, he needed this staff in order to authenticate his mission before the people (see *Shemos* 4:1-17). And now it hurt him to think that after all he had done during those forty years he had not yet won the trust and confidence of his people. In the bitterness of these emotions he forgot what he had been commanded to do and, instead of speaking calmly to the rock, he angrily rebuked the people. Agitated, he struck the rock — וירם וגו׳ ויך וגו׳ פעמים — whereupon water gushed forth from it in abundance and quenched the thirst of the people and their animals.

This is the rebuke that he addressed to them: שמעו נא המרים וגו׳.

We have already explained (Commentary, *Bereshis* 26:34-35) that from the root מרה we get מוֹרָה, a razor, which clashes with the hair, removing it at a right angle. Thus, the basic meaning of מרה is: going in the opposite direction and ultimately clashing. A term derived from a similar conception is the German "*widerhaarig*" [refractory, lit. "cross-haired"]. מרה refers primarily to actions and denotes positive or negative disobedience, but it also occurs in a more general sense, where it denotes behavior or a condition that is diametrically opposed to wishes and expectations. Thus, of a condition of wretchedness where everything wished for is denied, it says: עֳנִי יִשְׂרָאֵל מֹרֶה (*Melachim* II, 14:26). Iyov describes his complaint as מרי: גַּם־הַיּוֹם מְרִי שִׂחִי (*Iyov* 23:2); he could not formulate his complaint in accordance with the wishes of his friends, for יָדִי כָּבְדָה עַל־אַנְחָתִי, the trouble that had overtaken him was too heavy to be expressed by his groans. אֲדֹנָ-י יֱדֹוִד פָּתַח־לִי אֹזֶן וְאָנֹכִי לֹא מָרִיתִי (*Yeshayahu* 50:5): God opened his ear, and he did not turn a deaf ear to God's teaching. One who turns a deaf ear to teaching is called "מורה."

Here, too, המרים does not mean that they are disobedient, for in this incident no actual disobedience is displayed. Rather, Moshe's rebuke is that they are stiff-necked, and that their general behavior is contrary to justified expectations. In particular, his point is that they are inattentive to the lessons that should have been learned from their momentous experiences. In this light we can understand the various meanings — the שיטין הרבה, as *Bemidbar Rabbah* (19:9) puts it — found by our Sages in the term "המרים": סרבנים, שוטים, מלמדים את מלמדיהם, מורי חיצים; disobedience, lack of understanding, presumption, quarrelsomeness. For המרים does not denote disobedience in the narrow sense of the term; rather, it denotes general stiff-neckedness.

המן הסלע הזה נוציא לכם מים. In our view, this question should be understood as follows: Shall *we* bring forth water for you out of this rock? You have raised the accusation that it was *we* who brought you "to this wilderness," "to this evil place," where "there is not even any water to drink." Very well, but if then at a mere word from us, this very rock before which you are now standing should give you the water you need, will you then cease to be מרים? Will you then understand at last that wherever you have gone, it was not we, but *God,* that led you there?

By these words, Moshe had not yet deviated from his mission. By their content, these words were proper preparation for what should have taken place לעיניהם for their instruction. But the agitation in which they were spoken impelled him to raise the staff and strike the rock — and that was the deviation.

12 *And* God *said to Moshe and Aharon: Because you did not hold fast to Me, to sanctify Me before the eyes of the Children of Israel, therefore you shall not bring this community into the land that I have given them.*

יב וַיֹּאמֶר יְהוָה אֶל־מֹשֶׁה וְאֶל־אַהֲרֹן
יַעַן לֹא־הֶאֱמַנְתֶּם בִּי לְהַקְדִּישֵׁנִי
לְעֵינֵי בְּנֵי יִשְׂרָאֵל לָכֵן לֹא תָבִיאוּ
אֶת־הַקָּהָל הַזֶּה אֶל־הָאָרֶץ
אֲשֶׁר־נָתַתִּי לָהֶם׃

12 **יען לא האמנתם בי להקדישני**. If we are not mistaken in our whole approach thus far, Moshe's agitation sprang from the bitter feeling that his life work had been to no avail. All that he had done for the people had been in vain, for their attitude toward him was still that of stiff-necked מורים who paid no heed and were not open to persuasion.

On the one hand, this agitation is evidence that he had permitted his own personality to come to the fore, which is inappropriate for a man like Moshe; for the messenger's personality must recede in the face of the awareness of his mission. This is perhaps the most difficult of all trials: never to lose patience, but to hope in God and wait patiently for Him. On the other hand, this agitation attests to doubt — even if only for a fleeting moment — in the ultimate success of the Divine mission; for a moment, Moshe doubts whether the people will embrace its calling.

Does not all this constitute a momentary decline of אמונה? For he who trusts need not fear; he holds fast to God, no matter how antagonistic are the circumstances. Even if his mission stumbles, he does not question himself or his destiny — and this is the real test of his faith. A messenger of God is required to set God always before him, for there is nothing that can keep Him from accomplishing His absolute Will; He does whatever He pleases. This awareness should always remain with the messenger, and nothing that befalls him should demoralize him. Like the angels that sanctify God's Name, he should cover his eyes and cover his feet, and strictly by the winged power of his mission carry out God's service. Does not the fulfillment of this requirement constitute a קידוש השם in the midst of the people to whom this mission is directed? Hence, does not the charge לא האמנתם בי להקדישני strike at the very heart of Moshe's lapse? Does it not define the inner nature of Moshe's impatient agitation?

But who would dare to complete the unspoken link between the sin (יען) and its punishment (לכן)? And who would dare to define Aharon's part in this sin, whereby he was found deserving of the same punishment? In any event, in all its momentous significance, the fact remains: Because of one small and so easily understandable moment of weakness in אמונה, the leaders of the nation, standing at the borders of the Promised Land, received a punishment similar to that decreed upon the generation of the wilderness for their constant lack of אמונה. The leaders' graves beside those of the people bear eternal witness to the justice of the Divine rule, upon whose scales even the slightest misstep of men close to God, hallowed by their Divine service, weighs as heavily as the worst sins of ordinary mortals. God's rule completes its work on earth without the help of Moshe and Aharon, and thereby reveals itself in the whole קדושה of its absolute greatness. The accomplishment of its purposes is not dependent on any outside factor; even Moshe and Aharon are not indispensable to it.

And so we find in one of Israel's national hymns, which was written in a later period. The Psalmist (*Tehillim* 99) sings of God's קדושה, and he describes the exaltedness of God's kingship, before which every heart must tremble and every man must solemnly train himself to govern his actions with exceeding care. The Psalmist mentions the cherubim, which shield God's Torah, and in his song he says as follows: When God establishes His throne upon cherubim, the earth shakes on account of all its former ways. All who render homage to His Name recognize and acknowledge that God is great and awesome; He is holy. God's might loves justice, and He wishes to establish in us the attribute of equity, which is based on justice and righteousness. Because קדוש הוא, God is holy, we are obligated to devote the whole of ourselves to the Sanctuary of His Torah. The Psalmist then points to Moshe and Aharon, and asks us to consider that Moshe and Aharon were the most eminent among His priests, and Shemuel was among those who proclaim His Name; they called upon God to help others, and were sure of being answered. He spoke to them from a pillar of cloud, and they kept His testimonies and statutes, which He gave them. In their pleas for others, God listened to them and was a forgiving God — and yet for their own lapses He had no forgiveness: רוֹמְמוּ ה׳ אֱלֹקֵינוּ וְהִשְׁתַּחֲווּ לְהַר קָדְשׁוֹ כִּי־קָדוֹשׁ ה׳ אֱלֹקֵינוּ (cf. Commentary, ibid.).

13 *These are the waters of contention, where the Children of Israel contended with* God, *and He showed Himself in His holiness through them.*

יג הֵ֚מָּה מֵ֣י מְרִיבָ֔ה אֲשֶׁר־רָב֥וּ בְנֵֽי־יִשְׂרָאֵ֖ל אֶת־יְהֹוָ֑ה וַיִּקָּדֵ֖שׁ בָּֽם׃ ס

רביעי

14 *And Moshe sent messengers from Kadesh to the king of Edom: Thus says your brother, Israel, to you: You have learned about all the trouble that we have encountered.*

יד וַיִּשְׁלַ֨ח מֹשֶׁ֧ה מַלְאָכִ֛ים מִקָּדֵ֖שׁ אֶל־מֶ֣לֶךְ אֱד֑וֹם כֹּ֤ה אָמַר֙ אָחִ֣יךָ יִשְׂרָאֵ֔ל אַתָּ֣ה יָדַ֔עְתָּ אֵ֥ת כָּל־הַתְּלָאָ֖ה אֲשֶׁ֥ר מְצָאָֽתְנוּ׃

13 **ויקדש בם**. בם apparently refers to Moshe and Aharon of the previous verse, and the קידוש השם mentioned here is to be understood in the sense explained on verse 12. The death of Moshe and Aharon places an everlasting seal on the Divine origin of their mission. In addition, it attests to the inviolable holiness of God's Will. It was through Moshe and Aharon that God's Will was revealed to us, and it His Will that sets our course on earth. רוֹמְמוּ ה׳ אֱלֹקֵינוּ וְהִשְׁתַּחֲווּ לְהַר קָדְשׁוֹ כִּי־קָדוֹשׁ ה׳ אֱלֹקֵינוּ is the call that rings out from the graves of these *tzadikim*, and it warns all generations of Israel at all times and in every place.

Deeply significant is the juxtaposition in our verse of בני ישראל and בם. "The *Children of Israel* contended with God" — whereas *Moshe and Aharon* were stricken by the attribute of strict justice. This contrast attests to קדושת ה׳ in all its greatness (see Commentary, v. 12).

המה differentiates between these מי מריבה of the fortieth year and those of the first year (*Shemos* 17).

14 **וישלח**. It had already been decreed upon Moshe that he personally would not reach the long-pursued goal; nevertheless, he continued to carry out his task with vigor, for as long as God let him live in the midst of his people.

אחיך ישראל recalls their common descent. According to *Bemidbar Rabbah* (19:15), it also alludes to the different fortunes that had befallen the twin branches of the Abrahamitic line.

15 *Our fathers went down to Egypt, and we remained in Egypt for a long time, but the Egyptians did evil to us and to our fathers.*

טו וַיֵּרְדוּ אֲבֹתֵינוּ מִצְרַיְמָה וַנֵּשֶׁב בְּמִצְרַיִם יָמִים רַבִּים וַיָּרֵעוּ לָנוּ מִצְרַיִם וְלַאֲבֹתֵינוּ׃

16 *Then we cried to* God *and He heard our voice; He sent a messenger and led us out of Egypt. Now we are in Kadesh, a city on the border of your territory.*

טז וַנִּצְעַק אֶל־יְהוָה וַיִּשְׁמַע קֹלֵנוּ וַיִּשְׁלַח מַלְאָךְ וַיֹּצִאֵנוּ מִמִּצְרָיִם וְהִנֵּה אֲנַחְנוּ בְקָדֵשׁ עִיר קְצֵה גְבוּלֶךָ׃

17 *Please let us pass through your land. We will not pass through field or through vineyard, nor drink water from the wells. We will go by the king's highway, [and] will not turn aside to the right or to the left until we have passed through your territory.*

יז נַעְבְּרָה־נָּא בְאַרְצֶךָ לֹא נַעֲבֹר בְּשָׂדֶה וּבְכֶרֶם וְלֹא נִשְׁתֶּה מֵי בְאֵר דֶּרֶךְ הַמֶּלֶךְ נֵלֵךְ לֹא נִטֶּה יָמִין וּשְׂמֹאול עַד אֲשֶׁר־נַעֲבֹר גְּבֻלֶךָ׃

18 *Then Edom sent word to him: You shall not pass through me, or else I will come out to meet you with the sword.*

יח וַיֹּאמֶר אֵלָיו אֱדוֹם לֹא תַעֲבֹר בִּי פֶּן־בַּחֶרֶב אֵצֵא לִקְרָאתֶךָ׃

---

15 **ולאבתינו**: They did evil not just to the recent generation who left Egypt, a generation with whom you are not familiar and of whom you could possibly think that they somehow deserved the treatment they received; rather, they did evil already to our forefathers, whose honest characters are known to you by tradition. Thus, it was an injustice decreed against our people as a people, and the decree was bequeathed from one generation to the next.

17 **ולא נשתה מי באר**. We will not touch any private property.

דרך המלך: a road constructed by the "king" — i.e., by the nation, a

19 *The Children of Israel sent word to him in return: We will go up by the high road, and if we should drink from your waters, I or my livestock, then I will pay their purchase price — [I will do] nothing else whatsoever; only let me pass through with my feet.*

יט וַיֹּאמְר֨וּ אֵלָ֜יו בְּנֵֽי־יִשְׂרָאֵ֗ל בַּֽמְסִלָּ֣ה נַעֲלֶ֔ה וְאִם־מֵימֶ֤יךָ נִשְׁתֶּה֙ אֲנִ֣י וּמִקְנַ֔י וְנָתַתִּ֖י מִכְרָ֑ם רַ֥ק אֵין־דָּבָ֖ר בְּרַגְלַ֥י אֶֽעֱבֹֽרָה׃

public highway, one that is not private property, apparently not even the property of a local community.

19 **ויאמרו וגו׳ במסלה נעלה**. The meaning of הסתולל (Commentary, *Shemos* 9:17) is to exalt oneself; סַלְסְלֶהָ (*Mishlei* 4:8): to raise up; סֹלְלָה (*Yirmeyahu* 6:6): a high mound of earth cast up for military purposes; סֻלָּם (*Bereshis* 28:12; cf. Commentary there): a ladder; סַל (ibid. 40:17): a basket, used for lifting and carrying things. From all this it is evident that the basic meaning of סלל is ascent. Accordingly, מסלה is an uphill road. Indeed, here as well as elsewhere, we find עלייה construed with מסלה. Thus לִמְסִלָּה הָעֹלָה מִבֵּית־אֵל (*Shoftim* 21:19). The road going eastward from the Philistine coastal plain to בֵּית שֶׁמֶשׁ is uphill; hence it says: אִם־דֶּרֶךְ גְּבוּלוֹ יַעֲלֶה בֵּית שֶׁמֶשׁ (*Shemuel* I, 6:9), and that road is called "מְסִלָּה" (ibid. I, 6:12). Thus, too: בַּמְסִלָּה הָעוֹלָה מִשְׁמָר (*Divrei Ha-Yamim* I, 26:16). Also, it appears that מְסִלַּת שְׂדֵה כוֹבֵס (*Yeshayahu* 7:3; 36:2) was a road climbing uphill. In *Melachim* II, 18:17 it says of this road: וַיַּעֲלוּ וַיָּבֹאוּ יְרוּשָׁלַם וַיַּעֲלוּ וַיָּבֹאוּ וַיַּעַמְדוּ בִּתְעָלַת הַבְּרֵכָה הָעֶלְיוֹנָה אֲשֶׁר בִּמְסִלַּת שְׂדֵה כוֹבֵס. Thus, the road from Yerushalayim to שדה כובס is called an עלייה.

The מסלה mentioned in our verse may also be understood in this light. In the second petition, they proposed to travel on the mountain road. For the land of Edom and Se'ir is a mountainous region, which is why it is also called "הר שעיר."

There were two routes through Edom to the Land of Israel. The more convenient one, leading through valleys, was דרך המלך, to the right and to the left of which were fields and vineyards and wells that had been dug. First Moshe requested permission to travel on this road. He therefore prefaced this request with the self-imposed condition: לא נעבר בשדה ובכרם

20 *Then he sent word: You shall not pass through. And Edom went out to meet him with a massive complement of men and with enormous power.*

כ וַיֹּאמֶר לֹא תַעֲבֹר וַיֵּצֵא אֱדוֹם
לִקְרָאתוֹ בְּעַם כָּבֵד וּבְיָד חֲזָקָה׃

21 *Thus Edom refused to permit Israel to pass through his territory, and Israel turned aside from it.*

כא וַיְמָאֵן ׀ אֱדוֹם נְתֹן אֶת־יִשְׂרָאֵל
עֲבֹר בִּגְבֻלוֹ וַיֵּט יִשְׂרָאֵל מֵעָלָיו׃ פ

חמישי (שלישי כשהן מחוברין)

22 *They journeyed forth from Kadesh, and the Children of Israel, the whole community, came to Mount Hor.*

כב וַיִּסְעוּ מִקָּדֵשׁ וַיָּבֹאוּ בְנֵי־יִשְׂרָאֵל
כָּל־הָעֵדָה הֹר הָהָר׃

ולא נשתה מי באר, דרך המלך נלך לא נטה ימין ושמאל. When this request was refused, the people offered to take the more difficult route over the mountains: במסלה נעלה. There they would find mountain water, which was left at the disposal of travellers. Strictly speaking, however, this water, too, was מימיך, Edom's property. Hence, the people offered to pay for it, if they or their animals should drink of this water. Thus, nothing was asked of Edom except to permit their passage on foot.

21 **ויט ישראל מעליו**. From *Devarim* 2:4ff. we know that Israel was forbidden to provoke a war with Edom.

22 **כל העדה** — see Commentary, verse 1. This remark made here, just before Aharon's death, teaches us that although Aharon died in the wilderness, his death was not a consequence of the general decree that prevented the generation of the wilderness from entering the Land. When Israel reached the area of Mount Hor, that decree was no longer in effect. Aharon died solely on account of the sin of מי מריבה at Kadesh.

According to *Bemidbar Rabbah* (19:16), הר ההר means: הר על גבי הר כתפוח קטן על גבי תפוח גדול, a mount on top of a mount, a small mountain summit rising on the top of another mountain.

23 *And* God *said to Moshe and to Aharon on Mount Hor, on the border of the land of Edom:*

כג וַיֹּאמֶר יְהוָה אֶל־מֹשֶׁה וְאֶל־אַהֲרֹן בְּהֹר הָהָר עַל־גְּבוּל אֶרֶץ־אֱדוֹם לֵאמֹר׃

24 *Aharon shall be gathered unto his people, for he shall not enter into the land that I have given to the Children of Israel, because you have acted contrary to My word with regard to the waters of contention.*

כד יֵאָסֵף אַהֲרֹן אֶל־עַמָּיו כִּי לֹא יָבֹא אֶל־הָאָרֶץ אֲשֶׁר נָתַתִּי לִבְנֵי יִשְׂרָאֵל עַל אֲשֶׁר־מְרִיתֶם אֶת־פִּי לְמֵי מְרִיבָה׃

25 *Take Aharon and his son Elazar, and take them up Mount Hor.*

כה קַח אֶת־אַהֲרֹן וְאֶת־אֶלְעָזָר בְּנוֹ וְהַעַל אֹתָם הֹר הָהָר׃

26 *Divest Aharon of his garments and clothe his son Elazar with them, and Aharon will be gathered up and die there.*

כו וְהַפְשֵׁט אֶת־אַהֲרֹן אֶת־בְּגָדָיו וְהִלְבַּשְׁתָּם אֶת־אֶלְעָזָר בְּנוֹ וְאַהֲרֹן יֵאָסֵף וּמֵת שָׁם׃

27 *And Moshe did as* God *had commanded him. They went up Mount Hor before the eyes of the entire community.*

כז וַיַּעַשׂ מֹשֶׁה כַּאֲשֶׁר צִוָּה יְהוָה וַיַּעֲלוּ אֶל־הֹר הָהָר לְעֵינֵי כָּל־הָעֵדָה׃

23 **על גבול ארץ אדום**. Similarly, it says below (33:37): בקצה ארץ אדום. There is another Mount Hor at the northwest border of Eretz Yisrael (below, 34:7), hence the need to give the precise location.

24 **יאסף אהרן וגו׳** — see Commentary, *Bereshis* 25:8.

26 **והפשט וגו׳ והלבשתם וגו׳**. Thereby Elazar was inducted as כהן גדול in place of Aharon (see *Shemos* 29:29 and Commentary there). Thus, before his own death, Aharon merited to see himself living on in the person of his son.

כח וַיַּפְשֵׁט מֹשֶׁה אֶת־אַהֲרֹן אֶת־
בְּגָדָיו וַיַּלְבֵּשׁ אֹתָם אֶת־אֶלְעָזָר
בְּנוֹ וַיָּמָת אַהֲרֹן שָׁם בְּרֹאשׁ הָהָר
וַיֵּרֶד מֹשֶׁה וְאֶלְעָזָר מִן־הָהָר׃

28 *Moshe divested Aharon of his garments and clothed his son Elazar with them, and Aharon died there on the top of the mountain. Moshe and Elazar descended from the mountain.*

כט וַיִּרְאוּ כָּל־הָעֵדָה כִּי גָוַע אַהֲרֹן
וַיִּבְכּוּ אֶת־אַהֲרֹן שְׁלֹשִׁים יוֹם כֹּל
בֵּית יִשְׂרָאֵל׃ ס

29 *And the entire community saw that Aharon had expired, and the entire house of Israel wept for Aharon thirty days.*

29 **ויראו וגו׳**. Our Sages (*Ta'anis* 9a) teach us that even as, after the death of Miriam, the loss to the nation became manifest by the drying up of the well, so, too, the death of Aharon became "visible" to the nation by an external manifestation. With Aharon's death, the cloud that until then had protected and guided them in the wilderness departed, מת אהרן נסתלקו ענני הכבוד. Israel's resultant state of defenselessness immediately encouraged the Canaanite king Arad, who dwelled in the region, to launch an attack against them (see below, 21:1). (This external manifestation [the departure of the cloud] is alluded to in the text by the word "ויראו," and the Gemara's statement אל תקרי ויראו אלא וייראו [ibid.] is merely explanation.)

Our Sages say there: ג׳ פרנסים טובים עמדו לישראל אלו הן משה אהרן ומרים וג׳ מתנות טובות נתנו על ידם ואלו הן באר וענן ומן, באר בזכות מרים עמוד ענן בזכות אהרן מן בזכות משה וכו׳. The nation had their three leaders — Moshe, Aharon, and Miriam — to thank for three benefits which provided for their existence in the wilderness: the well, the cloud, and the manna. The well was due to the merit of Miriam, the cloud was due to the merit of Aharon, and the manna was due to the merit of Moshe.

Michah, too, directs the attention of his contemporaries to these three leaders of the nation. Israel cannot complain that God misled them and did not tell them what is good. It was always known to them that moral strength alone, and no other act, is the condition for their national existence. God says through the mouth of Michah: "My people, what have I done to you, and wherein have I wearied you? . . . When I brought you up out of the land of Egypt and redeemed you from the house of bondage, did I not send before you a Moshe, an Aharon, a Miriam?" (*Michah* 6:3-4). The work of these three personalities — the work for which they were qualified — was strictly their teaching and their influence on mind and heart. Their very personalities faithfully attested to the task whose accomplishment was crucial to our future.

Michah (ibid. 6:8) defines this task as follows: עֲשׂוֹת מִשְׁפָּט וְאַהֲבַת חֶסֶד וְהַצְנֵעַ לֶכֶת עִם־אֱלֹקֶיךָ. What immediately springs to mind is that these three elements of our moral mission also characterize the work of these three leaders. **משפט**, the norm of justice, which shapes one's whole life in accordance with God's Will, was the primary mission of *Moshe*. **חסד**, or more accurately אהבת חסד, the love of love: the heart's inclination to joyfully relinquish what one is rightfully entitled to, the attribute of compassion, the willingness to make sacrifices for others — these qualities characterize the activity of *Aharon*. Aharon's activity alongside of Moshe is described by our Sages as follows: משה היה אומר יקוב הדין את ההר אבל אהרן אוהב שלום ורודף שלום ומשים שלום בין אדם לחברו. "Moshe's principle was: 'The law must cut through the mountain,' but that of Aharon was: 'To love peace, pursue peace, and bring peace between one person and another'" (*Sanhedrin* 6b). הצנע לכת עם אלקים, walking with God unpretentiously, modestly, and in moral purity — the attribute of **צניעות**, which is the fundamental character of Jewish womanhood — was surely fostered under *Miriam*'s influence.

Now, those מתנות טובות that promoted the people's material well-being — do they not correspond to the spiritual מתנות fostered by the three פרנסים טובים to promote the people's spiritual well-being? Perhaps we do not err in saying: צניעות is the quiet, hidden "spring" from whose depths all holiness of life flows; חסד is the granting, cooling, and protecting "cloud," to which the clear penetrating rays of justice must be joined in order to mature the seeds of welfare and happiness in the field of mankind; whereas משפט, justice, is the bread from heaven, the "manna" [i.e., the granting of sustenance to each individual], on which the existence and endurance, the vigor and strength of all human and national life depend. Hence: באר through the זכות of Miriam, who cultivates צניעות; ענני הכבוד through the זכות of Aharon, who cultivates חסד; whereas מן through the זכות of Moshe, who transmits to Israel the Divine משפט.

ויבכו את אהרן שלשים יום כל בית ישראל. Our Sages (אבות דרבי נתן 12:3) note the difference between what is stated here and what is stated after

21 1 *The Canaanite king Arad, who dwelled in the south, heard that Israel was coming by the way of the scouts; he made war on Israel and took some of them captive.*

כא א וַיִּשְׁמַ֞ע הַכְּנַעֲנִ֤י מֶֽלֶךְ־עֲרָד֙ יֹשֵׁ֣ב הַנֶּ֔גֶב כִּ֚י בָּ֣א יִשְׂרָאֵ֔ל דֶּ֖רֶךְ הָאֲתָרִ֑ים וַיִּלָּ֙חֶם֙ בְּיִשְׂרָאֵ֔ל וַיִּ֥שְׁבְּ ׀ מִמֶּ֖נּוּ שֶֽׁבִי׃

the death of Moshe. There it says: ויבכו בני ישראל את משה וגו׳ (*Devarim* 34:8), whereas here — after the death of Aharon — it says: כל בית ישראל. Aharon was a devotee of lovingkindness, who loved peace and pursued peace; hence the magnitude of his loss was felt and appreciated by all. By contrast, Moshe's attribute — uncomfortable to some people — was godly truth and justice.

One should not overlook the following point. Only a few days earlier the people had heaped upon Aharon grave accusations and unjust complaints (v. 2ff.), yet now all classes of the people deeply mourned him. This deep mourning for Aharon teaches us that all those revolts that had troubled the lives of Aharon and Moshe were only passing incidents of unrest, brought about by momentary moods of despair. But, in its normal state, the people knew and appreciated the merits of its great leaders.

CHAPTER 21

1 **וישמע הכנעני** — see the Commentary on the previous verse.

הכנעני: apparently from the original nations living in Eretz Yisrael. It was as a Canaanite that he made war on Israel, for he felt threatened by Israel's intention to settle in the land of Canaan. For this reason he attacked Israel at the border.

ערד. According to *Targum Onkelos*, this is the name of a region. According to the Gemara in *Rosh Hashanah* 3a, this is the name of the king identical with סיחון. Some say that סיחון is the proper name, and he was called ערד, "the wild ass," because of his wildness: שדומה לערוד במדבר. Others say that ערד is the proper name, and he was called סיחון, "the young ass," because of his recklessness: שדומה לסייח במדבר. סיח is a young ass (*Bava Basra* 78b).

האתרים derives from the root תור with a prefixed א, like אגם and אגמון from the root גמא, אזן (אזנך [cf. *Devarim* 23:14]) from the root זון, אכן from the root כון, אכר from the root כור (כר), and so forth.

2 *Then Israel vowed a vow to* God *and said: If You will deliver this people into my hand, then I will place an interdiction upon their cities.*

ב וַיִּדַּ֨ר יִשְׂרָאֵ֥ל נֶ֛דֶר לַֽיהוָ֖ה וַיֹּאמַ֑ר אִם־נָתֹ֨ן תִּתֵּ֜ן אֶת־הָעָ֤ם הַזֶּה֙ בְּיָדִ֔י וְהַֽחֲרַמְתִּ֖י אֶת־עָרֵיהֶֽם׃

3 God *hearkened to the voice of Israel and delivered up the Canaanite[s]. [Israel] placed an interdiction upon them and upon their cities, and named the place Chormah.*

ג וַיִּשְׁמַ֨ע יְהוָ֜ה בְּק֣וֹל יִשְׂרָאֵ֗ל וַיִּתֵּן֙ אֶת־הַֽכְּנַעֲנִ֔י וַיַּחֲרֵ֥ם אֶתְהֶ֖ם וְאֶת־עָרֵיהֶ֑ם וַיִּקְרָ֥א שֵֽׁם־הַמָּק֖וֹם חָרְמָֽה׃ פ

2-3 **אם נתן תתן וגו׳ ויתן את הכנעני וגו׳**. The רמב״ן notes in his Commentary that the east bank of the Jordan is never called "ארץ כנען," and of this king Arad, whose people are called here "כנעני," it explicitly says: והוא ישב בנגב בארץ כנען (below, 33:40). The רמב״ן therefore holds that this king lived in the south, west of the Jordan, and that from there he launched an attack on Israel [who were traveling in the south, east of the Jordan]. Accordingly, the vow of verse 2 did not refer to the contemporary present, but to the future conquest. For this reason Scripture here employs a concise style — ויתן את הכנעני — and does not spell out to whom God delivered up the Canaanites, for the complete subjugation of the population was carried out only in a later period.

Thus, Israel vowed that if God would grant them victory over these attackers, they would place an interdiction upon their cities during the future conquest of the Land, in commemoration of their first victory over a Canaanite people; they would leave their cities uninhabited, but would give all the spoil to the Sanctuary treasury, as is stated in the case of Yericho. On this account they named the place of the victory חרמה.

Indeed, we do find מֶלֶךְ עֲרָד (*Yehoshua* 12:14) listed among the kings of Canaan defeated by Yehoshua in Western Eretz Yisrael, and from *Shoftim* 1:16 it is clear that ערד lay within the territory of Yehudah on the border of the wilderness of Yehudah. It also says there (v. 17): וַיַּכּוּ אֶת־הַכְּנַעֲנִי יוֹשֵׁב צְפַת וַיַּחֲרִימוּ אוֹתָהּ וַיִּקְרָא אֶת־שֵׁם־הָעִיר חָרְמָה, and according to the רמב״ן this was the final fulfillment of the vow. Nevertheless, we should note that in

ד וַיִּסְעוּ מֵהֹר הָהָר דֶּרֶךְ יַם־סוּף לִסְבֹב אֶת־אֶרֶץ אֱדוֹם וַתִּקְצַר נֶפֶשׁ־הָעָם בַּדָּרֶךְ׃

4 *They journeyed from Mount Hor toward the Red Sea, in order to bypass the land of Edom, and the people became impatient along the way.*

ה וַיְדַבֵּר הָעָם בֵּאלֹהִים וּבְמֹשֶׁה לָמָה הֶעֱלִיתֻנוּ מִמִּצְרַיִם לָמוּת בַּמִּדְבָּר כִּי אֵין לֶחֶם וְאֵין מַיִם וְנַפְשֵׁנוּ קָצָה בַּלֶּחֶם הַקְּלֹקֵל׃

5 *And the people spoke against God and against Moshe: Why have you brought us up from Egypt to die in the wilderness? For we have no bread and no water, and our soul is weary of this unsubstantial nourishment.*

Yehoshua 12:14 מֶלֶךְ חָרְמָה is mentioned next to מלך ערד, and this still requires explanation.

4 **דרך ים סוף**. It appeared as though they were retreating and turning back, and the detour was a long one. Similarly, in *Devarim* (2:1) it says: ונסב את הר שעיר ימים רבים.

ותקצר נפש העם בדרך — cf. *Shemos* 6:9, מקצר רוח. As we explained there, קצר רוח, and similarly here קצר נפש — which are apparently the opposite of ארך אפים — denote impatience. The רוח and the נפש are not sufficiently long-suffering to wait patiently for the goal they desire. Here, in particular, the נפש, the spirit of life, urges forward and cannot bear with patience the troubles of the long journey, out of longing for the desired goal. There was no real concrete cause for dissatisfaction; they had all their requirements.

5 **וידבר העם באלקים**. Their discontent turned also directly against God. They did not doubt the authenticity of Moshe's mission, but they were dissatisfied with God's guidance.

למה העליתֻנו: [The second person plural refers to] God and Moshe.

למות במדבר. If we continue in this way we will never reach our goal, but will end our days in the wilderness, under monotonous, utterly abnormal conditions.

6 *And* God *released the venomous snakes against the people; they bit the people and many people of Israel died.*

ו וַיְשַׁלַּח יְהֹוָה בָּעָם אֵת הַנְּחָשִׁים הַשְּׂרָפִים וַיְנַשְּׁכוּ אֶת־הָעָם וַיָּמָת עַם־רָב מִיִּשְׂרָאֵל׃

כי אין לחם ואין מים. This cannot mean that they lack the nourishment they require, for they immediately admit that they do have "לחם." What they miss is the kind of food and drink people normally have. The nourishment with which they had been provided by miracle, without any effort on their own part, had become monotonous to them. God's grace, His special providence, which had guided them daily for forty years, had become for them routine, and their discontent caused them to denigrate the nutritive value of the manna. They called it לחם הקלקל; according to the *Pesikta*, a light, easily digestible food, so easily digested that it was נימוח באברים (*Midrash Shochar Tov* 78:3, cited by *Yalkut Shimoni* ad loc.), נבלע ברמ"ח איברים (*Yoma* 75b); it was completely absorbed by the body and used up entirely to reproduce the body's tissues. In their sight, this excellent quality of the manna became a drawback; the manna was not substantial enough for them.

6 **וישלח ה' בעם**. שָׁלַח in the *kal* means: to send, to set something in motion toward a goal. שַׁלַּח in the *pi'el*, however, usually means: to dismiss something, to release it, not to hold it back, to let it go its natural way and move about as it pleases. Thus: וַיְשַׁלַּח את היונה, וַיְשַׁלַּח את הערב (*Bereshis* 8:7-8), וְשִׁלַּח לכם את אחיכם (ibid. 43:14), ויהי בְּשַׁלַּח פרעה (*Shemos* 13:17), וְשִׁלַּח את בעירה (ibid. 22:4), and elsewhere very frequently.

Here, too, the meaning is not: God sent snakes but, rather: He released the snakes, did not keep them back. Hence, it does not say here נחשים שרפים but הנחשים השרפים. These snakes had always existed in the wilderness. However, until this point, God, in His providence, had kept them away from the people. Now God removed this restraint, and the snakes of the wilderness reverted to their natural instincts — and bit the people. In *Devarim* 8:15, Moshe describes the wilderness, through which they had miraculously passed unscathed, as follows: המוליכך במדבר הגדל והנורא נחש שרף ועקרב וצמאון וגו'. Thus, נחשים שרפים are as natural to the wilderness as צמאון.

7 *And the people came to Moshe and said: We have sinned, for we have spoken against* God *and against you. Pray to* God *that He may turn away the snakes from us. And Moshe prayed for the people.*

ז וַיָּבֹא הָעָם אֶל־מֹשֶׁה וַיֹּאמְרוּ
חָטָאנוּ כִּי־דִבַּרְנוּ בַיהוָה וָבָךְ
הִתְפַּלֵּל אֶל־יְהוָה וְיָסֵר מֵעָלֵינוּ
אֶת־הַנָּחָשׁ וַיִּתְפַּלֵּל מֹשֶׁה בְּעַד
הָעָם׃

8 *And* God *said to Moshe: Make yourself a venomous snake and place it upon a tall pole, and it shall come to pass that anyone who is bitten, let him look upon it and he will live.*

ח וַיֹּאמֶר יְהוָה אֶל־מֹשֶׁה עֲשֵׂה לְךָ
שָׂרָף וְשִׂים אֹתוֹ עַל־נֵס וְהָיָה כָּל־
הַנָּשׁוּךְ וְרָאָה אֹתוֹ וָחָי׃

וינשכו. נשך is related to: נזק, to cause injury or loss; נשק, to burn; נֶשֶׁק, weapons (see Commentary, *Bereshis* 41:40).

8 **ויאמר ה׳ וגו׳ והיה כל הנשוך וגו׳**. The sole purpose of the snakebites was to make the people see the dangers that lie in wait for them at every step in the wilderness, and to make them realize that it was only God's miraculous power that had kept these dangers away from them, so far away that they did not even have an idea of their existence.

And now, anyone who was bitten must fix the image of the snake firmly in his mind, so that it should always remain before him, even after God, in His grace, would keep the snakes away from him once more. In this manner the victim will remain aware of the existence of the perils through which God's special protection guides us safely every day and at all times without our even knowing it, perils that demonstrate to us how each breath of our lives is a new gift of God's goodness and might.

A person is capable of reconciling himself to any fate — even the routine that makes him impatient because he did not "win the lottery" of a special gift from God — if only he will regard himself always as one who was saved from danger by God's grace and given back his life as a gift. A person will feel this way if he considers the precipice along whose

9 *And Moshe made a copper snake and placed it upon the tall pole, and it came to pass that if a snake had bitten a man, he would look upon the copper snake and live.*

ט וַיַּעַשׂ מֹשֶׁה נְחַשׁ נְחֹשֶׁת וַיְשִׂמֵהוּ
עַל־הַנֵּס וְהָיָה אִם־נָשַׁךְ הַנָּחָשׁ
אֶת־אִישׁ וְהִבִּיט אֶל־נְחַשׁ
הַנְּחֹשֶׁת וָחָי׃ ששי

10 *The Children of Israel journeyed on and camped in Ovos.*

י וַיִּסְעוּ בְּנֵי יִשְׂרָאֵל וַיַּחֲנוּ בְּאֹבֹת׃

narrow edge runs the path of all our lives, a precipice which the benevolent God screens from our view, lest we become dizzy, and over which He carries us in His power and goodness as on eagles' wings. A person would bless God for dealing kindly with him, if he would only see הנחשים השרפים which lurk on our path unseen, and which only God's almighty providence renders harmless.

Hence, this was the punishment of these כפויי טובה, as our Sages (*Avodah Zarah* 5a) call these sinners: God removed the protective screen which until that time had hidden the venomous fangs of the snakes in the wilderness and rendered them harmless. And, thus, the remedy for anyone bitten by a snake was to fix in his mind the image of the snake and to remember it always — והיה כל הנשוך וראה אתו וחי!

9 **ויעש משה נחש נחשת**: לשון נופל על לשון, a wordplay (רש״י). *Yerushalmi Rosh Hashanah* (3:9): עשה לך שרף, לא פירש, אמר משה עיקרה לא נחש הוא? לפיכך ויעש משה נחש נחשת. Moshe was not told out of which material he was to make the שרף. But just on that account Moshe concluded that it was self-understood that it was to be of copper, since שרף designates the kind of נחש, and so implies the material, too. And since the snake was made of נחושת, the material — by its very name — already called to mind the figure that was fashioned out of it. מכאן היה ר׳ מאיר דורש שמות: from this ר׳ מאיר proved that names have significance (ibid.).

If our interpretation is not mistaken, it is possible that the נחושת material of the נחש alludes from an additional standpoint to the purpose of this whole event. נחש הנחושת will lead them to sense [לנחש] the real נחשים which — unseen — lurk everywhere on the paths of the wilderness [cf. Commentary, *Bereshis* 44:5].

11 *They journeyed from Ovos and camped in the wastelands of the transitions in the wilderness that lies before Moav, toward sunrise.*

יא וַיִּסְע֖וּ מֵאֹבֹ֑ת וַֽיַּחֲנ֞וּ בְּעִיֵּ֣י הָעֲבָרִ֗ים
בַּמִּדְבָּר֙ אֲשֶׁר֙ עַל־פְּנֵ֣י מוֹאָ֔ב
מִמִּזְרַ֖ח הַשָּֽׁמֶשׁ׃

12 *From there they journeyed and camped in the basin of Zared.*

יב מִשָּׁ֖ם נָסָ֑עוּ וַֽיַּחֲנ֖וּ בְּנַ֥חַל זָֽרֶד׃

13 *From there they journeyed and camped on the other side of the Arnon, [the side] that is in the wilderness that extends from the territory of the Emori. For the Arnon forms the border of Moav, between Moav and the Emori.*

יג מִשָּׁם֮ נָסָ֒עוּ֒ וַֽיַּחֲנ֗וּ מֵעֵ֤בֶר אַרְנוֹן֙
אֲשֶׁ֣ר בַּמִּדְבָּ֔ר הַיֹּצֵ֖א מִגְּב֣וּל
הָאֱמֹרִ֑י כִּ֤י אַרְנוֹן֙ גְּב֣וּל מוֹאָ֔ב בֵּ֥ין
מוֹאָ֖ב וּבֵ֥ין הָאֱמֹרִֽי׃

---

11 **בעיי העברים**. עי is related to אי. אי — from the root איה — denotes an out-of-the-way, completely isolated place. Thus אַיֵּה, the question concerning a place unknown to the questioner (cf. Commentary, ibid. 4:9). Similarly, עי — from the root עיה — is an out-of-the-way, uninhabited place, a wasteland.

12 **בנחל זרד**. נחל denotes both the stream that flows from the heights to the valley, and also the channel of a watercourse. The basic concept is the natural movement from above to below — related to נהל. Hence נחל is the specific expression for the legal right of inheritance (see Commentary below, 27:7ff.). The opposite of נחל is נעל: to close, to shut in, to stem the natural forward movement.

13 **מעבר ארנון אשר וגו׳**. אשר refers to עבר. They travelled around the land of Moav and encamped on the north side of the Arnon, the side that is in the wilderness that extends from the territory of the Emori (רש״י). Thus they entered for the first time the land that was destined to be theirs, as is related below (v. 21ff.).

14 *Therefore it is said in the Book of the Wars of* God: *Vahev in Sufah, and the streams that form the Arnon.*

יד עַל־כֵּן יֵאָמַר בְּסֵפֶר מִלְחֲמֹת יְהוָה אֶת־וָהֵב בְּסוּפָה וְאֶת־הַנְּחָלִים אַרְנוֹן׃

15 *And the pouring forth of the streams that made a turn to give living space to Ar and then clings to the territory of Moav.*

טו וְאֶשֶׁד הַנְּחָלִים אֲשֶׁר נָטָה לְשֶׁבֶת עָר וְנִשְׁעַן לִגְבוּל מוֹאָב׃

14-15 **על כן**, since Arnon is the boundary between Moav and the Emori, its course is described in this way also in ספר מלחמת ה׳.

ספר מלחמת ה׳ — like סֵפֶר הַיָּשָׁר (*Yehoshua* 10:3; *Shemuel* II, 1:18) — proves that literary activity was not lacking in Israel in Moshe's time. Rather, great men of intellect — these would be המשלים of verse 27 — sang of the great events they witnessed and recorded them for the benefit of their contemporaries and for later generations. At the same time, these references to other books prove that God's holy Book, the Torah, is *not* a collection of such writings; for if that were the case, the supposed collector would have cited his sources also elsewhere in this collection, just as he did not conceal his source here. Furthermore, the incorporation of this citation from ספר מלחמות ה׳ in God's Book attests to the nature of that book, and teaches us that the records contained in that book are of value, and that it is worthwhile for the nation to pay attention to them.

את והב בסופה וגו׳. For us — members of a much later generation — the meaning of this citation is obscure. והב and סופה are apparently names of places to which the memory of great events is attached. Thus, the Gemara in *Berachos* 54a conveys to us the tradition that מעברות נחלי ארנון along with מעברות הים and מעברות הירדן are places where the one who beholds them recites the ברכה: ברוך שעשה נסים לאבותינו במקום הזה.

הנחלים ארנון apparently describes the Arnon as a stream formed of several streams; hence it says: ואשד הנחלים. אשד is phonetically related to חשד, חסד (see Commentary, *Vayikra* 20:17).

According to *Rashi* and *Targum Onkelos*, והב is a noun derived from the root יהב, "to give," like ולד, ועד, from ילד and יעד, whereas סופה refers to ים סוף. Accordingly, the translation of את והב בסופה ואת הנחלים ארנון would

16 *From there toward the well. This is the well of which* God *had said to Moshe: Gather the people; I will give them water.*

טז וּמִשָּׁם בְּאֵרָה הִוא הַבְּאֵר אֲשֶׁר
אָמַר יְהֹוָה לְמֹשֶׁה אֱסֹף אֶת־הָעָם
וְאֶתְּנָה לָהֶם מָיִם׃ ס

17 *It was then that Israel sang this song: Rise again, O well, sing responsively to it.*

יז אָז יָשִׁיר יִשְׂרָאֵל אֶת־הַשִּׁירָה
הַזֹּאת עֲלִי בְאֵר עֱנוּ־לָהּ׃

be: "What was granted at the Red Sea was also at the streams that form the Arnon." That is to say, the miracles that were performed at the Red Sea were repeated at the streams that form the Arnon.

ואשד הנחלים אשר נטה לשבת ער. ער is a Moabite city (v. 28). אשד הנחלים is the Arnon which is formed by several streams flowing together. After its formation, it makes a bend, and in the area enclosed by this bend lies the city of Ar. Thus, the Arnon bends away from its straight course לשבת ער — so that Ar can dwell there. For the term "ישב" is applied also to cities themselves: לֹא־תֵשֵׁב לָנֶצַח (*Yeshayahu* 13:20) is said of Bavel; פְּרָזוֹת תֵּשֵׁב יְרוּשָׁלַם (*Zecharyah* 2:8), and so forth. נטה לשבת ער: the Arnon bends for the settlement of Ar.

ונשען לגבול מואב: from there onward it flows along the boundary of Moav.

16 **ומשם בארה** can be interpreted: From there the Arnon flows to the well; or: from there one comes to the well.

הִוא הבאר. The place is called באר either because the well they received from Chorev forty years earlier (*Shemos* 17), the well whose waters then dried up after Miriam's death, was restored to them there; or, more probably, because the well that was given to them and that was later restored to them and that accompanied them until now, finally stopped there. באר would then be the name of the summit mentioned in verse 20 [see Commentary below, vv. 18-20].

17 **אז ישיר** — then, when the well was about to be restored to them.

עלי באר: the people bid it to raise its waters from the depths.

ענו לה: it is a well whose waters rise to the sound of responsive singing. It was created through the spirit; hence, it responds to a reawakening call.

18 *You are the well that was dug by princes, that the nobles of the people carved out with the stylus of the Law upon their staffs! And from the wilderness it was given again as a gift.*	יח בְּאֵ֞ר חֲפָר֣וּהָ שָׂרִ֗ים כָּר֙וּהָ֙ נְדִ֣יבֵי הָעָ֔ם בִּמְחֹקֵ֖ק בְּמִשְׁעֲנֹתָ֑ם וּמִמִּדְבָּ֖ר מַתָּנָֽה׃
19 *And from the renewed gift, a stream of* God, *and from the stream of* God *up to the high places.*	יט וּמִמַּתָּנָ֖ה נַחֲלִיאֵ֑ל וּמִנַּחֲלִיאֵ֖ל בָּמֽוֹת׃
20 *And from the high places [it went down] into the valley that is in the field of Moav, [and from there up] to the summit of the heights, and now overlooks the wasteland.*	כ וּמִבָּמ֗וֹת הַגַּיְא֙ אֲשֶׁר֙ בִּשְׂדֵ֣ה מוֹאָ֔ב רֹ֖אשׁ הַפִּסְגָּ֑ה וְנִשְׁקָ֖פָה עַל־פְּנֵ֥י הַיְשִׁימֹֽן׃ פ שביעי (רביעי כשהן מחוברין)
21 *And Israel sent messengers to Sichon, king of the Emori, saying:*	כא וַיִּשְׁלַ֤ח יִשְׂרָאֵל֙ מַלְאָכִ֔ים אֶל־סִיחֹ֥ן מֶֽלֶךְ־הָאֱמֹרִ֖י לֵאמֹֽר׃

18-20 **באר חפרוה**. It is a well that was not dug with working tools by workmen. Princes and nobles — משה וזקני העם (see Commentary, *Shemos* 17:5-6) — created it with the spiritual stylus of their scepter of law. It was given to them from Chorev, from the mountain of the Law.

וממדבר מתנה: and now this well was given to them a second time from the wilderness. It became a stream flowing down from God and accompanied them up the heights and down the valleys, into the field of Moav, and finally up to the summit of the heights, from where it now overlooks the wilderness through which it wandered. There, ראש הפסגה, it came to rest. Henceforth they would no longer require the miraculous well, for they had reached an inhabitable land which they conquered, as is immediately recorded.

22 *Let me pass through your land. We will not turn aside into field or into vineyard, nor drink water from the wells. We will go by the king's highway until we have passed through your territory.*

כב אֶעְבְּרָה בְאַרְצֶךָ לֹא נִטֶּה בְּשָׂדֶה
וּבְכֶרֶם לֹא נִשְׁתֶּה מֵי בְאֵר בְּדֶרֶךְ
הַמֶּלֶךְ נֵלֵךְ עַד אֲשֶׁר־נַעֲבֹר גְּבֻלֶךָ׃

23 *But Sichon did not permit Israel to pass through his territory. Sichon gathered all his people and went out to meet Israel, toward the wilderness. He came to Yahtzah and attacked Israel.*

כג וְלֹא־נָתַן סִיחֹן אֶת־יִשְׂרָאֵל עֲבֹר
בִּגְבֻלוֹ וַיֶּאֱסֹף סִיחֹן אֶת־כָּל־עַמּוֹ
וַיֵּצֵא לִקְרַאת יִשְׂרָאֵל הַמִּדְבָּרָה
וַיָּבֹא יָהְצָה וַיִּלָּחֶם בְּיִשְׂרָאֵל׃

24 *Israel struck him down with the edge of the sword and took possession of his land, from the Arnon to the Yabbok, as far as the sons of Ammon, for this territory of the sons of Ammon was firm.*

כד וַיַּכֵּהוּ יִשְׂרָאֵל לְפִי־חָרֶב וַיִּירַשׁ
אֶת־אַרְצוֹ מֵאַרְנֹן עַד־יַבֹּק עַד־
בְּנֵי עַמּוֹן כִּי עַז גְּבוּל בְּנֵי עַמּוֹן׃

---

24 **מארנן עד יבק**. From the Arnon to the Yabbok in the north, and to the territory of בני עמון in the east.

כי עז גבול בני עמון. As it is immediately explained, Cheshbon originally belonged to Moav, and since Israel was forbidden to provoke a war with Moav (*Devarim* 2:9), Israel could not conquer Cheshbon until after it was conquered by Sichon. A similar relationship existed between Israel and the land of the sons of Ammon (ibid. 2:19). Israel was forbidden to touch the land of the sons of Ammon, wherever the sons of Ammon controlled it and as long as they controlled it. At a former occasion, Sichon sought to conquer also the territory lying eastward to him, and had he done so, this territory, too, would have come into Israel's possession. However, עז גבול בני עמון: Ammon was able to withstand Sichon, and Sichon was unable to conquer this territory; hence, Israel was not allowed to touch it (see Commentary below, v. 30).

25 *Israel took all these cities, and Israel settled in all the cities of the Emori — in Cheshbon and in all its daughter cities.*

כה וַיִּקַּח יִשְׂרָאֵל אֵת כָּל־הֶעָרִים
הָאֵלֶּה וַיֵּשֶׁב יִשְׂרָאֵל בְּכָל־עָרֵי
הָאֱמֹרִי בְּחֶשְׁבּוֹן וּבְכָל־בְּנֹתֶיהָ׃

26 *For Cheshbon was then a city of Sichon, king of the Emori. He had overcome the earlier king of Moav with war and taken his entire land out of his hand as far as the Arnon.*

כו כִּי חֶשְׁבּוֹן עִיר סִיחֹן מֶלֶךְ הָאֱמֹרִי
הִוא וְהוּא נִלְחַם בְּמֶלֶךְ מוֹאָב
הָרִאשׁוֹן וַיִּקַּח אֶת־כָּל־אַרְצוֹ
מִיָּדוֹ עַד־אַרְנֹן׃

27 *Therefore the makers of parables say: Just go to Cheshbon! It has now been rebuilt as the city of Sichon and re-established.*

כז עַל־כֵּן יֹאמְרוּ הַמֹּשְׁלִים בֹּאוּ
חֶשְׁבּוֹן תִּבָּנֶה וְתִכּוֹנֵן עִיר סִיחוֹן׃

28 *For then fire went forth from*

כח כִּי־אֵשׁ יָצְאָה מֵחֶשְׁבּוֹן לֶהָבָה

---

26 **כי חשבון עיר סיחן** — see Commentary, verse 24.

הראשון — the one who was king of Cheshbon before him.

27 **על כן יאמרו המשלים** — see Commentary, verse 14.

המשלים — see Commentary, *Bereshis* 4:7. One who perceives and describes historical events, not as a chronicler but as one who tells of God's workings in history, is called a מושל. For he sees the solitary event in the generality of God's laws of world history, and a historical account related from this perspective is truly a משל.

באו חשבון: All those who do not yet know that dynasties rise and fall, and that power built on the illusion of the might of pagan gods will ultimately vanish, should go to Cheshbon. Let them see how Cheshbon, formerly the pride of Moav, is now rebuilt and fortified and is called "the city of Sichon" and even "the citadel of Sichon" (v. 28). From there Sichon goes on to capture a large part of the rest of Moav's territory!

28 **כי אש יצאה וגו׳**. By the fire of war, Sichon conquered the land of Moav from the Yabbok to the Arnon, with the flames belching forth precisely

Cheshbon, a flame from the citadel of Sichon; it consumed Ar of Moav, ruler of the Heights of Arnon.	מִקִּרְיַ֣ת סִיחֹ֑ן אָֽכְלָה֙ עָ֣ר מוֹאָ֔ב בַּעֲלֵ֖י בָּמ֥וֹת אַרְנֹֽן׃
29 *Woe to you, O Moav! You are lost, O people of Kemosh! He has given his sons as fugitives and his daughters into captivity to Sichon, king of the Emori.*	כט אוֹי־לְךָ֣ מוֹאָ֔ב אָבַ֖דְתָּ עַם־כְּמ֑וֹשׁ נָתַ֨ן בָּנָ֤יו פְּלֵיטִם֙ וּבְנֹתָ֣יו בַּשְּׁבִ֔ית לְמֶ֥לֶךְ אֱמֹרִ֖י סִיחֽוֹן׃
30 *And we overthrew them; Cheshbon has perished as far as Divon; we laid waste as far as Nofach, which reaches to Meideva.*	ל וַנִּירָ֛ם אָבַ֥ד חֶשְׁבּ֖וֹן עַד־דִּיבֹ֑ן וַנַּשִּׁ֣ים עַד־נֹ֔פַח אֲשֶׁר֖ עַד־מֵֽידְבָֽא׃ נָקוּד עַל ר׳

from the Moabite city of Cheshbon, which was transformed into "the citadel of Sichon."

בעלי במות ארנן is an attribute of Moav, which formerly was the ruler of the Heights of Arnon; alternatively, בעלי במות ארנון is an attribute of אש and להבה, which are the present rulers of the Heights of Arnon.

29 **אוי לך וגו׳**. In this defeat, the helplessness of Moav and its national god was demonstrated. The subject of נתן is כמוש.

30 **ונירם**: and now we came and overthrew them.

וַנִּירָם is the future *kal* of ירה with the convertive ו. Normally, the form of the suffix would be וַנִּירֵם, but the future does occasionally have the suffix of the past tense — e.g., יִלְבָּשָׁם הכהן (*Shemos* 29:30; see Commentary there). There we explained that the purpose of the apparent anomaly might be to emphasize an essential connection between what would happen in the future and what happened in the past. In our verse, the future tense is converted into the historical past, and the form of the suffix of the past gives it a concept of the past even more emphatically, such that it appears that the past is thereby converted into the pluperfect. The meaning of ונירָם is not "and now we overthrew them," but "it was we who had overthrown them"; that is to say, the truth is that it was not

31 *Israel settled in the land of the Emori.*	לא וַיֵּשֶׁב֙ יִשְׂרָאֵ֔ל בְּאֶ֖רֶץ הָאֱמֹרִֽי׃
32 *But Moshe sent to reconnoiter*	לב וַיִּשְׁלַ֤ח מֹשֶׁה֙ לְרַגֵּ֣ל אֶת־יַעְזֵ֔ר

Sichon but *we* who caused Moav's downfall. Sichon was only a tool for us; he overthrew Moav so that we could conquer Moav's land.

What is more, it is possible that the suffix ם refers to Sichon, and that ירה should be taken in its primary sense — namely, shooting an arrow: We shot Sichon at Moav; Sichon was our arrow. In this sense we could then also interpret the latter part of our verse as follows:

וַנַּשִּׁים is a regular *hif'il* of the root נשה with a suffix, like יַשִּׁימָוֶת עָלֵימוֹ (*Tehillim* 55:16): God will bring death upon them like a demanding creditor. So, too, here: we appointed them creditors to collect our debt. Sichon, as it were, collected a debt on our behalf. Otherwise, ונשים could also be the *hif'il* of the root שמם, as in אִם־לֹא יַשִּׁים עֲלֵיהֶם נְוֵהֶם (*Yirmeyahu* 49:20), and would mean: "we laid waste."

We have already explained that Israel benefited from Sichon's conquests, for if not for those conquests, Israel would not have been allowed to touch those territories as long as they were held by their previous owners. This is formulated in *Chullin* 60b as follows: עמון ומואב טיהרו בסיחון: The land of Ammon and Moav became accessible to Israel through Sichon.

Ammon is mentioned here beside Moav, even though it says above [v. 24; see Commentary there]: כי עז גבול בני עמון. For the territory conquered by Israel from Sichon included also a part that had formerly belonged to Ammon and was then conquered by Sichon. This is apparent from *Yehoshua* 13:25 and 13:27 and from *Shoftim* 11:13. From the latter it appears that the territory now conquered by Israel — from the Arnon to the Yabbok — included also parts formerly held by Ammon. Accordingly, the statement עז גבול בני עמון can refer only to the territory that still remained under Ammon's control because Sichon had been unable to conquer it (see רש"י on *Chullin* 60b).

32 **וישלח משה**. From *Yehoshua* 13:25 it appears that this was the territory that had previously belonged to Ammon.

וַיִּלְכְּדוּ בְּנֹתֶיהָ וַיּוֹרֶשׁ אֶת־הָאֱמֹרִי אֲשֶׁר־שָׁם׃
וירש קרי

Yazer, and they captured its daughter cities, and he drove out the Emori that lived there.

לג וַיִּפְנוּ וַיַּעֲלוּ דֶּרֶךְ הַבָּשָׁן וַיֵּצֵא עוֹג מֶלֶךְ־הַבָּשָׁן לִקְרָאתָם הוּא וְכָל־עַמּוֹ לַמִּלְחָמָה אֶדְרֶעִי׃ מפטיר

33 *They then turned and went up by the way of Bashan, and Og, king of the Bashan, went out to meet them, he and all his people, for war, to Edre'i.*

לד וַיֹּאמֶר יְהוָה אֶל־מֹשֶׁה אַל־תִּירָא אֹתוֹ כִּי בְיָדְךָ נָתַתִּי אֹתוֹ וְאֶת־כָּל־עַמּוֹ וְאֶת־אַרְצוֹ וְעָשִׂיתָ לּוֹ כַּאֲשֶׁר עָשִׂיתָ לְסִיחֹן מֶלֶךְ הָאֱמֹרִי אֲשֶׁר יוֹשֵׁב בְּחֶשְׁבּוֹן׃

34 *And* God *said to Moshe: Do not be afraid of him, for I have delivered him and all his people and his land into your hand. You shall do to him as you have done to Sichon, king of the Emori, who resided in Cheshbon.*

לה וַיַּכּוּ אֹתוֹ וְאֶת־בָּנָיו וְאֶת־כָּל־עַמּוֹ עַד־בִּלְתִּי הִשְׁאִיר־לוֹ שָׂרִיד וַיִּירְשׁוּ אֶת־אַרְצוֹ׃

35 *They struck him and his sons and all his people, so that none of him was left, and they took possession of his land.*

כב א וַיִּסְעוּ בְּנֵי יִשְׂרָאֵל וַיַּחֲנוּ בְּעַרְבוֹת מוֹאָב מֵעֵבֶר לְיַרְדֵּן יְרֵחוֹ׃ ססס

22 1 *Thereupon the Children of Israel journeyed on and camped in the wastelands of Moav, on the other side of the Yarden of Yericho.*

33 **ויפנו ויעלו דרך הבשן**: northward.

CHAPTER 22

1 **לירדן ירחו**. ירדן ירחו is the Yarden which flows opposite Yericho, as Onkelos translates: לירדנא דיריחא.

2 *When Balak, son of Tzippor, saw all that Israel had done to the Emori —*

ב וַיַּ֥רְא בָּלָ֖ק בֶּן־צִפּ֑וֹר אֵ֛ת כָּל־אֲשֶׁר־עָשָׂ֥ה יִשְׂרָאֵ֖ל לָאֱמֹרִֽי׃

3 *Moav had become terrified of the people because they were so powerful, and everything had become loathsome to Moav because of the presence of the Children of Israel.*

ג וַיָּ֨גָר מוֹאָ֜ב מִפְּנֵ֥י הָעָ֛ם מְאֹ֖ד כִּ֣י רַב־ה֑וּא וַיָּ֣קָץ מוֹאָ֔ב מִפְּנֵ֖י בְּנֵ֥י יִשְׂרָאֵֽל׃

בלק

2 **וירא בלק בן צפור** — see Commentary, verse 4.

לאמרי: to the nations controlled by Sichon and Og. Og's land, too, belonged to the Emori (see *Devarim* 3:8).

3 **ויגר מואב**. In the preceding verse, Balak is described merely as an individual, not as the king of Moav. Hence, "Moav" in this verse cannot be another term for King Balak. Rather, ויגר מואב is a continuation of what Balak saw. He saw the defeat of Sichon and Og, and also the effect these events were having on Moav — namely, that ויגר מואב, ויקץ מואב.

ויגר: they were seized with such terror that they lost all sense of stability, as though the ground had been cut from under their feet. As *Midrash Rabbah* puts it, they already regarded themselves as גֵּרים in their own land, as though the land no longer belonged to them and had already been conquered by Israel.

This terror seized them **מפני העם כי רב הוא**, because Israel had shown itself to be an overwhelmingly powerful people. רב does not just denote numerical greatness; it is also an expression for power: קִרְיַת מֶלֶךְ רָב (*Tehillim* 48:3), וְיִשְׁלַח לָהֶם מוֹשִׁיעַ וָרָב וְהִצִּילָם (*Yeshayahu* 19:20), et al. Indeed, they had good reason to be afraid. After all, Sichon, who had defeated Moav, had himself fallen before Israel!

ויקץ מואב מפני בני ישראל — see Commentary, *Shemos* 1:12. They sensed that these בני ישראל were endowed with a quality against which all power and might were meaningless. קוץ is the highest degree of contempt; everything they had became contemptible in their sight, even repulsive — מפני בני ישראל, because of the existence of the Children of Israel.

ד וַיֹּאמֶר מוֹאָב אֶל־זִקְנֵי מִדְיָן עַתָּה יְלַחֲכוּ הַקָּהָל אֶת־כָּל־סְבִיבֹתֵינוּ כִּלְחֹךְ הַשּׁוֹר אֵת יֶרֶק הַשָּׂדֶה וּבָלָק בֶּן־צִפּוֹר מֶלֶךְ לְמוֹאָב בָּעֵת הַהִוא׃

4 *Moav had already sent word to the elders of Midian: Now this united multitude will lick up all that is around us just as the ox licks up the herbs of the field. And yet Balak, son of Tzippor, was king for Moav at that time —*

4 **ויאמר מואב אל זקני מדין**. This fear had already driven them to take action. Moav — the people of Moav, ignoring their king — had sent a message to the elders of the people of Midyan, not to Midyan's kings (of whom there were five [below, 31:8]), telling them of their apprehensions. Since Sichon and Og, the mightiest kings of their time, had proven themselves utterly powerless against Israel, the people's confidence in the power of the kings to protect their peoples' independence had been undermined, and messengers went from nation [Moav] to nation [Midyan] — ignoring the kings — bearing invitations for consultations and joint action.

The message ran as follows: **עתה ילחכו וגו׳**. לחך means: to lick up, to lick up water or dust with the tongue: יְלַחֲכוּ עָפָר כַּנָּחָשׁ (*Michah* 7:17). Figuratively, it is applied to fire: הַמַּיִם אֲשֶׁר־בַּתְּעָלָה לִחֵכָה (*Melachim* I, 18:38). Now, as a matter of fact, an ox first grasps the grass with his tongue and then tears it off. Hence, one can literally say "the ox licks up the grass," and לחך here is the fitting expression. The sense of the message was: As naturally and effortlessly as the ox licks up the grass as food with his tongue, so, too, with the same ease, we will all become the prey of this קהל.

They intentionally do not call Israel an עם or a גוי. They do not regard Israel as a duly constituted nation because Israel has no land of its own, which — according to the normal conception — is an indispensable prerequisite for national existence. Nevertheless, they regard Israel as a קהל, a community united by some factor unknown to them.

את כל סביבתינו: not only us, opposite whom they are now encamped and who are the most immediately threatened by them, but also all the territories around us.

It is not clear why they sent precisely to Midyan, who were far away from them, and not to Edom, their immediate neighbors. Perhaps since

5 *He therefore sent messengers to* ה וַיִּשְׁלַח מַלְאָכִים אֶל־בִּלְעָם בֶּן־

Midyan was close to Egypt and particularly to the wilderness where Israel had stayed for many years, they therefore assumed that the Midianites might know more about this mysterious people. According to *Midrash Rabbah*, they sent to Midyan because the Midianites knew of Moshe's past in Midyan, and they therefore hoped to hear from them details about his qualities.

ובלק בן צפור מלך למואב בעת ההוא. The term used in Scripture for "king *of* Moav" is always מלך מואב, *never* מלך למואב, as in our verse. Consequently, the term מלך למואב denotes the position of king that someone has, or should have, as far as the land and people of Moav are concerned. Thus, בלק בן צפור מלך למואב וגו׳ means: Balak had the calling and the position of king for Moav; and in connection with the beginning of the verse, ובלק וגו׳ would mean: "And yet Balak, son of Tzippor, was king for Moav at that time!" The Moabite people should have discussed their apprehensions with him, the king, before communicating them to anyone else. After all, it was for just such a crisis that the king was expected to function as a king! When the people in their terror completely ignored his role of king, so that at a time such as this [בעת ההיא] he saw that he was merely Balak, son of Tzippor (as he is called in v. 2), not מלך מואב, he realized the full seriousness of the situation, and this realization explains all his subsequent actions.

Israel's mere presence and the wondrous victories they had already achieved had worked such a spell on his people that they had lost all confidence in the ordinary powers of nations and their rulers and did not expect the military prowess of their king to have any effect on Israel. This spell, or the conception of it in people's minds, had to be broken. No matter whether Balak himself shared this belief in magic powers, or whether — as it appears from verse 7 — he himself had been initiated into the secret tricks of the art, the spell had to be broken. It had to be countered with an equally mysterious power, one that acts secretly in the dark, before Balak could dare to lead his people into battle against Israel, or before he could even hope to succeed in doing so.

5 **וישלח מלאכים**. He therefore sent messengers to Aram in the Euphrates region, to the ancestral homeland of this dreaded wonder-working peo-

Bil'am, son of Be'or, to Pesor, which lies on the river in the land of his fellow citizens, in order to invite him to come to him; they were to say to him: Lo! A people has come out from Egypt. Lo! it has already covered the eye of the earth, and now it has settled opposite me.	בְּעוֹר פְּתוֹרָה אֲשֶׁר עַל־הַנָּהָר אֶרֶץ בְּנֵי־עַמּוֹ לִקְרֹא־לוֹ לֵאמֹר הִנֵּה עַם יָצָא מִמִּצְרַיִם הִנֵּה כִסָּה אֶת־עֵין הָאָרֶץ וְהוּא יֹשֵׁב מִמֻּלִי׃

ple. He sent them to the land of the east (below, 23:7), where, in former times, offspring of the nation's patriarch had been sent to settle (*Bereshis* 25:6; see Commentary there), and where, accordingly, beside idolatry and soothsaying (*Yeshayahu* 2:6), pure monotheistic ideas had been retained — so that this was also the homeland of Iyov and his friends (see *Iyov* 1:3). To this land, to which he, too, belonged by descent, Balak sent his messengers. There, they were to turn to Bil'am, the prophet to the nations, to invite him to come to Balak.

הנה עם וגו׳ הנה כסה וגו׳. The repetition of הנה indicates that עם יצא ממצרים expresses an independent consideration. These masses had already been absorbed both politically and socially in the power and nationality of Egypt, and yet they were able to go forth from there to freedom and independence as one people and one society. This marks them as a unique people, and it is to the cause of this uniqueness that you must give your full attention if you wish to help me attain my purpose!

הנה כסה את עין הארץ — cf. *Shemos* 10:5 and Commentary, there.

The very next sentence, והוא ישב ממלי, assigns the people a limited space; hence, its number, too, is limited. Therefore, כסה את עין הארץ cannot be hyperbole signifying numerical immensity. Rather, it probably describes the power already shown by this people and what can be expected from it in the future. "It has already covered the eye of the earth" — i.e., as far as the eye can gaze and the mind can absorb, this people has already taken over all the lands lying near to us. Wherever we look, we no longer see the old countries; rather, we see this people.

והוא ישב ממלי. יושב is not a threatening posture. Rather, what Balak means is as follows: It is uncertain whether this people will attack me, but its proximity intimidates me and is unsettling to me. And now I have

6 *So now, please come [and] curse this people for me, because they are too mighty for me; perhaps I will then be able to bring it about that we will deal them a blow and I will drive them out of the land, for I know that whomever you bless is blessed, and whomever you curse is cursed.*

ו וְעַתָּה לְכָה־נָּא אָרָה־לִּי אֶת־הָעָם הַזֶּה כִּי־עָצוּם הוּא מִמֶּנִּי אוּלַי אוּכַל נַכֶּה־בּוֹ וַאֲגָרְשֶׁנּוּ מִן־הָאָרֶץ כִּי יָדַעְתִּי אֵת אֲשֶׁר־תְּבָרֵךְ מְבֹרָךְ וַאֲשֶׁר תָּאֹר יוּאָר:

7 *And the elders of Moav and the elders of Midyan went with magic charms in their hands, came to Bil'am and told him the words of Balak.*

ז וַיֵּלְכוּ זִקְנֵי מוֹאָב וְזִקְנֵי מִדְיָן וּקְסָמִים בְּיָדָם וַיָּבֹאוּ אֶל־בִּלְעָם וַיְדַבְּרוּ אֵלָיו דִּבְרֵי בָלָק:

an excellent opportunity, if I can grasp it, to stand up to this people in the general interest [of the nations].

6 **ועתה לכה נא ארה לי וגו'**: Destroy the *inner* core of this people; bring destruction upon them by striking at them internally (see Commentary, *Bereshis* 12:3).

כי עצום הוא ממני: To defeat them by physical force alone is beyond my strength.

נַכֶּה could have been the infinitive of the *pi'el*, like נֻכּוּ, נֻכָּתָה (*Shemos* 9:31-32) from the *pu'al*. But then it should have been נַכֵּה. Rather, נַכֶּה is the future of the *hif'il*, and apparently means: Perhaps I will be able to bring it about that we — I and my people (רש"י), or I and you — נכה בו.

Had Balak meant to say that they would smite the people in battle and defeat them, he would have said נכה אותו; for הכאה — in this sense — is always construed with a direct object. Rather, נכה בו apparently means: we will deal them a blow, bring about their fall, ואגרשנו מן הארץ — not to destroy them, but only to drive them away to other regions. Balak does not venture to speak of complete annihilation — even with the help of Bil'am.

7 **זקני מואב וזקני מדין**. Balak chose as his emissaries not courtiers of high rank who were distant from the people but, in keeping with the purpose

8 *And he said to them: Spend the night here, and then I will give you an answer as* God *will speak to me. And the princes of Moav remained with Bil'am.*

ח וַיֹּאמֶר אֲלֵיהֶם לִינוּ פֹה הַלַּיְלָה וַהֲשִׁבֹתִי אֶתְכֶם דָּבָר כַּאֲשֶׁר יְדַבֵּר יְהוָה אֵלָי וַיֵּשְׁבוּ שָׂרֵי־מוֹאָב עִם־בִּלְעָם׃

of his mission, individuals who were close to the people and who enjoyed their confidence, individuals whom the people respected as their זקנים and advisers. For it was important to him that this whole process should gain the greatest possible amount of publicity among the people. זקני מדין, with whom the people had already been in consultation (v. 4), attached themselves to the delegation.

וקסמים בידם. We have already noted (Commentary, *Bereshis* 11:6) the connection between קסם and גזם, according to which קסם denotes causing an effect that goes beyond what is natural or possible. Thus, the word itself contains the implication of sham; it is mere גוזמא. In most of the cases where קסם occurs, it does not bring about a result; rather, its purpose is to predict the future, and especially to decide whether to undertake something one intends to do or to desist from doing it. Thus in *Yechezkel* 21:26 et al. Here, then, the קסמים were not meant to effect the curse. Besides, if that were the case, Bil'am would have needed them not in Aram but in Moav. Rather, the emissaries apparently assumed that Bil'am needed קסמים to decide whether to accept the proposal or to reject it.

Still, it is puzzling that the emissaries took the magic oracles with them. After all, they were going to a קוֹסֵם (*Yehoshua* 13:22) and could therefore assume that he would have all the tools required for his work. Perhaps it was part of the superstition that whoever sought the counsel of an oracle had to donate some of his own possessions for this purpose.

8 **ויאמר וגו׳ כאשר ידבר ה׳ אלי**. Already in Avraham's time, in the midst of a polytheistic world, there was Malki Tzedek, who was "a priest of God the Most High" — the same God Whom Avraham's descendants later accepted as the one and only God. Also Iyov and his friends served this one God. Here, too, we find that Bil'am considers himself a servant of the one God. For monotheism — as opposed to polytheism — is not the quintessence, and certainly not the whole essence, of Judaism. Rather,

9 *And God came to Bil'am and said: Who are these people with you?*

ט וַיָּבֹא אֱלֹהִים אֶל־בִּלְעָם וַיֹּאמֶר מִי הָאֲנָשִׁים הָאֵלֶּה עִמָּךְ׃

Judaism teaches monotheism with all of its ramifications for human life: the unity of God with the unity of life through God's Torah (cf. Commentary, *Bereshis* 14:17-19).

However, the spiritual level of Bil'am the monotheist is morally inferior, and in this respect he is far even from Malki Tzedek and far from Iyov and his friends. His spiritual aptitude to draw near to God is subordinated to his egoism; he places himself at the service of earthly powers and potentates and their base desires. The Sages say (*Tanchuma*): Look at what a difference there is between the prophets of Israel and the prophets of the nations. Compare a Bil'am with a Yeshayahu, a Yirmiyahu, a Yechezkel and their fellow prophets. The prophets of Israel, as G-d's watchmen, warned the nations against sin. Bil'am advised moral seduction so that people should lose their place in the world to come (see chap. 25). Israel's prophets were full of compassion for Israel and for the nations of the world — Yeshayahu says: "My heart throbs like a harp over Moav's woes" (*Yeshayahu* 16:11); Yechezkel says: "Wail lamentations over the fall of Tzor" (*Yechezkel* 27:2) — whereas the prophets of the nations were heartless. This man [Bil'am] rose up to uproot a whole nation — without cause, for nothing. Therefore the entire פרשה of Bil'am was written to reveal why God removed the holy spirit from the nations of the world. It was because this man [Bil'am] was one of those who received the holy spirit, and see how he misused his spiritual gift.

וישבו שרי מואב. It appears that the Midianites left. Bil'am did not expect to receive any benefits from them; hence, he did not treat them with the same consideration that he showed to זקני מואב. For it was זקני מואב whom he regarded as the main emissaries of Balak. Hence, he treated them as would befit שרי מואב.

9 **ויבא אלקים אל בלעם**. ויבא אלקים אל occurs elsewhere only in the cases of Avimelech (*Bereshis* 20:3) and Lavan (ibid. 31:24), and the common denominator of these two cases is that God came to them unexpectedly and prevented them from carrying out their intention.

Here, too, it is unnecessary to assume that Bil'am expected or prayed

10 *Bil'am said to God: Balak, son of Tzippor, king of Moav, has sent [a message] to me:*	י וַיֹּאמֶר בִּלְעָם אֶל־הָאֱלֹהִים בָּלָק בֶּן־צִפֹּר מֶלֶךְ מוֹאָב שָׁלַח אֵלָי׃
11 *Lo! this is the people that came out of Egypt, and it already covers the eye of the earth. Now, please come and curse them for me; perhaps I will then be able to wage war against them and drive them out.*	יא הִנֵּה הָעָם הַיֹּצֵא מִמִּצְרַיִם וַיְכַס אֶת־עֵין הָאָרֶץ עַתָּה לְכָה קָבָה־לִּי אֹתוֹ אוּלַי אוּכַל לְהִלָּחֶם בּוֹ וְגֵרַשְׁתִּיו׃

for this communication from God. What Bil'am said in the preceding verse, כאשר ידבר ה׳ אלי, appears to be just a phrase in Bil'am's mouth.

In any case, Balak's emissaries — and especially Balak himself — understood Bil'am's pronouncement "מאן ה׳ וגו׳" (v. 13) as meaning: "I do not intend to go with you, for to do so would be beneath my dignity and would not be in my interest." These elders surely belonged to the class of those who know and beguile rather than to those who are ignorant and beguiled. They knew what an appeal to the will of the gods means in the mouth of those who practice their art of divination in the service of rulers; they knew that מאן ה׳ — "God refuses" — in the mouth of Bil'am meant nothing other than מאן בלעם, "Bil'am refuses."

A decisive proof of the foregoing interpretation can be adduced from the question מי האנשים האלה עמך. If Bil'am truly had appealed to God for a decision on the matter, the question מי האנשים וגו׳ would be totally out of place. This question proves that the communication from God was Divine intervention which was completely unexpected by Bil'am. All his life, he had been playing a game and masquerading before his contemporaries. Now, suddenly, the game became actual reality — unexpectedly and, apparently, also undesirably.

11 **קבה לי**. The root קוב or קבב in the sense of cursing, invoking curses, occurs elsewhere only in this episode, in the mouths of Bil'am and Balak (cf. v. 17). The form is irregular. Derived from the root קבב, the form would normally be קֹבָּה or קָבָּה as in רָנּוּ לְיַעֲקֹב (*Yirmeyahu* 31:6); derived from the root קוב, the form would normally be קוּבָה. קָבָה, however, is a form for which there is no analogy.

12 *And God said to Bil'am: Do not go with them! You will not curse the people, for it is blessed.*

יב וַיֹּאמֶר אֱלֹהִים אֶל־בִּלְעָם לֹא תֵלֵךְ עִמָּהֶם לֹא תָאֹר אֶת־הָעָם כִּי בָרוּךְ הוּא׃ שני (חמישי כשהן מחוברין)

Below (23:8), אֶקֹּב occurs in the same sense, and the root is apparently נקב, which is used in a similar way in *Vayikra* 24:11 and 16 (see Commentary there). Just as נקב means "to make a hole," קבב apparently means "to hollow out"; hence, קַב is a measure of capacity, the amount of space that an object occupies (*Melachim* II, 6:25 and commonly in the Talmud).

Therefore, if נקב means: to harm someone through words, קבב would mean: to verbally attack someone until he becomes completely hollow, bereft of all content; to turn him into מוֹץ (*Tehillim* 1:4), "an empty husk," a mere shadow. Thus, מה אקב לא קבה א-ל (below, 23:8) would literally mean: Can I make in them even the slightest hole if God has not already completely hollowed them out? In *Bemidbar Rabbah* 20:9, קבב is taken to be a higher degree of ארר.

12 **לא תאר וגו'**. Do not go with them, because you will not be able to accomplish the purpose of your mission. You will not curse this people. Even if you should wish to do so, I will prevent it, because this people is blessed. The element that makes this people a people is precisely the purpose which I have determined to promote with My sovereignty. Even the nations of the world conceive of this people as destined to be blessed, not cursed.

If Bil'am had been a true prophet, he would have accurately conveyed this pronouncement by God to Balak's emissaries, and the purpose of God's intervention [in Bil'am's mission] would have been achieved without all the events narrated in the following episode. In that case, Balak, Moav and Midyan, instead of fearing Israel's conquering might, would have recognized the moral element inherent in this nation to which God had promised His blessing, and they would have befriended Israel, for their own good. However . . .

13 *Bil'am arose in the morning and said to the princes of Balak: Go to your land, for God has refused to allow me to go with you.*

יג וַיָּקָם בִּלְעָם בַּבֹּקֶר וַיֹּאמֶר אֶל־
שָׂרֵי בָלָק לְכוּ אֶל־אַרְצְכֶם כִּי
מֵאֵן יְהוָה לְתִתִּי לַהֲלֹךְ עִמָּכֶם׃

14 *And the princes of Moav set out and came to Balak and said: Bil'am refused to go with us.*

יד וַיָּקוּמוּ שָׂרֵי מוֹאָב וַיָּבֹאוּ אֶל־בָּלָק
וַיֹּאמְרוּ מֵאֵן בִּלְעָם הֲלֹךְ עִמָּנוּ׃

15 *But Balak still persisted; he sent princes, a large number and higher in rank than the former.*

טו וַיֹּסֶף עוֹד בָּלָק שְׁלֹחַ שָׂרִים רַבִּים
וְנִכְבָּדִים מֵאֵלֶּה׃

16 *They came to Bil'am and said to him: Thus says Balak, son of Tzippor: Please do not refuse to come to me.*

טז וַיָּבֹאוּ אֶל־בִּלְעָם וַיֹּאמְרוּ לוֹ כֹּה
אָמַר בָּלָק בֶּן־צִפּוֹר אַל־נָא תִמָּנַע
מֵהֲלֹךְ אֵלָי׃

---

13 **ויקם בלעם**. Bil'am tells them nothing about the second part, the essential element in God's warning. He mentions God's refusal, מאן ה׳, implying that he, Bil'am, would have liked to curse the people, only that מאן ה׳ לתתי להלוך עמכם: God does not consider it fitting that one like myself should go with people like yourselves. After all, they were only זקני מואב, not שרי מואב; they were only plebeians, not true princes.

14 **מאן בלעם הלך עמנו** — see Commentary, verse 9.

15 **ויסף עוד בלק**. Balak knew his man and was undeterred by the first refusal. ויסף עוד בלק is an independent sentence; hence the אתנחתא accent at the word בלק, and hence the use of the word עוד.

שלח שרים: This time he sent real princes, a larger delegation consisting of people of higher rank.

6-17 **אל נא תמנע**. מנע: to withhold, hold back — the opposite of מנה, מנח: to mete out, to give. אל נא תמנע: do not withhold yourself from me.

וכל אשר תאמר אלי אעשה: I will do everything necessary for the accomplishment of my purpose and all that is required for the satisfaction of your desires.

17 *For I will honor you beyond all measure, and whatever you will say I will do; so please come [and] curse this people for me.*

יז כִּֽי־כַבֵּ֤ד אֲכַבֶּדְךָ֙ מְאֹ֔ד וְכֹ֛ל אֲשֶׁר־
תֹּאמַ֥ר אֵלַ֖י אֶֽעֱשֶׂ֑ה וּלְכָה־נָּא֙
קָֽבָה־לִּ֔י אֵ֖ת הָעָ֥ם הַזֶּֽה׃

18 *Bil'am replied and said to the servants of Balak: Even if Balak were to give me his house full of silver and gold, I could not go beyond the word of* God, *my God, to do anything small or great.*

יח וַיַּ֣עַן בִּלְעָ֗ם וַיֹּ֙אמֶר֙ אֶל־עַבְדֵ֣י בָלָ֔ק
אִם־יִתֶּן־לִ֥י בָלָ֛ק מְלֹ֥א בֵית֖וֹ כֶּ֣סֶף
וְזָהָ֑ב לֹ֣א אוּכַ֗ל לַעֲבֹר֙ אֶת־פִּי֙
יְהוָ֣ה אֱלֹהָ֔י לַעֲשׂ֥וֹת קְטַנָּ֖ה א֥וֹ
גְדוֹלָֽה׃

19 *And now, you, too, please remain here this night; I will find out what else* God *will say to me.*

יט וְעַתָּ֗ה שְׁב֨וּ נָ֥א בָזֶ֛ה גַּם־אַתֶּ֖ם
הַלָּ֑יְלָה וְאֵֽדְעָ֔ה מַה־יֹּסֵ֥ף יְהוָ֖ה
דַּבֵּ֥ר עִמִּֽי׃

ולכה נא: From the formulation of these sentences, it appears that Balak expresses here two requests. First, to come to him in any case. For Balak felt that his standing among his people had weakened, and Bil'am's refusal would not serve to raise his prestige in their sight. Second, to fulfill his wish for the laying of a curse on Israel. Balak could not imagine the reason for Bil'am's refusal in this regard, for the fulfillment of this request would be well within the sphere of his profession.

18 **ויען וגו' אל עבדי בלק**. In contrast to his treatment of זקני מדין, he treated זקני מואב as though they were שרים (v. 8), and continued treating them as such (vv. 13-14), and this was not beneath his dignity. But the real שרים of the highest rank he treated as עבדים. This showed the true character of the man: He was condescending to the lowly and arrogant toward the high and the mighty.

אם יתן לי בלק מלא ביתו וגו'. This statement, too, shows Bil'am's character. As much as he seeks honor, he values money even more. Balak's message did not contain any reference to a monetary reward; it mentioned only great honor and expressed readiness to comply with all of Bil'am's wishes. But Bil'am translates honor into money; or he says that

20 *And God came to Bil'am at night and said to him: If the men have come to invite you, then arise and go with them; however, the word that I will speak to you, that you must do.*

כ וַיָּבֹא אֱלֹהִים ׀ אֶל־בִּלְעָם לַיְלָה
וַיֹּאמֶר לוֹ אִם־לִקְרֹא לְךָ בָּאוּ
הָאֲנָשִׁים קוּם לֵךְ אִתָּם וְאַךְ אֶת־
הַדָּבָר אֲשֶׁר־אֲדַבֵּר אֵלֶיךָ אֹתוֹ
תַעֲשֶׂה׃ שלישי

21 *And Bil'am arose in the morning, saddled his she-donkey, and went with the princes of Moav.*

כא וַיָּקָם בִּלְעָם בַּבֹּקֶר וַיַּחֲבֹשׁ אֶת־
אֲתֹנוֹ וַיֵּלֶךְ עִם־שָׂרֵי מוֹאָב׃

even if he were to receive the highest possible monetary reward, etc. In any case, money is more important to him than anything else. This is also how our Sages (*Avos* 5) characterize Bil'am: נפש רחבה along with רוח גבוהה — avarice side by side with a haughty spirit.

20 **ויבא וגו'**. We already noted on verses 16-17 that Balak's request had two parts: that Bil'am should come at his invitation, and that he should curse Israel. Permission to fulfill the first part is now granted. Fulfillment of the second part, however, which is Balak's real intended purpose, has already been forbidden to Bil'am in strong words at the first mission (v. 12): לא תאר את העם כי ברוך הוא. Here, it is only further indicated to him that if he does go, he will have to be the herald of God's Word; and since he has already been told כי ברוך הוא, Gods' Word could be nothing other than blessing. Thus, he was advised beforehand that his going would bring about the very opposite of Balak's intention. Nevertheless . . .

21 **ויקם וגו'**, nevertheless Bil'am arose in the morning, saddled his she-donkey and went — without saying a word — with the princes of Moav. He gave them no indication of what was told to him; moreover, his silence constituted implicit agreement to both parts of their request.

The continuation of the narrative (23:3 and 15; 24:1) shows that Bil'am — even after all that had happened to him, and certainly now at the start of his journey — still believed that, in spite of everything, he would succeed in pronouncing the curse. So little had the truth pene-

22 *And the anger of God was awakened because he had proceeded toward his own purpose in this manner, and an angel of* God *placed himself in the way to hinder him. And here he was riding on his she-donkey, and two of his attendants were with him.*

כב וַיִּֽחַר־אַ֣ף אֱלֹהִים֮ כִּֽי־הוֹלֵ֣ךְ הוּא֒ וַיִּתְיַצֵּ֞ב מַלְאַ֧ךְ יְהֹוָ֛ה בַּדֶּ֖רֶךְ לְשָׂטָ֣ן ל֑וֹ וְהוּא֙ רֹכֵ֣ב עַל־אֲתֹנ֔וֹ וּשְׁנֵ֥י נְעָרָ֖יו עִמּֽוֹ׃

trated his consciousness, that later on he was forced to proclaim: לא איש א-ל ויכזב ובן אדם ויתנחם (23:19). The pure conception of God, the consciousness of ה׳ — Whom he with prideful modesty called ה׳ אלקי (v. 18) — as one God, was so muddled in his mind; his idea of God had taken such a semi-heathen form in his mind, that he thought he could, through נחשים and magic charms, induce God to change His mind, nullify God's Will to accommodate his own base desire, or evade Him in an opportune moment when His power would weaken.

22 **ויחר וגו׳ כי הולך הוא**. Not כי הלך but כי הולך הוא. To be sure, permission had been granted to him to go with them. But he did not just go with them — הולך הוא, he was "a goer" with them; striving to reach his goal. In spite of the clear Divine warning, he thought in his arrogance that he would be able to achieve his purpose.

The angel, unseen by him, had already placed himself on the road to block his path, but Bil'am still rode proudly on *his* animal, with two of *his* attendants to wait on him! Surely, the royal delegation that had been sent to bring him must have brought a proper mount for him, along with a sufficient number of attendants to wait on him. Yet, in his arrogance, Bil'am indulged in the luxury of riding on his own animal which, cavalier-like, he had skillfully saddled that morning (v. 21), and he permitted only his own men — two of them, to be exact — to wait on him. This pride and arrogance had to be broken, so that he would become an obedient instrument of God's Word.

Bil'am wants to amend God's plan for the world, but he is blinder than his own animal. He seeks to overcome God's resistance, but finds that he must accommodate himself to the wishes of his own animal. He

23 *The she-donkey saw the angel of* God *standing in the way with his sword drawn in his hand, and the she-donkey turned aside from the way and went into the field. Then Bil'am struck the she-donkey to get her back upon the way.*

כג וַתֵּ֣רֶא הָאָתוֹן֩ אֶת־מַלְאַ֨ךְ יְהֹוָ֜ה
נִצָּ֣ב בַּדֶּ֗רֶךְ וְחַרְבּ֤וֹ שְׁלוּפָה֙ בְּיָד֔וֹ
וַתֵּ֤ט הָֽאָתוֹן֙ מִן־הַדֶּ֔רֶךְ וַתֵּ֖לֶךְ
בַּשָּׂדֶ֑ה וַיַּ֤ךְ בִּלְעָם֙ אֶת־הָ֣אָת֔וֹן
לְהַטֹּתָ֖הּ הַדָּֽרֶךְ׃

24 *And the angel of* God *placed himself in a footpath of the vineyards; there was a fence on one side and a fence on the other.*

כד וַֽיַּעֲמֹד֙ מַלְאַ֣ךְ יְהֹוָ֔ה בְּמִשְׁע֖וֹל
הַכְּרָמִ֑ים גָּדֵ֥ר מִזֶּ֖ה וְגָדֵ֥ר מִזֶּֽה׃

25 *The she-donkey saw the angel of* God, *and she pressed up against the wall and also pressed Bil'am's foot against the wall; and he struck her again.*

כה וַתֵּ֨רֶא הָאָת֜וֹן אֶת־מַלְאַ֣ךְ יְהֹוָ֗ה
וַתִּלָּחֵץ֙ אֶל־הַקִּ֔יר וַתִּלְחַ֛ץ אֶת־
רֶ֥גֶל בִּלְעָ֖ם אֶל־הַקִּ֑יר וַיֹּ֖סֶף
לְהַכֹּתָֽהּ׃

wants to destroy an entire nation by the words of his mouth, but finds himself forced to concede that his rage is impotent even when directed against a mere animal. He would strut before lords and princes, but finds that he has become a laughingstock among his own attendants.

לשטן לו. שטן is used here in its primary sense: to hinder, to stand in the way. It appears to be related to the Rabbinic term סדן, סדנא: wooden block; for סדנא occurs (*Pesachim* 28a) also in the sense of blocks attached to the legs of prisoners to hinder their walking.

23 **וחרבו שלופה**. שלף — see Commentary, *Shemos* 23:8.

24 **במשעול הכרמים**. The meaning of the root שעל is uncertain. From a comparison of our verse with אִם־יִשְׂפֹּק עֲפַר שֹׁמְרוֹן לִשְׁעָלִים לְכָל־הָעָם (*Melachim* I, 20:10) and מִי־מָדַד בְּשָׁעֳלוֹ מַיִם (*Yeshayahu* 40:12), it appears that שעל denotes a foot or step as a measure, and משעול is a narrow path along which one can proceed only step by step. But then the meaning of בְּשַׁעֲלֵי שְׂעֹרִים (*Yechezkel* 13:19) remains obscure. Perhaps a fox is called a שׁוּעָל because

26 *The angel continued to go ahead and placed himself in a narrow place where there was no way to turn to the right or to the left.*

כו וַיּוֹסֶף מַלְאַךְ־יְהוָה עֲבוֹר וַיַּעֲמֹד
בְּמָקוֹם צָר אֲשֶׁר אֵין־דֶּרֶךְ לִנְטוֹת
יָמִין וּשְׂמֹאול׃

27 *When the she-donkey saw the angel of* God, *she lay down under Bil'am. Bil'am's anger was stirred up, and he struck the she-donkey with the staff.*

כז וַתֵּרֶא הָאָתוֹן אֶת־מַלְאַךְ יְהוָה
וַתִּרְבַּץ תַּחַת בִּלְעָם וַיִּחַר־אַף
בִּלְעָם וַיַּךְ אֶת־הָאָתוֹן בַּמַּקֵּל׃

28 *And* God *opened the mouth of the she-donkey and she said to Bil'am: What have I done to you that you have struck me these three times?*

כח וַיִּפְתַּח יְהוָה אֶת־פִּי הָאָתוֹן
וַתֹּאמֶר לְבִלְעָם מֶה־עָשִׂיתִי לְךָ
כִּי הִכִּיתַנִי זֶה שָׁלֹשׁ רְגָלִים׃

it creeps stealthily through the paths between the vineyards, to which precisely foxes are so destructive.

גדר, to fence in, to form a boundary around, is related to כתר, a circlet which sets the wearer apart and shuts him off from the rest of the people, a crown (cf. זֵר from the root זור).

26 **ויוסף וגו' עבור**. עבר means: to cross over to the other side. Thus, too: to pass in front of someone and go in the direction he is facing.

27 **ויחר אף וגו'**. Bil'am was obsessed with the purpose of his journey and was quite sure that he would succeed. Otherwise, this man, who heeded מנחשים, would have noticed what had happened: Three times he had been delayed. He would have considered this a bad omen and would have wondered at its meaning.

במקל. Until now he had hit it only with the reins, to turn it in the right direction, but now he became angry and hit it with the stick, to punish it.

28 **ויפתח וגו'**. This man possessed superior intelligence and eloquence, but his greed and base desires confused him. When he was no longer worthy of his intellectual talent, God showed favor to the animal's intelligence and to its impulsive feelings and granted it the gift of human speech.

29 *And Bil'am said to the she-donkey: Because you have acted wilfully against me! If only I had a sword in my hand I would have killed you!*

כט וַיֹּאמֶר בִּלְעָם לָאָתוֹן כִּי הִתְעַלַּלְתְּ
בִּי לוּ יֶשׁ־חֶרֶב בְּיָדִי כִּי עַתָּה
הֲרַגְתִּיךְ׃

30 *And the she-donkey said to Bil'am: Am I not your she-donkey, on which you have ridden ever since you have been in existence, until this day? Have I ever been in the habit of doing this to you? And he answered: No.*

ל וַתֹּאמֶר הָאָתוֹן אֶל־בִּלְעָם הֲלוֹא
אָנֹכִי אֲתֹנְךָ אֲשֶׁר־רָכַבְתָּ עָלַי
מֵעוֹדְךָ עַד־הַיּוֹם הַזֶּה הַהַסְכֵּן
הִסְכַּנְתִּי לַעֲשׂוֹת לְךָ כֹּה וַיֹּאמֶר
לֹא׃

31 *And* God *unveiled the eyes of Bil'am, and he saw the angel of* God *standing in the way with his sword drawn in his hand. And he bowed down and threw himself upon his face.*

לא וַיְגַל יְהוָה אֶת־עֵינֵי בִלְעָם וַיַּרְא
אֶת־מַלְאַךְ יְהוָה נִצָּב בַּדֶּרֶךְ
וְחַרְבּוֹ שְׁלֻפָה בְּיָדוֹ וַיִּקֹּד וַיִּשְׁתַּחוּ
לְאַפָּיו׃

Thereby, He also prepared the man for what the future held in store for him. He, Bil'am, was endowed with the gift of eloquent human speech; and although he was unworthy of this Divine gift and had hitherto misused it, the human speech of his mouth would be placed in the service of Divine speech, and he — against his will — would lend his mouth to be the herald of Divine truth. He Who gives speech to an animal can also put His Word in the mouth of a Bil'am.

רגלים — see Commentary, *Shemos* 23:14.

29 **כי התעללת בי** — see Commentary, ibid. 10:2.

30 **הלוא אנכי וגו'**. Our Sages (in *Bemidbar Rabbah* 20:14) infer from here that Bil'am was not an old man. He was younger than his animal. His young age is entirely in keeping with the impetuous spirit that his behavior discloses.

32 *But the angel of* God *said to him: Why have you struck your she-donkey these three times? Lo! I have come out to hinder you, for the way was too abruptly contrary to me.*

לב וַיֹּ֤אמֶר אֵלָיו֙ מַלְאַ֣ךְ יְהֹוָ֔ה עַל־מָ֗ה הִכִּ֙יתָ֙ אֶת־אֲתֹ֣נְךָ֔ זֶ֖ה שָׁל֣וֹשׁ רְגָלִ֑ים הִנֵּ֤ה אָנֹכִי֙ יָצָ֣אתִי לְשָׂטָ֔ן כִּֽי־יָרַ֥ט הַדֶּ֖רֶךְ לְנֶגְדִּֽי׃

33 *And the she-donkey saw me and turned aside before me these three times. Perhaps she turned aside from fear of me. For otherwise I would have killed you also, but I would have let her live.*

לג וַתִּרְאַ֙נִי֙ הָֽאָת֔וֹן וַתֵּ֣ט לְפָנַ֔י זֶ֖ה שָׁלֹ֣שׁ רְגָלִ֑ים אוּלַי֙ נָטְתָ֣ה מִפָּנַ֔י כִּ֥י עַתָּ֛ה גַּם־אֹתְכָ֥ה הָרַ֖גְתִּי וְאוֹתָ֥הּ הֶחֱיֵֽיתִי׃

ההסכן וגו׳. We have already noted on *Bereshis* 19:4 that הסכן means paying constant attention to something. We find a similar conception in the German word *pflegen*, which denotes both "nursing" and "habit." For one who nurses a sick person extends to him constant care; and, similarly, one who develops a habit regularly directs his mind and will to the performance of a particular act.

32 **כי ירט הדרך לנגדי**. ירט occurs nowhere else. וְעַל־יְדֵי רְשָׁעִים יִרְטֵנִי (*Iyov* 16:11) derives — according to the form — from רטה. ירט is apparently a stronger form of ירד, and is applied to a road that descends in a steep slope.

לנגדי — as in אֵין חָכְמָה וְאֵין תְּבוּנָה וְאֵין עֵצָה לְנֶגֶד ה׳ (*Mishlei* 21:30).

I have no complaint against your going itself; after all, you had permission for that. My complaint is that you set out with an intention that is contrary to My intention, and that you are so confident of achieving *your* purpose — just as one who descends a steep slope is certain of reaching the bottom.

33 **אולי נטתה מפני**. We know of no instance in which אולי has the meaning of לולי, "unless." אולי always means "perhaps." But it appears that נטה מפני is to be distinguished from נטה לפני. נטה מפני denotes turning aside out of fear. Thus וַיִּסֹּב דָּוִד מִפָּנָיו פַּעֲמָיִם (*Shemuel* I, 18:11). By contrast, נטה לפני can mean simply to move out of the way in order to show honor. The angel says: Why did you strike your animal? It was for my sake that it turned

לד וַיֹּאמֶר בִּלְעָם אֶל־מַלְאַךְ יְהֹוָה
חָטָאתִי כִּי לֹא יָדַעְתִּי כִּי אַתָּה
נִצָּב לִקְרָאתִי בַּדָּרֶךְ וְעַתָּה אִם־
רַע בְּעֵינֶיךָ אָשׁוּבָה לִּי׃

34 *And Bil'am said to the angel of* God*: I have sinned, for I did not know that you stood in the way against me. And now, if it is displeasing in your eyes, I will gladly go back.*

לה וַיֹּאמֶר מַלְאַךְ יְהֹוָה אֶל־בִּלְעָם לֵךְ
עִם־הָאֲנָשִׁים וְאֶפֶס אֶת־הַדָּבָר
אֲשֶׁר־אֲדַבֵּר אֵלֶיךָ אֹתוֹ תְדַבֵּר
וַיֵּלֶךְ בִּלְעָם עִם־שָׂרֵי בָלָק׃

35 *But the angel of* God *said to Bil'am: Go with the men, but the word that I will speak to you, that you must speak. And Bil'am went with the princes of Balak.*

לו וַיִּשְׁמַע בָּלָק כִּי בָא בִלְעָם וַיֵּצֵא
לִקְרָאתוֹ אֶל־עִיר מוֹאָב אֲשֶׁר
עַל־גְּבוּל אַרְנֹן אֲשֶׁר בִּקְצֵה
הַגְּבוּל׃

36 *When Balak heard that Bil'am was coming, he went to meet him as far as the city of Moav, which is situated on the border of Arnon, which is at the extreme end of the territory.*

aside from the way three times. It did this out of respect for me: ותט לפני; perhaps it did so out of fear of me: אולי נטתה מפני. I would have killed you, but I would let it live.

גם אתכה הרגתי. This גם refers to Bil'am's statement: לו יש חרב בידי כי עתה הרגתיך (v. 29). You told your animal that you would have killed it for its behavior, but *you* are the one who would have been killed. Hence also the form that serves to emphasize and stress: אֹתְכָה.

34 **חטאתי**: It was unwittingly that I sinned.

ועתה אם רע וגו׳. Now Bil'am finally attained that spirit of meekness and humility in which he should have conducted himself toward God from the very outset. In this spirit he will be able to accomplish the mission that henceforth will devolve upon him.

36 **אשר בקצה הגבול**. He went out to meet him as far as he could possibly go. He received him at the very first place that lay in his territory.

37 *And Balak said to Bil'am: Have I not sent to you befittingly to invite you? Why did you not come to me? Do you really think that I cannot pay you [due] honor?*

לז וַיֹּאמֶר בָּלָק אֶל־בִּלְעָם הֲלֹא שָׁלֹחַ
שָׁלַחְתִּי אֵלֶיךָ לִקְרֹא־לָךְ לָמָּה
לֹא־הָלַכְתָּ אֵלָי הַאֻמְנָם לֹא אוּכַל
כַּבְּדֶךָ׃

38 *Bil'am replied to Balak: Lo! Now I have come to you; will I be able to say anything at all? The word that God will put into my mouth, that I will have to speak.*

לח וַיֹּאמֶר בִּלְעָם אֶל־בָּלָק הִנֵּה־
בָאתִי אֵלֶיךָ עַתָּה הֲיָכֹל אוּכַל
דַּבֵּר מְאוּמָה הַדָּבָר אֲשֶׁר יָשִׂים
אֱלֹהִים בְּפִי אֹתוֹ אֲדַבֵּר׃ רביעי
(ששי כשהן מחוברין)

39 *Thereupon Bil'am went with Balak, and they came to the City of Streets.*

לט וַיֵּלֶךְ בִּלְעָם עִם־בָּלָק וַיָּבֹאוּ קִרְיַת
חֻצוֹת׃

37 **הלא שלח שלחתי**. The emphasis does not refer to the repeated invitation, for he reproaches Bil'am for not responding immediately to the first invitation. Rather, the emphasis refers to the fact that he had implored Bil'am and acted fittingly toward him already in the first invitation.

39 **קרית חצות**. The term "חוצות" does occur — although seldom — in the sense of a military road, a thoroughfare. Thus, apparently: וְשֹׁלֵחַ מַיִם עַל־פְּנֵי חוצות (*Iyov* 5:10), וְחוצות תָּשִׂים לְךָ בְדַמֶּשֶׂק (*Melachim* I, 20:34). Hence, it is possible that קרית חצות is a fortified city that forms a central point from which roads radiate in all directions.

However, "חוצות" is more commonly found in the sense of a street that serves city traffic, and it is in this sense of a city of many streets that *Bemidbar Rabbah* (20:17) interprets קרית חוצות here: שעשה שווקים של מקח וממכר ועשה לו אטלית להראות לו אוכלוסין לומר ראה מה אלו באין להרוג בני אדם ותינוקות שלא חטאו להן. That is to say, Balak brought Bil'am to a city full of streets and markets, commercial traffic and throngs of people. For he wished to show him Moav in all the flower of its national prosperity, so that he should see with his own eyes the population whose survival was in danger.

מ וַיִּזְבַּח בָּלָק בָּקָר וָצֹאן וַיְשַׁלַּח לְבִלְעָם וְלַשָּׂרִים אֲשֶׁר אִתּוֹ׃

40 *Balak slaughtered cattle and sheep and sent this for Bil'am and for the princes who were with him.*

מא וַיְהִי בַבֹּקֶר וַיִּקַּח בָּלָק אֶת־בִּלְעָם וַיַּעֲלֵהוּ בָּמוֹת בָּעַל וַיַּרְא מִשָּׁם קְצֵה הָעָם׃

41 *In the morning Balak took Bil'am and led him up to the heights of Baal. From there he saw a part of the people.*

כג א וַיֹּאמֶר בִּלְעָם אֶל־בָּלָק בְּנֵה־לִי בָזֶה שִׁבְעָה מִזְבְּחֹת וְהָכֵן לִי בָּזֶה שִׁבְעָה פָרִים וְשִׁבְעָה אֵילִים׃

23 1 *And Bil'am said to Balak: Build me seven altars here and prepare for me here seven bulls and seven rams.*

ב וַיַּעַשׂ בָּלָק כַּאֲשֶׁר דִּבֶּר בִּלְעָם וַיַּעַל בָּלָק וּבִלְעָם פַּר וָאַיִל בַּמִּזְבֵּחַ׃

2 *And Balak did as Bil'am had spoken, and Balak and Bil'am offered one bull and one ram on each altar as an ascent offering.*

ג וַיֹּאמֶר בִּלְעָם לְבָלָק הִתְיַצֵּב עַל־עֹלָתֶךָ וְאֵלְכָה אוּלַי יִקָּרֵה יְהוָה לִקְרָאתִי וּדְבַר מַה־יַּרְאֵנִי וְהִגַּדְתִּי לָךְ וַיֵּלֶךְ שֶׁפִי׃

3 *And Bil'am said to Balak: Place yourself here next to your ascent offering. I will go there; perhaps* God *will bring it about that He will come to meet me, and whatever He will let me see I will give you word of it. And he went to the elevation.*

40 **ויזבח וגו' וישלח וגו'**. It does not say ויעש משתה; he did not invite them to a banquet; also, the *pi'el* form of וַיְשַׁלַּח is not indicative of a manner that shows honor. It appears that Balak was not pleased with what Bil'am said.

CHAPTER 23

1 **שבעה מזבחת**. The number seven signifies that the altars were erected for the invisible one God, and that the seven bulls and seven rams were dedicated to the invisible one God (cf. *Bereshis* 21:28).

3 **על עלתך**. As we indicated on verse 1, the seven offerings formed a single concept. [Hence, עֹלָתֶךָ, singular form.]

4 *God brought it about for Bil'am, and the latter said to Him: I have prepared the seven altars and have offered bulls and rams upon each altar as an ascent offering.*	ד וַיִּקָּר אֱלֹהִים אֶל־בִּלְעָם וַיֹּאמֶר אֵלָיו אֶת־שִׁבְעַת הַמִּזְבְּחֹת עָרַכְתִּי וָאַעַל פָּר וָאַיִל בַּמִּזְבֵּחַ׃
5 *And* God *put a word into Bil'am's mouth, and He said: Return to Balak and thus shall you speak.*	ה וַיָּשֶׂם יְהוָה דָּבָר בְּפִי בִלְעָם וַיֹּאמֶר שׁוּב אֶל־בָּלָק וְכֹה תְדַבֵּר׃
6 *He returned to him, and lo! he was still standing next to his ascent offering, he and all the princes of Moav.*	ו וַיָּשָׁב אֵלָיו וְהִנֵּה נִצָּב עַל־עֹלָתוֹ הוּא וְכָל־שָׂרֵי מוֹאָב׃
7 *And he took up his parable and*	ז וַיִּשָּׂא מְשָׁלוֹ וַיֹּאמַר מִן־אֲרָם

אולי יִקָּרֵה ה׳ וגו׳. See Commentary, *Vayikra* 1:1. The literal meaning here is: Perhaps God will allow Himself to be brought toward me — by the power of our offerings. The monotheistic idea of ה׳ was not foreign to Balak and Bil'am, as we have already noted above (22:5). However, this idea took a heathen form in their minds, and they thought that an offering could exert a compelling influence on God (cf. Commentary, *Shemos* 3:18).

ודבר מה יראני והגדתי לך: he expects a מראה אלקים, a prophetic revelation, and whatever he sees he will report.

4 **ויקר וגו׳**. God acceded to Bil'am's request. And Bil'am says: I have set up the altars for You, the invisible one God (שבעת), and solicited a revelation about man's doings and sufferings (פר ואיל).

5 **וישם ה׳ וגו׳**. God did not present to him a vision for him to then describe its meaning in words; rather, He put words in his mouth and commanded him to speak those words.

7 **וישא משלו**. משל — see Commentary above, 21:27, and *Bereshis* 4:7.

מן ארם וגו׳. By this statement, Balak himself declared that in the secrecy of his heart he knows that this people, from its very inception, was

said: From Aram has Balak, king of Moav, brought me, from the mountains of the east: Go, curse Ya'akov for me, and go, cast anger upon Israel.	יַנְחֵנִי בָלָק מֶלֶךְ־מוֹאָב מֵהַרְרֵי־ קֶדֶם לְכָה אָרָה־לִּי יַעֲקֹב וּלְכָה זֹעֲמָה יִשְׂרָאֵל׃
8 *Can I make a hole into what* God *has not hollowed? What can I strike with anger when* God *has not been angry?*	ח מָה אֶקֹּב לֹא קַבֹּה אֵל וּמָה אֶזְעֹם לֹא זָעַם יְהוָה׃

graced with a special quality, and that to ascertain the nature of this people and to assess its future one must investigate this quality. In particular, he thereby declared that this people's fate depends on that God of Whom the sages of Aram still retained some knowledge, and that since Aram was also his (Balak's) homeland, he, too, had heard of Him.

ארה לי יעקב וגו׳. According to its physical appearance, it is Ya'akov, the smallest and the weakest among all the peoples. According to what is godly in it and its spiritual importance, it is Yisrael, which proclaims God's rule on earth. Balak wants Bil'am's word to strike at the root of Ya'akov's hope for the future; Ya'akov shall be ארור, cut off from the source of blessing. And regarding Yisrael he seeks: זעמה ישראל.

Other terms denoting anger — כעס, אנף, קצף — are intransitive verbs and express the *mood* of the one who is angry; hence, they are construed with a preposition: -ב or על. By contrast, זעם is a transitive verb and is accompanied by a direct object: וְהָעָם אֲשֶׁר־זָעַם ה׳ (*Malachi* 1:4), יִזְעָמוּהוּ לְאֻמִּים (*Mishlei* 24:24), et al. Hence זעם also occurs in the passive: זעום ה׳ (ibid. 22:14), one who was stricken by God's wrath.

If Israel is to flourish, it must find favor before God. Bil'am's word is to cause the favor to turn into זעם, anger. Onkelos translates זעמה as תריך, the Aramaic for גרש: bring it about that God will banish Israel from His presence. זֹעֲמָה is the seldom-used פּוֹעֵל form, as in לִמְשֹׁפְטִי (*Iyov* 9:15).

8 **מה אקב וגו׳**. See Commentary above, 22:11.

קַבֹּה: the letter ה is indicative of the feminine, and the vowel (חולם) is indicative of the masculine. Bil'am says: My word cannot harm this people, if it has not first lost its virility by God's curse.

9 *For I see it from the top of the rocks, and I behold it from the hills; this is a people that will dwell apart and not count itself among the nations.*	ט כִּי־מֵרֹאשׁ צֻרִים֙ אֶרְאֶ֔נּוּ וּמִגְּבָע֖וֹת אֲשׁוּרֶ֑נּוּ הֶן־עָם֙ לְבָדָ֣ד יִשְׁכֹּ֔ן וּבַגּוֹיִ֖ם לֹ֥א יִתְחַשָּֽׁב׃
10 *Who would count the dust of Ya'akov and the number of the animal-like births of Israel? I myself would die the death of the straightforward and let my end be like his!*	י מִ֤י מָנָה֙ עֲפַ֣ר יַעֲקֹ֔ב וּמִסְפָּ֖ר אֶת־רֹ֣בַע יִשְׂרָאֵ֑ל תָּמֹ֤ת נַפְשִׁי֙ מ֣וֹת יְשָׁרִ֔ים וּתְהִ֥י אַחֲרִיתִ֖י כָּמֹֽהוּ׃

9 **כי מראש צרים וגו'**. When I look at it from a high vantage point, it appears near. From the perspective of a low lookout point, it appears to be still faraway. Just as distances seem to shrink from the perspective of a high lookout point, so does time. If one views history from an elevated perspective, high above one's own period, one can survey centuries in one glance. But if the viewer stands on the ground of the present reality, events appear distant from one another. שור is the far-reaching view which sees what others fail to see (Commentary, *Bereshis* 49:22). Bil'am says: I see this people, and I see that it is destined to attain the ideal of its purpose. This will not be in the near future; but within the framework of the development of time, the future is not distant (cf. below, 24:17).

הן עם לבדד ישכן וגו'. This people will dwell in its own delimited land, without much contact with other nations. It will fulfill its "internal" national mission as an "עם," as a people that forms a community, and will not seek its greatness as another "גוי" among גוים, as a national "body" that impresses by its power and might.

10 **מי מנה עפר יעקב וגו'**. You, Balak, count the numerical greatness of this people, the number of its fighters, and by that reckoning it seems to you to be too strong. You think that if its power in this respect were to weaken, you could defeat it; you think that you could strike at its very essence if you could succeed in bringing a curse against its physical growth. However, מי מנה עפר יעקב: Who would count the earthly element of Ya'akov? ומספר את רבע

11 *And Balak said to Bil'am: What have you done to me? I have fetched you to curse my enemies, but now you have, in fact, blessed them!*	יא וַיֹּאמֶר בָּלָק אֶל־בִּלְעָם מֶה עָשִׂיתָ לִי לָקֹב אֹיְבַי לְקַחְתִּיךָ וְהִנֵּה בֵּרַכְתָּ בָרֵךְ׃
12 *But he answered: Truly, I must be careful to say that which* God *puts into my mouth.*	יב וַיַּעַן וַיֹּאמַר הֲלֹא אֵת אֲשֶׁר יָשִׂים יְהוָה בְּפִי אֹתוֹ אֶשְׁמֹר לְדַבֵּר׃
	חמישי

ישראל: Who would count the births among God's people as one would count animal young produced by breeding? (**רבע** as in *Vayikra* 19:19 and 20:16.) The fortune of other nations depends on their number of "bodies"; therefore, other nations view a potential enemy's numerical increase as a cause for alarm and his numerical decrease as a reason for hope. It is not so with Ya'akov-Yisrael. Whether they are few in number as "Ya'akov" or numerous as "Yisrael," it is not the **עפר** element in them that determines their importance. The propagation of the body — whose basis is **עפר** — resembles animal breeding, and the bodies multiply or decrease in number; but that is not what Israel's weal or woe depends on. They need not fear even physical death, for not even death can affect their true essence.

תמת נפשי וגו': I would like to die as they do. I would like to know that my own death will be like theirs. Their death is more blessed than our lives, because these people are **ישרים**: they measure up to the purpose for which men were created human, and they strive toward that ideal in a "straight," undeviating line.

Let us now summarize Bil'am's first "parable." He pointed out the difference between Israel and all the peoples of history. He revealed to Balak that the future of this people does not depend on the physical-material conditions on which the success of other peoples depends; hence, neither is it harmed by the damaging influences to which all other peoples succumb. However, he thereby also revealed a general truth: The welfare of the peoples depends on the principle from which their success derives. Hence, his word is a true **משל**, for it transcends the concrete single case; inferring from the particular to the general, it derives a general truth which applies in all cases.

13 *And Balak said to him: Come with me to another place from where you will be able to see them. But you will see only a part of them; you will not see them all, and curse them for me from there.*

יג וַיֹּאמֶר אֵלָיו בָּלָק לְךָ־נָּא אִתִּי
אֶל־מָקוֹם אַחֵר אֲשֶׁר תִּרְאֶנּוּ
מִשָּׁם אֶפֶס קָצֵהוּ תִרְאֶה וְכֻלּוֹ לֹא
תִרְאֶה וְקָבְנוֹ־לִי מִשָּׁם׃

14 *He took him to the Field of Seers, to the top of the elevation. He built seven altars, and offered one bull and one ram as an ascent offering on each altar.*

יד וַיִּקָּחֵהוּ שְׂדֵה צֹפִים אֶל־רֹאשׁ
הַפִּסְגָּה וַיִּבֶן שִׁבְעָה מִזְבְּחֹת וַיַּעַל
פָּר וָאַיִל בַּמִּזְבֵּחַ׃

13-14 First Balak led Bil'am up to במות הבעל (22:41). Now he took him to שדה צופים. And when, here, too, his intention was thwarted and the curse turned into a blessing, he made one more attempt from ראש הפעור (v. 28). Let us compare the names of these three locations and compare them to the speeches Balak was forced to hear at each location. We will see that Balak took Bil'am from each one of these locations to the next in order to have him test various vantage points or perspectives from which the people might be cursed. Each time one of his attempts failed, Balak arranged for a change in the vantage point from which Bil'am was to view the Children of Israel.

בעל, צופים, פעור are the three mightiest powers which — in Balak's view — decide the weal or woe of nations.

בעל is the general Canaanite deity, the supreme "force of nature," who holds sway over the flourishing of material prosperity. According to the *Yerushalmi* (*Avodah Zarah* 3:6) — רב חמא בר גוריון בשם רב וכו׳ — the form in which he was represented was identical with the phallus, the symbol of the generative power in nature. (Also the name and conception בעל, פעל [phal, phallus] could be identical.)

In Balak's view, the first condition for a nation's survival is to find favor before "Baal," because Baal determines material growth and decay. By taking Bil'am to the Heights of Baal, he posed to him the question: Where does this nation stand in relation to the favor of the Divine power that can grant or withhold *material* prosperity? Could not its growth be

15 *And he said to Balak: Place yourself here next to your ascent offering, and I will submit myself there to what will be brought about.*

טו וַיֹּאמֶר אֶל־בָּלָק הִתְיַצֵּב כֹּה עַל־
עֹלָתֶךָ וְאָנֹכִי אִקָּרֶה כֹּה׃

16 *And* God *directed Himself to Bil'am and put a word into his mouth and said: Return to Balak and thus shall you speak.*

טז וַיִּקָּר יְהוָה אֶל־בִּלְעָם וַיָּשֶׂם דָּבָר
בְּפִיו וַיֹּאמֶר שׁוּב אֶל־בָּלָק וְכֹה
תְדַבֵּר׃

impeded from that direction? Bil'am answered this question in the negative, because the element of **עפר** and **רביעה** — which thrives under the influence of Baal — is not one of the basic conditions of Jewish national survival.

Balak's reaction to Bil'am's reply was to take him to **שדה צופים**, to the "Field of Seers and Watchmen," and there he led him to the top of the elevation. For it seemed to Balak that the second condition for a nation's survival is its intelligence, as demonstrated by the presence in its midst of an intellectual elite with insight into the counsel of the gods; individuals who could look into the future and who, as "seers and watchmen," could predict the future, and control and shape events to come. By taking Bil'am to this location, Balak posed to him the question: Where does this nation stand as regards the intellectual gifts that can decide and control the fate of nations by insight, prudence, foresight, and magic powers? Seen from the perspective of "seers and watchmen," might not this people have a weak spot which could be exploited to undermine its future?

Once again he builds seven altars, and through the ascent offerings of **פר ואיל** he presents the question to the invisible Deity on high, Who judges the actions and decides the fate of mortals.

15 **ויאמר וגו׳**. התיצב כה, אקרה כה — cf. ויפן כה וכה (*Shemos* 2:12), where כה likewise occurs as a description of place.

אִקָּרֶה, I will nullify all my aspirations. I will heed the "Divine call" and surrender myself to God's guidance, which directs events and occurrences (cf. Commentary, ibid. 3:18).

17 *He came to him and found him standing next to his ascent offering, and the princes of Moav with him. And Balak said to him: What has* God *spoken?*

יז וַיָּבֹא אֵלָיו וְהִנּוֹ נִצָּב עַל־עֹלָתוֹ וְשָׂרֵי מוֹאָב אִתּוֹ וַיֹּאמֶר לוֹ בָּלָק מַה־דִּבֶּר יְהוָה׃

18 *And he took up his parable and said: Arise, O Balak, and hear; incline your ear to me, [you] whom Tzippor calls his son.*

יח וַיִּשָּׂא מְשָׁלוֹ וַיֹּאמַר קוּם בָּלָק וּשְׁמָע הַאֲזִינָה עָדַי בְּנוֹ צִפֹּר׃

19 God *is not a man that He should deceive, a son of Adam that He should change His mind. Should He indeed make a promise and not do it, or speak and not uphold it?*

יט לֹא אִישׁ אֵל וִיכַזֵּב וּבֶן־אָדָם וְיִתְנֶחָם הַהוּא אָמַר וְלֹא יַעֲשֶׂה וְדִבֶּר וְלֹא יְקִימֶנָּה׃

17 **ושרי מואב**: not וכל שרי מואב as in verse 6. After the first attempt failed, several of them left.

18 **וישא משלו וגו'**. Balak had asked Bil'am to find the people's vulnerable point from the perspective of **צופים** (v. 14). Thereupon Bil'am proclaims his "words of rulership," saying: קום בלק וגו'. Stand up, Balak! You have inquired whether this people has an intellectual elite that can come close to the gods. Stand up and listen to what I shall tell you about this people. In all likelihood Balak and Tzippor were both well versed in the **צופים**-wisdom of Aram. The demand **קום בלק ושמע האזינה עדי בנו צפר** expresses right from the beginning the vast distance that separates the spiritual level of Israel and the wisdom of the Aramean **צופים**. "Balak, you must have respect, and you will get to hear things of which your father, whose worthy son and disciple you are, had no idea." **האזינה עדי**: it is worth your while to incline your ear most attentively. **בנו צפור** apparently means: Tzippor is proud to call you **בנו**, his son.

19 **לא איש וגו'**. Immediately upon your initial request through the first delegation, God said regarding this people **כי ברוך הוא** (22:12). If God says of something that it is blessed, then it *is* blessed, and it has no aspect to

20 *Lo! It is a blessing that I have received. He has blessed; I will not change it.*	כ הִנֵּה בָרֵךְ לָקָחְתִּי וּבֵרֵךְ וְלֹא אֲשִׁיבֶנָּה׃
21 *He has perceived no misuse of power in Ya'akov; therefore He has seen no misfortune in Israel;* God, *his God, is with him, and homage to the King is within him.*	כא לֹא־הִבִּיט אָוֶן בְּיַעֲקֹב וְלֹא־רָאָה עָמָל בְּיִשְׂרָאֵל יְהוָה אֱלֹהָיו עִמּוֹ וּתְרוּעַת מֶלֶךְ בּוֹ׃

which the curse can apply. And once God has said לא תאר את העם (ibid.), He does not afterward change His mind and permit one to do the opposite.

ויתנחם — see Commentary, *Bereshis* 6:6.

ההוא אמר וגו׳. By saying ברוך הוא, He already promised the people blessing, and shall He not do what He promised?

ודבר is a continuation of the question: if He says something — even if it is not a promise to anyone but only a categorical statement — shall He not keep His word? Such a statement was His לא תאור, which forbade me to issue a curse or deprived me of the possibility of issuing a curse.

20 **הנה ברך לקחתי**: I have received the mission and have been qualified for it. This is also the meaning of לֶקַח — teaching — from the standpoint of the student who receives the teaching. Now, too, I have received the mission to confer a blessing, **וברך** — He has already blessed this people in general, and in particular through the commission which has been assigned to me. My mouth merely expresses what He has already done. I can do nothing to alter that.

21 **לא הביט וגו׳** gives God's reason for blessing this people. אָוֶן is the misuse of אוֹן, of power and property (see Commentary, *Bereshis* 35:18). Before God blesses one of the nations, He finds out whether it will misuse the אוֹן that is to be granted to it. Before God promised to give אוֹן to Ya'akov — in order to raise him to the level of Yisrael — He found out whether in his possession the אוֹן would give rise to אָוֶן. לא הביט און ביעקב: God did not foresee in Ya'akov any misuse of the greatness that was to be given to him; therefore He saw no misfortune in Israel. That is to say, therefore

22 *The* God *Who brought them out from Egypt, He is to him like the ascending power of* re'em.	כב אֵל מוֹצִיאָם מִמִּצְרָיִם כְּתוֹעֲפֹת רְאֵם לוֹ:

He saw no need to bring upon him עמל to prevent him from becoming proud; He did not decree upon him hard struggle — sometimes in vain — against obstacles to success; for that is the meaning of עמל (see Commentary, ibid. 41:51). He saw no misfortune in Israel (that He could allow to be announced through my mouth).

ה' אלקיו עמו: ה', *the* Invisible One, Whom we know also from our native home as the Source of all existence and creation and as the Ruler over heaven and earth — He is the Owner, Guide, and Director of this people in their fate and in their actions. He, this God, is with them as their God, assisting them and accompanying them in their wanderings through the ages.

ותרועת מלך בו. תרועה, an alarming sound, also denotes a mood of shock, of fear and trembling; for the תרועה sound expresses emotional agitation and arouses such feelings in the hearts of men. Thus: וַיַּרְא פָּנָיו בִּתְרוּעָה (*Iyov* 33:26), וְאֶזְבְּחָה בְאָהֳלוֹ זִבְחֵי תְרוּעָה (*Tehillim* 27:6; see Commentary there). When used with reference to God, תרועה denotes the feeling of complete homage and submission, engendered by an overwhelming awareness of God's greatness. Thus, here we are told: God is *with* him [עמו], and *within* his heart [בו] there is nothing but homage to the King; i.e., Israel pays homage to God and acknowledges His kingship, and this homage pervades all of Israel's inner being. Perhaps the clause ותרועת מלך בו supplies the cause: God is *with* him because homage to the King is *in his heart.*

22 **א-ל מוציאם וגו'**. In Egypt they were still a loosely-knit, oppressed multitude (מוציאם, in the plural), and it was as such a multitude, unable to help themselves, that God brought them out of Egypt and made them into one united nation (לו, in the singular).

The God Who liberated them without any action taken on their part is the same God Who, again without any action on their part, will lead them to the heights of power and independence. This awareness gives them an impetus to power as awesome as [the horns of] the ראם. But

23 *For no divination is needed in Ya'akov, nor magic in Israel. At this very moment it is told to Ya'akov and Israel what* God *has wrought here.*	כג כִּ֤י לֹא־נַ֙חַשׁ֙ בְּיַעֲקֹ֔ב וְלֹא־קֶ֖סֶם בְּיִשְׂרָאֵ֑ל כָּעֵ֗ת יֵאָמֵ֤ר לְיַעֲקֹב֙ וּלְיִשְׂרָאֵ֔ל מַה־פָּ֖עַל אֵֽל׃

Israel does not have to seek this power; he need not apply his own physical and spiritual strength *toward this end*. Rather, the power will be given to him, ready and complete, by God. It is God's Will that they should be great and mighty. All He requires of them is תרועת מלך, "homage to the King," to be demonstrated by their keeping far from all אָוֶן, from all misuse of what was given to them by God.

תועפת — from the root יעף, which is identical with עיף and עוף (see Commentary, *Bereshis* 1:20 and 7:14) — denotes constant striving to ascend to the heights. Thus תוֹעֲפוֹת הָרִים, the striving of the mountains rising heavenward, in contrast to מֶחְקְרֵי־אָרֶץ, "the depths of the earth" (*Tehillim* 95:4).

23 **כי לא נחש וגו׳**. You inquire about this people's צופים-wisdom, and you project that its extent will determine the success or failure of this people's future position of power. You inquire about wisdom that gropes in the dark with occult divinations, about magicians who claim the ability to sway the fates in accordance with their own wishes. Ya'akov-Yisrael does *not* need these methods, to which people turn when helpless and at their wit's end. When in distress, Ya'akov does not hearken to divinations, and Israel's greatness does not result from magic arts. At this very moment — כעת — while we are talking together and becoming aware that we are powerless to initiate any action against God's people, Ya'akov and Yisrael are already receiving the revelation of what God has wrought here with us. They are told this so that they should understand it not only when they are in the position of "Ya'akov," but also so that they never forget it when they are in the [powerful] position of "Yisrael."

Instead of the paltry devices of divination and magic employed by the obscure צופים-wisdom, Ya'akov-Yisrael receives the bright, clear Word of God, without first having to inquire after it.

נחש — see Commentary, *Bereshis* 44:5. **קסם** — see Commentary, ibid. 11:6. **כעת** — as in וְכָעֵת לֹא הִשְׁמִיעָנוּ כָּזֹאת (*Shoftim* 13:23).

24 *Lo! As a people united he arises like a leopard, and he lifts himself up like a lion that does not lie down until he has devoured prey and drunk the blood of the slain.*

כד הֶן־עָם֙ כְּלָבִ֣יא יָק֔וּם וְכַאֲרִ֖י
יִתְנַשָּׂ֑א לֹ֤א יִשְׁכַּב֙ עַד־יֹ֣אכַל טֶ֔רֶף
וְדַם־חֲלָלִ֖ים יִשְׁתֶּֽה׃

25 *And Balak said to Bil'am: [If] you are not to curse them, [then] you should also not bless them.*

כה וַיֹּ֤אמֶר בָּלָק֙ אֶל־בִּלְעָ֔ם גַּם־קֹ֖ב
לֹ֣א תִקֳּבֶ֑נּוּ גַּם־בָּרֵ֖ךְ לֹ֥א תְבָרְכֶֽנּוּ׃

26 *But Bil'am answered and said to Balak: Have I not spoken to you and said: All that* God *will speak, that must I do?*

כו וַיַּ֣עַן בִּלְעָ֔ם וַיֹּ֖אמֶר אֶל־בָּלָ֑ק הֲלֹ֗א
דִּבַּ֤רְתִּי אֵלֶ֙יךָ֙ לֵאמֹ֔ר כֹּ֛ל אֲשֶׁר־
יְדַבֵּ֥ר יְהֹוָ֖ה אֹת֥וֹ אֶֽעֱשֶֽׂה׃ ששי
(שביעי כשהן מחוברין)

27 *And Balak said to Bil'am: Pray come, I will take you to yet another place; perhaps it will be right in the eyes of God that you should curse them for me from there.*

כז וַיֹּ֤אמֶר בָּלָק֙ אֶל־בִּלְעָ֔ם לְכָה־נָּא֙
אֶקָּ֣חֲךָ֔ אֶל־מָק֖וֹם אַחֵ֑ר אוּלַ֤י יִישַׁר֙
בְּעֵינֵ֣י הָֽאֱלֹהִ֔ים וְקַבֹּ֥תוֹ לִ֖י מִשָּֽׁם׃

24 **הן עם וגו'**. Ya'akov-Yisrael does not need our **צופים**-wisdom. Nor does he require **נחשים**; he is sure of his future. He does not need **קסמים**; by other means he will become master of his own fate. He will not fight to secure his position externally as a **גוי** among **גוים**, as a national power against other national powers. Rather, **הן עם**: He will fulfill his social mission internally, walk modestly with God and lead his own distinctive lifestyle. By virtue of the deeds that he will perform as an **עם**, he will be bold like a leopard and strong like a lion externally, and through these qualities he will overcome the world.

לא ישכב עד יאכל טרף וגו' is continued description of the lion's power, which Israel will attain in peaceful ways through its moral and social energies. The subject of **ישכב** is **ארי**.

27-28 It became clear to Balak that Israel was vulnerable neither from **במות בעל** nor from **שדה צופים**: neither from the standpoint of physical, material

28 *Balak took Bil'am to the Peak of Pe'or, which looks out upon the wasteland.*

כח וַיִּקַּח בָּלָק אֶת־בִּלְעָם רֹאשׁ הַפְּעוֹר הַנִּשְׁקָף עַל־פְּנֵי הַיְשִׁימֹן׃

power, nor from the standpoint of the spiritual, godly element. However, a nation may be blessed with an abundance of material and spiritual gifts, and still hasten headlong to its ruin. Providence may shower on it all the treasures, all the physical and spiritual wealth that heaven affords, and yet a worm will devour it from within and turn all the blessing into a curse, and it will ultimately become not only unworthy but also incapable of receiving and retaining God's blessings. This worm is called immorality; it is the shameless surrender to dissolute sensualism.

Hence, after Balak has had Bil'am look in vain from במות בעל and from שדה צופים for weak points in the nation of Israel, he says to him: לכה נא וגו׳ (cf. v. 13: לך נא וגו׳), I will make one more attempt; please come with me and let me show you the nation from yet another vantage point. Perhaps if you see them there, God Himself will permit you to cast a curse against this people. And so he took him to the peak of "shamelessness deified," which overlooks the wasteland. For that is the whole essence of the cult of Pe'or: It directs to the gods the animal side of human physicality, and says to man: Why do you dream of modesty and of an exalted moral calling? Your own body shows you that you are just like an animal, and you should not be ashamed of this before the gods! Thus, by taking Bil'am to the Peak of Pe'or, Balak put to him the question: What is the attitude of this people toward modesty and toward the holiness of sexual morality, on which the strength and prosperity of all nations ultimately depend?

Not without reason do our Sages (*Bemidbar Rabbah* 20:18) say: בלק היה בעל קסמים ובעל נחש יותר מבלעם שהיה נמשך אחריו כסומא. למה הדבר דומה? לאחד שיש בידו סכין ואינו מכיר את הפרקים וחבירו מכיר את הפרקים ואין בידו סכין, כך היו שניהם דומין וכו׳. Balak was even more deeply initiated into the arts of magic and divination than Bil'am, who let himself be led about like a blind man. To what may this be likened? To two men who wish to perform an operation. One of them has the instruments but has no knowledge of anatomy; the other has the knowledge but has no instruments. Thus Balak showed Bil'am where to direct the sharp point of his curse.

29 *And Bil'am said to Balak: Build me seven altars here and prepare for me here seven bulls and seven rams.*

כט וַיֹּ֤אמֶר בִּלְעָם֙ אֶל־בָּלָ֔ק בְּנֵה־לִ֥י בָזֶ֖ה שִׁבְעָ֣ה מִזְבְּחֹ֑ת וְהָכֵ֥ן לִי֙ בָּזֶ֔ה שִׁבְעָ֥ה פָרִ֖ים וְשִׁבְעָ֥ה אֵילִֽם׃

30 *Balak did as Bil'am had spoken, and he offered one bull and one ram on each altar as an ascent offering.*

ל וַיַּ֣עַשׂ בָּלָ֔ק כַּאֲשֶׁ֖ר אָמַ֣ר בִּלְעָ֑ם וַיַּ֛עַל פָּ֥ר וָאַ֖יִל בַּמִּזְבֵּֽחַ׃

24 1 *But Bil'am saw now that only to bless Israel would be good in* God's *eyes; so he did not go, as at other times, to meet divinations, but set his face toward the wilderness.*

כד א וַיַּ֣רְא בִּלְעָ֗ם כִּ֣י ט֞וֹב בְּעֵינֵ֤י יְהוָה֙ לְבָרֵ֣ךְ אֶת־יִשְׂרָאֵ֔ל וְלֹא־הָלַ֥ךְ כְּפַֽעַם־בְּפַ֖עַם לִקְרַ֣את נְחָשִׁ֑ים וַיָּ֥שֶׁת אֶל־הַמִּדְבָּ֖ר פָּנָֽיו׃

2 *When Bil'am lifted up his eyes and saw Israel camping according to its tribes, the spirit of God came upon him.*

ב וַיִּשָּׂ֨א בִלְעָ֜ם אֶת־עֵינָ֗יו וַיַּרְא֙ אֶת־יִשְׂרָאֵ֔ל שֹׁכֵ֖ן לִשְׁבָטָ֑יו וַתְּהִ֥י עָלָ֖יו ר֥וּחַ אֱלֹהִֽים׃

CHAPTER 24

1 **וירא וגו'**. Only now was the veil removed from over Bil'am's eyes, and he no longer believed that by magic arts he could change God's Will. What his mouth had uttered in verses 8 and 20 of the preceding chapter now became his own inner conviction. He therefore simply looked toward the wilderness — from the vantage point Balak had set for him — and waited to see whether God would continue to use him as His instrument.

2 **וישא וגו'**. But when he raised his eyes and saw Israel לשבטיו, encamped according to its tribes, grouped by households and families, this sight already gave him the answer to Balak's question. At that moment "the spirit of God came upon him": Now he was no longer an unwilling instrument for the words that God had put into his mouth. Whatever he will say henceforth he will utter in the pure spirit of prophecy.

3 *He took up his parable and said: Thus speaks Bil'am, whom Be'or calls his son; thus speaks the man whose eye has been opened.*	ג וַיִּשָּׂא מְשָׁלוֹ וַיֹּאמַר נְאֻם בִּלְעָם בְּנוֹ בְעֹר וּנְאֻם הַגֶּבֶר שְׁתֻם הָעָיִן:
4 *He speaks, hearing* God's *Words, [he] who beholds what* שדי *allows to behold, [he] who has fallen down yet has [his] eye unveiled:*	ד נְאֻם שֹׁמֵעַ אִמְרֵי־אֵל אֲשֶׁר מַחֲזֵה שַׁדַּי יֶחֱזֶה נֹפֵל וּגְלוּי עֵינָיִם:
5 *How good are your tents, O Ya'akov, your dwelling places, O Israel!*	ה מַה־טֹּבוּ אֹהָלֶיךָ יַעֲקֹב מִשְׁכְּנֹתֶיךָ יִשְׂרָאֵל:

3-4 וישא וגו'. This רוח אלקים was new to him, something he had never experienced before. For this reason he — unlike the prophets of Israel — focuses on *himself* first, and this thought totally preoccupies him. He is so busy describing his new state and the spiritual elevation of his personality that he does not get to what he really has to say.

נאם — see Commentary, *Bereshis* 5:30-31.

בנו בער — cf. 23:18 and Commentary there. In *Sanhedrin* 105a, the interpretation given to this expression is the opposite of the above: אביו בנו הוא לו בנביאות — i.e., his father Be'or compares to him like a son; as a prophet, Bil'am was superior to his father.

שתם. שתם occurs again only in the Mishnah (*Avodah Zarah* 69a) as the opposite of סתם: כדי שישתום ויסתום ויגוב. There, שתם denotes opening a stopper. שתם העין: now he feels that his eye has been opened.

מחזה ש-די: ש-די is God Who stands above the world order and assigns it measure and limit, law and order (see Commentary, *Bereshis* 17:1). מחזה ש-די: God allows a mortal to see something of the world order He has set.

נפל: רוח אלקים has overwhelmed and overpowered him; at the same time he is גלוי עינים: his mind is clear and alert.

5-6 מה טבו וגו'. Balak's question to Bil'am was: What view do you have of this people מראש הפעור? What is its attitude toward modesty and toward morality in sexual relations? The camp לשבטיו which he now beholds, אהלי

6 *Like brooks are they turned, like gardens by the river; like* ahol *trees planted by* God, *like cedars beside the waters.*

ו כִּנְחָלִ֣ים נִטָּ֔יוּ כְּגַנֹּ֖ת עֲלֵ֣י נָהָ֑ר כַּאֲהָלִים֙ נָטַ֣ע יְהוָ֔ה כַּאֲרָזִ֖ים עֲלֵי־מָֽיִם׃

יעקב and משכנות ישראל, which make it possible for every child to know who his father is; the fact that houses, families, and tribes are grouped according to paternal descent — משפחת האב קרויה משפחה (*Bava Basra* 109b) — these are the criteria by which the sexual morality of this people could be judged.

מה טבו: not "how beautiful" but "how good"; how good, how very much in accord with the ideal of morality and with the true welfare of a people, are your "houses," be they the transient tents of Ya'akov during his wanderings, or the proud permanent dwelling places of Yisrael (משכנתיך — cf. מִשְׁכְּנֹתָם לְדֹר וָדֹר [*Tehillim* 49:12], וְיָשַׁב עַמִּי בִּנְוֵה שָׁלוֹם וּבְמִשְׁכְּנוֹת מִבְטַחִים [*Yeshayahu* 32:18]). The homes of Israel's families are כנחלים, כגנת: They are like brooks that bring blessing and like gardens that are themselves blessed. Like a brook, each household and each family branch passes down to the next generation the blessings of material prosperity and spiritual and moral welfare. At the same time, each is in itself a "garden of man," blessed with material, intellectual, and moral abundance. Each is a brook unto itself, running its own particular course independently of all the others, but each one directs its attainments to flow, as it were, into the one river they all share in common. In addition, each is a garden that owes its abundance of fruit and flowers to one common river. They are כאהלים and at the same time כארזים; they combine the delicate ethereal essence of aloes with the firm strength of cedars; they combine refreshing, refined, and noble spirituality with strength and endurance.

אהלים as in מֹר אֲהָלִים וְקִנָּמוֹן (*Mishlei* 7:17), מֹר וַאֲהָלוֹת עִם כָּל־רָאשֵׁי בְשָׂמִים (*Shir Ha-Shirim* 4:14). The ethereal quality of the אהלים, representing the spiritual aptitude of the generations of Israel, is a Divine gift, which is dependent on planting in accordance with God's Will — hence: כאהלים נטע ה׳ — and on water, the source of life and strength, on which the human cedars grow.

7 *The water flows from* His *buckets, and it is* His *seed that is at the abundant flow. Therefore his king will be higher than Agag, and his kingdom will be exalted.*	ז יִזַּל־מַ֙יִם֙ מִדָּ֣לְיָ֔ו וְזַרְע֖וֹ בְּמַ֣יִם רַבִּ֑ים וְיָרֹ֤ם מֵֽאֲגַג֙ מַלְכּ֔וֹ וְתִנַּשֵּׂ֖א מַלְכֻתֽוֹ׃
8 *The* God *Who brought him out*	ח אֵ֚ל מוֹצִיא֣וֹ מִמִּצְרַ֔יִם כְּתוֹעֲפֹ֥ת

7 **יזל מים מדליו**. The water flows from God's buckets, and every human germ that is sown beside these streams is His seed.

We have seen that the tents of Ya'akov and the dwelling places of Yisrael are "good," and all the life that unfolds within them is a "garden of man," in which blessing resides and which is a source of blessing. The secret of this lies in the moral aspect, in the sanctity of family life. The sexual life of Israel is sanctified and immunized against all traces of the vulgarity symbolized by Pe'or. The people of Israel respect the power of man's seed as belonging to God and as sacred unto Him. Only in the Name of God and according to His teachings do they sow and plant human seed, so that the children should grow up by the wellsprings of His Teaching and laws, glorify His Name, and do His Will on earth. These truths are revealed to the onlooker by *the sight of the tents of Ya'akov and the dwelling places of Israel encamped — according to households, families, and tribes — around the Dwelling Place of God's Torah, which they all cherish in common*, the sight of ישראל שכן לשבטיו.

Israel's power of victory depends precisely on this moral aspect of private family and sexual life. יזל מים מדליו: God's laws of life are vessels containing pure water, and from these vessels emerges the river by whose banks the Jewish garden of man blossoms. Every pure Jewish human sprout is "זרעו": it is a product of sensuality subordinated to God's Torah. "Therefore his king shall be higher than Agag, and his kingdom shall be exalted"; for Israel's victory is the victory of the Divine law of morality, and the spread of the kingdom of Israel is the elevation of God's throne on earth.

8 **א-ל מוציאו וגו׳**. Above (23:22), it says: מוציאם. The sexual morality, the keeping far from גילוי עריות and from all the impurity of Pe'or, constituted already in Egypt the nobility shared by all the sons and daughters of Israel.

רְאֵ֫ם ל֑וֹ יֹאכַ֞ל גּוֹיִ֣ם צָרָ֗יו וְעַצְמֹתֵיהֶ֛ם יְגָרֵ֖ם וְחִצָּ֥יו יִמְחָֽץ׃	*from Egypt is to him as the ascending power of* re'em. *He [i.e., Israel] devours nations because they are His [God's] enemies, and he drains the marrow from their bones, and as His arrows does he wound them.*
ט כָּרַ֨ע שָׁכַ֧ב כַּאֲרִ֛י וּכְלָבִ֖יא מִ֣י	9 *When he kneels, he rests like a lion*

This common feature of moral purity formed a strong bond, which united them even in Egypt, when they still lacked all the external prerequisites of nationhood. The God Who redeemed them on the merit of their moral purity is the One Who will give them an impetus to power in the future as well, for on their merit God's law of morality will regain a place among men. They will defeat other nations, or, rather, God will destroy other nations before them, because these nations are צריו; they are the enemies of God's law of morality, and they oppose His Presence on earth. Indeed, it is repeatedly stated in the chapter on עריות (*Vayikra* 18) that the inhabitants of Canaan were doomed by God because of their excesses of immorality!

ועצמתיהם יגרם. We already noted on *Bereshis* 49:14 that גרם is to be distinguished from עצם. The עצם is so called because it is hard and strong, whereas the גרם is a limb, a joint. Accordingly, גֵּרֵם in the *pi'el* apparently means: to disjoint, to sever the joints, to deprive them of their power of leverage.

This, then, is the meaning of ועצמתיהם יגרם: All their strength will not help them against Israel, for they will lose their power of leverage; Israel will cause their bones to cease being גרמים, endowed with the power of leverage.

וחציו ימחץ: as the arrows of God, Israel will wound them. That is to say, Israel is an arrow in God's hand in His war against His enemies, against the enemies of the reign of His Law on earth. Only *because* Israel is an arrow in God's hand does it have the power to defeat the nations.

9 **כרע שכב וגו'**. After Israel defeats the nations and dwells among them in peace, it will command such respect that no one will dare to attack it.

and like a leopard — who would dare rouse him! Those who bless you are the blessed, and those who curse you are themselves laden with the curse.	יְקִימֶ֑נּוּ מְבָרְכֶ֣יךָ בָר֔וּךְ וְאֹרְרֶ֖יךָ אָרֽוּר׃
10 *Then Balak's anger was stirred against Bil'am and he struck his hands together. And Balak said to Bil'am: I have called you to curse my enemies, and now you have blessed them these three times.*	י וַיִּֽחַר־אַ֤ף בָּלָק֙ אֶל־בִּלְעָ֔ם וַיִּסְפֹּ֖ק אֶת־כַּפָּ֑יו וַיֹּ֨אמֶר בָּלָ֜ק אֶל־בִּלְעָ֗ם לָקֹ֤ב אֹֽיְבַי֙ קְרָאתִ֔יךָ וְהִנֵּה֙ בֵּרַ֣כְתָּ בָרֵ֔ךְ זֶ֖ה שָׁלֹ֥שׁ פְּעָמִֽים׃

מברכיך ברוך וגו'. Once again Bil'am looks down at Israel and now he makes the momentous statement, מברכיך וגו', which God made about Avraham when He first chose him (*Bereshis* 12:3), and which Yitzchak reiterated in his blessing (ibid. 27:29).

Here — as in Yitzchak's blessing — it says מברכיך, ואורריך, in the plural, whereas the predicates ברוך and ארור are in the singular. It appears, then, that this expression is to be taken as follows: "All those who bless you" — i.e., those who respect the principles for which you stand and who help promote them — are among the blessed and will be called blessed. That is to say, they are that to which God's blessing is assured and which will have a future under God's sovereignty. Conversely, "those who curse you" — i.e., those who are hostile to the principles you represent and who hope for your downfall, so that the values for which you stand may be destroyed along with you — ארור, are among the cursed. That is to say, they are that which will bear the curse within itself, that which God has doomed to destruction and which will have no future on God's earth.

10 **ויספק את כפיו**. ספק or שפק occurs — here and elsewhere — in the sense of striking one's hand together as an expression of surprise and dismay. It also occurs in the sense of striking one's thigh — סָפַקְתִּי עַל־יָרֵךְ (*Yirmeyahu* 31:18) — as an expression of grief. In addition, it also occurs in the sense of sufficing; thus: אִם־יִשְׂפֹּק עֲפַר שֹׁמְרוֹן (*Melachim* I, 20:10), et

11 *Now run away to your native place! I thought I would show you great honor, but lo!* God *has held you back from honor.*

יא וְעַתָּה בְּרַח־לְךָ אֶל־מְקוֹמֶךָ אָמַרְתִּי כַּבֵּד אֲכַבֶּדְךָ וְהִנֵּה מְנָעֲךָ יְהוָה מִכָּבוֹד׃

12 *And Bil'am said to Balak: Did I not even tell your messengers whom you sent to me, saying:*

יב וַיֹּאמֶר בִּלְעָם אֶל־בָּלָק הֲלֹא גַּם אֶל־מַלְאָכֶיךָ אֲשֶׁר־שָׁלַחְתָּ אֵלַי דִּבַּרְתִּי לֵאמֹר׃

13 *Even if Balak were to give me his house full of silver and gold, I could not go beyond the word of* God, *to do [anything] of my own accord, good or evil. What* God *will say, that will I have to say.*

יג אִם־יִתֶּן־לִי בָלָק מְלֹא בֵיתוֹ כֶּסֶף וְזָהָב לֹא אוּכַל לַעֲבֹר אֶת־פִּי יְהוָה לַעֲשׂוֹת טוֹבָה אוֹ רָעָה מִלִּבִּי אֲשֶׁר־יְדַבֵּר יְהוָה אֹתוֹ אֲדַבֵּר׃

שביעי

al. It is also the common expression — particularly in the Mishnah and Talmud — for doubt and uncertainty.

It appears that the basic meaning is striking the hands together. Stretching out the hand with the palm turned upward expresses the need to receive: one asks for a material gift, or for an intellectual gift, to understand something or to receive an answer. One who strikes his other hand against such an asking open hand — in reaction to an event or to things that were said — is saying: Is this what I asked? Is this what I expected? He is expressing surprise or even disgust. By extension, ספק, שפק came to mean: to put something in the palm of an outstretched hand — i.e., to satisfy a demand. One who lowers his palm — instead of extending it — in order to strike it against one's hip or thigh expresses hopelessness: We have nothing to hope for, we shall get nothing more. Finally, it appears that one who strikes his hands together is saying that the two things are equal, such that they balance each other and it is difficult to decide between them. Thus ספק in the sense of "doubt," "uncertainty."

14 *And now I go to my people. Come, I will give you a piece of advice. What this people will do to your people will be only in the end of days.*

יד וְעַתָּ֕ה הִנְנִ֥י הוֹלֵ֖ךְ לְעַמִּ֑י לְכָ֗ה אִיעָֽצְךָ֗ אֲשֶׁ֨ר יַעֲשֶׂ֜ה הָעָ֥ם הַזֶּ֛ה לְעַמְּךָ֖ בְּאַחֲרִ֥ית הַיָּמִֽים׃

15 *And he took up his parable and said: Thus speaks Bil'am, whom Be'or calls his son; thus speaks the man whose eye has been opened.*

טו וַיִּשָּׂ֥א מְשָׁל֖וֹ וַיֹּאמַ֑ר נְאֻ֤ם בִּלְעָם֙ בְּנ֣וֹ בְעֹ֔ר וּנְאֻ֥ם הַגֶּ֖בֶר שְׁתֻ֥ם הָעָֽיִן׃

14 **לכה איעצך**. Below (31:16), it says of the daughters of Midyan: הן הנה היו לבני ישראל בדבר בלעם למסר מעל בה׳ על דבר פעור. "They gave themselves up to the sons of Israel, on Bil'am's advice, to induce them to act faithlessly toward God by engaging in the cult of Pe'or" — an event that is described here immediately after Bil'am's departure (chap. 25). Hence, one is certainly justified in saying that **איעצך** refers to this. Bil'am advised Balak to entice Israel's youth to their downfall. For Bil'am had just declared in his last prophetic speech that the Pe'or aspect -- regarding which Bil'am had made his final attempt to uncover a vulnerable point in Israel — is this people's source of strength. Moreover, sexual purity is the fundamental condition for their closeness to God. It was reasonable, then, that Bil'am would now say to Balak: Your people is destined to suffer from this people, but the time for that has not yet come. At the moment you have nothing to fear from this people; on the contrary, according to the revelation that has just been granted to us, I have advice for you on how you can try to harm this people that you hate. We just heard that אלקיהם של אלו שונא זימה הוא, "the God of these people is an enemy of all unchastity" (*Sanhedrin* 106a), and He is the very antithesis of Pe'or. If you succeed in enticing them to sexual immorality, you will bring about their downfall, and you can make the attempt through the daughters of your people (see next chapter).

15-16 **וישא וגו׳** — see Commentary, vv. 3-4. Here, in addition to what was said above, he says of himself: **וידע דעת עליון**, because — as the רמב״ן explains

16 *He speaks, hearing the Words of* God, *and recognizing the thoughts of the Most High. What* שדי *allows to be beheld, he beholds, fallen down and yet eyes unveiled.*

טז נְאֻם שֹׁמֵעַ אִמְרֵי־אֵל וְיֹדֵעַ דַּעַת עֶלְיוֹן מַחֲזֵה שַׁדַּי יֶחֱזֶה נֹפֵל וּגְלוּי עֵינָיִם׃

17 *I see it, but not now; I behold it, but it is not near. A star has set out on its way from Ya'akov, and a scepter has arisen from Israel. It will strike the hinges of Moav and break down the walls of all the sons of Shes.*

יז אֶרְאֶנּוּ וְלֹא עַתָּה אֲשׁוּרֶנּוּ וְלֹא קָרוֹב דָּרַךְ כּוֹכָב מִיַּעֲקֹב וְקָם שֵׁבֶט מִיִּשְׂרָאֵל וּמָחַץ פַּאֲתֵי מוֹאָב וְקַרְקַר כָּל־בְּנֵי־שֵׁת׃

— he reveals here events of the distant future, which at present are mere thoughts in the mind of God Most High.

17 **אראנו וגו׳**. I see it clearly, as though it were before my eyes, even though it is not happening now but, rather, I am gazing into the distant future, whose events are not close at hand. By this he calms Balak's fears that Israel's growing strength is an immediate danger to him and his people. These words are a direct continuation of his previous statement: אשר יעשה העם הזה לעמך באחרית הימים (v. 14).

דרך כוכב וגו׳. Stars go along their appointed courses — הַכּוֹכָבִים מִמְּסִלּוֹתָם (*Shoftim* 5:20). Stars are signposts in the sky by which people find their way on earth וּמַצְדִּיקֵי הָרַבִּים כַּכּוֹכָבִים (*Daniyel* 12:3). Until now, because of his weakness,Ya'akov has been little respected. But a star will set out from Ya'akov and, keeping to the course set for it by God, it will show mankind the way.

וקם שבט מישראל: This star will also be a scepter; it will be invested with governing influence over the nations. It will arise as a scepter out of Israel, out of the people that proclaims and spreads "God's sovereignty." The very fact that a שבט will arise out of it turns יעקב into ישראל.

In his mind, Bil'am is present amidst these events while they are taking place. Hence he says דרך, not ידרוך.

ומחץ פאתי וגו׳ וקרקר וגו׳. The meaning of פאתי is questionable. By its form, it cannot be the plural construct state of פֵּאָה, unless we posit the

18 *And Edom will pass over to a master, to a master over Se'ir, his enemies, and Israel will grow in might.*	יח וְהָיָה אֱדוֹם יְרֵשָׁה וְהָיָה יְרֵשָׁה שֵׂעִיר אֹיְבָיו וְיִשְׂרָאֵל עֹשֶׂה חָיִל׃

existence of a dual plural form פְּאָתַיִם whose construct state would be פַּאֲתֵי. However, the meaning of such a dual plural form [a pair of corners] is obscure. In our view, פאתי is identical with פות, just as ראם derives from רום, for so we find וְרָאֲמָה (*Zecharyah* 14:10), רָאמוֹת (*Iyov* 28:18), which have an א instead of the quiescent ו. Accordingly, פאתי could be taken like וְהַפֹּתוֹת לְדַלְתוֹת (*Melachim* I, 7:50), door hinges, with the hinge representing the door. There would then be a conceptual relation between פאתי and what follows it: וקרקר וגו׳. For קרקר is a doubling of the *pi'el* form of קיר, and means: to demolish the קיר. Thus מְקַרְקַר קִר (*Yeshayahu* 22:5; cf. Commentary, *Vayikra* 19:28).

בני שת is the designation for all postdiluvian human beings, for they all are descendants of Noach, the last of the descendants of Seth.

This, then, is the meaning of our verse: This scepter-bearing star which came forth from Ya'akov-Yisrael will strike the gates of Moav and demolish the walls of all nations, for its Torah will show the nations the only way to salvation. By virtue of this Torah, Moav will no longer have any hinges to isolating gates — i.e., its pride in standing alone will cease; and all mankind will be "without walls" — i.e., material strongholds will no longer afford any protection and will not be considered a source of security.

18 **והיה אדום ירשה**. יְרֵשָׁה: something that is transferred into the possession of another. Edom is mentioned here beside שעיר, and of both it says: והיה ירשה. It appears, then, that Edom is the power and might of the Edomites, whereas Se'ir is their original homeland. Edom's sphere of power extends beyond the borders of its land. Until now, Edomite power has been a supreme national power with no master over it. Now it will become ירשה: it will receive a master, and it will be subordinate and subservient. As a result, the land of Se'ir, too, will undergo a change of ownership and will come into the possession of a new owner. Both will become ירשה, because both are אויביו, ancient enemies of Ya'akov-Yisrael. And when Edom-Se'ir loses its independence, Israel grows strong and gains power and influence.

19 *He will rule from out of Ya'akov and this shall cause the last [remnant] to be lost from the cities.*

יט וְיֵ֥רְדְּ מִֽיַּעֲקֹ֑ב וְהֶאֱבִ֥יד שָׂרִ֖יד
מֵעִֽיר׃

20 *He saw Amalek and took up his parable and said: Amalek is the first among the nations and his end — until he will be a lost one.*

כ וַיַּרְא֙ אֶת־עֲמָלֵ֔ק וַיִּשָּׂ֥א מְשָׁל֖וֹ
וַיֹּאמַ֑ר רֵאשִׁ֤ית גּוֹיִם֙ עֲמָלֵ֔ק
וְאַחֲרִית֖וֹ עֲדֵ֥י אֹבֵֽד׃

עשה חיל has two meanings: Yisrael creating and accumulating power, as in הנתן לך כח לעשות חיל (*Devarim* 8:18; see Commentary, *Shemos* 18:21-22), and also exercising this power, as in יְמִין ה׳ עֹשָׂה חָיִל (*Tehillim* 118:15).

19 **וירד מיעקב**. Precisely from powerless "Ya'akov" will emerge the power of the scepter, and all material power — even the Edomite scepter — will render homage to his spiritual loftiness. At that time, the last remnant of one-sided "worship of culture" will be wiped out: **והאביד שריד מעיר**. Since עיר is mentioned here in the absolute, it apparently refers to the culture of the cities, whose one-sided, self-sufficing development was the beginning of the historical development that led to the worship of man (Commentary, *Bereshis* 4:17 and 11:4). It is this that is destined to come to an end with the ultimate acknowledgement of the guiding scepter of the star that will set out from Ya'akov.

Yeshayahu, too, mentions the עִיר as the representative of one-sided worship of culture (*Yeshayahu* 32:14), and this is the hymn that will be sung "on that day": עִיר עָז־לָנוּ יְשׁוּעָה יָשִׁית חוֹמוֹת וָחֵל; "We have an invincible city, for it replaces walls and bulwarks with God's salvation" (ibid. 26:1).

20 **ראשית גוים**, the first in rank, not chronologically, for Moav was older. Amalek was also the first among the nations to make war against Israel, without any provocation on Israel's part.

ואחריתו, and his end will be **עדי אבד**: he goes on his way until he becomes אובד, one completely lost. Even his memory will disappear from the minds of men.

21 *And he saw the Keini and took up his parable and said: Let your seat remain very firm and build your nest in the rock.*	כא וַיַּרְא֙ אֶת־הַקֵּינִ֔י וַיִּשָּׂ֥א מְשָׁל֖וֹ וַיֹּאמַ֑ר אֵיתָן֙ מֽוֹשָׁבֶ֔ךָ וְשִׂ֥ים בַּסֶּ֖לַע קִנֶּֽךָ׃
22 *For if Kayin is laid waste, to what place would Asshur carry you off?*	כב כִּ֥י אִם־יִהְיֶ֖ה לְבָ֣עֵֽר קָ֑יִן עַד־מָ֖ה אַשּׁ֥וּר תִּשְׁבֶּֽךָּ׃
23 *And he took up his parable and said: Alas! Who will survive since* God *has founded him?*	כג וַיִּשָּׂ֥א מְשָׁל֖וֹ וַיֹּאמַ֑ר א֕וֹי מִ֥י יִחְיֶ֖ה מִשֻּׂמ֥וֹ אֵֽל׃

21-22 In *Shoftim* 4:11 it says that a branch of Kayin's line separated from Kayin — נִפְרָד מִקַּיִן — and settled in the midst of Israel. This branch was called "קיני" on account of its origin. This was the same branch to which Moshe's father-in-law belonged. Following his example, it attached itself to Israel (see Commentary above, 10:31-32).

Bil'am warns this branch not to sever its ties with Israel and not to cease dwelling in Israel's midst. Let his dwelling place remain firm there, let him build his nest in this rock he has chosen, and never return to the Kayinite race from which he came. For Kayin will be destroyed by Asshur and led away into captivity. Hence, if he returns to Kayin, he will suffer the same fate, and to what place will he then go in captivity? If he remains among Israel he will escape this fate. For it appears — as we already noted above (10:29) — that the קיני was not subjected to the Assyrian power that conquered Israel; rather, its freedom and independence were preserved. Indeed, in Israel its מושב was איתן.

תשבך. Asshur is referred to here in the feminine, which apparently alludes to the retribution that will also come upon Asshur, as immediately stated in the continuation [v. 24].

23 **אוי מי יחיה משמו א-ל**. Before God establishes Israel, no power will be able to preserve its independence if it opposes the principle that Israel's founding is destined to enforce. After God introduces Israel into world history, there will no longer be a future for that which opposes this Divine intention.

24 *Ships will come from the coast of the Kittim and weaken Asshur and weaken Ever, and he, too — until he will be one lost.*

כד וְצִים מִיַּד כִּתִּים וְעִנּוּ אַשּׁוּר וְעִנּוּ־עֵבֶר וְגַם־הוּא עֲדֵי אֹבֵד׃

24 **וצים וגו׳**. From וְצִי אַדִּיר לֹא יַעַבְרֶנּוּ (*Yeshayahu* 33:21) and יֵצְאוּ מַלְאָכִים מִלְּפָנַי בַּצִּים (*Yechezkel* 30:9) it is evident that צי — in the plural, צים — means "ship." On the other hand, צִיָּה means "wilderness," and צִיִּים are the inhabitants of the wilderness.

Analogous forms are בי (the word of petition) from the root בהה, בעה (see Commentary, *Bereshis* 1:2); הי (lament) from the root ההה, which is recognizable in אֲהָהּ (*Yehoshua* 7:7); מִי from the root מה, מהה; פי — in the plural, פִּים (*Shemuel* I, 13:21) — from the root פה, פהה, which is related to פעה, פחה; קי (in קִיקָלוֹן, *Chavakkuk* 2:16), from the root קאה.

From these forms it appears that the common root of צי and ציה is צאה, which is related to צעה, שאה, שהה, from which we get שַׁי. The basic meaning is long or strong movement toward a goal. Also related are זוע and יזע: movement and sweat. שהה, in Aramaic, means: to tarry a long time without reaching the goal. שאה denotes thinking a long time about something without getting at the knowledge you want; hence it also denotes desolation. שי: something whose delivery takes a long time, a large gift. צעה: to move with emphasis, with special attention; to march. צי: a ship that makes long journeys, overcoming difficulties; a large vessel. ציה: a region where one must wander for a long time and overcome difficulties before arriving at one's destination — i.e., a wilderness.

מיד כתים. The כתים (*Bereshis* 10:4) were descendants of Yavan. Tradition takes them to be the ancient Italian population of Greek ancestry — thus איטליא של יון: Greater Greece — and explains that the כתים are the Romans. Accordingly, יד כתים would be the Italian coast on the Mediterranean and יד כתים would be similar to יד הירדן (above, 13:29) and יַד אַשְׁדּוֹד (*Yehoshua* 15:46). מיד כתים could also mean from the power of the כתים.

עבר, according to *Targum Onkelos*: the lands on the far side of the Euphrates. It is possible that עבר includes all the descendants of Yoktan mentioned in *Bereshis* 10:26-30, for they all are descendants of Ever.

וגם הוא apparently refers to יד כתים. Accordingly, יד is construed here in the masculine, as it is in *Yechezkel* 2:9: וְהִנֵּה־יָד וגו׳ וְהִנֵּה־בוֹ וגו׳.

25 *Thereupon Bil'am arose, went, and returned to his native place, and Balak, too, went on his way.*

כה וַיָּקָם בִּלְעָם וַיֵּלֶךְ וַיָּשָׁב לִמְקֹמוֹ
וְגַם־בָּלָק הָלַךְ לְדַרְכּוֹ׃ פ

25 1 *Israel had settled in Shittim, and the people began to defect in immorality to the daughters of Moav.*

כה א וַיֵּשֶׁב יִשְׂרָאֵל בַּשִּׁטִּים וַיָּחֶל הָעָם
לִזְנוֹת אֶל־בְּנוֹת מוֹאָב׃

2 *They invited the people to the sacrificial feasts of their gods; the people ate with [them] and they bowed to their gods.*

ב וַתִּקְרֶאןָ לָעָם לְזִבְחֵי אֱלֹהֵיהֶן
וַיֹּאכַל הָעָם וַיִּשְׁתַּחֲווּ לֵאלֹהֵיהֶן׃

CHAPTER 25

1 Neither the sword nor the curse of a foe from without has the power to harm Israel. Only Israel itself can bring misfortune upon itself by forsaking God and His Torah.

וישב וגו׳. As our Sages say in *Midrash Rabbah*, after winning the war against Sichon and Og, the people wanted to settle down quietly and enjoy their booty.

בַּשִּׁטִּים, not בְּשִׁטִּים. The name of the place is הַשִּׁטִּים (*Michah* 6:5). It was a wooded shady region which offered a welcome rest after the long wandering in the burning sun of the desert.

ויחל העם. Our Sages (*Bemidbar Rabbah* 20:23) say: כל מקום שנאמר העם לשון גנאי הוא, וכל מקום שנאמר ישראל לשון שבח הוא. Wherever the term העם is used it is derogatory, whereas ישראל is an honorable appellation. Thus ויהי העם כמתאננים (above, 11:1), וידבר העם באלקים ובמשה (21:5), ויבכו העם בלילה ההוא (14:1), עד אנה ינאצני העם (14:11), et al.

לזנות אל וגו׳. They began to forsake the faithfulness to moral duty, which they had kept until then, and to give themselves up to the daughters of Moav. The אל already indicates that the initiative came from בנות מואב (see Commentary below, 25:18, 31:16, and above, 24:14).

2 **ותקראנה וגו׳**. After provoking them to sin, the daughters of Moav invited them to their sacrificial feasts and finally induced them to prostrate them-

3 *And Israel attached itself to the Ba'al Pe'or, and the anger of* God *was stirred against Israel.*	ג וַיִּצָּמֶד יִשְׂרָאֵל לְבַעַל פְּעוֹר וַיִּחַר־אַף יְהוָה בְּיִשְׂרָאֵל׃
4 *And* God *said to Moshe: Take all the heads of the people and hang them [i.e., the guilty] for* God *in the presence of the sun, and then the anger of* God *which has been stirred will turn away from Israel.*	ד וַיֹּאמֶר יְהוָה אֶל־מֹשֶׁה קַח אֶת־כָּל־רָאשֵׁי הָעָם וְהוֹקַע אוֹתָם לַיהוָה נֶגֶד הַשָּׁמֶשׁ וְיָשֹׁב חֲרוֹן אַף־יְהוָה מִיִּשְׂרָאֵל׃

selves before Pe'or deities, in whose cult licentiousness is not considered a sin but an act of surrender and homage to the power of the gods.

3 **ויצמד וגו'**. There were various **בעלים**, deified powers. There was **בעל צפן**, a midnight god of the desert (*Shemos* 14:2). In contrast, there was **בעל מעון** (below, 32:38), a god of dwelling places, and **בַּעַל בְּרִית** (*Shoftim* 8:33) a god of the union of people. There was also **בַּעַל זְבוּב** (*Melachim* II, 1:2), apparently a god of decay (cf. **זְבוּבֵי מָוֶת** [*Koheles* 10:1]), to whom they would turn in times of illness and inquire of him about life and death. And there was also **בעל פעור**, a god of shamelessness, who was worshipped by giving brazen prominence to the most bestial aspects of human life. Hence Hoshea says: **בָּאוּ בַעַל־פְּעוֹר וַיִּנָּזְרוּ לַבֹּשֶׁת** (*Hoshea* 9:10) — they came to Ba'al Pe'or and *dedicated themselves to shamefulness.*

צמד — see above, 19:15.

The cult of Pe'or is an illustration of the type of Darwinism that glories in man's descent to the level of the beast, where, stripping himself of his Divinely-given nobility, he comes to regard himself as merely a higher species of animal.

ויחר אף וגו'. Thereby the fundamental condition for Israel's future before God was abrogated. And thereby God's anger — which strikes the lives of the unworthy and destroys them with **מגפה** (cf. 17:11-12) — was stirred against Israel.

4 **ויאמר וגו'**. The criminal law of God's Torah is based entirely on the process of indictment. The court has no authority to act on its own initiative if there is no accuser. However, no public prosecutor is appointed to pre-

sent the indictment. Rather, the entire nation — all its independent men — acts as the prosecutor on behalf of the Torah. When a person is about to commit a crime, two men must warn him of the prohibition and of the punishment attached to it. If, despite these warnings, he commits the crime, they must bring the criminal to court and, in the name of the Torah, demand that he receive the punishment due him.

In this case, no witnesses brought the sinners to court; hence, the judges had no legal authority to adjudicate. This very fact, however, elicited God's anger; for in this widespread open defection from the Torah, no men intervened to warn the offenders, apprehend them after the act, and bring them to court in order to prevent the spread of the evil. This fact made every passive onlooker an accessory to the crime, and so the entire nation was responsible for what had happened. For this reason it says: ויחר אף ה׳ בישראל, and for this reason God gave Moshe the authority and the duty to adjudicate on the basis of a הוראת שעה.

קח את כל ראשי העם — these are the שפטי ישראל mentioned in the next verse.

קח וגו׳ is similar to what is stated above (1:17): ויקח משה ואהרן את האנשים וגו׳, where men who had been designated by name were coopted by Moshe and Aharon to assist in the performance of an official function that Moshe and Aharon had been commanded to carry out. Similarly here, Moshe, as the supreme authority of the Law, the personification of the Sanhedrin — משה במקום שבעים וחד קאי (*Sanhedrin* 16b) — was to coopt all the ראשי העם, the שרי אלפים וכו׳ who had been appointed as judges (*Devarim* 1:15-16), to assist him in administering justice. They were to inflict upon all those who had participated in the worship of פעור the penalty of סקילה prescribed for an עובד עבודה זרה. In the cases of מגדף ועובד עבודה זרה, this penalty also entails momentary תלייה after death (see *Sanhedrin* 46b; Commentary, *Vayikra* 20:2).

והוקע אותם. A large part of the people had become licentious and had attached itself to an idolatrous cult. That in such a moment God says to Moshe simply אותם without further specification is deeply significant. אותם refers to those people who were the focus of Moshe's attention at that time, those with whom he was preoccupied: the guilty ones who had brought his people to such a decline.

We have already analyzed, in our Commentary on *Vayikra* (ibid.), the meaning of the תלייה על העץ attached to the סקילה penalty of the מגדף and of the עובד עבודה זרה: It emphasizes the meaning of this punishment. For

5 *And Moshe said to the judges of Israel: Let each one execute those men turned over to him who attached themselves to Ba'al Pe'or.*

ה וַיֹּאמֶר מֹשֶׁה אֶל־שֹׁפְטֵי יִשְׂרָאֵל הִרְגוּ אִישׁ אֲנָשָׁיו הַנִּצְמָדִים לְבַעַל פְּעוֹר׃

the סקילה itself is actually execution by the earth, and it serves to define the nature of the crime for which this punishment is imposed. The earth, as it were, revolts against this crime and vomits out the criminal from its midst. This abhorrence of the criminal — at its height — is further demonstrated by תלייה for a moment between heaven and earth, to teach us that heaven and earth reject the מגדף and the עובד עבודה זרה and grant them no place in their midst.

It is precisely this concept that is given fitting expression by the term הוקע. For יקע appears to be a stronger form of יגע; the meaning of יגע is: to be without rest. הוקעה — the momentary hanging of the criminal's corpse — is a fitting expression for the seriousness of the crime: The sinner could not have found himself a place in the world, had his sin not been atoned for by the punishment now imposed on him (see *Sanhedrin* 47b).

לה׳: to satisfy thereby the demand of God, Who bases Israel's future on the principle of morality and on the purity of the idea of God. For by removing the criminals from earthly existence and by proclaiming — in practice — the depth of depravity of the sin committed, they reestablish this principle's idea of holiness, and ה׳ can continue to maintain His relationship with Israel.

נגד השמש: The whole procedure of criminal law — תחילת הדין, גמר דין, and carrying out the sentence — is performed ביום; it is connected with the clear, upright, free, social-human life of the daytime. It is not a result of a dark vindictive spirit. Rather, the nation, conscious of itself and of its mission, fulfills its duty and performs the procedure for the sake of the Torah, thereby atoning also for the criminal himself. Hence, לה׳ and נגד השמש.

וְיָשֹׁב — instead of the usual form וְיָשׁוּב — generally expresses a return to a previous condition which one had left only reluctantly. Thus: ילך וישב לביתו (*Devarim* 20:6ff.), וְיָשֹׁב לִמְקֹמוֹ (*Shemuel* I, 5:11), וְיָשֹׁב אֶל־מְקוֹמוֹ (ibid. 29:4), וְיָשֹׁב הֶעָפָר עַל־הָאָרֶץ (*Koheles* 12:7), et al.

5 **ויאמר וגו׳ אל שפטי ישראל** — see Commentary, verse 4.

6 *And lo! a man from among the Children of Israel came and brought the Midianite woman before the eyes of Moshe and the eyes of the whole community of the Children of Israel; and they were weeping at the entrance of the Tent of Appointed Meeting.*

ו וְהִנֵּה אִישׁ מִבְּנֵי יִשְׂרָאֵל בָּא וַיַּקְרֵב אֶל־אֶחָיו אֶת־הַמִּדְיָנִית לְעֵינֵי מֹשֶׁה וּלְעֵינֵי כָּל־עֲדַת בְּנֵי־יִשְׂרָאֵל וְהֵמָּה בֹכִים פֶּתַח אֹהֶל מוֹעֵד׃ מפטיר

אנשיו. In addition to the highest court of seventy-one, in every large city there was a criminal court of twenty-three members. Similarly, during Israel's wanderings in the wilderness, the people were divided into specific groups under the jurisdiction of specific courts (see *Shemos* 18:21-22 and Commentary there). Or, according to *Sanhedrin* 35a, חלק להם בתי דינין: For this purpose Moshe divided the people into groups, and each group was assigned its own court. Hence אנשיו וגו' are apparently the sinners found in the group assigned to each judge. Each court is to execute those of the people placed under its jurisdiction who had committed the crime of worshipping Pe'or.

איש apparently means not an individual judge but the presiding judge, אב בית דין, he and his colleagues on the bench.

6 **והנה**: before this order was carried out, while the nation's judges were gathering around Moshe.

איש מבני ישראל. From verse 14 we learn that he was one of the tribal princes. Nevertheless, here he is described simply as "a man from among the Children of Israel," this apparently in order to consider his act solely from the standpoint of a "Jewish man." The fact that he was a prince and should therefore have served as a model of moral purity certainly added to the seriousness of the crime. And Pinchas' act appears all the more exalted considering that the person from whom he exacted the Torah's vengeance was above him in rank. Hence, it is fitting that the Torah in verses 14-15 informs us of the ranks of both the man and the woman. Nevertheless, the seriousness of the crime committed here does not depend on the fact that the person who committed it was a prince. What makes the act so reprehensible is that it was committed by a "Jewish man."

7 *Pinchas, son of Elazar, son of Aharon the priest, saw it, arose from the midst of the community, took a spear in his hand,*	ז וַיַּרְא פִּינְחָס בֶּן־אֶלְעָזָר בֶּן־אַהֲרֹן הַכֹּהֵן וַיָּקָם מִתּוֹךְ הָעֵדָה וַיִּקַּח רֹמַח בְּיָדוֹ׃
8 *Followed the man of Israel into the alcove, and pierced both of them — the man of Israel, and the woman through her belly — and the dying was stopped from among the Children of Israel.*	ח וַיָּבֹא אַחַר אִישׁ־יִשְׂרָאֵל אֶל־הַקֻּבָּה וַיִּדְקֹר אֶת־שְׁנֵיהֶם אֵת אִישׁ יִשְׂרָאֵל וְאֶת־הָאִשָּׁה אֶל־קֳבָתָהּ וַתֵּעָצַר הַמַּגֵּפָה מֵעַל בְּנֵי יִשְׂרָאֵל׃

An איש מבני ישראל had, with the מדינית, flouted God, His Torah, and Israel. Therefore, he became liable to punishment at the hands of the קנאים who are moved by zeal for God, for the Torah, and for ישראל: הבועל את הארמית קנאין פוגעין בו (see *Sanhedrin* 82a and רש״י ד״ה העדה).

ויקרב: he brought her there in order to deride them thereby.

עדת בני ישראל — and also מתוך העדה (v. 7) — is the gathering of the judges called by Moshe (see *Sanhedrin* 82a).

והמה בכים: The sight was so painful to them that it broke their hearts and they could not summon the strength or collect themselves for manly action.

7 **מתוך העדה**: He was probably one of the judges assembled around Moshe.

רמח is related to רמה, to shoot an arrow; thus נוֹשְׁקֵי רוֹמֵי־קֶשֶׁת (*Tehillim* 78:9). רמח: a javelin.

8 **הקבה**: קבה stems from the root קבב: to hollow out (see Commentary above, 22:11). By extension, we get קֻבָּה, the small chamber of a tent. According to *Menachos* 31b, it is narrow above and wide below. The word is still preserved in the German word *Alkoven* [alcove].

קֳבָתָהּ derives from the root קוב, which is related to קבב. From this root we also get קֵבָה: the stomach, the abdominal cavity.

ותעצר המגפה, and there was no longer a need for the intervention of the courts, which were under orders to take action on the basis of a הוראת שעה (v. 4).

9 *But those who lost their lives in the death were twenty-four thousand.*	ט וַיִּהְיוּ הַמֵּתִים בַּמַּגֵּפָה אַרְבָּעָה וְעֶשְׂרִים אָלֶף׃ פפפ
10 God *spoke to Moshe, saying:*	י וַיְדַבֵּר יְהוָה אֶל־מֹשֶׁה לֵּאמֹר׃
11 *Pinchas, son of Elazar, son of Aharon the priest, has turned My anger away from the Children of Israel by bringing My rights to bear in their midst, so that I did not destroy the Children of Israel by bringing My rights to bear.*	יא פִּינְחָס בֶּן־אֶלְעָזָר בֶּן־אַהֲרֹן הַכֹּהֵן הֵשִׁיב אֶת־חֲמָתִי מֵעַל בְּנֵי־יִשְׂרָאֵל בְּקַנְאוֹ אֶת־קִנְאָתִי בְּתוֹכָם וְלֹא־כִלִּיתִי אֶת־בְּנֵי־יִשְׂרָאֵל בְּקִנְאָתִי׃
	י׳ זעירא

The רמב״ן refers to *Devarim* 4:3: כי כל האיש אשר הלך אחרי בעל פעור השמידו ה׳ אלקיך מקרבך, from which it is evident that all those who attached themselves to the cult of Pe'or met their death by the hand of God.

9 **ארבעה ועשרים אלף**. In the incident of the golden calf, only three thousand deaths are enumerated (see *Shemos* 32:28). Even though there were, in addition to these three thousand, other sinners who died by sudden death (ibid. v. 35), it seems that the number that died in the Ba'al Pe'or incident was substantially larger. A pagan cult of licentiousness is infinitely more serious than a mere metaphysical aberration into idolatry.

פינחס

11 **פינחס** — the י is זעירא, small. It is possible that his name was originally פנחס, but, after his bold display, a י was added to his name, and from then on he was called "פי נחס" — נחס being the same as נחץ — to explain that "My mouth urged him to it," he was "driven" to it by the mouth of God. For it was purely zeal for My Word that was the motive of his deed: בקנאו את קנאתי.

קנא — see Commentary, *Bereshis* 26:14 and *Shemos* 20:5.

בְּקַנְאוֹ is the *pi'el* form, but without a דגש in the נ, so that in its vowelization it resembles the *kal* form. קִנֵּא in the *pi'el* means: to bring to

12 *Therefore proclaim it: Lo! I give to him My covenant: Peace.*

יב לָכֵ֖ן אֱמֹ֑ר הִנְנִ֨י נֹתֵ֥ן ל֛וֹ אֶת־בְּרִיתִ֖י שָׁלֽוֹם׃

ו׳ קטיעא

bear the legal claim that one has "adopted." קָנָא in the *kal* expresses primarily an inner attitude: A person adopts in his mind someone else's cause and regards it as though it were his own.

This vowelization of the *kal* form indicates here that Pinchas' act was not merely an external exhibition, but the result of deep inner feeling, for the betrayal of God's Word was to him like a betrayal of his own cause.

בקנאו וגו׳ בתוכם ולא כליתי וגו׳. He asserted My rights and enforced them in the nation's midst, and thereby saved the whole nation from the destruction that would have befallen it had I been forced to assert My rights Myself.

A society in which there is no champion of God's Word is lost to God and thereby is lost also to itself and to its own future; for it is oblivious to God's rights over that society (cf. Commentary, *Shemos* 32:14). This is especially true of Jewish society, of Israel, whose very existence depends on the word "לי," which God pronounced upon Israel, thereby dedicating every member of Israel and all aspects of its existence to be His. For all eternity He will assert His right of ownership over Israel. Israel is "God's" — or it ceases to exist.

Pinchas was but one man, and it was but one manly deed that he performed; and although he was singular among his people, he saved the whole nation.

12 **לכן אמר וגו׳**. Not אמר לו or אליו, but generally proclaim it, so that all should know and take it to heart: הנני נתן לו את בריתי שלום!

In *Vayikra* 26:42 (see Commentary there) we find a ברית called "יעקב," a ברית called "יצחק," and a ברית called "אברהם"; thus, every relationship included in the concept "יעקב," "יצחק," "אברהם" is called a "ברית," and it is an absolute promise of God. Similarly, in our verse we find a ברית called "שלום." Thus, the formation of the most complete harmony of all the conditions on earth, among one another and with God, is a ברית, and it is an absolute promise of God; God aims to bring about the realization of His promise, and the world can rest assured that ultimately it will be realized (see Commentary, *Bereshis* 6:18).

Here, the realization of the supreme harmony of peace is entrusted by God precisely to that spirit and to that activism which thoughtless people — anxious to mask their passivity and neglect of duty as "love of peace" — like to brand and condemn as "disturbances of the peace." Peace is a precious thing for which one is obligated to sacrifice everything, all of one's own rights and possessions, but one may never sacrifice for it the rights of others, and one may never sacrifice for it what God has declared to be good and true. There can be true peace among men only if they all are at peace with God. One who dares to struggle against the enemies of what is good and true in the eyes of God is — by this very struggle — one of the fighters for the ברית שלום on earth. Conversely, one who, for the sake of what he imagines to be peace with his fellow men, cedes the field without protest and allows them to stir up strife with God makes common cause — by his very love of peace — with the enemies of the ברית שלום on earth. What saved the people was not the apathy of the masses, nor even the tears of sorrow shed by those who stood idly at the entrance to the Tent of Appointed Meeting. It was the brave act of Pinchas that saved the people and restored to them peace with God and His Law, thereby restoring the basis for true peace.

God calls the ברית entrusted generally to the *Levi'im* "Life and Peace": בְּרִיתִי הָיְתָה אִתּוֹ הַחַיִּים וְהַשָּׁלוֹם וָאֶתְּנֵם־לוֹ מוֹרָא וַיִּירָאֵנִי וּמִפְּנֵי שְׁמִי נִחַת הוּא, "My ברית was with him, Life and Peace . . ." (*Malachi* 2:5). I entrusted this covenant to him because the fear that he had was solely fear of Me, and he bowed his head first and foremost before My Name.

But the ו of שלום is a וי"ו קטיעא — according to most views a broken ו. For the covenant of Pinchas is שלום restored to its completeness. Where the zeal of Pinchas is required, the peace has been broken. And the struggle of Pinchas is aimed at restoring true peace; he fights so that שלום should again become שלם.

To this the Halachah (*Kiddushin* 66b) attaches the law that בעל מום שעבד עבודתו פסולה, the מום of an officiating כהן invalidates the עבודה. For it says here of Pinchas entering the priesthood: הנני נתן לו את בריתי שלום כשהוא שלם ולא כשהוא חסר, והא שלום כתיב, א"ר נחמן וי"ו דשלום קטיעה היא. He who wishes to restore the peace with God which was broken — and that is what every עבודה symbolizes — must himself be שלם.

יג וְהָ֤יְתָה לּוֹ֙ וּלְזַרְע֣וֹ אַחֲרָ֔יו בְּרִ֖ית כְּהֻנַּ֣ת עוֹלָ֑ם תַּ֗חַת אֲשֶׁ֤ר קִנֵּא֙ לֵֽאלֹהָ֔יו וַיְכַפֵּ֖ר עַל־בְּנֵ֥י יִשְׂרָאֵֽל׃

13 *And to him and to his descendants after him [this covenant] will be a covenant of everlasting priesthood, because he brought to bear the rights of his God and effected atonement for the Children of Israel.*

13 **והיתה לו וגו׳**. When Pinchas was born, his father Elazar was still a זר. Hence, until this point Pinchas had not yet attained the status of a כהן. However, just as the tribe of Levi attained the rank of the לוייה by its actions at the sin of the golden calf and then was expressly chosen for this office, the same happened here: In his act of rescue, Pinchas acted as a כהן who prepares the way for the people (see Commentary, *Bereshis* 14:18); he carried out in actual practice the atoning devotion which the עבודה of the כהן performs symbolically in the Sanctuary. That is why he was elevated to the rank of a כהן after this act.

The covenant of everlasting priesthood given here to him and to his descendants after him expressed itself in the fact that all the כהנים גדולים were descendants of Pinchas (see *Divrei Ha-Yamim* I, 5:29-41), and the כהנים גדולים of the Second Temple as well were, according to the *Sifre* (ad loc.), descendants of Pinchas (see תוספות *Yoma* 9a ד״ה ולא).

Pinchas himself was granted a very long life. As late as the time of פילגש בגבעה (*Shoftim* 20:28) we find פינחס בן אלעזר בן אהרן serving as the כהן גדול before the Ark of God's Covenant. Moreover, according to one opinion, Pinchas was identical with Eliyahu (*Yalkut Shimoni* ad loc.), whose zeal for God's Word was imbued with the spirit of Pinchas. In the future, Eliyahu will heal the brokenness of his people, which will be divided by a generation gap, and thereby he will pave the way for the realization of the ברית שלום on earth. For the future will be detached from the past, and Eliyahu's task will be to bridge the generation gap by restoring the Chorev spirit of God's Torah. As the last word of prophecy reads: זִכְרוּ תּוֹרַת מֹשֶׁה עַבְדִּי אֲשֶׁר צִוִּיתִי אוֹתוֹ בְחֹרֵב עַל־כָּל־יִשְׂרָאֵל חֻקִּים וּמִשְׁפָּטִים, הִנֵּה אָנֹכִי שֹׁלֵחַ לָכֶם אֵת אֵלִיָּה הַנָּבִיא לִפְנֵי בּוֹא יוֹם ה׳ הַגָּדוֹל וְהַנּוֹרָא, וְהֵשִׁיב לֵב־אָבוֹת עַל־בָּנִים וְלֵב בָּנִים עַל־אֲבוֹתָם פֶּן־אָבוֹא וְהִכֵּיתִי אֶת־הָאָרֶץ חֵרֶם (*Malachi* 3:22-24).

14 *The name of the slain man of Israel, who was slain along with the Midianite woman, was Zimri, son of Salu, a prince of a father's house of the tribe of Shimon.*	יד וְשֵׁם אִישׁ יִשְׂרָאֵל הַמֻּכֶּה אֲשֶׁר הֻכָּה אֶת־הַמִּדְיָנִית זִמְרִי בֶּן־סָלוּא נְשִׂיא בֵית־אָב לַשִּׁמְעֹנִי׃
15 *And the name of the slain Midianite woman [was] Kozbi, daughter of Tzur; he was the head of the peoples of a father's house in Midyan.*	טו וְשֵׁם הָאִשָּׁה הַמֻּכָּה הַמִּדְיָנִית כָּזְבִּי בַת־צוּר רֹאשׁ אֻמּוֹת בֵּית־אָב בְּמִדְיָן הוּא׃ פ
16 God *spoke to Moshe, saying:*	טז וַיְדַבֵּר יְהוָה אֶל־מֹשֶׁה לֵּאמֹר׃
17 *The Midianites are to be treated as enemies, and you shall strike them.*	יז צָרוֹר אֶת־הַמִּדְיָנִים וְהִכִּיתֶם אוֹתָם׃

14 **ושם איש ישראל** — see Commentary, verse 6. The exalted rank of the man against whom Pinchas took action added to the significance of the act. Pinchas gave no thought to the harm that might come to him personally as a result of his act; he thought only of God's Word.

אשר הֻכה את המדינית: Only את המדינית, only while the crime was being committed, was Pinchas's act a laudable one. Had the act been carried out after the crime was committed, it would have been a murder punishable by the court (see *Sanhedrin* 82a).

בית אב here is synonymous with משפחה: one of the tribal families into which the tribe branched off (see Commentary above, 1:2).

15 **ושם האשה וגו׳**. Not even the consideration that his act might stir up hostility against Israel deterred Pinchas from taking action, for the task at hand was to preserve the very life soul of his nation, in its faithfulness to God and to His Torah.

ראש אמות בית אב. Here בית אב is one of the tribes into which the Midianite nation branched off. He was the head of one of these tribes, and at the same time he was also ראש אמות: one who wielded influence over the united tribes.

17 **צרור וגו׳**. The primary meaning of צרור is to reduce, to compress, to limit someone's strength. The Midianites deserve צרור, that you break their

18 *For they treat you as enemies with the same tricks that they perpetrated against you in the matter of Pe'or and at the same time in the matter of Kozbi, the daughter of the Midianite prince, their sister, who was slain on the day of the plague that had come because of Pe'or.*

יח כִּי צֹרְרִים הֵם לָכֶם בְּנִכְלֵיהֶם אֲשֶׁר־נִכְּלוּ לָכֶם עַל־דְּבַר פְּעוֹר וְעַל־דְּבַר כָּזְבִּי בַת־נְשִׂיא מִדְיָן אֲחֹתָם הַמֻּכָּה בְיוֹם־הַמַּגֵּפָה עַל־דְּבַר־פְּעוֹר׃

26 1 *It came to pass after the plague:* God *said to Moshe and to Elazar, son of Aharon the priest, saying:*

כו א וַיְהִי אַחֲרֵי הַמַּגֵּפָה פ וַיֹּאמֶר יְהוָה אֶל־מֹשֶׁה וְאֶל אֶלְעָזָר בֶּן־אַהֲרֹן הַכֹּהֵן לֵאמֹר׃

פסקא באמצע פסוק

might. והכיתם אותם: it will yet devolve upon you to strike them in a war (see chap. 31).

18 **כי צררים וגו׳**: they still threaten you with the tricks of a hostile enemy. So it says of Haman: צֹרֵר הַיְּהוּדִים (*Esther* 8:1). They persist in their acts of seduction, which have already been crowned with great success. In this respect they differ from the Moabites, who brought trouble upon you once and then desisted. The Midianites, however, persist in this hostility, which threatens your faithfulness to God and your morality.

Their proven hostility toward you is further fueled by their desire for revenge. For the daughter of their prince did not die in the plague, but was killed by the hand of a Jew; hence they feel they must avenge the blood of their sister. Since her father is **ראש אמות**, the slain Kozbi is considered a sister to all of them.

CHAPTER 26

1 **ויהי אחרי המגפה**. [Our verse contains two sentences.] The preceding **פרשה** ends in the middle of the verse, after the opening sentence, whereas the verse's concluding sentence begins a new **פרשה**, to teach us that after the death of those who attached themselves to Ba'al Pe'or, a new and

2 *Take the total count of the entire community of the Children of Israel, from twenty years old and upward, according to their fathers' house, every one who goes forth into communal service in Israel.*

ב שְׂאוּ אֶת־רֹאשׁ ׀ כָּל־עֲדַת בְּנֵי־יִשְׂרָאֵל מִבֶּן עֶשְׂרִים שָׁנָה וָמַעְלָה לְבֵית אֲבֹתָם כָּל־יֹצֵא צָבָא בְּיִשְׂרָאֵל׃

3 *And Moshe and Elazar the priest proclaimed them in the wastelands of Moav, near the Yarden of Yericho, saying:*

ג וַיְדַבֵּר מֹשֶׁה וְאֶלְעָזָר הַכֹּהֵן אֹתָם בְּעַרְבֹת מוֹאָב עַל־יַרְדֵּן יְרֵחוֹ לֵאמֹר׃

4 *From twenty years old and upward, as* God *had commanded Moshe and the Children of Israel who had gone out of the land of Egypt.*

ד מִבֶּן עֶשְׂרִים שָׁנָה וָמָעְלָה כַּאֲשֶׁר צִוָּה יְהוָה אֶת־מֹשֶׁה וּבְנֵי יִשְׂרָאֵל הַיֹּצְאִים מֵאֶרֶץ מִצְרָיִם׃ שני

pure chapter in the life of the people began. Once all those corrupted by the sexual rites of Pe'or worship had died, Israel could again shine forth in their hereditary distinction of sexual purity, as the Moabite prophet had beheld them before the Pe'or seduction. This was faithfully demonstrated by every subsequent census taken of the people, and this was the reason a new census was taken after the מגפה. The fact that every individual could be counted למשפחתו לבית אביו, as had been done forty years earlier, following the exodus from Egypt, proved that there could be no doubt concerning the paternity of any child in Israel, and that the orgy of Pe'or worship had been only an isolated exception, whereas the prophecy regarding the households of Israel — יזל מים מדליו וזרעו במים רבים (above, 24:7; see Commentary there) — was a true reflection of reality (see מדרש אספה in *Yalkut Shimoni* on our verse).

3-4 **וידבר וגו׳ אתם**. Not ויפקד אתם but וידבר אתם: They called each individual by his name and related him to such-and-such a house and to such-and-such a family, as it says at the first census (above, chaps. 1 and 2): למשפחתם לבית אבתם במספר שמות כל זכר לגלגלתם. The main purpose was not

5 *Reuven, firstborn of Israel: The sons of Reuven: Chanoch, the family of the Chanochi branch; of Pallu, the family of the Pallu'i branch;*	ה רְאוּבֵן בְּכוֹר יִשְׂרָאֵל בְּנֵי רְאוּבֵן חֲנוֹךְ מִשְׁפַּחַת הַחֲנֹכִי לְפַלּוּא מִשְׁפַּחַת הַפַּלֻּאִי׃

to count them to determine their total number; rather, the main thing was to call each individual by his name and to relate him to his family and to his tribe, so that he should know his national task as יוצא צבא בישראל. Calling each individual by his name gave him a sense of self-worth and enabled him to recognize the importance of his contribution to his house, his family, and his tribe, which do their share in carrying out the general national mission.

What is spelled out there by the words למשפחתם וגו׳ במספר שמות וגו׳ is summarized here by the phrase וידבר אתם: they pronounced the name of each individual separately. The occasion that called for this census is also the reason that Scripture expressly points out that they pronounced the name of each individual separately. For this "announcement" of each one according to his descent attested to the sexual purity of the families. This is apparently also the reason why precisely at this census the families of each tribe are mentioned prominently.

There is no doubt, however, that this "calling out" of the six hundred thousand names was not done by just two people but, rather, Moshe and Elazar were assisted here by the נשיאים, just as we found at the first census. Accordingly, וידבר does not mean that they pronounced but that they ordered to pronounce, they brought to expression. Moshe and Elazar merely gave the order, as is made clear by the term לאמר at the end of the verse. They issued the order to announce every man of twenty years and upward — as they were commanded at the first census.

The accentuation of verse 3 is noteworthy, for the אתנח separates מואב from ירדן ירחו. Actually, the result is that two sentences are created, and the expression וידבר משה וגו׳ does double duty: וידבר וגו׳ אתם בערבת מואב and וידבר וגו׳ אתם על ירדן ירחו. This gives the census a dual purpose: בערבת מואב, referring to the Pe'or incident which took place there, and על ירדן ירחו, as preparation for the future conquest of the Land (see Commentary, v. 53).

5 **משפחת החנכי**. Each tribe branched off into family branches, the ancestor who gave the family its name being in most cases the eldest son of the

6 *Of Chetzron, the family of the Chetzroni branch; of Karmi, the family of the Karmi branch.*	ו לְחֶצְרֹן מִשְׁפַּחַת הַחֶצְרוֹנִי לְכַרְמִי מִשְׁפַּחַת הַכַּרְמִי:
7 *These are the families of the tribe of Reuven. Their numbered ones were forty-three thousand, seven hundred and thirty.*	ז אֵלֶּה מִשְׁפְּחֹת הָרְאוּבֵנִי וַיִּהְיוּ פְקֻדֵיהֶם שְׁלֹשָׁה וְאַרְבָּעִים אֶלֶף וּשְׁבַע מֵאוֹת וּשְׁלֹשִׁים:
8 *The sons of Pallu: Eli'av.*	ח וּבְנֵי פַלּוּא אֱלִיאָב:
9 *And the sons of Eli'av: Nemu'el, Dasan and Aviram. These are Dasan and Aviram, who had been designated by the community, who had incited strife against Moshe and Aharon with the community of Korach, when they incited strife against* God.	ט וּבְנֵי אֱלִיאָב נְמוּאֵל וְדָתָן וַאֲבִירָם הוּא־דָתָן וַאֲבִירָם קְרוֹאֵי הָעֵדָה אֲשֶׁר הִצּוּ עַל־מֹשֶׁה וְעַל־אַהֲרֹן בַּעֲדַת־קֹרַח בְּהַצֹּתָם עַל־יְהוָה: קריאי קרי

tribal ancestor, only that in some cases here the name is slightly changed, as so often happens with first names. In the case of several tribes — Yehudah, Efrayim, and Binyamin — the grandchildren, too, formed family branches which are named separately here, and in the case of Menashe even the great-grandchildren formed separate family branches.

The רמב"ן points out that the number of family branches does not depend on the size of the tribe's population. This is evident, for example, from a comparison of Binyamin and Dan. In the case of Binyamin, seven family branches are mentioned here, and it had a population of forty-five thousand, whereas in the case of Dan only one family branch is mentioned, and the tribe numbered sixty-four thousand.

9 **הוא דתן ואבירם**. According to *Bava Basra* 117b, all those who had taken part in the rebellion of Korach were considered, at the division of the Land, as non-existent, whereas all the other יוצאי מצרים — even though they had already died before the conquest of the Land — were considered as the ones taking possession of the Land; and the living descen-

י וַתִּפְתַּ֨ח הָאָ֜רֶץ אֶת־פִּ֗יהָ וַתִּבְלַ֥ע
אֹתָ֛ם וְאֶת־קֹ֖רַח בְּמ֣וֹת הָעֵדָ֑ה
בַּאֲכֹ֣ל הָאֵ֗שׁ אֵ֣ת חֲמִשִּׁ֤ים וּמָאתַ֙יִם֙
אִ֔ישׁ וַיִּהְי֖וּ לְנֵֽס׃

10 *And the earth opened its mouth and swallowed them and Korach, when the community died, when the fire devoured the two hundred and fifty men; then they became a sign [of admonition].*

יא וּבְנֵי־קֹ֖רַח לֹא־מֵֽתוּ׃ ס

11 *But the sons of Korach did not die.*

יב בְּנֵ֣י שִׁמְעוֹן֮ לְמִשְׁפְּחֹתָם֒ לִנְמוּאֵ֗ל
מִשְׁפַּ֙חַת֙ הַנְּמ֣וּאֵלִ֔י לְיָמִ֕ין מִשְׁפַּ֖חַת
הַיָּמִינִ֑י לְיָכִ֕ין מִשְׁפַּ֖חַת הַיָּכִינִֽי׃

12 *The sons of Shimon, according to their families: of Nemu'el, the family of the Nemu'eli branch; of Yamin, the family of the Yamini branch; of Yachin, the family of the Yachini branch;*

יג לְזֶ֕רַח מִשְׁפַּ֖חַת הַזַּרְחִ֑י לְשָׁא֕וּל
מִשְׁפַּ֖חַת הַשָּׁאוּלִֽי׃

13 *Of Zerach, the family of the Zarchi branch; of Sha'ul, the family of the Sha'uli branch.*

---

dants, who in reality took possession of the Land, received it only as the heirs of יוצאי מצרים (see Commentary, v. 53). עדת קרח לא היה להן חלק בארץ, הבנים נטלו בזכות אבי אביהן ובזכות אבי אמותיהן. According to the רמב"ן this is the reason Scripture mentions here the death of Dasan and Aviram.

אשר הצו וגו': The uprising against Moshe and Aharon was in reality an uprising against God. Hence —

10 **ותפתח וגו' ויהיו לנס**. נס is an emblem raised on high to direct someone who is headed in a certain direction, bound for a specific destination. The death of Dasan and Aviram was a conspicuous act of God, intended to show the way to all those requiring guidance as to the way of life they should follow or avoid. In the Hebrew of a later period, "נסים" is a common term for all prominent acts of God that were performed for our instruction.

11 **ובני קרח לא מתו** — see Commentary above, 16:5.

14 *These [are the] families of the tribe of Shimon: twenty-two thousand, two hundred.*

יד אֵ֛לֶּה מִשְׁפְּחֹ֖ת הַשִּׁמְעֹנִ֑י שְׁנַ֧יִם וְעֶשְׂרִ֛ים אֶ֖לֶף וּמָאתָֽיִם׃ ס

15 *The sons of Gad, according to their families: of Tzefon, the family of the Tzefoni branch; of Chaggi, the family of the Chaggi branch; of Shuni, the family of the Shuni branch;*

טו בְּנֵ֣י גָד֮ לְמִשְׁפְּחֹתָם֒ לִצְפ֗וֹן מִשְׁפַּ֙חַת֙ הַצְּפוֹנִ֔י לְחַגִּ֕י מִשְׁפַּ֖חַת הַֽחַגִּ֑י לְשׁוּנִ֕י מִשְׁפַּ֖חַת הַשּׁוּנִֽי׃

16 *Of Ozni, the family of the Ozni branch; of Eri, the family of the Eri branch;*

טז לְאׇזְנִ֕י מִשְׁפַּ֖חַת הָאׇזְנִ֑י לְעֵרִ֕י מִשְׁפַּ֖חַת הָעֵרִֽי׃

17 *Of Arod, the family of the Arodi branch; of Ar'eli, the family of the Ar'eli branch.*

יז לַֽאֲרוֹד֙ מִשְׁפַּ֣חַת הָֽאֲרוֹדִ֔י לְאַ֨רְאֵלִ֔י מִשְׁפַּ֖חַת הָֽאַרְאֵלִֽי׃

18 *These [are the] families of the sons of Gad, according to their numbered ones: forty thousand, five hundred.*

יח אֵ֛לֶּה מִשְׁפְּחֹ֥ת בְּנֵי־גָ֖ד לִפְקֻדֵיהֶ֑ם אַרְבָּעִ֥ים אֶ֖לֶף וַחֲמֵ֥שׁ מֵאֽוֹת׃ ס

---

14 **אלה משפחת השמעני**. Above, at the first census (1:22-23), when the honor of the tribe of Shimon had not yet been stained, the term פקודים is mentioned twice, פקדיהם, פקדיו, to teach us at once, in the case of the second tribe, that it — and likewise each of the following tribes — was not counted en masse; rather, the individuals were counted, just as they were counted in the case of the tribe of Reuven (see Commentary there).

Here, at the second census, it is different, for one of Shimon's princes had sinned, and the tribe had been dishonored. According to *Sanhedrin* 82a, the tribe itself actively participated in this sin. Hence the honorable term לפקדיהם or ופקדיהם is missing, and the report is made as curt as possible.

Strikingly, Shimon's population is the smallest of all the tribes and, compared with the first census, has decreased by thirty-seven thousand! It is not far-fetched to assume that a large part of the twenty-four thousand who died in the plague were from the tribe of Shimon.

19 *The sons of Yehudah: Er and Onan; Er and Onan died in the land of Canaan.*

יט בְּנֵי יְהוּדָה עֵר וְאוֹנָן וַיָּמָת עֵר
וְאוֹנָן בְּאֶרֶץ כְּנָעַן׃

20 *The sons of Yehudah, according to their families, were: of Shelah, the family of the Shelani branch; of Peretz, the family of the Partzi branch; of Zerach, the family of the Zarchi branch.*

כ וַיִּהְיוּ בְנֵי־יְהוּדָה לְמִשְׁפְּחֹתָם
לְשֵׁלָה מִשְׁפַּחַת הַשֵּׁלָנִי לְפֶרֶץ
מִשְׁפַּחַת הַפַּרְצִי לְזֶרַח מִשְׁפַּחַת
הַזַּרְחִי׃

21 *And the sons of Peretz were: of Chetzron, the family of the Chetzroni branch; of Chamul, the family of the Chamuli branch.*

כא וַיִּהְיוּ בְנֵי־פֶרֶץ לְחֶצְרֹן מִשְׁפַּחַת
הַחֶצְרֹנִי לְחָמוּל מִשְׁפַּחַת
הֶחָמוּלִי׃

22 *These [are the] families of Yehudah, according to their numbered ones: seventy-six thousand, five hundred.*

כב אֵלֶּה מִשְׁפְּחֹת יְהוּדָה לִפְקֻדֵיהֶם
שִׁשָּׁה וְשִׁבְעִים אֶלֶף וַחֲמֵשׁ
מֵאוֹת׃ ס

23 *The sons of Yissachar, according to their families: Tola, the family of the Tola'i branch; of Puvvah, the family of the Puni branch;*

כג בְּנֵי יִשָּׂשכָר לְמִשְׁפְּחֹתָם תּוֹלָע
מִשְׁפַּחַת הַתּוֹלָעִי לְפֻוָּה מִשְׁפַּחַת
הַפּוּנִי׃

24 *Of Yashuv, the family of the Yashuvi branch; of Shimron, the family of the Shimroni branch.*

כד לְיָשׁוּב מִשְׁפַּחַת הַיָּשֻׁבִי לְשִׁמְרֹן
מִשְׁפַּחַת הַשִּׁמְרֹנִי׃

25 *These [are the] families of Yissachar, according to their numbered ones: sixty-four thousand, three hundred.*

כה אֵלֶּה מִשְׁפְּחֹת יִשָּׂשכָר לִפְקֻדֵיהֶם
אַרְבָּעָה וְשִׁשִּׁים אֶלֶף וּשְׁלֹשׁ
מֵאוֹת׃ ס

26 *The sons of Zevulun, according to*

כו בְּנֵי זְבוּלֻן לְמִשְׁפְּחֹתָם לְסֶרֶד

their families: of Sered, the family of the Sardi branch; of Elon, the family of the Eloni branch; of Yachle'el, the family of the Yachle'eli branch.

מִשְׁפַּ֨חַת֙ הַסַּרְדִּ֔י לְאֵל֕וֹן מִשְׁפַּ֖חַת הָאֵלֹנִ֑י לְיַ֨חְלְאֵ֔ל מִשְׁפַּ֖חַת הַיַּחְלְאֵלִֽי׃

27 *These [are] the families of the tribe of Zevulun, according to their numbered ones: sixty thousand, five hundred.*

כז אֵ֛לֶּה מִשְׁפְּחֹ֥ת הַזְּבוּלֹנִ֖י לִפְקֻדֵיהֶ֑ם שִׁשִּׁ֥ים אֶ֖לֶף וַחֲמֵ֥שׁ מֵאֽוֹת׃ ס

28 *The sons of Yosef, according to their families: Menashe and Efrayim.*

כח בְּנֵ֥י יוֹסֵ֖ף לְמִשְׁפְּחֹתָ֑ם מְנַשֶּׁ֖ה וְאֶפְרָֽיִם׃

29 *The sons of Menashe: of Machir, the family of the Machiri branch; and Machir begot Gil'ad, and from Gil'ad [came] the family of the Gil'adi branch.*

כט בְּנֵ֣י מְנַשֶּׁ֗ה לְמָכִיר֙ מִשְׁפַּ֣חַת הַמָּכִירִ֔י וּמָכִ֖יר הוֹלִ֣יד אֶת־גִּלְעָ֑ד לְגִלְעָ֕ד מִשְׁפַּ֖חַת הַגִּלְעָדִֽי׃

30 *These [are] the sons of Gil'ad: I'ezer; the family of the I'ezri branch; of Chelek, the family of the Chelki branch;*

ל אֵ֚לֶּה בְּנֵ֣י גִלְעָ֔ד אִיעֶ֕זֶר מִשְׁפַּ֖חַת הָאִיעֶזְרִ֑י לְחֵ֕לֶק מִשְׁפַּ֖חַת הַֽחֶלְקִֽי׃

31 *And Asriel, the family of the Asrieli branch; and Shechem, the family of the Shichmi branch;*

לא וְאַ֨שְׂרִיאֵ֔ל מִשְׁפַּ֖חַת הָֽאַשְׂרְאֵלִ֑י וְשֶׁ֕כֶם מִשְׁפַּ֖חַת הַשִּׁכְמִֽי׃

32 *And Shemida, the family of the Shemida'i branch; and Chefer, the family of the Chefri branch.*

לב וּשְׁמִידָ֕ע מִשְׁפַּ֖חַת הַשְּׁמִידָעִ֑י וְחֵ֕פֶר מִשְׁפַּ֖חַת הַֽחֶפְרִֽי׃

33 *Tzelafchad, son of Chefer, had no sons, only daughters, and the name[s] of the daughters of Tzelafchad were: Machlah, No'ah, Choglah, Milkah and Tirtzah.*

לג וּצְלָפְחָ֣ד בֶּן־חֵ֗פֶר לֹא־הָ֥יוּ ל֛וֹ בָּנִ֖ים כִּ֣י אִם־בָּנ֑וֹת וְשֵׁם֙ בְּנ֣וֹת צְלָפְחָ֔ד מַחְלָ֣ה וְנֹעָ֔ה חׇגְלָ֥ה מִלְכָּ֖ה וְתִרְצָֽה׃

34 *These [are] the families of Menashe: their numbered ones were fifty-two thousand, seven hundred.*

לד אֵלֶּה מִשְׁפְּחֹת מְנַשֶּׁה וּפְקֻדֵיהֶם
שְׁנַיִם וַחֲמִשִּׁים אֶלֶף וּשְׁבַע
מֵאוֹת׃ ס

35 *These [are] the sons of Efrayim, according to their families: of Shuselach, the family of the Shusalachi branch; of Becher, the family of the Bachri branch; of Tachan, the family of the Tachani branch.*

לה אֵלֶּה בְנֵי־אֶפְרַיִם לְמִשְׁפְּחֹתָם
לְשׁוּתֶלַח מִשְׁפַּחַת הַשֻּׁתַלְחִי
לְבֶכֶר מִשְׁפַּחַת הַבַּכְרִי לְתַחַן
מִשְׁפַּחַת הַתַּחֲנִי׃

34 **ופקדיהם**. Whereas in the cases of most of the other tribes it says simply אלה משפחֹת וגו׳ לפקדיהם, here, in the case of Menashe, and also below, in the case of Binyamin, two sentences are formed: אלה משפחֹת וגו׳ ופקדיהם. This structure indicates that the results of the census should be carefully considered.

Bear in mind that the total population decreased by several thousand, that this census was preceded by the death of all the יוצאי מצרים over twenty years of age, and that many died at קברות התאוה, after the rebellion of Korach, by הנחשים השרפים, and because of the sin of Pe'or. From this it would appear that an increase in a tribe's population is honorable testimony to its faithfulness to duty. This applies especially to the two tribes, Menashe and Binyamin. At the first census their populations were smaller than all the other tribes, and now they show an increase. Menashe shows the largest increase, over twenty thousand, and Binyamin's increase is over ten thousand. This is probably the reason for the special sentence structure in the cases of Menashe and Binyamin.

In the case of Naftali (v. 50), too, it says ופקדיהם, even though there was a decrease of eight thousand, probably because the census concludes with Naftali, just as in the case of Reuven, with whom the census begins, the number of its population is reported in a separate sentence: ויהיו פקדיהם (v. 7).

36 *And the sons of Shuselach: of Eran, the family of the Erani branch.*

לו וְאֵ֖לֶּה בְּנֵ֣י שׁוּתָ֑לַח לְעֵרָ֕ן מִשְׁפַּ֖חַת הָעֵרָנִֽי׃

37 *These [are] the families of the sons of Efrayim, according to their numbered ones: thirty-two thousand, five hundred. These [are] the sons of Yosef, according to their families.*

לז אֵ֣לֶּה מִשְׁפְּחֹ֧ת בְּנֵֽי־אֶפְרַ֛יִם לִפְקֻדֵיהֶ֗ם שְׁנַ֨יִם וּשְׁלֹשִׁ֥ים אֶ֖לֶף וַחֲמֵ֣שׁ מֵא֑וֹת אֵ֥לֶּה בְנֵֽי־יוֹסֵ֖ף לְמִשְׁפְּחֹתָֽם׃ ס

38 *The sons of Binyamin, according to their families: of Bela, the family of the Bal'i branch; of Ashbel, the family of the Ashbeli branch; of Achiram, the family of the Achirami branch;*

לח בְּנֵ֣י בִנְיָמִן֮ לְמִשְׁפְּחֹתָם֒ לְבֶ֗לַע מִשְׁפַּ֙חַת֙ הַבַּלְעִ֔י לְאַשְׁבֵּ֕ל מִשְׁפַּ֖חַת הָֽאַשְׁבֵּלִ֑י לַאֲחִירָ֕ם מִשְׁפַּ֖חַת הָאֲחִירָמִֽי׃

39 *Of Shefufam, the family of the Shufami branch; of Chufam, the family of the Chufami branch.*

לט לִשְׁפוּפָ֕ם מִשְׁפַּ֖חַת הַשּֽׁוּפָמִ֑י לְחוּפָ֕ם מִשְׁפַּ֖חַת הַחוּפָמִֽי׃

40 *The sons of Bela were Ard and Na'aman; the family of the Ardi branch; of Na'aman, the family of the Na'ami branch.*

מ וַיִּהְי֥וּ בְנֵי־בֶ֖לַע אַ֣רְדְּ וְנַעֲמָ֑ן מִשְׁפַּ֙חַת֙ הָֽאַרְדִּ֔י לְנַֽעֲמָ֔ן מִשְׁפַּ֖חַת הַנַּעֲמִֽי׃

41 *These [are] the sons of Binyamin according to their families, and their numbered ones: forty-five thousand, six hundred.*

מא אֵ֥לֶּה בְנֵֽי־בִנְיָמִ֖ן לְמִשְׁפְּחֹתָ֑ם וּפְקֻדֵיהֶ֗ם חֲמִשָּׁ֧ה וְאַרְבָּעִ֛ים אֶ֖לֶף וְשֵׁ֥שׁ מֵאֽוֹת׃ ס

42 *These [are] the sons of Dan ac-*

מב אֵ֤לֶּה בְנֵי־דָן֙ לְמִשְׁפְּחֹתָ֔ם לְשׁוּחָ֕ם

---

42 **אלה משפחת דן למשפחתם** — and so it says in verse 50: אלה משפחת נפתלי למשפחתם.

We have already seen above — e.g., in the case of Menashe [see Commentary v. 5] — that the concept of משפחה can be taken in a *cording to their families; of Shucham, the family of the Shuchami branch. These [are] the families of Dan, according to their families.*

מִשְׁפַּ֖חַת הַשּׁוּחָמִ֑י אֵ֛לֶּה מִשְׁפְּחֹ֥ת
דָּ֖ן לְמִשְׁפְּחֹתָֽם׃

43 *All the families of the Shuchami branch, according to their numbered ones: sixty-four thousand, four hundred.*

מג כָּל־מִשְׁפְּחֹ֥ת הַשּׁוּחָמִ֖י לִפְקֻדֵיהֶ֑ם
אַרְבָּעָ֧ה וְשִׁשִּׁ֛ים אֶ֖לֶף וְאַרְבַּ֥ע
מֵאֽוֹת׃ ס

44 *The sons of Asher, according to their families: of Yimnah, the family of the Yimnah branch; of Yishvi, the family of the Yishvi branch; of Beri'ah, the family of the Beri'i branch.*

מד בְּנֵ֣י אָשֵׁר֮ לְמִשְׁפְּחֹתָם֒ לְיִמְנָ֗ה
מִשְׁפַּ֙חַת֙ הַיִּמְנָ֔ה לְיִשְׁוִ֕י מִשְׁפַּ֖חַת
הַיִּשְׁוִ֑י לִבְרִיעָ֕ה מִשְׁפַּ֖חַת הַבְּרִיעִֽי׃

45 *Of the sons of Beri'ah: of Chever, the family of the Chevri branch; of Malki'el, the family of the Malki'eli branch.*

מה לִבְנֵ֣י בְרִיעָ֔ה לְחֵ֕בֶר מִשְׁפַּ֖חַת
הַחֶבְרִ֑י לְמַ֨לְכִּיאֵ֔ל מִשְׁפַּ֖חַת
הַמַּלְכִּיאֵלִֽי׃

46 *And the name of one daughter of Asher was Serach.*

מו וְשֵׁ֥ם בַּת־אָשֵׁ֖ר שָֽׂרַח׃

---

narrower sense or in a wider sense. The subdivision of משפחת המכירי produced משפחת הגלעדי (v. 29), which in turn divided into six additional משפחות (vv. 30-32). For the primary meaning of משפחה — from the root שפח, which is related to שפע, ספח, and the like — is "group"; hence a משפחה can be a main group or a subgroup.

From the tribe of Dan, only one family group is mentioned: השוחמי, but this itself already consisted of several משפחות, which again branched into additional families. The same applies to משפחת נפתלי [where the formula אלה משפחת נפתלי למשפחתם signifies that משפחת היחצאלי, משפחת הגוני, etc., themselves branched into additional משפחות].

47 *These [are] the families of the sons of Asher, according to their numbered ones: fifty-three thousand, four hundred.*

מז אֵ֛לֶּה מִשְׁפְּחֹ֥ת בְּנֵֽי־אָשֵׁ֖ר לִפְקֻדֵיהֶ֑ם שְׁלֹשָׁ֧ה וַחֲמִשִּׁ֛ים אֶ֖לֶף וְאַרְבַּ֥ע מֵאֽוֹת׃ ס

48 *The sons of Naftali, according to their families: from Yachtze'el, the family of the Yachtze'eli branch; of Guni, the family of the Guni branch;*

מח בְּנֵ֤י נַפְתָּלִי֙ לְמִשְׁפְּחֹתָ֔ם לְיַ֨חְצְאֵ֔ל מִשְׁפַּ֖חַת הַיַּחְצְאֵלִ֑י לְגוּנִ֕י מִשְׁפַּ֖חַת הַגּוּנִֽי׃

49 *Of Yetzer, the family of the Yitzri branch; of Shillem, the family of the Shillemi branch.*

מט לְיֵ֕צֶר מִשְׁפַּ֖חַת הַיִּצְרִ֑י לְשִׁלֵּ֕ם מִשְׁפַּ֖חַת הַשִּׁלֵּמִֽי׃

50 *These [are] the families of Naftali, according to their families. And their numbered ones: forty-five thousand, four hundred.*

נ אֵ֛לֶּה מִשְׁפְּחֹ֥ת נַפְתָּלִ֖י לְמִשְׁפְּחֹתָ֑ם וּפְקֻדֵיהֶ֕ם חֲמִשָּׁ֧ה וְאַרְבָּעִ֛ים אֶ֖לֶף וְאַרְבַּ֥ע מֵאֽוֹת׃

51 *These numbered ones of the Children of Israel were: six-hundred-and-one thousand, seven hundred and thirty.*

נא אֵ֗לֶּה פְּקוּדֵי֙ בְּנֵ֣י יִשְׂרָאֵ֔ל שֵׁשׁ־מֵא֥וֹת אֶ֖לֶף וָאָ֑לֶף שְׁבַ֥ע מֵא֖וֹת וּשְׁלֹשִֽׁים׃ פ שלישי

52 God *spoke to Moshe, saying:*

נב וַיְדַבֵּ֥ר יְהֹוָ֖ה אֶל־מֹשֶׁ֥ה לֵּאמֹֽר׃

53 *To these shall the land be apportioned as an inheritance, according to the number of the names.*

נג לָאֵ֗לֶּה תֵּחָלֵ֥ק הָאָ֛רֶץ בְּנַחֲלָ֖ה בְּמִסְפַּ֥ר שֵׁמֽוֹת׃

53 **לאלה וגו'**. Those who were counted here על ירדן ירחו, in full view of the Land, are those to whom the Land shall be apportioned, all the male באי הארץ over the age of twenty. The division shall be done במספר שמות. If we understand this expression correctly, its meaning is as follows: All those whose names were pronounced at the census shall receive a plot of land which will be named after them and which will be their property. But at the census the names of the tribes, the names of the families,

54 *To the numerous you shall give a large inheritance, and to the few a small inheritance; to each according to his numbered ones shall his inheritance be given.*

נד לָרַב תַּרְבֶּה נַחֲלָתוֹ וְלַמְעַט תַּמְעִיט נַחֲלָתוֹ אִישׁ לְפִי פְקֻדָיו יֻתַּן נַחֲלָתוֹ׃

and the names of the individuals in each family, every male over twenty years of age, were pronounced: למשפחתם לבית אבתם כל זכר לגלגלתם (v. 4; above, 1:1). Accordingly, the Land shall be divided so that each tribe, and in each tribe every family, and in each family every individual — every male over twenty years of age — receives his own defined piece of land.

So we find later at the division of the Land by Yehoshua (*Yehoshua* 15): the rule of למשפחתם is kept in the case of each tribe. And שמיטין and יובלות are not in effect if the Land is only conquered in general or is even distributed among the tribes; rather, the division must be made to the families and to the heads of families and the individuals: מנין אתה אומר כבשו ולא חלקו, חלקו למשפחות ולא חלקו לבתי אבות, חלקו לבתי אבות ואין כל אחד ואחד מכיר את חלקו, יכול יהיו חייבים בשמטה ת״ל שדך, שיהא כל אחד ואחד מכיר שדהו, כרמך, שיהא כל אחד ואחד מכיר את כרמו (*Toras Kohanim, Vayikra*, 25:2).

This constitutes a realization of the fundamental character of the people of Israel, which we have already noted several times. Diversity of the tribes and families while maintaining spiritual and moral unity is essential to the calling of the people of God's Torah (see Commentary, *Bereshis* 35:11-12; 48:3-6). Each tribe, each branch, each home had its own distinctiveness, and this distinctiveness shall find the place that is right for it and shall develop on the common ground of the Torah. Indeed, the most beloved designation for Israel's installation in God's land is נטיעה, "planting" (cf. Commentary, *Shemos* 15:17; above, 24:6).

54 **לרב וגו׳ איש לפי פקדיו**. Since an individual has no פקודים, but is himself one of the פקודים, איש here cannot mean an individual but only the tribe and family — which are considered units — of which the twenty-year old men are numbered as members. Thus, the size of the territory to be allotted to a tribe or to a משפחה shall be determined by the size of that tribe or משפחה, and that shall be reckoned not by the total number

55 *Only by lot shall the land be divided; according to the names of the tribes of their fathers shall they receive it as a possession.*	נה אַךְ־בְּגוֹרָ֔ל יֵחָלֵ֖ק אֶת־הָאָ֑רֶץ לִשְׁמ֥וֹת מַטּֽוֹת־אֲבֹתָ֖ם יִנְחָֽלוּ׃

of people, but by the number of men aged twenty and over who were counted at the census. As the final result of the distribution, every twenty-year old man of באי הארץ will receive a piece of land, and all the men of the same family and all the families of the same tribe will receive their portions of contiguous plots of land which together form one inheritance.

55 **אך בגורל יחלק וגו׳**. However, the result of the division described in the preceding verses shall not be attained or determined by mutual compromise or by the decision of the national authority, but בגורל and על פי הגורל: by lot, whose results shall be confirmed by a declaration of the אורים ותומים (see *Bava Basra* 122a).

לשמות מטות אבתם ינחלו. According to ר׳ יונתן (ibid. 117a), this sentence indicates an important modification of the principle of division established in verse 53.

שמות מטות אבתם of באי הארץ, who actually took possession of the Land, are the fathers of this generation that is now reaching the Land, and these fathers were named in the first census as יוצאי מצרים. These fathers, who at יציאת מצרים had already reached the age of twenty, were supposed to take actual possession of the Land; it was to them that the promise was given: ונתתי אתה לכם מורשה (*Shemos* 6:8). However, these fathers sinned and rejected the Land and thus forfeited their right to actually take possession of it, and their children took possession of the Land in their stead.

According to verse 53, all the male descendants, aged twenty and over, of יוצאי מצרים are to have the right to receive their share in the possession of the Land. But according to verse 55 — לשמות מטות אבתם ינחלו — only for the names of their fathers and in the name of their fathers are they to take possession of the Land; they are to gain the Land only as their fathers' delegates, only as their heirs, just as they, too, the fathers, were promised the Land only as a מורשה, as a heritage from their forefathers: דכתיב ונתתי אותה לכם מורשה אני ה׳, ירושה היא לכם מאבותיכם, וליוצאי מצרים קאמר להו (*Bava Basra* 117b).

Accordingly, two principles come to expression in the division of the Land: מספר השמות of באי הארץ, who were included in the census of ערבות מואב, and שמות מטות אבתם, who were included in the first census of יוצאי מצרים.

For example, two brothers, A and B, were among those counted in the census of יוצאי מצרים. A had one son, and B had nine sons, and now these sons as באי הארץ take possession of the Land. Had the Land been divided only among יוצאי מצרים who were counted in the first census, and באי הארץ were to receive their shares solely as their heirs — which in fact is the opinion of ר׳ יאשיה (ibid. 117a) — the nine sons of B together would receive only one share, which would be no larger than the share of A's one son. If the division were to be conducted solely according to the principle of the census of באי הארץ, the nine sons of B would receive nine shares, and A's one son would receive only one share. Due to the combination of these two principles, the descendants of A and B received — as באי הארץ — ten shares: this one one share, and the others nine shares. However, they did not receive their shares solely on the basis of their own personal rights, but also as delegates and heirs of A and B. They received the ten shares לשמות מטות אבתם, in the name of their fathers, A and B; actually, they inherited the מורשה that fell to their fathers from their grandfather. Therefore A's one son inherited from him one half, which includes five shares, whereas B's nine sons inherited from him the other half, so that they, too, received only five shares.

This system of division is called "חזרה": what the sons take possession of "returns," as it were, to the deceased fathers, actually to the grandfather. Hence our Sages say: משונה נחלה זו מכל נחלות שבעולם, שכל נחלות שבעולם חיין יורשין מתים וכאן מתים יורשין חיין (ibid.). This case is an apparent paradox, for the deceased fathers and grandfather inherit, as it were, their living descendants.

Careful consideration of this system of division reveals that the Land was considered the legacy of the generation that preceded יוצאי מצרים, only that the fathers of יוצאי מצרים received a share in the Land according to the number of their grandsons, twenty years of age and older, who reached the Land. This legacy [of the generation that preceded יוצאי מצרים] was bequeathed only to those of the sons who were at least twenty years old at יציאת מצרים, and these sons in turn bequeathed it to their own sons who were at least twenty years old at the conquest of the Land.

Two distinct truths were thereby immortalized in the land register of our national land.

First, God's promise will definitely be fulfilled; hence, it is regarded as an accomplished fact even before it is fulfilled. Not only those who have already been redeemed, but even the members of the generation that still languishes beneath the Egyptian yoke are regarded as the owners of the land promised them by God, with legal rights assigned to their descendants accordingly. And so we find that Eretz Yisrael is considered actually מוחזקת by the fathers, not just ראויה to them by mere legal right. As a consequence, the legal right of בכור was applicable in the apportionment of the land (see Commentary below, 27:6, and *Devarim* 21:17).

Second, the greatest attainment of parents is children and grandchildren who prove themselves loyal and true to their heritage; for such children attest to the merits of the parents and atone for their shortcomings. Just as Ya'akov — according to our interpretation (*Bereshis* 48:21-22) — regarded his children as conquests he had wrested from the Emori, the spoils of victory of his life, so we find here that good and honest children and grandchildren are considered a credit to their fathers and grandfathers.

Notwithstanding all the trials devised by Egypt to break the spirit of the Children of Israel, more than 600,000 able-bodied men were worthy of redemption and ready to follow God. And again, notwithstanding all the aberrations and the attrition in the wilderness, more than 600,000 were found to be deserving of the land of the Torah, and Moshe was able to say to them: ואתם הדבקים בה׳ אלקיכם חיים כלכם היום (*Devarim* 4:4). All this was due to the spirit that the ancestors nurtured in their children even in the midst of Egyptian slavery. Each plot of God's land that the grandchildren received they then humbly placed at the feet of their grandfathers, and regained it only as the legacy of the grandfathers — through the mediation of the fathers, who likewise had already died.

Our Sages (*Bava Basra* 117a) say: אמשול לך משל למה הדבר דומה, לשני אחים כהנים שהיו בעיר אחת, לאחד יש לו בן אחד ואחד יש לו שני בנים, והלכו לגורן, זה שיש לו בן אחד נוטל חלק אחד וזה שיש לו שני בנים נוטל שני חלקים, ומחזירין אצל אביהן

56 *According to lot shall their inheritance be apportioned to them, with due regard for whether [they are] many or few.*

נו עַל־פִּי הַגּוֹרָל תֵּחָלֵק נַחֲלָתוֹ בֵּין רַב לִמְעָט: ס

וחוזרין וחולקין בשוה. "It is similar to two brothers who are priests and live in the same city, one of them having only one son, while the other has two. They go to a barn to receive their priestly portion. The one who sends his one son receives one portion. The other, who has two sons, receives two portions. But all that they have received they take home to their aged father, of whose household they still consider themselves members and on whose merits the grandsons were given their donated portions, and then they divide the whole amount equally." (This ברייתא is cited also in the *Yalkut*, where the text reads: אצל אבי אביהן. In the version of our ברייתא, the subject of מחזירין is the two brothers, and אביהן is the grandfather. This seems to have escaped the notice of several commentators.)

Although the sons were deemed worthy, in their own right, of taking possession of the Land, they received their portions only לשמות מטות אבתם, only as the heirs of their fathers and as the bearers of their names. This proves that these fathers, who had forfeited their right to the Land, had, during the thirty-eight years of wandering in the wilderness, succeeded in educating their children and had instilled in them the right spirit. And the fact that more than 600,000 men were found worthy of God's continued guidance in the Land proves that the fathers had understood how to atone for their own sins through their children, and that the דור המדבר was — as our Sages put it — a דור דעה (*Bemidbar Rabbah* 19:3). Indeed, the words of the prophet recall with love the generation of the wilderness: הָלֹךְ וְקָרָאתָ בְאָזְנֵי יְרוּשָׁלַם לֵאמֹר כֹּה אָמַר ה׳ זָכַרְתִּי לָךְ חֶסֶד נְעוּרַיִךְ אַהֲבַת כְּלוּלֹתָיִךְ לֶכְתֵּךְ אַחֲרַי בַּמִּדְבָּר בְּאֶרֶץ לֹא זְרוּעָה (*Yirmeyahu* 2:2), and to this our Sages note: ומה אחרים באים בזכותם הם עצמם לא כל שכן (*Sanhedrin* 110b). Thus, on the whole, despite all the repeated lapses, the image of Israel wandering through the wilderness is a worthy one.

56 **על פי הגורל**: באורים ותומים (*Bava Basra* 122a) — unlike בגורל (v. 55), which means simply "by lot."

57 *And these are the numbered ones of the* Levi'im, *according to their families: of Gershon, the family of the Gershuni branch; of Kehas, the family of the Kehasi branch; of Merari, the family of the Merari branch.*

נז וְאֵלֶּה פְקוּדֵי הַלֵּוִי לְמִשְׁפְּחֹתָם
לְגֵרְשׁוֹן מִשְׁפַּחַת הַגֵּרְשֻׁנִּי לִקְהָת
מִשְׁפַּחַת הַקְּהָתִי לִמְרָרִי מִשְׁפַּחַת
הַמְּרָרִי׃

58 *These [are] the families of Levi: the family of the Livni branch, the family of the Chevroni branch, the family of the Machli branch, the family of the Mushi branch, the family of the Korchi branch. And Kehas had begotten Amram.*

נח אֵלֶּה ׀ מִשְׁפְּחֹת לֵוִי מִשְׁפַּחַת
הַלִּבְנִי מִשְׁפַּחַת הַחֶבְרֹנִי מִשְׁפַּחַת
הַמַּחְלִי מִשְׁפַּחַת הַמּוּשִׁי מִשְׁפַּחַת
הַקָּרְחִי וּקְהָת הוֹלִד אֶת־עַמְרָם׃

59 *The name of Amram's wife was Yocheved, daughter of Levi, who had been borne to Levi in Egypt. She bore to Amram: Aharon and Moshe, and their sister Miriam.*

נט וְשֵׁם ׀ אֵשֶׁת עַמְרָם יוֹכֶבֶד בַּת־לֵוִי
אֲשֶׁר יָלְדָה אֹתָהּ לְלֵוִי בְּמִצְרָיִם
וַתֵּלֶד לְעַמְרָם אֶת־אַהֲרֹן וְאֶת־
מֹשֶׁה וְאֵת מִרְיָם אֲחֹתָם׃

נחלתו. Since ארץ as a rule is feminine, the pronominal suffix of נחלתו apparently refers to איש (v. 54).

בין רב למעט — according to one opinion (*Bava Basra* 122a), while retaining equal value. This corroborates Sforno's view that the twelve provinces of the tribes were not equal in size — the size of each province corresponded to the size of the population — but were equal in value. The smaller provinces were more valuable because of their location or because of the quality of the land.

In describing the system of the division, we primarily followed רש״י and רשב״ם. There are, however, other views (see תוספות *Bava Basra* 117a ד״ה ומחזירין and מזרחי here).

60 *To Aharon were born Nadav and Avihu, Elazar and Isamar.*

ס וַיִּוָּלֵד לְאַהֲרֹן אֶת־נָדָב וְאֶת־אֲבִיהוּא אֶת־אֶלְעָזָר וְאֶת־אִיתָמָר׃

61 *But Nadav and Avihu died when they brought near strange fire before* God.

סא וַיָּמָת נָדָב וַאֲבִיהוּא בְּהַקְרִיבָם אֵשׁ־זָרָה לִפְנֵי יְהוָה׃

62 *Their numbered ones were twenty-three thousand, all males from one month old upward; for they were not directed to number themselves among the Children of Israel, for no inheritance had been given to them among the Children of Israel.*

סב וַיִּהְיוּ פְקֻדֵיהֶם שְׁלֹשָׁה וְעֶשְׂרִים אֶלֶף כָּל־זָכָר מִבֶּן־חֹדֶשׁ וָמָעְלָה כִּי ׀ לֹא הָתְפָּקְדוּ בְּתוֹךְ בְּנֵי יִשְׂרָאֵל כִּי לֹא־נִתַּן לָהֶם נַחֲלָה בְּתוֹךְ בְּנֵי יִשְׂרָאֵל׃

63 *These are the ones numbered by Moshe and by Elazar the priest, who numbered the Children of Israel in the wastelands of Moav, on the Yarden of Yericho.*

סג אֵלֶּה פְּקוּדֵי מֹשֶׁה וְאֶלְעָזָר הַכֹּהֵן אֲשֶׁר פָּקְדוּ אֶת־בְּנֵי יִשְׂרָאֵל בְּעַרְבֹת מוֹאָב עַל יַרְדֵּן יְרֵחוֹ׃

64 *Among these there was not one man from those who had been numbered by Moshe and by Aharon the priest, who had numbered the Children of Israel in the wilderness of Sinai.*

סד וּבְאֵלֶּה לֹא־הָיָה אִישׁ מִפְּקוּדֵי מֹשֶׁה וְאַהֲרֹן הַכֹּהֵן אֲשֶׁר פָּקְדוּ אֶת־בְּנֵי יִשְׂרָאֵל בְּמִדְבַּר סִינָי׃

---

64 **ובאלה לא היה איש**. What applies to the golden calf applies also to the מרגלים: the women took no part in the sin; hence, neither did they incur its punishment. As our Sages say: אותו הדור היו הנשים גודרות מה שאנשים פורצים. In that generation of the wandering in the wilderness, the women upheld what the men tore down.

65 *For* God *had decreed concerning them: They shall die in the wilderness! Therefore none of them remained, except Kalev, son of Yefunneh, and Yehoshua, son of Nun.*

סה כִּֽי־אָמַ֤ר יְהוָה֙ לָהֶ֔ם מ֥וֹת יָמֻ֖תוּ
בַּמִּדְבָּ֑ר וְלֹֽא־נוֹתַ֤ר מֵהֶם֙ אִ֔ישׁ כִּ֚י
אִם־כָּלֵ֣ב בֶּן־יְפֻנֶּ֔ה וִיהוֹשֻׁ֖עַ בִּן־
נֽוּן׃ ס

27 1 *And the daughters of Tzelafechad, son of Chefer, son of Gil'ad, son of Machir, son of Menashe, of the families of Menashe, the son of Yosef came near — and these were the names of his daughters: Machlah, No'ah and Choglah, Milkah and Tirtzah*

כז א וַתִּקְרַ֜בְנָה בְּנ֣וֹת צְלָפְחָ֗ד בֶּן־חֵ֙פֶר֙
בֶּן־גִּלְעָ֤ד בֶּן־מָכִיר֙ בֶּן־מְנַשֶּׁ֔ה
לְמִשְׁפְּחֹ֖ת מְנַשֶּׁ֣ה בֶן־יוֹסֵ֑ף וְאֵ֙לֶּה֙
שְׁמ֣וֹת בְּנֹתָ֔יו מַחְלָ֣ה נֹעָ֔ה וְחָגְלָ֥ה
וּמִלְכָּ֖ה וְתִרְצָֽה׃

ובאלה here does not refer to the tribe of Levi mentioned in the immediately preceding verses; for the *Levi'im*, too, were not included in the fate of the מרגלים. Rather, ובאלה refers to פקודי בני ישראל who were mentioned beforehand [v. 51]. Establishing the number of the Children of Israel is the primary purpose of this second census, which is important for the apportionment of the Land, whereas the *Levi'im* did not receive a share of the Land.

CHAPTER 27

1 **למשפחת מנשה בן יוסף**. We have already noted above, on verse 5 [of chap. 26], that the branching off into separate family branches is most prominent in the tribe of Menashe. Whereas, for example, in the tribe of Reuven, only the immediate sons formed separate family branches, in the case of Menashe we find that Machir, Gil'ad, and Chefer — the son, the grandson, and the great-grandson — formed separate family branches, this despite the fact that Menashe himself was only a branch of the larger tribe of Yosef.

This tendency of the tribe to form separate and independent family branches throws light on the argument of Tzelafchad's daughters: למה יגרע שם אבינו מתוך משפחתו (v. 4). These words have an ethical meaning

2 *And they placed themselves before Moshe, before Elazar the priest, before the princes and the entire community in the entrance of the Tent of Appointed Meeting, and they said:*

ב וַתַּעֲמֹדְנָה לִפְנֵי מֹשֶׁה וְלִפְנֵי
אֶלְעָזָר הַכֹּהֵן וְלִפְנֵי הַנְּשִׂיאִם
וְכָל־הָעֵדָה פֶּתַח אֹהֶל־מוֹעֵד
לֵאמֹר׃

3 *Our father died in the wilderness; he was not among the company that banded together against* God*; he was not among Korach's allies. Rather, he died because of his own sin, and he had no sons.*

ג אָבִינוּ מֵת בַּמִּדְבָּר וְהוּא לֹא־הָיָה
בְּתוֹךְ הָעֵדָה הַנּוֹעָדִים עַל־יְהוָה
בַּעֲדַת־קֹרַח כִּי־בְחֶטְאוֹ מֵת
וּבָנִים לֹא־הָיוּ לוֹ׃

that goes beyond the mere desire to acquire land. The father, grandfather, and great-grandfather had all formed their own family branches, and their names will be perpetuated among their descendants through a special hereditary portion of land that will be allotted to them at the apportionment of the Land to families. As for Tzelafchad, however, the family name will come to an end already in the second generation, and the extraordinary opportunity for its perpetuation presented by the apportionment of the Land according to families and houses will be lost, and his name will cease to be remembered.

ואלה שמות בנתיו. Below, 36:11, they are mentioned in a different order, to indicate that they all were equally worthy: מלמד שכולן שקולות זו כזו (*Sifre*).

3 **אבינו מת במדבר וגו׳**. Our Sages say that the daughters of Tzelafchad were חכמניות ודרשניות (*Bava Basra* 119b). The clarity and sharpness of their minds are reflected by the manner in which they present their case, stating all the facts pertinent to their claim and not uttering an extraneous word.

אבינו מת במדבר: Our father was one of יוצאי מצרים, who were condemned to die in the wilderness; but according to the law of the Land's apportionment just now proclaimed — לשמות מטות אבתם ינחלו — they should be taken into consideration at the apportionment.

4 *Why should the name of our father disappear from the midst of his family just because he did not have a son? Please give us a possession among the brothers of our father.*	ד לָ֣מָּה יִגָּרַ֤ע שֵׁם־אָבִ֙ינוּ֙ מִתּ֣וֹךְ מִשְׁפַּחְתּ֔וֹ כִּ֛י אֵ֥ין ל֖וֹ בֵּ֑ן תְּנָה־לָּ֣נוּ אֲחֻזָּ֔ה בְּת֖וֹךְ אֲחֵ֥י אָבִֽינוּ׃
5 *Moshe brought their legitimate claim before* God.	ה וַיַּקְרֵ֥ב מֹשֶׁ֛ה אֶת־מִשְׁפָּטָ֖ן לִפְנֵ֥י יְהֹוָֽה׃ פ רביעי נו״ן רבתי

והוא לא היה בתוך העדה וגו׳: Had he been one of those who banded together against God, a member of Korach's party, we could not base a claim on his name.

Neither the descendants of the מרגלים nor the descendants of those who joined Korach's rebellion could present a claim based on the names of their fathers. These were the only ones who were excluded from the rule that מרגלים ומתלוננים שבעדת קרח לא היה להם חלק :לשמות מטות אבתם ינחלו בארץ (see *Bava Basra* 117b and 118b).

כי בחטאו מת: He — like every man — did not depart this world without having sinned, but his sin was undoubtedly only that of an individual. He never participated in any national sin.

ובנים לא היו לו: He never had any sons. Had he had sons, their descendants would take precedence over us, and our claim would be dismissed. But he never had any sons, and we are his sole descendants.

4 **למה יגרע וגו׳**. משפחת החפרי (above, 26:32) will divide its hereditary portion among the sons of Chefer, who are heads of this family, and if one of these sons had died but had left a son, that son would receive his father's portion as the bearer of his father's name. Why, then, should the name of our father disappear, just because he left no son but only daughters, and why should he not be counted among his family?

תנה לנו וגו׳. Let us stand in the place of our father and be counted among his brothers, and give us the hereditary portion to which he would be entitled were he still alive, for as a son of Chefer he was entitled to receive a hereditary portion among his brothers.

5 **את משפטן**. נו״ן רבתי — see verse 6.

6 *And* God *said to Moshe:* | ו וַיֹּאמֶר יְהוָה אֶל־מֹשֶׁה לֵּאמֹר׃

6 **ויאמר ה׳ אל משה לאמר**. Since the laws that now follow are introduced by ויאמר and not by וידבר, it appears that they do not deal with an entirely new subject but, rather, elaborate on a canon already communicated (cf. Commentary above, 15:37).

Indeed, two verses have already established the system of apportioning the Land: לאלה תחלק הארץ (above, 26:53), to the men, and לשמות מטות אבתם ינחלו (above, 26:55), indicating that this apportionment is a division of an inheritance. From the foregoing we learn the fundamental law that a legacy of land is inherited by the male descendants, as is also implied by what is stated in *Vayikra* (25:46): והתנחלתם אתם לבניכם אחריכם לרשת אחזה (see *Bava Basra* 110b).

This law must have been known also to the daughters of Tzelafchad, as is clear from the reasoning they adduced in support of their claim: כי אין לו בן (v. 4). If their father had left a son or — as implied by their words ובנים לא היו לו (v. 3) — a descendant of a son, they admittedly would have had no cause to make a claim.

It is possible that this is the reason for the prominent emphasis on the pronominal suffix ן of משפטן (v. 5): to indicate that Moshe knew the law of inheritance in general, but asked for a decision in this specific case. Moreover, if the Land was to be apportioned by the system of חזרה which we described above (26:55), it is possible that the law in ordinary cases was well known to Moshe; he, too, knew that, in the absence of a son or a descendant of a son, a daughter inherits, and the only doubt he had was to what extent this law applies to the apportionment of the Land. Thus, to him the question was only regarding משפטן, their special case. For it is possible that the question was as follows: In the division of an inheritance, the law in the case of five daughters is the same as in the case of five sons, provided that there is no son or descendant of a son. Hence, it is possible that the five daughters of Tzelafchad should be regarded as five באי הארץ and should receive five portions of land. These portions, together with those of all the other באי הארץ descended from Chefer, would then — in accordance with the principle of חזרה — return to Chefer, and as his legacy they would be divided among his heirs according to the ordinary law of inheritance. However, it is possible —

7 *The daughters of Tzelafchad speak justly. You shall certainly give them, according to the legal right of males, a hereditary possession among the brothers of their father, and transfer their father's inheritance to them.*	ז כֵּ֗ן בְּנ֣וֹת צְלָפְחָד֮ דֹּבְרֹת֒ נָתֹ֨ן תִּתֵּ֤ן לָהֶם֙ אֲחֻזַּ֣ת נַחֲלָ֔ה בְּת֖וֹךְ אֲחֵ֣י אֲבִיהֶ֑ם וְהַעֲבַרְתָּ֛ אֶת־נַחֲלַ֥ת אֲבִיהֶ֖ן לָהֶֽן׃

and this is actually how the apportionment was carried out (see *Bava Basra* 118b, רשב״ם ד״ה ותרי דידהו) — that the daughters of Tzelafchad are not to receive portions as באי הארץ, for only the male descendants of Chefer are to receive a נחלה as באי הארץ. That נחלה, therefore, returns to Chefer according to the principle of "חזרה," and is then divided into equal portions among Chefer's descendants — Tzelafchad and his brothers or their heirs. The daughters of Tzelafchad take part only in this latter division, and only as the heiresses of their father do they receive his share in the נחלה of Chefer.

7 **כן בנות וגו׳**. כן — cf. כנים אנחנו (*Bereshis* 42:11 and Commentary there). There, כן characterizes people; here, it characterizes a speech, a presentation. The daughters of Tzelafchad said what should have been said; their words correspond to the truth, to what is right.

דברת. The primary meaning of דִּבֵּר in the *pi'el* is to present a thought to the listener, audible expression, whereas דֹּבֵר in the *kal* relates primarily to the thought's content which comes to expression through words. Thus דובר צדק, דובר מישרים, דובר שלום, and the like. דַּבֵּר, to speak [enunciate]; אָמֹר, to say [explain]; דָּבוֹר, to specify a thought.

אחזת נחלה. נחלה: property that "flows down" like a stream from ancestors to descendants (cf. Commentary above, 21:12). אחזה — like גאולה, ישועה — is an active abstract concept: property that "holds" its owner, causing him to settle down and giving him a permanent place (see Commentary, *Bereshis* 47:27).

בתוך אחי אביהם: they take the place of a brother instead of their deceased father. If the Land was simply apportioned to יוצאי מצרים, then the daughters of Tzelafchad receive the share due to Tzelafchad, for Tzelafchad — like all his brothers — was one of יוצאי מצרים, and his daughters are his heiresses. It is different if the Land was apportioned according to the system of חזרה described above. According to this system, first the Land was apportioned to באי הארץ, and then it returned from them to יוצאי מצרים and was divided into equal parts among יוצאי מצרים as the legacy of their forefathers. Had Tzelafchad left five sons instead of five daughters, these five sons — like their cousins — would first have received five portions. These portions would then have returned to their grandfather Chefer and would have been divided into equal parts among his sons and their heirs. Hence, had the daughters of Tzelafchad been treated as sons also as regards this חזרה system of division, Scripture would have said here בתוך בני דודיהם and not בתוך אחי אביהם. Since, however, Scripture says בתוך אחי אביהם, the implication is as follows: Unlike their cousins, the daughters of Tzelafchad do not receive five shares for the חזרה system of division. Rather, only their cousins receive shares and return them to Chefer, whose legacy is then divided among his sons, who were of יוצאי מצרים. Tzelafchad was one of these sons, and his daughters receive his share, equal to that of his brothers, as we have already indicated in explaining verse 5.

The pronominal suffixes referring to the daughters are in the masculine: להם, אביהם. The implication is as follows: Give them a hereditary portion among the brothers of their father, as though they (the daughters) were sons; or, according to the system of "חזרה": Give them a hereditary portion as befits sons, but only among the brothers of their father; in relation to them they have the rights of sons.

והעברת את נחלת אביהן להן. נחלת אביהן, according to the system of apportionment to יוצאי מצרים, means: the portion due to their father as one of יוצאי מצרים; according to the system of חזרה, it means: their father's portion of the legacy divided between him and his brothers as a result of the חזרה.

A legacy bequeathed to an heiress is called העברה. For if she marries a man from one of the other tribes, this property will, after her death, pass over to her son who belongs to his father's tribe; or — if ירושת הבעל דאורייתא (see Commentary, vv. 9-11) — it will pass over to her husband. Thus, the property will pass into the possession of another tribe and will be lost to the tribe to which it originally belonged.

8 *And to the Children of Israel you shall say: If a man dies and has no son, you shall transfer his inheritance to his daughter.*

ח וְאֶל־בְּנֵי יִשְׂרָאֵל תְּדַבֵּר לֵאמֹר אִישׁ כִּי־יָמוּת וּבֵן אֵין לוֹ וְהַעֲבַרְתֶּם אֶת־נַחֲלָתוֹ לְבִתּוֹ׃

8 **ואל בני ישראל וגו׳**. The laws of inheritance set forth here apply for all time to come.

ובן אין לו. The negative word אין (here and in the following verses) is interpreted by the Halachah (*Bava Basra* 115a) in the widest sense. The right of inheritance transfers from son to daughter only if there is no son in existence in any respect — not even as an idea — and his existence is not represented by any offspring. Conversely, if the son left a son or daughter, grandson or granddaughter, etc., the right of inheritance passes through that line, and not to or through the sister. Similarly, the inheritance does not transfer from the daughter to the brothers (v. 9), or from the brothers to the father's brothers (v. 10), unless the daughter or the brothers left no descendants. Whoever is entitled to inherit is represented by his descendants, and the right of inheritance transfers to another line only if he left no descendants, not even a remote descendant: כל הקודם בנחלה יוצאי יריכו קודמין (*Bava Basra* 115a).

So we find also in the case treated here: As regards Chefer's legacy, which was divided between Tzelafchad and his brothers, Tzelafchad was represented by his daughters.

This sense of אין לו is expressed in the Halachah as עיין עליו. That is to say, before you say אין לו, עיין עליו; check whether the son exists through a living descendant. In such a case, the Torah's condition ובן אין לו is not met (see Commentary, *Devarim* 25:5).

והעברתם — see Commentary, verse 7.

The sense of the law is clear: The daughter inherits only where there is no son or descendant of a son. When a daughter — as opposed to a son — inherits, it is called "העברה." If the father leaves a son, the hereditary property remains in the father's tribe. If the property falls to a daughter, it might "pass over" to another tribe. For this reason a daughter inherits only במקום שאין בן. Even if the son predeceases his father, but leaves a daughter, who represents him according to the principle explained above, this granddaughter holds the rights of her father, and she takes prece-

9 *If he has no daughter, you shall give his inheritance to his brothers.*

ט וְאִם־אֵ֥ין ל֖וֹ בַּ֑ת וּנְתַתֶּ֥ם אֶת־נַחֲלָת֖וֹ לְאֶחָֽיו׃

10 *If he has no brothers, then you shall give his inheritance to his father's brothers.*

י וְאִם־אֵ֥ין ל֖וֹ אַחִ֑ים וּנְתַתֶּ֥ם אֶת־נַחֲלָת֖וֹ לַאֲחֵ֥י אָבִֽיו׃

11 *If his father has no brothers, you shall give his inheritance to his kin that is closest to him from among his family, and that one shall inherit it. This shall remain for Israel as a legal norm, as* God *had commanded Moshe.*

יא וְאִם־אֵ֣ין אַחִים֮ לְאָבִיו֒ וּנְתַתֶּ֣ם אֶת־נַחֲלָת֗וֹ לִשְׁאֵר֙וֹ הַקָּרֹ֥ב אֵלָ֛יו מִמִּשְׁפַּחְתּ֖וֹ וְיָרַ֣שׁ אֹתָ֑הּ וְֽהָיְתָ֞ה לִבְנֵ֤י יִשְׂרָאֵל֙ לְחֻקַּ֣ת מִשְׁפָּ֔ט כַּאֲשֶׁ֛ר צִוָּ֥ה יְהוָ֖ה אֶת־מֹשֶֽׁה׃ פ

dence over the daughter, her aunt. So, too, the daughter of a son has equal rights with the other sons, her uncles (as is clear from the case of בנות צלפחד), whereas the daughter is superseded by them, her brothers (see *Bava Basra* 115b, 116a).

9-11 **ואם אין לו בת וגו׳ ואם אין לו אחים וגו׳ ואם אין אחים לאביו ונתתם את נחלתו לשארו הקרב אליו ממשפחתו**. The cases discussed in verses 9-11 are merely examples for which finally the fundamental principle is stated, according to which these and all other cases not presented here are to be judged. This fundamental principle is formed by three concepts: **שארו**, blood relationship; הקרב, degree of closeness, as הקרוב קרוב קודם (*Bava Basra* 108b), the nearer relation has precedence over the more distant; and finally ממשפחתו, the relation must be a relation of משפחה, the relatives must be members of the deceased's משפחה.

The concept of משפחה is formed only by descent from the same father, not through the mother. For example: In the laws of inheritance, only sons of the same father are considered "אחים," but not sons of the same mother. Sons of the same mother who were born to different fathers belong to different משפחות, whereas sons of the same father from different mothers belong to the same משפחה: משפחת אב קרויה משפחה, משפחת אם אינה קרויה משפחה, דכתיב למשפחותם לבית אבותם (ibid. 109b).

For the purposes of the laws of inheritance, the deceased's nearest relations are his sons and daughters, and a son has precedence over a daughter. Similarly, a son takes the place of his father in יעוד (*Shemos* 21:9 and Commentary there) and in שדה אחוזה (*Vayikra* 25:25 and Commentary there; *Bava Basra* 108b). If there is no son and no descendant of a son, then the daughter or her descendants inherit (v. 8).

Where there are no children, the father is the שאר הקרב אליו ממשפחתו. As near as the son is to his deceased father in the descending line, the father is near to his deceased son in the ascending line. If the deceased left no descendants, the inheritance goes to the father, who is the nearest relative upward; or it goes to the father's descendants, who are the deceased's brothers or sisters, or to their descendants. If the deceased's father died and left no descendants, the inheritance goes to the next שאר הקרב אליו ממשפחתו, who is the father of the father, the deceased's paternal grandfather; or it goes to the grandfather's descendants, the father's brothers or his sisters, their descendants, and so on.

The inheritance always goes in a direct line — to descendants or to male forebears; it can come to a member of a parallel line, only because that member descends from the deceased's male forbears: It comes to the deceased brothers because they are descendants of the father; it comes to the deceased's uncles because they are descendants of the grandfather. Hence the brothers do not inherit in the father's lifetime, and the uncles do not inherit in the grandfather's lifetime, etc. סדר נחלות כך הוא, איש כי ימות ובן אין לו והעברתם נחלתו לבתו, בן קודם לבת, כל יוצאי ירכו של בן קודמין לבת, בת קודמת לאחין, יוצאי ירכה של בת קודמין לאחין, אחין קודמין לאחי האב, יוצאי ירכן של אחין קודמין לאחי האב, זה הכלל, כל הקודם בנחלה יוצאי ירכו קודמין, והאב קודם לכל יוצאי ירכו (ibid. 115a).

The principle of ונתתם את נחלתו לשארו הקרב אליו implicitly explains the statements ונתתם וגו׳ לאחיו (v. 9), ונתתם וגו׳ לאחי אביו (v. 10): In the former, the father has already died. In the latter, the grandfather has already died. אחי אביו are related to the deceased only through אביו [i.e., through his grandfather]; hence אביו is קרוב to him more than אחי אביו, and the inheritance goes first to the אב and his descendants, before it can come to אחי אביו.

It is possible that verses 8 and 9 are directly connected to the case that was brought here for a decision. For Chefer —the father of the deceased, Tzelafchad — had already died, and the question was whether the inheritance was to fall to Tzelafchad's daughters or to his brothers.

The answer given was that in this case of איש כי ימות ובן אין לו the נחלה is to be given to the daughters and not to the brothers — this despite the fact that property given to the brothers would remain in that tribe, whereas property given to the daughters might be transferred to another tribe — and that only where there is no daughter or descendants of a daughter ונתתם את נחלתו לאחיו.

This, then, is the rule of the laws of inheritance: The inheritance first seeks the nearest descendant; then it seeks the nearest male forebear or his descendants; then it seeks the next closest male forebear or his descendants, and so forth. In this order it continues to seek until it finds the שאר הקרוב אליו ממשפחתו. This "seeking" is called משמוש (from the root משש). [See *Bava Basra* 115b.]

What applies to the legacy of the father applies also to the legacy of the mother: it goes to her sons and to her daughters or to their descendants, and the sons have precedence over the daughters. If she dies without descendants, her legacy goes to her male forebears or to their descendants, and the father and his descendants have precedence over the grandfather. However, one qualification applies: If her descendants predecease her, her legacy does not go to their siblings from the father's side; rather, in such a case the legacy goes to משפחתה — i.e., to her nearest male forebear or to his descendants. This principle is called אין הבן יורש את אמו בקבר להנחיל לאחין מן האב (ibid. 114b).

In addition, although the son inherits his mother, the mother does not inherit her son (ibid. 115a). Rather, as already stated, if the son dies leaving no descendants, his legacy goes to his male forebears or to their descendants. This is already indicated in our verse by the term ממשפחתו, for משפחת אם אינה קרויה משפחה (ibid. 109b).

Our Sages say further (ibid. 111b) that the term לשארו of our verse includes primarily the relationship between husband and wife (see Commentary, *Vayikra* 21:2). Accordingly, we would have thought that a husband and wife inherit each other; the husband is the primary heir of his wife, and vice versa, and they take precedence over all the other relatives. However, the wife's right to inherit her husband is excluded by other indications in the Torah, and תוספות point out (*Bava Basra* 111b ד"ה הוא יורש אותה) that it is excluded by the very fact that the Torah is concerned about הסבה (the transference of hereditary property) only in the case of a woman who marries a man from another tribe, but not in the case of any man who marries a woman.

12 *And* God *said to Moshe: Go to this Mountain of Transitions, and look at the Land that I have given to the Children of Israel.*

יב וַיֹּאמֶר יְהוָה אֶל־מֹשֶׁה עֲלֵה אֶל־
הַר הָעֲבָרִים הַזֶּה וּרְאֵה אֶת־
הָאָרֶץ אֲשֶׁר נָתַתִּי לִבְנֵי יִשְׂרָאֵל׃

The husband's right to inherit his wife remains in force, but it is subject to the double limitation expressed in the sentence אין הבעל יורש את אשתו בקבר (ibid. 114b).

On the one hand, this sentence means: A husband does not inherit property that will come to his wife only after her death, since at the time of her death the property is only ראוי for her but not מוחזק. Rather, the property goes to her descendants or to her male forebears and their descendants.

On the other hand, it also means: The husband does not inherit his wife unless he outlives her — אין הבעל בקבר יורש את אשתו. According to the principle of משמוש, other heirs are represented "in the grave" by their descendants, who inherit the נחלה that would have come to their deceased forebear had he still been alive. However, this principle does not apply to the husband's right of inheritance. Just as a widow is entitled to marry another man, she is also independent as regards inheritance, and upon the death of her husband he loses the right to inherit her upon her death. Her inheritance therefore goes to her second husband if he outlives her, or, if she has no husband, it goes to her descendants or to her male forebears and their descendants (see תוספות ibid. 114b ד"ה מה אשה and רמב"ן there).

The question whether ירושת הבעל is דאורייתא or is only a תקנת חכמים is not clearly decided. According to one view, the husband's right of inheritance is only דרבנן (see *Kesubos* 83b, 84a).

For more on the laws of inheritance in Jewish Law, see Commentary, *Devarim* 21:15ff.

12 **ויאמר וגו'**. This is not yet the command to ascend the mountain. That command comes later: וידבר וגו' (ibid. 32:48). Here the command is mentioned only to explain what precedes and to give the reason for what follows (cf. Commentary above, v. 6). The immediately preceding passage concludes the instructions for the apportionment of the Land. To this

13 *And when you have seen it, you, too, shall be gathered to your people, just as your brother Aharon was gathered;*	יג וְרָאִ֣יתָה אֹתָ֔הּ וְנֶאֱסַפְתָּ֥ אֶל־עַמֶּ֖יךָ גַּם־אָ֑תָּה כַּאֲשֶׁ֥ר נֶאֱסַ֖ף אַהֲרֹ֥ן אָחִֽיךָ׃
14 *As you acted against My words in*	יד כַּאֲשֶׁ֨ר מְרִיתֶ֥ם פִּי֙ בְּמִדְבַּר־צִ֗ן

Scripture now adds and explains that Moshe himself will not enter the Land. His work on earth will be completed with his viewing the Land from a distance. Moshe's mission was to lead the people to the land of the Torah, to prepare them for taking possession of the Land and for fulfilling their mission there. But the realization itself did not devolve upon him. He is to die not in the land to which he led the people, but only within sight of that land.

This announcement did not come as a surprise to Moshe. He knew of this Divine decree ever since the incident at Kadesh. However, he was now made aware that he had now reached the end of his journey on earth, so that he should take the initiative to do whatever he wished to do before his death, and especially so that the appointment of his successor should fulfill the wishes of his own faithful heart; he himself should be able to appoint and install his successor.

הר העברים: the Mountain of Transitions — i.e., the mountain by which one crosses the Yarden and reaches the Land.

13 **וראיתה**. The addition of the ה at the end of the word indicates, apparently, that this viewing is not a command that is incumbent upon him immediately; rather, the time for its fulfillment is left to his own choice.[The addition of a letter, generally a ה, to a root indicates a desire or a request that some action be done; cf. קומה, above, 10:35.]

ונאספת אל עמיך — see Commentary, *Bereshis* 25:8.

14 **כאשר וגו'**. It seems to us that nowhere does כאשר occur in the sense of "because"; in any case, its predominant meaning is "just as." And since that is the meaning of כאשר in the preceding verse (v. 13), that is how it should be interpreted here as well. Still, it is difficult to understand the meaning of this comparison.

בִּמְרִיבַת֙ הָֽעֵדָ֔ה לְהַקְדִּישֵׁ֥נִי בַמַּ֖יִם לְעֵינֵיהֶ֑ם הֵ֛ם מֵֽי־מְרִיבַ֥ת קָדֵ֖שׁ מִדְבַּר־צִֽן׃ ס

the wilderness of Tzin during the contention of the community, [when you were] to sanctify Me before their eyes by means of the water. These are the waters of contention at Kadesh in the wilderness of Tzin.

Perhaps the intent is only to compare Moshe's fate with Aharon's fate. Just as you were both guilty of the same sin — and Aharon has already died because of it — you, too, shall die for the same reason.

It is possible, however, that the intent is to compare the cause and the effect, the sin — and the death of both of them in view of the longed-for Land. Their sin frustrated a Divine intention; their sin will be atoned for when they are prevented from reaching the goal for which they had longed for so many years.

מריתם פי במדבר צן במריבת העדה להקדישני וגו׳ — see Commentary above, 20:1-13.

להקדישני is the explanation of פי. God's command was intended להקדישני וגו׳, and they acted against this intention.

הם מי מריבת קדש מדבר צן — as opposed to מי מריבה of Refidim (*Shemos* 17:1-7), to which these מי מריבה of קדש מדבר צין are antithetical. In Refidim, at the outset of the wilderness journey, Moshe was commanded to bring forth water from the rock by a blow with the staff of God. This water was their guarantee for the whole period of their stay in the wilderness. It demonstrated to the people that they could expect the direct intervention of God's miraculous power, which would save them from all trouble and distress and would provide for all their urgent needs. Now, at the end of the journey, in קדש מדבר צין, at the edge of the desert and the beginning of habitable land, the mode of God's guidance would change: The very "non-striking of the rock," the effectiveness of the word beside the unused staff of God — that is what was to provide them with the guarantee for the new era which was now beginning. For they would henceforth lead their lives under normal conditions, and there would no longer be a need for the direct intervention of open miracles. They would no longer require the use of Moshe's *staff*; rather, Moshe's *word* would

15 *And Moshe spoke to* God, *saying:* טו וַיְדַבֵּר מֹשֶׁה אֶל־יְהוָה לֵאמֹר׃

suffice for finding the path of life and salvation, a path to be found by way of God's gifts which are hidden in the natural order of the world.

This truth came to expression in the very contrast between the Kadesh incident and the Refidim incident; the death of Moshe and Aharon, which is connected with the Kadesh incident, only adds clarity to this truth. When the people reached the border of the Land, the mission of Moshe and Aharon was concluded. For God had sent Moshe and Aharon to perform great deeds in the midst of the people, to enlighten their minds and to accustom them to a way of life. This mission was now accomplished, and it suffices for all time. There will no longer be a need for the miracles of יציאת מצרים and for the revelation of מתן תורה. Moshe and Aharon could be gathered unto their people in the world to come. The members of their people in this world will preserve the work and uphold the Torah that Moshe and Aharon accomplished and taught in their midst at God's command. Henceforth, after their deaths, לא בשמים היא (*Devarim* 30:12); henceforth, ושמרתם ועשיתם (ibid. 29:8) — "safeguarding and fulfilling" — will be the task of the people, a task for which they can be sure of God's help and blessing.

Not Moshe's *staff* but Moshe's *word* was to have brought forth water from the rock at the border of the Land, and this demonstration was nullified by the sin of Moshe and Aharon. Their death at the border of the Land expressed this truth with even greater clarity. Perhaps herein lies the true explanation of the word "כאשר" discussed above, which compares the death of Moshe and Aharon to their sin.

Thus one of the last prophets in the concluding period of prophecy says: "Your fathers, where are they? and will these prophets live forever? But My words and My statutes, which I have commanded to My servants, the prophets, indeed, they have become your fathers'" (*Zecharyah* 1:5-6).

15 **וידבר וגו' לאמר**. This form of introduction indicates that what follows is not a request, but a [necessary] measure. Moshe felt that it was necessary that his successor be appointed, now that he knew that he was about to die. Since what was at stake was not his own personal welfare but the

16 *Let* God, *the God of the spirits of all flesh, appoint a man over the community,*	טז יִפְקֹד יְהֹוָה אֱלֹהֵי הָרוּחֹת לְכָל־בָּשָׂר אִישׁ עַל־הָעֵדָה׃

future welfare of the community, he dared to couch his speech in these terms. כל מי שמבקש צרכי ציבור כאילו בא בזרוע (*Bemidbar Rabbah* here).

16 **אלקי הרוחת לכל בשר**: מגיד הכתוב שכל הרוחות אין יוצאות אלא מלפניו (*Sifre* here). It does not say here אלקי רוחות כל בשר but אלקי הרוחות לכל בשר. It is from God that every spirit is sent to the physical frame appropriate to it, and it is God Who joins the רוחות to all בשר. So it also says in *Yeshayahu* (57:16): כִּי־רוּחַ מִלְּפָנַי יַעֲטוֹף וּנְשָׁמוֹת אֲנִי עָשִׂיתִי — It is from Me that the spirit is sent to enter its case. ר׳ אליעזר בנו של ר׳ יוסי הגלילי adds (in the *Sifre*): סימן זה יהיה בידך: שכל זמן שאדם נתון בחיים נפשו פקודה ביד קונו שנאמר אשר בידו נפש כל חי, מת – נתונה באוצר שנאמר והיתה נפש אדוני צרורה בצרור החיים. "Hold fast to this idea: As long as a person is granted life, his soul is kept in the hand of his Creator and Owner, as it says: 'in Whose hand is the soul of every living thing' (*Iyov* 12:10). When he dies, however, his soul is stored in God's treasury, as it says: your soul is stored in the treasury of life" [cf. *Shemuel* I, 25:29].

Accordingly, God is אלקי הרוחות לכל בשר in two respects: It is He Who *grants* the spirit to every body, and it is He Who *keeps* the spirit in every body. He sends the spirit into the physical body and, as long as He is interested in the spirit's combination with the body, He maintains this combination; He protects the spirit, strengthens it, and nourishes it with talents and with the ability to grow and develop. Thus, He is personally nearer to every spirit during its life on earth than He will be to it after death, when the soul is stored away in the "bond of life" along with all the other ingathered souls, for a new future. According to ר׳ אליעזר, this truth is so important for us to keep in mind in this world that he admonishes us: סימן זה יהיה בידך! Let this truth be a sign in our hands to guide us on our way in life.

God, Who, as אלקי הרוחות לכל בשר, knows and watches over all the souls He has sent into material bodies, will also know how to find the right man to be Moshe's successor. Therefore, let God Himself appoint him. For even though Moshe and Aharon were no longer needed (see Commentary, v. 14), someone else will be needed to carry out the Divine mission whose realization now devolves upon the people.

יז אֲשֶׁר־יֵצֵא לִפְנֵיהֶם וַאֲשֶׁר יָבֹא לִפְנֵיהֶם וַאֲשֶׁר יוֹצִיאֵם וַאֲשֶׁר יְבִיאֵם וְלֹא תִהְיֶה עֲדַת יְהֹוָה כַּצֹּאן אֲשֶׁר אֵין־לָהֶם רֹעֶה׃	17 *Who will go out before them and come in before them, who will lead them out and bring them in, so that the community of* God *should not be like sheep that have no shepherd.*
יח וַיֹּאמֶר יְהֹוָה אֶל־מֹשֶׁה קַח־לְךָ אֶת־יְהוֹשֻׁעַ בִּן־נוּן אִישׁ אֲשֶׁר־רוּחַ בּוֹ וְסָמַכְתָּ אֶת־יָדְךָ עָלָיו׃	18 *And* God *said to Moshe: Take yourself Yehoshua, son of Nun, a man in whom there is spirit, and lean your hand upon him.*

17 **אשר יצא לפניהם וגו׳**. יצא ובא לפני- denotes more than just leading the troops into battle. When Shlomo seeks to fulfill his duty as king, he asks God for a לֵב שֹׁמֵעַ לִשְׁפֹּט אֶת־עַמְּךָ לְהָבִין בֵּין־טוֹב לְרָע, without which he will be unfit to carry out his duties, and he describes this state of unfitness as follows: וְאָנֹכִי נַעַר קָטֹן לֹא אֵדַע צֵאת וָבֹא (*Melachim* I, 3:7 and 9). יצא ובא, then, is an expression for the general activity of one placed at the head of a nation. Moreover, in *Yehoshua* (14:11) Kalev clearly distinguishes between going to war and לצאת ולבא, for he says: כְּכֹחִי אָז וּכְכֹחִי עָתָּה לַמִּלְחָמָה וְלָצֵאת וְלָבוֹא. Thus, in the expression לצאת ולבא he includes not only military prowess, but the general aptitude for public activity of every kind. **יצא** denotes going out into the public domain, in contrast to **בא**, which denotes returning to the private domain.

A man is required אשר יצא לפניהם ואשר יבא לפניהם. This man shall "go before" the people, setting an example for them in both his public and private life.

ואשר יוציאם ואשר יביאם: By the example he sets and through his general influence, he shall bring them, too, to fulfill all obligations, both public and personal, in accordance with the dictates of duty.

That the expression אשר יצא לפניהם וגו׳ involves more than just leadership in battle is corroborated by what is stated next: ולא תהיה וגו׳ כצאן אשר אין להם רעה, for the activity of a shepherd is devoted to the thriving and welfare of the flock.

18 **איש אשר רוח בו**. Like the wind (רוח), which is invisible and is discernible only by its effects as an active, moving power, the faculties of perception

19 *You shall present him to Elazar the priest and to the entire community, and charge him before their eyes.*

יט וְהַעֲמַדְתָּ אֹתוֹ לִפְנֵי אֶלְעָזָר הַכֹּהֵן וְלִפְנֵי כָּל־הָעֵדָה וְצִוִּיתָה אֹתוֹ לְעֵינֵיהֶם׃

and volition (רוח) reside in man (see Commentary, *Shemos* 25, end). This spiritual and moral element is present in every human being. Hence, if nevertheless it says here of Yehoshua that he is worthy of being Moshe's successor because he is "a man in whom there is רוח," it must be that רוח is mentioned here in an emphatic sense, even as we would use the expression "a man of spirit" to describe one who possesses this quality to an exceptional degree. Thus the prophet is called אִישׁ הָרוּחַ (*Hoshea* 9:7). Yehoshua possessed spirit that was not weakened by the tarnishing material of the body.

In *Devarim* (34:9) it says: ויהושע בן נון מלא רוח חכמה כי סמך משה את ידיו עליו. After he was appointed successor to Moshe, his natural gift of רוח was further enhanced; his רוח became רוח חכמה and filled his whole personality.

וסמכת את ידך עליו — see Commentary, *Vayikra* 1:4.

19 **והעמדת אתו וגו׳** (cf. above, 3:6, 5:16, and Commentary there). To place someone before someone else means to place him at his disposal, in his service. When Yehoshua was placed before Elazar the priest and before the whole community, he was placed in the service of the Sanctuary of the Torah and in the service of the national community. Thus said רבן גמליאל to two disciples who, out of modesty, hesitated to accept the high public position to which he had offered to raise them: כמדומין אתם ששררה אני נותן לכם, עבדות אני נותן לכם, "You imagine it is honor that I offer you; it is service that I offer you" (*Horayos* 10a).

וצויתה אתו לעיניהם. צוה is the special term for charging someone regarding an office to which he is to be appointed. Thus: וְצִוְּךָ לְנָגִיד עַל־יִשְׂרָאֵל (*Shemuel* I, 25:30), אֲשֶׁר צִוִּיתִי שֹׁפְטִים עַל־עַמִּי יִשְׂרָאֵל (ibid. II, 7:11), לְצַוֹּת אֹתִי נָגִיד (ibid. II, 6:21), ויצום אל בני ישראל (*Shemos* 6:13), and so also in *Devarim* (3:28): וצו את יהושע וחזקהו ואמצהו.

וצויתה: [For emphasis, the form וצויתה — rather than וצוית — is used.] *You* shall charge him with the duties of his office in the presence of the

20 *You will thus place [some] of your [own] prestige upon him, so that the entire community of the Children of Israel will obey [him].*

כ וְנָתַתָּ֥ה מֵהֽוֹדְךָ֖ עָלָ֑יו לְמַ֣עַן יִשְׁמְע֔וּ
כָּל־עֲדַ֖ת בְּנֵ֥י יִשְׂרָאֵֽל׃

21 *But he shall stand before Elazar the priest, and the latter shall make inquiry on his behalf through the judgment of the Urim before* God. *According to his word shall they go out, and according to his word shall they go in, he and all the Children of Israel with him, and the entire community.*

כא וְלִפְנֵ֨י אֶלְעָזָ֤ר הַכֹּהֵן֙ יַעֲמֹ֔ד וְשָׁ֥אַל
ל֛וֹ בְּמִשְׁפַּ֥ט הָאוּרִ֖ים לִפְנֵ֣י יְהוָ֑ה
עַל־פִּ֨יו יֵצְא֜וּ וְעַל־פִּ֤יו יָבֹ֙אוּ֙ ה֛וּא
וְכָל־בְּנֵֽי־יִשְׂרָאֵ֥ל אִתּ֖וֹ וְכָל־
הָעֵדָֽה׃

people. Thus he will appear as one commissioned by you, and his future activity will be supported by your authority.

20 **ונתתה מהודך עליו**. הוד is related to אוד, which is indicative of the active, moving force, and is related also to עוד, which is indicative of lasting existence. Accordingly, הוד is the outward appearance of fullness of existence and power. הוד is intensively what הדר means extensively. הוד is the greatness of the personality; הדר is the extent of its sphere of control.

למען ישמעו. שמע does occur in the absolute, without a preposition, in the sense of obeying. Thus: **והנה לא שמעת עד כה** (*Shemos* 7:16), **אִם־תֹּאבוּ וּשְׁמַעְתֶּם** (*Yeshayahu* 1:19), et al. But it is possible that Scripture employs here the verb "obey" in the absolute — instead of saying **למען ישמעו אליו** — because obedience to Yehoshua is really obedience to God's Word communicated to Yehoshua by Moshe.

21 **ולפני אלעזר הכהן יעמד**. He is not to be appointed as an autocratic ruler. In all public matters where the question is not about what is permissible or forbidden according to the revealed Law, but about the expediency or inexpediency of a plan of action, he is to seek, and act in accordance with, God's Word. This Word which will be communicated to him through the Urim borne over the heart of the כהן גדול, the national rep-

22 *Moshe did as* God *had commanded him. He took Yehoshua and presented him to Elazar the priest and to the entire community.*

כב וַיַּעַשׂ מֹשֶׁה כַּאֲשֶׁר צִוָּה יְהֹוָה אֹתוֹ וַיִּקַּח אֶת־יְהוֹשֻׁעַ וַיַּעֲמִדֵהוּ לִפְנֵי אֶלְעָזָר הַכֹּהֵן וְלִפְנֵי כָּל־הָעֵדָה׃

23 *He leaned his hands upon him and charged him, as* God *had commanded through Moshe.*

כג וַיִּסְמֹךְ אֶת־יָדָיו עָלָיו וַיְצַוֵּהוּ כַּאֲשֶׁר דִּבֶּר יְהֹוָה בְּיַד־מֹשֶׁה׃ פ

חמישי

resentative of the Sanctuary of the Torah. ולפני וגו׳ יעמוד — see Commentary, verse 19.

ושאל לו במשפט: Elazar shall make inquiry on his behalf before God to ascertain the decision of the Urim (see Commentary, *Shemos* 28, end).

שאל ב- is the usual expression for seeking God's decision about a plan of action. Thus: וַיִּשְׁאַל־לוֹ בה׳ ,וַיִּשְׁאֲלוּ בֵאלֹקִים (*Shoftim* 20:18ff.; *Shemuel* I, 10:22, 22:10, 23:2, 28:6, 30:8, et al.). Thus, too, עַמִּי בְּעֵצוֹ יִשְׁאָל (*Hoshea* 4:12). Since God's Word is not communicated to the inquirer directly by God nor directly by the Urim, this ב seems to indicate the idea of mediation, of cause. The inquirer seeks an answer which will be communicated to him not by God, but through His instrumentality; that is to say, God will cause an answer to be communicated to him. The question is directed to God, and God causes an answer to be communicated to him through the Urim and through Elazar. But it is not Elazar who causes the answer to be given. He is merely the passive instrument.

על פיו: according to Elazar.

וכל העדה: Since וכל בני ישראל have already been mentioned, העדה here is none other than בית דין הגדול, as in 25:6-7 (above) and *Vayikra* 4:13 (see Commentary there).

2-23 **ויעש וגו׳ ויסמך וגו׳**. It is possible that the instructions to appoint Yehoshua as his successor were given to Moshe as a general answer to his request, not as a command to be carried out at once. For after he was informed of his impending death, Moshe requested that a successor be appointed, and God's answer to Moshe was that, before his death, he should appoint Yehoshua before the eyes of all the people. But the actual

28 1 God *spoke to Moshe, saying:*

כח א וַיְדַבֵּר יְהוָה אֶל־מֹשֶׁה לֵּאמֹר׃

procedure was performed only just before Moshe's death (*Devarim* 31:7). In that case, ויעש וגו׳ ויסמך וגו׳ in our verse merely informs us that later on Moshe faithfully fulfilled God's Word.

It is possible, however, that Moshe was commanded to appoint Yehoshua immediately, and did so. In that case, ויקרא משה ליהושע וגו׳ in *Devarim* (31:7) is merely an additional admonition [to Yehoshua] to fulfill the duties already assigned to him, and that would also be the explanation of ויצו את יהושע וגו׳ (ibid. 31:23).

ויסמך את ידיו עליו. The command was only וסמכת את ידך עליו (v. 18), but Moshe fulfilled the mitzvah with all his heart and with "both hands," ידיו. He made Yehoshua — as the *Sifre* puts it — ככלי מלא וגדוש, "into a vessel filled to overflow": He made Yehoshua the bearer, in abundant measure, of his spirit and his prestige.

CHAPTER 28

1 In the preceding chapter God acceded to Moshe's request that, after his death, which was now close at hand, God's community should not remain without a leader who would go before the people as a model for private and public life, and who, through his personal influence, would guide and keep the individual and communal life of the people in the paths marked by God.

It was necessary, however, to ensure that the people and its leaders would never lose sight of their calling, but would always keep in mind Israel's eternal mission and its relationship to God in accordance with its unique destiny and duty. Toward this end they are charged here with קרבנות ציבור, תמידים ומוספים. These offerings are profound symbolic expressions of these relationships and their appropriate attitudes and resolves, and the offering procedures make the nation aware of them.

Thus, these offerings are a complement to the appointment of Yehoshua, for they, too, ensure the continuance of God's work which was begun by Moshe. The פרשה of the קרבנות is therefore a continuation of the פרשה of the appointment of Yehoshua. It can be said that, until now,

2 *Command the Children of Israel and say to them: That which is to be brought near to Me as My offering, for My fire offerings, the expressions of compliance due to Me, you shall keep, to bring near to Me in its season of appointed meeting.*

ב צַו אֶת־בְּנֵי יִשְׂרָאֵל וְאָמַרְתָּ אֲלֵהֶם אֶת־קָרְבָּנִי לַחְמִי לְאִשַּׁי רֵיחַ נִיחֹחִי תִּשְׁמְרוּ לְהַקְרִיב לִי בְּמוֹעֲדוֹ׃

God's work has been entrusted to Moshe. Before his death, Moshe hands it over to Yehoshua and to קרבנות ציבור.

The פרשה of קרבנות ציבור concludes the actual Lawgiving (see Commentary below, 30:2). We have already noted (Commentary, *Vayikra* 23:1) that this פרשה is presented only in the Book of Wanderings in the Wilderness, indeed only at the end of the book, because it required the experiences of forty years in the wilderness to make us aware of ourselves as a nation, and to make us feel the need for constant reminders of our relationship to God and of the attitudes and resolves on our part that this relationship demands of us.

2 **צו את בני ישראל וגו׳**. The first קרבן ציבור, which is the basis and foundation of all the offerings (see Commentary, *Vayikra* 6:5), is the תמיד, the daily ascent offering brought every morning and afternoon.

The mitzvah of the תמיד was stated (*Shemos* 29:38ff.) immediately after the sanctification of the altar, to show the altar at once in its living activity, in its fulfillment of the main purpose of its construction and dedication, and we refer the reader to the explanations given there [in the Commentary].

Here, the unceasing fulfillment of this mitzvah devolves upon Israel as a special national obligation, and the offering time of the קרבן תמיד is included — as a daily מועד (see Commentary above, 9:2) — among all the other מועדים and is even placed before them.

צו את בני ישראל — see Commentary above, 5:2-3. With the expression "ויצוהו" of the preceding section Yehoshua was placed in the service of the community, and with the expression "צו וגו׳" of this section the community is placed in the service of God. The תמיד offering constantly reminds the community that God's service devolves upon it. This is the meaning of the *Sifre* here: עד שאתה מפקדני על בני, פקוד בני עלי שלא ינהגו בי מנהג בזיון ושלא ימירו את כבודי באלהי נכר.

את קרבני וגו'. The תמיד offering is the foundation of all the offerings, and it is described here with all the main hallmarks of the relationships expressed by the offerings in general. **קרבני**: drawing near to God, attaining God's closeness; **לחמי**: by making all earthly endeavors fit for the Presence of God on earth; **לאשי**: by means of submitting them to the purifying and life-giving fire of the Torah (see Commentary, *Vayikra* 1:2 and 9; 3:11); **ריח ניחחי**: and all this is only an allusive expression of realizing God's Will in life. Hence our Sages say (in the *Sifre*): קרבני זה הדם, the נפש elevating itself to God; לחמי אלו אמורים, the submission of all aims and endeavors; לאשי אלו קמצים ולבונה, the means of subsistence, prosperity, and joy of life. (Although neither קומץ nor לבונה are offered in a תמיד offering but, rather, the entire מנחת נסכים is placed on the fire, the *Sifre* nevertheless mentions here those "gifts to the fire" that do not occur at the תמיד; for the תמיד is the foundation of all the other offerings, and the קומץ and לבונה of all מנחות are conceptually connected to מנחת התמיד.) Thus the whole earthly part of man and nations is transformed by the fire of the Torah into resources of God's kingdom on earth. ריח ניחחי אלו נסכים (גירסת הגר"א), the sum of our highest joy, rooted in the foundation of the Sanctuary of the Torah, rises in the consciousness of God's satisfaction with us.

Thus את קרבני לחמי לאשי ריח ניחחי, this most precise and concise expression of our whole Jewish national position and calling, **תשמרו להקריב לי במועדו**, we must offer to God at the time set by God for meeting with Him, and through this very offering we give expression to our meeting with God. This is the offering that devolves upon us here as מצוה and as שמירה: as an obligation to be fulfilled with due care.

And the Jewish people knew how to carry out this obligation! The communal offerings, and particularly the תמיד offerings (see *Menachos* 65a), were drawn strictly מתרומת הלשכה, from the annual half-shekel donation which attested to the ever-fresh devotion of every member of the nation. Six unblemished sheep were always kept ready in לשכת הטלאים four days before the offering (see *Arachin* 13a-b). In this respect the תמיד offering resembles the Pesach offering (*Shemos* 12:3), for the תמיד is basically a continuation of the Pesach offering. Thus the כהנים would each day offer the national offering on the heights of Mount Moriyah in Yerushalayim.

But Israel did not suffice themselves with this offering itself; they did not regard it merely as an act to be performed so that god — in the pagan sense — should be appeased. For in the Torah the mitzvah of offering the תמיד appears as follows: The singular form of תעשה (v. 4) conceives of the nation in the unity of its totality; hence the תמיד can be brought only by the national representative of the community [the כהן]. Nevertheless, the plural form of תשמרו (v. 2) obligates the nation in all its members to constantly watch over this national offering. Hence, Jewish minds have understood that the תמיד offering of the Sanctuary in Yerushalayim should be the offering of the entire nation. For the single act of offering the תמיד, performed each day on the heights of the national center, is not sufficient. Rather, it is necessary that the people residing throughout the national sphere direct its mind to this offering. As our Sages say: וכי היאך קרבנו של אדם קרב והוא אינו עומד על גביו! (*Ta'anis* 26a). How can an offering be brought on behalf of someone, if he is not present in person or at least in spirit? Does not the Torah say: תשמרו להקריב לי במועדו! The early prophets therefore divided the nation into twenty-four משמרות corresponding to the twenty-four משמרות כהונה (Commentary, *Devarim* 18:7-8). These משמרות כהונה took weekly turns serving in the Sanctuary. Each משמר of the people had members residing in Yerushalayim. These members were the deputies of the משמר, and during the week of that משמר they would come to the Sanctuary for the offering of the תמיד. At the same time, the other members of the משמר would gather in their cities and, through קריאת התורה and תענית, would attend the תמיד in spirit. In this way they would take to heart that the purpose of all the offerings is the purification of the mind and of conduct. This "standing" by the תמיד offering — in person or in spirit — is called "מעמד" (*Ta'anis* 26a). These מעמדות would heighten the awareness, in Yerushalayim and in the cities of the Land, of the entire nation's participation in the offering of the תמיד in Yerushalayim.

Thereby a twofold conviction was fostered in the people's hearts. First, every Jew recognized that the spiritual hold of his existence, thought, and deeds is in the Sanctuary of the Torah, the center point of the nation. For the Torah rests under the wings of the cherubim in the Sanctuary, and from there it goes forth to the people by means of the national representative of the community. The Jew's connection with God depends on this Torah. Second, the national vow, which comes to expression through the תמיד offering, concerns every member of the nation. For the nation vows every day to strive upward to God through faithfulness to the Torah, and the fulfillment of this vow devolves upon every one of the members of the people. Even those who reside in the far corners of the Land are required to fulfill it.

Thousands of years have now passed since this institution by the early prophets, and, in accordance with the legacy of the later leaders of our גלות, the whole nation, scattered all over the world, has become one מעמד. In the east and in the west, in the north and in the south, the time of the תמיד, which used to be offered in Yerushalayim, still stirs the heart of every loyal Jew as he turns to face the Moriyah district in Yerushalayim-Tziyon. At that time, he expresses anew the vow of the תמיד offering of שחרית and מנחה, which has been translated into words of prayer. This vow pledges loyalty to the Torah, which is a legacy to us from Mount Moriyah in Yerushalayim, and through this very vow we connect ourselves with God and with all our brethren all over the world. Basically, this is nothing other than the spiritual fulfillment of the mitzvah את קרבני לחמי לאשי ריח ניחחי תשמרו להקריב לי במועדו.

The day will yet come on which we fulfill this mitzvah in actual reality. We will build a new altar in Yerushalayim, and out of the communal shekels of the nation we will bring the תמיד offering, whose symbolical procedures, which were instituted by God, will express the eternal Jewish national vow.

The foregoing would explain the opposition of the Sadducees to providing for the תמיד offering out of public funds. For this is the idea that emerges from the תמיד offering of the nation:

Every individual among the people who wants to learn Torah and to sanctify his actions must turn to the representative of the community in the Sanctuary, to whom the Testimony and the teaching of God's Torah are entrusted (*Devarim* 17:10). It is this representative that is careful to offer in the name of the community the תמיד offering of the community, the offering that renews each day the vow of faithfulness to the Torah.

This idea, however, totally contradicts the doctrine of the Sadducees of every period. According to the Sadducean doctrine, Jewish man can connect himself with God only through the written letter of the Bible, which is accessible to everyone: כרוכה ומונחת בקרן זוית, כל הרוצה ללמוד יבוא וילמוד (*Kiddushin* 66b). Everyone may interpret Scripture as he pleases. He may take from it what appeals to him, regard that as God's Will, and fulfill it in accordance with his own understanding. The Sadducean doctrine abhors the spirit of the תמיד offering, because the תמיד teaches that the individual can find God only by attaching himself to the community of Israel, and that he will find favor before God only by fulfilling God's Word which was entrusted to the community.

Accordingly, one of the first objectives of the Sadducees was to enforce their position regarding the תמיד offering. For, in their view, the תמיד is not a national obligatory offering, but is left entirely to the subjective wishes of each individual. They superficially interpreted the singular form of את הכבש אחד תעשה בבקר ואת הכבש השני תעשה בין הערבים (v. 4), failing to consider that the plural form of תשמרו להקריב לי במועדו and of אשר תקריבו לה׳ (v. 3) indicates that the obligation devolves upon the community, only that the community must regard itself in this offering as one unified whole.

This attempt of the Sadducees touched upon a matter of critical importance. For this reason, when the Sages succeeded in convincing the people of the flimsiness of the Sadducean position, they included the days of "the vindication of the תמיד" — איתוקם תמידא — among the days listed in מגילת תענית. This מגילה of national remembrance lists all the days of deliverance to be celebrated by the prohibition of fasting and, in some cases, also by the prohibition of eulogizing, and not only does it include the days of "the vindication of the תמיד," it begins with them: אילין יומיא דלא להתענאה בהון ומקצתהון דלא למספד בהון, מריש ירחא דניסן עד תמניא ביה איתוקם תמידא וכו׳ שהיו הצדוקים אומרים יחיד מתנדב ומביא תמיד, מאי דרוש, את הכבש האחד תעשה בבקר ואת הכבש השני תעשה בין הערבים, מאי אהדרו, את קרבני לחמי לאשי תשמרו, שיהו כולן באין מתרומת הלשכה (*Menachos* 65a).

במועדו — see Commentary above, 9:2.

There is great importance in the fact that this section [on קרבנות ציבור] includes the *daily* occurrences of morning and evening with the *unique* events of human history, for it links sunrise and sunset with God's feats of יציאת מצרים, מתן תורה, and the wondrous journey in the wilderness, which attest to God and summon us to God. God's revelation in Egypt, at the Red Sea, at Mount Sinai, and in the wilderness was appointed a מועד, attesting to God and summoning us to God, at every anniversary of the event. So, too, God appointed sunrise and sunset — events that repeat themselves daily with regularity unsurpassed among all other natural phenomena — as a מועד.

Every rising or falling ray of light is a witness and a messenger, showing us God in the very midst of the course of the world and calling each

3 *And then say to them: This is the fire offering that you shall bring near to God: two yearling sheep that are whole, two per day, as a continual ascent offering.*

ג וְאָמַרְתָּ לָהֶם זֶה הָאִשֶּׁה אֲשֶׁר תַּקְרִיבוּ לַיהוָה כְּבָשִׂים בְּנֵי־שָׁנָה תְמִימִם שְׁנַיִם לַיּוֹם עֹלָה תָמִיד׃

one of us to Him. God's wondrous deeds in Egypt, which suspended the natural order of things, were signs attesting to God's presence. So, too, precisely the regularity of the changing times of the order of nature attests to God's presence. What is more, the whole purpose of God's wondrous deeds that suspended the laws of nature was to show that God is the Creator of this order and of these laws, and so that the regularity of the Divine order should not make us lose sight of the fact that God is the Creator of the laws of nature which govern the world. חָק־נָתַן וְלֹא יַעֲבוֹר (*Tehillim* 148:6), it is God Who established the law, and the law will not change as long as God wishes it to remain in force. Just as הוּא אָמַר וַיֶּהִי, so, too, הוּא־צִוָּה וַיַּעֲמֹד (ibid. 33:9): By His Will the world order was established, and by His Will it endures, so that יִירְאוּ מֵה׳ כָּל־הָאָרֶץ מִמֶּנּוּ יָגוּרוּ כָּל־יֹשְׁבֵי תֵבֵל (ibid. 33:8): Men should know that He is the Master of the earth and of the world of man, and they should understand that a bright future will dawn only on those deeds of men and nations that mesh harmoniously with His laws and with His Will.

The מועד of the daily creation of light heads the list here of all the historical מועדים, and so we find also in the case of these מועדים: the historical aspect is always connected with the natural aspect of the times of the year, so that we should see God in one glance both in nature and in history, and walk in the land of the living filled with the awareness of God.

3 **ואמרת להם**. This repetition indicates that צו וגו׳ ואמרת וגו׳ of the preceding verse is a separate pronouncement, and thereby we learn that the Torah attaches special importance to the duty of the community as regards the תמיד offering, a point already discussed above.

זה האשה אשר תקריבו לה׳. Let us compare what is stated here with what is stated in *Shemos* 29:38 [וזה אשר תעשה על המזבח]. There Scripture notes that the תמיד offering realizes the purpose of the altar, whereas here

4 *The one sheep you shall offer in the morning, and the other sheep you shall offer between the two evenings.*

ד אֶת־הַכֶּ֤בֶשׂ אֶחָד֙ תַּעֲשֶׂ֣ה בַבֹּ֔קֶר וְאֵת֙ הַכֶּ֣בֶשׂ הַשֵּׁנִ֔י תַּעֲשֶׂ֖ה בֵּ֥ין הָעַרְבָּֽיִם׃

Scripture discusses the meaning of the תמיד to the national consciousness. In this respect, the תמיד's character as אשה and as עולה is stressed: Devoting oneself to the fire of the Torah, to the illuminating, purifying, and vivifying power of the Torah, and thereby constantly advancing and ascending toward God and to the heights of the calling indicated by Him — אשה and עולה — these are the two basic ideas that the תמיד seeks to evoke in the mind of every Jew, so that they are embraced by the entire nation.

The phrase זה האשה indicates that the two sheep — that of the morning offering and that of the evening offering — are *one* offering, *one* fire offering, by which we seek God's closeness. One idea shall fill our minds day and night, for one God creates day and night, and to Him belong both forms of life, the day phase and the night phase of our earthly lives. Both together form a unified day of our life. In its changing times, it is divided into two; nevertheless, it is unified. The two sheep combining to form one offering express this aspect of the day, as is also indicated by the words שנים ליום (see Commentary, *Shemos* ibid.).

תמימם. In accordance with the aim of this repetition of the mitzvah of offering the תמיד, Scripture stresses here the תמימות of the offering: תמימם — our devotion must be complete.

4 **את הכבש אחד**. It does not say האחד [as in *Shemos* 29:39] but אחד; not "the one sheep" but "the sheep — and only one, אחד." Scripture thereby negates the Sadducean interpretation and explicitly says that the entire nation is to bring only *one* תמיד offering; thus, the תמיד is strictly a קרבן ציבור and cannot be brought by every individual as a נדבה.

ואת הכבש השני is not the command to offer the afternoon תמיד, for that command is mentioned only in verse 8. Rather, ואת הכבש השני serves to explain the preceding את הכבש אחד וגו׳: Not both but only *one* should be offered, for the second is to be offered only in the afternoon.

This necessary explanation emphasizes even more the unity of the תמיד offering. For one might have thought that the תמיד offering — even

5 *And [you shall offer] a tenth of an* eifah *of fine flour as an homage offering, mixed with a quarter* hin *of pressed oil.*	ה וַעֲשִׂירִ֧ית הָאֵיפָ֛ה סֹ֖לֶת לְמִנְחָ֑ה בְּלוּלָ֛ה בְּשֶׁ֥מֶן כָּתִ֖ית רְבִיעִ֥ת הַהִֽין׃
6 *A continual ascent offering that is made on Mount Sinai, as an expression of compliance, a fire offering to* God.	ו עֹלַ֖ת תָּמִ֑יד הָעֲשֻׂיָה֙ בְּהַ֣ר סִינַ֔י לְרֵ֣יחַ נִיחֹ֔חַ אִשֶּׁ֖ה לַיהוָֽה׃

though it is a קרבן ציבור — represents the ציבור by means of two sheep, as in the immediately following case of the Shabbos מוסף offering. But then the national community would be represented in the plurality of its members and not as one complete unit, whereas the תמיד offering is to represent Israel in the idea of the unity of the whole nation (see Commentary, vv. 9 and 10).

5 **ועשירית האיפה וגו׳**. In *Shemos* 29:40 it says only ועשרן סלת, and it does not say explicitly that the סולת is למנחה, whereas here it says למנחה, and the amount of סולת is set by the words עשירית האיפה. Both these points accord with the aim of the repetition of the mitzvah of the תמיד.

The nation must be made aware that the עולה idea must be supplemented by the מנחה concept. For the devotion of the whole personality is not sufficient. It must also be recognized and acknowledged that all of the nation's assets belong to God, and that the nation recognizes God as the Master over all the means of subsistence and prosperity on which its existence and prosperity depend.

And Scripture here does not use the term עשרן, which is the term consistently used in all the following offerings, but says ועשירית האיפה, alluding to what is stated in *Shemos* 16:36: והעמר עשרית האיפה הוא. Every מנחה-tenth shall remind the nation of the basic experience of the manna, for through the manna the nation experienced the providence of God, Who provides for all His creatures.

6 **עלת תמיד וגו׳**. In our Commentary on *Shemos* (27:8) we noted that in *Yechezkel* the altar is called "הראל," and we also cited there what is stated in *Tehillim* (68:18): אֲדֹנָ-י בָם סִינַי. On this basis we conjectured that the altar is

7 *And its libation [shall be] a quarter* hin *for each sheep, in the Sanctuary, to pour out a libation of strong wine before* God.

ז וְנִסְכּוֹ רְבִיעִת הַהִין לַכֶּבֶשׂ הָאֶחָד בַּקֹּדֶשׁ הַסֵּךְ נֶסֶךְ שֵׁכָר לַיהוָה׃

8 *The second sheep you shall offer*

ח וְאֵת הַכֶּבֶשׂ הַשֵּׁנִי תַּעֲשֶׂה בֵּין

called here "הר סיני," and that the altar, with its fire, represents—in the Sanctuary—Mount Sinai, on whose summit the "consuming fire" was revealed.

The foregoing corresponds entirely with the aim of this repetition of the mitzvah of the תמיד. Thus the תמיד offering symbolizes the everlasting daily renewal of the vow נעשה ונשמע, with which the nation responded to the revelation of the Torah on Mount Sinai and entered into the covenant of the Torah. Indeed, the עולה is nothing other than a vow to constantly advance in doing and in learning. But this devotion to the אש אוכלה בהר סיני is expressed only by delivering the עולה and the מנחה to the אש על המזבח; it is not expressed by ניסוך היין, for the wine is poured down to the base of the altar. Hence, in our verse, the summary "עלת תמיד" includes only the עולה and the מנחה, and only of them does it say that they are עלת תמיד העשיה בהר סיני, whereas the נסך is mentioned only in the next verse: ונסכו וגו׳.

7 **ונסכו וגו׳**. This devotion of all existence, all aspirations, and all possessions to the fire of God's Torah shall not be done out of constraint or unwillingly. Rather, Israel should find its highest joy in this calling. Israel's happiness has its roots in the base of the Sanctuary of the Torah, on which "God's Mountain" rises and presents its demands. Israel is filled with rapture when it pours out the expression of the joy of its life *inside* the Sanctuary *before* God (see Commentary above, 15:5ff.).

שכר is wine in its spiritual power. Superficially, it appears as though שכר and קדש are opposites. Scripture therefore puts בקדש first. The place that receives Israel's offerings is also the basis of Israel's highest joy. Israel may bring its שכר into the Sanctuary, and does not consider it שכר unless it [Israel] can pour it [the שכר] בקדש לפני ה׳.

8 **ואת הכבש השני** — see Commentary, *Shemos* 29:38-39 and 41.

וכנסכו refers to הבקר: the מנחה and the נסך of the afternoon are the

הָעַרְבָּ֑יִם כְּמִנְחַ֨ת הַבֹּ֤קֶר וּכְנִסְכּוֹ֙
תַּעֲשֶׂ֔ה אִשֵּׁ֛ה רֵ֥יחַ נִיחֹ֖חַ לַֽיהוָֽה׃ פ

between the two evenings; like the homage offering of the morning and its libation shall you offer to God *as a fire offering to express compliance.*

ט וּבְיוֹם֙ הַשַּׁבָּ֔ת שְׁנֵֽי־כְבָשִׂ֥ים בְּנֵֽי־
שָׁנָ֖ה תְּמִימִ֑ם וּשְׁנֵ֣י עֶשְׂרֹנִ֗ים סֹ֛לֶת
מִנְחָ֛ה בְּלוּלָ֥ה בַשֶּׁ֖מֶן וְנִסְכּֽוֹ׃

9 *And on the Sabbath day two yearling sheep that are whole and two tenths of fine flour as an homage offering, mixed with oil, and its libation.*

same as the מנחה and the נסך of the morning. (For more on the whole תמיד offering, see Commentary, *Shemos* 29:38-42.)

9 **וביום השבת וגו׳**. The ascent offering that is added on Shabbos to the תמיד offering expresses the special character of the day. This ascent offering resembles the תמיד offering. The only difference between them is that the תמיד offering includes *one* כבש, whereas the מוסף offering of Shabbos includes *two* כבשים. It follows, then, that the difference in meaning between the offerings resembles the difference in meaning between the numbers *one* and *two* in communal animal offerings.

Now, we have already analyzed the essential difference between an offering that represents the nation by means of one animal and an offering that represents it by means of two animals (*Vayikra* 23:12-13, 17, 19; et al.). The number one represents the nation *in its unity*, whereas the number two represents the nation *as a plurality of individuals*. This is also the difference between עולת התמיד and עולת השבת. The כבש אחד of the תמיד represents the nation *as a nation*. The Jewish nation approaches God, the Leader and Guide of its national fate, and whenever the light of day rises or falls, the nation renews its vow of faithfulness and obedience, and undertakes to devote itself to the goals mapped out for it by its Shepherd, Lord, and Master.

In the שני כבשים of the עולת שבת, all the *individuals* of the Jewish nation approach their *Creator* and *Master*. For on Shabbos they cease from all work, and through this שבתון they lay themselves and their world at God's feet. And just as they keep the שבתון of Shabbos, they also express through the עולה of Shabbos that רועה ישראל, the Shepherd of the Jewish nation as a whole, is also the Shepherd of every Jewish soul, for כְּרֹעֶה עֶדְרוֹ יִרְעֶה בִּזְרֹעוֹ יְקַבֵּץ טְלָאִים וּבְחֵיקוֹ יִשָּׂא עָלוֹת יְנַהֵל (*Yeshayahu* 40:11). Now they renew the vow of faithfulness and obedience to God Who shepherds all His creatures, and they undertake to devote themselves to the goals that He set for them. For the sake of these goals, He created them as Jewish men; and for this destiny He gave them a share of His world and of human powers of mastery over His world.

Thus, through the תמיד offering, Israel approaches God as one national unit — כבש אחד with one עשרון and with one רביעית יין; but on Shabbos Israel approaches God again, this time as a national *plurality*, representing all the souls included in the nation. Hence, on Shabbos Israel brings two כבשים with two עשרונים and with two רביעיות יין. Within the consciousness of the national community, Israel gives expression to each individual's relationship to God; and with the feeling of a created thing, a feeling evoked by Shabbos, Israel brings this relationship to living awareness.

The עולת שבת, then, is nothing but an עולת תמיד of a different nuance, and it differs from the תמיד only in the two כבשים instead of the one כבש of the תמיד. For this reason the mitzvah of the עולת שבת appears here without a special introduction such as וביום השבת תקריבו עולה לה׳ שני כבשים וגו׳; rather, it appears to be the continuation of the mitzvah of the תמיד offering: וביום השבת שני כבשים וגו׳. This wording emphasizes the two כבשים, which are characteristic of the מוסף of Shabbos — in contrast to the one כבש of the תמיד offering.

ונסכו. We do not know what the suffix ו refers to. If, as is usually the case, it had referred to כבשים, it would have said ונסכיהם. In the singular, the suffix can refer only to סלת or to יום השבת or to שבת, which in verse 10 occurs also in the masculine. Thus, the meaning could be: the נסך that accompanies all סולת of מנחת נסכים; for the expression of the means of subsistence and prosperity must be supplemented by the expression of the highest joy of life. Or the meaning could be: the joy that has already been expressed in the תמיד offering shall come to special expression also on Shabbos. For Shabbos seeks to fill the life every individual with the spirit of supreme joy; Shabbos says to each individual: וְקָרָאתָ לַשַּׁבָּת עֹנֶג (*Yeshayahu* 58:13). Thus, the refraining from producing on Shabbos the means of subsistence and prosperity — אִם־תָּשִׁיב מִשַּׁבָּת רַגְלֶךָ עֲשׂוֹת חֲפָצֶיךָ בְּיוֹם קָדְשִׁי — is not a tribute that is paid reluctantly; rather, it is a source of happiness and of supreme joy (ibid.).

10 *The ascent offering of the Sabbath on its Sabbath, over and above the continual ascent offering and its libation.*

י עֹלַ֥ת שַׁבַּ֖ת בְּשַׁבַּתּ֑וֹ עַל־עֹלַ֥ת הַתָּמִ֖יד וְנִסְכָּֽהּ׃ פ

10 **עלת שבת בשבתו**. In this expression — and also in the expression עלת חדש בחדשו (v. 14) — the words שבת and חדש refer to the *institutions* of the Sabbath and the New Moon in general, and these institutions come to expression בשבתו and בחדשו: every day on which the Sabbath or the New Moon falls. עלת שבת is the ascent offering corresponding to the meaning and purpose of the institution of the Sabbath, and שבתו is every seventh day which is dedicated to realizing the institution of the Sabbath. Perhaps that is why it says here שַׁבַּת in סמיכות without a נסמך: to express the generality of the concept designated by the first term, "שבת." It is the "Sabbath" concept which underlies every Sabbath day.

עלת שבת בשבתו ולא עולת חול בשבת (*Shabbos* 24b). On the Sabbath it is permissible to make an offering only so as to meet the obligations of the Sabbath institution; it is forbidden to offer חלבים ואיברים left over from before Sabbath.

על עלת התמיד ונסכה. The תמיד offering with its מנחה and its נסך is also offered on Shabbos (see Commentary above, 9:2). What is more, the שבת offering is only added to the תמיד offering: על עולת התמיד ונסכה מגיד שאין מקריבים מוספים אלא בינתים (*Sifre*); התמידין קודמין למוספין (*Zevachim* 89a).

The תמיד offering is the perpetual expression of the nation striving without letup to ascend to the heights of its calling, and for this reason it begins and concludes, daily, the service of the offerings in the Sanctuary. All the other offerings — including the Shabbos ascent-offering — are offered between the two תמידים, and their whole purpose is to proclaim this striving of the community to ascend, as we have already explained in our Commentary on *Vayikra* 6:5.

This institution of the Sabbath preceded the nation; conceptually, too, the Sabbath preceded the nation's election and mission, so much so that one could almost say that the realization of the institution of the Sabbath was the cause and the purpose of Israel's election. Nevertheless, the Sabbath is borne by the nation's devotion to its mission, of which the Sabbath is only one integral part. Hence על עלת התמיד ונסכה applies to עלת שבת בשבתו as well.

11 *And at the beginnings of your months you shall bring near to* God *an ascent offering: two young bulls and one ram, seven yearling sheep that are whole.*

יא וּבְרָאשֵׁי֙ חָדְשֵׁיכֶ֔ם תַּקְרִ֥יבוּ עֹלָ֖ה לַֽיהוָ֑ה פָּרִ֨ים בְּנֵֽי־בָקָ֤ר שְׁנַ֙יִם֙ וְאַ֣יִל אֶחָ֔ד כְּבָשִׂ֧ים בְּנֵֽי־שָׁנָ֛ה שִׁבְעָ֖ה תְּמִימִֽם׃

As a result of the foregoing, the priority of the Sabbath is, as it were, obscured here. Perhaps for this reason Scripture re-emphasizes the Sabbath's independence in regard to all the other *mitzvos*, and therefore refers to the Sabbath here in the masculine, even though it is usually treated as feminine: עלת שבת בְּשַׁבַּתּוֹ, not בְּשַׁבַּתָּהּ.

The מוסף of שבת consists solely of עולה, and, unlike all the other מוספים, a חטאת is not brought with it. If we recall what we said (Commentary, *Vayikra* 4:24) about the concept of חטאת and its relation to עולה, the absence of חטאת at the מוסף of שבת can be explained easily. For this is what we learned from the laws that characterize these two classes of offerings:

חטאת-consciousness — the depressing feeling of moral decline and inclination to sin — is not the normal state or mood of Jewish life. However, the מועדים are special days established mutually by God and the nation. On these days — and in this respect ראש חדש, too, is a מועד (see *Shevuos* 10a) — the nation meets with God, and in going to meet its God it gives expression, through its offering, to its ideal mission. Contemplating this ideal perfection, the nation feels the need to bring also a חטאת, for the חטאת represents the disparity between reality and those ideal heights.

The מוסף of שבת, on the other hand, is only a supplement to the תמיד offering; for the תמיד represents the acknowledgement of God that springs from the national consciousness, and the מוסף of שבת only adds to this the acknowledgement of God that springs from man's consciousness as a created being; from the two together is formed the spirit of devotion that strives for constant ascent. This spirit must fill us at every breath of our lives. Hence the חטאת must be excluded from the מוסף of שבת, just as it must be excluded from the תמיד itself.

11 **וּבראשי חדשיכם וגו׳**. ראש חדש is the cornerstone of the Jewish conception of God, of the world, and of man. With it God began to lay the foundation

of *His* nation, and with it He established the fact of חידוש as the pillar of the salvation of Israel and mankind. The fact of חידוש — the fact of the creation of the world and the redemption of man by a free act of God — is the antithesis of the erroneous notion of קדמות, which drags the world and man into the dark depths of guilt and wretchedness. We have already explained this in our Commentary on *Shemos* 12:1-2.

Self-renewal; reawakening to pure aspirations and a life of joy; redemption from all moral, social, and physical evil; reaching up to God's outstretched hand, to aspire to the ideal of morality and salvation; raising ourselves anew to the proximity of God's light, in order to extricate ourselves from the misery of the dark, distant places into which we have sunk — this is the call that is projected to us at the sight of every new moon. For God said: החדש הזה לכם ראש חדשים, and thereby made the renewal of the moon a model, a sign, that ensures our redemption, just as He made the rainbow a sign of the covenant ensuring the survival of mankind (see Commentary, ibid. 12:2).

Therefore, whenever the new moon invites us to create our חדשים, the periods of our renewal, we approach God in the Sanctuary of His Torah and bring before Him an offering. This offering represents the complete ideal of the calling He has ordained for us. Through the עולה we vow to strive to ascend to the heights of this calling, and through the חטאת we vow to remain strong and guard ourselves against any descent. This offering represents Israel's ideal calling, which was the purpose of the redemption from Egypt and of the Lawgiving at Sinai, and which is the purpose of God's further guidance throughout the ages. The offering that fully represents this calling is: פרים בני בקר שנים ואיל אחד כבשים בני שנה שבעה תמימם, and we have already analyzed its significance in our Commentary on *Vayikra* 23:18. At the announcement of the redemption, God said that its purpose is: ולקחתי אתכם לי לעם והייתי לכם לאלקים (*Shemos* 6:7; see Commentary there), and that purpose shall come to expression in this group of מועד offerings.

Israel shall be a nation *whose every member shall serve God with everlasting youthful freshness* (פרים בני בקר שנים), and *therefore* this is the nation's general appearance in God's *human flock*: Israel shall be a *model* for all the other nations and shall *stride before them with God-given strength* (איל אחד). Its whole *history* is nothing but the *finger of God attesting to God* in history. As a flock guided by God, the people of Israel proceeds with undying youthful freshness (כבשים בני שנה שבעה). (See Commentary, *Vayikra* 23:18.)

12 *Three tenths of fine flour as an homage offering, mixed with oil, for each bull; two tenths of fine flour as an homage offering mixed with oil for the one ram;*

יב וּשְׁלֹשָׁה עֶשְׂרֹנִים סֹלֶת מִנְחָה בְּלוּלָה בַשֶּׁמֶן לַפָּר הָאֶחָד וּשְׁנֵי עֶשְׂרֹנִים סֹלֶת מִנְחָה בְּלוּלָה בַשֶּׁמֶן לָאַיִל הָאֶחָד׃

This destiny of Israel shall come to expression on every ראש חדש, for it is Israel's goal of which it will never lose sight. Israel's pursuit of this destiny is perennially renewed, and all the מועדים that summon Israel to God express the aspiration to fulfill this destiny. For the sake of this destiny, the people of Israel were redeemed from Egypt, for its sake they received the Torah, for its sake God sheltered them in the wilderness, for its sake they are stirred by the sound of תרועה on Rosh Hashanah, and it is what opens for them the gates of atonement on יום הכיפורים.

Therefore, whenever the people of Israel appear before God on the מועדים, they bring the same group of offerings. The מועדים offerings differ one from the other in only one detail: On ראש השנה, יום הכיפורים, and שמיני עצרת, one פר is brought instead of two פרים. This difference is due to the special character of the respective days, as already noted in our Commentary on *Vayikra* 23:18.

We will see further here, in the continuation, that the ראש חדש group of offerings is also the basis of the group of offerings on the festival of Sukkos. Thus the ראש חדש offering is the archetype of all the מועדים offerings. Similarly, the קביעות, the קרא מקרא קדש, of all the מועדים depends on קידוש החדש and on the fixing of the ראש חדש.

12 **ושלשה וגו'**. As already stated in chapter 15, the nation as a whole and every individual in his individuality are obligated to add מנחה ונסך to the ascent offering. For the ascent offering, which represents the personal sanctification of deeds, must be supplemented by מנחה ונסך, which signify that all the means of subsistence, prosperity, and enjoyment of life belong to God and are rendered unto him with homage. This acknowledgement is expressed through the סולת, the שמן, and the יין נסכים, which correspond to the דגן תירוש ויצהר of the national wealth.

However, the importance of the personal standing in God's House

13 *And one tenth of fine flour as an homage offering, mixed with oil, for each sheep; an ascent offering as an expression of compliance, a fire offering to* God.

יג וְעִשָּׂרֹן עִשָּׂרוֹן סֹלֶת מִנְחָה בְּלוּלָה בַשֶּׁמֶן לַכֶּבֶשׂ הָאֶחָד עֹלָה רֵיחַ נִיחֹחַ אִשֶּׁה לַיהוָה׃

14 *And their libations: a half* hin *of wine for each bull, a third of a* hin *for the ram, and a quarter* hin *for each sheep. This [is] the ascent offering of the New Moon on its New Moon for the months of the year.*

יד וְנִסְכֵּיהֶם חֲצִי הַהִין יִהְיֶה לַפָּר וּשְׁלִישִׁת הַהִין לָאַיִל וּרְבִיעִת הַהִין לַכֶּבֶשׂ יָיִן זֹאת עֹלַת חֹדֶשׁ בְּחָדְשׁוֹ לְחָדְשֵׁי הַשָּׁנָה׃

differs in the various types of עולה. One who faithfully follows God's guidance is symbolized by a כבש. One who strides before God's flock as a model is symbolized by an איל. One who works energetically on God's soil, in the fields of the nation and humanity, is symbolized by a פר. And the higher the importance of the personal standing, the more important is the recognition that all the means of existence and achievement belong to God. Hence the prescribed measure of the מנחה and נסכים increases from the כבש to the איל to the פר. This has already been established in chapter 15, and is applied here at the מועדים offerings.

13 **עלה ריח ניחח וגו׳**. The מנחה of one's possessions is an essential complement of the פרים איל וכבשים. Like them, it, too, is given over to the אש המזבח, which awaits the devotion of the nation. Therefore, together with them, it forms the concept of the עולה.

The עולה expresses the vow of striving to ascend to the heights indicated by God. ריח ניחח: it [the עולה] signifies giving God satisfaction with one's active life. אשה לה׳: it [the עולה] represents drawing near to God by devotion to the purifying, vivifying, and formative power of His Torah.

14 **ונסכיהם**. This devotion is the source of Israel's purest joy, which increases with every higher degree of importance that the people perceive they have attained before God.

זאת עלת חדש בחדשו — see Commentary, verse 10. On every day of

15 *And one he-goat, as an offering that clears of sin, to* God, *over and above the continual ascent offering shall it be made, and its libation.*	טו וּשְׂעִיר עִזִּים אֶחָד לְחַטָּאת לַיהוָה עַל־עֹלַת הַתָּמִיד יֵעָשֶׂה וְנִסְכּוֹ׃ ס ששי

the new moon, the general idea of ראש חדש should be implemented. Hence עבר היום בטל קרבנו (*Sifre*): If a מועד offering is not offered on its designated day, there is no supplementary period for it. For the obligations of the *day* were not met, and expression was not given to the consciousness that should be aroused *on that very day and by that day. That* has no תשלומין; it cannot be made up. For it is not the purpose of the offerings to render unto God His due; hence, one cannot argue that it makes no difference to God when He receives His due, as long as He ultimately receives it. Rather, the purpose of the מועד offering is to elevate *our* consciousness and to direct it to the series of ideas appropriate to the מועד. And if this is not done on the day of the מועד, there is no making up for it on another day, for each day brings its own unique requirements, which must be met with all our energy and devotion. So it says also regarding the תמיד offering, the Shabbos מוסף offering, and all the other communal offerings that must be brought at a fixed time: עבר זמנו בטל קרבנו (*Temurah* 14a).

However, it is not sufficient that the national representative fulfills on each day the obligation of the day in the Sanctuary. Rather, the *entire nation* must constantly renew its *participation* in these offerings. So it says of all the מועדים offerings, including the תמיד, which heads their list (v. 2): Starting in Nissan, they are to be brought from the shekels collected each year לחדשי השנה: חדש והבא קרבן מתרומה חדשה (*Rosh Hashanah* 7a). In this respect, each year forms a special cycle of offerings, as already explained in our Commentary on *Shemos* 30:16.

15 **ושעיר עזים וגו׳**. שעיר החטאת is included in the group of offerings of all the מועדים. It gives expression to the consciousness that, until now, the reality has not met the requirements of the ideal perfection represented by the group of the עולות.

There is a special relationship between שעיר החטאת and ראש חדש, which signifies extricating oneself from all moral abasement. In all the מועדים offerings which follow, שעיר חטאת אחד is attached to the group of the עולות, the מנחה, and the נסכים, whereas here this group is first summarized by זאת עלת חדש וגו', and only then does Scripture add ושעיר עזים אחד לחטאת. What is more, Scripture adds לה' — just as in the case of עולה (v. 11) it adds לה' — and thereby gives this חטאת special importance of its own.

The meaning of this חטאת of ראש חדש is as follows: הקב"ה is the God of love Who educates man and mankind, and through the changing phases of the moon He has shown us a model of ourselves (see Commentary, *Shemos* 12:1-2). With each regularly recurring new moon, He has instituted for us a day of ראש חדש, to teach us that, like the moon, we are capable of renewing ourselves and of attaining light after any darkness. Thus He has taught us the great truth that the חוטא, too, is still לה', and that, moreover, even the חטאת is לה'; for חטאת is the *ability* to sin, the *need* for expiation, and the *possibility* of expiating oneself and of elevating oneself out of the depths of sin.

This חטאת is לה': it is a supreme gift of grace which God has granted to His noblest creation, man. For man's superiority and major distinction is freedom: By the exertion of his *free* will, he is capable of remaining on the heights of what is morally good; he can avoid evil and practice goodness in *freedom*. But this freedom is found only in man who also has the ability to sin. For sensuality entices man with its allurements, but he has been endowed with the power to resist it by the determination of his free will. By repeatedly exerting this power, he acquires the virtue of moral purity and attains closeness to God.

However, *were it not for man's ability to sin*, and were it not for sin's enticement to man, *he would not be a man* but an animal or an angel, "who do not deviate from their appointed path" [cf. *Yechezkel* 1]; he would not be a human being *who serves God in freedom*.

Man's ability to sin is innate in him and inseparable from him, whereas the חטאת teaches and effects that man can turn from his sin, and man's *self-elevation* from sin atones for his *ability to sin*. The free-willed virtue to which he raises himself through the חטאת is a Divinely-blessed result of his ability to sin. In the language of the mitzvah of ראש חדש: the glory of the moon's renewal reveals the wisdom of the Creator, Who endowed the moon with the capacity for temporary darkening.

Perhaps this is the meaning of the saying of our Sages on our verse: מה נשתנה שעיר של ר"ח שנאמר בו לה'? אמר הקב"ה, שעיר זה יהא כפרה על שמיעטתי את

הירח (*Shevuos* 9a). Sins committed by human beings are the only evil in God's world. Mindless people ask: Why did God give man the ability to sin? The answer to their question is given by the sinner who turns in freedom to moral purity; for he never would have reached this lofty level had he not been given the ability to sin. Thus, the sinner's repentance justifies, as it were, the Creator. Every victory over sin is an atonement for the ability to sin, with which the Creator has made man into man; and every ראש חדש requires of us to make such an "atonement for the work of the Creator." תוספות (ibid.) also cite the version: שעיר זה יהא כפרה עלי שמעטתי וכו׳; or as it says in *Chullin* 60b: הביאו כפרה עלי שמעטתי את הירח.

The ideal of our moral calling is given expression by מקדש וקדשיו, and the antithesis of this ideal — sinking into a lack of moral freedom — is represented by the states of טומאה. Hence the purity of the idea of מקדש וקדשיו is tarnished by contact with טומאה. The חטאת of the מועדים offerings nullifies the contrast between the reality of the present and the ideal of our calling represented by the עולות.

Accordingly, it may be said that the חטאת effects כפרה על טומאת מקדש וקדשיו, and therefore our Sages say in *Shevuos* 2a and 9a: שעירי רגלים ושעירי ראשי חדשים מכפרין על טומאת מקדש וקדשיו שאין בה ידיעה לא בתחילה ולא בסוף; "שעירי ראשי חדשים and רגלים effect atonement for טומאת מקדש וקדשיו [i.e., sins against the Sanctuary] that one committed unwittingly and about which one never became aware." (קרבן עולה ויורד, which atones for טומאת מקדש וקדשיו, is brought only where there is ידיעה בתחילה ובסוף; see *Vayikra* 5:2 and Commentary there, 5:13.) טומאת מקדש וקדשיו results from an act of the Creator, Who wedded the pure Divine soul to the physical, sensual side of man. טומאת מקדש וקדשיו in a case of אין בה ידיעה לא בתחילה ולא בסוף symbolizes the lack of moral freedom to which we so easily fall. For we inevitably come in contact with the unfree aspects of physical existence, and thus, unconsciously, we tend to become estranged from the purity and clarity of mind that must be maintained in the midst of physical, sensual life. מועדי ה׳ therefore come to us from time to time in order to bring us out of the stupor of servitude and to call us into the liberating and enlightening proximity of our God.

The liberation from טומאה that comes without our awareness is indicated by the addition of לה׳ to חטאת. As our Sages say: ושעיר עזים אחד לחטאת לה׳, חטא שאין מכיר בו אלא ה׳ יהא שעיר זה מכפר (*Shevuos* 9a). This statement basically overlaps the statement cited above: שעיר זה יהא כפרה על שמיעטתי את הירח. For the diminution of the moon — as understood from the פרשה of

16 *And in the first month, on the fourteenth day of the month, is a Pesach dedicated to* God.

טז וּבַחֹדֶשׁ הָרִאשׁוֹן בְּאַרְבָּעָה עָשָׂר יוֹם לַחֹדֶשׁ פֶּסַח לַיהוָה׃

17 *And on the fifteenth day of that month is a festival:* matzos *shall be eaten for seven days.*

יז וּבַחֲמִשָּׁה עָשָׂר יוֹם לַחֹדֶשׁ הַזֶּה חָג שִׁבְעַת יָמִים מַצּוֹת יֵאָכֵל׃

18 *On the first day is a convocation to the Sanctuary; you must not do any service work.*

יח בַּיּוֹם הָרִאשׁוֹן מִקְרָא־קֹדֶשׁ כָּל־מְלֶאכֶת עֲבֹדָה לֹא תַעֲשׂוּ׃

19 *And you shall bring near to* God *a fire offering as an ascent offering: two young bulls, one ram, and seven yearling sheep; in their completeness shall they be to you.*

יט וְהִקְרַבְתֶּם אִשֶּׁה עֹלָה לַיהוָה פָּרִים בְּנֵי־בָקָר שְׁנַיִם וְאַיִל אֶחָד וְשִׁבְעָה כְבָשִׂים בְּנֵי שָׁנָה תְּמִימִם יִהְיוּ לָכֶם׃

החדש הזה לכם — symbolizes the possibility that the Divine side of man will be temporarily eclipsed, a possibility that results from an act of the Creator, Who wedded the pure Divine soul to the physical, sensual side of man.

16-19 **ובחדש הראשון וגו׳**. When the anniversary of the first month of Jewish national birth comes round, then, on the fourteenth day of the month, in the afternoon before the redemption, the people of Israel offer the Pesach offering. Thereby, they re-enact the hour of redemption, and every Jewish household — with all the souls belonging to it — surrenders itself to God's decision whether to be or not to be, physically and nationally, and celebrates anew the establishment of the nation on the basis of its fundamental laws (see *Shemos* 12:3-14, 27, and Commentary there).

On the fifteenth, the nation gathers unto God in His Sanctuary and forms a *festive circle*, a **חג** (see Commentary, ibid. 5:1). By eating *matzos* for seven days, the nation acknowledges that God alone granted it freedom and independence, and therefore when it emerged from the depressing bondage of Pharaoh it entered the liberating service of God (*Shemos* 12:14-15; Commentary there).

20 *And their homage offering: fine flour mixed with oil; you shall make three tenths for each bull and two tenths for the ram.*

כ וּמִנְחָתָם סֹלֶת בְּלוּלָה בַשָּׁמֶן שְׁלֹשָׁה עֶשְׂרֹנִים לַפָּר וּשְׁנֵי עֶשְׂרֹנִים לָאַיִל תַּעֲשׂוּ׃

21 *You shall make one tenth for each sheep, for [all] the seven sheep.*

כא עִשָּׂרוֹן עִשָּׂרוֹן תַּעֲשֶׂה לַכֶּבֶשׂ הָאֶחָד לְשִׁבְעַת הַכְּבָשִׂים׃

At once, on the first day, the nation is called unto God in His Sanctuary and ceases from all creative work of earthly service (*Shemos* 12:16; Commentary there). And as it did on ראש חדש, so shall it do now. . .

והקרבתם: the nation draws near to God with the ideal expression of its mission, which derives from its whole relationship to God. This expression is: פרים בני בקר שנים ואיל אחד ושבעה כבשים. But as opposed to the ordinary statement "תמימם" of the ראש חדש section (cf. v. 11), the text here emphasizes the requirement of תמימות by means of a separate sentence: תמימם יהיו לכם. In accordance with the concepts of פסח and מצות, Scripture stresses the completeness of the devotion of our whole personalities: with the whole of ourselves we are to enter God's service, which was founded by יציאת מצרים. תמימם יהיו לכם: Only in a state of completeness can they give expression to the mission given to them with יציאת מצרים (see *Vayikra* 22:19ff.).

20-21 **ומנחתם**. Since, already in chapter 15, a general prescription is given that with every עולה the appropriate מנחה and נסכים must be added, it is self-understood that מנחה and נסכים must be brought also with the מועדים offerings. After the מנחה and נסכים are nevertheless mentioned in detail in the case of the מוסף of ראש חדש, in the case of the rest of the מועדים offerings they are treated in an abbreviated form: The מנחה is called מנחתם — the מנחה that, of course, is attached to them. The נסכים are not mentioned at all in the מועד offering of the festival of *matzos*, for they are self-understood, and in the rest of the offerings they are indicated only by the term "ונסכיהם," and Scripture does not specify the prescribed measures.

According to the רמב"ן in his Commentary, it is necessary to specially mention the מנחה and its prescribed measures, because the measure varies

22 *And one buck as an offering that clears of sin, to effect atonement for you.*

כב וּשְׂעִיר חַטָּאת אֶחָד לְכַפֵּר עֲלֵיכֶם׃

in some cases, as in the כבש brought with the עומר, which requires a מנחה of two tenths (*Vayikra* 23:12-13; Commentary there). By contrast, the prescribed measure of the נסכים is fixed and unchanging in every case; hence, it is not necessary to specially mention it here.

What requires special consideration is the sudden change from the plural to the singular (v. 21); for in the preceding verses and in the following verses the address is in the plural, whereas here in the מנחה of the כבשים it says תעשה in the singular. Moreover, the term תעשה itself requires explanation, for it establishes the מנחה of the כבשים as a separate command, whereas in all the other offerings Scripture simply adds עשרון עשרון לכבש to the עשרונים of the פרים and the איל. This variation in the wording can be explained by the meaning of the festival offering of יציאת מצרים. For the "seven" כבשים give expression to the God-revealing history of Israel, and this idea is renewed in our consciousness with the remembrance of יציאת מצרים of the nation as a whole. More than all the rest of God's benevolent deeds in our history, the redemption of יציאת מצרים conceives of Israel in its totality as one unit. יציאת מצרים revealed the love and the strong arm of the Father Who saved His child from death and imprisonment and delivered him to life and freedom. Therefore it says of Pesach: עשרון עשרון **תעשה** לכבש האחד לשבעת הכבשים. Furthermore, the law that only one עשרון is to be brought with the כבשים of the מוסף is stated here at the Pesach offering as an explicit command because precisely in the עומר which is brought on Pesach we find the anomaly of two עשרונים for one כבש [cf. Commentary, *Vayikra* 23:12-13].

22 **לכפר עליכם**. The עולות of the מוספים are the ideal expression of the nation, but on ראש חדש the nation is not present in God's House; only symbolically is it present there. Hence, on ראש חדש the nation's imperfection in actual reality is not apparent to all; only God is aware of it. Therefore it says there: ושעיר עזים אחד לחטאת לה׳ (v. 15; see Commentary there). On Pesach, however, the whole nation actually appears before God, and all can see that it has not yet attained its perfection and that it still requires atonement. Hence, it says here: ושעיר חטאת אחד לכפר עליכם.

23 *Apart from the ascent offering of the morning, which is for a continual ascent offering, shall you make these.*

כג מִלְּבַד֙ עֹלַ֣ת הַבֹּ֔קֶר אֲשֶׁ֖ר לְעֹלַ֣ת הַתָּמִ֑יד תַּעֲשׂ֖וּ אֶת־אֵֽלֶּה׃

23 **מלבד עלת הבקר**. In verse 24 it says, as it says in the case of ראש חדש and in the case of the other מועדים offerings: על עולת התמיד יעשה ונסכו. Here it says specially: מלבד עלת הבקר אשר לעלת התמיד תעשו את אלה. This verse does not serve to teach that the מוסף is to be brought after the תמיד offering, for that halachah is established by the usual formula in verse 24. Rather, our verse mentions these two offerings in their mutual relationship. First it treats the תמיד offering, which is stressed here in its meaning as עלת הבקר, an expression that occurs nowhere else in the entire section of the מועדים offerings.

There is no greater contrast than that between the תמיד offering and the מוסף of Pesach. For the תמיד offering is precipitated by the light of morning breaking forth in accordance with the natural order of things, whereas the מועד offerings of the festival of *matzos* commemorate יציאת מצרים, which came about through the suspension of the natural order. Nevertheless, these two facts are related here, one after the other, to the one and only God. The God Who reveals Himself to us through the shining rays of morning is the same God to Whom the remembrance of יציאת מצרים calls us. For the God Who regularly awakens the dawn in accordance with the natural order that He established is the same God Who in Egypt suspended this order and thus revealed Himself as the One Who established this order, the Master and Governor of nature and of history; and with that revelation He chose us as His people and He became our God.

For this reason it says here: מלבד עלת הבקר אשר לעלת התמיד תעשו את אלה; "Apart from the ascent offering of the *morning*, which is for a *daily* ascent offering, shall you make *these*." Moreover, you are to bring these in connection with the daily offering, which shall precede them. This is derived from the particles על and מלבד (see Commentary, v. 10).

It says here that עולת הבוקר precedes the מוספים because it is עולת התמיד. From this we derive the general halachah (*Zevachim* 89a; see also *Horayos* 12b and רש״י there) that כל התדיר מחבירו קודם את חבירו; the

24 *Like these you shall make daily, for seven days, an offering to* God *as a fire offering to express compliance; it shall be made over and above the continual ascent offering and its libation.*	כד כָּאֵ֫לֶּה תַּעֲשׂ֤וּ לַיּוֹם֙ שִׁבְעַ֣ת יָמִ֔ים לֶ֛חֶם אִשֵּׁ֥ה רֵֽיחַ־נִיחֹ֖חַ לַֽיהוָ֑ה עַל־עוֹלַ֧ת הַתָּמִ֛יד יֵעָשֶׂ֖ה וְנִסְכּֽוֹ׃
25 *On the seventh day there shall be*	כה וּבַיּוֹם֙ הַשְּׁבִיעִ֔י מִקְרָא־קֹ֖דֶשׁ

more frequently occurring has precedence over the less frequently occurring, the ordinary over the uncommon. This rule should be taken to heart, for people's tendency in the service of God is to pay more attention to the seldom occurring *mitzvos* than to the ordinary or daily *mitzvos*.

24 **כאלה תעשו ליום וגו׳**. The nation celebrating the festival of its establishment draws near to God for seven days, and on each of these seven days it gives expression to its raison d'être through the very same offering (as opposed to what is stated regarding the festival of Sukkos, on which the group of offerings changes from day to day [*Sifre*]). For on the festival of the nation's establishment, the people must be instilled with the idea of the nation's raison d'être; thus the offering shall be לחם אשה ריח ניחח לה׳. This purpose of the offering is not fully explained in the case of any other מועד.

לחם: All the conditions of the nation shall be ready and waiting for the Presence of God in its midst. **אשה ריח ניחח לה׳**: This will be achieved when the nation submits all that it has to the power of the fire of God's Torah, and thus demonstrates that it is doing God's Will in the active service of life.

ונסכו apparently refers to the תמיד offering, for that is how this term functions in the rest of the cases. Otherwise, one could interpret that נסכו refers to לחם [i.e., to the entire set of Pesach offerings], as the נסכים [of the offerings] have not been mentioned yet.

25 **וביום השביעי וגו׳**. What applies to the first day applies also to the seventh day: On this day as well you shall cease from all creative work of earthly

יִהְיֶה לָכֶם כָּל־מְלֶאכֶת עֲבֹדָה לֹא תַעֲשׂוּ׃ ס	*for you a convocation to the Sanctuary; you must not do any service work.*
כו וּבְיוֹם הַבִּכּוּרִים בְּהַקְרִיבְכֶם מִנְחָה חֲדָשָׁה לַיהוָה בְּשָׁבֻעֹתֵיכֶם מִקְרָא־קֹדֶשׁ יִהְיֶה לָכֶם כָּל־מְלֶאכֶת עֲבֹדָה לֹא תַעֲשׂוּ׃	26 *And on the day of first fruits, when you bring near to* God *a new homage offering, on your festival of weeks, there shall be for you a convocation to the Sanctuary; you must not do any service work.*

service, and you are called unto God and unto His Sanctuary. All the ideas and resolves acquired and reinforced under the influence of the seven days of the festival shall be collected and assimilated, and God's Sanctuary will send home all visitors to His House with a rich treasure of life (see Commentary, *Shemos* 12:16).

26 **וביום הבכורים**. After the festival of freedom has passed, you will finally reach the day that inaugurates the season of the "first fruits," the season in which you will be permitted to bring the first fruits of the year and lay them before God's altar. At that time, you shall acknowledge that God has kept His promise and blessed your land, as a result of your entering into the covenant of His Torah.

בהקריבכם מנחה חדשה לה׳: At the beginning of this season, before you bring near to God any homage offering from the new grain, you shall bring to His Sanctuary שתי הלחם, the two leavened loaves of wheat bread, representing the independence that is befitting for man, which is promised to every member of the people of the Torah if he keeps God's Torah.

This day will fall בשבעתיכם, upon the completion of *your* weeks, which you counted from the freedom and independence you attained. These weeks shall not be שְׁבֻעֹת חֻקּוֹת קָצִיר (*Yirmeyahu* 5:24), not the weeks of the ripening of the harvests, but שבעתיכם, *your* weeks. For it is *you* who are to mature spiritually and morally to become the receivers and bearers of the Torah (see *Vayikra* 23:15-22 and Commentary there). On this day you shall cease from all creative work of earthly service, and you will again be called to God's service in His Sanctuary.

27 *And you shall bring near to* God, *as an ascent offering to express compliance, two young bulls, one ram, seven yearling sheep.*

כז וְהִקְרַבְתֶּם עוֹלָה לְרֵיחַ נִיחֹחַ לַיהוָה פָּרִים בְּנֵי־בָקָר שְׁנַיִם אַיִל אֶחָד שִׁבְעָה כְבָשִׂים בְּנֵי שָׁנָה׃

28 *And their homage offering: fine flour mixed with oil, three tenths for each bull; two tenths for the one ram;*

כח וּמִנְחָתָם סֹלֶת בְּלוּלָה בַשָּׁמֶן שְׁלֹשָׁה עֶשְׂרֹנִים לַפָּר הָאֶחָד שְׁנֵי עֶשְׂרֹנִים לָאַיִל הָאֶחָד׃

29 *A tenth for each sheep, for [all] the seven sheep.*

כט עִשָּׂרוֹן עִשָּׂרוֹן לַכֶּבֶשׂ הָאֶחָד לְשִׁבְעַת הַכְּבָשִׂים׃

30 *One buck of the goat species, to effect atonement for you.*

ל שְׂעִיר עִזִּים אֶחָד לְכַפֵּר עֲלֵיכֶם׃

31 *Apart from the continual ascent offering and its homage offering shall you make them — in their completeness shall they be to you — and their libations.*

לא מִלְּבַד עֹלַת הַתָּמִיד וּמִנְחָתוֹ תַּעֲשׂוּ תְּמִימִם יִהְיוּ־לָכֶם וְנִסְכֵּיהֶם׃ פ

27-31 **והקרבתם וגו׳**. You shall again approach God with the ideal expression of your calling, which springs from all these relationships. Through the power of this calling, the life of every individual will be devoted to the active service of God; the nation as a whole will become an illuminating model for the nations; Jewish history will open the eyes of mankind to see God's works; your existence, prosperity, and happiness will be sanctified, so that they render homage to God. Out of the imperfection of every contemporary time, a gate will be opened to a new and pure future. Thus shall you approach God with two **פרים**, one **איל**, seven **כבשים**; with your **שמן**, your **יין נסכים**, and a **שעיר לכפר**.

Above, in the case of Pesach (v. 19), Scripture relates **תמימות** only to the offering animals that represent the personality liberated by God. It is different in the case of the festival of **שבועות**, on which we became worthy of receiving the Torah. Here, **תמימות** is mentioned only at the end, in

29 1 *And in the seventh month, on the first of the month, there shall be for you a convocation to the Sanctuary; you must not do any service work. It shall be to you a day of impressive sound.*

כט א וּבַחֹ֨דֶשׁ הַשְּׁבִיעִ֜י בְּאֶחָ֣ד לַחֹ֗דֶשׁ מִקְרָא־קֹ֙דֶשׁ֙ יִהְיֶ֣ה לָכֶ֔ם כָּל־מְלֶ֥אכֶת עֲבֹדָ֖ה לֹ֣א תַעֲשׂ֑וּ י֥וֹם תְּרוּעָ֖ה יִהְיֶ֥ה לָכֶֽם׃

a summarizing sentence referring to all the aspects represented by the offering. Of the פרים, the איל and the כבשים; of the סולת, the שמן and the יין, Scripture says: תמימם יהיו לכם — they all must be complete and must represent everything that is ours, with nothing left out. Only thus can they represent in an offering our true standing and our joy in them. For תמימות, unlimited and unconditional devotion to God, subordinating everything that we have to him, in the sense of ואהבת את ה׳ אלקיך בכל לבבך ובכל נפשך ובכל מאודך, the unity of our lives which stems from the unity of God — that is what comes to expression through the תמימות of the offerings (see Commentary, *Vayikra* 1:3), and this תמימות is the quintessence, the whole content of the Torah, which is תורת ה׳ תמימה משיבת נפש.

CHAPTER 29

1 **ובחדש השביעי**. Now comes the seventh month, which is similar in meaning to the seventh day of the week. The seventh day invites us to reflect upon ourselves and our world. On this day, we let go of our world and our power to control it and lay them at the feet of our Creator and Master, and thereby we attain vital energy in joy, earnestness, and recognition of duty. Similarly, the seventh month invites us to reflect upon ourselves and upon our lives retrospectively. In this month, we examine what has come to fruition in us through freedom, the Torah, and the blessing of material means; through the Sabbaths, the New Moons, the festivals, and the holy things of Israel. What is performed throughout the year symbolically in the offering procedures in the Sanctuary is now to be realized in life, in actual reality, in the life of every individual. In this month we return to closeness to God, we experience rebirth through atonement, and thereby we merit to serve God in joy.

At once באחד לחדש, on this profoundly significant New Moon, we

2 *And you shall make as an ascent offering to God, as an expression of compliance, one young bull, one ram, seven yearling sheep that are whole.*

ב וַעֲשִׂיתֶ֨ם עֹלָ֜ה לְרֵ֣יחַ נִיחֹ֗חַ לַֽיהוָ֔ה פַּ֧ר בֶּן־בָּקָ֛ר אֶחָ֥ד אַ֣יִל אֶחָ֑ד כְּבָשִׂ֧ים בְּנֵי־שָׁנָ֛ה שִׁבְעָ֖ה תְּמִימִֽם׃

3 *And their homage offering: fine flour mixed with oil, three tenths for the bull, two tenths for the ram;*

ג וּמִ֨נְחָתָ֔ם סֹ֖לֶת בְּלוּלָ֣ה בַשָּׁ֑מֶן שְׁלֹשָׁ֤ה עֶשְׂרֹנִים֙ לַפָּ֔ר שְׁנֵ֥י עֶשְׂרֹנִ֖ים לָאָֽיִל׃

4 *And one tenth for each sheep, for [all] the seven sheep.*

ד וְעִשָּׂר֣וֹן אֶחָ֔ד לַכֶּ֖בֶשׂ הָאֶחָ֑ד לְשִׁבְעַ֖ת הַכְּבָשִֽׂים׃

cease from all creative work of earthly service, and we are called to God's service in the Sanctuary.

But the call to repentance does not go forth from the Sanctuary. Rather, the alarming sound of the shofar calls us to return to our Master, and this sound is heard in every Jewish home and penetrates every Jewish heart.

2 **ועשיתם** — not והקרבתם. Do not yet approach God, do not yet dare to draw near to God, with the ideal expression of your calling, especially not with שני פרים, for שני פרים represent the fulfillment of this calling by every individual who serves God. Rather, all you can do is ועשיתם: through an objective act, give expression to the ideal of your calling, as set before you by the Sanctuary of the Torah. Now you shall bring only פר בן בקר אחד, representing the nation in its totality as an active worker in God's service. Only as part of this calling of the nation as a whole shall the individual, too, find his way, and shall the sound of the shofar call also the individual to return to God's service. Therefore —

4 **ועשרון אחד** — with special emphasis that it is *one* עשרון. This עשרון refers to the nation in its *totality*. Seven times the nation approaches God as a כבש following God's guidance, and each time it also brings one עשרון, thereby signifying that the material survival of the community — like the personal guidance of the community — reveals the finger of God in

5 *One buck of the goat species as an offering that clears of sin, to effect atonement for you.*	ה וּשְׂעִיר־עִזִּים אֶחָד חַטָּאת לְכַפֵּר עֲלֵיכֶם׃
6 *[These are] apart from the New Moon ascent offering and its homage offering, the continual ascent offering and its homage offering, and their libations according to their regulation, as an expression of compliance, a fire offering to* God.	ו מִלְּבַד עֹלַת הַחֹדֶשׁ וּמִנְחָתָהּ וְעֹלַת הַתָּמִיד וּמִנְחָתָהּ וְנִסְכֵּיהֶם כְּמִשְׁפָּטָם לְרֵיחַ נִיחֹחַ אִשֶּׁה לַיהוָה׃ ס

Jewish history. The material fate of the *individual* within the community is decided only by the day of תרועה and the day of כיפורים, and only on the festival of Sukkos does each individual build his hut on the earth given to him anew. Only then does he attain the gifts of the land, so as to lead a life of joy and of awareness of God.

5 **ושעיר וגו׳ לכפר עליכם**. However inadequate the nation as a whole stands at present in relation to the ideal expression of its mission, God's Sanctuary brings the nation atonement, thus securing the nation's survival and opening for it a gate to a new future. Within this framework the individual, too, should strive to atone for his past and to attain his own rebirth.

6 **מלבד עלת החדש**. The serious character of the day of תרועה comes to expression in the מועד offering of ראש השנה [see Commentary v. 2]. This offering is based on the idea of the offerings brought before it: the מוסף of ראש חדש, which is itself preceded by the תמיד offering (see the rule: כל התדיר מחבירו וכו׳ — Commentary above, 28:23). In all three offerings, the appropriate נסכים must not be lacking. For on this day the thoughts that lead joyfully to God spring from three sources: from the light of morning, which proclaims God's glory; from the new moon, which calls for renewal; and from the sound of תרועה, which stirs us to repentance. All three come to an expression of devotion, homage, and joy through עולה,

7 *And on the tenth [day] of that seventh month there shall be for you a convocation to the Sanctuary, and you shall let your souls starve; you must do no manner of work.*

ז וּבֶעָשׂוֹר לַחֹדֶשׁ הַשְּׁבִיעִי הַזֶּה מִקְרָא־קֹדֶשׁ יִהְיֶה לָכֶם וְעִנִּיתֶם אֶת־נַפְשֹׁתֵיכֶם כָּל־מְלָאכָה לֹא תַעֲשׂוּ׃

8 *And you shall bring to* God *as an ascent offering, to express compliance, one young bull, one ram, seven yearling sheep; in their completeness shall they be to you.*

ח וְהִקְרַבְתֶּם עֹלָה לַיהוָה רֵיחַ נִיחֹחַ פַּר בֶּן־בָּקָר אֶחָד אַיִל אֶחָד כְּבָשִׂים בְּנֵי־שָׁנָה שִׁבְעָה תְּמִימִם יִהְיוּ לָכֶם׃

9 *And their homage offering: fine flour mixed with oil, three tenths for the bull, two tenths for the one ram.*

ט וּמִנְחָתָם סֹלֶת בְּלוּלָה בַשָּׁמֶן שְׁלֹשָׁה עֶשְׂרֹנִים לַפָּר שְׁנֵי עֶשְׂרֹנִים לָאַיִל הָאֶחָד׃

10 *One tenth for each sheep, for [all] the seven sheep.*

י עִשָּׂרוֹן עִשָּׂרוֹן לַכֶּבֶשׂ הָאֶחָד לְשִׁבְעַת הַכְּבָשִׂים׃

11 *One buck of the goat species as an offering that clears of sin, apart from the sin offering of the atonements, the continual ascent offering and its homage offering, and their libations.*

יא שְׂעִיר־עִזִּים אֶחָד חַטָּאת מִלְּבַד חַטַּאת הַכִּפֻּרִים וְעֹלַת הַתָּמִיד וּמִנְחָתָהּ וְנִסְכֵּיהֶם׃ ס שביעי

מנחה, and נסכים; and ראש חדש and ראש השנה come to a special expression of atonement through חטאת (see תוספות *Rosh Hashanah* 8b ד"ה שהחדש).

Just as all three lead to God, so do all three unite in the sanctification of life to which they give expression. All these offerings represent doing God's Will by devoting oneself to the power of the fire of His Torah: לריח ניחח אשה לה'.

7-11 **ובעשור וגו'**. After these days of reflection and returning to God, the tenth of this month arrives. On this day, the miraculous power of Divine atonement was revealed, atonement that can wipe out any past, so that the person rises to a new future. This power was revealed after the incident of the golden calf, when Israel attained atonement for this sin, and the day of atonement for the sin of the עגל was sanctified for all time as a מועד ה׳, a day on which we meet again with God. The day of תרועה is merely an introduction and preparation for this Day of Atonement.

On this day, the momentous and unique עבודה is performed in the Sanctuary. Thanks to this עבודה, the connection is renewed with the Tablets of the Covenant, which were given anew after the atonement for the sin of the עגל. These Tablets of the Covenant of the Torah now rest under the wings of the cherubim beside the broken tablets, and from them begins the procedure of atonement that rebuilds all of Jewish life (*Vayikra* 16).

At this time, you are called to God, and you should hope to be reborn by His grace. For were it not for the gracious gift of the miraculous Divine power [of atonement], you would have already forfeited your whole future; your whole "existence" and "creativity" would have been "annihilated." This fact shall be given expression by עינוי and שביתה מכל מלאכה, by refraining from all eating, which sustains existence, and by ceasing from all work, which shapes the future.

והקרבתם. You should be confident about the promised future which will be granted to you anew, and thus with joy and confidence you shall approach God with the expression of your ideal calling. The ascent offering represents the vow that you will work faithfully in the fields of His human harvest (פר). You shall stride before the flock of nations as a model (איל). With everlasting freshness of youth you shall follow God's guidance, which reveals itself in your fate (כבשים בני שנה שבעה).

In all these respects you shall be תמימים and devote your whole being to these tasks. All the goods and enjoyments that can further these aims you shall take from God only for this purpose, and with שעיר-like firmness you shall remain on the heights of your calling.

מלבד וגו׳. The מועד offerings of יום הכיפורים are offered after עבודות היום and after the תמיד offering, as already explained in our Commentary on *Vayikra* 16:23.

12 *And on the fifteenth day of the seventh month there shall be for you a convocation to the Sanctuary; you must not do any service work, and you shall celebrate a festival to* God *for seven days.*

יב וּבַחֲמִשָּׁה עָשָׂר יוֹם לַחֹדֶשׁ
הַשְּׁבִיעִי מִקְרָא־קֹדֶשׁ יִהְיֶה לָכֶם
כָּל־מְלֶאכֶת עֲבֹדָה לֹא תַעֲשׂוּ
וְחַגֹּתֶם חַג לַיהוָה שִׁבְעַת יָמִים׃

13 *And you shall bring near an ascent offering, a fire offering, to express compliance, to* God: *thirteen young bulls, two rams, fourteen yearling sheep; they shall be complete.*

יג וְהִקְרַבְתֶּם עֹלָה אִשֵּׁה רֵיחַ נִיחֹחַ
לַיהוָה פָּרִים בְּנֵי־בָקָר שְׁלֹשָׁה
עָשָׂר אֵילִם שְׁנָיִם כְּבָשִׂים בְּנֵי־
שָׁנָה אַרְבָּעָה עָשָׂר תְּמִימִם יִהְיוּ׃

12 **ובחמשה עשר וגו׳**. Finally, the fifteenth of the seventh month arrives. On this day, all of Jewish life, which was planted on the fifteenth of the first month, blossoms and bears fruit. This day was preceded by the repentance of the day of תרועה, and on the day of כיפורים Israel was reborn through fasting and cessation from work. Now they remember their journey in the wilderness, when they were protected by God's cloud and nourished by manna. This memory becomes a מועד of joy in the building of a *sukkah* and in the enjoyment of God's blessing, and the people cease from all creative work of earthly service and are called to God's Sanctuary. Full of joy in God, they form "a circle around God and His Sanctuary" (וחגתם חג) as the people of God's Torah. They celebrate seven days before God and rejoice in their Jewish national existence.

13 **והקרבתם וגו׳**. On the festival of Sukkos, there is extraordinary joy, and the מועד offering of this festival includes an ascent offering of *thirteen* פרים, *two* אילים, and *fourteen* כבשים בני שנה. The number of אילים and כבשים offered each day does not change during the seven days of the festival, whereas the number of פרים diminishes by one each day. Thus, on the seventh day the group of offerings includes seven פרים, two אילים, and fourteen כבשים.

The *two* אילים and *fourteen* כבשים indicate, at first glance, that this מועד offering is a *double* offering. It follows, then, that also the *thirteen* פרים

of the first day divide into two groups of *seven* and *six* פרים. On this festival, Israel approaches God with a double ascent offering: with a group of offerings that includes *seven* פרים, one איל, and seven כבשים, and with a group of offerings that includes *six* פרים, one איל, and seven כבשים.

Accordingly, two communities are represented here, communities that are similar in the roles of "כבש" and "איל" but dissimilar in the role of "פר." The historical course of both communities relates to the one "Shepherd" of man (כבש), and both are blessed with immense power and strength, and they stride at the head of the flock (איל), but they differ in their creativity and activity (פר).

The members of the first group have entered into a covenant with God (seven) not only in their historical course (כבשים), but also in their creativity and activity (פרים). Not only does their history reveal the one God Who guides the events of the times, but also their creativity and activity constitute a revelation of God, for they subordinate their deeds to God's laws, and all that they do attests to His Will.

By contrast, the members of the second group are close to God in their fate alone; their history, their weal or woe, is a revelation of God, but their deeds do not attest to God. *Passively they belong to God, but not actively; they are "seven"* כבשים, *but as* פרים *they are only "six."* In their life of action they behave in accordance with the nature of creation, and they are subservient only to themselves; as creatures of creation they are controlled by their desires, and they follow their urges and inclinations, their opinions and whims. They do not shape their actions according to the dictates of the Will of their Creator and Master. Their life of action does not bear the signature of "seven." Their history is Divine, but their deeds are not Divine. They are שבעה כבשים — but only six פרים.

Clearly, what is depicted here is the difference between Israel and the nations. This contrast is not rooted in belief in or denial of God as the Director of man's fate; rather, it is rooted in belief in or denial of God as the Director of man's actions. The group that includes **שבעה** פרים, איל אחד, and שבעת כבשים represents Israel; the group that includes **ששה** פרים, איל אחד, and שבעת כבשים represents the rest of mankind.

On the festival of Sukkos, when Israel builds its *sukkah* "under the protection and blessing of God," a building that is the ultimate goal of the entire historical process of the nations — on this festival Israel approaches God with thirteen פרים, two אילים, and fourteen כבשים. Thus, it does not draw near to God just in its own name; rather, it gives expression to the totality of all the peoples as "Israel and the nations," and approaches God in the name of all mankind. At the same time, however, Israel marks *the contrast between action that serves God and action that does not serve Him*, and to this very day this contrast divides mankind into two camps.

But *this contrast diminishes more and more.* Under the influence of Israel's mission and under the influence of the example that Israel quietly sets among the nations, this contrast becomes smaller and smaller. At first, it is six to seven; on the second day, it is only five to seven; then it is four to seven, and so on. The seventh day is the goal of the development of mankind and of Israel's mission for it, and on this day the contrast will cease to exist. Israel and all of mankind will be united in their acknowledgement of God and in the life-service of deeds. They will stand before God as פרים שבעה, אילים שנים, כבשים בני שנה ארבעה עשר.

However, as regards the historical guidance and their role in fulfilling the mission of mankind, the special standing of Israel amidst the nations will not be discontinued. For Israel and the nations differ in their historical development and in their ability to realize the purposes of mankind; hence Israel and the nations, the nations and Israel, will continue to be separate and distinct, even though they will be equal in their value. Both will be close to God in His direction of their history, and both will lead the world for the achievement of mankind's purposes, but they will continue to be seven *and another* seven כבשים, one and another איל.

Nonetheless, they will be identical in rendering homage to God by fulfilling the commandments given to each respectively: the Sinaitic Teaching given to Israel, and the general Teaching given to mankind. *In rendering homage to God by doing His Will, Israel and mankind will become one.* The active life of all people will bear the stamp of faithfulness to moral duty, just like the active life of Israel; as פרים they will form only one set of "seven": וְהָיָה ה׳ לְמֶלֶךְ עַל־כָּל־הָאָרֶץ בַּיּוֹם הַהוּא יִהְיֶה ה׳ אֶחָד וּשְׁמוֹ אֶחָד (*Zecharyah* 14:9).

So, too, the saying of our Sages in *Sukkah* 55b — הני שבעים פרים כנגד מי כנגד שבעים אומות — regards the מוסף offerings of Sukkos as an offering-expression for all of mankind, and our Sages say there that Israel's offering represents a plea for the atonement of all mankind. If our interpretation is not mistaken, this plea is supported by the fact that, in the course of time, the contrast between Israel and the nations is disappearing, and that mankind is destined to return to God in its active life. On the merit of this future and for the sake of this future, may God preserve the nations!

The מועד offerings of the festival of Sukkos represent truths that were later stated by the prophets. For the prophets describe the historical goal of the nations' whole development and Israel's relationship to this goal, and for this reason the Prophet (*Zecharyah* 14:16) connects precisely the festival of Sukkos to the future goal of the nations. He describes the efforts of the nations employing their power to fight against their connections to God. Ultimately, they will pay homage to God in Yerushalayim, and all of mankind will celebrate the festival of Sukkos each year [וְהָיָה כָּל־הַנּוֹתָר מִכָּל־הַגּוֹיִם הַבָּאִים עַל־יְרוּשָׁלָם וְעָלוּ מִדֵּי שָׁנָה בְשָׁנָה לְהִשְׁתַּחֲוֹת לְמֶלֶךְ ה׳ צְבָאוֹת וְלָחֹג אֶת־חַג הַסֻּכּוֹת].

Moreover, we would venture to express the following idea: Yechezkel (*Yechezkel* 38, 39) describes the final wars that the nations will wage against God and against His workings, and the leader who wages these wars is called "גוג." It is not implausible to suggest that גוג stems from the root גגג and therefore denotes the formation of a roof. גוג, then, is the opposite of the *sukkah*, for the *sukkah* is unstable, weak roofing which is not installed by a craftsman. Indeed, the whole content of the world history of man is capsulized by this contrast. *One* erroneous notion leads mankind astray. Just as people have the power to put up "דפנות," strongly built artificial walls, to enclose their own sphere and safeguard it against their fellow earthly creatures, so they imagine that they should secure themselves against Heaven, against God and the effects of His power to direct matters. They think that they should take their fate into their own hands and protect themselves by their own power, and thus crown the building of human greatness with a gabled roof, rendering them independent of God. This is the struggle of the "גג" against the "סוכה." In the "roof-delusion" of human greatness, man will find no rest, whereas the truth of the *sukkah* teaches man to cheerfully rely on God's protection. World history begins with the building of the Tower and ends with the building of the *sukkah*. The builders of the Tower worshipped human power and sought to conquer heaven; the builders of the *sukkah* will render homage to God and rejoice in their lives on earth (cf. Commentary above, 11:29).

Other religions teach man how to merit the next world by renouncing this world. Judaism teaches man to perform his duty in his lifetime, so that he may attain bliss already in this world, and so that the life of the

14 *And their homage offering: fine flour mixed with oil, three tenths for each bull of the thirteen bulls, two tenths for each ram of the two rams;*

יד וּמִנְחָתָם סֹלֶת בְּלוּלָה בַשָּׁמֶן
שְׁלֹשָׁה עֶשְׂרֹנִים לַפָּר הָאֶחָד
לִשְׁלֹשָׁה עָשָׂר פָּרִים שְׁנֵי עֶשְׂרֹנִים
לָאַיִל הָאֶחָד לִשְׁנֵי הָאֵילִם׃

15 *And one tenth for each sheep of the fourteen sheep.*

טו וְעִשָּׂרוֹן עִשָּׂרוֹן לַכֶּבֶשׂ הָאֶחָד
לְאַרְבָּעָה עָשָׂר כְּבָשִׂים׃
נקוד על ו'

16 *And one buck of the goat species as an offering that clears of sin; apart from the continual ascent offering, its homage offering and its libation.*

טז וּשְׂעִיר־עִזִּים אֶחָד חַטָּאת מִלְּבַד
עֹלַת הַתָּמִיד מִנְחָתָהּ וְנִסְכָּהּ׃ ס

world to come should begin even during his life on earth. This is the teaching that emanates from the festival of Sukkos to Israel of every generation, and the מועד offerings of this festival make this teaching the universal hope for the future of all nations. From the pinnacle of its national joy, the people of God look to the future happiness of all mankind. Our Sages (*Yerushalmi, Sukkah* 5:1) say that at the peak of the joy of the festival of Sukkos, which embraces the hopes of Israel and all mankind, flowed the "wellsprings of salvation," from which the young disciples of prophecy drew the holy spirit (see Commentary, v. 19).

On the universal meaning of the festival of Sukkos and on the related concept of סוכתו של לויתן, cf. *Collected Writings,* vol. II, p.112.

תמימם יהיו. Everywhere else, תמימם is simply an attribute of the offering animals: פרים וגו' תמימם; and where the obligation of תמימות is stressed as a separate mitzvah, it says תמימם יהיו לכם. In our verse, the word "לכם" is missing — apparently because of the universal character of these offerings. There are not just לכם, they do not represent our national personality; rather, they represent Israel and all the nations.

17 *And on the second day: twelve young bulls, two rams, fourteen yearling sheep that are whole.*

יז וּבַיּוֹם הַשֵּׁנִי פָּרִים בְּנֵי־בָקָר שְׁנֵים
עָשָׂר אֵילִם שְׁנָיִם כְּבָשִׂים בְּנֵי־
שָׁנָה אַרְבָּעָה עָשָׂר תְּמִימִם׃

18 *And their homage offering and their libations for the bulls, for the rams and for the sheep according to their number as prescribed.*

יח וּמִנְחָתָם וְנִסְכֵּיהֶם לַפָּרִים לָאֵילִם
וְלַכְּבָשִׂים בְּמִסְפָּרָם כַּמִּשְׁפָּט׃

19 *And one buck of the goat species as an offering that clears of sin, apart from the continual ascent offering and its homage offering and their libations.*

יט וּשְׂעִיר־עִזִּים אֶחָד חַטָּאת מִלְּבַד
עֹלַת הַתָּמִיד וּמִנְחָתָהּ
וְנִסְכֵּיהֶם׃ ס

19 **ונסכיהם**. In *Sukkah* 44a, a הלכה למשה מסיני is transmitted: On the seven days of the festival of Sukkos, a libation of water was poured simultaneously with the libation of wine of the morning תמיד (see *Yoma* 26b; *Sukkah* 48b). In *Ta'anis* 2b, our Sages say that ניסוך המים is alluded to in Scripture in the terms נסכיה**ם**, נסכי**ה**, and כמשפט**ם** of the second, sixth, and seventh days, as the extra letters spell מים.

Let us consider the term ונסכיהם of our verse and seek the objects referred to by the plural suffix "הם." It is impossible to interpret that this suffix refers to the פרים אילים וכבשים, as it is interpreted in verse 31 of the preceding chapter and in verse 11 of this chapter, for here the נסכים of the פרים אילים וכבשים have already been expressly mentioned in verse 18: ומנחתם ונסכיהם. It must be that the suffix of ונסכיהם refers to the immediately preceding עלת התמיד ומנחתה. It appears, then, that Scripture ascribes a נסך to the עולה and a נסך to the מנחה.

The נסך of the עולה we know quite well. It is the libation of wine, which the personality represented by the עולה pours down to the base of the altar of the Torah, thus signifying that "every drop of his joy" comes from God and is dedicated to God. But *wine* is to the עולה as *water* is to the מנחה. For the *wine* relates to the עולה-personality, to the *person*, whereas the *water* relates to the means of subsistence and prosperity represented by the מנחה. The *flour* and the *oil* of the מנחה are products of the soil, whose growth depends on the blessing of rain.

Elsewhere we have already noted the parallel between the joyful blossoming in the human heart and the growth and blossoming of plants. This parallel is indicated by the relation of שמח and שוש to צמח and צוץ (see Commentary, *Bereshis* 2:5, et al.).

יין is משמח לבב אנוש, and מים is מצמיח צמחים; and if the נסך of the עולה is wine, *then the* נסך *ascribed here to the* מנחה *is none other than water.* On the festival of *sukkah* building and of joy in the blessing of our possessions, ניסוך המים is joined to ניסוך היין, signifying that not only "every drop of our wine" but also "every drop of our water" is God's. Not only the emotion of the joy of our hearts, but also the gifts of heaven, on which our earthly existence and prosperity depend, come from God and belong to God; the gifts of heaven, too, are dedicated to life lived according to God's Torah and their foundation is at the base of the altar of the Sanctuary of His Torah.

ניסוך המים, unique to the festival of Sukkos, is first alluded to on the *second* day. On this day, it becomes apparent for the *first* time that the nations' opposition to the will of God's Torah is gradually disappearing, and thus the door is opened for mankind's complete return to God.

It is only in anticipation of a humanity that will ultimately purify itself to reach the heights of its calling, that God causes every drop of rain to fall. Just as the very first rainfall waited for the creation of man — כי לא המטיר ה׳ אלקים על הארץ ואדם אין וגו׳ (*Bereshis* 2:5; see Commentary there) — so it was in later periods. When mankind strayed and placed itself in opposition to God, every raindrop fell from heaven only in anticipation of humanity of the future. The raindrops fall because every day of every contemporary time indicates gradual progress — even if only minor — toward that future.

The historical process of mankind is analogous to פרי החג: mankind's opposition to its exalted Divine calling is gradually disappearing, and thus mankind's moral progress becomes apparent. At the beginning of the period of this gradually disappearing opposition, ניסוך המים is connected more with the מנחה than with the עולה; it is connected with the עולה only indirectly, since the מנחה is the עולה's accompaniment. The rain falls by the זכות of the grain, which awaits man of the future, more than it falls by the זכות of man of the present, for "אדם" — who is worthy of the blessing of rain — is not yet there, as it says: ואדם אין. The נסך of the

20 *And on the third day: eleven bulls,* כ וּבַיּ֧וֹם הַשְּׁלִישִׁ֛י פָּרִ֥ים עַשְׁתֵּי־

מנחה is beside the נסך of the עולה, and of both it says: עלת התמיד ומנחתה ונסכיהם.

However, the more the contrast between mankind and its Divine calling disappears, the more pronounced becomes the worthiness of the human personality, and then the rain falls on the fields by the merit of man of the present. On the *sixth* day, the eve of the attainment of the goal, the two נסכים are no longer נסכיהם — distinct in their relationships — but נסכיה (v. 31): נסכים of man elevating himself toward God through the תמיד offering.

On the *seventh* day, these two נסכים — the נסך of man's flourishing and the נסך of the earth's flourishing — combine, and they are related to their uniform original source: משפטם (v. 33). All the נסכים together form just one נסך (״ונסכהם״ חסר), and ניסוך המים, too, is conceptually included in the group of מועד offerings, for the whole contrast has disappeared. Jewish humanity stands before God together with general humanity, both united in a bond of actions and represented by פרים שבעה אילם שנים כבשים בני שנה ארבעה עשר תמימם. "Man" who was lost is found again. The earth does not bear *him*; rather, *he*, as אדם, bears the אדמה, and God grants him the blessing of the earth, because he is His servant on earth. It will no longer be said, ואדם אין לעבד את האדמה; rather, ה׳ אלקים blesses אדם, who yearns for His grace and serves Him with joy; God grants him the rain of His blessing and the bliss of His joy.

Regarding the seven days of the festival of Sukkos, God says: ושמחתם לפני ה׳ אלקיכם שבעת ימים (*Vayikra* 23:40), and the nation — gathered into a festive circle (חג) about God and His Sanctuary — rejoices with great fervor in the עזרות of the Sanctuary. But the center point of all this rejoicing is the drawing of water for ניסוך המים, on account of which it is called שמחת בית השואבה.

It is characteristic that this Jewish rejoicing with its intense enthusiasm should be connected precisely with ניסוך המים. A person is not brought into a state of joy if he remembers only the kindness God showed him on special occasions. Rather, only the recognition that every drop of water that sustains our lives is a messenger of God's kindness capable of sending us into a rapture of God's nearness — only this recognition fills every breath of our lives with bliss.

עָשָׂ֖ר אֵילִ֣ם שְׁנָ֑יִם כְּבָשִׂ֧ים בְּנֵי־שָׁנָ֛ה אַרְבָּעָ֥ה עָשָׂ֖ר תְּמִימִֽם׃

two rams, fourteen yearling sheep that are whole.

כא וּמִנְחָתָ֣ם וְנִסְכֵּיהֶ֡ם לַפָּ֠רִים לָאֵילִ֧ם וְלַכְּבָשִׂ֛ים בְּמִסְפָּרָ֖ם כַּמִּשְׁפָּֽט׃

21 *And their homage offering and their libations for the bulls, for the rams and for the sheep according to their number as prescribed.*

כב וּשְׂעִ֥יר חַטָּ֖את אֶחָ֑ד מִלְּבַד֙ עֹלַ֣ת הַתָּמִ֔יד וּמִנְחָתָ֖הּ וְנִסְכָּֽהּ׃ ס

22 *And one buck to clear of sin, apart from the continual ascent offering and its homage offering and its libation.*

כג וּבַיּ֧וֹם הָרְבִיעִ֛י פָּרִ֥ים עֲשָׂרָ֖ה אֵילִ֣ם שְׁנָ֑יִם כְּבָשִׂ֧ים בְּנֵי־שָׁנָ֛ה אַרְבָּעָ֥ה עָשָׂ֖ר תְּמִימִֽם׃

23 *And on the fourth day: ten bulls, two rams, fourteen yearling sheep that are whole.*

כד מִנְחָתָ֣ם וְנִסְכֵּיהֶ֡ם לַפָּ֠רִים לָאֵילִ֧ם וְלַכְּבָשִׂ֛ים בְּמִסְפָּרָ֖ם כַּמִּשְׁפָּֽט׃

24 *Their homage offering and their libations for the bulls, for the rams and for the sheep according to their number as prescribed.*

כה וּשְׂעִיר־עִזִּ֥ים אֶחָ֖ד חַטָּ֑את מִלְּבַד֙ עֹלַ֣ת הַתָּמִ֔יד מִנְחָתָ֖הּ וְנִסְכָּֽהּ׃ ס

25 *And one buck of the goat species as an offering that clears of sin, apart from the continual ascent offering, its homage offering and its libation.*

כו וּבַיּ֧וֹם הַחֲמִישִׁ֛י פָּרִ֥ים תִּשְׁעָ֖ה אֵילִ֣ם שְׁנָ֑יִם כְּבָשִׂ֧ים בְּנֵי־שָׁנָ֛ה אַרְבָּעָ֥ה עָשָׂ֖ר תְּמִימִֽם׃

26 *And on the fifth day: nine bulls, two rams, fourteen yearling sheep that are whole.*

כז וּמִנְחָתָ֣ם וְנִסְכֵּיהֶ֡ם לַפָּ֠רִים לָאֵילִ֧ם וְלַכְּבָשִׂ֛ים בְּמִסְפָּרָ֖ם כַּמִּשְׁפָּֽט׃

27 *And their homage offering and their libations for the bulls, for the rams and for the sheep according to their number as prescribed.*

28 *And one buck to clear of sin, apart from the continual ascent offering, its homage offering and its libation.*

כח וּשְׂעִיר חַטָּאת אֶחָד מִלְּבַד עֹלַת
הַתָּמִיד וּמִנְחָתָהּ וְנִסְכָּהּ׃ ס

29 *And on the sixth day: eight bulls, two rams, fourteen yearling sheep that are whole.*

כט וּבַיּוֹם הַשִּׁשִּׁי פָּרִים שְׁמֹנָה אֵילִם
שְׁנָיִם כְּבָשִׂים בְּנֵי־שָׁנָה אַרְבָּעָה
עָשָׂר תְּמִימִם׃

30 *And their homage offering and their libations for the bulls, for the rams and for the sheep according to their number as prescribed.*

ל וּמִנְחָתָם וְנִסְכֵּיהֶם לַפָּרִים לָאֵילִם
וְלַכְּבָשִׂים בְּמִסְפָּרָם כַּמִּשְׁפָּט׃

31 *And one buck to clear of sin, apart from the continual ascent offering, its homage offering and its libations.*

לא וּשְׂעִיר חַטָּאת אֶחָד מִלְּבַד עֹלַת
הַתָּמִיד מִנְחָתָהּ וּנְסָכֶיהָ׃ ס

32 *And on the seventh day: seven bulls, two rams, fourteen yearling sheep that are whole.*

לב וּבַיּוֹם הַשְּׁבִיעִי פָּרִים שִׁבְעָה
אֵילִם שְׁנָיִם כְּבָשִׂים בְּנֵי־שָׁנָה
אַרְבָּעָה עָשָׂר תְּמִימִם׃

33 *And their homage offering and their libations for the bulls, for the rams and for the sheep according to their numbers as prescribed regarding them.*

לג וּמִנְחָתָם וְנִסְכֵּהֶם לַפָּרִים לָאֵילִם
וְלַכְּבָשִׂים בְּמִסְפָּרָם כְּמִשְׁפָּטָם׃
חסר י׳

34 *And one buck to clear of sin, apart from the continual ascent offering, its homage offering and its libation.*

לד וּשְׂעִיר חַטָּאת אֶחָד מִלְּבַד עֹלַת
הַתָּמִיד מִנְחָתָהּ וְנִסְכָּהּ׃ ס מפטיר

35 *On the eighth day there shall be for you a festival of abiding; you must not do any service work.*

לה בַּיּוֹם֙ הַשְּׁמִינִ֔י עֲצֶ֖רֶת תִּהְיֶ֣ה לָכֶ֑ם כָּל־מְלֶ֥אכֶת עֲבֹדָ֖ה לֹ֥א תַעֲשֽׂוּ׃

36 *And you shall bring near an ascent offering, a fire offering to express compliance, to* God*: one bull, one ram, seven yearling sheep that are whole.*

לו וְהִקְרַבְתֶּ֨ם עֹלָ֜ה אִשֵּׁ֨ה רֵ֤יחַ נִיחֹ֨חַ֙ לַֽיהוָ֔ה פַּ֥ר אֶחָ֖ד אַ֣יִל אֶחָ֑ד כְּבָשִׂ֧ים בְּנֵי־שָׁנָ֛ה שִׁבְעָ֖ה תְּמִימִֽם׃

37 *Their homage offering and their libations for the bull, for the ram and for the sheep according to their number as prescribed.*

לז מִנְחָתָ֣ם וְנִסְכֵּיהֶ֗ם לַ֠פָּר לָאַ֧יִל וְלַכְּבָשִׂ֛ים בְּמִסְפָּרָ֖ם כַּמִּשְׁפָּֽט׃

38 *And one buck that clears of sin, apart from the continual ascent offering and its homage offering and its libation.*

לח וּשְׂעִ֥יר חַטָּ֖את אֶחָ֑ד מִלְּבַד֙ עֹלַ֣ת הַתָּמִ֔יד וּמִנְחָתָ֖הּ וְנִסְכָּֽהּ׃

35-38 **ביום השמיני** — not וביום, as it says in the cases of all the preceding days, for the eighth day is a festival in its own right, רגל בפני עצמו (*Sukkah* 47a; see Commentary, *Vayikra* 23:36).

On the eighth day, the sounds of the public rejoicing of the Sukkos festival cease. No longer do we contemplate in a state of rapture the distant future of all mankind's salvation. Rather, we quietly assemble before God before we return to the reality of the still unrefined, imperfect present. Only then can we return to the service of God of everyday life, for our consciousness has been enriched and elevated by the whole cycle of the festivals, and the spirit that inspired us when we were before God will not depart from us in all the trials that we are likely to face.

On this eighth day, we renew, at the parting greeting in God's Sanctuary, the consciousness that all of us together belong to God and are bound in our destinies and endeavors to His Torah. As one community we shall work in the fields of the future of humanity; as one community we shall be guides leading the flock of nations; and God's guidance will be revealed through our destiny, for we are His covenantal people.

Thus [on this eighth day] we stand before God as פר אחד, איל אחד, and שבעת כבשים, with everlasting freshness of youth and with integrity: בני שנה תמימם; and all the means of subsistence and prosperity and all joy in life come to us and are dedicated for us only on the altar of God's Torah: מנחתם ונסכיהם. We will stubbornly resist all temptations so as to remain on the heights of our calling: ושעיר חטאת אחד.

If we consider once again the normal group of offerings that represents the eternal idea of the people of Israel at the uplifting times of the מועדים — שני פרים איל אחד שבעת כבשים and שעיר חטאת — we surprisingly discover that these are the same elements in which the foreign seer saw Israel at the height of their historical position in the world (above, chaps. 23-25).

From the Heights of Baal, the following questions were posed to him: What is this people's position from the standpoint of its material fate? How do the powers of nature, which determine the fate of every other people, relate to this people? The answer that was given was this: This unique people is not subject to the powers of nature; a different Power reveals Itself in this people's fate. In its historical course it is seven כבשים: it is the covenantal partner of the unique, invisible One.

From the "Field of Seers," this people was seen in its spiritual greatness, paying homage to God through faithfulness to duty in its social life. For this reason it is God's people among the nations. As God's people, it strides like an איל at the head of God's flock.

From the Peak of Pe'or, he looked down on the tents of Ya'akov and saw there family life sown with the spirit of God, borne and nurtured by God's spirit, blossoming like a garden of God. In the realization of this life, every father of a family is a dynamic worker in God's household, and the entire nation is in the category of "פרים" and appears as פרים שנים.

There is only one enemy that threatens this ideal of blessing and bliss, and this, too, was discovered by the seer, who then exploited it with fatal consequences. For Israel is threatened only by abandoning the lofty goal of moral purity. That is why, in spite of the vision revealed on במות בעל, at שדה צופים, and on ראש הפעור, the catastrophe of שיטים followed. Hence, it is not enough that Israel brings שבעה כבשים, איל אחד, and פרים שנים. Rather, to all these, Israel must also add שעיר חטאת אחד. This שעיר is to warn it of the single danger that threatens it, and whenever it focuses on its ideal greatness it should guard itself against the danger that lies in wait for it at the height of its calling.

39 *These you shall make to* God *at your times of appointed meeting, apart from your vows and your dedications, your ascent offerings and your homage offerings, your libations and your peace offerings.*

לט אֵלֶּה תַּעֲשׂוּ לַיהֹוָה בְּמוֹעֲדֵיכֶם
לְבַד מִנִּדְרֵיכֶם וְנִדְבֹתֵיכֶם
לְעֹלֹתֵיכֶם וּלְמִנְחֹתֵיכֶם וּלְנִסְכֵּיכֶם
וּלְשַׁלְמֵיכֶם׃

30 1 *Moshe explained to the Children of Israel all that* God *had commanded Moshe.*

ל א וַיֹּאמֶר מֹשֶׁה אֶל־בְּנֵי יִשְׂרָאֵל כְּכֹל
אֲשֶׁר־צִוָּה יְהֹוָה אֶת־מֹשֶׁה׃ פפפ

39 **אלה תעשו וגו׳**. The offerings mentioned in this chapter and in the preceding chapter are communal offerings, with which the nation as a whole approaches God on the מועדים, which summon the nation to meet with God. However, private offerings as well are offered on the מועדים. Not only עולות ראייה and שלמי חגיגה (see *Shemos* 23:15 and Commentary there), offerings that one is bound to bring on festivals, but also free-will offerings (see *Vayikra* 1:2ff.) and obligatory offerings of the individual, such as עולת יולדת and the like — all these are offered on the מועדים. עולות ראייה ושלמי חגיגה are offered even on יום טוב, whereas נדרים ונדבות are offered on חול המועד (see *Temurah* 14b, *Beitzah* 19a-b).

An individual who sanctifies his private life does not thereby reduce the national consciousness elevated by the spirit of the מועד. The reverse is true: The revitalization of the national relationship with God and His Sanctuary also benefits the life of the individual and his relationship with God. What is more, the rousing power of the מועדים reveals itself precisely in that they awaken the conscience of each individual to fulfill the duties he has neglected. If one neglects to fulfill an obligation and lets three רגלים pass without fulfilling it, he violates בל תאחר (see Commentary, *Vayikra* 23:38).

CHAPTER 30

1 **ויאמר משה**. The section on the מועדים offerings concludes the actual *mitzvos* of the Torah. What follows this section is only פרשת נדרים, but this פרשה deals with vows that a person accepts upon himself of his own

free will. It authorizes and limits a person's power to set for himself *mitzvos* not ordained by God, but established by man.

The principles set down in פרשת נדרים are also the basis for the תקנות and מנהגים of the communities, which serve to regulate and ensure the fulfillment of God's commandments according to the special circumstances of each place.

We therefore believe that the verse ויאמר משה אל בני ישראל ככל אשר צוה ה׳ את משה is a summarizing statement referring back to all of the Torah's commandments. If we are not mistaken, the wording of this verse is unique in Scripture. In various places the Torah reports that Moshe transmitted to the people a specific mitzvah he had received, but nowhere else is this worded as: ויאמר וגו׳ ככל וגו׳.

It is characteristic that it says here "ויאמר," which, as a rule, denotes the explanation of something already known, and it is especially characteristic that it says here "ככל," which indicates that the communication goes beyond the mere promulgation of the law in that it also includes the "how," the manner in which that law should be interpreted. Thus, this kind of expression [ככל אשר וגו׳] is used elsewhere in Scripture only for reporting *how* a law was observed in practice — e.g., ויעשו בני ישראל ככל אשר צוה ה׳ את משה כן עשו (above, 1:54, et al.). The expression denotes that the people did not just carry out a particular command in general, but carried it out in all its minute details, *in the manner* in which it was meant to be carried out.

This, then, is the literal meaning of our verse: Moshe explained to the Children of Israel the "how" of all that God had commanded Moshe. From this we learn, at the end of the whole Lawgiving until this point, that the people were not given only the verses of the Written Law, in which the *mitzvos* are formulated concisely; rather, Moshe explained to them each law with all the various aspects of its content.

As far as we know, there is only one other instance in Scripture where the expression "ככל" is used in connection with the communication of a mitzvah (*Devarim* 1:3; see Commentary there): ויהי וגו׳ דבר משה אל בני ישראל ככל אשר צוה ה׳ אתו אלהם. There, too, the expression refers to the whole giving of the *mitzvos* which Moshe reiterated (דבר) before his death, not merely in terse sentences but with the whole "how" of their content. They had already been transmitted to the people בדיבור and באמירה — in terse form and with detailed explanation. Now both modes of transmission were repeated.

2 *And Moshe spoke to the heads of the tribes of the Children of Israel, saying: This is the word that* God *has commanded:*	ב וַיְדַבֵּ֤ר מֹשֶׁה֙ אֶל־רָאשֵׁ֣י הַמַּטּ֔וֹת לִבְנֵ֥י יִשְׂרָאֵ֖ל לֵאמֹ֑ר זֶ֣ה הַדָּבָ֔ר אֲשֶׁ֖ר צִוָּ֥ה יְהוָֽה׃

מטות

2 **וידבר משה וגו'** Here, however, we have a new pronouncement. It introduces the *mitzvos* that a person accepts upon himself voluntarily, which are accordingly stated here as an appendix to the actual *mitzvos* of the Torah. For the Torah authorizes us to impose *mitzvos* upon ourselves, so that we should properly fulfill the *mitzvos* of the Torah. The Torah enables individuals, communities, and the entire nation to establish for themselves permanent norms for ensuring the faithful observance of the *mitzvos.*

For this reason this section is addressed particularly to the נשיאים, who, significantly, are called here ראשי המטות. As already noted in our Commentary on chapter 1, "מטה" conceives of the tribe as a "branch" of the larger whole, with each branch working, through its own unique characteristics, to carry out the mission shared in common by the entire nation. It was the task of ראשי המטות to attend to the customs arising from the individuality of each "branch," and to attend also to common activities, aspirations, and purposes. It was their responsibility to properly channel all of these to promote the fulfillment of the national mission in accordance with the unique characteristics of each "branch." The means for such activity, the prerequisite for the development of the nation as a whole and for communal life, is the binding force of vows and of regulations instituted by man — לא יחל דברו (v. 3) — which is what the laws that now follow deal with.

In addition, ראשי המטות are entrusted with היתר נדרים. They function as family counselors and spiritual advisors, coming *from among the people themselves.* It is for this reason, too, that the section on vows is addressed first to ראשי המטות.

זה הדבר אשר צוה ה'. This introductory formula is found primarily in connection with *mitzvos* applicable immediately, at that moment, as in the cases of the manna (*Shemos* 16:16 and 32), תרומת המשכן (ibid. 35:4), and

מילואים (*Vayikra* 8:5 and 9:6). So, too, the halachah that an heiress is not to marry out of her tribe (below, 36:6-8; see Commentary there) applied only in that generation, and this is derived from the introductory wording זה הדבר (see *Bava Basra* 120a). Only פרשת שחוטי חוץ (*Vayikra* 17:2; see Commentary there) is likewise introduced by זה הדבר, even though Scripture expressly states there (חקת עולם וגו'; v. 7) that it applies for all time.

Considering that a mitzvah that applies immediately, at that moment, requires the marshalling of all of one's mental energy and willpower, we can explain the use of this formula where it introduces a mitzvah for all time: The introductory formula stresses the significance and importance of that mitzvah.

פרשת נדרים, too, applies for all time, as we learn via a גזירה שוה from שחוטי חוץ (*Bava Basra* 120b). Accordingly, the use here of the introductory formula זה הדבר indicates the special importance of this פרשה.

From the גזירה שוה between פרשת נדרים and פרשת שחוטי חוץ we learn further (ibid.) that the address to ראשי המטות is directed also to אהרן ובניו וכל ישראל, who are mentioned in the case of שחוטי חוץ, and from this we derive that the absolution of vows can be effected by any three men, even if they are not מומחים, are not experts in the Law. According to the רמב"ם (הל' שבועות, 6:5), a יחיד מומחה, who can absolve vows, need not be a סמוך as in the case of other laws; rather, a חכם מובהק suffices, and the ר"ן (*Nedarim* 88b) explains that this is derived from the expression "ראשי המטות," for it does not say here "אלהים" as it says in other laws [where a סמוך is required].

All these *halachos* accord with our conception of פרשת נדרים: This פרשה deals with *mitzvos* that a person accepts upon himself voluntarily and with customs that he follows. Hence, it is different from the פרשיות that deal with the actual *mitzvos* and is secondary to them.

From the גזירה שוה between פרשת נדרים and פרשת שחוטי חוץ we learn further (ibid.) that the absolution of vows applies also to דברי הקדש: יש שאלה בהקדש. It appears that the analogy between these two פרשיות is based on a deep inner kinship. This inner relation is reflected already in the saying of our Sages: הנודר כאילו בנה במה והמקיימו כאילו מקריב עליו קרבן (*Nedarim* 22a). במה and נדר have a common denominator. They both sanction the subjective, arbitrary will, which stands outside and beside the Torah. שחוטי חוץ and במה give this subjectivity general sanction, and this is rejected by the Torah absolutely. The law of נדרים allows such subjectivity only limited and conditional room (see ר"ן there).

3 *If a man vows a vow to* God, *or swears an oath, to bind a bond for his will, he must not permit his word to remain unfulfilled; he shall do whatever has come forth from his mouth.*

ג אִישׁ כִּי־יִדֹּר נֶדֶר לַיהוָה אוֹ־
הִשָּׁבַע שְׁבֻעָה לֶאְסֹר אִסָּר עַל־
נַפְשׁוֹ לֹא יַחֵל דְּבָרוֹ כְּכָל־הַיֹּצֵא
מִפִּיו יַעֲשֶׂה׃

3 **איש כי ידר נדר לה׳ וגו׳** — see Commentary, *Bereshis* 28:20-21.

Except for the vow of נזירות, all the נדרים mentioned thus far have been נדרי הקדש: A person dedicates or vows to bring an object for an offering (קדשי מזבח) or for the Sanctuary (קדשי בדק הבית), using either the verbal formula of נדבה, "הרי זו," or the verbal formula of נדר, "הרי עלי" (see *Vayikra* 22:21 and Commentary, ibid. 7:16). In both these cases, the object affected by הקדש becomes prohibited to everyone for any profane use. If the verbal formula of נדבה is used, the object becomes prohibited immediately; if the verbal formula of נדר is used, the object becomes prohibited at the moment of the dedication.

Here Scripture treats the case where a person ידר נדר לה׳ לאסר אסר על נפשו: He expresses a vow that does not prohibit the object to everyone, but solely על נפשו, and in his vow he says that the object shall be prohibited to him as though it had been affected by a general נדר הקדש — i.e., the object shall be prohibited to him like a קרבן, like the מזבח, and so forth.

Hence, in our opinion, the halachah (*Nedarim* 14a): איש כי ידור נדר לה׳ :עד שידור בדבר הנדור. The vow does not take effect unless he prohibits the object as something prohibited by a vow (e.g., קדשי מזבח or קדשי בדק הבית). This excludes הנודר בדבר האסור — e.g., one says: the object shall be prohibited to me as דם or as נבילה; for the prohibition of דם or נבילה does not spring from a vow. Assigning the object a הקדש-like character is called התפסה (see ר״ן, beginning of *Nedarim*). Thus, a נדר is generally an איסור חפצא: it assigns to the object the consequences of the הקדש-character: דמיתסר חפצא עליה (ibid. 2b).

או השבע שבעה: or he expresses the vow as an oath. An oath is an איסור גברא: דקאסר נפשיה מן חפצא (ibid.), and it binds his will with respect to an object or action.

We have here, then, two categories: נדר לאסור איסר על נפשו and שבועה לאסור איסר על נפשו. If one says that wine shall be forbidden to him like a

קרבן, then drinking wine is forbidden to him by a נדר. If he says that he swears that he will not drink wine, then drinking wine is forbidden to him by a שבועה.

This difference between the concept of שבועה and the concept of נדר has several halachic ramifications.

A נדר can apply only to a concrete object, דבר שיש בו ממש; it cannot apply to something abstract, דבר שאין בו ממש. Accordingly, a נדר cannot apply to an action, whether this action is expressed as a noun or a verb — e.g., my sleeping, my walking, shall be to me as a קרבן; or, to sleep, to walk, shall be forbidden to me as a קרבן (see רמב״ם הל׳ נדרים, 3:10). However, a נדר can indirectly prohibit the fulfillment of a mitzvah — e.g., one says: the *sukkah* shall be prohibited to me as a קרבן (*Nedarim* 16a). For the mitzvah devolves on the person, not on the object.

As opposed to a נדר, a שבועה applies to the personality in the determination of its will. Hence, a שבועה can also apply to דבר שאין בו ממש — e.g., שבועה שלא אישן היום. But a שבועה to abstain from a mitzvah — e.g., שלא אשב בסוכה — is invalid, for the will is already bound to the mitzvah; relating to a mitzvah, a person is not free.

Thus the *halachos*: חומר בשבועות מבנדרים ובנדרים מבשבועות, חומר בנדרים שהנדרים חלין על המצוה כברשות מה שאין כן בשבועות, וחומר בשבועות שהשבועות חלות על דבר שיש בו ממש ושאין בו ממש מה שאין כן בנדרים (ibid. 13b). נדר a מדרבנן applies also to דבר שאין בו ממש (תוספות ibid. ד״ה באומר).

In popular language, כינויים, other terms, were used for נדרים and שבועות — e.g., קונם as another term for קרבן. The כינויים have the full force of נדרים and שבועות: כל כינויי נדרים כנדרים וכו׳ (ibid. 2a).

Also, it is not necessary to verbalize the full formula of the vow. It is sufficient to indicate the sense of the vow, so that what is said is like a יד, a handle that holds the vow: ידות נדרים כנדרים (ibid. 2b). Nor is it necessary to verbalize the התפסה. Simply saying "דבר זה אסור עלי" has the full force of a נדר (ר״ן ibid. 2a). Finally, only in optional matters must the explicit נדר or שבועה expression be pronounced. For mitzvah purposes, simply declaring one's intention is binding (see *Nedarim* 8a, ר״ן and רא״ש there). After all, the very first recorded נדר — עשר אעשרנו לך (*Bereshis* 28:22) — was not a correct נדר expression, but a נדר בלשון שבועה (see also יורה דעה 206:5). Moreover, even if one does not verbalize one's intention but does it [repeatedly] in practice, the law of נדר already applies to him (ibid. 214:1).

לאסר אסר. Elsewhere, אסר denotes only actual binding. Here, it is applied to the binding of the will by a vow or oath.

לא יחל דברו. יַחֵל is the *hif'il* of the root חלל, as in וְלֹא־אַחֵל אֶת־שֵׁם־קָדְשִׁי עוֹד (*Yechezkel* 39:7).

There appears to be a difference between the *pi'el* חִלֵּל and the *hif'il* הֵחֵל. חִלֵּל means: to act in opposition to the holiness of an object. The object remains in its holy state, but one treats it as though it were profane. Thus חלל שבת, חלל את השם, חלל ברית, and so forth. By contrast, הֵחֵל, in the *hif'il*, means: to leave something in a state of חולין, to prevent it from becoming holy. Thus the verse cited above from *Yechezkel*, וְלֹא־אַחֵל אֶת־שֵׁם־קָדְשִׁי עוֹד, does not mean: I will no longer desecrate My holy Name, but, rather: I will no longer leave it in the desecration to which it has come through Israel's sins and punishment.

Had it said here לא יחלל דברו, it would have meant: he must not make his word חולין; he must not act in opposition to the sanctity of his word. But it says לא יחל דברו, which means: he must not allow his word to remain without results; he must not *leave* it in a state of חולין; his word binds him.

This expression itself already points to the possibility that his word, although he has already spoken it, could be without results. The Halachah adds to this and teaches us to lay stress on the personal pronoun indicated here: הוא אינו מיחל אבל אחרים מחלין לו (such is the version in *Berachos* 32a). *He* may not leave his word without results, but others can cause his word to remain without results. Thus, this expression itself already defines the nature of the absolution of vows by the חכם: חכם עוקר את הנדר מעיקרו (*Kesubos* 74b). The investigation by the חכם clarifies that the vow was without effect from the very beginning. The investigation leads to the conclusion that the vow shall *remain* in its חולין-weakness. However, as long as the oath has not been subjected to this investigation, or if the investigation does not lead to such a conclusion, לא יחל דברו, *he* may not leave his word in a state of חולין; rather, ככל היצא מפיו יעשה.

We have already noted that ראשי המטות are mentioned in verse 2 because the absolution of vows is entrusted to them. Nevertheless, the absolution of vows is indicated in Scripture only by the slightest nuance, for the Torah seeks to prevent people from being careless in regard to the sanctity of vows; hence — as already noted by the רמב"ן in his Commentary — the absolution of vows is not expressly mentioned in the Written Law, which is available to everyone.

The absolution of vows is included among those *halachos* that are transmitted exclusively — or almost exclusively — in the Oral Law,

4 *But [as for] a woman, if she vows a vow to* God *and binds [herself] a bond in her father's house in her youth,*

ד וְאִשָּׁה כִּי־תִדֹּר נֶדֶר לַיהוָה וְאָסְרָה אִסָּר בְּבֵית אָבִיהָ בִּנְעֻרֶיהָ׃

halachos that are "פורחין באויר" (*Chagigah* 10a), without any literal support in Scripture and entirely dependent on the oral tradition. Or, the absolution of vows is included among those *halachos* that are כהררים התלויים בשערה (ibid.), large in scope and of great importance, yet whose indication in Scripture is as slight as a hairbreadth, שהן מקרא מועט והלכות מרובות. Other *halachos*, by contrast, are set down in the Written Law in great detail. Nevertheless הן הן גופי תורה (ibid.) — all of the *halachos* [transmitted in any form] are equally essential parts of the Torah.

This is the procedure of the absolution of נדרים, which is entrusted here to ראשי המטות. The vower regrets his vow to the point that he is sorry of having made the vow, and had he given the matter proper consideration, he would not have vowed at all (חרטה מעיקרא); or things happen which in normal circumstances could have been foreseen, and had he thought of them he would have refrained from taking the vow (פתח, but: אין פותחין בנולד — *Nedarim* 23a). He then submits his vow to the investigation of those who are qualified to examine it, and he asks them for a decision (שאלה). After cross-examining him, they say that the vow is null and void, for at the outset it was taken hastily, without due deliberation (מותר לך). However, the possibility of dissolving the vow depends on many conditions which must be carefully considered, and if the vower conceals from the חכם any relevant factor, the absolution of the vow has no effect and is nothing other than self-deception. A Jewish חכם has no power to bind or to absolve; he has only the ability and the duty to investigate and to attain true insight [whether a vow is null and void on its own, due to the circumstances under which it was made].

4 **ואשה וגו'**. A man's vow is binding on him from the outset. He can — and should (see ibid. 59a; cf. Commentary, *Devarim* 23:22ff.) — submit his vow to the national community and its representatives, so that they should examine the vow and decide on its fulfillment. Only in this way can a man dissolve his vow. For a man creates his position in life inde-

pendently, and if he binds himself with a vow that cannot be absolved, he introduces into his life a new element that is not ordinarily applicable. This element changes and individualizes his life, and, since he is independent, he is able to take this individuality into account when he shapes the conditions of his life.

Not so for a woman. The moral greatness of the woman's calling requires that she enter a position in life created by another. The woman does not build for herself her own home. She enters the home provided by the man, and she manages it, bringing happiness to the home and nurturing everything inside the home in a spirit of sanctity and orientation toward God. The woman — even more than the man — must avoid the constraint of extraordinary guidelines in her life, for they are likely to be an impediment to her in the fulfillment of her calling.

From this standpoint, one can understand the prescriptions instituted here out of concern for the woman. The Word of God seeks to insure the vowing woman against the consequences of her own words, and therefore confers on the father and on the husband a limited right to annul vows — on the father, as regards vows of a youthful daughter still under his care; on the father and on the fiancé, as regards vows of a betrothed daughter; on the husband, as regards vows of his wife.

בנעריה. There is a deep psychological basis for the following halachah, which has no parallel anywhere in the Torah: The age of maturity for vows starts earlier than that for all the other *mitzvos*.

In the case of the other *mitzvos*, this is the halachah: The male is considered an adult after his thirteenth year; the female is considered an adult after her twelfth year, for the Torah recognizes that her intelligence matures at an earlier age. Both are considered adults, only if — in addition — they have produced signs of puberty.

The binding force of vows, however, begins one year earlier: *in* the thirteenth year for boys, and *in* the twelfth year for girls, provided that יודעין לשם מי נדרו, they know that it is to God that vows are made (*Niddah* 45b).

This maturity as regards vows, which begins one year before regular maturity, is called "עונת נדרים," and one who has reached עונת נדרים is called "מופלא סמוך לאיש." This law is דאורייתא, and according to one opinion — which is not accepted as halachah, however — a מופלא סמוך לאיש is even liable to מלקות if he breaks his vow (ibid. 46a).

5 *And her father hears her vow and her bond which she bound for her will, and her father remains silent, then all her vows shall stand, and every bond that she has bound for her will shall stand.*

ה וְשָׁמַע אָבִיהָ אֶת־נִדְרָהּ וֶאֱסָרָהּ
אֲשֶׁר אָסְרָה עַל־נַפְשָׁהּ וְהֶחֱרִישׁ
לָהּ אָבִיהָ וְקָמוּ כָּל־נְדָרֶיהָ וְכָל־
אִסָּר אֲשֶׁר־אָסְרָה עַל־נַפְשָׁהּ
יָקוּם׃

6 *But if her father obstructed her on the day he heard it, none of her vows and her bonds that she bound for her will shall stand.* God *will forgive her, because her father has obstructed her.*

ו וְאִם־הֵנִיא אָבִיהָ אֹתָהּ בְּיוֹם
שָׁמְעוֹ כָּל־נְדָרֶיהָ וֶאֱסָרֶיהָ אֲשֶׁר־
אָסְרָה עַל־נַפְשָׁהּ לֹא יָקוּם וַיהוָה
יִסְלַח־לָהּ כִּי־הֵנִיא אָבִיהָ אֹתָהּ׃

In these years, the boy becomes a youth, and the girl becomes a maiden, and there is great significance to the resolutions that they vow in this period. These are resolutions uttered secretly, known only to God, but they are often decisive for a lifetime. The rich contents of the life of a noble man or noble woman are often only the ripened fruit of a resolution vowed to God in the dawn of youth. This would explain the loving seriousness with which God receives the vows of נערים and נערות who are maturing into His service.

Here it says: בבית אביה בנעריה, and similarly at the end of this chapter it says: בנעריה בית אביה (v. 17), and from this we learn that the נערה is under the care of her father as regards vows (*Kesubos* 46b and 47a).

The age of נערות begins when the girl produces [in her twelfth year] signs of puberty, and it ends after six months, when she ceases to be a נערה and becomes a בוגרת (see Commentary, *Shemos* 21:7).

5-6 **ושמע וגו׳ ואם הניא וגו׳**. On the day the father learns of the vow of his daughter who is still legally under his care, he can — via הפרה — annul the vow. But if he allows the day to pass and remains silent, any later attempt at הפרה has no effect, and in this regard the day ends at sundown (*Nedarim* 76b).

הניא — from נוא, which is also the root of נא (see Commentary,

Shemos 12:9) — is the specific term for the הפרה of the father or of the husband. He stops the vow's validity and prevents its continuance, מיגז גייז, as opposed to the התרה of the חכם, which does away with the whole existence of the vow from the beginning, עוקר נדר מעיקרו (*Nazir* 21b and 22a).

כל נדריה וגו׳. As noted in our Commentary on verses 14 and 17, the husband's veto power is limited to נדרי עינוי נפש and דברים שבינו לבינה; he is not entitled to annul his wife's vows unless they jeopardize her physical well-being or disturb the mutual relations of married life.

According to most commentators, the paternal veto is similarly limited, as the *Sifre* also expressly states.

Only the רמב״ם holds (הל׳ נדרים, 12:1) that the father's veto right is unlimited. In his recorded communication to חכמי לוניל, which is cited in the מגדל עוז (there), he tries to defend his position, and in particular he seeks to refute the proof brought against him from the *Sifre*. He bases his view also on the wording of Scripture, which does not limit the father's right, but his main argument is from the Talmud, which does not mention נדרי עינוי נפש and דברים שבינו לבינה in regard to annulment by the father. Had the Talmud held that the father's right, too, is limited, it should have specially defined the דברים שבינו לבינה, for clearly the relations בין אב לבתו are different from the relations בין בעל לאשתו.

However, in our Commentary on verse 4, we stated that the father is entitled to annul his daughter's vows only in consideration of her future calling in married life. If this is correct, the רמב״ם's question on the view of most commentators can be resolved. Perhaps the דברים שבינו לבינה, which the father can annul, are only דברים that are likely to interfere with a harmonious and intimate married life. In that case, the דברים שבינו לבינה that the father is entitled to annul are identical to those that the husband is entitled to annul.

Proof of this interpretation may be adduced from the following: The summarizing verse (v. 17) first mentions בין איש לאשתו and only then — almost as a consequence — adds בין אב לבתו. In fact, it is this sentence — אלה החקים וגו׳ בין איש לאשתו בין אב לבתו — from which the *Sifre* derives the limitation of the father's veto to the scope of the husband's veto: מקיש את האב לבעל, מה הבעל אינו מפר אלא נדרים שבינו לבינה ונדרים שיש בהם עינוי נפש, אף האב אינו מפר אלא נדרים שבינו לבינה ונדרים שיש בהם עינוי נפש.

ז וְאִם־הָי֤וֹ תִֽהְיֶה֙ לְאִ֔ישׁ וּנְדָרֶ֖יהָ עָלֶ֑יהָ א֚וֹ מִבְטָ֣א שְׂפָתֶ֔יהָ אֲשֶׁ֥ר אָסְרָ֖ה עַל־נַפְשָֽׁהּ׃

7 *And if she belongs to a man and has [taken] upon herself a vow or any utterance of her lips that she has bound for her will,*

ח וְשָׁמַ֥ע אִישָׁ֛הּ בְּי֥וֹם שָׁמְע֖וֹ וְהֶחֱרִ֣ישׁ לָ֑הּ וְקָ֣מוּ נְדָרֶ֗יהָ וֶֽאֱסָרֶ֛הָ אֲשֶׁר־אָסְרָ֥ה עַל־נַפְשָׁ֖הּ יָקֻֽמוּ׃

8 *And her husband heard it and remained silent for her on the day he heard it, then her vows shall stand, and her bonds that she has bound for her will shall stand.*

---

7 **ואם היו תהיה לאיש וגו'**. Only in verse 11 does Scripture come to the case of the נשואה, who has already entered her husband's home. Here, then, ואם היו תהיה לאיש refers only to the change of personal status, to קידושין, and it deals with a נערה המאורסה who is still living in the home of her father and who, as a נערה, is still under his care as regards vows.

In the case of such a נערה, the law is that אביה ובעלה מפירין נדריה (*Nedarim* 66b): the father and the ארוס can annul her vows only conjointly. Annulment by the father depends on annulment by the ארוס also as regards ונדריה עליה; that is to say, the ארוס can also annul — conjointly with the father — vows she made before the אירוסין, if the father did not hear of them before the אירוסין and did not annul them. By contrast, a husband can annul only vows that his wife makes after נישואין: אין הבעל מפר בקודמין (ibid. 67a).

ואם היו תהיה: even if she is betrothed again [היו תהיה], after the first ארוס dies. If she is still a נערה at the death of the ארוס, she reverts to her father's care as regards vows: מת הבעל נתרוקנה רשות לאב (ibid. 70a). If she is betrothed again while still a נערה, the father annuls her vows conjointly with the second ארוס (ibid. 71a). By contrast, if the father dies while she is an ארוסה, the ארוס cannot annul her vows by himself: מת האב לא נתרוקנה רשות לבעל (ibid. 70a).

8 **ושמע אישה**. According to the accepted halachah (ibid. 72b), both the father and the ארוס can annul the vows of the daughter and ארוסה respectively in a general manner, even if they did not hear of a particular vow. Hence our Sages say: דרך תלמידי חכמים עד שלא היתה בתו יוצאה מאצלו אמר לה כל

9 *But if on the day that her husband hears it, he obstructs her, he annuls her vow that she has [taken] upon herself and the utterance of her lips that she has bound for her will, and* God *will forgive her.*

ט וְאִם בְּיוֹם שְׁמֹעַ אִישָׁהּ יָנִיא אוֹתָהּ וְהֵפֵר אֶת־נִדְרָהּ אֲשֶׁר עָלֶיהָ וְאֵת מִבְטָא שְׂפָתֶיהָ אֲשֶׁר אָסְרָה עַל־נַפְשָׁהּ וַיהוָה יִסְלַח־לָהּ׃

10 *[As for] the vow of a widow or of a divorced woman — anything that she has bound for her will shall stand for her.*

י וְנֵדֶר אַלְמָנָה וּגְרוּשָׁה כֹּל אֲשֶׁר־אָסְרָה עַל־נַפְשָׁהּ יָקוּם עָלֶיהָ׃

נדרים שנדרת בתוך ביתי הרי הן מופרין, וכן הבעל עד שלא תכנס לרשותו אומר לה כל נדרים שנדרת עד שלא תכנסי לרשותי הרי הן מופרין, שמשתכנס לרשותו אינו יכול להפר (ibid.).

וקמו וגו׳: and then the father cannot annul her vows by himself.

9 **ואם ביום וגו׳**: But the vow is null and void if the annulment by the ארוס joins the annulment by the father.

10 **ונדר אלמנה וגרושה**. From the double הויה formulation of verse 7, we already know the law of an ארוסה who is widowed or divorced and who then is betrothed again. Our Sages (ibid. 70b) say: מקיש קודמי הויה שניה לקודמי הויה ראשונה — i.e., the daughter's relationship to her father before the second אירוסין resembles her relationship to her father before the first אירוסין: מה קודמי הויה ראשונה אב מיפר לחודיה אף קודמי הויה שניה אב מיפר לחודיה. That is to say, even after the אירוסין is broken, the father can again annul his daughter's vows, just as he annulled them before the אירוסין. היה תהיה: the two states of אירוסין are alike, and likewise the periods before them are alike. Thus, an אלמנה או גרושה מן האירוסין reverts to her father's care as regards vows, as long as she is a נערה.

Our verse, then, can be speaking only of an אלמנה או גרושה מן הנישואין. Once she has entered the home of her husband as a נשואה, she has — in a legal sense — left her father's home forever, and if the marriage is dissolved by death or divorce, she does not revert to her father's care as regards vows, even if she is still a נערה. Anything she vows as an אלמנה or גרושה shall stand for her, יקום עליה: The father cannot annul the vow now, nor can the husband in any future marriage annul this vow, for — as

11 *But if she made a vow in her husband's house, or has bound a bond for her will with an oath,*

יא וְאִם־בֵּית אִישָׁהּ נָדָרָה אוֹ־אָסְרָה
אִסָּר עַל־נַפְשָׁהּ בִּשְׁבֻעָה׃

12 *And her husband heard them and remained silent to her [and] has not obstructed her, then all her vows shall stand, and any bond that she has made for her will shall stand.*

יב וְשָׁמַע אִישָׁהּ וְהֶחֱרִשׁ לָהּ לֹא הֵנִיא
אֹתָהּ וְקָמוּ כָּל־נְדָרֶיהָ וְכָל־אִסָּר
אֲשֶׁר־אָסְרָה עַל־נַפְשָׁהּ יָקוּם׃

13 *But if her husband annuls them on the day he hears them, then whatever proceeded from her lips regarding her vows and the binding of her will shall not stand. Her husband has annulled them, and* God *will forgive her.*

יג וְאִם־הָפֵר יָפֵר אֹתָם | אִישָׁהּ בְּיוֹם
שָׁמְעוֹ כָּל־מוֹצָא שְׂפָתֶיהָ לִנְדָרֶיהָ
וּלְאִסַּר נַפְשָׁהּ לֹא יָקוּם אִישָׁהּ
הֲפֵרָם וַיהוָה יִסְלַח־לָהּ׃

14 *Every vow and every binding oath of self-denial — her husband can let it stand, and her husband can annul it.*

יד כָּל־נֵדֶר וְכָל־שְׁבֻעַת אִסָּר לְעַנֹּת
נָפֶשׁ אִישָׁהּ יְקִימֶנּוּ וְאִישָׁהּ יְפֵרֶנּוּ׃

---

already stated in our Commentary on verse 7 — אין הבעל מפר בקודמין. The husband can annul vows only אם בית אישה נדרה (v. 11): he can annul only vows she made after entering נישואין.

11 **ואם בית אישה נדרה** — see Commentary, verse 10.

13 **וה׳ יסלח לה**: even if she broke her vow without knowing that her husband had annulled it (see *Nazir* 23a). The הפרה by the husband makes the vow null and void for all time, or at any rate for the duration of the marriage (see Commentary, v. 14).

14 **כל נדר וגו׳**. The husband's right of annulment is limited here to נדרי עינוי נפש, vows that would cause her to neglect her health or that would afflict her spirit and prevent her from enjoying life. Furthermore, our Sages

15 *But if her husband remains silent for her from one day to the next, then he has caused all her vows and all her bonds which she has [taken] upon herself to stand; he has caused them to stand because he remained silent for her on the day he heard it.*	טו וְאִם־הַחֲרֵשׁ יַחֲרִישׁ לָהּ אִישָׁהּ מִיּוֹם אֶל־יוֹם וְהֵקִים אֶת־כָּל־נְדָרֶיהָ אוֹ אֶת־כָּל־אֱסָרֶיהָ אֲשֶׁר עָלֶיהָ הֵקִים אֹתָם כִּי־הֶחֱרִשׁ לָהּ בְּיוֹם שָׁמְעוֹ׃
16 *If he annuls them then, after he has heard them, he shall bear her iniquity.*	טז וְאִם־הָפֵר יָפֵר אֹתָם אַחֲרֵי שָׁמְעוֹ וְנָשָׂא אֶת־עֲוֺנָהּ׃
17 *These are the laws that* God *commanded Moshe, between a man and his wife, between a father and his daughter in her youth, in her father's house.*	יז אֵלֶּה הַחֻקִּים אֲשֶׁר צִוָּה יְהוָה אֶת־מֹשֶׁה בֵּין אִישׁ לְאִשְׁתּוֹ בֵּין־אָב לְבִתּוֹ בִּנְעֻרֶיהָ בֵּית אָבִיהָ׃ פ שני

derive from the phrase בין איש לאשתו (v. 17) that the husband can also annul vows affecting דברים שבינו לבינה — i.e., vows that disturb the mutual relations of husband and wife. נדרי עינוי נפש are invalidated for all time by the הפרה of the husband; vows affecting דברים שבינו לבינה are invalidated only for the period of the marriage with this husband (*Nedarim* 79b).

15 **ואם החריש יחריש לה**. Even בשותק על מנת למיקט (ibid. 79a), even if he remains silent, not so as to uphold the vow, but only to keep his wife in doubt and then to annul it later — even in this case, once the sun has set and the day on which he heard of the vow has passed, he cannot annul the vow.

If he remains silent out of agreement, the vow is upheld immediately, and he can no longer annul it, even on that same day: קיים בלבו קיים (ibid.).

16 **ואם הפר**: If he remains silent or expressly upholds the vow, and then he causes her to break her vow, he bears the blame.

17 **בין איש לאשתו** — see Commentary, verses 6 and 14.

בנעריה בית אביה, as long as she is a נערה and is still in her father's home — i.e., until she enters the home of her husband through נישואין.

31 1 God *spoke to Moshe, saying:* לא א וַיְדַבֵּר יְהֹוָה אֶל־מֹשֶׁה לֵּאמֹר:
2 *Accomplish the vengeance, in or-* ב נְקֹם נִקְמַת בְּנֵי יִשְׂרָאֵל מֵאֵת

For more on נדרים, see our Commentary on *Devarim* 23:22ff.

The summarizing verse — אלה החקים וגו׳ — mentions only the laws regulating the relationships of the daughter and the wife to her father and to her husband, but it does not mention the halachah stated in verse 3 about the sanctity of vows in general. From this it appears that the regulation of these relationships of the daughters and of the wives is the main content of this chapter, whereas the general statement about the binding force of vows is stated only as an introduction, whose purpose is to stress the contrast: A man cannot dissolve his own vows; the right to dissolve the man's vows is entrusted only to his fellows, the members of his people. By contrast, a man has a limited right of annulment as regards the vows of his daughter and his wife.

The foregoing suggests that this chapter on נדרים complements — and perhaps explains — the law of the daughter's right of inheritance, which is set forth in chapter 27. Woman's calling is to integrate into her husband's home as its most important factor, and her whole upbringing in her father's home prepares her for this. But it is not her calling to found a home independently. This is the source of her dependence on the agreement of her husband and her father as regards נדרי עינוי נפש and דברים שבינו לבינה (see Commentary, vv. 4-6). This also explains the law that normally a daughter does not inherit her father.

CHAPTER 31

1 It has already been stated above (25:16-18) that it was necessary to break the power of the Midianites in order to ensure the moral and spiritual integrity of the Jewish people, for the Midianites persisted in their attempts to seduce Israel with their wiles. Here the order was given to launch the war against the Midianites.

2 **נקם נקמת וגו׳**. Moshe transmitted to Israel God's Torah, which is based

הַמִּדְיָנִ֑ים אַחַ֖ר תֵּאָסֵ֥ף אֶל־עַמֶּֽיךָ׃

der to raise the Children of Israel from the Midianites; afterward, you shall be gathered to your peoples.

ג וַיְדַבֵּ֨ר מֹשֶׁ֤ה אֶל־הָעָם֙ לֵאמֹ֔ר
הֵחָלְצ֧וּ מֵאִתְּכֶ֛ם אֲנָשִׁ֖ים לַצָּבָ֑א
וְיִהְיוּ֙ עַל־מִדְיָ֔ן לָתֵ֥ת נִקְמַת־יְהֹוָ֖ה
בְּמִדְיָֽן׃

3 *And Moshe spoke to the people, saying: Detach from your midst men for the army, and let them be over Midyan, to bring the retribution of* God *to Midyan.*

on chastity and on loyalty to God. Now, before his death, Moshe was bidden to strike a blow against the Midianites, in order to safeguard these two pillars of his mission, to protect his people against גילוי עריות and עבודה זרה.

נקם וגו׳. We have already analyzed (Commentary, *Bereshis* 4:15) the relation of נקם to קום (cf. נפץ ,נסג סוג ,נזר זור ,נזל זול ,נהם הום ,נדח דוח ,נאץ אוץ פוץ, et al.). נקמה raises up justice which has been trampled underfoot, or it raises up a person who has been humbled to the ground. The נוקם identifies with the object that he seeks to raise up. That probably explains the reflexive form נְקֹם. The foregoing would also explain the prepositional letter מ: נקם נקמת בני ישראל מאת המדינים. The purpose is not to subdue the enemy and take revenge upon him; if that had been Scripture's intention, the construction would have been נקם ב-. Rather, the purpose is to raise Israel up *from* the Midianites, to effect Israel's spiritual and moral liberation from the power of Midyan's wiles.

3 **וידבר משה אל העם לאמר**. אל העם, not to the leaders, because the vindication of Israel's spiritual and moral integrity was to come from among the people themselves. The war was waged against Midyan and not against Moav, because Moav sought to weaken Israel physically but did not seek its moral and spiritual destruction. Hence, it was necessary to make the people aware of the moral and spiritual motivation of this campaign. Israel's true enemy is not the one who seeks its physical destruction but the one who plots its moral and spiritual demise.

4 *One thousand from each tribe, one thousand from each tribe, from all the tribes of Israel shall you send to the army.*	ד אֶ֚לֶף לַמַּטֶּ֔ה אֶ֖לֶף לַמַּטֶּ֑ה לְכֹל֙ מַטּ֣וֹת יִשְׂרָאֵ֔ל תִּשְׁלְח֖וּ לַצָּבָֽא׃

החלצו. חלץ means: to detach something from its connection — e.g., detaching stones from a wall (*Vayikra* 14:43); loosening shoe straps to take off the shoe from the foot to which it had been fastened (*Devarim* 25:9). By extension, חלץ commonly means: to save from danger, to deliver from dire straits, to extricate, to set free. In an army, הֶחָלוּץ is the body of troops sent ahead of and detached from the main force (*Yehoshua* 6:7ff.). Thus חלוצי צבא: those sent from the people's midst to serve in the army. The duty of army service devolves on everyone. The people send out of their midst a part of the whole population to fulfill this duty on behalf of the entire community.

Thus the unique construction החלצו מאתכם. The subject of החלצו is the community; מאתכם indicates that a selection of men is sufficient. החלצו presents a demand to all of them to detach themselves from the restraining bonds of the home and to join the army (see *Yevamos* 102b, שלופי מביתא לקרבא). מאתכם limits this duty to a chosen number from among the people, but החלצו shows that those who are chosen are considered representatives of the entire community. When they go forth, the whole community goes forth.

לתת נקמת ה׳ במדין. What is called in verse 2 "נקמת בני ישראל" is brought to the minds of the people as נקמת ה׳. Any defect in their moral and spiritual integrity severs the connection between them and God. Therefore God sends them to bring His retribution upon Midyan. By its policy of corrupting other nations, Midyan has been guilty of the gravest international crime and has therefore lost its right to exist as a nation among other nations before God.

4 **אלף למטה וגו׳**. This term, which is repeated in verses 5 and 6, expresses the idea already noted in our comments on verse 3: Those who went out to fight were emissaries of the whole community and fulfilled a duty that devolved on the whole community. Each tribe was represented by an equal number of men chosen from its midst.

5 *And from among the thousands of Israel, one thousand from each tribe were given over, twelve thousand fitted out for the army.*	ה וַיִּמָּסְרוּ֙ מֵאַלְפֵ֣י יִשְׂרָאֵ֔ל אֶ֖לֶף לַמַּטֶּ֑ה שְׁנֵים־עָשָׂ֥ר אֶ֖לֶף חֲלוּצֵ֥י צָבָֽא׃
6 *And Moshe sent them, one thousand from each tribe, to the army; them and Pinchas, son of Elazar the priest, to the army, with utensils of the Sanctuary and trumpets of the* teruah *in his hand.*	ו וַיִּשְׁלַ֨ח אֹתָ֥ם מֹשֶׁ֛ה אֶ֥לֶף לַמַּטֶּ֖ה לַצָּבָ֑א אֹ֠תָם וְאֶת־פִּ֨ינְחָ֜ס בֶּן־אֶלְעָזָ֤ר הַכֹּהֵן֙ לַצָּבָ֔א וּכְלֵ֥י הַקֹּ֛דֶשׁ וַחֲצֹצְר֥וֹת הַתְּרוּעָ֖ה בְּיָדֽוֹ׃
7 *They mounted a campaign against Midyan, as* God *had commanded Moshe, and they slew all the males.*	ז וַֽיִּצְבְּאוּ֙ עַל־מִדְיָ֔ן כַּאֲשֶׁ֛ר צִוָּ֥ה יְהֹוָ֖ה אֶת־מֹשֶׁ֑ה וַיַּֽהַרְג֖וּ כָּל־זָכָֽר׃

5 **וימסרו**. מסר occurs in תנ״ך only here and in verse 16. In Rabbinic Hebrew it means: to hand over, transfer. Here the term corresponds to the conditions already indicated. Each tribe transferred into Moshe's control a thousand men of its choosing, who represented the tribe in carrying out the common task of the whole nation.

6 **וישלח אתם וגו׳ ואת פינחס וגו׳**. In none of the accounts of earlier military campaigns — the wars against Sichon, Og, and the Emori — does Scripture explicitly mention that a כהן was present, along with the ארון and the חצוצרות. Those wars were wars of self-defense or conquest, fought for material reasons. This war, however, was waged for the most exalted moral and spiritual purposes. For such a war, it is especially fitting that a כהן should be there, along with the Testimony of the Torah and the חצוצרות calling for God's help.

וכלי הקדש: זה ארון ולוחות שבו (*Sotah* 43a). For they went out to fight for the sake of the לוחות and the ארון, for the sake of the Torah and its bearers. They fought this war to ensure that the Torah and its bearers could dwell securely in the midst of the nations.

וחצצרות התרועה — see above, 10:8-9, and Commentary there.

בידו: אין ידו אלא רשותו (*Sifre*).

8 *They slew the kings of Midyan upon their slain: Evi, Rekem, Tzur, Chur and Reva, five kings of Midyan; also Bil'am, son of Be'or did they slay with the sword.*

ח וְאֶת־מַלְכֵי מִדְיָן הָרְגוּ עַל־
חַלְלֵיהֶם אֶת־אֱוִי וְאֶת־רֶקֶם
וְאֶת־צוּר וְאֶת־חוּר וְאֶת־רֶבַע
חֲמֵשֶׁת מַלְכֵי מִדְיָן וְאֵת בִּלְעָם
בֶּן־בְּעוֹר הָרְגוּ בֶּחָרֶב׃

9 *The Children of Israel took captive the women of Midyan and their children, all their livestock and all their flocks and all their possessions did they take as booty.*

ט וַיִּשְׁבּוּ בְנֵי־יִשְׂרָאֵל אֶת־נְשֵׁי מִדְיָן
וְאֶת־טַפָּם וְאֵת כָּל־בְּהֶמְתָּם
וְאֶת־כָּל־מִקְנֵהֶם וְאֶת־כָּל־חֵילָם
בָּזָזוּ׃

10 *All their cities in their dwelling places and all their fortresses did they burn with fire.*

י וְאֵת כָּל־עָרֵיהֶם בְּמוֹשְׁבֹתָם וְאֵת
כָּל־טִירֹתָם שָׂרְפוּ בָּאֵשׁ׃

8 **על חלליהם** — the kings were not at the front of the battle.

ואת בלעם. After hearing of the success of his advice, he apparently returned from his homeland to Moav and Midyan, and he was the living spirit behind the seductive arts continued by the Midianites. According to *Sanhedrin* 106a, he came to collect his reward for his successful advice.

10 **ואת כל עריהם במושבתם**. In *Chavakkuk* 3:7 it says: יִרְגְּזוּן יְרִיעוֹת אֶרֶץ מִדְיָן, from which it appears that the Midianites were nomads and lived in tents. The same can be inferred, apparently, from *Shoftim* 6:5, where the Midianites are described — albeit in conjunction with other nations — as invading the Land of Israel with their tents, herds, and camels. Cf. also ibid. 7:12, 8:21 and 24, where the Midianites are characterized as יִשְׁמְעֵאלִים, by which probably nomads are to be understood. Nevertheless, our verse speaks of their cities and their castles.

It appears, then, that although the Midianites generally lived as nomads, they also settled in cities, which would explain the addition of במושבתם to עריהם: The cities were places where they had permanent dwell-

11 *They took all the booty and all that had been seized, of men and livestock.*

יא וַיִּקְחוּ֙ אֶת־כָּל־הַשָּׁלָ֔ל וְאֵ֖ת כָּל־
הַמַּלְק֑וֹחַ בָּאָדָ֖ם וּבַבְּהֵמָֽה׃

12 *And they brought to Moshe and to Elazar the priest and to the community of the Children of Israel the prisoners, those that had been seized, and the booty, to the camp, to the Moavi wastelands, which are on the Yarden near Yericho.*

יב וַ֠יָּבִאוּ אֶל־מֹשֶׁ֨ה וְאֶל־אֶלְעָזָ֜ר
הַכֹּהֵ֗ן וְאֶל־עֲדַ֣ת בְּנֵֽי־יִשְׂרָאֵ֡ל
אֶת־הַשְּׁבִ֛י וְאֶת־הַמַּלְק֥וֹחַ וְאֶת־
הַשָּׁלָ֖ל אֶל־הַֽמַּחֲנֶ֑ה אֶל־עַֽרְבֹ֣ת
מוֹאָ֔ב אֲשֶׁ֖ר עַל־יַרְדֵּ֥ן יְרֵחֽוֹ׃ ס

שלישי (שני כשהן מחוברין)

ings, and although generally they led nomadic lives, sometimes they would retire to these cities.

ואת כל טירתם — see *Bereshis* 25:16 and Commentary there. There, too, we see that the ישמעאלים also had permanent settlements.

11-12 **ויקחו וגו׳**. All the property that was captured in the war is called in verse 11 "שלל" and "מלקוח," and verse 12 further distinguishes between שבי and מלקוח.

In our Commentary on *Bereshis* 19:8, we have already analyzed the relation of שלל to זלל, סלל, צלל. The common basic conception is: to remove something from a realm. Hence, the root שלל does not always denote removal by force. Thus שֹׁל תָּשֹׁלּוּ (*Ruth* 2:16): Intentionally drop ears of corn that rightfully belong in stacks, and thereby increase the gleanings of the poor. The ears are removed from the possession of the owner of the field, but with his permission.

In general, שלל denotes all property captured in war, for the property is removed from the possession of its former owners. Thus, שלל also includes livestock, as in זֶה שְׁלַל דָּוִד (*Shemuel* I, 30:20). Where שלל appears beside מלקוח, שלל denotes inanimate property, whereas מלקוח denotes live property, which remains in the possession of its new owner only if he holds on to it and keeps it in his "grip."

In our verse, מלקוח denotes animals and people, whereas שבי specially denotes people taken captive in war.

13 *And Moshe and Elazar the priest and all the princes of the community went out to meet them, outside the camp.*

יג וַיֵּ֨צְא֜וּ מֹשֶׁ֨ה וְאֶלְעָזָ֧ר הַכֹּהֵ֛ן וְכָל־
נְשִׂיאֵ֥י הָעֵדָ֖ה לִקְרָאתָ֑ם אֶל־
מִח֖וּץ לַֽמַּחֲנֶֽה׃

14 *And Moshe was angry at the officers of the army — the princes of the thousands and the princes of the hundreds who had returned from the army service of the war.*

יד וַיִּקְצֹ֣ף מֹשֶׁ֔ה עַ֖ל פְּקוּדֵ֣י הֶחָ֑יִל שָׂרֵ֤י
הָאֲלָפִים֙ וְשָׂרֵ֣י הַמֵּא֔וֹת הַבָּאִ֖ים
מִצְּבָ֥א הַמִּלְחָמָֽה׃

15 *And Moshe said to them: So you allowed all the females to live?*

טו וַיֹּ֥אמֶר אֲלֵיהֶ֖ם מֹשֶׁ֑ה הַֽחִיִּיתֶ֖ם כָּל־
נְקֵבָֽה׃

16 *See, these are exactly the ones who, on Bil'am's advice, were to cause the Children of Israel to act faithlessly against* God *in the matter of Pe'or, so that the plague broke out within the community of* God*!*

טז הֵ֣ן הֵ֜נָּה הָי֨וּ לִבְנֵ֤י יִשְׂרָאֵל֙ בִּדְבַ֣ר
בִּלְעָ֔ם לִמְסָר־מַ֥עַל בַּֽיהוָ֖ה עַל־
דְּבַר־פְּע֑וֹר וַתְּהִ֥י הַמַּגֵּפָ֖ה בַּעֲדַ֥ת
יְהוָֽה׃

שבה — related to צבה, צבא, שבע, שׂבע, שפח (משפחה, שפחה; cf. Commentary, *Bereshis* 8:19), ספח — means: to expand the sphere of one's personal power by absorbing another person in it.

(שַׁבַּח means: to describe the abundant virtues of something, generally a person. It also means: to completely fulfill someone's aspirations; to assuage intense passion; and by extension: to calm the waves of the sea — בְּשׂוֹא גַלָּיו אַתָּה תְשַׁבְּחֵם [*Tehillim* 89:10; cf. Commentary ibid. 65:8].)

Where מלקוח appears beside שבי (as in verse 12), מלקוח refers to animals, and שבי to people.

14 **פקודי החיל** are those entrusted with leading the army; that is to say, those who are in charge of the army's actions and are responsible for them.

16 **הן הנה**. הן — as in הן נזבח (*Shemos* 8:22).

היו לבני ישראל. The meaning might be the same as in כי תהיה לאיש זר (*Vayikra* 22:12), הָיִיתִי הַלַּיְלָה לְאִישׁ (*Ruth* 1:12). They gave themselves up to

17 *And now, kill every male among the children, and kill every female who has known a man for sexual intercourse.*

יז וְעַתָּה הִרְגוּ כָל־זָכָר בַּטָּף וְכָל־אִשָּׁה יֹדַעַת אִישׁ לְמִשְׁכַּב זָכָר הֲרֹגוּ׃

18 *And all the children among the females who have not yet experienced sexual intercourse, keep alive for yourselves.*

יח וְכֹל הַטַּף בַּנָּשִׁים אֲשֶׁר לֹא־יָדְעוּ מִשְׁכַּב זָכָר הַחֲיוּ לָכֶם׃

19 *You shall camp outside the camp for seven days. Everyone who has slain a person and everyone who has touched a slain person — you must purify yourselves on the third day and on the seventh day, you and your prisoners.*

יט וְאַתֶּם חֲנוּ מִחוּץ לַמַּחֲנֶה שִׁבְעַת יָמִים כֹּל הֹרֵג נֶפֶשׁ וְכֹל ׀ נֹגֵעַ בֶּחָלָל תִּתְחַטְּאוּ בַּיּוֹם הַשְּׁלִישִׁי וּבַיּוֹם הַשְּׁבִיעִי אַתֶּם וּשְׁבִיכֶם׃

---

the sons of Israel, to cause them to act faithlessly against God in the matter of Pe'or — i.e., for the sake of Pe'or, so that they should attach themselves to the god of lechery.

17-18 The purpose of this act was to prevent Israel from absorbing heathen immoral elements. We must therefore assume that the national degeneration was rooted primarily in the males, whereas the females — if removed at an early age from impure influences and impressions — were able to attain pure morality. Similarly, in *Devarim* 23:4 (see Commentary there) the Halachah distinguishes between males and females regarding the acceptance of Ammonites and Moabites. The males are excluded, whereas the females may be admitted בקהל ה׳ even at a mature age.

19 **ואתם** — see above, 5:2-3; 19:11ff. and Commentary there.

אתם ושביכם. As נכריות, the captives could not be מקבל טומאה. טומאה applies only to a person who has a relation to the Jewish Sanctuary and to its holy things, מקדש וקדשיו. It must be, then, that שביכם, the captives, were susceptible to טומאה only לאחר שנתגיירו, after they converted, an act that could have been performed immediately with many of them.

20 *Every garment and every leather utensil and everything made out of goats' hair and every wooden utensil you must purify for yourselves.*

כ וְכָל־בֶּ֧גֶד וְכָל־כְּלִי־ע֛וֹר וְכָל־
מַעֲשֵׂ֥ה עִזִּ֖ים וְכָל־כְּלִי־עֵ֑ץ
תִּֽתְחַטָּֽאוּ׃ ס

21 *And Elazar the priest said to the men of the army who had gone to the war: This is a basic statute of the Teaching that* God *has commanded Moshe:*

כא וַיֹּ֨אמֶר אֶלְעָזָ֤ר הַכֹּהֵן֙ אֶל־אַנְשֵׁ֣י
הַצָּבָ֔א הַבָּאִ֖ים לַמִּלְחָמָ֑ה זֹ֚את
חֻקַּ֣ת הַתּוֹרָ֔ה אֲשֶׁר־צִוָּ֥ה יְהוָ֖ה
אֶת־מֹשֶֽׁה׃

22 *Only the gold and the silver, the copper and the iron, the tin and the lead —*

כב אַ֤ךְ אֶת־הַזָּהָב֙ וְאֶת־הַכָּ֔סֶף אֶֽת־
הַנְּחֹ֨שֶׁת֙ אֶת־הַבַּרְזֶ֔ל אֶת־הַבְּדִ֖יל
וְאֶת־הָעֹפָֽרֶת׃

כלי מתכות — according to one opinion all utensils except כלי חרס (see Commentary above, 19:16) — become אבי אבות הטומאה by contact with a corpse, and a person who touches them becomes אב הטומאה and requires הזיה. Hence, it is possible that שביכם, if they touched such a כלי after גיור, required הזיה.

20 **וכל בגד וגו׳** — see *Vayikra* 11:32 and Commentary there.

תתחטאו. Since כל בגד וגו׳ is the object of the sentence, the reflexive of תתחטאו can be explained only as in the case of והתנחלתם אותם (*Vayikra* 25:46): "Every garment . . . you must purify for yourselves." [See Commentary, *Bereshis* 37:18.]

21 **ויאמר וגו׳ הבאים למלחמה**. Since it does not say מן המלחמה but למלחמה, we can safely assume that this mitzvah was not communicated to them upon their return, but upon their departure for the war [see also Commentary above, 10:9].

זאת חקת התורה — see Commentary above, 19:2.

22 **אך את הזהב וגו׳**. We have already noted in our Commentary on *Vayikra* 11:32 that the term כלי from verse 20 should be supplied here, and thereby

כג כָּל־דָּבָר אֲשֶׁר־יָבֹא בָאֵשׁ תַּעֲבִירוּ בָאֵשׁ וְטָהֵר אַךְ בְּמֵי נִדָּה יִתְחַטָּא וְכֹל אֲשֶׁר לֹא־יָבֹא בָּאֵשׁ תַּעֲבִירוּ בַמָּיִם׃

23 *Everything that has entered by fire you shall cause to go out by fire, and then it can become pure; however, it must purify itself by the waters of separation; and everything that has not entered by fire you shall cause to go out by water.*

a close connection is formed between this verse and what is stated in verse 20: וכל בגד וגו׳ וכל כלי עץ requires only purification from טומאה by means of הזיה, whereas metal utensils require also הכשר (כל דבר אשר וגו׳) in addition to טבילה (אך במי וגו׳), as explained in verse 23.

23 **כל דבר וגו׳**. Everything that enters by fire shall be expelled by fire, and everything that does not enter by fire shall be expelled by water. תעבירו — as in הֶעֱבִיר חַטָּאתְךָ (*Shemuel* II, 12:13), הַעֲבֵר חֶרְפָּתִי (*Tehillim* 119:39), וַיַּעֲבֵר הַקְּדֵשִׁים מִן־הָאָרֶץ (*Melachim* I, 15:12).

This halachah deals with metal food-vessels into which איסור material has been absorbed. Before such vessels may be used, they must be freed of the איסור material. Material that is absorbed directly by fire — without the medium of liquid — shall be expelled by ליבון in fire; material that is not absorbed directly by fire shall be expelled by הגעלה in boiling water. This principle — that absorbed material can be expelled by the same medium that caused it to be absorbed — is formulated as follows: כבולעו כך פולטו (see *Avodah Zarah* 75b, et seq.).

This is the law of גיעולי נכרים, i.e., איסור material that comes out of food vessels that were in the possession of a non-Jew. געל means: to expel (*Iyov* 21:10; *Vayikra* 26:11). From here we learn that איסור material that is absorbed in a vessel remains אסור, even though its taste has been marred, and it is no longer pleasant to the taste: קדרה בת יומא אי אפשר דלא פגמה פורתא (*Avodah Zarah* 67b, תוספות there ד״ה ואידך). This halachah is based on a law that is borne out elsewhere as well (see Commentary above, 6:3), the law of טעם כעיקר: If איסור material [is absorbed into permitted material, and] is recognizable [there] by taste alone, its איסור remains in effect.

אך במי נדה יתחטא. The whole structure of these sentences indicates that these words cannot refer to the הזיה [whose purpose is to purify the vessel] from טומאת מת. If that were the case, these words — אך במי נדה יתחטא — would come after וכל אשר לא וגו׳. For even vessels that are not put on the fire — e.g., wooden vessels — require הזיה, as already stated in verse 20.

Clearly, then, אך במי נדה וגו׳ establishes a halachah that applies only to metal food-vessels. כל דבר אשר יבא באש of verse 23 is a summary that includes the metal vessels listed in verse 22. It says of them two things: If it is assumed that they were used directly on the fire, the איסור material that was absorbed by fire must also be expelled by fire. What is more, before these metal food-vessels may be used, they must undergo במי נדה יתחטא [see below].

The law is different in the case of כל אשר לא יבא באש, non-metallic vessels, which are not used on the fire. These vessels can be freed of the איסור material by water alone. What is more, they do not require the חיטוי במי נדה prescribed for metal vessels. The Halachah teaches (*Avodah Zarah* 75b) that this חיטוי is טבילה in a מקוה of ארבעים סאה (see *Vayikra* 11:36) — מים שנדה טובלת בהן — whereas for טבילת כלים מטומאתן even a רביעית suffices (see תוספות *Avodah Zarah* 75b ד״ה מים).

מי נדה would then be a general term for the מקוה that purifies people whose טומאה obligates them to "keep themselves away." Thus in *Zecharyah* (13:1): מָקוֹר וגו׳ לְחַטַּאת וּלְנִדָּה, where חטאת denotes הזיה on account of טומאת מת, and נדה denotes the general טבילה.

The halachah that metal food-vessels require a טבילה similar to that prescribed for people would explain the striking expression "יתחטא." In this expression, the vessel to be purified is not the object but the subject; thus the vessel is regarded as a person who is purifying himself, and טבילת כלי is considered as though it were טבילת אדם. The personality of Jewish man shall see in טבילת כלי מדין a טבילה for itself; hence יתחטא and hence ארבעים סאה (see Commentary, *Vayikra* 11:32).

This, then, is the halachah that is stated here: Metal food-vessels that pass from non-Jewish to Jewish possession require טבילה, even if they are free of all טומאה and they did not absorb any איסור. It is a halachah of קדושה, and its purpose is to teach Israel that even the sensual enjoyment of food must be sanctified. However, since this halachah is limited to food-vessels made of metal, it follows that the idea that is brought to mind by this טבילה has a special meaning.

A *metal* vessel represents man's *intellectual* mastery over the earth and its materials. Not only the vessel's shape but also its material attests

24 *And you shall rinse your clothes on the seventh day and become pure; after that you may come into the camp.*

כד וְכִבַּסְתֶּ֥ם בִּגְדֵיכֶ֛ם בַּיּ֥וֹם הַשְּׁבִיעִ֖י
וּטְהַרְתֶּ֑ם וְאַחַ֖ר תָּבֹ֥אוּ אֶל־
הַֽמַּחֲנֶֽה׃ ס רביעי

25 *And* God *said to Moshe:*

כה וַיֹּ֥אמֶר יְהֹוָ֖ה אֶל־מֹשֶׁ֥ה לֵּאמֹֽר׃

26 *Take up the sum of the booty seized, of what was captured in human beings and in animals, you and Elazar the priest and the heads of the fathers of the community.*

כו שָׂ֗א אֵ֣ת רֹ֤אשׁ מַלְק֙וֹחַ֙ הַשְּׁבִ֔י
בָּאָדָ֖ם וּבַבְּהֵמָ֑ה אַתָּה֙ וְאֶלְעָזָ֣ר
הַכֹּהֵ֔ן וְרָאשֵׁ֖י אֲב֥וֹת הָעֵדָֽה׃

to this mastery. Eating, on the other hand, is an activity that serves man's *physical-sensual* nature. A *metal* vessel used for *eating* represents — in and of itself — the *intellectual* side of man *in the service of* his sensual nature. But under the Torah's regime, even man's sensual life is removed from the sphere of physical compulsion and is put at the disposal of free moral action which constitutes the service of God.

Accordingly, one can well understand why the Torah ordains טבילה precisely for food vessels of *metal* that come into Jewish possession. So, too, one can well understand why this טבילה is also called "התחטא," for its purpose is to revive and strengthen the consciousness of moral freedom, which is none other than the ability to abstain from sin. Thus our Sages say (*Yerushalmi*, *Avodah Zarah* 5:15): לפי שיצאו מטומאת הנכרי ונכנסו לקדושת ישראל.

Glass vessels resemble metal vessels, for they too are made by an artisan who masters fire, and they too undergo melting. Hence, food vessels made of glass or covered with glass require טבילה מדרבנן (*Avodah Zarah* ibid.).

26 **מלקוח השבי**. They divided only the living spoil — animals and people — whereas inanimate booty was kept by the booty-takers. The reason for this may be as follows: Captured animals and people had to be guarded and looked after, and this required everyone's cooperation. Hence they were considered common spoil. Inanimate booty, however, could be guarded by each individual.

שא את ראש — see Commentary, *Shemos* 30:12.

27 *And you shall divide the seized booty among those who took the war in hand, who went forth into the army, and among the entire community.*

כז וְחָצִ֙יתָ֙ אֶת־הַמַּלְק֔וֹחַ בֵּ֚ין תֹּפְשֵׂ֣י הַמִּלְחָמָ֔ה הַיֹּצְאִ֖ים לַצָּבָ֑א וּבֵ֖ין כָּל־הָעֵדָֽה׃

28 *And you shall levy a tribute for* God *from the men of war who went forth into the army, one out of five hundred from the men, from the cattle, from the donkeys and from the sheep.*

כח וַהֲרֵמֹתָ֨ מֶ֜כֶס לַֽיהוָ֗ה מֵאֵ֞ת אַנְשֵׁ֤י הַמִּלְחָמָה֙ הַיֹּצְאִ֣ים לַצָּבָ֔א אֶחָ֣ד נֶ֔פֶשׁ מֵחֲמֵ֖שׁ הַמֵּא֑וֹת מִן־הָֽאָדָם֙ וּמִן־הַבָּקָ֔ר וּמִן־הַחֲמֹרִ֖ים וּמִן־הַצֹּֽאן׃

29 *Take from their half, and give to Elazar the priest the uplifted donation of* God.

כט מִמַּחֲצִיתָ֖ם תִּקָּ֑חוּ וְנָתַתָּ֛ה לְאֶלְעָזָ֥ר הַכֹּהֵ֖ן תְּרוּמַ֥ת יְהוָֽה׃

30 *And of the Children of Israel's half you shall take one taken out of fifty — from the men, from the cattle,*

ל וּמִמַּחֲצִ֨ת בְּנֵֽי־יִשְׂרָאֵ֜ל תִּקַּ֣ח ׀ אֶחָ֣ד ׀ אָחֻ֣ז מִן־הַחֲמִשִּׁ֗ים מִן־

---

27 **תפשי המלחמה** (cf. תופש כנור, *Bereshis* 4:21; וְתֹפְשֵׂי הַתּוֹרָה, *Yirmeyahu* 2:8) are all those who took on the task of fighting this war, all those who participated in the military campaign — officers as well as ordinary soldiers.

28 **מכס** — see Commentary, *Shemos* 12:5.

29 **תקחו**. In verse 28 it does not say אחד אחז, as in verse 30. For verse 28 deals with תרומת ה׳, which is not taken haphazardly but, rather, is to be selected, and this selection is indicated by תקחו in the absolute, without an object.

לאלעזר הכהן. The רמב״ן has already noted that this was a temporary measure, applicable only to this war, which had a holy moral purpose. As a rule, כהנים receive no share of the spoils of war (see above, 18:20, and Commentary there).

30 **אחז**: taken out, without selecting (see Commentary, v. 29).

from the donkeys and from the sheep, from all the animals — and give them to the Levi'im, *the keepers of the charge of the Dwelling Place of* God.

הָאָדָם מִן־הַבָּקָר מִן־הַחֲמֹרִים וּמִן־הַצֹּאן מִכָּל־הַבְּהֵמָה וְנָתַתָּה אֹתָם לַלְוִיִּם שֹׁמְרֵי מִשְׁמֶרֶת מִשְׁכַּן יְהוָה׃

31 *Moshe did — and [so did] Elazar the priest — as* God *had commanded Moshe.*

לא וַיַּעַשׂ מֹשֶׁה וְאֶלְעָזָר הַכֹּהֵן כַּאֲשֶׁר צִוָּה יְהוָה אֶת־מֹשֶׁה׃

32 *The booty that had been seized, apart from what the army people had plundered, was — sheep: six-hundred-and-seventy-five thousand;*

לב וַיְהִי הַמַּלְקוֹחַ יֶתֶר הַבָּז אֲשֶׁר בָּזְזוּ עַם הַצָּבָא צֹאן שֵׁשׁ־מֵאוֹת אֶלֶף וְשִׁבְעִים אֶלֶף וַחֲמֵשֶׁת אֲלָפִים׃

33 *Cattle: seventy-two thousand;*

לג וּבָקָר שְׁנַיִם וְשִׁבְעִים אָלֶף׃

34 *Donkeys: sixty-one thousand;*

לד וַחֲמֹרִים אֶחָד וְשִׁשִּׁים אָלֶף׃

35 *Human souls: of the females who had not yet experienced sexual intercourse, all the souls: thirty-two thousand.*

לה וְנֶפֶשׁ אָדָם מִן־הַנָּשִׁים אֲשֶׁר לֹא־יָדְעוּ מִשְׁכַּב זָכָר כָּל־נֶפֶשׁ שְׁנַיִם וּשְׁלֹשִׁים אָלֶף׃

36 *And the half, the portion of those who had gone forth into the army, was: the number of sheep — three-hundred-and-thirty-seven thousand, five hundred.*

לו וַתְּהִי הַמֶּחֱצָה חֵלֶק הַיֹּצְאִים בַּצָּבָא מִסְפַּר הַצֹּאן שְׁלֹשׁ־מֵאוֹת אֶלֶף וּשְׁלֹשִׁים אֶלֶף וְשִׁבְעַת אֲלָפִים וַחֲמֵשׁ מֵאוֹת׃

37 *Thus the tribute to* God *from the sheep was six hundred seventy-five.*

לז וַיְהִי הַמֶּכֶס לַיהוָה מִן־הַצֹּאן שֵׁשׁ מֵאוֹת חָמֵשׁ וְשִׁבְעִים׃

---

32 **יתר הבז** — cf. verse 53: אנשי הצבא בזזו איש לו. Inanimate valuables, which were kept by the booty-takers, are called "בז." The מלקוח which came to be divided here was over and above this בז.

38 *And the cattle: thirty-six thousand, and out of these the tribute to God [was] seventy-two.*

לח וְהַבָּקָר שִׁשָּׁה וּשְׁלֹשִׁים אָלֶף וּמִכְסָם לַיהוָה שְׁנַיִם וְשִׁבְעִים׃

39 *And donkeys: thirty thousand, five hundred, and out of these the tribute to God [was] sixty-one.*

לט וַחֲמֹרִים שְׁלֹשִׁים אֶלֶף וַחֲמֵשׁ מֵאוֹת וּמִכְסָם לַיהוָה אֶחָד וְשִׁשִּׁים׃

40 *Human souls: sixteen thousand, and out of these the tribute to God [was] thirty-two souls.*

מ וְנֶפֶשׁ אָדָם שִׁשָּׁה עָשָׂר אָלֶף וּמִכְסָם לַיהוָה שְׁנַיִם וּשְׁלֹשִׁים נָפֶשׁ׃

41 *Moshe gave the tribute, the uplifted donation of God, to Elazar the priest, as God had commanded Moshe.*

מא וַיִּתֵּן מֹשֶׁה אֶת־מֶכֶס תְּרוּמַת יְהוָה לְאֶלְעָזָר הַכֹּהֵן כַּאֲשֶׁר צִוָּה יְהוָה אֶת־מֹשֶׁה׃ חמישי

42 *And of the Children of Israel's half, which Moshe had divided off from the men who had gone into the army —*

מב וּמִמַּחֲצִית בְּנֵי יִשְׂרָאֵל אֲשֶׁר חָצָה מֹשֶׁה מִן־הָאֲנָשִׁים הַצֹּבְאִים׃

43 *The community's half was, of sheep: three-hundred-and-thirty-seven thousand, five hundred;*

מג וַתְּהִי מֶחֱצַת הָעֵדָה מִן־הַצֹּאן שְׁלֹשׁ־מֵאוֹת אֶלֶף וּשְׁלֹשִׁים אֶלֶף שִׁבְעַת אֲלָפִים וַחֲמֵשׁ מֵאוֹת׃

44 *Cattle: thirty-six thousand;*

מד וּבָקָר שִׁשָּׁה וּשְׁלֹשִׁים אָלֶף׃

45 *Donkeys: thirty thousand, five hundred;*

מה וַחֲמֹרִים שְׁלֹשִׁים אֶלֶף וַחֲמֵשׁ מֵאוֹת׃

46 *Human souls: sixteen thousand.*

מו וְנֶפֶשׁ אָדָם שִׁשָּׁה עָשָׂר אָלֶף׃

47 *And Moshe took from the Children of Israel's half, that which had been taken out, one out of every*

מז וַיִּקַּח מֹשֶׁה מִמַּחֲצִת בְּנֵי־יִשְׂרָאֵל אֶת־הָאָחֻז אֶחָד מִן־הַחֲמִשִּׁים

מִן־הָאָדָם וּמִן־הַבְּהֵמָה וַיִּתֵּן אֹתָם לַלְוִיִּם שֹׁמְרֵי מִשְׁמֶרֶת מִשְׁכַּן יְהוָה כַּאֲשֶׁר צִוָּה יְהוָה אֶת־מֹשֶׁה׃

fifty, from the men and from the animals, and gave it to the Levi'im, *the keepers of the charge of the Dwelling Place of* God, *as* God *had commanded Moshe.*

מח וַיִּקְרְבוּ אֶל־מֹשֶׁה הַפְּקֻדִים אֲשֶׁר לְאַלְפֵי הַצָּבָא שָׂרֵי הָאֲלָפִים וְשָׂרֵי הַמֵּאוֹת׃

48 *And the officers who were over the thousands of the army — the princes of the thousands and the princes of the hundreds — approached Moshe.*

מט וַיֹּאמְרוּ אֶל־מֹשֶׁה עֲבָדֶיךָ נָשְׂאוּ אֶת־רֹאשׁ אַנְשֵׁי הַמִּלְחָמָה אֲשֶׁר בְּיָדֵנוּ וְלֹא־נִפְקַד מִמֶּנּוּ אִישׁ׃

49 *And they said to Moshe: Your servants have taken up the sum of the men of war who were entrusted to our hand, and not one man of us is missing.*

נ וַנַּקְרֵב אֶת־קָרְבַּן יְהוָה אִישׁ אֲשֶׁר

50 *Therefore we have dedicated the*

---

49 **ולא נפקד**. We have already (Commentary, *Bereshis* 21:1) analyzed the relation of the root פקד to בגד and to בית, and remarked that פקד means: to mentally clothe something; the פוקד "clothes" — i.e., invests — an object with the attributes, conditions, and relationships that are fitting for it.

As a rule, the פוקד sees an object and mentally supplies it with the attributes that are fitting for it but that are still lacking. Sometimes the meaning is the opposite: The פוקד sees the relationships and the conditions, and he mentally supplies them with the object that is fitting for them but still lacking; that is to say, the relationships and conditions that are before his eyes cause him to recall the object that is fitting for them but missing. נפקד, then, means none other than: to perceive the absence of something.

50 **ונקרב את קרבן ה׳**. The wording is not ונקרב קרבן לה׳ but את קרבן ה׳. The obligation to offer this קרבן was self-evident. After all that had befallen them, they felt the need to offer a קרבן, and thus expressed that they had been saved thanks only to God's nearness — i.e., thanks to their relationship to God and to His Torah.

מָצָ֨א כְלִֽי־זָהָ֜ב אֶצְעָדָ֣ה וְצָמִ֔יד
טַבַּ֖עַת עָגִ֣יל וְכוּמָ֑ז לְכַפֵּ֥ר עַל־
נַפְשֹׁתֵ֖ינוּ לִפְנֵ֥י יְהֹוָֽה׃

offering of God, *every man who has acquired a gold article, an anklet or a bracelet, a finger ring, earring or clasp, to attain atonement for our souls before* God.

נא וַיִּקַּ֨ח מֹשֶׁ֜ה וְאֶלְעָזָ֧ר הַכֹּהֵ֛ן אֶת־
הַזָּהָ֖ב מֵאִתָּ֑ם כֹּ֖ל כְּלִ֥י מַעֲשֶֽׂה׃

51 *And Moshe and Elazar the priest took from them the gold, all articles wrought for [practical] use.*

נב וַיְהִ֣י ׀ כׇּל־זְהַ֣ב הַתְּרוּמָ֗ה אֲשֶׁ֤ר
הֵרִ֙ימוּ֙ לַיהֹוָ֔ה שִׁשָּׁ֨ה עָשָׂ֥ר אֶ֛לֶף
שְׁבַֽע־מֵא֥וֹת וַחֲמִשִּׁ֖ים שָׁ֑קֶל מֵאֵת֙
שָׂרֵ֣י הָאֲלָפִ֔ים וּמֵאֵ֖ת שָׂרֵ֥י
הַמֵּאֽוֹת׃

52 *And all the gold of the uplifted donation that they had dedicated to* God *was sixteen thousand, seven hundred and fifty shekels from the princes of the thousands and from the princes of the hundreds.*

נג אַנְשֵׁי֙ הַצָּבָ֔א בָּזְז֖וּ אִ֥ישׁ לֽוֹ׃

53 *The men of the army had seized booty, each man for himself.*

נד וַיִּקַּ֨ח מֹשֶׁ֜ה וְאֶלְעָזָ֤ר הַכֹּהֵן֙ אֶת־
הַזָּהָ֔ב מֵאֵ֛ת שָׂרֵ֥י הָאֲלָפִ֖ים
וְהַמֵּא֑וֹת וַיָּבִ֤אוּ אֹתוֹ֙ אֶל־אֹ֣הֶל

54 *Moshe and Elazar the priest took the gold from the princes of the thousands and of the hundreds, and brought it into the Tent of Ap-*

Thoughtfully, they chose for this purpose all the women's jewelry they had seized as booty, a choice that had perhaps dual significance: They sought to remove from their midst every reminder of the Midianite women. They also expressed thereby that thanks only to their adherence to moral purity did they merit God's miraculous protection. Our Sages interpret this קרבן in a similar vein (see *Shabbos* 64a-b).

וכומז — see Commentary, *Shemos* 35:22.

51 **כל כלי מעשה**. They brought these articles, not out of consideration of the value of the material, but with reference to their meaning for man's use (see Commentary, v. 50).

pointed Meeting as a remembrance for the Children of Israel before God.

מוֹעֵד זִכָּרוֹן לִבְנֵי־יִשְׂרָאֵל לִפְנֵי
יְהוָה׃ פ ששי (שלישי כשהן מחוברין)

32 1 *And the sons of Reuven had a wealth of herds, and the sons of Gad had a very great wealth. And they saw the land of Yazer and the land of Gil'ad, and lo! the region was a region [well suited] for herds.*

לב א וּמִקְנֶה ׀ רַב הָיָה לִבְנֵי רְאוּבֵן
וְלִבְנֵי־גָד עָצוּם מְאֹד וַיִּרְאוּ אֶת־
אֶרֶץ יַעְזֵר וְאֶת־אֶרֶץ גִּלְעָד וְהִנֵּה
הַמָּקוֹם מְקוֹם מִקְנֶה׃

2 *And the sons of Gad and the sons of Reuven came and said to Moshe and to Elazar the priest and to the princes of the community:*

ב וַיָּבֹאוּ בְנֵי־גָד וּבְנֵי רְאוּבֵן וַיֹּאמְרוּ
אֶל־מֹשֶׁה וְאֶל־אֶלְעָזָר הַכֹּהֵן
וְאֶל־נְשִׂיאֵי הָעֵדָה לֵאמֹר׃

3 *Ataros, Divon, Yazer, Nimrah, Cheshbon, El'aleh, Sevam, Nevo and Be'on;*

ג עֲטָרוֹת וְדִיבֹן וְיַעְזֵר וְנִמְרָה
וְחֶשְׁבּוֹן וְאֶלְעָלֵה וּשְׂבָם וּנְבוֹ
וּבְעֹן׃

54 **זכרון לבני ישראל לפני ה׳** — see Commentary, verse 50.

CHAPTER 32

1 **ומקנה רב**. From the accentuation it appears that **עצום מאד** refers to **בני גד**, implying that their herds far outnumbered those of בני ראובן. In any case, the רמב״ן has already noted that only here, in the introduction of this section, is the tribe of Reuven mentioned first, since Reuven is the firstborn, whereas in the continuation the sons of Gad are mentioned first. So we find also in *Devarim* (33:20-21): The sons of Gad are described there as the primary initiators of the idea. In addition, Scripture there describes their courage. Only by virtue of this trait could they have imagined that this idea was realizable. Were it not for this trait, they would not have dared to settle in a special portion outside the boundaries of the whole nation.

4 *The land that* God *has struck down before the community of Israel is a land for herds, and your servants have herds.*

ד הָאָ֗רֶץ אֲשֶׁ֨ר הִכָּ֤ה יְהוָה֙ לִפְנֵי֙ עֲדַ֣ת
יִשְׂרָאֵ֔ל אֶ֥רֶץ מִקְנֶ֖ה הִ֑וא וְלַעֲבָדֶ֖יךָ
מִקְנֶֽה׃ ס

5 *They said: If we have found favor in your eyes, let this land be given to your servants as a possession; do not let us cross the Yarden.*

ה וַיֹּאמְר֗וּ אִם־מָצָ֤אנוּ חֵן֙ בְּעֵינֶ֔יךָ
יֻתַּ֞ן אֶת־הָאָ֧רֶץ הַזֹּ֛את לַעֲבָדֶ֖יךָ
לַאֲחֻזָּ֑ה אַל־תַּעֲבִרֵ֖נוּ אֶת־הַיַּרְדֵּֽן׃

6 *And Moshe said to the sons of Gad and to the sons of Reuven: Shall your brothers come into war and you will sit here?*

ו וַיֹּ֣אמֶר מֹשֶׁ֔ה לִבְנֵי־גָ֖ד וְלִבְנֵ֣י
רְאוּבֵ֑ן הַאַחֵיכֶ֗ם יָבֹ֙אוּ֙ לַמִּלְחָמָ֔ה
וְאַתֶּ֖ם תֵּ֥שְׁבוּ פֹֽה׃

7 *And why do you restrain the heart of the Children of Israel from crossing over into the land that* God *has given them?*

ז וְלָ֣מָּה תְנוֹא֔וּן אֶת־לֵ֖ב בְּנֵ֣י יִשְׂרָאֵ֑ל
מֵֽעֲבֹר֙ אֶל־הָאָ֔רֶץ אֲשֶׁר־נָתַ֥ן לָהֶ֖ם
יְהוָֽה׃

°תניאון קרי

5 **ויאמרו**. The reiteration of this introductory formula implies that there was a pause in their speech. The implication is that they themselves were not at all sure how their proposal would be received. They needed a pause in which to compose themselves sufficiently to continue their presentation.

6 **האחיכם יבואו למלחמה וגו׳** — see Commentary above, 10:9.

7 **ולמה תנואון**. נוא denotes interruption of movement, and it mediates between נוע and נוח (see Commentary, *Bereshis* 28-31).

Here it is used in its primary sense. They and Israel are about to enter the Land. Suddenly, they halt and no longer mean to carry out this intention, and thereby they will also bring the people to refrain from carrying out its original intention. This double reproach is expressed by the קרי and the כתיב [תנואון means to come to a halt, whereas תניאון means to halt others].

8 *That is how your fathers acted when I sent them from Kadesh Barne'a to look at the land.*

ח כֹּה עָשׂוּ אֲבֹתֵיכֶם בְּשָׁלְחִי אֹתָם
מִקָּדֵשׁ בַּרְנֵעַ לִרְאוֹת אֶת־הָאָרֶץ׃

9 *They went up as far as the Valley of the Grapes and looked at the land, and restrained the heart of the Children of Israel so that they should not come into the land that* God *had given them.*

ט וַיַּעֲלוּ עַד־נַחַל אֶשְׁכּוֹל וַיִּרְאוּ אֶת־
הָאָרֶץ וַיָּנִיאוּ אֶת־לֵב בְּנֵי יִשְׂרָאֵל
לְבִלְתִּי־בֹא אֶל־הָאָרֶץ אֲשֶׁר־נָתַן
לָהֶם יְהֹוָה׃

10 *And the anger of* God *was stirred on that day and He swore:*

י וַיִּחַר־אַף יְהֹוָה בַּיּוֹם הַהוּא וַיִּשָּׁבַע
לֵאמֹר׃

11 *The men who came up from Egypt, from twenty years old and upward, will not see the land that I have sworn to Avraham, Yitzchak and Ya'akov, for they did not fulfill their duty [to] follow Me;*

יא אִם־יִרְאוּ הָאֲנָשִׁים הָעֹלִים
מִמִּצְרַיִם מִבֶּן עֶשְׂרִים שָׁנָה וָמַעְלָה
אֵת הָאֲדָמָה אֲשֶׁר נִשְׁבַּעְתִּי
לְאַבְרָהָם לְיִצְחָק וּלְיַעֲקֹב כִּי לֹא־
מִלְאוּ אַחֲרָי׃

12 *Except for Kalev, son of Yefunneh, the Kenizi, and Yehoshua, son of Nun, for they fulfilled their duty [by] following* God.

יב בִּלְתִּי כָּלֵב בֶּן־יְפֻנֶּה הַקְּנִזִּי וִיהוֹשֻׁעַ
בִּן־נוּן כִּי מִלְאוּ אַחֲרֵי יְהֹוָה׃

11-12 מלאו אחרי ה׳, לא מלאו אחרי — see Commentary above, 14:24.

The missing דגש [in מלאו] requires explanation. [מִלֵּא in the *pi'el*, the intense form, indicating a high degree of faithfulness, has a דגש; the less intense *kal* form מָלֵא lacks a דגש.] Perhaps in verse 11 it indicates the high degree of their unfaithfulness. It cannot be said of them that מלאו אחרי — not in the *pi'el* nor even in the *kal* [i.e., they did not even display the basic minimum of faith in His ways]. By contrast, it then says [in verse 12] of Yehoshua and Kalev that מלאו אחרי [the *pi'el* form without a דגש]. The fact that they are worthy of entering the Land does not yet prove a high degree of faithfulness to duty.

13 *So the anger of* God *was stirred against Israel, and He made them wander about in the wilderness for forty years, until that whole generation which had done what was evil in the eyes of* God *had come to an end.*

יג וַיִּחַר־אַף יְהוָה בְּיִשְׂרָאֵל וַיְנִעֵם
בַּמִּדְבָּר אַרְבָּעִים שָׁנָה עַד־תֹּם
כָּל־הַדּוֹר הָעֹשֶׂה הָרַע בְּעֵינֵי
יְהוָה׃

14 *And now you have arisen in the place of your fathers, [you] brood of sinful men, to add to the wrath of* God *that was kindled against Israel.*

יד וְהִנֵּה קַמְתֶּם תַּחַת אֲבֹתֵיכֶם
תַּרְבּוּת אֲנָשִׁים חַטָּאִים לִסְפּוֹת
עוֹד עַל חֲרוֹן אַף־יְהוָה אֶל־
יִשְׂרָאֵל׃

15 *If you hold back from following Him, He will make them remain in the wilderness even longer, and you will have prepared ruin for this whole people.*

טו כִּי תְשׁוּבֻן מֵאַחֲרָיו וְיָסַף עוֹד
לְהַנִּיחוֹ בַּמִּדְבָּר וְשִׁחַתֶּם לְכָל־
הָעָם הַזֶּה׃ ס

16 *And they came up to him and said: We want to build sheepfolds for our cattle [here] and cities for our children.*

טז וַיִּגְּשׁוּ אֵלָיו וַיֹּאמְרוּ גִּדְרֹת צֹאן
נִבְנֶה לְמִקְנֵנוּ פֹּה וְעָרִים לְטַפֵּנוּ׃

---

14 **קמתם תחת אבתיכם**. With this proposal of yours, you take the place of your fathers and continue their unfaithfulness to duty. You show yourselves as תרבות אנשים חטאים, sons brought up by sinful people (see Commentary, *Bereshis* 1:28).

16 **גדרת צאן נבנה למקננו וגו׳**. Our Sages in *Midrash Rabbah* say that the order in which בני גד ובני ראובן phrased their proposal shows that their property was dearer to them than anything else, and it was this pursuit of wealth that lay at the basis of their whole proposal. They cared about their cattle more than about their children; hence they first mentioned גדרת צאן למקננו and only then ערים לטפנו. Otherwise, they would have re-

17 *And we will go out quickly in the vanguard before the Children of Israel, until we have brought them to their place. Our children can remain in the fortified cities in the face of the inhabitants of the land.*

יז וַאֲנַחְנוּ נֵחָלֵץ חֻשִׁים לִפְנֵי בְּנֵי
יִשְׂרָאֵל עַד אֲשֶׁר אִם־הֲבִיאֹנֻם
אֶל־מְקוֹמָם וְיָשַׁב טַפֵּנוּ בְּעָרֵי
הַמִּבְצָר מִפְּנֵי יֹשְׁבֵי הָאָרֶץ׃

18 *We shall not return to our homes until the Children of Israel have taken over each one his inheritance.*

יח לֹא נָשׁוּב אֶל־בָּתֵּינוּ עַד הִתְנַחֵל
בְּנֵי יִשְׂרָאֵל אִישׁ נַחֲלָתוֹ׃

19 *For we do not want to inherit with them on the other side of the Yarden and beyond, if our inheritance has already come to us on the eastern side of the Yarden.*

יט כִּי לֹא נִנְחַל אִתָּם מֵעֵבֶר לַיַּרְדֵּן
וָהָלְאָה כִּי בָאָה נַחֲלָתֵנוּ אֵלֵינוּ
מֵעֵבֶר הַיַּרְדֵּן מִזְרָחָה׃ פ שביעי
(רביעי כשהן מחוברין)

20 *And Moshe said to them: If you will do this, if you will go forth to the war before* God, *in the vanguard,*

כ וַיֹּאמֶר אֲלֵיהֶם מֹשֶׁה אִם־תַּעֲשׂוּן
אֶת־הַדָּבָר הַזֶּה אִם־תֵּחָלְצוּ לִפְנֵי
יְהוָה לַמִּלְחָמָה׃

considered, if only for the sake of their children, before jeopardizing their spiritual connection with the rest of the nation and its Sanctuary because of the allurement of attractive pastureland.

In Moshe's reply (v. 24), he puts the care of the children first, and the petitioners obviously took due notice of this, for in their summation (v. 26) they, too, put the children and the women before the livestock.

Our Sages say further that this placing too much value in material wealth caused them to fare badly in the end. Just as they grasped at possession prematurely, they were the first to lose their possessions and their homeland. Of all the tribes, they were the first to be exiled by Pul and Tiglas Pileser (see *Divrei Ha-Yamim* I, 5:26).

17 **חשים**. חוש, עוש, אוץ: to hasten and push toward something, to hurry.

21 *And every one of you who goes out into the vanguard will cross the Yarden before* God, *until He has driven out His enemies from before Him,*

כא וְעָבַר לָכֶם כָּל־חָלוּץ אֶת־הַיַּרְדֵּן לִפְנֵי יְהוָה עַד הוֹרִישׁוֹ אֶת־אֹיְבָיו מִפָּנָיו׃

22 *And the land is conquered before* God, *and you will return only then, and you will thus be freed from your obligation by* God *and by Israel, then this land will become your property before* God.

כב וְנִכְבְּשָׁה הָאָרֶץ לִפְנֵי יְהוָה וְאַחַר תָּשֻׁבוּ וִהְיִיתֶם נְקִיִּם מֵיְהוָה וּמִיִּשְׂרָאֵל וְהָיְתָה הָאָרֶץ הַזֹּאת לָכֶם לַאֲחֻזָּה לִפְנֵי יְהוָה׃

23 *But if you will not do this, then lo! you [will] have sinned against* God, *and be aware of your sin that will befall you!*

כג וְאִם־לֹא תַעֲשׂוּן כֵּן הִנֵּה חֲטָאתֶם לַיהוָה וּדְעוּ חַטַּאתְכֶם אֲשֶׁר תִּמְצָא אֶתְכֶם׃

24 *Build yourselves cities for your children and sheepfolds for your sheep and that which has proceeded from your mouth you shall do.*

כד בְּנוּ־לָכֶם עָרִים לְטַפְּכֶם וּגְדֵרֹת לְצֹנַאֲכֶם וְהַיֹּצֵא מִפִּיכֶם תַּעֲשׂוּ׃

22 **והייתם נקים מה׳ ומישראל** — cf. והיית נקי מאלתי, אז תנקה מאלתי (*Bereshis* 24:41): The oath that you took will cause you no harm; it will not obligate you any further; you will have fulfilled your obligation (cf. Commentary, ibid. 24:8). Here, too, the meaning is: God and Israel will have no further demands of you.

23 **חטאתכם אשר תמצא**. Sin and its consequences strike the sinner. Not only will they not receive the transjordanic territory if they fail to fulfill the condition (v. 30), but they will be punished for breaking their promise.

24 **לצנאכם** — like לצאנכם; similarly, צֹנֶה in *Tehillim* 8:8 [is an unusual form of צאן]. Perhaps Moshe drew out the word in order to linger on it, and thus imply: "your sheep, about which you care too much." In any case,

25 *And the sons of Gad and the sons of Reuven said to Moshe in one accord: Your servants will do as my lord commands.*

כה וַיֹּאמֶר בְּנֵי־גָד וּבְנֵי רְאוּבֵן אֶל־
מֹשֶׁה לֵאמֹר עֲבָדֶיךָ יַעֲשׂוּ כַּאֲשֶׁר
אֲדֹנִי מְצַוֶּה׃

26 *Our children, our wives, our herds and all our livestock will remain there in the cities of Gil'ad,*

כו טַפֵּנוּ נָשֵׁינוּ מִקְנֵנוּ וְכָל־בְּהֶמְתֵּנוּ
יִהְיוּ־שָׁם בְּעָרֵי הַגִּלְעָד׃

27 *And your servants, every one who has gone forth into the army, will cross over before* God *to the war, just as my lord says.*

כז וַעֲבָדֶיךָ יַעַבְרוּ כָּל־חֲלוּץ צָבָא
לִפְנֵי יְהוָה לַמִּלְחָמָה כַּאֲשֶׁר אֲדֹנִי
דֹּבֵר׃

28 *Concerning them, Moshe then commanded Elazar the priest, Yehoshua, son of Nun, and the heads of the tribal fathers of the Children of Israel.*

כח וַיְצַו לָהֶם מֹשֶׁה אֵת אֶלְעָזָר הַכֹּהֵן
וְאֵת יְהוֹשֻׁעַ בִּן־נוּן וְאֶת־רָאשֵׁי
אֲבוֹת הַמַּטּוֹת לִבְנֵי יִשְׂרָאֵל׃

29 *Moshe said to them: If the sons of Gad and the sons of Reuven cross the Yarden with you, each one who has gone forth to war before* God, *and the land will be conquered before you, then you shall give them the land of Gil'ad as a possession.*

כט וַיֹּאמֶר מֹשֶׁה אֲלֵהֶם אִם־יַעַבְרוּ
בְנֵי־גָד וּבְנֵי־רְאוּבֵן ׀ אִתְּכֶם אֶת־
הַיַּרְדֵּן כָּל־חָלוּץ לַמִּלְחָמָה לִפְנֵי
יְהוָה וְנִכְבְּשָׁה הָאָרֶץ לִפְנֵיכֶם
וּנְתַתֶּם לָהֶם אֶת־אֶרֶץ הַגִּלְעָד
לַאֲחֻזָּה׃

---

converting צאן into צנא and צנה has the same sense of intensifying the concept. צאן — related to שאן — denotes animals that must be guarded by man (see Commentary, *Shemos* 21:37). צנא and צנה — related to צנע and צנח — denote intensive sheltering in a hiding place (see Commentary, v. 16).

29-30 This contract made with בני גד and בני ראובן was dependent on a condition, and it is the classic example in Jewish jurisprudence of an act that will

30 *But if they do not cross with you, ready for battle, then they shall settle down among you in the land of Canaan.*

ל וְאִם־לֹא יַעַבְרוּ חֲלוּצִים אִתְּכֶם וְנֹאחֲזוּ בְתֹכְכֶם בְּאֶרֶץ כְּנָעַן׃

take effect upon condition. The condition is valid if the following requirements (see *Kiddushin* 61a, *Gittin* 75a-b, *Kesubos* 74a) are met:

(a) תנאי כפול. Both cases — fulfillment and nonfulfillment of the condition — must be expressly stated. Thus here: אם יעברו וגו׳ ואם לא יעברו וגו׳. It is not sufficient that the alternative is self-understood, מכלל הן אתה שומע לאו and מכלל לאו אתה שומע הן.

(b) תנאי קודם למעשה. The condition must precede the contingent act: אם יעברו וגו׳ ונתתם וגו׳ ואם לא יעברו וגו׳ ונאחזו; and the order must not be reversed: תתנו אם יעברו. (According to the רמב״ם in הל׳ אישות, 6:4, this requirement does not apply to the formulation, but to the performance: The condition has no effect if one first performs the act and then meets the condition.)

(c) הן קודם ללאו. The case of the condition's fulfillment must precede the case of its nonfulfillment; first אם יעברו and then ואם לא יעברו.

(d) תנאי בדבר אחד ומעשה בדבר אחר. The fulfillment of the condition must not entail the nullification of the contingent act — e.g., אם תחזירי לי את הנייר הרי זה גיטך [*Gittin* 75a-b].

(e) אפשר לקיומיה על ידי שליח. The act which is dependent on the condition can be performed also by an agent, as in the division of the land by Yehoshua. This excludes, for example, חליצה, which is a mitzvah that must be done personally.

As our Sages say (*Kiddushin* 61a): כל תנאי שאינו כתנאי בני גד ובני ראובן אינו תנאי. Any condition that does not conform to these requirements is of no consequence; the condition is null and void, and the act remains binding: התנאי בטל והמעשה קיים. However, it is questionable whether this rule applies in all cases, and there are divergent opinions among the halachic authorities as to which *halachos* and to which cases this rule applies (see especially the commentators to *Gittin* 75a-b).

In any event, there are cases where גילוי מלתא בעלמא is sufficient; it suffices if, at the performance of the act, one indicates that the act is to take effect only conditionally, and it is not necessary to verbally spell out

לא וַיַּעֲנ֧וּ בְנֵי־גָ֛ד וּבְנֵ֥י רְאוּבֵ֖ן לֵאמֹ֑ר
אֵת֩ אֲשֶׁ֨ר דִּבֶּ֧ר יְהוָ֛ה אֶל־עֲבָדֶ֖יךָ
כֵּ֥ן נַעֲשֶֽׂה׃

31 *And the sons of Gad and the sons of Reuven answered: That which* God *has spoken to your servants, so we will do.*

לב נַ֣חְנוּ נַעֲבֹ֧ר חֲלוּצִ֛ים לִפְנֵ֥י יְהוָ֖ה
אֶ֣רֶץ כְּנָ֑עַן וְאִתָּ֙נוּ֙ אֲחֻזַּ֣ת נַחֲלָתֵ֔נוּ
מֵעֵ֖בֶר לַיַּרְדֵּֽן׃

32 *We will cross, ready for battle, before* God, *into the land of Canaan, and with us [will go] the occupancy of our inheritance on this side of the Yarden.*

לג וַיִּתֵּ֣ן לָהֶ֣ם ׀ מֹשֶׁ֡ה לִבְנֵי־גָ֡ד וְלִבְנֵ֣י
רְאוּבֵ֡ן וְלַחֲצִ֣י ׀ שֵׁ֣בֶט ׀ מְנַשֶּׁ֣ה בֶן־
יוֹסֵ֗ף אֶת־מַמְלֶ֙כֶת֙ סִיחֹן֙ מֶ֣לֶךְ
הָֽאֱמֹרִ֔י וְאֶ֨ת־מַמְלֶ֔כֶת ע֖וֹג מֶ֣לֶךְ
הַבָּשָׁ֑ן הָאָ֗רֶץ לְעָרֶ֙יהָ֙ בִּגְבֻלֹ֔ת עָרֵ֥י
הָאָ֖רֶץ סָבִֽיב׃

33 *And Moshe gave to them — to the sons of Gad and the sons of Reuven and the half-tribe of Menashe, son of Yosef — the realm of Sichon, king of the Emori, and the realm of Og, king of the Bashan, the land according to its cities within borders, the cities of the land round about.*

one's intention. Moreover, there are cases דאפילו גילוי מלתא לא בעי, for from the circumstances it is clear and apparent that the act is contingent, and in these cases it is not necessary even to indicate that one has in mind a condition (see תוספות *Kiddushin* 49b ד״ה דברים שבלב).

32 **ואתנו אחזת נחלתנו** apparently means: Our possession of our inheritance here will cross over with us to the other side of the Yarden. That is to say, we cannot take possession of this land while we are still here, on this side of the Yarden. Only by virtue of what we will do on the other side of the Yarden will we merit to take possession of our inheritance on this side.

33 **ולחצי שבט מנשה**. Scripture does not report the motives and factors that led to half the tribe of Menashe joining the transjordanic settlement. The רמב״ן speculates that when the time came to divide up the land, it proved to be too large for the needs of the two tribes, and consequently half the tribe of Menashe joined them.

34 *The sons of Gad built Divon and Ataros and Aro'er;*

לד וַיִּבְנוּ בְנֵי־גָד אֶת־דִּיבֹן וְאֶת־
עֲטָרֹת וְאֵת עֲרֹעֵר׃

35 *Atros Shofan, Yazer and Yagbehah;*

לה וְאֶת־עַטְרֹת שׁוֹפָן וְאֶת־יַעְזֵר
וְיָגְבְּהָה׃

36 *Beis Nimrah and Beis Haran, as fortified cities and sheepfolds.*

לו וְאֶת־בֵּית נִמְרָה וְאֶת־בֵּית הָרָן
עָרֵי מִבְצָר וְגִדְרֹת צֹאן׃

37 *The sons of Reuven built Cheshbon and El'ale and Kiryasayim;*

לז וּבְנֵי רְאוּבֵן בָּנוּ אֶת־חֶשְׁבּוֹן וְאֶת־
אֶלְעָלֵא וְאֵת קִרְיָתָיִם׃

38 *Nevo and Ba'al Me'on — their names being changed — and Sivmah; for the rest, they retained the names of the cities that they had constructed.*

לח וְאֶת־נְבוֹ וְאֶת־בַּעַל מְעוֹן מוּסַבֹּת
שֵׁם וְאֶת־שִׂבְמָה וַיִּקְרְאוּ בְשֵׁמֹת
אֶת־שְׁמוֹת הֶעָרִים אֲשֶׁר בָּנוּ׃

הארץ לעריה בגבלת: He gave them the land, dividing it among the tribes according to the cities and their defined districts. At that time it was already determined which cities would belong to the domain of Reuven, which to Gad, and which to the half tribe of Menashe.

ערי הארץ סביב: All the cities were marked off, including those cities that the population of that time could not occupy residentially.

34-36 **ויבנו וגו׳ את דיבן וגו׳ ערי מבצר וגו׳**: They rebuilt the cities, converting them into fortresses for their wives and children or into enclosures for their flocks.

38 **מוסבת שם**. Nevo and Ba'al Me'on — both names of gods — were renamed. **ויקראו בשמת**: As for the other cities, they retained the old names, even in the case of the cities they rebuilt into fortresses. According to the רמב״ן, however, מוסבת שם means that the cities had been renamed under Sichon's rule; ויקראו וגו׳: but the sons of Reuven restored to them their original names by which they were called under Moav.

39 *The sons of Machir, son of Menashe, went to Gil'ad and conquered it, and he drove out the Emori who dwelt there.*	לט וַיֵּלְכוּ בְּנֵי מָכִיר בֶּן־מְנַשֶּׁה גִּלְעָדָה וַיִּלְכְּדֻהָ וַיּוֹרֶשׁ אֶת־הָאֱמֹרִי אֲשֶׁר־בָּהּ: מפטיר
40 *And Moshe gave the Gil'ad to Machir, son of Menashe, and he settled there.*	מ וַיִּתֵּן מֹשֶׁה אֶת־הַגִּלְעָד לְמָכִיר בֶּן־מְנַשֶּׁה וַיֵּשֶׁב בָּהּ:
41 *Ya'ir, son of Menashe, went and conquered their villages and named them "Villages of Ya'ir."*	מא וְיָאִיר בֶּן־מְנַשֶּׁה הָלַךְ וַיִּלְכֹּד אֶת־חַוֹּתֵיהֶם וַיִּקְרָא אֶתְהֶן חַוֹּת יָאִיר:
42 *Novach went and conquered Kenas and its daughter cities, and named it Novach, after his own name.*	מב וְנֹבַח הָלַךְ וַיִּלְכֹּד אֶת־קְנָת וְאֶת־בְּנֹתֶיהָ וַיִּקְרָא לָה נֹבַח בִּשְׁמוֹ: פפפ

41 **חות יאיר**. The etymology of חוה — in the sense of village — is uncertain. One theory is that it derives from חיי with the י changed to ו, like הוה from היה. In that case, חוה resembles וְחַיַּת פְּלִשְׁתִּים [*Shemuel* II 23:13] and means "a circle of people" (cf. Commentary, *Bereshis* 18:10).

It is possible, however, that חוה is related to חבא ,חפא, which mean: to hide and cover up. In that case, חוה denotes the village as a place of protection, whose dwellings are meant primarily for residence and for the protection of people, but which are not the primary place of man's activity. This in contrast to the city, עיר, which encompasses human society organically, like skin (עור), and is the place of development of man's intellectual culture — עיר from the root עור (see Commentary, ibid. 4:17).

The other term for village is כְּפַר, from the root כפר, protective covering. This term is formed in accordance with the same train of thought [that a village is a place of protection].

42 **ויקרא לה**. לה has no מפיק in the ה. In this regard, our Sages (*Midrash Rabbah* on *Ruth* 2:13) comment: מלמד שלא עמד לה אותו השם. That is to say, Novach sought to immortalize himself in the name of the city and its daughter cities, but this name was not retained, and Novach did not attain his desire.

33 1 *These are the journeys of the Children of Israel, who had gone out of the land of Egypt according to their organized groups, under the guidance of Moshe and Aharon.*	**לג** א אֵ֣לֶּה מַסְעֵ֣י בְנֵֽי־יִשְׂרָאֵ֔ל אֲשֶׁ֥ר יָצְא֛וּ מֵאֶ֥רֶץ מִצְרַ֖יִם לְצִבְאֹתָ֑ם בְּיַד־מֹשֶׁ֖ה וְאַהֲרֹֽן׃
2 *Moshe recorded their decampments for their journeys at the command of* God, *and these are their journeys for their decampments.*	א וַיִּכְתֹּ֨ב מֹשֶׁ֜ה אֶת־מוֹצָאֵיהֶ֛ם לְמַסְעֵיהֶ֖ם עַל־פִּ֣י יְהֹוָ֑ה וְאֵ֥לֶּה מַסְעֵיהֶ֖ם לְמוֹצָאֵיהֶֽם׃

Does this perhaps imply a slight reproof of Novach? He sought to erect for himself an eternal memorial in structures of wood and stone, but that is not the way of a true Jew who seeks to immortalize himself on earth. For only through great feats of the spirit, through moral faithfulness to duty, and through the whole content of a noble life will one's name be perpetuated through the ages.

מסעי

CHAPTER 33

1-2 There could be various reasons for the Torah's inclusion of this list of the journeys and stopovers in the wilderness. These journeys and stopovers were associated with a whole series of events and experiences which were worthy of being remembered by the kinsmen, the fellow tribesmen, and the descendants of those directly affected by them. However, these events — experienced by particular families and tribes — are not recorded in the Torah, which addresses the nation as a whole. The memory of these events was therefore preserved by oral tradition, and this list includes signposts and signals by which to remember that tradition.

One can only surmise how many other traces of the wanderings and sojournings of our forefathers may have been preserved in these places in the wilderness for the immediate and more distant future, and what opportunities these could have offered to the children and the grandchildren of the generation of the wilderness to visit the places where God revealed Himself in His wondrous guidance. Visiting these places, future generations could contemplate the authenticity of God's presence on earth so eloquently expressed in the history of their forebears. The very barrenness and aridity of these localities in the wilderness, a desert so vast that even a caravan must carefully count the days in order to make its provisions hold out, a desert in which an entire people, at least two and a half million souls, lived for forty years — the very sight of these places in the wilderness (as the רמב"ם notes in *Moreh Nevuchim* III:50) provides ample documentation of the Divine nature of the history of Israel's establishment!

רש"י conveys to us a comment by ר' משה הדרשן: Of the forty-two journeys recorded in this register, fourteen — from Rameses to Ritmah — preceded the sending of the spies, and eight — from Mount Hor to the wastelands of Mo'av — were [undertaken] during the fortieth year, after the death of Aharon. This means that there were only twenty journeys during the thirty-eight years of wandering. Thus, God in His mercy mitigated the decree of wandering in the wilderness. They were not forced to wander interminably, without resting, for the average duration of their stay at each stopover was nearly two years.

ויכתב משה את מוצאיהם למסעיהם על פי ה' ואלה מסעיהם למוצאיהם. The change in the order of the words is certainly not without significance. God regarded their travels as מוצאיהם למסעיהם, whereas Israel regarded them as מסעיהם למוצאיהם.

The journey and the encampment were always at God's command (above, 9:17ff. and Commentary there). Whenever God ordered them to break camp, His intention was that they should *attain* a new goal, and God's educative guidance would seek out for them a new resting place which was suitable for the attainment of that goal. Each מסע entailed progress; the מסע was the purpose of the מוצא (decampment). Thus, all their decampments were מוצאיהם למסעיהם.

To the people, it was just the opposite. Wherever they stayed, they were dissatisfied. When the time came to leave a place, for them the decampment was the purpose. It did not matter to them where they were going next; the main thing was to leave the place in which they had been staying. They journeyed forth in order to leave their place of encampment. Thus, all their journeys were מסעיהם למוצאיהם.

3 *They journeyed from Rameses in the first month, on the fifteenth day of the first month. On the morning after the Pesach offering, the Children of Israel went out with a high hand, before the eyes of all the Egyptians.*

ג וַיִּסְעוּ מֵרַעְמְסֵס בַּחֹדֶשׁ הָרִאשׁוֹן
בַּחֲמִשָּׁה עָשָׂר יוֹם לַחֹדֶשׁ
הָרִאשׁוֹן מִמָּחֳרַת הַפֶּסַח יָצְאוּ
בְנֵי־יִשְׂרָאֵל בְּיָד רָמָה לְעֵינֵי כָּל־
מִצְרָיִם׃

4 *And the Egyptians buried what* God *had struck down from among them, every firstborn, and* God *had executed judgments also upon their gods.*

ד וּמִצְרַיִם מְקַבְּרִים אֵת אֲשֶׁר הִכָּה
יְהוָה בָּהֶם כָּל־בְּכוֹר וּבֵאלֹהֵיהֶם
עָשָׂה יְהוָה שְׁפָטִים׃

3-4 **ממחרת הפסח**, not in the night. In the night, the redemption was brought about by the death of the firstborn (*Shemos* 12:29). But the exodus took place in broad daylight, ביד רמה לעיני כל מצרים (*Berachos* 9a).

ומצרים מקברים. This contrast is integral to the ideas that the memory of the redemption from Egypt is to preserve and establish as fundamentals of faith. The rays of the morning sun showed the slave people raised to freedom and, beside it, the master race downcast and bewailing the loss of its most precious sons and assets. It showed the one and the same hand of the one sole God putting to death and bringing to life at the same time. Both together — fear and trust in the heart of man who faces the one and only God — form the foundation of Jewish consciousness of God. This came to heightened expression at the shore of the Red Sea: וירא ישראל וגו׳ וייראו העם את ה׳ ויאמינו בה׳ וגו׳ (*Shemos* 14:31; see Commentary there).

That is why the moment of the exodus, in its full characteristics, also appears in the list of the journeys and encampments of Israel's wanderings, and is also the cardinal point of פרשת קדש in תפלין (*Shemos* 13:1-10). It is the point of departure from which every Jewish man is to sanctify his "thoughts, desires, and deeds," a sanctification he is to renew each day.

ובאלהיהם עשה ה׳ שפטים. This whole event demonstrated the nullity of the supposed gods, as opposed to the reality and actuality of the one

5 *The Children of Israel journeyed from Rameses and camped in Sukkos.*

ה וַיִּסְעוּ בְנֵי־יִשְׂרָאֵל מֵרַעְמְסֵס וַיַּחֲנוּ
בְּסֻכֹּת׃

6 *They journeyed from Sukkos and camped in Esam, which lies at the edge of the wilderness.*

ו וַיִּסְעוּ מִסֻּכֹּת וַיַּחֲנוּ בְאֵתָם אֲשֶׁר
בִּקְצֵה הַמִּדְבָּר׃

7 *They journeyed from Esam, and it turned back toward Pi Hachiros, which lies before Ba'al Tzefon, and they camped before Migdol.*

ז וַיִּסְעוּ מֵאֵתָם וַיָּשָׁב עַל־פִּי הַחִירֹת
אֲשֶׁר עַל־פְּנֵי בַּעַל צְפוֹן וַיַּחֲנוּ
לִפְנֵי מִגְדֹּל׃

8 *They journeyed from before Hachiros and crossed through the midst of the sea toward the wilderness. They went a three days' journey in the wilderness of Esam and camped in Marah.*

ח וַיִּסְעוּ מִפְּנֵי הַחִירֹת וַיַּעַבְרוּ
בְתוֹךְ־הַיָּם הַמִּדְבָּרָה וַיֵּלְכוּ דֶּרֶךְ
שְׁלֹשֶׁת יָמִים בְּמִדְבַּר אֵתָם וַיַּחֲנוּ
בְּמָרָה׃

9 *They journeyed from Marah and came to Eilim, and in Eilim there were twelve springs of water and seventy date palms; there they camped.*

ט וַיִּסְעוּ מִמָּרָה וַיָּבֹאוּ אֵילִמָה
וּבְאֵילִם שְׁתֵּים עֶשְׂרֵה עֵינֹת מַיִם
וְשִׁבְעִים תְּמָרִים וַיַּחֲנוּ־שָׁם׃

---

sole God. Thus, the gods and their emblems likewise lay in ruins, like corpses, beside the Egyptian people, which was stricken with the loss of its dearest ones.

7 **וישב וגו'**. The switch to the singular requires explanation, for everything before and after is related in the plural. Perhaps Scripture's meaning is that they turned back with unanimous trust in God, even though the order to turn back must certainly have seemed odd to them.

9 **ובאילים שתים עשרה וגו'**. Such a place in which to encamp they did not find again in their whole journey through the wilderness.

10 *They journeyed from Eilim and camped by the Sea of Reeds.*

י וַיִּסְעוּ מֵאֵילִם וַיַּחֲנוּ עַל־יַם־סוּף׃

שני

11 *They journeyed from the Sea of Reeds and camped in the wilderness of Sin.*

יא וַיִּסְעוּ מִיַּם־סוּף וַיַּחֲנוּ בְּמִדְבַּר־סִין׃

12 *They journeyed from the wilderness of Sin and camped in Dofkah.*

יב וַיִּסְעוּ מִמִּדְבַּר־סִין וַיַּחֲנוּ בְּדָפְקָה׃

13 *They journeyed from Dofkah and camped in Alush.*

יג וַיִּסְעוּ מִדָּפְקָה וַיַּחֲנוּ בְּאָלוּשׁ׃

14 *They journeyed from Alush and camped in Refidim, where there was no water for the people to drink.*

יד וַיִּסְעוּ מֵאָלוּשׁ וַיַּחֲנוּ בִּרְפִידִם
וְלֹא־הָיָה שָׁם מַיִם לָעָם לִשְׁתּוֹת׃

15 *They journeyed from Refidim and camped in the wilderness of Sinai.*

טו וַיִּסְעוּ מֵרְפִידִם וַיַּחֲנוּ בְּמִדְבַּר סִינָי׃

16 *They journeyed from the wilderness of Sinai and camped in Kivros Hata'avah.*

טז וַיִּסְעוּ מִמִּדְבַּר סִינָי וַיַּחֲנוּ בְּקִבְרֹת הַתַּאֲוָה׃

17 *They journeyed from Kivros HaTaavah and camped in Chatzeros.*

יז וַיִּסְעוּ מִקִּבְרֹת הַתַּאֲוָה וַיַּחֲנוּ בַּחֲצֵרֹת׃

18 *They journeyed from Chatzeros and camped in Rismah.*

יח וַיִּסְעוּ מֵחֲצֵרֹת וַיַּחֲנוּ בְּרִתְמָה׃

---

14 **ולא היה שם מים**. Here began the terrors of the waterless desert, and here they were given the well of never-failing water, which flowed to them from Chorev. This well accompanied them through the wilderness from here onward.

19 *They journeyed from Rismah and camped in Rimmon Peretz.*

יט וַיִּסְעוּ מֵרִתְמָה וַיַּחֲנוּ בְּרִמֹּן פָּרֶץ׃

20 *They journeyed from Rimmon Peretz and camped in Livnah.*

כ וַיִּסְעוּ מֵרִמֹּן פָּרֶץ וַיַּחֲנוּ בְּלִבְנָה׃

21 *They journeyed from Livnah and camped in Rissah.*

כא וַיִּסְעוּ מִלִּבְנָה וַיַּחֲנוּ בְּרִסָּה׃

22 *They journeyed from Rissah and camped in Kehelasah.*

כב וַיִּסְעוּ מֵרִסָּה וַיַּחֲנוּ בִּקְהֵלָתָה׃

23 *They journeyed from Kehelasah and camped in Har Shefer.*

כג וַיִּסְעוּ מִקְּהֵלָתָה וַיַּחֲנוּ בְּהַר־שָׁפֶר׃

24 *They journeyed from Har Shefer and camped in Charadah.*

כד וַיִּסְעוּ מֵהַר־שָׁפֶר וַיַּחֲנוּ בַּחֲרָדָה׃

25 *They journeyed from Charadah and camped in Makhelos.*

כה וַיִּסְעוּ מֵחֲרָדָה וַיַּחֲנוּ בְּמַקְהֵלֹת׃

26 *They journeyed from Makhelos and camped in Tachas.*

כו וַיִּסְעוּ מִמַּקְהֵלֹת וַיַּחֲנוּ בְּתָחַת׃

27 *They journeyed from Tachas and camped in Terach.*

כז וַיִּסְעוּ מִתָּחַת וַיַּחֲנוּ בְּתָרַח׃

28 *They journeyed from Terach and camped in Miskah.*

כח וַיִּסְעוּ מִתָּרַח וַיַּחֲנוּ בְּמִתְקָה׃

29 *They journeyed from Miskah and camped in Chashmonah.*

כט וַיִּסְעוּ מִמִּתְקָה וַיַּחֲנוּ בְּחַשְׁמֹנָה׃

30 *They journeyed from Chashmonah and camped in Moseros.*

ל וַיִּסְעוּ מֵחַשְׁמֹנָה וַיַּחֲנוּ בְּמֹסֵרוֹת׃

31 *They journeyed from Moseros and camped in Benei Ya'akan.*

לא וַיִּסְעוּ מִמֹּסֵרוֹת וַיַּחֲנוּ בִּבְנֵי יַעֲקָן׃

32 *They journeyed from Benei Ya'akan and camped in Chor Hagidgad.*

לב וַיִּסְעוּ מִבְּנֵי יַעֲקָן וַיַּחֲנוּ בְּחֹר הַגִּדְגָּד׃

33 *They journeyed from Chor Hagidgad and camped in Yatvasah.*

לג וַיִּסְעוּ מֵחֹר הַגִּדְגָּד וַיַּחֲנוּ בְּיָטְבָתָה׃

34 *They journeyed from Yatvasah and camped in Avronah.*

לד וַיִּסְעוּ מִיָּטְבָתָה וַיַּחֲנוּ בְּעַבְרֹנָה׃

35 *They journeyed from Avronah and camped in Etzyon Gever.*

לה וַיִּסְעוּ מֵעַבְרֹנָה וַיַּחֲנוּ בְּעֶצְיֹן גָּבֶר׃

36 *They journeyed from Etzyon Gever and camped in the wilderness of Tzin, which is Kadesh.*

לו וַיִּסְעוּ מֵעֶצְיֹן גָּבֶר וַיַּחֲנוּ בְמִדְבַּר־צִן הִוא קָדֵשׁ׃

37 *They journeyed from Kadesh and camped on Mount Hor, at the edge of the land of Edom.*

לז וַיִּסְעוּ מִקָּדֵשׁ וַיַּחֲנוּ בְּהֹר הָהָר בִּקְצֵה אֶרֶץ אֱדוֹם׃

38 *Aharon the priest went up to Mount Hor at the command of* God *and died there, in the fortieth year after the exodus of the Children of Israel from the land of Egypt, in the fifth month, on the first of the month.*

לח וַיַּעַל אַהֲרֹן הַכֹּהֵן אֶל־הֹר הָהָר עַל־פִּי יְהוָה וַיָּמָת שָׁם בִּשְׁנַת הָאַרְבָּעִים לְצֵאת בְּנֵי־יִשְׂרָאֵל מֵאֶרֶץ מִצְרַיִם בַּחֹדֶשׁ הַחֲמִישִׁי בְּאֶחָד לַחֹדֶשׁ׃

39 *And Aharon was one hundred and twenty-three years old when he died on Mount Hor.*

לט וְאַהֲרֹן בֶּן־שָׁלֹשׁ וְעֶשְׂרִים וּמְאַת שָׁנָה בְּמֹתוֹ בְּהֹר הָהָר׃ ס

40 *And the Canaanite, the king of Arad — he dwelt in the south in the land of Canaan — heard that the Children of Israel were approaching.*

מ וַיִּשְׁמַע הַכְּנַעֲנִי מֶלֶךְ עֲרָד וְהוּא־יֹשֵׁב בַּנֶּגֶב בְּאֶרֶץ כְּנָעַן בְּבֹא בְּנֵי יִשְׂרָאֵל׃

40 **וישמע וגו'**. This was the first hostile encounter with the people of the land they were about to conquer.

מא וַיִּסְעוּ מֵהֹר הָהָר וַיַּחֲנוּ בְּצַלְמֹנָה׃

41 *They journeyed from Mount Hor and camped in Tzalmonah.*

מב וַיִּסְעוּ מִצַּלְמֹנָה וַיַּחֲנוּ בְּפוּנֹן׃

42 *They journeyed from Tzalmonah and camped in Punon.*

מג וַיִּסְעוּ מִפּוּנֹן וַיַּחֲנוּ בְּאֹבֹת׃

43 *They journeyed from Punon and camped in Ovos.*

מד וַיִּסְעוּ מֵאֹבֹת וַיַּחֲנוּ בְּעִיֵּי הָעֲבָרִים
בִּגְבוּל מוֹאָב׃

44 *They journeyed from Ovos and camped in the Wastelands of Transitions on the border of Moav.*

מה וַיִּסְעוּ מֵעִיִּים וַיַּחֲנוּ בְּדִיבֹן גָּד׃

45 *They journeyed from the Wastelands and camped in Divon Gad.*

מו וַיִּסְעוּ מִדִּיבֹן גָּד וַיַּחֲנוּ בְּעַלְמֹן
דִּבְלָתָיְמָה׃

46 *They journeyed from Divon Gad and camped in Almon-toward-Divlasayim.*

מז וַיִּסְעוּ מֵעַלְמֹן דִּבְלָתָיְמָה וַיַּחֲנוּ
בְּהָרֵי הָעֲבָרִים לִפְנֵי נְבוֹ׃

47 *They journeyed from Almon-toward-Divlosayim and camped at the Mountains of Transitions, before Nevo.*

מח וַיִּסְעוּ מֵהָרֵי הָעֲבָרִים וַיַּחֲנוּ
בְּעַרְבֹת מוֹאָב עַל יַרְדֵּן יְרֵחוֹ׃

48 *They journeyed from the Mountains of Transitions and camped in the wastelands of Moav, along the Yarden near Yericho.*

מט וַיַּחֲנוּ עַל־הַיַּרְדֵּן מִבֵּית הַיְשִׁמֹת
עַד אָבֵל הַשִּׁטִּים בְּעַרְבֹת מוֹאָב׃ ס
שלישי (חמישי כשהן מחוברין)

49 *They camped along the Yarden, from Beis Hayeshimos to Avel Hashittim, in the wastelands of Moav.*

49 **מבית הישימת עד אבל השטים**. According to *Yoma* 75b, the distance between them was 3 פרסאות = 12 מיל. Hence the measure of 12 מיל for the תחום, according to the view that תחומין דאורייתא (see Commentary, *Shemos* 16:29).

50 God *spoke to Moshe in the wastelands of Moav, along the Yarden before Yericho, saying:*

נ וַיְדַבֵּ֥ר יְהֹוָ֛ה אֶל־מֹשֶׁ֖ה בְּעַֽרְבֹ֣ת מוֹאָ֑ב עַל־יַרְדֵּ֥ן יְרֵח֖וֹ לֵאמֹֽר׃

51 *Speak to the Children of Israel and say to them: When you cross the Yarden into the land of Canaan,*

נא דַּבֵּר֙ אֶל־בְּנֵ֣י יִשְׂרָאֵ֔ל וְאָמַרְתָּ֖ אֲלֵהֶ֑ם כִּ֥י אַתֶּ֛ם עֹבְרִ֥ים אֶת־הַיַּרְדֵּ֖ן אֶל־אֶ֥רֶץ כְּנָֽעַן׃

51 **דבר וגו׳**. A similar warning had already been given in *Shemos* 34:12ff. (see Commentary there), after God's covenant was broken by the sin of the golden calf. At that time the people saw with their own eyes the powerful influence exerted by the alien elements among them, for these elements succeeded in leading Israel astray. And when God's covenant was reestablished, the people were warned that, when they settled in the Land, they were not to tolerate the existence of its pagan inhabitants in their midst; rather, they were to drive them out and get rid of all their idolatrous shrines.

Now they stood at the border and could see the Land with their own eyes. Before God sets the boundaries of the land to be dedicated to, and conquered for, the fulfillment of the Torah, He repeats this warning as the first basic condition for Israel's possession of the land.

What is more, in *Yehoshua* (4:10) it says: וְהַכֹּהֲנִים נֹשְׂאֵי הָאָרוֹן עֹמְדִים בְּתוֹךְ הַיַּרְדֵּן עַד תֹּם כָּל־הַדָּבָר אֲשֶׁר־צִוָּה ה׳ אֶת־יְהוֹשֻׁעַ לְדַבֵּר אֶל־הָעָם כְּכֹל אֲשֶׁר־צִוָּה מֹשֶׁה אֶת־יְהוֹשֻׁעַ. "The כהנים stood in the midst of the Yarden, bearing the Ark of the Covenant, waiting until Yehoshua had finished telling the people everything that God, through Moshe, had commanded him to say to them." According to our Sages (*Sotah* 34a), Yehoshua conveyed to them this warning that is connected here to the crossing of the Yarden. While they stood in the Yarden, at the critical moment when it would be decided whether they would be drowned in the waters of the Yarden or permitted to cross safely into the Land, Yehoshua repeated this warning, and whether or not they would retain possession of the Land depended on whether they would heed this warning.

52 *You shall drive out from before you all the inhabitants of the land and destroy all their symbols; you shall destroy all their molten [metal] images and demolish all their high places.*	נב וְהֽוֹרַשְׁתֶּ֞ם אֶת־כׇּל־יֹשְׁבֵ֤י הָאָ֙רֶץ֙ מִפְּנֵיכֶ֔ם וְאִ֨בַּדְתֶּ֔ם אֵ֖ת כׇּל־מַשְׂכִּיֹּתָ֑ם וְאֵ֨ת כׇּל־צַלְמֵ֤י מַסֵּֽכֹתָם֙ תְּאַבֵּ֔דוּ וְאֵ֥ת כׇּל־בָּמוֹתָ֖ם תַּשְׁמִֽידוּ׃

52 **והורשתם**. ירש is phonetically related to גרש, to force out. Thus תירוש, the juice pressed out of the hull. In the *kal*, ירש means: to possess something that until now has been in someone else's possession. The object of ירש can be the person who until now has been the owner, or it can be the property which until now has been under the person's ownership. One can inherit property, and one can inherit its owner. Thus במה אדע כי אירשנה (*Bereshis* 15:8) and thus בן ביתי יורש אתי (ibid. 15:3). In the *hif'il*, ירש means: to forcibly effect a change of possession, and the object of the verb can be either the property or its possessor: in our verse והורשתם את כל ישבי הארץ, to drive the inhabitants out of the Land, and in verse 53 והורשתם את הארץ, to remove the Land from the possession of its current inhabitants, to clear the Land of its inhabitants.

משכיתם. In our Commentary on *Vayikra* 26:1 we mentioned the possibility that the root of משכית is שכת. However, here it says מַשְׂכִּיֹּתָם, and this form of the plural [rather than מַשְׂכִּיתֹתָם] clearly indicates that the root is סכה [=שכה], not סכת [=שכת].

It does not say here אבני משכיתם but משכיתם, and this apparently includes all material representations designed to evoke certain thoughts. We have accordingly translated it as "symbols." Thus, too, מַשְׂכִּיּוֹת לֵבָב (*Tehillim* 73:7). The phonetically related roots שכה, שגה, שגח, שגע all denote intensive concentration of thought on something (see Commentary, *Bereshis* 8:1).

ואת כל צלמי מסכתם — see Commentary, *Vayikra* 19:4. משכיות are apparently the public means of teaching the polytheistic worldview; צלמי מסכתם are the graphic representations of their gods; במותם are the offering places of the nature cult.

53 *You shall first clear out the land for occupancy and [only] then settle in it, for to you have I given the land to take possession of it.*

נג וְהוֹרַשְׁתֶּם אֶת־הָאָרֶץ וִישַׁבְתֶּם־בָּהּ כִּי לָכֶם נָתַתִּי אֶת־הָאָרֶץ לָרֶשֶׁת אֹתָהּ׃

54 *You shall divide the land among yourselves by lot, according to your families; to the numerous you shall increase his inheritance, and to the fewer in numbers you shall diminish his inheritance. Wherever his lot comes out, that shall be his. According to the tribes of your fathers shall you divide the possession.*

נד וְהִתְנַחַלְתֶּם אֶת־הָאָרֶץ בְּגוֹרָל לְמִשְׁפְּחֹתֵיכֶם לָרַב תַּרְבּוּ אֶת־נַחֲלָתוֹ וְלַמְעַט תַּמְעִיט אֶת־נַחֲלָתוֹ אֶל אֲשֶׁר־יֵצֵא לוֹ שָׁמָּה הַגּוֹרָל לוֹ יִהְיֶה לְמַטּוֹת אֲבֹתֵיכֶם תִּתְנֶחָלוּ׃

53 **והורשתם את הארץ** — see Commentary, verse 52. You must first make the land fit to be your ירושה by removing all traces of polytheism, and only then will you be able to settle in it. As long as polytheistic inhabitants and polytheistic shrines are there, your ישיבה is not ישיבה (see Commentary, *Shemos* 34:11ff.).

כי לכם נתתי וגו׳: You are not inheriting the Land by your own power and might; rather, God's Will and God's power are giving you the Land. So, too, the division of the Land shall not be done according to arbitrary norms, but according to God's instructions and decision (v. 54). Hence, you will not be able to avoid fulfilling the first basic condition on which God makes the gift of the Land dependent.

54 **והתנחלתם וגו׳** — see Commentary above, 26:53-56.

בגורל — in a manner confirmed by the אורים ותומים (see ibid.). Everyone received his portion by lot, whose results were confirmed by God. Hence everyone was obligated to first drive out the inhabitants and their polytheistic shrines in order to make his portion fit for his possession.

55 *But if you will not drive out the inhabitants of the land from before you, then those whom you will leave over will become as hedges in your eyes and thorns in your sides; they will oppress you as enemies in the land in which you dwell.*

נה וְאִם־לֹא תוֹרִישׁוּ אֶת־יֹשְׁבֵי הָאָרֶץ מִפְּנֵיכֶם וְהָיָה אֲשֶׁר תּוֹתִירוּ מֵהֶם לְשִׂכִּים בְּעֵינֵיכֶם וְלִצְנִינִם בְּצִדֵּיכֶם וְצָרְרוּ אֶתְכֶם עַל־הָאָרֶץ אֲשֶׁר אַתֶּם יֹשְׁבִים בָּהּ׃

56 *It will then come to pass that what I had intended to do to them I will do to you.*

נו וְהָיָה כַּאֲשֶׁר דִּמִּיתִי לַעֲשׂוֹת לָהֶם אֶעֱשֶׂה לָכֶם׃ פ

55 **לשכים בעיניכם**. שוך and שכך — related to סכך and סוג -- denote a hedge of thorns designed to guard and protect. Thus הִנְנִי־שָׂךְ אֶת־דַּרְכֵּךְ בַּסִּירִים (*Hoshea* 2:8), הָסֵר מְשׂוּכָּתוֹ וְהָיָה לְבָעֵר (*Yeshayahu* 5:5), כִּמְשֻׂכַת חָדֶק (*Mishlei* 15:19).

This, apparently, is the meaning here: If you allow the pagan inhabitants to remain in the Land, they will become like a hedge around their pagan practices; the nature of these practices will be concealed from your perception and insight, and you will not find fault with them. Tolerance toward the pagan inhabitants will beget tolerance toward paganism (cf. *Shemos* 34:15-16 and Commentary there). If you tolerate paganism and find justification for it *within* God's land, you will cease to belong to God alone, and thus you will be deprived of your right to exist in the Land, and you will not be worthy of protection. And when God removes His protection of you, those toward whom you have been so tolerant will become your enemies and will oppress you in your own land. The whole book of *Shoftim* is nothing but a history of what befell the people of Israel when it disregarded this warning.

56 **והיה וגו'**. In the end, you will not be worthy of God's land, and God will expel you from the land as He had intended to expel the nations through you.

דמיתי. דמה — see Commentary, *Bereshis* 1:26. דַּמֵּה means: to recognize and express the similarity of something to some other *already existing*

34 1 God *spoke to Moshe [saying]:*	**לד** א וַיְדַבֵּר יְהוָה אֶל־מֹשֶׁה לֵּאמֹר׃
2 *Command the Children of Israel and say to them: When you come to the land of Canaan, this is the land that will fall to you as your possession, the land of Canaan according to its borders.*	ב צַו אֶת־בְּנֵי יִשְׂרָאֵל וְאָמַרְתָּ אֲלֵהֶם כִּי־אַתֶּם בָּאִים אֶל־הָאָרֶץ כְּנָעַן זֹאת הָאָרֶץ אֲשֶׁר תִּפֹּל לָכֶם בְּנַחֲלָה אֶרֶץ כְּנַעַן לִגְבֻלֹתֶיהָ׃

thing. And sometimes, as in our verse, it means: to form an idea of something not yet in existence, to envision what is destined to be — i.e., to intend to do something.

CHAPTER 34

2 **ארץ כנען לגבלתיה**. An exact definition of the borders of the Land is of importance also for the מצוות התלויות בארץ such as תרומות מעשרות ושביעית, for these *mitzvos* originally applied only within these borders. Only after the conquest of ארץ כנען — as defined here —was completed could also other conquered territories participate in קדושת הארץ and become subject to the duties stemming from that קדושה.

For this reason ארם צובה and דמשק, which were conquered by David (*Shemuel* II, 8:5-6) — and which are designated by the general term "סוריא" — are considered as having קדושת הארץ only מדרבנן. For the conquest of the main land of the Torah had not yet been completed, and even Yerushalayim was not yet entirely in Jewish hands. The conquest of Syria was thus not considered a national undertaking; it was termed "כיבוש יחיד" and by this designation was excluded from the legal קדושה-character.

Moreover, there is doubt even about the transjordanic land of the two and a half tribes: It is still not decided to what extent Trans-Jordan is included in the real קדושת הארץ. (See **תוספות** *Avodah Zarah* 21a ד"ה כיבוש יחיד; *Gittin* 8b and **תוספות** ibid. 8a ד"ה כיבוש יחיד; **תוספות** *Chagigah* 3b ד"ה עמון ומואב. See also Commentary above, 15:18; *Devarim* 30:5.)

3 *Your southernmost point will be from the wilderness of Tzin alongside Edom, and your southern border, to the east, will be at the edge of the Salt Sea.*

ג וְהָיָה לָכֶם פְּאַת־נֶגֶב מִמִּדְבַּר־צִן
עַל־יְדֵי אֱדוֹם וְהָיָה לָכֶם גְּבוּל נֶגֶב
מִקְצֵה יָם־הַמֶּלַח קֵדְמָה׃

4 *Then your border will turn from the south to the elevation of Akrabim; it will pass over to Tzin, and its ends will be in the south of Kadesh Barne'a. It will then extend to Chatzar Addar and over to Atzmon.*

ד וְנָסַב לָכֶם הַגְּבוּל מִנֶּגֶב לְמַעֲלֵה
עַקְרַבִּים וְעָבַר צִנָה וְהָיָה
תּוֹצְאֹתָיו מִנֶּגֶב לְקָדֵשׁ בַּרְנֵעַ
וְיָצָא חֲצַר־אַדָּר וְעָבַר עַצְמֹנָה׃
והיו קרי

5 *The border will then turn from Atzmon to the Brook of Egypt, and its ends will be at the sea.*

ה וְנָסַב הַגְּבוּל מֵעַצְמוֹן נַחְלָה
מִצְרָיִם וְהָיוּ תוֹצְאֹתָיו הַיָּמָּה׃

6 *And the western border: it will be for you the Great Sea and its territory. This will be your western border.*

ו וּגְבוּל יָם וְהָיָה לָכֶם הַיָּם הַגָּדוֹל
וּגְבוּל זֶה־יִהְיֶה לָכֶם גְּבוּל יָם׃

3 **פאת נגב**, the southernmost point on the east side (cf. Commentary, *Shemos* 27:9).

4 **ונסב וגו׳ ועבר וגו׳ ויצא וגו׳**. The translation of these terms relating to the borders of the Holy Land must waive claim to exactness, as it is impossible to determine the meaning of these terms on the basis of the topographical reality. The conventional identification of the places that form the border lines rests on suppositions that are by no means sure.

6 **הים הגדול וגבול**. According to *Gittin* 8a, this is the Mediterranean Sea and הנסין שבים — all the islands within the border of Eretz Yisrael. From the Amnon mountains, הר ההר (v. 7), the northwest corner of the border, a line is drawn cutting through the ים הגדול from north to south until נחל מצרים at the southwest corner of the border (v. 5). All that lies to the east of this line is ארץ ישראל, and all that lies to the west is חוצה לארץ.

7 *And this will be your northern border: From the Great Sea you shall draw a line extending to Mount Hor.*

ז וְזֶה־יִהְיֶה לָכֶם גְּבוּל צָפוֹן מִן־הַיָּם
הַגָּדֹל תְּתָאוּ לָכֶם הֹר הָהָר׃

8 *From Mount Hor you shall draw a line extending to the road [leading] to Chamas, and the ends of the border will be toward Tzedad.*

ח מֵהֹר הָהָר תְּתָאוּ לְבֹא חֲמָת וְהָיוּ
תּוֹצְאֹת הַגְּבֻל צְדָדָה׃

9 *Then the border will run out to Zifron, and its ends shall be Chatzar Einan. This will be your northern border.*

ט וְיָצָא הַגְּבֻל זִפְרֹנָה וְהָיוּ תוֹצְאֹתָיו
חֲצַר עֵינָן זֶה־יִהְיֶה לָכֶם גְּבוּל
צָפוֹן׃

10 *You shall then demarcate as your eastern border the territory from Chatzar Einan to Shefam.*

י וְהִתְאַוִּיתֶם לָכֶם לִגְבוּל קֵדְמָה
מֵחֲצַר עֵינָן שְׁפָמָה׃

---

7 **תְּתָאוּ** is the *pi'el* form of the root תאה. תאה means: to mark the direction from one point to another. Related to תאה is תעה, to constantly move from point to point, to wander about without knowing the right direction. Perhaps also related to תאה is דאה [cf. *Devarim* 28:49], the flight of the eagle which hovers to and fro before shooting down to a certain point (cf. Commentary, *Bereshis* 20:13).

הר ההר: not to be confused with the mountain by the same name in the southeast, on which Aharon died; הר ההר in our verse lies in the extreme northwest of the Land (cf. Commentary above, 20:23).

10 **והתאויתם לכם** — from the root אוה. התאוה — as in ולא תתאוה בית רעך (*Devarim* 5:18) — denotes the aspiration to expand the sphere of one's possession, to add an object to one's property. In our verse as well, התאוה means: to draw a line to demarcate how far our property — here the border of our land — will extend and what it will include. Perhaps at this point, in accordance with the lie of the land, the border curved outwardly, in which case the term would be all the more appropriate (cf. קוה and קו).

11 *The border will then run down from Shefam toward Rivlah, to the east of Ayin, and run down and strike upon the shore of Lake Kinneres to the east.*

יא וְיָרַד הַגְּבֻל מִשְּׁפָם הָרִבְלָה מִקֶּדֶם
לָעָיִן וְיָרַד הַגְּבֻל וּמָחָה עַל־כֶּתֶף
יָם־כִּנֶּרֶת קֵדְמָה׃

12 *Then the border will run down along the Yarden, and its ends shall be the Salt Sea. This will be the land for you according to its borders round about.*

יב וְיָרַד הַגְּבוּל הַיַּרְדֵּנָה וְהָיוּ
תוֹצְאֹתָיו יָם הַמֶּלַח זֹאת תִּהְיֶה
לָכֶם הָאָרֶץ לִגְבֻלֹתֶיהָ סָבִיב׃

13 *And Moshe commanded the Children of Israel, saying: This is the land that you are to divide among yourselves by lot as a possession that* God *has commanded to give to the nine and a half tribes.*

יג וַיְצַו מֹשֶׁה אֶת־בְּנֵי יִשְׂרָאֵל לֵאמֹר
זֹאת הָאָרֶץ אֲשֶׁר תִּתְנַחֲלוּ אֹתָהּ
בְּגוֹרָל אֲשֶׁר צִוָּה יְהֹוָה לָתֵת
לְתִשְׁעַת הַמַּטּוֹת וַחֲצִי הַמַּטֶּה׃

14 *For the tribe of the sons of Reuven according to their fathers' house, and the tribe of the sons of Gad according to their fathers' house, and the half-tribe of Menashe have [already] received their inheritance.*

יד כִּי לָקְחוּ מַטֵּה בְנֵי הָרְאוּבֵנִי לְבֵית
אֲבֹתָם וּמַטֵּה בְנֵי־הַגָּדִי לְבֵית
אֲבֹתָם וַחֲצִי מַטֵּה מְנַשֶּׁה לָקְחוּ
נַחֲלָתָם׃

15 *The two and a half tribes have received their inheritance on this side of the Yarden near Yericho, to the east, toward the sunrise.*

טו שְׁנֵי הַמַּטּוֹת וַחֲצִי הַמַּטֶּה לָקְחוּ
נַחֲלָתָם מֵעֵבֶר לְיַרְדֵּן יְרֵחוֹ קֵדְמָה
מִזְרָחָה׃ פ רביעי (ששי כשהן
מחוברין)

16 God *spoke to Moshe, saying:*

טז וַיְדַבֵּר יְהֹוָה אֶל־מֹשֶׁה לֵּאמֹר׃

17 *These are the names of the men who shall take possession of the land for you: Elazar the priest and Yehoshua, son of Nun.*

יז אֵלֶּה שְׁמוֹת הָאֲנָשִׁים אֲשֶׁר־יִנְחֲלוּ לָכֶם אֶת־הָאָרֶץ אֶלְעָזָר הַכֹּהֵן וִיהוֹשֻׁעַ בִּן־נוּן׃

18 *And one prince each from [each] tribe shall you take, to take possession of the land.*

יח וְנָשִׂיא אֶחָד נָשִׂיא אֶחָד מִמַּטֶּה תִּקְחוּ לִנְחֹל אֶת־הָאָרֶץ׃

19 *These are the names of the men: for the tribe of Yehudah: Kalev, son of Yefunneh.*

יט וְאֵלֶּה שְׁמוֹת הָאֲנָשִׁים לְמַטֵּה יְהוּדָה כָּלֵב בֶּן־יְפֻנֶּה׃

20 *And for the tribe of the sons of Shimon: Shemuel, son of Ammihud.*

כ וּלְמַטֵּה בְּנֵי שִׁמְעוֹן שְׁמוּאֵל בֶּן־עַמִּיהוּד׃

17-18 **אשר ינחלו לכם**. Elazar and Yehoshua shall be the representatives of the community. Under their supervision and guidance each tribal prince shall, on behalf of his tribe, "take possession" of the portion allocated to that tribe and divide the portion among the families and men entitled thereto. These princes are appointed here as representatives of the tribes, families, and individuals. They are the deputies of all those entitled to a portion, and everything the princes do on their behalf is legally binding (see רש״י).

In *Kiddushin* 42a our Sages derive from our verse the halachah that the court is to appoint guardians for orphans to look after their rights of inheritance. The decisions of duly-appointed guardians are binding and legally incontestable even after the orphans come of age: מנין ליתומים שבאו לחלוק בנכסי אביהן שבית דין מעמידין להם אפוטרופוס לחוב ולזכות? תלמוד לומר נשיא אחד נשיא אחד ממטה תקחו.

19-28 **ואלה שמות האנשים**. It is worthy of note that the order in which the tribes and their representatives are listed here, in connection with the division of the Land, corresponds exactly to the locations in the Land, from south to north, where the tribes settled in the Land, one beside the other, and one after the other. Yehudah, Shimon, and Binyamin settled in the south; Dan, Menashe, and between them Efrayim, in the center; Yissachar,

21 *For the tribe of Binyamin: Elidad, son of Kislon.*

כא לְמַטֵּה בִנְיָמִן אֱלִידָד בֶּן־כִּסְלוֹן׃

22 *And for the tribe of the sons of Dan, as prince: Bukki, son of Yogli.*

כב וּלְמַטֵּה בְנֵי־דָן נָשִׂיא בֻּקִּי בֶּן־יָגְלִי׃

23 *For the sons of Yosef, for the tribe of the sons of Menashe, as prince: Channi'el, son of Efod.*

כג לִבְנֵי יוֹסֵף לְמַטֵּה בְנֵי־מְנַשֶּׁה נָשִׂיא חַנִּיאֵל בֶּן־אֵפֹד׃

Zevulun, Asher, and Naftali, in the north. Later on, the allocation of the tribal territories would be determined by lot and confirmed by God through a declaration of the אורים ותומים (see Commentary above, 26:55); still, everything was foreseen, and is already indicated by the order of these verses.

Each tribe is referred to here as מטה בני־: ולמטה בני שמעון, ולמטה בני דן, and so forth. Only in the cases of Yehudah and Binyamin does it say: למטה יהודה, למטה בנימין. What underlies this difference is perhaps the following conception:

The designation "מטה בני" conceives of the tribe as a unit encompassing the individuals who are בני [the sons of] that tribe. But this does not apply to the tribes of Yehudah and Binyamin, on whose territory the national Sanctuary was to be erected. They are not conceived of as units that encompass their members, but only as parts of the national community, as "branches" of that whole which comprises the nation. Hence their designation here is not מטה בני יהודה, מטה בני בנימין, but מטה יהודה, מטה בנימין.

Perhaps this would also explain another difference. The representatives of all the other tribes are referred to by the honorable title of נשיא. The only exceptions are Yehudah, Shimon, and Binyamin. If we consider that the territory of Yehudah and Binyamin can be regarded as the immediate periphery of God's Sanctuary that is to be erected on their land, and that the territory of Shimon is included in the territory of Yehudah, the following idea automatically presents itself: In the face of the thought of the sovereignty of God and His Torah, represented by the Sanctuary, it is inappropriate to refer to anyone else by the grandeur of his sovereignty.

24 *And for the tribe of the sons of Efrayim, as prince: Kemuel, son of Shiftan.*	כד וּלְמַטֵּ֥ה בְנֵֽי־אֶפְרַ֖יִם נָשִׂ֑יא קְמוּאֵ֖ל בֶּן־שִׁפְטָֽן׃
25 *And for the tribe of the sons of Zevulun, as prince: Elitzafan, son of Parnach.*	כה וּלְמַטֵּ֥ה בְנֵֽי־זְבוּלֻ֖ן נָשִׂ֑יא אֱלִיצָפָ֖ן בֶּן־פַּרְנָֽךְ׃
26 *And for the tribe of the sons of Yissachar, as prince: Palti'el, son of Azzan.*	כו וּלְמַטֵּ֥ה בְנֵֽי־יִשָּׂשכָ֖ר נָשִׂ֑יא פַּלְטִיאֵ֖ל בֶּן־עַזָּֽן׃
27 *And for the tribe of the sons of Asher, as prince: Achihud, son of Shelomi.*	כז וּלְמַטֵּ֥ה בְנֵֽי־אָשֵׁ֖ר נָשִׂ֑יא אֲחִיה֖וּד בֶּן־שְׁלֹמִֽי׃
28 *And for the tribe of the sons of Naftali, as a prince: Pedah'el, son of Ammihud.*	כח וּלְמַטֵּ֥ה בְנֵֽי־נַפְתָּלִ֖י נָשִׂ֑יא פְּדַהְאֵ֖ל בֶּן־עַמִּיהֽוּד׃
29 *These are the ones whom* God *ordered to install the Children of Israel in the land of Canaan in their possession.*	כט אֵ֕לֶּה אֲשֶׁ֖ר צִוָּ֣ה יְהֹוָ֑ה לְנַחֵ֥ל אֶת־בְּנֵֽי־יִשְׂרָאֵ֖ל בְּאֶ֥רֶץ כְּנָֽעַן׃ פ
	חמישי
35 1 God *spoke to Moshe in the wastelands of Moav, at the Yarden before Yericho, saying:*	**לה** א וַיְדַבֵּ֧ר יְהֹוָ֛ה אֶל־מֹשֶׁ֖ה בְּעַרְבֹ֣ת מוֹאָ֑ב עַל־יַרְדֵּ֥ן יְרֵח֖וֹ לֵאמֹֽר׃
2 *Command the Children of Israel that they give to the* Levi'im, *from the inheritance of their possession, cities in which to dwell, and you shall grant the* Levi'im *open land around [these] cities.*	ב צַ֞ו אֶת־בְּנֵ֣י יִשְׂרָאֵ֗ל וְנָתְנ֤וּ לַלְוִיִּם֙ מִנַּחֲלַ֣ת אֲחֻזָּתָ֔ם עָרִ֖ים לָשָׁ֑בֶת וּמִגְרָ֗שׁ לֶֽעָרִים֙ סְבִיבֹ֣תֵיהֶ֔ם תִּתְּנ֖וּ לַלְוִיִּֽם׃

CHAPTER 35

2 **ומגרש לערים** — see Commentary, *Vayikra* 25:34.

3 *The cities shall be for them to dwell in, and their open areas shall be for their livestock, for their movable property and for all the needs of their life.*

ג וְהָי֧וּ הֶעָרִ֛ים לָהֶ֖ם לָשָׁ֑בֶת וּמִגְרְשֵׁיהֶ֗ם יִהְי֤וּ לִבְהֶמְתָּם֙ וְלִרְכֻשָׁ֔ם וּלְכֹ֖ל חַיָּתָֽם׃

4 *The open areas of the cities that you shall give to the* Levi'im *shall extend a thousand cubits from the wall of the city outward, all around.*

ד וּמִגְרְשֵׁי֙ הֶעָרִ֔ים אֲשֶׁ֥ר תִּתְּנ֖וּ לַלְוִיִּ֑ם מִקִּ֤יר הָעִיר֙ וָח֔וּצָה אֶ֥לֶף אַמָּ֖ה סָבִֽיב׃

סביבתיהם. Since עיר is feminine, סביבתיהם can refer only to the לויים. The open area (מגרש) is added to the cities so that the inheritance of the *Levi'im* should include not only cities but also an area around each city.

3 **ומגרשיהם** — of the *Levi'im*.

לכל חיתם. According to *Nedarim* 81a, this means: for any use that is necessary for the preservation of health — e.g., laundry. Thus it says in *Yeshayahu* (57:10): חַיַּת יָדֵךְ, the vitality of your hand. According to *Makkos* 12a, burial is forbidden in all the Levite domains (except for a רוצח בשגגה who fled to that city): לכל חיתם, לחיים נתנו ולא לקבורה.

4 **מקיר העיר וחוצה אלף אמה**. The thousand cubits do not begin next to the wall, but only וחוצה, beyond the outskirts of the town, which are considered part of the town: תן חוצה ואחר כך מדוד (*Eruvin* 57a). These are the "seventy cubits and a fraction," שבעים אמה ושיריים, which everywhere are considered part of the city: עיבורה של עיר (see ibid. 60a). So, too, the two thousand cubits of תחום שבת begin only after "seventy cubits and a fraction" (ibid. 57a).

"Seventy cubits and a fraction" is the length of the side of a square of five thousand square cubits, which corresponds to the total area of the חצר of the משכן, as the חצר is one hundred cubits long and fifty cubits wide. (Cf. Commentary, *Shemos* 27:18.)

5 *And you shall measure off outside the city, on the east side two thousand cubits, on the south side two thousand cubits, on the west side two thousand cubits, and on the north side two thousand cubits, with the city in the middle. These shall be for them the open areas around the cities.*

ה וּמַדֹּתֶם מִחוּץ לָעִיר אֶת־פְּאַת־
קֵדְמָה אַלְפַּיִם בָּאַמָּה וְאֶת־פְּאַת־
נֶגֶב אַלְפַּיִם בָּאַמָּה וְאֶת־פְּאַת־יָם ׀
אַלְפַּיִם בָּאַמָּה וְאֵת פְּאַת צָפוֹן
אַלְפַּיִם בָּאַמָּה וְהָעִיר בַּתָּוֶךְ זֶה
יִהְיֶה לָהֶם מִגְרְשֵׁי הֶעָרִים׃

6 *And [among] the cities that you shall give to the* Levi'im *there shall be, first of all, the six cities of reception which you shall designate, so that a manslayer can flee there; and to them you shall add another forty-two cities.*

ו וְאֵת הֶעָרִים אֲשֶׁר תִּתְּנוּ לַלְוִיִּם
אֵת שֵׁשׁ־עָרֵי הַמִּקְלָט אֲשֶׁר תִּתְּנוּ
לָנֻס שָׁמָּה הָרֹצֵחַ וַעֲלֵיהֶם תִּתְּנוּ
אַרְבָּעִים וּשְׁתַּיִם עִיר׃

5 **ומדתם**. In verse 4 it says that the מגרש of the city includes only one thousand cubits. Beyond this מגרש, a further thousand is added, designated for fields and vineyards (see Commentary, *Vayikra* 25:34). Altogether two thousand cubits are added to the city in each direction. This whole area outside the city is broadly referred to as מגרש.

6 **ואת הערים וגו׳ את שש ערי המקלט וגו׳**. This double accusative construction [את הערים and את שש ערי המקלט] apparently indicates that the six cities designated in the first instance as ערי מקלט (v. 13) are, in addition, to be handed over to the *Levi'im*. Their primary purpose, however, is to be ערי מקלט. Hence, an inadvertent manslayer who takes refuge in them pays no taxes to the *Levi'im* for his stay (see *Makkos* 13a and תוספות there ד״ה מעלים). From רש״י's wording (ibid.) it appears that the manslayer is entitled to free housing there.

ועליהם תתנו וגו׳. Apart from these six ערי מקלט, forty-two additional cities are to be given to the *Levi'im*. The term "ועליהם" indicates that the forty-two cities likewise provide מקלט to the manslayer, but that is only their secondary purpose; their primary purpose is to be Levite cities. This

ז כָּל־הֶעָרִים אֲשֶׁר תִּתְּנוּ לַלְוִיִּם אַרְבָּעִים וּשְׁמֹנֶה עִיר אֶתְהֶן וְאֶת־מִגְרְשֵׁיהֶן׃

7 *All the cities that you shall give to the* Levi'im *[will thus be] forty-eight cities, they and their open areas.*

ח וְהֶעָרִים אֲשֶׁר תִּתְּנוּ מֵאֲחֻזַּת בְּנֵי־יִשְׂרָאֵל מֵאֵת הָרַב תַּרְבּוּ וּמֵאֵת הַמְעַט תַּמְעִיטוּ אִישׁ כְּפִי נַחֲלָתוֹ אֲשֶׁר יִנְחָלוּ יִתֵּן מֵעָרָיו לַלְוִיִּם׃ פ

ששי (שביעי כשהן מחוברין)

8 *[As for] the cities that you will give from the possession of the Children of Israel, you shall take more from the larger and less from the smaller [holdings]. Each one shall give of his cities to the* Levi'im *according to his inheritance that is allotted to them.*

ט וַיְדַבֵּר יְהוָה אֶל־מֹשֶׁה לֵּאמֹר׃

9 God *spoke to Moshe, saying:*

י דַּבֵּר אֶל־בְּנֵי יִשְׂרָאֵל וְאָמַרְתָּ אֲלֵהֶם כִּי אַתֶּם עֹבְרִים אֶת־הַיַּרְדֵּן אַרְצָה כְּנָעַן׃

10 *Speak to the Children of Israel and say to them: When you cross the Yarden into the land of Canaan,*

---

accounts for the two differences between them and the six primary מקלט-cities: An inadvertent manslayer who takes refuge in one of the forty-two cities must pay taxes for his residence there, and they do not provide him with refuge unless he enters the city for the express purpose of protective asylum. By contrast, the six primary מקלט-cities provide refuge even if he just happens to be in one of them, even if he has no idea that they provide refuge (see ibid. 10a and 13a).

10 **כי אתם עברים וגו׳**. The land of God's Torah is given to God's people for the sake of man. Its most precious product, the purpose and goal of the blessing bestowed on it by God, is every human soul supported by it, for man realizes God's Torah through the means that the Land supplies. The Land is given to all of God's people only on condition that they respect the sanctity of every human life, which is sacred to the Torah. Innocent blood that is spilled and disregarded loosens a thread in the tie that con-

11 *You shall designate for yourselves cities in an accommodating location; cities of reception shall they be for you, so that a manslayer who committed manslaughter unintentionally can flee there.*

יא וְהִקְרִיתֶם לָכֶם עָרִים עָרֵי מִקְלָט תִּהְיֶינָה לָכֶם וְנָס שָׁמָּה רֹצֵחַ מַכֵּה־נֶפֶשׁ בִּשְׁגָגָה׃

nects the Land with the nation and both the Land and the nation with God (see vv. 33 and 34 and Commentary there). Safeguarding the sanctity of human life must come to expression immediately upon the conquest of the Land; and when the Land is divided, there shall be created that legal institution [עיר מקלט] to which reference has already been made in the fundamentals of social law (*Shemos* 21:13).

11 **והקריתם לכם וגו׳**. The cities shall be established in locations easily accessible to the fugitive, so that he will not have to search for them (see Commentary, *Bereshis* 24:12).

This והקריתם לכם is elaborated upon in *Devarim* 19:3 as follows: תכין לך הדרך ושלשת את גבול ארצך וגו׳. See to it that the roads are kept in good condition without any obstacles. According to *Makkos* 10b, signs should be posted on the roads, and the cities should be situated at equal distances from each other. The three transjordanic cities (*Devarim* 4:43) lie parallel to the three cities in Eretz Yisrael: Chevron in Yehudah parallel to Betzer in the wilderness, Shechem in the mountains of Efrayim parallel to Ramos in Gil'ad, Kadesh in the mountains of Naftali parallel to Golan in Bashan. From the southern border to Chevron is the same distance as from Chevron to Shechem; from Chevron to Shechem is the same distance as from Shechem to Kadesh; and from Shechem to Kadesh is the same distance as from Kadesh to the northern border. Thus, the distance from both borders to the first city is the same as from that city to the city closest to it.

Thus, three equal distances are given: the distance from the borders and the distance from the first city to the second, and from the second to the third. Or to put it differently, the whole country is divided into four equal parts by fixing three equidistant points in the land. Scripture terms this equal division "שַׁלֵּשׁ." In the terminology of חז״ל, dividing a given quantity into equal parts is termed שלש — e.g., משלשין בממון ואין משלשין במכות (*Makkos* 5a; see רש״י ibid. 3a).

ערי מקלט. In Scripture, קלט occurs only in the term מקלט in this connection, and in the expression שרוע וקלוט (*Vayikra* 22:23), where it denotes a hoof that is not split, in which the toes are grown together. In the terminology of חז״ל, קלט denotes absorbing foreign material to form a permanent junction, as in the absorption of dyes (*Shabbos* 17b) and in grafting (*Shevi'is* 2:6). However, it does occur in the sense of temporary reception: קלוטה כמי שהונחה דמיא (*Shabbos* 4a).

It appears that קלט is related to גלד, from which we get גֶּלֶד in the sense of skin (עֲלֵי גִלְדִּי [*Iyov* 16:15]), the organic casing enclosing the body; thus the Rabbinic term גלדאי, a tanner. Also, contracting, freezing frost is called "גליד."

From all this it appears that קלט in the term מקלט means: to receive and hold something permanently. Perhaps this is also the meaning of the phonetically related term ילד: to bring the young into the world, so that it should be received there permanently. Accordingly, the exile of the inadvertent manslayer to a מקלט-city is, as it were, a rebirth that adds restrictions: the מקלט-city shall henceforth be the whole world of the one exiled to it.

Hence, it says in the following verse: והיו לכם הערים למקלט; the word לכם is interpreted to mean לכל צרכיכם (*Makkos* 13a). The מקלט-city shall be for the fugitive a microcosm. It should contain all that he requires. Thus it says in *Devarim* (19:5): ינוס אל אחת הערים האלה וחי — i.e., עביד ליה מידי דתהוי ליה חיותא (*Makkos* 10a); see to it that he finds a "life" there.

The cities themselves should be of medium size, neither large nor small. According to the משנה למלך (on הל׳ רוצח, 8:8), they should not be enclosed by a wall. They should be located in areas where there are markets and sources of water. They should be settled with members of all the national categories — כהנים לויים וישראלים.

Even the spiritual needs of the fugitive must be provided for: If a disciple is exiled, his teacher must follow him there, and if a teacher is exiled, his students must follow him there (*Makkos* 10a).

Thus, the מקלט-city is truly a microcosm, as it contains all that a person needs.

מכה נפש בשגגה. The concept of שגגה applicable to a manslayer has already been defined in our Commentary on *Shemos* 21:13. The manslayer is not granted asylum in the עיר מקלט and is not exiled there unless

12 *The cities shall serve you as [a place of] reception from the advocate, so that the manslayer will not die until he has stood before the community for judgment.*

יב וְהָיוּ לָכֶם הֶעָרִים לְמִקְלָט מִגֹּאֵל וְלֹא יָמוּת הָרֹצֵחַ עַד־עָמְדוֹ לִפְנֵי הָעֵדָה לַמִּשְׁפָּט׃

the act is far from מזיד as well as from אונס — i.e., it is neither the result of criminal negligence nor the result of unforeseeable accident. Unintentional manslaughter which makes one liable to exile to an עיר מקלט is only where there was no reason to assume that the accident would occur, but a cautious person acting responsibly should have recognized the possibility of it occurring (see Commentary there).

בשגגה: מכלל דהוה ליה ידיעה (*Bava Kamma* 26b). The repeated term בשגגה excludes the case where the manslayer was never aware of the presence of the life-threatening object — e.g., היתה אבן מונחת לו בחיקו ולא הכיר בה ועמד ונפלה (ibid.).

12 **מגאל** — see Commentary, *Shemos* 6:6. Here, the גואל is one who takes up the cause of the person who was killed and requites the killer for his deed. This role is generally assumed by a relative of the victim. But the גואל's intervention is far from being a "vendetta," for our Sages say (*Sanhedrin* 45b) that if the victim has no blood relative, the court appoints a גואל for him: אם אין לו גואל בית דין מעמידין לו גואל. (According to רש״י there ד״ה גואל הדם, this law applies also in cases of הורג בשגגה, but the רמב״ן in ספר המצוות — in the addendum to the מצוות עשה, 13 — opposes this view, and in his view the law applies only to הורג במזיד.)

ולא ימות הרצח וגו׳. Any manslayer can take refuge in one of these cities, and this shall prevent the possibility of him being killed before he stands trial; for only the court may decide whether he is liable to capital punishment, or is liable to exile, or is to be exonerated and released. As the Mishnah says (*Makkos* 9b), based on verses 24 and 25: בתחילה אחד שוגג ואחד מזיד מקדימין לערי מקלט וב״ד שולחין ומביאין אותו משם, מי שנתחייב מיתה בב״ד הרגוהו ושלא נתחייב מיתה פטרוהו, מי שנתחייב גלות מחזירין אותו למקומו שנא׳ והשיבו אותו העדה אל עיר מקלטו.

In *Makkos* 12a our Sages derive from our verse a general law: Even if it is known with absolute certainty that the suspect is liable to the death

13 *The cities that you shall give them shall be for you six cities of reception.*

יג וְהֶעָרִים אֲשֶׁר תִּתֵּנוּ שֵׁשׁ־עָרֵי מִקְלָט תִּהְיֶינָה לָכֶם׃

14 *Three of the cities you shall give on this side of the Yarden, and three of the cities you shall give in the land of Canaan. Cities of reception shall they be.*

יד אֵת | שְׁלֹשׁ הֶעָרִים תִּתְּנוּ מֵעֵבֶר לַיַּרְדֵּן וְאֵת שְׁלֹשׁ הֶעָרִים תִּתְּנוּ בְּאֶרֶץ כְּנָעַן עָרֵי מִקְלָט תִּהְיֶינָה׃

penalty — e.g., he committed murder before the eyes of the court — the murderer may not be put to death without the proper legal procedure: מנין לסנהדרין שראו אחד שהרג את הנפש שאין ממיתין אותו עד שיעמוד בב״ד אחר תלמוד לומר עד עמדו לפני העדה למשפט עד שיעמוד בב״ד אחר. According to the foregoing, this legal procedure must be performed by other judges, who were not present when the act was committed. Those who were present can be witnesses, but not judges; for our Sages say in *Rosh Hashanah* 26a — based on verses 24 and 25 (see there) — that **בדיני נפשות**, in capital cases, אין עד הרואה נעשה דיין: One who witnessed the act cannot act as judge in the case. For the task of the court is to exonerate the accused, if possible, whereas כיון דחזיוהו דקטל נפשא לא מצי חזו ליה זכותא: The impression of actually seeing the murder committed prevents the witnesses from judging the accused impartially and finding reason to acquit him.

העדה here is the court, for the court represents the community to which God entrusted His Law and which He charged with the responsibility of carrying out justice.

13 **והערים וגו׳ שש ערי מקלט תהיינה**. Until the three cities in Eretz Yisrael were chosen, the three transjordanic cities did not provide refuge. The institution of ערי מקלט must come into force throughout the Jewish domain simultaneously (see *Makkos* 9b).

תהיינה לכם — see verse 11.

14 **ערי מקלט תהיינה**: Their primary purpose is to be ערי מקלט, whereas in the case of the other Levite cities, מקלט is only a secondary purpose (see Commentary, v. 6).

15 *For the Children of Israel and for those who have entered from abroad and for the settlers in their midst shall these six cities serve as [places of] reception, so that anyone who unintentionally committed manslaughter can flee there.*

טו לִבְנֵ֨י יִשְׂרָאֵ֜ל וְלַגֵּ֣ר וְלַתּוֹשָׁב֙ בְּתוֹכָ֔ם תִּהְיֶ֛ינָה שֵׁשׁ־הֶעָרִ֥ים הָאֵ֖לֶּה לְמִקְלָ֑ט לָנ֣וּס שָׁ֔מָּה כָּל־מַכֵּה־נֶ֖פֶשׁ בִּשְׁגָגָֽה׃

16 *If someone strikes another with an iron instrument so that he died, then he is a murderer, and the murderer must be executed.*

טז וְאִם־בִּכְלִ֨י בַרְזֶ֧ל ׀ הִכָּ֛הוּ וַיָּמֹ֖ת רֹצֵ֣חַ ה֑וּא מ֥וֹת יוּמַ֖ת הָרֹצֵֽחַ׃

17 *If he strikes someone with a rock that can be held in the hand, from which he may die, and he died, he is a murderer, and the murderer must be executed.*

יז וְאִ֡ם בְּאֶ֣בֶן יָד֩ אֲשֶׁר־יָמ֨וּת בָּ֥הּ הִכָּ֛הוּ וַיָּמֹ֖ת רֹצֵ֣חַ ה֑וּא מ֥וֹת יוּמַ֖ת הָרֹצֵֽחַ׃

18 *Or [if] someone strikes down another with a wooden instrument that can be held in the hand, from which he may die, and he died, he is a murderer, and the murderer must be executed.*

יח א֠וֹ בִּכְלִ֨י עֵֽץ־יָ֜ד אֲשֶׁר־יָמ֥וּת בּ֛וֹ הִכָּ֖הוּ וַיָּמֹ֑ת רֹצֵ֣חַ ה֔וּא מ֥וֹת יוּמַ֖ת הָרֹצֵֽחַ׃

16-18 **ואם בכלי ברזל וגו'**. Verses 16-21 list the criteria defining an act of deliberate murder, subject to punishment by a court of law. Apart from the subjective indications — confirmed by עדים והתראה (see Commentary above, 15:33) — that the accused was aware of what he was doing and had criminal intent, the objective factors must also be considered. One must consider the means set in motion or employed by the killer; one must determine the relation between them and the death that was caused; and one must decide, on the basis of human estimation, whether the death can be considered a direct result of the act. The court must take

19 *The blood advocate himself shall kill the murderer; wherever he meets him, he may kill him.*

יט גֹּאֵל הַדָּם הוּא יָמִית אֶת־הָרֹצֵחַ בְּפִגְעוֹ־בוֹ הוּא יְמִתֶנּוּ׃

into consideration the size of the weapon, the material from which the weapon was made, its properties, the amount of force exerted by the accused, the part of the victim's body that was struck, the physical condition of the victim, etc.

All these considerations are indicated here in Scripture. The various materials are mentioned: ברזל, אבן, עץ. In the cases of אבן and עץ, the word יד is added: באבן יד, בכלי עץ יד — i.e., a stone that can be manipulated, a wooden instrument that can be manipulated. Scripture thereby assumes that the size is sufficient [to cause a fatal blow] and indicates that one must estimate the amount of force required to set the article in motion [and whether the accused exerted that amount of force]. In the case of ברזל, this addition is missing, because with an iron or steel weapon, however small it may be, a fatal wound can be inflicted (*Sanhedrin* 76b; see תוספות there ד״ה שברזל). For this reason, also of the stone and of the wooden instrument, it says: אשר ימות בו; i.e., the instrument and the blow could cause death, and the death that occurred could be attributed to them. Finally, in all cases it says: הכהו וימות — i.e., according to expert opinion, death was caused as a result of the blow. In such a case the accused is a רוצח, a "murderer," and his punishment is death by human hands: רצח הוא מות יומת הרצח.

19 **גאל הדם וגו׳ בפגעו בו וגו׳**. It appears that this verse includes two directives. If the court, in accordance with the above (vv. 16-18), found the murderer guilty, it devolves first and foremost upon the גואל הדם to carry out the sentence. As already noted on verse 12, if the victim has no relative to serve as the גואל, the court appoints for him a גואל הדם to carry out the sentence (see *Sanhedrin* 45b). In addition, בפגעו בו וגו׳: If the court refrains from carrying out the sentence, or if the criminal escapes, the גואל הדם is authorized to carry out the death sentence wherever he meets him, even inside the ערי המקלט.

20 *Also if he pushes him down out of hatred, or throws something at him with deliberate aim, so that he died,*

כ וְאִם־בְּשִׂנְאָה יֶהְדָּפֶנּוּ אוֹ־הִשְׁלִיךְ
עָלָיו בִּצְדִיָּה וַיָּמֹת׃

21 *Or he struck him in enmity with his hand, so that he died, the one who struck him must be executed; he is a murderer. The blood advocate may kill the murderer wherever he meets him.*

כא אוֹ בְאֵיבָה הִכָּהוּ בְיָדוֹ וַיָּמֹת מוֹת־
יוּמַת הַמַּכֶּה רֹצֵחַ הוּא גֹּאֵל הַדָּם
יָמִית אֶת־הָרֹצֵחַ בְּפִגְעוֹ־בוֹ׃

22 *But if he pushed him down carelessly, without enmity, or if he threw at him some article without deliberate aim,*

כב וְאִם־בְּפֶתַע בְּלֹא־אֵיבָה הֲדָפוֹ
אוֹ־הִשְׁלִיךְ עָלָיו כָּל־כְּלִי בְּלֹא
צְדִיָּה׃

20-21 In the cases discussed in verses 16-18, where the act is committed by means of an instrument, it is easier to define the criteria that establish the killing as murder. That is why those cases are given first. To them Scripture now adds the verses ואם בשנאה וגו׳ או באיבה וגו׳, which teach us that also in cases of other ways of killing, one must consider the amount of force employed, the means used, and the result obtained, in order to decide whether the death occurred as a direct result of the act (see *Sanhedrin* 76b et seq.).

יהדפנו או השליך עליו. It makes no difference whether he threw the person at the fatal object, or threw the fatal object at the person.

הדף is related to עדף, חטף, חטב, עטף. The basic meaning: to be in excess or superfluous. This meaning is clear in the case of עדף. Thus הדף: to push something away from its place because it is superfluous in that place and should not be there. חטף: to grab something and hold on to it because it should not be in its former place. חטב עץ: to cut down trees in order to remove them from the forest. עטף: to isolate oneself by means of a cover.

בצדיה. צדה — see Commentary, *Shemos* 21:13.

22 **ואם בפתע** — see Commentary above, 6:9. ואם בפתע: פרט לקרן זוית (*Makkos* 7b). When the fatal movement occurred, the victim was going in a di-

23 *Or with any rock, from which he may die — without seeing him, he threw it on him — so that he died, but he was not an enemy to him and in no manner sought his hurt;*

כג אוֹ בְכָל־אֶבֶן אֲשֶׁר־יָמוּת בָּהּ בְּלֹא רְאוֹת וַיַּפֵּל עָלָיו וַיָּמֹת וְהוּא לֹא־אוֹיֵב לוֹ וְלֹא מְבַקֵּשׁ רָעָתוֹ׃

rection whereby it was possible for him to be seen in advance. Hence, the perpetrator was surprised by the encounter only בפתע — due to thoughtlessness. If, however, the perpetrator was going, for example, from west to east, and, facing east, he passed a side street corner, and at that moment the victim emerged [into the intersection] facing north, so that the victim could see the perpetrator, but could not be seen by him — in such a case the perpetrator is אנוס and is exempt from גלות (see ריטב״א there).

בלא איבה: פרט לשונא. In the case of one who kills a שונא, it can be assumed that there was negligence bordering on מזיד.

בלא צדיה: Since צדיה (v. 20) is definitely indicative of killing intentionally, of deliberately hitting the victim, the expression בלא צדיה can [by implication] exclude only the case of deliberately hitting the victim. However, in *Makkos* 7b our Sages say: בלא צדיה פרט למתכוון לצד זה והלכה לה לצד אחר — Scripture here [by the expression בלא צדיה] excludes the case of one who intends to throw a stone in one direction, but due to unforeseeable circumstances it flies in another direction. But this deviation from the intended direction cannot possibly be implied by the term צדיה. [That is, if צדיה means deliberately, and מתכוון לצד זה והלכה לה לצד אחר is not a case of deliberate hitting, then Scripture cannot exclude such a case by stating that the killing has to be without צדיה.] Rather, this case is excluded only by the [complete] expression בלא צדיה. [By this expression] Scripture means that only the intention, the aiming, is lacking. If, however, not only deliberate aiming is lacking, but he [positively] intends to throw the stone in another direction, he is קרוב לאונס and is exempt even from גלות.

23 **ויפל עליו**: עד שיפול דרך נפילה (ibid.). His action entailed carelessness if he directed the deadly object downward. Only in such a case is he liable to גלות, but not if he directed the object upward and, against his will, it

24 *The community shall then judge between the slayer and the blood advocate, on the basis of these [social] ordinances.*

כד וְשָׁפְטוּ֙ הָֽעֵדָ֔ה בֵּ֚ין הַמַּכֶּ֔ה וּבֵ֖ין גֹּאֵ֣ל
הַדָּ֑ם עַ֥ל הַמִּשְׁפָּטִ֖ים הָאֵֽלֶּה׃

25 *And the community shall rescue the manslayer from the hand of the blood advocate, and the community shall have him brought back to his city of reception to which he had fled. He must remain there until the death of the high priest whom he had anointed with the sacred oil.*

כה וְהִצִּ֨ילוּ הָֽעֵדָ֜ה אֶת־הָרֹצֵ֗חַ מִיַּד֮
גֹּאֵ֣ל הַדָּם֒ וְהֵשִׁ֤יבוּ אֹתוֹ֙ הָֽעֵדָ֔ה
אֶל־עִ֥יר מִקְלָט֖וֹ אֲשֶׁר־נָ֣ס שָׁ֑מָּה
וְיָ֣שַׁב בָּ֔הּ עַד־מוֹת֙ הַכֹּהֵ֣ן הַגָּדֹ֔ל
אֲשֶׁר־מָשַׁ֥ח אֹת֖וֹ בְּשֶׁ֥מֶן הַקֹּֽדֶשׁ׃

dropped and fell to the ground. So, too, he is liable to גלות only if, while descending a ladder, he fell on someone standing below, but he is not liable to גלות if, while ascending, he fell and killed someone thereby. זה הכלל כל שבדרך ירידתו גולה ושלא בדרך ירידתו אינו גולה (ibid.).

24-25 **ושפטו העדה וגו׳ והצילו העדה וגו׳**. We have already noted on verse 12 that the tendency to exonerate is an essential quality of Jewish criminal courts. This comes to expression in the court's very composition. The highest court, סנהדרי גדולה, consists of seventy-one members, whereas the smaller criminal courts, which are installed in every large city, consist of twenty-three members, a number derived in *Sanhedrin* 2a from our verse: ושפטו העדה, והצילו העדה. In every criminal trial there must be the possibility that the court will include an עדה שופטת and an עדה מצלת, so that both sides — the opinion to convict and the opinion to acquit — are represented by an עדה of ten men. Hence the court must consist of at least twenty men. However, since, in criminal cases, to convict the defendant requires a majority of at least two (see Commentary, *Shemos* 23:2), the court must consist of at least twenty-three judges.

This tendency to exonerate is stamped on the whole procedure of Jewish criminal law. A court that returns a unanimous verdict of guilty — שראו כולן לחובה — must let the accused go free (*Sanhedrin* 17a). A member of the court who, during the deliberation process, argued for conviction may change his opinion and argue for acquittal, but a member who argued for acquittal cannot change and argue for conviction (see ibid. 32a). At the גמר דין, however, he must vote in accordance with his final opinion (see ibid. and see also Commentary, *Shemos* 23:7).

על המשפטים האלה: They shall decide on the basis of these laws [vv. 16-23] whether the defendant is liable to the death penalty, is liable to גלות, or is completely exempt.

והשיבו וגו'. If he is found liable to גלות, the court sees to it that he returns to the מקלט-city and provides him with an escort for the journey (see *Makkos* 10b).

וישב בה עד מות וגו'. So it says also in verse 28: עד מות הכהן הגדל, and again in that same verse: ואחרי מות הכהן הגדל. These phrases extend the concept of the כהן גדול whose death releases the killer: Not only one who was anointed with the anointing oil, but also one who, in the absence of the anointing oil, was appointed כהן גדול by investment with the High-Priestly garments (see Commentary, *Shemos* 29:29-30 and Commentary, *Vayikra* 16:32), and also one who was appointed to fill in during the illness of a כהן גדול and then had to retire when the כהן גדול had recovered (עבר ממשיחתו) — all these are equal in this regard. אחד משוח בשמן המשחה ואחד המרובה בגדים ואחד שעבר ממשיחתו מחזירין את הרוצח (*Makkos* 11a).

It is not decided whether במיתת כולן הוא חוזר או במיתת אחד מהם — e.g., if there was both a כהן גדול and also a כהן שעבר ממשיחתו; in such a case it is open to question whether the killer returns already upon the death of one of them or only upon the death of both of them (see *Makkos* 11b, and see ריטב"א ibid. 11a, who discusses how it is possible for all three types of כהן גדול to be there at the same time).

(The relationship between כהן משיח and מרובה בגדים, and between כהן משמש and כהן שעבר is expressed in *Horayos* 11b as follows: אין בין כהן משוח בשמן המשחה למרובה בגדים אלא פר הבא על כל המצות [ויקרא ד, ג], ואין בין כהן משמש לכהן שעבר אלא פר יום הכיפורים [שם, טז, ג] ועשירית האיפה [שם ו, יג], זה וזה שוים בעבודת יום הכיפורים ומצווים על הבתולה ואסורים על האלמנה [שם כא, יד] ואינם מיטמאים בקרוביהם ולא פורעים ולא פורמים [שם כא, י-יא] ומחזירין את הרוצח.)

But only the death of one who was כהן גדול at the time of the גמר דין effects the return of the killer. It says (here): אשר משח אתו בשמן הקדש — i.e., in whose anointment the accused had participated. If we understand this correctly, it means: who was anointed when the accused was still part of the national community, in whose name every כהן גדול is appointed;

26 *But if the manslayer goes outside the boundaries of his city of reception to which he has fled,*	כו וְאִם־יָצֹא יֵצֵא הָרֹצֵחַ אֶת־גְּבוּל עִיר מִקְלָטוֹ אֲשֶׁר יָנוּס שָׁמָּה׃
27 *And the blood advocate finds him outside the boundaries of his city of reception, the blood advocate is permitted to kill the manslayer; there is no blood guilt on his account.*	כז וּמָצָא אֹתוֹ גֹּאֵל הַדָּם מִחוּץ לִגְבוּל עִיר מִקְלָטוֹ וְרָצַח גֹּאֵל הַדָּם אֶת־הָרֹצֵחַ אֵין לוֹ דָּם׃

who was anointed before the accused was banished from the national community by the very judgment pronounced against him — זה שנמשח בימיו (*Makkos* 11b). If the כהן גדול dies before the verdict is pronounced, and the verdict is pronounced only after a new כהן גדול is appointed, the accused may return only after the death of the second כהן גדול.

If the verdict is pronounced when there is no כהן גדול, or if someone kills a כהן גדול, or if a כהן גדול kills someone, he never leaves the city of refuge (ibid.). (According to תוספות *Sanhedrin* 18b ד״ה אינו יוצא, [the halachah that the killer never leaves the מקלט-city] applies in the last two cases — ההורג כהן גדול או כהן גדול שהרג — only if no other כהן גדול was appointed before the verdict. Thus, in this respect there is no difference between a כהן גדול and anyone else. This is also the view of the רמב״ם in הל׳ רוצח, 7:10.)

אשר נס שמה וישב בה. During the period of exile, the killer does not leave his מקלט-city under any circumstances, not even for the purpose of a mitzvah, not even in the highest interests of the community or state: אינו יוצא לא לעדות מצוה ולא לעדות ממון ולא לעדות נפשות ואפילו ישראל צריכין לו. After his death, too, he is buried there. What is more, if he dies in his homeland after the verdict is pronounced, his corpse is taken to the מקלט-city. He was commanded to dwell in the מקלט-city, and his burial is part of this dwelling. Only after the כהן גדול dies are his remains reinterred in the burial place of his ancestors: שם תהא דירתו שם תהא מיתתו שם תהא קבורתו (*Makkos* 11b).

26-27 **ואם יצא וגו׳ ורצח וגו׳**. Our Sages say (ibid.): כשם שהעיר קולטת כך תחומה קולט. Not only the city itself, but the city limits, too, afford refuge. That is

28 *For he has to remain in his city of reception until the death of the high priest, but after the death of the high priest the manslayer shall return to the land of his possession.*

כח כִּ֣י בְעִ֤יר מִקְלָטוֹ֙ יֵשֵׁ֔ב עַד־מ֖וֹת הַכֹּהֵ֣ן הַגָּדֹ֑ל וְאַחֲרֵי־מ֙וֹת֙ הַכֹּהֵ֣ן הַגָּדֹ֔ל יָשׁוּב֙ הָֽרֹצֵ֔חַ אֶל־אֶ֖רֶץ אֲחֻזָּתֽוֹ׃

apparently why it does not say here ואם יצא וגו׳ את עיר מקלטו, ומצא אתו וגו׳ את גבול עיר מקלטו, מחוץ לגבול עיר מקלטו but, rather, מחוץ לעיר מקלטו.

By contrast, in verse 28 it says כי בעיר מקלטו ישב, not בגבול עיר מקלטו, for his right of domicile is limited to the city itself, to the exclusion of the marked-off area around it (see ibid. 12a).

ואם יצא יצא. Only if he leaves the city limits במזיד is the גואל הדם permitted to kill him (ורצח וגו׳) and is anyone else who kills him not punished for doing so (אין לו דם): רשות ביד גואל הדם וכל אדם אין חייבין עליו (ibid. 11b, according to the accepted version). If, however, he leaves the city limits בשוגג, to kill him would be punishable murder (ibid. 12a). One who leaves בשוגג is only obligated to return to the city of refuge: במזיד נהרג בשוגג גולה, שלא יהא סופו (צאתו מחוץ לתחום) חמור מתחלתו (הרציחה).

28 **כי בעיר מקלטו ישב**. Scripture reemphasizes that his residence is limited to the city that has already received him. From this we derive (*Makkos* 12b) that if he kills בשגגה also in the מקלט-city, he does not flee to one of the other מקלט-cities; rather, he is exiled from one quarter to another quarter in the same city, משכונה לשכונה, and henceforth he is limited to that quarter of the city. בעיר מקלטו ישב עיר שקלטתו כבר (ibid.).

אל ארץ אחזתו: לארץ אחוזתו הוא שב ואינו שב למה שהחזיקו אבותיו, i.e., לא חוזר לשררה שהיה בה. He returns to his property, but he does not return to the social position or high office he may have held originally; nor does he return to a position or rank that had been his not by virtue of his personal achievements, but by inheritance (ibid. 13a; see *Shemos* 29:30; *Devarim* 17:20; *Vayikra* 25:41 and cf. Commentary, ibid. 16:32).

The ריטב״א on *Makkos* there [13a] remarks that this loss of positions and honors previously held is peculiar to the returned manslayer. All other lawbreakers, once they have received their punishment and corrected their actions, are qualified to resume their former positions and

29 *These regulations shall be for you a law of justice for your descendants in all your dwelling places.*	כט וְהָיוּ אֵלֶּה לָכֶם לְחֻקַּת מִשְׁפָּט לְדֹרֹתֵיכֶם בְּכֹל מוֹשְׁבֹתֵיכֶם׃
30 *Whoever slays another person, he may kill the murderer only on the basis of testimony from witnesses. However, one witness shall not testify against a person when the death penalty is involved.*	ל כָּל־מַכֵּה־נֶפֶשׁ לְפִי עֵדִים יִרְצַח אֶת־הָרֹצֵחַ וְעֵד אֶחָד לֹא־יַעֲנֶה בְנֶפֶשׁ לָמוּת׃

honors, and they may also follow their fathers in office and honors. What is more, they are eligible to be elected to any new honor and to any new position for which they are qualified.

29 **בכל מושבתיכם**: סנהדרין נוהגת בארץ ובחוצה לארץ (ibid. 7a). Capital cases are tried throughout Eretz Yisrael, as long as the highest court sits in the Stone Hall, the לשכת הגזית in the Sanctuary (see *Devarim* 17:10): ועשית על פי הדבר אשר יגידו לך מן המקום ההוא מלמד שהמקום גורם (*Avodah Zarah* 8b, תוספות there ד״ה מלמד). During the whole time that the סנהדרין sits in the לשכת הגזית, capital cases are tried also outside Eretz Yisrael in all places of Jewish settlement, and the members of the courts outside Eretz Yisrael act as delegates of the court in Eretz Yisrael, by virtue of authority conferred on them in the Land, סמיכה.

30 **כל מכה נפש וגו׳** as well as the following verses are apparently rules for the court. The court (vv. 12, 24-25) is commanded to judge — and, if need be, to condemn — and to appoint the גואל הדם as the one primarily responsible for carrying out the sentence. In our verse Scripture adds that the testimony of the גואל הדם is not sufficient; rather, לפי עדים — on the basis of testimony of two witnesses — is authorization to be given to the גואל הדם to kill the murderer as a רוצח.

The subject of the verb ירצח is the גואל הדם, of whom this whole chapter until now has been speaking. He is the one charged with carrying out the death sentence upon the murderer, and he is the one authorized to kill the inadvertent manslayer if the latter deliberately leaves his מקלט-city (see *Sifre* and cf. Commentary, *Shemos* 20:13).

ועד אחד לא יענה בנפש למות. In *Devarim* 17:6 and 19:15 it says explicitly that at least two witnesses are required in order to issue a death sentence, and that in general the court disregards a single witness testifying about a person's actions. It says there as follows: על פי שנים עדים או שלשה עדים יומת המת לא יומת על פי עד אחד and לא יקום עד אחד באיש לכל עון ולכל חטאת בכל חטא אשר יחטא על פי שני עדים או על פי שלשה עדים יקום דבר. Hence the Gemara in *Sanhedrin* 34a says that our verse does not deal with testimony, but with participation in the debate and deliberations that precede the verdict. Thus the meaning of לא יענה here resembles the meaning of ולא תענה על רִב (*Shemos* 23:2; see Commentary there).

[In a ברייתא] our Sages say there (*Sanhedrin* 34a) as follows: אמר אחד מן העדים יש לי ללמד עליו זכות, מנין שאין שומעין לו? ת"ל עד אחד לא יענה, מנין לאחד מן התלמידים שאמר יש לי ללמד עליו חובה, מנין שאין שומעין לו? ת"ל אחד לא יענה בנפש למות. Thereby the following rule is established:

The duty of the witnesses is to testify, but they are not permitted to influence in any other way the legal debate, neither in favor of the accused nor against him. The court may not hear their view, even if it is to the benefit of the accused.

With תלמידים, disciples, it is different. Every legal deliberation is attended by sixty-nine disciples who are seated in three rows of twenty-three each. These disciples are like apprentices who silently audit the legal deliberations, and if necessary the court chooses one of them to supplement its members (see ibid. 37a). If one of these disciples thinks he has an argument in favor of convicting the accused, they silence him; but if he has an argument in favor of acquitting the accused, he is listened to. In such a case they elevate him and seat him among the judges who are discussing the case. If there is substance to what he says, he remains permanently on the bench among the judges; if there is no substance to what he says, he remains there that day only (see ibid. 40a and 42a).

Thus, there are two *halachos*: the witnesses may not express any opinion at all during the deliberations, whereas the disciples may argue for acquittal; and [the ברייתא in] *Sanhedrin* 34a (cited above) derives both these laws from our verse.

It is extremely difficult, however, to interpret our verse in such a way that it serves as the source of both these laws. In our view, the real reason for prohibiting witnesses from expressing any opinion — בין לזכות בין לחובה — is stated by ריש לקיש: משום דמחזי כנוגע בעדותו (ibid.), a reason that applies all the more to an argument לחובה. Any participation of the witnesses in the deliberations raises the suspicion that they are prejudiced. Even if they wish to argue in favor of acquittal, it appears as though they are afraid of הזמה (see *Devarim* 19:19), for עדים זוממים are not punished unless a verdict of "guilty" has been delivered (see *Makkos* 5b). But — so it seems to us — all the more so do they appear prejudiced if they wish to argue in favor of conviction. In such a case, suspicion is cast on their testimony itself, and it appears as though their motive was not the objective presentation of the facts but the resulting punishment of the accused. ריש לקיש offers an explanation of the law that excludes witnesses from arguing לזכות, but in truth his explanation serves to exclude them entirely from participation in the deliberations. The derivation — from our verse — of this exclusion of witnesses from participation in the deliberations is merely an אסמכתא. Actually, our verse [i.e., the sentence ועד אחד לא יענה בנפש למות] deals not with עדים but with תלמידים, and it prohibits them from expressing an opinion לחובה.

Indeed, in criminal law, at least two witnesses are required for all testimony, whereas a single witness is *not* a witness at all, and what he says is of no more consequence than what anyone else says. Only as an *expert opinion* is his view of importance, and his words can have an influence just like those of any other expert.

Now here it says: Only a statement of *witnesses*, which by the statutes of criminal law means *two witnesses*, can influence the conviction of the accused. Their statement is taken as testimony testifying about a fact, and is the sole basis of the sentence. No one else, however, can influence the conviction, not even an individual who is a witness, for a single witness is *not* a witness at all. (It can happen that someone is present at an incident that is attested to by witnesses and that is brought before the court, and yet he is not counted among the witnesses and he cannot be counted among them [ibid. 6b].)

Other than witnesses, any other person can only express his private view, but as a single witness he cannot deliver testimony. Such a person *is* heard by the court if he wishes to provide reason to acquit, but he is not heard if he wishes to provide reason to convict: דיני נפשות הכל מלמדין זכות ואין הכל מלמדין חובה (*Sanhedrin* 32a). That is the meaning here of ועד אחד לא יענה בנפש למות; except for the members of the court, an individual is not permitted to argue for conviction, but he is permitted to argue לזכות, for acquittal.

This law — that the court is permitted to hear *any* view *in favor* of the accused, but is not permitted to hear *any* view *against* him — is char-

31 *You may not take ransom for the life of a murderer who has incurred the death penalty, for he must be executed.*	לא וְלֹא־תִקְחוּ כֹפֶר לְנֶפֶשׁ רֹצֵחַ אֲשֶׁר־הוּא רָשָׁע לָמוּת כִּי־מוֹת יוּמָת:
32 *And you may not take ransom in lieu of flight to his city of reception, [to permit him] to return to live in the land, until the death of the priest.*	לב וְלֹא־תִקְחוּ כֹפֶר לָנוּס אֶל־עִיר מִקְלָטוֹ לָשׁוּב לָשֶׁבֶת בָּאָרֶץ עַד־מוֹת הַכֹּהֵן:
33 *Do not turn the land in which you*	לג וְלֹא־תַחֲנִיפוּ אֶת־הָאָרֶץ אֲשֶׁר

acteristic of the whole of Jewish criminal law. More than the judge is obligated to guard against exonerating the guilty, he is obligated to guard against convicting the innocent (see Commentary, *Shemos* 23:7).

31 **ולא תקחו כפר וגו׳ אשר הוא רשע למות**. If, however, according to the evidence of the witnesses and the norms of justice, he is liable to the death penalty, you do not have the power to remit the sentence — e.g., by monetary redemption. Justice is not human law, which man enacts and man repeals. Rather, justice is God's Law, and you are merely instruments and executors in His service (see Commentary, *Vayikra* 27:29).

32 **ולא תקחו כפר לנוס וגו׳**. It is difficult to take נוס as anything other than the infinitive. Even if we assume, like רש״י, that what we have here is a noun [i.e, לנוס, meaning: for one who wants to flee] following the pattern of נוס — as in שׁוּבֵי מִלְחָמָה (*Michah* 2:8), מֻלִים הָיוּ (*Yehoshua* 5:5) — still, it should have said לַנוּס. Rather, it stands to reason that the meaning [of this verse] is as follows: You may not accept ransom in lieu of flight to a מקלט-city, and this prohibition applies in every case, even if he wants only to return home before the death of the High Priest.

33 **ולא תחניפו וגו׳**. In *Iyov* and in *Mishlei*, חָנֵף clearly denotes the hypocrite, who outwardly presents an appearance that is different from, and better than, his inner essence. Thus, one who turns another into a hypocrite removes the other's inner core while leaving his outer appearance unchanged.

Whereas the ענף (branch) and the ענב (grape) are true to themselves

are into a hypocrite, for the blood turns the land into a hypocrite, and there can be no atonement for the land for the blood that is spilled in it, except by the blood of the one who spilled it.	אַתֶּם֙ בָּ֔הּ כִּ֣י הַדָּ֔ם ה֖וּא יַחֲנִ֣יף אֶת־הָאָ֑רֶץ וְלָאָ֣רֶץ לֹֽא־יְכֻפַּ֗ר לַדָּם֙ אֲשֶׁ֣ר שֻׁפַּךְ־בָּ֔הּ כִּי־אִ֖ם בְּדַ֥ם שֹׁפְכֽוֹ׃

and actualize their inner being, the חנף is just the opposite. (This is a common phenomenon among ע and ח roots.) חנופה is the negation of the ענף and the ענב. Outwardly, it appears to be a branch, but it brings forth no blossom and no fruit. Outwardly, it appears to be a grape, but its inside is not as its outside; it contains no excellent juice.

If the Land is turned into a "hypocrite," this is חנופה in the literal sense of the term. It is still the same soil destined to bear abundant fruit beneath God's blessed dew and sunshine. But the soil, the dew, and the sunshine deceive, for no blessed seed germinates from within to give life and joy to mankind. And whatever sprouts the seeds do send forth is again deceiving, for there is no blessing in the pith of the sprouts and in the sap of the plants.

Now it says here: ולא תחניפו את הארץ. If you tolerate deliberate murder and careless manslaughter in your midst, you turn the land אשר אתם בה, "in which you *are*" (not merely אשר אתם ישבים בה as in verse 34), the land in which your whole earthly existence is rooted, the land of which you should be regarded as the most precious product, into a "hypocrite." The land will disappoint the expectations that you would otherwise be justified in placing in it; it will withhold the blessing that was meant to emanate from it. כי הדם הוא יחניף את הארץ: for blood, human blood, is the most precious sap nurtured by the land, and innocent human blood that is spilled turns the land into a "hypocrite."

Man, in his moral freedom, is meant to be close to God; he is the ultimate purpose of all earthly forces and developments. Living human blood, which bears within it the נפש, represents a point of contact between heaven and earth, a union of the terrestrial with the Divine. A human society that does not regard the blood of each of its members as sacred unto God, and that does not demand a reckoning for innocent human blood that is spilled — such a society breaks the terms under which it may possess its land and disappoints the expectations placed in it by the

34 *And do not defile the land in which you dwell, in whose midst I am present, for I,* God, *am present in the midst of the Children of Israel.*

לד וְלֹ֤א תְטַמֵּא֙ אֶת־הָאָ֗רֶץ אֲשֶׁ֤ר אַתֶּם֙ יֹשְׁבִ֣ים בָּ֔הּ אֲשֶׁ֥ר אֲנִ֖י שֹׁכֵ֣ן בְּתוֹכָ֑הּ כִּ֚י אֲנִ֣י יְהֹוָ֔ה שֹׁכֵ֕ן בְּת֖וֹךְ בְּנֵ֥י יִשְׂרָאֵֽל׃ פ שביעי

land when the land made its energies available to that society. Such a society becomes a "hypocrite" toward its land and at the same time turns the land into a "hypocrite" toward that society.

ולארץ לא יכפר לדם אשר שפך בה כי אם בדם שפכו: This חנופה can be purged from the Land only if human society demands a reckoning for the innocent blood that was spilled. The society must represent the person whose life was cut short, and the murderer must pay for the murder with his life; for by committing the murder, he forfeited his right to live. Since he spilled the blood of his fellow man, there is no blood guilt in his case; he has forfeited his own right to existence. The survival of a deliberate murderer is an affront to the higher dignity of man and is a breach of the contract [whose fulfillment is the condition] under which God gave the earth to man and the Land to Israel.

When God allowed Noach and his sons to set foot again on the earth, newly restored to man, and gave them dominion over the world of plants and animals, He declared: ואך את דמכם לנפשתיכם אדרש וגו׳ שפך דם האדם באדם דמו ישפך כי בצלם אלקים עשה את האדם (*Bereshis* 9:5-6; see Commentary there). Thereby, God proclaimed: Man, who was created in the image of God, is endowed with a higher dignity, and the recognition of this higher dignity is the basic condition for the gift of the earth and for man's dominion over the world. Similarly, when God gave Israel the Land in order to be blessed there and to develop there and to fulfill His Torah there, He reiterated: ולארץ לא יכפר לדם אשר שפך בה כי אם בדם שפכו. By this declaration, He renewed the principle of the dignity of man as the basic condition for Israel's right to possess the Land and to enjoy its fruits, and He extended it by establishing the institution through which atonement could be made for unpremeditated manslaughter.

34 **אשר אתם ישבים בה אשר אני שכן בתוכה**. The relationship described here between land and people is different from that described in verse 33 by

the words אשר אתם בה. There, the land is viewed as the basis for human existence. The soil will deny this existence to men if they will stand idly by while one man destroys the existence of another. Here, the land is viewed as the basis for ישיבה and שכינה, for the national human society and for the Presence of God on earth. Both — the nation's social welfare (which depends on allegiance to God and to His Torah) and the Presence of God on earth (which is promised to man if he elevates communal life to God [see *Shemos* 25:8]) — depend on the awareness and acknowledgement of the dignity of man who was created in His image.

The entire Torah rests on three pillars: justice, mercy in society, and moral sanctification of individual life. Hence, the entire Torah stands — or falls — on the recognition and acknowledgement — or the denial and repudiation — of the higher dignity of man who was created in God's image. Justice depends on man's recognition that his fellow man is created in the image of God; mercy and moral sanctification depend on man's awareness that he himself is created in the image of God.

If man is only another species of animal, only a physical creature like all other living things in creation, then likewise his life is motivated only by violence, selfishness, and the urge to gratify his animal drives. In that case, there can be no talk of justice, or mercy, or moral sanctification; in that case, the world of man bears only the imprint of טומאה, bondage to the physical and lack of freedom, which lead to violence and depravity. If individuals in their homes and nations in their states render homage to the false ideal of the animal, then there is no place on earth for God. For God demands that people do justice, love mercy, and walk modestly in moral sanctification [cf. *Michah* 6:8].

But indifference on the part of the community toward the shedding of innocent blood is a patent denial of man's Divine nature and proclaims טומאה as the principle of individual and national life. The Torah therefore says [in the singular] to the state of the Jewish nation: ולא תטמא את הארץ אשר אתם ישבים בה. Do not, by your indifference to the spilling of human blood, proclaim that the principle of טומאה rules the land; do not make טומאה the dominant principle in the land "in which you dwell [אשר אתם ישבים בה], in whose midst I am present [אשר אני שכן בתוכה]."

כי אני ה׳ שכן בתוך בני ישראל: For if Scripture has just said אשר אני שכן בתוכה, then the concern here is not with the land per se, but with people, with a nation, with the Children of Israel and the life they develop; for the nature of this life is what determines whether the conditions on earth are worthy of God's Presence. God is present in Israel's midst, even if the life of the people is still far — in various respects — from the goal of perfection. He is present among them, even if they still have various defects pertaining to טומאה. He is close to Israel at every present moment because His eye is on their future moral perfection, and this perfection will be attained through God's love, which trains them to attain it.

For the sake of this future perfection and for the sake of God's constant closeness, the nation as a whole must hold aloft the standard on which all progress toward the future attainment of this ideal depends. The human society in which God is present must reflect the dignity of man and must give expression to the fact that man was created in the image of God. Thus the society will preserve the principle of טהרה against all manifestations of טומאה, and the spirit of the nation will be worthy of the One Who said of Himself: אני ה׳ שכן בתוך בני ישראל (cf. Commentary, *Vayikra* 18:24-28 and 15:31).

These concluding sentences illuminate the laws of רוצח and ערי מקלט. Fulfillment of these laws was to be the first national duty upon the conquest of the Land. Indeed, Moshe had already implemented these laws in the transjordanic territory that he conquered. They are indicative of the sanctity of the life of even the lowliest citizens of the Land. With the very proclamation of the value of life, God's people shall take possession of its land. *This* state shall regard the lives of its citizens as its most precious and most sacred asset, and the nation as a whole is held responsible for every minute by which the life of any one of its members is prematurely curtailed.

A society that ascribes sanctity to human blood expresses the idea that man was created in the image of God. *God*, and the *Divine image in man* — these two factors are to form the basis of this state and of the private and public lives of all its members. Every individual is assured of life and land only on the condition that he respects the Divine image in every man, that he consequently recognizes that man has no right to harm human life, and that this recognition prompts him to be careful in all his actions.

The מקלט-cities, set at equal distances from one another throughout the Land, and becoming legally operative simultaneously (Commentary, v. 13), proclaim this principle throughout the Land and to all its inhabitants. The גואל הדם who is authorized by the state — and who sometimes is even appointed by the state — does not act only in his own name and in the name of his relatives. Rather, he acts in the name of the state; in its name he upholds this principle which was violated by the murder, or the killing, of one of its members.

The laws stated here regarding deliberate murder merely specify the rule already given to the Noachides: שפך דם האדם באדם דמו ישפך (*Bereshis* 9:6). In Jewish law, the limitation requiring עדים והתראה is added. This limitation applies throughout Jewish criminal law. A person is not put to death unless two witnesses testify to the crime. These witnesses must be present at the crime, and they must warn the criminal as he is about to commit it, also reminding him of the sin and its punishment as they are written in the Torah. (For more on this, see Commentary, *Shemos* 21:14 and 18; *Devarim* 17:6). Furthermore, the murderer is not liable to capital punishment unless the death undoubtedly occurred as a direct result of the criminal act. There is a decisive tendency to exonerate the accused. Capital punishment may be imposed only in the rare cases where the evidence is complete. In such cases, however, no authority is given to remit the sentence (see Commentary, vv. 31-32).

We have already noted (Commentary, *Bereshis* 4:13) the similarity of the punishment meted out to the careless manslayer and the punishment decreed upon the first murderer. The careless manslayer is banished from his home, excluded from the entire national soil, and bound to the single place that receives him and keeps him within its boundaries. If he deliberately leaves the city limits of his מקלט, he thereby makes light of the gravity of his crime, and the גואל הדם is entitled to kill him. All this suffering that he goes through is merely an example of the suffering he caused his brother, whom he uprooted from his home, his country, and his whole life on earth. Now he, too, is uprooted from the ground of his whole life thus far. All his ties with his home sphere, to which his heart goes out, are severed, and he lives in constant dread of the avenging sword which hangs over his head. In this way he will learn to appreciate the value of the life that his brother lost by his negligence.

However, the primary character of the exile to a מקלט-city is not punishment but כפרה; it frees him from the heavy burden of guilt which has come upon him (see *Makkos* 2b; תוספות ibid. 11b ד״ה מידי גלות). This character comes to expression also in the community's treatment of the fugitive. The community must lovingly look after his physical and spiritual welfare and provide for his needs in his place of exile (see Commentary, v. 11).

It remains for us to consider the relation between the כהן גדול and the exile of the inadvertent manslayer to a מקלט-city. The sentence passed on the manslayer is that he must remain in the מקלט-city "until the death of the כהן גדול," and the reference is to one who was כהן גדול at the time of the גמר דין. It cannot be that this is merely an external setting of a time; rather, it must be that there is an inner connection between the sin and the verdict. For if the כהן גדול dies after the verdict but before the criminal has fled to the מקלט-city, the sin is considered atoned for and the killer is exempt from exile. On the other hand, if there is no כהן גדול at the time of the verdict, the killer must remain in the מקלט-city until the end of his life.

As a matter of fact, our Sages say (*Makkos* 11b) that the death of the כהן גדול is the concluding כפרה, the final atonement of the sin: מידי גלות קא מכפרא? מיתת כהן הוא דמכפרא (see תוספות there ד"ה מידי גלות).

Our Sages also mention (ibid. 11a) the possibility that the כהנים גדולים, too, bear responsibility for the sin, and that their share in the sin is atoned for by their death; for they may have been indifferent to the welfare and innocence of their contemporaries, and may have failed to pray for them: שהיה להם לבקש רחמים על דורן ולא בקשו. The foregoing applies even to a כהן גדול who was elected between the sin and the verdict. He may have been indifferent to the fate of exile awaiting the accused, and may have failed to pray to God to enlighten the eyes of the judges, so that *if* there are any grounds to exonerate the accused, these should not escape their notice: היה לו לבקש רחמים שיגמור דינו לזכות ולא ביקש (ibid. 11b).

(In our view, both these statements should be understood in a hypothetical sense. Neither the misfortune that occurred nor the sentence that was pronounced constitutes positive proof that the כהן גדול of that time failed to pray for his contemporaries. After all, the efficacy of prayer depends on the Will of God. Particularly the second prayer — שיגמר דינו לזכות — can be understood only in a hypothetical sense, assuming the case to be that the accused is innocent; for otherwise it would be a prayer for the perversion of justice, or at any rate for an erroneous verdict.)

The כהנים's sharing in the offense and in the fate of exile of the inadvertent manslayer was so vivid in the minds of the people that, according to *Makkos* 11a, the mothers of the High Priests would look after those who were exiled and supply them with food and clothing so that they should not pray for the death of their sons: אימותיהן של כהנים מספקות להן מחיה וכסות כדי שלא יתפללו על בניהן שימותו (see there).

In the *Sifre*, our Sages explain the relationship between the High Priest and the exile of the inadvertent manslayer as follows: ר׳ מאיר אומר רוצח מקצר ימיו של אדם וכהן גדול מאריך ימיו של אדם, אין בדין שישב המקצר לפני המאריך; רבי אומר רוצח מטמא את הארץ ומסלק את השכינה וכהן גדול גורם לשכינה שתשרה על הארץ, אין בדין שיהא מי שמטמא את הארץ לפני מי שגורם להשרות את השכינה על הארץ (cf. *Yalkut Shimoni* ad loc.). That is to say, the murderer shortens life; the High Priest lengthens it. It is not right that the shortener of life should live in the presence of the one who lengthens it. The murderer brings טומאה upon the Land and drives away God's Presence; the High Priest causes God's Presence to dwell in the Land. It is not right that he who brings טומאה upon the Land should live in the presence of the one who causes God's Presence to dwell in the Land.

If we take all these statements together, the basic idea is apparently this: The inadvertent killing of a human being is an incident that stands in contradiction to the mission of the High Priest, and the High Priest who is in office shares, to a certain extent, in the responsibility for the incident.

Let us recall that the manslayer is exiled to the cities of the לויים, or, more accurately, to one of the Levite cities, so that he is entrusted entirely to the "לויים," who are attached to the כהן as his assistants. This fact emphasizes even more the connection with the mission of the כהנים and the לויים.

The emphasis in the whole task of the כהנים and לויים, whose supreme representative is the כהן גדול, is on two concepts: teaching and atonement. The atonement, which is effected in the Sanctuary, and the teaching, which is done outside the Sanctuary, are closely interrelated.

The atonement procedures performed by the כהן in the Sanctuary relate almost exclusively to שגגה, to unintentional deviations from the right path. זדון, acts committed in deliberate violation of the dictates of duty, in defiant disobedience, are not within the purview of the כהנים but, rather, are under the jurisdiction of the courts of justice.

Among the people, the essential function of the כהנים is to teach Torah. Under the influence of the כהנים, we are to place every aspect of our lives under the sovereignty of God's Law, and we are to weigh our every step and every action with care and circumspection, leaving no room for carelessness and thoughtlessness. We are to conduct our lives with the seriousness that saves a person even from שגגות. This is the main purpose of the priesthood among the people.

In sins against God, שבין אדם למקום, if a person sins בשגגה, thoughtlessly, and commits a serious offense שיש בה כרת, the כפרה is effected by the כהנים in the Sanctuary. (We have already noted the importance of אכילת בשר חטאת [see Commentary, *Vayikra* 4:11-12 and 6:19]. It may also entail a warning — to the כהנים who are partaking — that they should counteract the spirit of שגגה among the people.)

So, too, in sins of man against fellow man, שבין אדם לחבירו, if a person sins בשגגה, thoughtlessly, and commits the serious offense of killing a human being, this incident entails a reproach and warning to the כהנים, and there is a twofold connection between their highest representative — the High Priest, during whose tenure the verdict was given — and the verdict itself. The exile is regarded as a banishment from his [the כהן גדול's] presence; at the same time, the כהן גדול lives his life in sympathetic suffering with the condemned. For this reason the כהן גדול's subsequent death is regarded as a concluding atonement for the incident. The כהנים, led by the כהן גדול, must awaken and nurture among the people a spirit conducive to an ever-renewed life of duty lived under God's guidance and subject to His rule. An individual imbued with this spirit will not only let his own life run its appointed course until the end, but will also refrain from doing anything to shorten the lives of others. Concomitantly, the כהנים must awaken and nurture among the people the spirit of moral freedom. This spirit shall remove all of human life from the sphere of טומאה, the realm of bondage to blind physical forces. A person who lives in moral freedom becomes a bearer of God's Presence on earth. As it says in an old version of the *Sifre*: גורם שתשרה שכינה על האדם בארץ. Both of these [tasks of the priesthood] stand in screaming contrast to manslaughter; for the death was caused by a human act that was not subjected to the control of human intelligence and that was not performed in moral freedom, an act that was left to the play of physical, mechanical forces.

אין בדין, it is not right, say our Sages, that the killer should go about before the eyes of the כהן גדול; it is not in consonance with the principle of Jewish life, which the כהן גדול must represent and nurture. For the killer is מקצר ימים and is מסלק שכינה, whereas the כהן גדול teaches and fosters the spirit that causes אריכות ימים and השראת שכינה. If there is a כהן גדול at the time when the verdict is declared, the verdict is to be regarded as a banishment from the circle of the כהן גדול, and the condemnation of the act is brought to light from the standpoint of the כהן גדול. This standpoint

36 1 *The heads of the fathers of the family of the sons of Gil'ad, son of Machir, the son of Menashe, of the families of the sons of Yosef, approached and spoke before Moshe and before the princes, the heads of the fathers of the Children of Israel.*

לו א וַיִּקְרְב֞וּ רָאשֵׁ֣י הָאָב֗וֹת לְמִשְׁפַּ֤חַת בְּנֵֽי־גִלְעָד֙ בֶּן־מָכִ֣יר בֶּן־מְנַשֶּׁ֔ה מִֽמִּשְׁפְּחֹ֖ת בְּנֵ֣י יוֹסֵ֑ף וַֽיְדַבְּר֞וּ לִפְנֵ֤י מֹשֶׁה֙ וְלִפְנֵ֣י הַנְּשִׂאִ֔ים רָאשֵׁ֥י אָב֖וֹת לִבְנֵ֥י יִשְׂרָאֵֽל׃

is represented by him as the representative of the כהונה, and its spirit is sustained and fostered among the people by him and his fellow כהנים.

At the same time, it says here that the killer is to be exiled עד מות הכהן הגדול, and if the כהן גדול dies before him, his death concludes the כפרה that started with the sentence of exile. From that time onward the obligation of exile has already terminated, inasmuch as this death is a sign that the welfare of the people was not first on the minds of the כהנים, and they did not cultivate in the people the spirit of carefulness that would have prevented cases of שגגה of such serious consequences.

If, at the time the verdict is declared, there is no כהן גדול, the meaning of the exile should be understood differently. In such a case, there is no ideal representative who represents the nation and the כהונה; hence, the exile is a banishment from the midst of the actual nation. And since a nation does not die, the exile lasts until the death of the one who is exiled. Even if he dies outside the מקלט-city, his remains are brought there. Similarly, in the case where the exile is regarded as banishment from the proximity of the כהן גדול, and he dies before the death of the כהן גדול, when subsequently the כהן גדול dies, the remains of the exiled person are reinterred in the burial place of his ancestors.

For the continuation of the laws of רוצח בשגגה, see *Devarim* 19:1-10 and also ibid. 21:1-9.

CHAPTER 36

1 **ויקרבו**. We have already stated elsewhere (above, 26:42) that the concept of משפחה can be taken in a narrower sense and in a wider sense. The grandfather of Tzelafchad had six sons (see above, 26:30ff.), and each

2 *They said:* God *has commanded my lord to give the land, by lot, as an inheritance to the Children of Israel, and my lord was commanded by* God *to give the inheritance of our brother Tzelafchad to his daughters.*

ב וַיֹּאמְר֗וּ אֶת־אֲדֹנִי֙ צִוָּ֣ה יְהֹוָ֔ה לָתֵ֨ת אֶת־הָאָ֧רֶץ בְּנַחֲלָ֛ה בְּגוֹרָ֖ל לִבְנֵ֣י יִשְׂרָאֵ֑ל וַאדֹנִי֙ צֻוָּ֣ה בַֽיהֹוָ֔ה לָתֵ֗ת אֶת־נַחֲלַ֛ת צְלָפְחָ֥ד אָחִ֖ינוּ לִבְנֹתָֽיו׃

one of them was the head of a family. These six families were regarded as one family, one משפחה — in a wider sense. They formed משפחת הגלעדי, and the heads of the six branches of the Gil'adi family, who were great-uncles of Tzelafchad's daughters, approached Moshe and the princes with their objections.

2 **ויאמרו וגו׳**. As we will note below (vv. 6-7), the ruling issued here — in response to the initiative of the heads of the Gil'adi family — applied only to that generation among whom the land was divided for the first time. The request itself indicates such a limitation. The appeal submitted above (27:3) by the daughters of Tzelafchad is formulated in general terms; it opens with the personal matters of their father, and requests an inheritance for a daughter where there is no son. It contains not a word about the impending division of the land. Therefore the decision given there applies for all time and in all circumstances. The appeal submitted here, however, opens with the division of the land, and points out that the ruling issued there will have consequences for this division. Hence, it is logical to assume that the response given here applies only to the generation that participated in the division of the land. If the content of the appeal and response had extended beyond that period, there would be no reason to mention the fact with which the heads of the families began their appeal — viz., את אדני צוה ה׳ וגו׳. It would have sufficed to say: אדני צֻוה בה׳ לתת וגו׳; had they begun their appeal thus, it would have dealt with a problem that must be faced in all generations, whenever a daughter inherits a legacy.

את אדני צוה ה׳. . . ואדני צֻוה בה׳: the first command was given on God's initiative; the second command was given in the wake of a representation by Moshe.

3 *Now, if these should become wives to any of the sons of the [other] tribes of the Children of Israel, their inheritance will be deducted from the inheritance of our fathers and added to the inheritance of the tribe into which they marry, and it will be deducted from the lot of our inheritance.*

ג וְהָיוּ לְאֶחָד מִבְּנֵי שִׁבְטֵי בְנֵי־
יִשְׂרָאֵל לְנָשִׁים וְנִגְרְעָה נַחֲלָתָן
מִנַּחֲלַת אֲבֹתֵינוּ וְנוֹסַף עַל נַחֲלַת
הַמַּטֶּה אֲשֶׁר תִּהְיֶינָה לָהֶם וּמִגֹּרַל
נַחֲלָתֵנוּ יִגָּרֵעַ׃

לתת את הארץ בנחלה וגו׳: According to the first command, the land is to be given בנחלה; it shall be divided so that each portion resembles a stream, flowing down in its appointed channel. For that is the essence of the concept of inheritance in the sense of נחל (cf. Commentary above, 27:7). The fundamental intention, then, is that the נחלה should remain in the domain of the home, the family, and the tribe, and this applies all the more after the command to divide the land בגורל — with the co-operation of the אורים ותומים (see Commentary above, 26:55). Thus, each hereditary portion is assigned by Divine command. Hence, if a certain portion is assigned, for example, to the tribe of Yehudah, no other tribe may take possession of it.

ואדני צֻוה בה׳ וגו׳: This intention is evident in the whole system of dividing the land, but is contradicted by the second command, which gives the daughters of Tzelafchad the right to inherit their father at the division of the land. For —

3 **והיו וגו׳**. The right given to daughters to inherit (above, 27:8) contains also a general law: An inheritance they receive where there is no son will go, after their death, to their sons (or, according to one opinion, to their husbands — see Commentary above, 27:9-11); and if the husband is a member of a different tribe, the sons that she bears him likewise belong to a different tribe, and thus the inheritance will pass from one tribe to another tribe. For this reason the right of inheritance granted to daughters is called העברה (see Commentary, ibid.).

Now, if the daughters of Tzelafchad marry outside their tribe, and the above-mentioned right of inheritance is applied to them with all its

4 *Even if the* Yovel *will come for the Children of Israel, their inheritance will be added to the inheritance of the tribe into which they marry, and their inheritance will be deducted from the inheritance of the tribe of our fathers.*

ד וְאִם־יִהְיֶ֣ה הַיֹּבֵל֮ לִבְנֵ֣י יִשְׂרָאֵל֒ וְנֽוֹסְפָה֙ נַחֲלָתָ֔ן עַ֚ל נַחֲלַ֣ת הַמַּטֶּ֔ה אֲשֶׁ֥ר תִּהְיֶ֖ינָה לָהֶ֑ם וּמִֽנַּחֲלַת֙ מַטֵּ֣ה אֲבֹתֵ֔ינוּ יִגָּרַ֖ע נַחֲלָתָֽן׃

5 *And Moshe commanded the Children of Israel according to the word of* God*: The tribe of the sons of Yosef speaks justly.*

ה וַיְצַ֤ו מֹשֶׁה֙ אֶת־בְּנֵ֣י יִשְׂרָאֵ֔ל עַל־פִּ֥י יְהוָ֖ה לֵאמֹ֑ר כֵּ֛ן מַטֵּ֥ה בְנֵֽי־יוֹסֵ֖ף דֹּבְרִֽים׃

6 *This is the Word that* God *has*

ו זֶ֣ה הַדָּבָ֞ר אֲשֶׁר־צִוָּ֣ה יְהוָ֗ה לִבְנ֣וֹת

ramifications, the result will be that immediately upon the division of the land according to tribes, such a העברה will occur. Moreover, if the daughters of Tzelafchad marry now outside their tribe and die before the division, leaving descendants (or husbands), there will be a העברה already at the division of the land, and a portion of land assigned at God's command to the tribe of Menashe will be transferred to some other tribe.

4 **ואם יהיה היבל וגו׳**. This transfer will resemble the direct division determined by lot. It will not secure a temporary right, as in the right secured by sale; rather, it will entail a permanent transfer of a נחלה. A hereditary portion that should have fallen to the tribe of Menashe will be lost to it forever, as ירושה does not revert at the יובל. (The heads of the Gil'adi family speak [v. 3] of a loss to the inheritance of their fathers; they say מנחלת אבתינו and not מנחלתנו. This appears to be in agreement with the system of division according to which the land was apportioned to באי הארץ only as an inheritance from יוצאי מצרים. See Commentary above, 26:55.)

6-7 **זה הדבר וגו׳**. See Commentary above, 30:2. *Mitzvos* introduced by זה הדבר apply, as a rule, only temporarily, and we have already noted on verse 2 that the marriage limitation stated here regarding daughters who inherit applied only to the generation that participated in conquering the land.

צְלָפְחָד֙ לֵאמֹ֔ר לַטּ֥וֹב בְּעֵינֵיהֶ֖ם תִּהְיֶ֣ינָה לְנָשִׁ֑ים אַ֗ךְ לְמִשְׁפַּ֛חַת מַטֵּ֥ה אֲבִיהֶ֖ם תִּהְיֶ֥ינָה לְנָשִֽׁים׃

commanded concerning the daughters of Tzelafchad: Let them become wives to anyone who pleases them, but let them become wives, nevertheless, to the family of their paternal tribe.

ז וְלֹא־תִסֹּ֤ב נַחֲלָה֙ לִבְנֵ֣י יִשְׂרָאֵ֔ל מִמַּטֶּ֖ה אֶל־מַטֶּ֑ה כִּ֣י אִ֗ישׁ בְּנַחֲלַת֙ מַטֵּ֣ה אֲבֹתָ֔יו יִדְבְּק֖וּ בְּנֵ֥י יִשְׂרָאֵֽל׃

7 *So that no inheritance of the Children of Israel should be transferred from tribe to tribe; for the Children of Israel shall attach themselves, each one to the inheritance of the tribe of his fathers.*

What is more, according to *Bava Basra* 120a, the clause אך למשפחת מטה אביהם תהיינה לנשים does not constitute a dictate imposing a legal restriction; it is merely עצה טובה, good advice indicating that it is desirable that they marry within their own tribe. The statement לטוב בעיניהם תהיינה לנשים reserves for them their right [to marry outside the tribe] without any limitation, and it appears that this is also indicated by the clause והעברת את נחלת אביהן להן (above, 27:7), unless we assume that the העברה mentioned there in connection with the inheritance of the daughters of Tzelafchad is not to be taken literally, and that Scripture uses this term only because it generally is appropriate to the inheritance of daughters. According to the Gemara there in *Bava Basra*, the marriage limitation of a daughter who inherits applied to all the *other* heiresses of that generation [but not to בנות צלפחד].

Besides, it cannot be that ולא תסב נחלה וגו׳ lays down an absolute law, for in any case the נחלה will pass from tribe to tribe, if all the brothers die after the marriage of the daughter to a member of another tribe. It must be that Scripture's intention is only to prevent as much as possible the transfer of the נחלה from the original tribe.

Since the general section on the order of inheritance (chap. 27) uses the term העברת נחלה vis-à-vis the inheritance of daughters, and since here the section is introduced by the formula זה הדבר אשר צוה ה׳, we infer that the command to prevent as much as possible the transfer of the נחלה likewise applied only in that generation.

8 *And every daughter who inherits* ח וְכָל־בַּ֞ת יֹרֶ֣שֶׁת נַחֲלָ֗ה מִמַּטּוֹת֙ בְּנֵ֣י

What remains to be explained is this: What was Scripture's reason for enacting this temporary measure?

We have already seen, in our study of יובל (*Vayikra* 25:10), that the Torah assigns great value to the preservation of the tribal borders and to the settlement of each tribe in the territory of its portion. This promotes the fulfillment of the nation's one common calling in all the diversity of the unique characteristics of each tribe, and toward this end each tribe must be allowed to develop properly in the territory of its portion.

From this perspective, it is specially important to preserve the נחלות at the beginning of, and in the period immediately following, the possession of the Land. Each נחלה in its entirety should be handed over to the tribe for which it is suited, so that that tribe should maintain possession of it, and every possible precaution should be taken to avoid the intermingling of the tribes as a result of the laws of inheritance.

In all subsequent times, the tribes are not prohibited by the Torah to intermingle and to intermarry. On the contrary, three times a year the nation in its entirety is to assemble around the national Sanctuary, a mitzvah that is to bring about the actualization of complete national unity. But precisely for this reason it is necessary at the beginning that each נחלה be stamped with the specialty of its inhabitants, that the members of each tribe with their unique characteristics strike roots in the נחלה given to them, and that they both [people and נחלה] become interconnected and bound up with one another, so that the individual development of each tribe shall be assured forever.

The foregoing would explain the command that instructs the daughter who inherits to marry only within her own tribe, and would also explain why this command is limited to the first generation of those who took possession of the Land.

ידבקו: attach themselves, as in ודבק באשתו (*Bereshis* 2:24), וַתִּדְבַּק בְּנַעֲרוֹת בֹּעַז (*Ruth* 2:23).

8 **וכל בת ירשת נחלה ממטות בני ישראל**. According to *Bava Basra* 111a, this refers to a daughter who receives a legacy from two tribes, and from this we learn that a mother's legacy falls to her children, just as a father's

יִשְׂרָאֵל לְאֶחָד מִמִּשְׁפַּחַת מַטֵּה אָבִיהָ תִּהְיֶה לְאִשָּׁה לְמַעַן יִירְשׁוּ בְּנֵי יִשְׂרָאֵל אִישׁ נַחֲלַת אֲבֹתָיו׃

an inheritance from the tribes of the Children of Israel shall become a wife to one from the family of her paternal tribe, so that each of the Children of Israel inherit the inheritance of his fathers,

ט וְלֹא־תִסֹּב נַחֲלָה מִמַּטֶּה לְמַטֶּה אַחֵר כִּי־אִישׁ בְּנַחֲלָתוֹ יִדְבְּקוּ מַטּוֹת בְּנֵי יִשְׂרָאֵל׃

9 *And no inheritance be transferred from one tribe to another tribe; for each of the tribes of the Children of Israel shall attach itself to its own inheritance.*

legacy falls to his children. Accordingly, a daughter whose father and mother belong to different tribes receives a legacy from two tribes.

The Gemara (ibid. 112a) goes on to discuss what the law should be for such a daughter as regards her marriage. Perhaps the transference of a נחלה is a concern also as regards the maternal legacy; hence she must choose a husband whose father and mother belong to the same tribes to which her own father and mother belong. Or perhaps the transference of a נחלה is not a concern as regards the maternal legacy, שכבר הוסבה, for such a transference has already taken place, namely, when the maternal legacy fell to the daughter, who by law belongs to the tribe of her father.

This problem, too, proves what we have already stated: It is incorrect to assume that Scripture intended to prevent the transfer of the tribal נחלה absolutely.

9 **ולא תסב נחלה וגו׳**. The portion assigned to each tribe shall not, at first, be transferred in any part to any other tribe, כי איש בנחלתו ידבקו מטות בני ישראל: The members of each tribe shall be the first to be attached to the province assigned to them. Each נחלה shall first be stamped with the special imprint of the tribe to which it is assigned, and this specialty shall, as much as possible, be kept in its pure state. Each tribe with its special qualities shall — as much as possible, without exception — strike roots in its נחלה and, as it were, enter into a bond of "marriage" with it. There, in its נחלה, the tribe shall develop its special qualities on the basis of the general national mission (see Commentary, vv. 6-7).

10 *As* God *had commanded Moshe, so did the daughters of Tzelafchad do.*

י כַּאֲשֶׁר צִוָּה יְהֹוָה אֶת־מֹשֶׁה כֵּן
עָשׂוּ בְּנוֹת צְלָפְחָד: מפטיר

11 *Machlah, Tirtzah, Choglah, Milkah and No'ah, the daughters of Tzelafchad, became wives to the sons of their uncles.*

יא וַתִּהְיֶינָה מַחְלָה תִרְצָה וְחָגְלָה
וּמִלְכָּה וְנֹעָה בְּנוֹת צְלָפְחָד לִבְנֵי
דֹדֵיהֶן לְנָשִׁים:

12 *They became wives to [men] from the families of the sons of Menashe, son of Yosef, and so their inheritance remained in the tribe of their paternal families.*

יב מִמִּשְׁפְּחֹת בְּנֵי־מְנַשֶּׁה בֶן־יוֹסֵף
הָיוּ לְנָשִׁים וַתְּהִי נַחֲלָתָן עַל־מַטֵּה
מִשְׁפַּחַת אֲבִיהֶן:

13 *These are the commandments and the [social] ordinances that* God *commanded through Moshe to the Children of Israel, in the wastelands of Moav on the Yarden before Yericho.*

יג אֵלֶּה הַמִּצְוֺת וְהַמִּשְׁפָּטִים אֲשֶׁר
צִוָּה יְהֹוָה בְּיַד־מֹשֶׁה אֶל־בְּנֵי
יִשְׂרָאֵל בְּעַרְבֹת מוֹאָב עַל יַרְדֵּן
יְרֵחוֹ: חזק

10-12 **כאשר צוה וגו'**. Scripture recounts that all the daughters of Tzelafchad married within the tribe of their father, in accordance with the instruction that had been given to them. This confirms the interpretation cited above on verse 6, that this instruction was given only as "good advice," and had they decided on a different choice they would have suffered no loss and would not have been been acting against the law. They, however, chose in consideration of the national interest, and this was reckoned to their credit.

When the first generation that entered the Land had died, the limitation on marriages between the tribes was lifted, and the national authority of the Torah announced this on חמשה עשר באב, the fifteenth of Av. This יום שהותרו שבטים לבוא זה בזה was established as a permanent holiday, on which popular festivities were held (*Bava Basra* 121a).

13 **אלה המצות וגו'**. The commandments and ordinances set forth from chapter 26 until this point — the new census of the people; the regulations

pertaining to the division of the Land among the tribes; the appointment of Yehoshua [as Moshe's successor]; the obligatory offerings to be made by the nation as a whole; laws pertaining to self-imposed obligations; the treatment of food vessels that pass from non-Jewish to Jewish possession; the rights and duties of the tribes that received land in Trans-Jordan; the purging of the Land from pagan outrages; the boundaries of the Land; the מקלט-cities; temporary regulations regarding marriages of daughters who have inherited property — all these commandments and ordinances are connected, to a greater or lesser degree, with the conquest and possession of the Land. That is why they were given at the border of the Land and within sight of the Land, בערבת מואב על ירדן ירחו.

חזק